# *Essay and General Literature Index*

## *1980*

# PERMANENT CUMULATIONS

1900–1933

1934–1940

1941–1947

1948–1954

1955–1959

1960–1964

1965–1969

1970–1974

1975—1979

# Essay and General Literature Index
# 1980

AN INDEX TO 4,167 ESSAYS AND ARTICLES IN
300 VOLUMES OF COLLECTIONS OF ESSAYS
AND MISCELLANEOUS WORKS

EDITED BY
## Norma Freedman
and
## Juliette Yaakov

NEW YORK
THE H. W. WILSON COMPANY
1981

*International Standard Serial Number 0014-083X*

*Library of Congress Catalog Card Number 34-14581*

Printed in the United States of America

# Directions for Use

The Index is arranged in one alphabet and includes all author entries, subject entries, and such title entries as have been considered necessary.

For list of books indexed see pages at the end of the Index.

Full information, including pages, is given for all entries: author, subject, and occasional title entries. Material is arranged as follows:

1. Author's works

> **Vico, Giovanni Battista**
> On the heroic mind. *In* Conference on Vico and Contemporary Thought, New York, 1976. Vico and contemporary thought pt2 p228-45

2. Works about the author are listed under the heading **About**

> **Vico, Giovanni Battista**
> ### About
> Arieti, S. Vico and modern psychiatry. *In* Conference on Vico and Contemporary Thought, New York, 1976. Vico and contemporary thought pt2 p81-94

3. Criticism of an author's individual works is given under the heading **About individual works**

> **Vico, Giovanni Battista**
> ### About individual works
> *The new science*
> Stevenson, D. R. Vico's Scienza nuova: an alternative to the Enlightenment mainstream. *In* The Quest for the new science, ed. by K. J. Fink and J. W. Marchand p6-16

# Essay and General Literature Index
## 1980

**Aaron, M. Audrey**
 Garcia Marquez' mecedor as link between passage of time and presence of mind. *In* The Analysis of literary texts, ed. by R. D. Pope p21-30

**Abarbanel, Judah.** See Leo Hebraeus

**Abbé Loisy.** See Loisy, Alfred Firmin

**Abbey Theatre.** See Dublin. Abbey Theatre

**Abler, Lawrence**
 From Angel to Orpheus: mythopoesis in the late Rilke. *In* The Binding of Proteus, ed. by M. W. McCune, T. Orbison and P. M. Withim p197-219

**Abolition of slavery.** See Abolitionists

**Abolitionists**

### France
 Daget, S. A model of the French abolitionist movement and its variations. *In* Anti-slavery, religion, and reform: essays in memory of Roger Anstey, ed. by C. Bolt and S. Drescher p64-79

 Drescher, S. Two variants of anti-slavery: religious organization and social mobilization in Britain and France, 1780-1870. *In* Anti-slavery, religion, and reform: essays in memory of Roger Anstey, ed. by C. Bolt and S. Drescher p43-63

### Great Britain
 Anstey, R. The pattern of British abolitionism in the eighteenth and nineteenth centuries. *In* Anti-slavery, religion, and reform: essays in memory of Roger Anstey, ed. by C. Bolt and S. Drescher p19-42

 Ditchfield, G. M. Repeal, abolition, and reform: a study in the interaction of reforming movements in the Parliament of 1790-6. *In* Anti-slavery, religion, and reform: essays in memory of Roger Anstey, ed. by C. Bolt and S. Drescher p101-18

 Drescher, S. Two variants of anti-slavery: religious organization and social mobilization in Britain and France, 1780-1870. *In* Anti-slavery, religion, and reform: essays in memory of Roger Anstey, ed. by C. Bolt and S. Drescher p43-63

 Turley, D. M. 'Free air' and fugitive slaves: British abolitionists versus government over American fugitives, 1834-61. *In* Anti-slavery, religion, and reform: essays in memory of Roger Anstey, ed. by C. Bolt and S. Drescher p163-82

 Walvin, J. The rise of British popular sentiment for abolition, 1787-1832. *In* Anti-slavery, religion, and reform: essays in memory of Roger Anstey, ed. by C. Bolt and S. Drescher p149-62

### Netherlands
 Emmer, P. C. Anti-slavery and the Dutch: abolition without reform. *In* Anti-slavery, religion, and reform: essays in memory of Roger Anstey, ed. by C. Bolt and S. Drescher p80-98

### United States
 Foner, E. Abolitionism and the labor movement in antebellum America. *In* Anti-slavery, religion, and reform: essays in memory of Roger Anstey, ed. by C. Bolt and S. Drescher p254-71

 Wyatt-Brown, B. Conscience and career: young abolitionists and missionaries. *In* Anti-slavery, religion, and reform: essays in memory of Roger Anstey, ed. by C. Bolt and S. Drescher p183-203

**Abortion**
 Feinberg, J. Abortion. *In* Matters of life and death, ed. by T. Regan p183-217

 Parsons, K. J. P. Moral revolution. *In* The Prism of sex, ed. by J. A. Sherman and E. T. Beck p189-227

**Abraham, the patriarch**
 Schapiro, M. An Irish-Latin text on the angel with the ram in Abraham's sacrifice. *In* Schapiro, M. Selected papers v3: Late antique, early Christian and mediaeval art p307-18

### Art
 Schapiro, M. The angel with the ram in Abraham's sacrifice: a parallel in Western and Islamic art. *In* Schapiro, M. Selected papers v3: Late antique, early Christian and mediaeval art p289-306

**Abramsky, Chimen**
 The crisis of authority within European Jewry in the eighteenth century. *In* Studies in Jewish religious and intellectual history, ed. by S. Stein and R. Loewe p13-28

**Abramson, Glenda**
 Modern Hebrew drama
 *Contents*

 The development of the drama: Hascalah
 The development of the drama: Renaissance and Enlightenment
 The development of the drama: The theatres of Israel
 In search of the original play
 Modernism: A night in May
 Modernism: Hanoch Levin
 Modernism: Nissim Aloni
 Modernism: The inn of ghosts
 Modernism: The modern drama: the problem of imitation
 The problems of the Israeli drama: Audiences
 The problems of the Israeli drama: Criticism
 The problems of the Israeli drama: The director
 The problems of the Israeli drama: Tradition
 The state of Israel: Early social realism
 The state of Israel: Israel and the world
 The state of Israel: 1948 and after
 Thematic development: The Biblical-historical play
 Thematic development: The plays of the Holocaust

**Abravanel, Judah.** See Leo Hebraeus

**Academic freedom**

**United States**

Morowitz, H. J. Early warning. *In* Morowitz, H. J. The wine of life, and other essays on societies, energy & living things p168-71

**Accident law.** See Industrial safety—Law and legislation

**Acking, Carl-Axel**

Humanity in the built environment. *In* Architecture for people, ed. by B. Mikellides p101-14

**Acquisitions (Libraries)**

Munby, A. N. L. The acquisition of manuscripts by institutional libraries. *In* The Bibliographical Society of America, 1904-79 p384-98

**Act (Philosophy)**

Daly, G. The Blondelian challenge. *In* Daly, G. Transcendence and immanence p26-50

Hollis, M. Rational man and social science. *In* Rational action, ed. by R. Harrison p 1-15

Peacocke, C. Holistic explanation: an outline of a theory. *In* Rational action, ed. by R. Harrison p61-74

Striker, G. Sceptical strategies. *In* Doubt and dogmatism, ed. by M. Schofield, M. Burnyeat and J. Barnes p54-83

Tuck, R. Is there a free-rider problem, and if so, what is it? *In* Rational action, ed. by R. Harrison p147-56

Weale, A. Rational choice and political principles. *In* Rational action, ed. by R. Harrison p93-114

Williams, B. A. O. Internal and external reasons. *In* Rational action, ed. by R. Harrison p17-28

Wolheim, R. Wish-fulfilment. *In* Rational action, ed. by R. Harrison p47-60

*See also* Agent (Philosophy)

**Action (Philosophy)** See Act (Philosophy)

**Adams, Donald R.**

Prices and wages. *In* Encyclopedia of American economic history, ed. by G. Porter v 1 p229-46

**Adams, Robert Merrihew**

Authenticity-codes and sincerity-formulas. *In* The State of the language, ed. by L. Michaels and C. Ricks p579-92

In search of Baron Somers. *In* Culture and politics from Puritanism to the Enlightenment, ed. by P. Zagorin p165-202

Moral arguments for theistic belief. *In* Rationality and religious belief, ed. by C. F. Delaney p116-40

**Adams, Thomas Randolph**

Bibliotheca Americana: a merry maze of changing concepts. *In* The Bibliographical Society of America, 1904-79 p479-92

The British pamphlet press and the American controversy, 1764-1783. *In* American Antiquarian Society. Proceedings v89 pt 1 p33-88

**Adams, Willi Paul**

The colonial German-language press and the American Revolution. *In* The Press & the American Revolution, ed. by B. Bailyn and J. B. Hench p151-228

**Adaptability (Psychology)**

Pearlin, L. I. Life strains and psychological distress among adults. *In* Themes of work and love in adulthood, ed. by N. J. Smelser and E. H. Erikson p174-92

**Adaptation (Psychology)** See Adaptability (Psychology)

**Adaptive behavior.** See Adaptability (Psychology)

**Addams, Jane**

**About**

Cook, B. W. Female support networks and political activism: Lillian Wald, Crystal Eastman, Emma Goldman. *In* A Heritage of her own, ed. by N. F. Cott and E. H. Pleck p411-44

**Address, Forms of.** See Forms of address

**Ade, Femi Ojo-** See Ojo-Ade, Femi

**Adelman, Janet**

"Anger's my meat": feeding, dependency, and aggression in Coriolanus. *In* Representing Shakespeare, ed. by M. M. Schwartz and C. Kahn p129-49

**Adelman, Kenneth L.**

Revitalizing alliances. *In* National security in the 1980s: from weakness to strength, ed. by W. S. Thompson p295-317

**Adjustment (Psychology)** See Defense mechanisms (Psychology)

**Adler, Guido**

**About**

Carner, M. Guido Adler: a pioneer of musicology. *In* Carner, M. Major and minor p6-8

**Administrative agencies.** See Independent regulatory commissions

**Adolescence in literature**

Schyfter, S. E. Rites without passage: the adolescent world of Ana Maria Moix's Julia. *In* The Analysis of literary texts, ed. by R. D. Pope p41-50

**Adulthood**

Fiske, M. Changing hierarchies of commitment in adulthood. *In* Themes of work and love in adulthood, ed. by N. J. Smelser and E. H. Erikson p238-64

Giele, J. Z. Adulthood as transcendence of age and sex. *In* Themes of work and love in adulthood, ed. by N. J. Smelser and E. H. Erikson p151-73

Gould, R. L. Transformations during early and middle adult years. *In* Themes of work and love in adulthood, ed. by N. J. Smelser and E. H. Erikson p213-37

Levinson, D. J. Toward a conception of the adult life course. *In* Themes of work and love in adulthood, ed. by N. J. Smelser and E. H. Erikson p265-90

Pearlin, L. I. Life strains and psychological distress among adults. *In* Themes of work and love in adulthood, ed. by N. J. Smelser and E. H. Erikson p174-92

Smelser, N. J. Issues in the study of work and love in adulthood. *In* Themes of work and love in adulthood, ed. by N. J. Smelser and E. Erikson p 1-26

Swidler, A. Love and adulthood in American culture. *In* Themes of work and love in adulthood, ed. by N. J. Smelser and E. H. Erikson p120-47

**The adventures of Sherlock Holmes' smarter brother (Motion picture)**

Kael, P. Killing yourself with kindness. *In* Kael, P. When the lights go down p98-101

**Advertising**

**Food**

Fisher, M. F. K. As the lingo languishes. *In* The State of the language, ed. by L. Michaels and C. Ricks p267-76

Advertising—*Continued*

**United States—History**

Tedlow, R. S. Advertising and public relations. *In* Encyclopedia of American economic history, ed. by G. Porter v2 p677-95

**Advertising, Consumer.** See Advertising

**Æcerbot**

Niles, J. D. The Æcerbot ritual in context. *In* Old English literature in context, ed. by J. D. Niles p44-56

**Aelfric, abbot of Eynsham**

**About**

Scragg, D. G. The corpus of vernacular homilies and prose saints' lives before Ælfric. *In* Anglo-Saxon England 8 p223-77

**Aeschylus**

**About**

Knox, B. M. W. Aeschylus and the third actor. *In* Knox, B. M. W. Word and action p39-55

**About individual works**

*Agamemnon*

Knox, B. M. W. The lion in the house. Knox, B. M. W. Word and action p27-38

Knox, B. M. W. Review of Agamemnon (directed by Andrei Serban). *In* Knox, B. M. W. Word and action p70-78

*The Oresteia (tr. by Robert Fagles)*

Knox, B. M. W. Review of The Oresteia (tr. by Robert Fagles) and The Bacchae of Euripides, a communion rite (by Wole Soyinka). *In* Knox, B. M. W. Word and action p64-69

**Technique**

Knox, B. M. W. Review of The stagecraft of Aeschylus (by Oliver Taplin). *In* Knox, B. M. W. Word and action p79-84

**Translations, English**

Knox, B. M. W. Review of Aeschylus: Suppliants (tr. by Janet Lembke), Aeschylus: Seven against Thebes (tr. by Anthony Hecht and Helen Bacon), and Aeschylus: Prometheus bound (tr. by James Scully and C. John Herington). *In* Knox, B. M. W. Word and action p56-63

Knox, B. M. W. Review of The Oresteia (tr. by Robert Fagles) and The Bacchae of Euripides, a communion rite (by Wole Soyinka). *In* Knox, B. M. W. Word and action p64-69

**Aesthetics**

Alpers, S. Style is what you make it: the visual arts once again. *In* The Concept of style, ed. by B. Lang p95-117

Ashton, R. D. Coleridge and German 'aesthetics' (1802-18) *In* Ashton, R. D. The German idea p48-56

Ashton, R. D. Lewes and German aesthetics (1840-5) *In* Ashton, R. D. The German idea p112-25

Chatman, S. The styles of narrative codes. *In* The Concept of style, ed. by B. Lang p169-81

Gombrich, Sir E. H. J. Art and self-transcendence. *In* Gombrich, Sir E. H. J. Ideals and idols p123-30

Gombrich, Sir E. H. J. Art history and the social sciences. *In* Gombrich, Sir E. H. J. Ideals and idols p131-66

Gombrich, Sir E. H. J. The logic of vanity fair: alternatives to historicism in the study of fashions, style and taste. *In* Gombrich, Sir E. H. J. Ideals and idols p60-92

Hofstadter, A. On the interpretation of works of art. *In* The Concept of style, ed. by B. Lang p67-91

Humphrey, N. K. Natural aesthetics. *In* Architecture for people, ed. by B. Mikellides p59-73

Imbert, C. Stoic logic and Alexandrian poetics. *In* Doubt and dogmatism, ed. by M. Schofield, M. Burnyeat and J. Barnes p182-216

Kubler, G. Towards a reductive theory of visual style. *In* The Concept of style, ed. by B. Lang p119-27

Smith, P. F. Urban aesthetics. *In* Architecture for people, ed. by B. Mikellides p74-86

Walton, K. L. Style and the products and processes of art. *In* The Concept of style, ed. by B. Lang p45-66

Wollheim, R. Pictorial style: two views. *In* The Concept of style, ed. by B. Lang p129-45

*See also* Criticism; Painting

**Aesthetics, Ancient**

Manley, L. G. Art and convention in antiquity. *In* Manley, L. G. Convention, 1500-1750 p36-54

Manley, L. G. Art and nature in antiquity. *In* Manley, L. G. Convention, 1500-1750 p25-36

**Aesthetics, Communist.** See Communist aesthetics

**Aesthetics, Comparative**

Manley, L. G. "These broken ends": ancients, moderns, and modernity. *In* Manley, L. G. Convention, 1500-1750 p321-47

**Aesthetics, Medieval**

Manley, L. G. The medieval redefinition. *In* Manley, L. G. Convention, 1500-1750 p54-65

The ætheling: a study in Anglo-Saxon constitutional history. Dumville, D. N. *In* Anglo-Saxon England 8 p 1-33

**Affect (Psychology)** See Emotions

**Affection.** See Love

**Affirmative action programs**

**United States**

Glazer, N. American Jews: three conflicts of loyalties. *In* The Third century, ed. by S. M. Lipset p223-41

**Africa**

**Ethnic relations**

Cohen, R. Epilogue: integration, ethnicity, and stratification: focus and fashion in African studies. *In* Values, identities, and national integration, ed. by J. N. Paden p361-72

Morrison, D. G. and Stevenson, H. M. Cultural pluralism, modernization, and conflict: an empirical analysis of sources of political instability in African nations. *In* Values, identities, and national integration, ed. by J. N. Paden p11-23

Paden, J. N. Introduction. *In* Values, identities, and national integration, ed. by J. N. Paden p 1-7

**Ethnology**

*See* Ethnology—Africa

**Foreign relations—Cuba**

Gonzalez, E. Cuba, the Soviet Union, and Africa. *In* Communism in Africa, ed. by D. E. Albright p145-67

Africa—*Continued*

### Foreign relations—Russia

Albright, D. E. Moscow's African policy of the 1970s. *In* Communism in Africa, ed. by D. E. Albright p35-66

Gonzalez, E. Cuba, the Soviet Union, and Africa. *In* Communism in Africa, ed. by D. E. Albright p145-67

Legum, C. African outlooks toward the USSR. *In* Communism in Africa, ed. by D. E. Albright p7-34

Thompson, W. S. The African—American nexus in Soviet strategy. *In* Communism in Africa, ed. by D. E. Albright p189-218

Wilson, E. T. Russia's historic stake in black Africa. *In* Communism in Africa, ed. by D. E. Albright p67-92

### Foreign relations—United States

Thompson, W. S. The African—American nexus in Soviet strategy. *In* Communism in Africa, ed. by D. E. Albright p189-218

### Historiography

Curtin, P. D. African history. *In* The Past before us, ed. by M. Kammen p113-30

### Kings and rulers

Vaughan, J. H. A reconsideration of divine kingship. *In* Explorations in African systems of thought, ed. by I. C. Karp & C. S. Bird p120-42

### Politics and government

Cohen, R. Epilogue: integration, ethnicity, and stratification: focus and fashion in African studies. *In* Values, identities, and national integration, ed. by J. N. Paden p361-72

Fischer, L. F. Mass education and national conflict in thirty African states. *In* Values, identities, and national integration, ed. by J. N. Paden p261-69

Gann, L. H. and Duignan, P. Africa. *In* The United States in the 1980s, ed. by P. Duignan and A. Rabushka p827-58

Morrison, D. G. and Stevenson, H. M. Cultural pluralism, modernization, and conflict: an empirical analysis of sources of political instability in African nations. *In* Values, identities, and national integration, ed. by J. N. Paden p11-23

Paden, J. N. Conclusion: reformation of concepts and hypotheses. *In* Values, identities, and national integration, ed. by J. N. Paden p351-59

Paden, J. N. Introduction. *In* Values, identities, and national integration, ed. by J. N. Paden p 1-7

### Relations (general) with China

Yu, G. T. Sino—Soviet rivalry in Africa. *In* Communism in Africa, ed. by D. E. Albright p168-88

### Relations (general) with Russia

Yu, G. T. Sino—Soviet rivalry in Africa. *In* Communism in Africa, ed. by D. E. Albright p168-88

### Social conditions

Cohen, R. Epilogue: integration, ethnicity, and stratification: focus and fashion in African studies. *In* Values, identities, and national integration, ed. by J. N. Paden p361-72

Fischer, L. F. Mass education and national conflict in thirty African states. *In* Values, identities, and national integration, ed. by J. N. Paden p261-69

Morrison, D. G. and Stevenson, H. M. Cultural pluralism, modernization, and conflict: an empirical analysis of sources of political instability in African nations. *In* Values, identities, and national integration, ed. by J. N. Paden p11-23

Paden, J. N. Conclusion: reformation of concepts and hypotheses. *In* Values, identities, and national integration, ed. by J. N. Paden p351-59

Paden, J. N. Introduction. *In* Values, identities, and national integration, ed. by J. N. Paden p 1-7

### Africa, West

#### Social conditions

Hay, R. and Paden, J. N. A culture cluster analysis of six West African states. *In* Values, identities, and national integration, ed. by J. N. Paden p25-40

**African Americans.** See Afro-Americans

### African drama

#### History and criticism

Etherton, M. Trends in African theatre. *In* African literature today no. 10: Retrospect & prospect, ed. by E. D. Jones p57-85

### African fiction (English)

#### History and criticism

Izevbaye, D. Issues in the reassessment of the African novel. *In* African literature today no. 10: Retrospect & prospect, ed. by E. D. Jones p7-31

Knight, E. Popular literature in East Africa. *In* African literature no. 10: Retrospect & prospect, ed. by E. D. Jones p177-90

### African languages

Okonkwo, J. I. The missing link in African literature. *In* African literature today no. 10: Retrospect & prospect, ed. by E. D. Jones p86-105

### African literature

#### History and criticism

Jabbi, B. Influence and originality in African writing. *In* African literature today no. 10: Retrospect & prospect, ed. by E. D. Jones p106-23

Okonkwo, J. I. The missing link in African literature. *In* African literature today no. 10: Retrospect & prospect, ed. by E. D. Jones p86-105

### African literature (English)

#### History and criticism

[Jones, E. D.] Ten years of African literature today. *In* African literature today no. 10: Retrospect & prospect, ed. by E. D. Jones p 1-5

### African poetry

#### History and criticism

Wake, C. Poetry of the last five years. *In* African literature today no. 10: Retrospect & prospect, ed. by E. D. Jones p233-42

### African poetry (English)

#### History and criticism

Nwoga, D. I. Modern African poetry: the domestication of a tradition. *In* African literature today no. 10: Retrospect & prospect, ed. by E. D. Jones p32-56

### African studies

Cohen, R. Epilogue: integration, ethnicity, and stratification: focus and fashion in African studies. *In* Values, identities, and national integration, ed. by J. N. Paden p361-72

**Age groups**—*Continued*

Keller, M. Reflections on politics and generations in America. *In* Generations, ed. by S. R. Graubard p123-35

*See also* Age distribution (Demography); Conflict of generations

**Agee, James**

**About**

King, R. H. From theme to setting: Thomas Wolfe, James Agee, Robert Penn Warren. *In* King, R. H. A Southern Renaissance p194-241

*A death in the family*

Wyatt, D. Generating voice in A death in the family. *In* Wyatt, D. Prodigal sons p101-12

**Agee, James, and Evans, Walker**

**About individual works**

*Let us now praise famous men*

Trilling, L. An American classic. *In* Trilling, L. Speaking of literature and society p374-80

**Agent (Philosophy)**

Coleman, J. S. Rational actors in macro-sociological analysis. *In* Rational action, ed. by R. Harrison p75-91

Peacocke, C. Holistic explanation: an outline of a theory. *In* Rational action, ed. by R. Harrison p61-74

*See also* Act (Philosophy)

**Aggressive behavior.** See Aggressiveness (Psychology)

**Aggressive behavior in animals**

Flynn, J. P. [and others]. Anatomical pathways for attack behavior in cats. *In* Human ethology, ed. by M. von Cranach [and others] p301-15

**Aggressiveness (Psychology)**

Bandura, A. Psychological mechanisms of aggression. *In* Human ethology, ed. by M. von Cranach [and others] p316-56

Leyhausen, P. Aggression, fear and attachment: complexities and interdependencies. *In* Human ethology, ed. by M. von Cranach [and others] p253-64

*See also* Aggressive behavior in animals

**Agitprop theater**

**Great Britain**

Clark, J. Agitprop and Unity Theatre: Socialist theatre in the thirties. *In* Culture and crisis in Britain in the thirties, ed. by J. Clark [and others] p219-39

**United States**

Cosgrove, S. Prolet Buehne: agit-prop in America. *In* Performance and politics in popular drama, ed. by D. Bradby, L. James and B. Sharratt p201-12

**Agricultural associations.** See Agricultural societies

**Agricultural experiment stations**

**United States—History**

Rosenberg, C. E. Rationalization and reality in shaping American agricultural research, 1875-1914. *In* The Sciences in the American context: new perspectives, ed. by N. Reingold p143-63

**Agricultural experimentation.** See Agricultural experiment stations

**Agricultural research**

**United States—History**

Rosenberg, C. E. Rationalization and reality in shaping American agricultural research, 1875-1914. *In* The Sciences in the American context: new perspectives, ed. by N. Reingold p143-63

**Agricultural scientists.** See Agriculturists

**Agricultural societies**

**United States—History**

Saloutos, T. Farmers' movements. *In* Encyclopedia of American economic history, ed. by G. Porter v2 p562-74

**Agriculture**

**Experimentation**

*See* Agricultural experiment stations

**History**

*See* Agriculture—Origin

**Origin**

Clark, G. Primitive man as hunter, fisher, forager, and farmer. *In* The Origins of civilization, ed. by P. R. S. Moorey p 1-21

**Research**

*See* Agricultural research

**Northwestern states—History**

Danhof, C. H. Agriculture in the North and West. *In* Encyclopedia of American economic history, ed. by G. Porter v 1 p361-70

**Southern states—History**

Wright, G. Agriculture in the South. *In* Encyclopedia of American economic history, ed. by G. Porter v 1 p371-85

**United States—History**

Rasmussen, W. D. Agriculture. *In* Encyclopedia of American economic history, ed. by G. Porter v 1 p344-60

**The West—History**

Danhof, C. H. Agriculture in the North and West. *In* Encyclopedia of American economic history, ed. by G. Porter v 1 p361-70

**Agriculture, Primitive.** See Agriculture—Origin

**Agriculture and state**

*See also* Agricultural experiment stations

**Russia**

Millar, J. R. Post-Stalin agriculture and its future. *In* The Soviet Union since Stalin, ed. by S. F. Cohen, A. Rabinowitch and R. Sharlet p135-54

**Agriculturists**

**United States**

Rosenberg, C. E. Rationalization and reality in shaping American agricultural research, 1875-1914. *In* The Sciences in the American context: new perspectives, ed. by N. Reingold p143-63

**Agronomists.** See Agriculturists

**Ahearn, Marie Lucy**

David, the military exemplum. *In* The David myth in Western literature, ed. by R. J. Frontain and J. Wojcik p106-18

**Aichinger, Ilse**

**About**

Wolfschütz, H. Ilse Aichinger: the sceptical narrator. *In* Modern Austrian writing, ed. by A. Best and H. Wolfschütz p156-80

**Aid to underdeveloped areas.** See Economic assistance

**Aisenberg, Nadya**
A common spring
*Contents*
Dickens and the crime novel
Graham Greene and the modern thriller
Joseph Conrad and the thriller
Myth, fairy tale, and the crime novel

**Aithal, S. Krishnamoorthy**
The typewriters in the making of The waste
land. *In* Virginia. University. Bibliographical
Society. Studies in bibliography v33 p191-93

**Aïtmatov, Chingiz**
**About**
Shneidman, N. N. Chingiz Aitmatov: myth
and reality. *In* Shneidman, N. N. Soviet literature in the 1970s: artistic diversity and
ideological conformity p32-46

**Akans (African people)** See Ashantis; Fantis

**Alazraki, Jaime**
Neofantastic literature—a structuralist an-
swer. *In* The Analysis of literary texts, ed. by
R. D. Pope p286-90

**Alberti, Leone Battista**
**About**
Marsh, D. Leon Battista Alberti and the
volgare dialogue. *In* Marsh, D. The quattrocento dialogue p78-99

**Albrecht, Ulrich**
Militarism and underdevelopment. *In* Prob-
lems of contemporary militarism, ed. by A.
Eide and M. Thee p106-26

**Albright, David E.**
Moscow's African policy of the 1970s. *In*
Communism in Africa, ed. by D. E. Albright
p35-66

**Alcázar Alvarez, Juan**
**About individual works**
*Estudio filosófico del libro
"Progresso y miseria" de Henry George*
Busey, J. L. Alcázar's "most voluminous of
all assaults." *In* Critics of Henry George,
ed. by R. V. Andelson p326-41

**Alcoforado, Marianna**
**About individual works**
*Letters of a Portuguese nun*
Hagstrum, J. H. Woman in love: the
abandoned and passionate mistress. *In* Hag-
strum, J. H. Sex and sensibility p100-32

**Alcoholism**
**France**
Barrows, S. I. After the Commune: alcoholism, temperance, and literature in the early
Third Republic. *In* Consciousness and class
experience in nineteenth-century Europe, ed.
by J. M. Merriman p205-18

**Alcott, Louisa May**
**About**
Arms, G. W. The poet as theme reader:
William Vaughn Moody, a student, and Louisa
May Alcott. *In* Toward a new American
literary history, ed. by L. J. Budd, E. H.
Cady and C. L. Anderson p140-53

**Aldington and Craig**
Understanding people and developing a
brief. *In* Architecture for people, ed. by B.
Mikellides p27-33

**Aldington, Hilda Doolittle.** See Doolittle,
Hilda

**Aldis, Owen Franklin**
**About**
Gallup, D. C. Aldis, Foley, and the collec-
tion of American literature at Yale. In The
Bibliographical Society of America, 1904-79
p209-28

**Aldrich, Michele L.**
American state geological surveys, 1820-1845.
*In* New Hampshire Bicentennial Conference
on the History of Geology, University of
New Hampshire, 1976. Two hundred years
of geology in America p133-43

**Alemanno, Jochanan**
**About individual works**
*Sha'ar ha-heshek*
Rosenthal, E. I. J. Some observations on
Yohanan Alemanno's political ideas. *In* Studies
in Jewish religious and intellectual history,
ed. by S. Stein and R. Loewe p247-61

**Political science**
Rosenthal, E. I. J. Some observations on
Yohanan Alemanno's political ideas. *In* Studies
in Jewish religious and intellectual history, ed.
by S. Stein and R. Loewe p247-61

**Alembert, Jean Lerond d'.** See Diderot, D.
jt. auth.

**Alexander, Edward**
The resonance of dust
*Contents*
Between Diaspora and Zion: Israeli Holocaust
fiction
The destruction and resurrection of the Jews
in the fiction of Isaac Bashevis Singer
A dialogue of the mind with itself: Chaim
Grade's quarrel with Hersh Rasseyner
Holocaust and rebirth: Moshe Flinker, Nelly
Sachs, and Abba Kovner
The Holocaust and the God of Israel
The Holocaust in American Jewish fiction:
a slow awakening
The incredibility of the Holocaust
Saul Bellow: a Jewish farewell to the En-
lightenment

**Alexander, Nancy**
The work of Edwin Theodore Dumble on
the East Texas lignite deposits (1888-1892).
*In* New Hampshire Bicentennial Conference
on the History of Geology, University of New
Hampshire, 1976. Two hundred years of
geology in America p213-22

**Alexandria, Egypt**
**Description—Guide-books**
Shaheen, M. Forster's Alexandria: the
transitional journey. *In* E. M. Forster: a
human exploration, ed. by G. K. Das and J.
Beer p79-88

**Libraries**
Morowitz, H. J. Bibliophilia. *In* Morowitz, H. J. The wine of life, and other essays
on societies, energy & living things p204-07

**Alexandria, Egypt in literature**
Festa-McCormick, D. Durrell's Alexandria
quartet: "a whore among cities." *In* Festa-
McCormick, D. The city as catalyst p158-75

**Alexandrian school**
Imbert, C. Stoic logic and Alexandrian
poetics. *In* Doubt and dogmatism, ed. by M.
Schofield, M. Burnyeat and J. Barnes p182-216

**Alexandrov, Eugene Alexander**
100th anniversary of observations on petroleum geology in the U.S.A. by Dmitriy I. Mendeleyev. *In* New Hampshire Bicentennial Conference on the History of Geology, University of New Hampshire, 1976. Two hundred years of geology in America p285-88

**Alfred the Great, King of England, tr.**

### About individual works
*King Alfred's Orosius*

Bately, J. M. World history in the Anglo-Saxon Chronicle: its sources and its separateness from the Old English Orosius. *In* Anglo-Saxon England 8 p177-94

**Algebra**
Grosholz, E. R. Descartes' unification of algebra and geometry. *In* Descartes, ed. by S. Gaukroger p156-68

### History
Mahoney, M. S. The beginnings of algebraic thought in the seventeenth century *In* Descartes, ed. by S. Gaukroger p141-55

**al-Ghazzāli**

### About individual works
*Tahāfut al-Falāsifa*

Ivry, A. L. Averroes on causation. *In* Studies in Jewish religious and intellectual history, ed. by S. Stein and R. Loewe p143-55

**Alien and Sedition laws, 1798**
Buel, R. Freedom of the press in Revolutionary America: the evolution of libertarianism, 1760-1820. *In* The Press & the American Revolution, ed. by B. Bailyn and J. B. Hench p59-97

**Alienation (Philosophy)**
Collins, D. Proteus and the rat trap. *In* Collins, D. Sartre as biographer p31-59

**Alienation (Social psychology)**
Collins, D. Proteus and the rat trap. *In* Collins, D. Sartre as biographer p31-59

**Alienation (Social psychology) in literature**
Ojo-Ade, F. Madness in the African novel: Awoonor's This earth, my brother. In African literature today no. 10: Retrospect & prospect, ed. by E. D. Jones p134-52

**Alienation, Social..** See Alienation (Social psychology)

**Alison, William Pulteney**

### About
Leys, R. Background to the reflex controversy: William Alison and the doctrine of sympathy before Hall. *In* Studies in history of biology, v4 p 1-66

**Alkon, Paul K.**
The odds against Friday: Defoe, Bayes, and inverse probability. *In* Probability, time, and space in eighteenth-century literature, ed. by P. R. Backscheider p29-61

**All screwed up (Motion picture)**
Kauffmann, S. All screwed up. *In* Kauffmann, S. Before my eyes p28

**All the President's men (Motion picture)**
Kauffmann, S. All the President's men. *In* Kauffmann, S. Before my eyes p205-07

**Allegories.** See Parables

**Allegory**
Lutz, C. E. The symbol of the Y of Pythagoras in the ninth century. *In* Lutz, C. E. The oldest library motto, and other library essays p38-46

Manley, L. G. "Conveniency to nature" and the "secrets of privitie": nature and convention in defense of poetry. *In* Manley, L. G. Convention, 1500-1750 p158-75

Murrin, M. Epilogue: The disappearance of Homer and the end of Homeric allegory: Vico and Wolf. *In* Murrin, M. The allegorical epic p173-96

Murrin, M. The goddess of air. *In* Murrin, M. The allegorical epic p3-25

Murrin, M. Tasso's enchanted wood. *In* Murrin, M. The allegorical epic p87-127

Skura, M. A. Revisions and rereadings in dreams and allegories. *In* The Literary Freud: mechanisms of defense and the poetic will, ed. by J. H. Smith p345-79

*See also* Symbolism in literature

**Allen, Christine Garside**
Nietzsche's ambivalence about women. *In* The Sexism of social and political theory: women and reproduction from Plato to Nietzsche, ed. by L. M. G. Clark and L. Lange p117-33

**Allen, Garland E.**
The rise and spread of the classical school of heredity, 1910-1930; development and influence of the Mendelian chromosome theory. *In* The Sciences in the American context: new perspectives, ed. by N. Reingold p209-28

**Allen, Gay Wilson**
How Emerson, Thoreau, and Whitman viewed the "frontier." *In* Toward a new American literary history, ed. by L. J. Budd, Edwin H. Cady and C. L. Anderson p111-28

**Allen, Woody**

### About individual works
*Annie Hall*

Kauffmann, S. Annie Hall. *In* Kauffmann, S. Before my eyes p141-44

*Interiors*

Kauffmann, S. Interiors. *In* Kauffmann, S. Before my eyes p144-47

*Love and death*

Kauffmann, S. Love and death. *In* Kauffmann, S. Before my eyes p140-41

*Manhattan*

Kauffmann, S. Manhattan. *In* Kauffmann, S. Before my eyes p147-51

**Allingham, Anthony**
David as epic hero: Drayton's David and Goliah. *In* The David myth in Western literature, ed. by R. J. Frontain and J. Wojcik p86-94

**Allingham, William**

### About
Welch, R. William Allingham: 'the power and zest of all appearance.' *In* Welch, R. Irish poetry from Moore to Yeats p178-204

**Allsopp, Bruce**
Educating the client. *In* Architecture for people, ed. by B. Mikellides p41-43

**Allsopp, Harold B.** See Allsopp, Bruce

**Aloni, Nisim**

### About
Abramson, G. Modernism: Nissim Aloni. *In* Abramson, G. Modern Hebrew drama p147-61

### About individual works
*The king is the most cruel*

Abramson, G. Thematic development: The Biblical-historical play. *In* Abramson, G. Modern Hebrew drama p82-115

**Alós, Concha**

### About individual works
*Las hogueras*

Fox-Lockert, L. Concha Alos. *In* Fox-Lockert, L. Women novelists in Spain and Spanish America p114-24

**Alpers, Svetlana**
Style is what you make it: the visual arts once again. *In* The Concept of style, ed. by B. Lang p95-117

**Alphabet.** See Writing

**Alphaville (Motion picture)**
Thiher, A. Postmodern dilemmas: Godard's Alphaville and Deux ou trois choses que je sais d'elle. *In* Thiher, A. The cinematic muse p180-98

**Alterman, Nathan**

### About individual works
*The inn of ghosts*

Abramson, G. Modernism: The inn of ghosts. *In* Abramson, G. Modern Hebrew drama p162-70

**Altham, James Edward John**
Reflections on the state of nature. *In* Rational action, ed. by R. Harrison p133-45

**Althusser, Louis**

### About

Kurzweil, E. Louis Althusser: Marxism and structuralism. *In* Kurzweil, E. The age of structuralism p35-56

**Altman, Irwin**
Privacy as an interpersonal boundary process. *In* Human ethology, ed. by M. von Cranach [and others] p95-132

**Altman, Robert**

### About individual works
*Buffalo Bill and the Indians or, Sitting Bull's history lesson*

Kauffmann, S. Buffalo Bill. *In* Kauffmann, S. Before my eyes p38-40

*Nashville*

Kauffmann, S. Nashville. *In* Kauffmann, S. Before my eyes p35-38

*Quintet*

Kael, P. The Altman bunker. *In* Kael, P. When the lights go down p548-54
Kauffmann, S. Quintet. *In* Kauffmann, S. Before my eyes p46-48

*3 women*

Kauffmann, S. 3 women. *In* Kauffmann, S. Before my eyes p40-43

*A wedding*

Kauffmann, S. A wedding. *In* Kauffmann, S. Before my eyes p43-46

**Altmann, Alexander.** See Part 2 under title: Studies in Jewish religious and intellectual history

**Alvarez, Alfred**
The background; excerpt from "The savage god." *In* Suicide: the philosophical issues, ed. by M. P. Battin and D. J. Mayo p7-32

**Amarcord (Motion picture)**
Kauffmann, S. Amarcord. *In* Kauffmann, S. Before my eyes p52-55

**Amazon Valley**

### Economic conditions

Galvão, E. E. The encounter of tribal and national societies in the Brazilian Amazon. *In* Brazil, anthropological perspectives, ed. by M. L. Margolis and W. E. Carter p25-38
Moran, E. P. The trans-Amazonica: coping with a new environment. *In* Brazil, anthropological perspectives, ed. by M. L. Margolis and W. E. Carter p133-59

**Ambiguity**
Speier, H. The communication of hidden meaning. *In* Propaganda and communication in world history, ed. by H. D. Lasswell, D. Lerner and H. Speier v2 p261-300

**Ambivalence**
Greenspan, P. S. A case of mixed feelings: ambivalence and the logic of emotion. *In* Explaining emotions, ed. by A. O. Rorty p223-50

**Ament, Susan G.**
Music and art of the Holocaust. *In* Encountering the Holocaust: an interdisciplinary survey, ed. by B. L. Sherwin and S. G. Ament p383-406

**American Antiquarian Society, Worcester, Mass.**
Joyce, W. L. The manuscript collections of the American Antiquarian Society. *In* American Antiquarian Society. Proceedings v89 pt 1 p123-52

**American children's periodicals.** See Children's periodicals, American

**American drama**

### Bibliography

Frazer, W. L. Drama. *In* American literary scholarship, 1978 p365-79

### History and criticism—
Book reviews

Sidnell, M.J. The Revels history of drama in English volume VIII, American Drama. *In* Drama and mimesis, ed. by J. Redmond p227-42

### 20th century—History and criticism

Brown, J. Conclusion. *In* Brown, J. Feminist drama p133-46
Brown, J. Introduction. *In* Brown, J. Feminist drama p 1-21
Brown, J. Plays by feminist theatre groups. *In* Brown, J. Feminist drama p86-113
Weales, G. C. Drama. *In* Harvard Guide to contemporary American writing, ed. by D. Hoffman p396-438

**American English.** See English language in the United States

**American Federation of Labor**
Kessler-Harris, A. "Where are the organized women workers?" *In* A Heritage of her own, ed. by N. F. Cott and E. H. Pleck p343-66

**American Female Guardian Society and Home for the Friendless, New York**
Smith-Rosenberg, C. Beauty, the beast, and the militant woman: a case study in sex roles and social stress in Jacksonian America. *In* A Heritage of her own, ed. by N. F. Cott and E. H. Pleck p197-221

**American fiction**

### History and criticism

Kellman, S. G. The self-begetting novel and American literature. *In* Kellman, S. G. The self-begetting novel p101-28
Trilling, L. An American view of English literature. *In* Trilling, L. Speaking of literature and society p260-69

**American fiction**—*Continued*

### Jewish authors

Alexander, E. The Holocaust in American Jewish fiction: a slow awakening. *In* Alexander, E. The resonance of dust p121-46

Hellerstein, K. Yiddish voices in American English. *In* The State of the language, ed. by L. Michaels and C. Ricks p182-201

Shechner, M. E. Jewish writers. *In* Harvard Guide to contemporary American writing, ed. by D. Hoffman p91-239

### Mexican American authors

Lyon, T. "Loss of innocence" in Chicano prose. *In* The Identification and analysis of Chicano literature, ed. by F. Jiménez p254-62

Tatum, C. M. Contemporary Chicano prose fiction: a chronicle of misery. *In* The Identification and analysis of Chicano literature, ed. by F. Jiménez p241-53

Tatum, C. M. Contemporary Chicano prose fiction: its ties to Mexican literature. *In* The Identification and analysis of Chicano literature, ed. by F. Jiménez p47-57

### 20th century—Bibliography

Justus, J. H. Fiction: the 1950s to the present. *In* American literary scholarship, 1978 p283-322

Salzman, J. Fiction: the 1930s to the 1950s. *In* American literary scholarship, 1978 p247-82

Stouck, D. Fiction: 1900 to the 1930s. *In* American literary scholarship, 1978 p229-46

### 20th century—History and criticism

Braudy, L. B. Realists, naturalists, and novelists of manners. *In* Harvard Guide to contemporary American writing, ed. by D. Hoffman p84-152

Hendin, J. Experimental fiction. *In* Harvard Guide to contemporary American writing, ed. by D. Hoffman p240-86

Wagner, L. W. Tension and technique: the years of greatness. *In* Wagner, L. W. American modern p5-17

### Southern States—History and criticism

Simpson, L. P. Southern fiction. *In* Harvard Guide to contemporary American writing, ed. by D. Hoffman p153-90

**American folk-lore.** See Folk-lore, American

**The American friend (Motion picture)**
Kael, P. Heart/soul. *In* Kael, P. When the lights go down p310-16

**American hot wax (Motion picture)**
Kael, P. Shivers. *In* Kael, P. When the lights go down p418-24

**American literature**

### Afro-American authors

Scott, N. A. Black literature. *In* Harvard Guide to contemporary American writing, ed. by D. Hoffman p287-341

Turner, D. T. The Harlem Renaissance; one facet of an unturned kaleidoscope. *In* Toward a new American literary history, ed. by L. J. Budd, E. H. Cady and C. L. Anderson p195-210

*See also* Afro-American authors

### Afro-American authors—Bibliography

Turner, D. T. Black literature. *In* American literary scholarship, 1978 p381-411

### Bibliography

Anzilotti, R. Foreign scholarship: Italian contributions. *In* American literary scholarship, 1978 p465-75

Beppu, K. Foreign scholarship: Japanese contributions. *In* American literary scholarship, 1978 p475-82

Couturier, M. Foreign scholarship: French contributions. *In* American literary scholarship, 1978 p439-45

Galinsky, H. Foreign scholarship: German contributions. *In* American literary scholarship, 1978 p445-65

Lundén, R. Foreign scholarship: Scandinavian contributions. *In* American literary scholarship, 1978 p482-87

Robbins, J. A. Bibliographical addendum. *In* American literary scholarship, 1978 p489-93

Scheick, W. J. Literature to 1800. *In* American literary scholarship, 1978 p181-97

### History and criticism

Dean, D. R. The influence of geology on American literature and thought. *In* New Hampshire Bicentennial Conference on the History of Geology, University of New Hampshire, 1976. Two hundred years of geology in America p289-303

Leavis, F. R. "The Americanness of American literature." *In* Van Wyck Brooks: the critic and his critics, ed. by W. Wasserstrom p157-67

Miller, P. Europe's faith in American fiction. *In* Miller, P. The responsibility of mind in a civilization of machines p122-33

Riddel, J. N. Decentering the image: the "project" of "American" poetics? *In* Textual strategies, ed. by J. V. Harari p322-58

Spiller, R. E. The cycle and the roots; national identity in American literature. *In* Toward a new American literary history, ed. by L. J. Budd, E. H. Cady and C. L. Anderson p3-18

### Mexican American authors

Hinojosa, R. Chicano literature: an American literature in transition. *In* The Identification and analysis of Chicano literature, ed. by F. Jiménez p37-41

Hinojosa, R. Literatura chicana; background and present status of a bilcultural expression. *In* The Identification and analysis of Chicano literature, ed. by F. Jiménez p42-46

Hinojosa, R. Mexican-American literature: toward an identification. *In* The Identification and analysis of Chicano literature, ed. by F. Jiménez p7-18

Keller, G. D. The literary strategems available to the bilingual Chicano writer. *In* The Identification and analysis of Chicano literature, ed. by F. Jiménez p263-316

Leal, L. The problem of identifying Chicano literature. *In* The Identification and analysis of Chicano literature, ed. by F. Jiménez p2-6

Rivera, T. Chicano literature: fiesta of the living. *In* The Identification and analysis of Chicano literature, ed. by F. Jiménez p19-36

Salazar Parr, C. Current trends in Chicano literary criticism. *In* The Identification and analysis of Chicano literature, ed. by F. Jiménez p134-42

Salinas, J. The role of women in Chicano literature. *In* The Identification and analysis of Chicano literature, ed. by F. Jiménez p191-240

**American literature—**Mexican-American authors
—*Continued*

Sommers, J. Critical approaches to Chicano literature. *In* The Identification and analysis of Chicano literature, ed. by F. Jiménez p143-52

Villarreal, J. A. Chicano literature: art and politics from the perspective of the artist. *In* The Identification and analysis of Chicano literature, ed. by F. Jiménez p161-68

### Mexican American authors—Bibliography

Eger, E. N. A selected bibliography of Chicano criticism. *In* The Identification and analysis of Chicano literature, ed. by F. Jiménez p389-403

### Study and teaching

Trilling, L. Reflections on a lost cause: English literature and American education. *In* Trilling, L. Speaking of literature and society p343-60

### Women authors

Duncan, E. The hungry Jewish mother. *In* The Lost tradition: mothers and daughters in literature, ed. by C. N. Davidson and E. M. Broner p231-41

Janeway, E. H. Women's literature. *In* Harvard Guide to contemporary American writing, ed. by D. Hoffman p342-95

Maglin, N. B. "Don't never forget the bridge that you crossed over on": the literature of matrilineage. *In* The Lost tradition: mothers and daughters in literature, ed. by C. N. Davidson and E. M. Broner p257-67

### Women authors—Bibliography

Rudenstein, G. M.; Kessler, C. F. and Moore, A. M. Mothers and daughters in literature: a preliminary bibliography. *In* The Lost tradition: mothers and daughters in literature, ed. by C. N. Davidson and E. M. Broner p309-22

### Colonial period, ca. 1600-1775— History and criticism

Davis, R. B. The literary climate of Jamestown under the Virginia Company, 1607-1624. *In* Toward a new American literary history, ed. by L. J. Budd, E. H. Cady and C. L. Anderson p36-53

Elliott, E. The Puritan roots of American Whig rhetoric. *In* Puritan influences in American literature, ed. by E. Elliott p107-27

### 19th century

Blanck, J. N. Problems in the bibliographical description of nineteenth-century American books. *In* The Bibliographical Society of America, 1904-79 p188-200

### 19th century—Bibliography

Wortham, T. 19th-century literature. *In* American literary scholarship, 1978 p199-228

### 19th century—History and criticism

Bickman, M. Mythology: the symbol in Jungian thought and American romanticism. *In* Bickman, M. The unsounded centre p5-21

Bickman, M. One's self I sing: individuation and introjection. *In* Bickman, M. The unsounded centre p38-57

Davidson, C. N. Mothers and daughters in the fiction of the new Republic. *In* The Lost tradition: mothers and daughters in literature, ed. by C. N. Davidson and E. M. Broner p115-27

### 20th century—History and criticism

Wagner, L. W. Modern American literature: the poetics of the individual voice. *In* Wagner, L.W. American modern p95-114

### New England—History and criticism

Miller, P. Nineteenth-century New England and its descendants. *In* Miller, P. The responsibility of mind in a civilization of machines p161-75

### Southern States—History and criticism

Simpson, L. P. The Southern literary vocation. *In* Toward a new American literary history, ed. by L. J. Budd, E. H. Cady and C. L. Anderson p19-35

**American loyalists**

Norton, M. B. Eighteenth-century American women in peace and war: the case of the Loyalists. *In* A Heritage of her own, ed. by N. F. Cott and E. H. Pleck p136-61

Potter, J. and Calhoon, R. M. The character and coherence of the loyalist press. *In* The Press & the American Revolution p229-72

**American national characteristics.** See National characteristics, American

**American newspapers**

Bogart, L. Editorial ideals, editorial illusions. *In* Newspapers and democracy, ed. by A. Smith p247-67

Smith, A. The newspaper of the late twentieth century: the U.S. model. *In* Newspapers and democracy, ed. by A. Smith p5-48

**American nonsense-verses.** See Nonsense-verses, American

**American philosophy.** See Philosophy, American

**American poetry**

### Afro-American authors

Vendler, H. H. Broadsides. *In* Vendler, H. H. Part of nature, part of us p313-21

### History and criticism

Hartman, G. H. Purification and danger 1: American poetry. *In* Hartman, G. H. Criticism in the wilderness p115-32

### Women authors

Elias-Button, K. The muse as Medusa. *In* The Lost tradition: mothers and daughters in literature, ed. by C. N. Davidson and E. M. Broner p193-206

Ostriker, A. Body language: imagery of the body in women's poetry. *In* The State of the language, ed. by L. Michaels and C. Ricks p247-63

### 20th century—Bibliography

Breslin, J. E. Poetry: the 1930s to the present. *In* American literary scholarship, 1978 p343-63

Crowder, R. H. Poetry: 1900 to the 1930s. *In* American literary scholarship, 1978 p323-42

### 20th century—History and criticism

Hoffman, D. G. Poetry: after modernism. *In* Harvard Guide to contemporary American writing, ed. by D. G. Hoffman p439-95

Hoffman, D. G. Poetry: dissidents from schools. *In* Harvard Guide to contemporary American writing, ed. by D. G. Hoffman p564-606

Hoffman, D. G. Poetry: schools of dissidents. *In* Harvard Guide to contemporary American writing, ed. by D. G. Hoffman p496-563

Molesworth, C. The metaphors for the poem. *In* Molesworth, C. The fierce embrace p139-49

**American poetry**—20th century—History and criticism—*Continued*

Molesworth, C. The poet and the poet's generation. *In* Molesworth, C. The fierce embrace p77-84

Molesworth, C. Reflections in place of a conclusion. *In* Molesworth, C. The fierce embrace p196-204

Molesworth, C. "We have come this far": audience and form in contemporary poetry. *In* Molesworth, C. The fierce embrace p 1-21

Molesworth, C. "With your own face on": confessional poetry. *In* Molesworth, C. The fierce embrace p61-76

Vendler, H. H. Eight poets. *In* Vendler, H. H. Part of nature, part of us p337-53

Vendler, H. H. Ten poets. *In* Vendler, H. H. Part of nature, part of us p355-72

Wagner, L. W. Personism: some notes on the she and he of it. *In* Wagner, L. W. American modern p238-43

**New England**—19th century—
Illustrations

Tatham, D. Winslow Homer and the New England poets. *In* American Antiquarian Society. Proceedings v89 pt2 p241-60

**American prose literature**

Women authors—History and criticism

Edkins, C. Quest for community; spiritual autobiographies of eighteenth-century Quaker and Puritan women in America. *In* Women's autobiography, ed. by E. C. Jelinek, p39-52

**American religious literature.** See Religious literature, American

**Americans in Great Britain**

Sinclair, B. Americans abroad: science and cultural nationalism in the early nineteenth century. *In* The Sciences in the American context: new perspectives, ed. by N. Reingold p35-53

**Americans in literature**

Wilson, R. N. F. Scott Fitzgerald: personality and culture. *In* Wilson, R. N. The writer as social seer p17-41

**Ames, Bruce N.**

Environmental chemicals causing cancer and genetic birth defects. *In* The Condition of man, ed. by P. Hallberg p80-105

**Ames, Kenneth L.**

Folk art: the challenge and the promise. *In* Perspectives on American folk art, ed. by I. M. G. Quimby and S. T. Swank p293-324

**Amichai, Yehuda**

About

Flinker, N. Saul and David in the early poetry of Yehuda Amichai. *In* The David myth in Western literature, ed. by R. J. Frontain and J. Wojcik p170-78

About individual works

*Journey to Nineveh*

Abramson, G. Thematic development: The Biblical-historical play. *In* Abramson, G. Modern Hebrew drama p82-115

*Not of this time, not of this place*

Alexander, E. Between Diaspora and Zion: Israeli Holocaust fiction. *In* Alexander, E. The resonance of dust p73-118

**Aminzade, Ronald**

The transformation of social solidarities in nineteenth-century Toulouse. *In* Consciousness and class experience in nineteenth-century Europe, ed. by J. M. Merriman p85-105

**Amis, Kingsley**

Getting it wrong. *In* The State of the language, ed. by L. Michaels and C. Ricks p24-33

**Ammons, A. R.**

About

Howard, R. A. R. Ammons: "The spent seer consigns order to the vehicle of change." *In* Howard, R. Alone with America p 1-24

Vendler, H. H. Ammons, Berryman, Cummings. *In* Vendler, H. H. Part of nature, part of us p323-36

**Amundsen, Darrel W.**

Images of physicians in classical times. *In* 5000 years of popular culture, ed. by F. E. H. Schroeder p94-107

**Amur, G. S.**

Poetry as subterfuge: an introduction to Shiv K. Kumar's poetry. *In* Aspects of Indian writing in English, ed. by M. K. Naik p126-36

**Anabaptists**

Ozment, S. H. The sectarian spectrum: radical movements within Protestantism. *In* Ozment, S. H. The age of reform, 1250-1550 p340-51

**Analysis (Philosophy)**

Sen, A. K. Informational analysis of moral principals. *In* Rational action, ed. by R. Harrison p115-32

*See also* Ordinary-language philosophy

**Analytical geometry.** See Geometry, Analytic

**Anand, Mulk Raj**

Pigeon-Indian: some notes on Indian-English writing. *In* Aspects of Indian writing in English, ed. by M. K. Naik p24-44

**Anarchism and anarchists**

Hook, S. Law and anarchy. *In* Hook, S. Philosophy and public policy p16-37

Schwartzman, J. Ingalls, Hanson, and Tucker: nineteenth-century American anarchists. *In* Critics of Henry George, ed. by R. V. Andelson p234-53

**Anarchists.** See Anarchism and anarchists

**Anarchy.** See Anarchism and anarchists

**Ancients and moderns, Quarrel of**

Manley, L. G. "These broken ends": ancients, moderns, and modernity. *In* Manley, L. G. Convention, 1500-1750 p321-47

**Andelson, Robert V.**

Carver: reluctant demi-Georgist. *In* Critics of Henry George, ed. by R. V. Andelson p303-12

Cathrein's careless clerical critique. *In* Critics of Henry George, ed. by R. V. Andelson p126-36

Introduction. *In* Critics of Henry George, ed. by R. V. Andelson p15-28

Neo-Georgism. *In* Critics of Henry George, ed. by R. V. Andelson p381-93

Ryan and his domestication of natural law. *In* Critics of Henry George, ed. by R. V. Andelson p342-53

*See also* Cord, S. B. jt. auth.

**Andelson, Robert V. and Gaffney, Mason**

Seligman and his critique from social utility. *In* Critics of Henry George, ed. by R. V. Andelson p273-90

**Andersen, Arlow William**

Senator Knute Nelson: Minnesota's grand old man and the Norwegian immigrant press. *In* Makers of an American immigrant legacy, ed. by O. S. Lovoll p29-49

**Anderson, Martin,** 1936-
Welfare reform. *In* The United States in the 1980s, ed. by P. Duignan and A. Rabushka p139-79

**Anderson, Michael John**
Word and image: aspects of mimesis in contemporary British theatre. *In* Drama and mimesis, ed. by J. Redmond p 139-53

**Anderson, Sherwood**
About
Wagner, L. W. Sherwood, Stein, the sentence, and grape sugar and oranges. *In* Wagner, L. W. American modern p31-41

**Andersson, Theodore Murdock**
Tradition and design in Beowulf. *In* Old English literature in context, ed. by J. D. Niles p90-106

**Andreas (Anglo-Saxon poem)**
Earl, J. W. The typological structure of Andreas. *In* Old English literature in context, ed. by J. D. Niles p66-89

**Andrew, Saint, apostle in fiction, drama, poetry, etc.**
Cross, J. E. Cynewulf's traditions about the apostles in Fates of the apostles. *In* Anglo-Saxon England 8 p163-75

**Andrew, James Dudley**
About individual works
*André Bazin*
Kauffmann, S. André Bazin. *In* Kauffmann, S. Before my eyes p385-91

**Andrews, Malcolm**
A note on serialisation. *In* Reading the Victorian novel: detail into form, ed. by I. Gregor p243-47

**Androgyny (Psychology)**
Ferguson, A. Androgyny as an ideal for human development. *In* The Philosophy of sex, ed. by A. Soble p232-55

**Aneurin**
About individual works
*The Gododdin*
Jarman, A. O. H. Aneirin—the Gododdin. *In* A Guide to Welsh literature, ed. by A. O. H. Jarman and G. R. Hughes v 1 p68-80

**Angelou, Maya**
About individual works
*I know why the caged bird sings*
Demetrakopoulos, S. A. The metaphysics of matrilinearism in women's autobiography: studies of Mead's Blackberry winter, Hellman's Pentimento, Angelou's I know why the caged bird sings, and Kingston's The woman warrior. In Women's autobiography, ed. by E. C. Jelinek, p180-205

**Angels in literature**
Ellrodt, R. Angels and the poetic imagination from Donne to Traherne. *In* English Renaissance studies, ed. by J. Carey p164-79

**Anglican Church.** See Church of England

**Anglo-Saxon Chronicle**
Bately, J. M. World history in the Anglo-Saxon Chronicle: its sources and its separateness from the Old English Orosius. *In* Anglo-Saxon England 8 p177-94

**Anglo-Saxon civilization**
Bibliography
*See* Civilization, Anglo-Saxon—Bibliography

**Anglo-Saxon literature**
History and criticism
Opland, J. From horseback to monastic cell: the impact on English literature of the introduction of writing. *In* Old English literature in context, ed. by J. D. Niles p30-43
Robinson, F. C. Old English literature in its most immediate context. *In* Old English literature in context, ed. by J. D. Niles p11-29

**Anglo-Saxon manuscripts.** See Manuscripts, Anglo-Saxon

**Anglo-Saxon poetry**
Lally, T. D. P. Synchronic vs diachronic popular culture studies and the Old English elegy. *In* 5000 years of popular culture, ed. by F. E. H. Schroeder p203-12

Criticism, Textual
Leslie, R. F. The editing of Old English poetic texts: questions of style. *In* Old English poetry, ed. by D. G. Calder p111-25

History and criticism
Calder, D. G. The study of style in Old English poetry: a historical introduction. *In* Old English poetry, ed. by D. G. Calder p 1-65
Greenfield, S. B. Esthetics and meaning and the translation of Old English poetry. *In* Old English poetry, ed. by D. G. Calder p91-110
Robinson, F. C. Two aspects of variation in Old English poetry. *In* Old English poetry, ed. by D. G. Calder p127-45

**Anglo-Saxons**
Hills, C. The archaeology of Anglo-Saxon England in the pagan period: a review. *In* Anglo-Saxon England 8 p297-329

**Angoff, Charles**
"Van Wyck Brooks and our critical tradition." *In* Van Wyck Brooks: the critic and his critics, ed. by W. Wasserstrom p194-201

**Angola**
Foreign relations—Russia
Valenta, J. Soviet decision-making on the intervention in Angola. *In* Communism in Africa, ed. by D. E. Albright p93-117

History—Revolution, 1961-1975
Valenta, J. Soviet decision-making on the intervention in Angola. *In* Communism in Africa, ed. by D. E. Albright p93-117

**Animal experimentation.** See Laboratory animals

**Animal communication**
Chomsky, N. Human language and other semiotic systems. *In* Speaking of apes, ed. by T. A. Sebeok and J. Umiker-Sebeok p429-40
Lenneberg, E. H. A word between us. *In* Speaking of apes, ed. by T. A. Sebeok and J. Umiker-Sebeok p71-83
Savage-Rumbaugh, E. S.; Rumbaugh, D. M. and Boysen, S. Linguistically mediated tool use and exchange by chimpanzees (Pan troglodytes). *In* Speaking of apes, ed. by T. A. Sebeok and J. Umiker-Sebeok p353-83
Sebeok, T. A. Looking in the destination for what should have been sought in the source. *In* Speaking of apes, ed. by T. A. Sebeok and J. Umiker-Sebeok p407-27
Terrace, H. S. Is problem-solving language? *In* Speaking of apes, ed. by T. A. Sebeok and J. Umiker-Sebeok p385-405
Umiker-Sebeok, J. and Sebeok, T. A. Introduction: questioning apes. *In* Speaking of apes, ed. by T. A. Sebeok and J. Umiker-Sebeok p 1-59
*See also* Human-animal communication

**Animal communication with humans.** See Human-animal communication

**Animal-human communication.** See Human-animal communication

**Animal lore.** See Unicorns

**Animals, Cruelty to.** See Animals, Treatment of

**Animals, Experimental.** See Laboratory animals

**Animals, Legends and stories of.** See Fables

**Animals, Mythical.** See Dragons; Unicorns

**Animals, Treatment of**
Singer, P. Animals and the value of life. In Matters of life and death, ed. by T. Regan p218-59

**Animals in research.** See Laboratory animals

**Annan, Noel Gilroy**
"Our age": reflections on three generations in England. In Generations, ed. by S. R. Graubard p81-109

**Annas, Julia**
Truth and knowledge. In Doubt and dogmatism, ed. by M. Schofield, M. Burnyeat and J. Barnes p84-104

**Annie Hall (Motion picture)**
Kauffmann, S. Annie Hall. In Kauffmann, S. Before my eyes p141-44

**Annunzio, Gabriele d'**

### About individual works
*The child of pleasure*
Festa-McCormick, D. D'Annunzio's Child of pleasure: a city's power of seduction. In Festa-McCormick, D. The city as catalyst p49-68

**Anscombe, Gertrude Elizabeth Margaret**
What is it to believe someone? In Rationality and religious belief, ed. by C. F. Delaney p141-51

**Anselment, Raymond A.**
'Betwixt jest and earnest'
*Contents*
John Milton contra Hall
The Marprelate tracts
'Nor foolish talking, nor jesting, which are not convenient'
The rehearsal transpros'd
A tale of a tub

**Anstey, Roger**
The pattern of British abolitionism in the eighteenth and nineteenth centuries. In Anti-slavery, religion, and reform: essays in memory of Roger Anstey, ed. by C. Bolt and S. Drescher p19-42

### About
Davis, D. B. An appreciation of Roger Anstey. In Anti-slavery, religion, and reform: essays in memory of Roger Anstey, ed. by C. Bolt and S. Drescher p11-15

**Anthropo-geography**
Braudel, F. Is there a geography of biological man? In Braudel, F. On history p105-19

**Anthropological linguistics**
Arutiunov, S. Enthnography and linguistics. In Soviet and Western anthropology, ed. by E. Gellner p257-63

**Anthropology**
Fortes, M. Anthropology and the psychological disciplines. In Soviet and Western anthropology, ed. by E. Gellner p195-215
La Barre, W. The influence of Freud on anthropology. In La Barre, W. Culture in context p163-200

*See also* Archaeology; Ethnology

### History
Douglas, M. Judgments on James Frazer. In Generations, ed. by S. R. Graubard p151-64

### Methodology
La Barre, W. Clinic and field. In La Barre, W. Culture in context p3-34

### France
Godelier, M. The emergence and development of Marxism in anthropology in France. In Soviet and Western anthropology, ed. by E. Gellner p3-17

### Russia
Dragadze, T. The place of 'ethnos' theory in Soviet anthropology. In Soviet and Western anthropology, ed. by E. Gellner p161-70

**Anthropology, Structural.** See Structural anthropology

**Antipsychiatry**
Turkle, S. French anti-psychiatry. In Critical psychiatry, ed. by D. Ingleby p150-83

**Antiquities, Prehistoric.** See Man, Prehistoric

**Antisemitism**
Speier, H. The truth of hell: Maurice Joly on modern despotism. In Propaganda and communication in world history, ed. by H. D. Lasswell, D. Lerner and H. Speier v2 p301-16

### History
Sherwin, B. L. Ideological antecedents of the Holocaust. In Encountering the Holocaust: an interdisciplinary survey, ed. by B. L. Sherwin and S. G. Ament p23-51

### Southern States
Whitfield, S. J. Jews and other Southerners: counterpoint and paradox. In Conference on Southern Jewish History, Richmond, Va. 1976. "Turn to the South" p76-104

**Antisemitism in literature**
Steinberg, A. S. Dostoevski and the Jews. In The Jew, ed. by A. A. Cohen p158-70

**Antitrust law**

### United States—History
Hawley, E. W. Antitrust. In Encyclopedia of American economic history, ed. by G. Porter v2 p772-87

**Anton, John Peter**
A note toward a theory of political humanism. In Humanist ethics, ed. by M. B. Storer p272-80

**Antonia (Motion picture)**
Kauffmann, S. Antonia. In Kauffmann, S. Before my eyes p86-87

**Antonioni, Michelangelo**

### About individual works
*The passenger*
Kauffmann, S. The passenger/Story of a love. In Kauffmann, S. Before my eyes p121-26

*The red desert*
Arrowsmith, W. Antonioni's "Red desert" myth and fantasy. In The Binding of Proteus, ed. by M. W. McCune, T. Orbison and P. M. Withim p312-37

**Antraigues, Emmanuel Louis Henri de Launey, comte d'**

### About
Duckworth, C. D'Antraigues's feminism: where fact and fantasy meet. In Woman and society in eighteenth-century France, ed. by E. Jacobs and others p166-82

**The Antrobus soulcaking play**
Green, A. E. Popular drama and the mummers' play. *In* Performance and politics in popular drama, ed. by D. Bradby, L. James and B. Sharratt p139-66

**Anxiety**
Averill, J. R. Emotion and anxiety: sociocultural, biological, and psychological determinants. *In* Explaining emotions, ed. by A. O. Rorty p37-72

**Anzilotti, Rolando**
Foreign scholarship: Italian contributions. *In* American literary scholarship, 1978 p465-75

**Apes**
Morowitz, H. J. The crazy, hairy, naked ape. *In* Morowitz, H. J. The wine of life, and other essays on societies, energy & living things p155-58
*See also* Chimpanzees

**Apocalypse now (Motion picture)**
Kauffmann, S. Apocalypse now. *In* Kauffmann, S. Before my eyes p106-09

**Apocalypse of Gerona**
Schapiro, M. The Beatus Apocalypse of Gerona. *In* Schapiro, M. Selected papers v3: Late antique, early Christian and mediaeval art p319-28

**Apocryphal books (New Testament)**
Criticism, interpretation, etc.
Benko, S. Popular literature in early Christianity: the apocryphal New Testament. *In* 5000 years of popular culture, ed. by F. E. H. Schroeder p175-90

**Apologetics.** See Theodicy

**Appelbaum, Eileen**
The labor market. *In* A Guide to post-Keynesian economics, ed. by A. S. Eichner p100-19

**Applewhite, Harriet Verdier Branson.** See Levy, D. G. jt. auth.

**Applied science.** See Technology

**Appraisal of books.** See Criticism

**Appreciation of art.** See Art appreciation

**Apprehension.** See Perception (Philosophy)

**Apseloff, Marilyn**
Today's writers for children. *In* Children's literature v8 p164-67

**Aquinas, Thomas, Saint.** See Thomas Aquinas, Saint

**Aquirre, the wrath of God (Motion picture)**
Kauffmann, S. Aquirre, the wrath of God. *In* Kauffmann, S. Before my eyes p171-73

**Arabic language**
Rabin, D. Hebrew and Arabic in medieval Jewish philosophy. *In* Studies in Jewish religious and intellectual history, ed. by S. Stein and R. Loewe p235-45

**Arabs**
History—622-1517
*See* Islamic Empire

**Arcadia in literature.** See Pastoral literature

**Archaeology**
Moberg, C. A. What does mankind remember—and for how long? An archaeologist's reflections on some recent claims. *In* The Condition of man, ed. by P. Hallberg p60-79
*See also* Art, Prehistoric

**Archeology.** See Archaeology

**Archipoeta**
About individual works
*Lingua balbus*
Dronke, P. The art of the Archpoet: a reading of 'Lingua balbus'. *In* The Interpretation of medieval lyric poetry, ed. by W. T. H. Jackson p22-43

**Architects**
Language
Silver, N. Architect talk. *In* The State of the language, ed. by L. Michaels and C. Ricks p324-30

**Architects as artists**
Maguire, R. A conflict between art and life? *In* Architecture for people, ed. by B. Mikellides p122-33

**Architectural criticism**
Küller, R. Architecture and emotions. *In* Architecture for people, ed. by B. Mikellides p87-100
Smith, P. F. Urban aesthetics. *In* Architecture for people, ed. by B. Mikellides p74-86

**Architecture**
*See also* National Socialism and architecture
Criticism
*See* Architectural criticism
Human factors
Acking, C. A. Humanity in the built environment. *In* Architecture for people, ed. by B. Mikellides p101-14
Aldington and Craig. Understanding people and developing a brief. *In* Architecture for people, ed. by B. Mikellides p27-33
Allsopp, B. Educating the client. *In* Architecture for people, ed. by B. Mikellides p41-43
Darbourne and Darke. Social needs and landscape architecture. *In* Architecture for people, ed. by B. Mikellides p34-37
Egelius, M. Housing and human needs: the work of Ralph Erskine (with original sketches by Ralph Erskine). *In* Architecture for people, ed. by B. Mikellides p134-48
Ehrensvärd, G. The biosphere and man: some reflections on technology. *In* Architecture for people, ed. by B. Mikellides p187-90
Frampton, K. The disappearing factory: the Volvo experiment at Kalmar. *In* Architecture for people, ed. by B. Mikellides p149-61
Hertzberger, H. Shaping the environment. *In* Architecture for people, ed. by B. Mikellides p38-40
Kroll, L. Architecture and bureaucracy. *In* Architecture for people, ed. by B. Mikellides p162-70
Maguire, R. A conflict between art and life? *In* Architecture for people, ed. by B. Mikellides p122-33
Moore, C. W. Human energy. *In* Architecture for people, ed. by B. Mikellides p115-21
Stringer, P. Models of man in Casterbridge and Milton Keynes. *In* Architecture for people, ed. by B. Mikellides p176-86

Methodology
Aldington and Craig. Understanding people and developing a brief. *In* Architecture for people, ed. by B. Mikellides p27-33

Psychological aspects
Mikellides, B. Appendix on human needs. *In* Architecture for people, ed. by B. Mikellides p191-92
Mikellides, B. Architectural psychology and the unavoidable art. *In* Architecture for people, ed. by B. Mikellides p9-26

**Architecture, Church.** See Church architecture

**Architecture, Domestic**

Jones, M. O. L. A. add-ons and re-dos: renovation in folk art and architectural design. *In* Perspectives on American folk art, ed. by I. M. G. Quimby and S. T. Swank p325-63

### Great Britain

Egelius, M. Housing and human needs: the work of Ralph Erskine (with original sketches by Ralph Erskine). *In* Architecture for people, ed. by B. Mikellides p134-48

Stringer, P. Models of man in Casterbridge and Milton Keynes. *In* Architecture for people, ed. by B. Mikellides p176-86

**Architecture, Early Christian**

Krautheimer, R. Success and failure in late antique church planning. *In* Age of spirituality, ed. by K. Weitzmann p121-39

**Architecture, Ecclesiastical.** See Church architecture

**Architecture, French**

Kroll, L. Architecture and bureaucracy. *In* Architecture for people, ed. by B. Mikellides p162-70

**Architecture, Industrial**

### Sweden—Kalmar

Frampton, K. The disappearing factory: the Volvo experiment at Kalmar. *In* Architecture for people, ed. by B. Mikellides p149-61

**Architecture, Modern**

### 20th century

Newman, O. Whose failure is modern architecture? *In* Architecture for people, ed. by B. Mikellides p44-58

**Architecture and energy conservation**

Ehrensvärd, G. The biosphere and man: some reflections on technology. *In* Architecture for people, ed. by B. Mikellides p187-90

**Architecture and religion.** See Church architecture

**Architecture and society.** See Architecture—Human factors

**Archpoet.** See Archipoeta

**Arens, W.**

Taxonomy versus dynamics revisited: the interpretation of misfortune in a polyethnic community. *In* Explorations in African systems of thought, ed. by I. C. Karp & C. S. Bird p165-80

**Arequipa, Peru**

### History

Gallagher, M. A. Y. Aristocratic opposition to the establishment of a foundling home in Arequipa, Peru. *In* Studies in eighteenth-century culture v9 p45-58

**Arestad, Sverre**

What was Snus Hill? *In* Makers of an American immigrant legacy, ed. by O. S. Lovoll p159-72

**Argentine Republic**

### History

Naipaul, V. S. The corpse at the iron gate. *In* Naipaul, V. S. The return of Eva Perón p95-170

### Social conditions—1945-

Naipaul, V. S. The corpse at the iron gate. *In* Naipaul, V. S. The return of Evan Perón p95-170

**Argote, Luis de.** See Góngora y Argote, Luis de

**Argumentation.** See Logic

**Arias, Ron**

### About individual works

*The road to Tamazunchale*

Cárdenas de Dwyer, C. International literary metaphor and Ron Arias: an analysis of The road to Tamazunchale. *In* The Identification and analysis of Chicano literature, ed. by F. Jiménez p358-64

**Arieti, Silvano**

Vico and modern psychiatry. *In* Conference on Vico and Contemporary Thought, New York, 1976. Vico and contemporary thought pt2 p81-94

**Aristophanes**

### About

Dover, K. J. Comedy. *In* Ancient Greek literature, ed. by K. J. Dover p74-87

**Aristoteles**

### About

Montgomery, R. L. Faculty psychology and theories of imagination: Aristotle, Plato, Augustine, and Aquinas. *In* Montgomery, R. L. The reader's eye p13-49

### Ethics

Fox, M. The doctrine of the mean in Aristotle and Maimonides: a comparative study. *In* Studies in Jewish religious and intellectual history, ed. by S. Stein and R. Loewe p93-120

### Influence

Kristeller, P. O. The Aristotelian tradition. *In* Kristeller, P. O. Renaissance thought and its sources p32-49

### Teleology

Davidson, H. A. The principle that a finite body can contain only a finite power. *In* Studies in Jewish religious and intellectual history, ed. by S. Stein and R. Loewe p75-92

**Aristotle.** See Aristoteles

**Armah, Ayi Kwei**

### About

Nnolim, C. E. Dialectic as form: pejorism in the novels of Armah. *In* African literature today no. 10: Retrospect & prospect, ed. by E. D. Jones p207-23

### About individual works

*The beautiful ones are not yet born*

Nnolim, C. E. Dialectic as form: pejorism in the novels of Armah. *In* African literature today no. 10: Retrospect & prospect, ed. by E. D. Jones p207-23

**Armaments.** See Munitions

**Armed Forces.** See Sociology, Military

**Armies.** See Militarism; Sociology, Military

**Arms, George Warren**

The poet as theme reader: William Vaughn Moody, a student, and Louisa May Alcott. *In* Toward a new American literary history, ed. by L. J. Budd, E. H. Cady and C. L. Anderson p140-53

**Arms sales.** See Munitions

**Armstrong, David Malet**

Perception, sense data and causality. *In* Perception and identity, ed. by G. F. Macdonald p84-98

**Arnim, Bettina (Brentano) von**

### About

Kittler, F. Writing into the wind, Bettina. *In* Glyph 7 p32-69

Arnım, Ludwig Achim, Freiherr von

**About**

Hughes, G. T. The legacy of myth: the Grimms, Brentano and Arnim. *In* Hughes, G. T. Romantic German literature p79-77

Arnold, Matthew

**About**

McGhee, R. D. Arnold and Clough. *In* McGhee, R. D. Marriage, duty & desire in Victorian poetry and drama p99-138

**About individual works**

*Falkland*

Farrell, J. P. Arnold: tragic vision and the third host. *In* Farrell, J. P. Revolution as tragedy p247-80

**Influence**

Krieger, M. The critical legacy of Matthew Arnold; or, The strange brotherhood of T. S. Eliot, I. A. Richards, and Northrop Frye. *In* Krieger, M. Poetic presence and illusion p92-107

**Political and social views**

Farrell, J. P. Arnold: tragic vision and the third host. *In* Farrell, J. P. Revolution as tragedy p247-80

Arnstein, Walter L.

Edwardian politics: turbulent spring or Indian summer? *In* The Edwardian age: conflict and stability, 1900-1914, ed. by A. O'Day p60-78

Reflections on histories of childhood. *In* Research about nineteenth-century children and books, ed. by S. K. Richardson p41-60

Arrabal, Fernando

**About**

Lamont, R. C. A pack of cards. *In* The Analysis of literary texts, ed. by R. D. Pope p185-200

**About individual works**

*The solemn communion*

Orbison, T. T. Arrabal's The solemn communion as ritual drama. *In* The Binding of Proteus, ed. by M. W. McCune, T. T. Orbison, and P. M. Withim p280-96

Arrow, Kenneth Joseph

The economics of information. *In* The Computer age: a twenty-year view, ed. by M. L. Dertouzos and J. Moses p306-17

Arrowsmith, William

Antonioni's "Red desert" myth and fantasy. *In* The Binding of Proteus, ed. by M. W. McCune, T. T. Orbison and P. M. Withim p312-37

Arsenault, Raymond

Charles Jacobson of Arkansas: a Jewish politician in the land of the razorbacks, 1891-1915. *In* Conference on Southern Jewish History, Richmond, Va. 1976. "Turn to the South" p55-75

Art

Kubler, G. A. The arts: fine and plain. *In* Perspectives on American folk art, ed. by I. M. G. Quimby and S. T. Swank p234-46

*See also* Costume in art; National socialism and art; Painting

**Analysis, interpretation, appreciation**

*See* Aesthetics; Art—Study and teaching

**Criticism**

*See* Art criticism

**History**

Gombrich, Sir E. H. J. Art history and the social sciences. *In* Gombrich, Sir E. H. J. Ideals and idols p131-66

*See also* Art criticism

**Language**

Vaizey, Lady M. Art language. *In* The State of the language, ed. by L. Michaels and C. Ricks p331-42

**Museums**

*See* Art museums

**Study and teaching**

Gombrich, Sir E. H. J. The museum: past, present and future. *In* Gombrich, Sir E. H. J. Ideals and idols p189-204

Gombrich, Sir E. H. J. A plea for pluralism. *In* Gombrich, Sir E. H. J. Ideals and idols p184-88

Gombrich, Sir E. H. J. Reason and feeling in the study of art. *In* Gombrich, Sir E. H. J. Ideals and idols p205-07

Art, Akan (African people)

Ross, D. H. Cement lions and cloth elephants: popular arts of the Fante Asafo. *In* 5000 years of popular culture, ed. by F. E. H. Schroeder p290-317

Art, Ancient

Brown, P. R. L. Art and society in late antiquity. *In* Age of spirituality, ed. by K. Weitzmann p17-27

Weitzmann, K. Introduction. *In* Age of spirituality, ed. by K. Weitzmann p 1-5

Art, British

**History**

Mellor, D. British art in the 1930s: some economic, political and cultural structures. *In* Class, culture and social change, ed. by F. Gloversmith p185-207

Art, Christian. See Christian art and symbolism

Art, Classical

Hanfmann, G. M. A. The continuity of classical art: culture, myth, and faith. *In* Age of spirituality, ed. by K. Weitzmann p75-99

Weitzmann, K. Introduction. *In* Age of spirituality, ed. by K. Weitzmann p 1-5

Art, Computer. See Computer art

Art, Early Christian

Brenk, B. The imperial heritage of early Christian art. *In* Age of spirituality, ed. by K. Weitzmann p39-52

Brown, P. R. L. Art and society in late antiquity. *In* Age of spirituality, ed. by K. Weitzmann p17-27

Hanfmann, G. M. A. The continuity of classical art: culture, myth, and faith. *In* Age of spirituality, ed. by K. Weitzmann p75-99

Shepherd, M. H. Christology: a central problem of early Christian theology and art. *In* Age of spirituality, ed. by K. Weitzmann p101-20

Weitzmann, K. Introduction. *In* Age of spirituality, ed. by K. Weitzmann p 1-5

Art, Ecclesiastical. See Christian art and symbolism

Art, Folk. See Folk art

Art, Islamic. See Islamic art and symbolism

Art, Medieval

**English influences**

Schapiro, M. "Cain's jawbone that did the first murder." *In* Schapiro, M. Selected papers v3: Late antique, early Christian and mediaeval art p249-65

**Art, Modern**

Kepes, G. Private and public art. *In* Value and values in evolution, ed. by E. A. Maziarz p143-59

*See also* Neoclassicism (Art)

### 20th century

Barrett, C. Revolutions in the visual arts. *In* The Context of English literature, 1900-1930, ed. by M. Bell p218-40

*See* Computer art

**Art, Popular.** See Folk art

**Art, Prehistoric**

Sandars, N. K. The religious development of some early societies. *In* The Origins of civilization, ed. by P. S. R. Moorey p103-27

**Art, Primitive.** See Art, Prehistoric

**Art, Rococo**

### France

Harbison, R. Nature as a child. *In* Harbison, R. Deliberate regression p3-24

**Art, Roman**

Orr, D. G. Roman domestic religion: the archaeology of Roman popular art. *In* 5000 years of popular culture, ed. by F. E. H. Schroeder p156-72

**Art, Russian**

### History

Grossman, J. D. Feminine images in Old Russian literature and art. *In* California Slavic studies v11 p33-70

Harbison, R. Millennium. *In* Harbison, R. Deliberate regression p208-24

**Art and anthropology**

Fabian, J. and Szombati-Fabian, I. Folk art from an anthropological perspective. *In* Perspectives on American folk art, ed. by I. M. G. Quimby and S. T. Swank p247-92

**Art and literature**

Ashton, D. Cézanne in the shadow of Frenhofer. *In* Ashton, D. A fable of modern art p30-47

Ashton, D. Picasso and Frenhofer. *In* Ashton, D. A fable of modern art p75-95

Ashton, D. Rilke in search of the uttermost. *In* Ashton, D. A fable of modern art p48-74

Peyre, H. Symbolism, painting, and music. *In* Peyre, H. What is symbolism? p112-27

Tomlinson, C. The poet as painter. *In* Royal Society of Literature of the United Kingdom, London. Essays by divers hands: innovation in contemporary literature, new ser. v40 p147-62

**Art and mental illness**

Trilling, L. Literary pathology. *In* Trilling, L. Speaking of literature and society p392-97

Trilling, L. Neurosis and the health of the artist. *In* Trilling, L. Speaking of literature and society. p224-29

**Art and nature.** See Nature (Aesthetics)

**Art and religion**

Harbison, R. Religion as art. *In* Harbison, R. Deliberate regression p63-93

*See also* Christian art and symbolism

**Art and revolutions.** See Socialist realism in art

**Art and society**

Gombrich, Sir E. H. J. The logic of vanity fair: alternatives to historicism in the study of fashions, style and taste. *In* Gombrich, Sir E. H. J. Ideals and idols p60-92

Mellor, D. British art in the 1930s: some economic, political and cultural structures. *In* Class, culture and social change, ed. by F. Gloversmith p185-207

**Art and state.** See Art and society

**Art and technology**

Gorove, M. Computer impact on society: a personal view from the world of art. *In* Monster or messiah? Ed. by W. M. Mathews p 125-41

*See also* Computer art

**Art appreciation**

Duncan, R. F. H. Merit is always recognised. *In* Lying truth, ed. by R. Duncan and M. Weston-Smith p11-15

**Art criticism**

Alpers, S. Style is what you make it: the visual arts once again. *In* The Concept of style, ed. by B. Lang p95-117

Wollheim, R. Pictorial style: two views. *In* The Concept of style, ed. by B. Lang p129-45

**Art in literature**

Ashton, D. Who was Frenhofer? *In* Ashton, D. A fable of modern art p9-29

Cooke, J. 'Tis mysterious surely and fantastic strange: art and artists in three plays of George Fitzmaurice. *In* Irish Renaissance annual I p32-55

**Art museums**

Gombrich, Sir E. H. J. The museum: past, present and future. *In* Gombrich, Sir E. H. J. Ideals and idols p189-204

**Artaud, Antonin**

### About

Deleuze, G. The schizophrenic and language: surface and depth in Lewis Carroll and Antonin Artaud. *In* Textual strategies, ed. by J. V. Harari p277-95

**Arthurian romances**

Pickering, F. P. The 'fortune' of Hartmann's Erec. *In* Pickering, F. P. Essays on medieval German literature and iconography p110-29

Vinaver, E. Landmarks in Arthurian romance. *In* The Expansion and transformations of courtly literature, ed. by N. B. Smith and J. T. Snow p 17-31

Vinaver, E. The questioning knight. *In* The Binding of Proteus, ed. by M. W. McCune, T. Orbison and P. M. Withim p126-40

**Artificial intelligence**

Dennett, D. C. Artificial intelligence as philosophy and as psychology. *In* Philosophical perspectives in artificial intelligence, ed. by M. Ringle p57-78

Dreyfus, H. L. A framework for misrepresenting knowledge. *In* Philosophical perspectives in artificial intelligence, ed. by M. Ringle p124-56

Lehnert, W. Representing physical objects in memory. *In* Philosophical perspectives in artificial intelligence, ed. by M. Ringle p81-109

McCarthy, J. Ascribing mental qualities to machines. *In* Philosophical perspectives in artificial intelligence, ed. by M. Ringle p161-95

McDermott, J. Representing knowledge in intelligent systems. *In* Philosophical perspectives in artificial intelligence, ed. by M. Ringle p110-23

Minsky, M. L. Computer science and the representation of knowledge. *In* The Computer age: a twenty-year view, ed. by M. L. Dertouzos and J. Moses p393-421

Papert, S. The role of artificial intelligence in psychology. *In* Language and learning, ed. by M. Piattelli-Palmarini p90-99

**Artificial intelligence—**Continued

Pylyshyn, Z. W. Complexity and the study of artificial and human intelligence. In Philosophical perspectives in artificial intelligence, ed. by M. Ringle p23-56

Rey, G. Functionalism and the emotions. In Explaining emotions, ed. by A. O. Rorty p163-95

Ringle, M. Philosophy and artificial intelligence. In Philosophical perspectives in artificial intelligence, ed. by M. Ringle p 1-20

Sayre, K. M. The simulation of epistemic acts. In Philosophical perspectives in artificial intelligence, ed. by M. Ringle p139-60

Schank, R. C. Natural language, philosophy, and artificial intelligence. In Philosophical perspectives in artificial intelligence, ed. by M. Ringle p196-224

Simon, T. W. Philosophical objections to programs as theories. In Philosophical perspectives in artificial intelligence, ed. by M. Ringle p225-42

**Artificial satellites in telecommunication**

Coppa, F. J. The global impact of television: an overview. In Screen and society, ed. by F. J. Coppa p 1-29

**Artificial thinking.** See Artificial intelligence

**Artisans**

### New Jersey—Newark

Hirsch, S. E. From artisan to manufacturer: industrialization and the small producer in Newark, 1830-60. In Small business in American life, ed. by S. W. Bruchey p80-99

### South Carolina—Charleston

Walsh, R. The revolutionary Charleston mechanic. In Small business in American life, ed. by S. W. Bruchey p49-79

**Artists.** See Architects as artists

**Artists in literature**

Ashton, D. Who was Frenhofer? In Ashton, D. A fable of modern art p9-29

Cooke, J. 'Tis mysterious surely and fantastic strange: art and artists in three plays of George Fitzmaurice. In Irish Renaissance annual I p32-55

**Arts**

Meyer, L. B. The dilemma of choosing: speculations about contemporary culture. In Value and values in evolution, ed. by E. A. Maziarz p117-41

### Philosophy

Duncan, R. F. H. Merit is always recognised. In Lying truths, ed. by R. Duncan and M. Weston-Smith p11-15

Tomlin, E. W. F. Novelty is the chief aim in art. In Lying truths, ed. by R. Duncan and M. Weston-Smith p231-40

### Great Britain—History

Fehl, P. P. Poetry and the entry of the fine arts into England: ut pictura poesis. In The Age of Milton, ed. by C. A. Patrides and R. B. Waddington p273-306

**Arts, Classical**

Manley, L. G. Art and nature in antiquity. In Manley, L. G. Convention, 1500-1750 p25-36

**Arts, French**

Peyre, H. Symbolism, painting, and music. In Peyre, H. What is symbolism? p112-27

**Arts, Renaissance**

Manley, L. G. Art, nature, and convention. In Manley, L. G. Convention, 1500-1750 p15-25

**Arts and crafts movement**

Harbison, R. Art as religion. In Harbison, R. Deliberate regression p94-114

**Arts and society**

Brustein, R. S. The artist and the citizen. In Brustein, R. S. Critical moments p79-86

**Arts in the church.** See Christian art and symbolism

**Arutiunov, S.**

Enthnography and linguistics. In Soviet and Western anthropology, ed. by E. Gellner p257-63

**Arutyonov, S.** See Arutiunov, S.

**Ascension of Christ.** See Jesus Christ—Ascension

**Asch, Nathan**

### About individual works
*Pay day*

Trilling, L. The promise of realism. In Trilling, L. Speaking of literature and society p27-33

**Ashanti folk-lore.** See Folk-lore, Ashanti

**Ashantis**

### Religion

Pelton, R. D. Ananse: spinner of Ashanti doubleness. In Pelton, R. D. The trickster in West Africa p25-70

**Ashbery, John**

### About

Howard, R. John Ashbery: "You may never know how much is pushed back into the night, nor what may return." In Howard, R. Alone with America p25-56

Molesworth, C. "This leaving-out business": the poetry of John Ashbery. In Molesworth, C. The fierce embrace p163-83

**Ashton, Dore**

A fable of modern art

*Contents*

Arnold Schoenberg's ascent
Cézanne in the shadow of Frenhofer
Picasso and Frenhofer
Rilke in search of the uttermost
Who was Frenhofer?

**Ashton, Robert**

Tradition and innovation and the Great Rebellion. In Three British revolutions: 1641, 1688, 1776, ed. by J. G. A. Pocock p208-23

**Ashton, Rosemary D.**

The German idea

*Contents*

Carlyle and German philosophy (1824-34).
Carlyle and Goethe (1822-32)
Carlyle, the Germanist of the Edinburgh Review (1827)
Coleridge and Faust (1814-20)
Coleridge and German 'aesthetics' (1802-18)
Coleridge and Germany (1794-1800)
Coleridge and Kant (1801-25)
George Eliot and Goethe (1854-76)
George Eliot, translator of Strauss (1844-6)
Lewes and German aesthetics (1840-5)
Lewes and German philosophy
Lewes and Goethe (1843-55)
Lewes: one of Carlyle's 'young men' (1835-9)
More translation: Spinoza and Feuerbach (1849-54)
The pros and cons of the German genius
Sartor resartus, a beginning and an end (1830-4)

**Asia**

Foreign relations—United States

Scalapino, R. A. Asia. *In* The United States in the 1980s, ed. by P. Duignan and A. Rabushka p661-706

Literatures

*See* Oriental literature

**Asia, East.** See East Asia

**Asia, Southeastern**

Historiography

Hall, J. W. East, Southeast, and South Asia. *In* The Past before us, ed. by M. Kammen p157-86

**Asia, Western.** See Near East

**Asian literature.** See Oriental literature

**Asimakopulos, A.**

Tax incidence. *In* A Guide to post-Keynesian economics, ed. by A. S. Eichner p61-70

**Assessment, Landscape.** See Landscape assessment

**Associations, institutions, etc.**

United States

Steigerwalt, A. K. Organized business groups. *In* Encyclopedia of American economic history, ed. by G. Porter v2 p753-71

**Assyrian literature.** *See* Assyro-Babylonian literature

**Assyro-Babylonian civilization.** See Civilization, Assyro-Babylonian

**Assyro-Babylonian inscriptions.** See Cuneiform inscriptions

**Assyro-Babylonian literature**

*See also* Cuneiform inscriptions

History and criticism

Finkelstein, J. J. Early Mesopotamia, 2500-1000 B.C. *In* Propaganda and communication in world history, ed. by H. D. Lasswell, D. Lerner and H. Speier v 1 p50-110

Strand, W. E. In search of an Assyrian sense of humor. *In* 5000 years of popular culture, ed. by F. E. H. Schroeder p38-51

**Assyro-Babylonian propaganda.** See Propaganda, Assyro-Babylonian

**Astell, Mary**

About

Perry, R. The veil of chastity: Mary Astell's feminism. *In* Studies in eighteenth-century culture v9 p25-43

**Astrology in literature**

Loomis, D. B. Constance and stars. *In* Chaucerian problems and perspectives, ed. by E. Vasta and Z. P. Thundy p207-20

**Astronomy**

*See also* Radio astronomy

History—United States

Warner, D. J. Astronomy in antebellum America. *In* The Sciences in the American context: new perspectives, ed. by N. Reingold p55-75

**Athens**

History

Tracy, S. V. Athens in 100 B.C. *In* Harvard Studies in classical philology, v83 p213-35

**Atkinson, Edward**

About individual works

*A single tax upon land*

Truehart, W. B. Atkinson: an ill-informed assailant. *In* Critics of Henry George, ed. by R. V. Andelson p254-60

**Atkinson, Ross**

An application of semiotics to the definition of bibliography. *In* Virginia. University. Bibliographical Society. Studies in bibliography v33 p54-73

**Atkinson, Ti-Grace**

About

Rapaport, E. On the future of love: Rousseau and the radical feminists. *In* The Philosophy of sex, ed. by A. Soble p369-88

**Atomic warfare**

Hoeber, A. M. and Douglass, J. D. Soviet approach to global nuclear conflict. *In* The United States in the 1980s, ed. by P. Duignan and A. Rabushka p445-67

Speier, H. The chances for peace. *In* Propaganda and communication in world history, ed. by H. D. Lasswell, D. Lerner and H. Speier v2 p507-27

*See also* Atomic weapons

**Atomic weapons**

Teller, E. Technology: the imbalance of power. *In* The United States in the 1980s, ed. by P. Duignan and A. Rabushka p497-534

Van Cleave, W. R. Quick fixes to U.S. strategic nuclear forces. *In* National security in the 1980s: from weakness to strength, ed. by W. S. Thompson p89-107

Zumwalt, E. R. Heritage of weakness: an assessment of the 1970s. *In* National security in the 1980s: from weakness to strength, ed. by W. S. Thompson p17-51

**Atomic weapons and disarmament**

Moynihan, D. P. Cold dawn, high noon. *In* Moynihan, D. P. Counting our blessings p277-336

**Atonement, Day of.** See Yom Kippur

**Attitude (Psychology)** See Frustration

**Attman, Artur**

Man's use of nature's gifts: a historical survey. *In* The Condition of man, ed. by P. Hallberg p35-38

**Atuot (African people)** See Atwot (African people)

**Atwood, Margaret Eleanor**

About individual works

*Surfacing*

Christ, C. P. Refusing to be victim: Margaret Atwood. *In* Christ, C. P. Diving deep and surfacing p41-53

**Atwot (African people)**

Religion

Burton, J. W. The village and the cattle camp: aspects of Atuot religion. *In* Explorations in African systems of thought, ed. by I. C. Karp & C. S. Bird p268-97

**Auden, Wystan Hugh**

About

Gloversmith, F. Changing things: Orwell and Auden. *In* Class, culture and social change, ed. by F. Gloversmith p101-41

Kettle, A. W. H. Auden: poetry and politics in the thirties. *In* Culture and crisis in Britain in the thirties, ed. by J. Clark and others p83-101

About individual works

*City without walls, and other poems*

Vendler, H. H. W. H. Auden. *In* Vendler, H. H. Part of nature, part of us p91-95

**Audiences, Theater.** See Theater audiences

**Audiences, Television.** See Television audiences

**Auditory perception**

Marler, P. Development of auditory perception in relation to vocal behavior. *In* Human ethology, ed. by M. von Cranach [and others] p663-81

*See also* Speech perception

**Aue, Hartmann von.** See Hartmann von Aue

**Aufklärung (The German word)**

Rotenstreich, N. Enlightenment: between Mendelssohn and Kant. *In* Studies in Jewish religious and intellectual history, ed. by S. Stein and R. Loewe p263-79

**Augustine, fl. 655**

### About individual works
#### De mirabilus sacrae scripturae

Schapiro, M. An Irish-Latin text on the angel with the ram in Abraham's sacrifice. *In* Schapiro, M. Selected papers v3: Late antique, early Christian and mediaeval art p307-18

**Augustine, Saint, Bp. of Hippo.** See Augustinus, Aurelius, Saint, Bp. of Hippo

**Augustinus, fl. 655.** See Augustine, fl. 655

**Augustinus, Aurelius, Saint, Bp. of Hippo**

### About

Montgomery, R. L. Faculty psychology and theories of imagination: Aristotle, Plato, Augustine, and Aquinas. *In* Montgomery, R. L. The reader's eye p13-49

Ozment, S. H. The scholastic traditions. *In* Ozment, S. H. The age of reform, 1250-1550 p22-72

### About individual works
#### Confessions

Crosson, F. Religion and faith in St Augustine's Confessions. *In* Rationality and religious belief, ed. by C. F. Delaney p152-68

Spengemann, W. C. The formal paradigm. *In* Spengemann, W. C. The forms of autobiography p 1-33

**Aureola (Art)** See Nimbus (Art)

**Aurispa, Giovanni**

### About

Lutz, C. E. Two Renaissance dialogues in the manner of Lucian. *In* Lutz, C. E. The oldest library motto, and other library essays p92-98

**Aurobindo, Sri.** See Ghose, Aurobindo

**Austen, Jane**

### About

Macdonald, S. P. Jane Austen and the tradition of the absent mother. *In* The Lost tradition: mothers and daughters in literature, ed. by C. N. Davidson and E. M. Broner p58-69

### About individual works
#### Emma

Hilliard, R. F. Emma: dancing without space to turn in. *In* Probability, time, and space in eighteenth-century literature, ed. by P. R. Backscheider p275-98

Polhemus, R. M. Austen's Emma: the comedy of union. *In* Polhemus, R. M. Comic faith p24-59

Todd, J. Social friendship: Jane Austen's Emma. *In* Todd, J. Women's friendship in literature p274-301

#### Mansfield Park

Nabokov, V. V. Jane Austen: Mansfield Park. *In* Nabokov, V. V. Lectures on literature p9-61

Todd, J. Social friendship: Jane Austen's Mansfield Park. *In* Todd, J. Women's friendship in literature p246-74

#### Sense and sensibility

Hagstrum, J. H. The aftermath of sensibility: Sterne, Goethe, and Austen. *In* Hagstrum, J. H. Sex and sensibility p247-77

**Austin, Deborah**

Threefold Blake's divine vision, intention, and myth. *In* The Binding of Proteus, ed. by M. W. McCune, T. Orbison and P. M. Withim p79-96

**Austria**

### Civilization—History

Schorske, C. E. Generational tension and cultural change: reflections on the case of Vienna. *In* Generations, ed. by S. R. Graubard p111-22

### Politics and government—1945-

Mommsen-Reindl, M. Austria. *In* Western European party systems, ed. by P. H. Merkl p278-97

Wolfschütz, H. The emergence and development of the Second Republic. *In* Modern Austrian writing, ed. by A. Best and H. Wolfschütz p 1-22

### Social conditions

Wolfschütz, H. The emergence and development of the Second Republic. *In* Modern Austrian writing, ed. by A. Best and H. Wolfschütz p 1-22

**Authoritarianism**

Cardoso, F. H. On the characterization of authoritarian regimes in Latin America. *In* The New authoritarianism in Latin America, ed. by D. Collier p33-57

Collier, D. S. The bureaucratic-authoritarian model: synthesis and priorities for future research. *In* The New authoritarianism in Latin America, ed. by D. Collier p363-97

Collier, D. S. Overview of the bureaucratic-authoritarian model. *In* The New authoritarianism in Latin America, ed. by D. Collier p19-32

Hirschman, A. O. The turn to authoritarianism in Latin America and the search for its economic determinants. *In* The new authoritarianism in Latin America, ed. by D. Collier p61-98

Kaufman, R. R. Industrial change and authoritarian rule in Latin America: a concrete review of the bureaucratic-authoritarian model. *In* The New authoritarianism in Latin America, ed. by D. Collier p165-253

O'Donnell, G. A. Tensions in the bureaucratic-authoritarian state and the question of democracy. *In* The New authoritarianism in Latin America, ed. by D. Collier p285-318

Serra, J. M. Three mistaken theses regarding the connection between industrialization and authoritarian regimes. *In* The New authoritarianism in Latin America, ed. by D. Collier p99-163

*See also* Authority

**Authority**

Baum, R. C. Authority and identity: the case for evolutionary invariance. *In* Identity and authority, ed. by R. Robertson and B. Holzner p61-118

Fenn, R. K. Religion, identity and authority in the secular society. *In* Identity and authority, ed. by R. Robertson and B. Holzner p119-44

**Authority**—*Continued*

Holzner, B. and Robertson, R. Identity and authority; a problem analysis of processes of identification and authorization. *In* Identity and authority, ed. by R. Robertson and B. Holzner p1-39

Kavolis, V. Logics of selfhood and modes of order: civilizational structures for individual identities. *In* Identity and authority, ed. by R. Robertson and B. Holzner p40-62

La Barre, W. Authority, culture change, and the courts. *In* La Barre, W. Culture in context p215-24

Swanson, G. E. A basis of authority and identity in post-industrial society. *In* Identity and authority, ed. by R. Robertson and B. Holzner p190-217

*See also* Authoritarianism

**Authors**

*See also* Women authors

### Political and social views

Cunningham, V. Neutral?: 1930s writers and taking sides. *In* Class, culture and social change, ed. by F. Gloversmith p45-69

**Authors, Afro-American.** See Afro-American authors

**Authors, Black**

### Uruguay

Jackson, R. L. The black writer, the black press, and the black diaspora in Uruguay. *In* Jackson, R. L. Black writers in Latin America p93-111

**Authors, English**

### 19th century—History and criticism

Farrell, J. P. Tragedy and ideology. *In* Farrell, J. P. Revolution as tragedy p281-90

**Authors and patrons**

Ranum, O. Chapelain and the royal patronage of history. *In* Ranum, O. Artisans of glory p169-96

Ranum, O. Glancing backward and forward. *In* Ranum, O. Artisans of glory p333-40

Ranum, O. The historiographers royal. *In* Ranum, O. Artisans of glory p58-102

Ranum, O. Men of letters: sixteenth-century models of conduct. *In* Ranum, O. Artisans of glory p26-57

Ranum, O. Patronage and history from Richelieu to Colbert. *In* Ranum, O. Artisans of glory p148-68

**Authors and publishers**

### Germany

Unseld, S. Bertolt Brecht and his publishers. *In* Unseld, S. The author and his publisher p83-125

Unseld, S. Hermann Hesse and his publishers. *In* Unseld, S. The author and his publishers p45-81

Unseld, S. The responsibilities of a literary publisher. *In* Unseld, S. The author and his publisher p 1-44

Unseld, S. Robert Walser and his publishers. *In* Unseld, S. The author and his publisher p191-273

**Authors and readers**

Brooke-Rose, C. The readerhood of man. *In* The Reader in the text, ed. by S. R. Suleiman and I. Crosman p120-48

Crosman, R. T. Do readers make meaning? *In* The Reader in the text, ed. by S. R. Suleiman and I. Crosman p149-64

Iser, W. Interaction between text and reader. *In* The Reader in the text, ed. by S. R. Suleiman and I. Crosman p106-19

Valentine, R. Y. Cortazar's rhetoric of reader participation. *In* The Analysis of literary texts, ed. by R. D. Pope p212-23

*See also* Books and reading

**Authors as teachers**

Trilling, L. A valedictory. *In* Trilling, L. Speaking of literature and society p398-406

**Authors take sides on the Spanish War**

Cunningham, V. Neutral?: 1930s writers and taking sides. *In* Class, culture and social change, ed. by F. Gloversmith p45-69

**Authorship**

Blythe, R. The writer as listener. *In* Royal Society of Literature of the United Kingdom, London. Essays by divers hands: innovation in contemporary literature, new ser. v40 p 1-14

Collis, J. S. Forward to nature. *In* Royal Society of Literature of the United Kingdom, London. Essays by divers hands: innovation in contemporary literature, new ser. v40 p34-51

*See also* Autobiography; Biography (as a literary form); Children's literature—Technique; Imitation (in literature)

**Autobiography**

Bloom, L. Z. Heritages: dimensions of mother-daughter relationships in women's autobiographies. *In* The Lost tradition: mothers and daughters in literature, ed. by C. N. Davidson and E. M. Broner p291-303

Bruss, E. W. Eye for I: making and unmaking autobiography in film. *In* Autobiography: essays theoretical and critical, ed. by J. Olney p296-320

Gusdorf, G. Conditions and limits of autobiography. *In* Autobiography: essays theoretical and critical, ed. by J. Olney p28-48

Howarth, W. L. Some principles of autobiography. *In* Autobiography: essays theoretical and critical, ed. by J. Olney p84-114

Izevbaye, D. Issues in the reassessment of the African novel. *In* African literature today no. 10: Retrospect & prospect, ed. by E. D. Jones p7-31

Kazin, A. The self as history: reflections on autobiography. *In* Telling lives, ed. by M. Pachter p74-89

Mandel, B. J. Full of life now. *In* Autobiography: theoretical and critical, ed. by J. Olney p49-72

Mason, M. G. The other voice: autobiographies of women writers. *In* Autobiography: essays theoretical and critical, ed. by J. Olney p207-35

Olney, J. L. Autobiography and the cultural moment: a thematic, historical, and bibliographical introduction. *In* Autobiography: essays theoretical and critical, ed. by J. Olney p3-27

Olney, J. L. Some versions of memory/some versions of bios: the ontology of autobiography. *In* Autobiography: essays theoretical and critical, ed. by J. Olney p236-67

Renza, L. A. The veto of the imagination: a theory of autobiography. *In* Autobiography: essays theoretical and critical, ed. by J. Olney p268-95

Rosenblatt, R. Black autobiography: life as the death weapon. *In* Autobiography: essays theoretical and critical, ed. by J. Olney p169-80

Sayre, R. F. Autobiography and the making of America. *In* Autobiography: essays theoretical and critical, ed. by J. Olney p146-68

**Autobiography**—*Continued*

Spender, S. Confessions and autobiography; excerpt from "The making of a poem." *In* Autobiography: essays theoretical and critical, ed. by J. Olney p115-22

Spengemann, W. C. Afterword. *In* Spengemann, W. C. The forms of autobiography p166-69

Spengemann, W. C. Introduction. *In* Spengemann, W. C. The forms of autobiography p xi-xvii

Sprinker, J. M. Fictions of the self: the end of autobiography. *In* Autobiography: essays theoretical and critical, ed. by J. Olney p321-42

Starobinski, J. The style of autobiography. *In* Autobiography: essays theoretical and critical, ed. by J. Olney p73-83

### Bibliography

Spengemann, W. C. The study of autobiography: a bibliographical essay. *In* Spengemann, W. C. The forms of autobiography p170-213

### Friends (Quaker) authors

*See* Autobiography—Quaker authors

### History and criticism

*See* Autobiography

### Quaker authors

Edkins, C. Quest for community: spiritual autobiographies of eighteenth-century Quaker and Puritan women in America. *In* Women's autobiography, ed. by E. C. Jelinek p39-52

### Technique

*See* Autobiography

### Women authors

Blackburn, R. In search of the black female self: African-American women's autobiographies and ethnicity. *In* Women's autobiography, ed. by E. C. Jelinek p 133-48

Bloom, L. Z. and Holder, O. Anaïs Nin's Diary in context. *In* Women's autobiography, ed. by E. C. Jelinek p206-20

Jelinek, E. C. Introduction: women's autobiography and the male tradition. *In* Women's autobiography, ed. by E. C. Jelinek p 1-20

Juhasz, S. Towards a theory of form in feminist autobiography: Kate Millett's Flying and Sita; Maxine Hong Kingston's The woman warrior. *In* Women's autobiography, ed. by E. C. Jelinek p221-37

Pomerleau, C. S. The emergence of women's autobiography in England. *In* Women's autobiography, ed. by E. C. Jelinek p21-38

Spacks, P. M. Selves in hiding. *In* Women's autobiography, ed. by E. C. Jelinek p112-32

Winston, E. The autobiographer and her readers: from apology to affirmation. *In* Women's autobiography, ed. by E. C. Jelinek p93-111

**Automation**

### Social aspects

Bell, D. The social framework of the information society. *In* The Computer age: a twenty-year view, ed. by M. L. Dertouzos and J. Moses p163-211

Dertouzos, M. L. Individualized automation. *In* The Computer age: a twenty-year view, ed. by M. L. Dertouzos and J. Moses p38-55

**Automobile industry and trade**

### United States—History

Flink, J. J. Automobile. *In* Encyclopedia of American economic history, ed. by G. Porter v3 p1168-93

**Automobiles**

### Social aspects

*See* Automobile industry and trade

**Autumn sonata (Motion picture)**

Kael, P. Tentacles. *In* Kael, P. When the lights go down p476-81

Kauffmann, S. Autumn sonata. *In* Kauffmann, S. Before my eyes p79-86

**Avant-garde (Aesthetics)**

Stimpson, C. R. The power to name: some reflections on the avant-garde. *In* The Prism of sex, ed. by J. A. Sherman and E. T. Beck p55-77

**Avant-garde theater.** See Experimental theater

**Avellaneda, Gertrudis Gómez de.** See Gómez de Avellaneda y Artega, Gertrudis

**Average.** See Mean (Philosophy)

**Averill, James R.**

Emotion and anxiety: sociocultural, biological, and psychological determinants. *In* Explaining emotions, ed. by A. O. Rorty p37-72

**Averkieva, Yu Petrova-** See Petrova-Averkieva, Yu

**Averroës**

### About individual works

*Tahafut al-Tahafut (The incoherence of the incoherence)*

Ivry, A. L. Averroes on causation. *In* Studies in Jewish religious and intellectual history, ed. by S. Stein and R. Loewe p143-56

**Avery, Gillian Elise**

Children's books and social history. *In* Research about nineteenth-century children and books, ed. by S. K. Richardson p23-40

The researcher's craft: designs and implements. *In* Research about nineteenth-century children and books, ed. by S. K. Richardson p7-22

### Books and reading

Avery, G. E. The researcher's craft: designs and implements. *In* Research about nineteenth-century children and books, ed. by S. K. Richardson p7-22

**Avicebron.** See Ibn Gabirol, Solomon ben Judah

**Avineri, Shlomo**

The new Jerusalem of Moses Hess. *In* Powers, possessions and freedom, ed. by A. Kontos p107-18

**Awoonor, Kofi**

### About individual works

*This earth, my brother*

Ojo-Ade, F. Madness in the African novel: Awoonor's This earth, my brother. *In* African literature today no. 10: Retrospect & prospect, ed. by E. D. Jones p134-52

**Ayer, Sir Alfred Jules**

Replies. *In* Perception and identity, ed. by G. F. Macdonald p277-333

### Knowledge, Theory of

Pears, D. F. A comparison between Ayer's views about the privileges of sense-datum statements and the views of Russell and Austin. *In* Perception and identity, ed. by G. F. Macdonald p61-83

**Ayer, Sir Alfred J.**—Knowledge, Theory of
—*Continued*
Williams, B. A. O. Another time, another place, another person. *In* Perception and identity, ed. by G. F. Macdonald p252-61

### Logic
Wiggins, D. Ayer on monism, pluralism and essence. *In* Perception and identity, ed. by G. F. Macdonald p131-60

### Metaphysics
Körner, S. Ayer on metaphysics. *In* Perception and identity, ed. by G. F. Macdonald p262-76

**Aylmer, Gerald Edward**
Crisis and regrouping in the political elites: England from the 1630s to the 1660s. *In* Three British revolutions: 1641, 1688, 1776, ed. by J. G. A. Pocock p140-62
The historical background. *In* The Age of Milton, ed. by C. A. Patrides and R. B. Waddington p 1-33

**Aymara Indians**
La Barre, W. Aymara folklore and folk temperament. *In* La Barre, W. Culture in context p253-57

**Aymara folk-lore.** See Folk-lore, Aymara

**Azevedo, Thales de**
The "chapel" as symbol: Italian colonization in southern Brazil. *In* Brazil, anthropological perspectives, ed. by M. L. Margolis and W. E. Carter p86-95

# B

**Babilot, George**
Dixwell: animadversions of an admiring adversary. *In* Critics of Henry George, ed. by R. V. Andelson p165-77
Moffat's "unorthodox" critique. *In* Critics of Henry George, ed. by R. V. Andelson p109-25

**Babylonian civilization.** See Civilization, Assyro-Babylonian

**Babylonian inscriptions.** See Cuneiform inscriptions

**Babylonian literature.** See Assyro-Babylonian literature

**Bacarisse, Salvador**
Abaddón, el exterminador: Sabato's gnostic eschatology. *In* Contemporary Latin American fiction, ed. by S. Bacarisse p88-109

**Bacarisse, Pamela**
El obsceno pájaro de la noche: a willed process of evasion. *In* Contemporary Latin American fiction, ed. by S. Bacarisse p18-33

**Bache, Alexander Dallas**

### About
Post, R. C. Science, public policy, and popular precepts: Alexander Dallas Bache and Alfred Beach as symbolic adversaries. *In* The Sciences in the American context: new perspectives, ed. by N. Reingold p77-98

**Bäckström, Signe Landgren-** See Landgren-Bäckström, Signe

**Backward areas.** See Underdeveloped areas

**Bacteria**
Morowitz, H. J. Bulls, bears, and bacteria. *In* Morowitz, H. J. The wine of life, and other essays on societies, energy & living things p73-76

Morowitz, H. J. On first looking into Bergey's Manual. *In* Morowitz, H. J. The wine of life, and other essays on societies, energy & living things p103-06
Morowitz, H. J. Pumping iron. *In* Morowitz, H. J. The wine of life, and other essays on societies, energy & living things p99-102

**Baeck, Leo**

### About individual works
*The essence of Judaism*
Rosenzweig, F. Apologetic thinking. *In* The Jew, ed. by A. A. Cohen p262-72

**Baelz, P. R.**
Suicide: some theological reflections. *In* Suicide: the philosophical issues, ed. by M. P. Battin and D. J. Mayo p71-83

**Baganda**
Ray, B. The story of Kintu: myth, death, and ontology in Buganda. *In* Explorations in African systems of thought, ed. by I. C. Karp & C. S. Bird p60-79

**Bahm, Archie J.**
Humanist ethics as the science of oughtness. *In* Humanist ethics, ed. by M. B. Storer p210-26

**Baier, Annette**
Master passions. *In* Explaining emotions, ed. by A. O. Rorty p403-23

**Baier, Kurt Erich**
Freedom, obligation, and responsibility. *In* Humanist ethics, ed. by M. B. Storer p75-97

**Bailey, David Roy Shackleton**
On Cicero's speeches. *In* Harvard Studies in classical philology, v83 p237-85

**Bain, David**
Plautus uortit barbare: Plautus, Bacchides 526-61 and Menander, Dis exapaton 102-12. *In* Creative imitation and Latin literature, ed. by D. West and T. Woodman p17-34

**Bakshi, Ralph**

### About individual works
*Coonskin*
Kauffmann, S. Coonskin. *In* Kauffmann, S. Before my eyes p165-68

**Balance of power**
Teller, E. Technology: the imbalance of power. *In* The United States in the 1980s, ed. by P. Duignan and A. Rabushka p497-534

**Bald, Robert Cecil**
Early copyright litigation and its bibliographical interest. *In* The Bibliographical Society of America, 1904-79 p172-87

**Baldwin, James, 1924-**

### About individual works
*Another country*
Wilson, R. N. James Baldwin: relationships of love and race. *In* Wilson, R. N. The writer as social seer p89-104

*Go tell it on the mountain*
Wilson, R. N. James Baldwin: relationships of love and race. *In* Wilson, R. N. The writer as social seer p89-104

**Baldwin, John**
Ecological and areal studies in Great Britain and the United States. *In* Crime and justice v 1 p29-66

**Ball, Nicole.** See Leitenberg, M. jt. auth.

**Ballad-sheets.** See Broadsides

**Ballade**
Zumthor, P. A reading of a ballade by Jean Meschinot. *In* The Interpretation of medieval lyric poetry, ed. by W. T. H. Jackson p142-62

**Ballads, English**

### History and criticism
Waage, F. O. Social themes in urban broadsides of Renaissance England. *In* 5000 years of popular culture, ed. by F. E. H. Schroeder p242-54

**Balzac, Honoré de**

### About individual works
*The country doctor*
Plomer, W. C. F. Lenin's favourite novel. *In* Plomer, W. C. F. Electric delights p45-49

*The girl with the golden eyes*
Festa-McCormick, D. Balzac's Girl with the golden eyes: Parisian masks, not faces. *In* Festa-McCormick, D. The city as catalyst p19-32

*The unknown masterpieces*
Ashton, D. Who was Frenhofer? *In* Ashton, D. A fable of modern art p9-29

### Characters—Frenhofer
Ashton, D. Who was Frenhofer? *In* Ashton, D. A fable of modern art p9-29

**Bamborough, J. B.**
Burton and Cardan. *In* English Renaissance studies, ed. by J. Carey p180-93

**Bandura, Albert**
Psychological mechanisms of aggression. *In* Human ethology, ed. by M. von Cranach [and others] p316-56

**Banfield, Ann**
The nature of evidence in a falsifiable literary theory. *In* The Concept of style, ed. by B. Lang p183-211

**Banfield, Edward C.**
In defense of the American party system. *In* Political parties in the eighties, ed. by R. A. Goldwin p133-49
Party "reform" in retrospect. *In* Political parties in the eighties, ed. by R. A. Goldwin p20-33
Policy science as metaphysical madness. *In* Bureaucrats, policy analysts, statesmen: who leads? Ed. by R. A. Goldwin p 1-19

### About individual works
*Policy science as metaphysical madness*
Moore, M. H. Statesmanship in a world of particular substantive choices. *In* Bureaucrats, policy analysts, statesmen: who leads? Ed. by R. A. Goldwin p20-36

**Baniabungu (African people)** See Bashi (African people)

**Banim, John**

### About individual works
*The Nowlans*
Cronin, J. John Banim: The Nowlans. *In* Cronin, J. The Anglo-Irish novel, v 1 p41-58

**Banking.** See Banks and banking

**Banks, Central.** See Banks and banking, Central

**Banks and banking**
*See also* Banks and banking, Central

### State supervision
*See* Banks and banking, Central

**United States—History**
Green, G. D. Financial intermediaries. *In* Encyclopedia of American economic history, ed. by G. Porter v2 p707-26
Sylla, R. E. Small-business banking in the United States, 1780-1920. *In* Small business in American life, ed. by S. W. Bruchey p240-62

**Banks and banking, Central**

### United States—History
Trescott, P. Central banking. *In* Encyclopedia of American economic history, ed. by G. Porter v2 p737-52

**Banks of issue.** See Banks and banking, Central

**Bannan, Helen M.**
Spider Woman's web: mothers and daughters in Southwestern native American literature. *In* The Lost tradition: mothers and daughters in literature, ed. by C. N. Davidson and E. M. Broner p268-79

**Bantus.** See Baganda

**Banyaborgo (African people)** See Bashi (African people)

**Baptismal certificates**
Weiser, F. S. Baptismal certificate and gravemaker: Pennsylvania German folk art at the beginning and the end of life. *In* Perspectives on American folk art, ed. by I. M. G. Quimby and S. T. Swank p134-61

**Baraguyu (African people)**
Beidelman, T. O. Women and men in two East African societies. *In* Explorations in African systems of thought, ed. by I. C. Karp & C. S. Bird p143-64

**Baraka, Imamu Amiri.** See Jones, LeRoi

**Barbaro, Daniello**

### About individual works
*Della eloquenza*
Montgomery, R. L. Universals and particulars: Fracastoro and Barbaro. *In* Montgomery, R. L. The reader's eye p93-116

**Barbeau, Anne T.**
The disembodied rebels: psychic origins of rebellion in Absalom and Architophel. *In* Studies in eighteenth-century culture v9 p489-501

**Barber, Benjamin R.**
The undemocratic party system: citizenship in an elite/mass society. *In* Political parties in the eighties, ed. by R. A. Goldwin p34-49

**Barber, C. L.**
The family in Shakespeare's development: tragedy and sacredness. *In* Representing Shakespeare, ed. by M. M. Schwartz and C. Kahn p188-202

**Barbu, Zevedei**
The modern history of political fanaticism: a search for the roots. *In* Propaganda and communication in world history, ed. by H. D. Lasswell, D. Lerner and H. Spier v2 p112-44

**Bards and bardism**
Lewis, C. W. The content of poetry and the crisis in the bardic tradition. *In* A Guide to Welsh literature, ed. by A. O. H. Jarman and G. R. Hughes v2 p88-110
Lewis, C. W. Einion Offeiriad and the bardic grammar. *In* A Guide to Welsh literature, ed. by A. O. H. Jarman and G. R. Hughes v2 p58-86

**Barker, Eileen**
The limits of displacement: two disciplines face each other. *In* Sociology and theology: alliance and conflict, ed. by D. Martin; J. O. Mills and W. S. F. Pickering p 15-23

**Barlow, Joel**

### About individual works

*The Columbiad*

Sutton, W. Apocalyptic history and the American epic: Cotton Mather and Joel Barlow. *In* Toward a new American literary history, ed. by L. J. Budd, E. H. Cady and C. L. Anderson p69-83

**Barnes, Jonathan**

Proof destroyed. *In* Doubt and dogmatism, ed. by M. Schofield, M. Burnyeat and J. Barnes p161-81

Keith, W. J. William Barnes. *In* Keith, W. J. The poetry of nature p67-91

**Barnes, William**

### About

Sutton, M. K. Truth and the pastor's vision in George Crabbe, William Barnes, and R. S. Thomas. *In* Survivals of pastoral, ed. by R. F. Hardin p33-59

**Barnow, Jeffrey**

The philosophical achievement and historical significance of Johann Nicolas Tetens. *In* Studies in eighteenth-century culture v9 p301-35

**Baron, C. E.**

Forster on Lawrence. *In* E. M. Forster: a human exploration, ed. by G. K. Das and J. Beer p186-95

**Baron, Salo Wittmayer**

Civil versus political emancipation. *In* Studies in Jewish religious and intellectual history, ed. by S. Stein and R. Loewe p29-49

**Barrès, Maurice**

### About individual works

*Un homme libre*

Beaujour, M. Exemplary pornography: Barrès, Loyola, and the novel. *In* The Reader in the text, ed. by S. R. Suleiman and I. Crosman p325-49

**Barrett, Clifton Waller**

Some bibliographical adventures in Americana. *In* The Bibliographical Society of America, 1904-79 p229-40

**Barrett, Cyril**

Revolutions in the visual arts. *In* The Context of English literature, 1900-1930, ed. by M. Bell p218-40

**Barrington, Mary Rose**

Apologia for suicide. *In* Suicide: the philosophical issues, ed. by M. P. Battin and D. J. Mayo p90-103

**Barrow, Isaac**

### About

Anselment, R. A. 'Nor foolish talking, nor jesting, which are not convenient.' *In* Anselment, R. A. 'Betwixt jest and earnest' p8-32

**Barrows, Susanna I.**

After the Commune: alcoholism, temperance, and literature in the early Third Republic. *In* Consciousness and class experience in nineteenth-century Europe, ed. by J. M. Merriman p205-18

**Barry, Brian M.**

Justice as reciprocity. *In* Symposium on Theories and Justice in and for the Second Half of the Twentieth Century, Sydney, 1977. Justice p50-78

**Barry Lyndon (Motion picture)**

Kael, P. Kubrick's gilded age. *In* Kael, P. When the lights go down p101-07

Kauffmann, S. Barry Lyndon. *In* Kauffmann, S. Before my eyes p180-83

**Barthes, Roland**

From work to text. *In* Textual strategies, ed. by J. V. Harari p73-81

New critical essays

### Contents

Chateaubriand: life of Rancé
Flaubert and the sentence
Fromentin: Dominique
La Rochefoucauld: "Reflections or sentences and maxims"
Pierre Loti: Aziyadé
The plates of the Encyclopedia
Proust and names
Where to begin?

### About

Kurzweil, E. Roland Barthes: literary structuralism and erotics. *In* Kurzweil, E. The age of structuralism p165-91

Lentricchia, F. Uncovering history and the reader: structuralism. *In* Lentricchia, F. After the New Criticism p102-54

Sturrock, J. Roland Barthes. *In* Structualism and since, ed. by J. Sturrock p52-80

**Bartók, Bela**

### About

Carner, M. The string quartets of Bartók. *In* Carner, M. Major and minor p92-121

**Barton, Anne**

Leontes and the spider: language and speaker in Shakespeare's last plays. *In* Shakespeare's styles, ed. by P. Edwards; I. S. Ewbank, and G. K. Hunter p131-50

**Bartov, Hanokh**

### About individual works

*The brigade*

Alexander, E. Between Diaspora and Zion: Israeli Holocaust fiction. *In* Alexander, E. The resonance of dust p73-118

**Baruch, Elaine Hoffman**

Women and love: some dying myths. *In* The Analysis of literary texts, ed. by R. D. Pope p51-65

**Baruch, Geoff.** See Treacher, A. jt. auth.

**Bary, William Theodore de.** See De Bary, William Theodore

**Basaglia, Franco**

Breaking the circuit of control. *In* Critical psychiatry, ed. by D. Ingleby p184-92

**Bashi (African people)**

Packard, R. M. Social change and the history of misfortune among the Bashu of eastern Zaïre. *In* Explorations in African systems of thought, ed. by I. C. Karp & C. S. Bird p237-67

**Basilov, V.**

The study of religions in Soviet ethnography. *In* Soviet and Western anthropology, ed. by E. Gellner p231-42

**Bass, Nelson Estupiñán.** See Estaupiñán Bass, Nelson

**Bassetto, Corno di,** pseud. See Shaw, George Bernard

**Bassiouni, M. Cherif**

International law and the Holocaust. *In* Encountering the Holocaust: an interdisciplinary survey, ed. by B. L. Sherwin and S. G. Ament p146-88

**Bassnett-McGuire, Susan**

Art and life in Luigi Pirandello's Questa sera si recita a soggetto. *In* Drama and mimesis, ed. by J. Redmond p81-102

Bastos, Augusto Antonio Roa. See Roa Bastos, Augusto Antonio

Bataille, Georges

**About**

Stoekl, A. The death of Acephale and the will to chance: Nietzsche in the text of Bataille. *In* Glyph 6 p42-67

Bately, Janet M.
World history in the Anglo-Saxon Chronicle: its sources and its separateness from the Old English Orosius. *In* Anglo-Saxon England 8 p177-94

Bateso. See Teso tribe

Bateson, Frederick Noel Wilse
Myth—a dispensable critical term. *In* The Binding of Proteus, ed. by M. W. McCune, T. Orbison and P. M. Withim p98-109

Battersby, Christine
Hume, Newton and 'the hill called difficulty.' *In* Royal Institute of Philosophy. Philosophers of the Enlightenment p31-55

Battestin, Martin C.
A Fielding discovery, with some remarks on the canon. *In* Virginia. University. Bibliographical Society. Studies in bibliography v33 p131-43

Battin, M. Pabst
Manipulated suicide. *In* Suicide: the philosophical issues, ed. by M. P. Battin and D. J. Mayo p169-82
Suicide: a fundamental human right? *In* Suicide: the philosophical issues, ed. by M. P. Battin and D. J. Mayo p267-85

The battle of Chile (Motion picture)
Kael, P. The duellists/The battle of Chile. *In* Kael, P. When the lights go down p380-88
Kauffmann, S. The battle of Chile. *In* Kauffmann, S. Before my eyes p303-04

Baudelaire, Charles Pierre

**About**

Collins, D. Baudelaire and bad faith. *In* Collins, D. Sartre as biographer p60-79
Galand, R. Baudelaire and myth. *In* The Binding of Proteus, ed. by M. W. McCune, T. Orbison and P. M. Withim p174-95
Peyre, H. Baudelaire. *In* Peyre, H. What is symbolism? p21-32

**Criticism and interpretation**

Hartman, G. H. The sacred jungle 2: Walter Benjamin. *In* Hartman, G. H. Criticism in the wilderness p63-85

Bauer, Dan F. and Hinnant, John
Normal and revolutionary divination: a Kuhnian approach to African traditional thought. *In* Explorations in African systems of thought, ed. by I. C. Karp & C. S. Bird p213-36

Bauer, Pèter Tamàs
Foreign aid and the Third World. *In* The United States in the 1980s, ed. by P. Duignan and A. Rabushka p559-83

Bauer, Wolfgang

**About**

Rorrison, H. The 'Grazer Gruppe', Peter Handke and Wolfgang Bauer. *In* Modern Austrian writing, ed. by A. Best and H. Wolfschütz p252-66

Baugh, Edward
Since 1960: some highlights. *In* West Indian literature, ed. by B. King p78-94

Baughman, James P.
Management. *In* Encyclopedia of American economic history, ed. by G. Porter v2 p832-48

Baum, Gregory
The sociology of Roman Catholic theology. *In* Sociology and theology: alliance and conflict, ed. by D. Martin, J. O. Mills [and] W. S. F. Pickering p120-35

Baum, Lyman Frank

**About**

Sale, R. H. Baum's magic powder of life. *In* Children's literature v8 p157-63

Baum, Rainer C.
Authority and identity: the case for evolutionary invariance. *In* Identity and authority, ed. by R. Robertson and B. Holzner p61-118

Baumgardt, David
The inner structure of the Yom Kippur liturgy. *In* The Jew, ed. by A. A. Cohen p185-97

Bauschatz, Cathleen M.
Montaigne's conception of reading in the context of Renaissance poetics and modern criticism. *In* The Reader in the text, ed. by S. R. Suleiman and I. Crosman p264-91

Bawden, Nina

**About**

Rees, D. Making the children stretch: Nina Bawden. *In* Rees, D. The marble in the water p128-40
Townsend, J. R. Nina Bawden. *In* Townsend, J. R. A sounding of storytellers p18-29

Baxter, Richard

**About**

Knott, J. R. Richard Baxter and the Saints' rest. *In* Knott, J. R. The sword of the spirit p62-84

**About individual works**

*The Saints' everlasting rest*

Knott, J. R. Richard Baxter and the Saints' rest. *In* Knott, J. R. The sword of the spirit p62-84

Bay Psalm book
Miller, P. Religious background of the Bay Psalm book. *In* Miller, P. The responsibility of mind in a civilization of machines p15-25

Bayley, David H.
Police function, structure, and control in Western Europe and North America: comparative and historical studies. *In* Crime and justice v 1 p109-43

Baym, Nina Zippin
God, father, and lover in Emily Dickinson's poetry. *In* Puritan influences in American literature, ed. by E. Elliot p193-209

Bayo, Kalidu
Environment and national system formation: Gambian orientations toward Senegambia. *In* Values, identities, and national integration, ed. by J. N. Paden p105-19

Bazan, Emilia Pardo. See Pardo Bazán, Emilia, condesa de

Bazin, André

**About**

Kauffmann, S. André Bazin. *In* Kauffmann, S. Before my eyes p385-91

Beach, Alfred Ely

**About**

Post, R. C. Science, public policy, and popular precepts: Alexander Dallas Bache and Alfred Beach as symbolic adversaries. *In* The Sciences in the American context: new perspectives, ed. by N. Reingold p77-98

**Beaconsfield, Benjamin Disraeli, 1st Earl of**

#### About

Berlin, Sir I. Benjamin Disraeli, Karl Marx and the search for identity. *In* Berlin, Sir I. Against the current p252-86

Stone, D. D. Benjamin Disraeli and the romance of the will. *In* Stone, D. D. The romantic impulse in Victorian fiction p74-98

**Beardsley, Monroe Curtis**

Verbal style and illocutionary action. *In* The Concept of style, ed. by B. Lang p149-68

**Beat generation.** See Bohemianism

**Beatniks.** See Bohemianism

**Beats.** See Bohemianism

**Beatty, Richard Croom**

#### About individual works
*Lord Macaulay, Victorian liberal*

Trilling, L. The Victorians and democracy. *In* Trilling, L. Speaking of literature and society p135-40

**Beatus, Saint, presbyter of Liebana**

#### About individual works
*Sancti Beati a Liebana in Apocalypsin,
Codex Gerundensis*

Schapiro, M. The Beatus Apocalypse of Gerona. *In* Schapiro, M. Selected papers v3: Late antique, early Christian and mediaeval art p319-28

**Beauchamp, Tom L.**

Suicide. *In* Matters of life and death, ed. by T. Regan p67-108

**Beaujour, Michel**

Exemplary pornography: Barrès, Loyola, and the novel. *In* The Reader in the text, ed. by S. R. Suleiman and I. Crosman p325-49

Genus universum. *In* Glyph 7 p15-31

**Beautiful, The.** See Aesthetics

**Beauty.** See Aesthetics

**Beaver, Thomas Gordon.** See Terrace, H. S. jt. auth.

**Bechelloni, Giovanni**

The journalist as political client in Italy. *In* Newspapers and democracy, ed. by A. Smith p228-43

**Beck, Evelyn Torton.** See Lanser, S. S. jt. auth.

**Beck, Hans-Georg**

Constantinople: the rise of a new capital in the East. *In* Age of spirituality, ed. by K. Weitzmann p29-37

**Beck, Lewis White**

World enough, and time. *In* Probability, time, and space in eighteenth-century literature, ed. by P. R. Backscheider p113-39

**Becker, William H.**

Imperialism. *In* Encyclopedia of American economic history, ed. by G. Porter v2 p882-93

**Beckett, Samuel**

#### About

Leigh, J. Another Beckett: an analysis of Residua. *In* The Analysis of literary texts, ed. by R. D. Pope p314-30

#### About individual works
*Endgame*

Wilson, R. N. Samuel Beckett: the social psychology of emptiness. *In* Wilson, R. N. The writer as social seer p134-44

*Molloy, Malone dies, The unnamable:
a trilogy*

Kellman, S. G. Beckett's trilogy. *In* Kellman, S. G. The self-begetting novel p129-43

*More pricks than kicks*

Reid, A. Test flight: Beckett's More pricks than kicks. *In* The Irish short story, ed. by P. Rafroidi and T. Brown p227-35

*Watt*

Robinson, F. M. Samuel Beckett: Watt. *In* Robinson, F. M. The comedy of language p127-74

*Waiting for Godot*

Wilson, R. N. Samuel Beckett: the social psychology of emptiness. *In* Wilson, R. N. The writer as social seer p134-44

#### Criticism and interpretation

Pilling, J. Samuel Beckett: the critical heritage, edited by Lawrence Graver and Raymond Federman. *In* Drama and mimesis, ed. by J. Redmond p243-47

**Bécquer, Gustavo Adolfo**

#### About

Laguardia, G. Forbidden places: Becquer's scene of writing. *In* The Analysis of literary texts, ed. by R. D. Pope p31-40

**Beda Venerabilis**

#### About individual works
*Ecclesiastical history of the English
people (Leningrad State Public Library:
Latin Q, v. I, 18)*

Schapiro, M. The decoration of the Leningrad manuscript of Bede. *In* Schapiro, M. Selected papers v3: Late antique, early Christian and mediaeval art p199-224

*History of the abbots*

Meyvaert, P. Bede and the church paintings at Wearmouth—Jarrow. *In* Anglo-Saxon England 8 p63-77

**Bedau, Hugo Adam**

Capital punishment. *In* Matters of life and death, ed. by T. Regan p148-82

**Bede, The Venerable.** See Beda Venerabilis

**Beebe, Maurice**

The Portrait as portrait: Joyce and impressionism. *In* Irish Renaissance annual I p13-31

**Beer, John B.**

Coleridge and Wordsworth: the vital and the organic. *In* Reading Coleridge, ed. by W. B. Crawford p160-90

Introduction: the elusive Forster. *In* E. M. Forster: a human exploration, ed. by G. K. Das and J. Beer p 1-10

'The last Englishman': Lawrence's appreciation of Forster. *In* E. M. Forster: a human exploration, ed. by G. K. Das and J. Beer p245-68

**Beer**

#### Uganda

Karp, I. C. Beer drinking and social experience in an African society: an essay in formal sociology. *In* Explorations in African systems of thought, ed. by I. C. Karp & C. S. Bird p83-119

**Beerbohm, Sir Max**

#### About

Henkle, R. B. Wilde and Beerbohm: the wit of the avant-garde, the charm of failure. *In* Henkle, R. B. Comedy and culture p296-352

Pritchett, V. S. Max Beerbohm: a dandy. *In* Pritchett, V. S. The tale bearers p9-17

**Bees in literature**
 Scheinberg, S. The bee maidens of the Homeric Hymn to Hermes. *In* Harvard Studies in classical philology, v83 p 1-28

**Beethoven, Ludwig von**
### About individual works
*Fidelio*
 Carner, M. Fidelio. *In* Carner, M. Major and minor p186-252

#### Influence
 Carner, M. A Beethoven movement and its successors. *In* Carner, M. Major and minor p9-20

**Behan, Brendan**
### About
 Edwards, P. Nothing is concluded. *In* Edwards, P. Threshold of a nation p229-44

**Behavior (Psychology)** See Human behavior

**Behavior modification**
 Sutherland, N. S. The myth of mind control. *In* Lying truths, ed. by R. Duncan and M. Weston-Smith p107-20

**Behavioral pharmacology.** See Psychopharmacology

**Beichner, Paul E.** See Part 2 under title: Chaucerian problems and perspectives

**Beidelman, T. O.**
 Women and men in two East African societies. *In* Explorations in African systems of thought, ed. by I. C. Karp & C. S. Bird p143-64

**Beinart, Haim**
 The Jews in Spain. *In* The Jewish world, ed. by E. Kedourie p161-67

**Belief and doubt**
 Anscombe, G. E. M. What is it to believe someone? *In* Rationality and religious belief, ed. by C. F. Delaney p141-57
 Burnyeat, M. F. Can the sceptic live his scepticism? *In* Doubt and dogmatism, ed. by M. Schofield, M. Burnyeat and J. Barnes p20-53
 Gilkey, L. B. The dialectic of Christian belief: rational, incredible, credible. *In* Rationality and religious belief, ed. by C. F. Delaney p65-83
 Mavrodes, G. I. Rationality and religious belief—a perverse question. *In* Rationality and religious belief, ed. by C. F. Delaney p28-41
 Smith, J. E. Faith, belief, and the problem of rationality in religion. *In* Rationality and religious belief, ed. by C. F. Delaney p42-64
 *See also* Rationalism

**Bell, Clive**
### About
 Gloversmith, F. Defining culture: J. C. Powys, Clive Bell, R. H. Tawney & T. S. Eliot. *In* Class, culture and social change, ed. by F. Gloversmith p15-44

**Bell, Daniel**
 The social framework of the information society. *In* The Computer age: a twenty-year view, ed. by M. L. Dertouzos and J. Moses p163-211

**Bell, Michael**
 Introduction: modern movements in literature. *In* The Context of English literature, 1900-1930, ed. by M. Bell p 1-93

**Bellini, Vincenzo**
### About
 Dent, E. J. Bellini in England. *In* Dent, E. J. Selected essays p158-73

**Bellow, Saul**
### About
 Alexander, E. Saul Bellow: a Jewish farewell to the Enlightenment. *In* Alexander, E. The resonance of dust p172-92

### About individual works
*Herzog*
 Pritchett, V. S. Saul Bellow: jumbos. *In* Pritchett, V. S. The tale bearers p146-55
*Humboldt's gift*
 Pritchett, V. S. Saul Bellow: jumbos. *In* Pritchett, V. S. The tale bearers p146-55

**Bellugi, Ursula.** See Bronowski, J. jt. auth.

**Belov, Vasiliĭ Ivanovich**
### About
 Hosking, G. Village prose: Vasily Belov, Valentin Rasputin. *In* Hosking, G. Beyond Socialist realism p50-83

**Bely, Andrey,** pseud. See Bugaev, Boris Nikolaevich

**Ben-Amotz, Dan**
### About individual works
*To remember, to forget*
 Alexander, E. Between Diaspora and Zion: Israeli Holocaust fiction. *In* Alexander, E. The resonance of dust p73-118

**Benedetti, Mario**
### About individual works
*El cambiazo*
 Foster, D. W. The écriture of social protest in Mario Benedetti's "El cambiazo." *In* Foster, D. W. Studies in the contemporary Spanish-American short story p102-09

**Benedict, Philip Joseph**
 The Catholic response to Protestantism. *In* Religion and the people, 800-1700, ed. by J. Obelkevich p168-90

**Benedict Biscop, Saint**
### About
 Meyvaert, P. Bede and the church paintings at Wearmouth—Jarrow. *In* Anglo-Saxon England 8 p63-77

**Benjamin, Judah Philip**
### About
 Tedlow, R. S. Judah P. Benjamin. *In* Conference on Southern Jewish History, Richmond, Va. 1976. "Turn to the South" p44-54

**Benjamin, Walter**
### About
 Hartman, G. H. The sacred jungle 2: Walter Benjamin. *In* Hartman, G. H. Criticism in the wilderness p63-85
 Sandor, A. Rilke's and Walter Benjamin's conceptions of rescue and liberation. *In* Rilke: the alchemy of alienation, ed. by F. Baron, E. S. Dick and W. R. Maurer p223-42
 Slaughter, C. Against the stream: Walter Benjamin. *In* Slaughter, C. Marxism, ideology & literature p170-96
 Wohlfarth, I. The politics of prose and the art of awakening: Walter Benjamin's version of a German romantic motif. *In* Glyph 7 p131-48

**Benko, Stephen**

Popular literature in early Christianity: the apocryphal New Testament. *In* 5000 years of popular culture, ed. by F. E. H. Schroeder p175-90

**Benkovitz, Miriam J.**

### About individual works

*Frederick Rolfe, Baron Corvo*

Pritchett, V. S. Frederick Rolfe: the crab's shell. *In* Pritchett, V. S. The tale bearers p190-94

**Benn, Gottfried**

### About individual works

*Am Bruckenwehr*

Grundlehner, P. Gottfried Benn: "Am Bruckenwehr." *In* Grundlehner, P. The lyrical bridge p130-49

**Bennett, Benjamin**

Modern drama and German classicism

#### Contents

The assault upon the audience: types of modern drama

Breakthrough in theory: the philosophical background of modern drama

The classic modern: Brecht

Egmont and the maelstrom of the self

The importance of being Egmont

Iphigenie auf Tauris and Goethe's idea of drama

Lessing and the problem of drama

Nathan der Weise: breakthrough in practice

Prinz Friedrich von Homburg: theory in practice

Schiller's theoretical impasse and Maria Stuart

**Bennett, Jack Arthur Walter**

Some second thoughts on The parlement of foules. *In* Chaucerian problems and perspectives, ed. by E. Vasta and Z. P. Thundy p132-46

**Bensman, David**

Economics and culture in the gilded age hatting industry. *In* Small business in American life, ed. by S. W. Bruchey p352-65

**Benson, Edward Frederic**

### About individual works

*Make way for Lucia*

Pritchett, V. S. E. F. Benson: fairy tales. *In* Pritchett, V. S. The tale bearers p18-24

**Beowulf**

Andersson, T. M. Tradition and design in Beowulf. *In* Old English literature in context, ed. by J. D. Niles p90-106

Brady, C. A. V. 'Weapons' in Beowulf: an analysis of the nominal compounds and an evaluation of the poet's use of them. *In* Anglo-Saxon England 8 p79-141

Clemoes, P. Action in Beowulf and our perception of it. *In* Old English poetry, ed. by D. G. Calder p147-68

Damon, P. E. The middle of things: narrative patterns in the Iliad, Roland and Beowulf. *In* Old English literature in context, ed. by J. D. Niles p107-16

Foley, J. M. Beowulf and traditional narrative song: the potential and limits of comparison. *In* Old English literature in context, ed. by J. D. Niles p117-36

Hatto, A. T. Snake-swords and boar-helms in Beowulf. *In* Hatto, A. T. Essays on medieval German and other poetry p233-54

Lord, A. B. Interlocking mythic patterns in Beowulf. *In* Old English literature in context, ed. by J. D. Niles p137-42

Mellinkoff, R. D. Cain's monstrous progeny in Beowulf: part I, Noachic tradition. *In* Anglo-Saxon England 8 p143-62

Nagler, M. N. Beowulf in the context of myth. *In* Old English literature in context, ed. by J. D. Niles p143-56

Opland, J. From horseback to monastic cell: the impact on English literature of the introduction of writing. *In* Old English literature in context, ed. by J. D. Niles p30-43

Stanley, E. G. Two Old English poetic phrases insufficiently understood for literary criticism: Þing gehegan and seonoÞ gehegan. *In* Old English poetry, ed. by D. G. Calder p67-90

**Beppu, Keiko**

Foreign scholarship: Japanese contributions. *In* American literary scholarship, 1978 p475-82

**Bercovitch, Sacvan**

Rhetoric and history in early New England: the Puritan errand reassessed. *In* Toward a new American literary history, ed. by L. J. Budd, E. H. Cady and C. L. Anderson p36-53

**Berg, Alban**

#### About

Carner, M. Pfitzner versus Berg. *In* Carner, M. Major and minor p253-57

**Berg, Albert Ashton**

#### About

Gordan, J. D. A doctor's benefaction: the Berg collection at the New York Public Library. *In* The Bibliographical Society of America, 1904-79 p327-38

**Berger, Fred R.**

Pornography, sex and censorship. *In* The Philosophy of sex, ed. by A. Soble p322-47

**Berger, Peter L.**

Religion and the American future. *In* The Third century, ed. by S. M. Lipset p65-77

**Bergey's Manual of determinative bacteriology**

Morowitz, H. J. On first looking into Bergey's Manual. *In* Morowitz, H. J. The wine of life, and other essays on societies, energy & living things p103-06

**Bergman, Ingmar**

### About individual works

*Autumn sonata*

Kael, P. Tentacles. *In* Kael, P. When the lights go down p476-81

Kauffmann, S. Autumn sonata. *In* Kauffmann, S. Before my eyes p79-86

*Face to face*

Kauffmann, S. Face to face. *In* Kauffmann, S. Before my eyes p73-76

*The magic flute*

Kael, P. Walking into your childhood. *In* Kael, P. When the lights go down p72-79

Kauffmann, S. The magic flute. *In* Kauffmann, S. Before my eyes p69-72

*Scenes from a marriage*

Kauffmann, S. Scenes from a marriage. *In* Kauffmann, S. Before my eyes p66-69

*The serpent's egg*

Kael, P. More torment, or When they broke the silence. *In* Kael, P. When the lights go down p388-92

Kauffmann, S. The serpent's egg. *In* Kauffmann, S. Before my eyes p76-79

**Bergman, Ingrid**
A meeting with O'Neill. *In* Eugene O'Neill, ed. by V. Floyd p293-96

**Bergmark, Robert E.**
Computers and persons. *In* Monster or messiah? Ed. by W. M. Mathews p47-55

**Bergson, Henri Louis**

### About individual works

*Laughter*

Robinson, F. M. The comedy of language. *In* Robinson, F. M. The comedy of language p 1-24

**Berke, Jacqueline, and Berke, Laura**
Mothers and daughters in Wives and daughters: a study of Elizabeth Gaskell's last novel. *In* The Lost tradition: mothers and daughters in literature, ed. by C. N. Davidson and E. M. Broner p95-109

**Berke, Laura.** See Berke, J. jt. auth.

**Berkeley, George, Bp. of Cloyne**

### About

Schwartz, R. B. Berkeley, Newtonian space, and the question of evidence. *In* Probability, time, and space in eighteenth-century literature, ed. by P. R. Backscheider p259-73

**Berkhout, Carl Theodore [and others]**
Bibliography for 1978. *In* Anglo-Saxon England 8 p335-76

**Berlin, Sir Isaiah**
Against the current

*Contents*

Benjamin Disraeli, Karl Marx and the search for identity
The counter-Enlightenment
The divorce between the sciences and the humanities
Georges Sorel
Herzen and his memoirs
Hume and the sources of German anti-rationalism
The life and opinions of Moses Hess
Montesquieu
The 'naiveté' of Verdi
Nationalism: past neglect and present power
The originality of Machiavelli
Vico and the ideal of the Enlightenment
*Also in* Conference on Vico and Contemporary Thought, New York, 1976. Vico and contemporary thought pt 1 p250-63
Vico's concept of knowledge

### About

Hausheer, R. Introduction. *In* Berlin, Sir I. Against the current p xiii-liii

**Berman, Harold Joseph**
The weightier matters of the law. *In* Solzhenitsyn at Harvard, ed. by R. Berman p99-113

**Berman, Lawrence Victor**
The structure of the commandments of the Torah in the thought of Maimonides. *In* Studies in Jewish religious and intellectual history, ed. by S. Stein and R. Loewe p51-66

**Berman, Ronald S.**
Through Western eyes. *In* Solzhenitsyn at Harvard, ed. by R. Berman p75-84

**Bermel, Albert**
Poetry and mysticism in O'Neill. *In* Eugene O'Neill, ed. by V. Floyd p245-51

**Bern, Ronald Lawrence**
Utilizing the Southern-Jewish experience in literature. *In* Conference on Southern Jewish History, Richmond, Va. 1976. "Turn to the South" p151-57

### About individual works

*The legacy*

Bern, R. L. Utilizing the Southern-Jewish experience in literature. *In* Conference on Southern Jewish History, Richmond, Va. 1976. "Turn to the South" p151-57

**Bernard, Charles, 1571-1640**

### About

Ranum, O. Bernard and his history. *In* Ranum, O. Artisans of glory p103-28

**Bernard, Claude**

### About

Morowitz, H. J. The wine of life. *In* Morowitz, H. J. The wine of life, and other essays on societies, energy & living things p195-99

**Bernard, Jessie Shirley**
Afterword. *In* The Prism of sex, ed. by J. A. Sherman and E. T. Beck p267-75

**Bernard de Ventadour.** See Bernart de Ventadorn

**Bernart de Ventadorn**

### About individual works

*Ab joi mou lo vers e'l comens*

Ferrante, J. M. 'Ab joi mou lo vers e'l comens'. *In* The Interpretation of medieval lyric poetry, ed. by W. T. H. Jackson p113-41

**Bernhard, Thomas**

### About

Wolfschütz, H. Thomas Bernhard: the mask of death. *In* Modern Austrian writing, ed. by A. Best and H. Wolfschütz p214-35

**Bernstein, Gene Morrison**
The mediated vision: Eliade, Lévi-Strauss, and romantic mythopoesis. *In* The Binding of Proteus, ed. by M. W. McCune, T. Orbison and P. M. Withim p158-72

**Bernstein, Jerome S.**
In some cases jumps are made: "Axolotl" from an Eastern point of view. *In* The Analysis of literary texts, ed. by R. D. Pope p175-84

**Berryman, John**

### About

Vendler, H. H. Ammons, Berryman, Cummings. *In* Vendler, H. H. Part of nature, part of us p323-36
Wagner, L. W. Berryman: from the beginning. *In* Wagner, L. W. American modern p158-64

### About individual works

*His toy, his dream, his rest*

Vendler, H. H. John Berryman. *In* Vendler, H. H. Part of nature, part of us p119-23

**Berthoff, Rowland**
Independence and enterprise: small business in the American dream. *In* Small business in American life, ed. by S. W. Bruchey p28-48

**Bertolucci, Bernardo**

### About individual works

*1900*

Kael, P. Hail, folly! *In* Kael, P. When the lights go down p323-33
Kauffmann, S. 1900. *In* Kauffmann, S. Before my eyes p298-301

**Besserat, Denise Schmandt-** See Schmandt-Besserat, Denise

**Best, Alan**
The Austrian tradition: continuity and change. *In* Modern Austrian writing, ed. by A. Best and H. Wolfschütz p23-43

Bible. Old Testament. Genesis—*Continued*

### Illustrations

Schapiro, M. The angel with the ram in Abraham's sacrifice: a parallel in Western and Islamic art. *In* Schapiro, M. Selected papers v3: Late antique, early Christian and mediaeval art p289-306

Schapiro, M. "Cain's jawbone that did the first murder." *In* Schapiro, M. Selected papers v3: Late antique, early Christian and mediaeval art p249-65

Schapiro, M. An Irish-Latin text on the angel with the ram in Abraham's sacrifice. *In* Schapiro, M. Selected papers v3: Late antique, early Christian and mediaeval art p307-18

Bible. Old Testament. Joshua

### Illustrations

Schapiro, M. The place of the Joshua Roll in Byzantine history. *In* Schapiro, M. Selected papers v3: Late antique, early Christian and mediaeval art p49-66

Bible. Old Testament. Psalms

### Commentaries

Gosselin, E. A. Two views of the evangelical David: Lefèvre d'Etaples and Theodore Beza. *In* The David myth in Western literature, ed. by R. J. Frontain and J. Wojcik p56-67

### Liturgical use

Sarna, N. M. The psalm superscriptions and the guilds. *In* Studies in Jewish religious and intellectual history, ed. by S. Stein and R. Loewe p281-300

### Music

*See* Psalms—Music

Bible. Old Testament. 2 Samuel I, 17-27

### Homiletical use

Ahearn, M. L. David, the military exemplum. *In* The David myth in Western literature, ed. by R. J. Frontain and J. Wojcik p106-18

Bible. Old Testament. Song of Solomon

### Criticism, interpretation, etc., Jewish

Rosenthal, E. I. J. Some observations on Yohanan Alemanno's political ideas. *In* Studies in Jewish religious and intellectual history, ed. by S. Stein and R. Loewe p247-61

### Bible in literature

Murrin, M. The language of Milton's heaven. *In* Murrin, M. The allegorical epic p153-71

### Bible plays

Abramson, G. Thematic development: The Biblical-historical play. *In* Abramson, G. Modern Hebrew drama p82-115

### Bibliographical citations

Bühler, C. F. Literary research and bibliographical training. *In* The Bibliographical Society of America, 1904-79 p363-71

Butler, P. Bibliography and scholarship. *In* The Bibliographical Society of America, 1904-79 p40-50

### Bibliographical Society of America

### History

Van Hoesen, H. B. The Bibliographical Society of America—its leaders and activities, 1904-1939. *In* The Bibliographical Society of America, 1904-79 p139-71

### Bibliography

Tanselle, G. T. The state of bibliography today. *In* The Bibliographical Society of America, 1904-79 p542-57

### Indexes

McMullin, B. J. Indexing the periodical literature of Anglo-American bibliography. *In* Virginia. University. Bibliographical Society. Studies in bibliography v33 p 1-17

### Methodology

*See* Bibliography—Theory, methods, etc.

### Rare books

Carter, J. Bibliography and the rare book trade. *In* The Bibliographical Society of America, 1904-79 p307-17

Cole, G. W. Bibliography—a forecast. *In* The Bibliographical Society of America, 1904-79 p21-39

Ray, G. N. The changing world of rare books. *In* The Bibliographical Society of America, 1904-79 p416-54

### Societies, etc.

*See* Book clubs

### Theory, methods, etc.

Atkinson, R. An application of semiotics to the definition of bibliography. *In* Virginia. University. Bibliographical Society. Studies in bibliography v33 p54-73

Bühler, C. F. Literary research and bibliographical training. *In* The Bibliographical Society of America, 1904-79 p363-71

Butler, P. Bibliography and scholarship. *In* The Bibliographical Society of America, 1904-79 p40-50

Cole, G. W. Bibliography—a forecast. *In* The Bibliographical Society of America, 1904-79 p21-39

Hinman, C. Mechanized collation: a preliminary report. *In* The Bibliographical Society of America, 1904-79 p201-08

Paltsits, V. H. A plea for an anatomical method in bibliography. *In* The Bibliographical Society of America, 1904-79 p 1-2

Pantzer, K. F. The serpentine progress of the STC revision. *In* The Bibliographical Society of America, 1904-79 p455-69

Tanselle, G. T. The concept of ideal copy. *In* Virginia. University. Bibliographical Society. Studies in bibliography v33 p18-53

### United States—History

Adams, T. R. Bibliotheca Americana: a merry maze of changing concepts. *In* The Bibliographical Society of America, 1904-79 p479-92

Blanck, J. N. Problems in the bibliographical description of nineteenth-century American books. *In* The Bibliographical Society of America, 1904-79 p188-200

Silver, R. G. Problems in nineteenth-century American bibliography. *In* The Bibliographical Society of America, 1904-79 p126-38

Thwaites, R. G. Bibliographical activities of historical societies of the United States. *In* The Bibliographical Society of America, 1904-79 p3-8

### Bibliography, National

### United States

Blanck, J. N. Problems in the bibliographical description of nineteenth-century American books. *In* The Bibliographical Society of America, 1904-79 p188-200

### Bibliothèque universelle des dames

Mylne, V. The Bibliothèque universelle des dames. *In* Woman and society in eighteenth-century France, ed. by E. Jacobs and others p123-38

**Bickman, Martin**
The unsounded centre
*Contents*
Afterword
Animatopoeia: sirens of the self
The double consciousness revisited
Kora in heaven: Emily Dickinson
Mythodology: the symbol in Jungian thought and American romanticism
One's self I sing: individuation and introjection
Voyages of the mind's return: three paradigmatic works
Words out of the sea: Walt Whitman

**Big business**
*See also* Competition

### History
Chandler, A. D. and Daems, H. Introduction. *In* Managerial hierarchies, ed. by A. D. Chandler and H. Daems p 1-8
Daems, H. The rise of the modern industrial enterprise: a new perspective. *In* Managerial hierarchies, ed. by A. D. Chandler and H. Daems p203-23
Keller, M. Regulation of large enterprise: the United States experience in comparative perspective. *In* Managerial hierarchies, ed. by A. D. Chandler and H. Daems p161-81

### France—History
Lévy-Leboyer, M. The large corporation in modern France. *In* Managerial hierarchies, ed. by A. D. Chandler and H. Daems p117-60

### United States—History
Chandler, A. D. Rise and evolution of big business. *In* Encyclopedia of American economics history, ed. by G. Porter v2 p619-38

**The big fix (Motion picture)**
Kael, P. Detectives—the capon and the baby bowwow. *In* Kael, P. When the lights go down p462-69

**Bigger, Charles P.**
Walker Percy and the resonance of the word. *In* Walker Percy: art and ethics, ed. by J. Tharpe p43-54

**Bilingualism**
Miller, J. How do you spell Gujarati, sir? *In* The State of the language, ed. by L. Michaels and C. Ricks p140-51

**Bilingualism and literature**
Keller, G. D. The literary strategems available to the bilingual Chicano writer. *In* The Identification and analysis of Chicano literature, ed. by F. Jiménez p263-316

**Bill of rights (Great Britain)** See Great Britain. Bill of rights

**Billot, Louis, Cardinal**
### About
Daly, G. The integralist response (1): prelude to the Roman condemnation of Modernism. *In* Daly, G. Transcendence and immanence p165-89

**Billson, Marcus Kitchen, and Smith, Sidonie A.**
Lilian Hellman and the strategy of the "other." *In* Women's autobiography, ed. by E. C. Jelinek p163-79

**The Bingo long traveling all-Stars & motor kings (Motion picture)**
Kauffmann, S. The Bingo long traveling all-stars & motor kings. *In* Kauffmann, S. Before my eyes p225-26

**Biodegradation**
Morowitz, H. J. On riding a biocycle. *In* Morowitz, H. J. The wine of life, and other essays on societies, energy & living things p11-14

**Bioethics**
Malmström, B. G. Ethical implications of enzyme technology. *In* The Condition of man, ed. by P. Hallberg p162-69

**Biographical films**
Bruss, E. W. Eye for I: making and unmaking autobiography in film. *In* Autobiography: essays theoretical and critical, ed. by J. Olney p296-320

**Biography**
### History and criticism
*See* Biography (as a literary form)
### Technique
*See* Biography (as a literary form)

**Biography (as a literary form)**
Collins, D. Truth and alterity. *In* Collins, D. Sartre as biographer p 1-30
Edel, L. The figure under the carpet. *In* Telling lives, ed. by M. Pachter p16-34
Gittings, R. Artist upon oath. *In* Royal Society of Literature of the United Kingdom, London. Essays by divers hands: innovation in contemporary literature, new ser. v40 p67-82
Pachter, M. The biographer himself: an introduction. *In* Telling lives, ed. by M. Pachter p3-15
Tuchman, B. W. Biography as a prism of history. *In* Telling lives, ed. by M. Pachter p132-47
Wolff, G. Minor lives. *In* Telling lives, ed. by M. Pachter p56-72
*See also* Autobiography

**Biography, Writing of.** See Biography (as a literary form)

**Biological chemistry.** See Body composition

**Biological research.** See Cell research; Molecular biology—Research; Zoological research

**Biologists.** See Ecologists; Geneticists

**Biology.** See Genetics; Population biology

**Bionics.** See Artificial intelligence

**Bird, Charles Stephen, and Kendall, Martha B.**
The Mande hero. *In* Explorations in African systems of thought, ed. by I. C. Karp & C. S. Bird p13-26

**The Bird's Head Haggada.** See Jews. Liturgy and ritual. Hagadah. 1965

**Birje-Patil, J.**
Forster and Dewas. *In* E. M. Forster: a human exploration, ed. by G. K. Das and J. Beer p102-08

**Birnbaum, Pierre**
The state in contemporary France. *In* The State in Western Europe, ed. by R. Scase p94-114

**Birr, Kendall**
Industrial research laboratories. *In* The Sciences in the American context: new perspectives, ed. by N. Reingold p193-207

**Birth attendants.** See Midwives

**Birth control**
### United States—History
Gordon, L. Birth control and social revolution; excerpt from "Woman's body, woman's right." *In* A Heritage of her own, ed. by N. F. Cott and E. H. Pleck p445-75

**Birth of a nation (Motion picture)**
Fiedler, L. A. The anti-Tom novel and the First Great War: Thomas Dixon, Jr. and D. W. Griffith. *In* Fiedler, L. A. The inadvertent epic p43-57

**Bischof, Norbert**
Remarks on Lorenz and Piaget: how can "working hypotheses" be "necessary"? *In* Language and learning, ed. by M. Piattelli-Palmarini p233-41

**Biscop, Benedict.** See Benedict Biscop, Saint

**Bishop, Elizabeth**
**About**
Vendler, H. H. Elizabeth Bishop. *In* Vendler, H. H. Part of nature, part of us p97-110

**Bishop, Vaughn Frederick**
Language acquisition and value change in the Kano urban area. *In* Values, identities, and national integration, ed. by J. N. Paden p183-93

**Bisignano, Joseph**
The unemployment-inflation dilemma and the reemergence of classicism. *In* Economic issue of the eighties, ed. by N. M. Kamrany and R. M. Day p29-43

**The bitter tears of Petra von Kant (Motion picture)**
Kauffmann, S. The bitter tears of Petra von Kant. *In* Kauffmann, S. Before my eyes p216-18

**Bittner, Egon.** See Rumbaut, R. G. jt. auth.

**Bixler, Phyllis**
Idealization of the child and childhood in Frances Hodgson Burnett's Little Lord Fauntleroy and Mark Twain's Tom Sawyer. *In* Research about nineteenth-century children and books, ed. by S. K. Richardson p85-96

**Bjork, Kenneth O.**
**About**
Lovoll, O. S. Kenneth O. Bjork: teacher, scholar, and editor. *In* Makers of an American immigrant legacy, ed. by O. S. Lovoll p3-14

**Black, John W.**
Edward Wheeler Scripture, phonetician. *In* Psychology of language and thought, ed. by R. W. Rieber p225-38

**Black Americans.** See Afro-Americans

**Black authors.** See Authors, Black

**Black English**
Spears, M. K. Black English. *In* The State of the language, ed. by L. Michaels and C. Ricks p169-79

**Anecdotes, facetiae, etc.**
Smitherman, G. White English in blackface, or Who do I be? *In* The State of the language, ed. by L. Michaels and C. Ricks p168-68

**Black folk-lore.** See Folk-lore, Black

**Black literature (American)** See American literature—Afro-American authors

**Black poetry (American)** See American poetry—Afro-American authors

**Black poetry (Spanish American)** See Spanish American poetry—Black authors

**Black power**
**Trinidad**
Naipaul, V. S. Michael X and the Black power killings in Trinidad. *In* Naipaul, V. S. The return of Eva Perón p 1-91

**Blackburn, Regina**
In search of the black female self: African-American women's autobiographies and ethnicity. *In* Women's autobiography, ed. by E. C. Jelinek p133-48

**Blacks**
**Brazil**
Fernandes, F. The Negro in Brazilian society: twenty-five years later. *In* Brazil, anthropological perspectives, ed. by M. L. Margolis and W. E. Carter p96-113

**United States**
*See* Afro-Americans

**Uruguay**
Jackson, R. L. The black writer, the black press, and the black diaspora in Uruguay. *In* Jackson, R. L. Black writers in Latin America p93-111

**Blacks, Folk-lore.** See Folk-lore, Black

**Blacks in literature**
Jackson, R. L. Conclusion: prospects for a black aesthetic in Latin America. *In* Jackson, R. L. Black writers in Latin America p191-97 97

Jackson, R. L. Introduction: the problems of literary blackness in Latin America. *In* Jackson, R. L. Black writers in Latin America p 1-14

**Blackstone, William T.**
The search for an environmental ethic. *In* Matters of life and death, ed. by T. Regan p299-335

**Blair, David**
Wilkie Collins and the crisis of suspense. *In* Reading the Victorian novel, ed. by I. Gregor p32-50

**Blair, Walter**
Franklin's massacre of the Hessians. *In* Toward a new American literary history, ed. by L. J. Budd, E. H. Cady and C. L. Anderson p84-90

**Blake, William**
**About**
Austin, D. Threefold Blake's divine vision, intention and myth. *In* The Binding of Proteus, ed. by M. W. McCune, T. Orbison and P. M. Withim p79-96

Dickstein, M. The price of experience: Blake's reading of Freud. *In* The Literary Freud: mechanisms of defense and the poetic will, ed. by J. H. Smith p67-111

Harbison, R. The cult of death. *In* Harbison, R. Deliberate regression p25-62

Heinzelman, K. William Blake and "the price of experience." *In* Heinzelman, K. The economics of the imagination p110-33

**About individual works**
*London (I wander thro' each charter'd street)*
Culler, J. Prolegomena to a theory of reading. *In* The Reader in the text, ed. by S. R. Suleiman and I. Crosman p46-66

**Blanck, Jacob Nathaniel**
Problems in the bibliographical description of nineteenth-century American books. *In* The Bibliographical Society of America, 1904-79 p188-200

**Blasi, Augusto**
Vico, developmental psychology, and human nature. *In* Conference on Vico and Contemporary Thought, New York, 1976. Vico and contemporary thought pt2 p14-39

**Blasphemy.** See Trials (Blasphemy)

**Blau, Joseph Leon**

### About

Wohlgelernter, M. Introduction: Joseph Leon Blau: four ways of religion and philosophy. *In* History, religion, and spiritual democracy, ed. by M. Wohlgelernter [and others] p xxiii-lxxiv

**Blier, Bertrand**

### About

Kael, P. Bertrand Blier. *In* Kael, P. When the lights go down p454-62

### About individual works
*Get out your hankerchiefs*

Kauffmann, S. Get out your handkerchiefs. *In* Kauffmann, S. Before my eyes p14-16

**Blind children.** See Children, Blind

**Bloch, Jean Helen**

Women and the reform of the nation. *In* Woman and society in eighteenth-century France, ed. by E. Jacobs [and others] p3-18

**Blok, Aleksandr Aleksandrovich**

### About

Rosenthal, B. G. Eschatology and the appeal of revolution: Merezhkovsky, Bely, Blok. *In* California Slavic studies v11 p104-39

**Blondel, Maurice**

### About

Daly, G. The Blondelian challenge. *In* Daly, G. Transcendence and immanence p26-50

Daly, G. History and dogma: the debate between Alfred Loisy and Maurice Blondel. *In* Daly, G. Transcendence and immanence p69-90

**The blood of the poet (Motion picture)**

Thiher, A. Le sang d'un poète: film as Orphism. *In* Thiher, A. The cinematic muse p49-62

**Bloodbrothers (Motion picture)**

Kael, P. Forty-eight characters in search of a director. *In* Kael, P. When the lights go down p440-47

**Bloom, Allan**

The study of texts. *In* Political theory and political education, ed. by M. Richter p113-38

**Bloom, Harold**

Freud's concepts of defense and the poetic will. *In* The Literary Freud: mechanisms of defense and the poetic will, ed. by J. H. Smith p 1-28

### About

Hartman, G. H. The sacred jungle 1: Carlyle, Eliot, Bloom. *In* Hartman, G. H. Criticism in the wilderness p42-62

**Bloom, Lynn Z.**

Heritages: dimensions of mother-daughter relationships in women's autobiographies. *In* The Lost tradition: mothers and daughters in literature, ed. by C. N. Davidson and E. M. Broner p291-303

Lentricchia, F. Harold Bloom: the spirit of revenge. *In* Lentricchia, F. After the New Criticism p319-46

**Bloom, Lynn Z. and Holder, Orlee**

Anaïs Nin's Diary in context. *In* Women's autobiography, ed. by E. C. Jelinek p206-20

Kauffmann, S. Saturday night fever/Blue collar. *In* Kauffmann, S. Before my eyes p226-30

**Bloomfield, Morton Wilfred**

The wisdom of The nun's priest's tale. *In* Chaucerian problems and perspectives, ed. by E. Vasta and Z. P. Thundry p70-82

**Blue collar (Motion picture)**

Kael, P. The Cotton Mather of the movies. *In* Kael, P. When the lights go down p406-09

**Blum, Lawrence**

Compassion. *In* Explaining emotions, ed. by A. O. Rorty p507-17

**Blume, Bernhard**

Rilke's Letters. *In* Rilke: the alchemy of alienation, ed. by F. Baron, E. S. Dick and W. R. Maurer p3-14

**Blume, Judy**

### About

Rees, D. Not even for a one-night stand. *In* Rees, D. The marble in the water p173-84

**Blumin, Stuart M.**

Black coats to white collars: economic change, nonmanual work, and the social structure of industrializing America. *In* Small business in American life, ed. by S. W. Bruchey p100-21

**Blunden, Edmund Charles**

### About

Keith, W. J. The Georgians and after. *In* Keith, W. J. The poetry of nature p167-98

**Blunt, Wilfrid Scawen**

### About

Hourani, A. H. Wilfrid Scawen Blunt and the revival of the East. *In* Hourani, A. H. Europe and the Middle East p87-103

**Bly, Robert**

### About

Howard, R. Robert Bly: "Like those before, we move to the death we love." *In* Howard, R. Alone with America p57-67

Molesworth, C. "Rejoice in the gathering dark": the poetry of Robert Bly. *In* Molesworth, C. The fierce embrace p112-38

**Blythe, Ronald**

The writer as listener. *In* Royal Society of Literature of the United Kingdom, London. Essays by divers hands: innovation in contemporary literature, new ser. v40 p 1-14

**Boars in literature**

Hatto, A. T. Snake-swords and boar-helms in Beouwulf. *In* Hatto, A. T. Essays on medieval German and other poetry p233-54

Hatto, A. T. 'Venus and Adonis'—and the boar. *In* Hatto, A. T. Essays on medieval German and other poetry p221-32

### Adaptations

Jones, E. Dryden's Sigismonda. *In* English Renaissance studies, ed. by J. Carey p279-90

**Bobby Deerfield (Motion picture)**

Kael, P. The sacred oak. *In* Kael, P. When the lights go down p298-304

**Boccaccio, Giovanni**

### About individual works
*The Decameron*

Holloway, J. Supposition and supersession: a model of analysis for narrative structure. *In* Holloway, J. Narrative and structure: exploratory essays p 1-19

**Bockel, Pierre**

Malraux and death. *In* André Malraux, ed. by F. Dorenlot and M. Tison-Braun p75-82

**Bode, Carl**

Mencken in his letters. *In* On Mencken, ed. by J. Dorsey p241-50

**Bode, Kenneth A. and Casey, Carol F.**
Party reform: revisionism revised. *In* Political parties in the eighties, ed. by R. A. Goldwin p3-19

**Bodin, Jean**

**About individual works**

*Colloquim heptaplomeres de abditis rerum sublimium arcanis*

Pines, S. The Jewish religion after the destruction of Temple and state: the views of Bodin and Spinoza. *In* Studies in Jewish religious and intellectual history, ed. by S. Stein and R. Loewe p215-34

**Body, Human in literature**
Ostriker, A. Body language: imagery of the body in women's poetry. *In* The State of the language, ed. by L. Michaels and C. Ricks p247-63

**Body and soul (Philosophy)** See Mind and body

**Body composition**
Morowitz, H. J. The six million dollar man. *In* Morowitz, H. J. The wine of life, and other essays on societies, energy & living things p3-6

**Body language.** See Nonverbal communication (Psychology)

**Body weight**
Morowitz, H. J. Obesity: the erg to dyne. *In* Morowitz, H. J. The wine of life, and other essays on societies, energy & living things p52-56

**Boeschenstein, Hermann**
The First World War in German prose after 1945: some samples—some observations. *In* The First World War in German narrative prose, ed. by C. N. Genno and H. Wetzel p138-58

**Boethius**

**About individual works**

*The consolation of philosophy*

Robertson, D. W. Pope and Boethius. *In* Robertson, D. W. Essays in medieval culture p332-40

**Philosophy**

Pickering, F. P. Notes on fate and fortune. *In* Pickering, F. P. Essays on medieval German literature and iconography p95-109

**Bogart, Leo**
Editorial ideals, editorial illusions. *In* Newspapers and democracy, ed. by A. Smith p247-67

**Bogen, James**
Suicide and virtue. *In* Suicide: the philosophical issues, ed. by M. P. Battin and D. J. Mayo p286-92

**Boglioni, Pierre**
Some methodological reflections on the study of medieval popular religion. *In* 5000 years of popular culture, ed. by F. E. H. Schroeder p192-200

**Bogue, Allan G.**
Land policies and sales. *In* Encyclopedia of American economic history, ed. by G. Porter v2 p588-600

The new political history in the 1970s. *In* The Past before us, ed. by M. Kammen p231-57

**Bohemianism**
La Barre, W. Countertransference and the beatniks. *In* La Barre, W. Culture in context p276-85

**Bohl de Faber, Cecilia.** See Caballero, Fernán, pseud. of Cecilia Bohl de Faber

**Boiardo, Matteo Maria, conte di Scandiano.** See Bojardo, Matteo Maria, conte di Scandiano

**Bojardo, Matteo Maria, conte di Scandiano**

**About individual works**

*Orlando innamorato*

Murrin, M. Falerina's garden. *In* Murrin, M. The allegorical epic p53-85

**Bolamba, Antoine Roger**

**About individual works**

*Esanzo: Songs for my country*

Wright, L. Antoine-Roger Bolamba. Esanzo: Songs for my country. *In* African literature today no. 10: Retrospect & prospect, ed. by E. D. Jones p258-62

**Bolinger, Dwight Lemerton**
Fire in a wooden stove: on being aware in language. *In* The State of the language, ed. by L. Michaels and C. Ricks p379-88

**Bolt, Christine**
The anti-slavery origins of concern for the American Indians. *In* Anti-slavery, religion, and reform: essays in memory of Roger Anstey, ed. by C. Bolt and S. Drescher p233-53

**Bombal, María Luisa**

**About individual works**

*The shrouded woman*

Fox-Lockert, L. Maria Luisa Bombal. *In* Fox-Lockert, L. Women novelists in Spain and Spanish America p166-74

**Bonaventura, Saint, Cardinal**

**About individual works**

*The mind's road to God*

Ozment, S. H. The spiritual traditions. *In* Ozment, S. H. The age of reform, 1250-1550 p73-134

**Bond, Ralph**
Cinema in the thirties: documentary film and the labour movement. *In* Culture and crisis in Britain in the thirties, ed. by J. Clark and others p241-56

**Bond, William Henry**
Casting off copy of Elizabethan printers: a theory. *In* The Bibliographical Society of America, 1904-79 p218-28

**Bondarev, Iurii Vasel'evich**

**About**

Shneidman, N. N. Bondarev and Bykov: the war theme. *In* Shneidman, N. N. Soviet literature in the 1970s: artistic diversity and ideological conformity p47-60

**Bondi, Sir Hermann**
Religion is a good thing. *In* Lying truths, ed. by R. Duncan and M. Weston-Smith p203-10

**Book clubs**
Grannis, R. S. What bibliography owes to private book clubs. *In* The Bibliographical Society of America, 1904-79 p51-70

**Book collecting**
Barrett, C. W. Some bibliographical adventures in Americana. *In* The Bibliographical Society of America, 1904-79 p229-40

Taylor, R. H. Bibliothecohimatiourgomachia. *In* The Bibliographical Society of America, 1904-79 p318-26

**Book collectors**
Heaney, H. J. Thomas W. Streeter, collector, 1883-1965. *In* The Bibliographical Society of America, 1904-79 p500-13

**Book illustration.** See Illustration of books

**Book reviewing**
Wilmers, M. K. The language of novel reviewing. *In* The State of the language, ed. by L. Michaels and C. Ricks p313-23

**Book trade.** See Booksellers and bookselling

**Bookbinding**

### United States—Specimens
French, H. D. Notes on American bookbindings. *In* American Antiquarian Society. Proceedings v89 pt2 p369-70
Spawn, W. Notes on American bookbindings. *In* American Antiquarian Society. Proceedings v89 pt 1 p153-54

**Books**
### Appraisal
*See* Criticism
### Prices
Ray, G. N. The changing world of rare books. *In* The Bibliographical Society of America, 1904-79 p416-54
### Psychology
*See* Authors and readers

**Books and reading**
Kambouchner, D. The theory of accidents. *In* Glyph 7 p149-75
Lally, T. D. P. Synchronic vs diachronic popular culture studies and the Old English elegy. *In* 5000 years of culture, ed. by F. E. H. Shroeder p203-12
Rajo Rao. Books which have influenced me. *In* Aspects of Indian writing in English, ed. by M. K. Naik p45-49
Suleiman, S. R. Introduction: varieties of audience-oriented criticism. *In* The Reader in the text, ed. by S. R. Suleiman and I. Crosman p3-45
*See also* Authors and readers

**Books and reading for children.** See Children's literature

**Books for children.** See Children's literature

**Books of Hours.** See Hours, Books of

**Booksellers and bookselling**
Carter, J. Bibliography and the rare book trade. *In* The Bibliographical Society of America, 1904-79 p307-17
Ray, G. N. The changing world of rare books. *In* The Bibliographical Society of America, 1904-79 p416-54
Wroth, L. C. Lathrop Colgate Harper: a happy memory. *In* The Bibliographical Society of America, 1904-79 p372-83

**Boorstin, Daniel Joseph**
### About
Pole, J. R. Daniel J. Boorstin. *In* Pole, J. R. Paths to the American past p299-334

**Booth, James Curtis**
### About
Pickett, T. E. James C. Booth and the first Delaware geological survey, 1837-1841. *In* New Hampshire Bicentennial Conference on the History of Geology, University of New Hampshire, 1976. Two hundred years of geology in America p167-74

**Borges, Jorge Luis**
### About
Foster, D. W. Toward a characterization of écriture in the stories of Borges. *In* Foster, D. W. Studies in the contemporary Spanish-American short story p13-30

Naipaul, V. S. The corpse at the iron gate. *In* Naipaul, V. S. The return of Eva Perón p95-170

**Bornstein, George, and McDougal, Stuart Yeatman**
Pound and Eliot. *In* American literary scholarship, 1978 p111-25

**Borowski, Tadeusz**
### About individual works
*This way for the gas, ladies and gentlemen*
Bosmajian, H. The rage for order: autobiographical accounts of the self in the nightmare of history. *In* Bosmajian, H. Metaphors of evil p27-54

**Boskin, Michael J.**
Economic growth and productivity. *In* The Economy in the 1980s: a program for growth and stability, ed. by M. J. Boskin p23-50
Federal government spending and budget policy. *In* The Economy in the 1980s: a program for growth and stability, ed. by M. J. Boskin p255-90
An overview. *In* The Economy in the 1980s: a program for growth and stability, ed. by M. J. Boskin p421-25
Social security and the economy. *In* The United States in the 1980s, ed. by P. Duignan and A. Rabushka p181-95
U.S. economy at the crossroads. *In* The economy in the 1980s: a program for growth and stability, ed. by M. J. Boskin p3-20

**Bosmajian, Hamida**
Metaphors of evil
*Contents*
Günter Grass's Dog years: the dark side of utopia
Metaphors and myths of evil in history and literature: projections and reflections
The rage for order: autobiographical accounts of the self in the nightmare of history
Rituals of judgment: Hochhuth's The Deputy and Weiss's The investigation
Siegfried Lenz's The German lesson: metaphors of evil on a narrow ground
To the last syllable of recorded time: the dull, violent world of Uwe Johnson's Jahrestage
Towards the point of constriction: Nelly Sachs's "Landschaft aus Schreien" and Paul Celan's "Engführung"

**Boston, Lucy Marie**
### About individual works
*The children of Green Knowe*
Rosenthal, L. The development of consciousness in Lucy Boston's The children of Green Knowe. *In* Children's literature v8 p53-67

**Botany**
### Ecology—Study and teaching
Cittadino, E. Ecology and the professionalization of botany in America, 1890-1905. *In* Studies in history of biology, v4. p 171-98

**Botein, Stephen**
Printers and the American Revolution. *In* The Press and the American Revolution, ed. by B. Bailyn and J. B. Hench p11-57

**Botstein, Leon**
Outside in: music on language. *In* The State of the language, ed. by L. Michaels and C. Ricks p343-61

Bouchardy, Joseph
### About
McCormick, J. Joseph Bouchardy: a melodramatist and his public. *In* Performance and politics in popular drama, ed. by D. Bradby, L. James and B. Sharratt p33-48

Boucher, François
### About
Harbison, R. Nature as a child. *In* Harbison, R. Deliberate regression p3-24

Boué, André
William Carleton as a short-story writer. *In* The Irish short story, ed. by P. Rafroidi and T. Brown p81-89

Bourgeoisie. See Middle classes

Boulding, Kenneth Ewart
Prices and values: infinite worth in a finite world. *In* Value and values in evolution, ed. by E. A. Maziarz p31-46

Bound for glory (Motion picture)
Kael, P. Affirmation. *In* Kael, P. When the lights go down p224-30

Bourgeoisie. See Middle classes

Bourne, Randolph Silliman
### About
Foerster, N. "The literary prophets." *In* Van Wyck Brooks: the critic and his critics, ed. by W. Wasserstrom p56-68

Bouwsma, William James
Early modern Europe. *In* The Past before us, ed. by M. Kammen p78-94

The Renaissance and the broadening of communication. *In* Propaganda and communication in world history, ed. by H. D. Lasswell, D. Lerner and H. Speier v2 p3-40

Bowers, A. Joan
The fantasy world of Russell Hoban. *In* Children's literature v8 p80-97

Bowers, Edgar
### About
Howard, R. Edgar Bowers: "What seems won paid for as in defeat." *In* Howard, R. Alone with America p68-75

Bowers, Fredson Thayer
Establishing Shakespeare's text: notes on short lines and the problem of verse division. *In* Virginia. University. Bibliographical Society. Studies in bibliography v33 p74-130

Scholarship and editing. *In* The Bibliographical Society of America, 1904-79 p514-41

Shakespeare at work: the foul papers of All's well that ends well. *In* English Renaissance studies, ed. by J. Carey p56-73

Bowers, John M.
How Criseyde falls in love. *In* The Expansion and transformations of courtly literature, ed. by N. B. Smith and J. T. Snow p141-55

Bowie, E. L.
Greek literature after 50 B. C. *In* Ancient Greek literature, ed. by K. J. Dover p155-76

Bowie, Malcolm
Jacques Lacan. *In* Structualism and since ed. by J. Sturrock p81-115

Boxill, Anthony
The beginnings to 1929. *In* West Indian literature, ed. by B. King p30-44

Boyd, Julian, and Boyd, Zelda
Shall and will. *In* The State of the language, ed. by L. Michaels and C. Ricks p43-53

Boyd, Zelda. See Boyd, J. jt. auth.

Boyle, Patrick
### About
Paratte, H. D. Patrick Boyle's tragic humanity. *In* The Irish short story, ed. by P. Rafroidi and T. Brown p275-87

The boys from Brazil (Motion picture)
Kael, P. Furry freaks. *In* Kael, P. When the lights go down p448-54

Boysen, Sally. See Savage-Rumbaugh, E. S. jt. auth.

Boyson, Rhodes
Compulsory state education raises educational standards. *In* Lying truths, ed. by R. Duncan and M. Weston-Smith p61-69

Bracciolini, Poggio. See Poggio-Bracciolini

Bradbrook, Muriel Clara
Shakespeare's recollections of Marlowe. *In* Shakespeare's styles, ed. by P. Edwards; I. S. Ewbank, and G. K. Hunter p191-204

Bradby, David
The October group and theatre under the Front populaire. *In* Performance and politics in popular drama, ed. by D. Bradby, L. James and B. Sharratt p231-42

Bradshaigh, Dorothy, Lady
Wood, J. A. The chronology of the Richardson-Bradshaigh correspondence of 1751. *In* Virginia. University. Bibliographical Society. Studies in bibliography v33 p182-91

Bradstreet, Anne (Dudley)
### About
Mason, M. G. The other voice: autobiographies of women writers. *In* Autobiography: essays theoretical and critical, ed. by J. Olney p207-35

Watts, E. S. The posy UNITY: Anne Bradstreet's search for order. *In* Puritan influences in American literature, ed. by E. Elliott p23-37

Brady, Caroline Agnes Von Egmont
'Weapons' in Beowulf: an analysis of the nominal compounds and an evaluation of the poet's use of them. *In* Anglo-Saxon England 8 p79-141

Brain
Hydén, H. The adaptable brain during the stress of the life cycle. *In* The Condition of man, ed. by P. Hallberg p171-78

MacLean, P. D. Sensory and perceptive factors in emotional functions of the triune brain. *In* Explaining emotions, ed. by A. O. Rorty p9-36

*See also* Neuropsychology

Brain-washing
Sutherland, N. S. The myth of mind control. *In* Lying truths, ed. by R. Duncan and M. Weston-Smith p107-20

Brainwashing. See Brain-washing

Brandt, Richard B.
The rationality of suicide. *In* Suicide: the philosophical issues, ed. by M. P. Battin and D. J. Mayo p117-32

Branson, Clive
### About
Heinemann, M. Louis MacNeice, John Cornford and Clive Branson: three Left-wing poets. *In* Culture and crisis in Britain in the thirties, ed. by J. Clark [and others] p103-32

Brathwaite, Edward
### About
Dash, J. M. Edward Brathwaite. *In* West Indian literature, ed. by B. King p210-27

**Bratton, Jacqueline S.**
Theatre of war: the Crimea on the London stage, 1854-5. *In* Performance and politics in popular drama, ed. by D. Bradby, L. James and B. Sharratt p119-37

**Braudel, Fernand**
On history
*Contents*
Demography and the scope of the human sciences
History and sociology
History and the social sciences; the longue durée
The history of civilizations: the past explains the present
In Bahia, Brazil: the present explains the past
Is there a geography of biological man?
The Mediterranean and the Mediterranean world in the age of Philip II
On a concept of social history
The situation of history in 1950
Toward a historical economics
Toward a serial history: Seville and the Atlantic, 1504-1650
Unity and diversity in the human sciences

**Braudy, Leo Beal**
Realists, naturalists, and novelists of manners. *In* Harvard Guide to contemporary American writing, ed. by D. Hoffman p74-152

**Braun, Micheline Tison-** See Tison-Braun, Micheline

**Bray, Warwick**
From village to city in Mesoamerica. *In* The Origins of civilization, ed. by P. S. R. Moorey p78-102

**Brazeau, Peter Alden**
"A collect of philosophy": the difficulty of finding what would suffice. *In* Wallace Stevens, ed. by F. Doggett and R. Buttel p46-49
A trip in a balloon: a sketch of Stevens' later years in New York. *In* Wallace Stevens, ed. by F. Doggett and R. Buttel p114-29

**Brazil**

### Civilization

Wagley, C. Anthropology and Brazilian national identity. *In* Brazil, anthropological perspectives, ed. by M. L. Margolis and W. E. Carter p 1-18

### Emigration and immigration

Azevedo, T. de. The "chapel" as symbol: Italian colonization in southern Brazil. *In* Brazil, anthropological perspectives, ed. by M. L. Margolis and W. E. Carter p86-95

### Politics and government

Forman, S. and Riegelhaupt, J. F. The political economy of patron-clientship: Brazil and Portugal compared. *In* Brazil, anthropological perspectives, ed. by M. L. Margolis and W. E. Carter p379-400

### Race relations

Fernandes, F. The Negro in Brazilian society: twenty-five years later. *In* Brazil, anthropological perspectives, ed. by M. L. Margolis and W. E. Carter p96-113

### Social conditions

Brown, D. D. Umbanda and class relations in Brazil. *In* Brazil, anthropological perspectives, ed. by M. L. Margolis and W. E. Carter p270-304

### Social life and customs

Miller, C. I. The function of middle-class extended family networks in Brazilian urban society. *In* Brazil, anthropological perspectives, ed. by M. L. Margolis and W. E. Carter p305-16

**Brazilian national characteristics.** See National characteristics, Brazilian

**Break, George Farrington**
State and local finance in the 1980s. *In* The Economy in the 1980s: a program for growth and stability, ed. by M. J. Boskin p233-54

**Brecht, Bertolt**

### About

Bennett, B. The classic modern: Brecht. *In* Bennett, B. Modern drama and German classicism p315-33
Fuegi, J. Meditations on mimesis: the case of Brecht. *In* Drama and mimesis, ed. by J. Redmond p103-12
Unseld, S. Bertolt Brecht and his publishers. *In* Unseld, S. The author and his publisher p83-125

**Brée, Germaine**
Michel Leiris: mazemaker. *In* Autobiography: essays theoretical and critical, ed. by J. Olney p194-206

**Brenk, Beat**
The imperial heritage of early Christian art. *In* Age of spirituality, ed. by K. Weitzmann p39-52

**Brentano, Clemens Maria**

### About

Hughes, G. T. The legacy of myth: the Grimms, Brentano and Arnim. *In* Hughes, G. T. Romantic German literature p79-97

**Brentano, Robert**
Western civilization: the Middle Ages. *In* Propaganda and communication in world history, ed. by H. D. Lasswell, D. Lerner and H. Speier v 1 p552-95

**Breslin, James E.**
Gertrude Stein and the problems of autobiography. *In* Women's autobiography, ed. by E. C. Jelinek p149-62
Poetry: the 1930s to the present. *In* American literary scholarship, 1978 p343-63

**Bresson, Robert**

### About individual works

*A man escaped; or, The wind listeth where it will*
Thiher, A. Bresson's Un condamné à mort: the semiotics of grace. *In* Thiher, A. The cinematic muse p130-42

**Bretonne, Nicholus Edme Restif de la.** See Restif de la Bretonne, Nicholus Edme

**Breunig, Leroy C.**
Malraux's Storm in Shanghai. *In* André Malraux, ed. by F. Dorenlot and M. Tison-Braun p209-14

**Brewer, Derek Stanley**
The arming of the warrior in European literature and Chaucer. *In* Chaucerian problems and perspectives, ed. by E. Vasta and Z. P. Thundy p221-43

**Brewer, John**
English radicalism in the age of George III. *In* Three British revolutions: 1641, 1688, 1776, ed. by J. G. A. Pocock p323-67

**Bridges in literature**

Grundlehner, P. August Graf von Platen: "Wenn tiefe Schwermut meine Seele wieget. . . ." *In* Grundlehner, P. The lyrical bridge p41-52

Grundlehner, P. Conrad Ferdinand Meyer: "Auf Ponte Sisto." *In* Grundlehner, P. The lyrical bridge p69-77

Grundlehner, P. Conrad Ferdinand Meyer: "Die alte Brucke." *In* Grundlehner, P. The lyrical bridge p53-67

Grundlehner, P. Ernst Stadler: Fahrt über die Kölner Rheinbrücke bei Nacht." *In* Grundlehner, P. The lyrical bridge p119-29

Grundlehner, P. Friedrich Hölderlin: "Heidelberg." *In* Grundlehner, P. The lyrical bridge p27-40

Grundlehner, P. Friedrich Nietzsche: "Venedig." *In* Grundlehner, P. The lyrical bridge p97-107

Grundlehner, P. Gottfried Benn: "Am Bruckenwehr." *In* Grundlehner, P. The lyrical bridge p130-49

Grundlehner, P. Introduction. *In* Grundlehner, P. The lyrical bridge p13-25

Grundlehner, P. Rainer Maria Rilke: "Pont du Carrousel." *In* Grundlehner, P. The lyrical bridge p109-18

Grundlehner, P. Theodor Fontane: "Die Brück and Tay.' *In* Grundlehner, P. The lyrical bridge p81-95

**A brief vacation (Motion picture)**

Kauffmann, S. A brief vacation. *In* Kauffmann, S. Before my eyes p115-16

**Briffault, Robert**

### About individual works

*Europa in limbo*

Trilling, L. Marxism in limbo. *In* Trilling, L. Speaking of literature and society p100-03

**Briggs, E. R.**

Marie Huber and the campaign against eternal hell torments. *In* Woman and society in eighteenth-century France, ed. by E. Jacobs [and others] p218-28

**Briggs, Peter M.**

The Jonathan Richardsons as Milton critics. *In* Studies in eighteenth-century culture v9 p115-30

**Brighton, England**

### Description—Views

Plomer, W. C. F. Views of Brighton. *In* Plomer, W. C. F. Electric delights p212-14

**Brinkmeyer, Robert H.**

Percy's bludgeon: message and narrative strategy. *In* Walker Percy: art and ethics, ed. by J. Tharpe p80-90

**Brisman, Leslie.** See Brisman, S. H. jt. auth.

**Brisman, Susan Hawk, and Brisman, Leslie**

Lies against solitude: symbolic, imaginary, and real. *In* The Literary Freud: mechanisms of defense and the poetic will, ed. by J. H. Smith p29-65

**Britten, Edward Benjamin**

### About

Plomer, W. C. F. The church operas. *In* Plomer, W. C. F. Electric delights p190-92

### About individual works

*Gloriana*

Plomer, W. C. F. Let's crab an opera. *In* Plomer, W. C. F. Electric delights p180-85

Plomer, W. C. F. Notes on the libretto of Gloriana. *In* Plomer, W. C. F. Electric delights p175-79

*The war requiem*

Plomer, W. C. F. The war requiem. *In* Plomer, W. C. F. Electric delights p186-89

**Britwum, Kwabena**

Politics and literature. *In* African literature today no. 10: Retrospect & prospect, ed. by E. D. Jones p243-47

**Broadsides**

### 15th and 16th centuries

Waage, F. O. Social themes in urban broadsides of Renaissance England. *In* 5000 years of popular culture, ed. by F. E. H. Schroeder p242-54

**Brod, Max**

### About individual works

*Paganism—Christianity—Judaism*

Rosenzweig, F. Apologetic thinking. *In* The Jew, ed. by A. A. Cohen p262-72

**Brodsky, Louis Daniel.** See Hamblin, R. W. jt. auth.

**Brody, David**

Labor and small-scale enterprise during industrialization. *In* Small business in American life, ed. by S. W. Bruchey p263-79

Labor history in the 1970s: toward a history of the American worker. *In* The Past before us, ed. by M. Kammen p251-69

**Broe, Mary Lynn**

A subtle psychic bond: the mother figure in Sylvia Plath's poetry. *In* The Lost tradition: mothers and daughters in literature, ed. by C. N. Davidson and E. M. Broner p207-16

**The broken mirror: a collection of writing from contemporary Poland, ed. by Pawel Mayewski**

Trilling, L. Communism and intellectual freedom. *In* Trilling, L. Speaking of literature and society p300-09

**Bromlei, I͡Ulian Vladimirovich**

The object and the subject-matter of ethnography. *In* Soviet and Western anthropology, ed. by E. Gellner p151-60

**Bromley, Yu.** See Bromlei, I͡Ulian Vladimirovich

**Bromwich, Rachel**

Dafydd ap Gwilym. *In* A Guide to Welsh literature, ed. by A. O. H. Jarman and G. R. Hughes v2 p111-41

The earlier cywyddwyr: poets contemporary with Dafydd ap Gwilym. *In* A Guide to Welsh literature, ed. by A. O. H. Jarman and G. R. Hughes v2 p144-67

**Bronson, Charles**

### About

Kauffmann, S. Mr. Majestyk/Death wish. *In* Kauffmann, S. Before my eyes p31-34

**Brontë, Charlotte**

### About

Stone, D. D. Charlotte Brontë and the perils of romance. *In* Stone, D. D. The romantic impulse in Victorian fiction p99-132

### About individual works

*Jane Eyre*

Roberts, D. Jane Eyre and 'the warped system of things.' *In* Reading the Victorian novel: detail into form, ed. by I. Gregor p131-49

*Villette*

Kinkead-Weekes, M. The voicing of fictions. *In* Reading the Victorian novel: detail into form, ed. by I. Gregor p168-92

**Brontë, Emily Jane**
### About individual works
*Wuthering Heights*
Gregor, I. Reading a story: sequence, pace, and recollection. *In* Reading the Victorian novel: detail into form, ed. by I. Gregor p92-110
### Poetic works
Trilling, L. The poems of Emily Brontë. *In* Trilling, L. Speaking of literature and society p3-6

**Bronowski, Jacob, and Bellugi, Ursula**
Language, name, and concept. *In* Speaking of apes, ed. by T. A. Sebeok and J. Umiker-Sebeok p103-13

**Brook, Peter**
### About
Proudfoot, R. Peter Brook and Shakespeare. *In* Drama and mimesis, ed. by J. Redmond p157-89

**Brooke, Nicholas**
Language most shows a man. . . .? Language and speaker in Macbeth. *In* Shakespeare's styles, ed. by P. Edwards, I. S. Ewbank and G. K. Hunter p67-77

**Brooke-Rose, Christine**
The readerhood of man. *In* The Reader in the text, ed. by S. R. Suleiman and I. Crosman p120-48

**Brooks, Harold Fletcher**
'Richard III': antecedents of Clarence's dream. *In* Shakespeare survey 32 p145-50

**Brooks, Mel**
### About individual works
*High anxiety*
Kael, P. Fear of heights. *In* Kael, P. When the lights go down p371-76

*Silent movie*
Kauffmann, S. Silent movie. *In* Kauffmann, S. Before my eyes p111-13

*Young Frankenstein*
Kauffmann, S. Young Frankenstein. *In* Kauffmann, S. Before my eyes p110-11

**Brooks, Van Wyck**
### About
Angoff, C. "Van Wyck Brooks and our critical tradition." *In* Van Wyck Brooks: the critic and his critics, ed. by W. Wasserstrom p194-201
Cargill, O. "The ordeal of Van Wyck Brooks." *In* Van Wyck Brooks: the critic and his critics, ed. by W. Wasserstrom p129-36
Colum, M. "An American critic: Van Wyck Brooks." *In* Van Wyck Brooks: the critic and his critics, ed. by W. Wasserstrom p3-10
Cowley, M. "Van Wyck Brooks: a career in retrospect." *In* Van Wyck Brooks: the critic and his critics, ed. by W. Wasserstrom p189-93
Dupee, F. W. "The Americanism of Van Wyck Brooks." *In* Van Wyck Brooks: the critic and his critics, ed. by W. Wasserstrom p116-28
Foerster, N. "The literary prophets." *In* Van Wyck Brooks: the critic and his critics, ed. by W. Wasserstrom p56-68
Glicksberg, C. I. "Van Wyck Brooks." *In* Van Wyck Brooks: the critic and his critics, ed. by W. Wasserstrom p69-78
Hyman, S. E. "Van Wyck Brooks and biographical criticism"; excerpt from "The armed vision." *In* Van Wyck Brooks: the critic and his critics, ed. by W. Wasserstrom p137-56

Munson, G. B. "Van Wyck Brooks: his sphere and his encroachments." *In* Van Wyck Brooks: the critic and his critics, ed. by W. Wasserstrom p43-55
Paul, S. "The ordeal and the pilgrimage." *In* Van Wyck Brooks: the critic and his critics, ed. by W. Wasserstrom p206-10
Rosenfeld, P. "Van Wyck Brooks"; excerpt from "Port of New York." *In* Van Wyck Brooks: the critic and his critics, ed. by W. Wasserstrom p11-32
Smith, B. "Van Wyck Brooks"; excerpt from "After the genteel tradition." *In* Van Wyck Brooks: the critic and his critics, ed. by W. Wasserstrom p79-86
Wasserstrom, W. "Van Wyck Brooks." *In* Van Wyck Brooks: the critic and his critics, ed. by W. Wasserstrom p211-37
Wellek, F. "Van Wyck Brooks and a national literature." *In* Van Wyck Brooks: the critic and his critics, ed. by W. Wasserstrom p106-15
Wescott, G. "Van Wyck Brooks." *In* Van Wyck Brooks: the critic and his critics, ed. by W. Wasserstrom p202-05

### About individual works
*The confident years: 1885-1915*
Leavis, F. R. "The Americanness of American literature." *In* Van Wyck Brooks: the critic and his critics, ed. by W. Wasserstrom p157-67

*The times of Melville and Whitman*
Trilling, L. Family album. *In* Trilling, L. Speaking of literature and society p236-38

### Influence—Mumford
Dow, E. "Van Wyck Brooks and Lewis Mumford: a confluence in the 'twenties." *In* Van Wyck Brooks: the critic and his critics, ed. by W. Wasserstrom p238-51

**Brophy, Brigid**
The way of no flesh. *In* The Genius of Shaw, ed. by M. Holroyd p95-111

**Brothers and sisters in literature**
Neumann, E. Georg Trakl: the person and the myth. *In* Neumann, E. Creative man p138-231

**Brotherston, Gordon**
García Márquez and the secrets of Saturno Santos. *In* Contemporary Latin American fiction ed. by S. Bacarisse p48-53

**Broughton, Panthea Reid**
Faulkner. *In* American literary scholarship, 1978 p127-51

**Brown, Bertram Wyatt-** See Wyatt-Brown, Bertram

**Brown, Dianna DeGroat**
Umbanda and class relations in Brazil. *In* Brazil, anthropological perspectives, ed. by M. L. Margolis and W. E. Carter p270-304

**Brown, Janet**
Feminist drama
### Contents
The bed was full
Birth and after birth
For colored girls who have considered suicide/ when the rainbow is enuf
In the Boom Boom Room
Plays by feminist theatre groups
Wine in the wilderness

**Brown, Norman Oliver**
### About individual works
*Life against death*
Trilling, L. Paradise reached for. *In* Trilling, L. Speaking of literature and society p361-66

**Brown, Peter Robert Lamont**
Art and society in late antiquity. *In* Age of spirituality, ed. by K. Weitzmann p17-27

**Brown, Richard E.**
Rival socio-economic theories in two plays by George Lillo. *In* Tennessee Studies in literature v24 p94-110

**Brown, Roger**
The first sentences of child and chimpanzee. *In* Speaking of apes, ed. by T. A. Sebeok and J. Umiker-Sebeok p85-101

**Brown, Russell**
Ross Macdonald as Canadian mystery writer. *In* Seasoned authors for a new season: the search for standards in popular writing, ed. by L. Filler p164-69

**Brown, Stuart C.**
The 'principle' of natural order: or what the enlightened sceptics did not doubt. *In* Royal Institute of Philosophy. Philosophers of the Enlightenment p56-76

**Brown, Terence**
John McGahern's Nightlines: tone, technique and symbolism. *In* The Irish short story, ed. by P. Rafroidi and T. Brown p289-301

**Brown, William Wells**
### About individual works
*Narrative of the life and escape of William Wells Brown [appended to his novel, Clotel, or The president's daughter]*
Stepto, R. B. I rose and found my voice: narration, authentication, and authorial control in four slave narratives. *In* Stepto, R. B. From behind the veil p3-31

**Browne, Hablot Knight**
### About
Lutman, S. Reading illustrations: pictures in David Copperfield. *In* Reading the Victorian novel: detail into form, ed. by I. Gregor p196-225

**Browning, Elizabeth (Barrett)**
### About
McGhee, R. D. Elizabeth Barrett Browning and Oscar Wilde. *In* McGhee, R. D. Marriage, duty & desire in Victorian poetry and drama p233-97

**Browning, Robert**
### About
McGhee, R. D. Browning. *In* McGhee, R. D. Marriage, duty & desire in Victorian poetry and drama p67-98

**Bruce, Alvin King**
V. S. Naipaul. *In* West Indian literature, ed. by B. King p161-78

**Bruce, Lenny**
### About
Kauffmann, S. Lenny. *In* Kauffmann, S. Before my eyes p91-94

**Bruchey, Stuart Weems**
Introduction: a summary view of small business and American life. *In* Small business in American life, ed. by S. W. Bruchey p 1-27

**Bruckner, Anton**
### About
Carner, M. Bruckner's organ recitals in France and England. *In* Carner, M. Major and minor p40-44
Carner, M. Bruckner versus Mahler. *In* Carner, M. Major and minor p50-51

**Bruckner, Matilda Tomaryn**
Repetition and variation in twelfth-century French romance. *In* The Expansion and transformations of courtly literature, ed. by N. B. Smith and J. T. Snow p95-114

**Brumfitt, John Henry**
Cleopatra's nose and Enlightenment historiography. *In* Women and society in eighteenth-century France, ed. by E. Jacobs and others p183-94
Diderot: man and society. *In* Royal Institute of Philosophy. Philosophers of the Enlightenment p162-83

**Brun-Zejmis, Julia**
"A word on the Polish question" by P. Ya. Chaadaev. *In* California Slavic studies v11 p25-32

**Brunet, Marta**
### About individual works
*María Nadie*
Fox-Lockert, L. Marta Brunet. *In* Fox-Lockert, L. Women novelists in Spain and Spanish America p195-215

**Bruni, Leonardo Arentino**
### About
Marsh, D. Leonardo Bruni and the origin of humanist dialogue. *In* Marsh, D. The quattrocento dialogue p24-37

**Brunner, Otto**
### About individual works
*Neue Wege der Sozialgeschichte*
Braudel, F. On a concept of social history. *In* Braudel, F. On history p120-31

**Brunschwig, Jacques**
Proof defined. *In* Doubt and dogmatism, ed. by M. Schofield, M. Burnyeat and J. Barnes p125-60

**Bruss, Elizabeth W.**
Eye for I: making and unmaking autobiography in film. *In* Autobiography: essays theoretical and critical, ed. by J. Olney p296-320

**Brustein, Robert Sanford**
Critical moments
*Contents*
Art versus advocacy
The artist and the citizen
Broadway Anglophilia
Can the show go on?
The fate of Ibsenism
The future of the Endowments
H. L. Mencken (The new Mencken letters)
John Simon (Uneasy stages and singularities)
Pauline Kael (Reeling)
Remakes: the retread culture
Tennessee Williams (Letters to Donald Windham: 1940-1965)
The theatre audience: a house divided
Theatre in the age of Einstein: the crack in the chimney
Where are the repertory critics?

**Bryer, Jackson R.**
Fitzgerald and Hemingway. *In* American literary scholarship, 1978 p153-78

**Buache, Philippe**

### About individual works

*Carte minéralogique, où l'on voit la nature des terrains du Canada et de la Louisiane*

Cailleux, A. The geological map of North America (1752) of J.-E. Guettard. *In* New Hampshire Bicentennial Conference on the History of Geology, University of New Hampshire, 1976. Two hundred years of geology p43-52

**Buber, Martin**

Pharisaism. *In* The Jew, ed. by A. A. Cohen p223-31

Wyschogrod, E. Martin Buber and the no-self perspective. *In* History, religion, and spiritual demogracy, ed. by M. Wohlgelernter, [and others] p130-50

Zion, the state, and humanity: remarks on Hermann Cohen's answer. *In* The Jew, ed. by A. A. Cohen p85-96

**Buchanan, George**

### About individual works
*Jephtha*

Mueller, M. Buchanan's Jephtha. *In* Mueller, M. Children of Oedipus, and other essays on the imitation of Greek tragedy 1550-1800 p156-71

### Style

Reiss, T. J. Buchanan, Montaigne, and the difficulty of speaking. *In* Reiss, T. J. Tragedy and truth p40-77

**Buck, Philo Melvin**

### About individual works
*Directions in contemporary literature*

Trilling, L. Artists and the "societal function." *In* Trilling, L. Speaking of literature and society p186-91

**Buckingham, May**

Some reminiscences. *In* E. M. Forster: a human exploration, ed. by G. K. Das and J. Beer p183-85

**Buckingham, Willis J.**

Whitman and Dickinson. *In* American literary scholarship, 1978 p59-78

**Buckley, Suzann Caroline**

The family and the role of women. *In* The Edwardian age: conflict and stability, 1900-1914, ed. by A. O'Day p133-43

**Bucolic literature.** See Pastoral literature

**Budd, Louis J.**

Mark Twain. *In* American literary scholarship, 1978 p79-90

**Buddhism**

### China—History

Wright, A. F. On the spread of Buddhism to China. *In* Propaganda and communication in world history, ed. by H. D. Lasswell, D. Lerner and H. Speier v 1 p205-19

**Budé, Guillaume**

### About

Ranum, O. Men of letters: sixteenth-century models of conduct. *In* Ranum, O. Artisans of glory p26-57

**Budget**

### United States

Boskin, M. J. Federal government spending and budget policy. *In* The Economy in the 1980s: a program for growth and stability, ed. by M. J. Boskin p255-90

**Buel, Richard**

Freedom of the press in Revolutionary America: the evolution of libertarianism, 1760-1820. *In* The Press & the American Revolution, ed. by B. Bailyn and J. B. Hench p59-97

**Buero Vallejo, Antonio**

### About

Dixon, V. The 'immersion-effect' in the plays of Antonio Buero Vallejo. *In* Drama and mimesis, ed. by J. Redmond p113-37

**Buffalo Bill and the Indians or, Sitting Bull's history lesson (Motion picture)**

Kauffmann, S. Buffalo Bill. *In* Kauffmann, S. Before my eyes p38-40

**Bugaev, Boris Nikolaevich**

### About

Rosenthal, B. G. Eschatology and the appeal of revolution: Merezhkovsky, Bely, Blok. *In* California Slavic studies v11 p104-39

### About individual works
*Petersburg*

Festa-McCormick, D. Bely's Saint Petersburg: a city conjured by a visionary symbolist. *In* Festa-McCormick, D. The city as catalyst p108-23

**Bugsy Malone (Motion picture)**

Kael, P. Creamed. *In* Kael, P. When the lights go down p163-67

**Bühler, Curt Ferdinand**

Literary research and bibliographical training. *In* The Bibliographical Society of America, 1904-79 p363-71

**Buildings**

### Environmental engineering

*See* Architecture—Human factors

**Bullough, Geoffrey**

The defence of paradox. *In* Shakespeare's styles, ed. by P. Edwards, I. S. Ewbank and G. K. Hunter p163-82

**Bullrich, Sylvina.** See Bullrich Palenque, Sylvina

**Bullrich Palenque, Sylvina**

### About individual works
*Bodas de cristal*

Fox-Lockert, L. Silvina Bullrich. *In* Fox-Lockert, L. Women novelists in Spain and Spanish America p175-84

**Bulman, Raymond Francis**

"The God of our children": the humanist reconstruction of God. *In* History, religion, and spiritual democracy, ed. by M. Wohlgelernter, and others p35-52

**Bulwer-Lytton, Edward George Earle Lytton, 1st Baron Lytton.** See Lytton, Edward George Earle Lytton, Bulwer-Lytton, 1st Baron

**Bunin, Ivan Alekseevich**

### About individual works
*The well of days*

Plomer, W. C. F. Ivan Bunin. *In* Plomer, W. C. F. Electric delights p43-44

**Buñuel, Luis**

### About individual works
*Un chien andalou*

Thiher, A. Surrealism's enduring bite: Un chien andalou. *In* Thiher, A. The cinematic muse p24-37

**Buñuel, Luis**—About individual works—*Cont.*
*That obscure object of desire*
Kael, P. Cutting light. *In* Kael, P. When the lights go down p363-67

**Bunyan, John**
**About**
Knott, J. R. John Bunyan and the experience of the Word. *In* Knott, J. R. The sword of the spirit p131-63

**About individual works**
*Grace abounding to the chief of sinners*
Spengemann, W. C. Historical autobiography. *In* Spengemann, W. C. The forms of autobiography p34-61

*The Pilgrim's progress*
Miller, P. John Bunyan's Pilgrim's progress. *In* Miller, P. The responsibility of mind in a civilization of machines p61-77

**Bunzel, John H.**
Higher education: problems and prospects. *In* The United States in the 1980s, ed. by P. Duignan and A. Rabushka p391-415

**Burbidge, John B.**
The international dimension. *In* A Guide to post-Keynesian economics, ed. by A. S. Eichner p139-50

**Burchfield, Robert W.**
Dictionaries and ethnic sensibilities. *In* The State of the language, ed. by L. Michaels and C. Ricks p15-23

**Burckhardt, Jakob Christoph**
**About**
Gombrich, Sir E. H. J. In search of cultural history. *In* Gombrich, Sir E. H. J. Ideals and idols p24-59

**Bureaucracy**
Collier, D. S. The bureaucratic-authoritarian model: synthesis and priorities for future research. *In* The New authoritarianism in Latin America, ed. by D. Collier p363-97
Collier, D. S. Overview of the bureaucratic-authoritarian model. *In* The New authoritarianism in Latin America, ed. by D. Collier p19-32
Dannhauser, W. J. Reflections on statesmanship and bureaucracy. *In* Bureaucrats, policy analysts, statesmen: who leads? Ed. by R. A. Goldwin p114-32
Kaufman, R. R. Industrial change and authoritarian rule in Latin America: a concrete review of the bureaucratic-authoritarian model. *In* The New authoritarianism in Latin America, ed. by D. Collier p165-253
O'Donnell, G. A. Tensions in the bureaucratic-authoritarian state and the question of democracy. *In* The New authoritarianism in Latin America, ed. by D. Collier p285-318

**United States**
Silberman, L. H. Policy analysis: boon or curse for politicians? *In* Bureaucrats, policy analysts, statesmen: who leads? Ed. by R. A. Goldwin p37-43

**United States**—History
Yeaker, M. A. Bureaucracy. *In* Encyclopedia of American economic history, ed. by G. Porter v3 p894-926

**Burges, William**
**About**
Harbison, R. Art as religion. *In* Harbison, R. Deliberate regression p94-114

**Burgess, Anthony**
Dubbing. *In* The State of the language, ed. by L. Michaels and C. Ricks p297-303

**Burke, Edmund**
**About**
Janes, R. M. Edmund Burke's Indian idyll. *In* Studies in eighteenth-century culture v9 p3-13

**About individual works**
*Reflections on the Revolution in France*
Paulson, R. Burke's sublime and the representation of revolution. *In* Culture and politics from Puritanism to the Enlightenment, ed. by P. Zagorin p241-69

**Burke, Kenneth**
**About**
Brown, J. Introduction. *In* Brown, J. Feminist drama p 1-21
Hartman, G. H. The sacred jungle 3: Frye, Burke, and some conclusions. *In* Hartman, G. H. Criticism in the wilderness p86-114

**Burlesque (Literature)** See Parody

**Burne-Jones, Sir Edward Coley, bart**
**About**
Harbison, R. Turning against history. *In* Harbison, R. Deliberate regression p147-79

**Burnett, Anne Pippin**
**About individual works**
*Catastrophe survived: Euripides' plays of mixed reversal*
Knox, B. M. W. Review of Catastrophe survived (by Anne Pippin Burnett) *In* Knox, B. M. W. Word and action p329-42

**Burnett, Frances (Hodgson)**
**About individual works**
*Little Lord Fauntleroy*
Bixler, P. Idealization of the child and childhood in Frances Hodgson Burnett's Little Lord Fauntleroy and Mark Twain's Tom Sawyer. *In* Research about nineteenth-century children and books, ed. by S. K. Richardson p85-96

**Burns, Steven A. MacLeod**
The Humean female. *In* The Sexism of social and political theory: women and reproduction from Plato to Nietzsche, ed. by L. M. G. Clark and L. Lange p53-60

**Burnyeat, Miles F.**
Can the sceptic live his scepticism? *In* Doubt and dogmatism, ed. by M. Schofield, M. Burnyeat and J. Barnes p20-53

**Burrell, David B.**
Religious belief and rationality. *In* Rationality and religious belief, ed. by C. F. Delaney p84-115

**Burstyn, Harold Lewis, and Schlee, Susan B.**
The study of ocean currents in America before 1930. *In* New Hampshire Bicentennial Conference on the History of Geology, University of New Hampshire, 1976. Two hundred years of geology in America p145-55

**Burt, Richard R.**
Washington and the Atlantic alliance: the hidden crisis. *In* National security in the 1980s: from weakness to strength, ed. by W. S. Thompson p109-21

**Burton, John W.**
The village and the cattle camp: aspects of Atuot religion. *In* Explorations in African systems of thought, ed. by I. C. Karp & C. S. Bird p268-97

**Burton, Sir Richard Francis**

### About

Pritchett, V. S. Richard Burton: ruffian Dick. *In* Pritchett, V. S. The tale bearers p184-89

**Burton, Robert**

### About individual works
*The anatomy of melancholy*

Bamborough, J. B. Burton and Cardan. *In* English Renaissance studies. ed. by J. Carey p180-93

**Busey, James L.**

Alcázar's "most voluminous of all assaults." *In* Critics of Henry George, ed. by R. V. Andelson p326-41

**Bush, Douglas**

Literature, the academy, and the public. *In* Generations, ed. by S. R. Grabuard p165-74

**Bush, Vannevar**

### About

Pursell, C. W. Science agencies in World War II: the OSRD and its challengers. *In* The Sciences in the American context: new perspectives, ed. by N. Reingold p359-78

**Bushnell, John D.**

The "new Soviet man" turns pessimist. *In* The Soviet Union since Stalin, ed. by S. F. Cohen, A. Rabinowitch and R. Sharlet p179-99

**Business**

*See also* Business enterprise; Competition; Industrial management

### Data processing

Vyssotsky, V. A. The use of computers for business functions. *In* The Computer age: a twenty-year view, ed. by M. L. Dertouzas and J. Moses p130-45

### Language

Lundborg, L. B. The voices of business. *In* The State of the language, ed. by L. Michaels and C. Ricks p389-95

### Social aspects

*See* Industry—Social aspects

**Business and government.** See Industry and state

**Business cycles**

Keran, M. W. How the domestic business cycle is affected by the rest of the world. *In* Economic issues of the eighties, ed. by N. M. Kamrany and R. H. Day p58-68

Moore, G. H. Business cycles, panics, and depressions. *In* Encyclopedia of American economic history, ed. by G. Porter v 1 p151-56

### Mathematical models

Forrester, J. W. An alternative approach to economic policy: macrobehavior from microstructure. *In* Economic issues of the eighties, ed. by N. M. Kamrany and R. H. Day p80-108

**Business enterprises**

### History

Chandler, A. D. and Daems, H. Introduction. *In* Managerial hierarchies, ed. by A. D. Chandler and H. Daems p 1-8

Daems, H. The rise of the modern industrial enterprises: a new perspective. *In* Managerial hierarchies, ed. by A. C. Chandler and H. Daems p203-23

Williamson, O. E. Emergence of The visible hand: implications for industrial organization. *In* Managerial hierarchies, ed. by A. D. Chandler and H. Daems p182-202

### France—History

Lévy-Leboyer, M. The large corporation in modern France. *In* Managerial hierarchies, ed. by A. D. Chandler and H. Daems p117-60

### Germany—History

Kocka, J. The rise of the modern industrial enterprise in Germany. *In* Managerial hierarchies, ed. by A. D. Chandler and H. Daems p77-116

### Great Britain—History

Hannah, L. Visible and invisible hands in Great Britain. *In* Managerial hierarchies, ed. by A. D. Chandler and H. Daems p41-76

### United States—History

Chandler, A. D. The United States: seedbed of managerial capitalism. *In* Managerial hierarchies, ed. by A. D. Chandler and H. Daems p9-40

Hughes, J. R. T. Entrepreneurship. *In* Encyclopedia of American economic history, ed. by G. Porter v 1 p214-28

Salsbury, S. M. American business institutions before the railroad. *In* Encyclopedia of American economic history, ed. by G. Porter v2 p601-18

Steigerwalt, A. K. Organized business groups. *In* Encyclopedia of American economic history, ed. by G. Porter v2 p753-71

**Business enterprises, International.** See International business enterprises

**Business ethics.** See Competition

**Business mergers**

### United States

*See* Consolidation and merger of corporations

**Business organizations.** See Business enterprises

**Buslett, Ole Amundsen**

### About

Hustvedt, L. Ole Amundsen Buslett, 1855-1924. *In* Makers of an American immigrant legacy, ed. by O. S. Lovoll p131-58

**Busoni, Ferrucio Benvenuto**

### About individual works
*Doktor Faust*

Dent, E. J. Busoni's Doctor Faust. *In* Dent, E. J. Selected essays p118-32

**Butler, Colin**

Mr Britling sees it through: a view from the other side. *In* The First World War in German narrative prose, ed. by C. N. Genno and H. Wetzel p118-37

**Butler, Joseph, Bp. of Durham**

### About

Shiner, R. A. Butler's theory of moral judgment. *In* Royal Institute of Philosophy. Philosophers of the Enlightenment p199-225

**Butler, Michael**

From the 'Wiener Gruppe' to Ernst Jandl. *In* Modern Austrian writing, ed. by A. Best and H. Wolfschütz p236-51

**Butler, Pierce**

Bibliography and scholarship. *In* The Bibliographical Society of America, 1904-79 p40-50

**Butler, Samuel, 1612-1680**

### About individual works
*Hudibras*

Seidel, M. A. The internecine romance: Butler's Hudibras. *In* Seidel, M. A. Satiric inheritance, Rabelais to Sterne p95-134

**Butler, Samuel, 1835-1902**

### About

Henkle, R. B. Meredith and Butler: comedy as lyric, high culture, and the bourgeois trap. *In* Henkle, R. B. Comedy and culture p238-95

**Butor, Michel**

### About individual works
*Passing time*

Festa-McCormick, D. Butor's Passing time: the equivocal reality of a city. *In* Festa-McCormick, D. The city as catalyst p176-92

*Second thoughts*

Kellman, S. G. La modification and beyond. *In* Kellman, S. G. The self-begetting novel p49-76

**Button, Karen Elias-** See Elias-Button, Karen

**Buxton, John**

Two dead birds: a note on The phoenix and turtle. *In* English Renaissance studies, ed. by J. Carey p44-55

**Bykaŭ, Vasiliĭ Uladzimiravich**

### About

Shneidman, N. N. Bondarev and Bykov: the war theme. *In* Shneidman, N. N. Soviet literature in the 1970s. artistic diversity and ideological conformity p47-60

**Bykov, Vassily Vladimirovich.** See Bykaŭ Vasiliĭ Uladzimiravich

**Byron, George Gordon Noël Byron, 6th Baron**

### About

Mellor, A. K. Byron: 'half dust, half deity." *In* Mellor, A. K. English romantic irony p31-76

Stone, D. D. Trollope, Byron, and the conventionalities. *In* Stone, D. D. The romantic impulse in Victorian fiction p46-73

### About individual works
*Cain*

Farrell, J. P. Byron: rebellion and revolution. *In* Farrell, J. P. Revolution as tragedy p131-86

*Don Juan*

Mellor, A. K. Byron: "half dust, half deity." *In* Mellor, A. K. English romantic irony p31-76

*Marino Faliero*

Farrell, J. P. Byron: rebellion and revolution. *In* Farrell, J. P. Revolution as tragedy p131-86

*Sardanapalus*

Farrell, J. P. Byron: rebellion and revolution. *In* Farrell, J. P. Revolution as tragedy p131-86

### Political and social views

Farrell, J. P. Byron: rebellion and revolution. *In* Farrell, J. P. Revolution as tragedy p131-86

**Byzantine Empire**

Pickering, F. P. The Western image of Byzantium in the Middle Ages. *In* Pickering, F. P. Essays on medieval German literature and iconography p146-63

### Civilization

Brown, P. R. L. Art and society in late antiquity. *In* Age of spirituality, ed. by K. Weitzmann p17-27

### Study and teaching

Kristeller, P. O. Italian humanism and Byzantium. *In* Kristeller, P. O. Renaissance thought and its sources p137-50

**Byzantine illumination of books and manuscripts.** See Illumination of books and manuscripts, Byzantine

**Byzantine literature.** See Christian literature, Byzantine

**Byzantine mosaics.** See Mosaics, Byzantine

**Byzantine studies.** See Byzantine Empire—Study and teaching

# C

**CIA.** See United States. Central Intelligence Agency

**Caadaev, P. J.** See Chaadev, Petr Iakovlevich

**Caballero, Fernán, pseud. of Cecilia Bohl de Faber**

### About individual works
*Clemencia*

Fox-Lockert, L. Fernan Caballero (Cecilia Bohl de Faber). *In* Fox-Lockert, L. Women novelists in Spain and Spanish America p36-48

**Cabbala.** See Cabala

**Cabala**

Werblowsky, R. J. Z. O felix culpa: a cabbalistic version. *In* Studies in Jewish religious and intellectual history, ed. by S. Stein and R. Loewe p355-62

**Cabell, James Branch**

### About

Duke, M. "Cabell" rhymes with "rabble." *In* Seasoned authors for a new season: the search for standards in popular writings, ed. by L. Filler p117-26

**Cabello de Carbonera, Mercedes**

### About individual works
*Blanca Sol*

Fox-Lockert, L. Mercedes Cabello de Carbonera. *In* Fox-Lockert, L. Women novelists in Spain and Spanish America p147-55

**Cabrera Infante, Guillermo**

### About individual works
*Vista del amanecer en el trópico*

Foster, D. W. Guillermo Cabrera Infante's Vista del amanecer en el trópico and the generic ambiguity of narrative. *In* Foster, D. W. Studies in the contemporary Spanish-American short story p110-20

**Cadogan, Mary, and Craig, Patricia**

### About individual works
*You're a brick, Angela!: a new look at girls' fiction from 1839 to 1975*

Segel, E. Domesticity and the wide, wide world. *In* Children's literature v8 p168-75

**Cahan, Abraham**

### About individual works
*Yekl: a tale of the New York ghetto*

Miller, G. Jews without manners. *In* Miller, G. Screening the novel p 1-18

**Cahnman, Werner Jacob**
Vico and historical sociology. *In* Conference on Vico and Contemporary Thought, New York, 1976. Vico and contemporary thought pt2 p168-78

**Cailleux, André**
The geological map of North America (1752) of J.-E. Guettard. *In* New Hampshire Bicentennial Conference on the History of Geology, University of New Hampshire, 1976. Two hundred years of geology in America p39-41

**Cain**

### Art
Schapiro, M. "Cain's jawbone that did the first murder." *In* Schapiro, M. Selected papers v3: Late antique, early Christian and mediaeval art p249-65

**Cain, James Mallahan**

### About individual works
*The postman always rings twice*
Miller, G. Special delivery. *In* Miller, G. Screening the novel p46-63

**Cain, Peter**
Political economy in Edwardian England: the tariff-reform controversy. *In* The Edwardian age: conflict and stability, ed. by A. O'Day p35-59

**Cairns, Francis**
Self-imitation within a generic framework: Ovid, Amores 2.9 and 3.11 and the renuntiatio amoris. *In* Creative imitation and Latin literature, ed. by D. West and T. Woodman p121-41

**Cairns, Huntington**
Mencken of Baltimore. *In* On Mencken, ed. by J. Dorsey p51-83

**Calder, Daniel G.**
The study of style in Old English poetry: a historical introduction. *In* Old English poetry, ed. by D. G. Calder p 1-65

**Calendar of 354.** See Chronographis anni 354

**Calhoon, Robert McCluer.** See Potter, J. jt. auth.

**California split (Motion picture)**
Kauffmann, S. California split. *In* Kauffmann, S. Before my eyes p34-35

**California suite (Motion picture)**
Kael, P. Simon & Ross—the compassion boys. *In* Kael, P. When the lights go down p529-33

**Calin, William C.**
Defense and illustration of fin' amor: some polemical comments on the Robertsonian approach. *In* The Expansion and transformations of courtly literature, ed. by N. B. Smith and J. T. Snow p32-48

**Callanan, Jeremiah Joseph**

### About
Welch, R. J. J. Callanan: a provincial romantic. *In* Welch, R. Irish poetry from Moore to Yeats p46-75

**Callimachus**

### About
Thomas, R. F. New comedy, Callimachus, and Roman poetry. *In* Harvard Studies in classical philology, v83 p179-206

### About individual works
*Hymns and epigrams (Epigram no. 28)*
Henrichs, A. Callimachus Epigram 28: a fastidious priamel. *In* Harvard Studies in classical philology, v83 p207-12

**Calvary, Moses**
Yiddish. *In* The Jew, ed. by A. A. Cohen p31-42

**Calvin, Jean**

### About
Ozment, S. H. Calvin and Calvinism. *In* Ozment, S. H. The age of reform, 1250-1550 p352-80

**Calvin, John.** See Calvin, Jean

**Calvinism**
Ozment, S. H. Calvin and Calvinism. *In* Ozment, S. H. The age of reform, 1250-1550 p352-80
*See also* Puritans

### Netherlands
Mack, P. The wonderyear. *In* Religion and the people, 800-1700, ed. by J. Obelkevich p191-220

**Cambridge-Somerville Youth Study**
Morowitz, H. J. A controlled social experiment. *In* Morowitz, H. J. The wine of life, and other essays on societies, energy & living things p163-67

**Cambridge University**

### History
Westfall, R. S. Isaac Newton in Cambridge: the Restoration university and scientific creativity. *In* Culture and politics from Puritanism to the Enlightenment, ed. by P. Zagorin p135-64

**Cameroon**

### Ethnic relations
Kofele-Kale, N. The impact of environment on ethnic group values in Cameroon. *In* Values, identities, and national integration, ed. by J. N. Paden p121-50
Nwabuzor, E. J. O. Ethnic propensities for collaboration in Cameroon. *In* Values, identities, and national integration, ed. by J. N. Paden p231-58

### Politics and government
Kofele-Kale, N. The impact of environment on ethnic group values in Cameroon. *In* Values, identities, and national integration, ed. by J. N. Paden p121-50
Kofele-Kale, N. The impact of environment on national political culture in Cameroon. *In* Values, identities, and national integration, ed. by J. N. Paden p151-72
Nwabuzor, E. J. O. Ethnic value distance in Cameroon. *In* Values, identities, and national integration, ed. by J. N. Paden p205-29

### Social life and customs
Kofele-Kale, N. The impact of environment on ethnic group values in Cameroon. *In* Values, identities, and national integration, ed. by J. N. Paden p121-50
Nwabuzor, E. J. O. Ethnic propensities for collaboration in Cameroon. *In* Values, identities, and national integration, ed. by J. N. Paden p231-58
Nwabuzor, E. J. O. Ethnic value distance in Cameroon. *In* Values, identities, and national integration, ed. by J. N. Paden p205-29

**Cameroons.** See Cameroon

**Campbell, Joseph**
The interpretation of symbolic forms. *In* The Binding of Proteus, ed. by M. W. McCune, T. Orbison and P. M. Withim p35-59

**Campbell, Patricia B.**
Computer-assisted instruction in education: past, present and future. *In* Monster or messiah? Ed. by W. M. Mathews p89-98

**Campbell, Rita Ricardo**
Your health and the government. *In* The United States in the 1980s, ed. by P. Duignan and A. Rabushka p285-341

**Campin, Robert (Master of Flémalle)**

### About individual works
*Mérode altarpiece*
Schapiro, M. "Muscipula diaboli," the symbolism of the Mérode altarpiece. *In* Schapiro, M. Selected papers v3: Late antique, early Christian and mediaeval art p 1-11
Schapiro, M. A note on the Mérode altarpiece. *In* Schapiro, M. Selected papers v3: Late antique, early Christian and mediaeval art p12-19

**Camproux, Charles**
On the subject of an argument between Elias and his cousin. *In* The Interpretation of medieval lyric poetry, ed. by W. T. H. Jackson p61-90

**Camus, Albert**

### About individual works
*The plague*
Wilson, R. N. Albert Camus: personality as creative struggle. *In* Wilson, R. N. The writer as social seer p118-33

*The stranger*
Wilson, R. N. Albert Camus: personality as creative struggle. *In* Wilson, R. N. The writer as social seer p118-33

**Canada**
### Military policy
Regehr, E. What is militarism? In Problems of contemporary militarism, ed. by A. Eide and M. Thee p127-39

**Canadian fiction**
### Women authors
Irvine, L. A psychological journey: mothers and daughters in English-Canadian fiction. *In* The Lost tradition: mothers and daughters in literature, ed. by C. N. Davidson and E. M. Broner p242-52

**Canadian literature**
### Newfound—History and criticism
O'Flaherty, P. Visions and revisions: some writers in the new Newfoundland. *In* O'Flaherty, P. The rock observed p144-83

**Cancels (Printing)** See Printing—Cancels

**Cancer.** See Carcinogens

**Cancer causing agents.** See Carcinogens

**Canela Indians.** See Canelo Indians

**Canelo Indians**
Crocker, W. H. Canela kinship and the question of matrilineality. *In* Brazil, anthropological perspectives, ed. by M. L. Margolis and W. E. Carter p225-49

**Canetti, Elias**
### About
Turner, O. Elias Canetti: the intellectual as King Canute. *In* Modern Austrian writing, ed. by A. Best and H. Wolfschütz p79-96

**Cannabis**
La Barre, W. History and ethnography of cannabis. *In* La Barre, W. Culture in context p93-107

**Cantata**
Dent, E. J. Italian chamber cantatas. *In* Dent, E. J. Selected essays p58-84

**Capital formation.** See Saving and investment

**Capital output ratios.** See Capital productivity

**Capital productivity**
*See also* Labor productivity
### United States
Boskin, M. J. Economic growth and productivity. *In* The Economy in the 1980s: a program for growth and stability, ed. by M. J. Boskin p23-50

**Capital punishment**
Bedau, H. A. Capital punishment. *In* Matters of life and death, ed. by T. Regan p148-82

**Capitalism**
Hook, S. Capitalism, socialism, and freedom. *In* Hook, S. Philosophy and public policy p111-16
Senghaas, D. Militarism dynamics in the contemporary context of periphery capitalism. *In* Problems of contemporary militarism, ed. by A. Eide and M. Thee p195-206
*See also* Entrepreneur

**Car wash (Motion picture)**
Kael, P. No id. *In* Kael, P. When the lights go down p184-89

**Carabine, Keith**
Reading David Copperfield. *In* Reading the Victorian novel: detail into form, ed. by I. Gregor p150-67

**Carbonera, Mercedes Cabello de.** See Cabello de Carbonera, Mercedes

**Carcinogenicity testing**
Ames, B. N. Environmental chemicals causing cancer and genetic birth defects. *In* The Condition of man, ed. by P. Hallberg p80-105

**Carcinogens**
Ames, B. N. Environmental chemicals causing cancer and genetic birth defects. *In* The Condition of man, ed. by P. Hallberg p80-105

**Cardano, Girolamo**
### Influence—Burton, Robert
Bamborough, J. B. Burton and Cardan. *In* English Renaissance studies, ed. by J. Carey p180-93

**Cárdenas de Dwyer, Carlota**
International literary metaphor and Ron Arias: an analysis of The Road to Tamazunchale. *In* The Identification and analysis of Chicano literature, ed. by F. Jiménez p358-64

**Cardoso, Fernando Henrique**
On the characterization of authoritarian regimes in Latin America. *In* The New authoritarianism in Latin America, ed. by D. Collier p33-57

**Carduner, Jean.** See Carduner, Jean René

**Carduner, Jean René**
Metamorphosis and biography. *In* André Malraux, ed. by F. Dorenlot and M. Tison-Braun p37-54

**Carey, John**
Donne and coins. *In* English Renaissance studies, ed. by J. Carey p151-63

**Carey, Michael J.**
Ireland. *In* Western European party systems, ed. by P. H. Merkel p257-77

**Cargill, Oscar**
"The ordeal of Van Wyck Brooks." *In* Van Wyck Brooks: the critic and his critics, ed. by W. Wasserstrom p129-36

**Caribbean literature (English)** See West Indian literature (English)

**Carisoprodol**

La Barre, W. Soma: the three-and-one-half millennia mystery. *In* La Barre, W. Culture in context p108-15

**Carleton, William**

### About

Boué, A. William Carleton as a short-story writer. *In* The Irish short story, ed. by P. Rafroidi and T. Brown p81-89

### About individual works
*The black prophet*

Cronin, J. William Carleton: the black prophet. *In* Cronin, J. The Anglo-Irish novel, v 1 p83-98

**Carlton, Charles**

Three British revolutions and the personality of kingship. *In* Three British revolutions: 1641, 1688, 1776, ed. by J. G. A. Pocock p165-207

**Carlyle, Thomas**

### About

Mellor, A. K. Carlyle's Sartor resartus: a self-consuming artifact. *In* Mellor, A. K. English romantic irony p109-34

Stone, D. D. Introduction. *In* Stone, D. D. The romantic impulse in Victorian fiction p 1-45

### About individual works
*The French Revolution*

Farrell, J. P. Carlyle: the true man's tragedy. *In* Farrell, J. P. Revolution as tragedy p187-245

*The life of Friedrich Schiller*

Ashton, R. D. Carlyle and German philosophy (1824-34) *In* Ashton, R. D. The German idea p91-98

*On heroes, hero-worship,
and the heroic in history*

Farrell, J. P. Carlyle: the true man's tragedy. *In* Farrell, J. P. Revolution as tragedy p187-245

*Sartor resartus*

Ashton, R. D. Sartor resartus, a beginning and an end (1830-4). *In* Ashton, R. D. The German idea p99-104

Hartman, G. H. The sacred jungle 1: Carlyle, Eliot, Bloom. *In* Hartman, G. H. Criticism in the wilderness p42-62

Mellor, A. K. Carlyle's Sartor resartus: a self-consuming artifact. *In* Mellor, A. K. English romantic irony p109-34

Spengemann, W. C. Poetic autobiography. *In* Spengemann, W. C. The forms of autobiography p110-65

*Sartor resartus (Book III)*

Farrell, J. P. Carlyle: the true man's tragedy. *In* Farrell, J. P. Revolution as tragedy p187-245

*The state of German literature*

Ashton, R. D. Carlyle, the Germanist of the Edinburgh Review (1827) *In* Ashton, R. D. The German idea p67-76

**Carlyle, Thomas, tr**

### About individual works
*Wilhelm Meister*

Ashton, R. D. Carlyle and Goethe (1822-32) *In* Ashton, R. D. The German idea p76-91

### Influence—Lewes

Ashton, R. D. Lewes: one of Carlyle's 'young men' (1835-9). *In* Ashton, R. D. The German idea p105-11

### Political and social views

Farrell, J. P. Carlyle: the true man's tragedy. *In* Farrell, J. P. Revolution as tragedy p187-245

**Carmi, T.**

Jewish literature: poetry. *In* The Jewish world, ed. by E. Kedourie p258-63

**Carmina burana**

Hatto, A. T. An early 'Tagelied'. *In* Hatto, A. T. Essays on medieval German and other poetry p64-67

**Carmina burana. Dum Diane vitrea**

Jackson, W. T. H. Interpretation of Carmina burana 62, 'Dum Diane vitrea'. *In* The Interpretation of medieval lyric poetry, ed. by W. T. H. Jackson p44-60

Robertson, D. W. Two poems from the Carmina burana. *In* Robertson, D. W. Essays in medieval culture p131-50

**Carmina burana. Si Linguis angelicis**

Robertson, D. W. Two poems from the Carmina burana. *In* Robertson, D. W. Essays in medieval culture p131-50

**Carné, Marcel.** See Prévert, J. jt. auth.

**Carne-Ross, D. S.**

Instaurations

*Contents*

Center of resistance

Dante Antagonistes

Dark with excessive bright: four ways of looking at Góngora

Deianeira's dark cupboard: a question from Sophocles

Leopardi: the poet in a time of need

The music of a lost dynasty: Pound in the classroom

The scandal of necessity

Weaving with points of gold: Pindar's Sixth Olympian

**Carneades, 2d cent. B.C.**

### About

Striker, G. Sceptical strategies. *In* Doubt and dogmatism, ed. by M. Schofield, M. Burnyeat and J. Barnes p54-83

**Carner, Mosco**

Major and minor

*Contents*

A Beethoven movement and its successors

Bruckner versus Mahler

Bruckner's organ recitals in France and England

Composers as critics

Debussy and Puccini

Elgar and the symphony

Fidelio

Form and technique of Mahler's Lied von der Erde

Goethe and music

Guido Adler: a pioneer of musicology

Mahler's re-scoring of the Schumann symphonies

Mahler's visit to London

The mass from Rossini to Dvořák

Mátyás Seiber and his Ulysses

Pfitzner versus Berg

Schubert's orchestral music

Schumann as symphonist

The secret of Johann Strauss

Carner, Mosco
Major and minor
*Contents—Continued*
Simone Mayr and his L'amor coniugale
The string quartets of Bartók
The two 'Manons'
**Carnival plays.** See Mumming plays
**Carpentier, Alejo**

### About individual works
*The lost steps*
Macdonald, I. R. Magical electicism: Los pasos perdidos and Jean-Paul Sartre. *In* Contemporary Latin American fiction, ed. by S. Bacarisse p 1-17
**Carr, A. D.**
The historical background, 1282-1550. *In* A Guide to Welsh literature, ed. by A. O. H. Jarman and G. R. Hughes v2 p11-33
**Carr, Lois Green, and Menard, Russell R.**
Immigration and opportunity: the freedman in early colonial Maryland. *In* The Chesapeake in the seventeenth century, ed. by T. W. Tate and D. L. Ammerman p206-41
**Carr, Lois Green, and Walsh, Lorena S.**
The planter's wife: the experience of white women in seventeenth-century Maryland. *In* A Heritage of her own, ed. by N. F. Cott and E. H. Pleck p25-57
**Carrard, Philippe**
Life made into fiction. *In* André Malraux, ed. by F. Dorenlot and M. Tison-Braun p189-200
**Carrie (Motion picture)**
Kael, P. The curse. *In* Kael, P. When the lights go down p208-12
**Carroll, Lewis,** pseud. See Dodgson, Charles Lutwidge
**Carter, Angela**
The language of sisterhood. *In* The State of the language, ed. by L. Michaels and C. Ricks p226-34
**Carter, Frank W.**
Kafka's Prague. *In* The World of Franz Kafka, ed. by J. P. Stern p30-43
**Carter, John**
Bibliography and the rare book trade. *In* The Bibliographical Society of America, 1904-79 p307-17
**Cartesian linguistics**
Sullivan, J. J. Noam Chomsky and Cartesian linguistics. *In* Psychology of language and thought, ed. by R. W. Rieber p197-223
Uitti, K. D. Cordemoy and 'Cartesian linguistics.' *In* Psychology of language and thought, ed. by R. W. Rieber p53-76
**Cartwright, George**

### About
O'Flaherty, P. Walking new ground: books by two Newfoundland pioneers, 1770-1882. *In* O'Flaherty, P. The rock observed p32-48
**Carver, Thomas Nixon**

### About individual works
*The single tax*
Andelson, R. V. Carver: reluctant demi-Georgist. *In* Critics of Henry George, ed. by R. V. Andelson p303-12
**Casal, Julián del**

### About
Pearsall, P. Julian del Casal's portraits of women. *In* The Analysis of literary texts, ed. by R. D. Pope p78-88

**Casal, Lourdes**
Revolution and conciencia: women in Cuba. *In* Women, war, and revolution, ed. by C. R. Berkin and C. M. Lovett p183-206
**Casciato, Arthur D.**
His editor's hand: Hiram Haydn's changes in Styron's Lie down in darkness. *In* Virginia. University. Bibliographical Society. Studies in bibliography v33 p263-76
**Casey, Carol F.** See Bode, K. A. jt. auth.
**Cash, Wilbur Joseph**

### About individual works
*The mind of the South*
King, R. H. Narcissus grown analytical: Cash's Southern mind. *In* King, R. H. A Southern Renaissance p146-72
**Casimir, Louis John**
Dutchman: the price of culture is a lie. *In* The Binding of Proteus, ed. by M. W. McCune, T. Orbison and P. M. Withim p298-310
**Cassavetes, John**

### About individual works
*A woman under the influence*
Kauffmann, S. A woman under the influence/Murder on the Orient express. *In* Kauffmann, S. Before my eyes p94-97
**Castelseprio, Italy. Santa Maria (Church)**
Schapiro, M. The frescoes of Castelseprio. *In* Schapiro, M. Selected paper v3: Late antique, early Christian and mediaeval art p67-114
Schapiro, M. Notes on Castelseprio. *In* Schapiro, M. Selected papers v3: Late antique, early Christian and mediaeval art p115-42
**Cataloging of manuscripts**
Joyce, W. L. The manuscript collections of the American Antiquarian Society. *In* American Antiquarian Society. Proceedings v89 pt 1 p123-52
**Cather, Willa Sibert**

### About
Lilienfeld, J. Reentering paradise: Cather, Colette, Woolf and their mothers. *In* The Lost tradition: mothers and daughters in literature, ed. by C. N. Davidson and E. M. Broner p160-75
Trilling, L. Willa Cather. *In* Trilling, L. Speaking of literature and society p93-99
**Catholic Church**

### Doctrinal and controversial works
Daly, G. Alfred Loisy and the radicalization of the Modernistic movement. *In* Daly, G. Transcendence and immanence p51-68
Daly, G. History and dogma: the debate between Alfred Loisy and Maurice Blondel. *In* Daly, G. Transcendence and immanence p69-90
Daly, G. The integralist response (1): prelude to the Roman condemnation of Modernism. *In* Daly, G. Transcendence and immanence p165-89
Daly, G. The integralist response (2): Pascendi and after. *In* Daly, G. Transcendence and immanence p190-217

### History—Middle Ages, 600-1500
*See* Church History—Middle Ages, 600-1500

### Liturgy and ritual—Hours
*See* Hours, Books of

**Catholic Church and Communism.** See Communism and Christianity—Catholic Church

**Catholic Church in the United States**
Greeley, A. M. American Catholics: the post-immigrant century. *In* The Third century, ed. by S. M. Lipset p205-21

**Catholic theology.** See Theology, Catholic

**Catholics**
**United States**
Greeley, A. M. American Catholics: the post-immigrant century. *In* The Third century, ed. by S. M. Lipset p205-21

**Cathrein, Victor**
**About individual works**
*The champions of agrarian socialism: a refutation of Émile de Laveleye and Henry George*
Andelson, R. V. Cathrein's careless clerical critique. *In* Critics of Henry George, ed. by R. V. Andelson p126-36

**Cats as laboratory animals**
Flynn, J. P. [and others.] Anatomical pathways for attack behavior in cats. *In* Human ethology, ed. by M. von Cranach [and others] p301-15

**Causation**
Frede, M. The original notion of cause. *In* Doubt and dogmatism, ed. by M. Schofield, M. Burnyeat and J. Barnes p217-49

Ivry, A. L. Averroes on causation. *In* Studies in Jewish religious and intellectual history, ed. by S. Stein and R. Loewe p143-56

Sorabji, R. Causation, laws and necessity. *In* Doubt and dogmatism, ed. by M. Schofield, M. Burnyeat and J. Barnes p250-82

**Cause and effect.** See Causation

**Cavafy, Constantine P.** See Kabaphēs, Kōnstantinos Petrou

**Cavalieri, Emilio de'**
**About individual works**
*La rappresentazione di anima e di corpo*
Dent, E. J. La rappresentazione di anima e di corpo. *In* Dent, E. J. Selected essays p207-17

**Cavendish, Margaret, Duchess of Newcastle**
See Newcastle, Margaret (Lucas) Cavendish, Duchess of

**Caws, Mary Ann**
On one crossing-over: Valery's sea into Hart Crane's scene. *In* The Analysis of literary texts, ed. by R. D. Pope p100-06

Poetics and passion. *In* André Malraux, ed. by F. Dorenlot and M. Tison-Braun p143-48

**Ceadel, Martin**
Popular fiction and the next war, 1918-39. *In* Class, culture and social change, ed. by F. Gloversmith p161-84

**Ceaser, James W.**
Political change and party reform. *In* Political parties in the eighties, ed. by R. A. Goldwin p97-115

**Cech, John**
Notes on American children's folklore. *In* Children's literature v8 p176-83

**Celan, Paul**
**About**
Last, R. Paul Celan and the metaphorical poets. *In* Modern Austrian writing, ed. by A. Best and H. Wolfschütz p142-55

**About individual works**
*Engführung*
Bosmajian, H. Towards the point of constriction: Nelly Sachs's "Landschaft aus Schreien" and Paul Celan's "Engführung." *In* Bosmajian, H. Metaphors of evil p183-228

**Celibacy**
Ozment, S. H. Marriage and the ministry in the Protestant churches. *In* Ozment, S. H. The age of reform, 1250-1550 p381-96

**Cell research**
Morowitz, H. J. Manufacturing a living organism. *In* Morowitz, H. J. The wine of life, and other essays on societies, energy & living things p90-94

**Cellérier, Guy**
Cognitive strategies in problem solving. *In* Language and learning, ed. by M. Piatelli-Palmarini p67-72

Some clarifications on innatism and constructivism. *In* Language and learning, ed. by M. Piattelli-Palmarini p83-87

**Cells**
Morowitz, H. J. Cell types: the great divide. *In* Morowitz, H. J. The wine of life, and other essays on societies, energy & living things p95-98

**Research**
*See* Cell research

**Censorship**
Berger, F. R. Pornography, sex and censorship. *In* The Philosophy of sex, ed. by A. Soble p322-47

**Censorship of the press.** See Liberty of the press

**Cent, Sion.** See Kent, John

**Central America**
**Antiquities**
Bray, W. From village to city in Mesoamerica. *In* The Origins of civilization, ed. by P. S. R. Moorey p78-102

**Civilization**
Bray, W. From village to city in Mesoamerica. *In* The Origins of civilization, ed. by P. S. R. Moorey p78-102

**Central banking.** See Banks and banking, Central

**Central banks.** See Banks and banking, Central

**Central Intelligence Agency.** See United States. Central Intelligence Agency

**Certainty.** See Truth

**Cervantes Saavedra, Miguel de**
**About individual works**
*Don Quixote de la Mancha*
Seidel, M. A. The revisionary inheritance: Rabelais and Cervantes. *In* Seidel, M. A. Satiric inheritance, Rabelais to Sterne p60-94

**Cézanne, Paul**
**About**
Ashton, D. Cézanne in the shadow of Frenhofer. *In* Ashton, D. A fable of modern art p30-47

**Chaadev, Petr Íakovlevich**
**Manuscripts**
Brun-Zejmis, J. "A word on the Polish question" by P. Ya. Chaadaev. *In* California Slavic studies v11 p25-32

**Chabrol, Claude**

*About individual works*

*Wedding in blood*

Kauffmann, S. Wedding in blood. *In* Kauffmann, S. Before my eyes p8-10

**Chagall, Marc**

*About individual works*

*Illustrations for the Bible*

Neumann, E. Chagall and the Bible. *In* Neumann, E. Creative man p113-37

**Chakrabarti, Chandana.** See Hare, P. H. jt. auth.

**Chambers, Whittaker**

*About*

Hook, S. The case of Alger Hiss. *In* Hook, S. Philosophy and public policy p238-52

**Champion, Larry S.**

"Confound their skill in covetousness": the ambivalent perspective of Shakespeare's King John. *In* Tennessee Studies in literature v24 p36-55

**Champollion, Jean François**

*About*

Irwin, J. T. Champollion and the historical background; Emerson's hieroglyphical emblems. *In* Irwin, J. T. American hieroglyphics p3-14

**Chandler, Alfred Dupont**

The United States: seedbed of managerial capitalism. *In* Managerial hierarchies, ed. by A. D. Chandler and H. Daems p9-40

*About individual works*

*The visible hand: the managerial revolution in American business*

Williamson, O. E. Emergence of The visible hand: implications for industrial organization. *In* Managerial hierarchies, ed. by A. D. Chandler and H. Daems p182-202

**Chandler, Alfred Dupont, and Daems, Herman**

Introduction. *In* Managerial hierarchies, ed. by A. D. Chandler and H. Daems p 1-8

Rise and evolution of big business. *In* Encyclopedia of American economic history, ed. by G. Porter v2 p619-38

**Change, Linguistic.** See Linguistic change

**Change, Social.** See Social change

**Changeux, Jean-Pierre**

Genetic determinism and epigenesis of the neuronal network: is there a biological compromise between Chomsky and Piaget? *In* Language and learning, ed. by M. Piattelli-Palmarini p185-97

**Chaney, Jill**

*About*

Rees, D. The sadness of compromise: Robert Cormier and Jill Chaney. *In* Rees, D. The marble in the water p155-72

**Chanson de Roland**

Damon, P. W. The middle of things: narrative patterns in the Iliad, Roland and Beowulf. *In* Old English literature in context, ed. by J. D. Niles p107-16

Vance, E. Roland and the poetics of memory. *In* Textual strategies, ed. by J. V. Harari p374-403

**Chapelain, Jean**

*About*

Ranum, O. Chapelain and the royal patronage of history. *In* Ranum, O. Artisans of glory p169-96

**Chaplin, Sir Charles Spencer**

*About*

Kauffmann, S. Chaplin: history and mystery. *In* Kauffmann, S. Before my eyes p413-18

**Char, René**

*About*

Schürmann, R. Situating René Char: Hölderlin, Heidegger, Char and the "there is." *In* Martin Heidegger and the question of literature, ed. by W. V. Spanos p173-94

**Character**

Morton, A. Character and the emotions. *In* Explaining emotions, ed. by A. O. Rorty p153-61

*See also* Conduct of life

**Character and characteristics in literature**

Korshin, P. J. Probability and character in the eighteenth century. *In* Probability, time and space in eighteenth-century literature, ed. by P. R. Backscheider p63-77

Martin, T. The negative character in American fiction. *In* Toward a new American literary history p230-43

*See also* Characters under names of authors, e.g. Chaucer, Geoffrey—Characters

**Charleston, S.C.**

History—Colonial period, ca. 1600-1775

Walsh, R. The revolutionary Charleston mechanic. *In* Small business in American life, ed. by S. W. Bruchey p49-79

Industries—History

Walsh, R. The revolutionary Charleston mechanic. *In* Small business in American life, ed. by S. W. Bruchey p49-79

**Charlesworth, William R.**

Ethology: understanding the other half of intelligence. *In* Human ethology, ed. by M. von Cranach [and others] p491-529

**Charlton, Kenneth**

The educational background. *In* The Age of Milton, ed. by C. A. Patrides and R. B. Waddington p102-37

**Charney, Hanna.** See Charney, Hanna Kurz

**Charney, Hanna Kurz**

Dialectics of character in Malraux. *In* André Malraux, ed. by F. Dorenlot and M. Tison-Braun p15-20

**Chase, Richard Xavier**

Production theory. *In* A Guide to post-Keynesian economics, ed. by A. S. Eichner p71-86

**Chasidism.** See Hasidism

**Chassebœuf, Constantin François, comte de Volney.** See Volney, Constantin François Chassebœuf, comte de

**Chatalic, Roger**

Frank O'Connor and the desolation of reality. *In* The Irish short story, ed. by P. Rafroidi and T. Brown p189-204

**Chateaubriand, François Auguste René vicomte de**

*About individual works*

*Atala*

Harbison, R. Romantic localism. *In* Harbison, R. Deliberate regression p115-47

*Life of Rancé*

Barthes, R. Chateaubriand: life of Rancé. *In* Barthes, R. New critical essays p41-54

**Chatman, Seymour**

The styles of narrative codes. *In* The Concept of style, ed. by B. Lang p169-81

**Chaucer, Geoffrey**

## About

Middleton, A. Chaucer's "new men" and the good of literature in the Canterbury tales. *In* Literature and society, ed. by E. W. Said p15-56

### About individual works

*The book of the Duchess*

Robertson, D. W. The concept of courtly love as an impediment to the understanding of medieval texts. *In* Robertson, D. W. Essays in medieval culture p257-72

Robertson, D. W. The historical setting of Chaucer's Book of the Duchess. *In* Robertson, D. W. Essays in medieval culture p235-56

*Canterbury tales*

Middleton, A. Chaucer's "new men" and the good of literature in the Canterbury tales. *In* Literature and society, ed. by E. W. Said p15-56

Robertson, D. W. Some disputed Chaucerian terminology. *In* Robertson, D. W. Essays in medieval culture p291-301

*Canterbury tales—The franklin's tale*

Robertson, D. W. Chaucer's franklin and his tale. *In* Robertson, D. W. Essays in medieval culture p273-90

*Canterbury tales—The man of law's tale*

Manning, S. Chaucer's Constance, pale and passive. *In* Chaucerian problems and perspectives, ed. by E. Vasta and Z. P. Thundy p13-23

*Canterbury tales—The merchant's tale*

Donovan, M. J. Chaucer's January and May: counterparts in Claudian. *In* Chaucerian problems and perspectives, ed. by E. Vasta and Z. P. Thundy p59-69

*Canterbury tales—The miller's tale*

Reiss, E. Chaucer's deerne love and the medieval view of secrecy in love. *In* Chaucerian problems and perspectives, ed. by E. Vasta and Z. P. Thundy p164-79

*Canterbury tales—The nun's priest's tale*

Bloomfield, M. W. The wisdom of The nun's priest's tale. *In* Chaucerian problems and perspectives, ed. by E. Vasta and Z. P. Thundy p70-82

*Canterbury tales—The parson's tale*

Ruggiers, P. G. Serious Chaucer: The tale of Melibeus and The parson's tale. *In* Chaucerian problems and perspectives, ed. by E. Vasta and Z. P. Thundy p83-94

*Canterbury tales—The tale of Melibeus*

Ruggiers, P. G. Serious Chaucer: the tale of Melibeus and The parson's tale. *In* Chaucerian problems and perspectives, ed. by E. Vasta and Z. P. Thundy p83-94

*Canterbury tales—The wife of Bath's tale*

Thundy, Z. P. Matheolus, Chaucer, and The wife of Bath. *In* Chaucerian problems and perspectives, ed. by E. Vasta and Z. P. Thundy p24-58

*Chaucers words unto Adam, his owne scriveyn*

Kaske, R. E. Clericus Adam and Chaucer's Adam Scriveyn. *In* Chaucerian problems and perspectives, ed. by E. Vasta and Z. P. Thundy p114-18

*The house of fame*

Kratzmann, G. The palice of honour and The house of fame. *In* Kratzmann, G. Anglo-Scottish literary relations, 1430-1550 p104-28

*The parlement of foules*

Bennett, J. A. W. Some second thoughts on The parlement of foules. *In* Chaucerian problems and perspectives, ed. by E. Vasta and Z. P. Thundy p132-46

*To Rosemounde*

Vasta, E. To Rosemounde: Chaucer's "gentil" dramatic monologue. *In* Chaucerian problems and perspectives, ed. by E. Vasta and Z. P. Thundy p97-113

*Troilus and Criseyde*

Bowers, J. M. How Criseyde falls in love. *In* Expansion and transformations of courtly literature, ed. by N. B. Smith and J. T. Snow p141-55

Gransden, K. W. Lente currite, noctis equi: Chaucer, Troilus and Criseyde 3.1422-70, Donne, The sun rising and Ovid, Amores 1.13. *In* Creative imitation and Latin literature, ed. by D. West and T. Woodman p157-71

David, A. Chaucerian comedy and Criseyde. *In* Essays on Troilus and Criseyde, ed. by M. Salu p90-104

Frankis, J. Paganism and pagan love in Troilus and Criseyde. *In* Essays on Troilus and Criseyde, ed. by M. Salu p57-72

Gaylord, A. T. The lesson of the Troilus: chastisement and correction. *In* Essays on Troilus and Criseyde, ed. by M. Salu p23-42

Kratzmann, G. Henryson and English poetry. *In* Kratzmann, G. Anglo-Scottish literary relations, 1430-1550 p63-103

Lambert, M. Troilus, books I-III: a Criseydan reading. *In* Essays on Troilus and Criseyde, ed. by M. Salu p105-25

McKinnell, J. Letters as a type of the formal level in Troilus and Criseyde. *In* Essays on Troilus and Criseyde, ed. by M. Salu p73-89

Robertson, D. W. The concept of courtly love as an impediment to the understanding of medieval texts. *In* Robertson, D. W. Essays in medieval culture p257-72

Windeatt, B. The text of the Troilus. *In* Essays on Troilus and Criseyde, ed. by M. Salu p 1-22

Wimsatt, J. I. Realism in Troilus and Criseyde and the Roman de la Rose. *In* Essays on Troilus and Criseyde, ed. by M. Salu p43-56

## Characters

Middleton, A. Chaucer's "new men" and the good of literature in the Canterbury tales. *In* Literature and society, ed. by E. W. Said p15-56

Robertson, D. W. Some disputed Chaucerian terminology. *In* Robertson, D. W. Essays in medieval culture p291-301

### Characters—Constance

Loomis, D. B. Constance and the stars. *In* Chaucerian problems and perspectives, ed. by E. Vasta and Z. P. Thundy p207-20

Manning, S. Chaucer's Constance, pale and passive. *In* Chaucerian problems and perspectives, ed. by E. Vasta and Z. P. Thundy p13-23

### Characters—Criseyde

David, A. Chaucerian comedy and Criseyde. *In* Essays on Troilus and Criseyde, ed. by M. Salu p90-104

**Chaucer, Geoffrey—Characters—Criseyde—*Cont.***

Donaldson, E. T. Briseis, Briseida, Criseyde, Cresseid, Cressid: progress of a heroine. *In* Chaucerian problems and perspectives, ed. by E. Vasta and Z. P. Thundy p3-12

Lambert, M. Troilus, books I-III: a Criseydan reading. *In* Essays on Troilus and Criseyde, ed. by M. Salu p105-25

### Characters—Hodge

Hieatt, C. B. "To boille the chiknes with the marybones": Hodge's kitchen revisited. *In* Chaucerian problems and perspectives, ed. by E. Vasta and Z. P. Thundy p141-63

### Contemporary England

Robertson, D. W. Some disputed Chaucerian terminology. *In* Robertson, D. W. Essays in medieval culture p291-301

### Manuscripts

Windeatt, B. The text of the Troilus. *In* Essays on Troilus and Criseyde, ed. by M. Salu p 1-22

### Sources

Loomis, D. B. Constance and the stars. *In* Chaucerian problems and perspectives, ed. by E. Vasta and Z. J. Thundy p207-20

Wimsatt, J. I. Chaucer, Fortune, and Machaut's "Il m'est avis." *In* Chaucerian problems and perspectives, ed. by E. Vasta and Z. P. Thundy p119-31

**Chaudhuri, Nirad C.**

India in English literature. *In* Royal Society of Literature of the United Kingdom, London. Essays by divers hands: innovation in contemporary literature, new ser. v40 p15-33

**Chaunu, Huguette, and Chaunu, Pierre**

#### About individual works
*Séville et l'Atlantique, 1550-1650*

Braudel, F. Toward a serial history: Seville and the Atlantic, 1504-1650. *In* Braudel, F. On history p91-104

**Chaunu, Pierre.** See Chaunu, H. jt. auth.

**Chayefsky, Paddy**

#### About individual works
*Network*

Kael, P. Hot air. *In* Kael, P. When the lights go down p219-24

Kauffmann, S. Network. *In* Kauffmann, S. Before my eyes p101-04

**Chekhov, Anton Pavlovich**

#### About

Egri, P. The use of the short story in O'Neill's and Chekhov's one-act plays: a Hungarian view of O'Neill. *In* Eugene O'Neill, ed. by V. Floyd p115-44

McConkey, J. Two anonymous writers, E. M. Forster and Anton Chekhov. *In* E. M. Forster: a human exploration, ed. by G. K. Das and J. Beer p231-44

#### About individual works
*A boring story*

Holloway, J. Identity, inversion and density elements in narrative: three tales by Chekhov, James and Lawrence. *In* Holloway, J. Narrative and structure: exploratory essays p53-73

#### Influence—Yeh, Shao-chün

Prušek, J. Yeh Shao-chün and Anton Chekhov. *In* Prušek, J. The lyrical and the epic p178-94

**Chemistry**

#### History—Scotland

Donovan, A. L. Scottish responses to the new chemistry of Lavoisier. *In* Studies in eighteenth-century culture v9 p237-49

**Chen, Yen-ping.** See Shen, Yen-ping

**Chereb, David M.** See Kamrany, N. M. jt. auth.

**Chesapeake Bay region**

#### Emigration and immigration

Horn, J. P. P. Servant emigration to the Chesapeake in the seventeenth century. *In* The Chesapeake in the seventeenth century, ed. by T. W. Tate and D. L. Ammerman p51-95

#### Historiography

Tate, T. W. The seventeenth-century Chesapeake and its modern historians. *In* The Chesapeake in the seventeenth century, ed. by T. W. Tate and D. L. Ammerman p3-50

**Chester, Robert**

#### About individual works
*The phoenix and turtle*

Buxton, J. Two dead birds: a note on The phoenix and turtle. *In* English Renaissance studies, ed. by J. Carey p44-55

**Chevalier, Louis**

#### About individual works
*Laboring classes and dangerous classes in Paris during the first half of the nineteenth century*

Braudel, F. Demography and the scope of the human sciences. *In* Braudel, F. On history p132-61

**Chi, Madeleine**

Ts'ao Ju-lin (1876-1966): his Japanese connections. *In* The Chinese and the Japanese, ed. by A. Iriye p140-60

**Chicano literature (English)** See American literature—Mexican American authors

**Child, Lydia Maria (Francis)**

#### About

Karcher, C. L. Lydia Maria Child and The Juvenile Miscellany. *In* Research about nineteenth-century children and books, ed. by S. K. Richardson p67-84

**Child abuse in literature**

Fiedler, L. A. Child abuse and the literature of childhood. *In* Children's literature v8 p147-53

**Child analysis**

La Barre, M. B. "The worm in the honeysuckle": a case study of a child's hysterical blindness. *In* La Barre, W. Culture in context p233-46

**Child and parent.** See Parent and child

**Child development**

Coles, R. Children's stories: the link to a past. *In* Children's literature v8 p141-46

**Child health.** See Children—Care and hygiene

**Child psychoanalysis.** See Child analysis

**Child psychotherapy.** See Child analysis

**Child welfare.** See Foundlings

**Childbirth**

#### France

Lager, M. Childbirth in seventeenth-and eighteenth-century France: obstetrical practices and collective attitudes. *In* Medicine and society in France, ed. by R. Forester and O. Ranum p137-76

Childhood. See Children

**Children**

*See also* Child development

### Care and hygiene—France

Morel, M. F. City and country in eighteenth-century medical discussions about early childhood. *In* Medicine and society in France, ed. by R. Forester and O. Ranum p48-65

### Health

*See* Children—Care and hygiene

### History—Book reviews

Arnstein, W. L. Reflections on histories of childhood. *In* Research about nineteenth-century children and books, ed. by S. K. Richardson p41-60

### Language

Dunn, J. Playing in speech. *In* The State of the language, ed. by L. Michaels and C. Ricks p202-12

**Children, Blind**

La Barre, M. B. "The worm in the honeysuckle": a case study of a child's hysterical blindness. *In* La Barre, W. Culture in context p233-46

Children and adults. See Conflict of generations

**Children in art**

Harbison, R. Nature as a child. *In* Harbison, R. Deliberate regression p3-24

**Children in literature**

Bixler, P. Idealization of the child and childhood in Frances Hodgson Burnett's Little Lord Fauntleroy and Mark Twain's Tom Sawyer. *In* Research about nineteenth-century children and books, ed. by S. K. Richardson p85-96

Doll, C. The children of Sophie May. *In* Research about nineteenth-century children and books, ed. by S. K. Richardson p97-116

**Children in poetry.** See Children in literature

**The children of pride, ed. by Robert Manson Myers**

Pole, J. R. Of Mr. Booker T. Washington and others. *In* Pole, J. R. Paths to the American past p170-88

**Children's books.** See Children's literature

**Children's literature**

Fiedler, L. A. Child abuse and the literature of childhood. *In* Children's literature v8 p147-53

Hillman, J. The children, the children! *In* Children's literature v8 p3-6

Kuskin, K. The language of children's literature. *In* The State of the language, ed. by L. Michaels and C. Ricks p213-25

### Collectors and collecting

Coughlan, M. N. The Maxine Waldron collection of children's books and paper toys. *In* Research about nineteenth-century children and books, ed. by S. K. Richardson p61-66

### History and criticism

Egoff, S. Beyond the garden wall. *In* The Arbuthnot lectures, 1970-1979 p189-203

Fisher, M. Rights and wrongs. *In* The Arbuthnot lectures, 1970-1979 p3-20

Gardam, J. Writing for children: some wasps in the marmalade. *In* Royal Society of Literature of the United Kingdom, London. Essays by divers hands: innovation in contemporary literature, new ser. v40 p52-66

Townsend, J. R. Standards of criticism for children's literature. *In* The Arbuthnot lectures, 1970-1979 p23-36

Watanabe, S. One of the dozens. *In* The Arbuthnot lectures, 1970-1979 p141-63

### Periodicals—Bibliography

Silverman, J. A rack of journals: research in children's literature. *In* Children's literature v8 p193-204

### Technique

Gardam, J. Writing for children: some wasps in the marmalade. *In* Royal Society of Literature of the United Kingdom, London. Essays by divers hands: innovation in contemporary literature, new ser. v40 p52-66

McIllwraith, M. M. H. M. Talent is not enough. *In* Arbuthnot lectures, 1970-1979 p105-19

### England—History and criticism

Kramnick, L. Children's literature and bourgeois ideology: observations on culture and industrial capitalism in the later eighteenth century. *In* Culture and politics from Puritanism to the Enlightenment, ed. by P. Zagorin p203-40

### Europe—History and criticism

Orvig, M. One world in children's books? *In* The Arbuthnot lectures, 1970-1979 p39-59

### Germany—History and criticism

Hürlimann, B. Fortunate moments in children's books. *In* The Arbuthnot lectures, 1970-1979 p63-80

**Children's literature, American**

### History and criticism

Christy, H. R. First appearances: literature in nineteenth-century periodicals for children. *In* Research about nineteenth-century children and books, ed. by S. K. Richardson p117-32

Fritz, J. The education of an American. *In* The Arbuthnot lectures, 1970-1979 p123-38

### Translations into Hebrew

Ofek, U. Tom and Laura from right to left. *In* The Arbuthnot lectures, 1970-1979 p167-85

**Children's literature, English**

Avery, G. E. Children's books and social history. *In* Research about nineteenth-century children and books, ed. by S. K. Richardson p23-40

### Research

Avery, G. E. The researcher's craft: designs and implements. *In* Research about nineteenth-century children and books, ed. by S. K. Richardson p7-22

### Stories, plots, etc.

Kramnick, I. Children's literature and bourgeois ideology: observations on culture and industrial capitalism in the later eighteenth century. *In* Culture and politics from Puritanism to the Enlightenment, ed. by P. Zagorin p203-40

**Children's literature, Hebrew**

### History and criticism

Ofek, U. Tom and Laura from right to left. *In* The Arbuthnot lectures, 1970-1979 p167-85

**Children's periodicals, American**

### History

Christy, H. R. First appearances: literature in nineteenth-century periodicals for children. *In* Research about nineteenth-century children and books, ed. by S. K. Richardson p117-32

**Children's poetry, English**

### History and criticism

Shaw, J. M. Poetry for children of two centuries. *In* Research about nineteenth-century children and books, ed. by S. K. Richardson p133-42

**Children's stories.** See Story-telling

**Childress, Alice**

### About individual works

*Wine in the wilderness*

Brown, J. Wine in the wilderness. *In* Brown, J. Feminist drama p56-70

**Chimpanzees**

### Psychology

Bronowski, J. and Bellugi, U. Language, name, and concept. *In* Speaking of apes, ed. by T. A. Sebeok and J. Umiker-Sebeok p103-13

Brown, R. The first sentences of child and chimpanzee. *In* Speaking of apes, ed. by T. A. Sebeok and J. Umiker-Sebeok p85-101

Fouts, R. S. and Rigby, R. L. Man-chimpanzee communication. *In* Speaking of apes, ed. by T. A. Sebeok and J. Umiker-Sebeok p261-85

Gardner, R. A. and Gardner, B. T. Comparative psychology and language acquisition. *In* Speaking of apes, ed. by T. A. Sebeok and J. Umiker-Sebeok p287-330

Healy, A. F. Can chimpanzees learn a phonemic language? *In* Speaking of apes, ed. by T. A. Sebeok and J. Umiker-Sebeok p141-43

Hediger, H. Do you speak Yerkish? The newest colloquial language with chimpanzees. *In* Speaking of apes, ed. by T. A. Sebeok and J. Umiker-Sebeok p441-47

Hill, J. H. Apes and language. *In* Speaking of apes, ed. by T. A. Sebeok and J. Umiker-Sebeok p331-51

Kellogg, W. N. Communication and language in the home-raised chimpanzee. *In* Speaking of apes, ed. by T. A. Sebeok and J. Umiker-Sebeok p61-70

Limber, J. Language in child and chimp? *In* Speaking of apes, ed. by T. A. Sebeok and J. Umiker-Sebeok p197-220

McNeill, D. Sentence structure in chimpanzee communication. *In* Speaking of apes, ed. by T. A. Sebeok and J. Umiker-Sebeok p145-60

Malmi, W. A. Chimpanzees and language evolution. *In* Speaking of apes, ed. by T. A. Sebeok and J. Umiker-Sebeok p191-96

Marler, P. Primate vocalization: affective or symbolic? *In* Speaking of apes, ed. by T. A. Sebeok and J. Umiker-Sebeok p221-29

Mounin, G. Language, communication, chimpanzees. *In* Speaking of apes, ed. by T. A. Sebeok and J. Umiker-Sebeok p161-77

Premack, D. Representational capacity and accessibility of knowledge: the case of chimpanzees. *In* Language and learning, ed. by M. Piattelli-Palmarini p205-21

Rumbaugh, D. M. Language behavior of apes. *In* Speaking of apes, ed. by T. A. Sebeok and J. Umiker-Sebeok p231-59

Savage-Rumbaugh, E. S., Rumbaugh, D. M. and Boysen, S. Linguistically mediated tool use and exchange by chimpanzees (Pan troglodytes). *In* Speaking of apes, ed. by T. A. Sebeok and J. Umiker-Sebeok p353-83

Terrace, H. S. Is problem-solving language? *In* Speaking of apes, ed. by T. A. Sebeok and J. Umiker-Sebeok p385-405

Terrace, H. S. and Bever, T. G. What might be learned from studying language in the chimpanzee? The importance of symbolizing oneself. *In* Speaking of apes, ed. by T. A. Sebeok and J. Umiker-Sebeok p179-89

**Chimpanzees as laboratory animals**

Fouts, R. S. and Rigby, R. L. Man-chimpanzee communication. *In* Speaking of apes, ed. by T. A. Sebeok and J. Umiker-Sebeok p261-85

Gardner, R. A. and Gardner, B. T. Comparative psychology and language acquisition. *In* Speaking of apes, ed. by T. A. Sebeok and J. Umiker-Sebeok p287-330

Hediger, H. Do you speak Yerkish? The newest colloquial language with chimpanzees. *In* Speaking of apes, ed. by T. A. Sebeok and J. Umiker-Sebeok p441-47

Hill, J. H. Apes and language. *In* Speaking of apes, ed. by T. A. Sebeok and J. Umiker-Sebeok p331-51

Rumbaugh, D. M. Language behavior of apes. *In* Speaking of apes, ed. by T. A. Sebeok and J. Umiker-Sebeok p231-59

Savage-Rumbaugh, E. S., Rumbaugh, D. M. and Boysen, S. Linguistically mediated tool use and exchange by chimpanzees (Pan troglodytes). *In* Speaking of apes, ed. by T. A. Sebeok and J. Umiker-Sebeok p353-83

Terrace, H. S. Is problem-solving language? *In* Speaking of apes, ed. by T. A. Sebeok and J. Umiker-Sebeok p385-405

Umiker-Sebeok, J. and Sebeok, T. A. Introduction: questioning apes. *In* Speaking of apes, ed. by T. A. Sebeok and J. Umiker-Sebeok p 1-59

**China**

### Antiquities

Watson, W. The city in ancient China. *In* The Origins of civilization, ed. by P. S. R. Moorey p54-77

### Civilization

DeBary, W. T. Chinese values: the China problem and our problem. *In* Value and values in evolution, ed. by E. A. Maziarz p103-14

Watson, W. The city in ancient China. *In* The Origins of civilization, ed. by P. S. R. Moorey p54-77

Wright, A. F. Chinese civilization. *In* Propaganda and communication in world history, ed. by H. D. Lasswell, D. Lerner and H. Speier v 1 p220-56

Wright, A. F. On the spread of Buddhism to China. *In* Propaganda and communication in world history, ed. by H. D. Lasswell, D. Lerner and H. Speier v 1 p205-19

*See also* Japan—Civilization

### History—1862-1899

Chu, S. C. China's attitudes toward Japan at the time of the Sino-Japanese War. *In* The Chinese and the Japanese, ed. by A. Iriye p74-95

Oh, B. B. Sino-Japanese rivalry in Korea, 1876-1885. *In* The Chinese and the Japanese, ed. by A. Iriye p37-57

### History—1900-1949

Young, E. P. Chinese leaders and Japanese aid in the early Republic. *In* The Chinese and the Japanese, ed. by A. Iriye p124-39

### History—1937-1945

Iriye, A. Toward a new cultural order: the Hsin-Min Hui. *In* The Chinese and the Japanese, ed. by A. Iriye p254-74

*See also* Sino-Japanese Conflict, 1937-1945

**China**—*Continued*

**History**—Reform movement, 1898

Schrecker, J. E. The Reform movement of 1898 and the Meiji Restoration as ch'ing-i movements. *In* The Chinese and the Japanese, ed. by A. Iriye p96-106

**History**—Republic, 1912-1949

Chi, M. Ts'ao Ju-lin (1876-1966): his Japanese connections. *In* The Chinese and the Japanese, ed. by A. Iriye p140-60

Yue-Him Tam. An intellectual's response to Western intrusion: Naito Konan's view of Republican China. *In* The Chinese and the Japanese, ed. by A. Iriye p161-83

**Politics and government**

Wright, A. F. Chinese civilization. *In* Propaganda and communication in world history, ed. by H. D. Lasswell, D. Lerner and H. Speier v 1 p220-56

**Relations (general) with Africa**

Yu, G. T. Sino-Soviet rivalry in Africa. *In* Communism in Africa, ed. by D. E. Albright p168-88

**Relations (general) with India**

Wright, A. F. On the spread of Buddhism to China. *In* Propaganda and communication in world history, ed. by H. D. Lasswell, D. Lerner and H. Speier v 1 p205-19

**Relations (general) with Japan**

Chi, M. Ts'ao Ju-lin (1876-1966): his Japanese connections. *In* The Chinese and the Japanese, ed. by A. Iriye p140-60

Chu, S. C. China's attitudes toward Japan at the time of the Sino-Japanese War. *In* The Chinese and the Japanese, ed. by A. Iriye p74-95

Hashikawa, B. Japanese perspectives on Asia: from dissociation to coprosperity. *In* The Chinese and the Japanese, ed. by A. Iriye p328-55

Ikei, M. Ugaki Kazushige's view of China and his China policy, 1915-1930. *In* The Chinese and the Japanese, ed. by A. Iriye p199-219

Iriye, A. Toward a new cultural order: the Hsin-Min Hui. *In* The Chinese and the Japanese, ed. by A. Iriye p254-74

Nakamura, T. Japan's economic thrust into North China, 1933-1938: formation of the North China Development Corporation. *In* The Chinese and the Japanese, ed. by A. Iriye p220-53

Okamoto, S. Ishibashi Tanzan and the Twenty-One Demands. *In* The Chinese and the Japanese, ed. by A. Iriye p184-98

Young, E. P. Chinese leaders and Japanese aid in the early Republic. *In* The Chinese and the Japanese, ed. by A. Iriye p124-39

Yue-Him Tam. An intellectual's response to Western intrusion: Naito Konan's view of Republican China. *In* The Chinese and the Japanese, ed. by A. Iriye p161-83

**The China syndrome (Motion picture)**

Kauffmann, S. The China syndrome. *In* Kauffmann, S. Before my eyes p335-39

**Chinatown (Motion picture)**

Kauffmann, S. Chinatown. *In* Kauffmann, S. Before my eyes p16-18

**Chinese fiction**

**20th century**—History and criticism

Prušek, J. The changing role of the narrator in Chinese novels at the beginning of the twentieth century. *In* Prušek, J. The lyrical and the epic p110-20

**Chinese in Japan**

Kamachi, N. The Chinese in Meiji Japan: their interactions with the Japanese before the Sino-Japanese War. *In* The Chinese and the Japanese, ed. by A. Iriye p58-73

**Chinese-Japanese Conflict, 1937-1945.** See Sino-Japanese Conflict, 1937-1945

**Chinese literature**

**Ch'ing dynasty, 1644-1912**—History and criticism

Prušek, J. Subjectivism and individualism in modern Chinese literature. *In* Prušek, J. The lyrical and the epic p 1-28

**20th century**—History and criticism

Prušek, J. A confrontation of traditional Oriental literature with modern European literature in the context of the Chinese literary revolution. *In* Prušek, J. The lyrical and the epic p74-85

Prušek, J. Introduction to Studies in modern Chinese literature. *In* Prušek, J. The lyrical and the epic p29-73

Prušek, J. Reality and art in Chinese literature. *In* Prušek, J. The lyrical and the epic p86-101

Prušek, J. Subjectivism and individualism in modern Chinese literature. *In* Prušek, J. The lyrical and the epic p 1-28

**Chinese propaganda.** See Propaganda, Chinese

**Chitty, Thomas**

The novelist as victim. *In* Royal Society of Literature of the United Kingdom, London. Essays by divers hands: innovation in contemporary literature, new ser. v40 p101-16

**About**

Chitty, T. The novelist as victim. *In* Royal Society of Literature of the United Kingdom, London. Essays by divers hands: innovation in contemporary literature, new ser. v40 p101-16

**Chivalry**

*See also* Courtly love

**Romances**

*See* Romances

**Choderlos de Laclos, Pierre Ambroise François.** See Laclos, Pierre Ambroise François Choderlos de

**Choice, Social.** See Social choice

**Choice (Psychology)** See Social choice

**Chomsky, Noam**

Discussion of Putnam's comments. *In* Language and learning, ed. by M. Piattelli-Palmarini p310-24

Human language and other semiotic systems. *In* Speaking of apes, ed. by T. A. Seboek and J. Umiker-Sebeok p429-40

The linguistic approach. *In* Language and learning, ed. by M. Piattelli-Palmarini p109-17

opening the debate:

Opening the debate: On cognitive structures and their development: a reply to Piaget. *In* Language and learning, ed. by M. Piattelli-Palmarini p35-54

**Chomsky, Noam**—*Continued*

**About**

Gardner, H. Foreword: Cognition comes of age. *In* Language and learning, ed. by M. Piattelli-Palmarini p xix-xxxvi

Mehler, J. Psychology and psycholinguistics: the impact of Chomsky and Piaget. *In* Language and learning, ed. by M. Piattelli-Palmarini p341-53

Petitot, J. Localist hypothesis and theory of catastrophes: note on the debate. *In* Language and learning, ed. by M. Piattelli-Palmarini p372-79

|Piattelli-Palmarini, M. Introduction: How hard is the "hard core" of a scientific program? *In* Language and learning, ed. by M. Piattelli-Palmarini p 1-20

Putnam, H. Comments on Chomsky's and Fodor's replies. *In* Language and learning, ed. by M. Piattelli-Palmarini p335-40

Putnam, H. What is innate and why: comments on the debate. *In* Language and learning, ed. by M. Piattelli-Palmarini p287-309

**About individual works**
*Cartesian linguistics*

Sullivan, J. J. Noam Chomsky and Cartesian linguistics. *In* Psychology of language and thought, ed. by R. W. Rieber p197-223

**Chopin, Kate (O'Flaherty)**

**About individual works**
*The awakening*

Christ, C. P. Spiritual liberation, social defeat: Kate Chopin. *In* Christ, C. P. Diving deep and surfacing p27-40

**Chou, Fo-hai**

**About**

Marsh, S. H. Chou Fo-hai: the making of a collaborator. *In* The Chinese and the Japanese, ed. by A. Iriye p304-27

**Chou, Shu-jen**

**About individual works**
*The past (Huai-chiu)*

Prušek, J. Lu Hsün's "Huai chiu": a precursor of modern Chinese literature. *In* Prušek, J. The lyrical and the epic p102-09

**Chow Shou-jen.** See Chou, Shu-jen

**Chrestien de Troyes**

**About**

Robertson, R. D. Some medieval literary terminology, with special reference to Chrétien de Troyes. *In* Robertson, D. W. Essays in medieval culture p51-72

**About individual works**
*Cligés*

Robertson, D. W. Chrétien's Cligés and the Ovidian spirit. *In* Robertson, D. W. Essays in medieval culture p173-82

Robertson, D. W. The idea of fame in Chrétien's Cligés. *In* Robertson, D. W. Essays in medieval culture p183-201

*Erec and Enide*

Scully, T. P. The sen of Chrétien de Troyes's Joie de la cort. *In* The Expansion and transformations of courtly literature, ed. by N. B. Smith and J. T. Snow p71-94

*Perceval le Gallois*

Hatto, A. T. Some notes on Chrétien de Troyes and Wolfram von Eschenbach. *In* Hatto, A. T. Essays on medieval German and other poetry p151-64

Hatto, A. T. On Wolfram's conception of the 'Graal.' *In* Hatto, A. T. Essays on medieval German and other poetry p141-50 |

**Chrétien de Troyes.** See Chrestien de Troyes

**Christ, Carol P.**
Diving deep and surfacing

*Contents*

From motherhood to prophecy: Doris Lessing

Homesick for a woman, for ourselves: Adrienne Rich

"i found god in myself . . . & i loved her fiercely": Ntozake Shange

Nothingness, awakening, insight, new naming

Refusing to be victim: Margaret Atwood

Spiritual liberation, social defeat: Kate Chopin

Toward wholeness: a vision of women's culture

Women's stories, women's quest

**Christensen, Jerome C.**
Lancelot: sign for the times. *In* Walker Percy: art and ethics, ed. by J. Tharpe p107-20

**Christian art and symbolism**
Kitzinger, E. Christian imagery: growth and impact. *In* Age of spirituality, ed. by K. Weitzmann p141-63

Pickering, F. P. The Gothic image of Christ: the sources of medieval representations of The Crucifixion. *In* Pickering, F. P. Essays on medieval German literature and iconography p3-30

Robertson, D. W. In foraminibus petrae: a note on Leonardo's "Virgin of the rocks." *In* Robertson, D. W. Essays in medieval culture p305-07

Schapiro, M. The angel with the ram in Abraham's sacrifice: a parallel in Western and Islamic art. *In* Schapiro, M. Selected papers v3: Late antique, early Christian and mediaeval art p289-306

Schapiro, M. The bowman and the bird on the Ruthwell Cross and other works: the interpretation of secular themes in early mediaeval religious art. *In* Schapiro, M. Selected papers v3: Late antique, early Christian and mediaeval art p177-95

Schapiro, M. The frescoes of Castelseprio. *In* Schapiro, M. Selected papers v3: Late antique, early Christian and mediaeval art p67-114

Schapiro, M. The Joseph scenes on the Maximianus throne in Ravenna. *In* Schapiro, M. Selected papers v3: Late antique, early Christian and mediaeval art p35-47

Schapiro, M. "Muscipula diaboli," the symbolism of the Mérode altarpiece. *In* Schapiro, M. Selected papers v3: Late antique, early Christian and mediaeval art p 1-11

Schapiro, M. The religious meaning of the Ruthwell Cross. *In* Schapiro, M. Selected papers v3: Late antique, early Christian and mediaeval art p151-76

*See also* Art, Early Christian; Church architecture

**Classical influences**
Hanfmann, G. M. A. The continuity of classical art: culture, myth, and faith. *In* Age of spirituality, ed. by K. Weitzmann p75-99

**Christian communication.** See Communication (Theology)

**Christian Democrats (Italy)** See Partito della democrazia cristiana

**Christian literature**
Le Goff, J. Trades and professions as represented in medieval confessors' manuals. *In* Le Goff, J. Time, work, & culture in the Middle Ages p107-21

**Christian literature, Byzantine**

### History and criticism
Sevčenko, I. A shadow outline of virtue: the classical heritage of Greek Christian literature (second to seventh century) *In* Age of spirituality, ed. by K. Weitzmann p53-73

**Christian literature, Early**
*See also* Literature, Medieval

### Greek authors—History and criticism
Sevčenko, I. A shadow of virtue: the classical heritage of Greek Christian literature (second to seventh century) *In* Age of spirituality, ed. by K. Weitzmann p53-73

**Christian pilgrims and pilgrimages**

### Germany
Rothkrug, L. Popular religion and holy shrines. In Religion and the people, 800-1700, ed. by J. Obelkevich p20-86

**Christian sociology.** See Sociology, Christian

**Christian symbolism.** See Christian art and symbolism

**Christian theology.** See Theology

**Christianity**
Kristeller, P. O. Paganism and Christianity. *In* Kristeller, P. O. Renaissance thought and its sources p66-81
*See also* Reformation; Theology

### Philosophy
Colacurcio, M. J. The example of Edwards: idealist imagination and the metaphysics of sovereignty. *In* Puritan influences in American literature, ed. by E. Elliott p55-106

### Early church, ca. 30-600
Benko, S Popular literature in early Christianity: the apocryphal New Testament. *In* 5000 years of popular culture, ed. by F. E. H. Schroeder p175-90
Brown, P. R. L. Art and society in late antiquity. *In* Age of spirituality, ed. by K. Weitzmann p17-27
Momigliano, A. After Gibbon's Decline and fall. *In* Age of spirituality, ed. by K. Weitzmann p7-16

### Middle Ages, 600-1500
Boglioni, P. Some methodological reflections of the study of medieval popular religion. *In* 5000 years of popular culture, ed. by F. E. H. Schroeder p192-200

**Christianity and communication.** See Communication (Theology)

**Christianity and culture**

### Early church, ca. 30-600
Le Goff, J. Clerical culture and folklore traditions in Merovingian civilization. *In* Le Goff, J. Time, work, & culture in the Middle Ages p153-58
Le Goff, J. Ecclesiastical culture and folklore in the Middle Ages: Saint Marcellus of Paris and the dragon. *In* Le Goff, J. Time, work, & culture in the Middle Ages p159-88

Sevčenko, I. A shadow outline of virtue: the classical heritage of Greek Christian literature (second to seventh century) *In* Age of spirituality, ed. by K. Weitzmann p53-73

**Christianity and humor**
Anselment, R. A. 'Nor foolish talking, nor jesting, which are not convenient.' *In* Anselment, R. A. 'Betwixt jest and earnest' p8-32

**Christianity and literature**
Beaujour, M. Exemplary pornography: Barrès, Loyola, and the novel. *In* The Reader in the text, ed. by S. R. Suleiman and I. Crosman p325-49
*See also* Christianity in literature

**Christianity and other religions**

### Islam
Hourani, A. H. Western attitudes towards Islam. *In* Hourani, A. H. Europe and the Middle East p1-18

**Christianity and philosophy.** See Philosophy and religion

**Christianity and the arts.** See Christian art and symbolism

**Christianity in literature**
Brinkmeyer, R. H. Percy's bludgeon: message and narrative strategy. *In* Walker Percy: art and ethics, ed. by J. Tharpe p80-90
Kissel, S. S. Voices in the wilderness: the prophets of O'Connor, Percy, and Powers. *In* Walker Percy: art and ethics, ed. by J. Tharpe p91-98
Morrissey, T. J. The Good Shepherd and the Anti-Christ in Synge's The shadow of the glen. *In* Irish Renaissance annual I p157-67
Polhemus, R. M. Introduction: worlds without end. *In* Polhemus, R. M. Comic faith p3-23
Polhemus, R. M. Joyce's Finnegans wake: the comic gospel of "Shem." *In* Polhemus, R. M. Comic faith p294-337
Robertson, D. W. The doctrine of charity in medieval literary gardens: a topical approach through symbolism and allegory. *In* Robertson, D. W. Essays in medieval culture p21-50
Robertson, D. W. The "heresy" of the Pearl. *In* Robertson, D. W. Essays in medieval culture p215-17
Robertson, D. W. The Pearl as symbol. *In* Robertson, D. W. Essays in medieval culture p209-14
Sharma, G. N. Ngugi's Christian vision: theme and pattern in A grain of wheat. *In* African literature no. 10: Retrospect & prospect, ed. by E. D. Jones p167-76

**Christianson, J. R.**
Literary traditions of Norwegian-American women. *In* Makers of an American immigrant legacy, ed. by O. S. Lovoll p92-110

**Christmas books.** See Gift-books (Annuals, etc.)

**Christology.** See Jesus Christ

**Chromosomes.** See Genetics

**Chronographis anni 354**
Schapiro, M. The Carolingian copy of the Calendar of 354. *In* Schapiro, M. Selected papers v3: Late antique, early Christian and mediaeval art p143-49

**Chrysippus, the stoic**

### About
Frede, M. The original notion of cause. *In* Doubt and dogmatism, ed. by M. Schofield, M. Burnyeat and J. Barnes p217-49
Sorabji, R. Causation, laws and necessity. *In* Doubt and dogmatism, ed. by M. Schofield, M. Burnyeat and J. Barnes p250-82

**Christy, Harriett R.**
First appearances: literature in nineteenth-century periodicals for children. *In* Research about nineteenth-century children and books, ed. by S. K. Richardson p117-32

**Chu, Samuel C.**
China's attitudes toward Japan at the time of the Sino-Japanese War. *In* The Chinese and the Japanese, ed. by A. Iriye p74-95

**Chukovskiĭ, Korneĭ Ivanovich**
Excerpts from the diaries of Korney Chukovsky relating to Boris Pilnyak. *In* California Slavic studies v11 p187-99

**Chukovsky, Korney.** See Chukovskiĭ, Korneĭ Ivanovich

**Church and slavery.** See Slavery and the church

**Church and social problems.** See Slavery and the church

**Church and state**

### History

Ozment, S. H. The ecclesiopolitical traditions. *In* Ozment, S. H. The age of reform, 1250-1550 p135-81

**Church architecture**
Krautheimer, R. Success and failure in late antique church planning. *In* Age of spirituality, ed. by K. Weitzmann p121-39

### England—History

Schapiro, M. A note on the wall strips of Saxon churches. *In* Schapiro, M. Selected papers v3: Late antique, early Christian and mediaeval art p243-48

**Church buildings.** See Church architecture

**Church history**

### Primitive and early church, ca. 30-600

Forman, C. W. Christian missions in the ancient world. *In* Propaganda and communication in world history, ed. by H. D. Lasswell, D. Lerner and H. Speier v 1 p330-47

*See also* Christianity and culture—Early church, ca. 30-600

### Middle Ages, 600-1500

Geary, P. J. The ninth-century relic trade. *In* Religion and the people, 800-1700, ed. by J. Obelkevich p8-19

Le Goff, J. How did the medieval university conceive of itself? *In* Le Goff, J. Time, work, & culture in the Middle Ages p122-34

Le Goff, J. Trades and professions as represented in medieval confessors' manuals. *In* Le Goff, J. Time, work, & culture in the Middle Ages p107-21

Ozment, S. H. The ecclesiopolitical traditions. *In* Ozment, S. H. The age of reform, 1250-1550 p135-81

Ozment, S. H. On the eve of the Reformation. *In* Ozment, S. H. The age of reform, 1250-1550 p183-222

### Modern period, 1500-

Ozment, S. H. Catholic reform and Counter Reformation. *In* Ozment, S. H. The age of reform, 1250-1550 p397-418

*See also* Reformation

### Reformation, 1517-1648

*See* Reformation

**Church music**
*See also* Mass (Music)

### New England

Crawford, R. A. A historian's introduction to early American music. *In* American Antiquarian Society. Proceedings v89 pt2 p261-98

**Church of England**
Anselment, R. A. John Milton contra Hall. *In* Anselment, R. A. 'Betwixt jest and earnest' p61-93

Anselment, R. A. The rehearsal transpros'd. *In* Anselment, R. A. 'Betwixt jest and earnest' p94-125

*See also* Marprelate controversy

**Churches.** See Church architecture

**Chyet, Stanley F.**
Reflections on Southern-Jewish historiography. *In* Conference on Southern Jewish History, Richmond, Va. 1976. "Turn to the South" p13-20

**Cicero, Marcus Tullius**

### Influence

Marsh, D. Cicero and the humanist dialogue. *In* Marsh, D. The quattrocento dialogue p 1-23

### Oratory

Bailey, D. R. S. On Cicero's speeches. *In* Harvard Studies in classical philology, v83 p237-85

**Cimino, Michael**

### About individual works

*The deer hunter*

Kael, P. The God-bless-America symphony. *In* Kael, P. When the lights go down p512-19

**Circus**
Coxe, A. D. H. Equestrian drama and the circus. *In* Performance and politics in popular drama, ed. by D. Bradby, L. James and B. Sharratt p109-18

**Cities and towns**
*See also* Urbanization

### Economic aspects

*See* Urban economics

**Cities and towns, Ancient**

### Central America

Bray, W. From village to city in Mesoamerica. *In* The Origins of civilization, ed. by P. S. R. Moorey p78-102

### China

Watson, W. The city in ancient China. *In* The Origins of civilization, ed. by P. S. R. Moorey p54-77

### Europe

Piggott, S. Early towns in Europe? *In* The Origins of civilization, ed. by P. S. R. Moorey p34-53

### Near East

Mellaart, J. Early urban communities in the Near East, c9000-3400 B.C. *In* The Origins of civilization, ed. by P. S. R. Moorey p22-33

**Cities and towns, Movement to.** See Urbanization

**Cities and towns in literature**
Festa-McCormick, D. Butor's Passing time: the equivocal reality of a city. *In* Festa-McCormick, D. The city as catalyst p176-92

**Cittadino, Eugene**
Ecology and the professionalization of botany in America, 1890-1905. *In* Studies in history of biology, v4 p 171-98

**City and town life in literature**
Marchese, R. T. Urbanism in the classical world: some general considerations and remarks. *In* 5000 years of popular culture, ed. by F. E. H. Schroeder p55-91

**City-federal relations.** See Federal-city relations

**Civil disobedience.** See Government, Resistance to

**Civil liberty.** See Liberty

**Civil-military relations.** See Militarism; Sociology, Military

**Civil rights**
Hook, S. Reflections on human rights. *In* Hook, S. Philosophy and public policy p67-97
Moynihan, D. P. The politics of human rights. *In* Moynihan, D. P. Counting our blessings p85-105
Shinn, R L. Toward a post-Enlightenment doctrine of human rights. *In* History, religion, and spiritual democracy, ed. by M. Wohlgelernter p294-316
Taylor, C. Atomism. *In* Powers, possessions and freedom, ed. by A. Kontos p39-61
*See also* Equality before the law; Jews—Legal status, laws, etc.

**Underdeveloped areas**
*See* Underdeveloped areas—Civil rights

**Civil service.** See Bureaucracy

**Civil War**
**Great Britain**
*See* Great Britain—History—Civil War, 1642-1649

**Civilization**
*See also* Culture; Ethics; Progress

**History**
Braudel, F. The history of civilizations: the past explains the present. *In* Braudel, F. On history p177-218
Clark, G. Primitive man as hunter, fisher, forager, and farmer. *In* The Origins of civilization, ed. by P. S. R. Moorey p 1-21
*See also* Civilization, Medieval

**Civilization, Anglo-Saxon**
**Bibliography**
Berkhout, C. T. [and others]. Bibliography for 1978. *In* Anglo-Saxon England 8 p335-76

**Civilization, Arab.** See Civilization, Islamic

**Civilization, Assyro-Babylonian**
Oppenheim, A. L. Neo-Assyrian and neo-Babylonian empires. *In* Propaganda and communication in world history, ed. by H. D. Lasswell, D. Lerner and H. Speier v 1 p111-44

**Civilization, Babylonian.** See Civilization, Assyro-Babylonian

**Civilization, Greek**
Ferguson, J. Classical civilization. *In* Propaganda and communication in world history, ed. by H. D. Lasswell, D. Lerner and H. Speier v 1 p257-98
Nash, L. L. Concepts of existence: Greek origins of generational thought. *In* Generations, ed. by S. R. Graubard p 1-21

**Civilization, Islamic**
Hourani, A. H. Islam and the philosophers of history. *In* Hourani, A. H. Europe and the Middle East p19-73
Hourani, A. H. The present state of Islamic and Middle Eastern historiography. *In* Hourani, A. H. Europe and the Middle East p161-96

Kirk, G. Communication in classical Islam. *In* Propaganda and communication in world history, ed. by H. D. Lasswell, D. Lerner and H. Speier v 1 p348-80

**Civilization, Medieval**
Brentano, R. Western civilization: the Middle Ages. *In* Propaganda and communication in world history, ed. by H. D. Lasswell, D. Lerner, and H. Speier v 1 p552-95
Ozment, S. H. On the eve of the Reformation. *In* Ozment, S. H. The age of reform, 1250-1550 p182-222
*See also* Education, Medieval; Feudalism; Renaissance

**Civilization, Modern**
Kristol, I. The adversary culture of intellectuals. *In* The Third century, ed. by S. M. Lipset p327-43
*See also* Renaissance

**19th century**
Gay, P. On the bourgeoisie: a psychological interpretation. *In* Consciousness and class experience in nineteenth-century Europe, ed. by J. M. Merriman p187-203

**1950-**
Lipset, S. M. Predicting the future of post-industrial society: can we do it? *In* The Third century, ed. by S. M. Lipset p 1-35
Segerstedt, T. T. The condition of man in post-industrial society. *In* The Condition of man, ed. by P. Hallberg p152-60
Solzhenitsyn, A. I. A world split apart. *In* Solzhenitsyn at Harvard, ed. by R. Berman p3-20

**Civilization, Muslim.** See Civilization, Islamic

**Civilization, Occidental**
Berman, H. J. The weightier matters of the law. *In* Solzhenitsyn at Harvard, ed. by R. Berman p99-113
Hook, S. On Western freedom. *In* Solzhenitsyn at Harvard, ed. by R. Berman p85-97
McNeill, W. H. The decline of the West. *In* Solzhenitsyn at Harvard, ed. by R. Berman p122-30
Novak, M. On God and man. *In* Solzhenitsyn at Harvard, ed. by R. Berman p131-43
Pipes, R. In the Russian intellectual tradition. *In* Solzhenitsyn at Harvard, ed. by R. Berman p115-21
Solzhenitsyn, A. I. A world split apart. *In* Solzhenitsyn at Harvard, ed. by R. Berman p3-20

**Civilization and computers.** See Computers and civilization

**Civilization and technology.** See Technology and civilization

**Clair, René**
**About individual works**
*Entr'acte*
Thiher, A. From Entr'acte to A nous la liberté: René Clair and the order of farce. *In* Thiher, A. The cinematic muse p64-77

*A nous la liberté*
Thiher, A. From Entr'acte to A nous la liberté: René Clair and the order of farce. *In* Thiher, A. The cinematic muse p64-77

**Clare, John**
**About**
Keith, W. J. John Clare. *In* Keith, W. J. The poetry of nature p39-66

**Clark, Grahame**
Primitive man as hunter, fisher, forager, and farmer. *In* The Origins of civilization, ed. by P. S. R. Moorey p 1-21

**Clark, Jon**
Agitprop and Unity Theatre: Socialist theatre in the thirties. *In* Culture and crisis in Britain in the thirties, ed. by J. Clark and others p219-39

**Clark, Lorenne M. G.**
Women and Locke: who owns the apples in the Garden of Eden? *In* The Sexism of social and political theory: women and reproduction from Plato to Nietzsche, ed. by L. M. G. Clark and L. Lange p16-40

**Clark, Michael J.**
Jean Itard: a memoir on stuttering. *In* Psychology of language and thought, ed. by R. W. Rieber p153-84

**Clarke, Graham**
'Bound in moss and cloth': reading a long Victorian novel. *In* Reading the Victorian novel: detail into form, ed. by I. Gregor p54-71

**Clarke, Rebecca Sophia**

### About

Doll, C. The children of Sophie May. *In* Research about nineteenth-century children and books, ed. by S. K. Richardson p97-116

**Class distinction.** See Social classes

**Classes, Social.** See Social classes

**Classical antiquities.** See Art, Classical

**Classical art.** See Art, Classical

**Classical education**
Gombrich, Sir E. H. J. The tradition of general knowledge. *In* Gombrich, Sir E. H. J. Ideals and idols p9-23
*See also* Education, Humanistic

**Classical literature**
*See also* Latin literature

### Influence

Sevčenko, I. A shadow outline of virtue: the classical heritage of Greek Christian literature (second to seventh century) *In* Age of spirituality, ed. by K. Weitzmann p53-73

**Classical philology.** See Humanism

**Classicism.** See Neoclassicism (Literature)

**Classicism in art.** See Neoclassicism (Art)

**Claudian.** See Claudianus, Claudias

**Claudianus, Claudias**

### About individual works
#### The rape of Proserpine

Donovan, M. J. Chaucer's January and May: counterparts in Claudian. *In* Chaucerian problems and perspectives, ed. by E. Vasta and Z. P. Thundy p59-69

**Cleary, Beverly**

### About

Rees, D. Middle of the way: Rodie Sudbery and Beverly Cleary. *In* Rees, D. The marble in the water p90-103

**Cleave, William R. van.** See Van Cleave, William R.

**Cleaver, Bill**

### About

Townsend, J. R. Vera and Bill Cleaver. *In* Townsend, J. R. A sounding of storytellers p30-40

**Cleaver, Vera**

### About

Townsend, J. R. Vera and Bill Cleaver. *In* Townsend, J. R. A sounding of storytellers p30-40

**Cleland, John**

### About individual works
#### Memoirs of Fanny Hill

Miller, N. K. A harlot's progress: II, Fanny Hill. *In* Miller, N. K. The heroine's text p51-66

Todd, J. Erotic friendship: John Cleland's Fanny Hill. *In* Todd, J. Women's friendship in literature p69-100

Whitley, R. K. The libertine hero and heroine in the novels of John Cleland. *In* Studies in eighteenth-century culture v9 p387-404

**Clemen, Wolfgang H.**
Some aspects of style in the Henry VI plays. *In* Shakespeare's styles, ed. by P. Edwards, I. S. Ewbank and G. K. Hunter p9-24

**Clemens, Samuel Langhorne**

### About individual works
#### The adventures of Tom Sawyer

Bixler, P. Idealization of the child and childhood in Frances Hodgson Burnett's Little Lord Fauntleroy and Mark Twain's Tom Sawyer. *In* Research about nineteenth-century children and books, ed. by S. K. Richardson p85-96

### Bibliography

Budd, L. J. Mark Twain. *In* American literary scholarship, 1978 p79-90

### Characters—Huckleberry Finn

Martin, T. The negative character in American fiction. *In* Toward a new American literary history, ed. by L. J. Budd, E. H. Cady and C. L. Anderson p23-43

**Clements, Colleen D.**
The ethics of not-being: individual options for suicide. *In* Suicide: the philosophical issues, ed. by M. P. Battin and D. J. Mayo p104-14

**Clemoes, Peter**
Action in Beowulf and our perception of it. *In* Old English poetry, ed. by D. G. Calder p147-68

**Clerical celibacy.** See Celibacy

**Clergy.** See Rabbis

**Clignet, Remi**
Teachers and national values in Cameroon: an inferential analysis from census data. *In* Values, identities, and national integration, ed. by J. N. Paden p321-36

**Cline, Ray S.**
The future of U.S. foreign intelligence operations. *In* The United States in the 1980s, ed. by P. Duignan and A. Rabushka p469-96

**The Clockmaker (Motion picture)**
Kauffmann, S. The clockmaker. *In* Kauffmann, S. Before my eyes p232-34

**Clocks and watches.** See Time measurements

**Clopinel de Meun, Jean.** See Jean de Meun

**Clopinel, Jean de Meun.** See Jean de Meun

**Close encounters of the third kind (Motion picture)**
Kael, P. The greening of the solar system. *In* Kael, P. When the lights go down p348-54
Kauffmann, S. Close encounters of the third kind. *In* Kauffmann, S. Before my eyes p155-60

**Clothiers.** See Clothing trade

**Clothing and dress in art.** See Costume in art

**Clothing trade**

France

Johnson, C. H. Patterns of proletarianization: Parisian tailors and Lodève woolens workers. *In* Consciousness and class experience in nineteenth-century Europe, ed. by J. M. Merriman p65-84

**Clough, Arthur Hugh**

About

McGhee, R. D. Arnold and Clough. *In* McGhee, R. D. Marriage, duty & desire in Victorian poetry and drama p99-138

**Clune, Anne**

Seamus O'Kelly. *In* The Irish short story, ed. by P. Rafroidi and T. Brown p141-57

**Clytemnestra**

Washington, I. H. and Tobol, C. E. W. Kriemhild and Clytemnestra—sisters in crime or independent women? *In* The Lost tradition: mothers and daughters in literature, ed. by C. N. Davidson and E. M. Broner p15-21

**Coal.** See Lignite

**Coats, Alfred William**

Economic thought. *In* Encyclopedia of American economic history, ed. by G. Porter v 1 p468-83

**Cobb, Humphrey**

About individual works

*Paths of glory*

Miller, G. Murder in the first degree. *In* Miller, G. Screening the novel p116-42

**Coben, Stanley**

American foundations as patrons of science: the commitment to individual research. *In* The Sciences in the American context: new perspectives, ed. by N. Reingold p229-47

**Cobham, Rhonda**

The background. *In* West Indian literature, ed. by B. King p9-29

**Cocteau, Jean**

About individual works

*The blood of the poet*

Thiher, A. Le sang d'un poète: film as Orphism. *In* Thiher, A. The cinematic muse p49-62

**Coexistence.** See World politics—1945-

**Coffee**

Brazil

Margolis, M. Seduced and abandoned: agricultural frontiers in Brazil and the United States. *In* Brazil, anthropological perspectives, ed. by M. L. Margolis and W. E. Carter p160-79

**Cognition**

Bischof, N. Remarks on Lorenz and Piaget: how can "working hypotheses" be "necessary"? *In* Language and learning, ed. by M. Piattelli-Palmarini p233-41

Cellérier, G. Some clarification on innatism and constructivism. *In* Language and learning, ed. by M. Piattelli-Palmarini p83-87

Gardner, H. Foreword: Cognition comes of age. *In* Language and learning, ed. by M. Piatelli-Palmarini p xix-xxxvi

Inhelder, B. Language and knowledge in a constructivist framework. *In* Language and learning, ed. by M. Piatelli-Palmarini p132-37

Mason, W. A. Maternal attributes and primate cognitive development. *In* Human ethology, ed. by M. von Cranach [and others] p437-55

Papert, S. The role of artificial intelligence in psychology. *In* Language and learning, ed. by M. Piatelli-Palmarini p90-99

Piaget, J. Afterthoughts. *In* Language and learning, ed. by M. Piatelli-Palmarini p278-84

Piaget, J. Introductory remarks. *In* Language and learning, ed. by M. Piatelli-Palmarini p57-61

Piaget, J. Opening the debate: the psychogenesis of knowledge and its epistemological significance. *In* Language and learning, ed. by M. Piatelli-Palmarini p23-34

Premack, D. Representational capacity and accessibility of knowledge: the case of chimpanzees. *In* Language and learning, ed. by M. Piatelli-Parmarini p205-21

Sperber, D. Remarks on the lack of positive contributions from anthropologists to the problem of innateness. *In* Language and learning, ed. by M. Piatelli-Palmarini p245-49

*See also* Knowledge, Theory of; Perception; Thought and thinking

**Cohan, George Michael**

About individual works

*The phantom president*

Kauffmann, S. The phantom president. *In* Kauffmann, S. Before my eyes p345-49

**Cohen, Amnon**

The Jews under Islam: part two c. 1500-today. *In* The Jewish world, ed. by E. Kedourie p186-91

**Cohen, Arthur A.**

About

Alexander, E. The Holocaust in American Jewish fiction: a slow awakening. *In* Alexander, E. The resonance of dust p121-46

**Cohen, Estelle Jelinek.** See Jelinek, Estelle Cohen

**Cohen, Hermann**

The Polish Jew. *In* The Jew, ed. by A. A. Cohen p52-60

About

Buber, M. Zion, the state, and humanity: remarks on Hermann Cohen's answer. *In* The Jew, ed. by A. A. Cohen p85-96

Klatzkin, J. Hermann Cohen. *In* The Jew, ed. by A. A. Cohen p251-61

**Cohen, Lester H.**

Narrating the Revolution: ideology, language, and form. *In* Studies in eighteenth-century culture v9 p455-76

**Cohen, Ronald**

Epilogue: integration, ethnicity, and stratification: focus and fashion in African studies. *In* Values, identities, and national integration, ed. by J. N. Paden p361-72

**Cohen, Stephen F.**

The friends and foes of change: reformism and conservatism in the Soviet Union. *In* The Soviet Union since Stalin, ed. by S. F. Cohen, A. Rabinowitch and R. Sharlet p11-31

**Coins in literature**

Carey, J Donne and coins. *In* English Renaissance studies, ed. by J. Carey p151-63

**Coke, Sir Edward**

About

Gray, C. W. Reason, authority, and imagination: the jurisprudence of Sir Edward Coke. *In* Culture and politics from Puritanism to the Enlightenment, ed. by P. Zagorin p25-66

**Colleges.** See Universities and colleges

**Collier, Charles F.**
Harris and his anachronistic attack. *In* Critics of Henry George, ed. by R. V. Andelson p187-95

Rutherford: the Devil quotes scriptures. *In* Critics of Henry George, ed. by R. V. Andelson p222-33

**Collier, David S.**
The bureaucratic-authoritarian model: synthesis and priorities for future research. *In* The New authoritarianism in Latin America, ed. by D. Collier p363-97

Overview of the bureaucratic authoritarian model. *In* The New authoritarianism in Latin America, ed. by D. Collier p19-32

**Collier, John Payne**
**About**
Foakes, R. A. What did Coleridge say? John Payne Collier and the reports of the 1811-12 lectures. *In* Reading Coleridge, ed. by W. B. Crawford p191-210

**Collins, Douglas**
Sartre a as biographer
*Contents*
Baudelaire and bad faith
The dialectic of narcissism
Flaubert and the objective neurosis
Flaubert and the subjective neurosis
Genet and the just
Proteus and the rat trap
The tribunal of crabs
Truth and alterity

**Collins, Randall**
Erving Goffman and the development of modern social theory. *In* The View from Goffman, ed. by J. Ditton p170-209

**Collins, Wilkie**
**About**
Blair, D. Wilkie Collins and the crisis of suspense. *In* Reading the Victorian novel, ed. by I. Gregor p32-50

**Collins, William**
**About**
Fry, P. H. The tented sky in the odes of Collins. *In* Fry, P. H. The poet's calling in the English ode p97-132

**About individual works**
*Persian eclogues*
Eversole, R. L. Collins and the end of the shepherd pastoral. *In* Survivals of pastoral, ed. by R. F. Hardin p19-32

**Collis, John Stewart**
Forward to nature. *In* Royal Society of Literature of the United Kingdom, London. Essays by divers hands: innovation in contemporary literature, new ser. v40 p34-51

Religion and philosophy. *In* The Genius of Shaw, ed. by M. Holroyd p79-93

**Collodi, Carlo,** pseud. See Lorenzini, Carlo

**Colmer, John**
Promise and withdrawal in A passage to India. *In* E. M. Forster: a human exploration, ed. by G. K. Das and J. Beer p117-28

**Cologne. Universität. Mani Codex**
Henrichs, A. The Cologne Mani Codex reconsidered. *In* Harvard Studies in classical philology, v83, p339-67

**Colonialism.** See Imperialism

**Colored people (U.S.)** See Afro-Americans

**Colum, Mary**
"An American critic: Van Wyck Brooks." *In* Van Wyck Brooks: the critic and his critics, ed. by W. Wasserstrom p3-10

**Columnists.** See Journalists

**Coma (Motion picture)**
Kael, P. Soul-snatching and body-snatching. *In* Kael, P. When the lights go down p392-96

Kauffmann, S. Coma. *In* Kauffmann, S. Before my eyes p304-06

**Comes a horseman (Motion picture)**
Kael, P. Enfant terrible. *In* Kael, P. When the lights go down p482-88

**Comedy**
Robinson, F. M. Afterword. *In* The comedy of language p175-77

Robinson, F. M. The comedy of language. *In* Robinson, F. M. The comedy of language p 1-24

*See also* Comic, The; Greek drama (Comedy)

**Comes a horseman (Motion picture)**
Kauffmann, S. Comes a horseman. *In* Kauffmann, S. Before my eyes p207-09

**Comfort, Standard of.** See Cost and standard of living

**Comic, The**
Henkle, R. B. 1820-1845: the anxieties of sublimation, and middle-class myths. *In* Henkle, R. B. Comedy and culture p20-57

Henkle, R. B. Hood, Gilbert, Carroll, Jerrold, and the Grossmiths: comedy from inside. *In* Henkle, R. B. Comedy and culture p185-237

Henkle, R. B. Introduction. *In* Henkle, R. B. Comedy and culture p3-19

Henkle, R. B. Meredith and Butler: comedy as lyric, high culture, and the bourgeois trap. *In* Henkle, R. B. Comedy and culture p238-95

Henkle, R. B. Peacock, Thackeray, and Jerrold: the comedy of "radical" disaffection. *In* Henkle, R. B. Comedy and culture p58-110

Henkle, R. B. Wilde and Beerbohm: the wit of the avant-garde, the charm of failure. *In* Henkle, R. B. Comedy and culture p296-352

Polhemus, R. M. Introduction: worlds without end. *In* Polhemus, R. M. Comic faith p3-23

**Comic literature.** See Comedy; Satire

**Coming home (Motion picture)**
Kael, P. Mythologizing the sixties. *In* Kael, P. When the lights go down p402-05

Kauffmann, S. Coming home. *In* Kauffmann, S. Before my eyes p118-21

**Commandments (Judaism)** See Commandments, Six hundred and thirteen; Commandments, Ten

**Commandments, Six hundred and thirteen**
Berman, L. V. The structure of the commandments of the Torah in the thought of Maimonides. *In* Studies in Jewish religious and intellectual history, ed. by S. Stein and R. Loewe p51-66

**Commandments, Ten**
Robertson, D. W. Certain theological conventions in Mannyng's treatment of the Commandments. *In* Robertson, D. W. Essays in medieval culture p105-13

**Commerce**
Burbidge, J. B. The international dimension. *In* A Guide to post-Keynesian economics, ed. by A. S. Eichner p139-50

*See also* Merchants

**Commercial law.** See Antitrust law

**Commercial policy.** See Tariff

**Commission on Party Structure and Delegate Selection.** See Democratic Party. National Committee. Commission on Party Structure and Delegate Selection

**Commissions of the federal government.** See Independent regulatory commissions

**Commitment (Psychology)**
Fiske, M. Changing hierarchies of commitment in adulthood. *In* Themes of work and love in adulthood, ed. by N. J. Smelser and E. H. Erikson p238-64

**Commodity exchanges**

United States—History

Sobel, R. Exchanges. *In* Encyclopedia of American economic history, ed by G. Porter v2 p696-706

**Common law**
Tay, A. E. The sense of justice in the common law. *In* Symposium on Theories of Justice in and for the Second Half of the Twentieth Century, Sydney, 1977. Justice p79-96
*See also* Law—Great Britain—History and criticism

**Common sense**
Nabokov, V. V. The art of literature and commonsense. *In* Nabokov, V. V. Lectures on literature p371-80

**Communication**
Bouwsma, W. J. The Renaissance and the broadening of communication. *In* Propaganda and communication in world history, ed. by H. D. Lasswell, D. Lerner and H. Speier v2 p3-40

Eisenstadt, S. N. Communication patterns in centralized empires. *In* Propaganda and communication in world history, ed. by H. D. Lasswell, D. Lerner and H. Speier v 1 p536-51

Evans, B. O. Computers and communications. *In* The Computer age: a twenty-year view, ed. by M. L. Dertouzas and J. Moses p338-66

Guerra, D. M. Computer technology and the mass media: interacting communication environments. *In* Monster or Messiah? Ed. by W. M. Mathews p99-112

Lasswell, H. D. The future of world communication and propaganda. *In* Propaganda and communication in world history, ed. by H. D. Lasswell, D. Lerner and H. Speier v3 p516-34

Lasswell, H. D.; Lerner, D. and Speier, H. Introduction. *In* Propaganda and communication in world history, ed. by H. D. Lasswell, D. Lerner and H. Speier v 1 p 1-20

Martin, L. J. The moving target: general trends in audience composition. *In* Propaganda and communication in world history, ed. by H. D. Lasswell, D. Lerner and H. Speier v3 p249-94

Mead, M. Continuities in communication from early man to modern times. *In* Propaganda and communication in world history, ed. by H. D. Lasswell, D. Lerner and H. Speier v 1 p21-49

Roelker, N. L. The impact of the Reformation era on communication and propaganda. *In* Propaganda and communication in world history, ed. by H. D. Lasswell, D. Lerner and H. Speier v2 p41-84

Speier, H. The communication of hidden meaning. *In* Propaganda and communication in world history, ed. by H. D. Lasswell, D. Lerner and H. Speier v2 p261-300

Weston-Smith, M. Mass media assist communication. *In* Lying truths, ed. by R. Duncan and M. Weston-Smith p31-33
*See also* Human-animal communication; Language and languages; Mass media

Political aspects

*See* Communication in politics

Social aspects

Bell, D. The social framework of the information society. *In* The Computer age: a twenty-year view, ed. by M. L. Dertouzos and J. Moses p163-211

Goldhamer, H. The social effects of communication technology. *In* Propaganda and communication in world history, ed. by H. D. Lasswell, D. Lerner and H. Speier v3 p346-400

Lerner, D. The revolutionary elites and world symbolism. *In* Propaganda and communication in world history, ed. by H. D. Lasswell, D. Lerner and H. Speier v2 p371-94

India

Sharma, R. S. Indian civilization. *In* Propaganda and communication in world history, ed. by H. D. Lasswell, D. Lerner and H. Speier v1 p175-204

Iraq

Finklestein, J. J. Early Mesopotamia, 2500-1000 B.C. *In* Propaganda and communication in world history v 1 p50-110

Oppenheim, A. L. Neo-Assyrian and neo-Babylonian empires. *In* Propaganda and communication in world history, ed. by H. D. Lasswell; D. Lerner and H. Speier v 1 p111-44

Islamic Empire

Kirk, G. Communication in classical Islam. *In* Propaganda and communication in world history, ed. by H. D. Lasswell, D. Lerner and H. Speier v 1 p348-80

Turkey

Mardin, S. A. The modernization of social communication. *In* Propaganda and communication in world history, ed. by H. D. Lasswell, D. Lerner and H. Speier v 1 p381-443

United States—History

Madison, J. H. Communications. *In* Encyclopedia of American economic history, ed. by G. Porter v 1 p335-43

**Communication (Theology)**
Roelker, N. L. The impact of the Reformation era on communication and propaganda. *In* Propaganda and communication in world history, ed. by H. D. Lasswell, D. Lerner and H. Speier v2 p41-84
*See also* Mass media in religion

**Communication, Primitive**
Mead, M. Continuities in communication from early man to modern times. *In* Propaganda and communication in world history, ed. by H. D. Lasswell, D. Lerner and H. Speier v 1 p21-49

**Communication in politics**
Eisenstadt, S. N. Communication patterns in centralized empires. *In* Propaganda and communication in world history, ed. by H. D. Lasswell, D. Lerner and H. Speier v 1 p536-51

Lasswell, H. D. The future of world communication and propaganda. *In* Propaganda and communication in world history, ed. by H. D. Lasswell, D. Lerner and H. Speier v3 p516-34

**Communication in politics**—*Continued*

Lerner, D. The revolutionary elites and world symbolism. *In* Propaganda and communication in world history, ed. by H. D. Lasswell, D. Lerner and H. Speier v2 p371-94

Speier, H. The communication of hidden meaning. *In* Propaganda and communication in world history, ed. by H. D. Lasswell, D. Lerner and H. Speier v2 p261-300

*See also* Mass media—Political aspects; Propaganda

### Turkey

McGowan, B. W. Ottoman political communication. *In* Propaganda and communication, ed. by H. D. Lasswell, D. Lerner and H. Speier v 1 p444-92

**Communication systems.** See Telecommunication systems

### Communism

Kurzweil, E. Henri Lefebvre: a Marxist against structuralism. *In* Kurzweil, E. The age of structuralism p57-85

Kurzweil, E. Louis Althusser: Marxism and structuralism. *In* Kurzweil, E. The age of structuralism p35-56

Marković, M. Marxism as a political philosophy. *In* Political theory and political education, ed. by M. Richter p94-112

*See also* Propaganda, Communist; Women and socialism

### Angola

Valenta, J. Soviet decision-making on the intervention in Angola. *In* Communism in Africa, ed. by D. E. Albright p93-117

### Ethiopia

Ottaway, M. The theory and practice of Marxism-Leninism in Mozambique and Ethiopia. *In* Communism in Africa, ed. by D. E. Albright p118-44

### Great Britain

Howkins, A. Class against class: the political culture of the Communist Party of Great Britain, 1930-35. *In* Class, culture and social change, ed. by F. Gloversmith p240-57

### Mozambique

Ottaway, M. The theory and practice of Marxism-Leninism in Mozambique and Ethiopia. *In* Communism in Africa, ed. by D. E. Albright p118-44

### Poland

Trilling, L. Communism and intellectual freedom. *In* Trilling, L. Speaking of literature and society p300-09

**Communism and anthropology**

Godelier, M. The emergence and development of Marxism in anthropology in France. *In* Soviet and Western anthropology, ed. by E. Gellner p3-17

**Communism and art.** See Socialist realism in art

**Communism and Christianity**

### Catholic Church

Lion, A. Theology and sociology: what point is there in keeping the distinction? *In* Sociology and theology: alliance and conflict, ed. by D. Martin; J. O. Mills [and] W. S. F. Pickering p163-82

**Communism and family**

Juviler, P. H. The Soviet family in post-Stalin perspective. *In* The Soviet Union since Stalin, ed. by S. F. Cohen, A. Rabinowitch, and R. Sharlet p227-51

**Communism and law.** See Law and socialism

**Communism and literature**

Gibian, G. New aspects of Soviet Russian literature. *In* The Soviet Union since Stalin, ed. by S. F. Cohen, A. Rabinowitch, and R. Sharlet p252-75

Slaughter, C Conclusions: literature and dialetical materialism. *In* Slaughter, C. Marxism, ideology & literature. p197-213

Slaughter, C. The legacy of Marx. *In* Slaughter, C. Marxism, ideology & literature. p21-85

**Communism and religion**

Basilov, V. The study of religions in Soviet ethnography. *In* Soviet and Western anthropology, ed. by E. Gellner p231-42

**Communist aesthetics**

Slaughter, C. The legacy of Marx. *In* Slaughter, C. Marxism, ideology & literature. p21-85

### Communist countries

#### Propaganda

*See* Propaganda, Communist

**Communist Party of China**

Maloney, J. M. Women in the Chinese Communist revolution: the question of political equality. *In* Women, war, and revolution, ed. by C. R. Bergin and C. M. Lovett p165-81

**Communist Party of Russia**

Hoffmann, E. P. Changing Soviet perspectives on leadership and administration. *In* The Soviet Union since Stalin, ed. by S. F. Cohen, A. Rabinowitch, and R. Sharlet p71-92

**Communist propaganda.** See Propaganda, Communist

**Community organization.** See Local government

**Community plays, etc.**

Huerta, J. A. From the temple to the arena: Teatro Chicano today. *In* The Identification and analysis of Chicano literature, ed. by F. Jiménez p90-116

Jiménez, F. Dramatic principles of the Teatro Campesino. *In* The Identification and analysis of Chicano literature, ed. by F. Jiménez p117-32

**Community theater.** See Community plays, etc.

**Comparative government**

Scase, R. Introduction. *In* The State in Western Europe, ed. by R. Scase p11-22

**Comparative literature.** See Literature, Comparative

**Comparative psychology.** See Psychology, Comparative

**Comparative religion.** See Religions

**Compassion (Ethics)** See Sympathy

**Compensation.** See Wages

**Competition**

Kenyon, P. Pricing. *In* A Guide to post-Keynesian economics, ed. by A. S. Eichner p34-45

#### United States—History

Eichner, A. S. and Ross, D. R. B. Competition. *In* Encyclopedia of American economic history, ed by G. Porter v2 p661-76

**Composers**

Carner, M. Composers as critics. *In* Carner, M. Major and minor p 1-5

**Composition (Music)** See Counterpoint; Melody; Musical form

**Compulsory education.** See Education, Compulsory

**Compulsory school attendance.** See Education, Compulsory

**Computer art**

Negroponte, N. The return of the Sunday painter. *In* The Computer age: a twenty-year view, ed. by M. L. Dertouzos and J. Moses p21-37

**Computer assisted instruction**

Campbell, P. B. Computer-assisted instruction in education: past, present and future. *In* Monster or messiah? Ed. by W. M. Mathews p89-98

Papert, S. A. Computers and learning. *In* The Computer age: a twenty-year view, ed. by M. L. Dertouzos and J. Moses p73-86

**Computer control.** See Automation

**Computer engineering**

Noyce, R. N. Hardware prospects and limitations. *In* The Computer age: a twenty-year view, ed. by M. L. Dertouzos and J. Moses p321-37

**Computer languages.** See Programming languages (Electronic computers)

**Computer simulation**

Simon, T. W. Philosophical objections to programs as theories. *In* Philosophical perspectives in artificial intelligence, ed. by M. Ringle p225-42

**Computers**

Bergmark, R. E. Computers and persons. *In* Monster or messiah? Ed. by W. M. Mathews p47-55

Denicoff, M. Sophisticated software: the road to science and Utopia. *In* The Computer age: a twenty-year view, ed. by M. L. Dertouzos and J. Moses p367-91

Evans, B. O. Computers and communications. *In* The Computer age: a twenty-year view, ed. by M. L. Dertouzos and J. Moses p338-66

Guerra, D. M. Computer technology and the mass media: interacting communication environments. *In* Monster or messiah? Ed. by W. M. Mathews p99-112

Johnson, R. B. Printout appeal. *In* Monster or messiah? Ed. by W. M. Mathews p62-71

Landon, M de L. A historian looks at the computer's impact on society. *In* Monster or messiah? Ed. by W. M. Mathews p13-22

Minsky, M. L. Computer science and the representation of knowledge. *In* The Computer age: a twenty-year view, ed. by M. L. Dertouzos and J. Moses p393-421

Mooers, G. R. Computer impact and the social welfare sector. *In* Monster or messiah? Ed. by W. M. Mathews p113-24

Morowitz, H. J. On computers, free will, and creativity. *In* Morowitz, H. J. The wine of life, and other essays on societies, energy & living things p28-32

Perlis, A. J. Current research frontiers in computer science. *In* The Computer age: a twenty-year view, ed. by M. L. Dertouzos and J. Moses p422-36

Shubik, M. Computers and modeling. *In* The Computer age: a twenty-year view, ed. by M. L. Dertouzos and J. Moses p285-305

Tolliver, J. E. The computer and the Protestant ethic: a conflict. *In* Monster or messiah? Ed. by W. M. Mathews p156-64

Vyssotsky, V. A. The use of computers for business functions. *In* The Computer age: a twenty-year view, ed. by M. L. Dertouzos and J. Moses p130-45

Williams, P. F. Reflection on computers as daughters of memory. *In* Monster or messiah? Ed. by W. M. Mathews p165-74

*See also* Computer art

**Appraisal**

*See* Computers—Valuation

**Design and construction**

*See* Computer engineering

**Law and legislation**

Noll, R. G. Regulation and computer services. *In* The Computer age: a twenty-year view, ed. by M. L. Dertouzos and J. Moses p254-84

**Scientific applications**

Fernbach, S. Scientific use of computers. *In* The Computer age: a twenty-year view, ed. by M. L. Dertouzos and J. Moses p146-60

**Valuation**

Dolin, E. F. Computers—for better and for worse. *In* Monster or messiah? Ed. by W. M. Mathews p37-44

**Computers and civilization**

Gilpin, R. G. The computer and world affairs. *In* The Computer age: a twenty-year view, ed. by M. L. Dertouzos and J. Moses p229-53

Gorove, M. Computer impact on society: a personal view from the world of art. *In* Monster or messiah? Ed. by W. M. Mathews p125-41

Hallblade, S. and Mathews, W. M. Computers and society: today and tomorrow. *In* Monster or messiah? Ed. by W. M. Mathews p25-36

Kibler, T. R. While debating the philosophy we accept the practice. *In* Monster or messiah? Ed. by W. M. Mathews p56-61

Laurenzo, F. E. Computers and the idea of progress. *In* Monster or messiah? Ed. by W. M. Mathews p3-12

Licklider, J. C. R. Computers and government. *In* The Computer age: a twenty-year view, ed. by M. L. Dertouzos and J. Moses p87-126

Moses, J. The computer in the home. *In* The Computer age: a twenty-year view, ed. by M. L. Dertouzos and J. Moses p3-20

Simon, H. A. The consequences of computers for centralization and decentralization. *In* The Computer age: a twenty-year view, ed. by M. L. Dertouzos and J. Moses p212-28

Weizenbaum, J. Once more: the computer revolution. *In* The Computer age: a twenty-year view, ed. by M. L. Dertouzos and J. Moses p439-58

**Computational linguistics.** See Linguistics—Data processing

**Conduct of life**

Nisbet, L. Kulturkampf. *In* Humanist ethics, ed. by M. B. Storer p242-52

*See also* Culture; Ethics; Pride and vanity; Sympathy

**Conacher, Desmond John**

**About individual works**

*Euripidean drama*

Knox, B. M. W. Review of Euripidean drama (by D. J. Conacher). *In* Knox, B. M. W. Word and action p323-28

**Concord, Mass.**

Howarth, W. L. Travelling in Concord: the world of Thoreau's Journal. *In* Puritan influences in American literature, ed. by E. Elliott p143-66

**Condorcet, Marie Jean Antoine Nicolas Caritat, marquis de**

### About

Gardner, E. J. The philosophes and women: sensationalism and sentiment. *In* Woman and society in eighteenth-century France, ed. by E. Jacobs and others p19-27

White, I. Condorcet: politics and reason. *In* Royal Institute of Philosophy. Philosophers of the Enlightenment p110-39

**Conduct of life.** See Culture; Ethics

**Conduct unbecoming (Motion picture)**

Kael, P. Horseplay. *In* Kael, P. When the lights go down p62-68

**Confession in literature**

Molesworth, C. "With your own face on": confessional poetry. *In* Molesworth, C. The fierce embrace p61-76

Raleigh, J. H. The last confession: O'Neill and the Catholic confessional. *In* Eugene O'Neill, ed. by V. Floyd p212-28

Spender, S. Confessions and autobiography; excerpt from "The making of a poem." *In* Autobiography: essays theoretical and critical, ed. by J. Olney p115-22

**The confessions of Winifred Wagner (Motion picture)**

Kauffmann, S. The confessions of Winifred Wagner. *In* Kauffmann, S. Before my eyes p306-09

**Conflict, Social.** See Social conflict

**Conflict of generations**

Kriegel, A. Generational difference: the history of an idea. *In* Generations, ed. by S. R. Graubard p23-38

La Barre, W. Authority, culture change, and the courts. *In* La Barre, W. Culture in context p215-24

Letwin, S. R. Trollope on generations without gaps. *In* Generations, ed. by S. R. Graubard p53-70

**Conformity.** See Deviant behavior

**Congregationalism.** See Puritans

**Conley, Tom**

Framing Malraux. *In* André Malraux, ed. by F. Dorenlot and M. Tison-Braun p125-40

**Conner, Lester Irwin**

A matter of character: Red Hanrahan and Crazy Jane. *In* Yeats, Sligo and Ireland, ed. by A. N. Jeffares p 1-16

**Connotation (Linguistics)**

Crosman, R. T. Do readers make meaning? *In* The Reader in the text, ed. by S. R. Suleiman and I. Crosman p149-64

Michaels, W. B. Against formalism: chickens and rocks. *In* The State of the language, ed. by L. Michaels and C. Ricks p410-20

Speier, H. The communication of hidden meaning. *In* Propaganda and communication in world history, ed. by H. D. Lasswell, D. Lerner and H. Speier v2 p261-300

**Connotative meaning.** See Connotation (Linguistics)

**Conrad, Joseph**

### About

Aisenberg, N. Joseph Conrad and the thriller. *In* Aisenberg, N. A common spring p111-67

Naipaul, V. S. Conrad's darkness. *In* Naipaul, V. S. The return of Eva Perón p207[28]

Pritchett, V. S. Joseph Conrad: a moralist of exile. *In* Pritchett, V. S. The tale bearers p43-53

### About individual works

*Nostromo*

Visser, N. W. The novel and the concept of social network. *In* The Analysis of literary texts, ed. by R. D. Pope p268-85

### Criticism and interpretation

Trilling, L. Literary pathology. In Trilling, L. Speaking of literature and society p392-97

**Conrad, Peter**

On the medicalization of deviance and social control. *In* Critical psychiatry, ed. by D. Ingleby p102-19

**Conscience**

Miller, P. The New England conscience. *In* Miller, P. The responsibility of mind in a civilization of machines p176-85

Shiner, R. A. Butler's theory of moral judgment. *In* Royal Institute of Philosophy. Philosophers of the Enlightenment p199-225

**Consciousness**

*See also* Subconsciousness

### Language

Kukla, A. The modern language of consciousness. *In* The State of the language, ed. by L. Michaels and C. Ricks p516-23

**Consensus (Social sciences)**

Manley, L. G. "A latitude of sense": testing for truth. *In* Manley, L. G. Convention, 1500-1750 p241-64

White, I. Condorcet: politics and reason. *In* Royal Institute of Philosophy. Philosophers of the Enlightenment p110-39

*See also* Authority

**Conservationists.** See Ecologists

**Conservative Party (Great Britain)**

Searle, G. R. Critics of Edwardian society: the case of the Radical Right. *In* The Edwardian age: conflict and stability, 1900-1914, ed. by A. O'Day p79-96

**Consolidation and merger of corporations**

### United States—History

Hannah, L. Mergers. *In* Encyclopedia of American economic history, ed. by G. Porter v2 p639-51

**Constance, Council of, 1414-1418**

Ozment, S. H. The ecclesiopolitical traditions. *In* Ozment, S. H. The age of reform, 1250-1550 p135-81

**Constant, Benjamin** See Constant de Rebecque, Henri Benjamin

**Constant de Rebecque, Henri Benjamin**

### About individual works

*Adolphe*

Todorov, T. Reading as construction. *In* The Reader in the text, ed. by S. R. Suleiman and I. Crosman p67-82

**Constantinople.** See Istanbul

**Constitutional law.** See Federal government; Judicial power

**Consumption (Economics)**

*See also* Demand (Economic theory)

### Surveys

*See* Cost and standard of living

**Consumption of energy.** See Energy consumption

**Contaminated food.** See Food contamination

**Contemporary art.** See Art, Modern—20th century

Contentment. See Happiness

Continental drift. See Plate tectonics

Contraception. See Birth control

Conundrums. See Riddles

Convention (Philosophy)

Manley, L. G. Art and convention in antiquity. *In* Manley, L. G. Convention, 1500-1750 p36-54

Manley, L. G. The "duble name" of custom: the Reformation attack on convention. *In* Manley, L. G. Convention, 1500-1750 p67-90

Manley, L. Historical rhetoric and historical explanation. *In* Manley, L. Convention, 1500-1750 p203-15

Manley, L. G. Introduction. *In* Manley, L. G. Convention, 1500-1750 p 1-14

Manley, L. G. "A latitude of sense": testing for truth. *In* Manley, L. G. Convention, 1500-1750 p241-64

Manley, L. G. Neo-Stoic and Baconian nature: seventeenth century prospects. *In* Manley, L. G. Convention, 1500-1750 p133-36

Manley, L. G. "The separation of opinions": the role of convention in criticism and controversy. *In* Manley, L. G. Convention, 1500-1750 p188-202

Manley, L. G. "Use becomes another nature": custom in sixteenth-century politics and law. *In* Manley, L. G. Convention, 1500-1750 p90-106

Manley, L. G. A world on wheels: convention in sixteenth-century moral philosophy. *In* Manley, L. G. Convention, 1500-1750 p106-36

Nussbaum, M. C. Eleatic conventionalism and Philolaus on the conditions of thought. *In* Harvard Studies in classical philology, v83 p63-108

Conversation

Williams, R. M. Goffman's sociology of talk. *In* The View from Goffman, ed. by J. Ditton p210-32

Conversation piece (Motion picture)

Kael, P. Lazarus laughs. *In* Kael, P. When the lights go down p35-40

Convicts. See Prisoners

Conzen, Kathleen Neils

Community studies, urban history, and American local history. *In* The Past before us, ed. by M. Kammen p270-91

Cook, Albert Spaulding

Myth & language

*Contents*

Between prose and poetry: the speech and silence of the proverb

Heraclitus and the conditions of utterance

Inquiry: Herodotus

Language and myth

The large phases of myth

Lévi-Strauss, myth, and the Neolithic revolution

Metaphor: literature's access to myth

Ovid: the dialectics of recovery from atavism

Parable

Pindar: "great deeds of prowess are always many-mythed"

The self-enclosure of the riddle

Cook, Blanche Wiesen

Female support networks and political activism: Lillian Wald, Crystal Eastman, Emma Goldman. *In* A Heritage of her own, ed. by N. F. Cott and E. H. Peck p411-44

Cooke, Alistair Alfred

Mencken and the English language. *In* On Mencken, ed. by J. Dorsey p 84-113

Cooke, John

'Tis mysterious surely and fantastic strange: art and artists in three plays of George Fitzmaurice. *In* Irish Renaissance annual I p32-55

Cookery in literature

Hieatt, C. B. "To boille the chiknes with the marybones": Hodge's kitchen revisited. *In* Chaucerian problems and perspectives, ed. by E. Vasta and Z. P. Thundy p149-63

Cooley, Charles Horton

About

Fuhrman, E. R. Charles H. Cooley. *In* Fuhrman, E. R. The sociology of knowledge in America, 1883-1915 p186-211

Coombes, John

British intellectuals and the Popular Front. *In* Class, culture and social change, ed. by F. Gloversmith p70-100

Coonskin (Motion picture)

Kauffmann, S. Coonskin. *In* Kauffmann, S. Before my eyes p165-68

Cooper, James Fenimore

About individual works

*Home as found*

Sundquist, E. J. "The home of my childhood": incest and imitation in Cooper's Home as found. *In* Sundquist, E. J. Home as found p 1-40

Characters—Natty Bumpo

Martin, T. The negative character in American fiction. *In* Toward a new American literary history, ed. by L. J. Budd, E. H. Cady and C. L. Anderson p230-43

Coote, Mary Putney

The singer's themes in Serbocroatian heroic song. *In* California Slavic studies v11 p201-35

Copernicus, Nicolaus

About

Lutz, C. E. Copernicus' stand for humanism. *In* Lutz, C. E. The oldest library motto, and other library essays p75-82

Coping behavior. See Adaptability (Psychology)

Coppa, Frank J.

The explosion of the eye: an introduction to the promise and problems of television. *In* Screen and society, ed. by F. J. Coppa p ix-xxvii

The global impact of television: an overview. *In* Screen and society, ed. by F. J. Coppa p 1-29

Coppola, Francis Ford

About individual works

*Apocalypse now*

Kauffmann, S. Apocalypse now. *In* Kauffmann, S. Before my eyes p106-09

Copyright

Cases

Bald, R. C. Early copyright litigation and its bibliographical interest. *In* The Bibliographical Society of America, 1904-79 p172-87

Copyright infringement

Cases

*See* Copyright—Cases

Cord, Steven B.

Walker: the general leads the charge. *In* Critics of Henry George, ed. by R. V. Andelson p178-86

**Cord, Steven B. and Andelson, Robert V.**
Ely: a liberal economist defends landlordism. *In* Critics of Henry George, ed. by R. V. Andelson p313-25

**Cordemoy, Géraud de**

### About individual works
*A philosophicall discourse concerning speech*

Uitti, K. D. Cordemoy and 'Cartesian linguistics.' *In* Psychology of language and thought, ed. by R. W. Rieber p53-76

**Corkery, Daniel**

### About

Lucy, S. Place and people in the short stories of Daniel Corkery. *In* The Irish short story, ed. by P. Rafroidi and T. Brown p159-73

**Cormack, William Epps**

### About

O'Flaherty, P. Walking new ground: books by two Newfoundland pioneers, 1770-1882. *In* O'Flaherty, P. The rock observed p32-48

**Cormier, Robert**

### About

Rees, D. The sadness of compromise: Robert Cormier and Jill Chaney. *In* Rees, D. The marble in the water p155-72

**Corneille, Pierre**

### About individual works
*Oedipe*

Mueller, M. Oedipus Rex as tragedy of fate: Corneille's Oedipe and Schiller's Die Braut von Messina. *In* Mueller, M. Children of Oedipus, and other essays on the imitation of Greek tragedy, 1550-1800 p129-46

**Cornford, John**

### About

Heinemann, M. Louis MacNeice, John Cornford and Clive Branson: three Left-wing poets. *In* Culture and crisis in Britain in the thirties, ed. by J. Clark and others p103-32

**Corngold, Stanley**
Sein und Zeit: implications for poetics. *In* Martin Heidegger and the question of literature, ed. by W. V. Spanos p99-114

**Corno di Basseto,** pseud. See Shaw, George Bernard

**Cornwall, John**
Macrodynamics. *In* A Guide to post-Keynesian economics, ed. by A. S. Eichner p19-33

**Corporate mergers.** See Consolidation and merger of corporations

**Corporations**
*See also* International business enterprises

### Merger
*See* Consolidation and merger of corporations

**Corporations, International.** See International business enterprise

**Corrections.** See Juvenile corrections

**Corso, Gregory**

### About

Howard, R. Gregory Corso: "Surely there'll be another table . . ." *In* Howard, R. Alone with America p76-83

**Cortázar, Julio**

### About

Valentine, R. Y. Cortazar's rhetoric of reader participation. *In* The Analysis of literary texts, ed. by R. D. Pope p212-23

### About individual works
*Las armas secretas*

Foster, D. W. Cortázar's "Las armas secretas" and structurally anomalous narratives. *In* Foster, D. W. Studies in the contemporary Spanish-American short story p83-101

*Axolotl*

Bernstein, J. S. In some cases jumps are made: "Axolotl" from an Eastern point of view. *In* The Analysis of literary texts, ed. by R. D. Pope p175-84

*Historias de cronopios y famas*

Foster, D. W. The écriture of rupture and subversion of language in Cortázar's Historias de cronopios y famas. *In* Foster, D. W. Studies in the contemporary Spanish-American short story p63-82

**Corvo, Frederick, Baron,** pseud. See Rolfe, Frederick William

**Cosgrove, Stuart**
Prolet Buehne: agit-prop in America. *In* Performance and politics in popular drama, ed. by D. Bradby, L. James and B. Sharratt p201-12

**Cosmology**
Davies, P. C. W. Reality exists outside us? *In* Lying truth, ed. by R. Duncan and M. Weston-Smith p143-58

Eliade, M. The world, the city, and the house; excerpt from "Occultism, witchcraft, and cultural fashions." *In* Value and values in evolution, ed. by E. A. Maziarz p3-16

**Cost and standard of living**
Spengler, J. J. Rising expectations: frustrations. *In* Propaganda and communication in world history, ed. by H. D. Lasswell, D. Lerner and H. Speier v3 p37-92

### Great Britain—History
Gourvish, T. R. The standard of living, 1890-1914. *In* The Edwardian age: conflict and stability, 1900-1914, ed. by A. O'Day p13-34

**Cost of living.** See Cost and standard of living

**Cost of medical care.** See Medical care, Cost of

**Costa, Gustavo**
Vico's political thought in his time and ours. *In* Conference on Vico and Contemporary Thought, New York, 1976. Vico and contemporary thought pt 1 p222-34

**Costa-Gavras**

### About individual works
*Special section*

Kael, P. Political acts. *In* Kael, P. When the lights go down p95-98

**Costick, Miles M.**
Soviet military posture and strategic trade. *In* National security in the 1980s: from weakness to strength, ed. by W. S. Thompson p189-213

**Costume**

### Great Britain—History
Owen, G. R. Wynflæd's wardrobe. *In* Anglo-Saxon England 8 p195-222

**Costume in art**
Schapiro, M. Notes on Castelseprio. *In* Schapiro, M. Selected papers v3: Late antique, early Christian and mediaeval art p115-42

**Cothi, Lewis Glyn.** See Lewis Glyn Cothi

**Cotler, Julio**
State and regime: comparative notes on the southern cone and the "enclave" societies. *In* The New authoritarianism in Latin America, ed. by D. Collier p255-82

**Cott, Nancy F.**
Eighteenth-century family and social life revealed in Massachusetts divorce records. *In* A Heritage of her own, ed. by N. F. Cott and E. H. Pleck p107-35

Passionlessness: an interpretation of Victorian sexual ideology, 1790-1850. *In* A Heritage of her own, ed. by N. F. Cott and E. H. Pleck p162-81

**Cottle, Basil**
Names. *In* The State of the language, ed. by L. Michaels and C. Ricks p98-107

**Cotton growing**
### Southern States
Margolis, M. Seduced and abandoned: agricultural frontiers in Brazil and the United States. *In* Brazil, anthropological perspectives, ed. by M. L. Margolis and W. E. Carter p160-79

**Cottrell, Sir Alan**
Science is objective. *In* Lying truths, ed. by R. Duncan and M. Weston-Smith p159-69

The **counter**-Enlightenment. Berlin, Sir I. *In* Berlin, Sir I. Against the current p 1-24

**Coughlan, Margaret N.**
The Maxine Waldron collection of children's books and paper toys. *In* Research about nineteenth-century children and books, ed. by S. K. Richardson p61-66

**Council of Constance.** See Constance, Council of, 1414-1418

**Council of Trent.** See Trent, Council of, 1545-1563

**Counter culture.** See Conflict of generations

**Counter-Reformation**
Ozment, S. H. Catholic reform and Counter Reformation. *In* Ozment, S. H. The age of reform, 1250-1550 p397-418
*See also* Reformation

### France—Rouen
Benedict, P. J. The Catholic response to Protestantism. *In* Religion and the people, 800-1700, ed. by J. Obelkevich p168-90

**Counterpoint**
Dent, E. J. The teaching of strict counterpoint. *In* Dent, E. J. Selected essays p218-31

**Country life**
### Great Britain
Lowerson, J. Battles for the countryside. *In* Class, culture and social change, ed. by F. Gloversmith p258-80

**Country life in literature**
Sutton, M. K. Truth and the pastor's vision in George Crabbe, William Barnes, and R. S. Thomas. *In* Survivals of pastoral, ed. by R. Hardin p33-59
*See also* Pastoral literature

**Couperus, Louis Marie Anne**
#### About individual works
*The hidden force*
Plomer, W. C. F. Louis Couperus. *In* Plomer, W. C. F. Electric delights p58-65

**Coups d'état**
Senghaas, D. Militarism dynamics in the contemporary context of periphery capitalism. *In* Problems of contemporary militarism, ed. by A. Eide and M. Thee p195-206

**Courcel, Martine Hallade de**
Timeless geography. *In* André Malraux, ed. by F. Dorenlot and M. Tison-Braun p67-74

**Courtly love**
Calin, W. C. Defense and illustration of fin' amor: some polemical comments on the Robertsonian approach. *In* The Expansion and transformations of courtly literature, ed. by N. B. Smith and J. T. Snow p32-48

Camproux, C. On the subject of an argument between Elias and his cousin. *In* The Interpretation of medieval lyric poetry, ed. by W. T. H. Jackson p91-112

Cropp, G. M. The partimen between Folquet de Marseille and Tostemps. *In* The Interpretation of medieval lyric poetry, ed. by W. T. H. Jackson p91-112

Robbins, R. H. The Middle English court love lyric. *In* The Interpretation of medieval lyric poetry, ed. by W. T. H. Jackson p205-32

Robertson, D. W. The concept of courtly love as an impediment to the understanding of medieval texts. *In* Robertson, D. W. Essays in medieval culture p257-72

Robertson, D. W. Five poems by Marcabru. *In* Robertson, D. W. Essays in medieval culture p151-65

Smith, N. B. and Snow, J. T. Courtly love and courtly literature. *In* The Expansion and transformations of courtly literature, ed. by N. B. Smith and J. T. Snow p3-14
*See also* Troubadors

**Courts**
*See also* Judicial power

### United States
Moynihan, D. P. The iron law of emulation. *In* Moynihan, D. P. Counting our blessings p115-37

**Courts and courtiers in literature**
Melczer, W. The war of the carrots and the onions or concentration versus dispersion: the methodology of interdisciplinary studies applied to the European courts. *In* The Expansion and transformations of courtly literature, ed. by N. B. Smith and J. T. Snow p207-26

Ridley, F. H. Scottish transformations of courtly literature: William Dunbar and the court of James IV. *In* The Expansion and transformations of courtly literature, ed. by N. B. Smith and J. T. Snow p171-84

**Couturier, Maurice**
Foreign scholarship: French contributions. *In* American literary scholarship, 1978 p439-45

**Covenant theology.** See Covenants (Theology)

**Covenants (Theology)**
Hill, J. E. C. Covenant theology and the concept of 'a public person.' *In* Powers, possessions and freedom, ed. by A. Kontos p3-22

**Cowley, Abraham**
#### About individual works
*Davideis*
Pebworth, T. L. Cowley's Davideis and the exaltation of friendship. *In* The David myth in Western literature, ed. by R. J. Frontain and J. Wojcik p96-104

**Cowley, Malcolm**
"Van Wyck Brooks: a career in retrospect." *In* Van Wyck Brooks: the critic and his critics, ed. by W. Wasserstrom p189-93

**Cox, James Melville**
Recovering literature's lost ground through autobiography. *In* Autobiography: essays theoretical and critical, ed. by J. Olney p123-45

**Cox, John F.**
The stage representation of the 'kill Claudio' sequence in 'Much ado about nothing.' *In* Shakespeare survey 32 p27-36

**Cox, William A.**
The U.S. economy in the eighties. *In* Economic issues of the eighties, ed. by N. Kamrany and R. H. Day p69-79

**Coxe, Antony D. Hippisley**
Equestrian drama and the circus. *In* Performance and politics in popular drama, ed. by D. Bradby, L. James and B. Sharratt p109-18

**Crabbe, George, 1754-1832**

### About

Sutton, M. K. Truth and the pastor's vision in George Crabbe, William Barnes, and R. S. Thomas. *In* Survivals of pastoral, ed. by R. F. Hardin p33-59

**Craftsmen.** See Artisans

**Craig, Patricia.** See Cadogan, M. jt. auth.

**Crane, Hart**

### About individual works

*The bridge*

Irwin, J. T. Figurations of the writer's death: Freud and Hart Crane. *In* The Literary Freud: mechanisms of defense and the poetic will, ed. by J. H. Smith p217-60

*Passage*

Caws, M. A. On one crossing-over: Valery's sea into Hart Crane's scene. *In* The Analysis of literary texts, ed. by R. D. Pope p100-06

**Crane, Stephen**

### Influence—Berryman

Wagner, L. W. Berryman: from the beginning. *In* Wagner, L. W. American modern p158-64

**Crawford, Richard Arthur**
A historian's introduction to early American music. *In* American Antiquarian Society. Proceedings v89 pt2 p261-98

**Creation**

### Art

Pickering, F. P. Trinitas creator: word and image. *In* Pickering, F. P. Essays on medieval German literature and iconography p46-58

**Creation (Literary, artistic, etc.)**
Fehrman, C. A. D. Concluding unscientific postscript. *In* Fehrman, C. A. D. Poetic creation p197-202

Fehrman, C. A. D. Documentation and experimentation. *In* Fehrman, C. A. D. Poetic creation p3-34

Fehrman, C. A. D. Periodicity and the stages of literary creativity. *In* Fehrman, C. A. D. Poetic creation p137-58

Nabokov, V. V. The art of literature and commonsense. *In* Nabokov, V. V. Lectures on literature p371-80

Tison-Braun, M. The artist as exemplar of humanity. *In* André Malraux, ed. by F. Dorenlot and M. Tison-Braun p155-64

*See also* Inspiration

**Creative ability**
Morowitz, H. J. On computers, free will, and creativity. *In* Morowitz, H. J. The wine of life, and other essays on societies, energy & living things p28-32

**Creativity.** See Creation (Literary, artistic, etc.); Creative ability

**Credit.** See Banks and banking

**Creeley, Robert**

### About

Howard, R. Robert Creeley; "I begin where I can, and end when I see the whole thing returning." *In* Howard, R. Alone with America p84-93

Wagner, L. W. Creeley's late poems: contexts. *In* Wagner, L. W. American modern p178-86

Wagner, L. W. The latest Creeley. *In* Wagner, L. W. American modern p165-77

**Creevey, Thomas**

### About

Blythe, R. The writer as listener. *In* Royal Society of Literature of the United Kingdom, London. Essays by divers hands: innovation in contemporary literature, new ser. v40 p 1-14

**Crestien de Troyes.** See Chrestien de Troyes

**Crick, Joyce**
Kafka and the Muirs. *In* The World of Franz Kafka, ed. by J. P. Stern p159-74

**Crime and criminals**
Durkheim, E. Crime and social health. *In* Durkheim, E. Emile Durkheim on institutional analysis p181-88

*See also* Prisoners

### Research

Baldwin, J. Ecological and areal studies in Great Britain and the United States. *In* Crime and justice v 1 p29-66

Farrington, D. P. Longitudinal research on crime and delinquency. *In* Crime and justice v 1 p289-348

### Massachusetts

Frye, J. Class, generation and social change: a case in Salem, Massachusetts, 1636-1656. *In* 5000 years of popular culture, ed. by F. E. H. Schroeder p278-85

### United States

Hook, S. The rights of the victims. *In* Hook, S. Philosophy and public policy p130-37

Zimring, F. E. American youth violence: issues and trends. *In* Crime and justice v 1 p67-107

**Crime in literature**
Aisenberg, N. Dickens and the crime novel. *In* Aisenberg, N. A common spring p68-110

**Crime stories.** See Detective and mystery stories

**Crimean War, 1853-1856**

### Drama

Bratton, J. S. Theatre of war: the Crimea on the London stage, 1854-5. *In* Performance and politics in popular drama, ed. by D. Bradby, L. James and B. Sharratt p119-37

**Criminal anthropology.** See Criminal behavior, Prediction of

**Criminal behavior, Prediction of**
Glaser, D. A review of crime-causation theory and its application. *In* Crime and justice v 1 p203-37

**Criminal law**
Durkheim, E. Two laws of penal evolution. *In* Durkheim, E. Emile Durkheim on institutional analysis p153-80

**Criminal psychology.** See Criminal behavior, Prediction of

**Critchfield, Richard**
The search for an enlightened sovereign in Lessing's drama. *In* Studies in eighteenth-century culture v9 p251-67

**Criterion (Theory of knowledge)**

Annas, J. Truth and knowledge. *In* Doubt and dogmatism ed. by M. Shofield, M. Burnyeat and J. Barnes p84-104

Taylor, C. C. W. 'All perceptions are true.' *In* Doubt and dogmatism, ed. by M. Schofield, M. Burnyeat and J. Barnes p105-24

**Criticism**

Barthes, R. From work to text. *In* Textual strategies, ed. by J. V. Harari p73-81

Culler, J. Prolegomena to a theory of reading. *In* The Reader in the text, ed. by S. R. Suleiman and I. Crosman p46-66

Eagleton, T. Text, ideology, realism. *In* Literature and society, ed. by E. W. Said p149-73

Eldridge, R. Criticism and its objects. *In* Glyph 6 p158-76

Foucault, M. What is an author? excerpt from "Language, counter-memory, practice." *In* Textual strategies, ed. by J. V. Harari p141-60

Gasché, R. Deconstruction as criticism. *In* Glyph 6 p177-215

Harari, J. V. Critical factions/critical fictions. *In* Textual strategies, ed. by J. V. Harari p17-72

Hartman, G. H. Centaur: on the psychology of the critic. *In* Hartman, G. H. Criticism in the wilderness p214-25

Hartman, G. H. Criticism, indeterminacy, irony. *In* Hartman, G. H. Criticism in the wilderness p265-83

Hartman, G. H. Introduction. *In* Hartman, G. H. Criticism in the wilderness p 1-15

Hartman, G. H. Literary commentary as literature. *In* Hartman, G. H. Criticism in the wilderness p189-213

Hartman, G. H. Past and present. *In* Hartman, G. H. Criticism in the wilderness p226-49

Hartman, G. H. Purification and danger 2: critical style. *In* Hartman, G. H. Criticism in the wilderness p133-57

Hartman, G. H. The recognition scene of criticism. *In* Hartman, G. H. Criticism in the wilderness p253-64

Hartman, G. H. The sacred jungle 1: Carlyle, Eliot, Bloom. *In* Hartman, G. H. Criticism in the wilderness p42-62

Hartman, G. H. A short history of practical criticism. *In* Hartman, G. H. Criticism in the wilderness p284-301

Hartman, G. H. Understanding criticism. *In* Hartman, G. H. Criticism in the wilderness p19-41

Hartman, G. H. The work of reading. *In* Hartman, G. H. Criticism in the wilderness p161-88

Holloway, J. Conclusion: structure and the critic's art. *In* Holloway, J. Narrative and structure: exploratory essays p100-17

Holloway, J. Poetic analysis and the idea of the transformation-rule: some examples from Herbert, Wordsworth, Pope and Shakespeare. *In* Holloway, J. Narrative and structure: exploratory essays p118-36

Krieger, M. Literary analysis and evaluation—and the ambidextrous critic. *In* Krieger, M. Poetic presence and illusion p303-22

Krieger, M. Literature, criticism, and decision theory. *In* Krieger, M. Poetic presence and illusion p238-69

Krieger, M. Literature versus ecriture: constructions and deconstructions in recent critical theory. *In* Krieger, M. Poetic presence and illusion p169-87

Krieger, M. Mediation, language, and vision in the reading of literature. *In* Krieger, M. Poetic presence and illusion p270-302

Krieger, M. Poetic presence and illusion II: Formalist theory and the duplicity of metaphor. *In* Krieger, M. Poetic presence and illusion p139-68

Krieger, M. A scorecard for the critics. *In* Krieger, M. Poetic presence and illusion p211-37

Lentricchia, F. Afterword. *In* Lentricchia, F. After the New Criticism. p348-51

Lentricchia, F. History or the abyss: post-structuralism. *In* Lentricchia, F. After the New Criticism p156-210

Nabokov, V. V. Good readers and good writers. *In* Nabokov, V. V. Lectures on literature p 1-6

Peyre, H. On the arrogance of criticism. *In* The Analysis of literary texts, ed. by R. D. Pope p 1-8

Robertson, D. W. The allegorist and the aesthetician. *In* Robertson, D. W. Essays in medieval culture p85-101

Robertson, D. W. Some observations on method in literary studies. *In* Robertson, D. W. Essays in medieval culture p73-84

Said, E. W. The text, the world, the critic. *In* Textual strategies, ed. by J. V. Harari p161-88

Suleiman, S R. Introduction: varieties of audience-oriented criticism. *In* The Reader in the text, ed. by S. R. Suleiman and I. Crosman p3-45

Uphaus, R. W. The impossible observer. *In* Uphaus, R. W. The impossible observer p 1-8

*See also* Aesthetics; Architectural criticism; Art criticism; Hermeneutics; New Criticism; Poetry—History and criticism; Structuralism (Literary analysis); Style, Literary

### Bibliography

Crosman, I. K. Annotated bibliography of audience-oriented criticism. *In* The Reader in the text, ed. by S. R. Suleiman and I. Crosman p401-24

### History

Lanser, S. S. and Beck, E. T. [Why] are there no great women critics? And what difference does it make? *In* The Prism of sex, ed. by J. A. Sherman and E. T. Beck p79-91

Manley, L. G. Introduction. *In* Manley, L. G. Convention, 1500-1750 p1-14

### France

Couturier, M. Foreign scholarship: French contributions. *In* American literary scholarship, 1978 p439-45

### Germany

Galinsky, H. Foreign scholarship: German contributions. *In* American literary scholarship, 1978 p445-65

### Great Britain

Wright, I. F. R. Leavis, the Scrutiny movement and the crisis. *In* Culture and crisis in Britain in the thirties, ed. by J. Clark and others p37-65

### Italy

Anzilotti, R. Foreign scholarship: Italian contributions. *In* American literary scholarshp, 1978 p465-75

Della Terza, D. Methodology and exegesis: the Italian side. *In* The Analysis of literary texts, ed. by R. D. Pope p9-20

Criticism—*Continued*

### Japan

Beppu, K. Foreign scholarship: Japanese contributions. *In* American literary scholarship, 1978 p475-82

### Scandinavia

Lundén, R. Foreign scholarship: Scandinavian contributions. *In* American literary scholarship, 1978 p482-87

### United States

Bush, D. Literature, the academy, and the public. *In* Generations, ed. by S. R. Graubard p165-74

Krieger, M. Reconsideration—the New Critics. *In* Krieger, M. Poetic presence and illusion p108-14

Litz, A. W. Literary criticism. *In* Harvard Guide to contemporary American writing, ed. by D. Hoffman p51-83

### United States—Bibliography

Hoffman, M. J. Themes, topics, criticism. *In* American literary scholarship, 1978 p413-38

### Criticism (Philosophy)

Manley, L. G. The possibilities of discourse: Renaissance logic, rhetoric, and poetics. *In* Manley, L. G. Convention, 1500-1750 p137-58

### Criticism, Textual

Prince, G. Notes on the text as reader. *In* The Reader in the text, ed. by S. R. Suleiman and I. Crosman p225-40

*See also* Anglo-Saxon poetry—Criticism, Textual; Semiotics and literature; Structuralism (Literary analysis); and subdivision Criticism, Textual under individual authors and literatures, e.g. Shakespeare, William—Criticism, Textual

### Critics

### Psychology

Hartman, G. H. Centaur: on the psychology of the critic. *In* Hartman, G. H. Criticism in the wilderness p214-25

### Crocker, William Henry

Canela kinship and the question of matrilineality. *In* Brazil, anthropological perspectives, ed. by M. L. Margolis and W. E. Carter p225-49

### Crockett, David

### About

Seelye, J. A well-wrought Crockett: or, How the fakelorists passed through the credibility gap and discovered Kentucky. *In* Toward a new American literary history, ed. by L. J. Budd, E. H. Cady and C. L. Anderson p91-110

### Cronin, John

The Anglo-Irish novel

*Contents*

Charles Kickham: Knocknagow
George Moore: A drama in muslin
Gerald Griffin: The collegians
John Banim: The Nowlans
Maria Edgeworth: Castle Rackrent
Somerville and Ross: The real Charlotte
William Carleton: the black prophet

George Moore: The untilled field. *In* The Irish short story, ed. by P. Rafroidi and T. Brown p113-25

### Crook, Steve, and Taylor, Laurie

Goffman's version of reality. *In* The View from Goffman, ed. by J. Ditton p233-51

### Cropp, Glynnis M.

The partimen between Folquet de Marseille and Tostemps. *In* The Interpretation of medieval lyric poetry, ed. by W. T. H. Jackson p91-112

### Crosby, Harry

### About

Wolff, G. Minor lives. *In* Telling lives, ed. by M. Pachter p56-72

### Crosman, Inge Karalus

Annotated bibliography of audience-oriented criticism. *In* The Reader in the text, ed. by S. R. Suleiman and I. Crosman p401-24

### Crosman, Robert True

Do readers make meaning? *In* The Reader in the text, ed. by S. R. Suleiman and I. Crosman p149-64

### Cross, James E.

Cynewulf's traditions about the apostles in Fates of the apostles. *In* Anglo-Saxon England 8 p163-75

**Cross, Mary Ann (Evans)** See Eliot, George, pseud.

**Cross-cultural psychology.** See Ethnopsychology

### Crosses

Schapiro, M. The bowman and the bird on the Ruthwell Cross and other works: the interpretation of secular themes in early mediaeval religious art. *In* Schapiro, M. Selected papers v3: Late antique, early Christian and mediaeval art p177-95

Schapiro, M. The religious meaning of the Ruthwell Cross. *In* Schapiro, M. Selected papers v3: Late antique, early Christian and mediaeval art p151-76

*See also* Symbolism

### Crosson, Frederick

Religion and faith in St Augustine's Confessions. *In* Rationality and religious belief, ed. by C. F. Delaney p152-68

### Crowder, Richard H.

Poetry: 1900 to the 1930s. *In* American literary scholarship, 1978 p323-42

### Crowley, Joseph Donald

Hawthorne. *In* American literary scholarship, 1978 p17-28

### Crozier, Brian

The Cold War is over. *In* Lying truths, ed. by R. Duncan and M. Weston-Smith p35-46

### Cuba

### Foreign relations—Africa

Gonzalez, E. Cuba, the Soviet Union, and Africa. *In* Communism in Africa, ed. by D. E. Albright p145-67

**Cubena.** See Wilson, Carlos Guillermo

### Cuchulain in literature

Wyatt, D. Yeats and Synge: the Cuchulain complex. *In* Wyatt, D. Prodigal sons p26-51

### Cuddington, John T. and McKinnon, Ronald I.

The United States and the world economy. *In* The Economy in the 1980s: a program for growth and stability, ed. by M. J. Boskin p161-95

### Cuff, Robert D.

Herbert Hoover, the ideology of voluntarism and war organization during the Great War. *In* Herbert Hoover, ed. by L. E. Gelfand p21-39

**Culler, Jonathan D.**

Jacques Derrida. *In* Structuralism and since, ed. by J. Sturrock p154-80

Prolegomena to a theory of reading. *In* The Reader in the text, ed. by S. R. Suleiman and I. Crosman p46-66

### About individual works
*Structuralist poetics*

Lentricchia, F. Uncovering history and the reader: structuralism. *In* Lentricchia, F. After the New Criticism p102-54

**Cultural anthropology.** See Ethnology

**Cultural pluralism.** See Pluralism (Social sciences)

**Cultural relativism**

La Barre, W. Obscenity: an anthropological appraisal. *In* La Barre, W. Culture in context p258-68

La Barre, W. Paralinguistics, kinesics, and cultural anthropology. *In* La Barre, W. Culture in context p289-332

*See also* Ethnocentrism

**Culture**

Braudel, F. The history of civilizations: the past explains the present. *In* Braudel, F. On history p177-218

Gloversmith, F. Defining culture: J. C. Powys, Clive Bell, R. H. Tawney & T. S. Eliot. *In* Class, culture and social change, ed. by F. Gloversmith p15-44

Gombrich, Sir E. H. J. In search of cultural history. *In* Gombrich, Sir E. H. J. Ideals and idols p24-59

Kristol, I. The adversary culture of intellectuals. *In* The Third century, ed. by S. M. Lipset p327-43

Meyer, L. B. The dilemma of choosing: speculations about contemporary culture. *In* Value and values in evolution, ed. by E. A. Maziarz p117-41

Rotenstreich, N. Enlightenment: between Mendelssohn and Kant. *In* Studies in Jewish religious and intellectual history, ed. by S. Stein and R. Loewe p263-79

*See also* Humanism; Language and culture; Learning and scholarship; Politics and culture

**Culture and Christianity.** See Christianity and culture

**Cummings, Edward Estlin**

#### About

Vendler, H. H. Ammons, Berryman, Cummings. *In* Vendler, H. H. Part of nature, part of us p323-36

**Cuneiform inscriptions**

Oppenheim, A. L. Neo-Assyrian and neo-Babylonian empires. *In* Propaganda and communication in world history, ed. by H. D. Lasswell, D. Lerner and H. Speier v 1 p111-44

*See also* Assyro-Babylonian literature

**Cunningham, Valentine**

Neutral?: 1930s writers and taking sides. *In* Class, culture and social change, ed. by F. Gloversmith p45-69

**Curran, James; Douglas, Angus, and Whannel, Garry**

The political economy of the human-interest story. *In* Newspapers and democracy, ed. by A. Smith p288-347

**Currency question.** See Banks and banking, Central; Finance

**Currimbhoy, Asif**

### About individual works
*The doldrummers*

Venugopal, C. V. Asif Currimbhoy's 'The doldrummers': a glimpse into the Bombay shacks. *In* Aspects of Indian writing in English, ed. by M. K. Naik p262-67

**Curtin, Philip D.**

African history. *In* The Past before us, ed. by M. Kammen p113-30

**Curtius, Ernest Robert**

### About individual works
*European literature and The Latin Middle Ages*

Pickering, F. P. On coming to terms with Curtius. *In* Pickering, F. P. Essays on medieval German literature and iconography p177-90

**Cusa, Nicolaus de.** See Nicolaus Cusanus, Cardinal

**Cusanus, Nicolas.** See Nicolaus Cusanus, Cardinal

**Cushing, John Daniel**

American bibliographical notes. *In* American Antiquarian Society. Proceedings v89 pt2 p371-74

**Cynewulf**

### About individual works
*The fates of the apostles*

Cross, J. E. Cynewulf's traditions about the apostles in Fates of the apostles. *In* Anglo-Saxon England 8 p163-75

**Cyr, Arthur Irving**

Great Britain. *In* Western European party systems, ed. by P. H. Merkl p61-86

**Czech drama**

#### 20th century—History and criticism

Goetz-Stankiewicz, M. Aspects of history. *In* Goetz-Stankiewicz, M. The silenced theatre: Czech playwrights without a stage p224-38

Goetz-Stankiewicz, M. East meets West. *In* Goetz-Stankiewicz, M. The silenced theatre: Czech playwrights without a stage p239-71

Goetz-Stankiewicz, M. Life in a group. *In* Goetz-Stankiewicz, M. The silenced theatre: Czech playwrights without a stage p190-223

# D

**Daems, Herman**

The rise of the modern industrial enterprise: a new perspective. *In* Managerial hierarchies, ed. by A. D. Chandler and H. Daems p203-23

*See also* Chandler, A. D. jt. auth.

**Dafydd ap Gwilym**

#### About

Bromwich, R. Dafydd ap Gwilym. *In* A Guide to Welsh literature, ed. by A. O. H. Jarman and G. R. Hughes v2 p111-41

**Dafydd Nanmor**

#### About

Lloyd, D. M. Dafydd Nanmor. *In* A Guide to Welsh literature, ed. by A. O. H. Jarman and G. R. Hughes v2 p189-200

**Daget, Serge**
A model of the French abolitionist movement and its variations. *In* Anti-slavery, religion, and reform: essays in memory of Roger Anstey, ed. by C. Bolt and S. Drescher p64-79

**Dahl, Hans**
The press, most national of media: a report from Norway. *In* Newspapers and democracy, ed. by A. Smith p95-103

**Dahl, Robert Alan**
On removing certain impediments to democracy in the United States. *In* The Moral foundations of the American Republic, ed. by R. H. Horwitz p234-56

**Dahlberg, Edward**
### About individual works
*Bottom dogs*
Trilling, L. The promise of realism. *In* Trilling, L. Speaking of literature and society p27-33

**Dahomans.** See Fon (African people)

**Dahomeyans.** See Fon (African people)

**Daisy Miller (Motion picture)**
Kauffmann, S. Daisy Miller. *In* Kauffmann, S. Before my eyes p5-7

**Dale, Corinne**
Lancelot and the medieval quests of Sir Lancelot and Dante. *In* Walker Percy: art and ethics, ed. by J. Tharpe p99-106

**Dallmayr, Fred R.**
"Natural history" and social evolution: reflections on Vico's corsi e ricorsi. *In* Conference on Vico and Contemporary Thought, New York, 1976. Vico and contemporary thought pt2 p199-215

**Daly, Gabriel**
Transcendence and immanence
*Contents*
Alfred Loisy and the radicalization of the Modernist movement
The Blondelian challenge
Friedrich von Hügel: experience and transcendence
George Tyrrell: revelation as experience
History and dogma: the debate between Alfred Loisy and Maurice Blondel
The integralist response (1): Prelude to the Roman condemnation of Modernism
The integralist response (2): Pascendi and after
Lucien Laberthonnière's 'critical mysticism'
Modernism in retrospect
Roman fundamental theology in the last quarter of the nineteenth century

**Damon, Phillip W.**
The middle of things: narrative patterns in the Iliad, Roland and Beowulf. *In* Old English literature in context, ed. by J. D. Niles p107-16

**Dan, Joseph**
The concept of knowledge in the Shi'ur qomah. *In* Studies in Jewish religious and intellectual history, ed. by S. Stein and R. Loewe p67-73

**Danchin, Antoine**
A critical note on the use of the term "phenocopy". *In* Language and learning, ed. by M. Piatelli-Palmarini p356-60

**Danforth, Samuel**
### About individual works
*A brief recognition of New England's errand into the wilderness*
Bercovitch, S. Rhetoric and history in early New England: the Puritan errand reassessed. *In* Toward a new American literary history, ed. by L. J. Budd, E. H. Cady and C. L. Anderson p54-68

**Danhof, Clarence H.**
Agriculture in the North and West. *In* Encyclopedia of American economic history, ed. by G. Porter v 1 p361-70

**Dannhauser, Werner J.**
Reflections on statesmanship and bureaucracy. *In* Bureaucrats, policy analysts, statesmen: who leads? Ed. by R. A. Goldwin p114-32

**D'Annunzio, Gabriele.** See Annunzio, Gabriele d'

**Dante Alighieri**
### About
Montgomery, R. L. Dante's esthetic of grace and the reader's imagination. *In* Montgomery, R. L. The reader's eye p50-92

### About individual works
*The Divine comedy*
Carne-Ross, D. S. Dante Antagonistes. *In* Carne-Ross, D. S. Instaurations p116-32
Dale, C. Lancelot and the medieval quests of Sir Lancelot and Dante. *In* Walker Percy: art and ethics, ed. by J. Tharpe p99-106

*The new life*
Spengemann, W. C. Historical autobiography. *In* Spengemann, W. C. The forms of autobiography p34-61
Sturm, S. Transformations of courtly love poetry: Vita nouva and Canzoniere. *In* The Expansion and transformations of courtly literature, ed. by N. B. Smith and J. T. Snow p128-40

**D'Antraigues, Emmanuel Louis Henri de Launey, comte.** See Antraigues, Emmanuel Louis Henri de Launey, comte d'

**Danzig.** See Gdansk, Poland

**Darbourne and Darke**
Social needs and landscape architecture. *In* Architecture for people, ed. by B. Mikellides p34-37

**Darnton, Robert**
Intellectual and cultural history. *In* The Past before us, ed. by M. Kammen p327-54

**Darwin, Charles Robert**
### About
Kohn, D. Theories to work by: rejected theories, reproduction, and Darwin's path to natural selection. *In* Studies in history of biology, v4 p67-170

**Das, G. K.**
E. M. Forster, T. S. Eliot, and the 'Hymn before action.' *In* E. M. Forster: a human exploration, ed. by G. K. Das and J. Beer p208-15

**Dash, Cheryl M. L.**
Jean Rhys. *In* West Indian literature, ed. by B. King p196-209

**Dash, Irene G.; Kushner, Deena Dash, and Moore, Deborah Dash**
"How light a lighthouse for today's women?" *In* The Lost tradition: mothers and daughters in literature, ed. by C. N. Davidson and E. M. Broner p176-88

**Dash, J. Michael**
Edward Brathwaite. *In* West Indian literature, ed. by B. King p210-27

**Data display systems.** *See* Information display systems

**Data retrieval.** *See* Information retrieval

**Davenport, Herbert Joseph**

### About

Fuller, A. B. Davenport: "Single taxer of the looser observance." *In* Critics of Henry George, ed. by R. V. Andelson p293-302

**David, King of Israel**
Gosselin, E. A. Two views of the evangelical David: Lefèvre d'Etaples and Theodore Beza. *In* The David myth in Western literature, ed. by R. J. Frontain and J. Wojcik p56-67
Veith, G. E. "Wait upon the Lord": David, Hamlet, and the problem of revenge. *In* The David myth in Western literature, ed. by R. J. Frontain and J. Wojcik p70-83
Wojcik, J. Discriminations against David's tragedy in ancient Jewish and Christian literature. *In* The David myth in Western literature, ed. by R. J. Frontain and J. Wojcik p12-35

### Sermons

Ahearn, M. L. David, the military exemplum. *In* The David myth in Western literature, ed. by R. J. Frontain and J. Wojcik p106-18
Huttar, C. A. Frail grass and firm tree: David as a model of repentance in the Middle Ages and early Renaissance. *In* The David myth in Western literature, ed. by R. J. Frontain and J. Wojcik p38-54

**David, King of Israel, in literature**
Allingham, A. David as epic hero: Drayton's David and Goliath. *In* The David myth in Western literature, ed. by R. J. Frontain and J. Wojcik p86-94
Dillingham, T. F. "Blest light": Christopher Smart's myth of David. *In* The David myth in Western literature, ed. by R. J. Frontain and J. Wojcik p120-33
Flinker, N. Saul and David in the early poetry of Yehuda Amichai. *In* The David myth in Western literature, ed. by R. J. Frontain and J. Wojcik p170-78
Lewandowska, M. L. The words of their roaring: Roethke's use of the Psalms of David. *In* The David myth in Western literature, ed. by R. J. Frontain and J. Wojcik p156-67
Pebworth, T. L. Cowley's Davideis and the exaltation of friendship. *In* The David myth in Western literature, ed. by R. J. Frontain and J. Wojcik p96-104
Ross, S. M. Faulkner's Absalom, Absalom! And the David story: a speculative contemplation. *In* The David myth in Western literature, ed. by R. J. Frontain and J. Wojcik p136-53

**David, Alfred**
Chaucerian comedy and Criseyde. *In* Essays on Troilus and Criseyde, ed. by M. Salu p90-104

**David, Jacques-Louis**

### About

Harbison, R. The cult of death. *In* Harbison, R. Deliberate regression p25-62

**Davidson, Cathy N.**
Mothers and daughters in the fiction of the new Republic. *In* The Lost tradition: mothers and daughters in literature, ed. by C. N. Davidson and E. M. Broner p115-27

**Davidson, Edward Hutchins.** See Part 2 under title: Puritan influences in American literature

**Davidson, Herbert Alan**
The principle that a finite body can contain only a finite power. *In* Studies in Jewish religious and intellectual history, ed. by S. Stein and R. Loewe p75-92

**Davidson, Paul**
Natural resources. *In* A Guide to post-Keynesian economics, ed. by A. S. Eichner p151-64

**Davies, P. C. W.**
Reality exists outside us? *In* Lying truths, ed. by R. Duncan and M. Weston-Smith p143-58

**Davies, Robertson.** See Davies, William Robertson

**Davies, William Robertson**

### About

Wyatt, D. Davies and the middle of the journey. *In* Wyatt, D. Prodigal sons p129-49

**Da Vinci, Leonardo.** See Leonardo da Vinci

**Davis, David Brion**
An appreciation of Roger Anstey. *In* Anti-slavery, religion, and reform: essays in memory of Roger Anstey, ed. by C. Bolt and S. Drescher p11-15
Slavery and 'progress.' *In* Anti-slavery, religion, and reform: essays in memory of Roger Anstey, ed. by C. Bolt and S. Drescher p351-66

### About

Pole, J. R. Slavery and revolution: the conscience of the rich. *In* Pole, J. R. Paths to the American past p55-74

**Davis, Jeff, 1862-1913**

### About

Arsenault, R. Charles Jacobson of Arkansas: a Jewish politician in the land of the razorbacks, 1891-1915. *In* Conference on Southern Jewish History, Richmond, Va. 1976. "Turn to the South" p55-75

**Davis, Kingsley**
The continuing demographic revolution in industrial societies. *In* The Third century, ed. by S. M. Lipset p37-64

**Davis, Lance Edwin**
Savings and investment. *In* Encyclopedia of American economic history, ed. by G. Porter v 1 p183-201

**Davis, Lennard J.**
A social history of fact and fiction: authorial disavowal in the early English novel. *In* Literature and society, ed. by E. W. Said p120-48

**Davis, Ralph**
The European background. *In* Encyclopedia of American economic history, ed. by G. Porter v 1 p19-33

**Davis, Richard Beale**
The literary climate of Jamestown under the Virginia Company, 1607-1624. *In* Toward a new American literary history, ed. by L. J. Budd, E. H. Cady and C. L. Anderson p36-53

**Davison, Walter Phillips**
The media kaleidoscope: general trends in the channels. *In* Propaganda and communication in world history, ed. by H. D. Lasswell, D. Lerner and H. Speier v3 p191-248

**Dawn in poetry**
Hatto, A. T. And early 'Tagelied'. *In* Hatto, A. T. Essays on medieval German and other poetry p64-67

**Day, Richard Hollis**

Technology, population, and the agro-industrial complex: a global view. *In* Economic issues of the eighties, ed. by N. M. Kamrany and R. H. Day p146-62

**Day of Atonement (Jewish holiday).** See Yom Kippur

**The day of the locust (Motion picture)**

Kauffmann, S. The day of the locust. *In* Kauffmann, S. Before my eyes p151-53

**Days of heaven (Motion picture)**

Kauffmann, S. Days of heaven. *In* Kauffmann, S. Before my eyes p321-23

**Deaf**

### Means of communication

Wollock, J. William Thornton and the practical applications of new writing systems. *In* Psychology of language and thought, ed. by R. W. Rieber p121-51

**Dean, Dennis Richard**

The character of the early Labour Party 1900-14. *In* The Edwardian age: conflict and stability, 1900-1914, ed. by A. O'Day p97-112

The influence of geology on American literature and thought. *In* New Hampshire Bicentennial Conference on the History of Geology, University of New Hampshire, 1976. Two hundred years of geology in America p289-303

**Deane, Séamus**

Mary Lavin. *In* The Irish short story, ed. by P. Rafroidi and T. Brown p237-47

**Death**

*See also* Right to die

### Causes

*See* Mortality

### Psychological aspects

*See* Death instinct

**Death (African religion)**

Ray, B. The story of Kintu: myth, death, and ontology in Buganda. *In* Explorations in African systems of thought, ed. by I. C. Karp & C. S. Bird p60-79

**Death in art**

Harbison, R. The cult of death. *In* Harbison, R. Deliberate regression p25-62

**Death in literature**

Bickman, M. Kora in heaven: Emily Dickinson. *In* Bickman, M. The unsounded centre p117-46

Bockel, P. Malraux and death. *In* André Malraux, ed. by F. Dorenlot and M. Tison-Braun p75-82

Hayes, J. J. Gothic love and death: Francois Villon and the city of Paris. *In* 5000 years of popular culture, ed. by F. E. H. Schroeder p228-39

Irwin, J. T. Figurations of the writer's death: Freud and Hart Crane. *In* The Literary Freud: mechanisms of defense and the poetic will, ed. by J. H. Smith p217-60

James, W. L. G. The portrayal of death and 'substance of life': aspects of the modern reader's response to 'Victorianism.' *In* Reading the Victorian novel: detail into form, ed. by I. Gregor p226-42

Rees, D. Timor mortis conturbat me: E. B. White and Doris Buchanan Smith. *In* Rees, D. The marble in the water p68-77

Wolfschütz, H. Thomas Bernhard: the mask of death. *In* Modern Austrian writing, ed. by A. Best and H. Wolfschütz p214-35

**Death, Right to.** See Right to die

**Death instinct**

Irwin, J. T. Figurations of the writer's death: Freud and Hart Crane. *In* The Literary Freud: mechanisms of defense and the poetic will, ed. by J. H. Smith p217-60

**Death of God theology in literature**

Donato, E. U. Divine agonies: of representation and narrative in romantic poetics. *In* Glyph 6 p90-122

**Death on the Nile (Motion picture)**

Kael, P. Detectives—the capon and the baby bowwow. *In* Kael, P. When the lights go down p462-69

**Death penalty.** See Capital punishment

**Death rate.** See Mortality; Vital statistics

**Death wish (Motion picture)**

Kauffmann, S. Mr. Majestyk/Death wish. *In* Kauffmann, S. Before my eyes p31-34

**De Azevedo, Thales.** See Azevedo, Thales de

**De Balzac, Honoré.** See Balzac, Honoré de

**DeBary, William Theodore**

Chinese values: the China problem and our problem. *In* Value and values in evolution, ed. by E. A. Maziarz p103-14

**Debussy, Claude**

### About

Carner, M. Debussy and Puccini. *In* Carner, M. Major and minor p139-47

**Decadence.** See Degeneration

**Decadence (Literary movement)**

### History and criticism

Peyre, H. In search of the morbid and the strange: the decadents and Laforgue. *In* Peyre, H. What is symbolism? p98-111

**Decadence in literature**

Nnolim, C. E. Dialectic as form: pejorism in the novels of Armah. *In* African literature today no. 10: Retrospect & prospect, ed. by E. D. Jones p207-23

**Decentralization in government.** See Federal government

**Decision-making**

Simon, H. A. The consequences of computers for centralization and decentralization. *In* The Computer age: a twenty-year view, ed. by M. L. Dertouzos and J. Moses p212-28

Walzer, M. Political decision-making and political education. *In* Political theory and political education, ed. by M. Richter p159-76

*See also* Social choice

**Decision-making, Group**

White, I. Condorcet: politics and reason. *In* Royal Institute of Philosophy. Philosophers of the Enlightenment p110-39

**Decision-making in literature**

Krieger, M. Literature, criticism, and decision theory. *In* Krieger, M. Poetic presence and illusion p238-69

**Decomposition (Biology)** See Biodegradation

**Decomposition (Chemistry)**

Morowitz, H. J. Christ, Clausius, and corrosion. *In* Morowitz, H. J. The wine of life, and other essays on societies, energy & living things p43-47

**De Courcel, Martine Hallade.** See Courcel, Martine Hallade de

**De Dwyer, Carlota Cárdenas.** See Cárdenas de Dwyer, Carlota

**The deer hunter (Motion picture)**
Kael, P. The God-bless-America symphony. *In* Kael, P. When the lights go down p512-19
Kauffmann, S. The deer hunter. *In* Kauffmann, S. Before my eyes p324-30

**Deerne (The Middle English word)**
Reiss, E. Chaucer's deerne love and the medieval view of secrecy in love. *In* Chaucerian problems and perspectives, ed. by E. Vasta and Z. P. Thundy p164-79

**Defense contracts**

**United States**
Pursell, C. W. Military-industrial complex. *In* Encyclopedia of American economic history, ed. by G. Porter v3 p926-34

**Defense mechanisms (Psychology)**
Bloom, H. Freud's concepts of defense and the poetic will. *In* The Literary Freud: mechanisms of defense and the poetic will, ed. by J. H. Smith p 1-28

**Defense mechanisms (Psychology) in literature.** See Repression (Psychology) in literature

**Defensiveness (Psychology)** See Aggressiveness (Psychology)

**Defoe, Daniel**

**About**
Uphaus, R. W. Defoe, deliverance, and dissimulation. *In* Uphaus, R. W. The impossible observer p46-70

**About individual works**
*Moll Flanders*
Miller, N. K. A harlot's progress: I, Moll Flanders. *In* Miller, N. K. The heroine's text p3-20

*Robinson Crusoe*
Alkon, P. K. The odds against Friday: Defoe, Bayes, and inverse probability. *In* Probability, time, and space in eighteenth-century literature, ed. by P. R. Backscheider p29-61

**De Freitas, Michael.** See Malik, Michael Abdul

**Degeneration**
Harbison, R. Turning against history. *In* Harbison, R. Deliberate regression p147-79

**Degler, Carl Neumann**
Women. *In* Encyclopedia of American economic history, ed. by G. Porter v3 p988-1000
Women and the family. *In* The Past before us, ed. by M. Kammen p308-26

**De Heusch, Luc.** See Heusch, Luc de

**Deira, The dates of.** Miller, M. *In* Anglo-Saxon England 8 p35-61

**De La Bretonne, Nicolas Edmé Restif.** See Restif de La Bretonne, Nicolas Edmé

**Deleuze, Gilles**
The schizophrenic and language: surface and depth in Lewis Carroll and Antonin Artaud. *In* Textual strategies, ed. by J. V. Harari p277-95

**Deleuze, Gilles, and Guattari, Félix**

**About individual works**
*Anti-Oedipus: capitalism and schizophrenia*
Turkle, S. French anti-psychiatry. *In* Critical psychiatry, ed. by D. Ingleby p150-83

**Delgado, Martin Morúa.** See Morúa Delgado, Martin

**Della Terza, Dante**
Methodology and exegesis: the Italian side. *In* The Analysis of literary texts, ed. by R. D. Pope p9-20

**Delusions.** See Hallucinations and illusions

**De Man, Paul**
Allegories of reading
*Contents*
Allegory (Julie)
Allegory of reading (Profession de foi)
Excuses (Confessions)
Genesis and genealogy (Nietzsche)
Metaphor (Second discourse)
Promises (Social contract)
Reading (Proust)
Rhetoric of persuasion (Nietzsche)
Rhetoric of tropes (Nietzsche)
Self (Pygmalion)
Semiology and rhetoric
*Also in* Textual strategies, ed. by J. V. Harari p121-40
Tropes (Rilke)

**About**
Ferguson, F. C. Reading Heidegger: Paul De Man and Jacques Derrida. *In* Martin Heidegger and the question of literature, ed. by W. V. Spanos p253-70
Lentricchia, F. Paul de Man: the rhetoric of authority. *In* Lentricchia, F. After the New Criticism p283-317
Riddel, J. N. From Heidegger to Derrida to chance: doubling and (poetic) language. *In* Martin Heidegger and the question of literature, ed. by W. V. Spanos p231-52

**Demand (Economic theory)**
Spengler, J. J. Rising expectations: frustrations. *In* Propaganda and communication in world history, ed. by H. D. Lasswell, D. Lerner and H. Speier v3 p37-92

**Dembo, L. S.**
The socialist and socialite heroes of Upton Sinclair. *In* Toward a new American literary history, ed. by L. J. Budd, E. H. Cady and C. L. Anderson p164-80

**Demetrakopoulos, Stephanie A.**
The metaphysics of matrilinearism in women's autobiography: studies of Mead's Blackberry winter, Hellman's Pentimento, Angelou's I know why the caged bird sings, and Kingston's The woman warrior. *In* Women's autobiography, ed. by E. C. Jelinek p180-205

**Democracy**
Dahl, R. A. On removing certain impediments to democracy in the United States. *In* The Moral foundations of the American Republic, ed. by R. H. Horwitz p234-56
Hook, S. The autonomy of the democratic faith. *In* Hook, S. Philosophy and public policy p272-78
Hook, S. The ethics of controversy. *In* Hook, S. Philosophy and public policy p117-23
Lukes, S. The real and ideal worlds of democracy. *In* Powers, possessions and freedom, ed. by A. Kontos p139-52
Norton, D. L. Equality and excellence in the democratic ideal. *In* History, religion, and spiritual democracy, ed. by M. Wohlgelernter p273-93
Pole, J. R. Historians and the problem of early American democracy. *In* Pole, J. R. Paths to the American past p223-49
*See also* Equality; Federal government; Liberty; Representative government and representation; Socialism

**Democratic Party**

Fraser, D. M. Democratizing the Democratic Party. *In* Political parties in the eighties, ed. by R. A. Goldwin p116-32

Polsby, N. W. The news media as an alternative to party in the Presidential selection process. *In* Political parties in the eighties, ed. by R. A. Goldwin p50-66

**National Committee. Commission on Party Structure and Delegate Selection**
**About individual works**
*Mandate for reform; a report to the Democratic National Committee*

Bode, K. A. and Casey, C. F. Party reform: revisionism revised. *In* Political parties in the eighties, ed. by R. A. Goldwin p3-19

**National Convention, Chicago, 1968**

Bode, K. A. and Casey, C. F. Party reform: revisionism revised. *In* Political parties in the eighties, ed. by R. A. Goldwin p3-19

**Demography**

Braudel, F. Demography and the scope of the human sciences. *In* Braudel, F. On history p132-61

Davis, K. The continuing demographic revolution in industrial societies. *In* The Third century, ed. by S. M. Lipset p37-64

Kozlov, V. I. Ethnography and demography. *In* Soviet and Western anthropology, ed. by E. Gellner p265-74

**Demoniac possession**

Erickson, G. Possession, sex and hysteria: the growth of demonism in later antiquity. *In* 5000 years of popular culture, ed. by F. E. H. Schroeder p110-35

**Denicoff, Marvin**

Sophisticated software: the road to science and Utopia. *In* The Computer age: a twenty-year view, ed. by M. L. Dertouzos and J. Moses p367-91

**Denmark**

**Politics and government—1947-**

Nilson, S. S. Norway and Denmark. *In* Western European party systems, ed. by P. H. Merkl p205-34

**Dennett, Daniel Clement**

Artificial intelligence as philosophy and as psychology. *In* Philosophical perspectives in artificial intelligence, ed. by M. Ringle p57-78

**Dent, Edward Joseph**

Selected essays

*Contents*

Bellini in England
Binary and ternary form
Busoni's Doctor Faust
Cecil Armstrong Gibbs
Corno di Bassetto
The historical approach to music
Italian chamber cantatas
Leonardo Leo
Looking backward
[Melody and harmony]
[Music for the Cambridge Greek plays]
On the composition of English songs
A pastoral opera by Alessandro Scarlatti
[The problems of modern music]
La rappresentazione di anima e di corpo
The style of Schubert
The teaching of strict counterpoint
The translation of operas
Verdi in English
The Victorians and opera

**De Pixérécourt, René Charles Guilbert.** See Pixérécourt, René Charles Guilbert de

**DePrano, Michael**

The untidy state of macroeconomic analysis. *In* Economic issues of the eighties, ed. by N. M. Kamrany and R. H. Day p5-28

**Depressions**

Moore, G. H. Business cycles, panics and depressions. *In* Encyclopedia of American economic history, ed. by G. Porter v 1 p151-56

**1929—United States**

Milkman, R. Women's work and the economic crisis: some lessons from the Great Depression. *In* A Heritage of her own, ed. by N. F. Cott and E. H. Pleck p507-41

**De Quincey, Thomas**

**About individual works**
*Confessions of an English opium eater*

Spengemann, W. C. Philosophical autobiography. *In* Spengemann, W. C. The forms of autobiography p62-109

**De Robespierre, Maximilien Marie Isidore.** See Robespierre, Maximilien Marie Isidore de

**Derrida, Jacques**

The law of genre. *In* Glyph 7 p202-29

The supplement of copula: philosophy before linguistics. *In* Textual strategies, ed. by J. V. Harari p82-120

**About**

Culler, J.D. Jacques Derrida. *In* Structuralism and since, ed. by J. Sturrock p154-80

Lentricchia, F. History or the abyss: poststructuralism. *In* Lentricchia, F. After the New Criticism p156-210

Riddel, J. N. From Heidegger to Derrida to chance: doubling and (poetic) language. *In* Martin Heidegger and the question of literature, ed. by W. V. Spanos p231-52

**About individual works**
*De la grammatologie*

Ferguson, F. C. Reading Heidegger: Paul De Man and Jacques Derrida. *In* Martin Heidegger and the question of literature, ed. by W. V. Spanos p253-70

*Glas*

Hartman, G. H. Literary commentary as literature. *In* Hartman, G. H. Criticism in the wilderness p189-213

**Dertouzos, Michael L.**

Individualized automation. *In* The Computer age: a twenty-year view, ed. by M. L. Dertouzos and J. Moses p38-55

**Desai, S. K.**

Tagore's 'Red oleanders': a revaluation. *In* Aspects of Indian writing in English, ed. by M. K. Naik p232-47

**De Saint-Just, Louis Antoine Léon.** See Saint-Just, Louis Antoine Léon de

**Descartes, René**

**About**

Funkenstein, A. Descartes, eternal truths and the divine omnipotence. *In* Descartes, ed. by S. Gaukroger p181-95

Gabbey, A. Force and inertia in the seventeenth century: Descartes and Newton. *In* Descartes, ed. by S. Gaukroger p230-320

Gaukroger, S. Descartes' project for a mathematical physics. *In* Descartes, ed. by S. Gaukroger p97-140

Manley, L. G. Real and mental theater: the complex of classicism. *In* Manley, L. G. Convention, 1500-1750 p264-90

Descartes, René—About—*Continued*

Maull, N. L. Cartesian optics and the geometrization of nature. *In* Descartes, ed. by S. Gaukroger p23-40

Sullivan, J. J. Noam Chomsky and Cartesian linguistics. *In* Psychology of language and thought, ed. by R. W. Rieber p197-223

### About individual works
#### Geometry

Grosholz, E. R. Descartes' unification of algebra and geometry. *In* Descartes, ed. by S. Gaukroger p156-68

#### Rules for the direction of the mind

Schuster, J. A. Descartes' mathesis universalis: 1619-28. *In* Descartes, ed. by S. Gaukroger p41-96

### Knowledge, Theory of

Hacking, I. Proof and eternal truths: Descartes and Leibniz. *In* Descartes, ed. by S. Gaukroger p169-80

Larmore, C. Descartes' empirical epistemology. *In* Descartes, ed. by S. Gaukroger p6-22

### Logic

Hacking, I. Proof and eternal truths: Descartes and Leibniz. *In* Descartes, ed. by S. Gaukroger p169-80

### Mathematics

Grosholz, E. R. Descartes' unification of algebra and geometry. *In* Descartes, ed. by S. Gaukroger p156-68

Mahoney, M. S. The beginnings of algebraic thought in the seventeenth century. *In* Descartes, ed. by S. Gaukroger p141-55

Schuster, J. A. Descartes' mathesis universalis: 1619-28. *In* Descartes, ed. by S. Gaukroger p41-96

De Sica, Vittorio

### About individual works
#### A brief vacation

Kauffmann, S. A brief vacation. *In* Kauffmann, S. Before my eyes p115-16

Desire

Wollheim, R. Wish-fulfilment. *In* Rational action, ed. by R. Harrison p47-60

Desire in literature

McGhee, R. D. Rossetti and Meredith. *In* McGhee, R. D. Marriage, duty & desire in Victorian poetry and drama p139-76

McGhee, R. D. Swinburne and Hopkins. *In* McGhee, R. D. Marriage, duty & desire in Victorian poetry and drama p177-232

De Sola Pool, Ithiel. See Pool, Ithiel de Sola

De Sousa, Ronald. See Sousa, Ronald de

De Spinoza, Benedictus. See Spinoza, Benedicus de

Despotism

Giner, S. and Seville-Guzman, E. From despotism to parliamentarianism; class domination and political order in the Spanish state. *In* The State in Western Europe, ed. by R. Scase p197-229

Dessner, Lawrence Jay

The Salinger story, or, Have it your way. *In* Seasoned authors for a new season: the search for standards in popular writing, ed. by L. Filler p91-97

Destitution. See Poverty

Destruction of the Jews (1939-1945) See Holocaust, Jewish (1939-1945)

De Tarlé, Antoine. See Tarlé, Antoine de

Detective and mystery stories

### History and criticism

Aisenberg, N. Graham Greene and the modern thriller. *In* Aisenberg, N. A common spring p223-55

Aisenberg, N. Introduction. *In* Aisenberg, N. A common spring p 1-15

Aisenberg, N. Myth, fairy tale, and the crime novel. *In* Aisenberg, N. A common spring p16-67

Miller, D. A. Language of detective fiction: fiction of detective language. *In* The State of the language, ed. by L. Michaels and C. Ricks p478-99

Detectives

### Fiction

*See* Detective and mystery stories

Detente

Sakharov, A. D. Thoughts on progress, peaceful coexistence and intellectual freedom. *In* Propaganda and communication in world history, ed. by H. D. Lasswell, D. Lerner and H. Speier v2 p471-506

Determinism (Philosophy)

Sorabji, R. Causation, laws and necessity. *In* Doubt and dogmatism, ed. by M. Schofield, M. Burnyeat and J. Barnes p250-82

Determinism and indeterminism. See Free will and determinism

Deutscher, Isaac

### About

Hook, S. Leon Trotsky and the cunning of history. *In* Hook, S. Philosophy and public policy p181-89

Developing countries. See Underdeveloped areas

Development, Economic. See Economic development

Developmental linguistics. See Language acquisition

Developmental psychobiology. See Developmental psychology

Developmental psycholinguistics. See Language acquisition

Developmental psychology

Blasi, A. Vico, developmental psychology, and human nature. *In* Conference on Vico and Contemporary Thought, New York, 1976. Vico and contemporary thought pt2 p14-39

Dunn, J. Understanding human development: limitations and possibilities in an ethological approach. *In* Human ethology, ed. by M. von Cranach [and others] p623-41

White, S. H. Developmental psychology and Vico's concept of universal history. *In* Conference on Vico and Contemporary Thought, New York, 1976. Vico and contemporary thought pt2 p 1-13

De Vere, Aubrey Thomas

### About

Welch, R. Aubrey de Vere: an attempt at a Catholic humanity. *In* Welch, R. Irish poetry from Moore to Yeats p156-77

De Vere White, Terence. See White, Terence de Vere

Deviance. See Deviant behavior

Deviant behavior

Conrad, P. On the medicalization of deviance and social control. *In* Critical psychiatry, ed. by D. Ingleby p102-19

**Deviant behavior—**Continued

Hepworth, M. Deviance and control in everyday life: the contribution of Erving Goffman. *In* The View from Goffman, ed. by J. Ditton p80-99

**Deviation, Sexual.** See Sexual deviation

**Devine, Philip E.**

On choosing death. *In* Suicide: the philosophical issues, ed. by M. P. Battin and D. J. Mayo p138-43

**De Voltaire, François Marie Arouet.** See Voltaire, François Marie Arouet de

**Devotion.** See Prayer

**Devotional literature**

**Manuscripts**

Scragg, D. G. The corpus of vernacular homilies and prose saints' lives before Ælfric. *In* Anglo-Saxon England 8 p223-77

**Dewas Senior, India (State) in literature**

Birje-Patil, J. Forster and Dewas. *In* E. M. Forster: a human exploration, ed. by G. K. Das and J. Beer p102-08

**Dewey, John**

**About**

Hook, S. The relevance of John Dewey's thought. *In* Hook, S. Philosophy and public policy p165-80

Martin, J. A. The esthetic, the religious, and the natural. *In* History, religion, and spiritual democracy, ed. by M. Wohlgelernter p76-91

Rockefeller, S. C. John Dewey: the evolution of a faith. *In* History, religion, and spiritual democracy, ed. by M. Wohlgelernter p5-34

Shea, W. M. The supernatural in the naturalists. *In* History, religion, and spiritual democracy, ed. by M. Wohlgelernter p53-75

**Dewhurst, C. Kurt**

Expanding frontiers: the Michigan Folk Art Project. *In* Perspectives on American folk art, ed. by I. M. G. Quimby and S. T. Swank p54-78

**Dezayas, Maria.** See Zayas y Sotomayor, María de

**Dho Luo (African people)** See Luo (African people)

**D'Holbach, Paul Henri Thiry.** See Holbach, Paul Henri Thiry, baron d'

**Dialogue**

Marsh, D. Cicero and the humanist dialogue. *In* Marsh, D. The quattrocento dialogue p 1-23

Marsh, D. Leon Battista Alberti and the volgare dialogue. *In* Marsh, D. The quattrocento dialogue p78-99

**Diaspora.** See Israel and the Diaspora

**Diaspora of the Jews.** See Jews—Diaspora

**Di Battista, Maria Alba**

To the lighthouse: Virginia Woolf's winter's tale. *In* Virginia Woolf, ed. by R. Friedman p161-88

**Dickens, Charles**

**About**

Aisenberg, N. Dickens and the crime novel. *In* Aisenberg, N. A common spring p68-110

Andrews, M. A note on serialisation. *In* Reading the Victorian novel: detail into form, ed. by I. Gregor p243-47

Garrett, P. K. Dickens: he mounts a high tower in his mind. *In* Garrett, P. K. The Victorian multiplot novel p23-51

Garrett, P. K. Dickens: machinery in motion. *In* Garrett, P. K. The Victorian multiplot novel p52-94

Stone, D. D. Death and circuses: Charles Dickens and the byroads of romanticism. *In* Stone, D. D. The romantic impulse in Victorian fiction p249-83

**About individual works**

*Bleak House*

Nabokov, V. V. Charles Dickens: Bleak House. *In* Nabokov, V. V. Lectures on literature p63-124

*David Copperfield*

Carabine, K. Reading David Copperfield. *In* Reading the Victorian novel: detail into form, ed. by I. Gregor p150-67

Kinkead-Weekes, M. The voicing of fictions. *In* Reading the Victorian novel: detail into form, ed. by I. Gregor p168-92

Spengemann, W. C. Poetic autobiography. *In* Spengemann, W. C. The forms of autobiography p110-65

*David Copperfield—Illustrations*

Lutman, S. Reading illustrations: pictures in David Copperfield. *In* Reading the Victorian novel: detail into form, ed. by I. Gregor p196-225

*Martin Chuzzlewit*

Polhemus, R. M. Dickens's Martin Chuzzlewit: the comedy of expression. *In* Polhemus, R. M. Comic faith p88-123

*The Old Curiosity Shop*

James, W. L. G. The portrayal of death and 'substance of life': aspects of the modern reader's response to 'Victorianism.' *In* Reading the Victorian novel: detail into form, ed. by I. Gregor p226-42

**Characters**

Henkle, R. B. Early Dickens: metamorphosis, psychic disorientation, and the small fry. *In* Henkle, R. B. Comedy and culture p111-44

**Humor, satire, etc.**

Henkle, R. B. Early Dickens: metamorphosis, psychic disorientation, and the small fry. *In* Henkle, R. B. Comedy and culture p111-44

Henkle, R. B. Later Dickens: disenchantment, transmogrification, and ambivalence. *In* Henkle, R. B. Comedy and culture p145-84

**Political and social views**

Henkle, R. B. Later Dickens: disenchantment, transmogrification, and ambivalence. *In* Henkle, R. B. Comedy and culture p145-84

**Satire**

*See* Dickens, Charles—Humor, satire, etc.

**Social views**

*See* Dickens, Charles—Political and social views

**Dickey, James**

**About**

Howard, R. James Dickey: "We never can really tell whether nature condemns us or loves us." *In* Howard, R. Alone with America p94-122

**About individual works**

*Deliverance*

Schecter, H. The eye and the nerve: a psychological reading of James Dickey's Deliverance. *In* Seasoned authors for a new season: the search for standards in popular writing, ed. by L. Filler p4-19

Wagner, L. W. Deliverance: initiation and possibility. *In* Wagner, L. W. American modern p76-84

**Dickinson, Emily**

**About**

Baym, N. Z. God, father, and lover in Emily Dickinson's poetry. *In* Puritan influences in American literature, ed. by E. Elliott p193-209

Bickman, M. Kora in heaven: Emily Dickinson. *In* Bickman, M. The unsounded centre p117-46

Hartman, G. H. Purification and danger 1: American poetry. *In* Hartman, G. H. Criticism in the wilderness p115-32

Mossberg, B. A. C. Reconstruction in the house of art: Emily Dickinson's "I never had a mother." *In* The Lost tradition: mothers and daughters in literature, ed. by C. N. Davidson and E. M. Broner p128-38

**Bibliography**

Buckingham, W. J. Whitman and Dickinson. *In* American literary scholarship, 1978 p59-78

**Language**

Lair, R. L. Emily Dickinson's fracture of grammar: syntactic ambiguity in her poems. *In* The Analysis of literary texts, ed. by R. D. Pope p158-64

**Dickinson, Goldsworthy Lowes**

**About**

Trilling, L. Politics and the liberal. *In* Trilling, L. Speaking of literature and society p89-91

**Dickinson, Peter**

**About**

Townsend, J. R. Peter Dickinson. *In* Townsend, J. R. A sounding of storytellers p41-54

**Dickstein, Morris**

The price of experience: Blake's reading of Freud. *In* The Literary Freud: mechanisms of defense and the poetic will, ed. by J. H. Smith p67-111

**Didactic poetry**

**History and criticism**

Montgomery, R. L. Conclusion. *In* Montgomery, R. L. The reader's eye p169-85

**Diderot, Angélique.** See Vandeul, Marie Angélique (Diderot) de

**Diderot, Denis**

**About**

Brumfitt, J. H. Diderot: man and society. *In* Royal Institute of Philosophy. Philosophers of the Enlightenment p162-83

Gardner, E. J. The philosophes and women: sensationalism and sentiment. *In* Woman and society in eighteenth-century France, ed. by E. Jacobs and others p19-27

Jacobs, E. Diderot and the education of girls. *In* Woman and society in eighteenth-century France, ed. by E. Jacobs and others p83-95

Niklaus, R. Diderot and women. *In* Woman and society in eighteenth-century France, ed. by E. Jacobs and others p69-82

**About individual works**

*Letter on the blind*

Seigel, J. P. The perceptible and the imperceptible: Diderot's speculation on language in his Letters on the deaf and blind. *In* Psychology of language and thought, ed. by R. W. Rieber p91-102

*Letter on the deaf and dumb*

Seigel, J. P. The perceptible and the imperceptible: Diderot's speculation on language in his Letters on the deaf and blind. *In* Psychology of language and thought, ed. by R. W. Rieber p91-102

*The nun*

Todd, J. Erotic friendship: Denis Diderot's The nun. *In* Todd, J. Women's friendship in literature p100-31

**Diderot, Denis, and Alembert, Jean Lerond d'**

**About individual works**

*Encyclopaedia*—Illustrations

Barthes, R. The plates of the Encyclopedia. *In* Barthes, R. New critical essays p23-39

**Dido, Queen of Carthage**

**About**

Hagstrum, J. H. Woman in love: the abandoned and passionate mistress. *In* Hagstrum, J. H. Sex and sensibility p100-32

**Dierick, Augustinus P.**

Two representative expressionist responses to the challenge of the First World War: Carl Sternheim's eigene Nuance and Leonhard Frank's utopia. *In* The First World War in German narrative prose, ed. by C. N. Genno and H. Wetzel p16-33

**Dietmar von Aist.** See Dietmar von Eist

**Dietmar von Eist**

**About individual works**

*Nu ist ez an ein Ende komen*

Wapnewski, P. Dietmar von Eist XII: 'Nu ist ez an ein Ende komen'. *In* The Interpretation of medieval lyric poetry, ed. by W. T. H. Jackson p163-75

**Dillingham, Thomas Forcey**

"Blest light": Christopher Smart's myth of David. *In* The David myth in Western literature, ed. by R. J. Frontain and J. Wojcik p120-33

**Dillon, John M.**

Antaeus and Hercules: some notes on the Irish predicament. *In* The State of the language, ed. by L. Michaels and C. Ricks p553-59

**Dilworth, Thomas**

David Jones's glosses on the Anathemata. *In* Virginia. University. Bibliographical Society. Studies in bibliography v33 p239-53

**Dinnage, Rosemary**

Under the harrow. *In* The World of Franz Kafka, ed. by J. P. Stern p69-78

**Disarmament.** See Militarism; Peace

**Disarmament and atomic weapons.** See Atomic weapons and disarmament

**Disasters in motion pictures**

Roddick, N. Only the stars survive: disaster movies in the seventies. *In* Performance and politics in popular drama, ed. by D. Bradby, L. James and B. Sharratt p243-69

**Discoverers.** See Explorers

**Discoveries (in geography)** See Scientific expeditions

**Discrimination**

Hook, S. Reverse discrimination. *In* Hook, S. Philosophy and public policy p138-50

**Discrimination in employment.** See Affirmative action programs

**Diseases, Mental.** See Mental illness

**Dispersion of the Jews.** See Jews—Diaspora

**Disputations, Religious**

Daly, G. The integralist response (1): prelude to the Roman condemnation of modernism. *In* Daly, G. Transcendence and immanence p165-89

Daly, G. The integralist response (2): Pascendi and after. *In* Daly, G. Transcendence and immanence p190-217

**Display systems, Information.** See Information display systems

**Disraeli, Benjamin.** See Beaconsfield, Benjamin Disraeli, 1st Earl of

**Dissenters, Religious**

Ozment, S. H. The sectarian spectrum: radical movements within Protestantism. *In* Ozment, S. H. The age of reform, 1250-1550 p340-51

**Distant thunder (Motion picture)**

Kael, P. A dream of women. *In* Kael, P. When the lights go down p68-72

**Distribution of wealth.** See Wealth

**Ditchfield, G. M.**

Repeal, abolition, and reform: a study in the interaction of reforming movements in the Parliament of 1790-6. *In* Anti-slavery, religion, and reform: essays in memory of Roger Anstey, ed. by C. Bolt and S. Drescher p101-18

**Division of powers.** See Federal government

**Divorce**

Durkheim, E. Divorce by mutual consent. *In* Durkheim, E. Emile Durkheim on institutional analysis p240-52

### United States—History

Cott, N. F. Eighteenth-century family and social life revealed in Massachusetts divorce records. *In* A Heritage of her own, ed. by N. F. Cott and E. H. Pleck p107-35

**Dixon, Thomas**

#### About individual works
*The clansman: an historical romance of the Ku Klux Klan*

Fiedler, L. A. The anti-Tom novel and the First Great War: Thomas Dixon, Jr. and D. W. Griffith. *In* Fiedler, L. A. The inadvertent epic p43-57

**Dixon, Victor**

The 'immersion-effect' in the plays of Antonio Buero Vallejo. *In* Drama and mimesis, ed. by J. Redmond p113-37

**Dixwell, George Basil**

#### About individual works
*"Progress and poverty." A review of the doctrines of Henry George*

Babilot, G. Dixwell: animadversions of an admiring adversary. *In* Critics of Henry George, ed. by R. V. Andelson p165-77

**Do-it-yourself work.** See Self-service (Economics)

**Döblin, Alfred**

#### About

Riley, A. W. The aftermath of the First World War; Christianity and revolution in Alfred Döblin's November 1918. *In* The First World War in German narrative prose, ed. by C. N. Genno and H. Wetzel p93-117

#### About individual works
*November 1918*

Riley, A. W. The aftermath of the First World War: Christianity and revolution in Alfred Döblin's November 1918. *In* The First World War in German narrative prose, ed. by C. N. Genno and H. Wetzel p93-117

**Doctors.** See Physicians

**Documentary films.** See Moving pictures, Documentary

**Doderer, Heimito von**

#### About

Pabisch, P. and Best, A. The 'total novel': Heimito von Doderer and Albert Paris Gütersloh. *In* Modern Austrian writing, ed. by A. Best and H. Wolfschütz p63-78

**Dodgson, Charles Lutwidge**

#### About

Mellor, A. K. Feat and trembling: from Lewis Carroll to existentialism. *In* Mellor, A. K. English romantic irony p165-84

#### About individual works
*Through the looking-glass*

Polhemus, R. M. Carroll's Through the looking-glass: the comedy of regression. *In* Polhemus, R. M. Comic faith p245-93

#### Language

Deleuze, G. The schizophrenic and language: surface and depth in Lewis Carroll and Antonin Artaud. *In* Textual strategies, ed. by J. V. Harari p277-95

**Dodsley, Robert**

#### About individual works
*A collection of poems by several hands*

Todd, W. B. Concurrent printing: an analysis of Dodsley's Collection of poems by several hands. *In* The Bibliographical Society of America, 1904-79 p276-88

**Dog day afternoon (Motion picture)**

Kauffmann, S. Dog day afternoon. *In* Kauffmann, S. Before my eyes p97-101

**Dogma.** See Theology, Doctrinal

**Dogons (African people)**

#### Religion

Pelton, R. D. Ogo-Yurugu: lord of the random, servant of wholeness. *In* Pelton, R.D. The trickster in West Africa p164-222

**Dogs in literature**

Lutz, C. E. Le bon chien Soullart. *In* Lutz, C. E. The oldest library motto, and other library essays p109-14

**Dolin, Edwin Francis**

Computers—for better and for worse. *In* Monster or messiah? Ed. by W. M. Mathews p37-44

**Doll, Carol**

The children of Sophie May. *In* Research about nineteenth-century children and books, ed. by S. K. Richardson p97-116

**Dollimore, Jonathan**

Two concepts of mimesis: Renaissance literary theory and The revenger's tragedy. *In* Drama and mimesis, ed. by J. Redmond p25-50

**Domestic architecture.** See Architecture, Domestic

**Domestic relations.** See Family

**Domestication.** See Agriculture—Origin

**Donaldson, Ethelbert Talbot**

Briseis, Briseida, Criseyde, Cresseid, Cressid: progress of a heroine. *In* Chaucerian problems and perspectives, ed. by E. Vasta and Z. P. Thundy p3-12

**Donat, Alexander**

### About individual works

*The Holocaust kingdom, a memoir*

Alexander, E. The incredibility of the Holocaust. *In* Alexander, E. The resonance of dust p3-28

**Donato, Eugenio Umberto**

Divine agonies: of representation and narrative in romantic poetics. *In* Glyph 6 p90-122

The museum's furnace: notes toward a contextual reading of Bouvard and Pécuchet. *In* Textual strategies, ed. by J. V. Harari p213-38

**Donne, John, 1573-1631**

### About

Ellrodt, R. Angels and the poetic imagination from Donne to Traherne. *In* English Renaissance studies, ed. by J. Carey p164-79

### About individual works

*The ecstasy*

Perry, T. A. John Donne's philosophy of love in "The ecstasy." *In* Perry, T. A. Erotic spirituality p89-98

*Elegy on the L.C.*

Shapiro, I. A. The date of a Donne elegy, and its implications. *In* English Renaissance studies, ed. by J. Carey p141-50

*The sun rising*

Gransden, K. W. Lente currite, noctis equi: Chaucer, Troilus and Criseyde 3.1422-70, Donne, The sun rising and Ovid, Amores 1.13. *In* Creative imitation and Latin literature, ed. by D. West and T. Woodman p157-71

### Technique

Carey, J. Donne and coins. *In* English Renaissance studies, ed. by J. Carey p151-63

**Donoghue, Denis**

Radio talk. *In* The State of the language, ed. by L. Michaels and C. Ricks p539-52

Romantic Ireland. *In* Yeats, Sligo and Ireland, ed. by A. N. Jeffares p17-30

**Donolo, Carlo**

Social change and transformation of the state of Italy. *In* The State in Western Europe, ed. by Richard Scase p164-96

**Donoso, José**

### About

Magnarelli, S. From El obsceno pajaro to Tres novelitas burguesas: development of a semiotic theory in the works of Donoso. *In* The Analysis of literary texts, ed. by R. D. Pope p224-35

### About individual works

*The obscene bird of night*

Bacarisse, P. El obsceno pájaro de la noche: a willed process of evasion. *In* Contemporary Latin American fiction, ed. by S. Bacarisse p18-33

**Donovan, Arthur L.**

Scottish responses to the new chemistry of Lavoisier. *In* Studies in eighteenth-century culture v9 p237-49

**Donovan, Mortimer J.**

Chaucer's January and May: counterparts in Claudian. *In* Chaucerian problems and perspectives, ed. by E. Vasta and Z. P. Thundy p59-69

**Doody, Margaret Anne**

"How shall we sing the Lord's song upon an alien soil?": The new Episcopalian liturgy. *In* The State of the language, ed. by L. Michaels and C. Ricks p108-24

**Dooley, Patricia**

Magic and art in Ursula Le Guin's Earthsea trilogy. *In* Children's literature v8 p103-10

**Doolittle, Hilda**

### About individual works

*Helen in Egypt*

Wagner, L. W. Helen in Egypt: a culmination. *In* Wagner, L. W. American modern p199-212

**Dos Passos, John**

### About

Wagner, L. W. The poetry in American fiction. *In* Wagner, L. W. American modern p18-30

### About individual works

*Manhattan transfer*

Festa-McCormick, D. Dos Passos's Manhattan transfer: the death of a metropolis. *In* Festa-McCormick, D. The city as catalyst p141-57

*U.S.A.*

Trilling, L. The America of John Dos Passos. *In* Trilling, L. Speaking of literature and society p104-12

**Dostoevskiĭ, Fedor Mikhaĭlovich**

### About

Steinberg, A. S. Dostoevski and the Jews. *In* The Jew, ed. by A. A. Cohen p158-70

### About individual works

*The short novels of Dostoevsky*

Trilling, L. A comedy of evil. *In* Trilling, L. Speaking of literature and society p387-91

**Dostoevsky, Fyodor Mikhailovich.** See Dostoevskiĭ, Fedor Mikhaĭlovich

**Dott, Robert H.**

The geosyncline—first major geological concept "made in America." *In* New Hampshire Bicentennial Conference on the History of Geology, University of New Hampshire, 1976. Two hundred years of geology in America p239-64

**Dotterer, Ronald L.**

The fictive and the real: myth and form in the poetry of Wallace Stevens and William Carlos Williams. *In* The Binding of Proteus, ed. by M. W. McCune, T. Orbison and P. M. Withim p221-48

**Douglas, Angus.** See Curran, J. jt. auth.

**Douglas, Gawin, Bp. of Dunkeld**

### About individual works

*The palice of honour*

Kratzmann, G. The palice of honour and The hous of fame. *In* Kratzmann, G. Anglo-Scottish literary relations. 1430-1550 p104-28

**Douglas, Gawin, Bp. of Dunkeld, tr.**

### About individual works

*The Aeneid of Virgil translated into Scottish verse*

Kratzmann, G. Two Aeneid translators—Surrey's debt to Douglas: Wyatt and Henryson. *In* Kratzmann, G. Anglo-Scottish literary relations, 1430-1550 p169-94

**Douglas, Mary**

Judgments of James Frazer. *In* Generations, ed. by S. R. Graubard p151-64

**Douglas, Roy**

Huxley's critique from social Darwinism. *In* Critics of Henry George, ed. by R. V. Andelson p137-52

Laveleye: the critic ripe for conversion. *In* Critics of Henry George, ed. by R. V. Andelson p47-55

Mallock and the "most elaborate answer." *In* Critics of Henry George, ed. by R. V. Andelson p95-108

**Douglass, Frederick**

### About individual works

*Narrative of the life of Frederick Douglass, an American slave, written by himself*

Stepto, R. B. I rose and found my voice: narration, authentication, and authorial control in four slave narratives. *In* Stepto, R. B. From behind the veil p3-31

**Douglass, Joseph D.** See Hoeber, A. M. jt. auth.

**Doulis, Thomas**

John D. MacDonald: the liabilities of professionalism. *In* Seasoned authors for a new season: the search for standards in popular writing, ed. by L. Filler p170-86

**Dover, Kenneth James**

The classical historians. *In* Ancient Greek literature, ed. by K. J. Dover p88-104

Classical oratory. *In* Ancient Greek literature, ed. by K. J. Dover p122-33

Classical science and philosophy. *In* Ancient Greek literature, ed. by K. J. Dover p105-21

Comedy. *In* Ancient Greek literature, ed. by K. J. Dover p74-87

Introduction. *In* Ancient Greek literature, ed. by K. J. Dover p 1-9

Tragedy. *In* Ancient Greek literature, ed. by K. J. Dover p50-73

**Dow, Eddy**

"Van Wyck Brooks and Lewis Mumford: a confluence in the 'twenties." *In* Van Wyck Brooks: the critic and his critics, ed. by W. Wasserstrom p238-51

**Dowling, John Clarkson**

Smallpox and literature in eighteenth-century Spain. *In* Studies in eighteenth-century culture v9 p59-77

**Doyle, Elisabeth Joan**

Commercial and noncommercial television in America and Europe. *In* Screen and society, ed. by F. J. Coppa p185-210

**Dragadze, Tamara**

The place of 'ethnos' theory in Soviet anthropology. *In* Soviet and Western anthropology, ed. by E. Gellner p161-70

**Dragons**

Le Goff, J. Ecclesiastical culture and folklore in the Middle Ages: Saint Marcellus of Paris and the dragon. *In* Le Goff, J. Time, work, & culture in the Middle Ages p159-88

**Dragons in literature**

Hatto, A. T. Herzeloyde's dragon-dream. *In* Hatto, A. T. Essays on medieval German and other poetry p182-99

**Drama**

*See also* Theater; Tragedy

#### Plots

*See* Plots (Drama, novel, etc.)

### 15th and 16th centuries

*See also* European drama—Renaissance, 1450-1600

### 20th century—History and criticism

Goetz-Stankiewicz, M. East meets West. *In* Goetz-Stankiewicz, M. The silenced theatre: Czech playwrights without a stage p239-71

**Drama, Renaissance.** See European drama—Renaissance, 1450-1600

**Dramatic criticism.** See Theatre critics

**Dramatic music.** See Music, Incidental; Music in theaters

**Dramatists, American**

### 20th century

Brustein, R. S. Theatre in the age of Einstein: the crack in the chimney. *In* Brustein, R. S. Critical moments p107-23

**Drayton, Michael**

#### About

Fry, P. H. The pressure of sense in some odes of Jonson and Drayton. *In* Fry, P. H. The poet's calling in the English ode p15-36

#### About individual works

*David and Goliath*

Allingham, A. David as epic hero: Drayton's David and Goliah. *In* The David myth in Western literature, ed. by R. J. Frontain and J. Wojcik p86-94

**Dreams**

Le Goff, J. Dreams in the culture and collective psychology of the medieval West. *In* Le Goff, J. Time, work, & culture in the Middle Ages p201-04

Skura, M. A. Revisions and rereadings in dreams and allegories. *In* The Literary Freud: mechanisms of defense and the poetic will, ed. by J. H. Smith p345-79

**Dreams in literature**

Hatto, A. T. Herzeloyde's dragon-dream. *In* Hatto, A. T. Essays on medieval German and other poetry p182-99

Katz, M. R. Dreams in Pushkin. *In* California Slavic studies v11 p71-103

Norwood, H. N. Hermia's dream. *In* Representing Shakespeare, ed. by M. M. Schwartz and C. Kahn p 1-20

Novak, M. E. The extended moment: time, dream, history, and perspective in eighteenth-century fiction. *In* Probability, time, and space in eighteenth-century literature, ed. by P. R. Backscheider p141-66

Simenauer, E. R. M. Rilke's dreams and his conception of dream. *In* Rilke: the alchemy of alienation, ed. by F. Baron, E. S. Dick and W. R. Maurer p243-62

Skura, M. A. Interpreting Posthumus' dream from above and below: families, psychoanalysts, and literary critics. *In* Representing Shakespeare, ed. by M. M. Schwartz and C. Kahn p203-16

**Dreiser, Theodore**

#### About

Shapiro, C. On our own: Trilling vs. Dreiser. *In* Seasoned authors for a new season: the search for standards in popular writing, ed. by L. Filler p152-56

**Drescher, Seymour**

Two variants of anti-slavery: religious organization and social mobilization in Britain and France, 1780-1870. *In* Anti-slavery, religion, and reform: essays in memory of Roger Anstey, ed. by C. Bolt and S. Drescher p43-63

**Drew, John**
A passage via Alexandria? *In* E. M. Forster: a human exploration, ed. by G. K. Das and J. Beer p89-101

**Drexler, Rosalyn**

### About individual works
*The bed was full*

Brown, J. The bed was full. *In* Brown, J. Feminist drama p22-36

**Dreyfus, Hubert L.**
A framework for misrepresenting knowledge. *In* Philosophical perspectives in artificial intelligence, ed. by M. Ringle p124-36

**Drobizheva, L.**
Ethnic sociology of present-day life. *In* Soviet and Western anthropology, ed. by E. Gellner p171-80

**Dronke, Peter**
The art of the Archpoet: a reading of 'Lingua balbus'. *In* The Interpretation of medieval lyric poetry, ed. by W. T. H. Jackson p22-43

**Drury, Patricia, and Enthoven, Alain C.**
Competition and health care costs. *In* The Economy in the 1980s: a program for growth and stability, ed. by M. J. Boskin p393-417

**Dryden, John**

### About

Hagstrum, J. H. John Dryden: sensual, heroic, and "pathetic" love. *In* Hagstrum, J. H. Sex and sensibility p50-71

Manley, L. G. "Betwixt two ages cast": Dryden's criticism. *In* Manley, L. G. Convention, 1500-1750 p290-321

Wallace, J. M. John Dryden's play and the conception of a heroic society. *In* Culture and politics from Puritanism to the Enlightenment, ed. by P. Zagorin p113-34

### About individual works
*Absalom and Achitophel*

Barbeau, A. T. The disembodied rebels: psychic origins of rebellion in Absalom and Achitophel. *In* Studies in eighteenth-century culture v9 p489-501

Seidel, M. A. A house divided: Marvell's last instructions and Dryden's Absalom and Achitophel. *In* Seidel, M. A. Satiric inheritance, Rabelais to Sterne p135-68

*Alexander's feast*

Fry, P. H. "Alexander's feast" and the tyranny of music. *In* Fry, P. H. The poet's calling in the English ode p49-62

*All for love*

Lamb, M. All for love and the theatrical arts. *In* The Analysis of literary texts, ed. by R. D. Pope p236-43

Reiss, T. J. A new time and the glory that was Egypt. *In* Reiss, T. J. Tragedy and truth p204-18

*Aureng-Zebe*

Tarbet, D. W. Reason dazzled: perspective and language in Dryden's Aureng-Zebe. *In* Probability, time, and space in eighteenth-century literature, ed. by P. R. Backscheider p187-205

Vieth, D. M. Shadwell in acrostic land: the reversible meaning of Dryden's Mac Flecknoe. *In* Studies in eighteenth-century culture v9 p503-16

*Sigismonda and Guiscardo*

Jones, E. Dryden's Sigismonda. *In* English Renaissance studies, ed. by J. Carey p279-90

**Dubbing of moving-pictures**
Burgess, A. Dubbing. *In* The State of the language p297-303

**Dublin. Abbey Theatre**
Saddlemyer, A. The 'dwarf-dramas' of the early Abbey Theatre. *In* Yeats, Sligo and Ireland, ed. by A. N. Jeffares p197-215

**Dubofsky, Melvyn**
Labor organizations. *In* Encyclopedia of American economic history, ed. by G. Porter v2 p524-51

**Du Bois, William Edward Burghardt**

### About individual works
*The souls of black folk*

Stepto, R. B. The quest of the weary traveler: W. E. B. Du Bois's The souls of black folk. *In* Stepto, R. B. From behind the veil p52-91

**Dubos, René Jules**
Richer life through less energy consumption. *In* The Condition of man, ed. by P. Hallberg p23-33

**Ducasse, Isidore Lucien**

### About individual works
*The lay of Maldoror*

Riffaterre, M. Generating Lautréamont's text. *In* Textual strategies, ed. by J. V. Harari p404-20

**Duccio di Buoninsegna**

### About

Cole, B. Duccio and his school. *In* Cole, B. Sienese painting p24-67

Schapiro, M. On an Italian painting of the Flagellation of Christ in the Frick Collection. *In* Schapiro, M. Selected papers v3: Late antique, early Christian and mediaeval art p355-79

**Duckworth, Colin**
D'Antraigues's feminism: where fact and fantasy meet. *In* Woman and society in eighteenth-century France, ed. by E. Jacobs and others p166-82

**Duclos, Charles Pinot**

### About individual works
*Histoire de Madame de Luz*

Hall, P. M. Duclos's Histoire de Madame de Luz: woman and history. *In* Woman and society in eighteenth-century France, ed. by E. Jacobs and others p139-51

**The duellists (Motion picture)**
Kael, P. The duellists/The battle of Chile. *In* Kael, P. When the lights go down p380-88

**Duffey, Bernard**
Ezra Pound and the attainment of imagism. *In* Toward a new American literary history, ed. by L. J. Budd, E. H. Cady and C. L. Anderson p181-94

**Dugan, Alan**

### About

Howard, R. Alan Dugan: "Possessed of an echo but not a fate." *In* Howard, R. Alone with America p122-30

**Du Guillet, Pernette**

### About

Perry, T. A. Pernette du Guillet's poetry of love and desire. *In* Perry, T. A. Erotic spirituality p53-67

**Duignan, Peter James, and Gann, Lewis Henry**
Middle East. *In* The United States in the 1980s, ed. by P. Duignan and A. Rabushka p757-96
*See also* Gann, L. H. jt. auth.

**Duke, Jean Maurice.** See Duke, Maurice

**Duke, Maurice**
"Cabell" rhymes with "rabble." *In* Seasoned authors for a new season: the search for standards in popular writing, ed. by L. Filler p117-26

**Duley, Margaret**
#### About
O'Flaherty, P. Bridging two worlds: Margaret Duley's fiction, 1936-42. *In* O'Flaherty, P. The rock observed p127-43

**Dumble, Edwin Theodore**
#### About
Alexander, N. The work of Edwin Theodore Dumble on the East Texas lignite deposits (1888-1892). *In* New Hampshire Bicentennial Conference on the History of Geology, University of New Hampshire, 1976. Two hundred years of geology in America p213-22

**Dumfriesshire, Scotland. Ruthwell Cross**
Schapiro, M. The bowman and the bird on the Ruthwell Cross and other works: the interpretation of secular themes in early mediaeval religious art. *In* Schapiro, M. Selected papers v3: Late antique, early Christian and mediaeval art p177-95
Schapiro, M. The religious meaning of the Ruthwell Cross. *In* Schapiro, M. Selected papers v3: Late antique, early Christian and mediaeval art p151-76

**Dummett, Michael A. B.**
Common sense and physics. *In* Perception and identity, ed. by G. F. Macdonald p 1-40

**Du Moulin of Nîmes, Milton's admirer.**
Duncan-Jones, E. E. *In* English Renaissance studies, ed. by J. Carey p245-53

**Dumville, David N.**
The ætheling: a study in Anglo-Saxon constitutional history. *In* Anglo-Saxon England 8 p 1-33

**Dunbar, William**
#### About
Kratzmann, G. Dunbar and Skelton. *In* Kratzmann, G. Anglo-Scottish literary relations, 1430-1550 p129-68
Ridley, F. H. Scottish transformations of courtly literature: William Dunbar and the court of James IV. *In* The Expansion and transformations of courtly literature, ed. by N. B. Smith and J. T. Snow p171-84

**Duncan, Erika**
The hungry Jewish mother. *In* The Lost tradition: mothers and daughters in literature, ed. by C. N. Davidson and E. M. Broner p231-41

**Duncan, Quince**
#### About
Jackson, R. L. Return to the origins: the Afro-Costa Rican literature of Quince Duncan. *In* Jackson, R. L. Black writers in Latin America p171-79

**Duncan, Ronald Frederick Henry**
Merit is always recognized. *In* Lying truths, ed. by R. Duncan and M. Weston-Smith p11-15

**Duncan-Jones, E. E.**
Milton's admirer, Du Moulin of Nimes. *In* English Renaissance studies, ed. by J. Carey p245-53

**Duncan-Jones, Katherine**
Sidney and Titian. *In* English Renaissance studies, ed. by J. Carey p 1-11

**Dundes, Alan**
Interpreting folklore
*Contents*
The crowing hen and the Easter bunny: male chauvinism in American folklore
The curious case of the wide-mouth frog
The hero pattern and the life of Jesus
Into the endzone for a touchdown: a psychoanalytic consideration of American football
The number three in American culture
Projection in folklore: a plea for psychoanalytic semiotics
A psychoanalytic study of the bullroarer
Seeing is believing
Texture, text, and context
Thinking ahead: a folkloristic reflection of the future orientation in American worldview
"To love my father all": a psychoanalytic study of the folktale source of King Lear
Wet and dry, the evil eye: an essay in Indo-European and Semitic worldview
Who are the folk?

**Dunn, Charles James**
The Japanese puppet theatre. *In* Drama and mimesis, ed. by J. Redmond p65-80

**Dunn, Judy**
Playing in speech. *In* The State of the language, ed. by L. Michaels and C. Ricks p202-12
Understanding human development: limitations and possibilities in an ethological approach. *In* Human ethology, ed. by M. von Cranach [and others] p623-41

**Dunlop, John Thomas**
The future of the American labor movement. *In* The Third century, ed. by S. M. Lipset p183-203

**Dupee, Frederick Wilcox**
"The Americanism of Van Wyck Brooks." *In* Van Wyck Brooks: the critic and his critics, ed. by W. Wasserstrom p116-28

**Du Quesnay, Ian M. Le M.**
From Polyphemus to Corydon: Virgil, Eclogue 2 and the Idylls of Theocritus. *In* Creative imitation and Latin literature, ed. by D. West and T. Woodman p35-69

**Durkheim, Emile**
Emile Durkheim on institutional analysis
*Contents*
The conjugal family
Course in sociology: opening lecture
Crime and social health
Divorce by mutual consent
Introduction to morality
Introduction to the sociology of the family
Note on social morphology
Review of Albert Schaeffle, Bau und Leben des sozialen Körpers: erster Band
Review of Antonio Labriola, Essais sur la conception matérialiste de l'histoire
Review of Ferdinand Tönnies, Gemeinschaft und Gesellschaft
Review of Gaston Richard, Le socialisme et la science sociale
Review of Lucien Levy-Bruhl, Les fonctions mentales dans les sociétés inférieures and Emile Durkheim, Les formes élémentaires de la vie religieuse
Review of Marianne Weber, Ehefrau und Mutter in der Rechtsentwickelung
Sociology and the social sciences
Two laws of penal evolution

**Durkheim, Emile**—*Continued*

**About**

Collins, R. Erving Goffman and the development of modern social theory. *In* The View from Goffman, ed. by J. Ditton p170-209

**About individual works**
*The elementary forms of the religious life*

Durkheim, E. Review of Lucien Levy-Bruhl, Les fonctions mentales dans les sociétés inférieures. *In* Durkheim, E. Emile Durkheim on institutional analysis p145-49

**Durrell, Lawrence**

**About individual works**
*The Alexandria quartet*

Festa-McCormick, D. Durrell's Alexandria quartet: "a whore among cities." *In* Festa-McCormick, D. The city as catalyst p158-75

**Dürrenmatt, Friedrich**

**About individual works**
*The visit*

Kontos, A. The dialectics of domination: an interpretation of Friedrich Dürrenmatt's The visit. *In* Powers, possessions and freedom, ed. by A. Kontos p153-65

**Dusek, Val**

Geodesy and the earth sciences in the philosophy of C. S. Peirce. *In* New Hampshire Bicentennial Conference on the History of Geology, University of New Hampshire, 1976. Two hundred years of geology in America p265-75

**Duty in literature**

McGhee, R. D. Arnold and Clough. *In* McGhee, R. D. Marriage, duty & desire in Victorian poetry and drama p99-138

McGhee, R. D. Browning. *In* McGhee, R. D. Marriage, duty & desire in Victorian poetry and drama p67-98

McGhee, R. D. Elizabeth Barrett Browning and Oscar Wilde. *In* McGhee, R. D. Marriage, duty & desire in Victorian poetry and drama p233-97

McGhee, R. D. Introduction. *In* McGhee, R. D. Marriage, duty & desire in Victorian poetry and drama p 1-28

McGhee, R. D. Swinburne and Hopkins. *In* McGhee, R. D. Marriage, duty & desire in Victorian poetry and drama p177-232

McGhee, R. D. Tennyson. *In* McGhee, R. D. Marriage, duty & desire in Victorian poetry and drama p29-66

**Dwellings**

**Remodeling**

Jones, M. O. L. A. add-ons and re-dos: renovation in folk art and architectural design. *In* Perspectives on American folk art, ed. by I. M. G. Quimby and S. T. Swank p325-63

**Los Angeles**

Jones, M. O. L. A. add-ons and re-dos; renovation in folk art and architectural design. *In* Perspectives on American folk art, ed. by I. M. G. Quimby and S. T. Swank p325-63

**Texas**

Taylor, L. W. Fachwerk and Brettstuhl: the rejection of traditional folk culture. *In* Perspectives on American folk art, ed. by I. M. G. Quimby and S. T. Swank p162-76

**Dworkin, Ronald Myles**

Political theory and legal education. *In* Political theory and political education, ed. by M. Richter p177-89

**Dwyer, Carlota Cárdenas de.** See Cárdenas de Dwyer, Carlota

**Dye, Nancy Schrom**

Clio's American daughters: male history, female reality. *In* The Prism of sex, ed. by J. A. Sherman and E. T. Beck p9-31

**Dynamics.** See Force and energy

# E

**Eagleton, Terence**

Text, ideology, realism. *In* Literature and society, ed. by E. W. Said p149-73

**About individual works**
*Criticism and ideology*

Slaughter, C. Conclusions: literature and dialectical materialism. *In* Slaughter, C. Marxism, ideology & literature p197-213

**Eagleton, Terry.** See Eagleton, Terence

**Eakin, Paul John**

Malcolm X and the limits of autobiography. *In* Autobiography: essays theoretical and critical, ed. by J. Olney p180-93

**Earl, James W.**

The typological structure of Andreas. *In* Old English literature in context, ed. by J. D. Niles p66-89

**Earle, Carville E.**

Environment, disease, and mortality in early Virginia. *In* The Chesapeake in the seventeenth century, ed. by T. W. Tate and D. L. Ammerman p96-125

**Early Christian architecture.** See Architecture, Early Christian

**Early Christian art.** See Art, Early Christian

**Early Christian literature.** See Christian literature, Early

**Early Christian mosaics.** See Mosaics, Early Christian

**Earth**

*See also* Cosmology

**Crust**

*See* Plate tectonics

**Earth sciences**

**History**

Pyne, S. J. From the Grand Canyon to the Marianas Trench: the earth sciences after Darwin. *In* The Sciences in the American context: new perspectives, ed. by N. Reingold p165-92

**United States**—History

Pyne, S. J. From the Grand Canyon to the Marianas Trench: the earth sciences after Darwin. *In* The Sciences in the American context: new perspectives, ed. by N. Reingold p165-92

**East (Near East)** See Near East

**East Asia**

**Historiography**

Hall, J. W. East, Southeast, and South Asia. *In* The Past before us, ed. by M. Kammen p157-86

East Indian literature. See Indic literature

**Easterlin, Richard Ainley**
Population. *In* Encyclopedia of American economic history, ed. by G. Porter v 1 p167-82

**Eastern Empire.** See Byzantine Empire

**Eastern Europe.** See Europe, Eastern

**Eastman, Crystal**
### About
Cook, B. W. Female support networks and political activism: Lillian Wald, Crystal Eastman, Emma Goldman. *In* A Heritage of her own, ed. by N. F. Cott and E. H. Pleck p411-44

**Eastmon, Lloyd E.**
Facets of an ambivalent relationship;smuggling, puppets, and atrocities during the war, 1937-1945. *In* The Chinese and the Japanese, ed. by A. Iriye p275-303

**Easton, Barbara**
Feminism and the contemporary family. *In* A Heritage of her own, ed. by N. F. Cott and E. H. Pleck p555-77

**Ebreo, Leone.** See Leo Hebraeus

**Ecclesiastical architecture.** See Church architecture

**Ecclesiastical art.** See Christian art and symbolism

**Eckhardt, William**
The causes and correlates of Western militarism. *In* Problems of contemporary militarism, ed. by A. Eide and M. Thee p323-55

**Eckhart, Johannes.** See Eckhart, Meister

**Eckhart, Meister**
### About
Ozment, S. H. The spiritual traditions. *In* Ozment, S. H. The age of reform, 1250-1550 p73-134

**Ecologists**
Morowitz, H. J. Fair is foul, and foul is fair. *In* Morowitz, H. J. The wine of life, and other essays on societies, energy & living things p176-78

**Ecology.** See Botany—Ecoolgy; Population biology

**Economic anthropology.** See Economics, Primitive

**Economic assistance**
Bauer, P. T. Foreign aid and the Third World. *In* The United States in the 1980s, ed. by P. Duignan and A. Rabushka p559-83

**Economic concentration.** See Big business

**Economic conditions.** See Economic history

**Economic cycles.** See Business cycles

**Economic depressions.** See Depressions

**Economic development**
Boskin, M. J. Economic growth and productivity. *In* The Economy in the 1980s: a program for growth and stability, ed. by M. J. Boskin p23-50

Olmstead, A. L. The costs of economic growth. *In* Encyclopedia of American economic history, ed. by G. Porter v2 p863-81

Pye, L. W. Communication, development, and power. *In* Propaganda and communication in world history, ed. by H. D. Lasswell, D. Lerner and H. Speier v2 p424-45

*See also* Underdeveloped areas

### Social aspects
Leiss, W. Marx and Macpherson: needs, utilities, and self-development. *In* Powers, possessions and freedom, ed. by A. Kontos p119-38

Lipset, S. M. Predicting the future of post-industrial society: can we do it? *In* The Third century, ed. by S. M. Lipset p 1-35

**Economic equilibrium.** See Equilibrium (Economics)

**Economic fluctuations.** See Business cycles

**Economic growth.** See Economic development

**Economic history**
Braudel, F. Toward a historical economics. *In* Braudel, F. On history p83-90

Day, R. H. Technology, population, and the agro-industrial complex: a global view. *In* Economic issues of the eighties, ed. by N. M. Kamrany and R. H. Day p146-62

### 1945-
Cuddington, J. T. and McKinnon, R. I. The United States and the world economy. *In* The Economy in the 1980s: a program for growth and stability. ed. by M. J. Boskin p161-95

**Economic planning.** See subdivision Economic policy under names of countries, e.g. France—Economic policy

**Economic policy.** See Economic development; Industrial laws and legislation; Industry and state; International economic relations; Underdeveloped areas—Economic policy; also subdivision Economic policy under names of countries, regions, cities, etc. e.g. France—Economic policy

**Economic policy, Foreign.** See International economic relations

**Economic security.** See Public welfare

**Economic statistics.** See Statistics

**Economic theory.** See Economics

**Economics**
Arrow, K. J. The economics of information. *In* The Computer age: a twenty-year view, ed. by M. L. Dertouzos and J. Moses p306-17

Cornwall, J. Macrodynamics. *In* A Guide to post-Keynesian economics, ed. by A. S. Eichner p19-33

Eichner, A. S. Introduction. *In* A Guide to post-Keynesian economics, ed. by A. S. Eichner p3-18

Eichner, A. S. A look ahead. *In* A Guide to post-Keynesian economics, ed. by A. S. Eichner p165-84

Flew, A. G. N. Intended conduct and unintended consequences. *In* Lying truths, ed. by R. Duncan and M. Weston-Smith p17-30

See also Capitalism; Commerce; Cost and standard of living; Demography; Depressions; Economic development; Economic history; Equilibrium (Economics); Finance, Public; Income; Industry; Labor and laboring classes; Land use; Macroeconomics; Money; Prices; Property; Regional economics; Statistics; Taxation; Value

### Terminology
Heinzelman, K. "Unreal words": language in political economy. *In* Heinzelman, K. The economics of the imagination p70-109

### United States—History
Coats, A. W. Economic thought. *In* Encyclopedia of American economic history, ed. by G. Porter v 1 p468-83

**Economics, International.** See International economic relations

**Economics, Medical.** See Medical economics

**Economics, Primitive**

Woodburn, J. Hunters and gatherers today and reconstruction of the past. *In* Soviet and Western anthropology, ed. by E. Gellner p95-117

**Economics in literature**

Brown, R. E. Rival socio-economic theories in two plays by George Lillo. *In* Tennessee Studies in literature v24 p94-110

Heinzelman, K. Afterword: the merchant as poet. *In* Heinzelman, K. The economics of the imagination p276-82

Heinzelman, K. Economics in Mammon's cave. *In* Heinzelman, K. The economics of the imagination p35-69

Heinzelman, K. "Getting it" in Paterson: the increment defended. *In* Heinzelman, K. The economics of the imagination p234-75

Heinzelman, K. "The mouth-tale of the giants": an introduction to the economics of the imagination. *In* Heinzelman, K. The economics of the imagination p3-34

Heinzelman, K. William Blake and "the price of experience." *In* Heinzelman, K. The economics of the imagination p110-33

*See also* Money in literature

**Edari, Ronald S.**

Social distance and social change among four ethnic groups in Mombasa. *In* Values, identities, and national integration, ed. by J. N. Paden p197-203

**Edel, Leon**

The figure under the carpet. *In* Telling lives, ed. by M. Pachter p16-34

**About individual works**

*Henry James: the conquest of London, 1870-1881*

Pritchett, V. S. Henry James: birth of a hermaphrodite. *In* Pritchett, V. S. The tale bearers p120-37

*Henry James: the treacherous years, 1895-1901*

Pritchett, V. S. Henry James: birth of a hermaphrodite. *In* Pritchett, V. S. The tale bearers p120-37

**Edelson, Marshall**

Two questions about psychoanalysis and poetry. *In* The Literary Freud: mechanisms of defense and the poetic will, ed. by J. H. Smith p113-18

**Edgeworth, Maria**

**About individual works**

*Castle Rackrent*

Cronin, J. Maria Edgeworth: Castle Rackrent. *In* Cronin, J. The Anglo-Irish novel, v 1 p19-40

**Editing**

Bowers, F. Scholarship and editing. *In* The Bibliographical Society of America, 1904-79 p514-41

**Editors (Journalism)** See Journalists

**Edkins, Carol**

Quest for community: spiritual autobiographies of eighteenth-century Quaker and Puritan women in America. *In* Women's autobiography, ed. by E. C. Jelinek p39-52

**Edmond, Rod**

'The past-marked prospect': reading The Mayor of Casterbridge. *In* Reading the Victorian novel: detail into form, ed. by I. Gregor p111-27

**Education**

*See also* Culture; Learning and scholarship

**Aims and objectives**

*See* Educational sociology

**Costs**

Le Goff, J. Academic expenses at Padua in the fifteenth century. *In* Le Goff, J. Time, work, & culture in the Middle Ages p101-06

**Experimental methods**

Radest, H. B. Schooling and the search for a usable politics. *In* History, religion, and spiritual democracy, ed. by M. Wohlgelernter p317-40

**History—Medieval, 500-1500**

*See* Education, Medieval

**Philosophy**

Perkinson, H. J. Vico and the methods of study of our time. *In* Conference on Vico and Contemporary Thought, New York, 1976. Vico and contemporary thought pt2 p95-109

**Standards**

Boyson, R. Compulsory state education raises educational standards. *In* Lying truths, ed. by R. Duncan and M. Weston-Smith p61-69

**Africa**

Fischer, L. F. Mass education and national conflict in thirty African states. *In* Values, identities, and national integration, ed. by J. N. Paden p261-69

**Cameroon**

Clignet, R. Teachers and national values in Cameroon: an inferential analysis from census data. *In* Values, identities, and national integration, ed. by J. N. Paden p321-36

**Great Britain—History**

Charlton, K. The educational background. *In* The Age of Milton, ed. by C. A. Patrides and R. B. Waddington p102-37

**United States**

Miller, P. Education under cross fire. *In* Miller, P. The responsibility of mind in a civilization of machines p78-97

**United States—History**

Solmon, L. C. and Tierney, M. Education. *In* Encyclopedia of American economic history, ed. by G. Porter v3 p1012-27

**Education, Classical.** See Classical education

**Education, Compulsory**

**Great Britain—History**

Boyson, R. Compulsory state education raises educational standards. *In* Lying truths, ed. by R. Duncan and M. Weston-Smith p61-69

**Education, Elementary**

**India**

Narayan, R. K. English in India: the process of transmutation. *In* Aspects of Indian writing in English, ed. by M. K. Naik p19-23

**Education, Ethical.** See Moral education

**Education, Higher**

*See also* Classical education; Science—Study and teaching (Higher); Universities and colleges

Education Higher—*Continued*

### Aims and objectives

Nisbet, R. A. The future of the university. *In* The Third century, ed. by S. M. Lipset p303-25

### United States

Bunzel, J. H. Higher education: problems and prospects. *In* The United States in the 1980s, ed. by P. Duignan and A. Rabushka p391-415

Trilling, L. Reflections on a lost cause: English literature and American education. *In* Trilling, L. Speaking of literature and society p343-60

Education, Humanistic

Carne-Ross, D. S. Center of resistance. *In* Carne-Ross, D. S. Instaurations p 1-28

Carne-Ross, D. S. The scandal of necessity. *In* Carne-Ross, D. S. Instaurations p218-42

### History

Ozment, S. H. Humanism and the Reformation. *In* Ozment, S. H. The age of reform, 1250-1550 p290-317

Education, Liberal. See Education, Humanistic

Education, Medieval

Le Goff, J. Academic expenses at Padua in the fifteenth century. *In* Le Goff, J. Time, work, & culture in the Middle Ages p101-06

Le Goff, J. How did the medieval university conceive of itself? *In* Le Goff, J. Time, work, & culture in the Middle Ages p122-34

### Social aspects

Le Goff, J. The universities and the public authorities in the Middle Ages and the Renaissance. *In* Le Goff, J. Time, work, & culture in the Middle Ages p135-49

Education, Moral. See Moral education

Education and nationalism. See Nationalism and education

Education and politics. See Politics and education

Education and sociology. See Educational sociology

Education and state. See Endowment of research; Nationalism and education; Politics and education

Education of girls. See Education of women

Education of women

### France

Bloch, J. H. Women and the reform of the nation. *In* Woman and society in eighteenth-century France, ed. by E. Jacobs and others p3-18

Jacobs, E. Diderot and the education of girls. *In* Woman and society in eighteenth-century France, ed. by E. Jacobs and others p83-95

Mylne, V. The Bibliothèque universelle des dames. *In* Woman and society in eighteenth-century France, ed. by E. Jacobs and others p123-38

Educational aims and objectives. See Education, Higher

Educational endowments. See Endowment of research

Educational freedom. See Academic freedom

Educational innovations. See Education—Experimental methods

Educational laws and legislation. See Education, Compulsory

Educational sociology

Elton, L. R. B. Education can change society? *In* Lying trusts, ed. by R. Duncan and M. Weston-Smith p71-83

Radest, H. B. Schooling and the search for a usable politics. *In* History, religion, and spiritual democracy, ed. by M. Wohlgelernter and others p317-40

Rodriguez, R. An education in language. *In* The State of the language, ed. by L. Michaels and C. Ricks p129-39

Educational technology. See Computer-assisted instruction

Edwards, Jonathan

### About

Colacurcio, M. J. The example of Edwards: idealist imagination and the metaphysics of sovereignty. *In* Puritan influences in American literature, ed. by E. Elliott p55-106

Martin, J. A. The esthetic, the religious, and the natural. *In* History, religion, and spiritual democracy, ed. by M. Wohlgelernter and others p76-91

Edwards, Philip

The declaration of love. *In* Shakespeare's styles, ed. by P. Edwards; I. S. Ewbank, and G. K. Hunter p39-50

Threshold of a nation

*Contents*

Astraea and Chrisoganus

Ben Jonson

The hidden king: Shakespeare's history plays

Introduction: The king's threshold

Nation and empire

Nothing is concluded

Our Irish theatre

A play-house in the waste: George Moore and the Irish theatre

The royal pretenders: Ford's Perkin Warbeck and Massinger's Believe as you list

A superfluous sort of men: the rise and fall of the professional theatre

Effi Briest (Motion picture)

Kauffmann, S. Effi Briest. *In* Kauffmann, S. Before my eyes p22-25

Efficiency, Industrial. See Capital productivity; Labor productivity

Egelius, Mats

Housing and human needs: the work of Ralph Erskine (with original sketches by Ralph Erskine) *In* Architecture for people, ed. by B. Mikellides p134-48

Eger, Ernestina N.

A selected bibliography of Chicano criticism. *In* The Identification and analysis of Chicano literature, ed. by F. Jiménez p389-403

Ego (Psychology) in literature

Kerrigan, W. The articulation of the ego in the English Renaissance. *In* The Literary Freud: mechanisms of defense and the poetic will, ed. by J. H. Smith p261-308

Egoff, Sheila

Beyond the garden wall. *In* The Arbuthnot lectures, 1970-1979 p189-203

Egri, Péter

The use of the short story in O'Neill's and Chekhov's one-act plays: a Hungarian view of O'Neill. *In* Eugene O'Neill, ed. by V. Floyd p115-44

Egypt

### Civilization

Wilson, J. A. Egyptian civilization. *In* Propaganda and communication in world history, ed. by H. D. Lasswell, D. Lerner and H. Speier v 1 p145-74

## Egyptian language

### Inscriptions

Lutz, C. E. The oldest library motto. *In* Lutz, C. E. The oldest library motto, and other library essays p17-21

## Ehrenpreis, Irvin

Strange relation: Stevens' nonsense. *In* Wallace Stevens, ed. by F. Doggett and R. Buttel p219-34

## Ehrenreich, Bernard C.

### About

Sherwin, B. L. Portrait of a romantic rebel Bernard C. Ehrenreich. *In* Conference on Southern Jewish History, Richmond, Va. 1976. "Turn to the South" p 1-12

## Ehrensvvärd, Gösta

The biosphere and man: some reflections on technology. *In* Architecture for people, ed. by B. Mikellides p187-90

**Eibesfeldt, Irenäus Eibl-** See Eibl-Eibesfeldt, Irenäus

## Eibl-Eibesfeldt, Irenäus

Ritual and ritualization from a biological perspective. *In* Human ethology, ed. by M. von Cranach [and others] p3-55

## Eichendorff, Joseph Karl Benedikt, Freiherr von

### About

Hughes, G. T. Natural and supernatural: Eichendorff, with Görres. *In* Hughes, G. T. Romantic German literature p98-111

## Eichner, Alfred S.

Introduction. *In* A Guide to post-Keynesian economics, ed. by A. S. Eichner p3-18

A look ahead. *In* A Guide to post-Keynesian economics, ed. by A. S. Eichner p165-84

## Eichner, Alfred S. and Ross, Davis, R. B.

Competition. *In* Encyclopedia of American economic history, ed. by G. Porter v2 p661-76

## Eide, Asbjørn

Militarisation with a global reach: a challenge to sovereignty, security and the international legal order. *In* Problems of contemporary militarism, ed. by A. Eide and M. Thee p299-322

## Eide, Asbjørn, and Thee, Marek

Introduction. *In* Problems of contemporary militarism, ed. by A. Eide and M. Thee p9-11

## 8 1/2 (Motion picture)

Kauffmann, S. 8 1/2. *In* Kauffmann, S. Before my eyes p356-67

**Eighteenth century.** See Enlightenment

## Eisenstadt, Samuel Noah

Communication patterns in centralized empires. *In* Propaganda and communication in world history, ed. by H. D. Lasswell, D. Lerner and H. Speier v 1 p536-51

## Eisenstein, Sergei Mikhailovich

### About

Worrall, N. Meyerhold and Eisenstein. *In* Performance and politics in popular drama, ed. by D. Bradby, L. James and B. Sharratt p173-87

## Ekman, Paul

About brows: emotional and conversational signals. *In* Human ethology, ed. by M. von Cranach [and others] p169-202

Biological and cultural contributions to body and facial movement in the expression of emotions. *In* Explaining emotions, ed. by A. O. Rorty p73-101

## Ekwensi, Cyprian

### About individual works

#### *Jagua Nana*

Hawkins, L. A. The free spirit of Ekwensi's Jagua Nana. *In* African literature today no. 10: Retrospect & prospect, ed. by E. D. Jones p202-06

## Elazar, Daniel J.

Constitutionalism, federalism, and the post-industrial American polity. *In* The Third century, ed. by S. M. Lipset p79-107

## Eldridge, Richard

Criticism and its objects. *In* Glyph 6 p158-76

## Eleatics

Nussbaum, M. C. Eleatic conventionalism and Philolaus on the conditions of thought. *In* Harvard Studies in classical philology, v83, p63-108

**Elections.** See Representative government and representation

**Electric communication.** See Telecommunication

**Electronic brains.** See Artificial intelligence

## Elegiac poetry, Irish

Vendler, H. H. Four elegies. *In* Yeats, Sligo and Ireland, ed. by A. N. Jeffares p216-31

**Elegies.** See Elegiac poetry, Irish

**Elementary education.** See Education, Elementary

## Elephants in art

Ross, D. H. Cement lions and cloth elephants: popular arts of the Fante Asafo. *In* 5000 years of culture, ed. by F. E. H. Schroeder p290-317

## Elgar, Sir Edward William

### About

Carner, M. Elgar and the symphony. *In* Carner, M. Major and minor p183-85

## Eliach, Yaffa

Holocaust literature III: poetry and drama. *In* Encountering the Holocaust: an interdisciplinary survey, ed. by B. L. Sherwin and S. G. Ament p316-50

## Eliade, Mircea

The world, the city, and the house; excerpt from "Occultism, witchcraft, and cultural fashions." *In* Value and values in evolution, ed. by E. A. Maziarz p3-16

### About

Bernstein, G. M. The mediated vision: Eliade, Lévi-Strauss, and romantic mythopoesis. *In* The Binding of Proteus, ed. by M. W. McCune, T. Orbison and P. M. Withim p158-72

## Elias-Button, Karen

The muse of Medusa. *In* The Lost tradition: mothers and daughters in literature, ed. by C. N. Davidson and E. M. Broner p193-206

## Eliot, George, pseud

### About

Ashton, R. D. More translations: Spinoza and Feuerbach (1894-54) *In* Ashton, R. D. The German idea p155-66

Ashton, R. D. The pros and cons of the German genius. *In* Ashton, R. D. The German idea p173-77

Garrett, P. K. George Eliot: equivalent centers. *In* Garrett, P. K. The Victorian multiplot novel p135-79

**Eliot, George, pseud.**—*Continued*

Stone, D. D. George Eliot: the romantic legacy. *In* Stone, D. D. The romantic impulse in Victorian fiction p173-248

Zimmerman, B. "The mother's history" in George Eliot's life, literature and political ideology. *In* The Lost tradition: mothers and daughters in literature, ed. by C. N. Davidson and E. M. Broner p81-94

### About individual works
#### Daniel Deronda
Raider, R. 'The flash of fervour': Daniel Deronda. *In* Reading the Victorian novel: detail into form, ed. by I. Gregor p253-73

#### Middlemarch
Hertz, N. H. Recognizing Casaubon. *In* Glyph 6 p24-41

Holloway, J. Narrative process in 'Middlemarch.' *In* Holloway, J. Narrative and structure: exploratory essays p38-52

#### The mill on the Floss
Gregor, I. Reading a story: sequence, pace, and recollection. *In* Reading the Victorian novel: detail into form, ed. by I. Gregor p92-110

Lee, A. R. The mill on the Floss: 'memory' and the reading experience. *In* Reading the Victorian novel: detail into form, ed. by I. Gregor p72-91

#### The morality of Wilhelm Meister
Ashton, R. D. George Eliot and Goethe (1854-76) *In* Ashton, R. D. The German idea p166-77

**Eliot, George, pseud., tr.**

#### The essence of Christianity
Ashton, R. D. More translations: Spinoza and Feuerbach (1849-54) *In* Ashton, R. D. The German idea p155-66

#### The life of Jesus critically examined
Ashton, R. D. George Eliot, translator of Strauss (1844-6) *In* Ashton, R. D. The German idea p147-55

**Eliot, Thomas Stearns**

### About
Gloversmith, F. Defining culture: J. C. Powys, Clive Bell, R. H. Tawney & T. S. Eliot. *In* Class, culture and social change, ed. by F. Gloversmith p15-44

Hartman, G. H. The sacred jungle 1: Carlyle, Eliot, Bloom. *In* Hartman, G. H. Criticism in the wilderness p42-62

Hook, S. Religion and culture: the dilemma of T. S. Eliot. *In* Hook, S. Philosophy and public policy p255-61

Krieger, M. The critical legacy of Matthew Arnold; or, The strange brotherhood of T. S. Eliot, I. A. Richards, and Northrop Frye. *In* Krieger, M. Poetic presence and illusion p92-107

### About individual works
#### Four quartets
Spender, S. Rilke and Eliot. *In* Rilke: the alchemy of alienation, ed. by F. Baron, E. S. Dick and W. R. Maurer p47-62

#### The idea of a Christian society
Trilling, L. T. S. Eliot's politics. *In* Trilling, L. Speaking of literature and society p156-69

#### The waste land
Aithal, S. K. The typewriters in the making of The waste land. *In* Virginia. University. Bibliographical Society. Studies in bibliography v33 p191-93

Das, G. K. E. M. Forster, T. S. Eliot, and the 'Hymn before action.' *In* E. M. Forster: a human exploration, ed by G. K. Das and J. Beer p208-15

Kirk, R. Pilgrims in The waste land. *In* Seasoned authors for a new season: the search for standards in popular writing, ed. by L. Filler p20-32

Vendler, H. H. T. S. Eliot. *In* Vendler, H. H. Part of nature, part of us p77-85

### Bibliography
Bornstein, G. and McDougal, S. Y. Pound and Eliot. *In* American literary scholarship, 1978, p111-25

### Political and social views
Cunningham, V. Neutral?: 1930s writers and taking sides. *In* Class, culture and social change, ed. by F. Gloversmith p45-69

Trilling, L. T. S. Eliot's politics. *In* Trilling, L. Speaking of literature and society p156-69

### Social views
*See* Eliot, Thomas Stearns—Political and social views

**Elite (Social sciences) in literature**
Gloversmith, F. Defining culture: J. C. Powys, Clive Bell, R. H. Tawney & T. S. Eliot. *In* Class, culture and social change, ed. by F. Gloversmith p15-44

**Elizabeth I, Queen of England**

### About
Edwards, P. Astraea and Christoganus. *In* Edwards, P. Threshold of a nation p38-65

**Elliott, Emory**
The Puritan roots of American Whig rhetoric. *In* Puritan influences in American literature, ed. by E. Elliott p107-27

**Ellison, Ralph**

### About individual works
#### Invisible man
Stepto, R. B. Literacy and hibernation: Ralph Ellison's Invisible man. *In* Stepto, R. B. From behind the veil p163-94

**Ellmann, Richard**
How Wallace Stevens saw himself. *In* Wallace Stevens, ed. by F. Doggett and R. Buttel p149-70

**Ellrodt, Robert**
Angels and the poetic imagination from Donne to Traherne. *In* English Renaissance studies, ed. by J. Carey p164-79

**Ellsworth, Robert F.**
Quick fixes in intelligence. *In* National security in the 1980s: from weakness to strength, ed. by W. S. Thompson p173-87

**Elshtain, Jean Bethke**
Methodological sophistication and conceptual confusion: a critique of mainstream political science. *In* The Prism of sex, ed. by J. A. Sherman and E. T. Beck p229-52

**Eltis, David.** See Engerman, S. L. jt. auth.

**Elton, Lewis Richard Benjamin**
Education can change society? *In* Lying truths, ed. by R. Duncan and M. Weston-Smith p71-83

Éluard, Paul

### About

Maranda, P. The dialectic of metaphor: an anthropological essay on hermeneutics. *In* The Reader in the text, ed. by S. R. Suleiman and I. Crosman p183-204

Ely, Richard Theodore

### About

Cord, S. B. and Andelson, R. V. Ely: a liberal economist defends landlordism. *In* Critics of Henry George, ed. by R. V. Andelson p313-25

Emancipation. See Liberty

Emancipation of Jews. See Jews—Emancipation

Emerson, Ralph Waldo

### About

Allen, G. W. How Emerson, Thoreau, and Whitman viewed the "frontier." *In* Toward a new American literary history, ed. by L. J. Budd, E. H. Cady and C. L. Anderson p111-28

Bickman, M. The double consciousness revisited. *In* Bickman, M. The unsounded centre p80-94

Bickman, M. Mythology: the symbol in Jungian thought and American romanticism. *In* Bickman, M. The unsounded centre p5-21

Irwin, J. T. Champollion and the historical background; Emerson's hieroglyphical emblems. *In* Irwin, J. T. American hieroglyphics p3-14

#### About individual works
*Plato*

Bickman, M. Voyages of the mind's return: three paradigmatic works. *In* Bickman, M. The unsounded centre p22-37

#### Bibliography

Glick, W. Emerson, Thoreau, and transcendentalism. *In* American literary scholarship, 1978, p3-16

#### Influence

McDermott, J. J. Spires of influence: the importance of Emerson for classical American philosophy. *In* History, religion, and spiritual democracy, ed. by M. Wohlgelernter and others p181-202

Emerson, Roger L.

American Indians, Frenchmen, and Scots philosophers. *In* Studies in eighteenth-century culture v9 p211-36

Emigration and immigration. See Brazil—Emigration and immigration; Chesapeake Bay region—Emigration and immigration

Emmer, Pieter C.

Anti-slavery and the Dutch: abolition without reform. *In* Anti-slavery, religion, and reform: essays in memory of Roger Anstey, ed. by C. Bolt and S. Drescher p80-98

Emotional stress. See Stress (Psychology)

Emotions

Averill, J. R. Emotion and anxiety: socio-cultural, biological, and psychological determinants. *In* Explaining emotions, ed. by A. O. Rorty p37-72

Baier, A. Master passions. *In* Explaining emotions, ed. by A. O. Rorty p403-23

Ekman, P. Biological and cultural contributions to body and facial movement in the expression of emotions. *In* Explaining emotions, ed. by A. O. Rorty p73-101

MacLean, P. D. Sensory and perceptive factors in emotional functions of the triune brain. *In* Explaining emotions, ed. by A. O. Rorty p9-36

Marshall, G. Overdetermination and the emotions. *In* Explaining emotions, ed. by A. O. Rorty p197-222

Matthews, G. B. Ritual and the religious feelings. *In* Explaining emotions, ed. by A. O. Rorty p339-53

Morton, A. Character and the emotions. *In* Explaining emotions, ed. by A. O. Rorty p153-61

Rey, G. Functionalism and the emotions. *In* Explaining emotions, ed. by A. O. Rorty p163-95

Rorty, A. O. Agent regret. *In* Explaining emotions, ed. by A. O. Rorty p489-506

Rorty, A. O. Explaining emotions. *In* Explaining emotions, ed. by A. O. Rorty p103-26

Scruton, R. Emotion, practical knowledge and common culture. *In* Explaining emotions, ed. by A. O. Rorty p519-36

Solomon, R. C. Emotions and choice. *In* Explaining emotions, ed. by A. O. Rorty p251-81

Sousa, R. de. The rationality of emotions. *In* Explaining emotions, ed. by A. O. Rorty p127-51

Sousa, R. de Self-deceptive emotions. *In* Explaining emotions, ed. by A. O. Rorty p283-97

Stocker, M. Intellectual desire, emotion, and action. *In* Explaining emotions, ed. by A. O. Rorty p323-38

*See also* Ambivalence; Facial expression; Jealousy; Shame; Sympathy

Empiricism

Rogers, G. A. J. The empiricism of Locke and Newton. *In* Royal Institute of Philosophy. Philosophers of the Enlightenment p 1-30

Employee-employer relations. See Industrial relations

Employer-employee relations. See Industrial relations

Employers' liability. See Industrial safety—Law and legislation

Employment of women. See Women—Employment

Encyclopedia Britannica. 15th ed. See The New Encyclopaedia Britannica. 15th ed.

The end of the world in our usual bed in a night full of rain (Motion picture)

Kael, P. Soul-snatching and body-snatching. *In* Kael, P. When the lights go down p392-96

Kauffmann, S. Night full of rain. *In* Kauffmann, S. Before my eyes p29-31

Endowment of research

*See also* Technology and state

#### United States—History

Coben, S. American foundations as patrons of science: the commitment to individual research. *In* The Sciences in the American context: new perspectives, ed. by N. Reingold p229-47

Kohler, R. E. Warren Weaver and the Rockefeller Foundation program in molecular biology: a case study in the management of science. *In* The Sciences in the American context: new perspectives, ed. by N. Reingold p249-93

Sapolsky, H. M. Academic science and the military: the years since the Second World War. *In* The Sciences in the American context: new perspectives, ed. by N. Reingold p379-99

**Endowments**
Brustein, R. S. Can the show go on? *In* Brustein, R. S. Critical moments p44-57

Brustein, R. S. The future of the Endowments. *In* Brustein, R. S. Critical moments p58-78

See also Endowment of research

**Energy.** See Force and energy; Power resources

**Energy (The English word)**
Morowitz, H. J. Whose energy? *In* Morowitz, H. J. The wine of life, and other essays on societies, energy & things p62-66

**Energy and state.** See Energy policy

**Energy conservation.** See Architecture and energy conservation; Energy consumption; Energy policy

**Energy consumption**
Dubos, R. Richer life through less energy consumption. *In* The Condition of man, ed. by P. Hallberg p23-33

**Energy industries**
*See also* Petroleum industry and trade

United States—History
Pratt, J. A. Natural resources and energy. *In* Encyclopedia of American economic history, ed. by G. Porter v 1 p202-13

**Energy policy**
United States
Moore, T. G. Energy options. *In* The United States in the 1980s, ed. by P. Duignan and A. Rabushka p221-51

Pindyck, R. S. The critical issues in U.S. energy policy. *In* Economic issues of the eighties, ed. by N. M. Kamrany and R. H. Day p135-45

Rowen, H. S. The threatened jugular: oil supply of the West. *In* National security in the 1980s: from weakness to strength, ed. by W. S. Thompson p275-94

Sweeney, J. L. Energy problems and policies. *In* The Economy in the 1980s: a program for growth and stability, ed. by M. J. Boskin p353-92

**Energy resources.** See Power resources

**The enforcer (Motion picture)**
Kael, P. Harlan County. *In* Kael, P. When the lights go down p249-55

**Engelhardt, H. Tristram.** See Lebacqz, K. jt. auth.

**Engerman, Stanley L. and Eltis, David**
Economic aspects of the abolition debate. *In* Anti-slavery, religion, and reform: essays in memory of Roger Anstey, ed. by C. Bolt and S. Drescher p272-93

**England**
Industries—History
Kramnick, I. Children's literature and bourgeois ideology: observations on culture and industrial capitalism in the later eighteenth century. *In* Culture and politics from Puritanism to the Enlightenment, ed. by P. Zagorin p203-40

Intellectual life
Pocock, J. G. A. Post-Puritan England and the problem of the Enlightenment. *In* Culture and politics from Puritanism to the Enlightenment, ed. by P. Zagorin p91-111

Social life and customs—
18th century
Kramnick, I. Children's literature and bourgeois ideology: observations on culture and industrial capitalism in the later eighteenth century. *In* Culture and politics from Puritanism to the Enlightenment, ed. by P. Zagorin p203-40

**England, Church of.** See Church of England

**England in literature**
Avery, G. E. Children's books and social history. *In* Research about nineteenth-century children and books, ed. by S. K. Richardson p23-40

**English ballads.** See Ballads, English

**English children's literature.** See Children's literature, English

**English children's poetry.** See Children's poetry, English

**English drama**
To 1500—History and criticism
Robertson, D. W. The question of typology and the Wakefield Mactacio Abel. *In* Robertson, D. W. Essays in medieval culture p218-32

Early modern and Elizabethan,
1500-1600—History and criticism
Edwards, P. Astraea and Chrisoganus. *In* Edwards, P. Threshold of a nation p38-65

Edwards, P. Introduction: The king's threshold. *In* Edwards, P. Threshold of a nation p 1-14

Edwards, P. Nation and empire. *In* Edwards, P. Threshold of a nation p66-109

Hawkins, H. The morality of Elizabethan drama: some footnotes to Plato. *In* English Renaissance studies, ed. by J. Carey p12-32

Restoration, 1660-1700—History
and criticism
Hagstrum, J. H. Restoration love and the tears of morbidity. *In* Hagstrum, J. H. Sex and sensibility p72-99

Restoration, 1660-1700—
History and criticism—Book reviews
Gibbons, B. The Revels history of drama in English volume V, 1660-1750. *In* Drama and mimesis, ed. by J. Redmond p191-206

19th century—History and criticism
James, L. Was Jerrold's Black ey'd Susan more popular than Wordsworth's Lucy? *In* Performance and politics in popular drama, ed. by D. Bradby, L. James and B. Sharratt p3-16

20th century—History and criticism
Anderson, M. J. Word and image: aspects of mimesis in contemporary British theatre. *In* Drama and mimesis, ed. by J. Redmond p139-53

Brustein, R. S. Broadway Anglophila. *In* Brustein, R. S. Critical moments p89-94

**English drama (Tragedy)**
History and criticism
Reiss, T. J. A new time and the glory that was Egypt. *In* Reiss, T. J. Tragedy and truth p204-18

**English fiction**
African authors
*See* African fiction (English)

English fiction—*Continued*

**Indic authors**

*See* Indic fiction (English)

**Irish authors**—History and criticism

Cronin, J. Introduction. *In* Cronin, J. The Anglo-Irish novel, v 1 p7-18

**18th century**—History and criticism

Davis, L. J. A social history of fact and fiction: authorial disavowal in the early English novel. *In* Literature and society, ed. by E. W. Said p120-48

Hilliard, R. F. Desire and the structure of eighteenth-century fiction. *In* Studies in eighteenth-century culture v9 p357-70

Novak, M. E. The extended moment: time, dream, history, and perspective in eighteenth-century fiction. *In* Probability, time, and space in eighteenth-century literature, ed. by P. R. Backscheider p141-66

Todd, J. The biographical context. *In* Todd, J. Women's friendship in literature p359-402

Todd, J. The literary context. *In* Todd, J. Women's friendship in literature p305-58

**19th century**—History and criticism

Clarke, G. 'Bound in moss and cloth': reading a long Victorian novel. *In* Reading the Victorian novel: detail into form, ed. by I. Gregor p54-71

Henkle, R. B. Introduction. *In* Henkle, R. B. Comedy and culture p3-19

Irwin, M. Readings of melodrama. *In* Reading the Victorian novel: detail into form, ed. by I. Gregor p15-31

Polhemus, R. M. Introduction: worlds without end. *In* Polhemus, R. M. Comic faith p3-23

Stone, D. D. Introduction. *In* Stone, D. D. The romantic impulse in Victorian fiction p 1-45

**20th century**—History and criticism

Ceadel, M. Popular fiction and the next war, 1918-39. *In* Class, culture and social change, ed. by F. Gloversmith p161-84

Kellman, S. G. The self-begetting novel and the English tradition. *In* Kellman, S. G. The self-begetting novel p77-100

Snee, C. A. Working-class literature or proletarian writing? *In* Culture and crisis in Britain in the thirties, ed. by J. Clark and others p165-91

Widdowson, P. Between the acts? English fiction in the thirties. *In* Culture and crisis in Britain in the thirties, ed. by J. Clark and others p133-64

**English language**

Dillon, J. M. Antaeus and Hercules: some notes on the Irish predicament. *In* The State of the language, ed. by L. Michaels and C. Ricks p553-59

Donoghue, D. Radio talk. *In* The State of the language, ed. by L. Michaels and C. Ricks p539-52

Hudson, L. Language, truth, and psychology. *In* The State of the language, ed. by L. Michaels and C. Ricks p449-57

Karlinsky, S. "More piercing than a whistle": notes on English sounds in Russian ears. *In* The State of the language, ed. by L. Michaels and C. Ricks p532-38

Quirk, R. Sound barriers and Gangbangsprache. *In* The State of the language, ed. by L. Michaels and C. Ricks p3-14

**Dictionaries**—History and criticism

*See* English language—Lexicography

**Errors**

*See* English language—Idioms, corrections, errors

**Grammar**

Boyd, J. and Boyd, Z. Shall and will. *In* The State of the language, ed. by L. Michaels and C. Ricks p43-53

**Idioms, corrections, errors**

Simon, J. The corruption of English. *In* The State of the language, ed. by L. Michaels and C. Ricks p35-42

*See also* English language—Usage

**Lexicography**

Burchfield, R. W. Dictionaries and ethnic responsibilities. *In* The State of the language, ed. by L. Michaels and C. Ricks p15-23

**Liturgical use**

*See* Liturgical language—English

**Names**

*See* Names, English

**Rhetoric**

Sloane, T. O. Rhetoric, 'logic' and poetry: the formal cause. *In* The Age of Milton, ed. by C. A. Patrides and R. B. Waddington p307-37

**Sex differences**

Carter, A. The language of sisterhood. *In* The State of the language, ed. by L. Michaels and C. Ricks p226-34

**Slang**

McConville, S. Prison language. *In* The State of the language, ed. by L. Michaels and C. Ricks p524-31

**Social aspects**

*See* English language—Sex differences

**Study and teaching**—Foreign students

Miller, J. How do you spell Gujarati, sir? *In* The State of the language, ed. by L. Michaels and C. Ricks p140-51

**Terms and phrases**

Ricks, C. Clichés. *In* The State of the language, ed. by L. Michaels and C. Ricks p54-63

**Usage**

Amis, K. Getting it wrong. *In* The State of the language, ed. by L. Michaels and C. Ricks p24-33

**Vocabulary**

*See* Vocabulary

**English language in India**

Anand, M. R. Pigeon-Indian: some notes on Indian-English writing. *In* Aspects of Indian writing in English, ed. by M. K. Naik p24-44

Narayan, R. K. English in India: the process of transmutation. *In* Aspects of Indian writing in English, ed. by M. K. Naik p19-23

**English language in the United States**

**Dialects**

Hellerstein, K. Yiddish voices in American English. *In* The State of the language, ed. by L. Michaels and C. Ricks p182-201

**English language in the United States**—*Cont.*

### Dialects—California
Lodge, D. Where it's at: California language. *In* The State of the language, ed. by L. Michaels and C. Ricks p503-13

## English literature

### History and criticism
Hagstrum, J. H. Introduction. *In* Hagstrum, J. H. Sex and sensibility p 1-23

Trilling, L. The changing myth of the Jew. *In* Trilling, L. Speaking of literature and society p50-76

### Indic authors
*See* Indic literature (English)

### Study and teaching—United States
Trilling, L. Reflections on a lost cause: English literature and American education. *In* Trilling, L. Speaking of literature and society p343-60

### West Indian authors
*See* West Indian literature (English)

### To 1100
*See* Anglo-Saxon literature

### Middle English, 1100-1500—
History and criticism
Stiller, N. Eve's orphans: mothers and daughters in medieval English literature. *In* The Lost tradition: mothers and daughters in literature, ed. by C. N. Davidson and E. M. Broner p22-32

### Early modern, 1500-1700—
History and criticism
Kerrigan, W. The articulation of the ego in the English Renaissance. *In* The Literary Freud: mechanisms of defense and the poetic will, ed. by J. H. Smith p261-308

Mackenzie, E. The growth of plants: a seventeenth-century metaphor. *In* English Renaissance studies, ed. by J. Carey p194-211

Manley, L. G. "The separation of opinions": the role of convention in criticism and controversy. *In* Manley, L. G. Convention, 1500-1750 p188-202

O'Flaherty, P. 'It passeth England': literature of discovery and early settlement, 1497-1670. *In* O'Flaherty, P. The rock observed p3-15

Sloane, T. O. Rhetoric, 'logic' and poetry: the formal cause. *In* The Age of Milton, ed. by C. A. Patrides and R. B. Waddington p307-37

Sternfeld, F. W. Repetition and echo in Renaissance poetry and music. *In* English Renaissance studies, ed. by J. Carey p33-43

Travitsky, B. S. The new mother of the English Renaissance: her writings on motherhood. *In* The Lost tradition: mothers and daughters in literature, ed. by C. N. Davidson and E. M. Broner p33-43

### 18th century—History and criticism
Korshin, P. J. Probability and character in the eighteenth century. *In* Probability, time, and space in eighteenth-century literature, ed. by P. R. Backscheider p63-77

Krieger, M. "Trying experiments upon our sensibility": the art of dogma and doubt in eighteenth-century literature. *In* Krieger, M. Poetic presence and illusion p70-91

Selby, H. "Never finding full repast:" satire and self-extension in the early eighteenth century. *In* Probability, time, and space in eighteenth-century literature, ed. by P. R. Backscheider p217-47

Uphaus, R. W. Criticism and the idea of nature. *In* Uphaus, R. W. The impossible observer p137-42

### 19th century—History and criticism
Ashton, R. D. Introduction. *In* Ashton, R. D. The German idea p 1-26

Henkle, R. B. 1820-1845: the anxieties of sublimation, and middle-class myths. *In* Henkle, R. B. Comedy and culture p20-57

Henkle, R. B. Hood, Gilbert, Carroll, Jerrold, and the Grossmiths: comedy from inside. *In* Henkle, R. B. Comedy and culture p185-237

Stone, D. D. Trollope, Byron, and the conventionalities. *In* Stone, D. D. The romantic impulse in Victorian fiction p46-73

### 20th century—History and criticism
Bell, M. Introduction: modern movements in literature. *In* The Context of English literature, 1900-1930, ed. by M. Bell p 1-93

Gekoski, R. A. Freud and English literature, 1900-30. *In* The Context of English literature, 1900-30, ed. by M. Bell p186-217

**English mysteries and miracle-plays.** See Mysteries and miracle-plays, English

**English names.** See Names, English

## English newspapers
Curran, J., Douglas, A. and Whannel, G. The political economy of the human-interest story. *In* Newspapers and democracy, ed. by A. Smith p288-347

**English pastoral poetry.** See Pastoral poetry, English

## English periodicals

### Abstracting and indexing
McMullin, B. J. Indexing the periodical literature of Anglo-American bibliography. *In* Virginia. University. Bibliographical Society. Studies in bibliography v33 p 1-17

## English poetry
### African authors
*See* African poetry (English)

### History and criticism
Miles, J. Values in language; or, Where have goodness, truth, and beauty gone? *In* The State of the language, ed. by L. Michaels and C. Ricks p362-76

### Indic authors
*See* Indic poetry (English)

### To 1100
*See* Anglo-Saxon poetry

### Middle English, 1100-1500—
History and criticism
Kratzmann, G. Influences and perspectives. *In* Kratzmann, G. Anglo-Scottish literary relations, 1430-1550 p 1-32

Kratzmann, G. The two traditions. *In* Kratzmann, G. Anglo-Scottish literary relations, 1430-1550 p227-61

Robbins, R. H. The Middle English court love lyric. *In* The Interpretation of medieval lyric poetry, ed. by W. T. H. Jackson p205-32

**English poetry—Middle English, 1100-1500—**
History and criticism—*Continued*

Robbins, R. H. The structure of longer Middle English court poems. *In* Chaucerian problems and perspectives, ed. by E. Vasta and Z. P. Thundy p244-64

**Early modern, 1500-1700—History and criticism**

Ellrodt, R. Angels and the poetic imagination from Donne to Traherne. *In* English Renaissance studies, ed. by J. Carey p164-79

Manley, L. G. The artlessness of art: convention in Renaissance poetics. *In* Manley, L. G. Convention, 1500-1750 p175-88

Waddington, R. B. Milton among the Carolines. *In* The Age of Milton, ed. by C. A. Patrides and R. B. Waddington p338-64

**20th century—History and criticism**

Heinemann, M. Louis MacNeice, John Cornford and Clive Branson: three Left-wing poets. *In* Culture and crisis in Britain in the thirties, ed. by J. Clark and others p103-32

**English prose literature**

**Women authors—History and criticism**

Pomerleau, C. S. The emergence of women's autobiography in England. *In* Women's autobiography, ed. by E. C. Jelinek p 21-38

**English songs.** See Songs, English

**Enigmas.** See Riddles

**Enlightenment**

Berlin, Sir I. The counter--Enlightenment. *In* Berlin, Sir I. Against the current p 1-24

Berlin, Sir I. Vico and the ideal of the Enlightenment. *In* Berlin, Sir I. Against the current p120-29

*Also in* Conference on Vico and Contemporary Thought, New York, 1976, Vico and contemporary thought pt I p250-63

Gay, P. The Enlightenment as a communication universe. *In* Propaganda and communication in world history, ed. by H. D. Lasswell, D. Lerner and H. Speier v2 p85-111

*See also* Haskalah

**England**

Pocock, J. G. A. Post-Puritan England and the problem of the Enlightenment. *In* Culture and politics from Puritanism to the Enlightenment, ed. by P. Zagorin p91-111

**The entertainer (Motion picture)**

Kael, P. A bit of Archie Rice. *In* Kael, P. When the lights go down p148-52

**Entr'acte (Motion picture)**

Thiher, A. From Entr'acte to A nous la liberté: René Clair and the order of farce. *In* Thiher, A. The cinematic muse p64-77

**Entrepreneur**

Hughes, J. R. T. Entrepreneurship. *In* Encyclopedia of American economic history, ed. by G. Porter v 1 p214-28

**Entropy**

Morowitz, H. J. Entropy crisis. *In* Morowitz, H. J. The wine of life, and other essays on societies, energy & living things p48-51

Morowitz, H. J. Women's lib and the battle against entropy. *In* Morowitz, H. J. The wine of life, and other essays on societies, energy & living things p67-70

**Environment.** See Anthropo-geography; Nature and nurture

**Environment and state.** See Environmental policy

**Environment perception.** See Landscape assessment

**Environmental control.** See Environmental policy

**Environmental policy**

**United States**

Kneese, A. V. Environmental policy. *In* The United States in the 1980s, ed. by P. Duignan and A. Rabushka p253-83

Teece, D. J. The new social regulation: implications and alternatives. *In* The Economy in the 1980s: a program for growth and stability, ed. by M. J. Boskin p119-58

**United States—History**

Olmstead, A. L. The costs of economic growth. *In* Encyclopedia of American economic history v2 p863-81

**Environmental protection.** See Environmental policy

**Envy.** See Jealousy

**Epic poetry**

**History and criticism**

Hatto, A. T. Shamanism and epic poetry in northern Asia. *In* Hatto, A. T. Essays on medieval German and other poetry p117-38

Pickering, F. P. Historical thought and moral codes in medieval epic. *In* Pickering, F. P. Essays on medieval German literature and iconography p130-45

**Epicurus**

**About**

Taylor, C. C. W. 'All perceptions are true.' *In* Doubt and dogmatism, ed. by M. Schofield, M. Burnyeat and J. Barnes p105-24

**Epistemology.** See Knowledge, Theory of

**Epstein, Jean**

**About individual works**

*Fall of the House of Usher*

Thiher, A. The impressionist avant-garde. *In* Thiher, A. The cinematic muse p16-23

**Equal employment opportunity.** See Affirmative action programs

**Equal opportunity in employment.** See Affirmative action programs

**Equality**

Feher, F. and Heller, A. Forms of equality. *In* Symposium on Theories of Justice in and for the Second Half of the Twentieth Century, Sydney, 1977. Justice p149-71

Killian, L. M. The respect revolution: freedom and equality. *In* Propaganda and communication in world history, ed. by H. D. Lasswell, D. Lerner and H. Speier v3 p93-147

Miller, P. Equality in the American setting. *In* Miller, P. The responsibility of mind in a civilization of machines p142-60

Norton, D. L. Equality and excellence in the democratic ideal. *In* History, religion, and spiritual democracy, ed. by M. Wohlgelernter and others p273-93

*See also* Democracy; Social justice

**Equality before the law**

Stone, J. Justice not equality. *In* Symposium on Theories of Justice in and for the Second Half of the Twentieth Century, Sydney, 1977. Justice p97-115

Equestrian drama and the circus. Coxe, A. D. H. *In* Performance and politics in popular drama, ed. by D. Bradby, L. James and B. Sharratt p109-18

**Equilibrium (Economics)**
Keran, M. W. How the domestic business cycle is affected by the rest of the world. *In* Economic issues of the eighties, ed. by N. M. Kamrany and R. H. Day p58-68

**Equus (Motion picture)**
Kael, P. The lower trash/the higher trash. *In* Kael, P. When the lights go down p333-39

**Erasmus, Desiderius**

### Theology

Ozment, S. H. Humanism and the Reformation. *In* Ozment, S. H. The age of reform, 1250-1550 p290-317

**Erickson, Gerald**
Possession, sex and hysteria: the growth of demonism in later antiquity. *In* 5000 years of popular culture, ed. by F. E. H. Schroeder p110-35

**Erikson, Erik Homburger**
Themes of adulthood in the Freud-Jung correspondence. *In* Themes of work and love in adulthood, ed. by N. J. Smelser and E. H. Erikson p43-74

### About individual works

*Young man Luther*

Ozment, S. H. The mental world of Martin Luther. *In* Ozment, S. H. The age of reform, 1250-1550 p223-44

**Erotic literature.** See Love in literature; Sex in literature

**Errors, Popular.** See Medical delusions

**Errors, Scientific**
Medawar, Sir P. B. A bouquet of fallacies from medicine and medical science with a sideways glance at mathematics and logic. *In* Lying truths, ed. by R. Runcan and M. Weston-Smith p97-105

**Erskine, Ralph, 1914-**

### About

Egelius, M. Housing and human needs: the work of Ralph Erskine (with original sketches by Ralph Erskine). *In* Architecture for people, ed. by B. Mikellides p134-48

**Escape from Alcatraz (Motion picture)**
Kauffmann, S. Escape from Alcatraz. *In* Kauffmann, S. Before my eyes p240-42

**Eschatology.** See Time (Theology)

**Eschatology, Jewish.** See Messianic era (Judaism)

**Espina, Concha.** See Espina de Serna, Concha

**Espina de Serna, Concha**

### About individual works

*La esfinge maragata*

Fox-Lockert, L. Concha Espina. *In* Fox-Lockert, L. Women novelists in Spain and Spanish America p66-72

**Essence (Philosophy)**
Wiggins, D. Ayer on monism, pluralism and essence. *In* Perception and identity, ed. by G. F. Macdonald p131-60

**Esthetics.** See Aesthetics

**Estrangement (Philosophy).** See Alienation (Philosophy)

**Estrangement (Social psychology).** See Alienation (Social psychology)

**Estupiñán Bass, Nelson**
Jackson, R. L. Literary blackness and Third Worldism in recentt Ecuadorian fiction: the novels of Nelson Estupiñán Bass. *In* Jackson, R. L. Black writers in Latin America p153-59

**Étaples, Jacques, Le Fèvre d'.** See Le Fèvre, Jacques, d'Étaples

**Etherton, Michael**
Trends in African theatre. *In* African literature today no. 10: Retrospect and prospect, ed. by E. D. Jones p57-85

**Ethical education.** See Moral education

**Ethical relativism**
Radest, H. B. Relativism and responsibility. *In* Humanist ethics, ed. by M. B. Storer p228-41

**Ethics**
Blackstone, W. T. The search for an environmental ethic. *In* Matters of life and death, ed. by T. Regan p299-335

Durkheim, E. Introduction to morality. *In* Durkheim, E. Emile Durkheim on institutional analysis p191-202

Kohl, M. On suffering. *In* Humanist ethics, ed. by M. B. Storer p173-78

Manley, L. G. A world on wheels: convention in sixteenth-century moral philosophy. *In* Manley, L. G. Convention, 1500-1750 p106-36

Neilsen, K. Morality and the human situation. *In* Humanist ethics, ed. by M. B. Storer p58-74

Parsons, K. J. P. Moral revolution. *In* The Prism of sex, ed. by J. A. Sherman and E. T. Beck p189-227

Phillipson, N. T. Hume as moralist: a social historian's perspective. *In* Royal Institute of Philosophy. Philosophers of the Enlightenment p140-61

Regan, T. Introduction. *In* Matters of life and death, ed. by T. Regan p3-27

Schneider, H. W. Morality as an art. *In* Humanist ethics, ed. by M. B. Storer p98-103

White, N. P. The basis of Stoic ethics. *In* Harvard Studies in classical philology, v83 p143-78

*See also* Animals, Treatment of; Conduct of life; Ethical relativism; God—Proof, Moral; Humanistic ethics; Justice; Political ethics; Pride and vanity; Responsibility; Self-sacrifice; Social ethics; Spirituality; Suicide; Sympathy

**Ethics, Humanistic.** See Humanistic ethics

**Ethics, Jewish.** See Sin (Judaism)

**Ethics, Political.** See Political ethics

**Ethics, Sexual.** See Sexual ethics

**Ethics, Social.** See Social ethics

**Ethics and science.** See Science and ethics

**Ethiopia**

### Politics and government

Ottaway, M. The theory and practice of Marxism-Leninism in Mozambique and Ethiopia. *In* Communism in Africa, ed. by D. E. Albright p118-44

**Ethnic attitudes in literature**
Marx, P. Hemingway and ethics. *In* Seasoned authors for a new season: the search for standards in popular writing, ed. by L. Filler p43-50

**Ethnic relations.** See subdivision under names of regions, countries, cities, etc. e.g. Africa—Ethnic relations

**Ethnicity.** See Pluralism (Social sciences)

**Ethnocentrism**

Isaacs, H. R. Changing arenas and identities in world affairs. *In* Propaganda and communication in world history, ed. by H. D. Lasswell, D. Lerner and H. Speier v2 p395-423

Merton, R. K. Insiders and outsiders: an essay in the sociology of knowledge. *In* Value and values in evolution, ed. by E. A. Maziarz p47-69

**Ethnography.** See Ethnology

**Ethnologists**

Arens, W. Taxonomy versus dynamics revisited: the interpretation of misfortune in a polyethnic community. *In* Explorations in African systems of thought, ed. by I. C. Karp & C. S. Bird p165-80

**Ethnology**

Altman, I. Privacy as an interpersonal boundary process. *In* Human ethology, ed. by M. von Cranach [and others] p95-132

Arutiunov, S. Ethnography and linguistics. *In* Soviet and Western anthropology, ed. by E. Gellner p257-63

Godelier, M. Territory and property in primitive society. *In* Human ethology, ed. by M. von Cranach [and others] p133-55

Harbison, R. Tribe and race. *In* Harbison, R. Deliberate regression p180-205

Kozlov, V. I. Ethnography and demography. *In* Soviet and Western anthropology, ed. by E. Gellner p265-74

Le Goff, J. The historian and the ordinary man. *In* Le Goff, J. Time, work, & culture in the Middle Ages p225-36

Woodburn, J. Hunters and gatherers today and reconstruction of the past. *In* Soviet and Western anthropology, ed. by E. Gellner p95-117

*See also* Cultural relativism; Ethnopsychology; Structural anthropology

**Methodology**

Fernandez, J. W. Edification by puzzlement. *In* Explorations in African systems of thought, ed. by I. C. Karp & C. S. Bird p44-49

**Africa**

MacGaffey, W. African religions: types and generalizations. *In* Explorations in African systems of thought, ed. by I. C. Karp & C. S. Bird p301-28

**Africa, West**

Hay, R. and Paden, J. N. A culture cluster analysis of six West African states. *In* Values, identities, and national integration, ed. by J. N. Paden p25-40

**Brazil**

Gross, D. R. A new approach to central Brazilian social organization. *In* Brazil, anthropological perspectives, ed. by M. L. Margolis and W. E. Carter p321-42

**Cameroon**

Kofele-Kale, N. The impact of environment on ethnic group values in Cameroon. *In* Values, identities, and national integration, ed. by J. N. Paden p121-50

Nwabuzor, E. J. O. Ethnic propensities for collaboration in Cameroon. *In* Values, identities, and national integration, ed. by J. N. Paden p231-58

Nwabuzor, E. J. O. Ethnic value distance in Cameroon. *In* Values, identities, and national integration, ed. by J. N. Paden p205-29

**Ghana**

Kaufert, J. M. Ethnic unit definition in Ghana: a comparison of culture cluster analysis and social distance measures. *In* Values, identities, and national integration, ed. by J. N. Paden p41-51

Kaufert, J. M. Situational ethnic identity in Ghana: a survey of university students. *In* Values, identities, and national integration, ed. by J. N. Paden p53-74

**Kenya**

Laughlin, T. Environment, political culture, and national orientations: a comparison of settled and pastoral Masai. *In* Values, identities, and national integration, ed. by J. N. Paden p91-103

**Kenya—Mombasa**

Edari, R. S. Social distance and social change among four ethnic groups in Mombasa. *In* Values, identities, and national integration, ed. by J. N. Paden p197-203

**Mozambique**

*See* Thonga tribe

**Nigeria**

Vaughan, J. H. A reconsideration of divine kingship. *In* Explorations in African systems of thought, ed. by I. C. Karp & C. S. Bird p120-42

**Russia**

Basilov, V. The study of religions in Soviet ethnography. *In* Soviet and Western anthropology, ed. by E. Gellner p231-42

Bromlei, I. V. The object and the subject-matter of ethnography. *In* Soviet and Western anthropology, ed. by E. Gellner p151-60

Drobizheva, L. Ethnic sociology of present-day life. *In* Soviet and Western anthropology, ed. by E. Gellner p171-80

Fortes, M. Introduction. *In* Soviet and Western anthropology, ed. by E. Gellner p xix-xxv

Pershits, A. I. Ethnographic reconstruction of the history of primitive society. *In* Soviet and Western anthropology, ed. by E. Gellner p85-94

Petrova-Averkieva, Y. Historicism in Soviet ethnographic science. *In* Soviet and Western anthropology, ed. by E. Gellner p19-27

**South Africa**

*See* Thonga tribe

**Tanganyika**

*See* Kaguru (Bantu tribe); Suku (African tribe)

**Tanzania**

Arens, W. Taxonomy versus dynamics revisited: the interpretation of misfortune in a polyethnic community. *In* Explorations in Africans systems of thought, ed. by I. C. Karp & C. S. Bird p165-80

**United States**

*See* Norwegian Americans

**Zaire**

*See* Bashi (African people)

**Ethnopsychology**

Fernandez, J. W. Edification by puzzlement. *In* Explorations in African systems of thought, ed. by I. C. Karp & C. S. Bird p44-49

Fortes, M. Anthropology and the psychological disciplines. *In* Soviet and Western anthropology, ed. by E. Gellner p195-215

**Ethnopsychology**—*Continued*

Kon, I. S. Ethnography and psychology. *In* Soviet and Western anthropology, ed. by E. Gellner p217-27

*See also* Ethnocentrism

**Ethology.** See Human behavior

**Ettinger, Samuel**

The Jews and the Enlightenment. *In* The Jewish world, ed. by E. Kedourie p224-31

**Eubanks, Cecil Lenard**

Walker Percy: eschatology and the politics of grace. *In* Walker Percy: art and ethics, ed. by J. Tharpe p121-36

**Eugenics.** See Heredity, Human

**Euripides**

### About

Knox, B. M. W. Euripidean comedy. *In* Knox, B. M. W. Word and action p250-74

Knox, B. M. W. Review of Catastrophe survived (by Anne Pippin Burnett). *In* Knox, B. M. W. Word and action p329-42

Knox, B. M. W. Review of Euripidean drama (by D. J. Conacher). *In* Knox, B. M. W. Word and action p323-28

### About individual works

#### Alcestis

Scodel, R. ΑΔΜΗΤΟΥ ΛΟΓΟΣ and the Alcestis. *In* Harvard Studies in classical philology, v83 p51-62

#### The Bacchae (tr. by Wole Soyinka)

Knox, B. M. W. Review of The Oresteia (tr. by Robert Fagles) and The Bacchae of Euripides, a communion rite (by Wole Soyinka). *In* Knox, B. M. W. Word and action p64-69

#### Hippolytus

Knox, B. M. W. The Hippolytus of Euripides. *In* Knox, B. M. W. Word and action p205-30

#### Iphigenia in Aulide

Knox, B. M. W. Euripides' Iphigenia in Aulide 1-163 (in that order). *In* Knox, B. M. W. Word and action p275-94

Knox, B. M. W. Review of Euripides: Iphigeneia at Aulis (tr. by W. S. Merwin and George E. Dimock, Jr.) and Iphigenia (directed by Michael Cacoyannis). *In* Knox, B. M. W. Word and action p343-54

#### Medea

Knox, B. M. W. The Medea of Euripides. *In* Knox, B. M. W. Word and action p295-322

### Film adaptations

Knox, B. M. W. Review of Euripides: Iphigeneia at Aulis(tr.by W. S. Merwin and George E. Dimock, Jr.) and Iphigenia (directed by Michael Cacoyannis). *In* Knox, B. M. W. Word and action p343-54

**Europe**

### Antiquities

Piggott, S. Early towns in Europe? *In* The Origins of civilization, ed. by P. S. R. Moorey p34-53

### Civilization

Piggott, E. Early towns in Europe? *In* The Origins of civilization, ed. by P. S. R. Moorey p34-53

### Defenses

Burt, R. R. Washington and the Atlantic alliance: the hidden crisis. *In* National security in the 1980s: from weakness to strength, ed. by W. S. Thompson p109-21

### Economic conditions—History

Davis, R. The European background. *In* Encyclopedia of American economic history, ed. by G. Porter v 1 p19-33

### Foreign relations—United States

Grosser, A. Western Europe. *In* The United States in the 1980s, ed. by P. Duignan and A. Rabushka p707-34

### Historiography

Bouwsma, W. J. Early modern Europe. *In* The Past before us, ed. by M. Kammen p78-94

McNeill, W. H. Modern European history. *In* The Past before us, ed. by M. Kammen p95-112

Schulenburg, J. A. T. Clio's European daughters: myopic modes of perception. *In* The Prism of sex, ed. by J. A. Sherman and E. T. Beck p33-53

### Industries

Kurth, J. R. Industrial change and political change: a European perspective. *In* The New authoritarianism in Latin America, ed. by D. Collier p319-62

### Intellectual life

Miller, P. Europe's faith in American fiction. *In* Miller, P. The responsibility of mind in a civilization of machines p122-33

Miller, P. What drove me crazy in Europe. *In* Miller, P. The responsibility of mind in a civilization of machines p98-109

### Occupations

Le Goff, J. Labor, techniques, and craftsmen in the value systems of the early Middle Ages (fifth to tenth centuries). *In* Le Goff, J. Time, work, & culture in the Middle Ages p71-86

Le Goff, J. Licit and illicit trades in the medieval West. *In* Le Goff, J. Time, work, & culture in the Middle Ages p58-70

### Politics and government

Kurth, J. R. Industrial change and political change: a European perspective. *In* The New authoritarianism in Latin America, ed. by D. Collier p319-62

Merkl, P. H. The sociology of European parties: members, voters, and social groups. *In* Western European party systems, ed. by P. Merkl p614-67

### Politics and government—476-1492

Ozment, S. H. On the eve of the Reformation. *In* Ozment, S. H. The age of reform. 1250-1550 p182-222

### Politics and government—1945-

Scase, R. Introduction. *In* The State in Western Europe, ed. by Richard Scase p11-22

### Religious life and customs

Boglioni, P. Some methodological reflections of the study of medieval popular religion. *In* 5000 years of popular culture, ed. by F. E. H. Schroeder p192-200

### Social conditions

Merkl, P. H. The sociology of European parties: members, voters, and social groups. *In* Western European party systems, ed. by P. Merkl p614-67

Tilly, C. Did the cake of custom break? *In* Consciousness and class experience in nineteenth-century Europe, ed. by J. M. Merriman p17-44

**Europe**—*Continued*

### Social conditions—History

Braudel, F. On a concept of social history. *In* Braudel, F. On history p120-31

### Europe, Eastern

#### Foreign relations—Russia

Kanet, R. E. and Robertson, J. D. The Soviet Union and Eastern Europe. *In* The Soviet Union since Stalin, ed. by S. F. Cohen, A. Rabinowitch, and R. Sharlet p312-23

### European Communities

Ward, Z. A. Pan-European parties: proselytes of the European Community. *In* Western European party systems, ed. by P. H. Merkl p552-75

### European drama

#### Renaissance, 1450-1600—History and criticism

Mueller, M. Humanist tragedy as the mediator between ancient and modern tragedy. *In* Mueller, M. Children of Oedipus, and other essays on the imitation of Greek tragedy 1550-1800 p3-17

Reiss, T. J. Buchanan, Montaigne, and the difficulty of speaking. *In* Reiss, T. J. Tragedy and truth p40-77

#### 19th century—History and criticism

Bennett, B. Breakthrough in theory: the philosophical background of modern drama. *In* Bennett, B. Modern drama and German classicism p229-81

#### 20th century—History and criticism

Bennett, B. The assault upon the audience: types of modern drama. *In* Bennett, B. Modern drama and German classicism p282-314

Bennett, B. Breakthrough in theory: the philosophical background of modern drama. *In* Bennett, B. Modern drama and German classicism p229-81

### European drama (Tragedy)

#### Greek influences

Mueller, M. Humanist tragedy as the mediator between ancient and modern tragedy. *In* Mueller, M. Children of Oedipus, and other essays on the imitation of Greek tragedy 1550-1800 p3-17

### European literature

#### Medieval, 500-1500

*See* Literature, Medieval

### European Parliament

Ward, Z. A. Pan-European parties: proselytes of the European Community. *In* Western European party systems, ed. by P. H. Merkl p552-75

### European poetry

#### Medieval, 500-1500

*See* Poetry, Medieval

### European War, 1914-1918

#### Food question

Cuff, R. D. Herbert Hoover, the ideology of voluntarism and war organization during the Great War. *In* Herbert Hoover, ed. by L. E. Gelfand p21-39

Rothbard, M. N. Hoover's 1919 food diplomacy in retrospect. *In* Herbert Hoover, ed. by L. E. Gelfand p87-110

#### Literature and the war

Boeschenstein, H. The First World War in German prose after 1945: some samples—some observations. *In* The First World War in German narrative prose, ed. by C. N. Genno and H. Wetzel p138-58

Butler, C. Mr Britling sees it through: a view from the other side. *In* The First World War in German narrative prose, ed. by C. N. Genno and H. Wetzel p118-37

Dierick, A. P. Two representative expressionist responses to the challenge of the First World War: Carl Sternheim's eigene Nuance and Leonhard Frank's utopia. *In* The First World War in German narrative prose, ed. by C. N. Genno and H. Wetzel p16-33

Genno, C. N . The anatomy of pre-war society in Robert Musil's Der Mann ohne Eigenschaften. *In* The First World War in German narrative prose, ed. by C. N. Genno and H. Wetzel p3-15

John, D. The Sperber in Hesse's Demian. *In* The First World War in German narrative prose, ed. by C. N. Genno and H. Wetzel p34-49

Riley, A. W. The aftermath of the First World War: Christianity and revolution in Alfred Döblin's November 1918. *In* The First World War in German narrative prose, ed. by C. N. Genno and H. Wetzel p93-117

Wetzel, H. War and the destruction of moral principles in Arnold Zweig's Der Streit un den Sergeanten Grischa and Erziehung vor Verdun. *In* The First World War in German narrative prose, ed. by C. N. Genno and H. Wetzel p50-70

#### Reconstruction

*See* Reconstruction (1914-1939)

#### Supplies

*See* European War, 1914-1918—Food question

#### Treaties

*See* Versailles, Treaty of, June 28, 1919 (Germany)

#### Women

Steinson, B. J. "The mother half of humanity": American women in the peace and preparedness movements in World War I. *In* Women, war, and revolution, ed. C. R. Berkin and C. M. Lovett p259-84

#### Great Britain

Nicolson, C. Edwardian England and the coming of the First World War. *In* The Edwardian age: conflict and stability, ed. by A. O'Day p144-68

**Euthanasia**

Rachels, J. Euthanasia. *In* Matters of life and death, ed. by T. Regan p28-66

*See also* Right to die

**Evaluation of literature.** See Criticism

**Evangelicalism**

#### Southern States

Mathews, D. G. Religion and slavery—the case of the American South. *In* Anti-slavery, religion, and reform: essays in memory of Roger Anstey, ed. by C. Bolt and S. Drescher p207-32

**Evangelistic work.** See Communication (Theology)

**Evans, Bob Overton**

Computers and communications. *In* The Computer age: a twenty-year view, ed. by M. L. Dertouzos and J. Moses p338-66

**Evans, Charles**

### About individual works
*American bibliography*

Shipton, C. K. Bibliotheca Americana. *In* The Bibliographical Society of America, 1904-79 p470-78

**Evans, Clifford.** See Meggers, B. J. jt. auth.

**Evans, Eli N.**
Southern-Jewish history alive and unfolding. *In* Conference on Southern Jewish History, Richmond, Va. 1976. "Turn to the South" p158-67

**Evans, J. Martin**
Lycidas, Daphnis, and Gallus. *In* English Renaissance studies, ed. by J. Carey p228-44

**Evans, Mary Ann.** See Eliot, George, pseud.

**Evans, R. Wallis**
Prophetic poetry. *In* A Guide to Welsh literature, ed. by A. O. H. Jarman and G. R. Hughes v2 p278-96

**Everett, Barbara**
The end of the big names: Milton's epic catalogues. *In* English Renaissance studies, ed. by J. Carey p254-70

**Eversole, Richard Langley**
Collins and the end of the shepherd pastoral. *In* Survivals of pastoral, ed. by R. F. Hardin p19-32

**Everson v. Board of Education of Ewing Township.** *In* Moynihan, D. P. Counting our blessings p162-90

**Every man for himself and God against all (Motion picture)**
Kauffmann, S. Every man for himself and God against all. *In* Kauffmann, S. Before my eyes p169-71

**Evidence**
Barnes, J. Proof destroyed. *In* Doubt and dogmatism, ed. by M. Schofield, M. Burnyeat and J. Barnes p161-81

Brunschwig, J. Proof defined. *In* Doubt and dogmatism, ed. by M. Schofield, M. Burnyeat and J. Barnes p125-60

**Evil eye**
Dundes, A. Wet and dry, the evil eye: an essay in Indo-European and Semitic world-view. *In* Dundes, A. Interpreting folklore p93-133

**Evolution**
Morowitz, H. J. The crazy, hairy, naked ape. *In* Morowitz, H. J. The wine of life, and other essays on societies, energy & living things p155-58

*See also* Natural selection

**Ewbank, Inga-Stina**
'My name is Marina': the language of recognition. *In* Shakespeare's styles, ed. by P. Edwards; I. S. Ewbank, and G. K. Hunter p111-30

**Exchange theory (Sociology)**
Maguire, J. D. Contract, coercion, and consciousness. *In* Rational action, ed. by R. Harrison p157-73

*See also* Social interaction

**Exchanges, Commodity.** See Commodity exchanges

**Exchanges, Stock.** See Stock-exchange

**Executive power**
### United States
Moynihan, D. P. The iron law of emulation. *In* Moynihan, D. P. Counting our blessings p115-37

Weiner, S. L. and Wildavsky, A. B. The prophylactic Presidency. *In* The Third century, ed. by S. M. Lipset p133-52

**Existential psychology**
Frankl, V. E. Meaninglessness: a challenge to psychiatry. *In* Value and values in evolution, ed. by E. A. Maziarz p71-91

**Existentialism**
Lentricchia, F. Versions of existentialism. *In* Lentricchia, F. After the New Criticism p28-60

*See also* Existential psychology

**Exodus (Anglo-Saxon poem)**
Hill, T. D. The virga of Moses and the Old English Exodus. *In* Old English literature in context, ed. by J. D. Niles p57-65

**Expansion (United States politics)** See Imperialism

**Expectation (Psychology)**
Spengler, J. J. Rising expectations: frustrations. *In* Propaganda and communication in world history, ed. by H. D. Lasswell, D. Lerner and H. Speier v3 p37-92

**Expeditions, Scientific.** See Scientific expeditions

**Expenditures, Public.** See Budget

**Experience**
Crook, S. and Taylor, L. Goffman's version of reality. *In* The View from Goffman, ed. by J. Ditton p233-51

Daly, G. Friedrich von Hügel: experience and transcendence. *In* Daly, G. Transcendence and immanence p117-39

**Experience (Religion) and hallucinogenic drugs.** *See* Hallucinogenic drugs and religious experience

**Experimental animals.** See Laboratory animals

**Experimental farms.** See Agricultural experiment stations

**Experimental theater**
### Czechoslovakia
Goetz-Stankiewicz, M. Responses: East and West. *In* Goetz-Stankiewicz, M. The silenced theatre: Czech playwrights without a stage p17-42

**Explorers**
Goetzmann, W. H. Paradigm lost. *In* The Sciences in the American context: new perspectives, ed. by N. Reingold p21-34

**Exports.** See Tariff

**Expression**
Goffman, E. Response cries. *In* Human ethology, ed. by M. von Cranach [and others] p203-40

*See also* Facial expression

**Extermination, Jewish (1939-1945)** See Holocaust, Jewish (1939-1945)

**Extinct animals.** See Paleontology

**Extinct languages.** See Writing

**Eye (in religion, folk-lore, etc.)** See Evil eye

**Ezekiel, Nissim**
### About
Walsh, W. Small observations on a large subject. *In* Aspects of Indian writing in English, ed. by M. K. Naik p101-19

# F

**F is for fake (Motion picture)**
Kauffmann, S. F is for fake. *In* Kauff-mann, S. Before my eyes p282-84

**FRELIMO.** See Liberation Front of Mozambique

**Fabian, Ilona Szombati-** See Szombati-Fabian, Ilona

**Fabian, Johannes, and Szombati-Fabian, Ilona**
Folk art from an anthropological perspective. *In* Perspectives on American folk art, ed. by I. M. G. Quimby and S. T. Swank p247-92

**Fabian Society, London**
Skidelsky, R. J. A. The Fabian ethic. *In* The Genius of Shaw, ed. by M. Holroyd p113-28

**Fables**
Bloomfield, M. W. The wisdom of The nun's priest's tale. *In* Chaucerian problems and perspectives, ed. by E. Vasta and Z. P. Thundy p70-82
*See also* Parables

**Fabre, Michel Henry**
Samuel Selvon. *In* West Indian literature, ed. by B. King p111-25

**Face**

### Expression

*See* Facial expression

**Face to face (Motion picture)**
Kauffmann, S. Face to face. *In* Kauffmann, S. Before my eyes p73-76

**Facial expression**
Ekman, P. About brows: emotional and conversational signals. *In* Human ethology, ed. by M. von Cranach [and others] p169-202

**Factories**

### Design and construction

Frampton, K. The disappearing factory: the Volvo experiment at Kalmar. *In* Architecture for people, ed. by B. Mikellides p149-61

**Factory construction.** See Factories—Design and construction

**Factory design.** See Factories—Design and construction

**Factory laws and legislation.** See Industrial safety—Law and legislation

**Fadeev, Aleksandr Aleksandrovich**

### About individual works

#### The nineteen

Trilling, L. The social emotions. *In* Trilling, L. Speaking of literature and society p34-36

**Fadeyev, A.** See Fadeev, Aleksandr Aleksandrovich

**Fairness.** See Justice

**Fairy tales**
Cook, A. S. Parable. *In* Cook, A. S. Myth & language p234-47

**Faith.** See Faith and reason

**Faith and reason**
Hudson, W. D. The rational system of beliefs. *In* Sociology and theology: alliance and conflict, ed. by D. Martin; J. O. Mills [and] W. S. F. Pickering p80-101

**Faith in literature**
Rosenthal, B. Herman Melville's Wandering Jews. *In* Puritan influences in American literature, ed. by E. Elliott p167-92

**Fajardo, Salvador Jiménez-** See Jiménez-Fajardo, Salvador

**Falcoff, Mark**
Latin America. *In* The United States in the 1980s, ed. by P. Duignan and A. Rabushka p797-826

**Falconry in literature**
Hatto, A. T. Poetry and the hunt in medieval Germany. *In* Hatto, A. T. Essays on medieval German and other poetry p298-322

**Falk, Richard Anderson**
Militarisation and human rights in the Third World. *In* Problems of contemporary militarism, ed. by A. Eide and M. Thee p207-25

**Fall of man**
Werblowsky, R. J. Z. O felix culpa: a cabbalistic version. *In* Studies in Jewish religious and intellectual history, ed. by S. Stein and R. Loewe p355-62

**Fall of the House of Usher (Motion picture)**
Thiher, A. The impressionist avant-garde. *In* Thiher, A. The cinematic muse p16-23

**Fallacies (Logic)**
Medawar, Sir P. B. A bouquet of fallacies from medicine and medical science with a sideways glance at mathematics and logic. *In* Lying truths, ed. by R. Duncan and M. Weston-Smith p97-105

**Falvey, John**
Women and sexuality in the thought of La Mettrie. *In* Woman and society in eighteenth-century France, ed. by E. Jacobs [and others] p55-68

**Fame in literature**
Robertson, D. W. The idea of fame in Chrétien's Cligés. *In* Robertson, D. W. Essays in medieval culture p183-201

**Families, Afro-American.** See Afro-American families

**Family**
Durkheim, E. The conjugal family. *In* Durkheim, E. Emile Durkheim on institutional analysis p229-39

Durkheim, E. Introduction to the sociology of the family. *In* Durkheim, E. Emile Durkheim on institutional analysis p205-28
*See also* Marriage; Parent and child

### Historiography

Degler, C. N. Women and the family. *In* The Past before us, ed. by M. Kammen p308-26

### Brazil

Miller, C. I. The function of middle-class extended family networks in Brazilian urban society. *In* Brazil, anthropological perspectives, ed. by M. L. Margolis and W. E. Carter p305-16

### Russia

Juviler, P. H. The Soviet family in post-Stalin perspective. *In* The Soviet Union since Stalin, ed. by S. F. Cohen, A. Rabinowitch and R. Sharlet p227-51

### Southern States

King, R. H. The Southern family romance and its context. *In* King, R. H. A Southern Renaissance p20-38

### United States

Easton, B. Feminism and contemporary family. *In* A Heritage of her own, ed. by N. F. Cott and E. H. Pleck p555-77
*See also* Afro-American families

Family—*Continued*

### United States—Case studies

Smith, J. E. Our own kind: family and community networks in Providence. *In* A Heritage of her own, ed. by N. F. Cott and E. H. Pleck p393-411

### United States—History

Cott, N. F. Eighteenth-century family and social life revealed in Massachusetts divorce records. *In* A Heritage of her own, ed. by N. F. Cott and E. H. Pleck p107-35

Smith, D. B. Family. *In* Encyclopedia of American economic history, ed. by G. Porter v3 p974-87

Smith, D. S. Family limitation, sexual control, and domestic feminism in Victorian America. *In* A Heritage of her own, ed. by N. F. Cott and E. H. Pleck p222-45

**Family histories.** See Southern States—Genealogy

**Family in literature**

Barber, C. L. The family in Shakespeare's development: tragedy and sacredness. *In* Representing Shakespeare, ed. by M. M. Schwartz and C. Kahn p188-202

Kahn, C. The providential tempest and the Shakespearean family. *In* Representing Shakespeare, ed. by M. M. Schwartz, and C. Kahn p217-43

Wilson, R. N. Arthur Miller: the salesman and society. *In* Wilson, R. N. The writer as social seer p56-71

Wilson, R. N. Eugene O'Neill: the web of family. *In* Wilson, R. N. The writer as social seer p72-88

**Family planning.** See Birth control

**Family plot (Motion picture)**

Kauffman, S. Family plot. *In* Kauffman, S. Before my eyes p209-10

**Fanaticism**

Barbu, Z. The modern history of political fanaticism: a search for the roots. *In* Propaganda and communication in world history, ed. by H. D. Lasswell, D. Lerner and H. Speier v2 p112-44

Harrison, B. J. Kant and the sincere fanatic. *In* Royal Institute of Philosophy. Philosophers of the Enlightenment p226-61

**Fantasy in literature**

Alazraki, J. Neofantastic literature—a structuralist answer. *In* The Analysis of literary texts, ed. by R. D. Pope p286-90

**Fantes.** See Fantis

**Fantis**

Ross, D. H. Cement lions and cloth elephants: popular arts of the Fante Asafo. *In* 5000 years of popular culture, ed. by F. E. H. Schroeder p290-317

**Faragher, Johnny, and Stansell, Christine**

Women and their families on the Overland Trail to California and Oregon, 1842-1867. *In* A Heritage of her own, ed. by N. F. Cott and E. H. Pleck p246-67

**Farge, Arlette**

Work-related diseases of artisans in eighteenth-century France. *In* Medicine and society in France, ed. by R. Forster and O. Ranum p89-103

**Farigoule, Louis.** See Romains, Jules

**Farmer, Penelope**

#### About

Rees, D. The marble in the water: Penelope Farmer. *In* Rees, D. The marble in the water p 1-13

**Farmers' organizations.** See Agricultural societies

**Farming.** See Agriculture

**Farms, Experimental.** See Experimental farms

**Farnsworth, Beatrice Brodsky**

Communist feminism: its synthesis and demise. *In* Women, war, and revolution, ed. by E. Jacobs and others p145-63

**Farrell, John P.**

Revolution in tragedy

*Contents*

Arnold: tragic vision and the third host
Byron: rebellion and revolution
Carlye: the true man's tragedy
Revolution as tragedy: being at the center
Scott: the implicit note of tragedy
Tragedy and ideology

**Farrington, David P.**

Longitudinal research on crime and delinquency. *In* Crime and justice v 1 p289-348

**Fassbinder, Rainer Werner**

#### About individual works

*The bitter tears of Petra von Kant*

Kauffmann, S. The bitter tears of Petra von Kant. *In* Kauffmann, S. Before my eyes p216-18

*Effi Briest*

Kauffmann, S. Effi Briest. *In* Kauffmann, S. Before my eyes p222-25

**Fathers**

Isaacs, H. R. Bringing up the father question. *In* Generations, ed. by S. R. Graubard p189-203

**Fathers and sons in literature**

Wyatt, D. Faulkner and the burdens of the past. *In* Wyatt, D. Prodigal sons p72-100

**Fathers in literature**

Sundelson, O. So rare a wonder'd father: Prospero's Tempest. *In* Representing Shakespeare, ed. by M. M. Schwartz and C. Kahn p33-53

Tennenhouse, L. The counterfeit order of The merchant of Venice. *In* Representing Shakespeare. ed. by M. M. Schwartz and C. Kahn p54-69

**Faulkner, William**

#### About

King, R. H. Repetition and despairing monumentalism: William Faulkner and Will Percy. *In* King, R. H. A Southern Renaissance p77-98

Wagner, L. W. The poetry in American fiction. *In* Wagner, L. W. American modern p18-30

Wyatt, D. Faulkner and the burdens of the past. *In* Wyatt, D. Prodigal sons p72-100

#### About individual works

*Absalom, Absalom!*

Ross, S. M. Faulkner's Absalom, Absalom! and the David story: a speculative contemplation. *In* The David myth in Western literature, ed. by R. J. Frontain and J. Wojcik p136-53

*As I lay dying*

Robinson, F. M. Faulkner: As I lay dying. *In* Robinson, F. M. The comedy of language p51-88

*L'apres-midi d'un faune*

Hamblin, R. W. and Brodsky, L. D. Faulkner's "L'apres-midi d'un faune": the evolution of a poem. *In* Virginia. University. Bibliographical Society. Studies in bibliography v33 p254-63

**Faulkner, William**—About individual works
—*Continued*

*Go down, Moses*

King, R. H. Working through: Faulkner's Go down Moses. *In* King, R. H. A Southern Renaissance p130-45

**Bibliography**

Broughton, P. R. Faulkner. *In* American literary scholarship, 1978 p127-51

**Characters**—Isaac McCaslin

Martin, T. The negative character in American fiction. *In* Toward a new American literary history, ed. by L. J. Budd, E. H. Cady and C. L. Anderson p230-43

**Characters**—Quentin Compson

King, R. H. Between repetition and recollection: Allen Tate and William Faulkner. *In* King, R. H. A Southern Renaissance p99-129

**Characters**—Women

Wagner, L. W. Faulkner and (Southern) women. *In* Wagner, L. W. American modern p42-55

**Fear.** See Anxiety

**February, Vernie**

Sipho Sepamla: The Soweto I love. *In* African literature today no. 10: Retrospect & prospect, ed. by E. D. Jones p256-58

**Fecher, Charles A.**

The comfortable bourgeois: the thought of H. L. Mencken. *In* On Mencken, ed. by J. Dorsey p114-27

**Federal aid to education.** See Federal aid to private schools

**Federal aid to private schools**

Moynihan, D. P. Government and the ruin of private education. *In* Moynihan, D. P. Counting our blessings p235-56

**Federal aid to the arts**

Brustein, R. S. The artist and the citizen. *In* Brustein, R. S. Critical moments p79-86

Brustein, R. S. The future of the Endowments. *In* Brustein, R. S. Critical moments p58-78

**Federal aid to the performing arts**

Brustein, R. S. Introduction. *In* Brustein, R. S. Critical moments p xii-xx

**Federal-city relations**

**New York (City)**

Moynihan, D. P. The politics of regional growth. *In* Moynihan, D. P. Counting our blessings p216-34

**Federal government**

**United States**

Elazar, D. J. Constitutionalism, federalism, and the post-industrial American polity. *In* The Third century, ed. by S. M. Lipset p79-107

**Federal-state fiscal relations.** See Intergovernmental fiscal relations

**Federal-state relations.** See Federal government

**Federalism.** See Federal government

**Federman, Raymond** (ed.) See Samuel Beckett: the critical heritage, ed. by Lawrence Graver and Raymond Federman

**Feelings.** See Emotions

**Feher, Ferenc, and Heller, Agnes**

Forms of equality. *In* Symposium on Theories of Justice in and for the Second Half of the Twentieth Century, Sydney, 1977. Justice p149-71

**Fehl, Philipp P.**

Poetry and the entry of the fine arts into England: ut pictura poesis. *In* The Age of Milton, ed. by C. A. Patrides and R. B. Waddington p273-306

**Fehlmann, Guy**

The composition of Somerville and Ross's Irish R.M. *In* The Irish short story, ed. by P. Rafroidi and T. Brown p103-11

**Fehrman, Carl Abraham Daniel**

Poetic creation

*Contents*

Concluding unscientific postscript
Documentation and experimentation
E. A. Poe and the aesthetics of work
Gösta Berlings saga and its transformations
Improvisation—rite and myth
Inspiration disputed
Paul Valéry and Le cimetière marin
Periodocity and the stages of literary creativity
The writing of Ibsen's Brand

**Fein, Helen**

Socio-political responses during the Holocaust: actions and reactions of Allies, Axis partners and neutrals to the destruction of European Jewry. *In* Encountering the Holocaust: an interdisciplinary survey, ed. by B. L. Sherwin and S. G. Ament p84-145

**Feinberg, Joel**

Abortion. *In* Matters of life and death, ed. by T. Regan p183-217

Suicide and the inalienable right to life. *In* Suicide: the philosophical issues, ed. by M. P. Battin and D. J. Mayo p223-28

**Feldman, Irving**

**About**

Howard, R. Irving Feldman: "Who will call these things his own"? *In* Howard, R. Alone with America p131-42

**Fellini, Federico**

**About individual works**

*Amarcord*

Kauffmann, S. Amarcord. *In* Kauffmann, S. Before my eyes p52-55

*8 1/2*

Kauffmann, S. 8½. *In* Kauffmann, S. Before my eyes p356-67

*Fellini's Casanova*

Kauffmann, S. Fellini's Casanova. *In* Kauffmann, S. Before my eyes p56-58

*Orchestra rehearsal*

Kauffmann, S. Orchestra rehearsal. *In* Kauffmann, S. Before my eyes p58-60

**Fellini's Casanova (Motion picture)**

Kauffmann, S. Fellini's Casanova. *In* Kauffmann, S. Before my eyes p56-58

**Felman, Shoshana**

On reading poetry: reflections on the limits and possibilities of psychoanalytical approaches. *In* The Literary Freud: mechanisms of defense and the poetic will, ed. by J. H. Smith p119-48

**Feminism**

Christ, C. P. Nothingness, awakening, insight, new naming. *In* Christ, C. P. Diving deep and surfacing p13-26

**Feminism**—*Continued*

Christ, C. P. Toward wholeness: a vision of women's culture. *In* Christ, C. P. Diving deep and surfacing p119-31

### Italy—History

Howard, J. J. Patriot mothers in the post-Risorgimento: women after the Italian revolution. *In* Women, war, and revolution, ed. by C. R. Berkin and C. M. Lovett p237-58

### United States

Easton, B. Feminism and the contemporary family. *In* A Heritage of her own, ed. by N. F. Cott and E. H. Pleck p555-77

### United States—History

Cook, B. W. Female support networks and political activism: Lillian Wald, Crystal Eastman, Emma Goldman. *In* A Heritage of her own, ed. by N. F. Cott and E. H. Pleck p411-44

**Feminism and literature**

Baruch, E. H. Women and love: some dying myths. *In* The Analysis of literary texts, ed. by R. D. Pope p51-65

Gohlke, M. S. "I wooed thee with my sword": Shakespeare's tragic paradigms. *In* Representing Shakespeare, ed. by M. M. Schwartz and C. Kahn p170-87

**Feminism in literature**

Brown, J. Conclusion. *In* Brown, J. Feminist drama p133-46

Brown, J. Introduction. *In* Brown, J. Feminist drama p 1-21

Brown, J. Plays by feminist theatre groups. *In* Brown, J. Feminist drama p86-113

Janeway, E. H. Women's literature. *In* Harvard Guide to contemporary American writing, ed. by D. Hoffman p342-95

**Feminist studies.** See Women's studies

**Fences**

Stein, S. The concept of the "fence": observations on its origin and development. *In* Studies in Jewish religious and intellectual history, ed. by S. Stein and R. Loewe p301-29

**Fenn, Richard K.**

Religion, identity and authority in the secular society. *In* Identity and authority, ed. by R. Robertson and B. Holzner p119-44

**Fenno, John**

#### About

Hench, J. B. ed. Letters of John Fenno and John Ward Fenno, 1779-1800—Part 1: 1779-1790. *In* American Antiquarian Society. Proceedings v89 pt2 p299-368

**Fenno, John Ward**

#### About

Hench, J. B. ed. Letters of John Fenno and John Ward Fenno, 1779-1800—Part 1: 1779-1790. *In* American Antiquarian Society. Proceedings v89 pt2 p299-368

**Ferguson, Ann**

Androgyny as an ideal for human development. *In* The Philosophy of sex, ed. by A. Soble p232-55

**Ferguson, Frances C.**

Reading Heidegger: Paul De Man and Jacques Derrida. *In* Martin Heidegger and the question of literature, ed. by W. V. Spanos p253-70

The unfamiliarity of familiar letters. *In* The State of the language, ed. by L. Michaels and C. Ricks p78-88

**Ferguson, John**

Classical civilization. *In* Propaganda and communication in world history, ed. by H. D. Lasswell, D. Lerner and H. Speier v 1 p257-98

**Ferguson, Margaret W.**

Border territories of defense: Freud and defenses of poetry. *In* The Literary Freud: mechanisms of defense and the poetic will, ed. by J. H. Smith p149-80

**Ferguson, Sir Samuel**

#### About

Welch, R. Sir Samuel Ferguson: the two races of Ireland. *In* Welch, R. Irish poetry from Moore to Yeats p116-55

**Fernandes, Florestan**

The Negro in Brazilian society: twenty-five years later. *In* Brazil, anthropological perspectives, ed. by M. L. Margolis and W. E. Carter p96-113

**Fernandez, James W.**

Edification by puzzlement. *In* Explorations in African systems of thought, ed. by I. C. Karp & C. S. Bird p44-59

**Fernbach, Sidney**

Scientific use of computers. *In* The Computer age: a twenty-year view, ed. by M. L. Dertouzos and J. Moses p146-60

**Ferrante, Joan M.**

'Ab joi mou lo vers e'l comens'. *In* The Interpretation of medieval lyric poetry, ed. by W. T. H. Jackson p113-41

**Fertile crescent.** See Near East

**Fertility cults**

Oberhelman, S. Greek and Roman witches: literary conventions or agrarian fertility priestesses? *In* 5000 years of popular culture, ed. by F. E. H. Schroeder p138-53

**Festa-McCormick, Diana**

The city as catalyst

*Contents*

Balzac's Girl with the golden eyes: Parisian masks, not faces

Bely's Saint Petersburg: a city conjured by a visionary symbolist

Butor's Passing time: the equivocal reality of a city

D'Annunzio's Child of pleasure: a city's power of seduction

Dos Passos's Manhattan transfer: the death of a metropolis

Durrell's Alexandria quartet: "a whore among cities"

Proust's Remembrance of things past: Venice and the reality within the dream

Rilke's Notebooks: Paris and the phantoms of the past

Romain's Death of a nobody: a city's collective soul

Zola's L'assommoir: Paris's stranglehold on the lives of the poor

**Feu Mathias Pascal (Motion picture)**

Thiher, A. The impressionist avant-garde. *In* Thiher, A. The cinematic muse p16-23

**Feudal law.** See Homage (Feudal law)

**Feudalism**

#### Europe

Le Goff, J. The symbolic ritual of vassalage. *In* Le Goff, J. Time, work, & culture in the Middle Ages p237-87

**Feuerbach, Ludwig Andreas**

### About individual works

*The essence of Christianity*

Ashton, R. D. More translations: Spinoza and Feuerbach (1894-54) *In* Ashton, R. D. The German idea p155-66

**Fèvre, Jacques le.** See Le Fèvre, Jacques, d'Étaples

**Ficino, Marsilio**

### About

Kristeller, P. O. The dignity of man. *In* Kristeller, P. O. Renaissance thought and its sources p169-81

**Fiction**

Stierle, K. The reading of fictional texts. *In* The Reader in the text, ed. by S. R. Suleiman and I. Crosman p83-105

*See also* Detective and mystery stories

### History and criticism

Schor, N. A. Fiction as interpretation/interpretation as fiction. *In* The Reader in the text, ed. by S. R. Suleiman and I. Crosman p165-82

### Moral and religious aspects

Beaujour, M. Exemplary pornography: Barrès, Loyola, and the novel. *In* The Reader in the text, ed. by S. R. Suleiman and I. Crosman p325-49

### 20th century—History and criticism

Baruch, E. H. Women and love: some dying myths. *In* The Analysis of literary texts, ed. by R. D. Pope p51-65

Kellman, S. G. The fiction of self-begetting. *In* Kellman, S. G. The self-begetting novel p 1-11

Kronegger, M. E. From the impressionist to the phenomenological novel. *In* The Analysis of literary texts, ed. by R. D. Pope p129-37

**Fiction, Serialized.** See Serialized fiction

**Fiedler, Leslie Aaron**

Child abuse and the literature of childhood. *In* Children's literature v8 p147-53

The inadvertent epic

*Contents*

Anti-anti-Tom novels and the decline of the American empire: Alex Haley's Roots

The anti-Tom novel and the First Great War: Thomas Dixon, Jr. and D. W. Griffith

The anti-Tom novel and the Great Depression: Margaret Mitchell's Gone with the wind

Uncle Tom as white mother

Uncle Tom's cabin: the invisible masterpiece

**Fiefs.** See Feudalism

**Field, Edward**

### About

Howard, R. Edward Field: "His body comes together joyfully from all directions." *In* Howard, R. Alone with America, p143-57

**Field, George Wallis.** See Part 2 under title: The First World War in German narrative prose

**Fielding, Henry**

### About individual works

*Amelia*

Hagstrum, J. H. Sentimental love and marriage "esteem enliven'd by desire." *In* Hagstrum, J. H. Sex and sensibility p160-85

Uphaus, R. W. 'Clarissa,' 'Amelia,' and the state of probation. *In* Uphaus, R. W. The impossible observer p71-88

**Manuscripts**

Battestin, M. C. A Fielding discovery, with some remarks on the canon. *In* Virginia. University. Bibliographical Society. Studies in bibliography v33 p131-43

**Fighting.** See War

**Fighting (Psychology)** See Aggressiveness (Psychology)

**Figures of speech**

De Man, P. Rhetoric of tropes (Nietzsche). *In* De Man, P. Allegories of reading p103-18

De Man, P. Tropes (Rilke). *In* De Man, P. Allegories of reading p20-56

**Film adaptations.** See under authors, e.g. Euripides—Film adaptations

**Filstrup, Jane Merrill**

Thirst for enchanted views in Ruskin's The king of the Golden River. *In* Children's literature v8 p68-79

**Final cause.** See Causation

**Finance**

*See also* Commerce

### United States—History

Green, G. D. Financial intermediaries. *In* Encyclopedia of American economic history, ed. by G. Porter v2 p707-26

**Finance, Local.** See Local finance

**Finance, Personal.** See Insurance

**Finance, Public**

*See also* Budget; Taxation

### United States—1933-

Boskin, M. J. Federal government spending and budget policy. *In* The Economy in the 1980s: a program for growth and stability, ed. by M. J. Boskin p233-54

Break, G. F. State and local finance in the 1980s. *In* The Economy in the 1980s: a program for growth and stability, ed. by M. J. Boskin p233-54

### United States—States

Break, G. F. State and local finance in the 1980s. *In* The Economy in the 1980s: a program for growth and stability, ed. by M. J. Boskin p233-54

**Financial institutions.** See Banks and banking

**Fine arts.** See Art; Arts

**Fineman, Joel**

Fratricide and cuckoldry: Shakespeare's doubles. *In* Representing Shakespeare, ed. by M. M. Schwartz and C. Kahn p70-109

**Fingers (Motion picture)**

Kael, P. "What symmetrical digits!" *In* Kael, P. When the lights go down p414-18

**Fink, Karl J.**

The metalanguage of Goethe's history of color theory. *In* The Quest for the new science, ed. by K. J. Fink and J. W. Marchand p41-55

**Finkel, Donald**

### About

Howard, R. Donald Finkel: "There is no perfection possible. But there is tomorrow." *In* Howard, R. Alone with America p158-75

**Finklestein, Jacob J.**

Early Mesopotamia, 2500-1000 B.C. *In* Propaganda and communication in world history, ed. by H. D. Lasswell, D. Lerner and H. Speier v 1 p50-110

**Finland**

**Politics and government—1917-**

Suhonen, P. Finland. *In* Western European party systems, ed. by P. H. Merkl p235-56

**Fire walking**

Morowitz, H. J. Sole on fire. *In* Morowitz, H. J. The wine of life, and other essays on societies, energy & living things p15-19

**Firestone, Shulamith**

**About individual works**
*The dialectic of sex*

Rapaport, E. On the future of love: Rousseau and the radical feminists. *In* The Philosophy of sex, ed. by A. Soble p369-88

**Fisch, Max Harold**

What has Vico to say to philosophers of today? *In* Conference on Vico and Contemporary Thought, New York, 1916. Vico and contemporary thought pt 1 p9-19

**Fischer, Lynn F.**

Mass education and national conflict in thirty African states. *In* Values, identities, and national integration, ed. by J. N. Paden p261-69

Student orientations toward nation-building in Ghana. *In* Values, identities, and national integration, ed. by J. N. Paden p271-84

**Fischer, Wolfgang**

Kafka without a world. *In* The World of Franz Kafka, ed. by J. P. Stern p223-28

**Fishburn, Katherine**

The nightmare repetition: the mother-daughter conflict in Doris Lessing's Children of violence. *In* The Lost tradition: mothers and daughters in literature, ed. by C. N. Davidson and E. M. Broner p207-16

**Fisher, Margery**

Rights and wrongs. *In* The Arbuthnot lectures, 1970-1979 p3-20

**Fisher, Mary Frances Kennedy**

As the lingo languishes. *In* The State of the language, ed. by L. Michaels and C. Ricks p267-75

**Fisher, Stephen L.**

The "decline of parties" thesis and the role of minor parties. *In* Western European party systems, ed. by P. H. Merkl p609-13

**Fishermen**

**Brazil**

Kottak, C. P. Ecology, behavior, and the spirit of fishermen. *In* Brazil, anthropological perspectives, ed. by M. L. Margolis and W. E. Carter p180-209

**Fiske, Marjorie**

Changing hierarchies of commitment in adulthood. *In* Themes of work and love in adulthood, ed. by N. J. Smelser and E. H. Erikson p238-64

**FitzGerald, Edward**

**About**

Plomer, W. C. F. Edward FitzGerald. *In* Plomer, W. C. F. Electric delights p87-105

**Fitzgerald, Francis Scott Key**

**About**

Trilling, L. Fitzgerald plain. *In* Trilling, L. Speaking of literature and society p255-59

Wilson, R. N. F. Scott Fitzgerald: personality and culture. *In* Wilson, R. N. The writer as social seer p17-41

**About individual works**
*The great Gatsby*

Gross, B. R. "Would 25-cent press keep Gatsby in the public eye—or is the book unpopular?" *In* Seasoned authors for a new season: the search for standards in popular writing, ed. by L. Filler p51-57

**Bibliography**

Bryer, J. R. Fitzgerald and Hemingway. *In* American literary scholarship, 1978 p153-78

**Fitzgerald, Geraldine**

Another neurotic Electra: a new look at Mary Tyrone. *In* Eugene O'Neill, ed. by V. Floyd p290-92

**Fitzmaurice, George**

**About**

Cooke, J. 'Tis mysterious surely and fantastic strange: art and artists in three plays of George Fitzmaurice. *In* Irish Renaissance annual I p32-55

**Flagellation of Christ (Frick Collection)**

Schapiro, M. On an Italian painting of the Flagellation of Christ in the Frick Collection. *In* Schapiro, M. Selected papers v3: Late antique, early Christian and mediaeval art p355-79

**Flaubert, Gustave**

**About**

Collins, D. Flaubert and the objective neurosis. *In* Collins, D. Sartre as biographer p151-83

Collins, D. Flaubert and the subjective neurosis. *In* Collins, D. Sartre as biographer p111-50

**About individual works**
*Bouvard and Pécuchet*

Donato, E. U. The museum's furnace: notes toward a contextual reading of Bouvard and Pécuchet. *In* Textual strategies, ed. by J. V. Harari p213-38

*Madame Bovary*

Nabokov, V. V. Gustave Flaubert: Madame Bovary. *In* Nabokov, V. V. Lectures on literature p125-77

*Sentimental education*

White, H. W. The problem of style in realistic representation: Marx and Flaubert. *In* The Concept of style, ed. by B. Lang p213-29

**Style**

Barthes, R. Flaubert and the sentence. *In* Barthes, R. New critical essays p69-78

**Fleishman, Avrom**

Forms of the Woolfian short story. *In* Virginia Woolf, ed. by R. Freedman p44-70

**Fletcher, Dennis**

Restif de la Bretonne and woman's estate. *In* Woman and society in eighteenth-century France, ed. by E. Jacobs and others p96-109

**Fletcher, Joseph Francis**

Humanist ethics: the groundwork. *In* Humanist ethics, ed. by M. B. Storer p253-61

**Flew, Antony Garrard Newton**

Intended conduct and unintended consequences. *In* Lying truths, ed. by R. Duncan and M. Weston-Smith p17-30

**Flink, James J.**

Automobile. *In* Encyclopedia of American economic history, ed. by G. Porter v3 p1168-93

Flinker, Moses

### About individual works

*Young Moshe's diary*

Alexander, E. Holocaust and rebirth: Moshe Flinker, Nelly Sachs, and Abba Kovner. *In* Alexander, E. The resonance of dust p31-71

Flinker, Noam

Saul and David in the early poetry of Yehuda Amichai. *In* The David myth in Western literature, ed. by R. J. Frontain and J. Wojcik p170-78

Floors, Mosaic

Schapiro, M. Ancient mosaics in Israel: late antique art—pagan, Jewish, Christian. *In* Schapiro, M. Selected papers v3: Late antique, early Christian and mediaeval art p20-33

Flynn, John Paul [and others]

Anatomical pathways for attack behavior in cats. *In* Human ethology, ed. by M. von Cranach [and others] p301-15

Foakes, Reginald Anthony

Poetic language and dramatic significance in Shakespeare. *In* Shakespeare's styles, ed. by P. Edwards; I. S. Ewbank, and G. K. Hunter p79-93

What did Coleridge say? John Payne Collier and the reports of the 1811-12 lectures. *In* Reading Coleridge, ed. by W. B. Crawford p191-210

Fodor, Jerry

Fixation of belief and concept acquisition. *In* Language and learning, ed. by M. Piattelli-Palmarini p143-49

Reply to Putnam. *In* Language and learning, ed. by M. Piattelli-Palmarini p325-34

### About

Putnam, H. Comments on Chomsky's and Fodor's replies. *In* Language and learning, ed. by M. Piattelli-Palmarini p335-40

Putnam, H. What is innate and why: comments on the debate. *In* Language and learning, ed. by M. Piattelli-Palmarini p287-309

Foerster, Norman

"The literary prophets." *In* Van Wyck Brooks: the critic and his critics, ed. by W. Wasserstrom p56-68

Fogelmark, Staffan

A troublesome antithesis: Lysias 12.88. *In* Harvard Studies in classical philology, v83 p109-41

Fogle, Richard Harter

Hawthorne's sketches and the English romantics. *In* Toward a new American literary history, ed. by L. J. Budd, E. H. Cady and C. L. Anderson p129-39

Foley, John Miles

Beowulf and traditional narrative song: the potential and limits of comparison. *In* Old English literature in context, ed. by J. D. Niles p117-36

Foley, Patrick Kevin

### About

Gallup, D. C. Aldis, Foley, and the collection of American literature at Yale. *In* The Bibliographical Society of America, 1904-79 p209-28

Folk art

Ames, K. L. Folk art: the challenge and the promise. *In* Perspectives on American folk art, ed. by I. M. G. Quimby and S. T. Swank p293-324

Fabian, J. and Szombati-Fabian, I. Folk art from an anthropological perspective. *In* Perspectives on American folk art, ed. by I. M. G. Quimby and S. T. Swank p247-92

Harbison, R. Romantic localism. *In* Harbison, R. Deliberate regression p115-47

Jones, M. O. L. A. add-ons and re-dos: renovation in folk art and architectural design. *In* Perspectives on American folk art, ed. by I. M. G. Quimby and S. T. Swank p325-63

Kubler, G. A. The arts: fine and plain. *In* Perspectives on American folk art, ed. by I. M. G. Quimby and S. T. Swank p234-46

Swank, S. T. Introduction. *In* Perspectives on American folk art, ed. by I. M. G. Quimby and S. T. Swank p 1-12

Welsch, R. L. Beating a live horse: yet another note on definitions and defining. *In* Perspectives of American folk art, ed. by I. M. G. Quimby and S. T. Swank p218-33

#### Mexico

Kubler, G. A. The arts: fine and plain. *In* Perspectives on American folk art, ed. by I. M. G. Quimby and S. T. Swank p234-46

#### Michigan

Dewhurst, C. K. Expanding frontiers: the Michigan Folk Art Project. *In* Perspectives on American folk art, ed. by I. M. G. Quimby and S. T. Swank p54-78

#### Middle West

Nelson, M. J. The material culture and folk arts of the Norwegians in America. *In* Perspectives on American folk art, ed. by I. M. G. Quimby and S. T. Swank p79-133

#### Pennsylvania

Weiser, F. S. Baptismal certificate and gravemarker: Pennsylvania German folk art at the beginning and the end of life. *In* Perspectives on American folk art, ed. by I. M. G. Quimby and S. T. Swank p134-61

#### Southern States

Vlach, J. M. Arrival and survival: the maintenance of an Afro-American tradition in folk art and craft. *In* Perspectives of American folk art, ed. by I. M. G. Quimby and S. T. Swank p127-217

#### Texas

Taylor, L. W. Fachwerk and Brettstuhl: the rejection of traditional folk culture. *In* Perspectives of American folk art, ed. by I. M. G. Quimby and S. T. Swank p162-76

#### United States—Collectors and collecting

Rumford, B. T. Uncommon art of the common people: a review of trends in the collecting and exhibiting of American folk art. *In* Perspectives on American folk art, ed. by I. M. G. Quimby and S. T. Swank p13-53

Folk drama, English. See Mumming plays

Folk literature. See Fairy tales; Folk-lore in literature

Folk-lore

*See also* Dragons; Evil Eye; Oral tradition; Story-telling; Trickster

#### Methodology

*See* Folk-lore—Theory, methods, etc.

#### Theory, methods, etc.

Dundes, A. Projection in folklore: a plea for psychoanalytic semiotics. *In* Dundes, A. Interpreting folklore p33-61

**Folk-lore**—Theory, methods, etc.—*Continued*

Dundes, A. Texture, text, and context. *In* Dundes, A. Interperting folklore p20-32

Dundes, A. Who are the folk? *In* Dundes, A. Interpreting folklore p 1-19

**Folk-lore, American**

Dundes, A. The crowing hen and the Easter bunny: male chauvinism in American folklore. *In* Dundes, A. Interpreting folklore p160-75

Dundes, A. The number three in American culture. *In* Dundes, A. Interpreting folklore p134-59

Dundes, A. Seeing is believing. *In* Dundes, A. Interpreting folklore p86-92

Dundes, A. Thinking ahead: a folkloristic reflection of the future orientation in American worldview. *In* Dundes, A. Interpreting folklore p69-85

**Folk-lore, Ashanti**

Pelton, R. D. Ananse: spinner of Ashanti doubleness. *In* Pelton, R. D. The trickster in West Africa p25-70

**Folk-lore, Aymara**

La Barre, W. Aymara folklore and folk temperament. *In* La Barre, W. Culture in context p253-57

**Folk-lore, Black**

Jackson, R. L. In the beginning: oral literature and the "true black experience." *In* Jackson, R. L. Black writers in Latin America p16-24

**Folk-Lore, Fon (African people)**

Pelton, R. D. Legba: master of the Fon dialetic. *In* Pelton, R. D. The trickster in West Africa p71-112

**Folk-lore, Germanic**

Hatto, A. T. Folk ritual and the Minnesang. *In* Hatto, A. T. Essays on medieval German and other poetry p42-63

**Folk-lore, Yoruba**

Pelton, R. D. Legba and Eshu: writers of destiny. *In* Pelton, R. D. The trickster in West Africa p113-63

**Folk-lore in literature**

Dundes, A. "To love my father all": a psychoanalytic study of the folktale source of King Lear. *In* Dundes, A. Interpreting folklore p211-22

**Folk-lore of initiations.** See Initiations (in religion, folk-lore, etc.)

**Folk-songs, Spanish**

*Themes, Motives*

Wardropper, B. W. Meaning in medieval Spanish folk song. *In* The Interpretation of medieval lyric poetry, ed. by W. T. H. Jackson p176-93

**Folklore.** See Folk-lore

**Folquet de Marseille, Bp. of Toulouse**

*About*

Cropp, G. M. The partimen between Folquet de Marseille and Tostemps. *In* The Interpretation of medieval lyric poetry, ed. by W. T. H. Jackson p91-112

**Fon (African people)**

*Religion*

Pelton, R. D. Legba: master of the Fon dialetic. *In* Pelton, R. D. The trickster in West Africa p71-112

**Foner, Eric**

Abolitionism and the labor movement in antebellum America. *In* Anti- slavery, religion, and reform: essays in memory of Roger Anstey, ed. by C. Bolt and S. Drescher p254-71

**Fontane, Theodor**

*About individual works*

*Die Brück am Tay*

Grundlehner, P. Theodor Fontane: "Die Brück am Tay." *In* Grundlehner, P. The lyrical bridge p8)-95

**Food**

*See also* Gastronomy

*Contamination*

*See* Food contamination

**Food (in religion, folklore, etc.)**

Jacobs, L. Eating as an act of worship in Hasidic thought. *In* Studies in Jewish religious and intellectual history, ed. by S. Stein and R. Loewe p157-66

**Food Administration.** See United States. Food Administration

**Food conservation.** See Food contamination

**Food contamination**

Morowitz, H. J. Dull realities. *In* Morowitz, H. J. The wine of life, and other essays on societies, energy & living things p246-50

**Food industry and trade**

*Advertising*

*See* Advertising—Food

**Food relief**

*Moral and religious aspects*

O'Neill, O. The moral perplexities of famine relief. *In* Matters of life and death, ed. by T. Regan p260-98

**Foods, Contaminated.** See Food contamination

**Foot-ball.** See Football

**Football**

*Psychological aspects*

Dundes, A. Into the endzone for a touchdown: a psychoanalytic consideration of American football. *In* Dundes, A. Interpreting folklore p199-210

**Footnotes, Bibliographical.** See Bibliographical citations

**Foppa, Klaus**

Language acquisition: a human ethological problem? *In* Human ethology, ed. by M. von Cranach [and others] p729-38

**Forbes, Derek**

Water drama. *In* Performance and politics in popular drama, ed. by D. Bradby, L. James and B. Sharratt p91-107

**Forbes, Duncan**

Hume and the Scottish Enlightenment. *In* Royal Institute of Philosophy. Philosophers of the Enlightenment p94-109

**Force and energy**

Gabbey, A. Force and inertia in the seventeenth century: Descartes and Newton. *In* Descartes, ed. by S. Gaukroger p230-320

Gueroult, M. The metaphysics and physics of force in Descartes. *In* Descartes, ed. by S. Gaukroger p196-229

**Ford, Ford Madox**
### About
Lurie, A. Ford Madox Ford's fairy tales. *In* Children's literature v8 p7-21

**Ford, John,** 1586-1640?
### About individual works
*Perkin Warbeck*
Edwards, P. The royal pretenders: Ford's Perkin Warbeck and Massinger's Believe as you list. *In* Edwards, P. Threshold of a nation p174-87

**Forecasting**
Segerstedt, T. T. The condition of man in post-industrial society. *In* The Condition of man, ed. by P. Hallberg p152-60
*See also* Social prediction

**Foreign aid program.** See Economic assistance

**Foreign economic relations.** See International economic relations

**Foreign military sales.** See Munitions

**Foreign trade.** See Commerce

**Forgery of manuscripts**
Lutz, C. E. A forged manuscript in boustrophedon. *In* Lutz, C. E. The oldest library motto, and other library essays p65-72

**Form (Philosophy)** See Structuralism

**Form, Literary.** See Literary form

**Forman, Charles W.**
Christian missions in the ancient world. *In* Propaganda and communication in world history, ed. by H. D. Lasswell, D. Lerner and H. Speier v 1 p330-47

**Forman, Shepard, and Riegelhaupt, Joyce Firstenberg**
The political economy of patron-clientship: Brazil and Portugal compared. *In* Brazil, anthropological perspectives, ed. by M. L. Margolis and W. E. Carter p379-400

**Forms of addresses**
Whitcut, J. The language of address. *In* The State of the language, ed. by L. Michaels and C. Ricks p89-97

**Forrester, Jay Wright**
An alternative approach to economic policy: macrobehavior from microstructure. *In* Economic issues of the eighties, ed. by N. M. Kamrany and R. H. Day p80-108

**Forster, Edward Morgan**
### About
Baron, C. E. Forster on Lawrence. *In* E. M. Forster: a human exploration, ed. by G. K. Das and J. Beer p186-95

Beer, J. B. Introduction: the elusive Forster. *In* E. M. Forster: a human exploration ed. by G. K. Das and J. Beer p 1-10

Buckingham, M. Some reminiscences. *In* E. M. Forster: a human exploration, ed. by G. K. Das and J. Beer p183-85

Hanquart, E. E. M. Forster's travelogue from the Hill of Devi to the Bayreuth Festival. *In* E. M. Forster: a human exploration, ed. by G. K. Das and J. Beer p167-82

Herz, J. S. The narrator as Hermes: a study of the early short fiction. *In* E. M. Forster: a human exploration, ed. by G. K. Das and J. Beer p17-27

McConkey, J. Two anonymous writers, E. M. Forster and Anton Chekhov. *In* E. M. Forster: a human exploration, ed. by G. K. Das and J. Beer p231-44

Pritchett, V. S. E. M. Forster: the private voice. *In* Pritchett, V. S. The tale bearers p64-77

Stallybrass, O. A quorum of quotations. *In* E. M. Forster: a human exploration, ed. by G. K. Das and J. Beer p11-16

Stone, W. H. Forster on profit and loss. *In* E. M. Forster: a human exploration, ed. by G. K. Das and J. Beer p69-78

Wilde, A. The naturalisation of Eden. *In* E. M. Forster: a human exploration, ed. by G. K. Das and J. Beer p196-207

### About individual works
*Alexandria: a history and a guide*
Shaheen, M. Forster's Alexandria: the transitional journey. *In* E. M. Forster: a human exploration, ed. by G. K. Das and J. Beer p79-88

*Goldsworthy Lowes Dickinson*
Trilling, L. Politics and the liberal. *In* Trilling, L. Speaking of literature and society p89-91

*The hill of Devi*
Birje-Patil, J. Forster and Dewas. *In* E. M. Forster: a human exploration, ed. by G. K. Das and J. Beer p102-08

*Howards End*
Parkinson, R. N. The inheritors; or A single ticket for Howards End. *In* E. M. Forster: a human exploration, ed. by G. K. Das and J. Beer p55-68

*Hymn before action*
Das, G. K. E. M. Forster, T. S. Eliot, and the 'Hymn before action.' *In* E. M. Forster: a human exploration, ed by G. K. Das and J. Beer p208-15

*The longest journey*
Rosenbaum, S. P. The longest journey: E. M. Forster's refutation of idealism. *In* E. M. Forster: a human exploration, ed. by G. K. Das and J. Beer p32-54

*A passage to India*
Chaudhuri, N. C. India in English literature. *In* Royal Society of Literature of the United Kingdom, London. Essays by divers hands: innovation in contemporary literature, new ser. v40 p15-33

Colmer, J. Promise and withdrawal in A passage to India. *In* E. M. Forster: a human exploration, ed. by G. K. Das and J. Beer p117-28

Drew, J. A passage via Alexandria? *In* E. M. Forster: a human exploration, ed. by G. K. Das and J. Beer p89-101

Orange, M. Language and silence in A passage to India. *In* E. M. Forster: a human exploration, ed. by G. K. Das and J. Beer p142-60

Parry, B. A passage to India: epitaph or manifesto? *In* E. M. Forster: a human exploration, ed. by G. K. Das and J. Beer p129-41

Shahane, V. A. Life's walking shadows in A passage to India. *In* E. M. Forster: a human exploration, ed. by G. K. Das and J. Beer p109-16

*The road from Colonus*
Thomson, G. H. Where was the road from Colonus? *In* E. M. Forster: a human exploration, ed. by G. K. Das and J. Beer p28-31

**Forster, Edward M.**—*Continued*

### Bibliography
McDowell, F. P. W. Forster scholarship and criticism for the desert islander. *In* E. M. Forster: a human exploration, ed. by G. K. Das and J. Beer p269-82

### Characters
Shahane, V. A. Life's walking shadows in A passage to India. *In* E. M. Forster: a human exploration, ed. by G. K. Das and J. Beer p109-16

### Criticism and interpretation
Beer, J. B. 'The last Englishman': Lawrence's appreciation of Forster. *In* E. M. Forster: a human exploration, ed. by G. K. Das and J. Beer p245-68

Trivedi, H. K. Forster and Virginia Woolf: the critical friends. *In* E. M. Forster: a human exploration, ed. by G. K. Das and J. Beer p216-30

### Language—Style
*See* Forster, Edward Morgan—Style

### Philosophy
Drew, J. A passage via Alexandria? *In* E. M. Forster: a human exploration, ed. by G. K. Das and J. Beer p89-101

### Style
Furbank, P. N. Forster and 'Bloomsbury' prose. *In* E. M. Forster: a human exploration, ed. by G. K. Das and J. Beer p161-66

**Fortes, Meyer**
Anthropology and the psychological disciplines. *In* Soviet and Western anthropology, ed. by E. Gellner p195-215

Introduction. *In* Soviet and Western anthropology, ed. by E. Gellner p xix-xxv

**Fortunata, Jacqueline**
Masturbation and women's sexuality. *In* The Philosophy of sex, ed. by A. Soble p389-408

**Fortunatus, Venantius Honorius Clementianus, Bp.**

### Manuscripts
Hunt, R. W. Manuscript evidence for knowledge of the poems of Venantius Fortunatus in late Anglo-Saxon England. *In* Anglo-Saxon England 8 p279-95

**The fortune (Motion picture)**
Kauffmann, S. The fortune. *In* Kauffmann, S. Before my eyes p138-39

**Fortune in literature**
Wimsatt, J. I. Chaucer, fortune, and Machaut's "Il m'est avis." *In* Chaucerian problems and perspectives, ed. by E. Vasta and Z. P. Thundy p119-31

**Fortune Theatre, London**
Limon, J. Pictorial evidence for a possible replica of the London Fortune Theatre in Gdansk. *In* Shakespeare survey 32 p189-99

**Fossils.** See Paleontology

**Foster, David William**
Studies in the contemporary Spanish-American short story
*Contents*
Cortázar's "Las armas secretas" and structurally anomalous narratives
The double inscription of the narrataire in "Los funerales de la Mamá Grande"
The écriture of rupture and subversion of language in Cortázar's Historias de cronopios y famas
The écriture of social protest in Mario Benedetti's "El cambiazo"
García Márquez and the écriture of complicity: "La prodigiosa tarde de Baltazar"
Guillermo Cabrera Infante's Vista del amanecer en el trópico and the generic ambiguity of narrative
Introduction: the écriture of literary texts
Rulfo's "Luvina" and structuring figures of diction
Toward a characterization of écriture in the stories of Borges

**Foster, John**
In self-defence. *In* Perception and identity, ed. by G. F. Macdonald p161-85
Private worlds: the stories of Michael McLaverty. *In* The Irish short story, ed. by P. Rafroidi and T. Brown p249-61

**Foucault, Michel**
What is an author? excerpt from "Language, counter-memory, practice." *In* Textual strategies, ed. by J. V. Harari p141-60

### About
Kurzweil, E. Michel Foucault: structuralism and structures of knowledge. *In* Kurzweil, E. The age of structuralism p193-226

Lentricchia, F. History or the abyss: poststructuralism. *In* Lentricchia, F. After the New Criticism p156-210

White, H. V. Michel Foucault. *In* Structuralism and since, ed. by J. Sturrock p81-115

**Foulques of Marseilles.** See Folquet de Marseille, Bp. of Toulouse

**Foundations (Endowments)** See Endowments

**Foundlings**

### Peru—Arequipa—History
Gallagher, M. A. Y. Aristocratic opposition to the establishment of a foundling home in Arequipa, Peru. *In* Studies in eighteenth-century culture v9 p45-58

**The 400 blows (Motion picture)**
Thiher, A. The existential play in Truffaut's early films. *In* Thiher, A. The cinematic muse p143-63

**Fourteenth century**
Le Goff, J. Labor time in the "crisis" of the fourteenth century: from medieval time to modern time. *In* Le Goff, J. Time, work, & culture in the Middle Ages p43-52

**Fouts, Roger S. and Rigby, Randall L.**
Man-chimpanzee communication. *In* Speaking of apes, ed. by T. A. Sebeok and J. Umiker-Sebeok p261-85

**Fox, Lucía.** See Fox-Lockert, Lucía

**Fox, Marvin**
The doctrine of the mean in Aristotle and Maimonides: a comparative study. *In* Studies in Jewish religious and intellectual history, ed. by S. Stein and R. Loewe p93-120

**Fox, Paula**

### About
Rees, D. "The colour of saying": Paula Fox. *In* Rees, D. The marble in the water p114-27
Townsend, J. R. Paula Fox. *In* Townsend, J. R. A sounding of storytellers p55-65

**Fox-Lockert, Lucía**
    Women novelists in Spain and Spanish
America
    *Contents*
Beatriz Guido
Carmen Laforet
Clara Silva
Clorinda Matto de Turner
Concha Alos
Concha Espina
Dolores Medio
Elena Garro
Elena Poniatowska
Elena Quiroga
Elena Soriano
Emilia Pardo Bazan
Fernan Caballero (Cecilia Bohl de Faber)
Gertrudiz Gomez de Avellaneda
Luisa Josefina Hernandez
Maria de Zayas
Maria Luisa Bombal
Marta Brunet
Mercedes Cabello de Carbonera
Silvina Bullrich
Teresa de la Parra (Ana Teresa Parra Sanojo)
**Fracastoro, Girolamo**
    **About**
    Montgomery, R. L. Universals and particu-
lars: Fracastoro and Barbaro. *In* Montgomery,
R. L. The reader's eye p93-116
**Fragonard, Jean Honoré**
    **About**
    Harbison, R. Nature as a child. *In* Harbi-
son, R. Deliberate regression p3-24
**Frampton, Kenneth**
    The disappearing factory: the Volvo experi-
ment at Kalmar. *In* Architecture for people,
ed. by B. Mikellides p149-61
**France**
    **Economic policy**
    Birnbaum, P. The state in contemporary
France. *In* The State in Western Europe
ed. by R. Scase p94-114

    **Historiography**
    Ranum, O. The historiographers royal. *In*
Ranum, O. Artisan of glory p58-102

    **History—To 987**
    *See* Merovingians

    **History—Medieval period, 987-1515—**
        **Historiography**
    Le Goff, J. The several Middle Ages of
Jules Michelet. *In* Le Goff, J. Time, work, &
culture in the Middle Ages p3-28

    **History—17th century—Historiography**
    Ranum, O. Chapelain and the royal patron-
age of history. *In* Ranum, O. Artisans of glory
p169-96

    **History—18th century—Historiography**
    Brumfitt, J. H. Cleopatra's nose and En-
lightenment historiography. *In* Woman and
society in eighteenth-century France, ed. by E.
Jacobs and others p183-94

    **History—Revolution, 1789-1799**
    Johnson, M. D. Old wine in new bottles: the
institutional changes for women of the people
during the French Revolution. *In* Women, war,
and revolution, ed. by C. R. Berkin and C. H.
Lovett p107-43

    Levy, D. G. and Applewhite, H. V. B.
Women of the popular classes in revolutionary
Paris, 1789-1795. *In* Women, war, and revolution, ed. by C. R. Berkin and C. M. Lovett
p9-35

    **History—Revolution, 1789-1799—Clubs**
    *See* Montagnards

    **History—19th century**
    Sewell, W. H. Property, labor, and the
emergence of socialism in France, 1789-1848.
*In* Consciousness and class experience in nineteenth-century Europe, ed. by J. M. Merriman
p45-63

    **History—Third Republic, 1870-1940**
    Barrows, S. I. After the Commune: alcohol-
ism, temperance, and literature in the early
Third Republic. *In* Consciousness and class
experience in nineteenth-century Europe, ed. by
J. M. Merriman p205-18

    **Intellectual life**
    Ranum, O. Men of letters: sixteenth-cen-
tury models of conduct. *In* Ranum, O. Artisans
of glory p26-57
    Ranum, O. Patronage and history from
Richelieu to Colbert. *In* Ranum, O. Artisans
of glory p148-68

    **Politics and government**
    Wilson, F. L. Sources of party transforma-
tion: the case of France. *In* Western European
party systems, ed. by P. H. Merkl p526-51

    **Politics and government—1789-1900**
    Daget, S. A model of the French abolition-
ist movement and its variations. *In* Anti-
slavery, religion, and reform: essays in memory
of Roger Anstey, ed. by C. Bolt and S.
Drescher p64-79

    **Politics and government—1945-**
    Birnbaum, P. The state in contemporary
France. *In* The State in Western Europe
p94-114
    Noonan, L. G. France. *In* Western European
party systems, ed. by P. H. Merkl p87-121

    **Social conditions**
    Farge, A. Work-related diseases of artisans
in eighteenth-century France. *In* Medicine and
society in France, ed. by R. Forster and O.
Ranum p89-103
    Goubert, J. P. The art of healing: learned
medicine and popular medicine in the France
of 1790. *In* Medicine and society in France, ed.
by R. Forster and O. Ranum p 1-23
    Joerger, M. The structure of the hospital
system in France in the ancient regime. *In*
Medicine and society in France, ed. by R.
Forster and O. Ranum p104-36
    Laget, M. Childbirth in seventeenth--and
eighteenth-century France: obstetrical practices and collective attitudes. *In* Medicine and
society in France, ed. by R. Forster and O.
Ranum p137-76
    Léonard, J. Women, religion, and medicine.
*In* Medicine and society in France, ed. by R.
Forster and O. Ranum p24-47
    Morel, M. F. City and country in eighteenth-
century medical discussions about early childhood. *In* Medicine and society in France, ed.
by R. Forster and O. Ranum p48-65

**France—Social conditions—*Continued***

Perrot, M. The three ages of industrial discipline in nineteenth-century France. *In* Consciousness and class experience in nineteenth-century Europe, ed. by J. H. Merriman p149-68

Roche, D. Talent, reason, and sacrifice: the physician during the Enlightenment. *In* Medicine and society in France, ed. by R. Forster and O. Ranum p66-88

**Francis, Leslie Pickering**

Assisting suicide: a problem for the criminal law. *In* Suicide: the philosophical issues, ed. by M. P. Battin and D. J. Mayo p254-66

**Franciscans**

Ozment, S. H. The spiritual traditions. *In* Ozment, S. H. The age of reform, 1250-1550 p73-134

**Frank, Leonhard**

**About**

Dierick, A. F. Two representative expressionist responses to the challenge of the First World War: Carl Sternheim's eigene Nuance and Leonhard Frank's utopia. *In* The First World War in German narrative prose, ed. by C. N. Genno and H. Wetzel p16-33

**Frank, Manfred**

The infinite text. *In* Glyph 7 p70-101

**Frankel, Henry**

Why drift theory was accepted with the confirmation of Harry Hess's concept of seafloor spreading. *In* New Hampshire Bicentennial Conference on the History of Geology, University of New Hampshire, 1976. Two hundred years of geology in America p337-53

**Frankis, John**

Paganism and pagan love in Troilus and Criseyde. *In* Essays on Troilus and Criseyde, ed. by M. Salu p57-72

**Frankl, Viktor Emil**

Meaninglessness: a challenge to psychiatry. *In* Value and values in evolution, ed. by E. A. Maziarz p71-91

**Franklin, Benjamin**

**About**

Botein, S. Printers and the American Revolution. *In* The Press & the American Revolution, ed. by B. Bailyn and J. B. Hench p11-57

**About individual works**

*Autobiography*

Spengemann, W. C. Historical autobiography. *In* Spengemann, W. C. The forms of autobiography p34-61

*The sale of the Hessians*

Blair, W. Franklin's massacre of the Hessians. *In* Toward a new American literary history, ed. by L. J. Budd, E. H. Cady and C. L. Anderson p84-90

**Library**

Wolf, E. The reconstruction of Benjamin Franklin's library: an unorthodox jigsaw puzzle. *In* The Bibliographical Society of America, 1904-79 p399-415

**Fraser, Donald McKay**

Democratizing the Democratic Party. *In* Political parties in the eighties, ed. by R. A. Goldwin p116-32

**Frazer, Sir James George**

**About**

Douglas, M. Judgments on James Frazer. *In* Generations, ed. by S. R. Graubard p151-64

**Frazer, Winifred L.**

Drama. *In* American literary scholarship, 1978 p365-79

**Frede, Michael**

The original notion of cause. *In* Doubt and dogmatism, ed. by M. Schofield, M. Burnyeat and J. Barnes p217-49

**Fredrickson, George M.**

Comparative history. *In* The Past before us, ed. by M. Kammen p457-73

**Free agency.** See Free will and determinism

**Free trade and protection.** See Tariff

**Free will and determinism**

Madden, E. H. Asa Mahan and the Oberlin philosophy. *In* History, religion, and spiritual democracy, ed. by M. Wohlgelernter and others p155-80

Ozment, S. H. Humanism and the Reformation. *In* Ozment, S. H. The age of reform, 1250-1550 p290-317

**Freedman, Ralph**

The form of fact and fiction: Jacob's room as paradigm. *In* Virginia Woolf, ed. by R. Freedman p123-40

Introduction: Virginia Woolf, the novel, and a chorus of voices. *In* Virginia Woolf, ed. by R. Freedman p3-12

**Freedmen**

Carr, L. G. and Menard, R. R. Immigration and opportunity: the freedman in early colonial Maryland. *In* The Chesapeake in the seventeenth century, ed. by T. W. Tate and D. L. Ammerman p206-41

**Freedom.** See Liberty

**Freedom, Academic.** See Academic freedom

**Freedom of information.** See Government and the press

**Freedom of the press.** See Liberty of the press

**Freedom of the will.** See Free will and determinism

**Freeman, Gillian**

**About individual works**

*The schoolgirl ethic: the life and work of Angela Brazil*

Segel, E. Domesticity and the wide, wide world. *In* Children's literature v8 p168-75

**Freidin, Gregory**

Osip Mandelstam: the poetry of time (1908-1916). *In* California Slavic studies v11 p141-86

**Freitas, Michael de.** See Malik, Michael Abdul

**French, Hannah Dustin**

Notes on American bookbindings. *In* American Antiquarian Society. Proceedings v89 pt2 p369-70

**French architecture.** See Architecture, French

**French connection (Motion picture)**

Kauffmann, S. French connection II/Night moves. *In* Kauffmann, S. Before my eyes p131-34

**French drama**

**17th century—History and criticism**

Mueller, M. Dramaturgical and thematic aspects of versions in seventeenth-century France. *In* Mueller, M. Children of Oedipus, and other essays on the imitation of Greek tragedy 1550-1800 p33-45

French drama—*Continued*

**18th century—History and criticism**

Mueller, M. Moral and aesthetic tendencies in eighteenth-century adaptations of Greek tragedy. *In* Mueller, M. Children of Oedipus, and other essays on the imitation of Greek tragedy 1550-1800 p65-79

**French drama (Tragedy)**
**Greek influences**

Mueller, M. Dramaturgical and thematic aspects of versions in seventeenth-century France. *In* Mueller, M. Children of Oedipus, and other essays on the imitation of Greek tragedy 1550-1800 p33-45

Mueller, M. Moral and aesthetic tendencies in eighteenth-century adaptations of Greek tragedy. *In* Mueller, M. Children of Oedipus, and other essays on the imitation of Greek tragedy 1550-1800 p65-79

**French fiction**
**Women authors**

Jones, S. Madame de Tencin: an eighteenth-century woman novelist. *In* Woman and society in eighteenth-century France, ed. by E. Jacobs and others p207-17

**18th century—History and criticism**

Todd, J. The biographical context. *In* Todd, J. Women's friendship in literature p359-402

Todd, J. The literary context. *In* Todd, J. Women's friendship in literature p305-58

**French poetry**
*See also* Romances; Troubadors

**To 1500—History and criticism**

Lutz, C. E. Le bon chien Soullart. *In* Lutz, C. E. The oldest library motto, and other library essays p109-14

**19th century—History and criticism**

Peyre, H. Introduction. *In* Peyre, H. What is symbolism? p 1-5

Peyre, H. The symbolists. *In* Peyre, H. What is symbolism? p82-97

**French provincial (Motion picture)**

Kael, P. Lion-hearted women. *In* Kael, P. When the lights go down p143-48

**Frente de Libertação de Moçambique.** See Liberation Front of Mozambique

**Frenz, Horst**

Eugene O'Neill and Georg Kaiser. *In* Eugene O'Neill, ed. by V. Floyd p172-85

**Freud, Sigmund**
**About**

Bloom, H. Freud's concepts of defense and the poetic will. *In* The Literary Freud: mechanisms of defense and the poetic will, ed. by J. H. Smith p 1-28

Dickstein, M. The price of experience: Blake's reading of Freud. *In* The Literary Freud: mechanisms of defense and the poetic will, ed. by J. H. Smith p67-111

Ferguson, M. W. Border territories of defense: Freud and defenses of poetry. *In* The Literary Freud: mechanisms of defense and the poetic will, ed. by J. H. Smith p149-80

Gekoski, R. A. Freud and English literature, 1900-30. *In* The Context of English literature, 1900-1930, ed. by M. Bell p186-217

Hale, N. G. Freud's reflections on work and love. *In* Themes of work and love in adulthood, ed. by N. J. Smelser and E. H. Erikson p29-42

Irwin, J. T. Figurations of the writer's death: Freud and Hart Crane. *In* The Literary Freud: mechanisms of defense and the poetic will, ed. by J. H. Smith p217-60

La Barre, W. Personality from a psychoanalytic viewpoint. *In* La Barre, W. Culture in context p119-40

Morris, H. The need to connect: representations of Freud's psychical apparatus. *In* The Literary Freud: mechanisms of defense and the poetic will, ed. by J. H. Smith p309-44

Neumann, E. Freud and the father image. *In* Neumann, E. Creative man p232-45

Skura, M. A. Revisions and rereadings in dreams and allegories. *In* The Literary Freud: mechanisms of defense and the poetic will, ed. by J. H. Smith p345-79

Sokel, W. H. Freud and the magic of Kafka's writing. *In* The World of Franz Kafka, ed. by J. P. Stern p145-58

Sprinker, J. M. Fictions of the self: the end of autobiography. *In* Autobiography: essays theoretical and critical, ed. by J. Olney p321-42

Trilling, L. The formative years. *In* Trilling, L. Speaking of literature and society p270-74

Trilling, L. Last years of a Titan. *In In* Trilling, L. Speaking of literature and society p295-99

Trilling, L. The progressive psyche. *In* Trilling, L. Speaking of literature and society p181-85

Trilling, L. The years of maturity. *In* Trilling, L. Speaking of literature and society p275-78

**About individual works**
*Leonardo da Vinci*

Trilling, L. Neurosis and the health of the artist. *In* Trilling, L. Speaking of literature and society p224-29

*The uncanny*

Hertz, N. H. Freud and The sandman. *In* Textual strategies, ed. by J. V. Harari p296-319

**Influence**

La Barre, W. The influence of Freud on anthropology. *In* La Barre, W. Culture in context p163-200

Trilling, L. The problem of influence. *In* Trilling, L. Speaking of literature and society p217-19

**Freud, Sigmund, and Jung, Carl Gustav**
**About individual works**
*The Freud/Jung letters*

Erikson, E. H. Themes of adulthood in the Freud-Jung correspondence. *In* Themes of work and love in adulthood, ed. by N. J. Smelser and E. H. Erikson p43-74

**Frey, R. G.**

Did Socrates commit suicide? *In* Suicide: the philosophical issues, ed. by M. P. Battin and D. J. Mayo p35-38

**Fried, Erich**
**About**

Last, R. Erich Fried: poetry and politics. *In* Modern Austrian writing, ed. by A. Best and H. Wolfschütz p181-96

**Friedlaender, Salomo**

### About

Kuxdorf, M. Mynona versus Remarque, Tucholsky, Mann, and others: not so quiet on the literary front. *In* The First World War in German narrative prose, ed. by C. N. Genno and H. Wetzel p71-92

**Friedman, Lawrence Meir**

Law and small business in the United States: one hundred years of struggle and accommodation. *In* Small business in American life, ed. by S. W. Bruchey p305-18

**Friedman, Melvin J.**

The enigma of unpopularity and critical neglect: the case for Wallace Markfield. *In* Seasoned authors for a new season: the search for standards in popular writing, ed. by L. Filler p33-42

**Friedman, Milton, and Friedman, Rose**

The tide is turning; excerpt "From free to choose: a personal statement." *In* The United States in the 1980s, ed. by P. Duignan and A. Rabushka p3-30

**Friedman, Rose.** See Friedman, M. jt. auth.

**Friedrich, David Caspar**

### About

Harbison, R. The cult of death. *In* Harbison, R. Deliberate regression p25-62

**Friends, Society of**

Wells, R. V. Quaker marriage patterns in a colonial perspective. *In* A Heritage of her own, ed. by N. F. Cott and E. H. Pleck p81-106

**Friends, Society of in literature**

Reisler, M. Voltaire's Quaker letters as strategical truth: altering the reader's structure of perception in the service of a higher vision. *In* Studies in eighteenth-century culture v9 p429-54

**Friendship**

Smith-Rosenberg, C. The female world of love and ritual: relations between women in nineteenth-century America. *In* A Heritage of her own, ed. by N. F. Cott and E. H. Pleck p311-42

*See also* Sympathy

**Friendship in literature**

Pebworth, T. L. Cowley's Davideis and the exaltation of friendship. *In* The David myth in Western literature, ed. by R. J. Frontain and J. Wojcik p96-104

Scodel, R. ΑΔΜΗΤΟΥ ΛΟΓΟΣ and the Alcestis. *In* Harvard Studies in classical philology, v83, p51-62

Todd, J. The biographical context. *In* Todd, J. Women's friendship in literature p359-402

Todd, J. Erotic friendship: Denis Diderot's The nun. *In* Todd, J. Women's friendship in literature p100-31

Todd, J. Erotic friendship: John Cleland's Fanny Hill. *In* Todd, J. Women's friendship in literature p69-100

Todd, J. The literary context. *In* Todd, J. Women's friendship in literature p305-58

Todd, J. Manipulative friendship: Jean-Jacques Rousseau's Julie. *In* Todd, J. Women's friendship in literature p132-67

Todd, J. Political friendship: Mary Wollstonecraft's Mary, a fiction. *In* Todd, J. Women's friendship in literature p191-226

Todd, J. Sentimental friendship: Samuel Richardson's Clarissa. *In* Todd, J. Women's friendship in literature p9-68

**Frisch, Otto Robert**

You can prove anything with statistics. *In* Lying truths, ed. by R. Duncan and M. Weston-Smith p171-79

**Fritz, Jean**

The education of an American. *In* The Arbuthnot lectures, 1970-1979 p123-38

**Frohock, William Merrill**

The voice of the poet. *In* André Malraux, ed, by F. Dorenlot and M. Tison-Braun p3-14

**Fromentin, Eugène**

### About individual works

*Dominique*

Barthes, R. Fromentin: Dominique. *In* Barthes, R. New critical essays p91-104

**The front (Motion picture)**

Kael, P. Charmed lives. *In* Kael, P. When the lights go down p167-72

Kauffmann, S. The front. *In* Kauffmann, S. Before my eyes p242-44

**Front populaire**

Bradby, D. The October group and theatre under the Front populaire. *In* Performance and politics in popular drama, ed. by D. Bradby, L. James and B. Sharratt p231-42

**Frontier and pioneer life**

*See also* Overland journeys to the Pacific

#### California

Scott, F. D. Peter Lassen: Danish pioneer of California, 1800-1859. *In* Makers of an American immigrant legacy, ed. by O. S. Lovoll p186-209

**Frontier and pioneer life in literature**

Allen, G. W. How Emerson, Thoreau, and Whitman viewed the "frontier." *In* Toward a new American literary history, ed. by L. J. Budd, E. H. Cady and C. L. Anderson p111-28

**Frost, Robert**

### About

Heinzelman, K. The psychomachia of labor. *In* Heinzelman, K. The economics of the imagination p166-95

Keith, W. J. Robert Frost. *In* Keith, W. J. The poetry of nature p119-40

**Frustration**

Spengler, J. J. Rising expectations: frustrations. *In* Propaganda and communication in world history, ed. by H. D. Lasswell, D. Lerner and H. Speier v3 p37-92

**Fry, Paul H.**

The poet's calling in the English ode

*Contents*

"Alexander's feast" and the tyranny of music
Introduction: the man at the gate
Milton's light-harnessed ode
Postscript: the ode after "Autumn"
The pressure of sense in some odes of Jonson and Drayton
Shelley and the celebration of power
The tented sky in the odes of Collins
Thomas Gray's feather'd cincture
"To autumn" and the sound of being
Voice in the leaves: three odes of Keats
The wedding guest in "Dejection"
Wordsworth's severe Intimations

**Frye, Herman Northrop.** See Frye, Northrop

**Frye, John**

Class, generation and social change: a case in Salem, Massachusetts, 1636-1656. *In* 5000 years of popular culture, ed. by F. E. H. Schroeder p278-85

**Frye, Northrop**

**About**

Hartman, G. H. The sacred jungle 3: Frye, Burke, and some conclusions. *In* Hartman, G. H. Criticism in the wilderness p86-114

Krieger, M. The critical legacy of Matthew Arnold; or, The strange brotherhood of T. S. Eliot, I. A. Richards, and Northrop Frye. *In* Krieger, M. Poetic presence and illusion p92-107

**About individual works**

*Anatomy of criticism*

Lentricchia, F. The place of Northrop Frye's "Anatomy of criticism." *In* Lentricchia, F. After the New Criticism p2-26

**Fryxell, Fritiof Melvin.** See Nelson, C. M. jt. auth.

**Fuchs, Daniel**

**About individual works**

*Low company*

Miller, G. The gangster as existential hero. *In* Miller, G. Screening the novel p143-66

**Fuegi, John**

Meditations on mimesis: the case of Brecht. *In* Drama and mimesis, ed. by J. Redmond p103-12

**Fuentes, Carlos**

**About individual works**

*The death of Artemio Cruz*

Shaw, D. L. Narrative arrangement in La muerte de Artemio Cruz. *In* Contemporary Latin American fiction, ed. by S. Bacarisse p34-47

**Fuhrman, Ellsworth R.**

The sociology of knowledge in America, 1883-1915

*Contents*

Albion W. Small
Charles H. Cooley
Coleridge and his dream poem
Critical-emancipatory and social-technological themes in the sociology of knowledge
Edward A. Ross
Franklin H. Giddings
Lester F. Ward
On the cognitive superiority of the sociology of knowledge
Social context and early American sociology: the Progressive era
William G. Sumner

**Fulfillment (Ethics).** See Self-realization

**Fulk of Toulouse.** See Folquet de Marseille, Bp. of Toulouse

**Fuller, Aaron B.**

Davenport: "Single taxer of the looser observance." *In* Critics of Henry George, ed. by R. V. Andelson p293-302

Rae: a journalist out of his depth. *In* Critics of Henry George, ed. by R. V. Andelson p153-61

**Fuller, Roy**

A normal enough dog: Kafka and the office. *In* The World of Franz Kafka, ed. by J. P. Stern p191-201

**Funkenstein, Amos**

Descartes, eternal truths and the divine omnipotence. *In* Descartes, ed. by S. Gaukroger p181-95

**Furbank, Philip Nicholas**

Forster and 'Bloomsbury' prose. *In* E. M. Forster: a human exploration, ed. by G. K. Das and J. Beer p161-66

**Furniture, German-American**

**Texas**

Taylor, L. W. Fachwerk and Brettstuhl: the rejection of traditional folk culture. *In* Perspectives on American folk art, ed. by I. M. G. Quimby and S. T. Swank p162-76

**Furniture, Norwegian-American**

**Middle West**

Nelson, M. J. The material culture and folk arts of the Norwegians in America. *In* Perspectives on American folk art, ed. by I. M. G. Quimby and S. T. Swank p79-133

**The fury (Motion picture)**

Kael, P. Shivers. *In* Kael, P. When the lights go down p418-24

**Fussell, B. H.**

Woolf's peculiar comic world: Between the acts. *In* Virginia Woolf, ed. by R. Freedman p262-83

**Futabatei, Shemei, pseud.**

**About individual works**

*The drifting clouds*

Walker, J. A. Futabatei's Ukigumo (The floating clouds): the first novel of the individual. *In* Walker, J. A. The Japanese novel of the Meiji and the ideal of individualism p30-61

**Futility.** See Frustration

**Futures.** See Commodity exchanges

**Futurology.** See Forecasting

# G

**Gabbey, Alan**

Force and inertia in the seventeenth century: Descartes and Newton. *In* Descartes, ed. by S. Gaukroger p230-320

**Gabirol, Solomon ibn.** See Ibn Gabirol, Solomon ben Judah

**Gable and Lombard (Motion picture)**

Kael, P. Libel. *In* Kael, P. When the lights go down p140-43

**Gabriel (Archangel)**

Schapiro, M. An Irish-Latin text on the angel with the ram in Abraham's sacrifice. *In* Schapiro, M. Selected papers v3: Late antique, early Christian and mediaeval art p307-18

**Art**

Schapiro, M. The angel with the ram in Abraham's sacrifice: a parallel in Western and Islamic art. *In* Schapiro, M. Selected papers v3: Late antique, early Christian and mediaeval art p289-306

**Gaffney, Mason.** See Andelson, R. V. jt. auth.

**Gago, Serras.** See Portas N. jt. auth.

**Galand, René**

Baudelaire and myth. *In* The Binding of Proteus, ed. by M. W. McCune, T. Orbison and P. M. Withim p174-95

**Gale, Robert L.**

Henry James. *In* American literary scholarship, 1978 p91-110

**Galileo (Motion picture)**

Kauffmann, S. Galileo. *In* Kauffmann, S. Before my eyes p113-14

**Galinsky, Hans**
Foreign scholarship: German contributions. *In* American literary scholarship, 1978 p445-65

**Gallagher, Mary Ann Y.**
Aristocratic opposition to the establishment of a foundling home in Arequipa, Peru. *In* Studies in eighteenth-century culture v9 p45-58

**Gallas**
Bauer, D. F. and Hinnant, J. Normal and revolutionary divination: a Kuhnian approach to African traditional thought. *In* Explorations in African systems of thought, ed. by I. C. Karp & C. S. Bird p213-36

**Gallman, Robert E.**
Economic growth. *In* Encyclopedia of American economic history, ed. by G. Porter v 1 p133-50

**Gallup, Donald Clifford**
Aldis, Foley, and the collection of American literature at Yale. *In* The Bibliographical Society of America, 1904-79 p209-28

**Galuth.** See Jews—Diaspora

**Galvão, Eduardo Eneas**
The encounter of tribal and national societies in the Brazilian Amazon. *In* Brazil, anthropological perspectives, ed. by M. L. Margolis and W. E. Carter p25-38

**Gambia**
### Foreign relations—Senegal
Bayo, K. Environment and national system formation: Gambian orientations toward Senegambia. *In* Values, identities, and national integration, ed. by J. N. Paden p105-19

### Politics and government
Bayo, K. Environment and national system formation: Gambian orientations toward Senegambia. *In* Values, identities, and national integration, ed. by J. N. Paden p105-19

**The gambler (Motion picture)**
Kauffmann, S. The gambler. *In* Kauffmann, S. Before my eyes p87-88

**Ganda.** See Baganda

**The gangster (Motion picture)**
Miller, G. The gangster as existential hero. *In* Miller, G. Screening the novel p143-66

**Gann, Daniel H.** See Weixlmann, J. jt. auth.

**Gann, Lewis Henry, and Duignan, Peter James**
Africa. *In* The United States in the 1980s, ed. by P. Duignan and A. Rabushka p827-58
*See also* Duignan, P. J. jt. auth.

**Gannon, Susan**
A note on Collodi and Lucian. *In* Children's literature v8 p98-102

**Garaudy, Roger**
Values in a Marxist perspective. *In* Value and values in evolution, ed. by E. A. Maziarz p95-102

**García Márquez, Gabriel**
#### About individual works
*The autumn of the patriarch*
Brotherston, G. García Márquez and the secrets of Saturno Santos. *In* Contemporary Latin American fiction, ed. by S. Bacarisse p48-53
*"Los funerales de la Mamá Grande"*
Foster, D. W. The double inscription of the narrataire in "Los funerales de la Mamá Grande." *In* Foster, D. W. Studies in the contemporary Spanish-American short story p51-62

*One hundred years of solitude*
Aaron, M. A. Garcia Marquez' mecedor as link between passage of time and presence of mind. *In* The Analysis of literary texts, ed. by R. D. Pope p21-30
Brotherston, G. García Márquez and the secrets of Saturno Santos. *In* Contemporary Latin American fiction, ed. by S. Bacarisse p48-53
*La prodigiosa tarde de Baltazar*
Foster, D. W. García Márquez and the écriture of complicity: "La prodigiosa tarde de Baltazar." *In* Foster, D. W. Studies in the contemporary Spanish-American short story p39-50

**Gardam, Jane**
Writing for children: some wasps in the marmalade. *In* Royal Society of Literature of the United Kingdom, London. Essays by divers hands: innovation in contemporary literature, new ser. v40 p52-66
#### About
Gardam, J. Writing for children: some wasps in the marmalade. *In* Royal Society of Literature of the United Kingdom, London. Essays by divers hands: innovation in contemporary literature, new ser. v40 p52-66

**Gardening.** See Landscape gardening

**Gardens**
#### Symbolic aspects
Robertson, D. W. The doctrine of charity in medieval literary gardens: a topical approach through symbolism and allegory. *In* Robertson, D. W. Essays in medieval culture p21-50

**Gardner, Beatrice T.** See Gardner, R. A. jt. auth.

**Gardner, Elizabeth J.**
The philosophes and women: sensationalism and sentiment. *In* Woman and society in eighteenth-century France, ed. by E. Jacobs and others p19-27

**Gardner, Dame Helen Louise.** See Part 2 under title: English Renaissance studies

**Gardner, Howard**
Foreword: Cognition comes of age. *In* Language and learning, ed. by M. Piattelli-Palmarini p xix-xxxvi

**Gardner, Richard Allen, and Gardner, Beatrice T.**
Comparative psychology and language acquisition. *In* Speaking of apes, ed. by T. A. Sebeok and J. Umiker-Sebeok p287-330

**Garfield, Leon**
#### About
Townsend, J. R. Leon Garfield. *In* Townsend, J. R. A sounding of storytellers p66-80

**Garner, Alan**
#### About
Rees, D. Hanging in their true shapes: Alan Garner. *In* Rees, D. The marble in the water p56-67
Townsend, J. R. Alan Garner. *In* Townsend, J. R. A sounding of storytellers p81-96

**Garner, Stanton B.**
'The tempest': language and society. *In* Shakespeare survey 32 p177-87

**Garnier, Robert**
#### About individual works
*Antigone*
Mueller, M. The historical vision of tragedy: Garnier's Antigone. *In* Mueller, M. Children of Oedipus, and other essays on the imitation of Greek tragedy 1550-1800 p17-32

**Garnier, Robert**—About individual works—*Cont.*

### Les Juifves

Mueller, M. The scriptural tragedies of De la Taille and Garnier. *In* Mueller, M. Children of Oedipus, and other essays on the imitation of Greek tragedy 1550-1800 p172-82

Reiss, T. J. Les Juifves: possession and the willful eye. *In* Reiss, T. J. Tragedy and truth p137-61

**Garrett, Peter K.**
The Victorian multiplot novel

*Contents*

Dickens: he mounts a high tower in his mind
Dickens: machinery in motion
George Eliot: equivalent centers
Thackeray: seeing double
Trollope: eccentricities

**Garro, Elena**

### About individual works
*Los recuerdos del porvenir*

Fox-Lockert, L. Elena Garro. *In* Fox-Lockert, L. Women novelists in Spain and Spanish America p228-40

**Gas, Natural**

### Law and legislation—United States

Malbin, M. J. Congress, policy analysis, and natural gas deregulation: a parable about fig leaves. *In* Bureaucrats, policy analysts, statesmen: who leads? Ed. by R. A. Goldwin p62-87

**Gas warfare.** See Gases, Asphixiating and poisonous—War use

**Gasché, Rodolphe**
Deconstruction as criticism. *In* Glyph 6 p177-215

The mixture of genres, the mixture of styles, and figural interpretation: Sylvie, by Gerard de Nerval. *In* Glyph 7 p102-30

**Gases, Asphixiating and poisons**

### War use

Ceadel, M. Popular fiction and the next war, 1918-39. *In* Class, culture and social change, ed. by F. Gloversmith p161-84

**Gaskell, Elizabeth Cleghorn (Stevenson)**

### About

Stone, D. D. Elizabeth Gaskell, Wordsworth, and the burden of reality. *In* Stone, D. D. The romantic impulse in Victorian fiction p133-72

### About individual works
*Mary Barton*

James, W. L. G. The portrayal of death and 'substance of life': aspects of the modern reader's response to 'Victorianism.' *In* Reading the Victorian novel: detail into form, ed. by I. Gregor p226-42

*Wives and daughters*

Berke, J. and Berke, L. Mothers and daughters in Wives and daughters: a study of Elizabeth Gaskell's last novel. *In* The Lost tradition: mothers and daughters in literature, ed. by C. N. Davidson and E. M. Broner p95-109

**Gastronomy**

### Language

Fisher, M. F. K. As the lingo languishes. *In* The State of the language, ed. by L. Michaels and C. Ricks p267-76

**Gati, Charles**
The Stalinist legacy in Soviet foreign policy. *In* The Soviet Union since Stalin, ed. by S. F. Cohen, A. Rabinowitch, and R. Sharlet p279-301

**Gaukroger, Stephen**
Descartes' project for a mathematical physics. *In* Descartes, ed. by S. Gaukroger p97-140

**Gay, Peter**
The Enlightenment as a communication universe. *In* Propaganda and communication in world history, ed. by H. D. Lasswell, D. Lerner and H. Speier v2 p85-111

On the bourgeoisie: a psychological interpretation. *In* Consciousness and class experience in nineteenth-century Europe, ed. by J. M. Merriman p187-203

**Gaylord, Alan T.**
The lesson of the Troilus: chastisement and correction. *In* Essays on Troilus and Criseyde, ed. by M. Salu p23-42

**Gays, Male.** See Homosexuals, Male

**Gdansk, Poland**

### Theaters—History

Limon, J. Pictorial evidence for a possible replica of the London Fortune Theatre in Gdansk. *In* Shakespeare survey 32 p189-99

**Geary, Patrick J.**
The ninth-century relic trade. *In* Religion and the people, 800-1700, ed. by J. Obelkevich p8-19

**Geiger, George Raymond**

### About individual works
*The philosophy of Henry George*

Fuller, A. B. Davenport: "Single taxer of the looser observance." *In* Critics of Henry George, ed. by R. V. Andelson p293-302

**Geismar, Maxwell David**

### About individual works
*Writers in crisis*

Trilling, L. Artists and the "societal function." *In* Trilling, L. Speaking of literature and society p186-91

**Gekoski, R. A.**
Freud and English literature, 1900-30. *In* The Context of English literature, 1900-1930, ed. by M. Bell p186-217

**Gellie, George Henry**

### About individual works
*Sophocles*

Knox, B. M. W. Review of Sophocles: a reading (by G. H. Gellie). *In* Knox, B. M. W. Word and action p194-97

**Gellner, Ernest**
A Russian Marxist philosophy of history. *In* Soviet and Western anthropology, ed. by E. Gellner p59-82

**Gelven, Michael**
Heidegger and tragedy. *In* Martin Heidegger and the question of literature, ed. by W. V. Spanos p215-28

**Gendron, Bernard**
Sexual alienation. *In* The Philosophy of sex, ed. by A. Soble p281-98

**Genealogy.** See Southern States—Genealogy

**Genealogy in literature**
Sundquist, E. J. Preface. *In* Sundquist, E. J. Home as found p xi-xx

**Generation gap.** See Conflict of generations

**Genêt, Jean**

### About

Collins, D. Genet and the just. *In* Collins, D. Sartre as biographer p80-110

**Genetic engineering.** See Recombinant DNA

**Genetic recombination.** Recombinant DNA

**Geneticists**

### United States

Allen, G. E. The rise and spread of the classical school of heredity, 1910-1930; development and influence of the Mendelian chromosome theory. *In* The Sciences in the American context: new perspectives, ed. by N. Reingold p209-28

**Genetics**

Danchin, A. A critical note on the use of the term "phenocopy". *In* Language and learning, ed. by M. Piattelli-Palmarini p356-60

*See also* Heredity; Nature and nurture

### History

Allen, G. E. The rise and spread of the classical school of heredity, 1910-1930; development and influence of the Mendelian chromosome theory. *In* The Sciences in the American context: new perspectives, ed. by N. Reingold p209-28

**Genetics and environment.** See Nature and nurture

**Genette, Gérard**

Valéry and the poetics of language. *In* Textual strategies, ed. by J. V. Harari p359-73

**Genno, Charles N.**

The anatomy of pre-war society in Robert Musil's Der Mann ohne Eigenschaften. *In* The First World War in German narrative prose, ed. by C. N. Genno and H. Wetzel p3-15

**Genocide.** See Holocaust, Jewish (1939-1945)

**Genovese, Eugene D.**

Life in the big house; excerpts from "Roll, Jordan, roll." *In* A Heritage of her own, ed. by N. F. Cott and E. H. Pleck p290-97

**Genre (Literature).** See Literary form

**Geographical distribution of man.** See Anthropo-geography

**Geography, Social.** See Anthropo-geography

**Geology**

Dean, D. R. The influence of geology on American literature and thought. *In* New Hampshire Bicentennial Conference on the History of Geology, University of New Hampshire, 1976. Two hundred years of geology in America p289-303

*See also* Paleontology; Submarine geology

### Bibliography

Hazen, R. M. and Hazen, M. H. Neglected geological literature: an introduction to a bibliography by American-published geology, 1669 to 1850 (abstract). *In* New Hampshire Bicentennial Conference in the History of Geology, University of New Hampshire, 1976. Two hundred years of geology in America p33-36

### History

Taylor, K. L. Geology in 1776: some notes on the character of an incipient science. *In* New Hampshire Bicentennial Conference on the History of Geology, University of New Hampshire, 1976. Two hundred years of geology in America p75-90

### Maps

Cailleux, A. The geological map of North America (1752) of J.-E. Guettard. *In* New Hampshire Bicentennial Conference on the History of Geology, University of New Hampshire, 1976. Two hundred years of geology in America p43-52

### Delaware

Pickett, T. E. James C. Booth and the first Delaware geological survey, 1837-1841. *In* New Hampshire Bicentennial Conference on the History of Geology, University of New Hampshire, 1976. Two hundred years of geology in America p167-74

### Louisiana

Skinner, H. C. Raymond Thomassy and the practical geology of Louisiana. *In* New Hampshire Bicentennial Conference on the History of Geology, University of New Hampshire, 1976. Two hundred years of geology in America p201-11

### Pennsylvania

Jordan, W. M. Geology and the industrial-transportation revolution in early to mid nineteenth-century Pennsylvania. *In* New Hampshire Bicentennial Conference on the History of Geology, University of New Hampshire, 1976. Two hundred years of geology in America p91-103

### Texas

Alexander, N. The work of Edwin Theodore Dumble on the East Texas lignite deposits (1882-1892). *In* New Hampshire Bicentennial Conference on the History of Geology, University of New Hampshire 1976. Two hundred years of geology in America p213-22

### United States—History

Mirsky, A. Geologic resources of the original thirteen United States (summary). *In* New Hampshire Bicentennial Conference on the History of Geology, University of New Hampshire, 1976. Two hundred years of geology in America p39-41

### United States—Surveys

Aldrich, M. L. American state geological surveys, 1820-1845. *In* New Hampshire Bicentennial Conference on the History of Geology, University of New Hampshire, 1976. Two hundred years of geology in America p133-43

**Geology, Stratigraphic**

Gerstner, P. A. Henry Darwin Rogers and William Barton Rogers on the nomenclature of the American Paleozoic rocks. *In* New Hampshire Bicentennial Conference on the History of Geology, University of New Hampshire, 1976. Two hundred years of geology in America p175-86

Nelson, C. M. and Fryxell, F. M. The antebellum collaboration of Meek and Hayden in stratigraphy. *In* New Hampshire Bicentennial Conference on the History of Geology. University of New Hampshire, 1976. Two hundred years of geology in America p187-200

**Geology, Structural.** See Plate tectonics

**Geology, Submarine.** See Submarine geology

**Geometry, Algebraic.** See Geometry, Analytic

**Geometry, Analytic**

Grosholz, E. R. Descartes' unification of algebra and geometry. *In* Descartes, ed. by S. Gaukroger p156-68

**Geophysics.** See Plate tectonics

**Geopolitics**

Kemp, G. T. H. Defense innovation and geopolitics: from the Persian Gulf to outer space. *In* National security in the 1980s: from weakness to strength, ed. by W. S. Thompson p69-87

*See also* Demography

**George, Henry**

### About individual works
*Progress and poverty*

Andelson, R. V. Carver: reluctant demi-Georgist. *In* Critics of Henry George, ed. by R. V. Andelson p303-12

Andelson, R. V. Cathrein's careless clerical critique. *In* Critics of Henry George, ed. by R. V. Andelson p126-36

Andelson, R. V. Introduction. *In* Critics of Henry George, ed. by R. V. Andelson p15-28

Andelson, R. V. Neo-Georgism. *In* Critics of Henry George, ed. by R. V. Andelson p381-93

Andelson, R. V. Ryan and his domestication of natural law. *In* Critics of Henry George, ed. by R. V. Andelson p342-53

Andelson, R. V. and Gaffney, M. Seligman and his critique from social utility. *In* Critics of Henry George, ed. by R. V. Andelson p273-90

Babilot, G. Dixwell: animadversions of an admiring adversary. *In* Critics of Henry George, ed. by R. V. Andelson p165-77

Babilot, G. Moffat's "unorthodox" critique. *In* Critics of Henry George, ed. by R. V. Andelson p109-25

Busey, J. L. Alcázar's "most voluminous of all assaults." *In* Critics of Henry George, ed. by R. V. Andelson p326-41

Collier, C. F. Harris and his anachronistic attack. *In* Critics of Henry George, ed. by R. V. Andelson p187-95

Collier, C. F. Rutherford: the Devil quotes scripture. *In* Critics of Henry George, ed. by R. V. Andelson p222-33

Cord, S. B. Walker: the general leads the charge. *In* Critics of Henry George, ed. by R. V. Andelson p178-86

Cord, S. B. and Andelson, R. V. Ely: a liberal economist defends landlordism. *In* Critics of Henry George, ed. by R. V. Andelson p313-25

Douglas, R. Huxley's critique from social Darwinism. *In* Critics of Henry George, ed. by R. V. Andelson p137-52

Douglas, R. Laveleye: the critic ripe for conversion. *In* Critics of Henry George, ed. by R. V. Andelson p47-55

Douglas, R. Mallock and the "most elaborate answer." *In* Critics of Henry George, ed. by R. V. Andelson p95-108

Fuller, A. B. Davenport: "Single taxer of the looser observance." *In* Critics of Henry George, ed. by R. V. Andelson p293-302

Fuller, A. B. Rae: a journalist out of his depth. *In* Critics of Henry George, ed. by R. V. Andelson p153-61

Harrison, F. Gronlund and other Marxists. *In* Critics of Henry George, ed. by R. V. Andelson p196-221

Harrison, F. Longe and Wrightson: conservative critics of George's wage theory. *In* Critics of Henry George, ed. by R. V. Andelson p72-94

Harriss, C. L. Rothbard's **anarcho-capitalist** critique. *In* Critics of Henry George, ed. by R. V. Andelson p354-70

Hébert, R. F. Marshall: a professional economist guards the purity of his discipline. *In* Critics of Henry George, ed. by **R. V.** Andelson p56-71

Johannsen, O. B. Oser: reservations of a friendly commentator. *In* Critics of Henry George, ed. by R. V. Andelson p371-77

Schwartzman, J. Ingalls, Hanson, and Tucker: nineteenth-century American anarchists. *In* Critics of Henry George, ed. by R. V. Andelson p234-53

Truehart, W. B. Atkinson: an ill-informed assailant. *In* Critics of Henry George, ed. by R. V. Andelson p254-60

Wasserman, L. The essential Henry George. *In* Critics of Henry George, ed. by R. V. Andelson p29-43

**Georgia (Transcaucasia)**

Suny, R. G. Georgia and Soviet nationality policy. *In* The Soviet Union since Stalin, ed. by S. F. Cohen, A. Rabinowitch, and R. Sharlet p200-26

**Geoscience.** See Earth sciences

The **geosyncline**—first major geological concept "made in America." Dott, R. H. *In* New Hampshire Bicentennial Conference on the History of Geology, University of New Hampshire, 1976. Two hundred years of geology in America p239-64

**Gérard de Nerval, Gérard Labrunie, known as**

### About individual works
*Sylvie*

Gasché, R. The mixture of genres, the mixture of styles, and figural interpretation: Sylvie, by Gerard de Nerval. *In* Glyph 7 p102-30

**German-American newspapers**

### History
Adams, W. P. The colonial German-language press and the American Revolution. *In* The Press & the American Revolution, ed. by B. Bailyn and J. B. Hench p151-228

**German Americans**
### Texas
Taylor, L. W. Fachwerk and Brettstuhl: the rejection of traditional folk culture. *In* Perspectives on American folk art, ed. by I. M. G. Quimby and S. T. Swank p162-76

**German drama**

#### 18th century—History and criticism
Bennett, B. Introduction. *In* Bennett, B. Modern drama and German classicism p15-21

#### 19th century—History and criticism
Bennett, B. The importance of being Egmont. *In* Bennett, B. Modern drama and German classicism p151-87

Bennett, B. Introduction. *In* Bennett, B. Modern drama and German classicism p15-21

#### 20th century—History and criticism
Bennett, B. The importance of being Egmont. *In* Bennett, B. Modern drama and German classicism p151-87

**German language**
Calvary, M. Yiddish. *In* The Jew, ed. by A. A. Cohen p31-42

**Gerson, John.** See Gerson, Joannes

**Gerstner, Patsy A.**
Henry Darwin Rogers and William Barton Rogers on the nomenclature of the American Paleozoic rocks. *In* New Hampshire Bicentennial Conference on the History of Geology, University of New Hampshire, 1976. Two hundred years of geology in America p175-86

**Get out your handkerchiefs (Motion picture)**
Kael, P. Bertrand Blier. *In* Kael, P. When the lights go down p454-62
Kauffmann, S. Get out your handkerchiefs. *In* Kauffmann, S. Before my eyes p14-16

**Ghana**
### Ethnic relations
Fischer, L. F. Student orientations toward nation-building in Ghana. *In* Values, identities, and national integration, ed. by J. N. Paden p271-84
Kaufert, J. M. Ethnic unit definition in Ghana: a comparison of culture cluster analysis and social distance measures. *In* Values, identities, and national integration, ed. by J. N. Paden p41-51
Kaufert, J. M. Situational ethnic identity in Ghana: a survey of university students. *In* Values, identities, and national integration, ed. by J. N. Paden p53-74

### Politics and government
Fischer, L. F. Student orientations toward nation-building in Ghana. *In* Values, identities, and national integration, ed. by J. N. Paden p271-84

### Social conditions
Kaufert, J. M. Ethnic unit definition in Ghana: a comparison of culture cluster analysis and social distance measures. *In* Values, identities, and national integration, ed. by J. N. Paden p41-51

**Ghazali.** See al-Ghazzālī

**al-Ghazzālī**
### About individual works
*Tahāfut al-Falāsifa*
Ivry, A. L. Averroes on causation. *In* Studies in Jewish religious and intellectual history, ed. by S. Stein and R. Loewe p143-56

**Ghertman, Sharon**
Language as protagonist in Sarduy's De donde son los cantantes: a linguistic approach to narrative structure. *In* The Analysis of literary texts, ed. by R. D. Pope p145-52

**Ghose, Aurobindo**
### About
Naik, M. K. Idylls of the occult: the short stories of Sri Aurobindo. *In* Aspects of Indian writing in English, ed. by M. K. Naik p150-61

### About individual works
*The mother*
Nandakumar, P. Sri Aurobindo's 'The mother.' *In* Aspects of Indian writing in English, ed. by M. K. Naik p279-93

*Savitri*
Godak, V. K. Doctrine as imagination in Sri Aurobindo's Savitri. *In* Aspects of Indian writing in English, ed. by M. K. Naik p50-63
Raghavacharyulu, D. V. K. The immense journey: an outline of Aswapathy's Sadhana. *In* Aspects of Indian writing in English, ed. by M. K. Naik p64-79

*Vasavadutta*
Bhatta, S. K. Sri Aurobindo's 'Vasavadutta'. *In* Aspects of Indian writing in English, ed. by M. K. Naik p248-61

### Characters—Aswapathy
Raghavacharyulu, D. V. K. The immense journey: an outline of Aswapathy's Sadhana. *In* Aspects of Indian writing in English, ed. by M. K. Naik p64 79

### Philosophy
Ghose, S. K. Sri Aurobindo and the spiritual society. *In* Aspects of Indian writing in English, ed. by M. K. Naik p268-78

**Ghose, Sisir Kumar**
Sri Aurobindo and the spiritual society. *In* Aspects of Indian writing in English, ed. by M. K. Naik p268-78

**Ghose, Sudhindra Nath**
### About
Narayan, S. A. Reality and fantasy in the novels of Sudhin N. Ghose. *In* Aspects of Indian writing in English, ed. by M. K. Naik p162-71

**Gibb, Hamilton Alexander Rosskeen**
### About
Hourani, A. H. H. A. R. Gibb: the vocation of an Orientalist. *In* Hourani, A. H. Europe and the Middle East. p104-34

**Gibbon, Edward**
### About individual works
*The decline and fall of the Roman Empire*
Momigliano, A. After Gibbon's Decline and fall. *In* Age of spirituality, ed. by K. Weitzmann p7-16

**Gibbons, Brian**
The Revels history of drama in English volume V, 1660-1750. *In* Drama and mimesis, ed. by J. Redmond p191-206

**Gibbs, Cecil Armstrong**
### About
Dent, E. J. Cecil Armstrong Gibbs. *In* Dent, E. J. Selected essays p85-91

**Gibbs, Josiah Willard, 1839-1933**
### About
Morowitz, H. J. Let free energy ring. *In* Morowitz, H. J. The wine of life, and other essays on societies, energy & living things p57-61

**Gibian, George**
New aspects of Soviet Russian literature. *In* The Soviet Union since Stalin, ed. by S. F. Cohen, A. Rabinowitch, and R. Sharlet p252-75

**Gibson, Charles**
Latin America and the Americas. *In* The Past before us, ed. by M. Kammen p187-202

**Giddings, Franklin Henry**
### About
Fuhrman, E. R. Franklin H. Giddings. *In* Fuhrman, E. R. The sociology of knowledge in America, 1883-1915 p100-28

**Giele, Janet Zollinger**
Adulthood as transcendence of age and sex. *In* Themes of work and love in adulthood, ed. by N. J. Smelser and E. H. Erikson p151-73

**Gielgud, Sir John**

### About

Kauffmann, S. John Gielgud: the actor as paragon. *In* Kauffmann, S. Before my eyes p405-13

**Gift-books (Annuals, etc.)**

Tatham, D. Winslow Homer and the New England poets. *In* American Antiquarian Society. Proceedings v89 pt2 p241-60

**Gilbert, Grove Karl**

### About

Pyne, S. J. Certain allied problems in mechanics: Grove Karl Gilbert at the Henry Mountains. *In* New Hampshire Bicentennial Conference on the History of Geology, University of New Hampshire, 1976. Two hundred years of geology in America p225-38

**Gildner, Gary**

### About individual works
#### Nails

Wagner, L. W. Nails: Gary Gildner's house of poetry. *In* Wagner, L. W. American modern p194-98

**Gilkes, Michael**

Edgar Mittelholzer. *In* West Indian literature, ed. by B. King p95-110

**Gilkey, Langdon Brown**

The dialectic of Christian belief: rational, incredible, credible. *In* Rationality and religious belief, ed. by C. F. Delaney p65-83

The religious dilemmas of a scientific culture: the interface of technology, history and religion. *In* Being human in a technological age, ed. by D. M. Borchert and D. Stewart p73-88

**Gill, Robin**

From sociology to theology. *In* Sociology and theology: alliance and conflict, ed. by D. Martin; J. O. Mills [and] W. S. F. Pickering p102-19

**Gilpin, Robert G.**

The computer and world affairs. *In* The Computer age: a twenty-year view, ed. by M. L. Dertouzos and J. Moses p229-53

**Gilson, Étienne Henry**

### About

Ozment, S. H. The interpretation of medieval intellectual history. *In* Ozment, S. H. The age of reform, 1250-1550 p 1-21

**Giner, Francisco.** See Giner de los Rios, Francisco

**Giner, Salvador, and Sevilla-Guzman, Eduardo**

From despotism to parliamentarianism: class domination and political order in the Spanish state. *In* The State in Western Europe, ed. by Richard Scase p197-229

**Giner de los Rios, Francisco**

### About

López-Morillas, J. Francisco Giner and the redemption of Spain. *In* The Analysis of literary texts, ed. by R. D. Pope p244-55

**Ginsberg, Allen**

### About

Howard, R. Allen Ginsberg: "O brothers of the laurel, is the world real? Is the laurel a joke or a crown of thorns?" *In* Howard, R. Alone with America p176-83

Molesworth, C. Republican objects and utopian moments: the poetry of Robert Lowell and Allen Ginsberg. *In* Molesworth, C. The fierce embrace p37-60

Vendler, H. H. Allen Ginsberg. *In* Vendler, H. H. Part of nature, part of us p195-203

**Ginzberg, Eli**

The role of small business in the process of skill acquisition. *In* Small business in American life, ed. by S. W. Bruchey p366-79

**Ginzburg, Carlo**

Cheese and worms. *In* Religion and the people, 800-1700, ed. by J. Obelkevich p87-167

**Giorgi, Amedeo**

Vico and humanistic psychology. *In* Conference on Vico and Contemporary Thought, New York, 1976. Vico and contemporary thought pt2 p69-78

**Girard, René**

Myth and ritual in Shakespeare: A midsummer night's dream. *In* Textual strategies, ed. by J. V. Harari p189-212

"To entrap the wisest": a reading of The merchant of Venice. *In* Literature and society, ed. by E. W. Said p100-19

**Girlfriends (Motion picture)**

Kauffmann, S. Girlfriends. *In* Kauffmann, S. Before my eyes p318-21

**Girls series books**

Segel, E. Domesticity and the wide, wide world. *In* Children's literature v8 p168-75

**Gissing, George Robert**

### About

Plomer, W. C. F. George Gissing. *In* Plomer, W. C. F. Electric delights p66-86

**Gittings, Robert**

Artist upon oath. *In* Royal Society of Literature of the United Kingdom, London. Essays by divers hands: innovation in contemporary literature, new ser. v40 p67-82

### About

Gittings, R. Artist upon oath. *In* Royal Society of Literature of the United Kingdom, London. Essays by divers hands: innovation in contemporary literature, new ser. v40 p67-82

**Givaro Indians.** See Jivaro Indians

**Gladness.** See Happiness

**Gladstone, Jacob**

### About

Alexander, E. The Holocaust and the God of Israel. *In* Alexander, E. The resonance of dust p195-230

**Glasco, Laurence Admiral**

The life cycles and household structure of American ethnic groups: Irish, Germans, and native-born whites in Buffalo, New York, 1855. *In* A Heritage of her own, ed. by N. F. Cott and E. H. Pleck p268-89

**Glaser, Daniel**

A review of crime-causation theory and its application. *In* Crime and justice v 1 p203-37

**Glasgow, Ellen Anderson Gholson**

### About

Wagner, L. W. Ellen Glasgow: daughter as justified. *In* The Lost tradition: mothers and daughters in literature, ed. by C. N. Davidson and E. M. Broner p140-46

### About individual works
#### Barren ground

Wagner, L. W. Barren ground's vein of iron: Dorinda Oakley and some concepts of heroine in 1925. *In* Wagner, L. W. American modern p56-66

**Glasgow, Ellen A. G.**—About individual works
—*Continued*

*The romance of a plain man*

Holman, C. H. The tragedy of self-entrapment: Ellen Glasgow's The romance of a plain man. *In* Toward a new American literary history, ed. by L. Budd, E. H. Cady and C. L. Anderson p154-63

**Characters**—Dorinda Oakley

Wagner, L. W. Barren ground's vein of iron: Dorinda Oakley and some concepts of heroine in 1925. *In* Wagner, L. W. American modern p56-66

**Glatstein, Jacob.** See Gladstone, Jacob

**Glatzer, Nahum Norbert**

Was Franz Rosenzweig a mystic? *In* Studies in Jewish religious and intellectual history, ed. by S. Stein and R. Loewe p121-32

**Glazer, Nathan**

American Jews: three conflicts of loyalties. *In* The Third century, ed. by S. M. Lipset p223-41

**Glazier Psalter.** See Pierpont Morgan Library, New York. Glazier Psalter Ms. G. 25

**Glick, Wendell**

Emerson, Thoreau, and transcendentalism. *In* American literary scholarship, 1978 p3-16

**Glicksberg, Charles Irving**

"Van Wyck Brooks." *In* Van Wyck Brooks: the critic and his critics, ed. by W. Wasserstrom p69-78

**Gloversmith, Frank**

Changing things: Orwell and Auden. *In* Class, culture and social change, ed. by F. Gloversmith p101-41

Defining culture: J. C. Powys, Clive Bell, R. H. Tawney & T. S. Eliot. *In* Class, culture and social change, ed. by F. Gloversmith p15-44

**Glück, Louise**

Vendler, H. H. Louise Glück. *In* Vendler, H. H. Part of nautre, part of us p303-11

**Go tell the Spartans (Motion picture)**

Kauffmann, S. Go tell the Spartans. *In* Kauffmann, S. Before my eyes p313-15

**The goalie's anxiety at the penalty kick (Motion picture)**

Kauffmann, S. The goalie's anxiety at the penalty kick. *In* Kauffmann, S. Before my eyes p276-79

**God**

Plantinga, A. Is belief in God rational? *In* Rationality and religious belief, ed. by C. F. Delaney p7-27

*See also* Causation; Rationalism; Religion

**Attributes**

Davidson, H. A. The principle that a finite body can contain only finite power. *In* Studies in Jewish religious and intellectual history, ed. by S. Stein and R. Loewe p75-92

**Omnipotence**

Funkenstein, A. Descartes, eternal truths and the divine omnipotence. *In* Descartes, ed. by S. Gaukroger p181-95

**Proof**

Burrell, D. B. Religious belief and rationality. *In* Rationality and religious belief, ed. by C. F. Delaney p84-115

**Proof, Moral**

Adams, R. M. Moral arguments for theistic belief. *In* Rationality and religious belief, ed. by C. F. Delaney p116-40

**God (Greek religion)**

Schofield, M. Preconception, argument, and God. *In* Doubt, and dogmatism, ed. by M. Schofield, M. Burnyeat and J. Barnes p283-308

**God (Judaism)**

**Attributes**

Davidson, H. A. The principle that a finite body can contain only finite power. *In* Studies in Jewish religious and intellectual history, ed. by S. Stein and R. Loewe p75-92

**God in literature**

Baym, N. Z. God, father, and lover in Emily Dickinson's poetry. *In* Puritan influences in American literature, ed. by E. Elliott p193-209

**Godard, Jean-Luc**

**About individual works**

*Alphaville*

Thiher, A. Postmodern dilemmas: Godard's Alphaville and Deux ou trois choses que je sais d'elle. *In* Thiher, A. The cinematic muse p180-98

*Two or three things I know about her*

Thiher, A. Postmodern dilemmas: Godard's Alphaville and Deux ou trois choses que je sais d'elle. *In* Thiher, A. The cinematic muse p180-98

**Godelier, Maurice**

The emergence and development of Marxism in anthropology in France. *In* Soviet and Western anthropology, ed. by E. Gellner p3-17

Territory and property in primitive society. *In* Human ethology, ed. by M. von Cranach [and others] p133-55

**The godfather part II (Motion picture)**

Kauffmann, S. The godfather part II. *In* Kauffmann, S. Before my eyes p104-06

**Godwin, Mary (Wollstonecraft)**

**About individual works**

*Mary*

Todd, J. Political friendship: Mary Wollstonecraft's Mary, a fiction. *In* Todd, J. Women's friendship in literature p191-226

**Godwin, William**

**About individual works**

*Caleb Williams*

Uphaus, R. W. Moral and tendency in 'Caleb Williams.' *In* Uphaus, R. W. The impossible observer p123-36

**Goethe, Johann Wolfgang von**

**About**

Ashton, R. D. Lewes and Goethe (1843-55) *In* Ashton, R. D. The German idea p131-46

Carner, M. Goethe and music. *In* Carner, M. Major and minor p85-91

**About individual works**

*Alexis und Dora*

Pickering, F. P. Goethe's 'Alexis und Dora': an interpretation. *In* Pickering, F. P. Essays on medieval German literature and iconography p75-92

*Egmont*

Bennett, B. Egmont and the maelstrom of the self. *In* Bennett, B. Modern drama and German classicism p121-50

Bennett, B. The importance of being Egmont. *In* Bennett, B. Modern drama and German classicism p151-87

**Goethe, Johann W. von**—About individual works—*Continued*

*Elective affinities*

Miller, J. H. A "buchstabliches" reading of The elective affinities. *In* Glyph 6 p 1-23

*Faust*

Ashton, R. D. Coleridge and Faust (1814-20) *In* Ashton, R. D. The German idea p56-66

*Iphigenia in Tauris*

Bennett, B. Iphigenie auf Tauris and Goethe's idea of drama. *In* Bennett, B. Modern drama and German classicism p97-120

Mueller, M. The internalization of eighteenth-century patterns of transformation in Iphigenie auf Tauris. *In* Children of Oedipus, and other essays on the imitation of Greek tragedy 1550-1800 p79-92

*Theory of colours*

Fink, K. J. The metalanguage of Goethe's history of color theory. *In* The Quest for the new science, ed. by K. J. Fink and J. W. Marchand p41-55

*Wilhelm Meister*

Ashton, R. D. Carlyle and Goethe (1822-32) *In* Ashton, R. D. The German idea p76-91

Ashton, R. D. George Eliot and Goethe (1854-76) *In* Ashton, R. D. The German idea p166-77

*Young Werther*

Hagstrum, J. H. The aftermath of sensibility: Sterne, Goethe, and Austen. *In* Hagstrum, J. H. Sex and sensibility p247-77

**Influence—Carlyle**

Ashton, R. D. Carlyle and Goethe (1822-32) *In* Ashton, R. D. The German idea p76-91

**Influence—Schiller**

Bennett, B. The importance of being Egmont. *In* Bennett, B. Modern drama and German classicism p151-87

**Translations, English**

Ashton, R. D. Coleridge and Faust (1814-20) *In* Ashton, R. D. The German idea p56-66

**Goetz-Stankiewicz, Marketa**

The silenced theatre: Czech playwrights without a stage

*Contents*

Aspects of history
East meets West
Ivan Klima
Josef Topol
Ladislav Smoček
Life in a group
Pavel Kohout
Responses: East and West
Václav Havel

**Goetzmann, William H.**

Paradigm lost. *In* The Sciences in the American context: new perspectives, ed. by N. Reingold p21-34

**Goff, Frederick Richmond**

The preparation of the Third census of incunabula in American libraries. *In* The Bibliographical Society of America, 1904-79 p493-99

**About individual works**

*Incunabula in American libraries; a third census of fifteenth-century books recorded in North American collections*

Goff, F. R. The preparation of the Third census of incunabula in American libraries. *In* The Bibliographical Society of America, 1904-79 p493-99

**Goffman, Erving**

Response cries. *In* Human ethology, ed. by M. von Cranach [and others] p203-40

**About**

Collins, R. Erving Goffman and the development of modern social theory. *In* The View from Goffman, ed. by J. Ditton p170-209

Gonos, G. The class position of Goffman's sociology: social origins of an American structuralism. *In* The View from Goffman, ed. by J. Ditton p134-69

Hepworth, M. Deviance and control in everyday life: the contribution of Erving Goffman. *In* The View from Goffman, ed. by J. Ditton p80-99

Lofland, J. Early Goffman: style, structure, substance, soul. *In* The View from Goffman, ed. by J. Ditton p24-51

Manning, P. K. Goffman's framing order: style as structure. *In* The View from Goffman, ed. by J. Ditton p252-84

Rogers, M. F. Goffman on power, hierarchy, and status. *In* The View from Goffman, ed. by J. Ditton p100-33

Williams, R. M. Goffman's sociology of talk. *In* The View from Goffman, ed. by J. Ditton p210-32

**About individual works**

*Frame analysis: an essay on the organization of experience*

Crook, S. and Taylor, L. Goffman's version of reality. *In* The View from Goffman, ed. by J. Ditton p233-51

Manning, P. K. Goffman's framing order: style as structure. *In* The View from Goffman, ed. by J. Ditton p252-84

*Strategic interaction*

Psathas, G. Early Goffman and the analysis of face-to-face interaction in Strategic interaction. *In* The View from Goffman, ed. by J. Ditton p52-79

**Gogynfeirdd (Welsh poets)**

Lewis, C. W. The court poets: their function, status and craft. *In* A Guide to Welsh literature, ed. by A. O. H. Jarman and G. R. Hughes v 1 p123-56

Lloyd, D. M. The later Gogynfeirdd. *In* A Guide to Welsh literature, ed. by A. O. H. Jarman and G. R. Hughes v2 p36-57

**Gohlke, Madelon Sprengnether**

"I wooed thee with my sword": Shakespeare's tragic paradigms. *In* Representing Shakespeare, ed. by M. M. Schwartz and C. Kahn p 170-87

**Goin' south (Motion picture)**

Kael, P. Manic/depressive. *In* Kael, P. When the lights go down p507-11

**Going places (Motion picture)**

Kauffmann, S. Going places. *In* Kauffmann, S. Before my eyes p11-13

**Goitein, Shelomo Dov.** See Goitein, Solomon Dob Fritz

**Goitein, Solomon Dob Fritz**

The Jews under Islam: part one 6th-16th centuries. *In* The Jewish world, ed. by E. Kedourie p178-85

**Gokak, Vinayak Krishna**

Doctrine as imagination in Sri Aurobindo's Savitri. *In* Aspects of Indian writing in English, ed. by M. K. Naik p50-63

**The Gold** effect. Lyttleton, R. A. *In* Lying truths, ed. by R. Duncan and M. Weston-Smith p181-98

**Goldberg, Leah**

### About individual works

*The lady of the castle*

Abramson, G. Thematic development: The plays of the Holocaust. *In* Abramson, G. Modern Hebrew drama p116-40

**Goldhamer, Herbert**

The social effects of communication technology. *In* Propaganda and communication in world history, ed. by H. D. Lasswell, D. Lerner and H. Speier v3 p346-400

**Goldin, Claudia D.**

War. *In* Encyclopedia of American economic history, ed. by G. Porter v3 p935-57

**Goldman, Alan Harris**

Plain sex. *In* The Philosophy of sex, ed. by A. Soble p119-38

**Goldman, Emma**

### About

Cook, B. W. Female support networks and political activism: Lillian Wald, Crystal Eastman, Emma Goldman. *In* A Heritage of her own, ed. by N. F. Cott and E. H. Pleck p411-44

**Goldmann, Lucien**

### About

Slaughter, C. The hidden structure: Lucien Goldmann. *In* Slaughter, C. Marxism, ideology & literature p150-69

**Golem**

Urzidil, J. Two recollections. *In* The World of Franz Kafka, ed. by J. P. Stern p56-68

**Gombrich, Sir Ernst Hans Josef**

Ideals and idols

#### Contents

Art and self-transcendence

Art history and the social sciences

In search of cultural history

The logic of vanity fair: alternatives to historicism in the study of fashions, style and taste

The museum: past, present and future

Myth and reality in German wartime broadcasts

A plea for pluralism

Reason and feeling in the study of art

Research in the humanities: ideals and idols

The tradition of general knowledge

**Gómez de Avellaneda y Artega, Gertrudis**

### About individual works

*Sab*

Fox-Lockert, L. Gertrudiz Gomez de Avellaneda. *In* Fox-Lockert, L. Women novelists in Spain and Spanish America p127-36

**Góngora, Luis de. See Góngora y Argote, Luis de**

**Góngora y Argote, Luis de**

### About individual works

*El Polifemo*

Carne-Ross, D. S. Dark with excessive bright: four ways of looking at Góngora. *In* Carne-Ross, D. S. Instaurations p133-66

*Soledades*

Carne-Ross, D. S. Dark with excessive bright: four ways of looking at Góngora. *In* Carne-Ross, D. S. Instaurations p133-36

**Gonos, George**

The class position of Goffman's sociology: social origins of an American structuralism. *In* The View from Goffman, ed. by J. Ditton p134-69

**Gonzalez, Edward**

Cuba, the Soviet Union, and Africa. *In* Communism in Africa, ed. by D. E. Albright p145-67

**The goodbye girl (Motion picture)**

Kael, P. Regressions. *In* Kael, P. When the lights go down p376-80

Kauffmann, S. The goodbye girl. *In* Kauffmann, S. Before my eyes p256-75

**Goodman, Paul, 1911-1972**

### About

Howard, R. Paul Goodman: "The form of life, the art of dissidence." *In* Howard, R. Alone with America p184-94

**Goody, John Rankine**

Thought and writing. *In* Soviet and Western anthropology, ed. by E. Gellner p119-33

**Gopaleen, Myles, pseud. See O'Nolan, Brian**

**Gordan, John Dozer**

A doctor's benefaction: the Berg collection at the New York Public Library. *In* The Bibliographical Society of America, 1904-79 p327-38

**Gordon, David J.**

Literature and repression: the case of Shavian drama. *In* The Literary Freud: mechanisms of defense and the poetic will, ed. by J. H. Smith p181-203

**Gordon, Linda**

Birth control and social revolution; excerpt from "Woman's body, woman's right." *In* A Heritage of her own, ed. by N. F. Cott and E. H. Pleck p445-75

**Gorove, Margaret**

Computer impact on society: a personal view from the world of art. *In* Monster or messiah? Ed. by W. M. Mathews p 125-41

**Goshen-Gottstein, M. H.**

Maimonides' Guide of the perplexed: towards a critical edition. *In* Studies in Jewish religious and intellectual history, ed. by S. Stein and R. Loewe p133-42

**Gosselin, Edward Alberic**

Two views of the evangelical David: Lefèvre d'Etaples and Theodore Beza. *In* The David myth in Western literature, ed. by R. J. Frontain and J. Wojcik p56-67

**Gothic illumination of books and manuscripts.** See Illumination of books and manuscripts, Gothic

**Gothic revival (Architecture)**

Harbison, R. Art as religion. *In* Harbison, R. Deliberate regression p94-114

Harbison, R. Religion as art. *In* Harbison, R. Deliberate regression p63-93

**Gothic revival (Art)**

Harbison, R. Art as religion. *In* Harbison, R. Deliberate regression p94-114

Harbison, R. Religion as art. *In* Harbison, R. Deliberate regression p63-93

*See also* Romanticism in art

**Gottstein, M. H. Goshen-** See Goshen-Gottstein, M. H.

**Goubert, Jean-Pierre**

The art of healing: learned medicine and popular medicine in the France of 1790. *In* Medicine and society in France, ed. by R. Forster and O. Ranum p 1-23

**Gould, Roger L.**
Transformations during early and middle adult years. *In* Themes of work and love in adulthood, ed. by N. J. Smelser and E. H. Erikson p213-37

**Gould, Stephen Jay**
Agassiz' later, private thoughts on evolution: his marginalia in Haeckel's Natürliche Schöpfungsgeschichte. *In* New Hampshire Bicentennial Conference on the History of Geology, University of New Hampshire, 1976. Two hundred years of geology in America p277-82

**Gouri, Haim.** See Guri, Haim

**Gourvish, Terence Richard**
The standard of living, 1890-1914. *In* The Edwardian age: conflict and stability, 1900-1914, ed. by A. O'Day p13-34

**Government, Comparative.** *See* Comparative government

**Government, Resistance to**
Ozment, S. H. Protestant resistance to tyranny: the career of John Knox. *In* Ozment, S. H. The age of reform, 1250-1550 p419-33
*See also* Revolutions

**Government and business.** See Industry and state

**Government and the press**

### France
Tarlé, A. de. The press and state in France. *In* Newspapers and democracy, ed. by A. Smith p127-48

### Sweden
Gustafsson, K. E. The press subsidies of Sweden: a decade of experiment. *In* Newspapers and democracy, ed. by A. Smith p104-26

**Government information.** See Government and the press

**Government regulation of commerce.** See Industrial laws and legislation; Industry and state

**Grade, Chaim**

### About individual works
*My quarrel with Hersh Rasseyner*
Alexander, E. A dialogue of the mind with itself: Chaim Grade's quarrel with Hersh Rasseyner. *In* Alexander, E. The resonance of dust p233-47

**Graduate work.** See Universities and colleges

**Graetz, Heinrich Hirsch**

### About
Meisl, J. Graetz and national Judaism. *In* The Jew, ed. by A. A. Cohen p43-51

**Graham, Tom,** pseud. See Lewis, Sinclair

**Grail**

### Legends—History and criticism
Hatto, A. T. On Wolfram's conception of the 'Graal'. *In* Hatto, A. T. Essays on medieval German and other poetry p141-50

**Grajeda, Rafael F.**
Jose Antonio Villarreal and Richard Vasquez: the novelist against himself. *In* The Identification and analysis of Chicano literature, ed. by F. Jiménez p329-57

**Grammar, Comparative and general**

### Sentences
Michaels, L. Legible death. *In* The State of the language, ed. by L. Michaels and C. Ricks p594-600

**The grand illusion (Motion picture)**
Thiher, A. Jean Renoir and the mimesis of history. *In* Thiher, A. The cinematic muse p92-112

**Granniss, Ruth Shepard**
What bibliography owes to private book clubs. *In* The Bibliographical Society of America, 1904-79 p51-70

**Gransden, Karl Watts**
Lente currite, noctis equi: Chaucer, Troilus and Criseyde 3.1422-70, Donne, The sun rising and Ovid, Amores 1.13. *In* Creative imitation and Latin literature, ed. by D. West and T. Woodman p157-71

**Grant, Cary**

### About
Kael, P. The man from dream city. *In* Kael, P. When the lights go down p3-32

**Grants.** See Subsidies

**The grapes of wrath (Motion picture)**
Kauffmann, S. The grapes of wrath. *In* Kauffmann, S. Before my eyes p349-50

**Grass, Günter**

### About individual works
*Dog years*
Bosmajian, H. Günter Grass's Dog years: the dark side of utopia. *In* Bosmajian, H. Metaphors of evil p82-114

**Grassi, Ernesto**
The priority of common sense and imagination: Vico's philosophical relevance today. *In* Conference on Vico and Contemporary Thought, New York, 1976. Vico and contemporary thought pt 1 p163-85

**Graver, Lawrence,** (ed.). See Samuel Beckett: the critical heritage, ed. by Lawrence Graver and Raymond Federman

**Gravestones.** See Sepulchral monuments

**Gray, Charles Wright**
Reason, authority, and imagination: the jurisprudence of Sir Edward Coke. *In* Culture and politics from Puritanism to the Enlightenment, ed. by P. Zagorin p25-66

**Gray, Robert**
Sex and sexual perversion. *In* The Philosophy of sex, ed. by A. Soble p 158-68

**Gray, Ronald**
Ibsen: a reply to James Walter McFarlane. *In* Drama and mimesis, ed. by J. Redmond p251-57

**Gray, Thomas**

### About
Fry, P. H. Thomas Gray's feather'd cincture. *In* Fry, P. H. The poet's calling in the English ode p63-96

**Great Britain**

### Antiquities, Saxon
Hills, C. The archaeology of Anglo-Saxon England in the pagan period: a review. *In* Anglo-Saxon England 8 p297-329

### Bill of rights
Schwoerer, L. The Bill of rights: epitome of the Revolution of 1688-89. *In* Three British revolutions: 1641, 1688, 1776, ed. by J. G. A. Pocock p224-43

### Church history—Anglo-Saxon period, 449-1066
Meyvaert, P. Bede and the church paintings at Wearmouth—Jarrow. *In* Anglo-Saxon England 8 p63-77

**Great Britain**—*Continued*

**Church history**—Medieval period,
1066-1485—Sources

Robertson, D. W. Frequency of preaching in thirteenth century England. *In* Robertson, D. W. Essays in medieval culture p114-28

**Civilization**—History

Annan, N. G. "Our age": reflections on three generations in England. *In* Generations, ed. by S. R. Graubard p81-109

**Civilization**—20th century

Klugmann, J. Introduction: The crisis of the thirties: a view from the Left. *In* Culture and crisis in Britain in the thirties, ed. by J. Clark and others p13-36

**Colonies**—Administration

Lovejoy, D. S. Two American revolutions, 1689 and 1776. *In* Three British revolutions: 1641, 1688, 1776, ed. by J. G. A. Pocock p244-62

Olson, A. G. Parliament, Empire, and Parliamentary law, 1776. *In* Three British revolutions: 1641, 1688, 1776, ed. by J. G. A. Pocock p289-322

**Colonies**—Politics and government

*See* Great Britain—Colonies—Administration

**Colonies**—America

Lovejoy, D. S. Two American revolutions, 1689 and 1776. *In* Three British revolutions: 1641, 1688, 1776, ed. by J. G. A. Pocock p244-62

**Commercial policy**

Cain, P. Political economy in Edwardian England: the tariff-reform controversy. *In* The Edwardian age: conflict and stability, 1900-1914, ed. by A. O'Day p35-59

**Economic conditions**

Gourvish, T. R. The standard of living, 1890-1914. *In* The Edwardian age: conflict and stability, 1900-1914, ed. by A. O'Day p13-34

Rabb, T. K. Population, economy and society in Milton's England. *In* The Age of Milton, ed. by C. A. Patrides and R. B. Waddington p72-101

**Economic conditions**—1760-1860

Brewer, J. English radicalism in the age of George III. *In* Three British revolutions: 1641, 1688, 1776, ed. by J. G. A. Pocock p323-67

**Economic policy**—1945-

Jessop, B. The transformation of the state in post-war Britain. *In* The State in Western Europe, ed. by Richard Scase p23-93

**Foreign relations**—1910-1936

Nicolson, C. Edwardian England and the coming of the First World War. *In* The Edwardian age: conflict and stability, 1900-1914, ed. by A. O'Day p144-68

**History**—Philosophy

Manley, L. G. The emergence of historical consciousness. *In* Manley, L. G. Convention, 1500-1750 p215-26

Manley, L. G. "A genius of times": the contexts of historical periods. *In* Manley, L. G. Convention, 1500-1750 p226-31

**History**—Anglo-Saxon period,
449-1066

Dumville, D. N. The ætheling: a study in Anglo-Saxon constitutional history. *In* Anglo-Saxon England 8 p 1-33

**History**—Anglo-Saxon period,
449-1066—Sources

Miller, M. The dates of Deira. *In* Anglo-Saxon England 8 p35-61

**History**—Tudors, 1485-1603

Ozment, S. H. Protestant resistance to tyranny: the career of John Knox. *In* Ozment, S. H. The age of reform, 1250-1550 p419-33

**History**—17th century

*See* Great Britain—History—Stuarts, 1603-1714

**History**—Stuarts, 1603-1714

Aylmer, G. E. The historical backgrounds. *In* The Age of Milton, ed. by C. A. Patrides and R. B .Waddington p 1-33

Charlton, K. The educational background. *In* The Age of Milton, ed. by C. A. Patrides and R. B. Waddington p102-37

Fehl, P. P. Poetry and the entry of the fine arts into England: ut pictura poesis. *In* The Age of Milton, ed. by C. A. Patrides and R. B. Waddington p273-306

Hill, J. E. C. A bourgeois revolution? *In* Three British revolutions: 1641, 1688, 1776, ed. by J. G. A. Pocock p109-39

Le Huray, P. The fair musick that all creatures made. *In* The Age of Milton, ed. by C. A. Patrides and R. B. Waddington p241-72

Rattansi, P. M. The scientific background. *In* The Age of Milton, ed. by C. A. Patrides and R. B. Waddington p197-240

Stone, L. The results of the English revolutions of the seventeenth century. *In* Three British revolutions: 1641, 1688, 1776, ed. by J. G. A. Pocock p23-108

**History**—Charles I, 1625-1649

Ashton, R. Tradition and innovation and the Great Rebellion. *In* Three British revolutions: 1641, 1688, 1776, ed. by J. G. A. Pocock p208-23

Carlton, C. Three British revolutions and the personality of kingship. *In* Three British revolutions: 1641, 1688, 1776, ed. by J. G. A. Pocock p165-207

**History**—Civil War, 1642-1649

Hill, J. E. C. A bourgeois revolution? *In* Three British revolutions: 1641, 1688, 1776, ed. by J. G. A. Pocock p109-39

**History**—Puritan Revolution, 1642-1660

Ashton, R. Tradition and innovation and the Great Rebellion. *In* Three British revolutions: 1641, 1688, 1776, ed. by J. G. A. Pocock p208-23

Stone, L. The results of the English revolutions of the seventeenth century. *In* Three British revolutions, 1641,1688, 1776, ed. by J. G. A. Pocock p23-108

**History**—James II, 1685-1688

Carlton, C. Three British revolutions and the personality of kingship. *In* Three British revolutions: 1641, 1688, 1776, ed. by J. G. A. Pocock p165-207

**History**—Revolution of 1688

Murrin, J. M. The great inversion, or court versus country: a comparison of the Revolution settlements in England (1688-1721) and America (1776-1816) *In* Three British revolutions: 1641, 1688, 1776, ed. by J. G. A. Pocock p368-453

**Great Britain**—History—Revolution of 1688
—*Continued*

Schwoerer, L. G. The Bill of rights: epitome of the Revolution of 1688-89. *In* Three British revolutions: 1641, 1688, 1776, ed. by J. G. A. Pocock p224-43

Stone, L. The results of the English revolutions of the seventeenth century. *In* Three British revolutions: 1641, 1688, 1776, ed. by J. G. A. Pocock p23-108

### History—1689-1714

Murrin, J. M. The great inversion, or court versus country: a comparison of the revolution settlements in England (1688-1721) and America (1776-1816) *In* Three British revolutions: 1641, 1688, 1776, ed. by J. G. A. Pocock p368-453

### History—George III, 1760-1820

Brewer, J. English radicalism in the age of George III. *In* Three British revolutions: 1641, 1688, 1776, ed. by J. G. A. Pocock p323-67

Carlton, C. Three British revolutions and the personality of kingship. *In* Three British revolutions: 1641, 1688, 1776, ed. by J. G. A. Pocock p165-207

Langford, P. British correspondence in the colonial press, 1763-1775: a study in Anglo-American misunderstanding before the American Revolution. *In* The Press & the American Revolution, ed. by B. Bailyn and J. B. Hench p273-313

Pocock, J. G. A. 1776: the revolution against Parliament. *In* Three British revolutions: 1641, 1688, 1776, ed. by J. G. A. Pocock p265-88

### Intellectual life

Annan, N. G. "Our age": reflections on three generations in England. *In* Generations, ed. by S. R. Graubard p81-109

Mintz, S. I. The motion of thought: intellectual and philosophical backgrounds. *In* The Age of Milton, ed. by C. A. Patrides and R. B. Waddington p138-69

Wright, I. F. R. Leavis, the Scrutiny movement and the crisis. *In* Culture and crisis in Britain in the thirties, ed. by J. Clark and others p37-65

### Intellectual life—20th century

Coombes, J. British intellectuals and the Popular Front. *In* Class, culture and social change, ed. by F. Gloversmith p70-100

### Kings and rulers—Succession

Dumville, D. N. The ætheling: a study in Anglo-Saxon constitutional history. *In* Anglo-Saxon England 8 p 1-33

### Moral conditions

Radner, J. B. The art of sympathy in eighteenth-century British moral thought. *In* Studies in eighteenth-century culture v9 ,p189-210

### Parliament—History

Ditchfield, G. M. Repeal, abolition, and reform: a study in the interaction of reforming movements of the Parliament of 1790-6. *In* Anti-slavery, religion, and reform: essays in memory of Roger Anstey, ed. by C. Bolt and S. Drescher p101-18

### Parliament. House of Commons

Robinson, I. Parliamentary expressions. *In* The State of the language, ed. by L. Michaels and C. Ricks p64-75

### Politics and government—1603-1714

Woolrych, A. Political theory and political practice. *In* The Age of Milton, ed. by C. A. Patrides and R. B. Waddington p34-71

### Politics and government—1625-1649

Aylmer, G. E. Crisis and regrouping in the political elites: England from the 1630s to the 1660s. *In* Three British revolutions: 1641, 1688, 1776, ed. by J. G. A. Pocock p140-62

### Politics and government—1642-1660

Alymer, G. E. Crisis and regrouping in the political elites: England from the 1630s to the 1660s. *In* Three British revolutions: 1641, 1688, 1776, ed. by J. G. A. Pocock p140-62

### Politics and government—18th century

Olson, A. G. Parliament, Empire, and Parliamentary law, 1776. *In* Three British revolutions: 1641, 1688, 1776, ed. by J. G. A. Pocock p289-322

### Politics and government—1760-1820

Brewer, J. English radicalism in the age of George III. *In* Three British revolutions: 1641, 1688, 1776, ed. by J. G. A. Pocock p323-67

### Politics and government—1789-1820

Ditchfield, G. M. Repeal, abolition, and reform: a study in the interaction of reforming movements of the Parliament of 1790-6. *In* Anti-slavery, religion, and reform: essays in memory of Roger Anstey, ed. by C. Bolt and S. Drescher p101-18

### Politics and government—19th century

Anstey, R. The pattern of British abolitionism in the eighteenth and nineteenth centuries. *In* Anti-slavery, religion, and reform: essays in memory of Roger Anstey, ed. by C. Bolt and S. Drescher p19-42

Turley, D. M. 'Free air' and fugitive slaves: British abolitionists versus government over American fugitives, 1834-61. *In* Anti-slavery, religion, and reform: essays in memory of Roger Anstey, ed. by C. Bolt and S. Drescher p163-82

### Politics and government—1837-1901

Reid, F. The disintegration of Liberalism, 1895-1931. *In* The Context of English literature, 1900-1930, ed. by M. Bell p94-125

### Politics and government—1901-1936

Arnstein, W. L. Edwardian politics: turbulent spring or Indian summer? *In* The Edwardian age: conflict and stability, 1900-1914, ed. by A. O'Day p60-78

Dean, D. R. The character of the early Labour Party, 1900-14. *In* The Edwardian age: conflict and stability, 1900-1914, ed. by A. O'Day p97-112

Reid, F. The disintegration of Liberalism, 1895-1931. *In* The Context of English literature, 1900-1930, ed. by M. Bell p94-125

Searle, G. R. Critics of Edwardian society: the case of the Radical Right. *In* The Edwardian age: conflict and stability, 1900-1914, ed. by A. O'Day p79-96

### Politics and government—1910-1936

Howkins, A. Class against class: the political culture of the Communist Party of Great Britain, 1930-35. *In* Class, culture and social change, ed. by F. Gloversmith p240-57

**Great Britain**—*Continued*

### Politics and government—1936-1945

Coombes, J. British intellectuals and the Popular Front. *In* Class, culture and social change, ed. by F. Gloversmith p70-100

### Politics and government—1945-

Cyr, A. I. Great Britain. *In* Western European party systems, ed. by P. H. Merkl p61-86

Jessop, B. The transformation of the state in post-war Britain. *In* The State in Western Europe, ed. by Richard Scase p23-93

### Population

Rabb, T. K. Population, economy and society in Milton's England. *In* The Age of Milton, ed. by C. A. Patrides and R. B. Waddington p72-101

### Social conditions

Smelser, N. J. Vicissitudes of work and love in Anglo-American society. *In* Themes of work and love in adulthood, ed. by N. J. Smelser and E. H. Erikson p105-19

### Social conditions—17th century

Rabb, T. K. Population, economy and society in Milton's England. *In* The Age of Milton, ed. by C. A. Patrides and R. B. Waddington p72-101

### Social conditions—18th century

Temperley, H. Anti-slavery as a form of cultural imperialism. *In* Anti-slavery, religion, and reform: essays in memory of Roger Anstey, ed. by C. Bolt and S. Drescher p335-50

### Social conditions—19th century

Harrison, B. A genealogy of reform in modern Britain. *In* Anti-slavery, religion, and reform: essays in memory of Roger Anstey, ed. by C. Bolt and S. Drescher p119-48

Hollis, P. Anti-slavery and British working-class radicalism in the years of reform. *In* Anti-slavery, religion, and reform: essays in memory of Roger Anstey, ed. by C. Bolt and S. Drescher p294-315

Temperley, H. Anti-slavery as a form of cultural imperialism. *In* Anti-slavery, religion, and reform: essays in memory of Roger Anstey, ed. by C. Bolt and S. Drescher p335-50

Walvin, J. The rise of British popular sentiment for abolition, 1787-1832. *In* Anti-slavery, religion, and reform: essays in memory of Roger Anstey, ed. by C. Bolt and S. Drescher p149-62

### Social conditions—20th century

Lowerson, J. Battles for the countryside. *In* Class, culture and social change, ed. by F. Gloversmith p258-80

Segal, W. The housing crisis in Western Europe: Britain—assessment and options. *In* Architecture for people, ed. by B. Mikellides p171-75

### Social conditions—1945-

Walker, P. E. Charity begins at home. *In* Lying truths, ed. by R. Duncan and M. Weston-Smith p219-29

### Social life and customs— Medieval period, 1066-1485

Niles, J. D. The Æcerbot ritual in context. *In* Old English literature in context, ed. by J. D. Niles p44-56

### Social policy

Jessop, B. The transformation of the state in post-war Britain. *In* The State in Western Europe, ed. by R. Scase p23-93

**Great Plains in literature**

Gridley, R. E. Some versions of the primitive and the pastoral on the Great Plains of America. *In* Survivals of pastoral, ed. by R. F. Hardin p61-85

**Great Schism.** See Schism, The Great Western, 1378-1417

**The great train robbery (Motion picture)**

Kael, P. Steam engines. *In* Kael, P. When the lights go down p538-42

**Great Western Schism.** See Schism, The Great Western, 1378-1417

**Greece**

### Civilization

*See* Civilization, Greek

### Historiography

Momigliano, A. The rediscovery of Greek history in the eighteenth century: the case of Sicily. *In* Studies in eighteenth-century culture v9 p167-87

### Religion

Schofield, M. Preconception, argument and God. *In* Doubt and dogmatism, ed. by M. Schofield, M. Burnyeat and J. Barnes p283-308

**Greece, Modern**

### Economic conditions—1918-

Mouzelis, N. Capitalism and the development of the Greek state. *In* The State in Western Europe, ed. by R. Scase p241-73

### Politics and government—20th century

Mouzelis, N. Capitalism and the development of the Greek state. *In* The State in Western Europe, ed. by R. Scase p241-73

**Greek civilization.** See Civilization, Greek

**Greek drama**

### Presentation, Modern

Dent, E. J. [Music for the Cambridge Greek plays] *In* Dent, E. J. Selected essays p26-36

**Greek drama (Comedy)**

### History and criticism

Bain, D. Plautus uortit barbare: Plautus, Bacchides 526-61 and Menander, Dis exapaton 102-12. *In* Creative imitation and Latin literature, ed. by D. West and T. Woodman p17-34

Dover, K. J. Comedy. *In* Ancient Greek literature, ed. by K. J. Dover p74-87

Thomas, R. F. New comedy, Callimachus, and Roman poetry. *In* Harvard Studies in classical philology, v83 p179-206

**Greek drama (Tragedy)**

### History and criticism

Dover, K. J. Tragedy. *In* Ancient Greek literature, ed. by K. J. Dover p50-73

Knox, B. M. W. Aeschylus and the third actor. *In* Knox, B. M. W. Word and action p39-55

Knox, B. M. W. Myth and Attic tragedy. *In* Knox, B. M. W. Word and action p3-24

Knox, B. M. W. Review of The stagecraft of Aeschylus (by Oliver Taplin). *In* Knox, B. M. W. Word and action p79-84

**Greek drama (Tragedy)**—History and criticism
—*Continued*

Knox, B. M. W. Second thoughts in Greek tragedy. *In* Knox, B. M. W. Word and action p231-49

Mueller, M. Humanist tragedy as the mediator between ancient and modern tragedy. *In* Mueller, M. Children of Oedipus, and other essays on the imitation of Greek tragedy 1550-1800 p3-17

Reiss, T. J. A hypothesis and its prehistory. *In* Reiss, T. J. Tragedy and truth p 1-39

**Greek literature**

### History and criticism

Amundsen, D. W. Images of physicians in classical times. *In* 5000 years of popular culture, ed. by F. E. H. Schroeder p94-107

Bowie, E. L. Greek literature after 50 B. C. *In* Ancient Greek literature, ed. by K. J. Dover p155-76

Cook, A. S. Pindar: "Great deeds of prowess are always many-mythed." *In* Cook, A. S. Myth & language p108-44

Dover, K. J. Introduction. *In* Ancient Greek literature, ed. by K. J. Dover p 1-9

Griffin, J. Greek literature 300-50 B.C. *In* Ancient Greek literature, ed. by K. J. Dover p134-54

Marchese, R. T. Urbanism in the classical world: some general considerations and remarks. *In* 5000 years of popular culture, ed. by F. E. H. Schroeder p55-91

Oberhelman, S. Greek and Roman witches: literary conventions or agrarian fertility priestesses? *In* 5000 years of popular culture, ed. by F. E. H. Schroeder p13-53

**Greek philology**

Fogelmark, S. A troublesome antithesis: Lysias 12.88. *In* Harvard Studies in classical philology, v83 p109-41

**Greek philosophy.** See Philosophy, Ancient

**Greek poetry**

### History and criticism

West, M. L. Other early poetry. *In* Ancient Greek literature, ed. by K. J. Dover p29-49

**Greek propaganda.** See Propaganda, Greek

**Greek rhetoric.** See Rhetoric, Ancient

**Greeley, Andrew M.**
American Catholics: the post-immigrant century. *In* The Third century, ed. by S. M. Lipset p205-21

**Green, A. E.**
Popular drama and the mummers' play. *In* Performance and politics in popular drama, ed. by D. Bradby, L. James and B. Sharratt p139-66

**Green, Benny**
A funny man. *In* The Genius of Shaw, ed. by M. Holroyd p201-11

**Green, George D.**
Financial intermediaries. *In* Encyclopedia of American economic history, ed. by G. Porter v2 p707-26

**Green, Henry,** 1905-1974

#### About individual works
*Blindness*

Pritchett, V. S. Henry Green: in the echo chamber. *In* Pritchett, V. S. The tale bearers p115-19

**Green, William H.**
The four-part structure of Bilbo's education. *In* Children's literature v8 p133-40

**Greenaway, Kate**

### About

Hearn, M. P. Mr Ruskin and Miss Greenaway. *In* Children's literature v8 p22-34

**Greenblatt, Stephen Jay**
Improvisation and power. *In* Literature and society, ed. by E. W. Said p57-99

**Greene, Graham**

### About

Aisenberg, N. Graham Greene and the modern thriller. *In* Aisenberg, N. A common spring p168-222

Pritchett, V. S. Graham Greene: disloyalties. *In* Pritchett, V. S. The tale bearers p78-91

#### About individual works
*The power and the glory*

Higdon, D. L. A textual history of Graham Greene's The power and the glory. *In* Virginia. University. Bibliographical Society. Studies in bibliography v33 p222-39

#### Criticism, Textual

Higdon, D. L. A textual history of Graham Greene's The power and the glory. *In* Virginia. University. Bibliographical Society. Studies in bibliography v33 p222-39

**Greene, Larry A.**
Blacks. *In* Encyclopedia of American economic history, ed. by G. Porter v3 p1001-11

**Greenfield, Sidney Martin**
Patron-client exchanges in southeastern Minas Gerais. *In* Brazil, anthropological perspectives, ed. by M. L. Margolis and W. E. Carter p362-78

**Greenfield, Stanley B.**
Esthetics and meaning and the translation of Old English poetry. *In* Old English poetry, ed. by D. G. Calder p91-110

**Greenlee, Douglas**
Santayana and the ideal of reason. *In* History, religion, and spiritual democracy, ed. by M. Wohlgelernter and others p203-30

**Greenspan, Alan**
Economic policy. *In* The United States in the 1980s, ed. by P. Duignan and A. Rabushka p31-48

**Greenspan, Patricia Susan**
A case of mixed feelings: ambivalence and the logic of emotion. *In* Explaining emotions, ed. by A. O. Rorty p223-50

**Greg, Sir Walter Wilson**
The printing of Shakespeare's Troilus and Cressida in the First Folio. *In* The Bibliographical Society of America, 1904-79 p266-75

**Gregor, Ian**
Reading a story: sequence, pace, and recollection. *In* Reading the Victorian novel: detail into form, ed. by I. Gregor p92-110

**Gregor, Thomas Arthur**
Secrets, exclusion, and the dramatization of men's roles. *In* Brazil, anthropological perspectives, ed. by M. L. Margolis and W. E. Carter p250-69

**Gregory, Horace**

### About

Wagner, L. W. Horace Gregory: voice in action. *In* Wagner, L. W. American modern p125-33

**Gregory, Isabella Augusta Persse, Lady**

**About**

Saddlemyer, A. The 'dwarf-dramas' of the early Abbey Theatre. *In* Yeats, Sligo and Ireland, ed. by A. N. Jeffares p197-215

**Gregory, Joseph T.**

North American vertebrate paleontology, 1776-1976. *In* New Hampshire Bicentennial Conference on the History of Geology, University of New Hampshire, 1976. Two hundred years of geology in America p305-35

**Greuze, Jean Baptiste**

**About**

Hagstrum, J. H. Love in painting and music: an appended survey. *In* Hagstrum, J. H. Sex and sensibility p278-331

Harbison, R. Nature as a child. *In* Harbison, R. Deliberate regression p3-24

**Gridley, Roy E.**

Some versions of the primitive and the pastoral on the Great Plains of America. *In* Survivals of pastoral, ed. by R. F. Hardin p61-85

**Griffen, Clyde, and Griffen, Sally**

Small business and occupational mobility in mid-nineteenth-century Poughkeepsie. *In* Small business in American life, ed. by S. W. Bruchey p122-41

**Griffen, Sally.** See Griffen, C. jt. auth.

**Griffin, Gerald**

**About individual works**

*The collegians*

Cronin, J. Gerald Griffin: The collegians. *In* Cronin, J. The Anglo-Irish novel, v 1 p59-82

**Griffin, Jasper**

Greek literature 300-50 B. C. *In* Ancient Greek literature, ed. by K. J. Dover p134-54

**Griffith, David Wark**

**About individual works**

*The birth of a nation*

Fiedler, L. A. The anti-Tom novel and the First Great War: Thomas Dixon, Jr. and D. W. Griffith. *In* Fiedler, L. A. The inadvertent epic p43-57

**Griffith, John**

Charlotte's web: a lonely fantasy of love. *In* Children's literature v8 p111-17

**Griffith, William E.**

Communist propaganda. *In* Propaganda and communication in world history, ed. by H. D. Lasswell, D. Lerner and H. Speier v2 p239-58

**Griggs, Earl Leslie.** See Part 2 under title: Reading Coleridge

**Grillet, Alain Robbe-** See Robbe-Grillet, Alain

**Grimm, Jakob Ludwig Karl**

**About**

Harbison, R. Romantic localism. *In* Harbison, R. Deliberate regression p115-47

**Grimm, Wilhelm Karl**

**About**

Harbison, R. Romantic localism. *In* Harbison, R. Deliberate regression p115-47

**Grimsley, Ronald**

Jean-Jacques Rousseau, philosopher of nature. *In* Royal Institute of Philosophy. Philosophers of the Enlightenment p184-98

**Griselda**

Maddox, D. L. Early secular courtly drama in France: L'estoire de Griseldis. *In* The Expansion and transformations of courtly literature, ed. by N. B. Smith and J. T. Shaw p157-70

**Gronlund, Laurence**

**About**

Harrison, F. Gronlund and other Marxists. *In* Critics of Henry George, ed. by R. V. Andelson p196-221

**Grosholz, Emily R.**

Descartes' unification of algebra and geometry. *In* Descartes, ed. by S. Gaukroger p156-68

**Gross, Barry R.**

"Would 25-cent press keep Gatsby in the public eye—or is the book unpopular?" *In* Seasoned authors for a new season: the search for standards in popular writing, ed. by L. Filler p51-57

**Gross, Daniel Russell**

A new approach to central Brazilian social organization. *In* Brazil, anthropological perspectives, ed. by M. L. Margolis and W. E. Carter p321-42

**Gross national product.** See Income

**Grosser, Alfred**

Western Europe. *In* The United States in the 80s, ed. by P. Duignan and A. Rabushka p707-34

**Grossman, Avraham**

The Jews in Byzantium and medieval Europe. *In* The Jewish world, ed. by E. Kedourie p168-77

**Grossman, Joan Delaney**

Feminine images in Old Russian literature and art. *In* California Slavic studies v11 p33-70

**Group dynamics.** See Social groups

**La Groupe Octobre.** See October (Theater group)

**Groups, Social.** See Social groups

**Growth, Personal.** See Self-actualization (Psychology)

**Grundlehner, Philip**

The lyrical bridge

*Contents*

August Graf von Platen: "When tiefe Schwermut meine Seele wieget . . ."

Conrad Ferdinand Meyer: "Auf Ponte Sisto"

Conrad Ferdinand Meyer: "Die alte Brücke"

Ernst Stadler: Fahrt über die Kölner Rheinbrücke bei Nacht"

Friedrich Hölderlin: "Heidelberg"

Friedrich Nietzsche: "Venedig"

Gottfried Benn: "Am Brückenwehr"

Theodor Fontane: "Die Brück am Tay"

Rainer Maria Rilke: "Pont du Carrousel"

**Gueroult, Martial**

The metaphysics and physics of force in Descartes. *In* Descartes, ed. by S. Gaukroger p196-229

**Guerra, David M.**

Computer technology and the mass media: interacting communication environments. *In* Monster or messiah? Ed. by W. M. Mathews p99-112

**Guido, Beatriz**

### About individual works
*Fin de fiesta*

Fox-Lockert, L. Beatriz Guido. *In* Fox-Lockert, L. Women novelists in Spain and Spanish America p216-27

**Guillaume de Lorris.** See Roman de la Rose

**Guillaume de Machaut**

### About individual works
*Il m'est avis*

Wimsatt, J. I. Chaucer, fortune, and Machaut's "Il m'est avis." *In* Chaucerian problems and perspectives, ed. by E. Vasta and Z. P. Thundy p119-31

**Guillén, Nicolás**

### About

Jackson, R. L. The turning point: the blackening of Nicolás Guillén and the impact of his Motivos de son. *In* Jackson, R. L. Black writers in Latin America p80-92

**Guilleragues, Gabriel Joseph, de Lavergne, Vicomte de**

### About individual works
*Letters of a Portuguese nun*

Hagstrum, J. H. Woman in love: the abandoned and passionate mistress. *In* Hagstrum, J. H. Sex and sensibility p100-32

**Guillet, Pernette du.** See Du Guillet, Pernette

**Guilt in literature**

Mellor, A. K. Guilt and Samuel Taylor Coleridge. *In* Mellor A. K. English romantic irony p137-64

**Guji Oromo.** See Gallas

**Gunderson, Gerald**

Slavery. *In* Encyclopedia of American economic history, ed. by G. Porter v2 p552-61

**Gupta, G. S. Balarama**

Bhabani Bhattacharya's 'So many hungers!': a study. *In* Aspects of Indian writing in English, ed. by M. K. Naik p209-21

**Guralnick, Stanley M.**

The American scientist in higher education, 1820-1910. *In* The Sciences in the American context: new perspectives, ed. by N. Reingold p99-141

**Guri, Haim**

### About individual works
*The chocolate deal*

Alexander, E. Between Diaspora and Zion: Israeli Holocaust fiction. *In* Alexander, E. The resonance of dust p73-118

**Gusdorf, Georges**

Conditions and limits of autobiography. *In* Autobiography: essays theoretical and critical, ed. by J. Olney p28-48

**Gusii (Bantu tribe)**

Levine, R. A. Adulthood among the Gusii of Kenya. *In* Themes of work and love in adulthood, ed. by N. J. Smelser and E. H. Erikson p77-104

**Gustafsson, Karl-Erik**

The press subsidies of Sweden: a decade of experiment. *In* Newspapers and democracy, ed. by A. Smith p104-26

**Gütersloh, Albert Paris, pseud.**

### About

Pabisch, P. and Best, A. The 'total novel': Heimito von Doderer and Albert Paris Gütersloh. *In* Modern Austrian writing, ed. by A. Best and H. Wolfschütz p63-78

**Gutman, Herbert George**

Marital and sexual norms among slave women. *In* A Heritage of her own, ed. by N. F. Cott and E. H. Pleck p298-310

**Guto'r Glyn**

### About

Williams, J. E. C. Guto'r Glyn. *In* A Guide to Welsh literature, ed. by A. O. H. Jarman and G. R. Hughes v2 p218-41

**Gutun Owain**

### About

Williams, J. E. C. Gutun Owain. *In* A Guide to Welsh literature, ed. by A. O. H. Jarman and C. R. Hughes v2 p262-77

**Guyana**

### Antiquities

Meggers, B. J. and Evans, C. An experimental reconstruction of Taruma Village succession and some implications. *In* Brazil, anthropological perspectives, ed. by M. L. Margolis and W. E. Carter p39-60

**Guzman, Eduardo Sevilla.** See Sevilla-Guzman, Eduardo

**Gyseghem, André van**

British theatre in the thirties: an autobiographical record. *In* Culture and crisis in Britain in the thirties, ed. by J. Clark and others p209-18

# H

**H. D.** pseud. See Doolittle, Hilda

**Habe (African people)** See Dogons (African people)

**Hacking, Ian**

Proof and eternal truths: Descartes and Leibniz. *In* Descartes, ed. by S. Gaukroger p169-80

**Haddock, Bruce Adrian**

Vico and the problem of historical reconstruction. *In* Conferences on Vico and Contemporary Thought, New York, 1976. Vico and contemporary thought pt 1 p122-29

Vico: the problem of interpretation. *In* Conference on Vico and Contemporary Thought, New York, 1976. Vico and contemporary thought pt 1 p145-62

**Haeckel, Ernst Heinrich Philipp August**

### About individual works
*Natürliche Schöpfungsgeschichte*

Gould, S. J. Agassiz' later, private thoughts on evolution: his marginalia in Haeckel's Natürliche Schöpfungsgeschichte. *In* New Hampshire Bicentennial Conference on the History of Geology, University of New Hampshire, 1976. Two hundred years of geology in America p277-82

**Haezrachi, Yehuda.** See Haezrahi, Yehuda

**Haezrahi, Yehuda**

### About individual works
*The refusal*

Abramson, G. The state of Israel: Early social realism. *In* Abramson, G. Modern Hebrew drama p59-76

**Hafley, James**

Virginia Woolf's narrators and the art of "life itself." *In* Virginia Woolf, ed. by R. Freedman p29-43

**Haggard, Sir Henry Rider**

**About**

Pritchett, V. S. Rider Haggard: still riding. *In* Pritchett, V. S. The tale bearers p25-30

**Hagstrum, Jean H.**

Sex and sensibility

*Contents*

The aftermath of sensibility: Sterne, Goethe, and Austen

Friends and lovers: the witty and the wise

John Dryden: sensual, heroic, and "pathetic" love

Love in painting and music: an appended survey

Milton and the ideal of heterosexual friendship

Restoration love and the tears of morbidity

Richardson

Rousseau

Sentimental love and marriage "esteem enliven'd by desire"

Woman in love: the abandoned and passionate mistress

**Hair**

**Care and hygiene**

*See* Hair preparations

**Hair (Motion picture)**

Kauffmann, S. Hair. *In* Kauffmann, S. Before my eyes p178-80

**Hair preparations**

Morowitz, H. J. Molecular cosmetology. *In* Morowitz, H. J. The wine of life, and other essays on societies, energy & living things p262-65

**Halakha.** See Talmud

**Hale, Nathan G.**

Freud's reflections on work and love. *In* Themes of work and love in adulthood, ed. by N. J. Smelser and E. H. Erikson p29-42

**Haley, Alex**

**About**

Fiedler, L. A. Anti-anti-Tom novels and the decline of the American empire: Alex Haley's Roots. *In* Fiedler, L. A. The inadvertent epic p71-85

**Hall, James, 1811-1898**

**About**

Dott, R. H. The geosyncline—first major geological concept "made in America." *In* New Hampshire Bicentennial Conference on the History of Geology, University of New Hampshire, 1976. Two hundred years of geology in America p239-64

**Hall, John Whitney**

East, Southeast, and South Asia. *In* The Past before us, ed. by M. Kammen p157-86

**Hall, Joseph, Bp. of Norwich**

**About**

Anselment, R. A. John Milton contra Hall. *In* Anselment, R. A. 'Betwixt jest and earnest' p61-93

**Hall, P. M.**

Duclos's Histoire de Madame de Luz: woman and history. *In* Woman and society in eighteenth-century France, ed. by E. Jacobs and others p139-51

**Hall, Wayne**

Esther Waters: an Irish story. *In* Irish Renaissance annual I p137-56

**Hallblade, Shirley, and Mathews, Walter M.**

Computer and society: today and tomorrow. *In* Monster or messiah? Ed. by W. M. Mathews p25-36

**Hallucinations and illusions**

La Barre, W. Anthropological perspectives on hallucination, hallucinogens, and the shamanic origins of religion. *In* La Barre, W. Culture in context p37-92

**Hallucinogenic drugs.** See Cannabis

**Hallucinogenic drugs and religious experience**

La Barre, W. Anthropological perspectives on hallucination, hallucinogens, and the shamanic origins of religion. *In* La Barre, W. Culture in context p37-92

**Halman, Talat Sait**

Propaganda functions of poetry. *In* Propaganda and communication in world history, ed. by H. D. Lasswell, D. Lerner and H. Speier v 1 p493-535

**Halo (Art)** See Nimbus (Art)

**Halophytes**

Morowitz, H. J. Deep purple. *In* Morowitz, H. J. The wine of life, and other essays on societies, energy & living things p145-48

**Hamblin, Robert W. and Brodsky, Louis Daniel**

Faulkner's "L'apres-midi d'un faune": the evolution of a poem. *In* Virginia. University. Bibliographical Society. Studies in bibliography v33 p254-63

**Hamilton, Virginia**

**About**

Townsend, J. R. Virginia Hamilton. *In* Townsend, J. R. A sounding of storytellers p97-110

**Hammack, David C.**

Small business and urban power: some notes on the history of economic policy in nineteenth-century American cities. *In* Small business in American life, ed. by S. W. Bruchey p319-37

**Hammond, Paul**

**About individual works**

*Marvellous Méllies*

Kauffmann, S. Marvellous Méllies. *In* Kauffmann, S. Before my eyes p371-72

**Hammond Report**

Morowitz, H. J. Hiding in the Hammond Report. *In* Morowitz, H. J. The wine of life, and other essays on societies, energy & living things p241-45

**Hancock, M. Donald**

Sweden. *In* Western European party systems, ed. by P. H. Merkl p185-204

**Handel, Georg Friedrich**

**About**

Hagstrum, J. H. Love in painting and music: an appended survey. *In* Hagstrum, J. H. Sex and sensibility p278-331

**Handke, Peter**

**About**

Rorrison, H. The 'Grazer Gruppe', Peter Handke and Wolfgang Bauer. *In* Modern Austrian writing, ed. by A. Best and H. Wolfschütz p252-66

**Handle with care (Motion picture)**

Kael, P. Goodbar, or How nice girls go wrong. *In* Kael, P. When the lights go down p316-23

**Handlin, Oscar**
American Jewry. *In* The Jewish world, ed. by E. Kedourie p274-83

**Hanfmann, George Maxim Anossov**
The continuity of classical art: culture, myth, and faith. *In* Age of spirituality, ed. by K. Weitzmann p75-99

**Hannah, Leslie**
Mergers. *In* Encyclopedia of American economic history, ed. by G. Porter v2 p639-51
Visible and invisible hands in Great Britain. *In* Managerial hierarchies, ed. by A. D. Chandler and H. Daems p41-76

**Hanquart, Evelyne**
E. M. Forster's travelogue from the Hill of Devi to the Bayreuth Festival. *In* E. M. Forster: a human exploration, ed. by G. K. Das and J. Beer p167-82

**Hanson, William**

### About individual works
*The fallacies in "Progress and poverty"*
Schwartzman, J. Ingalls, Hanson, and Tucker: nineteenth-century American anarchists. *In* Critics of Henry George, ed. by R. V. Andelson p234-53

**Happiness**
Mosley, N. Human beings desire happiness. *In* Lying truths, ed. by R. Duncan and M. Weston-Smith p211-17
Rescher, N. Social values and technological change. *In* Value and values in evolution, ed. by E. A. Maziarz p163-78

**Harari, Josué V.**
Critical factions/critical fictions. *In* Textual strategies, ed. by J. V. Harari p17-72

**Harbison, Robert**
Deliberate regression
*Contents*
Art as religion
The cult of death
Millennium
Nature as a child
Religion as art
Romantic localism
Tribe and race
Turning against history

**Hard times (Motion picture)**
Kael, P. The visceral poetry of pulp. *In* Kael, P. When the lights go down p40-45

**Hardcore (Motion picture)**
Kael, P. No contest. *In* Kael, P. When the lights go down p543-48
Kauffmann, S. Hardcore. *In* Kauffmann, S. Before my eyes p230-32

**Hardenberg, Friedrich Leopold, Freiherr von**
### About
Hughes, G. T. Poetry in metaphysics: Novalis. *In* Hughes, G. T. Romantic German literature p61-78

**Hardin, Richard Francis**
The pastoral moment. *In* Survivals of pastoral, ed. by R. F. Hardin p 1-17

**Harding, Anthony John**
James Marsh as editor of Coleridge. *In* Reading Coleridge, ed. by W. B. Crawford p223-51

**Hardt, John P.**
Stages in Soviet economic development: a sixty-year record. *In* Economic issues of the eighties, ed. by N. Reingold p199-225

**Hardy, Barbara (Nathan)**
The wildness of Crazy Jane. *In* Yeats, Sligo and Ireland, ed. by A. N. Jeffares p31-55

**Hardy, John Edward**
Percy and place: some beginnings and endings. *In* Walker Percy: art and ethics, ed. by J. Tharpe p5-25

**Hardy, Thomas**
### About
Keith, W. J. Thomas Hardy. *In* Keith, W. J. The poetry of nature p93-117

### About individual works
*Far from the madding crowd*
Gregor, I. Reading a story: sequence, pace, and recollection. *In* Reading the Victorian novel: detail into form, ed. by I. Gregor p92-110

*The Mayor of Casterbridge*
Edmond, R. 'The past-marked prospect': reading The Mayor of Casterbridge. *In* Reading the Victorian novel: detail into form, ed. by I. Gregor p111-27
Gregor, I. Reading a story: sequence, pace, and recollection. *In* Reading the Victorian novel: detail into form, ed. by I. Gregor p92-110
Stringer, P. Models of man in Casterbridge and Milton Keynes. *In* Architecture for people, ed. by B. Mikellides p176-86

**Hare, Peter H. and Chakrabarti, Chandana**
The development of William James's epistemological realism. *In* History, religion, and spiritual democracy, ed. by M. Wohlgelernter and others p231-45

**Hare, Richard Mervyn**
### About individual works
*Freedom and reason*
Harrison, B. J. Kant and the sincere fanatic. *In* Royal Institute of Philosophy. Philosophers of the Enlightenment p226-61

**Hareven, Tamara K.**
The search for generational memory: tribal rites in industrial society. *In* Generations, ed. by S. R. Graubard p137-49

**Harlan, Louis R.**
### About individual works
*Booker T. Washington: the making of a black leader, 1856-1901*
Pole, J. R. Of Mr. Booker T. Washington and others. *In* Pole, J. R. Paths to the American past p170-88

**Harlan County, U.S.A. (Motion picture)**
Kael, P. Harlan County. *In* Kael, P. When the lights go down p249-55
Kauffmann, S. Harlan County, U.S.A. *In* Kauffmann, S. Before my eyes p279-80

**Harmon, Maurice**
First impressions: 1968-78. *In* The Irish short story, ed. by P. Rafroidi and T. Brown p63-77

**Harmond, Richard Peter**
Sugar daddy or ogre? The impact of commercial television on professional sports. *In* Screen and society, ed. by F. J. Coppa p81-108

**Harmony**
Dent, E. J. [Melody and harmony] *In* Dent, E. J. Selected essays p142-57

**Harootunian, Harry D.**
The functions of China in Tokugawa thought. *In* The Chinese and the Japanese, ed. by A. Iriye p9-36

**Harper, Lathrop Colgate**

### About

Wroth, L. C. Lathrop Colgate Harper: a happy memory. *In* The Bibliographical Society of America, 1904-79 p372-83

**Harries, Karsten**
Language and silence: Heidegger's dialogue with Georg Trakl. *In* Martin Heidegger and the question of literature, ed. by W. V. Spanos p155-71

**Harrington, Michael**
Socialism. *In* Encyclopedia of American economic history, ed. by G. Porter v2 p851-62

**Harris, Alice Kessler-** See Kessler-Harris, Alice

**Harris, Christopher W. J.**
Displacements and reinstatements: the relations between sociology and theology considered in their changing intellectual context. *In* Sociology and theology: alliance and conflict, ed. by D. Martin, J. O. Mills and W. S. F. Pickering p24-36

**Harris, Marvin**
The Yanomamö and the causes of war in band and village societies. *In* Brazil, anthropological perspectives, ed. by M. L. Margolis and W. E. Carter p121-32

### About individual works
*Town and country in Brazil*

Braudel, F. In Bahia, Brazil: the present explains the past. *In* Braudel, F. On history p165-76

**Harris, William Torrey**

### About individual works
*The right of property and the ownership of land*

Collier, C. F. Harris and his anachronistic attack. *In* Critics of Henry George, ed. by R. V. Andelson p187-95

**Harris, Wilson**

### About

Maes-Jelinek, H. Wilson Harris. *In* West Indian literature, ed. by B. King p179-95

**Harrison, Bernard Joseph**
Kant and the sincere fanatic. *In* Royal Institute of Philosophy. Philosophers of the Enlightenment p226-61

**Harrison, Brian**
A genealogy of reform in modern Britain. *In* Anti-slavery, religion, and reform: essays in memory of Roger Anstey, ed. by C. Bolt and S. Drescher p119-48

**Harrison, Fred**
Gronlund and other Marxists. *In* Critics of Henry George, ed. by R. V. Andelson p196-221
Longe and Wrightson: conservative critics of George's wage theory. *In* Critics of Henry George, ed. by R. V. Andelson p72-94

**Harrison, Ross**
Ethical consistency. *In* Rational action, ed. by R. Harrison p29-45

**Harriss, Clement Lowell**
Rothbard's anarcho-capitalist critique. *In* Critics of Henry George, ed. by R. V. Andelson p354-70

**Harry and Tonto (Motion picture)**
Kauffmann, S. Harry and Tonto. *In* Kauffmann, S. Before my eyes p49-51

**Hart, David J.**
Changing relationships between publishers and journalists: an overview. *In* Newspapers and democracy, ed. by A. Smith p268-87

**Hartman, Geoffrey**
Criticism in the wilderness
*Contents*
Centaur: on the psychology of the critic
Criticism, indeterminacy, irony
Literary commentary as literature
Past and present
Purification and danger 1: American poetry
Purification and danger 2: critical style
The recognition scene of criticism
The sacred jungle 1: Carlyle, Eliot, Bloom
The sacred jungle 2: Walter Benjamin
The sacred jungle 3: Frye, Burke, and some conclusions
A short history of practical criticism
Understanding criticism
The work of reading

Diction and defense in Wordsworth. *In* The Literary Freud: mechanisms of defense and the poetic will, ed. by J. H. Smith p205-15

**Hartmann von Aue**

### About individual works
*Erec*

Pickering, F. P. The 'fortune' of Hartmann's Erec. *In* Pickering, F. P. Essays on medieval German literature and iconography p110-29

**Harwood, Ronald**
The language of screenwriting. *In* The State of the language, ed. by L. Michaels and C. Ricks p290-96

**Hasegawa, Tatsunosuke.** See Futabatei, Shimei, pseud.

**Hashikawa, Bunso**
Japanese perspectives on Asia: from dissociation to coprosperity. *In* The Chinese and the Japanese, ed. by A. Iriye p328-55

**Hasidism**
Jacobs, L. Eating as an act of worship in Hasidic thought. *In* Studies in Jewish religious and intellectual history, ed. by S. Stein and R. Loewe p157-66

**Haskalah**
Abramson, G. The development of the drama: Hascalah. *In* Abramson, G. Modern Hebrew drama p24-27
Ettinger, S. The Jews and the Enlightenment. *In* The Jewish world, ed. by E. Kedourie p224-31

**Hat trade**

### United States—History

Bensman, D. Economics and culture in the gilded age hatting industry. *In* Small business in American life, ed. by S. W. Bruchey p352-65

**Hatto, Arthur Thomas**
Essays on medieval German and other poetry
*Contents*
An early 'Tagelied'
Folk ritual and the Minnesang
Herzeloyde's dragon-dream
The lime-tree and early German, Goliard and English lyric poetry
Neidhart von Reuental
A note on Walther's song 'Madam, accept this garland' (A May dance for the court)

**Hatto, Arthur T.**
Essays on medieval German and other poetry
*Contents—Continued*

On the excellence of the 'Hildebrandslied': a comparative study in dynamics
On Wolfram's conception of the 'Graal'
Poetry and the hunt in medieval Germany
Shamanism and epic poetry in northern Asia
Snake-swords and boar-helms in Beowulf
Some notes on Chrétien de Troyes and Wolfram von Eschenbach
The swan maiden: a folk-tale of North Eurasian origin?
'Venus and Adonis'—and the boar
Wolfram von Eschenbach and the chase

**Haugen, Einar Ingvald**
Norway in America: the hidden heritage. *In* Makers of an American immigrant legacy, ed. by O. S. Lovoll p15-28

**Haugsgjerd, Svein**
Report from Norway. *In* Critical psychiatry, ed. by D. Ingleby p193-208

**Hauptmann, Gerhart Johann Robert**

### About individual works
#### The weavers

Bennett, B. The assault upon the audience: types of modern drama. *In* Bennett, B. Modern drama and German classicism p282-314

**Hausheer, Roger**
Introduction. *In* Berlin, Sir I. Against the current p xiii-liii

**Havel, Václav**

### About

Goetz-Stankiewicz, M. Václav Havel. *In* Goetz-Stankiewicz, M. The silenced theatre: Czech playwrights without a stage p43-88

**Hawkins, Harriett**
The morality of Elizabethan drama: some footnotes to Plato. *In* English Renaissance studies, ed. by J. Carey p12-32

**Hawkins, J. David**
The origin and dissemination of writing in western Asia. *In* The Origins of civilization, ed. by P. S. R. Moorey p128-65

**Hawkins, Loretta A.**
The free spirit of Ekwensi's Jagua Nana. *In* African literature today no. 10: Retrospect & prospect, ed. by E. D. Jones p202-06

**Hawley, Ellis Wayne**
Antitrust. *In* Encyclopedia of American economic history, ed. by G. Porter v2 p772-87

**Hawthorne, Nathaniel**

### About

Fogle, R. H. Hawthorne's sketches and the English romantics. *In* Toward a new American literary history, ed. by L. J. Budd, E. H. Cady and C. L. Anderson p129-39
Irwin, J. T. Hawthorne: the ambiguity of the hieroglyphics; the unstable self and its roles; mirror image and phonetic veil; the feminine role of the artist; veil and phallus; the book as partial object. *In* Irwin, J. T. American hieroglyphics p239-84
Johnson, C. D. Resolution in The marble faun: a minority view. *In* Puritan influences in American literature, ed. by E. Elliott p128-42

### About individual works
#### The House of the Seven Gables

Sundquist, E. J. "The home of the dead": representation and speculation in Hawthorne and The House of the Seven Gables. *In* Sundquist, E. J. Home as found p86-142

#### The marble faun

Johnson, C. D. Resolution in The marble faun: a minority view. *In* Puritan influence in American literature, ed. by E. Elliott p128-42

#### The scarlet letter

Spengemann, W. C. Afterword. *In* Spengemann, W. C. The forms of autobiography p166-69
Spengemann, W. C. Poetic autobiography. *In* Spengemann, W. C. The forms of autobiography p110-65

### Bibliography

Crowley, J. D. Hawthorne. *In* American literary scholarship, 1978 p17-28

**Hay, Richard, and Paden, John N.**
A culture cluster analysis of six West African states. *In* Values, identities, and national integration, ed. by J. N. Paden p25-40

**Hayden, Ferdinand Vandeveer**

### About

Nelson, C. M. and Fryxell, F. M. The antebellum collaboration of Meek and Hayden in stratigraphy. *In* New Hampshire Bicentennial Conference on the History of Geology, University of New Hampshire, 1976. Two hundred years of geology in America p187-200

**Haydn, Hiram Collins**

### About

Casciato, A. D. His editor's hand: Hiram Haydn's changes in Styron's Lie down in darkness. *In* Virginia. University, Bibliographical Society. Studies in bibliography v33 p263-76

**Hayes, Joseph J.**
Gothic love and death: Francois Villon and the city of Paris. *In* 5000 years of popular culture, ed. by F. E. H. Schroeder p228-39

**Hayles, Nancy K.**
Sexual disguise in 'As you like it' and 'Twelfth night.' *In* Shakespeare survey 32 p63-72

**Hazen, Margaret H.** See Hazen, R. M. jt. auth.

**Hazen, Robert M. and Hazen, Margaret H.**
Neglected geological literature: an introduction to a bibliography of American-published geology, 1669 to 1850 (abstract). *In* New Hampshire Bicentennial Conference on the History of Geology, University of New Hampshire, 1976. Two hundred years of geology in America p33-36

**Health, Public.** See Public health

**Health care costs.** See Medical care, Cost of

**Health economics.** See Medical economics

**Health insurance.** See Insurance, Health

**Health misconceptions.** See Medical delusions

**Health of children.** See Children—Care and hygiene

**Health plans, Prepaid.** See Insurance, Health

**Health policy.** See Medical policy

**Health services.** See Public health

**Healy, Alice F.**
Can chimpanzees learn a phonemic language? *In* Speaking of apes, ed. by T. A. Sebeok and J. Umiker-Sebeok p141-43

**Heaney, Howell J.**
Thomas W. Streeter, collector, 1883-1965. *In* The Bibliographical Society of America, 1904-79 p500-13

**Heaney, Seamus**
Feeling into words. *In* Royal Society of Literature of the United Kingdom, London. Essays by divers hands: innovation in contemporary literature, new ser. v40 p83-100
Yeats as an example? *In* Yeats, Sligo and Ireland, ed. by A. N. Jeffares p56-72

**About**
Heaney, S. Feeling into words. *In* Royal Society of Literature of the United Kingdom, London. Essays by divers hands: innovation in contemporary literary, new ser. v40 p83-100

**Hearing.** See Auditory perception

**Hearn, Michael Patrick**
Mr Ruskin and Miss Greenaway. *In* Children's literature v8 p22-34

**Hearts of the West (Motion picture)**
Kael, P. Living inside a movie. *In* Kael, P. When the lights go down p45-51

**Hébert, Robert F.**
Marshall: a professional economist guards the purity of his discipline. *In* Critics of Henry George, ed. by R. V. Andelson p56-71

**Hebreo, León.** See Leo Hebraeus

**Hebrew drama**
Abramson, G. Thematic development: The plays of the Holocaust. *In* Abramson, G. Modern Hebrew drama p116-40

**History and criticism**
Abramson, G. The development of the drama: Hascalah. *In* Abramson, G. Modern Hebrew drama p24-27
Abramson, G. The development of the drama: Renaissance and Enlightenment. *In* Abramson, G. Modern Hebrew drama p16-23
Abramson, G. In search of the original play. *In* Abramson, G. Modern Hebrew drama p209-13
Abramson, G. Introduction. *In* Abramson, G. Modern Hebrew drama p9-14
Abramson, G. Modernism: The modern drama: the problem of imitation. *In* Abramson, G. Modern Hebrew drama p141-46
Abramson, G. The problems of the Israeli drama: Tradition. *In* Abramson, G. Modern Hebrew drama p205-207
Abramson, G. The state of Israel: Early social realism. *In* Abramson, G. Modern Hebrew drama p59-76
Abramson, G. The state of Israel: Israel and the world. *In* Abramson, G. Modern Hebrew drama p77-80
Abramson, G. The state of Israel: 1948 and after. *In* Abramson, G. Modern Hebrew drama p48-58

**Hebrew fiction**

**History and criticism**
Spicehandler, E. Jewish literature: fiction. *In* The Jewish world, ed. by E. Kedourie p253-58

**Hebrew language**
Kaufmann, Y. The Hebrew language and our national future. *In* The Jew, ed. by A. A. Cohen p97-111
Rabin, C. Hebrew and Arabic in medieval Jewish philosophy. *In* Studies in Jewish religious and intellectual history, ed. by S. Stein and R. Loewe p235-45

**Hebrew literature.** See Talmud

**Hebrew poetry**

**History and criticism**
Carmi, T. Jewish literature: poetry. *In* The Jewish world, ed. by E. Kedourie p258-63

**Hecht, Anthony**
**About**
Howard, R. Anthony Hecht: "What do we know of lasting since the Fall?" *In* Howard, R. Alone with America p195-208

**Hediger, Heini**
Do you speak Yerkish? The newest colloquial language with chimpanzees. *In* Speaking of apes, ed. by T. A. Sebeok and J. Umiker-Sebeok p441-47

**Hefzi-Bah, Israel. Beth Alpha Synagogue**
Schapiro, M. Ancient mosaics in Israel: late antique art—pagan, Jewish, Christian. *In* Schapiro, M. Selected papers v3: Late antique, early Christian and mediaeval art p20-33

**Hegel, Georg Wilhelm Friedrich**
**About**
Gombrich, Sir E. H. J. In search of cultural history. *In* Gombrich, Sir E. H. J. Ideals and idols p24-59
Hoy, D. C. The owl and the poet: Heidegger's critique of Hegel. *In* Martin Heidegger and the question of literature, ed. by W. V. Spanos p53-70
Mills, P. J. Hegel and 'the woman question': recognition and intersubjectivity. *In* The Sexism of social and political theory: women and reproduction from Plato to Nietzsche, ed. by L. M. G. Clark and L. Lange p74-98

**About individual works**
*Aesthetics*
Ashton, R. D. Lewes and German aesthetics (1840-5) *In* Ashton, R. D. The German idea p112-25

**Influence**
Bennett, B. Breakthrough in theory: the philosophical background of modern drama. *In* Bennett, B. Modern drama and German classicism p229-81

**Heidegger, Martin**
The age of the world view. *In* Martin Heidegger and the question of literature, ed. by W. V. Spanos p 1-15

**About**
Gelven, M. Heidegger and tragedy. *In* Martin Heidegger and the question of literature, ed. by W. V. Spanos p215-28
Hartman, G. H. The work of reading. *In* Hartman, G. H. Criticism in the wilderness p161-88
Hofstadter, A. Enownment. *In* Martin Heidegger and the question of literature, ed. by W. V. Spanos p17-37
Krell, D. F. Art and truth in raging discord: Heidegger and Nietzsche on the will to power. *In* Martin Heidegger and the question of literature, ed. by W. V. Spanos p39-52

**Heidegger, Martin**—About—Continued

Lentricchia, F. Versions of phenomenology. *In* Lentricchia, F. After the New Criticism p62-100

Marshall, D. G. The ontology of the literary sign: notes toward a Heideggerian revision of semiology. *In* Martin Heidegger and the question of literature, ed. by W. V. Spanos p271-94

Palmer, R. E. The postmodernity of Heidegger. *In* Martin Heidegger and the question of literature, ed. by W. V. Spanos p71-92

Rosenfeld, A. H. "The being of language and the language of being": Heidegger and modern poetics. *In* Martin Heidegger and the question of literature, ed. by W. V. Spanos p195-213

Spanos, W. V. Heidegger, Kierkegaard, and the hermeneutic circle: towards a postmodern theory of interpretation as dis-closure. *In* Martin Heidegger and the question of literature, ed. by W. V. Spanos p115-48

### About individual works
*Being and time*

Corngold, S. Sein und Zeit: implications for poetics. *In* Martin Heidegger and the question of literature, ed. by W. V. Spanos p99-114

*On the way to language*

Harries, K. Language and silence: Heidegger's dialogue with Georg Trakl. *In* Martin Heidegger and the question of literature, ed. by W. V. Spanos p155-71

### Aesthetics

Hoy, D. C. The owl and the poet: Heidegger's critique of Hegel. *In* Martin Heidegger and the question of literature, ed. by W. V. Spanos p53-70

Riddel, J. N. From Heidegger to Derrida to chance: doubling and (poetic) language. *In* Martin Heidegger and the question of literature, ed. by W. V. Spanos p231-52

Stahl, G. Attuned to being: Heideggerian music in technological society. *In* Martin Heidegger and the question of literature, ed. by W. V. Spanos p297-324

### Influence—Stevens

Kermode, F. Dwelling poetically in Connecticut. *In* Wallace Stevens, ed. by F. Doggett and R. Buttel p256-73

**Heinemann, Margot**

Louis MacNeice, John Cornford and Clive Branson: three Left-wing poets. *In* Culture and crisis in Britain in the thirties, ed. by J. Clark and others p103-32

**Heinzelman, Kurt**

The economics of the imagination

*Contents*

Afterword: the merchant as poet
The art of labor
Economics in Mammon's cave
"Getting it" in Paterson: the increment defended
"The mouth-tale of the giants": an introduction to the economics of the imagination
The psychomachia of labor
"Unreal words": language in political economy
William Blake and "the price of experience"
Wordsworth's labor theory: an economics of compensation

**Hellenism.** See Neoplatonism

**Heller, Agnes.** See Feher, F. jt. auth.

**Heller, Erich**

Investigations of a dog and other matters. *In* The World of Franz Kafka, ed. by J. P. Stern p103-11

**Hellerstein, Kathryn**

Yiddish voices in American English. *In* The State of the language, ed. by L. Michaels and C. Ricks p182-201

**Hellman, Lillian**

### About

Hook, S. The scoundrel in the looking glass. *In* Hook, S. Philosophy and public policy p218-37

### About individual works
*Pentimento*

Billson, M. K. and Smith, S. A. Lillian Hellman and the strategy of the "other." *In* Women's autobiography, ed. by E. C. Jelinek p 163-79

Demetrakopoulos, S. A. The metaphysics of matrilinearism in women's autobiography: studies of Mead's Blackberry winter, Hellman's Pentimento, Angelou's I know why the caged bird sings, and Kingston's The woman warrior. *In* Women's autobiography, ed. by E. C. Jelinek, p180-205

*An unfinished woman—a memoir*

Billson, M. K. and Smith, S. A. Lillian Hellman and the strategy of the "other." *In* Women's autobiography, ed. by E. C. Jelinek p163-79

**Helm, Jutta A.**

Citizen lobbies in West Germany. *In* Western European party systems, ed. by P. H. Merkl p576-96

**Helmets in art**

Hatto, A. T. Snake-swords and boar-helms in Beowulf. *In* Hatto, A. T. Essays on medieval German and other poetry p233-54

**Helmholtz, Hermann Ludwig Ferdinand von**

### About

Morowitz, H. J. Helmholtz, Mayer, and the M.D.-Ph.D program. *In* Morowitz, H. J. The wine of life, and other essays on societies, energy & living things p125-28

**Helvetius, Claude Adrien**

### About

Gardner, E. J. The philosophes and women: sensationalism and sentiment. *In* Woman and society in eighteenth-century France, ed. by E. Jacobs and others p19-27

**Hemingway, Ernest**

### About

Marx, P. Hemingway and ethnics. *In* Seasoned authors for a new season: the search for standards in popular writing, ed. by L. Filler p43-50

Wagner, L. W. The poetry in American fiction. *In* Wagner, L. W. American modern p18-30

Wyatt, D. Hemingway's uncanny beginnings. *In* Wyatt, D. Prodigal sons p52-71

Wilson, R. N. Ernest Hemingway: competence and character. *In* Wilson, R. N. The writer as social seer p42-55

### About individual works
*The fifth column, and the first forty-nine stories*

Trilling, L. Hemingway and his critics. *In* Trilling, L. Speaking of literature and society p123-34

**Hemingway, Ernest**—About individual works
—*Continued*

*For whom the bell tolls*

Trilling, L. An American in Spain. *In* Trilling, L. Speaking of literature and society p170-76

**Bibliography**

Bryer, J. R. Fitzgerald and Hemingway. *In* American literary scholarship, 1978 p153-78

**Hench, John B.** ed.

Letters of John Fenno and John Ward Fenno, 1779-1800—Part 1: 1779-1790. *In* American Antiquarian Society. Proceedings v89 pt2 p299-368

**Hendin, Josephine**

Experimental fiction. *In* Harvard Guide to contemporary American writing, ed. by D. Hoffman p240-86

**Henkle, Roger B.**

Comedy and culture

*Contents*

Early Dickens: metamorphosis, psychic disorientation, and the small fry

1820-1845: the anxieties of sublimation, and middle-class myths

Hood, Gilbert, Carroll, Jerrold, and the Grossmiths: comedy from inside

Later Dickens: disenchantment, transmogrification, and ambivalence

Meredith and Butler: comedy as lyric, high culture, and the bourgeois trap

Peacock, Thackeray, and Jerrold: the comedy of "radical" disaffection

Wilde . and Beerbohm: the wit of the avant-garde, the charm of failure

**Henn, Thomas Rice**

The place of shells. *In* Yeats, Sligo and Ireland, ed. by A. N. Jeffares p73-88

**Henrichs, Albert**

Callimachus Epigram 28: a fastidious priamel. *In* Harvard Studies in classical philology, v83 p207-12

The Cologne Mani Codex reconsidered. *In* Harvard Studies in classical philology p339-67

**Henry Francis DuPont Winterthur Museum**

Coughlan, M. N. The Maxine Waldron collection of children's books and paper toys. *In* Research about nineteenth-century children and books, ed. by S. K. Richardson p61-66

**Henryson, Robert**

*About individual works*

*The testament of Cresseid*

Kratzmann, G. Henryson and English poetry. *In* Kratzmann, G. Anglo-Scottish literary relations, 1430-1550 p63-103

**Hepworth, Mike**

Deviance and control in everyday life: the contribution of Erving Goffman. *In* The View from Goffman, ed. by J. Ditton p80-99

**Heraclitus of Ephesus**

*About*

Cook, A. S. Heraclitus and the conditions of utterance. *In* Cook, A. S. Myth & language p69-107

**Herder, Johann Gottfried von**

*About*

Seibt, K. M. Einfühlung, language, and Herder's philosophy of history. *In* The Quest for the new science, ed. by K. J. Fink and J. W. Marchand p17-27

**Heredity**

Cellérier, G. Cognitive strategies in problem solving. *In* Language and learning, ed. by M. Piattelli-Palmarini p67-72

Cellérier, G. Some clarification on innatism and constructivism. *In* Language and learning, ed. by M. Piattelli-Palmarini p83-87

Piaget, J. Introductory remarks. *In* Language and learning, ed. by M. Piattelli-Palmarini p57-61

*See also* Genetics

**Heredity, Human**

Purcell, H. D. The fallacy of environmentalism. *In* Lying truths, ed. by R. Duncan and M. Weston-Smith p85-96

**Heredity and environment.** See Nature and nurture

**Heredity in man.** See Heredity, Human

**Hermeneutics**

Brooke-Rose, C. The readerhood of man. *In* The Reader in the text, ed. by S. R. Suleiman and I. Crosman p120-48

Crosman, R. T. Do readers make meaning? *In* The Reader in the text, ed. by S. R. Suleiman and I. Crosman p149-64

Ferguson, F. C. Reading Heidegger: Paul de Man and Jacques Derrida. *In* Martin Heidegger and the question of literature, ed. by W. V. Spanos p253-70

Hartman, G. H. Understanding criticism. *In* Hartman, G. H. Criticism in the wilderness p19-41

Kurzweil, E. Paul Ricoeur: hermeneutics and structuralism. *In* Kurzweil, E. The age of structuralism p87-112

Maranda, P. The dialectic of metaphor: an anthropological essay on hermeneutics. *In* The Reader in the text, ed. by S. R. Suleiman and I. Crosman p183-204

Palmer, R. E. The postmodernity of Heidegger. *In* Martin Heidegger and the question of literature, ed. by W. V. Spanos p71-92

Rabinowitz, P. J. "What's Hecuba to us?" The audience's experience of literary borrowing. *In* The Reader in the text, ed. by S. R. Suleiman and I. Crosman p241-63

Rosenfeld, A. H. "The being of language and the language of being": Heidegger and modern poetics. *In* Martin Heidegger and the question of literature, ed. by W. V. Spanos p195-213

Schor, N. A. Fiction as interpretation/interpretation as fiction. *In* The Reader in the text, ed. by S. R. Suleiman and I. Crosman p165-82

Spanos, W. V. Heidegger, Kierkegaard, and the hermeneutic circle: towards a postmodern theory of interpretation as dis-closure. *In* Martin Heidegger and the question of literature, ed. by W. V. Spanos p115-48

**Hermes in literature**

Herz, J. S. The narrator as Hermes: a study of the early short fiction. *In* E. M. Forster: a human exploration, ed. by G. K. Das and J. Beer p17-27

**Hernández, Gaspar Octavio**

*About*

Jackson, R. L. The black swan: Gaspar Octavio Hernández, Panama's black modernist poet. *In* Jackson, R. L. Black writers in Latin America p63-77

**Hernández, Luisa Josefina**

### About individual works
*La cólera secreta*

Fox-Lockert, L. Luisa Josefina Hernandez. *In* Fox-Lockert, L. Women novelists in Spain and Spanish America p241-59

**Hero, Alfred O.**

Southern Jews and public policy. *In* Conference on Southern Jewish History, Richmond, Va. 1976. "Turn to the South" p143-50

**Herodotus**

### About

Cook, A. S. Inquiry: Herodotus. *In* Cook, A. S. Myth & language p145-89

Dover, K. J. The classical historians. *In* Ancient Greek literature, ed. by K. J. Dover p88-104

**Heroes**

Dundes, A. The hero pattern and the life of Jesus. *In* Dundes, A. Interpreting folklore p223-61

Hook, S. The hero in history: myth, power, or moral ideal? *In* Hook, S. Philosophy and public policy p153-64

**Heroes in literature**

Bennett, B. The importance of being Egmont. *In* Bennett, B. Modern drama and German classicism p151-87

Hagstrum, J. H. John Dryden: sensual, heroic, and "pathetic" love. *In* Hagstrum, J. H. Sex and sensibility p50-71

Horton, A. S. Ken Kesey, John Updike and the Lone Ranger. *In* Seasoned authors for a new season: the search for standards in popular writing, ed. by L. Filler p83-90

Wallace, J. M. John Dryden's play and the conception of a heroic society. *In* Culture and politics from Puritanism to the Enlightenment, ed. by P. Zagorin p113-34

**Héroët, Antoine**

### About

Perry, T. A. Erotic experiment and androgynous integration: Héroët's poetry. *In* Perry, T. A. Erotic spirituality p68-77

**Heroic poetry.** See Epic poetry

**Heroines.** See Women in literature

**Heroism.** See Heroes

**Hertz, Neil H.**

Freud and The sandman. *In* Textual strategies, ed. by J. V. Harari p296-319

Recognizing Casaubon. *In* Glyph 6 p24-41

**Hertzberg, Arthur**

Judaism and modernity. *In* The Jewish world, ed. by E. Kedourie p301-08

**Hertzberg, Hazel Whitman**

The teaching of history. *In* The Past before us, ed. by M. Kammen p474-504

**Hertzberger, Herman**

Shaping the environment. *In* Architecture for people, ed. by B. Mikellides p38-40

**Hertzen, Aleksandr Ivanovich**

### About

Berlin, Sir I. Herzen and his memoirs. *In* Berlin, Sir I. Against the current p188-212

### About individual works
*My past and thoughts*

Berlin, Sir I. Herzen and his memoirs. *In* Berlin, Sir I. Against the current p188-212

**Herz, Judith Scherer**

The narrator as Hermes: a study of the early short fiction. *In* E. M. Forster: a human exploration, ed. by G. K. Das and J. Beer p17-27

**Herzen, Alexander.** See Hertzen, Aleksandr Ivanovich

**Herzog, Werner**

### About individual works
*Aquirre, the wrath of God*

Kauffmann, S. Aquirre, the wrath of God. *In* Kauffmann, S. Before my eyes p171-73

**Hesiod.** See Hesiodus

**Hesiodus**

### About

West, M. L. Homeric and Hesiodic poetry. *In* Ancient Greek literature, ed. by K. J. Dover p 10-28

**Hess, Henry Hammond**

### About

Frankel, H. Why drift theory was accepted with the confirmation of Harry Hess's concept of sea-floor spreading. *In* New Hampshire Bicentennial Conference on the History of Geology, University of New Hampshire, 1976. Two hundred years of geology in America p337-53

**Hess, Moses**

### About

Avineri, S. The new Jerusalem of Moses Hess. *In* Powers, possessions and freedom, ed. by A. Kontos p107-18

Berlin, Sir I. The life and opinions of Moses Hess. *In* Berlin, Sir I. Against the current p213-51

### About individual works
*Rome and Jerusalem*

Berlin, Sir I. The life and opinions of Moses Hess. *In* Berlin, Sir I. Against the current p213-51

**Hesse, Hermann**

### About

John, D. The Sperber in Hesse's Demian. *In* The First World War in German narrative prose, ed. by C. N. Genno and H. Wetzel p34-49

Unseld, S. Hermann Hesse and his publishers. *In* Unseld, S. The author and his publishers p45-81

### About individual works
*Demian*

John, D. The Sperber in Hesse's Demian. *In* The First World War in German narrative prose, ed. by C. N. Genno and H. Wetzel p34-49

**Hester Street (Motion picture)**

Kael, P. Becoming an American. *In* Kael, P. When the lights go down p79-84

Miller, G. Jews without manners. *In* Miller, G. Screening the novel p1-18

**Heusch, Luc de**

Heat, physiology, and cosmogony: rites de passage among the Thonga. *In* Explorations in African systems of thought, ed. by I. C. Karp & C. S. Bird p27-43

**Hewitt, James Robert**

"Figures in the carpet" of Malraux's Le miroir des limbes. *In* André Malraux, ed. by F. Dorenlot and M. Tison-Braun p55-66

**Hexter, Jack H.**
Property, monopoly, and Shakespeare's Richard II. *In* Culture and politics from Puritanism to the Enlightenment, ed. by P. Zagorin p 1-24

**Hibbard, George Richard**
Feliciter audax: Antony and Cleopatra, I,i, 1-24. *In* Shakespeare's styles, ed. by P. Edwards, I. S. Ewbank and G. K. Hunter p95-109

**Hickey, William**

### About individual works

*The memoirs of William Hickey*
Plomer, W. C. F. William Hickey. *In* Plomer, W. C. F. Electric delights p106-12

**Hieatt, Constance B.**
"To boille the chiknes with the marybones": Hodge's kitchen revisited. *In* Chaucerian problems and perspectives, ed. by E. Vasta and Z. P. Thundy p149-63

**Hieroglyphic Bibles**
Irwin, J. T. Whitman: hieroglyphic Bibles and phallic songs. *In* Irwin, J. T. American hieroglyphics p20-40

**Hieroglyphics**
Irwin, J. T. Champollion and the historical background; Emerson's hieroglyphical emblems. *In* Irwin, J. T. American hieroglyphics p3-14

**Hieroglyphics in literature**
Irwin, J. T. Hawthorne: the ambiguity of the hieroglyphics; the unstable self and its roles; mirror image and phonetic veil; the feminine role of the artist; veil and phallus; the book as partial object. *In* Irwin, J. T. American hieroglyphics p239-84
Irwin, J. T. The hieroglyphics and the quest for origins: the myth of hieroglyphics p43-235
Irwin, J. T. Melville: the indeterminate ground; a conjunction of fountain and vortex; the myth of Isis and Osiris; master oppositions; the doubleness of the self and the illusion of consistent character; Dionysus and Apollo; mask and phallus; the chain of partial objects. *In* Irwin, J. T. American hieroglyphics p285-349
Irwin, J. T. Thoreau: the single, basic form—patenting a leaf. *In* Irwin, J. T. American hieroglyphics p14-20

**Higdon, David Leon**
A textual history of Graham Greene's The power and the glory. *In* Virginia. University. Bibliographical Society. Studies in bibliography v33 p222-39

**High anxiety (Motion picture)**
Kael, P. Fear of heights. *In* Kael, P. When the lights go down p371-76

**High Holy Days.** See Yom Kippur

**Hiking**

### Great Britain
Lowerson, J. Battles for the countryside. *In* Class, culture and social change, ed. by F. Gloversmith p258-80

**Hilar, Karel Hugo**

### About
Jařab, J. The lasting challenge of Eugene O'Neill: a Czechoslovak view. *In* Eugene O'Neill, ed. by V. Floyd p84-100

**Hildebrandslied**
Hatto, A. T. On the excellence of the 'Hildebrandslied': a comparative study in dynamics. *In* Hatto, A. T. Essays on medieval German and other poetry p93-116

**Hill, Christopher.** See Hill, John Edward Christopher

**Hill, Jane H.**
Apes and language. *In* Speaking of apes, ed. by T. A. Sebeok and J. Umiker-Sebeok p331-51

**Hill, John Edward Christopher**
A bourgeois revolution? *In* Three British revolutions: 1641, 1688, 1776, ed. by J. G. A. Pocock p109-39
Covenant theology and the concept of 'a public person.' *In* Powers, possessions and freedom, ed. by A. Kontos p3-22
George Wither and John Milton. *In* English Renaissance studies, ed. by J. Carey p212-27

**Hill, R. F.**
Critical studies. *In* Shakespeare survey 32 p211-27

**Hill, Thomas Dana**
The virga of Moses and the Old English Exodus. *In* Old English literature in context, ed. by J. N. Niles p57-65

**Hill, William Speed**
Casting off copy and the composition of Hooker's Book V. *In* Virginia. University. Bibliographical Society. Studies in bibliography v33 p144-61

**Hilliard, Raymond Francis**
Desire and the structure of eighteenth-century fiction. *In* Studies in eighteenth-century culture v9 p357-70
Emma: dancing without space to turn in. *In* Probability, time, and space in eighteenth-century literature, ed. by P. R. Backscheider p275-98

**Hillman, James**
The children, the children! *In* Children's literature v8 p3-6

**Hills, Catherine**
The archaeology of Anglo-Saxon England in the pagan period: a review. *In* Anglo-Saxon England 8 p297-329

**Hiltner, Seward**
Theological perspectives on humanness. *In* Being human in a technological age, ed. by D. M. Borchert and D. Stewart p51-71

**Himes, Chester B.**

### About
Reilly, J. M. Chester Himes' Harlem tough guys. *In* Seasoned authors for a new season: the search for standards in popular writing, ed. by L. Filler p58-69

**Himmelberg, Robert F.**
Hoover's public image, 1919-20: the emergence of a public figure and a sign of the times. *In* Herbert Hoover, ed. by L. E. Gelfand p207-32

**Hinde, Thomas,** pseud. See Chitty, Thomas

**The Hindenburg (Motion picture)**
Kael, P. Kaputt. *In* Kael, P. When the lights go down p119-23

**Hinduism.** See Vedanta

**Hinduism in literature**
Das, G. K. E. M. Forster, T. S. Eliot, and the 'Hymn before action.' *In* E. M. Forster: a human exploration, ed. by G. K. Das and J. Beer p208-15

**Hine, Daryl**

### About
Howard, R. Daryl Hine: "Between dream and doing, meaning lurks." *In* Howard, R. Alone with America p209-21

**Hinman, Charlton**
Mechanized collation: a preliminary report. *In* The Bibliographical Society of America, 1904-79 p201-08

**Hinnant, John.** See Bauer, D. F. jt. auth.

**Hinojosa, Rolando**
Chicano literature: an American literature in transition. *In* The Identification and analysis of Chicano literature, ed. by F. Jiménez p37-41

Literatura chicana: background and present status of a bicultural expression. *In* The Identification and analysis of Chicano literature, ed. by F. Jiménez p42-46

Mexican-American literature: toward an identification. *In* The Identification and analysis of Chicano literature, ed. by F. Jiménez p7-18

**Hippodrome.** See Circus

**Hirsch, Eric Donald**
### About
Lentricchia, F. E. D. Hirsch: the hermeneutics of innocence. *In* Lentricchia, F. After the New Criticism p256-80

### About individual works
*Validity in interpretation*
Crosman, R. T. Do readers make meaning? *In* The Reader in the text, ed. by S. R. Suleiman and I. Crosman p149-64

**Hirsch, Jerrold**
Ludwig Lewisohn: can he still help us? A reconsideration of expression in America. *In* Seasoned authors for a new season: the search for standards in popular writing, ed. by L. Filler p98-116

**Hirsch, Joachim**
Developments in the political system of West Germany since 1945. *In* The State in Western Europe, ed. by Richard Scase p115-41

**Hirsch, Samson Raphael**
### About
Thieberger, F. Samson Raphael Hirsch (1808-1888) *In* The Jew, ed. by A. A. Cohen p237-50

**Hirsch, Susan Eleanor**
From artisan to manufacturer: industrialization and the small producer in Newark, 1830-60. *In* Small business in American life, ed. by S. W. Bruchey p80-99

**Hirschman, Albert O.**
The turn to authoritarianism in Latin America and the search for its economic determinants. *In* The New authoritarianism in Latin America, ed. by D. Collier p61-98

**Hiss, Alger**
### About
Hook, S. The case of Alger Hiss. *In* Hook, S. Philosophy and public policy p238-52

**Historians**
Dye, N. S. Clio's American daughters: male history, female reality. *In* The Prism of sex, ed. by J. A. Sherman and E. T. Beck p9-31

Kammen, M. G. Introduction: the historian's vocation and the state of the discipline in the United States, ed. by M. Kammen p19-46

*See also* Medievalists

### France
Ranum, O. Glancing backward and forward. *In* Ranum, O. Artisans of glory p333-40

Ranum, O. The historiographers royal. *In* Ranum, O. Artisans of glory p58-102

### Great Britain
Pole, J. R. Introduction. *In* Pole, J. R. Paths to the American past pxi-xxiii

### United States
Pole, J. R. The American past: is it still usable? *In* Pole, J. R. Paths to the American past p250-70

Pole, J. R. The new history and the sense of social purpose in American historical writing. *In* Pole, J. R. Paths to the American past p271-98

**Historical drama.** See English drama—Early modern and Elizabethan, 1500-1600

**Historical fiction, French**
Hall, P. M. Duclos's Histoire de Madame de Luz: woman and history. *In* Woman and society in eighteenth-century France, ed. by E. Jacobs and others p139-51

**Historical linguistics.** See Linguistic change

**Historical research**
Landon, M. de L. A historian looks at the computer's impact on society. *In* Monster or messiah? Ed. by W. M. Mathews p13-22

*See also* Historiography

**Historical sociology.** See Culture

**Historicism**
Petrova-Averkieva, Y. Historicism in Soviet ethnographic science. *In* Soviet and Western anthropology, ed. by E. Gellner p19-27

**Historiography**
Braudel, F. The situation of history in 1950. *In* Braudel, F. On history p6-22

Manley, L. G. The emergence of historical consciousness. *In* Manley, L. G. Convention, 1500-1750 p215-26

Manley, L. G. Historical rhetoric and historical explanation. *In* Manley, L. G. Convention, 1500-1750 p203-15

Manley, L. G. "A passable contexture": convention and the practice of contextualism. *In* Manley, L. G. Convention, 1500-1750 p231-40

Tuchman, B. W. Biography as a prism of history. *In* Telling lives, ed. by M. Pachter p132-47

*See also* Historians; Psychohistory; also subdivision Historiography under subjects, e.g. Europe—Historiography; Holocaust, Jewish (1939-1945)—Historiography; Islamic Empire—Historiography; Newfoundland—Historiography; United States—Historiography

### United States
Fredrickson, G. M. Comparative history. *In* The Past before us, ed. by M. Kammen p457-73

Kammen, M. G. Introduction: the historian's vocation and the state of the discipline in the United States, ed. by M. Kammen p19-46

### Wales
Roberts, B. F. Historical writing. *In* A Guide to Welsh literature, ed. by A. O. H. Jarman and G. R. Hughes v 1 p244-47

**History**
Braudel, F. The Mediterranean and the Mediterranean world in the age of Philip II; excerpt. *In* Braudel, F. On history p3-5

Le Goff, J. The historian and the ordinary man. *In* Le Goff, J. Time, work, & culture in the Middle Ages p225-36

Moynihan, R. D. "Dwarfs of wit and learning": problems of historical time. *In* Probability, time, and space in eighteenth-century literature, ed. by P. R. Backscheider p167-85

History—*Continued*

Pickering, F. P. Economies of history. What is fiction? *In* Pickering, F. P. Essays on medieval German literature and iconography p164-74

*See also* Coups d'état; Heroes; Historians; Revolutions

### Criticism

*See* Historiography

### Errors, inventions, etc.

*See* Indian Ocean region—History—Errors, inventions, etc.

### Historiography

*See* Historiography

### Methodology

*See* Oral history

### Periodization

Manley, L. G. "A genius of times": the contexts of historical periods. *In* Manley, L. G. Convention, 1500-1750 p226-31

### Philosophy

Braudel, F. History and sociology. *In* Braudel, F. On history p64-82

Braudel, F. History and the social sciences; the longue durée. *In* Braudel, F. On history p25-54

Braudel, F. The situation of history in 1950. *In* Braudel, F. On history p6-22

*See also* History—Periodization

### Psychological aspects

*See* Psychohistory

### Research

*See* Historical research

### Study and teaching—United States

Hertzberg, H. W. The teaching of history. *In* The Past before us, ed. by M. Kammen p474-504

History (Theology)

Daly, G. History and dogma: the debate between Alfred Loisy and Maurice Blondel. *In* Daly, G. Transcendence and immanence p69-90

History, Ancient

Bately, J. M. World history in the Anglo-Saxon Chronicle: its sources and its separateness from the Old English Orosius. *In* Anglo-Saxon England 8 p177-94

History, Economic. See Economic history

History, Modern

*See also* Reformation

### Philosophy

*See* History—Philosophy

History and social sciences. See Social sciences and history

Histrio-Mastix

Edwards, P. A superfluous sort of men: the rise and fall of the professional theatre. *In* Edwards, P. Threshold of a nation p17-37

Hitchcock, Alfred Joseph

### About individual works
#### Family plot

Kauffmann, S. Family plot. *In* Kauffmann, S. Before my eyes p209-10

Hitler, Adolf

### About

Harbison, R. Tribe and race. *In* Harbison, R. Deliberate regression p180-205

Hoban, Russell C.

### About

Bowers, A. J. The fantasy world of Russell Hoban. *In* Children's literature v8 p80-97

Hobsbawn, Eric J.

Pre-political movements in modern politics. *In* Powers, possessions and freedom, ed. by A. Kontos p89-106

Hochhuth, Rolf

### About individual works
#### The Deputy

Bosmajian, H. Rituals of judgment: Hochhuth's The Deputy and Weiss's The investigation. *In* Bosmajian. M. Metaphors of evil p147-82

Hochwaelder, Fritz. See Hochwälder, Fritz

Hochwälder, Fritz

### About

Best, A. Shadows of the past: the drama of Fritz Hochwälder. *In* Modern Austrian writing, ed. by A. Best and H. Wolfschütz p44-62

Hocutt, Max

Toward an ethic of mutual accommodation. *In* Humanist ethics, ed. by M. B. Storer p137-53

Hoeber, Amoretta M. and Douglass, Joseph D.

Soviet approach to global nuclear conflict. *In* The United States in the 1980s, ed. by P. Duignan and A. Rabushka p445-67

Hoffman, Bryant E.

All imaginable things: Yeats's Per amica silentia lunae. *In* Irish Renaissance annual I p56-72

Hoffman, Daniel Gerard

Poetry: after modernism. *In* Harvard Guide to contemporary American writing, ed. by D. G. Hoffman p439-95

Poetry: dissidents from schools. *In* Harvard Guide to contemporary American writing, ed. by D. G. Hoffman p564-606

Poetry: schools of dissidents. *In* Harvard Guide to contemporary American writing, ed. by D. G. Hoffman p564-606

### About

Howard, R. Daniel Hoffman: "A testament of change, melting into song." *In* Howard, R. Alone with America p222-38

Hoffmann, Erik P.

Changing Soviet perspectives on leadership and administration. *In* The Soviet Union since Stalin, ed. by S. F. Cohen; A. Rabinowitch, and R. Sharlet p71-92

Hoffmann, Ernst Theodor Amadeus

### About

Hughes, G. T. The risks of the imagination: Hoffmann, with Chamisso, Fouqué and Werner. *In* Hughes, G. T. Romantic German literature p112-26

### About individual works
#### The sandman

Hertz, N. H. Freud and The sandman. *In* Textual strategies, ed. by J. V. Harari p296-319

Hoffman, Frederick John

### About individual works
#### Freudianism and the literary mind

Trilling, L. The problem of influence. *In* Trilling, L. Speaking of literature and society p217-19

**Hoffman, Michael J.**
Themes, topics, criticism. *In* American literary scholarship, 1978 p413-38

**Hofstadter, Albert**
Enownment. *In* Martin Heidegger and the question of literature, ed. by W. V. Spanos p17-37
On the interpretation of works of art. *In* The Concept of style, ed. by B. Lang p67-91

**Hofstadter, Richard**
**About**
Pole, J. R. Richard Hofstadter, 1916-1970. *In* Pole, J. R. Paths to the American past p335-37

**Hogenkamp, Bert**
Making films with a purpose: film-making and the working class. *In* Culture and crisis in Britain in the thirties, ed. by J. Clark and others p257-69

**Holbach, Paul Henri Thiry, baron d'**
**About**
Gardner, E. J. The philosophes and women: sensationalism and sentiment. *In* Woman and society in eighteenth-century France, ed. by E. Jacobs and others p19-27

**Holdcroft, David**
From the one to the many: philosophy, 1900-30. *In* The Context of English literature, 1900-1930, ed. by M. Bell p126-59

**Holder, Orlee.** See Bloom, L. Z. jt. auth.

**Hölderlin, Friedrich**
**About**
Schürman, R. Situating René Char: Hölderlin, Heidegger, Char and the "there is." *In* Martin Heidegger and the question of literature, ed. by W. V. Spanos p173-94

**About individual works**
*Heidelberg*
Grundlehner, P. Friedrich Hölderlin: "Heidelberg." *In* Grundlehner, P. The lyrical bridge p27-40

**Influence—Stevens**
Kermode, F. Dwelling poetically in Connecticut. *In* Wallace Stevens, ed. by F. Doggett and R. Buttel p256-73

**Holding, Edith**
'As you like it' adapted: Charles Johnson's 'Love in a forest.' *In* Shakespeare survey 32 p37-48

**Holland, Norman Norwood**
Hermia's dream. *In* Representative Shakespeare, ed. by M. M. Schwartz and C. Kahn p 1-20
Re-covering "The purloined letter": reading as a personal transaction. *In* The Reader in the text, ed. by S. R. Suleiman and I. Crosman p350-70

**Hollander, John**
The sound of the music of music and sound. *In* Wallace Stevens, ed. by F. Doggett and R. Buttel p235-55
**About**
Howard, R. John Hollander: "Between the deed and the dream is the life remembered." *In* Howard, R. Alone with America p239-75

**Hollander, Stanley C.**
The effects of industrialization of small retailing in the United States in the twentieth century. *In* Small business in American life, ed. by S. W. Bruchey p212-39

**Hollis, Martin**
Rational man and social science. *In* Rational action, ed. by R. Harrison p 1-15

**Hollis, Patricia**
Anti-slavery and British working-class radicalism in the years of reform. *In* Anti-slavery, religion, and reform: essays in memory of Roger Anstey, ed. by C. Bolt and S. Drescher p294-315

**Holloway, John**
How goes the weather? *In* Yeats, Sligo and Ireland, ed. by A. N. Jeffares p89-97
Narrative and structure: exploratory essays
*Contents*
Conclusion: structure and the critic's art
Effectively complete enumeration in 'Phèdre'
Identity, inversion and density elements in narrative: three tales by Chekhov, James and Lawrence
Logic, feeling and structure in nineteenth-century political oratory: a primer of analysis
Narrative process in 'Middlemarch'
Narrative structure and text structure: Isherwood's A meeting by the river and Muriel Spark's The prime of Miss Jean Brodie
Poetic analysis and the idea of the transformation-rule: some examples from Herbert, Wordsworth, Pope and Shakespeare
Supposition and supersession: a model of analysis for narrative structure

**Hollywood, Calif.**
Kauffmann, S. Welcome to L.A. *In* Kauffmann, S. Before my eyes p286-89

**Holman, C. Hugh.** See Holman, Clarence Hugh

**Holman, Clarence Hugh**
The tragedy of self-entrapment: Ellen Glasgow's The romance of a plain man. *In* Toward a new American literary history, ed. by L. J. Budd, E. H. Cady and C. L. Anderson p154-63

**Holmes, Abiel**
**About**
Lutz, C. E. A family tablet. *In* Lutz, C. E. The oldest library motto, and other library essays p140-47

**About individual works**
*The life of Ezra Stiles*
Lutz, C. E. Abiel Holmes' life of Ezra Stiles. *In* Lutz, C. E. The oldest library motto, and other library essays p125-39

**Holocaust (Jewish theology)**
Alexander, E. The Holocaust and the God of Israel. *In* Alexander, E. The resonance of dust p195-230
Sherwin, B. L. Jewish and Christian theology encounters the Holocaust. *In* Encountering the Holocaust: an interdisciplinary survey, ed. by B. L. Sherwin and S. G. Ament p407-42

**Holocaust, Jewish (1939-1945)**
Bassiouni, M. C. International law and the Holocaust. *In* Encountering the Holocaust: an interdisciplinary survey, ed. by B. L. Sherwin and S. G. Ament p146-88
Fein, H. Socio-political responses during the Holocaust: actions and reactions of Allies, Axis partners and neutrals to the destruction of European Jewry. *In* Encountering the Holocaust: an interdisciplinary survey, ed. by B. L. Sherwin and S. G. Ament p84-145

**Holocaust, Jewish (1939-1945)**—*Continued*
Lustig, A. and Lustig, J. The Holocaust and the film arts. *In* Encountering the Holocaust: an interdisciplinary survey, ed. by B. L. Sherwin and S. G. Ament p351-82

Sherwin, B. L. Philosophical reactions to and moral implications of the Holocaust. *In* Encountering the Holocaust: an interdisciplinary survey, ed. by B. L. Sherwin and S. G. Ament p443-72

Weinberg, D. H. and Sherwin, B. L. The Holocaust: an historical overview. *In* Encountering the Holocaust: an interdisciplinary survey, ed. by B. L. Sherwin and S. G. Ament p12-22

### Historiography
Sherwin, B. L. Ideological antecedents of the Holocaust. *In* Encountering the Holocaust: an interdisciplinary survey, ed. by B. L. Sherwin and S. G. Ament p23-51

Weinberg, D. H. The Holocaust in historical perspective. *In* Encountering the Holocaust: an interdisciplinary survey, ed. by B. L. Sherwin and S. G. Ament p52-83

### Psychological aspects
Porter, J. N. Social-psychological aspects of the Holocaust. *In* Encountering the Holocaust: an interdisciplinary survey, ed. by B. L. Sherwin and S. G. Ament p189-222

**Holocaust, Jewish (1939-1945) in art**
Ament, S. G. Music and art of the Holocaust. *In* Encountering the Holocaust: an interdisciplinary survey, ed. by B. L. Sherwin and S. G. Ament p383-406

**Holocaust, Jewish (1939-1945) in literature**
Abramson, G. Thematic development: The plays of the Holocaust. *In* Abramson, G. Modern Hebrew drama p116-40

Alexander, E. Between Diaspora and Zion: Israeli Holocaust fiction. *In* Alexander, E. The resonance of dust p73-118

Alexander, E. A dialogue of the mind with itself: Chaim Grade's quarrel with Hersh Rasseyner. *In* Alexander, E. The resonance of dust p233-47

Alexander, E. The destruction and resurrection of the Jews in the fiction of Isaac Bashevis Singer. *In* Alexander, E. The resonance of dust p149-69

Alexander, E. Holocaust and rebirth: Moshe Flinker, Nelly Sachs, and Abba Kovner. *In* Alexander, E. The resonance of dust p31-71

Alexander, E. The Holocaust and the God of Israel. *In* Alexander, E. The resonance of dust p195-230

Alexander, E. The Holocaust in American Jewish fiction: a slow awakening. *In* Alexander, E. The resonance of dust p121-46

Alexander, E. The incredibility of the Holocaust. *In* Alexander, E. The resonance of dust p3-28

Alexander, E. Saul Bellow: a Jewish farewell to the Enlightenment. *In* Alexander, E. The resonance of dust p172-92

Eliach, Y. Holocaust literature III: poetry and drama. *In* Encountering the Holocaust: an interdisciplinary survey, ed. by B. L. Sherwin and S. G. Ament p316-50

Knopp, J. Z. and Lustig, A. Holocaust literature II: novels and short stories. *In* Encountering the Holocaust: an interdisciplinary survey, ed. by B. L. Sherwin and S. G. Ament p267-315

Syrkin, M. and Kunzer, R. G. Holocaust literature I: diaries and memoirs. *In* Encountering the Holocaust: an interdisciplinary survey, ed. by B. L. Sherwin and S. G. Ament p226-66

**Holroyd, Michael**
Introduction. *In* The Genius of Shaw, ed. by M. Holroyd p9-11

Women and the body politic. *In* The Genius of Shaw, ed. by M. Holroyd p167-83

**Holthusen, Hans Egon**
The poet and the Lion of Toledo. *In* Rilke: the alchemy of alienation, ed. by F. Baron, E. S. Dick and W. R. Maurer p29-45

**Holy Roman Empire**

### History—Charles V, 1519-1556
Ozment, S. H. Society and politics in the German Reformation. *In* Ozment, S. H. The age of reform, 1250-1550 p245-89

**Holzner, Burkart, and Robertson, Roland**
Identity and authority: a problem analysis of processes of identification and authorization. *In* Identity and authority, ed. by R. Robertson and B. Holzner p1-39

**Homage (Feudal law)**
Le Goff, J. The symbolic ritual of vassalage. *In* Le Goff, J. Time, work, & culture in the Middle Ages p237-87

**Home.** See Home in literature

**Home economics**

### United States
Vanek, J. Time spent in housework. *In* A Heritage of her own, ed. by N. F. Cott and E. H. Pleck p499-506

**Home in literature**
Sopher, D. E. The landscape of home: myth, experience, social meaning. *In* The Interpretation of ordinary landscapes, ed. by D. W. Meinig p129-49

**Home remodeling.** See Dwellings—Remodeling

**Home rule (Ireland)** See Irish question

**The home treasury**
Summerfield, G. The making of The home treasury. *In* Children's literature v8 p35-52

**Homer.** See Homerus

**Homer, Winslow**

### About
Tatham, D. Winslow Homer and the New England poets. *In* American Antiquarian Society. Proceedings v89 pt2 p241-60

**Homerus**

### About
Renner, T. Three new Homerics on papyrus. *In* Harvard Studies in classical philology, v83, p311-37

West, M. L. Homeric and Hesiodic poetry. *In* Ancient Greek literature, ed. by K. J. Dover p 10-28

### About individual works
*Hymn to Aphrodite*
Smith, P. M. Notes on the text of the fifth Homeric Hymn. *In* Harvard Studies in classical philology, v83 p29-50

*Hymn to Hermes*
Scheinberg, S. The bee maidens of the Homeric Hymn to Hermes. *In* Harvard Studies in classical philology, v83 1-28

**Horn, James P. P.**

Servant emigration to the Chesapeake in the seventeenth century. *In* The Chesapeake in the seventeenth century, ed. by T. W. Tate and D. L. Ammerman p51-95

**Horney, Karen**

### About individual works
*Self-analysis*

Trilling, L. The progressive psyche. *In* Trilling, L. Speaking of literature and society p181-85

**Horse sense.** See Common sense

**Horsley, William**

The press as loyal opposition in Japan. *In* Newspapers and democracy, ed. by A. Smith p200-27

**Horton, Andrew S.**

Ken Kesey, John Updike and the Lone Ranger. *In* Seasoned authors for a new season: the search for standards in popular writing, ed. by L. Filler p83-90

**Horváth, Odön**

### About

Best, A. Odön von Horváth: the Volksstück revived. *In* Modern Austrian writing, ed. by A. Best and H. Wolfschütz p108-27

**Hosking, Geoffrey**

Beyond Socialist realism

*Contents*

Alexander Solzhenitsyn
The Socialist realist tradition
Two key works: Doctor Zhivago and One day in the life of Ivan Denisovich
Vasily Shukshin
Village prose: Vasily Belov, Valentin Rasputin
Vladimir Maximov
Vladimir Tendryakov
Vladimir Voinovich, Georgy Vladimov
Yury Trifonov

**Hoskins, William George**

### About individual works
*The making of the English landscape*

Meinig, D. W. Reading the landscape: an appreciation of W. G. Hoskins and J. B. Jackson. *In* The Interpretation of ordinary landscapes, ed. by D. W. Meinig p195-244

**Hospitals**

### France

Joerger, M. The structure of the hospital system in France during the ancien régime. *In* Medicine and society in France, ed. by R. Forster and O. Ranum p104-36

**Hostilities.** See War

**Hourani, Albert Habib**

Europe and the Middle East

*Contents*

H. A. R. Gibb: the vocation of an Orientalist
Islam and the philosophers of history
Muslims and Christians
The present state of Islamic and Middle Eastern historiography
Toynbee's vision of history
Volney and the ruin of empires
Western attitudes towards Islam
Wilfrid Scawen Blunt and the revival of the East

**Hours, Books of**

Schapiro, M. A note on the Mérode altarpiece. *In* Schapiro, M. Selected papers v3: Late antique, early Christian and mediaeval art p12-19

**Hours of labor**

### History

Le Goff, J. Labor time in the "crisis" of the fourteenth century: from medieval time to modern time. *In* Le Goff, J. Time, work, & culture in the Middle Ages p43-52

**Household shrines**

Orr, D. G. Roman domestic religion: the archaeology of Roman popular art. *In* 5000 years of popular culture, ed. by F. E. H. Schroeder p156-72

**Housing and state.** See Housing policy

**Housing policy**

### Great Britain

Segal, W. The housing crisis in Western Europe: Britain—assessment and options. *In* Architecture for people, ed. by B. Mikellides p171-75

### United States

Muth, R. F. National housing policy. *In* The United States in the 1980s, ed. by P. Duignan and A. Rabushka p343-66

**Houston, John**

### About individual works
*The man who would be king*

Kauffmann, S. The man who would be king. *In* Kauffmann, S. Before my eyes p193-95

**Houthakker, Hendrik S.**

World energy sources. *In* The United States in the 1980s, ed. by P. Duignan and A. Rabushka p535-58

**Howard, Judith Jeffrey**

Patriot mothers in the post-Risorgimento: women after the Italian revolution. *In* Women, war, and revolution, ed. by C. R. Berkin and C. M. Lovett p237-58

**Howard, Richard**

Alone with America

*Contents*

A. R. Ammons: "The spent seer consigns order to the vehicle of change"
Adrienne Rich: "What lends us anchor but the mutable?"
Alan Dugan: "Possessed of an echo but not a fate"
Allen Ginsberg: "O brothers of the laurel, is the world real? Is the laurel a joke or a crown of thorns?"
Anne Sexton: "Some tribal female who is known but forbidden"
Anthony Hecht: "What do we know of lasting since the Fall?"
Carolyn Kizer: "Our masks keep us in thrall to ourselves . . ."
Daniel Hoffman: "A testament of change, melting into song"
Daryl Hine: "Between dream and doing, meaning lurks"
David Wagoner: "It dawns on us that we must come apart"
Denise Levertov: "I don't want to escape, only to see the enactment of rites"
Donald Finkel: "There is no perfection possible. But there is tomorrow"
Donald Justice: "As the butterfly longs for the cocoon or the looping net"
Edgar Bowers: "What seems won paid for as in defeat"
Edward Field: "His body comes together joyfully from all directions"
Frank O'Hara: "Since once we are we always will be in this life come what may"

**Howard, Richard**
Alone with America
*Contents—Continued*

Galway Kinnell: "Everything that may abide the fire was made to go through the fire"

Gary Snyder: "To hold both history and wilderness in mind"

Gregory Corso: "Surely there'll be another table . . ."

Howard Moss: "Beginnings spin a web where endings spawn"

Irving Feldman: "Who will call these things his own?"

James Dickey: "We never can really tell whether nature condemns us or loves us"

James Merrill: "Masked, as who was not, in laughter, pain and love"

James Wright: "The body wakes to burial"

John Ashbery: "You may never know how much is pushed back into the night, nor what may return"

John Hollander: "Between the deed and the dream is the life remembered"

John Logan: "I am interested in the unicorn underneath the wound"

Kenneth Koch: "What was the ecstasy, and what the stricture?"

Louis Simpson: "The hunger in my vitals is for some credible extravaganza"

Mark Strand: "The mirror was nothing without you"

May Swenson: "Turned back to the wild by love"

Paul Goodman: "The form of life, the art of dissidence"

Richard Hugo: "Why track down unity when the diffuse is so exacting?"

Robert Bly: "Like those before, we move to the death we love"

Robert Creeley: "I begin where I can, and end when I see the whole thing returning"

Sylvia Plath: "And I have no face, I have wanted to efface myself . . ."

Theodore Weiss: "No shore beyond our own"

W. D. Snodgrass: "There's something beats the same in opposed hearts"

W. S. Merwin: "We survived the selves that we remembered"

William Meredith: "All of a piece and clever and at some level, true"

William Stafford: " 'Tell us what you deserve,' the whole world said"

**Howard, Victor**
J. S. Pennell's The history of Rome Hanks: contributions toward perspectives. *In* Seasoned authors for a new season: the search for standards in popular writing, ed. by L. Filler p127-38

**Howarth, William Driver**
Word and image in Pixérécourt's melodramas: the dramaturgy of the strip-cartoon. *In* Performance and politics in popular drama, ed. by D. Bradby, L. James and B. Sharratt p17-32

**Howarth, William L.**
Some principles of autobiography. *In* Autobiography: essays theoretical and critical, ed. by J. Olney p84-114

Travelling in Concord: the world of Thoreau's Journal. *In* Puritan influences in American literature, ed. by E. Elliott p143-66

**Howe, Tina**
### About individual works
*Birth and after birth*
Brown, J. Birth and after birth. *In* Brown, J. Feminist drama p71-85

**Howkins, Alun**
Class against class: the political culture of the Communist Party of Great Britain, 1930-35. *In* Class, culture and social change, ed. by F. Gloversmith p240-57

**Hoy, David Couzens**
The owl and the poet: Heidegger's critique of Hegel. *In* Martin Heidegger and the question of literature, ed. by W. V. Spanos p53-70

**Hsia, C. T.** See Hsia, Chih-tsing

**Hsia, Chih-tsing**
### About individual works
*A history of modern Chinese literature, 1917-1957*
Prušek, J. Basic problems of the history of modern Chinese literature: a review of C. T. Hsia, A history of modern Chinese fiction. *In* Prušek, J. The lyrical and the epic p195-230

**Hsüw, Lu,** pseud. See Chou, Shu-jen

**Huber, Marie**
### About
Briggs, E. R. Marie Huber and the campaign against eternal hell torments. *In* Woman and society in eighteenth-century France, ed. by E. Jacobs and others p218-28

**Hudson, Liam**
Language, truth, and psychology. *In* The State of the language, ed. by L. Michaels and C. Ricks p449-57

**Hudson, William Donald**
The rational system of beliefs. *In* Sociology and theology: alliance and conflict, ed. by D. Martin, J. O. Mills [and] W. S. F. Pickering p80-101

**Hueffer, Ford Madox.** See Ford, Ford Madox

**Huerta, Jorge A.**
From the temple to the arena: Teatro Chicano today. *In* The Identification and analysis of Chicano literature, ed. by F. Jiménez p90-116

**Hügel, Friedrich Freiherr von**
### About
Daly, G. Friedrich von Hügel: experience and transcendence. *In* Daly, G. Transcendence and immanence p117-39

**Hughes, Glyn Tegai**
Romantic German literature
*Contents*
Background and backbone
Coda: the Swabians
The legacy of myth: the Grimms, Brentano and Arnim
Natural and supernatural: Eichendorff, with Görres
New ways of feeling: Wackenroder, Tieck and 'the night watches'
Poetry in metaphysics: Novalis
Profusion and order: the brothers Schlegel
The risks of the imagination: Hoffmann, with Chamisso, Fouqué and Werner

**Hughes, Jonathan Roberts Tyson**
Entrepreneurship. *In* Encyclopedia of American economic history, ed. by G. Porter v 1 p214-28

**Hughes, Robert P. comp.**
Gleb Struve: a bibliography. *In* California Slavic studies v11 p269-317

**Hugo, Richard F.**
### About
Howard, R. Richard Hugo: "Why track down unity when the diffuse is so exacting?" *In* Howard, R. Alone with America p276-91

**Human acts.** See Free will and determinism

**Human-animal communication**
Bronowski, J. and Bellugi, U. Language, name, and concept. *In* Speaking of apes, ed. by T. A. Sebeok and J. Umiker-Sebeok p103-13

Brown, R. The first sentences of child and chimpanzee. *In* Speaking of apes, ed. by T. A. Sebeok and J. Umiker-Sebeok p85-101

Fouts, R. S. and Rigby, R. L. Man-chimpanzee communication. *In* Speaking of apes, ed. by T. A. Sebeok and J. Umiker-Sebeok p261-85

Gardner, R. A. and Gardner, B. T. Comparative psychology and language acquisition. *In* Speaking of apes, ed. by T. A. Sebeok and J. Umiker-Sebeok p287-330

Healy, A. F. Can chimpanzees learn a phonemic language? *In* Speaking of apes, ed. by T. A. Sebeok and J. Umiker-Sebeok p141-43

Hediger, H. Do you speak Yerkish? The newest colloquial language with chimpanzees. *In* Speaking of apes, ed. by T. A. Sebeok and J. Umiker-Sebeok p441-47

Hill, J. H. Apes and language. *In* Speaking of apes, ed. by T. A. Sebeok and J. Umiker-Sebeok p331-51

Kellogg, W. N. Communication and language in the home-raised chimpanzee. *In* Speaking of apes, ed. by T. A. Sebeok and J. Umiker-Sebeok p61-70

Limber, J. Language in child and chimp? *In* Speaking of apes, ed. by T. A. Sebeok and J. Umiker-Sebeok p197-220

McNeill, D. Sentence structure in chimpanzee communication. *In* Speaking of apes, ed. by T. A. Sebeok and J. Umiker-Sebeok p145-60

Marler, P. Primate vocalization: affective or symbolic? *In* Speaking of apes, ed. by T. A. Sebeok and J. Umiker-Sebeok p221-29

Mounin, G. Language, communication, chimpanzees. *In* Speaking of apes, ed. by T. A. Sebeok and J. Umiker-Sebeok p161-77

Rumbaugh, D. M. Language behavior of apes. *In* Speaking of apes, ed. by T. A. Sebeok and J. Umiker-Sebeok p231-59

Terrace, H. S. and Bever, T. G. What might be learned from studying language in the chimpanzee? The importance of symbolizing oneself. *In* Speaking of apes, ed. by T. A. Sebeok and J. Umiker-Sebeok p179-89

**Human behavior**
Charlesworth, W. R. Ethology: understanding the other half of intelligence. *In* Human ethology, ed. by M. von Cranach [and others] p491-529

Dunn, J. Understanding human development: limitations and possibilities in an ethological approach. *In* Human ethology, ed. by M. von Cranach [and others] p623-41

Eibl-Eibesfeldt, I. Ritual and ritualization from a biological perspective. *In* Human ethology, ed. by M. von Cranach [and others] p3-55

Leyhausen, P. Aggression, fear and attachment: complexities and interdependencies. *In* Human ethology, ed. by M. von Cranach [and others] p253-64

Masters, R. D. Beyond reductionism: five basic concepts in human ethology. *In* Human ethology, ed. by M. von Cranach [and others] p265-84

Salzen, E. A. Social attachment and a sense of security. *In* Human ethology, ed. by M. von Cranach [and others] p595-622
*See* also Behavior modification

**Human biology.** See Human behavior

**Human communication with animals.** See Human-animal communication

**Human ecology.** See Anthropo-geography; Landscape assessment

**Human engineering.** See Architecture—Human factors

**Human factors in architecture.** See Architecture—Human factors

**Human geography.** See Anthropo-geography

**Human intelligence.** See Intellect

**Human interaction.** See Social interaction

**Human relations.** See Interpersonal relations

**Human relations in literature.** See Interpersonal relations in literature

**Human rights.** See Civil rights

**Humanism**
Bouwsma, W. J. The Renaissance and the broadening of communication. *In* Propaganda and communication in world history, ed. by H. D. Lasswell, D. Lerner and H. Speier v2 p3-40

Kristeller, P. O. Humanism and scholasticism in the Italian Renaissance. *In* Kristeller, P. O. Renaissance thought and its sources p85-105

Kristeller, P. O. The humanist movement. *In* Kristeller, P. O. Renaissance thought and its sources p21-32

Levinas, E. The contemporary criticism of the idea of value and the prospects for humanism. *In* Value and values in evolution, ed. by E. A. Maziarz p179-87

Lutz, C. E. Copernicus' stand for humanism. *In* Lutz, C. E. The oldest library motto, and other library essays p75-82

Ozment, S. H. Humanism and the Reformation, 1250-1550. *In* Ozment, S. H. The age of reform, 1250-1550 p290-317
*See also* Culture; Humanistic ethics

**Humanism, Religious**
Bulman, R. F. "The God of our children": the humanist reconstruction of God. *In* History, religion, and spiritual democracy, ed. by M. Wohlgelernter and others p35-52

**Humanism in literature**
Marsh, D. Cicero and the humanist dialogue. *In* Marsh, D. The quattrocento dialogue p1-23

**Humanist ethics.** See Humanistic ethics

**Humanist Manifesto II**
Simpson, J. R. Toward a humanist consensus on ethics of international development. *In* Humanist ethics, ed. by M. B. Storer p122-36

**Humanistic education.** See Education, Humanistic

**Humanistic ethics**
Anton, J. P. A note toward a theory of political humanism. *In* Humanist ethics, ed. by M. B. Storer p272-80

Bahm, A. J. Humanist ethics as the science of oughtness. *In* Humanist ethics, ed. by M. B. Storer p210-26

**Humanistic ethics**—*Continued*

Fletcher, J. F. Humanist ethics: the groundwork. *In* Humanist ethics, ed. by M. B. Storer p253-61

Hocutt, M. Toward an ethic of mutual accommodation. *In* Humanist ethics, ed. by M. B. Storer p137-53

Kirkendall, L. A. An ethical system for now and the future. *In* Humanist ethics, ed. by M. B. Storer p193-209

Kurtz, P. W. Does humanism have an ethic of responsibility? *In* Humanist ethics, ed. by M. B. Storer p11-35

Manley, L. G. A world on wheels: convention in sixteenth-century moral philosophy. *In* Manley, L. G. Convention, 1500-1750 p106-36

Marković, M. Historical praxis as the ground of morality. *In* Humanist ethics, ed. by M. B. Storer p36-57

Simpson, J. R. Toward a humanist consensus on ethics of international development. *In* Humanist ethics, ed. by M. B. Storer p122-36

Storer, M. B. A factual investigation of the foundations of morality. *In* Humanist ethics, ed. by M. B. Storer p281-300

Tarkunde, V. M. Towards a fuller consensus in humanistic ethics. *In* Humanist ethics, ed. by M. B. Storer p154-72

Zimmerman, M. How "humanistic" are humanists? *In* Humanist ethics, ed. by M. B. Storer p262-71

**Humanistic psychology**

Giorgi, A. Vico and humanistic psychology. *In* Conference on Vico and Contemporary Thought, New York, 1976. Vico and contemporary thought pt2 p69-78

**Humanities**

*See also* Education, Humanistic; Science and the humanities

### Methodology

Gombrich, Sir, E. H. J. Research in the humanities: ideals and idols. *In* Gombrich, Sir E. H. J. Ideals and idols p112-22

### Study and teaching

Hartman, G. H. A short history of practical criticism. *In* Hartman, G. H. Criticism in the wilderness p284-301

**Humanities and science.** See Science and the humanities

**Humanity.** See Sympathy

**Humans.** See Man

**Hume, David**

### About

Baier, A. Master passions. *In* Explaining emotions, ed. by A. O. Rorty p403-23

Battersby, C. Hume, Newton and 'the hill called difficulty.' *in* Royal Institute of Philosophy. Philosophers of the Enlightenment p31-55

Brown, S. C. The 'principle' of natural order: or what the enlightened sceptics did not doubt. *In* Royal Institute of Philosophy. Philosophers of the Enlightenment p56-76

Burns, S. A. M. The Humean female. *In* The Sexism of social and political theory: women and reproduction from Plato to Nietzsche, ed. by L. M. G. Clark and L. Lange p53-60

Forbes, D. Hume and the Scottish Enlightenment. *In* Royal Institute of Philosophy. Philosophers of the Enlightenment p94-109

Marcil-Lacoste, L. Hume's method in moral reasoning. *In* The Sexism of social and political theory: women and reproduction from Plato to Nietzsche, ed. by L. M. G. Clark and L. Lange p60-73

Phillipson, N. T. Hume as moralist: a social historian's perspective. *In* Royal Institute of Philosophy. Philosophers of the Enlightenment p140-61

Taylor, G. Pride. *In* Explaining emotions, ed. by A. O. Rorty p385-402

### Influence

Berlin, Sir I. Hume and the sources of German anti-rationalism. *In* Berlin, Sir I. Against the current p162-87

**Humor.** See Wit and humor

**Humphrey, Colin**

Theories of North Asian shamanism. *In* Soviet and Western anthropology, ed. by E. Gellner p243-54

**Humphrey, Nicholas K.**

Natural aesthetics. *In* Architecture for people, ed. by B. Mikellides p59-73

**Humphreys, David**

### About

Lutz, C. E. Colonel David Humphreys and the Stiles family. *In* Lutz, C. E. The oldest library motto, and other library essays p149-55

**Hunsaker, O. Glade**

Roger Williams and John Milton: the calling of the Puritan writer. *In* Puritan influences in American literature, ed. by E. Elliott p3-22

**Hunt, Richard William**

Manuscript evidence for knowledge of the poems of Venantius Fortunatus in late Anglo-Saxon England. *In* Anglo-Saxon England 8 p279-95

**Hunter, George Kirkpatrick**

Poem and context in Love's labour's lost. *In* Shakespeare's styles, ed. by P. Edwards, I. S. Ewbank and G. K. Hunter p25-38

**Hunter, Mollie,** pseud. See McIllwraith, Maureen Mollie Hunter (McVeigh)

**Hunting, Primitive**

Clark, G. Primitive man as hunter, fisher, forager, and farmer. *In* The Origins of civilization, ed. by P. S. R. Moorey p 1-21

**Hunting in literature**

Hatto, A. T. Poetry and the hunt in medieval Germany. *In* Hatto, A. T. Essays on medieval German and other poetry p298-322

Hatto, A. T. Wolfram von Eschenbach and the chase. *In* Hatto, A. T. Essays on medieval German and other poetry p200-17

**Hürlimann, Bettina**

Fortunate moments in children's books. *In* The Arbuthnot lectures, 1970-1979 p63-80

**Husayn, Muhammad Kāmil**

### About individual works

*City of wrong*

Hourani, A. H. Muslims and Christians. *In* Hourani, A. H. Europe and the Middle East p74-80

**Hussein, Muhammad Kāmil.** See Husayn, Muhammad Kāmil

**Hustle (Motion picture)**

Kael, P. Dirty Harry with Weltschmerz. *In* Kael, P. When the lights go down p124-27

**Huston, John**

### About individual works
*The treasure of the Sierra Madre*
Miller, G. The wages of sin. *In* Miller, G. Screening the novel p84-115

**Hustvedt, Lloyd**
Ole Amundsen Buslett, 1855-1924. *In* Makers of an American immigrant legacy, ed. by O. S. Lovoll p131-58

**Hutchinson, Stuart**
Beyond the Victorians: The portrait of a lady. *In* Reading the Victorian novel: detail into form, ed. by I. Gregor p274-87

**Huttar, Charles Adolph**
Frail grass and firm tree: David as a model of repentance in the Middle Ages and early Renaissance. *In* The David myth in Western literature, ed. by R. J. Frontain and J. Wojcik p38-54

**Huxley, Thomas Henry**

### About individual works
*Collected essays*
Douglas, R. Huxley's critique from social Darwinism. *In* Critics of Henry George, ed. by R. V. Andelson p137-52

**Hyde, Mary Morley (Crapo)**
The history of the Johnson papers. *In* The Bibliographical Society of America, 1904-79 p252-65

**Hydén, Holger**
The adaptable brain during the stress of the life cycle. *In* The Condition of man, ed. by P. Hallberg p171-78

**Hygiene.** See Travel—Hygienic aspects

**Hyman, Arthur**
Jewish philosophy. *In* The Jewish world, ed. by E. Kedourie p209-16

**Hyman, Stanley Edgar**
"Van Wyck Brooks and biographical criticism"; excerpt from "The armed vision." *In* Van Wyck Brooks: the critic and his critics, ed. by W. Wasserstrom p137-56

**Hypocrisy in literature**
Steiger, R. "Wit in a corner": hypocrisy in The country wife. *In* Tennessee Studies in literature v24 p56-70

**Hysteria**
Erickson, G. Possession, sex and hysteria: the growth of demonism in later antiquity. *In* 5000 years of popular culture, ed. by F. E. H. Schroeder p110-35

**Hysteria (Social psychology)**
Morowitz, H. J. Extraordinary popular delusions. *In* Morowitz, H. J. The wine of life, and other essays on societies, energy & living things p183-86

# I

**Ibn Gabirol, Solomon ben Judah**

### About individual works
*Keter malkut*
Loewe, R. Ibn Gabirol's treatment of sources in the Kether Malkhuth. *In* Studies in Jewish religious and intellectual history, ed. by S. Stein and R. Loewe p183-94

### Sources
Loewe, R. Iban Gabirol's treatment of sources in the Kether Malkhuth. *In* Studies in Jewish religious and intellectual history, ed. by S. Stein and R. Loewe p183-94

**Ibsen, Henrik**

### About
Brustein, R. S. The fate of Ibsenism. *In* Brustein, R. S. Critical moments p124-38
Johnston, B. The critical writings. *In* Johnston, B. To the third empire p3-27
Johnston, B. Epilogue: toward the realistic cycle. *In* Johnston, B. To the third empire p272-82
Johnston, B. The recovery of the past: St. John's night to The Vikings at Helgeland. *In* Johnston, B. To the third empire p58-101

### About individual works
*Brand*
Fehrman, C. A. D. The writing of Ibsen's Brand. *In* Fehrman, C. A. D. Poetic creation p105-18
Johnston, B. Brand: the tragedy of vocation. *In* Johnston, B. To the third empire p130-63

*Catiline*
Johnston, B. The subjectivity of Catiline/the objectivity of The burial mound. *In* Johnston, B. To the third empire p28-57

*Emperor and Galilean*
Johnston, B. The third empire: Emperor and Galilean. *In* Johnston, B. To the third empire p224-71

*Ghosts*
Mueller, M. Oedipus Rex and modern analytical drama: Ibsen's Ghosts. *In* Mueller, M. Children of Oedipus, and other essays on the imitation of Greek tragedy 1550-1800 p146-52

*The league of youth*
Johnston, B. The mediocre angels of The league of youth. *In* Johnston, B. To the third empire p208-23

*Love's comedy*
Johnston, B. The achieved art: Love's comedy and The pretenders. *In* Johnston, B. To the third empire p102-29

*The Oxford Ibsen v8*
Leland, C. The Oxford Ibsen, volume VIII, translated and edited by James Walter McFarlane. *In* Drama and mimesis, ed. by J. Redmond p207-25

*Peer Gynt*
Johnston, B. The parable of Peer Gynt. *In* Johnston, B. To the third empire p164-207

*The pretenders*
Johnston, B. The achieved art: Love's comedy and The pretenders. *In* Johnston, B. To the third empire p102-29

*The warrior's barrow*
Johnston, B. The subjectivity of Catiline/the objectivity of The burial mound. *In* Johnston, B. To the third empire p28-57

**Iconoclasm**
Mack, P. The wonderyear. *In* Religion and the people, 800-1700, ed. by J. Obelkevich p191-220

**Iconography.** See Christian art and symbolism

**Idealism in literature**

Rosenbaum, S. P. The longest journey: E. M. Forster's refutation of idealism. *In* E. M. Forster: a human exploration, ed. by G. K. Das and J. Beer p32-54

*See also* Romanticism

**Identity**

Baum, R. C. Authority and identity: the case for evolutionary invariance. *In* Identity and authority, ed. by R. Robertson and B. Holzner p61-118

Fenn, R. K. Religion, identity and authority in the secular society. *In* Identity and authority, ed. by R. Robertson and B. Holzner p119-44

Holzner, B. and Robertson, R. Identity and authority: a problem analysis of processes of identification and authorization. *In* Identity and authority, ed. by R. Robertson and B. Holzner p1-39

Marx, J. H. The ideological construction of post-modern identity models in contemporary cultural movements. *In* Identity and authority, ed. by R. Robertson and B. Holzner p145-89

Robertson, R. Aspects of identity and authority in sociological theory. *In* Identity and authority, ed. by R. Robertson and B. Holzner p218-65

Swanson, G. E. A basis of authority and identity in post-industrial society. *In* Identity and authority, ed. by R. Robertson and B. Holzner p190-217

Wollheim, R. Memory, experiential memory, and personal identity. *In* Perception and identity, ed. by G. F. Macdonald p186-234

**Identity (Psychology)**

Kavolis, V. Logics of selfhood and modes of order: civilizational structures for individual identities. *In* Identity and authority, ed. by R. Robertson and B. Holzner p40-60

Luckmann, T. Personal identity as an evolutionary and historical problem. *In* Human ethology, ed. by M. von Cranach [and others] p56-74

Wollheim, R. On persons and their lives. *In* Explaining emotions, ed. by A. O. Rorty p299-321

**Ideology**

Farrell, J. P. Tragedy and ideology. *In* Farrell, J. P. Revolution as tragedy p281-90

Ricoeur, P. Ideology and utopia as cultural imagination. *In* Being human in a technological age, ed. by D. M. Borchert and D. Stewart p107-25

**Ideology in literature**

Eagleton, T. Text, ideology, realism. *In* Literature and society, ed. by E. W. Said p149-73

Kramnick, I. Children's literature and bourgeois ideology: observations on culture and industrial capitalism in the later eighteenth century. *In* Culture and politics from Puritanism to the Enlightenment, ed. by P. Zagorin p203-40

**Ignacio de Loyola, Saint.** See Loyola, Ignacio de, Saint

**Ignatow, David**

**About**

Wagner, L. W. On David Ignatow. *In* Wagner, L. W. American modern p134-39

**Ikei, Masaru**

Ugaki Kazushige's view of China and his China policy, 1915-1930. *In* The Chinese and the Japanese, ed. by A. Iriye p199-219

**Iklé, Fred Charles**

Arms control and national defense. *In* The United States in the 1980s, ed. by P. Duignan and A. Rabushka p419-43

Preparing for industrial mobilization: the first step toward full strength. *In* National security in the 1980s: from weakness to strength, ed. by W. S. Thompson p55-68

**Illuminati.** See Enlightenment

**Illumination of books and manuscripts**

*See also* Initials

**Ireland**

Schapiro, M. The place of Ireland in Hiberno-Saxon art. *In* Schapiro, M. Selected papers v3: Late antique, early Christian and mediaeval art p225-41

**Illumination of books and manuscripts, Byzantine**

Schapiro, M. The place of the Joshua Roll in Byzantine history. *In* Schapiro, M. Selected papers v3: Late antique, early Christian and mediaeval art p49-66

**Illumination of books and manuscripts, English**

Schapiro, M. The image of the disappearing Christ. *In* Schapiro, M. Selected papers v3: Late antique, early Christian and mediaeval art p266-87

**Illumination of books and manuscripts, Gothic**

Schapiro, M. Marginal images and drôlerie. *In* Schapiro, M. Selected papers v3: Late antique, early Christian and mediaeval art p197-98

**Illumination of books and manuscripts, Jewish**

Schapiro, M. The Bird's Head Haggada, an illustrated Hebrew manuscript of ca. 1300. *In* Schapiro, M. Selected papers v3: Late antique, early Christian and mediaeval art p381-86

**Illumination of books and manuscripts, Medieval**

Schapiro, M. The Beatus Apocalypse of Gerona. *In* Schapiro, M. Selected papers v3: Late antique, early Christian and mediaeval art p319-28

Schapiro, M. An illuminated English psalter of the early thirteenth century. *In* Schapiro, M. Selected papers v3: Late antique, early Christian and mediaeval art p329-54

**Illusion in literature.** See Reality in literature

**Illusions.** See Hallucinations and illusions

**Illustration of books**

**19th century—New England**

Tatham, D. Winslow Homer and the New England poets. *In* American Antiquarian Society. Proceedings v89 pt2 p241-60

**Imagination.** See Creation (Literary, artistic, etc.)

**Imagism.** See Imagist poetry

**Imagist poetry**

Duffey, B. Ezra Pound and the attainment of imagism. *In* Toward a new American literary history, ed. by L. J. Budd, E. H. Cady and C. L. Anderson p181-94

Wagner, L. W. The poetry in American fiction. *In* Wagner, L. W. American modern p18-30

**Imbert, Claude**

Stoic logic and Alexandrian poetics. *In* Doubt and dogmatism, ed. by M. Schofield, M. Burnyeat and J. Barnes p182-216

**Imitation (in literature)**
Cairns, F. Self-imitation within a generic framework: Ovid, Amores 2.9 and 3.11 and the renuntiatio amoris. *In* Creative imitation and Latin literature, ed. by D. West and T. Woodman p121-41

Rabinowitz, P. J. "What's Hecuba to us?" The audience's experience of literary borrowing. *In* The Reader in the text, ed. by S. R. Suleiman and I. Crosman p241-63

Russell, D. A. De imitatione. *In* Creative imitation and Latin literature, ed. by D. West and T. Woodman p 1-16

Sundquist, E. J. "The home of my childhood": incest and imitation in Cooper's Home as found. *In* Sundquist, E. J. Home as found p 1-40

Sundquist, E. J. "The home of the dead": representation and speculation in Hawthorne and The House of the Seven Gables. *In* Sundquist, E. J. Home as found p86-142
*See also* Mimesis in literature

**Immanence (Philosophy)**
Daly, G. The Blondelian challenge. *In* Daly, G. Transcendence and immanence p26-50

**Immanence of God**
Daly, G. Friedrich von Hügel: experience and transcendence. *In* Daly, G. Transcendence and immanence p117-39

Daly, G. George Tyrrell: revelation as experience. *In* Daly, G. Transcendence and immanence p140-64

Daly, G. Lucien Laberthonnière's 'critical mysticism.' *In* Daly, G. Transcendence and immanence p91-116

**Immortality**
Kristeller, P. O. The immortality of the soul. *In* Kristeller, P. O. Renaissance thought and its sources p181-96

Kristeller, P. O. The immortality of the soul. *In* Kristeller, P. O. Renaissance thought and its sources p181-96

**Imperialism**
Wolpin, M. D. Arms transfer and dependency in the Third World. *In* Problems of contemporary militarism, ed. by A. Eide and M. Thee p248-60
*See also* Militarism

### History
Becker, W. H. Imperialism. *In* Encyclopedia of American economic history, ed. by G. Porter v2 p882-93

**Impermanence (Buddhism)**
Morowitz, H. J. Christ, Clausius, and corrosion. *In* Morowitz, H. J. The wine of life, and other essays on societies, energy & living things p43-47

**Impersonation in literature**
Hayles, N. K. Sexual disguise in 'As you like it' and 'Twelfth night.' *In* Shakespeare survey 32 p63-72

**Implication (Linguistics)** See Connotation (Linguistics)

**Implied powers (Constitutional law)** See Judicial power

**Imports.** See Tariff

**Impressionism (Art)**

### Influence
Beebe, M. The Portrait as portrait: Joyce and impressionism. *In* Irish Renaissance annual I p13-31

**Improvisation**—rite and myth. Fehrman, C. A. D. *In* Fehrman, C. A. D. Poetic creation p35-54

**In the realm of the senses (Motion picture)**
Kauffmann, S. In the realm of the senses. *In* Kauffmann, S. Before my eyes p291-93

**Incest in literature**
Sundquist, E. J. "At home in his words": parody and parricide in Melville's Pierre. *In* Sundquist, E. J. Home as found p143-85

Sundquist, E. J. "The home of my childhood": incest and imitation in Cooper's Home as found. *In* Sundquist, E. J. Home as found p 1-40

**Incidental music.** See Music, Incidental

**Income**
Kregel, J. A. Income distribution. *In* A Guide to post-Keynesian economics, ed. by A. S. Eichner p46-60

### United States—History
Soltow, L. Distribution of income and wealth. *In* Encyclopedia of American economic history, ed. by G. Porter v3 p1087-1119

**Income distribution.** See Income

**The incredible Sarah (Motion picture)**
Kael, P. Travesties. *In* Kael, P. When the lights go down p204-07

**Incunabula**
Goff, F. R. The preparation of the Third census of incunabula in American libraries. *In* The Bibliographical Society of America, 1904-79 p493-99

Klebs, A. C. Gleanings from incunabula of science and medicine. *In* The Bibliographical Society of America, 1904-79 p71-109

**Indentured servants**
Horn, J. P. P. Servant emigration to the Chesapeake in the seventeenth century. *In* The Chesapeake in the seventeenth century, ed. by T. W. Tate and D. L. Ammerman p51-95

**Independent regulatory commissions**

### United States—History
McCraw, T. W. Regulatory agencies. *In* Encyclopedia of American economic history, ed. by G. Porter v2 p788-807

**Indexes.** See Bibliography—Indexes

**India**

### Civilization
Sharma, R. S. Indian civilization. *In* Propaganda and communication in world history, ed. by H. D. Lasswell, D. Lerner and H. Speier v 1 p175-204

### Relations (general) with China
Wright, A. F. On the spread of Buddhism to China. *In* Propaganda and communication in world history, ed. by H. D. Lasswell, D. Lerner and H. Speier v 1 p205-19

### Social conditions
Organ, T. W. Humanness in neo-Vedāntism. *In* Being human in a technological age, ed. by D. M. Borchert and D. Stewart p127-64

**India in literature**
Chaudhuri, N. C. India in English literature. *In* Royal Society of Literature of the United Kingdom, London. Essays by divers hands: innovation in contemporary literature, new ser. v40 p15-33

Drew, J. A passage via Alexandria? *In* E. M. Forster: a human exploration, ed. by G. K. Das and J. Beer p89-101

India in literature—*Continued*

Orange, M. Language and silence in A passage to India. *In* E. M. Forster: a human exploration, ed. by G. K. Das and J. Beer p142-60

Parry, B. A passage to India: epitaph or manifesto? *In* E. M. Forster: a human exploration, ed. by G. K. Das and J. Beer p129-41

**Indian literature (East Indian)** See Indic literature

**Indian Ocean region**

### History—Errors, inventions, etc.

Le Goff, J. The medieval West and the Indian Ocean: an oneiric horizon. *In* Le Goff, J. Time, work, & culture in the Middle Ages p189-200

**Indians of Central America**

### Antiquities

Bray, W. From village to city in Mesoamerica. *In* The Origins of civilization, ed. by P. R. S. Moorey p78-102

**Indians of North America**

### History

Bolt, C. The anti-slavery origins of concern for the American Indians. *In* Anti-slavery, religion, and reform: essays in memory of Roger Anstey, ed. by C. Bolt and S. Drescher p233-53

### Slaves, Ownership of

Bolt, C. The anti-slavery origins of concern for the American Indians. *In* Anti-slavery, religion, and reform: essays in memory of Roger Anstey, ed. by C. Bolt and S. Drescher p233-53

### Sources

Emerson, R. L. American Indians, Frenchmen, and Scots philosophers. *In* Studies in eighteenth-century culture v9 p211-36

### Women

Bannan, H. M. Spider Woman's web: mothers and daughters in Southwestern native American literature. *In* The Lost tradition: mothers and daughters in literature, ed. by C. N. Davidson and E. M. Broner p268-79

**Indians of South America**

*See also* Aymara Indians; Canelo Indians; Jivaro Indians; Tarirapé Indians; Yanoama Indians

### Kinship

Crocker, W. H. Canela kinship and the question of matrilineality. *In* Brazil, anthropological perspectives, ed. by M. L. Margolis and W. E. Carter p225-49

Murphy, R. F. Lineage and lineality in lowland South America. *In* Brazil, anthropological perspectives, ed. by M. L. Margolis and W. E. Carter p217-24

### Brazil

Gross, D. R. A new approach to central Brazilian social organization. *In* Brazil, anthropological perspectives, ed. by M. L. Margolis and W. E. Carter p321-42

### Brazil—Amazon Valley

Galvão, E. E. The encounter of tribal and national societies in the Brazilian Amazon. *In* Brazil, anthropological perspectives, ed. by M. L. Margolis and W. E. Carter p25-38

**Guyana**

Meggers, B. J. and Evans, C. An experimental reconstruction of Taruma Village succession and some implications. *In* Brazil, anthropological perspectives, ed. by M. L. Margolis and W. E. Carter p39-60

**Indic fiction (English)**

### History and criticism

Riemenschneider, D. British characters in Indo-English fiction. *In* Aspects of Indian writing in English, ed. by M. K. Naik p137-49

**Indic literature**

### History and criticism

Sharma, R. S. Indian civilization. *In* Propaganda and communication in world history, ed. by H. D. Lasswell, D. Lerner and H. Speier v 1 p175-204

**Indic literature (English)**

### History and criticism

Anand, M. R. Pigeon-Indian: some notes on Indian-English writing. *In* Aspects of Indian writing in English, ed. by M. K. Naik p24-44

Lal, P. Myth and the Indian writer in English: a note. *In* Aspects of Indian writing in English, ed. by M. K. Naik p15-18

Singh, A. Contemporary Indo-English literature: an approach. *In* Aspects of Indian writing in English, ed. by M. K. Naik p 1-14

**Indic poetry (English)**

### History and criticism

Walsh, W. Small observations on a large subject. *In* Aspects of Indian writing in English, ed. by M. K. Naik p101-19

**Indic propaganda.** See Propaganda, Indic

**Individualism**

Taylor, C. Atomism. *In* Powers, possessions and freedom, ed. by A. Kontos p39-61

*See also* Self (Philosophy)

**Individualism in literature**

Walker, J. A. Futabatei's Ukigumo (The floating clouds): the first novel of the individual. *In* Walker, J. A. The Japanese novel of the Meiji period and the ideal of individualism p30-61

Walker, J. A. Hakai (Breaking the commandment): a novel of the inner life. *In* Walker, J. A. The Japanese novel of the Meiji period and the ideal of individualism p156-93

Walker, J. A. Katai's Futon (The quilt): the birth of the I-novel. *In* Walker, J. A. The Japanese novel of the Meiji period and the ideal of individualism p93-120

Walker, J. A. Kitamura Tōkoku and the ideal of the inner life: the interiorization of the ideal of individualism. *In* Walker, J. A. The Japanese novel of the Meiji period and the ideal of individualism p62-92

**Individualists.** See Identity

**Individuality**

Bickman, M. One's self I sing: individuation and introjection. *In* Bickman, M. The unsounded centre p38-57

**Individuation.** See Self (Philosophy)

**Indo-English fiction.** See Indic fiction (English)

**Indo-English literature.** See Indic literature (English)

**Indo-English poetry.** See Indic poetry (English)

**Induction (Logic)**
Mackie, J. L. A defence of induction. *In* Perception and identity, ed. by G. F. Macdonald p113-30

**Industrial architecture.** See Architecture, Industrial

**Industrial concentration.** See Consolidation and merger of corporations

**Industrial discipline.** See Labor discipline

**Industrial laboratories.** See Research, Industrial—Laboratories

**Industrial laws and legislation**

### United States—History
Jones, B. L. Government management of the economy. *In* Encyclopedia of American economic history, ed. by G. Porter v2 p808-31

**Industrial management**
*See also* Big business; Industrial organization; Marketing

### United States—History
Baughman, J. P. Management. *In* Encyclopedia of American economic history v2 p832-48

**Industrial mobilization**

### United States
Iklé, F. C. Preparing for industrial mobilization: the first step toward full strength. *In* National security in the 1980s: from weakness to strength, ed. by W. S. Thompson p55-68

**Industrial organization**

### History
Daems, H. The rise of the modern industrial enterprises: a new perspective. *In* Managerial hierarchies, ed. by A. C. Chandler and H. Daems p203-23

Williamson, O. E. Emergence of The visible hand: implications for industrial organization. In Managerial hierarchies, ed. by A. D. Chandler and H. Daems p182-202

### Europe—History
Chandler, A. D. The United States: seedbed of managerial capitalism. *In* Managerial hierarchies, ed. by A. D. Chandler and H. Daems p9-40

### Germany—History
Kocka, J. The rise of the modern industrial enterprise in Germany. *In* Managerial hierarchies, ed. by A. D. Chandler and H. Daems p77-116

### Great Britain—History
Hannah, L. Visible and invisible hands in Great Britain. *In* Managerial hierarchies, ed. by A. D. Chandler and H. Daems p41-76

### United States—History
Chandler, A. D. The United States: seedbed of managerial capitalism. *In* Managerial hierarchies, ed. by A. D. Chandler and H. Daems p9-40

**Industrial productivity.** See Labor productivity

**Industrial relations**
*See also* Trade-unions

### United States—History
Brody, D. Labor and small-scale enterprise during industrialization. *In* Small business in American life, ed. by S. W. Bruchey p263-79

**Industrial research.** See Research, Industrial

**Industrial sociology.** See Industry—Social aspects

**Industrial safety**

### Law and legislation
Teece, D. J. The new social regulation: implication and alternatives. *In* The Economy in the 1980s: a program for growth and stability, ed. by M. J. Boskin p119-58

**Industrial unions.** See Trade-unions

**Industrialization**
Kaufman, R. R. Industrial change and authoritarian rule in Latin America: a concrete review of the bureaucratic-authoritarian model. *In* The New authoritarianism in Latin America, ed. by D. Collier p165-253

Serra, J. M. Three mistaken theses regarding the connection between industrialization an authoritarian regimes. *In* The New authoritarianism in Latin America, ed. by D. Collier p99-163

**Industries, Service.** See Service industreis

**Industries, Size of.** See Big business

**Industry**
Roncaglia, A. The Sraffian contribution. *In* A Guide to post-Keynesian economics, ed. by A. S. Eichner p87-99

*See also* Big business; Entrepreneur; Industrial organization; Technology

### Organization
*See* Industrial organization

### Social aspects—United States
Blumin, S. M. Black coats to white collars: economic change, nonmanual work, and the social structure of industrializing America, ed. by S. W. Bruchey p100-21

**Industry (Psychology)** See Work

**Industry and state**
*See also* Industrial laws and legislation

### History
Keller, M. Regulation of large enterprise: the United States experience in comparative perspective. *In* Managerial hierarchies, ed. by A. D. Chandler and H. Daems p161-81

### Greece, Modern
Mouzelis, N. Capitalism and the development of the Greek state. *In* The State of Western Europe, ed. by Richard Scase p241-73

### United States
Pursell, C. W. Military-industrial complex. *In* Encyclopedia of American economic history, ed. by G. Porter v3 p926-34

Teece, D. J. The new social regulation: implications and alternatives. *In* The Economy in the 1980s: a program for growth and stability, ed. by M. J. Boskin p119-58

Weidenbaum, M. L. Government power and business performance. *In* The United States in the 1980s, ed. by P. Duignan and A. Rabushka p197-220

**Inequality.** See Equality

**Inertia (Mechanics)**
Gabbey, A. Force and inertia in the seventeenth century: Descartes and Newton. *In* Descartes, ed. by S. Gaukroger p230-320

**Infant psychology**
Papoušek, H. and Papoušek, M. Early ontogeny of human social interaction: its biological roots and social dimensions. *In* Human ethology, ed. by M. von Cranach [and others] p456-78

**Infant psychology**—*Continued*

Trevarthen, C. Instincts for human understanding and for cultural cooperation: their development in infancy. *In* Human ethology, ed. by M. von Cranach [and others] p530-71

**Infante, Guillermo Cabrera.** See Cabrera Infante, Guillermo

**Infants**

*See also* Infant psychology

#### Psychology

*See* Infant psychology

**Inference (Logic)** See Induction (Logic)

**Inflation (Finance)**

#### Mathematical models

*See* Phillips curve

#### United States

Scadding, J. L. Inflation: a perspective from the 1970s. *In* The Economy in the 1980s: a program for growth and stability, ed. by M. J. Boskin p53-81

**Inflation (Finance) and unemployment**

Bisignano, J. The unemployment-inflation dilemma and the reemergence of classicism. *In* Economic issues of the eighties, ed. by N. M. Kamrany and R. H. Day p29-43

**Influence (Literary, artistic, etc.)**

Jabbi, B. Influence and originality in African writing. *In* African literature today no. 10: Retrospect & prospect, ed. by E. D. Jones p106-23

Rabinowitz, P. J. "What's Hecuba to us?" The audience's experience of literary borrowing. *In* The Reader in the text, ed. by S. R. Suleiman and I. Crosman p241-63

**Information display systems**

Tomita, T. The new electronic media and their place in the information market of the future. *In* Newspapers and democracy, ed. by A. Smith p49-62

**Information retrieval**

Arrow, K. J. The economics of information. *In* The Computer age: a twenty-year view, ed. by M. L. Dertouzos and J. Moses p306-17

**Ingalls, Joshua King**

##### About individual works

*Social wealth*

Schwartzman, J. Ingalls, Hanson, and Tucker: nineteenth-century American anarchists. *In* Critics of Henry George, ed. by R. V. Andelson p234-53

**Ingleby, David**

Understanding 'mental illness.' *In* Critical psychiatry, ed. by D. Ingleby p23-71

**Inhelder, Bärbel**

Language and knowledge in a constructivist framework. *In* Language and learning, ed. by M. Piattelli-Palmarini p132-37

**Inheritance and succession in literature**

Seidel, M. A. Inheritance and narrative mode. *In* Seidel, M. A. Satiric inheritance, Rabelais to Sterne p26-59

**Initials**

Schapiro, M. The decoration of the Leningrad manuscript of Bede. *In* Schapiro, M. Selected papers v3: Late antique, early Christian and mediaeval art p199-224

**Initiations (in religion, folk-lore, etc.)**

Dundes, A. A psychoanalytic study of the bullroarer. *In* Dundes, A. Interpreting folklore p176-98

**Inkeles, Alex**

Continuity and change in the American national character. *In* The Third century, ed. by S. M. Lipset p389-416

The emerging social structure of the world. *In* Propaganda and communication in world history, ed. by H. D. Lasswell, D. Lerner and H. Speier v3 p482-515

**Innateness hypothesis (Linguistics).** See Cartesian linguistics

**The innocent (Motion picture)**

Kael, P. Steam engines. *In* Kael, P. When the lights go down p538-42

Kauffmann, S. The innocent. *In* Kauffmann, S. Before my eyes p334-35

**Insanity and art.** See Art and mental illness

**Inscriptions, Assyrian.** See Cuneiform inscriptions

**Inscriptions, Babylonian.** See Cuneiform inscriptions

**Inscriptions, Cuneiform.** See Cuneiform inscriptions

**Inscriptions, Egyptian.** See Egyptian language—Inscriptions

**Insel-Verlag**

Unseld, S. Rainer Maria Rilke and his publishers. *In* Unseld, S. The author and his publishers p127-89

**Inspiration**

Fehrman, C. A. D. Inspiration disputed. *In* Fehrman, C. A. D. Poetic creation p159-96

*See also* Creation (Literary, artistic, etc.)

**Institutions, associations, etc.** See Associations, institutions, etc.

**Instruments of war.** See Munitions

**Insurance**

##### United States—History

Williamson, H. F. Insurance. *In* Encyclopedia of American economic history, ed. by G. Porter v2 p727-36

**Insurance, Health**

##### United States

Drury, P. and Enthoven, A. C. Competition and health care costs. *In* The Economy in the 1980s: a program for growth and stability, ed. by M. J. Boskin p393-417

**Insurance, Mutual.** See Insurance

**Insurance, Sickness.** See Insurance, Health

**Insurance, Social.** See Social security

**Insurance, State and compulsory.** See Social security

**Insurance, Working-men's.** See Social security

**Insurrections.** See Revolutions

**Integration, Social.** See Social integration

**Intellect**

Charlesworth, W. R. Ethology: understanding the other half of intelligence. *In* Human ethology, ed. by M. von Cranach [and others] p491-529

Morowitz, H. J. Bulls, bears, and bacteria. *In* Morowitz, H. J. The wine of life, and other essays on societies, energy & living things p73-76

Stocker, M. Intellectual desire, emotion, and action. *In* Explaining emotions, ed. by A. O. Rorty p323-38

**Intellect**—*Continued*

Thorpe, W. H. The problem of purpose in evolution. *In* The Condition of man, ed. by P. Hallberg p128-49

*See also* Thought and thinking

**Intellectual life**

*See also* Learning and scholarship; also subdivision Intellectual life under names of countries, cities, etc. e.g. Europe—Intellectual life; France—Intellectual life; Ireland—Intellectual life; Vienna—Intellectual life

### Historiography

Darnton, R. Intellectual and cultural history. *In* The Past before us, ed. by M. Kammen p327-54

**Intellectuals**

Kristol, I. The adversary culture of intellectuals. *In* The Third century, ed. by S. M. Lipset p327-43

### Great Britain

Annan, N. G. "Our age": reflections on three generations in England. *In* Generations, ed. by S. R. Graubard p81-109

### Russia

Bushnell, J. D. The "new Soviet man" turns pessimist. *In* The Soviet Union since Stalin, ed. by S. F. Cohen; A. Rabinowitch, and R. Sharlet p179-99

**Intelligence.** See Intellect

**Intelligence, Artificial.** See Artificial intelligence

**Intelligence service**

### United States

Cline, R. S. The future of U.S. foreign intelligence operations. *In* The United States in the 1980s, ed. by P. Duignan and A. Rabushka p469-96

Ellsworth, R. F. Quick fixes in intelligence. *In* National security in the 1980s: from weakness to strength, ed. by W. S. Thompson p173-87

**Intelligent machines.** See Artificial intelligence

**Intelligentsia.** See Intellectuals

**Interaction, Social.** See Social interaction

**Interdependence of nations.** See International economic relations; International relations

**Interest groups.** See Pressure groups

**Intergovernmental fiscal relations**

### New York (City)

Moynihan, D. P. The politics of regional growth. *In* Moynihan, D. P. Counting our blessings p216-34

**Interiors (Motion picture)**

Kauffmann, S. Interiors. *In* Kauffmann, S. Before my eyes p144-47

**Internal migration.** See Migration, Internal

**International agencies**

### Rules and practice

Schachter, O. Rhetoric and law in international political organs .*In* Propaganda and communication in world history, ed. by H. D. Lasswell, D. Lerner and H. Speier v2 p446-57

**International business enterprises**

Vernon, R. and Wortzel, H. Multinational enterprise. *In* Encyclopedia of American economic history, ed. by G. Porter v2 p652-60

**International corporations.** See International business enterprises

**International cooperation in science.** See Science—International cooperation

**International economic relations**

Cuddington, J. T. and McKinnon, R. I. The United States and the world economy. *In* The Economy in the 1980s: a program for growth and stability, ed. by M. J. Boskin p161-95

Strange, S. The management of surplus productive capacity. *In* Economic issues of the eighties, ed. by N. M. Kamrany and R. H. Day p226-46

*See also* International business enterprises

**International economics.** See International economic relations

**International law**

Eide, A. Militarisation with a global reach: a challenge to sovereignty, security and the international legal order. *In* Problems of contemporary militarism, ed. by A. Eide and M. Thee p299-322

Schachter, O. Rhetoric and law in international political organs. *In* Propaganda and communication in world history, ed. by H. D. Lasswell, D. Lerner, and H. Speier v2 p446-57

**International organization.** See International law

**International organizations.** See International agencies

**International politics.** See World politics

**International relations**

Eide, A. Militarisation with a global reach: a challenge to sovereignty, security and the international legal order. *In* Problems of contemporary militarism, ed. by A. Eide and M. Thee p299-322

Inkeles, A. The emerging social structure of the world. *In* Propaganda and communication in world history, ed. by H. D. Lasswell, D. Lerner and H. Speier v3 p482-515

Øberg, J. The new international order: a threat to human security. *In* Problems of contemporary militarism, ed. by A. Eide and M. Thee p47-74

Speier, H. The chances for peace. *In* Propaganda and communication in world history, ed. by H. D. Lasswell, D. Lerner and H. Speier v2 p507-27

Thee, M. Militarism and militarisation in contemporary international relations. *In* Problems of contemporary militarism, ed. by A. Eide and M. Thee p15-35

Wolpin, M. D. Arms transfer and dependency in the Third World. *In* Problems of contemporary militarism, ed. by A. Eide and M. Thee p248-60

*See also* Balance of power; Detente; International economic relations; International law; Munitions; National security; Peace; World politics

### Historiography

Maier, C. S. Marking time: the historiography of international relations. *In* The Past before us, ed. by M. Kammen p355-87

### Moral and religious aspects

Hook, S. Intelligence, morality, and foreign policy. *In* Hook, S. Philosophy and public policy p54-63

Kolenda, K. Globalism vs. consensual pluralism. *In* Humanist ethics, ed. by M. B. Storer p104-21

**International trade.** See Commerce

**Internationalism.** See Nationalism

**Interpersonal communication.** See Nonverbal communication (Psychology)

**Interpersonal relations**

Salzen, E. A. Social attachment and a sense of security. *In* Human ethology, ed. by M. von Cranach [and others] p595-622

Trevarthen, C. Instincts for human understanding and for cultural cooperation: their development in infancy. *In* Human ethology, ed. by M. von Cranach [and others] p530-71

*See also* Conflict of generations; Medical personnel and patient; Parent and child

**Interpersonal relations in literature**

Visser, N. W. The novel and the concept of social network. *In* The Analysis of literary texts, ed. by R. D. Pope p268-85

**Interpretation.** See Hermeneutics

**Interstellar communication.** See Radio astronomy

**Intolerance.** See Fanaticism

**Intrilligator, Michael D.**

Issues in the economics of health. *In* Economic issues of the eighties, ed. by N. M. Kamrany and R. H. Day p119-34

**Invasion of the body snatchers (Motion picture)**

Kael, P. Pods. *In* Kael, P. When the lights go down p520-23

**Invective.** See Satire

**Investment and saving.** See Saving investment

**Iphigenia (Motion picture)**

Knox, B. M. W. Review of Euripides: Iphigeneia at Aulis (tr. by W. S. Merwin and George E. Dimock, Jr.) and Iphigenia (directed by Michael Cacoyannis). *In* Knox, B. M. W. Word and action p343-54

**Iraq**

**Civilization—To 634**

Finklestein, J. J. Early Mesopotamia, 2500-1000 B.C. *In* Propaganda and communication in world history, ed. by H. D. Lasswell, D. Lerner and H. Speier v 1 p50-110

**History—To 634**

Finklestein, J. J. Early Mesopotamia, 2500-1000 B.C. *In* Propaganda and communication in world history, ed. by H. D. Lasswell, D. Lerner and H. Speier v 1 p50-110

**Kings and rulers**

Oppenheim, A. L. Neo-Assyrian and neo-Babylonian empires. *In* Propaganda and communication in world history, ed. by H. D. Lasswell, D. Lerner and H. Speier v 1 p111-44

**Politics and government—To 634**

Oppenheim, A. L. Neo-Assyrian and neo-Babylonian empires. *In* Propaganda and communication in world history, ed. by H. D. Lasswell, D. Lerner and H. Speier v 1 p111-44

**Iraq**

**Religion**

Sandars, N. K. The religious development of some early societies. *In* The Origins of civilization, ed. by P. R. S. Moorey p103-27

**Ireland**

**Description**

Plomer, W. C. F. Notes on a visit to Ireland. *In* Plomer, W. C. F. Electric delights p195-201

**History—1837-1901**

Lyons, F. S. L. Yeats and Victorian Ireland. *In* Yeats, Sligo and Ireland, ed. by A. N. Jeffares p115-38

**Intellectual life**

Edwards, P. A play-house in the waste: George Moore and the Irish theatre. *In* Edwards, P. Threshold of a nation p212-28

**Politics and government—1949-**

Carey, M. J. Ireland. *In* Western European party systems, ed. by P. H. Merkl p257-77

**Ireland in literature**

Donoghue, D. Romantic Ireland. *In* Yeats, Sligo and Ireland, ed. by A. N. Jeffares p17-30

Henn, T. R. The place of shells. *In* Yeats, Sligo and Ireland, ed. by A. N. Jeffares p73-88

**Irish drama**

**History and criticism**

Edwards, P. Introduction: The king's threshold. *In* Edwards, P. Threshold of a nation p 1-14

**Irish drama (English)**

**History and criticism**

Saddlemeyer, A. The 'dwarf-dramas' of the early Abbey Theatre. *In* Yeats, Sligo and Ireland, ed. by A. N. Jeffares p197-215

**Irish elegiac poetry.** See Elegiac poetry, Irish

**Irish fiction (English)** See English fiction—Irish authors

**Irish in the United States**

Glasco, L. A. The life cycles and household structures of American ethnic groups: Irish, Germans, and native-born whites in Buffalo, New York, 1855. *In* A Heritage of her own, ed. by N. F. Cott and E. H. Pleck p268-89

**Irish national characteristics.** See National characteristics, Irish

**Irish question**

O'Day, A. Irish home rule and liberalism. *In* The Edwardian age: conflict and stability, 1900-1914, ed. by A. O'Day p113-32

**Iriye, Akira**

Toward a new cultural order: the Hsin-Min Hui. *In* The Chinese and the Japanese, ed. by A. Iriye p254-74

**Iron metabolism**

Morowitz, H. J. Pumping iron. *In* Morowitz, H. J. The wine of life, and other essays on societies, energy & living things p99-102

**Irony**

Hartman, G. H. Criticism, indeterminacy, irony. *In* Hartman, G. H. Criticism in the wilderness p265-83

Mellor, A. K. The paradigm of romantic irony. *In* Mellor, A. K. English romantic irony p3-30

**Irony in literature**

Mellor, A. K. Byron: "half dust, half deity." *In* Mellor, A. K. English romantic irony p31-76

Mellor, A. K. Carlyle's Sartor resartus: a self-consuming artifact. *In* Mellor, A. K. English romantic irony p109-34

Mellor, A. K. A conclusion in which nothing is concluded. *In* Mellor, A. K. English romantic irony p185-89

Mellor, A. K. Fear and trembling: from Lewis Carroll to existentialism. *In* Mellor, A. K. English romantic irony p165-84

Mellor, A. K. Guilt and Samuel Taylor Coleridge. *In* Mellor, A. K. English romantic irony p137-64

Mellor, A. K. Keats and the vale of soul-making. *In* Mellor, A. K. English romantic irony p77-108

Irony in literature—*Continued*

Mellor, A. K. The paradigm of romantic irony. *In* Mellor, A. K. English romantic irony p3-30

**Irreligion.** See Secularism

**Irvine, Lorna**

A psychological journey: mothers and daughters in English-Canadian fiction. *In* The Lost tradition: mothers and daughters in literature, ed. by C. N. Davidson and E. M. Broner p242-52

**Irving, Washington**

*About individual works*

*Rip Van Winkle*

Brooke-Rose, C. The readerhood of man. *In* The Reader in the text, ed. by S. R. Suleiman and I. Crosman p120-48

**Irwin, Galen Arnold**

The Netherlands. *In* Western European party systems, ed. by P. H. Markl p161-84

**Irwin, John T.**

American hieroglyphics

*Contents*

Champollion and the historical background; Emerson's hieroglyphical emblems

Hawthorne: the ambiguity of the hieroglyphics; the unstable self and its roles; mirror image and phonetic veil; the feminine role of the artist; veil and phallus; the book as partial object

The hieroglyphics and the quest for origins: the myth of hieroglyphic doubling

Melville: the indeterminate ground; a conjunction of fountain and vortex; the myth of Isis and Osiris; master oppositions; the doubleness of the self and the illusion of consistent character; Dionysus and Apollo; mask and phallus; the chain of partial objects

Thoreau: the single, basic form—patenting a leaf

Whitman: hieroglyphic Bibles and phallic songs

Figurations of the writer's death: Freud and Hart Crane. *In* The Literary Freud: mechanisms of defense and the poetic will, ed. by J. H. Smith p217-60

**Irwin, Michael**

Readings of melodrama. *In* Reading the Victorian novel: detail into form, ed. by I. Gregor p15-31

**Isaacs, Harold Robert**

Bringing up the father question. *In* Generations, ed. by S. R. Graubard p189-203

**Isenberg, Arnold**

Changing arenas and identities in world affairs. *In* Propaganda and communication in world history, ed. by H. D. Lasswell, D. Lerner and H. Speier v2 p395-423

Natural pride and natural shame. *In* Explaining emotions, ed. by A. O. Rorty p355-83

**Iser, Wolfgang**

Interaction between text and reader. *In* The Reader in the text, ed. by S. R. Suleiman and I. Crosman p106-19

**Isherwood, Christopher**

*About individual works*

*A meeting by the river*

Holloway, J. Narrative structure and text structure: Isherwood's A meeting by the river and Muriel Spark's The prime of Miss Jean Brodie. *In* Holloway, J. Narrative and structure: exploratory essays p74-99

**Ishibashi, Tanzan**

*About*

Okamoto, S. Ishibashi Tanzan and the Twenty-One Demands. *In* The Chinese and the Japanese, ed. by A. Iriye p184-98

**Isla, José Francisco de**

*About individual works*

*Historia del famoso predicador Fray Gerundio de Campazas, alias Zotes*

Polt, J. H. R. The ironic narrator in the novel: Isla. *In* Studies in eighteenth-century culture v9 p371-86

**Islam**

Hourani, A. H. Islam and the philosophers of history. *In* Hourani, A. H. Europe and the Middle East p19-73

*History*

Kirk, G. Communication in classical Islam. *In* Propaganda and communication in world history, ed. by H. D. Lasswell, D. Lerner and H. Speier v 1 p348-80

*Relations—Christianity*

Hourani, A. H. Western attitudes towards Islam. *In* Hourani, A. H. Europe and the Middle East p1-18

**Islamic art and symbolism**

Schapiro, M. The angel with the ram in Abraham's sacrifice: a parallel in Western and Islamic art. *In* Schapiro, M. Selected papers v3: Late antique, early Christian and mediaeval art p289-306

**Islamic civilization.** See Civilization, Islamic

**Islamic countries**

*Historiography*

Keddie, N. R. The history of the Muslim Middle East. *In* The Past before us, ed. by M. Kammen p131-56

**Islamic Empire**

*Historiography*

Hourani, A. H. Islam and the philosophers of history. *In* Hourani, A. H. Europe and the Middle East p19-73

*History*

Kirk, G. Communication in classical Islam. *In* Propaganda and communication in world history, ed. by H. D. Lasswell, D. Lerner and H. Speier v 1 p348-80

**Islamic symbolism.** See Islamic art and symbolism

**Islamism.** See Islam

**Islands in the stream (Motion picture)**

Kael, P. Stag show. *In* Kael, P. When the lights go down p278-83

Kauffmann, S. Islands in the stream. *In* Kauffmann, S. Before my eyes p284-86

**Israel and the Diaspora**

Vital, D. Zionism and Israel. *In* The Jewish world, ed. by E. Kedourie p309-17

*See also* Jews—Attitudes toward Israel

**Israel and the Diaspora in literature**

Abramson, G. The state in Israel: Israel and the world. *In* Abramson, G. Modern Hebrew drama p77-80

**Israel in literature**

Abramson, G. Modernism: Hanoch Levin. *In* Abramson, G. Modern Hebrew drama p171-80

Israel in literature—*Continued*

Abramson, G. Modernism: A night in May. *In* Abramson, G. Modern Hebrew drama p181-88

Abramson, G. The state of Israel: Early social realism. *In* Abramson, G. Modern Hebrew drama p59-76

Abramson, G. The state of Israel: 1948 and after. *In* Abramson, G. Modern Hebrew drama p48-58

Alexander, E. Holocaust and rebirth: Moshe Flinker, Nelly Sachs, and Abba Kovner. *In* Alexander, E. The resonance of dust p31-71

**Israeli drama**

### History and criticism

Abramson, G. In search of the original play. *In* Abramson, G. Modern Hebrew drama p209-13

Abramson, G. Modernism: The modern drama: the problem of imitation. *In* Abramson, G. Modern Hebrew drama p141-46

Abramson, G. The state of Israel: Early social realism. *In* Abramson, G. Modern Hebrew drama p59-76

Abramson, G. The state of Israel: Israel and the world. *In* Abramson, G. Modern Hebrew drama p77-80

Abramson, G. The state of Israel: 1948 and after. *In* Abramson, G. Modern Hebrew drama p48-58

Abramson, G. Thematic development: The plays of the Holocaust. *In* Abramson, G. Modern Hebrew drama p116-40

**Istanbul**

### Church history

Beck, H. G. Constantinople: the rise of a new capital in the East. *In* Age of spirituality, ed. by K. Weitzmann p29-37

### History

Beck, H. G. Constantinople: the rise of a new capital in the East. *In* Age of spirituality, ed. by K. Weitzmann p29-37

### Intellectual life

Beck, H. G. Constantinople: the rise of a new capital in the East. *In* Age of spirituality, ed. by K. Weitzmann p29-37

**Italians in Brazil**

Azevedo, T. de. The "chapel" as symbol: Italian colonization in southern Brazil. *In* Brazil, anthropological perspectives, ed. by M. L. Margolis and W. E. Carter p86-95

**Italians in the United States**

Pleck, E. H. A mother's wages; income earning among married Italian and black women, 1896-1911. *In* A Heritage of her own, ed. by N. F. Cott and E. H. Pleck p367-92

Smith, J. E. Our own kind: family and community networks in Providence. *In* A Heritage of her own, ed. by N. F. Cott and E. H. Pleck p393-411

**Italy**

### Politics and government—1945-

Donolo, C. Social change and transformation of the state of Italy. *In* The State in Western Europe, ed. by Richard Scase p164-96

Zariski, R. Italy. *In* Western European party systems, ed. by P. H. Merkl p122-52

### Social conditions—1945-

Donolo, C. Social change and transformation of the state of Italy. *In* The State in Western Europe, ed. by Richard Scase p164-96

**Itard, Jean Marc Gaspard**

### About individual works
*A memoir on stuttering*

Clark, M. J. Jean Itard: a memoir on stuttering. *In* Psychology of language and thought, ed. by R. W. Rieber p153-84

**Iteso.** See Teso tribe

**Ivory Coast**

### Ethnic relations

Lewis, B. C. Ethnicity and occupational specialization in the Ivory Coast: the Transporters' Association. *In* Values, identities, and national integration, ed. by J. N. Paden p75-87

**Ivry, Alfred Lyon**

Averroes on causation. *In* Studies in Jewish religious and intellectual history, ed. by S. Stein and R. Loewe p143-56

**Iyengar, K. R. Srinivasa.** See Part 2 under title: Aspects of Indian writing in English

**Izevbaye, Daniel S.**

Issues in the reassessment of the African novel. *In* African literature today no. 10: Retrospect & prospect, ed. by E. D. Jones p7-31

# J

**Jabbi, Bu-Buakei**

Influence and originality in African writing. *In* African literature today no. 10: Retrospect & prospect, ed. by E. D. Jones p106-23

**Jackson, Esther Merle**

O'Neill the humanist. *In* Eugene O'Neill, ed. by V. Floyd p252-56

**Jackson, J. B.** See Jackson, John Brinckerhoff

**Jackson, John Brinckerhoff**

The order of a landscape: reason and religion in Newtonian America. *In* The Interpretation of ordinary landscapes, ed. by D. W. Meinig p153-62

### About

Meinig, D. W. Reading the landscape: an appreciation of W. G. Hoskins and J. B. Jackson. *In* The Interpretation of ordinary landscapes, ed. by D. W. Meinig p195-244

**Jackson, Richard L.**

Black writers in Latin America

*Contents*

Adalberto Ortiz and his black Ecuadorian classic

The black swan: Gaspar Octavio Hernández, Panama's black modernist poet

The black writer, the black press, and the black diaspora in Uruguay

Conclusion: prospects for a black aesthetic in Latin America

Cultural nationalism and the emergence of literary blackness in Colombia: the originality of Candelario Obeso

Ebe yiye—"the future will be better": an update on Panama from black Cubena

Folk forms and formal literature: revolution and the black poet-singer in Ecuador, Peru, and Cuba

From antislavery to antiracism: Martín Morúa Delgado, black novelist, politician, and critic of postabolitionist Cuba

In the beginning: oral literature and the "true black experience"

Jackson, Richard L.
Black writers in Latin America
*Contents—Continued*

Introduction: the problems of literary blackness in Latin America

Juan Pablo Sojo and the black novel in Venezuela

Literary blackness and Third Worldism in recent Ecuadorian fiction: the novels of Nelson Estupiñan Bass

Literary blackness in Colombia: the ideological development of Manuel Zapata Olivella

Literary blackness in Colombia: the novels of Arnold Palacios

Return to the origins: the Afro-Costa Rican literature of Quince Duncan

Slave poetry and slave narrative: Juan Francisco Manzano and black autobiography

Slave societies and the free black writer: José Manual Valdés and "Plácido"

The turning point: the blackening of Nicolás Guillén and the impact of his Motivos de son

Jackson, Russell
'Perfect types of womanhood': Rosalind, Beatrice and Viola in Victorian criticism and performance. *In* Shakespeare survey 32 p15-26

Jackson, W. A.
Variant entry fees of the Stationers' company. *In* The Bibliographical Society of America, 1904-79 p355-62

Jackson, William Thomas Hobdell
Interpretation of Carmina Burana 62, 'Dum Diane vitrea.' *In* The Interpretation of medieval lyric poetry, ed. by W. T. H. Jackson p44-60

Introduction. *In* The Interpretation of medieval lyric poetry, ed. by W. T. H. Jackson p 1-21

Jacobs, Eva
Diderot and the education of girls. *In* Woman and society in eighteenth-century France, ed. by E. Jacobs and others p83-95

Jacobs, James B.
Race relations and the prisoner subculture. *In* Crime and justice v 1 p 1-27

Jacobs, Lewis
**About individual works**
*The compound cinema*
Kauffmann, S. The compound cinema. *In* Kauffmann, S. Before my eyes p376-85

Jacobs, Louis
Eating as an act of worship in Hasidic thought. *In* Studies in Jewish religious and intellectual history, ed. by S. Stein and R. Loewe p157-66

Jacobson, Charles
**About**
Arsenault, R. Charles Jacobson of Arkansas: a Jewish politician in the land of the razorbacks, 1891-1915. *In* Conference on Southern Jewish History, Richmond, Va. 1976. "Turn to the South" p55-75

Jagger, Alison Mary
Prostitution. *In* The Philosophy of sex, ed. by A. Soble p348-68

Jail bait (Motion picture)
Kauffmann, S. Mother Kusters goes to heaven/Jail bait. *In* Kauffmann, S. Before my eyes p218-21

Jaluo (African people) See Luo (African people)

James I, King of Scotland
**About individual works**
*The kingis quair*
Kratzmann, G. The kingis quair and English poetry. *In* Kratzmann, G. Anglo-Scottish literary relations, 1430-1550 p33-62

James IV, King of Scotland
**About**
Ridley, F. H. Scottish transformations of courtly literature: William Dunbar and the court of James IV. *In* The Expansion and transformations of courtly literature, ed. by N. B. Smith and J. T. Snow p171-84

James, Henry, 1843-1916
**About**
Pritchett, V. S. Henry James: birth of a hermaphrodite. *In* Pritchett, V. S. The tale bearers p120-37

Wyatt, D. Modernity and paternity: James's The American. *In* Wyatt, D. Prodigal sons p 1-25

**About individual works**
*The American*
Wyatt, D. Modernity and paternity: James's The American. *In* Wyatt, D. Prodigal sons p 1-25

*The American scene*
Pritchett, V. S. Henry James: birth of a hermaphrodite. *In* Pritchett, V. S. The tale bearers p120-37

*The lesson of the master*
Holloway, J. Identity, inversion and density elements in narrative: three tales by Chekhov, James and Lawrence. *In* Holloway, J. Narrative and structure: exploratory essays p53-73

*The portrait of a lady*
Hutchinson, S. Beyond the Victorians: The portrait of a lady. *In* Reading the Victorian novel: detail into form, ed. by I. Gregor p274-87

**Bibliography**
Gale, R. L. Henry James. *In* American literary scholarship, 1978 p91-110

James, Louis
Was Jerrold's Black ey'd Susan more popular than Wordsworth's Lucy? *In* Performance and politics in popular drama, ed. by D. Bradby, L. James and B. Sharratt p3-16

James, W. L. G.
The portrayal of death and 'substance of life': aspects of the modern reader's response to 'Victorianism.' *In* Reading the Victorian novel: detail into form, ed. by I. Gregor p226-42

James, William
**Epistemology**
*See* James, William—Knowledge, Theory of

**Influence**
Crook, S. and Taylor, L. Goffman's version of reality. *In* The View from Goffman, ed. by J. Ditton p233-51

**Knowledge, Theory of**
Hare, P. H. and Chakrabarti, C. The development of William James's epistemological realism. *In* History, religion, and spiritual democracy, ed. by M. Wohlgelernter p231-45

**Jamestown, Va.**

### Intellectual life

Davis, R. B. The literary climate of Jamestown under the Virginia Company, 1607-1624. *In* Toward a new American literary history, ed. by L. J. Budd, E. H. Cady and C. L. Anderson p36-53

**Jandl, Ernst**

### About

Butler, M. From the 'Wiener Gruppe' to Ernst Jandl. *In* Modern Austrian writing, ed. by A. Best and H. Wolfschütz p236-51

**Janes, Regina M.**

Edmund Burke's Indian idyll. *In* Studies in eighteenth-century culture v9 p3-13

**Janeway, Elizabeth Hall**

Women's literature. *In* Harvard Guide to contemporary American writing, ed. by D. Hoffman p342-95

**Jankofsky, Klaus P.**

Entertainment, edification and popular education in the South English legendary. *In* 5000 years of popular culture, ed. by F. E. H. Schroeder p214-25

**Jansen, Marius B.**

Konoe Atsumaro. *In* The Chinese and the Japanese, ed. by A. Iriye p107-23

**Japan**

### Civilization—Chinese influences

Harootunian, H. D. The functions of China in Tokugawa thought. *In* The Chinese and the Japanese, ed. A. Iriye p9-36

### History—Tokugawa period, 1600-1868

Harootunian, H. D. The functions of China in Tokugawa thought. *In* The Chinese and the Japanese, ed. by A. Iriye p9-36

### History—Restoration, 1853-1870

Schrecker, J. E. The Reform movement of 1898 and the Meiji Restoration as ch'ing-i movements. *In* The Chinese and the Japanese, ed. by A. Iriye p96-106

### History—Meiji period, 1868-1912

Oh, B. B. Sino-Japanese rivalry in Korea, 1876-1885. *In* The Chinese and the Japanese, ed. by A. Iriye p37-57

Kamachi, N. The Chinese in Meiji Japan: their interactions with the Japanese before the Sino-Japanese War. *In* The Chinese and the Japanese, ed. by A. Iriye p58-73

### History—1912-1945

*See* Sino-Japanese Conflict, 1937-1945

### History—1926-1945

Iriye, A. Toward a new cultural order: the Hsin-Min Hui. *In* The Chinese and the Japanese, ed. by A. Iriye p254-74

Nakamura, T. Japan's economic thrust into North China, 1933-1938: formation of the North China Development Corporation. *In* The Chinese and the Japanese, ed. by A. Iriye p220-53

### Relations (general) with China

Chi, M. Ts'ao Ju-lin (1876-1966): his Japanese connections. *In* The Chinese and the Japanese, ed. by A. Iriye p140-60

Chu, S. C. China's attitudes toward Japan at the time of the Sino-Japanese War. *In* The Chinese and the Japanese, ed. by A. Iriye p74-95

Hashikawa, B. Japanese perspectives on Asia: from dissociation to coprosperity. *In* The Chinese and the Japanese, ed. by A. Iriye p328-55

Ikei, M. Ugaki Kazushige's view of China and his China policy, 1915-1930. *In* The Chinese and the Japanese, ed. by A. Iriye p199-219

Iriye, A. Toward a new cultural order: the Hsin-Min Hui. *In* The Chinese and the Japanese, ed. by A. Iriye p254-74

Nakamura, T. Japan's economic thrust into North China, 1933-1938: formation of the North China Development Corporation. *In* The Chinese and the Japanese, ed. by A. Iriye p220-53

Okamoto, S. Ishibashi Tanzan and the Twenty-one Demands. *In* The Chinese and Japanese, ed. by A. Iriye p184-98

Young, E. P. Chinese leaders and Japanese aid in the early Republic. *In* The Chinese and the Japanese, ed. by A. Iriye p124-39

Yue-Him Tam. An intellectual's response to Western intrusion: Naitō Konan's view of Republican China. *In* The Chinese and the Japanese, ed. by A. Iriye p161-83

**Japanese-Chinese Conflict, 1937-1945.** See Sino-Japanese Conflict, 1937-1945

**Japanese in foreign countries**

Jansen, M. B. Konoe Atsumaro. *In* The Chinese and the Japanese, ed. by A. Iriye p107-23

**Japanese newspapers**

Horsley, W. The press as loyal opposition in Japan. *In* Newspapers and democracy, ed. by A. Smith p200-27

Tomita, T. The new electronic media and their place in the information market of the future. *In* Newspapers and democracy, ed. by A. Smith p49-62

**Jařab, Josef**

The lasting challenge of Eugene O'Neill: a Czechoslovak view. *In* Eugene O'Neill, ed. by V. Floyd p84-100

**Jarman, Alfred Owen Hughes**

Aneirin—the Gododdin. *In* A Guide to Welsh literature, ed. by A. O. H. Jarman and G. R. Hughes v 1 p68-80

The later Cynfeirdd. *In* A Guide to Welsh literature, ed. by A. O. H. Jarman and G. R. Hughes v 1 p98-122

Saga poetry—the cycle of Llywarch Hen. *In* A Guide to Welsh literature, ed. by A. O. H. Jarman and G. R. Hughes v 1 p81-97

Taliesin. *In* A Guide to Welsh literature, ed. by A. O. H. Jarman and G. R. Hughes v 1 p51-67

**Jarrell, Randall**

### About individual works

*The complete poems*

Vendler, H. H. Randall Jarrell. *In* Vendler, H. H. Part of nature, part of us p111-18

**Jarrow monastery**

Meyvaert, P. Bede and the church paintings at Wearmouth—Jarrow. *In* Anglo-Saxon England 8 p63-77

**Jaws (Motion picture)**

Kael, P. Notes on evolving heroes, morals, audiences. *In* Kael, P. When the lights go down p195-204

**Jaws (Motion picture)**—*Continued*
Kauffmann, S. Jaws. *In* Kauffmann, S. Before my eyes p154

**Jaws 2 (Motion picture)**
Kauffmann, S. Jaws 2. *In* Kauffmann, S. Before my eyes p315-17

**Jayne, Richard**
Rilke and the problem of poetic inwardness. *In* Rilke: the alchemy of alienation, ed. by F. Baron, E. S. Dick and W. R. Maurer p191-222

**Jealousy**
Neu, J. Jealous thoughts. *In* Explaining emotions, ed. by A. O. Rorty p425-63
Tov-Ruach, L. Jealousy, attention, and loss. *In* Explaining emotions, ed. by A. O. Rorty p465-88

**Jean Clopinel de Meun.** See Jean de Meun

**Jean de Meun.** See Roman de la Rose

**Jean de Savoie**

### About individual works
*Partitura amorosa*
Robertson, D. W. The Partitura amorosa of Jean de Savoie. *In* Robertson, D. W. Essays in medieval culture p166-72

**Jeffares, Alexander Norman**
Yeats and the wrong Lever. *In* Yeats, Sligo and Ireland, ed. by A. N. Jeffares p98-111

**Jefferson, Thomas, President U.S.**

### About individual works
*The autobiography of Thomas Jefferson*
Cox, J. M. Recovering literature's lost ground through autobiography. *In* Autobiography: essays theoretical and critical, ed. by J. Olney p123-45

### Library
Sowerby, E. M. Thomas Jefferson and his library. *In* The Bibliographical Society of America, 1904-79 p339-54

**Jelinek, Estelle Cohen**
Introduction: women's autobiography and the male tradition. *In* Women's autobiography, ed. by E. C. Jelinek p 1-20
The paradox and success of Elizabeth Cady Stanton. *In* Women's autobiography, ed. by E. C. Jelinek p71-92

**Jelinek, Hena Maes-** See Maes-Jelinek, Hena

**Jennings, Paul Francis**
Humor: the modern religion? *In* Royal Society of Literature of the United Kingdom, London. Essays by divers hands: innovation in contemporary literature, new ser. v40 p117-31

**Jerrold, Douglas**

### About
Henkle, R. B. Peacock, Thackeray, Jerrold: the comedy of "radical" disaffection. *In* Henkle, R. B. Comedy and culture p58-110

**Jessop, Bob**
The transformation of the state in post-war Britain. *In* The State in Western Europe, ed. by R. Scase p23-93

**Jesuits**

### History
Ozment, S. H. Catholic reform and Counter Reformation. *In* Ozment, S. H. The age of reform, 1250-1550 p376-418

**Jesus Christ**
Pickering, F. P. Exegesis and imagination: a contribution to the study of Rupert of Deutz. *In* Pickering, F. P. Essays on medieval German literature and iconography p31-45

### Art
Lutz, C. E. The letter of Lentulus describing Christ. *In* Lutz, C. E. The oldest library motto, and other library essays p49-56
Schapiro, M. The bowman and the bird on the Ruthwell Cross and other works: the interpretation of secular themes in early medieval religious art. *In* Schapiro, M. Selected papers v3: Late antique, early Christian and mediaeval art p177-95
Schapiro, M. The image of the disappearing Christ. *In* Schapiro, M. Selected papers v3: Late antique, early Christian and mediaeval art p266-87
Schapiro, M. On a Italian painting of the Flagellation of Christ in the Frick Collection. *In* Schapiro, M. Selected papers v3: Late antique, early Christian and mediaeval art p355-79
Schapiro, M. The religious meaning of the Ruthwell Cross. *In* Schapiro, M. Selected papers v3: Late antique, early Christian and mediaeval art p151-76
Shepherd, M. H. Christology: a central problem of early Christian theology and art. *In* Age of spirituality, ed. by K. Weitzmann p101-20

### Ascension
Schapiro, M. The image of the disappearing Christ. *In* Schapiro, M. Selected papers v3: Late antique, early Christian and mediaeval art p266-87

### Biography
Dundes, A. The hero pattern and the life of Jesus. *In* Dundes, A. Interpreting folklore p223-61

### Crucifixion
Pickering, F. P. The Gothic image of Christ: the sources of medieval representations of The Crucifixion. *In* Pickering, F. P. Essays on medieval German literature and iconography p3-30

### History of doctrines—Early church, ca. 30-600
Shepherd, M. H. Christology: a central problem of early Christian theology and art. *In* Age of spirituality, ed. by K. Weitzmann p101-20

### Life
*See* Jesus Christ—Biography

### Passion—Art
*See* Jesus Christ—Art

### Pictures, illustrations, etc.
*See* Jesus Christ—Art

### Teachings
Morowitz, H. J. Christ, Clausius, and corrosion. *In* Morowitz, H. J. The wine of life, and other essays on societies, energy & living things p43-47

**Jesus Christ in art.** See Jesus Christ—Art

**Jeux-partis**
Cropp, G. M. The partimen between Folquet de Marseille and Tostemps. *In* The Interpretation of medieval lyric poetry, ed. by W. T. H. Jackson p91-112

**Jewish-Afro-American relations.** See Afro-Americans—Relations with Jews

**Jewish art and symbolism**
Schapiro, M. Ancient mosaics in Israel: late antique art—pagan, Jewish, Christian. *In* Schapiro, M. Selected papers v3: Late antique, early Christian and mediaeval art p20-33

Jewish art and symbolism—*Continued*
Schapiro, M. The Bird's Head Haggada, an illustrated Hebrew manuscript of ca. 1300. *In* Schapiro, M. Selected papers v3: Late antique, early Christian and mediaeval art p381-86

**Jewish Christians.** See Maranos

**Jewish drama**

### History and criticism
Abramson, G. The development of the drama: Renaissance and Enlightenment. *In* Abramson, G. Modern Hebrew drama p16-23

**Jewish emancipation.** See Jews—Emancipation

**Jewish holocaust (1939-1945)** See Holocaust, Jewish (1939-1945)

**Jewish identity.** See Jews—Identity

**Jewish illumination of books and manuscripts.** See Illumination of books and manuscripts, Jewish

**Jewish language.** See Yiddish language

**Jewish leadership**
Abramsky, C. The crisis of authority within European Jewry in the eighteenth century. *In* Studies in Jewish religious and intellectual history, ed. by S. Stein and R. Loewe p13-28

**Jewish literature.** See Talmud

**Jewish liturgical music.** See Synagogue music

**Jewish philosophy.** See Philosophy, Jewish

**Jewish poetry.** See Hebrew poetry

**Jewish question**
Springer, A. R. Enlightened absolutism and Jewish reform: Prussia, Austria, and Russia. *In* California Slavic studies v11 p237-67
*See also* Antisemitism; Zionism

**Jewish rabbis.** See Rabbis

**Jewish sects.** See Hasidism; Pharisees

**Jewish symbolism in art.** See Jewish art and symbolism

**Jewish theology.** See Judaism

**Jews**
*See also* Prophets

### Attitudes toward Israel
Glazer, N. American Jews: three conflicts of loyalties. *In* The Third century, ed. by S. M. Lipset p223-41

### Cabala
*See* Cabala

### Civil rights
*See* Jews—Legal status, laws, etc.

### Diaspora
Kaufmann, Y. The Hebrew language and our national future. *In* The Jew, ed. by A. A. Cohen p97-111
Schwadron, A. The dogma of the eternal Galut: a cardinal issue in Zionist ideology. *In* The Jew, ed. by A. A. Cohen p112-19
*See also* Israel and the Diaspora

### Dispersion
*See* Jews—Diaspora

### Emancipation
Baron, S. W. Civil versus political emancipation. *In* Studies in Jewish religious and intellectual history, ed. by S. Stein and R. Loewe p29-49

### Historiography
Meisl, J. Jewish historical writing. *In* The Jew, ed. by A. A. Cohen p198-211

### History—To 586 B.C.
Saggs, H. W. F. Pre-exilic Jewry. *In* The Jewish world, ed. by E. Kedourie p37-51

### History—To 70 A.D.
Yavetz, Z. The Jews and the great powers of the ancient world. *In* The Jewish world, ed. by E. Kedourie p89-107

### History—1789-1945
*See* Jews—Emancipation

### Identity
Berlin, Sir I. Benjamin Disraeli, Karl Marx and the search for identity. *In* Berlin, Sir I. Against the current p252-86

### Intellectual life
Hertzberg, A. Judaism and modernity. *In* The Jewish world, ed. by E. Kedourie p301-08

### Languages
*See* Hebrew language; Yiddish language

### Law
*See* Jews—Legal status, laws, etc.

### Legal status, laws, etc.
Baron, S. W. Civil versus political emancipation. *In* Studies in Jewish religious and intellectual history, ed. by S. Stein and R. Loewe p29-49

### Liturgy and ritual
Shiloah, A. The ritual and music of the synagogue. *In* The Jewish world, ed. by E. Kedourie p120-27

### Liturgy and ritual—Day of Atonement prayers
Baumgardt, D. The inner structure of the Yom Kippur liturgy. *In* The inner structure of the Yom Kippur liturgy. *In* The Jew, ed. by A. A. Cohen p185-97

### Liturgy and ritual—Hagadah 1965
Schapiro, M. The Bird's Head Haggada, an illustrated Hebrew manuscript of ca. 1300. *In* Schapiro, M. Selected papers v3: Late antique, early Christian and mediaeval art p381-86

### Nationalism
*See* Nationalism—Jews

### Persecution
*See* Holocaust, Jewish (1939-1945)

### Philosophy
*See* Philosophy, Jewish

### Relations with Afro-Americans
*See* Afro-Americans—Relations with Jews

### Religion
*See* Judaism

### Restoration
*See* Jews—Diaspora; Messianic era (Judaism); Zionism

### Zionism
*See* Zionism

**Jews in Byzantium**
Grossman, A. The Jews in Byzantium and medieval Europe. *In* The Jewish world, ed. by E. Kedourie p168-77

**Jews in Europe**

### History
Abramsky, C. The crisis of authority within European Jewry in the eighteenth century. *In* Studies in Jewish religious and intellectual history, ed. by S. Stein and R. Lowe p13-28

**Jews in Europe**—History—*Continued*

Baron, S. W. Civil versus political emancipation. *In* Studies in Jewish religious and intellectual history, ed. by S. Stein and R. Loewe p29-49

Grossman, A. The Jews in Byzantium and medieval Europe. *In* The Jewish world, ed. by E. Kedourie p168-77

Kochman, L. European Jewry in the 19th and 20th centuries. *In* The Jewish world, ed. by E. Kedourie p264-73

**Jews in Germany**

### History—1933-1945

Weinberg, D. H. The Holocaust in historical perspective. *In* Encountering the Holocaust: an interdisciplinary survey, ed. by B. L. Sherwin and S. G. Ament p52-83

**Jews in Islamic countries**

### History

Cohen, A. The Jews under Islam: part two c. 1500-today. *In* The Jewish world, ed. by E. Kedourie p186-91

Goitein, S. D. F. The Jews under Islam: part one 6th-16th centuries. *In* The Jewish world, ed. by E. Kedourie p178-85

**Jews in literature**

Abramson, G. The state of Israel: Israel and the world. *In* Abramson, G. Modern Hebrew drama p77-80

Bern, R. L. Utilizing the Southern-Jewish experience in literature. *In* Conference on Southern Jewish History, Richmond, Va. 1976. "Turn to the South" p151-57

Girard, R. "To entrap the wisest": a reading of The merchant of Venice. *In* Literature and society, ed. by E. W. Said p100-19

Shechner, M. E. Jewish writers. *In* Harvard Guide to contemporary American writing, ed. by D. Hoffman p91-239

Trilling, L. Another Jewish problem novel. *In* Trilling, L. Speaking of literature and society p16-20

Trilling, L. The changing myth of the Jew. *In* Trilling, L. Speaking of literature and society p50-76

Trilling, L. Flawed instruments. *In* Trilling, L. Speaking of literature and society p21-26

*See also* Holocaust, Jewish (1939-1945) in literature

**Jews in Miami**

Rosen, G. The rabbi in Miami—a case history. *In* Conference on Southern Jewish History, Richmond, Va. 1976. "Turn to the South" p33-40

**Jews in Poland**

Cohen, H. The Polish Jew. *In* The Jew, ed. by A. A. Cohen p52-60

**Jews in Prague**

Carter, F. W. Kafka's Prague. *In* The World of Franz Kafka, ed. by J. P. Stern p30-43

Urzidil, J. Two recollections. *In* The World of Franz Kafka, ed. by J. P. Stern p56-68

Weltsch, F. The rise and fall of the Jewish-German symbiosis: the case of Franz Kafka. *In* The World of Franz Kafka, ed. by J. P. Stern p47-55

**Jews in Spain**

### History

Beinart, H. The Jews in Spain. *In* The Jewish world, ed. by E. Kedourie p161-67

**Jews in the Southern States**

Bern, R. L. Utilizing the Southern-Jewish experience in literature. *In* Conference on Southern Jewish History, Richmond, Va. 1976. "Turn to the South" p151-57

Hero, A. O. Southern Jews and public policy. *In* Conference on Southern Jewish History, Richmond, Va. 1976. "Turn to the South" p143-50

Lavender, A. D. Jewish values in the Southern milieu. *In* Conference on Southern Jewish History, Richmond, Va. 1976. "Turn to the South" p124-34

Reed, J. S. Ethnicity in the South: observations on the acculturation of Southern Jews. *In* Conference on Southern Jewish History, Richmond, Va. 1976. "Turn to the South" p135-42

Stern, M. H. The role of the rabbi in the South. *In* Conference on Southern Jewish History, Richmond, Va. 1976. "Turn to the South" p21-32

Whitfield, S. J. Jews and other Southerners: counterpoint and paradox. *In* Conference on Southern Jewish History, Richmond, Va. 1976. "Turn to the South" p76-104

### Historiography

Chyet, S. F. Reflections on Southern-Jewish historiography. *In* Conference on Southern Jewish History, Richmond, Va. 1976. "Turn to the South" p13-20

Evans, E. N. Southern-Jewish history alive and unfolding. *In* Conference on Southern Jewish History, Richmond, Va. 1976. "Turn to the South" p158-67

**Jews in the United States**

Glazer, N. American Jews: three conflicts of loyalties. *In* The Third century, ed. by S. M. Lipset p223-41

Smith, J. E. Our own kind: family and community networks in Providence. *In* A Heritage of her own, ed. by N. F. Cott and E. H. Pleck p393-411

### History

Handlin, O. American Jewry. *In* The Jewish world, ed. by E. Kedourie p274-83

**Jhabvala, Ruth Prawer**

### About individual works

*Heat and dust*

Shahane, V. A. Jhabvala's 'Heat and dust': a cross-cultural encounter. *In* Aspects of Indian writing in English, ed. by M. K. Naik p222-31

*A new dominion*

Pritchett, V. S. Ruth Prawer Jhabvala: snares and delusions. *In* Pritchett, V. S. The tale bearers p206-12

**Jimack, Peter David**

The paradox of Sophie and Julie: contemporary response to Rousseau's ideal wife and ideal mother. *In* Woman and society in eighteenth-century France, ed. by E. Jacobs and others p152-65

**Jiménez, Francisco**

Dramatic principles of the Teatro Campesino. *In* The Identification and analysis of Chicano literature, ed. by F. Jiménez p117-32

**Jiménez-Fajardo, Salvador**

A descriptive approach to Claude Simon's novel Leçon de choses. *In* The Analysis of literary texts, ed. by R. D. Pope p298-313

**Jivaro Indians**

Morowitz, H. J. Shrinks. *In* Morowitz, H. J. The wine of ilfe, and other essays on societies, energy & living things p149-52

**Jo Luo (African people)** See Luo (African people)

**Job satisfaction**

Kohn, M. L. Job complexity and adult personality. *In* Themes of work and love in adulthood, ed. by N. J. Smelser and E. H. Erikson p193-210

**Jodelle, Étienne**

### About individual works
*Cléopâtre captive*

Reiss, T. J. Jodelle's Cléopâtre and the enchanted circle. *In* Reiss, T. J. Tragedy and truth p78-102

**Joerger, Muriel**

The structure of the hospital system in France during the ancien régime. *In* Medicine and society in France, ed. by R. Forster and O. Ranum p104-36

**Johannsen, Oscar B.**

Oser: reservations of a friendly commentator. *In* Critics of Henry George, ed. by R. V. Andelson p371-77

**John, David**

The Sperber in Hesse's Demian. *In* The First World War in German narrative prose, ed. by C. N. Genno and H. Wetzel p34-49

**Johnson, Arthur Menzies**

Economy since 1914. *In* Encyclopedia of American economic history, ed. by G. Porter v 1 p110-30

**Johnson, Charles, 1679-1748**

### About individual works
*Love in a forest*

Holding, E. 'As you like it' adapted: Charles Johnson's 'Love in a forest.' *In* Shakespeare survey 32 p37-48

**Johnson, Christopher H.**

Patterns of proletarianization: Paris tailors and Lodève woolens workers. *In* Consciousness and class experience in nineteenth-century Europe, ed. by J. M. Merriman p65-84

**Johnson, Claudia D.**

Resolution in The marble faun: a minority view. *In* Puritan influences in American literature, ed. by E. Elliott p128-42

**Johnson, Diane**

Doctor talk. *In* The State of the language, ed. by L. Michaels and C. Ricks p396-99

**Johnson, James Weldon**

### About individual works
*The autobiography of an ex-coloured man*

Steptoe, R. B. Lost in a quest: James Weldon Johnson's The autobiography of an ex-coloured man. *In* Steptoe, R. B. From behind the veil p95-127

**Johnson, Lyndon Baines, President U.S.**

### About

Kearns, D. Angles of vision. *In* Telling lives, ed. by M. Pachter p90-103

**Johnson, Mary Durham**

Old wine in new bottles: the institutional changes for women of the people during the French Revolution. *In* Women, war, and revolution, ed. by C. R. Berkin and C. M. Lovett p107-43

**Johnson, Roger Barton**

Printout appeal. *In* Monster or messiah? ed. by W. M. Mathews p62-71

**Johnson, Samuel, 1709-1784**

### About

Krieger, M. "Trying experiments upon our sensibility": the art of dogma and doubt in eighteenth-century literature. *In* Krieger, M. Poetic presence and illusion p70-91

### About individual works
*The life of Mr Richard Savage*

Uphaus, R. W. Johnson's equipoise and the state of man. *In* Uphaus, R. W. The impossible observer p89-107

*Preface to Shakespeare*

Krieger, M. Fiction, nature and literary kinds in Johnson's criticism of Shakespeare. *In* Krieger, M. Poetic presence and illusion p55-69

*Rasselas*

Uphaus, R. W. Johnson's equipoise and the state of man. *In* Uphaus, R. W. The impossible observer p89-107

*The vanity of human wishes*

MacAndrew, E. Life in the maze—Johnson's use of chiasmus in The vanity of human wishes. *In* Studies in eighteenth-century culture v9 p517-27

### Manuscripts

Hyde, M. M. C. The history of the Johnson papers. *In* The Bibliographical Society of America, 1904-79 p252-65

**Johnson, Sheila K.**

The future of women in America's third century. *In* The Third century, ed. by S. M. Lipset p285-301

**Johnson, Uwe**

### About individual works
*Anniversaries: from the life of Gesine Cresspahl*

Bosmajian, H. To the last syllable of recorded time: the dull, violent world of Uwe Johnson's Jahrestage. *In* Bosmajian, H. Metaphors of evil p115-43

**Johnston, Brian**

To the third empire

*Contents*

The achieved art: Love's comedy and The pretenders

Brand: the tragedy of vocation

The critical writings

Epilogue: toward the realistic cycle

The mediocre angels of The league of youth

The parable of Peer Gynt

The recovery of the past: St. John's night to The Vikings at Helgeland

The subjectivity of Catiline/the objectivity of The burial mound

The third empire: Emperor and Galilean

**Johnston, Denis**

### About

Edwards, P. Nothing is concluded. *In* Edwards, P. Threshold of a nation p229-44

**Jokes.** See Wit and humor

**Joly, Maurice**

### About individual works

*Dialogue in hell between Machiavelli and Montesquieu*

Speier, H. The truth in hell: Maurice Joly on modern despotism. *In* Propaganda and communication in world history, ed. by H. D. Lasswell, D. Lerner and H. Speier v2 p301-16

**Jonah who will be 25 in the year 2000 (Motion picture)**

Kael, P. A cuckoo clock that laughs. *In* Kael, P. When the lights go down p179-84

**Jonathan, son of Saul, in literature**

Pebworth, T. L. Cowley's Davideis and the exaltation of friendship. *In* The David myth in Western literature, ed. by R. J. Frontain and J. Wojcik p96-104

**Jones, Byrd L.**

Government management of the economy. *In* Encyclopedia of American economic history, ed. by G. Porter v2 p808-31

**Jones, David, 1895-1974**

### About individual works

*Anathemata*

Dilworth, T. David Jones's glosses on the Anathemata. *In* Virginia. University. Bibliographical Society. Studies in bibliography v33 p239-53

**Jones, Emrys**

Dryden's Sigismonda. *In* English Renaissance studies, ed. by J. Carey p279-90

**Jones, Ernest**

### About individual works

*The life and work of Sigmund Freud (v 1, The formative years and the great discoveries)*

Trilling, L. The formative years. *In* Trilling, L. Speaking of literature and society p270-74

*The life and work of Sigmund Freud (v2, Years of maturity, 1901-1919)*

Trilling, L. The years of maturity. *In* Trilling, L. Speaking of literature and society p275-78

*The life and work of Sigmund Freud (v3, The last phase, 1919-1939)*

Trilling, L. Last years of a Titan. *In* Trilling, L. Speaking of literature and society p295-99

**Jones, Evan David**

Lewis Glyn Cothi. *In* A Guide to Welsh literature, ed. by A. O. H. Jarman and G. R. Hughes v2 p243-61

**Jones, Glyn E.**

Early prose: the mabinogi. *In* A Guide to Welsh literature, ed. by A. O. H. Jarman and G. R. Hughes v 1 p189-202

**Jones, Jim**

### About

Reid, D. At home in the abyss: Jonestown and the language of enormity. *In* The State of the language, ed. by L. Michaels and C. Ricks p277-88

**Jones, Katherine Duncan-** See Duncan-Jones, Katherine

**Jones, LeRoi**

### About individual works
*Dutchman*

Casimir, L. J. Dutchman: the price of culture is a lie. *In* The Binding of Proteus, ed. by M. W. McCune, T. Orbison and P. M. Withim p298-310

**Jones, Lowanne E.**

Narrative transformations of twelfth-century troubadour lyric. *In* The Expansion and transformation of courtly literature, ed. by N. B. Smith and J. T. Snow p118-27

**Jones, Maldwyn A.**

Immigration. *In* Encyclopedia of American economic history, ed. by G. Porter v3 p1068-86

**Jones, Michael Owen**

L. A. add-ons and re-dos: renovation in folk art and architectural design. *In* Perspectives on American folk art, ed. by I. M. G. Quimby and S. T. Swank p325-63

**Jones, Shirley**

Madame de Tencin: an eighteenth-century woman novelist. *In* Woman and society in eighteenth-century France, ed. by E. Jacobs and others p207-17

**Jonson, Ben**

### About

Edwards, P. Ben Jonson. *In* Edwards, P. Threshold of a nation p131-73

Fry, P. H. The pressure of sense in some odes of Jonson and Drayton. *In* Fry, P. H. The poet's calling in the English ode p15-36

**Jordan, David William**

Political stability and the emergence of a native elite in Maryland. *In* The Chesapeake in the seventeenth century, ed. by T. W. Tate and D. L. Ammerman p243-73

**Jordan, Robert Welsh**

Vico and the phenomenology of the moral sphere. *In* Conference on Vico and Contemporary Thought, New York, 1976. Vico and contemporary thought pt 1 p130-41

**Jordan, William Malcolm**

Geology and the industrial-transportation revolution in early to mid nineteenth-century Pennsylvania. *In* New Hampshire Bicentennial Conference on the History of Geology, University of New Hampshire, 1976. Two hundred years of geology in America p91-103

**Joseph, Saint**

### Art

Schapiro, M. "Muscipula diaboli," the symbolism of the Mérode altarpiece. *In* Schapiro, M. Selected papers v3: Late antique, early Christian and mediaeval art p 1-11

**Joseph, the patriarch**

### Art

Schapiro, M. The Joseph scenes on the Maximianus throne in Ravenna. In Schapiro, M. Selected papers v3: Late antique, early Christian and mediaeval art p35-47

**Josephson, Matthew**

### About individual works

*Portrait of the artist as American*

Trilling, L. The problem of the American artist. *In* Trilling, L. Speaking of literature and society p46-49

**The Joshua Roll.** See Vatican. Biblioteca Vaticana. Mss. (Pal. Graec. 431)

**Le jour se lève (Motion picture)**

Thiher, A. Prévert and Carné's Le jour se lève: proletarian tragedy. *In* Thiher, A. The cinematic muse p113-28

**Journalism**

See also Government and the press; Newspaper publishing; Press; Reporters and reporting

### Political aspects

See Press and politics

### Political aspects—Italy

Bechelloni, G. The journalist as political client in Italy. In Newspapers and democracy, ed. by A. Smith p228-43

### Political aspects—Japan

Horsley, W. The press as loyal opposition in Japan. In Newspapers and democracy, ed. by A. Smith p200-27

### Political aspects—Portugal

Seaton, J. and Pimlott, B. The role of the media in the Portuguese revolution. In Newspapers and democracy, ed. by A. Smith p174-99

### England—History

Davis, L. J. A social history of fact and fiction: authorial disavowal in the early English novel. In Literature and society, ed. by E. W. Said p120-48

### Great Britain

Curran, J., Douglas, A. and Whannel, G. The political economy of the human-interest story. In Newspapers and democracy, ed. by A. Smith p288-347

### Italy

Bechelloni, G. The journalist as political client in Italy. In Newspapers and democracy, ed. by A. Smith p228-43

### United States

Bogart, L. Editorial ideals, editorial illusions. In Newspapers and democracy, ed. by A. Smith p247-67

### United States—Correspondence, Reminiscences, etc.

Hench, J. B. ed. Letters of John Fenno and John Ward Fenno, 1779-1800—Part 1: 1779-1790. In American Antiquarian Society. Proceedings v89 pt2 p299-368

**Journalists**

Hart, D. J. Changing relationships between publishers and journalists: an overview. In newspapers and democracy, ed. by A. Smith p268-87

### United States

Bogart, L. Editorial ideals, editorial illusions. In Newspapers and democracy, ed. by A. Smith p247-67

**Joy.** See Happiness

**Joyce, James**

### About

Bell, M. Introduction: modern movements in literature. In The Context of English literature, 1900-1930, ed. by M. Bell p 1-93

### About individual works

#### Dubliners

Torchiana, D. T. James Joyce's method in Dubliners. In The Irish short story, ed. by P. Rafroidi and T. Brown p127-40

#### Finnegans wake

Polhemus, R. M. Joyce's Finnegans wake: the comic gospel of "Shem." In Polhemus, R. M. Comic faith p294-337

#### Letters (ed. by Stuart Gilbert)

Trilling, L. The person of the artist. In Trilling, L. Speaking of literature and society p285-94

#### A portrait of the artist as a young man

Beebe, M. The Portrait as portrait: Joyce and impressionism. In Irish Renaissance annual I p13-31

#### Ulysses

Nabokov, V. V. James Joyce: Ulysses. In Nabokov, V. V. Lectures on literature p285-370

Robinson, F. M. Joyce: Ulysses. In Robinson, F. M. The comedy of language p25-50

Senn, F. Bloom among the orators: the why and the wherefore and all the codology. In Irish Renaissance annual I p168-90

#### Characters—Leopold Bloom

Senn, F. Bloom among the orators: the why and the wherefore of all the codology. In Irish Renaissance annual I p168-90

### Style

Beebe, M. The Portrait as portrait: Joyce and impressionism. In Irish Renaissance annual I p13-31

**Joyce, William Leonard**

The manuscript collections of the American Antiquarian Society. In American Antiquarian Society. Proceedings v89 pt 1 p123-52

**Judaism**

Klatzkin, J. Germanism and Judaism: a critique. In The Jew, ed. by A. A. Cohen p63-84

Meisl, J. Graetz and national Judaism. In The Jew, ed. by A. A. Cohen p43-51

Wiener, M. Secularized religion. In The Jew, ed. by A. A. Cohen p215-22

See also Commandments, Six hundred and thirteen; Haskalah; Mysticism—Judaism

### Functionaries

See Rabbis

### History

Hertzberg, A. Judaism and modernity. In The Jewish world, ed. by E. Kedourie p301-08

Weber, M. Judaism: the psychology of the Prophets; excerpt from "Ancient Judaism." In Propaganda and communication in world history, ed. by H. D. Lasswell, D. Lerner and H. Speier v 1 p299-329

### History of doctrines

Pines, S. The Jewish religion after the destruction of Temple and state: the views of Bodin and Spinoza. In Studies in Jewish religious and intellectual history, ed. by S. Stein and R. Loewe p215-34

### Liturgy and ritual

See Jews—Liturgy and ritual

**Judaism and philosophy**

Hyman, A. Jewish philosophy. In The Jewish world, ed. by E. Kedourie p209-16

**Judaism and state**

Buber, M. Zion, the state, and humanity: remarks on Hermann Cohen's answer. In The Jew, ed. by A. A. Cohen p85-96

See also Zionism

**Judge-made law**

### United States

Schapiro, M. M. Judicial activism. In The Third century, ed. by S. M. Lipset p109-31

**Judgment (Ethics)**
Shiner, R. A. Butler's theory of moral judgment. *In* Royal Institute of Philosophy. Philosophers of the Enlightenment p199-225

**Judgment (Logic)**
Harrison, R. Ethical consistency. *In* Rational action, ed. by R. Harrison p29-45

**Judicial law.** See Judge-made law

**Judicial legislation.** See Judge-made law

**Judicial power**

### United States
Shapiro, M. M. Judicial activism. *In* The Third century, ed. by S. M. Lipset p109-31

**Judiciary.** See Judicial power

**Juhasz, Suzanne**
Towards a theory of form in feminist autobiography: Kate Millett's Flying and Sita; Maxine Hong Kingston's The woman warrior. *In* Women's autobiography, ed. by E. C. Jelinek p221-37

**Jules and Jim (Motion picture)**
Thiher, A. The existential play in Truffaut's early films. *In* Thiher, A. The cinematic muse p143-63

**Julia (Motion picture)**
Kael, P. A woman for all seasons? *In* Kael, P. When the lights go down p304-10
Kauffmann, S. Julia. *In* Kauffmann, S. Before my eyes p293-96

**Julian of Norwich, Lady.** See Juliana, anchoret

**Juliana, anchoret**

### About
Mason, M. G. The other voice: autobiographies of women writers. *In* Autobiography: essays theoretical and critical, ed. by J. Olney p207-35

**Jung, Carl Gustav**
*See also* Freud, S. jt. auth.

### About
Bickman, M. Afterword. *In* Bickman, M. The unsounded centre p147-49
Bickman, M. Animatopoeia: sirens of the self. *In* Bickman, M. The unsounded centre p58-79
Bickman, M. The double consciousness revisited. *In* Bickman, M. The unsounded centre p80-94
Bickman, M. Mythology: the symbol in Jungian thought and American romanticism. *In* Bickman, M. The unsounded centre p5-21
Bickman, M. One's self I sing: individuation and introjection. *In* Bickman, M. The unsounded centre p38-57
Neumann, E. C. G. Jung: 1955. *In* Neumann, E. Creative man p246-56

**Junggrammatikire.** See Neogrammarians

**Jurisprudence**
*See also* Law

### Great Britain—History
Gray, C. W. Reason, authority, and imagination: the jurisprudence of Sir Edward Coke. *In* Culture and politics from Puritanism to the Enlightenment, ed. by P. Zagorin p25-66

**Justice, Donald Rodney**

### About
Howard, R. Ronald Justice: "As the butterfly longs for the cocoon or the looping net." *In* Howard, R. Alone with America p291-303

**Justice**
Barry, B. M. Justice as reciprocity. *In* Symposium on Theories of Justice in and for the Second Half of the Twentieth Century, Sydney, 1977. Justice p50-78
Kamenka, E. What is justice? In Symposium on Theories of Justice in and for the Second Half of the Twentieth Century, Sydney, 1977. Justice p 1-24
Stone, J. Justice not equality. *In* Symposium on Theories of Justice in and for the Second Half of the Twentieth Century, Sydney, 1977. Justice p97-115
Tay, A. E. The sense of justice in the common law. *In* Symposium on Theories of Justice in and for the Second Half of the Twentieth Century, Sydney, 1977. Justice p79-96
*See also* Social justice

**Justus, James Huff**
Fiction: the 1950s to the present. *In* American literary scholarship, 1978 p283-322

**Juvenile corrections**

### United States
Klein, M. W. Deinstitutionalization and diversion of juvenile offenders: a litany of impediments. *In* Crime and justice v 1 p145-201

**Juvenile delinquency**
*See also* Criminal behavior, Prediction of; Juvenile corrections

### Research
Farrington, D. P. Longitudinal research on crime and delinquency. *In* Crime and justice v 1 p289-348

### United States
Zimring, F. E. American youth violence: issues and trends. *In* Crime and justice v 1 p67-107

**Juvenile delinquents**

### United States
Klein, M. W. Deinstitutionalization and diversion of juvenile offenders: a litany of impediments. *In* Crime and justice v 1 p145-201

**Juvenile justice, Administration of.** See Juvenile corrections

**Juvenile literature.** See Children's literature

**The Juvenile Miscellany (Periodical)**
Karcher, C. L. Lydia Maria Child and The Juvenile Miscellany. *In* Research about nineteenth-century children and books, ed. by S. K. Richardson p67-84

**Juviler, Peter H.**
The Soviet family in post-Stalin perspective. *In* the Soviet Union since Stalin, ed. by S. F. Cohen, A. Rabinowitch and R. Sharlet p227-51

# K

**Kabaphēs, Kōnstantinos Petrou**

### About individual works
*Poems, translated into English, with a few notes by John Mavrogordato*
Plomer, W. C. F. C. P. Cavafy. *In* Plomer, W. C. F. Electric delights p151-54

**Kabbala.** See Cabala

**Kael, Pauline**
When the lights go down

*Contents*

Affirmation
All for love
The Altman bunker
The artist as a young comedian
Bertrand Blier
Becoming an American
A bit of Archie Rice
Boss ladies
Brotherhood is powerful
The bull goose loony
The calvary gig
Charmed lives
Contempt for the audience
Contrasts
The Cotton Mather of the movies
Creamed
A cuckoo clock that laughs
The curse
Cutting light
Detectives—the capon and the baby bowwow
Dirty Harry with Weltschmerz
Doused
A dream of women
Drip-dry comedy
The duellists/The battle of Chile
Empathy, and its limits
Enfant terrible
Fear of heights
Fear of movies
Forty-eight characters in search of a director
Furry freaks
The God-bless-America symphony
Goodbar, or How nice girls go wrong
The greening of the solar system
Hail, folly!
Harlan County
Heart/soul
Here's to the big one
Hill's pâté
Horseplay
Hot air
The hundred-per-cent solution
Kaputt
Killing yourself with kindness
Kubrick's gilded age
The late show
Lazarus laughs
Libel
Lion-hearted women
Living inside a movie
The lower trash/the higher trash
The man from dream city
Manic/depressive
More torment, or When they broke the silence
Movie yellow journalism
Mythologizing the sixties
Nirvana
No contest
No id
Notes on evolving heroes, morals, audiences
Notes on the nihilist poetry of Sam Peckinpah
Oh, anomie, I love you
The package
A piece of music
Pods
Political acts
Poses
Processing sludge
Regressions
Rocky's knucklehead progeny
Rumbling
Running into trouble
The sacred oak
Saint Dorothy
Scrambled eggs

Seven fatties
Shivers
Shouldn't old acquaintance be forgot?
Simon & Ross—the compassion boys
Soul-snatching and body-snatching
Stag show
Stallone and Stahr
Steam engines
Suicide is painless
Taming the movies
Tentacles
This is my beloved
Travesties
Underground man
The unjoy of sex
The visceral poetry of pulp
Walking into your childhood
Werewolf, mon amour
"What symmetrical digits!"
Where we are now
A woman for all seasons?

**About individual works**
*Reeling*

Brustein, R. S. Pauline Kael (Reeling). *In* Brustein, R. S. Critical moments p18-24

**Kafka, Franz**

**About**

Beug, J. The cunning of a writer. *In* The World of Franz Kafka, ed. by J. P. Stern p122-32

Fischer, W. Kafka without a world. *In* The World of Franz Kafka, ed. by J. P. Stern p223-28

Parry, I. A path in autumn. *In* The World of Franz Kafka, ed. by J. P. Stern p229-37

Pascal, R. Kafka's parables. *In* The World of Franz Kafka, ed. by J. P. Stern p112-19

Roth, P. 'I always wanted you to admire my fasting', or, Looking at Kafka; excerpt from "Reading myself and others." *In* The World of Franz Kafka, ed. by J. P. Stern p202-22

Sokel, W. H. Freud and the magic of Kafka's writing. *In* The World of Franz Kafka, ed. by J. P. Stern p145-58

Urzidil, J. Two recollections. *In* The World of Franz Kafka, ed. by J. P. Stern p56-68

Walser, M. On Kafka's novels. *In* The World of Franz Kafka, ed. by J. P. Stern p87-101

**About individual works**
*Investigations of a dog*

Heller, E. Investigations of a dog and other matters. *In* The World of Franz Kafka, ed. by J. P. Stern p103-11

*The metamorphosis*

Nabokov, V. V. Franz Kafka: "The metamorphosis." *In* Nabokov, V. V. Lectures on literature p251-83

*The trial*

Neumann, E. Kafka's "The trial": an interpretation through depth psychology. *In* Neumann, E. Creative man p3-112

Sewall, R. B. The trial. *In* Sewall, R. B. The vision of tragedy p148-60

**Biography**—Character

Dinnage, R. Under the harrow. *In* The World of Franz Kafka, ed. by J. P. Stern p69-78

Fuller, R. A normal enough dog: Kafka and the office. *In* **The World of Franz Kafka,** ed. by J. P. Stern p191-201

**Kaplan, Chaim Aron**

### About individual works
*Scroll of agony*

Alexander, E. The Holocaust and the God of Israel. *In* Alexander, E. The resonance of dust p195-230

Bosmajian, H. The rage for order: autobiographical accounts of the self in the nightmare of history. *In* Bosmajian, M. Metaphors of evil p27-54

**Kaplan, Justin**
The naked self and other problems. *In* Telling lives, ed. by M. Pachter p36-55

**Karcher, Carolyn L.**
Lydia Maria Child and The Juvenile Miscellany. *In* Research about nineteenth-century children and books, ed. by S. K. Richardson p67-84

**Karlinsky, Simon**
"More piercing than a whistle": notes on English sounds in Russian ears. *In* The State of the language, ed. by L. Michaels and C. Ricks p532-38

**Karp, Ivan C.**
Beer drinking and social experience in an African society: an essay in formal sociology. *In* Explorations in African systems of thought, ed. by I. C. Karp & C. S. Bird p83-119

**Kaske, Robert E.**
Clericus Adam and Chaucer's Adam Scriveyn. *In* Chaucerian problems and perspectives, ed. by E. Vasta and Z. P. Thundy p114-18

**Katai.** See Tayama, Katai

**Katz, Michael R.**
Dreams in Pushkin. *In* California Slavic studies v11 p71-103

**Kaufert, Joseph M.**
Ethnic unit definition in Ghana: a comparison of culture cluster analysis and social distance measures. *In* Values, identities, and national integration, ed. by J. N. Paden p41-51

Situational ethnic identity in Ghana: a survey of university students. *In* Values, identities, and national integration, ed. by J. N. Paden p53-74

**Kaufman, Robert R.**
Industrial change and authoritarian rule in Latin America: a concrete review of the bureaucratic-authoritarian model. *In* The New authoritarianism in Latin America, ed. by D. Collier p165-253

**Kauffmann, Stanley**
Before my eyes
*Contents*
Aguirre, the wrath of God
A la recherche du temps perdu: the Proust screenplay
All screwed up
Amarcord
American to the world
André Bazin
Annie Hall
Antonia
Apocalypse now
Autumn sonata
Barry Lyndon
The battle of Chile
The Bingo traveling all-stars & motor kings
The bitter tears of Petra von Kant
Blood on the screen
A brief vacation

All the President's men
Buffalo Bill
California split
Chaplin: history and mystery
The China syndrome
Chinatown
The clockmaker
Close encounters of the third kind
Coma
Comes a horseman
Coming home
The compound cinema
The confessions of Winifred Wagner
Coonskin
Daisy Miller
The day of the locust
Days of heaven
The deer hunter
Dog day afternoon
Effi Briest
8½
1894-1979
Escape from Alcatraz
Every man for himself and God against all
F is for fake
Face to face
Family plot
Fellini's Casanova
The films in my life
The fortune
French connection II/Night moves
The front
Galileo
The gambler
Get out your handkerchiefs
Girlfriends
Go tell the Spartans
The goalie's anxiety at the penalty kick
The godfather part II
Going places
The goodbye girl
The grapes of wrath
Hair
Hardcore
Harlan County, U.S.A.
Harry and Tonto
In the realm of the senses
The innocent
Interiors
Islands in the stream
Jaws
Jaws 2
John Gielgud: the actor as paragon
Julia
King Lear
Lacombe Lucien
The last supper/Pirosmani
The last tycoon
The last woman/A piece of pleasure
Le petit théâtre de Jean Renoir
Lenny
Let joy reign supreme
Love and death
Love on the run
The magic flute
The maids
The man loved women
The man who would be king
Manhattan
The Marquise of O . . .
Marvellous Méliès
The memory of justice
The middle of the world
Mikey and Nicky
The Missouri breaks
Mr Majestyk/Death wish
Money in focus
Mother Kusters goes to heaven/Jail bait

**Kauffmann, Stanley**
  Before my eyes
    *Contents—Continued*
My love has been burning
Nashville
Network
New York, New York
Next stop, Greenwich Village
Night full of rain
1900
Norma Rae
One flew over the cuckoo's nest
Orchestra rehearsal
The Oxford Companion to film
Padre padrone
The passenger/Story of a love
Perceval
A perfect couple
The phantom president
Pretty baby
Providence
Quintet
Remembrance of films past
Rocky
Rocky II
Roman holiday
Salò
The saphead
Saturday night fever/Blue collar
Scenes from a marriage
The seduction of Mimi
The serpent's egg
Seven beauties
The seven-per-cent solution
Shampoo
The shootist
Silent movie
Slave of love
Small change
Smile
Star wars
Stay hungry
The story of Adéle H.
Swept away
Taxi driver
3 women
The tree of wooden clogs
The turning point
An unmarried woman
Voyage of the damned
A wedding
Wedding in blood
Welcome to L.A.
Why I'm not bored
Who'll stop the rain?
A woman under the influence/Murder on the
  Orient express
Woyzeck
Young Frankenstein

**Kaufmann, Walter Arnold**
  Rilke: Nirvana or creation. *In* Rilke: the alchemy of alienation, ed. by F. Baron, E. S. Dick and W. R. Maurer p15-28

**Kaufmann, Yehezkel**
  The Hebrew language and our national future. *In* The Jew, ed. by A. A. Cohen p97-111

**Kavolis, Vytautas**
  Logics of selfhood and modes of order: civilizational structures for individual identities. *In* Identity and authority, ed. by R. Robertson and B. Holzner p40-62

**Kazin, Alfred**
  The self as history: reflections on autobiography. *In* Telling lives, ed. by M. Pachter p74-89

**Keane, John B.**
  **About**
  Rafroidi, P. From Listowel with love: John B. Keane and Bryan MacMahon. *In* The Irish short story, ed. by P. Rafroidi and T. Brown p263-73

**Keaney, Winifred Gleeson**
  A courtly paradox in book IV of Spenser's Faerie Queene. *In* The Expansion and transformations of courtly literature, ed. by N. B. Smith and J. T. Snow p185-203

**Kearns, Doris**
  Angles of vision. *In* Telling lives, ed. by M. Pachter p90-103
  **About idividual works**
    *Lyndon Johnson and the American dream*
  Kearns, D. Angles of vision. *In* Telling lives, ed. by M. Pachter p90-103

**Keaton, Buster**
  **About individual works**
    *The saphead*
  Kauffmann, S. The saphead. *In* Kauffmann, S. Before my eyes p52

**Keats, John, 1795-1821**
  **About**
  Fry, P. H. Voice in the leaves: three odes of Keats. *In* Fry, P. H. The poet's calling in the English ode p218-57
  Mellor, A. K. Keats and the vale of soulmaking. *In* Mellor, A. K. English romantic irony p77-108
  **About individual works**
    *To autumn*
  Fry, P. H. "To autumn" and the sound of being. *In* Fry, P. H. The poet's calling in the English ode p258-74
  Vendler, H. H. Stevens and Keats' "To autumn." *In* Wallace Stevens, ed. by F. Doggett and R. Buttel p171-95
  **Biography**
  Gittings, R. Artist upon oath. *In* Royal Society of Literature of the United Kingdom, London. Essays by divers hands: innovation in contemporary literature, new ser. v40 p67-82
  **Influence—Stevens**
  Vendler, H. H. Stevens and Keats' "To autumn." *In* Wallace Stevens, ed. by F. Doggett and R. Buttel p171-95

**Keddie, Nikki R.**
  The history of the Muslim Middle East. *In* The Past before us, ed. by M. Kammen p131-56

**Keener, Frederick Michael**
  Candide: structure and motivation. *In* Studies in eighteenth-century culture v9 p405-27

**Keith, William J.**
  The poetry of nature
    *Contents*
The Georgians and after
John Clare
Robert Frost
Thomas Hardy
William Barnes
William Wordsworth

**Keller, Gary D.**

The literary strategems available to the bilingual Chicano writer. *In* The Identification and analysis of Chicano literature, ed. by F. Jiménez p263-316

**Keller, Morton**

Reflections on politics and generations in America. *In* Generations, ed. by S. R. Graubard p123-35

Regulation of large enterprise: the United States experience in comparative perspective. *In* Managerial hierarchies, ed. by A. D. Chandler and H. Daems p161-81

**Kelley, Donald R.**

In Vico veritas: the true philosophy and the new science. *In* Conference on Vico and Contemporary Thought, New York, 1976. Vico and contemporary thought pt 1 p211-21

**Kellman, Steven G.**

The self-begetting novel

Contents

Beckett's trilogy

The fiction of self-begetting

Marcel's self-begetting novel

La nausée

The self-begetting novel and American literature

The self-begetting novel and the English tradition

**Kellogg, Winthrop N.**

Communication and language in the home-raised chimpanzee. *In* Speaking of apes, ed. by T. A. Sebeok and J. Umiker-Sebeok p61-70

**Kelly, Kevin Peter**

"In dispers'd country plantations": settlement patterns in seventeenth-century Surry County, Virginia. *In* The Chesapeake in the seventeenth century, ed. by T. W. Tate and D. L. Ammerman p183-205

**Kemp, Geoffrey T. H.**

Defense innovation and geopolitics: from the Persian Gulf to outer space. *In* National security in the 1980s: from weakness to strength, ed. by W. S. Thompson p69-87

**Kempe, Margery (Burnham)**

About individual works

*The book of Margery Kempe*

Mason, M. G. The other voice: autobiographies of women writers. *In* Autobiography: essays theoretical and critical, ed. by J. Olney p207-35

**Kendall, Martha B.** See Bird, C. S. jt. auth.

**Kende, Istvan**

Local wars 1945-76. *In* Problems of contemporary militarism, ed. by A. Eide and M. Thee p261-85

**Kendrick, John W.**

Productivity. *In* Encyclopedia of American economic history, ed. by G. Porter v 1 p157-66

**Kennelly, Brendan**

Liam O'Flaherty: the unchained storm. A view of his short stories. *In* The Irish short story, ed. by P. Rafroidi and T. Brown p175-87

**Kenner, Hugh**

Machinespeak. *In* The State of the language, ed. by L. Michaels and C. Ricks p467-77

**Kenner, William Hugh.** See Kenner, Hugh

**Kenney, Edwin James**

Iudicium transferendi: Virgil, Aeneid 2.469-505 and its antecedents. *In* Creative imitation and Latin literature, ed. by D. West and T. Woodman p103-20

**Kent, John**

About

Ruddock, G. E. Sion Cent. *In* A Guide to Welsh literature, ed. by A. O. H. Jarman and G. R. Hughes v2 p169-87

**Kentucky and Virginia resolutions of 1798.**

See Alien and Sedition laws, 1798

**Kenya**

Ethnic relations

Edari, R. S. Social distance and social change among four ethnic groups in Mombasa. *In* Values, identities, and national integration, ed. by J. N. Paden p197-203

Laughlin, T. Environment, political culture, and national orientations: a comparison of settled and pastoral Masai. *In* Values, identities, and national integration, ed. by J. N. Paden p91-103

Ross, M. H. Political alienation, participation, and ethnicity in the Nairobi urban area. *In* Values, identities, and national integration, ed. by J. N. Paden p173-81

Social conditions

Edari, R. S. Social distance and social change among four ethnic groups in Mombasa. *In* Values, identities, and national integration, ed. by J. N. Paden p197-203

Social life and customs

Levine, R. A. Adulthood among the Gusii of Kenya. *In* Themes of work and love in adulthood, ed. by N. J. Smelser and E. H. Erikson p77-104

**Kenyon, Peter**

Pricing. *In* A Guide to post-Keynesian economics, ed. by A. S. Eichner p34-45

**Kepes, Gyorgy**

Private and public art. *In* Value and values in evolution, ed. by E. A. Maziarz p143-59

**Keran, Michael William**

How the domestic business cycle is affected by the rest of the world. *In* Economic issues of the eighties, ed. by N. M. Kamrany and R. H. Day p58-68

**Kermode, John Frank**

Dwelling poetically in Connecticut. *In* Wallace Stevens, ed. by F. Doggett and R. Buttel p256-73

About individual works

*The sense of an ending*

Lentricchia, F. Versions of existentialism. *In* Lentricchia, F. After the New Criticism p28-60

**Kermode, Frank.** See Kermode, John Frank

**Kerrigan, William**

The articulation of the ego in the English Renaissance. *In* The Literary Freud: mechanisms of defense and the poetic will, ed. by J. H. Smith p261-308

**Kesey, Ken**

About individual works

*One flew over the cuckoo's nest*

Horton, A. S. Ken Kesey, John Updike and the Lone Ranger. *In* Seasoned authors for a new season: the search for standards in popular writing, ed. by L. Filler p83-90

Characters—Randall McMurphy

Martin, T. The negative character in American fiction. *In* Toward a new American literary history, ed. by L. J. Budd, E. H. Cady and C. L. Anderson p230-43

**Kessler, Carol Farley.** See Rudenstein, G. M. jt. auth.

**Kessler-Harris, Alice**
"Where are the organized women workers?" *In* A Heritage of her own, ed. by N. F. Cott and E. H. Pleck p343-66

**Ketchum, Sara Ann**
The good, the bad and the perverted: sexual paradigms revisited. *In* The Philosophy of sex, ed. by A. Soble p139-57

**Kettle, Arnold**
W. H. Auden: poetry and politics in the thirties. *In* Culture and crisis in Britain in the thirties, ed. by J. Clark and others p83-101

**Key, Valdimer Orlando**

### About individual works
#### *Southern politics*
King, R. H. The new Southern liberalism: V.O. Key, Vann Woodward, Robert Penn Warren. *In* King, R. H. A Southern Renaissance p242-86

**Keynes, John Maynard**

### About
Skidelsky, R. J. A. Keynes and his parents. *In* Generations, ed. by S. R. Graubard p71-79

**Kiberd, Declan**
Story-telling: the Gaelic tradition. *In* The Irish short story, ed. by P. Rafroidi and T. Brown p13-25

**Kibler, Tom R.**
While debating the philosophy we accept the practice. *In* Monster or messiah? Ed. by W. M. Mathews p56-61

**Kickham, Charles Joseph**

### About individual works
#### *Knocknagow*
Cronin, J. Charles Kickham: Knocknagow. *In* Cronin, J. The Anglo-Irish novel, v 1 p99-113

**Kierkegaard, Søren Aabye**

### About
Mellor, A. K. Fear and trembling: from Lewis Carroll to existentialism. *In* Mellor, A. K. English romantic irony p165-84

Spanos, W. V. Heidegger, Kierkegaard, and the hermeneutic circle: towards a postmodern theory of interpretation as dis-closure. *In* Martin Heidegger and the question of literature, ed. by W. V. Spanos p115-48

**Kikuyu tribe**
Ross, M. H. Political alienation, participation, and ethnicity in the Nairobi urban area. *In* Values, identities, and national integration, ed. by J. N. Paden p173-81

**The killer elite (Motion picture)**
Kael, P. Notes on the nihilist poetry of Sam Peckinpah. *In* Kael, P. When the lights go down p112-19

**Killian, Lewis Martin**
The respect revolution: freedom and equality. *In* Propaganda and communication in world history, ed. by H. D. Lasswell, D. Lerner and H. Speier v3 p93-147

**Killigrew, Sir William,** 1606-1695

### Bibliography
Motten, J. P. V. Some problems of attribution in the canon of Sir William Killigrew's works. *In* Virginia. University. Bibliographical Society. Studies in bibliography v33 p161-68

**The killing of Abel**
Robertson, D. W. The question of typology and the Wakefield Mactacio Abel. *In* Robertson, D. W. Essays in medieval culture p218-32

**Kilvert, Robert Francis**

### About individual works
#### *Kilvert's diary*
Plomer, W. C. F. Francis Kilvert. *In* Plomer, W. C. F. Electric delights p126-42

**Kinesics.** See Nonverbal communication (Psychology)

**King, Bruce Alvin**
Introduction. *In* West Indian literature, ed. by B. King p 1-8

**King, Richard H.**
A Southern Renaissance

#### Contents
Between repetition and recollection: Allen Tate and William Faulkner

From theme to setting: Thomas Wolfe, James Agee, Robert Penn Warren

From therapy to morality: the example of Lillian Smith

Modernizers and monumentalists: social thought in the 1930s

Narcissus grown analytical: Cash's Southern mind

The new Southern liberalism: V. O. Key, C. Vann Woodward, Robert Penn Warren

Repetition and despairing monumentalism: William Faulkner and Will Percy

The Southern family romance and its context

A Southern Renaissance

Working through: Faulkner's Go down Moses

**King Kong (Motion picture, 1976)**
Kael, P. Here's to the big one. *In* Kael, P. When the lights go down p234-39

**King Lear (Motion picture by Grigory Kozintsev)**
Kauffmann, S. King Lear. *In* Kauffmann, S. Before my eyes p163-65

**Kings and rulers.** See subdivision Kings and rulers under names of geographic areas, e.g. Africa—Kings and rulers

**Kings and rulers in literature**
Edwards, P. Astraea and Chrisoganus. *In* Edwards, P. Threshold of a nation p38-65
*See also* Shakespeare, William—Characters—Kings and rulers

**Kingston, Maxine Hong**
"How are you?" I am fine, thank you. And you?" *In* The State of the language, ed. by L. Michaels and C. Ricks p152-57

### About individual works
#### *The woman warrior*
Demetrakopoulos, S. A. The metaphysics of matrilinearism in women's autobiography: studies of Mead's Blackberry winter, Hellman's Pentimento, Angelou's I know why the caged bird sings, and Kingston's The woman warrior. *In* Women's autobiography, ed. by E. C. Jelinek p180-205

Juhasz, S. Towards a theory of form in feminist autobiography: Kate Millett's Flying and Sita; Maxine Hong Kingston's The woman warrior. *In* Women's autobiography, ed. by E. C. Jelinek, p221-37

**Kinkead-Weekes, Mark**
The voicing of fictions. *In* Reading the Victorian novel: detail into form, ed. by I. Gregor p168-92

**Kinnell, Galway**

Howard, R. Galway Kinnell: "Everything that may abide the fire was made to go through the fire." *In* Howard, R. Alone with America p304-19

**About**

Molesworth, C. "The rank flavor of blood": the poetry of Galway Kinnell. *In* Molesworth, C. The fierce embrace p98-111

**About individual works**

*Spindrift*

Wagner, L. W. Spindrift: the world in a seashell. *In* Wagner L. W. American modern p187-93

**Kinship**

*See also* Indians of South America—Kinship

**Brazil**

Miller, C. I. The function of middle-class extended family networks in Brazilian urban society. *In* Brazil, anthropological perspectives, ed. by M. L. Margolis and H. E. Carter p305-16

**Kintu,** The story of. Ray, B. *In* Explorations in African systems of thought p60-79

**Kipling, Rudyard**

**About**

Pritchett, V. S. Rudyard Kipling: a Pre-Raphaelite's son. *In* Pritchett, V. S. The tale bearers p31-42

**Kippenberg, Anton**

**About**

Unseld, S. Rainer Maria Rilke and his publishers. *In* Unseld, S. The author and his publishers p127-89

**Kirby, Winston L.**

The influence of television on social relations: some personal reflections. *In* Screen and society, ed. by F. J. Coppa p137-56

**Kirk, George**

Communication in classical Islam. *In* Propaganda and communication in world history, ed. by H. D. Lasswell, D. Lerner and H. Speier v 1 p348-69

**Kirk, Russell**

Pilgrims in The waste land. *In* Seasoned authors for a new season: the search for standards in popular writing, ed. by L. Filler p20-32

**Kirkendall, Lester Allen**

An ethical system for now and the future. *In* Humanist ethics, ed. by M. B. Storer p193-209

**Kirkpatrick, Daniel Lane, ed.** See Twentieth-century children's writers

**Kisii (Bantu tribe)** See Gusii (Bantu tribe)

**Kissel, Susan S.**

Voices in the wilderness: the prophets of O'Connor, Percy, and Powers. *In* Walker Percy; art and ethics, ed. by J. Tharpe p91-98

**Kitamura, Tōkoku**

**About**

Walker, J. A. Kitamura Tōkoku and the ideal of the inner life: the interiorization of the ideal of individualism. *In* Walker, J. A. The Japanese novel of the Meiji period and the ideal of individualism p62-92

**Kittler, Friedrich**

Writing into the wind, Bettina. *In* Glyph 7 p32-69

**Kitzinger, Ernst**

Christian imagery: growth and impact. *In* Age of spirituality, ed. by K. Weitzmann p141-63

**Kizer, Carolyn**

**About**

Howard, R. Carolyn Kizer: "Our masks keep us in thrall to ourselves . . ." *In* Howard, R. Alone with America p320-30

**Klare, Michael T.**

Militarism: the issues today. *In* Problems of contemporary militarism, ed. by A. Eide and M. Thee p36-46

**Klassen, Peter, J.**

The role of the masses in shaping the Reformation. *In* 5000 years of popular culture, ed. by F. E. H. Schroeder p257-75

**Klatzkin, Jacob**

Germanism and Judaism: a critique. *In* The Jew, ed. by A. A. Cohen p63-84

Hermann Cohen. *In* The Jew, ed. by A. A. Cohen p251-61

**Klebs, Arnold Carl**

Gleanings from incunabula of science and medicine. *In* The Bibliographical Society of America, 1904-79 p71-109

**Klein, Joan Larsen**

'What is't to leave betimes?' Proverbs and logic in 'Hamlet.' *In* Shakespeare survey 32 p163-76

**Klein, Malcolm W.**

Deinstitutionalization and diversion of juvenile offenders: a litany of impediments. *In* Crime and justice v 1 p145-201

**Kleist, Heinrich von**

**About individual works**

*The broken jug*

Mueller, M. Oedipus Rex as tragedy of knowledge: Voltaire's Oedipe and Kleist's Der zerbrochene Krug. *In* Mueller, M. Children of Oedipus, and other essays on the imitation of Greek tragedy, 1550-1800 p109-28

*Penthesilea*

Mueller,. M. The fall of an ideal: Kleist's Penthesilea. *In* Mueller, M. Children of Oedipus, and other essays on the imitation of Greek tragedy, 1550-1800 p92-104

*The Prince of Homburg*

Bennett, B. Prinz Friedrich von Homburg: theory in practice. *In* Bennett, B. Modern drama and German classicism p22-56

**Klíma, Ivan**

**About**

Goetz-Stankiewicz, M. Ivan Klíma. *In* Goetz-Stankiewicz, M. The silenced theatre: Czech playwrights without a stage p116-45

**Klossowski, Pierre**

**About**

Lasowski, P. W. Un souffle unique. *In* Glyph 6 p68-89

**Klugmann, James**

Introduction: The crisis of the thirties: a view from the Left. *In* Culture and crisis in Britain in the thirties, ed. by J. Clark and others p13-36

**Knapp, Bettina Liebowitz**

Archetypes: dissolution as creation. *In* André Malraux, ed. by F. Dorenlot and M. Tison-Braun p149-54

**Knapp, Herbert.** See Knapp, M. jt. auth.

**Knapp, Mary, and Knapp, Herbert**

### About individual works

*One potato, two potato . . . : the secret education of American children*

Cech, J. Notes on American children's folklore. *In* Children's literature v8 p176-83

**Kneese, Allen V.**

Environmental policy. *In* The United States in the 1980s, ed. by P. Duignan and A. Rabushka p253-83

**Knight, Elizabeth**

Popular literature in East Africa. *In* African literature no. 10: Retrospect & prospect, ed. by E. D. Jones p177-90

**Knight, George Wilson**

Caliban as a Red Man. *In* Shakespeare's styles, ed. by P. Edwards, I. S. Ewbank and G. K. Hunter p205-20

**Knights, Lionel Charles**

Rhetoric and insincerity. *In* Shakespeare's styles, ed. by P. Edwards, I. S. Ewbank and G. K. Hunter p 1-8

**Knights and knighthood in literature**

Vinaver, E. The questing knight. *In* The Binding of Proteus, ed. by M. W. McCune, J. Orbison and P. M. Withim p126-40

**Knopf, Alfred A.**

H. L. Mencken: a memoir. *In* On Mencken, ed. by J. Dorsey p283-313

**Knopp, Josephine Zadovsky, and Lustig, Arnost**

Holocaust literature II: novels and short stories. *In* Encountering the Holocaust: an interdisciplinary survey, ed. by B. L. Sherwin and S. G. Ament p267-315

**Knott, John Ray**

The sword of the spirit

*Contents*

Gerrard Winstanley's Land of Righteousness
John Bunyan and the experience of the Word
The Living Word
Milton and the spirit of truth
Richard Baxter and the Saints' rest
Richard Sibbes and spiritual preaching

**Knowledge, Sociology of**

Fuhrman, E. R. Critical-emancipatory and social-technological themes in the sociology of knowledge. *In* Fuhrman, E. R. The sociology of knowledge in America, 1883-1915 p 1-20

Furhman, E. R. On the cognitive superiority of the sociology of knowledge. *In* Fuhrman, E. R. The sociology of knowledge in America, 1883-1915 p212-29

Gombrich, Sir E. H. J. The tradition of general knowledge. *In* Gombrich, Sir E. H. J. Ideals and idols p9-23

Merton, R. K. Insiders and outsiders: an essay in the sociology of knowledge. *In* Value and values in evolution, ed. by E. A. Maziarz p47-69

**Knowledge, Theory of**

Annas, J. Truth and knowledge. *In* Doubt and dogmatism, ed. by M. Schofield, M. Burnyeat and J. Barnes p84-104

Morowitz, H. J. Drinking hemlock and other nutritional matters. *In* Morowitz, H. J. The wine of life, and other essays on societies, energy & living things p231-35

Pears, D. F. A comparison between Ayer's views about the privileges of sense-datum statements and the views of Russell and Austin. *In* Perception and identity, ed. by G. F. Macdonald p61-83

Scruton, R. Emotion, practical knowledge and common culture. 6 Explaining emotions, ed. by A. O. Rorty p519-36

Tagliacozzo, G. General education as unity of knowledge: a theory based on Vichian principles. *In* Conference on Vico and Contemporary Thought, New York, 1976. Vico and contemporary thought pt2 p110-38

*See also* Cognition; Experience; Identity; Intellect; Objectivity; Perception; Reality; Truth

**Knowledge, Theory of (Religion)**

Dan, J. The concept of knowledge in the Shi'ur qomah. *In* Studies in Jewish religious and intellectual history. ed. by S. Stein and R. Loewe p67-73

*See also* Truth (Theology)

**Knox, Bernard MacGregor Walker**

Word and action

*Contents*

Aeschylus and the third actor
The Ajax of Sophocles
The date of the Oedipus Tyrannus of Sophocles
Euripidean comedy
Euripides' Iphigenia in Aulide 1-163 (in that order)
The Hippolytus of Euripides
The lion in the house
The Medea of Euripides
La modification and beyond
Myth and Attic tragedy
Review of Aeschylus: Suppliants (tr. by Janet Lembke), Aeschylus: Seven against Thebes (tr. by Anthony Hecht and Helen Bacon), and Aeschylus: Prometheus bound (tr. by James Scully and C. John Herington)
Review of Agamemnon (directed by Andrei Serban)
Review of Catastrophe survived (by Anne Pippin Burnett)
Review of Euripidean drama (by D. J. Conacher)
Review of Euripides: Iphigeneia at Aulis (tr. by W. S. Merwin and George E. Dimock, Jr.) and Iphigenia (directed by Michael Cacoyannis)
Review of The Oresteia (tr. by Robert Fagles) and The Bacchae of Euripides, a communion rite (by Wole Soyinka)
Review of Sophocle, poète tragique (by Gilberte Ronnet)
Review of Sophocles: a reading (by G. H. Gellie)
Review of Sophocles' Ajax (ed. by W. B. Stanford)
Review of Sophocles, Women of Trachis (tr. by C. K. Williams and Gregory W. Dickerson) and Sophocles, Oedipus the King (tr. by Steven Berg and Diskin Clay)
Review of Sophokles, Antigone (by Gerhard Müller)
Review of The stagecraft of Aeschylus (by Oliver Taplin)
Second thoughts in Greek tragedy
Sophocles' Oedipus
The Tempest and the ancient comic tradition
Why is Oedipus called tyrannos?

**Knox, John,** 1505-1572

About

Ozment, S. H. Protestant resistance to tyranny: the career of John Knox. *In* Ozment, S. H. The age of reform, 1250-1550 p419-33

**Koch, Kenneth**

About

Howard, R. Kenneth Koch: "What was the ecstasy, and what the stricture?" *In* Howard, R. Alone with America p331-41

**Kochan, Lionel**
European Jewry in the 19th and 20th centuries. *In* The Jewish world, ed. by E. Kedourie p264-73

**Kocka, Jürgen**
The rise of the modern industrial enterprise in Germany. *In* Managerial hierarchies, ed. by A. D. Chandler and H. Daems p77-116

**Koestler, Arthur**
Nothing but . . . ? *In* Lying truths, ed. by R. Duncan and M. Weston-Smith p199-201

**Kofele-Kale, Ndiva**
The impact of environment on ethnic group values in Cameroon. *In* Values, identities, and national integration, ed. by J. N. Paden p121-50
The impact of environment on national political culture in Cameroon. *In* Values, identities, and national integration, ed. by J. N. Paden p151-72

**Kohl, Marvin**
On suffering. *In* Humanist ethics, ed. by M. B. Storer p173-78

**Kohler, Robert E.**
Warren Weaver and the Rockefeller Foundation program in molecular biology: a case study in the management of science. *In* The Sciences in the American context: new perspectives, ed. by N. Reingold p249-93

**Kohn, David**
Theories to work by: rejected theories, reproduction, and Darwin's path to natural selection. *In* Studies in history of biology, v4 p67-170

**Kohn, Hans**
Nationalism. *In* The Jew, ed. by A. A. Cohen p19-30

**Kohn, Melvin L.**
Job complexity and adult personality. *In* Themes of work and love in adulthood, ed. by N. J. Smelser and E. H. Erikson p193-210

**Kohout, Pavel**

About

Goetz-Stankiewicz, M. Pavel Kohout. *In* Goetz-Stankiewicz, M. The silenced theatre: Czech playwrights without a stage p89-115

**Koht, Halvdan**

About

Leiren, T. I. Halvdan Koht's America. *In* Makers of an immigrant legacy, ed. by O. S. Lovoll p173-85

**Kolenda, Konstantin**
Globalism vs. consensual pluralism. *In* Humanist ethics, ed. M. B. Storer p104-21

**Kolodny, Annette**
The lady's not for spurning: Kate Millett and the critics. *In* Women's autobiography, ed. by E. C. Jelinek p238-59

**Kon, I. S.**
Ethnography and psychology. *In* Soviet and Western anthropology, ed. by E. Gellner p217-27

**Konigsburg, Elaine (Lobl)**

About

Rees, D. Your arcane novelist: E. L. Konigsburg. *In* Rees, D. The marble in the water p14-24
Townsend, J. R. E. L. Konigsburg. *In* Townsend, J. R. A sounding of storytellers p111-24

**Konoe, Atsumaro**

About

Jansen, M. B. Konoe Atsumaro. *In* The Chinese and the Japanese, ed. by A. Iriye p107-23

**Kontos, Alkis**
The dialectics of domination: an interpretation of Friedrich Dürrenmatt's The visit. *In* Powers, possessions and freedom, ed. by A. Kontos p153-65

**Kopelev, Lev Zalmanovich**
Rilke and Russia. *In* Rilke: the alchemy of alienation, ed. by F. Baron, E. S. Dick and W. R. Maurer p113-36

**Kopytoff, Igor**
Revitalization and the genesis of cults in pragmatic religion: the Kita rite of passage among the Suku. *In* Explorations in African systems of thought, ed. by I. C. Karp & C. S. Bird p183-212

**Koreneva, Maya**
One hundred percent American tragedy: a Soviet view. *In* Eugene O'Neill, ed. by V. Floyd p145-71

**Korea**

History—1864-1910

Oh, B. B. Sino-Japanese rivalry in Korea, 1876-1885. *In* The Chinese and the Japanese, ed. by A. Iriye p37-57

**Körner, Stephan**
Ayer on metaphysics. *In* Perception and identity, ed. by G. F. Macdonald p262-76

**Korshin, Paul J.**
Probability and character in the eighteenth century. *In* Probability, time, and space in eighteenth-century literature, ed. by P. R. Backscheider p63-77

**Kotlikoff, Laurence J.**
Social Security and welfare: what we have, want, and can afford. *In* The Economy in the 1980s: a program for growth and stability, ed. by M. J. Boskin p293-324

**Kottak, Conrad Phillip**
Ecology, behavior, and the spirit of fishermen. *In* Brazil, anthropological perspectives, ed. by M. L. Margolis and W. E. Carter p180-209

**Kousser, J. Morgan**
Quantitative social-scientific history. *In* The Past before us, ed. by M. Kammen p433-56

**Kovaleff, Theodore P.**
Television as big business. *In* Screen and society, ed. by F. J. Coppa p173-83

**Kovel, Joel**
The American mental health industry. *In* Critical psychiatry, ed. by D. Ingleby p72-101

**Kovner, Abba**

About

Alexander, E. Holocaust and rebirth: Moshe Flinker, Nelly Sachs, and Abba Kovner. *In* Alexander, E. The resonance of dust p31-71

**Kozlov, Vasily Ivanovich**
Ethnography and demography. *In* Soviet and Western anthropology, ed. by E. Gellner p265-74

**Kozlovskiĭ, Petr Borisovich, Kniâz**
### About
Struve, G. Towards a biography of Prince Peter Kozlovsky: Kozlovsky's letter to Countess Lieven. *In* California Slavic studies v11 p 1-24

**Kozlovsky, Peter.** See Kozlovskiĭ, Petr Borisovich Kniâz

**Krader, Lawrence**
The origins of the state among the nomads of Asia. *In* Soviet and Western anthropology, ed. by E. Gellner p135-47

**Kramnick, Isaac**
Children's literature and bourgeois ideology: observations on culture and industrial capitalism in the later eighteenth century. *In* Culture and politics from Puritanism to the Enlightenment, ed. by P. Zagorin p203-40

**Kratzmann, Gregory**
Anglo-Scottish literary relations, 1430-1550
### Contents
Ane satyre of the thrie estaitis and English drama
Dunbar and Skelton
Henryson and English poetry
Influences and perspectives
The kingis quair and English poetry
The palice of honour and The hous of fame
Two Aeneid translators—Surrey's debt to Douglas: Wyatt and Henryson
The two traditions

**Krautheimer, Richard**
Success and failure in late antique church planning. *In* Age of spirituality, ed. by K. Weitzmann p121-39

**Kregel, J. A.**
Income distribution. *In* A Guide to post-Keynesian economics, ed. by A. S. Eichner p46-60

**Krell, David Farrell**
Art and truth in raging discord: Heidegger and Nietzsche on the will to power. *In* Martin Heidegger and the question of literature, ed. by W. V. Spanos p39-52

**Kreyche, Gerald F.**
The meaning of humanness: a philosophical perspective. *In* Being human in a technological age, ed. by D. M. Borchert and D. Stewart p37-50

**Kriegel, Annie**
Generational difference: the history of an idea. *In* Generations, ed. by S. R. Graubard p23-38

**Krieger, Elliot**
Social relations and the social order in 'Much ado about nothing.' *In* Shakespeare survey 32 p49-61

**Krieger, Murray**
Poetic presence and illusion
### Contents
The critical legacy of Matthew Arnold; or, The strange brotherhood of T. S. Eliot, I. A. Richards, and Northrop Frye
Fiction, nature, and literary kinds in Johnson's criticism of Shakespeare
Jacopo Mazzoni, repository of diverse critical traditions or source of a new one?
Literary analysis and evaluation—and the ambidextrous critic
Literature as illusion, as metaphor, as vision
Literature, criticism, and decision theory
Literature versus ecriture: constructions and deconstructions in recent critical theory

Mediation, language, and vision in the reading of literature
Poetic presence and illusion I: Renaissance theory and the duplicity of metaphor
Poetic presence and illusion II: Formalist theory and the duplicity of metaphor
Reconsideration—the New Critics
A scorecard for the critics
Shakespeare and the critic's idolatry of the word
The theoretical contributions of Eliseo Vivas
Theories about theories about Theory of criticism
The tragic vision, twenty years after
"Trying experiments upon our sensibility": the art of dogma and doubt in eighteenth-century literature
### About
Lentricchia, F. Murray Krieger's last romanticism. *In* Lentricchia, F. After the New Criticism p212-54

### About individual works
*Theory of criticism*
Krieger, M. Theories about theories about Theory of criticism. *In* Krieger, M. Poetic presence and illusion p197-210

*The tragic vision*
Kreiger, M. The tragic vision, twenty years after. *In* Krieger, M. Poetic presence and illusion p129-35

**Kristeller, Paul Oskar**
Renaissance thought and its sources
### Contents
The Aristotelian tradition
Byzantine and Western Platonism in the fifteenth century
Classical antiquity
The dignity of man
Humanism and scholasticism in the Italian Renaissance
The humanist movement
The immortality of the soul
Italian humanism and Byzantium
The Middle Ages
Paganism and Christianity
The Renaissance
Renaissance philosophy and the medieval tradition
Renaissance Platonism
The unity of truth

**Kristol, Irving**
The adversary culture of intellectuals. *In* The Third century, ed by S. M. Lipset p327-43

**Kroll, Lucien**
Architecture and bureaucracy. *In* Architecture for people, ed. by B. Mikellides p162-70

**Kronegger, Maria Elisabeth**
From the impressionist to the phenomenological novel. *In* The Analysis of literary texts, ed. by R. D. Pope p129-37

**Kubler, George A.**
The arts: fine and plain. *In* Perspectives on American folk art, ed. by I. M. G. Quimby and S. T. Swank p234-46

Towards a reductive theory of visual style. *In* The Concept of style, ed. by B. Lang p119-27

**Kubrick, Stanley**

### About individual works
*Barry Lyndon*
Kael, P. Kubrick's gilded age. *In* Kael, P. When the lights go down p101-07

Kubrick, Stanley—About individual works—
Barry Lyndon—*Continued*

Kauffmann, S. Barry Lyndon. *In* Kauffmann, S. Before my eyes p180-83

Miller, G. Murder in the first degree. *In* Miller, G. Screening the novel p116-42

Kučuk, Ejub

The socio-class determinants of militarism.
*In* Problems of contemporary militarism, ed.
by A. Eide and M. Thee p148-72

Kuhn, Thomas S.

### About individual works
*The structure of scientific revolutions*

Morowitz, H. J. Puzzle solving science. *In*
Morowitz, H. J. The wine of life, and other
essays on societies, energy & living things
p212-16

Kukla, André. See Kukla, Andy

Kukla, Andy

The modern language of consciousness. *In*
The State of the language, ed. by L. Michaels
and C. Ricks p516-23

Küller, Rikard

Architecture and emotions. *In* Architecture
for people, ed. by B. Mikellides p87-100

Kumar, Shiv Kumar

### About

Amur, G. S. Poetry as subterfuge: an introduction to Shiv K. Kumar's poetry. *In* Aspects
of Indian writing in English, ed. by M. K.
Naik p126-36

Kummer, Hans

On the value of social relationships to nonhuman primates: a heuristic scheme. *In* Human
ethology, ed. by M. von Cranach [and oth-
ers] p381-95

Kunzer, Ruth Goldschmidt. See Syrkin, M. jt.
auth.

Kurth, James Ransom

Industrial change and political change: a
European perspective. *In* The New authoritarianism in Latin America, ed. by D. Collier
p319-62

Kurtz, Paul W.

Does humanism have an ethic of responsibility? *In* Humanist ethics, ed. by M. B. Storer
p11-35

Kurzweil, Edith

The age of structuralism

*Contents*

Alain Touraine: structures without structuralism

Claude Lévi-Strauss: the father of structuralism

Henri Lefebvre: a Marxist against structuralism

Jacques Lacan: structuralist psychoanalysis

Louis Althusser: Marxism and structuralism

Michel Foucault: structuralism and structures
of knowledge

Paul Ricoeur: hermeneutics and structuralism

Roland Barthes: literary structuralism and
erotics

Kushner, Deena Dash. See Dash, I. G. jt. auth.

Kuskin, Karla

The language of children's literature. *In*
The State of the language, ed. by L. Michaels
and C. Ricks p213-25

Kuxdorf, Manfred

Mynona versus Remarque, Tucholsky, Mann,
and others: not so quiet on the literary front.
*In* The First World War in German narrative
prose, ed. by C. N. Genno and H. Wetzel
p71-92

# L

La Barre, Maurine Boie

"The worm in the honeysuckle": a case study
of a child's hysterical blindness. *In* La
Barre, W. Culture in context p233-46

La Barre, Weston

Culture in context

*Contents*

Anthropological perspectives on hallucination,
hallucinogens, and the shamanic origins of
religion

Anthropological perspectives on sexuality

Authority, culture change, and the courts

Aymara folklore and folk temperament

Clinic and field

Countertransference and the beatniks

History and ethnography of Cannabis

The influence of Freud on anthropology

Obscenity: an anthropological appraisal

Paralinguistics, kinesics, and cultural anthropology

The patient and his families

Personality from a psychoanalytic viewpoint

Psychoanalysis and the biology of religion

Social cynosure and social structure

Soma: the three-and-one-half millennia mystery

Labarthe, Philippe Lacoue- See Lacoue-Labarthe, Philippe

Laberthonnière, Lucien

### About

Daly, G. Lucien Laberthonnière's 'critical
mysticism'. *In* Daly, G. Transcendence and
immanence p91-116

Labor, Organized. See Trade-unions

Labor, Hours of. See Hours of labor

Labor, Right to. See Right to labor

Labor and laboring classes

*See also* Artisans; Cost and standard of living;
Hours of labor; Industrial relations; Middle
classes; Right to labor; Trade-unions

### Historiography

Brody, D. Labor history in the 1970s: toward a history of the American worker. *In* The
Past before us, ed. by M. Kammen p251-69

### Medical care—France

Farge, A. Work-related diseases of artisans
in eighteenth-century France. *In* Medicine and
society in France, ed. by R. Forster and O.
Ranum p89-103

### Wages

*See* Wages

### Europe—History

Le Goff, J. Labor, techniques, and craftsmen
in the value systems of the early Middle Ages
(fifth to tenth centuries) *In* Le Goff, J. Time,
work, & culture in the Middle Ages p71-86

Le Goff, J. A note on tripartite society,
monarchical ideology, and economic renewal
in ninth- to twelfth-century Christendom. *In*
Le Goff, J. Time, work, & culture in the Middle Ages p53-57

Labor and laboring classes—*Continued*

### France

Barrows, S. I. After the Commune: alcoholism, temperance, and literature in the early Third Republic. *In* Consciousness and class experience in nineteenth-century Europe, ed. by J. M. Merriman p205-18

Perrot, M. The three ages of industrial discipline in nineteenth-century France. *In* Consciousness and class experience in nineteenth-century Europe, ed. by J. M. Merriman p149-68

Sewell, W. H. Property, labor, and the emergence of socialism in France, 1789-1848. *In* Consciousness and class experience in nineteenth-century Europe, ed. by J. M. Merriman p45-63

### France—Case studies

Johnson, C. H. Patterns of proletarianization: Parisian tailors and Lodève woolens workers. *In* Consciousness and class experience in nineteenth-century Europe, ed. by J. M. Merriman p65-84

### France—Limoges

Merriman, J. M. Incident at the statue of the Virgin Mary: the conflict of old and new in nineteenth-century Limoges. *In* Consciousness and class experience in nineteenth-century Europe, ed. by J. M. Merriman p129-48

### France—Lyons

Sheridan, G. J. Household and craft in an industrializing economy: the case of the silk weavers of Lyons. *In* Consciousness and class experience in nineteenth-century Europe, ed. by J. M. Merriman p107-28

### France—Toulouse

Aminzade, R. The transformation of social solidarities in nineteenth-century Toulouse. *In* Consciousness and class experience in nineteenth-century Europe, ed. by J. M. Merriman p85-105

### Great Britain

Bond, R. Cinema in the thirties: documentary film and the labour movement. *In* Culture and crisis in Britain in the thirties, ed. by J. Clark and others p241-56

Hogenkamp, B. Making films with a purpose: film-making and the working class. *In* Culture and crisis in Britain in the thirties, ed. by J. Clark and others p257-69

Lees, L. H. Getting and spending: the family budgets of English industrial workers in 1890. *In* Consciousness and class experience in nineteenth-entury Europe, ed. by J. M. Merriman p169-86

Pole, J. R. Abraham Lincoln and the working classes of Britain. *In* Pole, J. R. Paths to the American past p111-45

### Great Britain—History

Hollis, P. Anti-slavery and British working-class radicalism in the years of reform. *In* Anti-slavery, religion, and reform: essays in memory of Roger Anstey, ed. by C. Bolt and S. Drescher p294-315

### United States

Dunlop, J. T. The future of the American labor movement. *In* The Third century, ed. by S. M. Lipset p183-203

Ginzberg, E. The role of small business in the process of skill acquisition. *In* Small business in American life, ed. by S. W. Bruchey p366-79

### United States—History

Foner, E. Abolitionism and the labor movement in antebellum America. *In* Anti-slavery, religion, and reform: essays in memory of Roger Anstey, ed. by C. Bolt and S. Drescher p254-71

Montgomery, D. Work. *In* Encyclopedia of American economic history, ed. by G. Porter v3 p958-73

### Labor and laboring classes in literature

Snee, C. A. Working-class literature or proletarian writing? *In* Culture and crisis in Britain in the thirties, ed. by J. Clark and others p165-91

**Labor costs.** See Wages

### Labor discipline

### France—History

Perrot, M. The three ages of industrial discipline in nineteenth-century France. *In* Consciousness and class experience in nineteenth-century Europe, ed. by J. M. Merriman p149-68

**Labor economics.** See Labor and laboring classes

### Labor economics in literature

Heinzelman, K. The art of labor. *In* Heinzelman, K. The economics of the imagination p137-65

Heinzelman, K. The psychomachia of labor. *In* Heinzelman, K. The economics of the imagination p166-95

Heinzelman, K. Wordsworth's labor theory: an economics of compensation. *In* Heinzelman, K. The economics of the imagination p196-233

**Labor-management relations.** See Industrial relations

**Labor market.** See Labor supply

**Labor organizations.** See Trade-unions

**Labor output.** See Labor productivity

### Labor productivity

Kendrick, J. W. Productivity. *In* Encyclopedia of American economic history, ed. by G. Porter v 1 p157-66

### United States

Boskin, M. J. Economic growth and productivity. *In* The Economy in the 1980s: a program for growth and stability, ed. by M. J. Boskin p23-50

**Labor relations.** See Industrial relations

### Labor supply

Appelbaum, E. The labor market. *In* A Guide to post-Keynesian economics, ed by A. S. Eichner p100-19

**Labor-unions.** See Trade-unions

**Laboratories, Industrial research.** See Research, Industrial—Laboratories

**Laboratories, Technical.** See Research, Industrial—Laboratories

### Laboratory animals

Morowitz, H. J. Sacred cows and sacrificial guinea pigs. *In* Morowitz, H. J. The wine of life, and other essays on societies, energy & living things p129-32

Sebeok, T. A. Looking in the destination for what should have been sought in the source. *In* Speaking of apes, ed. by T. A. Sebeok and J. Umiker-Sebeok p407-27

**Laborers.** See Labor and laboring classes

**Labour Party (Great Britain)**
Dean, D. R. The character of the early Labour Party, 1900-14. *In* The Edwardian age: conflict and stability, 1900-1914, ed. by A. O'Day p97-112

**Labrador**
Description and travel
O'Flaherty, P. Walking new ground: books by two Newfoundland pioneers, 1770-1882. *In* O'Flaherty, P. The rock observed p32-48

**Labrador in literature**
O'Flaherty, P. The lure of the north: fiction and travel literature, 1850-1905. *In* O'Flaherty, P. The rock observed p82-110

**La Bretonne, Nicolas Edme Restif de.** See Restif de La Bretonne, Nicolas Edme

**Labriola, Antonio**
About individual works
*Essais sur la conception matérialiste de l'histoire*
Durkheim, E. Review of Antonio Labriola, Essais sur la conception matérialiste de l'histoire. *In* Durkheim, E. Emile Durkheim on institutional analysis p123-30

**Lacan, Jacques**
About
Bowie, M. Jacques Lacan. *In* Structuralism and since, ed. by J. Sturrock p116.53
Kerrigan, W. The articulation of the ego in the English Renaissance. *In* The Literary Freud: mechanisms of defense and the poetic will, ed. by J. H. Smith p261-308
Kurzweil, E. Jacques Lacan: structuralist psychoanalysis. *In* Kurzweil, E. The age of structuralism p135-64
Turkle, S. French anti-psychiatry. *In* Critical psychiatry, ed. by D. Ingleby p150-83

**Laclos, Pierre Ambroise François Choderlos de**
About individual works
*Dangerous acquaintances*
Mellor, N. K. The misfortunes of virtue: III, Les liaisons dangereuses. *In* Mellor, N. K. The heroine's text p116-35
Mellor, N. K. The negative heroine: Les liasons dangereuses. *In* Mellor, N. K. The heroine's text p136-48

**Lacombe Lucien (Motion picture)**
Kauffmann, S. Lacombe Lucien. *In* Kauffmann, S. Before my eyes p60-62

**Lacoste, Louise Marcil-** See Marcil-Lacoste, Louise

**Lacoue-Labarthe, Philippe, and Nancy, Jean-Luc**
Genre. *In* Glyph 7 p 1-14

**Ladd, Everett Carll**
The American party system today. *In* The Third century, ed. by S. M. Lipset p153-82

**Ladd, Everett Carll, and Lipset, Seymour Martin**
Public opinion and public policy. *In* The United States in the 1980s, ed. by P. Duignan and A. Rabushka p49-84

**Laffer, Arthur B.**
An equilibrium rational macroeconomic framework. *In* Economic issues of the eighties, ed. by N. M. Kamrany and R. H. Day p44-57

**Laforet, Carmen**
About individual works
*Nada*
Fox-Lockert, L. Carmen Laforet. *In* Fox-Lockert, L. Women novelists in Spain and Spanish America p73-84

**Laforgue, John**
About
Peyre, H. In search of the morbid and the strange: the decadents and Laforgue. *In* Peyre, H. What is symbolism? p98-111

**Lagerlöf, Selma Ottiliana Louise**
About individual works
*Gösta Berlings saga*
Fehrman, C. A. D. Gösta Berlings saga and its transformations. *In* Fehrman, C. A. D. Poetic creation p119-36

**Laget, Mireille**
Childbirth in seventeenth-and eighteenth-century France: obstetrical practices and collective attitudes. *In* Medicine and society in France, ed. by R. Forster and O. Ranum p137-76

**Laguardia, Gari**
Forbidden places: Bacquer's scene of writing. *In* The Analysis of literary texts, ed. by R. D. Pope p31-40

**Laing, Stuart**
Presenting 'things as they are': John Sommerfield's May Day and mass observation. *In* Class, culture and social change, ed. by F. Gloversmith p142-60

**Lair, Robert L.**
Emily Dickinson's fracture of grammar: syntactic ambiguity in her poems. *In* The Analysis of literary texts, ed. by R. D. Pope p158-64

**Laissez-faire.** See Competition

**Lakoff, Robin Tolmach**
When talk is not cheap: psychotherapy as conversation. *In* The State of the language, ed. by L. Michaels and C. Ricks p440-48

**Lal, P.**
Myth and the Indian writer in English: a note. *In* Aspects of Indian writing in English, ed. by M. K. Naik p15-18

**Lally, Timothy Douglas Patrick**
Synchronic vs diachronic popular culture studies and the old English elegy. *In* 5000 years of popular culture, ed. by F. E. H. Schroeder p203-12

**Lamb, Margaret**
All for love and the theatrical arts. *In* The Analysis of literary texts, ed. by R. D. Pope p236-43

**Lambert, Mark**
Troilus, books I-III: a Criseydan reading. *In* Essays on Troilus and Criseyde, ed. by M. Salu p105-25

**La Mettrie, Julien Offray de**
About
Falvey, J. Women and sexuality in the thought of La Mettrie. *In* Woman and society in eighteenth-century France, ed. by E. Jacobs and others p55-68

**Lamming, George**
About
Munro, I. George Lamming. *In* West Indian literature, ed. by B. King p126-43

**Lamont, Rosette C.**
A pack of cards. *In* The Analysis of literary texts, ed. by R. D. Pope p185-200

**Lampard, Eric E.**
Urbanization. *In* Encyclopedia of American economic history, ed. by G. Porter v3 p1028-57

**Lancelot**
Dale, C. Lancelot and the medieval quests of Sir Lancelot and Dante. *In* Walker Percy: art and ethics, ed. by J. Tharpe p99-106

**Land.** See Land use

**Land use**
Douglas, R. Laveleye: the critic ripe for conversion. *In* Critics of Henry George, ed. by R. V. Andelson p47-55
*See also* Landscape assessment; Public lands

**Land value taxation.** See Single tax

**Landauer, Gustav**
Strindberg's Historical miniatures: a lecture. *In* The Jew, ed. by A. A. Cohen p171-84

### About

Simon, E. The maturing of man and the maturing of the Jew. *In* The Jew, ed by A. A. Cohen p127-46

**Landgren-Backström, Signe**
Arms trade and transfer of military technology to Third World countries. *In* Problems of contemporary militarism, ed. by A. Eide and M. Thee p230-47

**Landino, Cristoforo**

### About individual works
*Disputationes Camaldulenses*

Murrin, M. Appendix: Landino's Camaldulensian dialogues. *In* Murrin, M. The allegorical epic p197-202
Murrin, M. Landino's Virgil. *In* Murrin, M. The allegorical epic p27-50

**Landon, Michael de L.**
A historian looks at the computer's impact on society. *In* Monster or messiah? Ed. by W. M. Mathews p13-22

**Landscape**
Lowenthal, D. Age and artifact: dilemmas of appreciation. *In* The Interpretation of ordinary landscapes, ed. by D. W. Meinig p103-28
Meinig, D. W. The beholding eye: ten versions of the same scene. *In* The Interpretation of ordinary landscapes, ed. by D. W. Meinig p33-48
Samuels, M. S. The biography of landscape: cause and culpability. *In* The Interpretation of ordinary landscapes, ed. by D. W. Meinig p51-88
Tuan, Yi-Fu. Thought and landscape: the eye and the mind's eye. *In* The Interpretation of ordinary landscapes, ed. by D. W. Meinig p89-102

### United States

Jackson, J. B. The order of a landscape: reason and religion in Newtonian America. *In* The Interpretation of ordinary landscapes, ed. by D. W. Meinig p153-62
Lewis, P. F. Axioms for reading the landscape: some guides to the American scene. *In* The Interpretation of ordinary landscapes, ed. by D. W. Meinig p11-32
Meinig, D. W. Symbolic landscapes: some idealizations of American communities. *In* The Interpretation of ordinary landscapes, ed. by D. W. Meinig p164-92

**Landscape architecture**
Darbourne and Darke. Social needs and landscape architecture. *In* Architecture for people, ed. by B. Mikellides p34-37

**Landscape assessment**
Jackson, J. B. The order of a landscape: reason and religion in Newtonian America. *In* The Interpretation of ordinary landscapes, ed. by D. W. Meinig p153-62
Lewis, P. F. Axioms for reading the landscape: some guides to the American scene. *In* The Interpretation of ordinary landscapes, ed. by D. W. Meinig p11-32
Meinig, D. W. The beholding eye: ten versions of the same scene. *In* The Interpretation of ordinary landscapes, ed. by D. W. Meinig p33-48
Meinig, D. W. Reading the landscape: an appreciation of W. G. Hoskins and J. B. Jackson. *In* The Interpretation of ordinary landscapes, ed. by D. W. Meinig p195-244
Meinig, D. W. Symbolic landscapes: some idealizations of American communities. *In* The Interpretation of ordinary landscapes, ed. by D. W. Meinig p164-92
Samuels, M. S. The biography of landscape: cause and culpability. *In* The Interpretation of ordinary landscapes, ed. by D. W. Meinig p51-88
Sopher, D. E. The landscape of home: myth, experience, social meaning. *In* The Intepretation of ordinary landscapes, ed. by D. W. Meinig p129-49
Tuan, Yi-Fu. Thought and landscape: the eye and the mind's eye. *In* The Interpretation of ordinary landscapes, ed. by D. W. Meinig p89-102

**Landscape evaluation.** See Landscape assessment

**Landscape gardening**

### Great Britain—History
Quaintance, R. E. Walpole's Whig interpretation of landscaping history. *In* Studies in eighteenth-century culture v9 p285-300

**Landscape; magazine of human geography**
Meinig, D. W. Reading the landscape: an appreciation of W. G. Hoskins and J. B. Jackson. *In* The Interpretation of ordinary landscapes, ed. by D. W. Meinig p195-244

**Landscape painting, American**
Parry, E. C. Acts of God, acts of man: geological ideas and the imaginary landscapes of Thomas Cole. *In* New Hampshire Bicentennial Conference on the History of Geology, University of New Hampshire, 1976. Two hundred years of geology in America p53-71

**Lang, Wiesław**
Marxism, liberalism and justice. *In* Symposium on Theories of Justice in and for the Second Half of the Twentieth Century, Sydney, 1977. Justice p116-48

**Lange, Lynda**
The function of equal education in Plato's Republic and Laws. *In* The Sexism of social and political theory: women and reproduction from Plato to Nietzsche, ed. by L. M. G. Clark and L. Lange p3-15
Rousseau: women and the general will. *In* The Sexism of social and political theory: women and reproduction from Plato to Nietzsche, ed. by L. M. G. Clark and L. Lange p41-52

**Langford, Paul**

British correspondence in the colonial press, 1763-1775: a study in Anglo-American misunderstanding before the American Revolution. *In* The Press & the American Revolution, ed. by B. Bailyn and J. B. Hench p273-313

**Langlois, Walter G.**

Malraux and Medellin. *In* André Malraux, ed. by F. Dorenlot and M. Tison-Braun p167-88

**Language, Legal.** See Law—Language

**Language, Philosophy of.** See Languages—Philosophy

**Language, Psychology of.** See Psycholinguistics

**Language acquisition**

Bronowski, J. and Bellugi, U. Language, name, and concept. *In* Speaking of apes, ed. by T. A. Sebeok and J. Umiker-Sebeok p103-13

Brown, R. The first sentences of child and chimpanzee. *In* Speaking of apes, ed. by T. A. Sebeok and J. Umiker-Sebeok p85-101

Foppa, K. Language acquisition: a human ethological problem? *In* Human ethology, ed. by M. von Cranach [and others] p729-38

Gardner, R. A. and Gardner, B. T. Comparative psychology and language acquisition. *In* Speaking of apes, ed. by T. A. Sebeok and J. Umiker-Sebeok p287-330

Limber, J. Language in child and chimp? *In* Speaking of apes, ed. by T. A. Sebeok and J. Umiker Sebeok p197-220

**Language and culture**

Cook, A. S. Introduction. *In* Cook, A. S. Myth & language p 1-10

Cook, A. S. Language and myth. *In* Cook, A. S. Myth & language p260-83

Cook, A. S. The large phases of myth. *In* Cook, A. S. Myth & language p37-66

Cook, A. S. Lévi-Strauss, myth, and the Neolithic revolutions. *In* Cook, A. S. Myth & language p13-36

*See also* Sociolinguistics

**Language and languages**

Adams, R. M. Authenticity-codes and sincerity-formulas. *In* The State of the language, ed. by L. Michaels and C. Ricks p579-92

Chomsky, N. Human language and other semiotic systems. *In* Speaking of apes, ed. by T. A. Sebeok and J. Umiker-Sebeok p429-40

Hudson, L. Language, truth, and psychology. *In* The State of the language, ed. by L. Michaels and C. Ricks p449-57

Kukla, A. The modern language of consciousness. *In* The State of the language, ed. by L. Michaels and C. Ricks p516-23

Lenneberg, E. H. A word between us. *In* Speaking of apes, ed. by T. A. Sebeok and J. Umiker-Sebeok p71-83

Malmi, W. A. Chimpanzees and language evolution. *In* Speaking of apes, ed. by T. A. Sebeok and J. Umiker-Sebeok p191-96

Marler, P. Primate vocalization: affective or symbolic? *In* Speaking of apes, ed. by T. A. Sebeok and J. Umiker-Sebeok p211-29

Reid, D. At home in the abyss: Jonestown and the language of enormity. *In* The State of the language, ed. by L. Michaels and C. Ricks p277-88

Rumbaugh, D. M. Language behavior of apes. *In* Speaking of apes, ed. by T. A. Sebeok and J. Umiker-Sebeok p231-59

Tanner, M. The language of philosophy. *In* The State of the language, ed. by L. Michaels and C. Ricks p458-66

Terrace, H. S. and Bever, T. G. What might be learned from studying language in the chimpanzee? The importance of symbolizing oneself. *In* Speaking of apes, ed. by T. A. Sebeok and J. Umiker-Sebeok p179-89

*See also* Bilingualism; Communication; Multilingualism; Psycholinguistics; Schizophrenics—Language; Sociolinguistics; Writing; names of particular languages, e.g. English

### Anecdotes, facetiae, satire, etc.

Kingston, M. H. "How are you?" I am fine, thank you. And you?" *In* The State of the language, ed. by L. Michaels and C. Ricks p152-57

### Data processing

*See* Linguistics—Data processing

### Origin

McNeill, D. Language origins. *In* Human ethology, ed. by M. von Cranach [and others] p715-27

### Political aspects

*See* Languages—Political aspects

### Psychology

*See* Psycholinguistics

### Style

Beardsley, M. C. Verbal style and illocutionary action. *In* The Concept of style, ed by B. Lang p149-68

**Language and logic**

Manley, L. G. The possibilities of discourse: Renaissance logic, rhetoric, and poetics. *In* Manley, L. G. Convention, 1500-1750 p137-58

**Language and society.** See Sociolinguistics

**Language arts.** See Reading

**Language data processing.** See Linguistics—Data processing

**Language development in children.** See Language acquisition

**Language learning by animals.** See Animal communication; Human-animal communication

**Languages**

### Origin

*See* Language and languages—Origin

### Philosophy

Derrida, J. The supplement of copula: philosophy before linguistics. *In* Textual strategies, ed. by J. V. Harari p82-120

*See also* Ordinary-language philosophy

### Political aspects

Powell, J. E. The language of politics. *In* The State of the language, ed. by L. Michaels and C. Ricks p432-39

### Psychology

*See* Psycholinguistics

**Lanser, Susan Sniader, and Beck, Evelyn Torton**

[Why] are there no great women critics? And what difference does it make? *In* The Prism of sex, ed. by J. A. Sherman and E. T. Beck p79-91

**LaRochefoucauld, Francois VI, duc de, prince de Marsillac**

### About individual works

*Maxims*

Barthes, R. La Rochefoucauld: "reflections or sentences and maxims." *In* Barthes, R. New critical essays p3-22

**Larmore, Charles**
Descartes' empirical epistemology. *In* Descartes, ed. by S. Gaukroger p6-22

**Lasowski, Patrick Wald**
Un souffle unique. *In* Glyph 6 p68-89

**Lassen, Peter**

### About

Scott, F. D. Peter Lassen: Danish pioneer of California, 1800-1859. *In* Makers of an immigrant legacy, ed. by O. S. Lovoll p186-209

**Lasswell, Harold Dwight**
The future of world communication and propaganda. *In* Propaganda and communication in world history, ed. by H. D. Lasswell, D. Lerner and H. Speier v3 p516-34

Must science serve political power? *In* Propaganda and communication in world history, ed. by H. D. Lasswell, D. Lerner and H. Speier v3 p3-15

**Lasswell, Harold Dwight; Lerner, Daniel, and Speier, Hans**
Introduction. *In* Propaganda and communication in world history, ed. by H. D. Lasswell, D. Lerner and H. Speier v 1 p 1-20

**Last, Rex**
Erich Fried: poetry and politics. *In* Modern Austrian writing, ed. by A. Best and H. Wolfschütz p181-96

Paul Celan and the metaphorical poets. *In* Modern Austrian writing, ed. by A. Best and H. Wolfschütz p142-55

**The last supper (Motion picture)**
Kauffmann, S. The last supper/Pirosmani. *In* Kauffmann, S. Before my eyes p310-13

**The last tycoon (Motion picture)**
Kael, P. Stallone and Stahr. *In* Kael, P. When the lights go down p213-19

Kauffmann, S. The last tycoon. *In* Kauffmann, S. Before my eyes p266-69

**The last wave (Motion picture)**
Kael, P. Doused. *In* Kael, P. When the lights go down p533-37

**The last woman (Motion picture)**
Kauffmann, S. The last woman/A piece of pleasure. *In* Kauffmann, S. Before my eyes p213-16

**Last year at Marienbad (Motion picture)**
Thiher, A. L'année dernière à Marienbad: the narration of narration. *In* Thiher, A. The cinematic muse p166-79

**La Taille, Jean de**

### About

Mueller, M. The scriptural tragedies of De la Taille and Garnier. *In* Mueller, M. Children of Oedipus, and other essays on the imitation of Greek tragedy, 1550-1800 p172-82

**The late show (Motion picture)**
Kael, P. The late show. *In* Kael, P. When the lights go down p259-62

**Latin America**

### Armed Forces—Political activity

Cardosa, F. H. On the characterization of authoritarian regimes in Latin America. *In* The New authoritarianism in Latin America, ed. by D. S. Collier p33-57

### Economic conditions

Cotler, J. State and regime: comparative notes on the southern cone and the "enclave" societies. *In* The New authoritarianism in Latin America, ed. by D. S. Collier p255-82

### Economic policy

Hirschman, A. O. The turn to authoritarianism in Latin America and the search for its economic determinants. *In* The New authoritarianism in Latin America, ed. by D. S. Collier p61-98

Kaufman, R. R. Industrial change and authoritarian rule in Latin America: a concrete review of the bureaucratic-authoritarian model. *In* The New authoritarianism in Latin America, ed. by D. S. Collier p165-253

Serra, J. M. Three mistaken theses regarding the connection between industrialization and authoritarian regimes. *In* The New authoritarianism in Latin America, ed. by D. S. Collier p99-163

### Foreign relations—United States

Falcoff, M. Latin America. *In* The United States in the 1980s, ed. by P. Duignan and A. Rabushka p797-826

### Historiography

Gibson, C. Latin America and the Americas. *In* The Past before us, ed. by M. Kammen p187-202

### Industries

Kurth, J. R. Industrial change and political change: a European perspective. *In* The New authoritarianism in Latin America, ed. by D. S. Collier p319-62

### Politics and government

Cardoso, F. H. On the characterization of authoritarian regimes in Latin America. *In* The New authoritarianism in Latin America, ed. by D. S. Collier p33-57

Collier, D. S. The bureaucratic-authoritarian model: synthesis and priorities for future research. *In* The New authoritarianism in Latin America, ed. by D. S. Collier p363-97

Collier, D. S. Overview of the bureaucratic-authoritarian model. *In* The New authoritarianism in Latin America, ed. by D. S. Collier p19-32

Cotler, J. State and regime: comparative notes on the southern cone and the "enclave" societies. *In* The New authoritarianism in Latin America, ed. by D. S. Collier p255-82

Hirschman, A. O. The turn to authoritarianism in Latin America and the search for its economic determinants. *In* The New authoritarianism in Latin America, ed. by D. S. Collier p61-98

Kaufman, R. R. Industrial change and authoritarian rule in Latin America: a concrete review of the bureaucratic-authoritarian model. *In* The New authoritarianism in Latin America, ed. by D. S. Collier p165-253

Kurth, J. R. Industrial change and political change: a European perspective. *In* The New authoritarianism in Latin America, ed. by D. S. Collier p319-62

O'Donnell, G. A. Tensions in the bureaucratic-authoritarian state and the question of democracy. *In* The New authoritarianism in Latin America, ed. by D. S. Collier p285-318

Serra, J. M. Three mistaken theses regarding the connection between industrialization and authoritarian regimes. *In* The New authoritarianism in Latin America, ed. by D. S. Collier p99-163

**Latin drama (Comedy)**

### History and criticism

Bain, D. Plautus uortit barbare: Plautus, Bacchides 526-61 and Menander, Dis exapaton 102-12. *In* Creative imitation and Latin literature. ed. by D. West and T. Woodman p17-34

## Latin literature

### History and criticism

Amundsen, D. W. Images of physicians in classical times. *In* 5000 years of popular culture, ed. by F. E. H. Schroeder p94-107

Cook, A. S. Ovid: the dialetics of recovery from atavism. *In* Cook, A. S. Myth & language p190-206

Marchese, R. T. Urbanism in the classical world: some general considerations and remarks. *In* 5000 years of popular culture, ed. by F. E. H. Schroeder p55-91

Oberhelman, S. Greek and Roman witches: literary conventions or agrarian fertility priestesses? *In* 5000 years of popular culture, ed. by F. E. H. Schroeder p138-53

Russell, D. A. De imitatione. *In* Creative imitation and Latin literature, ed. by D. West and T. Woodman p 1-16

## Latin philology

Bailey, D. R. S. On Cicero's speeches. *In* Harvard Studies in classical philology, v83 p237-85

## Latin poetry

Thomas, R. F. New comedy, Callimachus, and Roman poetry. *In* Harvard Studies in classical philogy, v83 p179-206

**Latin proverbs.** See Proverbs, Latin

**Latin rhetoric.** See Rhetoric. Ancient

## Latrobe, Benjamin Henry

### About

Lintner, S. F. and Stapleton, D. H. Geological theory and practice in the career of Benjamin Henry Latrobe. *In* New Hampshire Bicentennial Conference on the History of Geology, University of New Hampshire, 1976. Two hundred years of geology in America p107-19

## Laughlin, Thomas

Environment, political culture, and national orientations: a comparison of settled and pastoral Masai. *In* Values, identities, and national integration, ed. by J. N. Paden p91-103

## Laurenzo, Frederick E.

Computers and the idea of progress. *In* Monster or messiah? Ed. by W. M. Mathews p3-12

**Lautréamont, comte de,** pseud. See Ducasse, Isidore Lucien

## Laveleye, Émile Louis Victor, baron de

### About

Douglas, R. Laveleye: the critic ripe for conversion. *In* Critics of Henry George, ed. by R. V. Andelson p47-55

## Lavender, Abraham Donald

Jewish values in the Southern milieu. *In* Conference on Southern Jewish History, Richmond, Va. 1976. "Turn to the South" p124-34

## Lavin, Mary

### About

Deane, S. Mary Lavin. *In* The Irish short story, ed. by P. Rafroidi and T. Brown p237-47

## Lavoisier, Antoine Laurent

### About

Donovan, A. L. Scottish responses to the new chemistry of Lavoisier. *In* Studies in eighteenth-century culture v9 p237-49

## Law

*See also* Justice

### Interpretation and construction

*See* Judge-made law

### Jews

*See* Jews—Legal status, laws, etc.

### Language

Levine, D. S. "My client has discussed your proposal to fill the drainage ditch with his partners": legal language. *In* The State of the language, ed. by L. Michaels and C. Ricks p400-09

Schachter, O. Rhetoric and law in international political organs. *In* Propaganda and communication in world history, ed. by H. D. Lasswell, D. Lerner and H. Speier v2 p446-57

### Philosophy

Berman, H. J. The weightier matters of the law. *In* Solzhenitsyn at Harvard, ed. by R. Berman p99-113

### Religious aspects

*See* Religion and law

### Study and teaching

Dworkin, R. M. Political theory and legal education. *In* Political theory and political education, ed. by M. Richter p177-89

### Brazil

Shirley, R. W. Law in rural Brazil. *In* Brazil, anthropological perspectives, ed. by M. L. Margolis and W. E. Carter p343-59

### Great Britain—History and criticism

Manley, L. G. "Use becomes another nature": custom in sixteenth-century politics and law. *In* Manley, L. G. Convention, 1500-1750 p90-106

### Russia

Sharlet, R. S. De-Stalinization and Soviet constitutionalism. *In* The Soviet Union since Stalin, ed. by S. F. Cohen, A. Rabinowitch, and R. Sharlet p93-110

### United States—History

Scheiber, H. N. Law and political institutions. *In* Encyclopedia of American economic history, ed. by G. Porter v2 p487-508

**Law, Anglo-American.** See Common law

**Law, Industrial.** See Industrial laws and legislation

**Law, International.** See International law

**Law, Judge-made.** See Judge-made law

**Law and communism.** See Law and socialism

## Law and socialism

Sharlet, R. S. De-Stalinization and Soviet constitutionalism. *In* The Soviet Union since Stalin, ed. by S. F. Cohen, A. Rabinowitch, and R. Sharlet p93-110

**Law of nations.** See International law

## Lawrence, David Herbert

### About

Beer, J. B. 'The last Englishman': Lawrence's appreciation of Forster. *In* E. M. Forster: a human exploration, ed. by G. K. Das and J. Beer p245-68

Bell, M. Introduction: modern movements in literature. *In* The Context of English literature, 1900-1930, ed. by M. Bell p 1-93

Harbison, R. Tribe and race. *In* Harbison, R. Deliberate regression p180-205

Lawrence, David H.—*Continued*

### About individual works
*Fantasia of the unconscious*

Trilling, L. D. H. Lawrence: a neglected aspect. *In* Trilling, L. Speaking of literature and society p37-45

*The fox*

Ruderman, J. G. Tracking Lawrence's fox: an account of its composition, evolution, and publication. *In* Virginia. University. Bibliographical Society. Studies in bibliography v33 p206-21

*Love among the haystacks*

Holloway, J. Identity, inversion and density elements in narrative: three tales by Chekhov, James and Lawrence. *In* Holloway, J. Narrative and structure: exploratory essays p53-73

### Criticism and interpretation

Baron, C. E. Forster on Lawrence. *In* E. M. Forster: a human exploration, ed. by G. K. Das and J. Beer p186-95

### Manuscripts

Steele, B. The manuscript of D. H. Lawrence's Saga of Sigmund. *In* Virginia. University. Bibliographical Society. Studies in bibliography v33 p193-205

### Political and social views

Trilling, L. D. H. Lawrence: a neglected aspect. *In* Trilling, L. Speaking of literature and society p37-45

### Social views

*See* Lawrence, David Herbert—Political and social views

Lawrence, Thomas Edward

### About

Pritchett, V. S. T. E. Lawrence: the aesthete in war. *In* Pritchett, V. S. The tale bearers p54-63

Lawrenson, Thomas Edward
The ideal theatre in the eighteenth century: Paris and Venice. *In* Drama and mimesis, ed. by J. Redmond p51-64

Lawson, Lewis A.
Moviegoing in The moviegoer. *In* Walker Percy: art and ethics, ed. by J. Tharpe p26-42

Lea, Kathleen Marguerite
Shakespeare's inner stage. *In* English Renaissance studies, ed. by J. Carey p132-40

Leach, Sir Edmund
Vico and the future of anthropology. *In* Conference on Vico and Contemporary Thought, New York, 1976. Vico and contemporary thought pt2 p149-59

Leadership, Jewish. See Jewish leadership

Leal, Luis
The problem of identifying Chicano literature. *In* The Identification and analysis of Chicano literature, ed. by F. Jiménez p2-6

Lear, Jonathan
Going native. *In* Generations, ed. by S. R. Graubard p175-88

Learning
### Psychological aspects
*See* Learning, Psychology of

Learning, Psychology of
Fodor, J. Fixation of belief and concept acquisition. *In* Language and learning, ed. by M. Piattelli-Palmarini p143-49

Fodor, J. Reply to Putnam. *In* Language and learning, ed. by Piattelli-Palmarini p325-34

Piaget, J. Schemes of action and language learning. *In* Language and learning, ed. by M. Piattelli-Palmarini p164-67

Learning and scholarship
Morowitz, H. J. Splitters and lumpers. *In* Morowitz, H. J. The wine of life, and other essays on societies, energy & living things p200-03

Vico, G. B. On the heroic mind. *In* Conference on Vico and Contemporary Thought, New York, 1976. Vico and contemporary thought pt2 p228-45

*See also* Culture; Education

### Europe

Miller, P. What drove me crazy in Europe. *In* Miller, P. The responsibility of mind in a civilization of machines p98-109

### United States

Bush, D. Literature, the academy, and the public. *In* Generations p165-74

Miller, P. Liberty and conformity. *In* Miller, P. The responsibility of mind in a civilization of machines p186-94

Miller, P. The plight of the lone wolf. *In* Miller, P. The responsibility of mind in a civilization of machines p8-14

Leavis, Frank Raymond
"The Americanness of American literature." *In* Van Wyck Brooks: the critic and his critics, ed. by W. Wasserstrom p157-67

### About

Wright, I. F. R. Leavis, the Scrutiny movement and the crisis. *In* Culture and crisis in Britain in the thirties, ed. by J. Clark and others p37-65

Lebacqz, Karen, and Englehardt, H. Tristram
Suicide and covenant. *In* Suicide: the philosophical issues, ed. by M. P. Battin and D. J. Mayo p84-89

Leboyer, Maurice Levy- See Levy-Leboyer, Maurice

Leclerc, Ivor
Concepts of space. *In* Probability, time, and space in eighteenth-century literature, ed. by P. R. Backscheider p209-16

Lee, A. Robert
The mill on the Floss: 'memory' and the reading experience. *In* Reading the Victorian novel: detail into form, ed. by I. Gregor p72-91

Leech, Clifford
O'Neill in England—from Anna Christie to Long day's journey into night, 1923-1958. *In* Eugene O'Neill, ed. by V. Floyd p68-72

Leenhardt, Jacques
Toward a sociology of reading. *In* The Reader in the text, ed. by S. R. Suleiman and I. Crosman p205-24

Lees, Lynn Hollen
Getting and spending: the family budgets of English industrial workers in 1890. *In* Consciousness and class experience in nineteenth-century Europe, ed. by J. M. Merriman p169-86

Le Fanu, Joseph Sheridan

### About

Lozes, J. Joseph Sheridan Le Fanu. The prince of the invisible. *In* The Irish short story, ed. by P. Rafroidi and T. Brown p91-101

**Lefebvre, Henri**
### About
Kurzweil, E. Henri Lefebvre: a Marxist against structuralism. *In* Kurzweil, E. The age of structuralism p57-85

**Le Fèvre, Jacques, d'Étaples**
### About
Gosselin, E. A. Two views of the evangelical David: Lefèvre d'Etaples and Theodore Beza. *In* The David myth in Western literature, ed. by R. J. Frontain and J. Wojcik p56-67

**Le Fèvre d'Étaples, Jacques.** See Le Févre, Jacques, d'Étaples

**Left (Political science).** See Right and left (Political science)

**Left Book Club, London**
Reid, B. The Left Book Club in the thirties. *In* Culture and crisis in Britain in the thirties, ed. by J. Clark and others p193-207

**The Left Review**
Margolies, D. N. Left Review and Left literary theory. *In* Culture and crisis in Britain in the thirties, ed. by J. Clark and others p67-82

**Legal education.** See Law—Study and teaching

**Legal language.** See Law—Language

**Legal style.** See Law—Language

**Legends.** See Fairy tales; Romances; subdivision Legends under special subjects e.g. Marcellus, Saint, Bp. of Paris—Legends

**Legends, Jewish.** See Golem

**Legislation.** See Law; Judge-made law

**Legislative power.** See Judge-made law

**Le Goff,, Jacques**
Time, work, & culture in the Middle Ages
*Contents*
Academic expenses at Padua in the fifteenth century
Clerical culture and folklore traditions in Merovingian civilization
Dreams in the culture and collective psychology of the medieval West
Ecclesiastical culture and folklore in the Middle Ages: Saint Marcellus of Paris and the dragon
The historian and the ordinary man
How did the medieval university conceive of itself?
Labor, techniques, and craftsmen in the value systems of the early Middle Ages (fifth to tenth centuries)
Labor time in the "crisis" of the fourteenth century: from medieval time to modern time
Licit and illicit trades in the medieval West
The medieval West and the Indian Ocean: an oneiric horizon
Melusina: mother and pioneer
Merchant's time and church's time in the Middle Ages
A note on tripartite society, monarchical ideology, and economic renewal in ninth- to twelfth-century Christendom
Peasants and the rural world in the literature of the early Middle Ages (fifth and sixth centuries)
The several Middle Ages of Jules Michelet
The symbolic ritual of vassalage
Trades and professions as represented in medieval confessors' manuals
The universities and the public authorities in the Middle Ages and the Renaissance

**Le Guin, Ursula K.**
### About individual works
*Earthsea trilogy*
Dooley, P. Magic and art in Ursula Le Guin's Earthsea trilogy. *In* Children's literature v8 p103-10
Rees, D. Earthsea revisited: Ursula K. Le Guin. *In* Rees, D. The marble in the water p78-89

**Legum, Colin**
African outlooks toward the USSR. *In* Communism in Africa, ed. by D. E. Albright p7-34

**Lehnert, Herbert**
Alienation and transformation: Rilke's poem "Der Schwan." *In* Rilke: the alchemy of alienation, ed. by F. Baron, E. S. Dick and W. R. Maurer p95-112

**Lehnert, Wendy**
Representing physical objects in memory. *In* Philosophical perspectives in artificial intelligence, ed. by M. Ringle p81-109

**Lehrman, Irving**
### About
Rosen, G. The rabbi in Miami—a case history. *In* Conference on Southern Jewish History, Richmond, Va. 1976. "Turn to the South" p33-40

**Le Huray, Peter**
The fair musick that all creatures made. *In* The Age of Milton, ed. by C. A. Patrides and R. B. Waddington p241-72

**Leibniz, Gottried Wilhelm, Freiherr von**
### Knowledge, Theory of
Hacking, I. Proof and eternal truths: Descares and Leibniz. *In* Descartes, ed. by S. Gaukroger p169-80
### Logic
Hacking, I. Proof and eternal truths: Descartes and Leibniz. *In* Descartes, ed. by S. Gaukroger p169-80

**Leigh, James**
Another Beckett: an analysis of Residua. *In* The Analysis of literary texts, ed. by R. D. Pope p314-30

**Leiren, Terje I.**
Halvdan Koht's America. *In* Makers of an American immigrant legacy, ed. by O. S. Lovoll p173-85

**Leiris, Michel**
### About
Brée, G. Michael Leiris: mazemaker. *In* Autobiography: essays theoretical and critical, ed. by J. Olney p194-206

**Leiss, William**
Marx and Macpherson: needs, utilities, and self-development. *In* Powers, possessions and freedom, ed. by A. Kontos p119-38

**Leitch, R. G.**
Nortje: poet at work. *In* African literature today no. 10: Retrospect & prospect, ed. by E. D. Jones p224-32

**Leitenberg, Milton, and Ball, Nicole**
The military expenditures of less developed nations as a proportion of their state budgets: a research note. *In* Problems of contemporary militarism, ed. by A. Eide and M. Thee p286-96

**Leland, Charles**
The Oxford Ibsen, volume VIII, translated and edited by James Walter McFarlane. *In* Drama and mimesis, ed by J. Redmond p207-25

**Lemius, Joseph**

**About**

Daly, G. The integralist response (1): prelude to the Roman condemnation of Modernism. *In* Daly, G. Transcendence and immanence p165-89

**Le Moigne, Guy**

Sean O'Faolain's short stories and tales. *In* The Irish short story, ed. by P. Rafroidi and T. Brown p205-26

**Lenclos, Anne, called Ninon de**

**About**

Waddicor, M. Voltaire and Ninon de Lenclos. *In* Woman and society in eighteenth-century France, ed. by E. Jacobs and others p197-206

**Lenclos, Ninon de.** See Lenclos, Anne, called Ninon de

**Leningrad in literature**

Festa-McCormick, D. Bely's Saint Petersburg: a city conjured by a visionary symbolist. *In* Festa-McCormick, D. The city as catalyst p108-23

**Lenneberg, Eric Heinz**

Of language knowledge, apes, and brains. *In* Speaking of apes, ed. by T. A. Sebeok and J. Umiker-Sebeok p115-40

A word between us. *In* Speaking of apes, ed. by T. A. Sebeok and J. Umiker-Sebeok p71-83

**Lenny (Motion picture)**

Kauffmann, S. Lenny. *In* Kauffmann, S. Before my eyes p91-94

**Lensing, George S.**

Wallace Stevens in England. *In* Wallace Stevens, ed. by F. Doggett and R. Buttel p130-48

**Lentricchia, Frank**

After the New Criticism

*Contents*

Afterword
E. D. Hirsch: the hermeneutics of innocence
Harold Bloom: the spirit of revenge
History or the abyss: poststructuralism
Murray Krieger's last romanticism
Paul de Man: the rhetoric of authority
The place of Northrop Frye's "Anatomy of criticism"
Uncovering history and the reader: structuralism
Versions of existentialism
Versions of phenomenology

**Lentulus, Publius**

**About**

Lutz, C. E. The letter of Lentulus describing Christ. *In* Lutz, C. E. The oldest library motto, and other library essays p49-56

**Lenz, Siegfried**

**About individual works**

*The German lesson*

Bosmajian, H. Siegfried Lenz's The German lesson: metaphors of evil on a narrow ground. *In* Bosmajian, H. Metaphors of evil p57-81

**Leo Hebraeus**

**About individual works**

*The philosophy of love*

Perry, T. A. The Dialoghi d'amore as literature: the uses of dialogue. *In* Perry, T. A. Erotic spirituality p25-34

Perry, T. A. Introduction. *In* Perry, T. A. Erotic spirituality p 1-9

Perry, T. A. Leone Ebreo's Dialoghi d'amore: the argument. *In* Perry, T. A. Erotic spirituality p10-24

Perry, T. A. Return and reincarnation in Scève's Délie. *In* Perry, T. A. Erotic spirituality p44-52

**Influence**

Perry, T. A. Introduction. *In* Perry, T. A. Erotic spirituality p 1-9

**Influence—Donne**

Perry, T. A. John Donne's philosophy of love in "The ecstasy." *In* Perry, T. A. Erotic spirituality p89-98

**Influence—Scève**

Perry, T. A. Return and reincarnation in Scève's Délie. *In* Perry, T. A. Erotic spirituality p44-52

**Leo, Leonardo**

**About**

Dent, E. J. Leonardo Leo. *In* Dent, E. J. Selected essays p37-57

**Leon Hebreo.** See Leo Hebraeus

**Léonard, Jacques**

Women, religion, and medicine. *In* Medicine and society in France, ed. by R. Forster and O. Ranum p24-47

**Leonard, Robert Z.**

**About individual works**

*Susan Lenox: her fall and rise*

Miller, G. The new woman gets the old treatment. *In* Miller, G. Screening the novel p19-45

**Leonardo da Vinci**

**About individual works**

*Mona Lisa*

Conley, T. Framing Malraux. *In* André Malraux p125-40

*Virgin of the rocks*

Robertson, D. W. In foraminibus petrae: a note on Leonardo's "Virgin of the rocks." *In* Robertson, D. W. Essays in medieval culture p305-07

**Leone Ebreo.** See Leo Hebraeus

**Leopardi, Giacomo, conte**

**About**

Carne-Ross, D. S. Leopardi: the poet in a time of need. *In* Carne-Ross, D. S. Instaurations p167-92

**About individual works**

*Il passero solitario*

Carne-Ross, D. S. Leopardi: the poet in a time of need. *In* Carne-Ross, D. S. Instaurations p167-92

**Le petit théâtre de Jean Renior (Motion picture)**

Kauffmann, S. Le petit théâtre de Jean Renoir. *In* Kauffmann, S. Before my eyes p3-5

**Lerner, Daniel**

The revolutionary elites and world symbolism. *In* Propaganda and communication in world history, ed. by H. D. Lasswell, D. Lerner and H. Speier v2 p371-94

See also Lasswell, H. D. jt. auth.

**Lerner, Gerda**

The lady and the mill girl: changes in the status of women in the age of Jackson, 1800-1840. *In* A Heritage of her own, ed. by N. F. Cott and E. H. Pleck p182-96

**Le Roy, Edouard Louis Emmanuel Julien**

### About

Daly, G. Lucien Laberthonnière's critical mysticism.' *In* Daly, G. Transcendence and immanence p91-116

**Leslie, Roy F.**

The editing of Old English poetic texts: questions of style. *In* Old English poetry, ed. by D. G. Calder p111-25

**Less developed countries.** See Underdeveloped areas

**Lessing, Doris May**

### About individual works
*Children of violence*

Fishburn, K. The nightmare repetition: the mother-daughter conflict in Doris Lessing's Children of violence. *In* The Lost tradition: mothers and daughters in literature, ed. by C. N. Davidson and E. M. Broner p207-16

*The four-gated city*

Christ, C. P. From motherhood to prophecy: Doris Lessing. *In* Christ, C. P. Diving deep and surfacing p55-73

**Lessing, Gotthold Ephraim**

### About

Critchfield, R. The search for an enlightened sovereign in Lessing's drama. *In* Studies in eighteenth-century culture v9 p251-67

Saine, T. P. Gotthold Ephraim Lessing's views on theological issues as reflected in his early book reviews. *In* Studies in eighteenth-century culture v9 p269-84

### About individual works
*Hamburg dramaturgy*

Bennett, B. Lessing and the problem of drama. *In* Bennett, B. Modern drama and German classicism p57-73

*Nathan the Wise*

Bennett, B. Nathan der Weise: breakthrough in practice. *In* Bennett, B. Modern drama and German classicism p74-96

**L'estoire de Griseldis.** See Griselda

**Let joy reign supreme (Motion picture)**

Kauffmann, S. Let joy reign supreme. *In* Kauffman, S. Before my eyes p234-37

**L'etoile de mer (Motion picture)**

Thiher, A. The surrealist film: Man Ray and the limits of metaphor. *In* Thiher, A. The cinematic muse p38-48

**Let's do it again (Motion picture)**

Kael, P. Horseplay. *In* Kael, P. When the lights go down p62-68

**Letter-writing**

Ferguson, F. C. The unfamiliarity of familiar letters. *In* The State of the language, ed. by L. Michaels and C. Ricks p78-88

**Letters as a theme in literature.** See Letters´ in literature

**Letters in literature**

McKinnell, J. Letters as a type of the formal level in Troilus and Criseyde. *In* Essays on Troilus and Criseyde, ed. by M. Salu p73-89

**Letwin, Shirley Robin**

Trollope on generations without gaps. *In* Generations, ed. by S. R. Graubard p53-70

**Le Veness, Frank Paul**

The political use and abuse of television in America and abroad. *In* Screen and society, ed. by F. J. Coppa p59-80

**Lever, Charles James**

### About

Jeffares, A. N. Yeats and the wrong Lever. *In* Yeats, Sligo and Ireland, ed. by A. N. Jeffares p98-111

**Leverenz, David**

The woman in Hamlet: an interpersonal view. *In* Representing Shakespeare, ed. by M. M. Schwartz and C. Kahn p110-28

**Levertov, Denise**

### About

Howard, R Denise Levertov: "I don't want to escape, only to see the enactment of rites." *In* Howard, R. Alone with America p342-55

Wagner, L. W. Levertov and Rich: the later poems. *In* Wagner, L. W. American modern p221-30

### About individual works
*O taste and see*

Wagner, L. W. The sound of direction. *In* Wagner, L. W. American modern p213-20

**Lévi-Strauss, Claude**

### About

Bernstein, G. M. The mediated vision: Eliade, Lévi-Strauss, and romantic mythopoesis. *In* The Binding of Proteus, ed. by M. W. McCune, T. Orbison, and P. M. Withim p158-72

Cook, A. S. The large phases of myth. *In* Cook, A. S. Myth & language p37-66

Cook, A. S. Lévi-Strauss, myth, and the Neolithic revolution. *In* Cook, A. S. Myth & language p13-36

Harbison, R. Tribe and race. *In* Harbison, R. Deliberate regression p180-205

Kurzweil, E. Claude Lévi-Strauss: the father of structuralism. *In* Kurzweil, E. The age of structuralism p13-34

Sperber, D. Claude Lévi-Strauss. *In* Structuralism and since, ed. by J. Sturrock p19-51

### About individual works
*Tristes tropiques*

O'Donnell, T. J. "Une exploration des déserts de ma mémoire": pastoral aspects of Lévi-Strauss's Tristes tropiques. *In* Survivals of pastoral, ed. by R. F. Hardin p87-102

**Levin, Hanoch.** See Levin, Hanokh

**Levin, Hanokh**

### About

Abramson, G. Modernism: Hanoch Levin. *In* Abramson, G. Modern Hebrew drama p171-80

**Levin, Harry Tuckman**

The wages of satire. *In* Literature and society, ed. by E. W. Said p 1-14

**Levin, Meyer**

### About individual works
*Frankie and Johnnie, a love story*

Trilling, L. The promise of realism. *In* Trilling, L. Speaking of literature and society p27-33

**Levinas, Emmanuel**

The contemporary criticism of the idea of value and the prospects for humanism. *In* Value and values in evolution, ed. by E. A. Maziarz p179-87

**Levine, David S.**

"My client has discussed your proposal to fill the drainage ditch with his partners": legal language. *In* The State of the language, ed. by L. Michaels and C. Ricks p400-09

**Levine, Isaac Don**

**About individual works**

*The mind of an assassin*

Trilling, L. The assassination of Leon Trotsky. *In* Trilling, L. Speaking of literature and society p367-73

**Levine, Philip, 1928-**

**About**

Molesworth, C. "The burned essential oil": the gestures of Philip Levine. *In* Molesworth, C. The fierce embrace p150-62

**Levine, Robert Alan**

Adulthood among the Gusii of Kenya. *In* Themes of work and love in adulthood, ed. by N. J. Smelser and E. H. Erikson p77-104

**Levinson, Daniel J.**

Toward a conception of the adult life course. *In* Themes of work and love in adulthood, ed. by N. J. Smelser and E. H. Erikson p265-90

**Levy, Darlene Gay, and Applewhite, Harriet Verdier Branson**

Women of the popular classes in revolutionary Paris, 1789-1795. *In* Women, war, and revolution, ed. by C. R. Berkin and C. M. Lovett p9-35

**Levy, Donald**

Perversion and the unnatural as moral categories. *In* The Philosophy of sex, ed. by A. Soble p158-68

**Lévy-Bruhl, Lucien**

**About individual works**

*Les fonctions mentales dans les sociétés inférieures*

Durkheim, E. Review of Lucien Levy-Bruhl, Les fonctions mentales dans les sociétés inférieures. *In* Durkheim, E. Emile Durkheim on institutional analysis p145-49

**Lévy-Leboyer, Maurice**

The large corporation in modern France. *In* Managerial hierarchies, ed. by A. D. Chandler and H. Daems p117-60

**Lewandowska, M. L.**

The words of their roaring: Roethke's use of the Psalms of David. *In* The David myth in Western literature, ed. by R. J. Frontain and J. Wojcik p156-67

**Lewes, George Henry**

**About**

Ashton, R. D. Lewes: one of Carlyle's 'young men' (1835-9). *In* Ashton, R. D. The German idea p105-11

**About individual works**

*The biographical history of philosophy from its origin in Greece down to the present day*

Ashton, R. D. Lewes and German philosophy. *In* Ashton, R. D. The German idea p126-31

*Hegel's aesthetics*

Ashton, R. D. Lewes and German aesthetics (1840-5) *In* Ashton, R. D. The German idea p112-25

*The life and works of Goethe*

Ashton, R. D. Lewes and Goethe (1843-55) *In* Ashton, R. D. The German idea p131-46

**Lewis, Barbara Caroline**

Ethnicity and occupational specialization in the Ivory Coast: the Transporters' Association. *In* Values, identities, and national integration, ed. by J. N. Paden p75-87

**Lewis, Ceri W.**

The content of poetry and the crisis in the bardic tradition. *In* A Guide to Welsh literature, ed. by A. O. H. Jarman and G. R. Hughes v2 p88-110

The court poets: their function, status and craft. *In* A Guide to Welsh literature, ed. by A. O. H. Jarman and G. R. Hughes v 1 p123-56

Einion Offeiriad and the bardic grammar. *In* A Guide to Welsh literature, ed. by A. O. H. Jarman and G. R. Hughes v2 p58-86

The historical background of early Welsh verse. *In* A Guide to Welsh literature, ed. by A. O. H. Jarman and G. R. Hughes v 1 p11-50

**Lewis, Jane**

In search of a real equality: women between the Wars. *In* Class, culture and social change, ed. by F. Gloversmith p208-39

**Lewis, Peirce Fee**

Axioms for reading the landscape: some guides to the American scene. *In* The Interpretation of ordinary landscapes, ed. by D. W. Meinig p11-32

**Lewis, Sinclair**

**About**

Miller, P. The incorruptible Sinclair Lewis. *In* Miller, P. The responsibility of mind in a civilization of machines p110-21

Trilling, L. The unhappy story of Sinclair Lewis. *In* Trilling, L. Speaking of literature and society p141-45

**Lewis Glyn Cothi**

**About**

Jones, E D. Lewis Glyn Cothi. *In* A Guide to Welsh literature, ed. by A. O. H. Jarman and G. R. Hughes v2 p243-61

**Lewisohn, Ludwig**

**About**

Trilling, L. Flawed instruments. *In* Trilling, L. Speaking of literature and society p21-26

**About individual works**

*Expression in America*

Hirsch, J. Ludwig Lewisohn: can he still help us? A reconsideration of expression in America. *In* Seasoned authors for a new season: the search for standards in popular writing, ed. by L. Filler p98-116

**Lewy, Guenter**

Millenarianism as a revolutionary force. *In* Propaganda and communication in world history, ed. by H. D. Lasswell, D. Lerner and H. Speier v2 p168-209

**Leys, Ruth**

Background to the reflex controversy: William Alison and the doctrine of sympathy before Hall. *In* Studies in history of biology, v4. p 1-66

**Leyhausen, Paul**

Aggression, fear and attachment: complexities and interdependencies. *In* Human ethology, ed. by M. von Cranach [and others] p253-64

**L'Herbier, Marcel**

**About individual works**

*Feu Mathias Pascal*

Thiher, A. The impressionist avant-garde. *In* Thiher, A. The cinematic muse p16-23

**Liberal education.** See Education, Humanistic

**Liberal Party (Great Britain)**

Reid, F. The disintegration of Liberalism, 1895-1931. *In* The Context of English literature, 1900-1930, ed. by M. Bell p94-125

**Liberalism**

**Great Britain**

O'Day, A. Irish home rule and liberalism. *In* The Edwardian age: conflict and stability, 1900-1914, ed. by A. O'Day p113-32

**Southern States**

King, R. H. The new Southern liberalism: V. O. Key, C. Vann Woodward, Robert Penn Warren. *In* King, R. H. A Southern Renaissance p242-86

**Liberalism (Religion)** See Haskalah

**Liberation Front of Mozambique**

Ottaway, M. The theory and practice of Marxism-Leninism in Mozambique and Ethiopia. *In* Communism in Africa, ed. by D. E. Albright p118-44

**Liberia**

**Politics and government**

Sawyer, A. C. Social stratification and national orientations: students and nonstudents in Liberia. *In* Values, identities, and national integration, ed. by J. N. Paden p285-303

Sawyer, A. C. Social stratification, social change, and political socialization: students and nonstudents in Liberia. *In* Values, identities, and national integration, ed. by J. N. Paden p305-20

**Social conditions**

Sawyer, A. C. Social stratification and national orientations: students and nonstudents in Liberia. *In* Values, identities, and national integration, ed. by J. N. Paden p285-303

Sawyer, A. C. Social stratification, social change, and political socialization: students and nonstudents in Liberia. *In* Values, identities, and national integration, ed. by J. N. Paden p305-20

**Liberman, Alvin M.**

An ethological approach to language through the study of speech perception. *In* Human ethology, ed. by M. von Cranach [and others] p682-704

**Libertarianism.** See Liberty

**Liberty**

Baier, K. E. Freedom, obligation, and responsibility. *In* Humanist ethics, ed. by M. B. Storer, p75-97

Hook, S. Capitalism, socialism, and freedom. *In* Hook, S. Philosophy and public policy p111-16

Hook, S. The social democratic prospect. *In* Hook, S. Philosophy and public policy p98-110

Killian, L. M. The respect revolution: freedom and equality. *In* Propaganda and communication in world history, ed. by H. D. Lasswell, D. Lerner and H. Speier v3 p93-147

Sakharov, A. D. Thoughts on progress, peaceul coexistence and intellectual freedom. *In* Propaganda and communication in world history, ed. by H. D. Lasswell, D. Lerner and H. Speier v2 p471-506

Wilson, C. Man is born free, and he is everywhere in chains. *In* Lying truths, ed. by R. Duncan and M. Weston-Smith p3-7

*See also* Anarchism and anarchists; Civil rights; Equality; Human rights

**Liberty of speech**

**United States**

Hook, S. Are there limits to freedom of expression? *In* Hook, S. Philosophy and public policy p124-29

**Liberty of the press**

**Portugal**

Seaton, J. and Pimlott, B. The role of the media in the Portuguese revolution. *In* Newspapers and democracy, ed. by A. Smith p174-99

**Spain**

Soler, J. A. M. The paradoxes of press freedom: the Spanish case. *In* Newspapers and democracy, ed. by A. Smith p153-73

**United States—History**

Buel, R. Freedom of the press in Revolutionary America: the evolution of libertarianism, 1760-1820. *In* The Press & the American Revolution, ed. by B. Bailyn and J. B. Hench p59-97

Wiggins, J. R. Afterword: the legacy of the Press in the American Revolution. *In* The Press & the American Revolution, ed. by B. Bailyn and J. B. Hench p365-72

**Liberty of the will.** See Free will and determinism

**Libraries**

Morowitz, H. J. Bibliophilia. *In* Morowitz, H. J. The wine of life, and other essays on societies, energy & living things p204-07

**Special collections**

Munby, A. N. L. The acquisition of manuscripts by institutional libraries. *In* The Bibliographical Society of America, 1904-79 p384-98

**Licht, Robert A.**

On the three parties in America. *In* Political parties in the eighties, ed. by R. A. Goldwin p66-96

**Licklider, Joseph Carl Robnett**

Computers and government. *In* The Computer age: a twenty-year review, ed. by M. L. Dertouzos and J. Moses p87-126

**Lider, Julian**

The critique of militarism in Soviet studies. *In* Problems of contemporary militarism, ed. by A. Eide and M. Thee p173-91

**Lieven, Dar'ia Khristoforovna (Benckendorff) Kniaginia**

**About**

Struve, G. Towards a biography of Prince Peter Kozlovsky: Kozlovsky's letter to Countess Lieven. *In* California Slavic studies v11 p 1-24

**Life**

Morowitz, H. J. All the world's a stage. *In* Morowitz, H. J. The wine of life, and other essays on societies, energy & living things p7-10

Singer, P. Animals and the value of life. *In* Matters of life and death, ed. by T. Regan p218-59

**Lignite**

**Texas**

Alexander, N. The work of Edwin Theodore Dumble on the East Texas lignite deposits (1888-1892). *In* New Hampshire Bicentennial Conference on the History of Geology, University of New Hampshire, 1976. Two hundred years of geology in America p213-22

**Lilienfeld, Jane**

Reentering paradise: Cather, Colette, Woolf and their mothers. *In* The Lost tradition: mothers and daughters in literature, ed. by C. N. Davidson and E. M. Broner p160-75

**Lillo, George**

### About individual works

*Fatal curiosity*

Brown, R. E. Rival socio-economic theories in two plays by George Lillo. *In* Tennessee Studies in literature v24 p94-110

*The London merchant; or, The history of George Barnwell*

Brown, R. E. Rival socio-economic theories in two plays by George Lillo. *In* Tennessee Studies in literature v24 p94-110

**Limber, John**

Language in child and chimp? *In* Speaking of apes, ed. by T. A. Sebeok and J. Umiker-Sebeok p197-220

**Limoges**

### History

Merriman, J. M. Incident at the statue of the Virgin Mary: the conflict of old and new in nineteenth-century Limoges. *In* Consciousness and class experience in nineteenth-century Europe, ed. by J. M. Merriman p129-48

**Limon, Jerzy**

Pictorial evidence for a possible replica of the London Fortune Theatre in Gdansk. *In* Shakespeare survey 32 p189-99

**Lincoln, Abraham, President U.S.**

### About

Pole, J. R. Abraham Lincoln and the American commitment. *In* Pole, J. R. Paths to the American past p146-69

Pole, J. R. Abraham Lincoln and the working classes of Britain. *In* Pole, J. R. Paths to the American past p111-45

**Lindsay, Sir David**

### About individual works

*Ane satyre of the thrie estaitis*

Kratzmann, G. Ane satyre of the thrie estaitis and English drama. *In* Kratzmann, G. Anglo-Scottish literary relations, 1430-1550 p195-226

**Lindstrom, Diane**

Domestic trade and regional specialization. *In* Encyclopedia of American economic history, ed. by G. Porter v 1 p264-80

**Linguistic analysis (Literature)**

Bolinger, D. L. Fire in a wooden stove: on being aware in language. *In* The State of the language, ed. by L. Michaels and C. Ricks p379-88

**Linguistic anthropology.** See Anthropological linguistics

**Linguistic change**

Percival, W. K. Hermann Paul's view of the nature of language. *In* Psychology of language and thought, ed. by R. W. Rieber p187-96

Quirk, R. Sound barriers and Gangbangsprache. *In* The State of the language, ed. by L. Michaels and C. Ricks p3-14

**Linguistic connotation.** See Connotation (Linguistics)

**Linguistics**

Hill, J. H. Apes and language. *In* Speaking of apes, ed. by T. A. Sebeok and J. Umiker-Sebeok p331-51

McNeill, D. Sentence structure in chimpanzee communication. *In* Speaking of apes, ed. by T. A. Sebeok and J. Umiker-Sebeok p145-60

*See also* Connotation (Linguistics); Paralinguistics; Psycholinguistics

### Data processing

Lehnert, W. Representing physical objects in memory. *In* Philosophical perspectives in artificial intelligence, ed. by M. Ringle p81-109

Schank, R. C. Natural language, philosophy, and artificial intelligence. *In* Philosophical perspectives in artificial intelligence, ed. by M. Ringle p196-224

**Lintner, Stephen F. and Stapleton, Darwin H.**

Geological theory and practice in the career of Benjamin Henry Latrobe. *In* New Hampshire Bicentennial Conference on the History of Geology, University of New Hampshire, 1976. Two hundred years of geology in America p107-19

**Lion, Antoine**

Theology and sociology: what point is there in keeping the distinction? *In* Sociology and theology: alliance and conflict, ed. by D. Martin, J. O. Mills [and] W. S. F. Pickering p163-82

**Lions in art**

Ross, D. H. Cement lions and cloth elephants: popular arts of the Fante Asafo. *In* 5000 years of culture, ed. by F. E. H. Schroeder p290-317

**Lippincott, Benjamin Evans**

### About individual works

*Victorian critics of democracy*

Trilling, L. The Victorians and democracy. *In* Trilling, L. Speaking of literature and society p135-40

**Lipset, Seymour Martin**

Predicting the future of post-industrial society: can we do it? *In* The Third century, ed. by S. M. Lipset p 1-35

*See also* Ladd, E. C. jt. auth.

**Lipsius, Justus**

### About individual works

*De Cruce libri tres*

Pickering, F. P. Justus Lipsius' De Cruce libri tres, or the historian's dilemma. *In* Pickering, F. P. Essays on medieval German literature and iconography p59-74

**Lipski, John M.**

Split signifiers in La pasión de Urbino. *In* The Analysis of literary texts, ed. by R. D. Pope p165-74

**Lisztomania (Motion picture)**

Kael, P. Becoming an American. *In* Kael, P. When the lights go down p79-84

**Literary criticism.** See Criticism

**Literary form**

Beaujour, M. Genus universum. *In* Glyph 7 p15-31

Derrida, J. The law of genre. *In* Glyph 7 p202-29

Kambouchner, D. The theory of accidents. *In* Glyph 7 p149-75

Lacoue-Labarthe, P. and Nancy, J. L. Genre. *In* Glyph 7 p 1-14

Sloane, T. O. Rhetoric, 'logic' and poetry: the formal cause. *In* The Age of Milton, ed. by C. A. Patrides and R. B. Waddington p307-37

**Literary influence.** See Influence (Literary, artistic, etc.)

**Literary research**

Bühler, C. F. Literary research and bibliographical training. *In* The Bibliographical Society of America, 1904-79 p363-71

Literary style. See Style, Literary

Literary tradition. See Influence (Literary, artistic, etc.)

# Literature

See also Art and literature; Bilingualism and literature; Christian literature, Early; Creation (Literary, artistic, etc.); Criticism; Imitation (in literature); Nationalism and literature; Poetry; Romances; Satire; Semiotics and literature; also Individualism in literature; Mothers and daughters in literature; Naturalism in literature; Paris in literature and similar headings; Poetry; also national literatures, e.g. American literature, English literature, French literature

### Aesthetics
See Style, Literary

### Evaluation
See Criticism

### Forms
See Literary form

### History and criticism
Rabinowitz, P. J. "What's Hecuba to us?" The audience's experience of literary borrowing. In The Reader in the text, ed. by S. R. Suleiman and I. Crosman p241-63

Robinson, F. M. Afterword. In Robinson, F. M. The comedy of language p175-77

Seidel, M. A. Inheritance and narrative mode. In Seidel, M. A. Satiric inheritance, Rabelais to Sterne p26-59

### History and criticism—Theory, etc.
Kambouchner, D. The theory of accidents. In Glyph 7 p149-75

Robertson, D. W. The allegorist and the aesthetician. In Robertson, D. W. Essays in medieval culture p85-101

Robertson, D. W. Some observations on method in literary studies. In Robertson, D. W. Essays in medieval culture p73-84

### Philosophy
Cook, A. S. Language and myth. In Cook, A. S. Myth & language p260-83

Krieger, M. Literature as illusion, as metaphor, as vision. In Krieger, M. Poetic presence and illusion p188-96

Trilling, L. Literature and power. In Trilling, L. Speaking of literature and society p146-55

See also Phenomenology and literature

### Political aspects
See Politics and literature

### Research
See Literary research

### Study and teaching
Carne-Ross, D. S. Center of resistance. In Carne-Ross, D. S. Instaurations p 1-28

Robertson, D. W. Some observations on method in literary studies. In Robertson, D. W. Essays in medieval culture p73-84

### Style
See Style, Literary

Literature, Comic. See Comedy; Satire

# Literature, Comparative

## Chinese and European
Průšek, J. A confrontation of traditional Oriental literature with modern European literature in the context of the Chinese literary revolution. In Průšek, J. The lyrical and the epic p74-85

## Classical and modern
Mueller, M. Oedipus Rex and modern analytical drama: Ibsen's Ghosts. In Mueller, M. Children of Oedipus, and other essays on the imitation of Greek tragedy, 1550-1800 p146-52

## English and German
Ashton, R. D. Carlyle, the Germanist of the Edinburgh Review (1827) In Ashton, R. D. The German idea p67-76

Ashton, R. D. Introduction. In Ashton, R. D. The German idea p 1-26

Ashton, R. D. The pros and cons of the German genius. In Ashton, R. D. The German idea p173-77

## English and Scottish
Kratzmann, G. Influences and perspectives. In Kratzmann, G. Anglo-Scottish literary relations, 1430-1550 p 1-32

Kratzmann, G. The two traditions. In Kratzmann, G. Anglo-Scottish literary relations, 1430-1550 p227-61

## European and Chinese
Průšek, J. A confrontation of traditional Oriental literature with modern European literature in the context of the Chinese literary revolution. In Průšek, J. The lyrical and the epic p74-85

## German and English
Ashton, R. D. Carlyle, the Germanist of the Edinburgh Review (1827) In Ashton, R. D. The German idea p67-76

Ashton, R. D. Introduction. In Ashton, R. D. The German idea p 1-26

Ashton, R. D. The pros and cons of the German genius. In Ashton, R. D. The German idea p173-77

## Greek and Latin
Bain, D. Plautus uortit barbare: Plautus, Bacchides 526-61 and Menander, Dis exapaton 102-12. In Creative imitation and Latin literature, ed. by D. West and T. Woodman p17-34

## Latin and Greek
Bain, D. Plautus uortit barbare: Plautus, Bacchides 526-61 and Menander, Dis exapaton 102-12. In Creative imitation and Latin literature, ed. by D. West and T. Woodman p17-34

## Modern and classical
Mueller, M. Oedipus Rex and modern analytical drama: Ibsen's Ghosts. In Mueller, M. Children of Oedipus, and other essays on the imitation of Greek tragedy, 1550-1800 p146-52

## Scottish and English
Kratzmann, G. Influences and perspectives. In Kratzmann, G. Anglo-Scottish literary relations, 1430-1550 p 1-32

Kratzmann, G. The two traditions. In Kratzmann, G. Anglo-Scottish literary relations, 1430-1550 p227-61

## Themes, motives
Egri, P. The use of the short story in O'Neill's and Chekhov's one-act plays: a Hungarian view of O'Neill. In Eugene O'Neill, ed. by V. Floyd p115-44

Maddox, D. L. Early secular courtly drama in France: L'estoire de Griseldis. In The Expansion and transformations of courtly literature, ed. by N. B. Smith and J. T. Snow p157-70

## Literature, Medieval

*See also* Romances

### History and criticism

Calin, W. C. Defense and illustration of fin' amor: some polemical comments on the Robertsonian approach. *In* The Expansion and transformations of courtly literature, ed. by N. B. Smith and J. T. Snow p32-48

Le Goff, J. Dreams in the culture and collective psychology of the medieval West. *In* Le Goff, J. Time, work, & culture in the Middle Ages p201-04

Le Goff, J. Melusina: mother and pioneer. *In* Le Goff, J. Time, work, & culture in the Middle Ages p205-22

Le Goff, J. Peasants and the rural world in the literature of the early Middle Ages (fifth and sixth centuries). *In* Le Goff, J. Time, work, & culture in the Middle Ages p87-97

Lutz, C. E. Some medieval impressions of the ostrich. *In* Lutz, C. E. The oldest library motto, and other library essays p101-06

Melczer, W. The war of the carrots and the onions or concentration versus dispersion: the methodology of interdisciplinary studies applied to the European courts. *In* The Expansion and transformations of courtly literature, ed. by N. B. Smith and J. T. Snow p207-26

Pickering, F. P. Notes on fate and fortune. *In* Pickering, F. P. Essays on medieval German literature and iconography p95-109

Reiss, E. Chaucer's deerne love and the medieval view of secrecy in love. *In* Chaucerian problems and perspectives, ed. by E. Vasta and Z. P. Thundy p164-79

Renoir, A. The inept lover and the reluctant mistress: remarks on sexual inefficiency in medieval literature. *In* Chaucerian problems and perspectives, ed. by E. Vasta and Z. P. Thundy p180-206

Robertson, D. W. Historical criticism. *In* Robertson, D. W. Essays in medieval culture p3-20

Smith, N. B. and Snow, J. T. Courtly love and courtly literature. *In* The Expansion and transformations of courtly literature, ed. by N. B. Smith and J. T. Snow p3-14

### History and criticism—Theory, etc,

Robertson, D. W. Some medieval literary terminology, with special reference to Chrétien de Troyes. *In* Robertson, D. W. Essays in medieval culture p51-72

## Literature, Modern

### History and criticism

Farrell, J. P. Revolution as tragedy: being at the center. *In* Farrell, J. Revolution as tragedy p17-68

### 19th century—History and criticism

McGhee, R. D. Introduction. *In* McGhee, R. D. Marriage, duty & desire in Victorian poetry and drama p 1-28

*See also* Decadence (Literary movement)

### 20th century—History and criticism

Robinson, F. M. The comedy of language. *In* Robinson, F. M. The comedy of language p 1-24

Wilson, R. N. Reflections on the sociology of literature. *In* Wilson, R. N. The writer as social seer p145-53

**Literature, Pastoral.** See Pastoral literature

**Literature and art.** See Art and literature

**Literature and Christianity.** See Christianity and literature

**Literature and communism.** See Communism and literature

**Literature and folk-lore.** See Folk-lore in literature

**Literature and music.** See Music and literature

**Literature and painting.** See Art and literature

**Literature and politics.** See Politics and literature

**Literature and psychoanalysis.** See Psychoanalysis and literature

### Literature and revolutions

Farrell, J. P. Revolution as tragedy: being at the center. *In* Farrell, J. Revolution as tragedy

### Literature and science

Collis, J. S. Forward to nature. *In* Royal Society of Literature of the United Kingdom, London. Essays by divers hands: innovation in contemporary literature, new ser. v40 p34-51

### Literature and society

Izevbaye, D. Issues in the reassessment of the African novel. *In* African literature today no. 10: Retrospect & prospect, ed. by E. D. Jones p7-31

Trilling, L. Artists and the "societal function." *In* Trilling, L. Speaking of literature and society p186-91

Trilling, L. Literature and power. *In* Trilling, L. Speaking of literature and society p146-55

Wilson, R. N. Literature, society and personality. *In* Wilson, R. N. The writer as social seer p3-16

Wilson, R. N. Reflections on the sociology of literature. *In* Wilson, R. N. The writer as social seer p145-53

#### Turkey

Halman, T. S. Propaganda functions of poetry. *In* Propaganda and communication in world history, ed. by H. D. Lasswell, D. Lerner and H. Speier v 1 p493-535

**Literature and sociology.** See Literature and society

### Literature and state

*See also* Authors and patrons

#### France—History

. Ranum, O. Patronage and history from Richelieu to Colbert. *In* Ranum, O. Artisans of glory p148-68

**Literature teachers.** See Authors as teachers

**Little, Malcolm.** See Malcolm X

**Liturgical English.** See Liturgical language—English

### Liturgical language

#### English

Doody, M. A. "How shall we sing the Lord's song upon an alien soil?": The new Episcopalian liturgy. *In* The State of the language, ed. by L. Michaels and C. Ricks p108-24

### Litz, Arthur Walton

Literary criticism. *In* Harvard Guide to contemporary American writing, ed. by D. Hoffman p51-83

Particles of order: the unpublished Adagia. *In* Wallace Stevens, ed. by F. Doggett and R. Buttel p57-77

**Lively, Penelope**

### About

Rees, D. Time present and time past: Penelope Lively. *In* Rees, D. The marble in the water p185-98

Townsend, J. R. Penelope Lively. *In* Townsend, J. R. A sounding of storytellers p125-38

**Livesay, Harold C.**

Lilliputians in Brobdingnag: small business in late-nineteenth-century America. *In* Small business in American life, ed. by S. W. Bruchey p338-51

**Living, Cost of.** See Cost and standard of living

**Living, Standard of.** See Cost and standard of living

**Livingston, Luther Samuel**

### About

Winship, G. P. Luther S. Livingston: a biographical sketch. *In* The Bibliographical Society of America, 1904-79 p9-20

**Lloyd, D. Myrddin**

Dafydd Nanmor. *In* A Guide to Welsh literature, ed. by A. O. H. Jarman and G. R. Hughes v2 p189-200

The later Gogynfeirdd. *In* A Guide to Welsh literature, ed. by A. O. H. Jarman and G. R. Hughes v2 p36-57

The poets of the princes. *In* A Guide to Welsh literature, ed. by A. O. H. Jarman and G. R. Hughes v 1 p157-88

**Llywarch Hen**

### About

Jarman, A. O. H. Saga poetry—the cycle of Llywarch Hen. *In* A Guide to Welsh literature, ed. by A. O. H. Jarman and G. R. Hughes v 1 p81-97

**Local administration.** See Local government

**Local finance**

### United States

Break, G. F. State and local finance in the 1980s. *In* The Economy in the 1980s: a program for growth and stability. ed. by M. J. Boskin p223-54

**Local government**

### United States—History

Nash, G. D. State and local governments. *In* Encyclopedia of American economic history, ed. by G. Porter v2 p509-23

**Local history**

### Historiography

Conzen, K. N. Community studies, urban history, and American local history. *In* The Past before us, ed. by M. Kammen p270-91

**Locke, John**

### About

Clark, L. M. G. Women and Locke: who owns the apples in the Garden of Eden? *In* The Sexism of social and political theory: women and reproduction from Plato to Nietzsche, ed. by L. M. G. Clark and L. Lange p16-40

Mansfield, H. C. On the political character of property in Locke. *In* Powers, possessions and freedom, ed. by A. Kontos p23-38

Rogers, G. A. J. The empiricism of Locke and Newton. *In* Royal Institute of Philosophy. Philosophers of the Enlightenment p 1-30

**Lockert, Lucía.** See Fox-Lockert, Lucía

**Lockridge, Laurence S.**

Explaining Coleridge's explanation: toward a practical methodology for Coleridge studies. *In* Reading Coleridge, ed. by W. B. Crawford p23-55

**Lodève, France**

### Social conditions

Johnson, C. H. Patterns of proletarianization: Parisian tailors and Lodève woolens workers. *In* Consciousness and class experience in nineteenth-century Europe, ed. by J. M. Merriman p65-84

**Lodge, David**

Where it's at: California language. *In* The State of the language, ed. by L. Michaels and C. Ricks p503-13

**Loewe, Raphael**

Ibn Gabirol's treatment of sources in the Kether Malkhuth. *In* Studies in Jewish religious and intellectual history, ed. by S. Stein and R. Loewe p183-94

**Loewenberg, Peter J.**

Psychohistory. *In* The Past before us, ed. by M. Kammen p408-32

**Lofland, John**

Early Goffman: style, structure, substance, soul. *In* The View from Goffman, ed. by J. Ditton p24-51

**Logan, John**

### About

Howard, R. John Logan: "I am interested in the unicorn underneath the wound." *In* Howard, R. Alone with America p356-71

**Logic**

Barnes, J. Proof destroyed. *In* Doubt and dogmatism, ed. by M. Schofield, M. Burnyeat and J. Barnes p161-81

Brunschwig, J. Proof defined. *In* Doubt and dogmatism, ed. by M. Schofield, M. Burnyeat and J. Barnes p125-60

Holloway, J. Logic, feeling and structure in nineteenth-century political oratory: a primer of analysis. *In* Holloway, J. Narrative and structure: exploratory essays p137-56

Imbert, C. Stoic logic and Alexandrian poetics. *In* Doubt and dogmatism, ed. by M. Schofield, M. Burnyeat and J. Barnes p182-216

Schofield, M. Preconception, argument and God. *In* Doubt and dogmatism, ed. by M. Schofield, M. Burnyeat and J. Barnes p283-308

Sloane, T. O. Rhetoric 'logic' and poetry: the formal cause. *In* The Age of Milton, ed. by C. A. Patrides and R. B. Waddington p307-37

*See also* Identity; Induction (Logic); Judgment (Logic); Reasoning

**Logic and faith.** See Faith and reason

**Logic machines.** See Artificial intelligence

**Loisy, Alfred Firmin**

### About

Daly, G. Alfred Loisy and the radicalization of the Modernist movement. *In* Daly, G. Transcendence and immanence p51-68

Daly, G. History and dogma: the debate between Alfred Loisy and Maurice Blondel. *In* Daly, G. Transcendence and immanence p69-90

**London Fortune Theatre.** See Fortune Theatre, London

The **Lone** Ranger, Ken Kesey, John Updike and. Horton, A. S. *In* Seasoned authors for a new season: the search for standards in popular writing, ed. by L. Filler p83-90

**Longe, Francis Davey**

**About individual works**

*A critical examination of Mr George's "Progress and poverty" and Mr. Mill's theory of wages*

Harrison, F. Longe and Wrightson: conservative critics of George's wage theory. *In* Critics of Henry George, ed. by R. V. Andelson p72-94

**Lönnrot Elias**

**About**

Harbison, R. Romantic localism. *In* Harbison, R. Deliberate regression p115-47

**Looking for Mr Goodbar (Motion picture)**

Kael, P. Goodbar, or How nice girls go wrong. *In* Kael, P. When the lights go down p316-23

**Loomis, Dorothy Bethurum**

Constance and the stars. *In* Chaucerian problems and perspectives, ed. by E. Vasta and Z. P. Thundy p207-20

**López-Morillas, Juan**

Francisco Giner and the redemption of Spain. *In* The Analysis of literary texts, ed. by R. D. Pope p244-55

**Lord, Albert Bates**

Interlocking mythic patterns in Beowulf. *In* Old English literature in context, ed. by J. D. Niles p137-42

**Lorenz, Konrad Zacharias**

**About**

Bischof, N. Remarks on Lorenz and Piaget: how can "working hypotheses" be "necessary"? *In* Language and learning, ed. by M. Piattelli-Palmarini p233-41

**Lorenzetti, Ambrogio**

**About**

Cole, B. Ambrogio Lorenzetti. *In* Cole, B. Sienese painting p137-79

**Lorenzetti, Pietro**

**About**

Cole, B. Pietro Lorenzetti. *In* Cole, B. Sienese painting p103-36

**Lorenzini, Carlo**

**About individual works**

*The adventures of Pinocchio*

Gannon, S. A note on Collodi and Lucian. *In* Children's literature v8 p98-102

**Lorretto Indians.** See Canelo Indians

**Lorris, Guillaume de.** See Guillame de Lorris

**Lorris, W.** See Guillaume de Lorris

**Loti, Pierre,** pseud. See Viaud, Julien

**Lough, John**

Women in Mercier's Tableau de Paris. *In* Woman and society in eighteenth-century France, ed. by E. Jacobs and others p110-22

**Louis XIII, King of France**

**About**

Ranum, O. Bernard and his history. *In* Ranum, O. Artisans of glory p103-28

**Louis XIV, King of France**

**About**

Ranum, O. Chapelain and the royal patronage of history. Ranum, O. Artisans of glory p169-96

Ranum, O. Pellisson-Fontanier: from Protestant judge to historiographer royal. *In* Ranum, O. Artisans of glory p234-77

Ranum, O. Racine learns to be a historiographer. *In* Ranum, O. Artisans of glory p278-332

**Love, Jean O.**

Orlando and its genesis: venturing and experimenting in art, love, and sex. *In* Virginia Woolf, ed. by R. Freedman p188-218

**Love**

Rapaport, E. On the future of love: Rousseau and the radical feminist. *In* The Philosophy of sex, ed. by A. Soble p369-88

Smelser, N. J. Vicissitudes of work and love in Anglo-American society. *In* Themes of work and love in adulthood, ed. by N. J. Smelser and E. H. Erikson p105-19

Swidler, A. Love and adulthood in American culture. *In* Themes of work and love in adulthood, ed. by N. J. Smelser and E. H. Erikson p120-47

Taylor, R. J. Sexual experiences. *In* The Philosophy of sex, ed. by A. Soble p59-75

**Songs and music**

Hagstrum, J. H. Love in painting and music: an appended survey. *In* Hagstrum, J. H. Sex and sensibility p278-331

**Love, Courtly.** See Courtly love

**Love and death (Motion picture)**

Kauffmann, S. Love and death. *In* Kauffmann, S. Before my eyes p140-41

**Love in art**

Hagstrum, J. H. Love in painting and music: an appended survey. *In* Hagstrum, J. H. Sex and sensibility p278-331

**Love in literature**

Baym, N. Z. God, father, and lover in Emily Dickinson's poetry. *In* Puritan influences in American literature, ed. by E. Elliott p193-209

Bickman, M. Kora in heaven: Emily Dickinson. *In* Bickman, M. The unsounded centre p117-46

Edwards, P. The declaration of love. *In* Shakespeare's styles, ed. by P. Edwards, I. S. Ewbank J. and G. K. Hunter p39-50

Hagstrum, J. H. The aftermath of sensibility: Sterne, Goethe, and Austen. *In* Hagstrum, J. H. Sex and sensibility p247-77

Hagstrum, J. H. Friends and lovers: the witty and the wise. *In* Hagstrum, J. H. Sex and sensibility p133-59

Hagstrum, J. H. Introduction. *In* Hagstrum, J. H. Sex and sensibility p 1-23

Hagstrum, J. H. John Dryden: sensual, heroic, and "pathetic" love. *In* Hagstrum, J, H. Sex and sensibility p50-71

Hagstrum, J. H. Milton and the ideal of heterosexual friendship. *In* Hagstrum, J. H. Sex and sensibility p24-49

Hagstrum, J. H. Restoration love and the tears of morbidity. *In* Hagstrum, J. H. Sex and sensibility p72-99

Hagstrum, J. H. Richardson. *In* Hagstrum, J. H. Sex and sensibility p186-218

Hagstrum, J. H. Rousseau. *In* Hagstrum, J. H. Sex and sensibility p219-46

**Love in literature**—*Continued*

Hagstrum, J. H. Woman in love: the abandoned and passionate mistress. *In* Hagstrum, J. H. Sex and sensibility p100-32

Hayes, J. J. Gothic love and death: Francois Villon and the city of Paris. *In* 5000 years of popular culture, ed. by F. E. H. Schroeder p228-39

Perry, T. A. Introduction. *In* Perry, T. A. Erotic spirituality p 1-9

Reiss, E. Chaucer's deerne love and the medieval view of secrecy in love. *In* Chaucerian problems and perspectives, ed. by E. Vasta and Z. P. Thundy p164-79

Robertson, D. W. Love conventions in Marie's Equitan. *In* Robertson, D. W. Essays in medieval culture p202-06

Robertson, D. W. The Partitura amorosa of Jean de Savoie. *In* Robertson, D. W. Essays in medieval culture p166-72

Robertson, D. W. Two poems from the Carmina burana. *In* Robertson, D. W. Essays in medieval culture p131-50

Swidler, A. Love and adulthood in American culture. *In* Themes of work and love in adulthood, ed. by N. J. Smelser and E. H. Erikson p120-47

*See also* Sex in literature

**Love on the run (Motion picture)**

Kauffmann, S. Love on the run. *In* Kauffmann, S. Before my eyes p190-93

**Love poetry**

### History and criticism

Hatto, A. T. The lime-tree and early German, Goliard and English lyric poetry. *In* Hatto, A. T. Essays on medieval German and other poetry p17-41

Perry, T. A. Introduction. *In* Perry, T. A. Erotic spirituality p 1-9

**Love poetry, English**

Robbins, R. H. The structure of longer Middle English court poems. *In* Chaucerian problems and perspectives, ed. by E. Vasta and Z. P. Thundy p244-64

### History and criticism

Robbins, R. H. The Middle English court love lyric. *In* The Interpretation of medieval lyric poetry, ed. by W. T. H. Jackson p205-32

**Lovejoy, David Sherman**

Two American revolutions, 1689 and 1776. *In* Three British revolutions: 1641, 1688, 1776, ed. by G. A. Pocock p244-62

**Lovoll, Odd S.**

Kenneth O. Bjork: teacher, scholar, and editor. *In* Makers of an American immigrant legacy, ed. by O. S. Lovell p3-14

**Lowell, Robert**

### About

Molesworth, C. Republican objects and utopian moments: the poetry of Robert Lowell and Allen Ginsberg. *In* Molesworth, C. The fierce embrace p37-60

Vendler, H. H. Robert Lowell. *In* Vendler, H. H. Part of nature, part of us p125-73

**Lowenthal, David**

Age and artifact: dilemmas of appreciation. *In* The Interpretation of ordinary landscapes, ed. by D. W. Meinig p103-28

**Lowerson, John**

Battles for the countryside. *In* Class, culture and social change, ed. by F. Gloversmith p258-80

**Loyalists, American.** See American loyalists

**Loyola, Ignacio de, Saint**

### About

Ozment, S. H. Catholic reform and Counter Reformation. *In* Ozment, S. H. The age of reform, 1250-1550 p397-418

### About individual works
*Spiritual exercises*

Beaujour, M. Exemplary pornography: Barrès, Loyola, and the novel. *In* The Reader in the text, ed. by S. R. Suleiman and I. Crosman p325-49

**Lozès, Jean**

Joseph Sheridan Le Fanu. The prince of the invisible. *In* The Irish short story, ed. by P. Rafroidi and T. Brown p91-101

**Lu, Hsün,** pseud. See Chou, Shu-jen

**Lu-hsün,** pseud. See Chou, Shu-jen

**Lucian.** See Lucianus Samosatensis

**Lucianus Samosatensis**

### About

Lutz, C. E. Two Renaissance dialogues in the manner of Lucian. *In* Lutz, C. E. The oldest library motto, and other library essays p92-98

### Influence—Lorenzini

Gannon, S. A note on Collodi and Lucian. *In* Children's literature v8 p98-102

**Luckmann, Thomas**

Personal identity as an evolutionary and historical problem. *In* Human ethology, ed. by M. von Cranach [and others] p56-74

**Lucretius Carus, Titus**

### About individual works
*On the nature of things*

West, D. A. Two plagues: Virgil, Georgics 3.478-566 and Lucretius 6.1090-1286. *In* Creative imitation and Latin literature, ed. by D. West and T. Woodman p71-88

**Lucy, Sean**

Place and people in the short stories of Daniel Corkery. *In* The Irish short story, ed. by P. Rafroidi and T. Brown p159-73

**Luft, Sandra Rudnick**

Creative activity in Vico and the secularization of providence. *In* Studies in eighteenth-century culture v9 p337-55

**Lukács, Georg.** See Lukács, György

**Lukács, György**

### About

Hartman, G. H. Literary commentary as literature. *In* Hartman, G. H. Criticism in the wilderness p189-213

Slaughter, C. A man for all seasons: Georg Lukács. *In* Slaughter, C. Marxism, ideology & literature p114-49

**Lukes, Steven**

The real and ideal worlds of democracy. *In* Powers, possessions and freedom, ed. by A. Kontos p139-52

**Lumet, Sidney**

### About individual works
*The pawnbroker*

Miller, G. Those who walk in darkness. *In* Miller, G. Screening the novel p167-89

**Lumière (Motion picture)**
Kael, P. This is my beloved. *In* Kael, P. When the lights go down p230-33

**Lumsden, Malvern**
Militarism: cultural dimensions of militarisation. *In* Problems of contemporary militarism, ed. by A. Eide and M. Thee p356-69

**Lundborg, Louis B.**
The voices of business. *In* The State of the language, ed. by L. Michaels and C. Ricks p389-95

**Lundén, Rolf**
Foreign scholarship: Scandinavian contributions. *In* American literary scholarship, 1978 p482-87

**Luo (African people)**
Ross, M. H. Political alienation, participation, and ethnicity in the Nairobi urban area. *In* Values, identities, and national integration, ed. by J. N. Paden p173-81

**Lurie, Alison**
Ford Madox Ford's fairy tales. *In* Children's literature v8 p7-21

**Lustig, Arnost.** See Knopp, J. Z. jt. auth.

**Lustig, Arnost, and Lustig, Joseph**
The Holocaust and the film arts. *In* Encountering the Holocaust: an interdisciplinary survey, ed. by B. L. Sherwin and S. G. Ament p351-82

**Lustig, Joseph.** See Lustig, A. jt. auth.

**Luther, Martin**
### About
Ozment, S. H. The mental world of Martin Luther. *In* Ozment, S. H. The age of reform, 1250-1550 p223-44

### Political science
Ozment, S. H. Society and politics in the German Reformation. *In* Ozment, S. H. The age of reform, 1250-1550 p245-89

### Theology
Ozment, S. H. Humanism and the Reformation. *In* Ozment, S. H. The age of reform, 1250-1550 p290-317
Ozment, S. H. Marriage and the ministry in the Protestant churches. *In* Ozment, S. H. The age of reform, 1250-1550 p381-96

**Lutheran Church in Norway**
### History
Munch, P. A. Pastor Munch of Wiota, 1827-1908. *In* Makers of an American immigrant legacy, ed. by O. S. Lovoll p62-91

**Lutheran Church in Wisconsin**
### History
Munch, P. A. Pastor Munch of Wiota, 1827-1908. *In* Makers of an American immigrant legacy, ed. by O. S. Lovoll p62-91

**Lutherans, Norwegian**
### United States
Munch, P. A. Pastor Munch of Wiota, 1827-1908. *In* Makers of an American immigrant legacy, ed. by O. S. Lovoll p62-91

**Lüthi, Max**
### About individual works
*Once upon a time*
Nodelman, P. Defining children's literature. *In* Children's literature v8 p184-90

**Lutman, Stephen**
Reading illustrations: pictures in David Copperfield. *In* Reading the Victorian novel: detail into form, ed. by I. Gregor p196-225

On the meaning of strategy . . . for the United States in the 1980s. *In* National security in the 1980s: from weakness to strength, ed. by W. S. Thompson p259-73

**Lutz, Cora Elizabeth**
The oldest library motto, and other library essays
*Contents*
Abiel Holmes' life of Ezra Stiles
The American unicorn
Le bon chien Soullart
The clock of eternal wisdom
Colonel David Humphreys and the Stiles family
Copernicus' stand for humanism
A family tablet
A forged manuscript in boustrophedon
The "gentle Puritan" and the "angelic doctor"
The letter of Lentulus describing Christ
The mystical symbol of the beryl
The oldest library motto
A Roman proverb in sixteenth-century England
Some medieval impressions of the ostrich
The symbol of the Y of Pythagoras in the ninth century
Two Renaissance dialogues in the manner of Lucian

**Lynn, Joanne L.**
Hyacinths and biscuits in the village of liver and onions: Sandburg's Rootabaga stories. *In* Children's literature v8 p118-32

**Lyon, Ted**
"Loss of innocence" in Chicano prose. *In* The Identification and analysis of Chicano literature, ed. by F. Jiménez p254-62

**Lyons, Francis Stewart Leland**
Yeats and Victorian Ireland. *In* Yeats, Sligo and Ireland, ed. by A. N. Jeffares p115-38

**Lyons**
### Social conditions
Sheridan, G. J. Household and craft in an industrializing economy: the case of the silk weavers of Lyons. *In* Consciousness and class experiences in nineteenth-century Europe, ed. by J. M. Merriman p107-28

**Lyric poetry**
*See also* Odes
### History and criticism
Jackson, W. T. H. Introduction. *In* The Interpretation of medieval lyric poetry, ed. by W. T. H. Jackson p 1-21

**Lysias**
*Orations (12.88)*
Fogelmark, S. A troublesome antithesis: Lysias 12.88. *In* Harvard Studies in classical philology, v83 p109-41

**Lyttleton, Raymond Arthur**
The Gold effect. *In* Lying truths, ed. by R. Duncan and M. Weston-Smith p181-98

**Lytton, Edward George Earle Lytton, Baron Lytton, 1st Baron**
### About
Stone, D. D. Introduction. *In* Stone, D. D. The romantic impulse in Victorian fiction p 1-45
*Pelham; or, The adventures of a gentleman*
Henkle, R. B. 1820-1845: the anxieties of sublimation, and middle-class myths. *In* Henkle, R. B. Comedy and culture p20-57

# M

**MacAndrew, Elizabeth**
Life in the maze—Johnson's use of chiasmus in The vanity of human wishes. *In* Studies in eighteenth-century culture v9 p517-27

**MacCaffrey, Isabel Gambel**
The ways of truth in "Le monocle de mon oncle." *In* Wallace Stevens, ed. by F. Doggett and R. Buttel p196-218

**McCarthy, John**
Ascribing mental qualities to machines. *In* Philosophical perspectives in artificial intelligence, ed. by M. Ringle p161-95

**McCarthy, Mary Therese**

### About individual works
*Birds of America*

Pritchett, V. S. Mary McCarthy: a quiet American. *In* Pritchett, V. S. The tale bearers p156-63

**McClaughry, John**
Neighborhood revitalization. *In* The United States in the 1980s, ed. by P. Duignan and A. Rabushka p367-90

**McClelland, Peter D.**
Transportation. *In* Encyclopedia of American economic history, ed. by G. Porter v 1 p309-34

**Maccoby, Hyam**
The Bible. *In* The Jewish world, ed. by E. Kedourie p52-67

**McConkey, James**
Two anonymous writers, E. M. Forster and Anton Chekhov. *In* E. M. Forster: a human exploration, ed. by G. K. Das and J. Beer p231-44

**McConville, Sean**
Prison language. *In* The State of the language, ed. by L. Michaels and C. Ricks p524-31

**McCorison, Marcus Allen**
Foreword *In* The Press & the American Revolution, ed. by B. Bailyn and J. B. Hench p 1-10

**McCormick, Diana Festa-** See Festa-McCormick, Diana

**McCormick, John**
Joseph Bouchardy: a melodramatist and his public. *In* Performance and politics in popular drama, ed. by D. Bradby, L. James and B. Sharratt p33-48

**McCoy, Horace**

### About individual works
*They shoot horses, don't they?*

Miller, G. Marathon man/marathon woman. *In* Miller, G. Screening the novel p64-83

**McCrann, Anthony T.**
Frank O'Connor and the silence. *In* Irish Renaissance annual I p113-36

**McCraw, Thomas K.**
Regulatory agencies. *In* Encyclopedia of American economic history, ed. by G. Porter v2 p788-807

**McDermott, John**
Representing knowledge in intelligent systems. *In* Philosophical perspectives in artificial intelligence, ed. by M. Ringle p110-23

**McDermott, John J.**
Spires of influence: the importance of Emerson for classical American philosophy. *In* History, religion, and spiritual democracy, ed. by M. Wohlgelernter p181-202

**Macdonald, Ian R.**
Magical eclecticism: Los pasos perdidos and Jean-Paul Sartre. *In* Contemporary Latin American fiction, ed. by S. Bacarisse p 1-17

**MacDonald, John Dann**

### About

Doulis, T. John D. MacDonald: the liabilities of professionalism. *In* Seasoned authors for a new season: the search for standards in popular writing, ed. by L. Filler p170-86

**Macdonald, Ross,** pseud. See Millar, Kenneth

**MacDonald, Susan Peck**
Jane Austen and the tradition of the absent mother. *In* The Lost tradition: mothers and daughters in literature, ed. by C. N. Davidson and E. M. Broner p58-69

**McDougal, Stuart Yeatman.** See Bornstein, G. jt. auth.

**McDowell, Frederick Peter Woll**
Forster scholarship and criticism for the desert islander. *In* E. M. Forster: a human exploration, ed. by G. K. Das and J. Beer p269-82
"Surely order did prevail": Virginia Woolf and The voyage out. *In* Virginia Woolf, ed. by R. Freedman p73-96

**McFadden, Cyra**

### About individual works
*The serial: a year in the life of Marin County*

Lodge, D. Where it's at: California language. *In* The State of the language, ed. by L. Michaels and C. Ricks p503-13

**McFarland, Thomas Alfred**
A complex dialogue: Coleridge's doctrine of polarity and its European contexts. *In* Reading Coleridge, ed. by W. B. Crawford p56-115

**MacFarlane, James Walter**

### About individual works
*Ronald Gray's Ibsen—a dissenting view*

Gray, R. Ibsen: a reply to James Walter McFarlane. *In* Drama and mimesis, ed. by J. Redmond p 251-57

**McFarlane, James Walter, ed. and tr.**

### About individual works
*The Oxford Ibsen*

Leland, C. The Oxford Ibsen, volume VIII, translated and edited by James Walter McFarlane. *In* Drama and mimesis, ed. by J. Redmond p207-25

**MacGaffey, Wyatt**
African religions: types and generalizations. *In* Explorations in African systems of thought, ed. by I. C. Karp & C. S. Bird p301-28

**McGahern, John**

### About

Brown, T. John McGahern's Nightlines: tone, technique and symbolism. *In* The Irish short story, ed. by P. Rafroidi and T. Brown p289-301

**McGhee, Richard D.**
Marriage, duty & desire in Victorian poetry and drama

*Contents*

Arnold and Clough
Browning
Elizabeth Barrett Browning and Oscar Wilde
Rossetti and Meredith
Swinburne and Hopkins
Tennyson

McGovern, George Stanley. See Democratic Party. National Committee. Commission on Party Structure and Delegate Selection

**McGowan, Bruce William**
Ottoman political communication. *In* Propaganda and communication in world history, ed. by H. D. Lasswell, D. Lerner and H. Speier v 1 p444-92

**McGuane, Thomas**

### About individual works
*The Missouri breaks*
Kauffmann, S. The Missouri breaks. *In* Kauffmann, S. Before my eyes p134-37

McGuire, Susan Bassnett- See Bassnett-McGuire, Susan

**Mach, Ernest**

### About individual works
*The analysis of sensations*
Irwin, J. T. Figurations of the writer's death: Freud and Hart Crane. *In* The Literary Freud: mechanisms of defense and the poetic will, ed. by J. H. Smith p217-60

Machaut, Guillaume de. See Guillaume de Machaut

**Machiavelli, Niccoló**

### About
Berlin, Sir I. The originality of Machiavelli. *In* Berlin, Sir I. Against the current p25-79

**Machine intelligence.** See Artificial intelligence

**Machine language.** See Programming languages (Electronic computers)

**McIllwraith, Maureen Mollie Hunter (McVeigh)**
Talent is not enough. *In* The Arbuthnot lectures, 1970-1979 p105-19

### About
McIllwraith, M. M. H. M. Talent is not enough. *In* The Arbuthnot lectures, 1970-1979 p105-19

**Mack, Phyllis**
The wonderyear. *In* Religion and the people, 800-1700, ed. by J. Obelkevich p191-220

**Mackie, John Leslie**
A defence of induction. *In* Perception and identity, ed. by G. F. Macdonald p113-30

**Mackenzie, Elizabeth**
The growth of plants: a seventeenth-century metaphor. *In* English Renaissance studies, ed. by J. Carey p194-211

**Mckinnell, John**
Letters as a type of the formal level in Troilus and Criseyde. *In* Essays on Troilus and Criseyde, ed. by M. Salu p73-89

**McKinnon, Ronald I.** See Cuddington, J. T. jt. auth.

**McLaverty, Michael**

### About
Foster, J. Private worlds: the stories of Michael McLaverty. The Irish short story, ed. by P. Rafroidi and T. Brown p249-61

**MacLean, Paul D.**
Sensory and perceptive factors in emotional functions of the triune brain. *In* Explaining emotions, ed. by A. O. Rorty p9-36

**Macleod, C. W.**
Horatian imitatio and Odes 2.5. *In* Creative imitation and Latin literature, ed. by D. West and T. Woodman p89-102

**MacMahon, Bryan**

### About
Rafroidi, P. From Listowel with love: John B. Keane and Bryan MacMahon. *In* The Irish short story, ed. by P. Rafroidi and T. Brown p263-73

**McMullin, B. J.**
Indexing the periodical literature of Anglo-American bibliography. *In* Virginia. University. Bibliographical Society. Studies in bibliography v33 p 1-17

**McMullin, Ernan**
Vico's theory of science. *In* Conference on Vico and Contemporary Thought, New York, 1976. Vico and contemporary thought pt 1 p60-90

**McMurtry, Larry**

### About
Morrow, P. D. Larry McMurtry: the first phase. *In* Seasoned authors for a new season: the search for standards in popular writing, ed. by L. Filler p70-82

**MacNeice, Louis**

### About
Heinemann, M. Louis MacNeice, John Cornford and Clive Branson: three Left-wing poets. *In* Culture and crisis in Britain in the thirties, ed. by J. Clark and others p103-32

**McNeill, David**
Language origins. *In* Human ethology, ed. by M. von Cranach [and others] p715-28
Sentence structure in chimpanzee communication. *In* Speaking of apes, ed. by T. A. Sebeok and J. Umiker-Sebeok p145-60

**McNeill, William Hardy**
The decline of the West. *In* Solzhenitsyn at Harvard, ed. by R. Berman p122-30
Modern European history. *In* The Past before us, ed. by M. Kammen p95-112

**Macpherson, Crawford Brough**

### About
Leiss, W. Marx and Macpherson: needs utilities, and self-development. *In* Powers, possessions and freedom, ed. by A. Kontos p119-38
Lukes, S. The real and ideal worlds of democracy. *In* Powers, possessions and freedom, ed. by A. Kontos p139-52

**Macpherson, James**

### About
Harbison, R. Romantic localism. *In* Harbison, R. Deliberate regression p115-47

**Macroeconomics**

### Mathematical models
DePrano, M. The untidy state of macroeconomic analysis. *In* Economic issues of the eighties, ed. by N. M. Kamrany and R. H. Day p5-28
Laffer, A. B. An equilibrium rational macroeconomic framework. *In* Economic issues of the eighties, ed. by N. M. Kamrany and R. H. Day p44-57

**Mactacio Abel.** See The killing of Abel

**Madden, Edward Harry**
Asa Mahan and the Oberlin philosophy. *In* History, religion, and spiritual democracy, ed. by M. Wohlgelernter p155-80

**Maddox, Donald L.**
Early secular courtly drama in France: L'estoire de Griseldis. *In* The Expansion and transformations of courtly literature, ed. by N. B. Smith and J. T. Snow p157-70

**Maddox, Sara Sturm-** See Sturm, Sara

**Madison, James Henry**
Communications. *In* Encyclopedia of American economic history, ed. by G. Porter v 1 p335-43

**Madrigal**
Dent, E. J. Italian chamber cantatas. *In* Dent E. J. Selected essays p58-84

**Maes-Jelinek, Hena**
Wilson Harris. *In* West Indian literature, ed. by B. King p179-95

**Magic.** See Witchcraft

**The magic flute (Motion picture)**
Kael, P. Walking into your childhood. *In* Kael, P. When the lights go down p72-79
Kauffmann, S. The magic flute. *In* Kauffmann, S. Before my eyes p69-72

**Maglin, Nan Bauer**
"Don't never forget the bridge that your crossed over on": the literature of matrilineage. *In* The Lost tradition: mothers and daughters in literature, ed. by C. N. Davidson and E. M. Broner p257-67

**Magnarelli, Sharon**
From El obsceno pajaro to Tres novelitas burguesas: development of a semiotic theory in the works of Donoso. The Analysis of literary texts, ed. by R. D. Pope p224-35

**Maguire, John David**
Contract, coercion, and consciousness. *In* Rational action, ed. by R. Harrison p157-73

**Maguire, Robert**
A conflict between art and life? *In* Architecture for people, ed. by B. Mikellides p122-33

**Mahan, Asa**
### About
Madden, E. H. Asa Mahan and the Oberlin philosophy. *In* History, religion, and spiritual democracy, ed. by M. Wohlgelernter p155-80

**Mahler, Gustav**
### About
Carner, M. Mahler's re-scoring of the Schumann symphonies. *In* Carner, M. Major and minor p71-84
Carner, M. Mahler's visit to London. *In* Carner, M. Major and minor p45-49

#### About individual works
*Lied von der Erde*
Carner, M. Form and technique of Mahler's Lied von der Erde. *In* Carner, M. Major and minor p52-55

**Mahogany (Motion picture)**
Kael, P. All for love. *In* Kael, P. When the lights go down p55-61

**Mahoney, Michael S.**
The beginnings of algebraic thought in the seventeenth century. *In* Descartes, ed. by S. Gaukroger p141-55

**Mahood, Molly Maureen**
Shakespeare's middle comedies: a generation of criticism. *In* Shakespeare survey 32 p 1-13

#### About individual works
*The colonial encounter, a reading of six novels*
Palmer, E. Novels and the colonial experience. *In* African literature today no. 10; Retrospect & prospect, ed. by E. D. Jones p248-52

**The maids (Motion picture)**
Kauffmann, S. The maids. *In* Kauffmann, S. Before my eyes p128-31

**Maier, Charles Steven**
Marking time: the historiography of international relations. *In* The Past before us, ed. by M. Kammen p355-87

**Maier, Joseph Ben**
Vico and critical theory. *In* Conference on Vico and Contemporary Thought, New York, 1976. Vico and contemporary thought pt2 p187-98

**Maimonides, Moses.** See Moses ben Maimon

**Maksimov, Vladimir Emelianovich**
### About
Hosking, G. Vladimir Maximov. *In* Hosking, G. Beyond Socialist realism p123-35

**Malbin, Michael Jacob**
Congress, policy analysis, and natural gas deregulation: a parable about fig leaves. *In* Bureaucrats, policy analysts, statesmen: who leads? Ed. by R. A. Goldwin p62-87

**Malcolm X**
#### About individual works
*The autobiography of Malcolm X*
Eakin, P. J. Malcolm X and the limits of autobiography. *In* Autobiography: essays theoretical and critical, ed. by J. Olney p180-93

**Mali empire**
Bird, C. S. and Kendall, M. B. The Mande hero. *In* Explorations in African systems of thought, ed. by I. C. Karp & C. S. Bird p13-26

**Malick, Terrence**
#### About individual works
*Days of heaven*
Kauffmann, S. Days of heaven. *In* Kauffmann, S. Before my eyes p321-23

**Malik, Michael Abdul**
### About
Naipaul, V. S. Michael X and the Black Power killings in Trinidad. *In* Naipaul, V. S. The return of Eva Perón p 1-91

**Malinke empire.** See Mali empire

**Malinowski, Bronislaw**
### About
Harbison, R. Tribe and race. *In* Harbison, R. Deliberate regression p180-205

**Mallarmé, Stéphanie**
### About
Genette, G. Valéry and the poetics of language. *In* Textual strategies, ed. by J. V. Harari p359-73
Peyre, H. Mallarmé. *In* Peyre, H. What is symbolism? p63-81

**Malle, Louis**
#### About individual works
*Lacombe Lucien*
Kauffmann, S. Lacombe Lucien. *In* Kauffmann, S. Before my eyes p60-62

*Pretty baby*
Kauffmann, S. Pretty baby. *In* Kauffmann, S. Before my eyes p63-66

**Mallock, William Hurrell**
#### About individual works
*Property and progress*
Douglas, R. Mallock and the "most elaborate answer." *In* Critics of Henry George, ed. by R. V. Andelson p95-108

**Malmi, William A.**
Chimpanzees and language evolution. *In* Speaking of apes, ed. by T. A. Sebeok and J. Umiker-Sebeok p191-96

**Malmström, Bo G.**
Ethical implications of enzyme technology. *In* The Condition of man, ed. by P. Hallberg p162-69

**Maloney, Joan M.**
Women in the Chinese Communist Revolution: the question of political equality. *In* Women, war, and revolution, ed. by C. R. Berkin and C. M. Lovett p165-81

**Malraux, André**

### About

Conley, T. Framing Malraux. *In* André Malraux, ed. by F. Dorenlot and M. Tison-Braun p125-40

#### About individual works

*Anti-memoirs*

Carduner, J. R. Metamorphosis and biography. *In* André Malraux, ed. by F. Dorenlot and M. Tison-Braun p37-54

*Lazarus*

Bockel, P. Malraux and death. *In* André Malraux, ed. by F. Dorenlot and M. Tison-Braun p75-82

*L'homme précaire et la littérature*

Peyre, H. M. André Malraux and the metamorphosis of literature. *In* André Malraux, ed. by F. Dorenlot and M. Tison-Braun p27-34

*Man's fate*

Breunig, L. C. Malraux's Storm in Shanghai. *In* André Malraux, ed. by F. Dorenlot and M. Tison-Braun p209-14

*Man's hope*

Carrard, P. Life made into fiction. *In* André Malraux, ed. by F. Dorenlot and M. Tison-Braun p189-200

Langlois, W. G. Malraux and Medellin. *In* André Malraux, ed. by F. Dorenlot and M. Tison-Braun p167-88

Thompson, B. Visual imagination in L'espoire. *In* André Malraux, ed. by F. Dorenlot and M. Tison-Braun p201-08

*Le miroir des limbes*

Hewitt, J. R. "Figures in the carpet" of Malraux's Le miroir des limbes. *In* André Malraux, ed. by F. Dorenlot and M. Tison-Braun p55-66

*The voices of silence*

Caws, M. A. Poetics and passion. *In* André Malraux, ed. by F. Dorenlot and M. Tison-Braun p143-48

Knapp, B. L. Archetypes: dissolution as creation. *In* André Malraux, ed. by F. Dorenlot and M. Tison-Braun p149-54

#### Aesthetics

Caws, M. A. Poetics and passion. *In* André Malraux, ed. by F. Dorenlot and M. Tison-Braun p143-48

Frohock, W. M. The voice of the poet. *In* André Malraux, ed. by F. Dorenlot and M. Tison-Braun p3-14

Knapp, B. L. Archetypes: dissolution as creation. *In* André Malraux, ed. by F. Dorenlot and M. Tison-Braun p149-54

Tison-Braun, M. The artist as exemplar of humanity. *In* André Malraux, ed. by F. Dorenlot and M. Tison-Braun p155-64

#### Appreciation—United States

Breunig, L. C. Malraux's Storm in Shanghai. *In* André Malraux, ed. by F. Dorenlot and M. Tison-Braun p209-14

#### Biography

Courcel, M. H. de. Timeless geography. *In* André Malraux, ed. by F. Dorenlot and M. Tison-Braun p67-74

Hewitt, J. R. "Figures in the carpet" of Malraux's Le miroir des limbes. *In* André Malraux, ed. by F. Dorenlot and M. Tison-Braun p55-66

#### Biography—Character

Bockel, P. Malraux and death. *In* André Malraux, ed. by F. Dorenlot and M. Tison-Braun p75-82

Carduner, J. R. Metamorphosis and biography. *In* André Malraux, ed. by F. Dorenlot and M. Tison-Braun p37-54

#### Characters

Charney, H. K. Dialectics of character in Malraux. *In* André Malraux, ed. by F. Dorenlot and M. Tison-Braun p15-20

#### Language

Charney, H. K. Dialectics of character in Malraux. *In* André Malraux, ed. by F. Dorenlot and M. Tison-Braun p15-20

Morot-Sir, E. Agnosticism and the gnosis of the imaginary. *In* André Malraux, ed. by F. Dorenlot and M. Tison-Braun p85-124

#### Philosophy

Courcel, M. H. de. Timeless geography. *In* André Malraux, ed. by F. Dorenlot and M. Tison-Braun p67-74

Frohock, W. M. The voice of the poet. *In* André Malraux, ed. by F. Dorenlot and M. Tison-Braun p3-14

#### Psychology

*See* Malraux, André—Biography—Character

**Mammals**

#### Physiology

Morowitz, H. J. Of mammals great and small. *In* Morowitz, H. J. The wine of life, and other essays on societies, energy & living things p81-85

**Mammies**
Genovese, E. D. Life in the big house; excerpts from "Roll, Jordan, roll." *In* A Heritage of her own, ed. by N. F. Cott and E. H. Pleck p290-97

**Man, Paul de.** See De Man, Paul

**Man**
Kreyche, G. F. The meaning of humanness: a philosophical perspective. *In* Being human in a technological age, ed. by D. M. Borchert and D. Stewart p37-50

Mikellides, B. Appendix on human needs. *In* Architecture for people, ed. by B. Mikellides p191-92

Morowitz, H. J. De motu animalium. *In* Morowitz, H. J. The wine of life, and other essays on societies, energy & living things p24-27

Yankelovich, D. Two truths: the view from the social science. *In* Being human in a technological age, ed. by D. M. Borchert and D. Stewart p89-105

*See also* Ethnology; Men

#### Animal nature

Carne-Ross, D. S. Deianeria's dark cupboard: a question from Sophocles. *In* Carne-Ross, D. S. Instaurations p61-115

#### Influence of environment

*See* Anthropo-geography; Architecture

Man—*Continued*

### Influence on nature

Blackstone, W. T. The search for an environmental ethic. *In* Matters of life and death, ed. by T. Regan p299-335

Lowenthal, D. Age and artifact: dilemmas of appreciation. *In* The Interpretation of ordinary landscapes, ed. by D. W. Meinig p103-28

### Man (Christian theology)

Hill, J. E. C. Covenant theology and the concept of 'a public person.' *In* Powers, possessions and freedom, ed. by A. Kontos p3-22

Hiltner, S. Theological perspectives on humanness. *In* Being human in a technological age, ed. by D. M. Borchert and D. Stewart p51-71

**Man (Jewish theology).** See Sin (Judaism)

### Man (Theology)

Kristeller, P. O. The dignity of man. *In* Kristeller, P. O. Renaissance thought and its sources p169-81

**Man, Doctrine of.** See Man (Theology)

**Man, Fall of.** See Fall of man

### Man, Prehistoric

Clark G. Primitive man as hunter, fisher, forager, and farmer. *In* The Origins of civilization, ed. by P. R. S. Moorey p 1-21

*See also* Art, Prehistoric

**Man, Primitive.** See Ethnology

**Man-animal communication.** See Human-animal communication

### A man escaped; or, The wind listeth where it will (Motion picture)

Thiher, A. Bresson's Un condamné à mort: the semiotics of grace. *In* Thiher, A. The cinematic muse p130-42

### The man who loved women (Motion picture)

Kael, P. The unjoy of sex. *In* Kael, P. When the lights go down p354-58

Kauffmann, S. The man who loved women. *In* Kauffmann, S. Before my eyes p193-95

### The man who would be king (Motion picture)

Kael, P. Brotherhood is powerful. *In* Kael, P. When the lights go down p107-12

Kauffmann, S. The man who would be king. *In* Kauffmann, S. Before my eyes p189-90

**Management.** See Industrial management; Theater management

**Management, Industrial.** See Industrial management

### Manchester, William Raymond

Mencken in person. *In* On Mencken, ed. by J. Dorsey p3-13

**Mandé (African people)** See Mandingo (African people)

### Mandel, Barrett J.

Full of life now. *In* Autobiography: essays theoretical and critical, ed. by J. Olney p49-72

**Mandel'shtam, Osip Emil'evich**

### About

Freidin, G. Osip Mandelstam: the poetry of time (1908-1916). *In* California Slavic studies v11 p141-86

**Mandelstam, Osip.** See Mandel'shtam, Osip Emil'evich

### Mandeville, Bernard

### About individual works

*The fable of the bees*

Uphaus, R. W. Mandeville and the force of prejudice. *In* Uphaus, R. W. The impossible observer p28-45

### Mandingo (African people)

Bird, C. S. and Kendall, M. B. The Mande hero. *In* Explorations in African systems of thought, ed. by I. C. Karp & C. S. Bird p13-26

**Mandingo empire.** See Mali empire

### Mandingo poetry

### History and criticism

Bird, C. S. and Kendall, M. B. The Mande hero. *In* Explorations in African systems of thought, ed. by I. C. Karp & C. S. Bird p13-26

**Mangan, James Clarence**

### About

Welch, R. James Clarence Mangan: 'apples from the Dead sea shore.' *In* Welch, R. Irish poetry from Moore to Yeats p76-115

### Manhattan (Motion picture)

Kauffmann, S. Manhattan. *In* Kauffmann, S. Before my eyes p147-51

### Mani, 3d cent

### About

Henrichs, A. The Cologne Mani Codex reconsidered. *In* Harvard Studies in classical philology p339-67

### Manichaeism

### Manuscripts

Henrichs, A. The Cologne Mani Codex reconsidered. *In* Harvard Studies in classical philology p339-67

**Manichaeus.** See Mani, 3d cent.

### Manley, Lawrence Gordon

Convention, 1500-1750

*Contents*

Art and convention in antiquity

Art and nature in antiquity

Art, nature, and convention

The artlessness of art: convention in Renaissance poetics

"Betwixt two ages cast": Dryden's criticism

"Conveniency to nature" and the "secrets of privitie": nature and convention in defense of poetry

The "duble name" of custom: the Reformation attack on convention

The emergence of historical consciousness

"A genius of times": the contexts of historical periods

Historical rhetoric and historical explanation

"A latitude of sense": testing for truth

The medieval redefinition

Neo-Stoic and Baconian nature: seventeenth century prospects

"A passable contexture": convention and the practice of contextualism

The possibilities of discourse: Renaissance logic, rhetoric, and poetics

Real and mental theater: the complex of classicism

"The separation of opinions": the role of convention in criticism and controversy

"These broken ends": ancients, moderns, and modernity

"Use becomes another nature": custom in sixteenth-century politics and law

A world on wheels: convention in sixteenth-century moral philosophy

**Manners and customs.** See Rites and ceremonies; Taboo

### Manning, Peter K.

Goffman's framing order: style as structure. *In* The View from Goffman, ed. by J. Ditton p252-84

**Manning, Stephen**
Chaucer's Constance, pale and passive. *In* Chaucerian problems and perspectives, ed. by E. Vasta and Z. P. Thundy p13-23

**Manning, Thomas G.**
George Otis Smith as fourth director of the U.S. Geological Survey. *In* New Hampshire Bicentennial Conference on the History of Geology, University of New Hampshire, 1976. Two hundred years of geology in America p157-64

**Mannyng, Robert, of Brune**

### About individual works

*Handlyng synne*

Robertson, D. W. Certain theological conventions in Mannyng's treatment of the Commandments. *In* Robertson, D. W. Essays in medieval culture p105-13

**Mansfield, Edwin**
Major issues concerning U.S. technology policy. *In* Economic issues of the eighties, ed. by N. M. Kamrany and R. H. Day p185-98

**Mansfield, Harvey C.**
On the political character of property in Locke. *In* Powers, possessions and freedom, ed. by A. Kontos p23-38

**Manuscripts**
Munby, A. N. L. The acquisition of manuscripts by institutional libraries. *In* The Bibliographical Society of America, 1904-79 p384-98

*See also* subdivision Manuscripts under subjects and names of authors, e.g. Chaadev, Petr IAkovlevich—Manuscripts; Fielding, Henry—Manuscripts

### Cataloging

*See* Cataloging of manuscripts

### Forgeries

*See* Forgery of manuscripts

### United States—Catalogs

Joyce, W. L. The manuscript collections of the American Antiquarian Society. *In* American Antiquarian Society. Proceedings v89 pt 1 p123-52

**Manuscripts, American**
Joyce, W. L. The manuscript collections of the American Antiquarian Society. *In* American Antiquarian Society. Proceedings v89 pt 1 p123-52

**Manuscripts, Anglo-Saxon**
Owen, G. R. Wynflæd's wardrobe. *In* Anglo-Saxon England 8 p195-222

Schapiro, M. The decoration of the Leningrad manuscript of Bede. *In* Schapiro, M. Selected papers v3: Late antique, early Christian and mediaeval art p199-224

Scragg, D. G. The corpus of vernacular homilies and prose saints' lives before Ælfric. *In* Anglo-Saxon England 8 p223-77

**Manuscripts, Biblical.** See Bible—Manuscripts

**Manuscripts, Carolingian**
Schapiro, M. The Carolingian copy of the Calendar of 354. *In* Schapiro, M. Selected papers v3: Late antique, early Christian and mediaeval art p143-49

**Manuscripts, Forgery of.** See Forgery of manuscripts

**Manuscripts, French**
Lutz, C. E. Le bon chien Soullart. *In* Lutz, C. E. The oldest library motto, and other library essays p109-14

**Manuscripts, Greek (Papyri)**
Henrichs, A. The Cologne Mani Codex reconsidered. *In* Harvard Studies in classical philology, v83 p339-67

Renner, T. Three new Homerica on papyrus. *In* Harvard Studies in classical philology, v83 p311-37

**Manzano, Juan Francisco**

### About

Jackson, R. L. Slave poetry and slave narrative: Juan Francisco Manzano and black autobiography. *In* Jackson, R. L. Black writers in Latin America p25-35

**Mao, Dun,** pseud. See Shen, Yen-ping

**Mao, Toen,** pseud. See Shen, Yen-ping

**Mao, Tun.** See Shen, Yen-ping

**Maps, Geological.** See Geology—Maps

**Maranda, Pierre**
The dialectic of metaphor: an anthropological essay on hermeneutics. *In* The Reader in the text, ed. by S. R. Suleiman and I. Crosman p183-204

**Maranos**

### Influence

Pines, S. The Jewish religion after the destruction of Temple and state: the views of Bodin and Spinoza. *In* Studies in Jewish religious and intellectual history, ed. by S. Stein and R. Loewe p215-34

**Marathon man (Motion picture)**
Kael, P. Running into trouble. *In* Kael, P. When the lights go down p172-79

**Marcabru.** See Marcabrun

**Marcabrun**

### About

Robertson, D. W. Five poems by Marcabru. *In* Robertson, D. W. Essays in medieval culture p151-65

**Marcellus, Saint, Bp. of Paris, d. 436?**

### Legends

Le Goff, J. Ecclesiastical culture and folklore in the Middle Ages: Saint Marcellus of Paris and the dragon. *In* Le Goff, J. Time, work, & culture in the Middle Ages p159-88

**Marchese, Ronald T.**
Urbanism in the classical world: some general considerations and remarks. *In* 5000 years of popular culture, ed. by F. E. H. Schroeder p55-91

**Marcil-Lacoste, Louise**
Hume's method in moral reasoning. *In* The Sexism of social and political theory: women and reproduction from Plato to Nietzsche, ed. by L. M. G. Clark and L. Lange p60-73

**Mardin, Serif Arif**
The modernization of social communication. *In* Propaganda and communication in world history, ed. by H. D. Lasswell, D. Lerner and H. Speier v 1 p381-443

**Marcus, Jane**
Enchanted organs, magic bells: Night and day as comic opera. *In* Virginia Woolf, ed. by R. Freedman p97-122

**Margolies, David N.**
Left Review and Left literary theory. *In* Culture and crisis in Britain in the thirties, ed. by J. Clark and others p67-82

**Margolis, Maxine**
Seduced and abandoned: agricultural frontiers in Brazil and the United States. *In* Brazil, anthropological perspectives, ed. by M. L. Margolis and W. E. Carter p160-79

**Marie de France**

### About individual works
*Equitan*

Robertson, D. W. Love conventions in Marie's Equitan. *In* Robertson, D. W. Essays in medieval culture p202-06

**Marin, Louis**

On the interpretation of ordinary language: a parable of Pascal. *In* Textual strategies, ed. by J. V. Harari p239-59

Toward a theory of reading in the visual arts: Poussin's The Arcadian shepherds. *In* The Reader in the text, ed. by S. R. Suleiman and I. Crosman p293-324

**Marivaux, Pierre Carlet de Chamblain de**

### About

Mason, H. T. Women in Marivaux: journalist to dramatist. *In* Woman and society in eighteenth-century France, ed. by E. Jacobs and others p42-54

### About individual works
*The virtuous orphan, or,*
*The life of Marianne*

Miller, N. K. The virtuous orphan. *In* Miller, N. K. The heroine's text p21-36

**Mark Twain**, pseud. See Clemens, Samuel Langhorne

**Marketing**

*See also* Commodity exchanges

### United States—History

Porter, G. Marketing. *In* Encyclopedia of American economic history, ed. by G. Porter v 1 p386-96

**Markfield, Wallace**

### About

Friedman, M. J. The enigma of unpopularity and critical neglect: the case for Wallace Markfield. *In* Seasoned authors for a new season: the search for standards in popular writing, ed. by L. Filler p33-42

Marxism as a political philosophy. *In* Political theory and political education, ed. by M. Richter p94-112

**Marković, Mihailo.** See Markovic, Mihajlo

**Marković, Mihajlo**

Historical praxis as the ground of morality. *In* Humanist ethics, ed. by M. B. Storer p36-57

**Marler, Peter**

Development of auditory perception in relation to vocal behavior. *In* Human ethology, ed. by M. von Cranach [and others] p663-81

Primate vocalization: affective or symbolic? *In* Speaking of apes, ed. by T. A. Sebeok and J. Umiker-Sebeok p221-29

**Marlowe, Christopher**

### About individual works
*Doctor Faustus*

Reiss, T. J. Power and fallibility (Tamburlaine and Faustus). *In* Reiss, T. J. Tragedy and truth p103-36

*Tamburlaine*

Reiss, T. J. Power and fallibility (Tamburlaine and Faustus). *In* Reiss, T. J. Tragedy and truth p103-36

### Influence—Shakespeare

Bradbrook, M. C. Shakespeare's recollections of Marlowe. *In* Shakespeare's styles, ed. by P. Edwards, I. S. Ewbank and G. K. Hunter p191-204

**Marprelate, Martin, pseud.**

### About

Anselment, R. A. The Marprelate tracts. *In* Anselment, R. A. 'Betwixt jest and earnest' p33-60

**Marprelate controversy**

Anselment, R. A. The Marprelate tracts. *In* Anselment, R. A. 'Betwixt jest and earnest' p33-60

**Márquez, Gabriel García.** See García Márquez, Gabriel

**The Marquise of O (Motion picture)**

Kael, P. No id. *In* Kael, P. When the lights go down p184-89

Kauffmann, S. The Marquise of O. . . . *In* Kauffmann, S. Before my eyes p258-61

**Marranos.** See Maranos

**Marriage**

*See also* Family

### History

Ozment, S. H. Marriage and the ministry in the Protestant churches. *In* Ozment, S. H. The age of reform, 1250-1550 p381-96

### United States—History

Wells, R. V. Quaker marriage patterns in a colonial perspective. *In* A Heritage of her own, ed. by N. F. Cott and E. H. Pleck p81-106

**Marriage in literature**

Hagstrum, J. H. Sentimental love and marriage "esteem enliven'd by desire." *In* Hagstrum, J. H. Sex and sensibility p160-85

McGhee, R. D. Browning. *In* McGhee, R. D. Marriage, duty & desire in Victorian poetry and drama p67-98

McGhee, R. D. Elizabeth Barrett Browning and Oscar Wilde. *In* McGhee, R. D. Marriage, duty & desire in Victorian poetry and drama p233-97

McGhee, R. D. Introduction. *In* McGhee, R. D. Marriage, duty & desire in Victorian poetry and drama p 1-28

McGhee, R. D. Tennyson. *In* McGhee, R. D. Marriage, duty & desire in Victorian poetry and drama p29-66

**Marriage statistics.** See Vital statistics

**Marsh, David**

The quattrocento dialogue

*Contents*

Cicero and the humanist dialogue
Giovanni Pontano and the academic gathering
Leon Battista Alberti and the volgare dialogue
Leonardo Bruni and the origin of humanist dialogue
Lorenzo Valla and the rhetorical dialogue
Poggio Bracciolini and the moral debate

**Marsh, James**

### About

Harding, A. J. James Marsh as editor of Coleridge. *In* Reading Coleridge, ed. by W. B. Crawford p223-51

**Marsh, Susan H.**

Chou Fo-hai: the making of a collaborator. *In* The Chinese and the Japanese, ed. by A. Iriye p304-27

**Marshall, Alfred**

### About individual works
*Three lectures on Progress and poverty*

Hébert, R. F. Marshall: a professional economist guards the purity of his discipline. *In* Critics of Henry George, ed. by R. V. Andelson p56-71

**Marshall, Charles Burton**
Strategy: the emerging dangers. *In* National security in the 1980s: from weakness to strength, ed. by W. S. Thompson p423-41

**Marshall, David**
Reading tasting. *In* Glyph 6 p123-40

**Marshall, Donald G.**
The ontology of the literary sign: notes toward a Heideggerian revision of semiology. *In* Martin Heidegger and the question of literature, ed. by W. V. Spanos p271-94

**Marshall, Graeme**
Overdetermination and the emotions. *In* Explaining emotions, ed. by A. O. Rorty p197-222

**Marshall, W. Gerald**
Pope's Windsor-Forest as providential history. *In* Tennessee Studies in literature v24 p82-93

**Marsilius of Padua**
### About
Ozment, S. H. The ecclesiopolitical traditions. *In* Ozment, S. H. The age of reform, 1250-1550 p135-81

**Martin, Albro**
Economy from Reconstruction to 1914. *In* Encyclopedia of American economic history, ed. by G. Porter v 1 p91-109

**Martin, Augustine**
Hound voices were they all: an experiment in Yeats criticism. *In* Yeats, Sligo and Ireland, ed. by A. N. Jeffares p139-52

**Martin, David A.**
The sociological mode and the theological vocabulary. *In* Sociology and theology: alliance and conflict, ed. by D. Martin, J. O. Mills [and] W. S. F. Pickering p46-58

**Martin, Gerald**
Yoel Supremo: the dictator and his script. *In* Contemporary Latin American fiction, ed. by S. Bacarisse p73-87

**Martin, James Alfred**
The esthetic, the religious, and the natural. *In* History, religion, and spiritual democracy, ed. by M. Wohlgelernter p76-91

**Martin, Leslie John**
The moving target: general trends in audience composition. *In* Propaganda and communication in world history, ed. by H. D. Lasswell, D. Lerner and H. Speier v3 p249-94

**Martin, Robert M.**
Suicide and false desires. *In* Suicide: the philosophical issues, ed. by M. P. Battin and D. J. Mayo p144-50
Suicide and self-sacrifice. *In* Suicide: the philosophical issues, ed. by M. P. Battin and D. J. Mayo p48-68

**Martin, Terence**
The negative character in American fiction. *In* Toward a new American literary history, ed. by L. J. Budd, E. H. Cady and C. L. Anderson p230-43

**Martin, Violet Florence.** See Somerville, E. A. Œ. jt. auth.

**Martineau, Harriet**
### About
Myers, M. Unmothered daughter and radical reformer: Harriet Martineau's career. *In* The Lost tradition: mothers and daughters in literature, ed. by C. N. Davidson and E. M. Broner p70-89

### About individual works
*Harriet Martineau's autobiography*
Myers, M. Harriet Martineau's autobiography: the making of a female philosopher. *In* Women's autobiography, ed. by E. C. Jelinek p53-70

**Martini, Simone.** See Simone di Martino

**Martz, Louis Lohr**
"From the journal of Crispin": an early version of "The comedian as the letter C." *In* Wallace Stevens, ed. by F. Doggett and R. Buttel p3-29
Shakespeare's humanist enterprise: The winter's tale. *In* English Renaissance studies, ed. by J. Carey p114-31

**Marvell, Andrew**
### About individual works
*The last instructions to a painter*
Seidel, M. A. A house divided: Marvell's Last instructions and Dryden's Absalom and Achitophel. *In* Seidel, M. A. Satiric inheritance, Rabelais to Sterne p135-68

*The rehearsal transpros'd*
Anselment, R. A. The rehearsal transpros'd. *In* Anselment, R. A. 'Betwixt jest and earnest' p94-125

**Marx, Joan Carolyn**
The encounter of genres: Cymbeline's structure of juxtaposition. *In* The Analysis of literary texts, ed. by R. D. Pope p138-44

**Marx, John H.**
The ideological construction of post-modern identity models in contemporary cultural movements. *In* Identity and authority, ed. by R. Robertson and B. Holzner p145-89

**Marx, Karl**
### About
Berlin, Sir I. Benjamin Disraeli, Karl Marx and the search for identity. *In* Berlin, Sir I. Against the current p252-86
Harrison, F. Gronlund and other Marxists. *In* Critics of Henry George, ed. by R. V. Andelson p196-221
Leiss, W. Marx and Macpherson: needs, utilities, and self-development. *In* Powers, possessions and freedom, ed. by A. Konto p119-38
Maguire, J. D. Contract, coercion, and consciousness. *In* Rational action, ed. by R. Harrison p157-73
Mansfield, H. C. On the political character of property in Locke. *In* Powers, possessions and freedom, ed. by A. Kontos p23-38
O'Brien, M. Reproducing Marxist man. *In* The Sexism of social and political theory: women and reproduction from Plato to Nietzsche, ed. by L. M. G. Clark and L. Lange p99-116
O'Neill, J. On the history of the human senses in Vico and Marx. *In* Conference on Vico and Contemporary Thought, New York, 1976. Vico and contemporary thought pt2 p179-86
Padover, S. K. Karl Marx—the propagandist as prophet. *In* Propaganda and communication in world history, ed. by H. D. Lasswell, D. Lerner and H. Speier v2 p210-38
Ritter, H. Science and the imagination in the thought of Schiller and Marx. *In* The Quest for the new science, ed. by K. J. Fink and J. W. Marchand p28-40
Slaughter, C. The legacy of Marx. *In* Slaughter, C. Marxism, ideology & literature p21-85

**Marx, Karl**—*Continued*

### About individual works
*Capital*

Heinzelman, K. The psychomachia of labor. *In* Heinzelman, K. The economics of the imagination p166-95

Padover, S. K. Karl Marx—the propagandist as prophet. *In* Propaganda and communication in world history, ed. by H. D. Lasswell, D. Lerner and H. Speier v2 p210-38

*The eighteenth Brumaire of Napoleon Bonaparte*

White, H. W. The problem of style in realistic representation: Marx and Flaubert. *In* The Concept of style, ed. by B. Lang p213-29

**Marx, Paul**

Hemingway and ethnics. *In* Seasoned authors for a new season: the search for standards in popular writing, ed. by L. Filler p43-50

**Marxian economics**

Harrison, F. Gronlund and other Marxists. *In* Critics of Henry George, ed. by R. V. Andelson p196-221

Semenov, Y. I. The theory of socio-economic formations and world history. *In* Soviet and Western anthropology, ed. by E. Gellner p29-58

**Marxian school of sociology**

Gellner, E. A Russian Marxist philosophy of history. *In* Soviet and Western anthropology, ed. by E. Gellner p59-82

Semenov, Y. I. The theory of socio-economic formations and world history. *In* Soviet and Western anthropology, ed. by E. Gellner p29-58

**Marxian sociology.** See Marxian school of sociology

**Marxism.** See Communism; Socialism

**Marxist sociology.** See Marxian school of sociology

**Maryland**

### Historiography

Tate, T. W. The seventeenth-century Chesapeake and its modern historians. *In* The Chesapeake in the seventeenth century, ed. by T. W. Tate and D. L. Ammerman p3-50

### History—Colonial period, ca. 1600-1775

Carr, L. G. and Menard, R. R. Immigration and opportunity: the freedman in early colonial Maryland. *In* The Chesapeake in the seventeenth century, ed. by T. W. Tate and D. L. Ammerman p206-41

Carr, L. G. and Walsh, L. S. The planter's wife: the experience of white women in seventeenth-century Maryland. *In* A Heritage of her own, ed. by N. F. Cott and E. H. Pleck p25-57

Jordan, D. W. Political stability and the emergence of a native elite in Maryland. *In* The Chesapeake in the seventeenth century, ed. by T. W. Tate and D. L. Ammerman p243-73

Walsh, L. S. "Till death us do part": marriage and family in seventeenth-century Maryland. *In* The Chesapeake in the seventeenth century, ed. by T. W. Tate and D. L. Ammerman p126-52

**Masai**

Laughlin, T. Environment, political culture, and national orientations: a comparison of settled and pastoral Masai. *In* Values, identities, and national integration, ed. by J. N. Paden p91-103

**Masai, François**

### About individual works
*Essai sur les origines de la miniature dite irlandaise*

Schapiro, M. The place of Ireland in Hiberno-Saxon art. *In* Schapiro, M. Selected papers v3: Late antique, early Christian and mediaeval art p225-41

**Mason, H. T.**

Women in Marivaux: journalist to dramatist. *In* Woman and society in eighteenth-century France, ed. by E. Jacobs and others p42-54

**Mason, Mary Gertrude**

The other voice: autobiographies of women writers. *In* Autobiography: essays theoretical and critical, ed. by J. Olney p207-35

**Mason, Sheila Mary**

The riddle of Roxane. *In* Woman and society in eighteenth-century France, ed. by E. Jacobs and others p28-41

**Mason, William A.**

Maternal attributes and primate cognitive development. *In* Human ethology, ed. by M. von Cranach [and others] p437-55

**Mass (Music)**

Carner, M. The mass from Rossini to Dvořák. *In* Carner, M. Major and minor p122-35

**Mass (Physics)** See Inertia (Mechanics)

**Mass communication.** See Communication; Mass media; Telecommunication

**Mass culture.** See Popular culture

**Mass hysteria.** See Hysteria (Social psychology)

**Mass media**

Davison, W. P. The media kaleidoscope: general trends in the channels. *In* Propaganda and communication in world history, ed. by H. D. Lasswell, D. Lerner and H. Speier v3 p191-248

Martin, L. J. The moving target: general trends in audience composition. *In* Propaganda and communication in world history, ed. by H. D. Lasswell, D. Lerner and H. Speier v3 p249-94

Schramm, W. L. The effects of mass media in an information era. *In* Propaganda and communication in world history, ed. by H. D. Lasswell, D. Lerner and H. Speier v3 p295-345

Weston-Smith, M. Mass media assist communication. *In* Lying truths, ed. by R. Duncan and M. Weston-Smith p31-33

### Political aspects

Pye, L. W. Communication, development, and power. *In* Propaganda and communication in world history, ed. by H. D. Lasswell, D. Lerner and H. Speier v2 p424-45

### Political aspects—Italy

Bechelloni, G. The journalist as political client in Italy. *In* Newspapers and democracy, ed. by A. Smith p228-43

### Political aspects—Portugal

Seaton, J. and Pimlott, B. The role of the media in the Portuguese revolution. *In* Newspapers and democracy, ed. by A. Smith p174-99

### Political aspects—United States

Rothman, S. The mass media in post-industrial society. *In* The Third century, ed. by S. M. Lipset p345-88

**Mass media**—*Continued*

**Social aspects**—United States

Rothman, S. The mass media in post-industrial society. *In* The Third century, ed. by S. M. Lipset p345-88

**Italy**

Bechelloni, G. The journalist as political client in Italy. *In* Newspapers and democracy, ed. by A. Smith p228-43

**Japan**

Tomita, T. The new electronic media and their place in the information market of the future. *In* Newspapers and democracy, ed. by A. Smith p49-62

**Norway**

Dahl, H. The press, most national of media: a report from Norway. *In* Newspapers and democracy, ed. by A. Smith p95-103

**Scandinavia**

Dahl, H. The press, most national of media: a report from Norway. *In* Newspapers and democracy, ed. by A. Smith p95-103

**Underdeveloped areas**

*See* Underdeveloped areas—Mass media

**United States**

Rogow, A. A. Love and intimacy: mass media and phallic culture. *In* Propaganda and communication in world history, ed. by H. D. Lasswell, D. Lerner and H. Speier v3 p148-67

**Mass media in religion**

Mills, J. O. God, man and media: on a problem arising when theologians speak of the modern world. *In* Sociology and theology: alliance and conflict, ed. by D. Martin, J. O. Mills [and] W. S. F. Pickering p136-50

**Mass society.** See Mass media

**Massachusetts**

**History**—Colonial period, ca. 1600-1775

Frye, J. Class, generation and social change: a case in Salem, Massachusetts, 1636-1656. *In* 5000 years of popular culture, ed. by F. E. H. Schroeder p278-85

**Politics and government**—Revolution, 1775-1783

Pole, J. R. The emergence of the majority principle in the American Revolution. *In* Pole, J. R. Paths to the American past p41-54

**Social conditions**

Cott, N. F. Eighteenth-century family and social life revealed in Massachusetts divorce records. *In* A Heritage of her own, ed. by N. F. Cott and E. H. Pleck p107-35

**Massai.** See Masai

**Massenet, Jules**

**About individual works**

*Manon*

Carner, M. The two 'Manons.' *In* Carner, M. Major and minor p136-38

**Massinger, Philip**

**About individual works**

*Believe as you list*

Edwards, P. The royal pretenders: Ford's Perkin Warbeck and Massinger's Believe as you list. *In* Edwards, P. Threshold of a nation p174-87

**Master and servant**

Genovese, E. D. Life in the big house; excerpts from "Roll, Jordan, roll." *In* A Heritage of her own, ed. by N. F. Cott and E. H. Pleck p290-97

**Master of Flémalle.** See Campin, Robert (Master of Flémalle)

**Masters, Roger D.**

Beyond reductionism: five basic concepts in human ethology. *In* Human ethology, ed. by M. von Cranach [and others] p265-84

**Masturbation**

Fortunata, J. Masturbation and women's sexuality. *In* The Philosophy of sex, ed. by A. Soble p389-408

**Materialism.** See Naturalism

**Mathematical linguistics.** See Linguistics—Data processing

**Mathematical physics**

Gaukroger, S. Descartes' project for a mathematical physics. *In* Descartes, ed. by S. Gaukroger p97-140

**Mathematical statistics.** See Statistics

**Mathematics**

**Philosophy**

Morowitz, H. J. A new math for the CNS? *In* Morowitz, H. J. The wine of life, and other essays on societies, energy & living things p208-11

**Matheolus**

**About individual works**

*Lamentations*

Thundy, Z. P. Matheolus, Chaucer, and The wife of Bath. *In* Chaucerian problems and perspectives, ed. by E. Vasta and Z. P. Thundy p24-58

**Mather, Cotton**

**About individual works**

*Magnalia Christi Americana; or, The ecclesiastical history of New-England*

Sutton, W. Apocalyptic history and the American epic: Cotton Mather and Joel Barlow. *In* Toward a new American literary history, ed. by L. J. Budd, E. H. Cady and C. L. Anderson p69-83

**Mathews, Donald G.**

Religion and slavery—the case of the American South. *In* Anti-slavery, religion, and reform: essays in memory of Roger Anstey, ed. by C. Bolt and S. Drescher p207-32

**Mathews, Walter M.** See Hallblade, S. jt. auth.

**Matricide in literature.** See Parricide in literature

**A matter of time (Motion picture)**

Kael, P. The hundred-per-cent solution. *In* Kael, P. When the lights go down p190-95

**Matthews, Gareth Blanc**

Ritual and the religious feelings. *In* Explaining emotions, ed. by A. O. Rorty p339-53

**Matthews, James H.**

Women, war, and words: Frank O'Connor's first confessions. *In* Irish Renaissance annual I p73-112

**Matthews, Robert D.**

National security: propaganda or legitimate concern? *In* Problems of contemporary militarism, ed. by A. Eide and M. Thee p140-47

**Matthiessen, Francis Otto**

### About individual works

*Henry James, the major phase*

Trilling, L. The head and heart of Henry James. *In* Trilling, L. Speaking of literature and society p202-06

**Mattiussi, Guido**

### About

Daly, G. The integralist response (1): prelude to the Roman condemnation of Modernism. *In* Daly, G. Transcendence and immanence p165-89

**Matto de Turner, Clorinda**

### About individual works

*Aves sin nido*

Fox-Lockert, L. Clorinda Matta de Turner. *In* Fox-Lockert, L. Women novelists in Spain and Spanish America p137-46

**Mau-dun,** pseud. See Shen, Yen-ping

**Maull, Nancy L.**

Cartesian optics and the geometrization of nature. *In* Descartes, ed. by S. Gaukroger p23-40

**Maximov, Vladimir.** See Maksimov, Vladimir Emelíanovich

**Maxims**

Barthes, R. La Rochefoucauld: "reflections or sentences and maxims." *In* Barthes, R. New critical essays p3-22

**Maxwell, Desmond Ernest Stewart**

The shape-changers. *In* Yeats, Sligo and Ireland, ed. by A. N. Jeffares p153-69

**May, Elaine**

### About individual works

*Mikey and Nicky*

Kauffmann, S. Mikey and Nicky. *In* Kauffmann, S. Before my eyes p272-75

**May, Sophie,** pseud. See Clarke, Rebecca Sophia

**Mayer, David**

The music of melodrama. *In* Performance and politics in popular drama, ed. by D. Bradley, L. James and B. Sharratt p49-63

**Mayer, Julius Robert von**

### About

Morowitz, H. J. Helmholtz, Mayer, and the M.D.-Ph.D. program. *In* Morowitz, H. J. The wine of life, and other essays on societies, energy & living things p125-28

**Mayer, Lawrence C.**

A note on the aggregation of party systems. *In* Western European party systems, ed. by P. H. Merkl p515-20

Party systems and cabinet stability. *In* Western European party systems, ed. by P. H. Merkl p335-47

**Mayne, William**

### About

Townsend, J. R. William Mayne. *In* Townsend, J. R. A sounding of storytellers p139-52

**Mayo, David James**

Irrational suicide. *In* Suicide: the philosophical issues, ed. by M. P. Battin and D. J. Mayo p133-37

**Mayr, Simone**

### About individual works

*L'amor coniugale*

Carner, M. Simone Mayr and his L'amor coniugale. *In* Carner, M. Major and minor p148-71

**Mayrodes, George I.**

Rationality and religious belief—a perverse question. *In* Rationality and religious belief, ed. by C. F. Delaney p28-41

**Mazursky, Paul**

### About individual works

*An unmarried woman*

Kauffmann, S. An unmarried woman. *In* Kauffmann, S. Before my eyes p197-200

**Mazzoni, Jacopo**

Krieger, M. Jacopo Mazzoni, repository of diverse critical traditions or source of a new one? *In* Krieger, M. Poetic presence and illusion p28-38

**Mead, Margaret**

Continuities in communication from early man to modern times. *In* Propaganda and communication in world history, ed. by H. D. Lasswell, D. Lerner and H. Speier v 1 p21-49

### About individual works

*Blackberry winter*

Demetrakopoulos, S. A. The metaphysics of matrilinearism in women's autobiography: studies of Mead's Blackberry winter, Hellman's Pentimento, Angelou's I know why the caged bird sings, and Kingston's The woman warrior. *In* Women's autobiography, ed. by E. C. Jelinek p180-205

**Mean (Philosophy)**

Fox, M. The doctrine of the mean in Aristotle and Maimonides: a comparative study. *In* Studies in Jewish religious and intellectual history, ed. by S. Stein and R. Loewe p93-120

**Meaning (Psychology)** See Connotations (Linguistics)

**Mechanics.** See Force and energy; Inertia (Mechanics); Mathematical physics

**Mechanisms of defense.** See Defense mechanisms (Psychology)

**Medawar, Sir Peter Brian**

A bouquet of fallacies from medicine and medical science with a sideways glance at mathematics and logic. *In* Lying truths, ed. by R. Duncan and M. Weston-Smith p97-105

**Medical care**

*See also* Insurance, Health

#### Costs

*See* Medical care, Cost of

#### Economic aspects

*See* Medical economics

#### France

Drury, P. and Enthoven, A. C. Competition and health care costs. *In* The Economy in the 1980s: a program for growth and stability, ed. by M. J. Boskin p393-417

Léonard, J. Women, religion, and medicine. *In* Medicine and society in France, ed. by R. Forster and O. Ranum p24-47

**Medical care, Cost of**

#### United States

Campbell, R. R. Your health and the government. *In* The United States in the 1980s, ed. by P. Duignan and A. Rabushka p285-341

**Medical college applicants.** See Medical colleges—Admission

**Medical colleges**

**Admission**

Morowitz, H. J. Zen and the art of getting into medical school. *In* Morowitz, H. J. The wine of life, and other essays on societies, energy & living things p115-19

**Medical delusions**

Medawar, Sir P. B. A bouquet of fallacies from medicine and medical science with a sideways glance at mathematics and logic. *In* Lying truths, ed. by R. Duncan and M. Weston-Smith p97-105

**Medical economics**

*See also* Medical care, Cost of

**United States**

Intriligator, M. D. Issues in the economics of health. *In* Economic issues of the eighties, ed. by N. M. Kamrany and R. H. Day p119-34

**Medical education**

Morowitz, H. J. Helmholtz, Mayer, and the M.D.-Ph.D. program. *In* Morowitz, H. J. The wine of life, and other essays on societies, energy & living things p125-28

**Medical ethics.** See Euthanasia

**Medical literature**

Klebs, A. C. Gleanings from incunabula of science and medicine. *In* The Bibliographical Society of America, 1904-79 p71-107

**Medical personnel and patient**

La Barre, W. The patient and his families. *In* La Barre, W. Culture in context p225-32

**Medical policy**

**United States**

Campbell, R. R. Your health and the government. *In* The United States in the 1980s, ed. by P. Duignan and A. Rabushka p285-341

Drury, P. and Enthoven, A. C. Competition and health care costs. *In* The Economy in the 1980s: a program for growth and stability, ed. by M. J. Boskin p393-417

**Medical profession.** See Physicians

**Medical service, Cost of.** See Medical care, Cost of

**Medical service, Prepaid.** See Insurance, Health

**Medical superstitions.** See Medical delusions

**Medication, Self.** See Self medication

**Medicine**

*See also* Hospitals

**History**

Morowitz, H. J. The Merck of time. *In* Morowitz, H. J. The wine of life, and other essays on societies, energy & living things p120-24

**Language**

Johnson, D. Doctor talk. *In* The State of the language, ed. by L. Michaels and C. Ricks p396-99

**France**

Goubert, J. P. The art of healing: learned medicine and popular medicine in the France of 1790. *In* Medicine and society in France, ed. by R. Forster and O. Ranum p 1-23

**United States—History**

Meeker, E. F. Medicine and public health. *In* Encyclopedia of American economic history, ed. by G. Porter v3 p1058-67

**Medicine, Ancient**

Erickson, G. Possession, sex and hysteria: the growth of demonism in later antiquity. *In* 5000 years of popular culture, ed. by F. E. H. Schroeder p110-35

**Medicine, Popular**

Goubert, J. P. The art of healing: learned medicine and popular medicine in the France of 1790. *In* Medicine and society in France, ed. by R. Forster and O. Ranum p 1-23

**Medicine, State.** See Public health

**Medicine and state.** See Medical policy

**Medieval literature.** See Literature, Medieval

**Medieval rhetoric.** See Rhetoric, Medieval

**Medieval sermons.** See Sermons, Medieval

**Medievalists**

Le Goff, J. The several Middle Ages of Jules Michelet. *In* Le Goff, J. Time, work, & culture in the Middle Ages p3-28

Morrison, K. F. Fragmentation and unity in "American medievalism." *In* The Past before us, ed. by M. Kammen p49-77

**Medio, Dolores**

**About individual works**

*Diario de una maestra*

Fox-Lockert, L. Dolores Medio. *In* Fox-Lockert, L. Women novelists in Spain and Spanish America p107-13

**Mediterranean region**

**History**

Braudel, F. The Mediterranean and the Mediterranean world in the age of Philip II; excerpt. *In* Braudel, F. On history p3-5

**Medvedev, Roĭ Aleksandrovich**

The Stalin question. *In* The Soviet Union since Stalin, ed. by S. F. Cohen, A. Rabinowitch and R. Sharlet p32-49

**Medvedev, Roy A.** See Medvedev, Roĭ Aleksandrovich

**Meeker, Edward Franklin**

Medicine and public health. *In* Encyclopedia of American economic history, ed. by G. Porter v3 p1058-67

**Meged, Aron.** See Megged, Aharon

**Megged, Aharon**

**About individual works**

*Genesis*

Abramson, G. Thematic development: The Biblical-historical play. *In* Abramson, G. Modern Hebrew drama p82-115

**Meggers, Betty Jane, and Evans, Clifford**

An experimental reconstruction of Taruma Village succession and some implications. *In* Brazil, anthropological perspectives, ed. by M. L. Margolis and W. E. Carter p39-60

**Mehinacu Indians**

Gregor, T. A. Secrets, exclusion, and the dramatization of men's roles. *In* Brazil, anthropological perspectives, ed by M. L. Margolis and W. E. Carter p250-69

**Mehinkaku Indians.** See Mehinacu Indians

**Mehler, Jacques**

Psychology and psycholinguistics: the impact of Chomsky and Piaget. *In* Language and learning, ed. by M. Piattelli-Palmarini p341-53

**Meier, Gerald M.**

U.S. foreign economic policies. *In* The United States in the 1980s, ed. by P. Duignan and A. Rabushka p585-611

**Meiji Restoration.** See Japan—History—Restoration, 1853-1870

**Meinig, Donald William**

The beholding eye: ten versions of the same scene. *In* The Interpretation of ordinary landscapes, ed. by D. W. Meinig p33-48

Reading the landscape: an appreciation of W. C. Heskins and J. B. Jackson. *In* The Interpretation of ordinary landscapes, ed. by D. H. Meinig p195-244

Symbolic landscapes: some idealizations of American communities. *In* The Interpretation of ordinary landscapes, ed. by D. W. Meinig p164-92

**Meisl, Josef**

Graetz, and national Judaism. *In* The Jew, ed. by A. A. Cohen p43-51

Jewish historical writing. *In* The Jew, ed. by A. A. Cohen p198-211

**Meiss, Millard**

**About**

Schapiro, M. On an Italian painting of the Flagellation of Christ in the Frick Collection. *In* Schapiro, M. Selected papers v3: Late antique, early Christian and mediaeval art p355-79

**Melczer, William.** See Melczer, Willy

**Melczer, Willy**

The war of the carrots and the onions or concentration versus dispersion: the methodology of interdisciplinary studies applied to the European courts. *In* The Expansion and transformations of courtly literature, ed. by N. B. Smith and J. T. Snow p207-26

**Mellaart, James**

Early urban communities in the Near East, c9000-3400 BC. *In* The Origins of civilization, ed. by P. R. S. Moorey p22-33

**Mellinkoff, Ruth Delores**

· Cain's monstrous progeny in Beowulf: part I, Noachic tradition. *In* Anglo-Saxon ,England 8 p143-62

**Mellor, Anne Kostelanetz**

English romantic irony

*Contents*

Byron: "half dust, half deity"

Carlyle's Sartor resartus: a self-consuming artifact

A conclusion in which nothing is concluded

Fear and trembling: from Lewis Carroll to existentialism

Guilt and Samuel Taylor Coleridge

Keats and the vale of soul-making

The paradigm of romantic irony

**Mellor, David**

British art in the 1930s: some economic, political and cultural structures. *In* Class, culture and social change, ed. by F. Glover-smith p185-207

**Melodrama**

Irwin, M. Readings of melodrama. *In* Reading the Victorian novel: detail into form, ed. by I. Gregor p15-31

James, L. Was Jerrold's Black ey'd Susan more popular than Wordsworth's Lucy? *In* Performance and politics in popular drama, ed. by D. Bradby, L. James and B. Sharratt p3-16

Mayer, D. The music of melodrama. *In* Performance and politics in popular drama, ed. by D. Bradby, L. James and B. Sharratt p49-63

**Mélusine in literature**

Le Goff, J. Melusina: mother and pioneer. *In* Le Goff, J. Time, work, & culture in the Middle Ages p205-22

**Melody**

Dent, E. J. [Melody and harmony] *In* Dent, E. J. Selected essays p142-57

**Melville, Herman**

**About**

Irwin, J. T. Melville: the indeterminate ground; a conjunction of fountain and vortex; the myth of Isis and Osiris; master oppositions; the doubleness of the self and the illusion of consistent character; Dionysus and Apollo; mask and phallus; the chain of partial objects. *In* Irwin, J. T. American hieroglyphics p285-349

Plomer, W. C. F. Herman Melville. *In* Plomer, W. C. F. Electric delights p50-57

**About individual works**

*Clarel*

Rosenthal, B. Herman Melville's Wandering Jews. *In* Puritan influences in American literature, ed. by E. Elliott p167-92

*The confidence-man*

Irwin, J. T. Melville: the indeterminate ground; a conjunction of fountain and vortex; the myth of Isis and Osiris; master oppositions; the doubleness of the self and the illusion of consistent character; Dionysus and Apollo; mask and phallus; the chain of partial objects. *In* Irwin, J. T. American hieroglyphics p285-349

*Moby Dick*

Irwin, J. T. Melville: the indeterminate ground; a conjunction of fountain and vortex; the myth of Isis and Osiris; master oppositions; the doubleness of the self and the illusion of consistent character; Dionysus and Apollo; mask and phallus; the chain of partial objects. *In* Irwin, J. T. American hieroglyphics p285-349

*Pierre*

Sundquist, E. J. "At home in his words": parody and parricide in Melville's Pierre. *In* Sundquist, E. J. Home as found p143-85

**Bibliography**

Parker, H. Melville. *In* American literary scholarship, 1978 p43-58

**Memoirs.** See Autobiography

**Memory**

Moberg, C. A. What does mankind remember—and for how long? An archaeologist's reflections on some recent claims. *In* The Condition of man, ed. by P. Hallberg p60-79

**The memory of justice (Motion picture)**

Kael, P. Running into trouble. *In* Kael, P. When the lights go down p172-79

Kauffmann, S. The memory of justice. *In* Kauffmann, S. Before my eyes p248-51

**Men**

Dundes, A. A psychoanalytic study of the bullroarer. *In* Dundes, A. Interpreting folklore p176-98

**Menander, of Athens**

**About**

Bain, D. Plautus uortit barbare: Plautus, Bacchides 526-61 and Menander, Dis exapaton 102-12. *In* Creative imitation and Latin literature, ed. by D. West and T. Woodman p17-34

Turner, E. G. The rhetoric of question and answer in Menander. *In* Drama and mimesis, ed. by J. Redmond p 1-23

**Menard, Henry William**

Very like a spear. *In* New Hampshire Bicentennial Conference on the History of Geology, University of New Hampshire, 1976. Two hundred years of geology in America p19-30

**Menard, Russell R.** See Carr, L. G. jt. auth.

**Menasseh ben Joseph ben Israel**

### About

Popkin, R. H. Jewish messianism and Christian millenarianism. *In* Culture and politics from Puritanism to the Enlightenment, ed. by P. Zagorin p67-90

**Mencken, Henry Louis**

### About

Cairns, H. Mencken of Baltimore. *In* On Mencken, ed. by J. Dorsey p51-83

Knopf, A. A. H. L. Mencken: a memoir. *In* On Mencken, ed. by J. Dorsey p283-313

Manchester, W. R. Mencken in person. *In* On Mencken, ed. by J. Dorsey p3-13

Nolte, W. H. The literary critic. *In* On Mencken, ed. by J. Dorsey p196-205

### About individual works
#### The new Mencken letters

Brustein, R. S. H. L. Mencken (The new Mencken letters). *In* Brustein, R. S. Critical moments p25-29

### Biography—Character

Bode, C. Mencken in his letters. *In* On Mencken, ed. by J. Dorsey p241-50

### Biography—Personality

*See* Mencken, Henry Louis—Biography—Character

### Language—Style

*See* Mencken, Henry Louis—Style

### Philosophy

Fecher, C. A. The comfortable bourgeois: the thought of H. L. Mencken. *In* On Mencken, ed. by J. Dorsey p114-27

*See also* Mencken, Henry Louis—Political and social views

### Political and social views

Moos, M. Mencken, politics, and politicians. *In* On Mencken, ed. by J. Dorsey p150-65

### Social views

*See* Mencken, Henry Louis—Political and social views

### Style

Cooke, A. A. Mencken and the English language. *In* On Mencken, ed. by J. Dorsey p84-113

### Technique

*See* Mencken, Henry Louis—Style

**Mendeleejj, D. I.** See Mendeleev, Dmitrii Ivanovich

**Mendeleev, Dmitrii Ivanovich**

### About

Alexandrov, E. A. 100th anniversary of observations on petroleum geology in the U.S.A. by Dmitriy I. Mendeleyev. *In* New Hampshire Bicentennial Conference on the History of Geology, University of New Hampshire, 1976. Two hundred years of geology in America p285-88

**Mendeleyev, Dmitriy I.** See Mendeleev, Dmitrii Ivanovich

**Mendel's law.** See Genetics

**Mendelssohn, Moses**

### About

Abramsky, C. The crisis of authority within European Jewry in the eighteenth century. *In* Studies in Jewish religious and intellectual history, ed. by S. Stein and R. Loewe p13-28

### About individual works
#### Über de Frage: Was heisst Aufklären?

Rotenstreich, N. Enlightenment: between Mendelssohn and Kant. *In* Studies in Jewish religious and intellectual history, ed. by S. Stein and R. Loewe p263-79

**Menocchio.** See Scandella, Domenico

**Mental disorders.** See Mental illness

**Mental health.** See Mental illness

**Mental health policy**

### Great Britain

Treacher, A. and Baruch, G. Towards a critical history of the psychiatric profession. *In* Critical psychiatry, ed. by D. Ingleby p120-49

### Norway

Haugsgjerd, S. Report from Norway. *In* Critical psychiatry, ed. by D. Ingleby p193-208

### Trieste

Basaglia, F. Breaking the circuit of control. *In* Critical psychiatry, ed. by D. Ingleby p184-92

### United States

Conrad, P. On the medicalization of deviance and social control. *In* Critical psychiatry, ed. by D. Ingleby p102-19

Kovel, J. The American mental health industry. *In* Critical psychiatry, ed. by D. Ingleby p72-101

**Mental health and state.** See Mental health policy

**Mental hygiene.** See Mental illness

**Mental illness**

Ingleby, D. Understanding 'mental illness.' *In* Critical psychiatry, ed. by D. Ingleby p23-71

Szasz, T. S. The lying truths of psychiatry. *In* Lying truths, ed. by R. Duncan and M. Weston-Smith p121-42

### United States

Kovel, J. The American mental health industry. *In* Critical psychiatry, ed. by D. Ingleby p72-101

**Mental illness and art.** See Art and mental illness

**Mercador del Rio Hernández, Jaime Ramón**

### About

Trilling, L. The assassination of Leon Trotsky. *In* Trilling, L. Speaking of literature and society p367-73

**Merchants**

### Europe

Le Goff, J. Merchant's time and church's time in the Middle Ages. *In* Le Goff, J. Time, work, & culture in the Middle Ages p29-42

### United States—History

Salsbury, S. M. American business institutions before the railroad. *In* Encyclopedia of American economic history, ed. by G. Porter v2 p601-18

**Mercier, Louis Sébastien**

### About individual works
#### Paris

Lough, J. Women in Mercier's Tableau de Paris. *In* Woman and society in eighteenth-century France, ed. by E. Jacobs and others p110-22

**Mercier, Sébastien.** See Mercier, Louis Sébastien

**The Merck manual of diagnosis and therapy**

Morowitz, H. J. The Merck of time. *In* Morowitz, H. J. The wine of life, and other essays on societies, energy & living things p120-24

**Mercy death.** See Euthanasia

**Meredith, George**

### About

Henkle, R. B. Meredith and Butler: comedy as lyric, high culture, and the bourgeois trap. *In* Henkle, R. B. Comedy and culture p238-95

McGhee, R. D. Rossetti and Meredith. *In* McGhee, R. D. Marriage, duty & desire in Victorian poetry and drama p139-76

Stone, D. D. George Meredith: a romantic in spite of himself. *In* Stone, D. D. The romantic impulse in Victorian fiction p284-316

### About individual works
#### The egoist

Polhemus, R. M. Meredith's The egoist: the comedy of egoism. *In* Polhemus, R. M. Comic faith p204-44

**Meredith, William**

### About

Howard, R. William Meredith: "All of a piece and clever and at some level, true." *In* Howard, R. Alone with America p372-85

**Merger of corporations.** See Consolidation and merger of corporations

**Merezhkovskiĭ, Dmitriĭ Sergeevich**

### About

Rosenthal, B. G. Eschatology and the appeal of revolution: Merezhkovsky, Bely, Blok. *In* California Slavic studies v11 p104-39

**Merezhkovsky, D. S.** See Merezhkovskiĭ, Dmitriĭ Sergeevich

**Merkl, Peter H.**

Attitudes, ideology, and politics of party members. *In* Western European party systems, ed. by P. H. Merkl p402-89

Introduction: the study of party systems. *In* Western European party systems, ed. by P. H. Merkl p 1-19

The sociology of European parties: members, voters, and social groups. *In* Western European party systems, ed. by P. H. Merkl p614-67

West Germany. *In* Western European party systems, ed. by P. H. Merkl p21-60

**Merovingians**

Le Goff, J. Clerical culture and folklore traditions in Merovingian civilization. *In* Le Goff, J. Time, work, & culture in the Middle Ages p153-58

**Merrill, James Ingram**

### About

Howard, R. James Merrill: "Masked, as who was not, in laughter, pain and love." *In* Howard, R. Alone with America p386-411

Howard, R. W. S. Merwin: "We survived the selves that we remembered." *In* Howard, R. Alone with America p412-49

Vendler, H. H. James Merrill. *In* Vendler, H. H. Part of nature, part of us p205-32

**Merriman, John M.**

Incident at the statue of the Virgin Mary: the conflict of old and new in nineteenth-century Limoges. *In* Consciousness and class experience in nineteenth-century Europe, ed. by J. M. Merriman p129-48

**Merton, Robert King**

Insiders and outsiders: an essay in the sociology of knowledge. *In* Value and values in evolution, ed. by E. A. Maziarz p47-69

**Merwin, William Stanley**

### About

Vendler, H. H. W. S. Merwin. *In* Vendler, H. H. Part of nature, part of us p233-36

**Meschinot, Jean**

### About

Zumthor, P. A reading of a ballade by Jean Meschinot. *In* The Interpretation of medieval lyric poetry, ed. by W. T. H. Jackson p142-62

**Mesoamerica.** From village to city in. Bray, W. *In* The Origins of civilization, ed. by P. R. S. Moorey p78-102

**Mesopotamia.** See Iraq

**Messiah.** See Messianic era (Judaism)

**Messianic era (Judaism)**

Popkin, R. H. Jewish messianism and Christian millenarianism. *In* Culture and politics from Puritanism to the Enlightenment, ed. by P. Zagorin p67-90

**Messianism in literature**

Wohlfarth, I. The politics of prose and the art of awakening: Walter Benjamin's version of a German romantic motif. *In* Glyph 7 p131-48

**Metal industries.** See Metal trade

**Metal trade**

#### New England—History

Soltow, J. H. Origins of small business and the relationships between large and small firms: metal fabricating and machinery making in New England, 1890-1957. *In* Small business in American life, ed. by S. W. Bruchey p192-211

**Metalanguage**

Bolinger, D. L. Fire in a wooden stove: on being aware in language. *In* The State of the language, ed. by L. Michaels and C. Ricks p379-88

**Metaphor**

Cook, A. S. Metaphor: literature's access to myth. *In* Cook, A. S. Myth & language p248-59

De Man, P. Metaphor (Second discourse) *In* De Man, P. Allegories of reading p139-59

De Man, P. Self (Pygmalion). *In* De Man, P. Allegories of reading p160-87

Ruegg, M. Metaphor and metonymy: the logic of a structuralist rhetoric. *In* Glyph 6 p141-57

Mackenzie, E. The growth of plants: a seventeenth-century metaphor. *In* English Renaissance studies, ed. by J. Carey p194-211

**Metaphysics.** See Causation

**Metcalf, Rosamund**

West Indian literature. *In* African literature today no. 10: Retrospect & prospect, ed. by E. D. Jones p253-55

**Methodist Church**

#### Missions

O'Flaherty, P. Fishers of men: three missionaries in eighteenth-century Newfoundland, 1764-98. *In* O'Flaherty, P. The rock observed p16-31

**Metropolitan areas**

#### Historiography

Conzen, K. N. Community studies, urban history, and American local history. *In* The Past before us, ed. by M. Kammen p270-91

**Mexican American literature (Spanish)**
Hinojosa, R. Chicano literature: an American literature in transition. *In* The Identification and analysis of Chicano literature, ed. by F. Jiménez p37-41
Rivera, T. Chicano literature: fiesta of the living. *In* The Identification and analysis of Chicano literature, ed. by F. Jiménez p19-36

**Mexican Americans**
Huerta, J. A. From the temple to the arena: Teatro Chicano today. *In* The Identification and analysis of Chicano literature, ed. by F. Jiménez p90-116
Jiménez, F. Dramatic principles of the Teatro Campesino. *In* The Identification and analysis of Chicano literature, ed. by F. Jiménez p117-32

**Education—Personal narratives**
Rodriguez, R. An education in language. *In* The State of the language, ed. by L. Michaels and C. Ricks p129-39

**Mexican Americans in literature**
Cárdenas de Dwyer, C. International literary metaphor and Ron Arias: an analysis of The road to Tamazunchale. *In* The Identification and analysis of Chicano literature, ed. by F. Jiménez p358-64
Grajeda, R. F. Jose Antonio Villarreal and Richard Vasquez: the novelist against himself. *In* The Identification and analysis of Chicano literature, ed. by F. Jiménez p329-57
Lyon, T. "Loss of innocence" in Chicano prose. *In* The Identification and analysis of Chicano literature, ed. by F. Jiménez p254-62
Tatum, C. M. Contemporary Chicano prose fiction: a chronicle of misery. *In* The Identification and analysis of Chicano literature, ed. by F. Jiménez p241-53
Tatum, C. M. Contemporary Chicano prose fiction: its ties to Mexican literature. *In* The Identification and analysis of Chicano literature, ed. by F. Jiménez p47-57

**Meyer, Bernard C.**
**About**
Trilling, L. Literary pathology. *In* Trilling, L. Speaking of literature and society p392-97

**Meyer, Conrad Ferdinand**
**About individual works**
*Auf Ponte Sisto*
Grundlehner, P. Conrad Ferdinand Meyer: "Auf Ponte Sisto." *In* Grundlehner, P. The lyrical bridge p69-77

*Die alte Brücke*
Grundlehner, P. Conrad Ferdinand Meyer: "Die alte Brücke." *In* Grundlehner, P. The lyrical bridge p53-67

**Meyer, Leonard B.**
The dilemma of choosing: speculations about contemporary culture. *In* Value and values in evolution, ed. by E. A. Maziarz p117-41
Toward a theory of style. *In* The Concept of style, ed. by B. Lang p3-44

**Meyerhold, Vsevolod Emilievich**
**About**
Worrall, N. Meyerhold and Eisenstein. *In* Performance and politics in popular drama, ed. by D. Bradby, L. James and B. Sharratt p173-87

**Meyvaert, Paul**
Bede and the church paintings at Wearmouth—Jarrow. *In* Anglo-Saxon England 8 p63-77

**Mézerai, François Eudes de.** See Mezeray, François Eudes de
**Mézeray, François Eudes de**
**About**
Ranum, O. Mézerai: a libertin historiographer royal. *In* Ranum, O. Artisans of glory p197-232

**Michael X.** See Malik, Michael Abdul

**Michelet, Jules**
**About**
Le Goff, J. The several Middle Ages of Jules Michelet. *In* Le Goff, J. Time, work, & culture in the Middle Ages p3-28

**Michaels, Leonard**
Legible death. *In* The State of the language, ed. by L. Michaels and C. Ricks p594-600

**Michaels, Walter Benn**
Against formalism: chickens and rocks. *In* The State of the language, ed. by L. Michaels and C. Ricks p410-20

**Michigan Folk Art Project**
Dewhurst, C. K. Expanding frontiers: the Michigan Folk Art Project. *In* Perspectives on American folk art, ed. by I. M. G. Quimby and S. T. Swank p54-78

**Microbiologists.** See Geneticists

**Microeconomics.** See Production (Economic theory)

**Micro-organisms.** See Mycoplasmatales

**Microsurgery**
Morowitz, H. J. On swallowing the surgeon. *In* Morowitz, H. J. The wine of life, and other essays on societies, energy & living things p141-44

**Middle age**
**Psychological aspects**
Gould, R. L. Transformations during early and middle adult years. *In* Themes of work and love in adulthood, ed. by N. J. Smelser and E. H. Erikson p213-37

**Middle Ages**
*See also* Church history—Middle Ages, 600-1500; Civilization, Medieval; Education, Medieval; Literature, Medieval and similar headings

**Historiography**
Morrison, K. F. Fragmentation and unity in "American medievalism." *In* The Past before us, ed. by M. Kammen p49-77
Ozment, S. H. The interpretation of medieval intellectual history. *In* Ozment, S. H. The age of reform, 1250-1550 p 1-21
Pickering, F. P. Notes on fate and fortune. *In* Pickering, F. P. Essays on medieval German literature and iconography p95-109
Pickering, F. P. The Western image of Byzantium in the Middle Ages. *In* Pickering, F. P. Essays on medieval German literature and iconography p146-63

**History**
Le Goff, J. Merchant's time and church's time in the Middle Ages. *In* Le Goff, J. Time, work, & culture in the Middle Ages p29-42
*See also* Civilization, Medieval; Feudalism; Fourteenth century

**History—476-1492**
Ozment, S. H. On the eve of the Reformation. *In* Ozment, S. H. The age of reform, 1250-1550 p182-222

**Middle classes**

Gay, P. On the bourgeoisie: a psychological interpretation. *In* Consciousness and class experience in nineteenth-century Europe, ed. by J. M. Merriman p187-203

### England

Henkle, R. B. 1820-1845: the anxieties of sublimation, and middle-class myths. *In* Henkle, R. B. Comedy and culture p20-57

Henkle, R. B. Hood, Gilbert, Carroll, Jerrold, and the Grossmiths: comedy from inside. *In* Henkle, R. B. Comedy and culture p185-237

### Russia

Bushnell, J. D. The "new Soviet man" turns pessimist. *In* The Soviet Union since Stalin, ed. by S. F. Cohen, A. Rabinowitch and R. Sharlet p179-99

### United States

Gonos, G. The class position of Goffman's sociology: social origins of an American structuralism. *In* The View from Goffman, ed. by J. Ditton p134-69

**Middle East.** See Near East

**The middle of the world (Motion picture)**

Kauffmann, S. The middle of the world. *In* Kauffmann, S. Before my eyes p126-28

**Middlesex County, Va.**

### Statistics, Vital

Rutman, D. B. and Rutman, A. H. "Now-wives and sons-in-law": parental death in a seventeenth-century Virginia county. *In* The Chesapeake in the seventeenth century, ed. by T. W. Tate and D. L. Ammerman p153-82

**Middletown, Anne**

Chaucer's "new men" and the good of literature in the Canterbury tales. *In* Literature and society, ed. by E. W. Said p15-56

**Midelfort, H. C. Erik**

Witch hunting and the domino theory. *In* Religion and the people, 800-1700 p277-88

**Midnight express (Motion picture)**

Kael, P. Movie yellow journalism *In* Kael, P. When the light go down p496-501

**Midwives**

### France

Lager, M. Childbirth in seventeenth-and eighteenth-century France: obstetrical practices and collective attitudes. *In* Medicine and society in France, ed. by R. Forster and O. Ranum p137-76

**Migration, Internal**

### United States—History

Ridge, M. Westward movement. *In* Encyclopedia of American economic history, ed. by G. Porter v2 p575-87

**Mikellides, Byron**

Appendix on human needs. *In* Architecture for people, ed. by B. Mikellides p191-92

Architectural psychology and the unavoidable art. *In* Architecture for people, ed. by B. Mikellides p9-26

**Mikey and Nicky (Motion picture)**

Kauffmann, S. Mikey and Nicky. *In* Kauffmann, S. Before my eyes p272-75

**Miles, Josephine**

Values in language; or, Where have goodness, truth, and beauty gone? *In* The State of the language, ed. by L. Michaels and C. Ricks p362-76

**Milic, Louis Tonko**

The metaphor of time as space. *In* Probability, time, and space in eighteenth-century literature, ed. by P. R. Backscheider p249-58

**Militarism**

Albrecht, U. Militarism and underdevelopment. *In* Problems of contemporary militarism, ed. by A. Eide and M. Thee p106-26

Eckhardt, W. The causes and correlates of Western militarism. *In* Problems of contemporary militarism, ed. by A. Eide and M. Thee p323-55

Eide, A. Militarisation with a global reach: a challenge to sovereignty, security and the international legal order. *In* Problems of contemporary militarism, ed. by A. Eide and M. Thee p299-322

Eide, A. and Thee, M. Introduction. *In* Problems of contemporary militarism, ed. by A. Eide and M. Thee p9-11

Klare, M. T. Militarism: the issues today. *In* Problems of contemporary militarism, ed. by A. Eide and M. Thee p36-46

Kučuk, E. The socio-class determinants of militarism. *In* Problems of contemporary militarism, ed. by A. Eide and M. Thee p148-72

Lider, J. The critique of militarism in Soviet studies. *In* Problems of contemporary militarism, ed. by A. Eide and M. Thee p173-91

Lumsden, M. Militarism: cultural dimensions of militarisation. *In* Problems of contemporary militarism, ed. by A. Eide and M. Thee p356-69

Øberg, J. The new international order: a threat to human security. *In* Problems of contemporary militarism, ed. by A. Eide and M. Thee p47-74

Skjelsbæk, K. Militarism, its dimensions and corollaries: an attempt at conceptual clarification. *In* Problems of contemporary militarism, ed. by A. Eide and M. Thee p77-105

Thee, M. Militarism and militarisation in contemporary international relations. *In* Problems of contemporary militarism, ed. by A. Eide and M. Thee p15-35

*See also* Imperialism

### North America

Regehr, E. What is militarism? *In* Problems of contemporary militarism, ed. by A. Eide and M. Thee p127-39

### Underdeveloped areas

Albrecht, U. Militarism and underdevelopment. *In* Problems of contemporary militarism, ed. by A. Eide and M. Thee p106-26

Falk, R. A. Militarisation and human rights in the Third World. *In* Problems of contemporary militarism, ed. by A. Eide and M. Thee p207-25

Senghaas, D. Militarism dynamics in the contemporary context of periphery capitalism. *In* Problems of contemporary militarism, ed. by A. Eide and M. Thee p195-206

**Military art and science.** See Strategy

**Military-civil relations.** See Militarism

**Military contracts.** See Defense contracts

**Military government**

Falk, R. A. Militarisation and human rights in the Third World. *In* Problems of contemporary militarism, ed. by A. Eide and M. Thee p207-25

Senghaas, D. Militarism dynamics in the contemporary context of periphery capitalism. *In* Problems of contemporary militarism, ed. by A. Eide and M. Thee p195-206

**Military history, Modern**
Whaley, B. Deception—its decline and revival in international conflict. *In* Propaganda and communication in world history, ed. by H. D. Lasswell, D. Lerner and H. Speier v2 p339-67

**20th century**
Kende, I. Local wars, 1945-76. *In* Problems of contemporary militarism, ed. by A. Eide and M. Thee p261-85

**Military policy.** See Militarism; National security; subdivision Military policy under names of countries, e.g. Canada—Military policy

**Military research**

**United States—History**
Sapolsky, H. M. Academic science and the military: the years since the Second World War. *In* The Sciences in the American context: new perspectives, ed. by N. Reingold p379-99

**Military sales.** See Munitions

**Military sociology.** See Sociology, Military

**Military strategy.** See Strategy

**Milkman, Ruth**
Women's work and the economic crisis: some lessons from the Great Depression. *In* A Heritage of her own, ed. by N. F. Cott and E. H. Pleck p507-41

**Mill, John Stuart**

**About**
Norton, D. L. Equality and excellence in the democratic ideal. *In* History, religion, and spiritual democracy, ed. by M. Wohlgelernter p273-93

**About individual works**
*Principles of political economy*
Heinzelman, K. "Unreal words": language in political economy. *In* Heinzelman, K. The economics of the imagination p70-109

**Millar, James R.**
Post-Stalin agriculture and its future. *In* The Soviet Union since Stalin, ed. by S. F. Cohen, A. Rabinowitch and R. Sharlet p113-34

**Millar, Kenneth**

**About**
Brown, R. Ross Macdonald as Canadian mystery writer. *In* Seasoned authors for a new season: the search for standards in popular writing, ed. by L. Filler p164-69

**Millenarianism.** See Millennialism

**Millennialism**
Lewy, G. Millenarianism as a revolutionary force. *In* Propaganda and communication in world history, ed. by H. D. Lasswell, D. Lerner and H. Speier v2 p168-209
Popkin, R. H. Jewish messianism and Christian millenarianism. *In* Culture and politics from Puritanism to the Enlightenment, ed. by P. Zagorin p67-90

**Millennianism.** See Millenialism

**Millennium.** See Millennialism

**Miller, Arthur, 1915-**

**About individual works**
*Death of a salesman*
Wilson, R. N. Arthur Miller: the salesman and society. *In* Wilson, R. N. The writer as social seer p56-71

**Miller, Charlotte I.**
The function of middle-class extended family networks in Brazilian urban society. *In* Brazil, anthropological perspectives, ed. by M. L. Margolis and W. E. Carter p305-16

**Miller, D. A.**
Language of detective fiction: fiction of detective language. *In* The State of the language, ed. by L. Michaels and C. Ricks p478-99

**Miller, Gabriel**
Screening the novel
*Contents*
The gangster as existential hero
Jews without manners
Marathon man/marathon woman
Murder in the first degree
The new woman gets the old treatment
Special delivery
Those who walk in darkness
The wages of sin

**Miller, Jane**
How do you spell Gujarati, sir? *In* The State of the language, ed. by L. Michaels and C. Ricks p140-51

**Miller, John Henry**

**About**
Adams, W. P. The colonial German-language press and the American Revolution. *In* The Press & the American Revolution, ed. by B. Bailyn and J. B. Hench p151-228

**Miller, Joseph Hillis**
A "buchstabliches" reading of The elective affinities. *In* Glyph 6 p 1-23
Theoretical and atheoretical in Stevens. *In* Wallace Stevens, ed. by F. Doggett and R. Buttel p274-85

**Miller, Molly**
The dates of Deira. In Anglo-Saxon England 8 p35-61

**Miller, Nancy K.**
The heroine's text
*Contents*
Epilogue
A harlot's progress: I, Moll Flanders
A harlot's progress: II, Fanny Hill
Love for a harlot
The misfortunes of virtue: I, Clarissa
The misfortunes of virtue: II, La nouvelle Heloïse
The misfortunes of virtue: III, Les liaisons dangereuses
The negative heroine: Les liasons dangereuses
The rewards of virtue
The virtuous orphan

**Miller, Perry**
The responsibility of mind in a civilization of machines
*Contents*
The Cambridge Platform in 1648
Education under cross fire
Equality in the American setting
Europe's faith in American fiction
The incorruptible Sinclair Lewis
Individualism and the New England tradition
John Bunyan's Pilgrim's progress
Liberty and conformity
The New England conscience
Nineteenth-century New England and its descendants
The plight of the lone wolf
Religious background of the Bay Psalm book

**Miller, Perry**
The responsibility of mind in a civilization of machines

*Contents—Continued*

The responsibility of mind in a civilization of machines
The social context of the covenant
What drove me crazy in Europe

### About individual works
*Errand into the wilderness*

Bercovitch, S. Rhetoric and history in early New England: the Puritan errand re-assessed. *In* Toward a new American literary history, ed. by L. J. Budd, E. H. Cady and C. L. Anderson p54-68

**Millett, Kate**

### About individual works
*Flying*

Juhasz, S. Towards a theory of form in feminist autobiography: Kate Millett's Flying and Sita; Maxine Hong Kingston's The woman warrior. *In* Women's autobiography, ed. by E. C. Jelinek p221-37

Kolodny, A. The lady's not for spurning: Kate Millett and the critics. *In* Women's autobiography, ed. by E. C. Jelinek p238-59

*Sita*

Juhasz, S. Towards a thory of form in feminist autobiography: Kate Millett's Flying and Sita; Maxine Hong Kingston's The woman warrior. *In* Women's autobiography, ed. by E. C. Jelinek p221-37

**Mills, Charles Wright**

### About individual works
*White collar*

Gonos, G. The class position of Goffman's sociology: social origins of an American structuralism. *In* The View from Goffman, ed. by J. Ditton p134-69

**Mills, John Orme**
God, man and media: on a problem arising when theologians speak of the modern world. *In* Sociology and theology: alliance and conflict, ed. by D. Martin, J. O. Mills [and] W. S. F. Pickering p136-50

Introduction: of two minds. *In* Sociology and theology: alliance and conflict, ed. by D. Martin, J. O. Mills [and] W. S. F. Pickering p 1-14

**Mills, Patricia Jagentowicz**
Hegel and 'the woman question': recognition and intersubjectivity. *In* The Sexism of social and political theory: women and reproduction from Plato to Nietzsche, ed. by L. M. G. Clark and L. Lange p74-98

**Milton, John**

### About

Hagstrum, J. H. Milton and the ideal of heterosexual friendship. *In* Hagstrum, J. H. Sex and sensibility p24-49

Hill, J. E. C. George Wither and John Milton. *In* English Renaissance studies, ed. by J. Carey p212-27

Knott, J. R. Milton and the spirit of truth. *In* Knott, J. R. The sword of the spirit p106-30

Waddington, R. B. Milton among the Carolines. *In* The Age of Milton, ed. by C. A. Patrides and R. B. Waddington p338-64

### About individual works
*Animadversions upon the remonstrants defense against Smectymnuus*

Anselment, R. A. John Milton contra Hall. *In* Anselment, R. A. 'Betwixt jest and earnest' p61-93

*An apology against a pamphlet call'd A modest confutation of the animadversions upon a remonstrant against Smectymnuus*

Anselment, R. A. John Milton contra Hall. *In* Anselment, R. A. 'Betwixt jest and earnest' p61-93

*Lycidas*

Evans, J. M. Lycidas, Daphnis, and Gallus. *In* English Renaissance studies, ed. by J. Carey p228-44

*On the morning of Christ's nativity*

Fry, P. H. Milton's light-harnessed ode. *In* Fry, P. H. The poet's calling in the English ode p37-48

*Paradise lost*

Briggs, P. M. The Jonathan Richardsons as Milton critics. *In* Studies in eighteenth-century culture v9 p115-30

Moyles, R. G. The text of Paradise lost: a stemma for the early editions. *In* Virginia. University. Bibliographical Society. Studies in bibliography v33 p168-82

Mueller, M. The tragic epic: Paradise lost and the Iliad. *In* Mueller, M. Children of Oedipus, and other essays on the imitation of Greek tragedy, 1550-1800 p213-30

Murrin, M. The language of Milton's heaven. *In* Murrin, M. The allegorical epic p153-71

Wilkes, G. A. 'Full of doubt I stand': the final implications of Paradise lost. *In* English Renaissance studies, ed. by J. Carey p271-78

*Samson Agonistes*

Hartman, G. Diction and defense in Wordsworth. *In* The Literary Freud: mechanisms of defense and the poetic will, ed. by J. H. Smith p205-15

Mueller, M. The tragedy of deliverance: Samson Agonistes. *In* Mueller, M. Children of Oedipus, and other essays on the imitation of Greek tragedy, 1550-1800 p193-212

### Criticism, Textual

Moyles, R. G. The text of Paradise lost: a stemma for the early editions. *In* Virginia. University. Bibliographical Society. Studies in bibliography v33 p168-82

### Religion and ethics

Hunsaker, O. G. Roger Williams and John Milton: the calling of the Puritan writer. *In* Puritan influences in American literature, ed. by E. Elliott p3-22

### Style
*See* Milton, John—Technique

### Technique

Everett, B. The end of the big names: Milton's epic catalogues. *In* English Renaissance studies, ed. by J. Carey p254-70

**Mimesis in literature**
Dollimore, J. Two concepts of mimesis: Renaissance literary theory and The revenger's tragedy. *In* Drama and mimesis, ed. by J. Redmond p25-50

Fuegi, J. Meditations on mimesis: the case of Brecht. *In* Drama and mimesis, ed. by J. Redmond p103-12

**Mimesis in literature**—*Continued*

Maxwell, D. E. S. The shape-changers. *In* Yeats, Sligo and Ireland, ed. by A. N. Jeffares p153-69

*See also* Imitation (in literature)

**Minaco Indians.** See Mehinacu Indians

**Minas Gerais, Brazil**

### Social conditions

Greenfield, S. M. Patron-client exchanges in southeastern Minas Gerais. *In* Brazil, anthropological perspectives, ed. by M. L. Margolis and W. E. Carter p362-78

**Minas Velhas, Brazil**

### Social conditions

Braudel, F. In Bahia, Brazil: the present explains the past. *In* Braudel, F. On history p165-76

**Mind.** See Intellect

**Mind and body**

Morowitz, H. J. Good news for humanists. *In* Morowitz, H. J. The wine of life, and other essays on societies, energy & living things p33-36

Selby, H. "Never finding full repast:" satire and self-extension in the early eighteenth century. *In* Probability, time, and space in eighteenth-century literature, ed. by P. R. Backscheider p217-47

**Minnesinger**

Wapnewski, P. Dietmar von Eist XII: 'Nu ist ez an ein Ende komen.' *In* The Interpretation of medieval lyric poetry, ed. by W. T. H. Jackson p163-75

**Minorities**

*See also* Nationalism

### Employment

*See* Affirmative action programs

### Russia

Suny, R. G. Georgia and Soviet nationality policy. *In* The Soviet Union since Stalin, ed. by S. F. Cohen, A. Rabinowitch and R. Sharlet p200-26

### United States

Harevan, T. K. The search for generational memory: tribal rites in industrial society. *In* Generations, ed. by S. R. Graubard p137-49

**Minsky, Marvin Lee**

Computer science and the representation of knowledge. *In* The Computer age: a twenty-year view, ed. by M. L. Dertouzos and J. Moses p392-421

**Mintz, Samuel I.**

The motion of thought: intellectual and philosophical backgrounds. *In* The Age of Milton, ed. by C. A. Patrides and R. B. Waddington p138-69

**Mirandola, Giovanni Pico della.** See Pico della Mirandola, Giovanni

**Mirsky, Arthur**

Geologic resources of the original thirteen United States (summary). *In* New Hampshire Bicentennial Conference on the History of Geology, University of New Hampshire, 1976. Two hundred years of geology in America p39-41

**Mishna. Tamid**

Neusner, J. Dating a Mishnah-Tractate: the case of Tamid. *In* History, religion, and spiritual democracy, ed. by M. Wohlgelernter p97-113

**Missionaries**

Wyatt-Brown, B. Conscience and career: young abolitionists and missionaries. *In* Antislavery, religion, and reform: essays in memory of Roger Anstey, ed. by C. Bolt and S. Drescher p183-203

**Missions**

### History—Early church, ca. 30-600

Forman, C. W. Christian missions in the ancient world. *In* Propaganda and communication in world history, ed. by H. D. Lasswell, D. Lerner and H. Speier v 1 p330-47

### Newfoundland

O'Flaherty, P. Fishers of men: three missionaries in eighteenth-century Newfoundland, 1864-98. *In* O'Flaherty, P. The rock observed p16-31

**The Missouri breaks (Motion picture)**

Kauffmann, S. The Missouri breaks. *In* Kauffmann, S. Before my eyes p134-37

**Mistacco, Vicki E.**

The theory and practice of reading nouveaux romans: Robbe-Grillet's Topologie d'une cité fantôme. *In* The Reader in the text, ed. by S. R. Suleiman and I. Crosman p371-400

**Mr Majestyk (Motion picture)**

Kauffmann, S. Mr. Majestyk/Death wish. *In* Kauffmann, S. Before my eyes p31-34

**Mitchell, Margaret**

### About individual works
*Gone with the wind*

Fiedler, L. A. The anti-Tom novel and the Great Depression: Margaret Mitchell's Gone with the wind. *In* Fiedler, L. A. The inadvertent epic p59-70

**Mittelhölzer, Edgar**

### About

Gilkes, M. Edgar Mittelholzer. *In* West Indian literature, ed. by B. King p95-110

**Mizener, Arthur**

### About individual works
*The far side of Paradise*

Trilling, L. Fitzgerald plain. *In* Trilling, L. Speaking of literature and society p255-59

**Mizoguchi, Kenji**

### About individual works
*My love has been burning*

Kauffmann, S. My love has been burning. *In* Kauffmann, S. Before my eyes p330-33

**Mizwahs, Six hundred and thirteen.** See Commandments, Six hundred and thirteen

**Moberg, Carl-Axel**

What does mankind remember—and for how long? An archaeologist's reflections on some recent claims. *In* The Condition of man, ed. by P. Hallberg p60-79

**Mobility.** See Social mobility

**Mobutu, Joseph Désiré.** See Mobutu, Sese Seko

**Mobutu, Sese Seko**

### About

Naipaul, V. S. A new king for the Congo: Mobutu and the nihilism of Africa. *In* Naipaul, V. S. The return of Eva Perón p173-204

**Moderation.** See Mean (Philosophy)

**Modern architecture.** See Architecture, Modern

**Modern civilization.** See Civilization, Modern

**Modern Language Association. Publications.** See PMLA

**Modern music.** See Music—History and criticism—20th century

**Modernism**

### Catholic Church

Daly, G. Introduction. *In* Daly, G. Transcendence and immanence p 1-6

Daly, G. Modernism in retrospect. *In* Daly, G. Transcendence and immanence p218-31

Daly, G. The integralist response (1): prelude to the Roman condemnation of Modernism. *In* Daly, G. Transcendence and immanence p165-89

**Modernism (Art)** See Art, Modern—20th century

**Moffat, Robert Scott**

### About individual works
*Mr Henry George, the "orthodox"*

Babilot, G. Moffat's "unorthodox" critique. *In* Critics of Henry George, ed. by R. V. Andelson p109-25

**Mohammedanism.** See Islam

**Moix, Ana Maria**

### About individual works
*Julia*

Schyfter, S. E. Rites without passage: the adolescent world of Ana Maria Moix's Julia. *In* The Analysis of literary texts, ed. by R. D. Pope p41-50

**Molecular biology**

### Research—United States

Kohler, R. E. Warren Weaver and the Rockefeller Foundation program in molecular biology: a case study in the management of science. *In* The Sciences in the American context: new perspectives, ed. by N. Reingold p249-93

**Molesworth, Charles**
The fierce embrace

*Contents*

"The burned essential oil": the gestures of Philip Levine
"The clear architecture of the nerves": the poetry of Frank O'Hara
Magazines and magazine verse
The metaphors for the poem
The poet and the poet's generation
"The rank flavor of blood": the poetry of Galway Kinnell
Reflections in place of a conclusion
"Rejoice in the gathering dark": the poetry of Robert Bly
Republican objects and utopian moments: the poetry of Robert Lowell and Allen Ginsberg
"Songs of a happy man": the poetry of Theodore Roethke
"This leaving-out business": the poetry of John Ashbery
"We have come this far": audience and form in contemporary poetry
"With your own face on": confessional poetry

**Momigliano, Arnaldo**
After Gibbon's Decline and fall. *In* Age of spirituality, ed. by K. Weitzmann p7-16

The rediscovery of Greek history in the eighteenth century: the case of Sicily. *In* Studies in eighteenth-century culture v9 p167-87

**Mommsen-Reindl, Margareta**
Austria. *In* Western European party system, ed. by P. H. Merkl p278-97

**Monastic and religious life**
Ozment, S. H. The spiritual traditions. *In* Ozment, S. H. The age of reform, 1250-1550 p73-134

**Monastic life.** See Monastic and religious life

**Monastic orders.** See Monasticism and religious orders

**Monasticism and religious orders**

### Middle Ages, 600-1500

Ozment, S. H. The spiritual traditions. *In* Ozment, S. H. The age of reform, 1250-1550 p73-134

**Monetary policy.** See Money supply

**Money**
Moore, B. J. Monetary factors. *In* A Guide to post-Keynesian economics, ed. by A. S. Eichner p120-38

*See also* Finance; Money supply

**Money in literature**
Stone, W. Forster on profit and loss. *In* E. M. Forster: a human exploration, ed. by G. K. Das and J. Beer p69-78

**Money supply**

### United States—History

Rockoff, H. Money supply. *In* Encyclopedia of American economic history, ed. by G. Porter v 1 p424-38

**Monkeys as laboratory animals**
Mason, W. A. Maternal attributes and primate cognitive development. *In* Human ethology, ed. by M. von Cranach [and others] p437-55

**Monopolies.** See Competition

**Monroe, Nellie Elizabeth**

### About individual works
*The novel and society*

Trilling, L. Artists and the "societal function." *In* Trilling, L. Speaking of literature and society p186-91

**Monsters.** See Dragons

**Montagnards**
Barbu, Z. The modern history of political fanaticism: a search for the roots. *In* Propaganda and communication in world history, ed. by H. D. Lasswell, D. Lerner and H. Speier v2 p112-44

**Montaigne, Michel Eyquem de**

### About individual works
*Essays*

Bauschatz, C. M. Montaigne's conception of reading in the context of Renaissance poetics and modern criticism. *In* The Reader in the text, ed. by S. R. Suleiman and I. Crosman p264-91

Reiss, T. J. Buchanan, Montaigne, and the difficulty of speaking. *In* Reiss, T. J. Tragedy and truth p40-77

**Montemayor, Jorge de**

### About individual works
*Diana*

Perry, T. A. Ideal love and human reality: Montemayor's pastoral philosophy. *In* Perry, T. A. Erotic spirituality p78-88

**Montesquieu, Charles Louis de Secondat, baron de La Brede et de**

### About

Berlin, Sir I. Montesquieu. *In* Berlin, Sir I. Against the current p130-61

Montesquieu Charles Louis de Secondat, baron
de La Brede et de—*Continued*

### About individual works
*The Persian letters*

Mason, S. M. The riddle of Roxane. *In*
Woman and society in eighteenth-century
France, ed. by E. Jacobs and others p28-41

*The spirit of the laws*

Mason, S. M. The riddle of Roxane. *In*
Woman and society in eighteenth-century
France, ed. by .E. Jacobs and others p28-41

Montesquieu, Jeanne (Lartique) baronne de la
Brède et de

### About

Shackleton, R. Madame de Montesquieu
with some considerations on Thérése de
Secondat. *In* Woman and society in eighteenth-
century France, ed. by E. Jacobs and others
p229-42

Montgomery, David
Work. *In* Encyclopedia of American economic history, ed. by G. Porter v3 p958-73

Montgomery, Robert Lawrence
The reader's eye

*Contents*

Conclusion
Dante's esthetic of grace and the reader's
imagination
Faculty psychology and theories of imagin-
ation: Aristotle, Plato, Augustine, and
Aquinas
"The gates of popular judgments": Sidney's
Apology for poetry (ca. 1581-1583)
Universals and particulars: Fracastoro and
Barbaro
Verisimilar things: Tasso's Discourses on the
heroic poem (1594)

Monuments, Sepulchral. See Sepulchral monuments

Moody, William Vaughn

### About

Arms, G. W. The poet as theme reader:
William Vaughn Moody, a student, and Louisa
May Alcott. *In* Toward a new American literary history, ed. by L. J. Budd, E. H. Cady
and C. L. Anderson p140-53

Mooers, Gary Royal
Computer impact and the social welfare
sector. *In* Monster or messiah? Ed. by W. M.
Mathews p 113-24

Mooney, Michael
The primacy of language in Vico. *In* Conference on Vico and Contemporary Thought,
New York, 1976. Vico and contemporary
thought pt 1 p191-210

Moore, Ann M. See Rudenstein, G. M. jt. auth.

Moore, Basil J.
Monetary factors. *In* A Guide to post-Keynesian economics, ed. by A. S. Eichner p120-38

Moore, Charles Willard
Human energy. *In* Architecture for people,
ed. by B. Mikellides p115-21

Moore, Deborah Dash. See Dash, I. G. jt. auth.

Moore, Geoffrey Hoyt
Business cycles, panics, and depressions. *In*
Encyclopedia of American economic history,
ed. by G. Porter v 1 p151-56

Moore, George

### About

Edwards, P. A play-house in the waste:
George Moore and the Irish theatre. *In* Edwards, P. Threshold of a nation p212-28

### About individual works
*A drama in muslin*

Cronin, J. George Moore: A drama in muslin.
*In* Cronin, J. The Anglo-Irish novel v 1
p115-34

*Esther Waters*

Hall, W. Esther Waters: an Irish story. *In*
Irish Renaissance annual I p137-56

*The untilled field*

Cronin, J. George Moore: The untilled
field. *In* The Irish short story, ed. by P.
Rafroidi and T. Brown p113-25

Moore, George Edward

### Influence

Rosenbaum, S. P. The longest journey:
E. M. Forster's refutation of idealism. *In*
E. M. Forster: a human exploration, ed. by
G. K. Das and J. Beer p32-54

Moore, Madeline
Nature and community: a study of cyclical
reality in The waves. *In* Virginia Woolf, ed.
by R. Freedman p219-40

Moore, Marianne

### About

Vendler, H. H. Marianne Moore. *In* Vendler, H. H. Part of nature, part of us p59-76

Moore, Mark Harrison
Statesmanship in a world of particular substantive choices. *In* Bureaucrats, policy analysts,
statesmen: who leads? Ed. by R. A. Goldwin
p20-36

Moore, Thomas

### About individual works
*Irish melodies*

Welch, R. Thomas Moore: an elegiac
silence. *In* Welch, R. Irish poetry from Moore
to Yeats p17-45

Moore, Thomas Gale
.Energy options. *In* The United States in the
1980s, ed. by P. Duignan and A. Rabushka
p221-51

Moorman, Charles
Comparative mythography: a fungo to the
outfield. *In* The Binding of Proteus, ed. by
M. W. McCune, T. Orbison and P. M. Withim
p63-77

Moos, Malcolm
Mencken, politics, and politicians. *In* On
Mencken, ed. by J. Dorsey p150-65

Mora, George
Vico and Piaget: parallels and différences.
*In* Conference on Vico and Contemporary
Thought, New York, 1976. Vico and contem-
porary thought pt2 p40-54

Morace, Robert A.
The writer and his middle class audience:
Frank Norris: a case in point. *In* Seasoned
authors for a new season: the search for standards in popular writing, ed. by L. Filler
p144-51

Moral conditions. See Sex customs

Moral education
Kurtz, P. W. Does humanism have an ethic
of responsibility? *In* Humanist ethics, ed. by
M. B. Storer p11-35

Moral philosophy. See Ethics

Moral proof of God. See God—Proof, Moral

Morality. See Ethics

Morals. See Conduct of life

**Moran, Emilio F.**

The trans-Amazonica: coping with a new environment. *In* Brazil, anthropological perspectives, ed. by M. L. Margolis and W. E. Carter p133-59

**Moreau, Jeanne**

### About individual works

*Lumière*

Kael, P. This is my beloved. *In* Kael, P. When the lights go down p230-33

**Morel, Marie-France**

City and country in eighteenth-century medical discussions about early childhood. *In* Medicine and society in France, ed. by R. Forster and O. Ranum p48-65

**Morgan, Edmund Sears**

### About

Pole, J. R. Slavery and revolution: the conscience of the rich. *In* Pole, J. R. Paths to the American past p55-74

**Morgan, Thomas Hunt**

### About

Allen, G. E. The rise and spread of the classical school of heredity, 1910-1930; development and influence of the Mendelian chromosome theory. *In* The Sciences in the American context: new perspectives, ed. by N. Reingold p209-28

**Morgner, Aurelius.** See Kamrany, N. M. jt. auth.

**Morillas, Juan López-** See López-Morillas, Juan

**Morot-Sir, Edouard**

Agnosticism and the gnosis of the imaginary. *In* André Malraux, ed. by F. Dorenlot and M. Tison-Braun p85-124

**Morowitz, Harold J.**

The wine of life, and other essays on societies, energy & living things

*Contents*

All the world's a stage
Bay to Breakers
Bibliophilia
Bulls, bears, and bacteria
Cell types: the great divide
Change four sparkplugs and take two aspirin
Christ, Clausius, and corrosion
A controlled social experiment
The crazy, hairy, naked ape
Deep purple
Drinking hemlock and other nutritional matters
Dull realities
Early warning
The entropy crisis
Extraordinary popular delusions
Fair is foul, and foul is fair
Food for thought
Frankenstein and recombinant DNA
From Aalto to Zwingli
Good news for humanists
Grant us this day our daily bread
Helmholtz, Mayer, and the M.D.-Ph.D. program
Hiding in the Hammond Report
High in the Andes
Let free energy ring
Loch Ness to Lahaina
Lox et veritas
Manufacturing a living organism
The Merck of time
Molecular cosmetology

De motu animalium
A new math for the CNS?
Obesity. the erg to dyne
Of mammals great and small
On computers, free will, and creativity
On first looking into Bergey's Manual
On riding a biocycle
On swallowing the surgeon
Psychosclerosis
Pumping iron
Puzzle solving in science
Return of the six million dollar man
The roots of prejudice
Sacred cows and sacrificial guinea pigs
Shrinks
The six million dollar man
The smallest free living cell
Social implications of a biological principle
Sole on fire
Splitters and lumpers
Stalking the heffalump
Who are the standard bearers?
Whose energy?
The wine of life
Women's lib and the battle against entropy
Yellow is mellow
Zen and the art of getting into medical school

**Morris, Humphrey**

The need to connect: representations of Freud's psychical apparatus. *In* The Literary Freud: mechanisms of defense and the poetic will, ed. by J. H. Smith p309-44

**Morris, Mervyn**

Derek Walcott. *In* West Indian literature, ed. by B. King p144-60

**Morris, William, 1834-1896**

### About

Harbison, R. Art as religion. *In* Harbison, R. Deliberate regression p94-114

### About individual works

*News from nowhere*

Sharratt, B. News from nowhere: detail and desire. *In* Reading the Victorian novel: detail into form, ed. by I. Gregor p288-305

**Morrissey, Thomas J.**

The Good Shepherd and the Anti-Christ in Synge's The shadow of the glen. *In* Irish Renaissance annual I p157-67

**Morrison, Donald G. and Stevenson, Hugh Michael**

Cultural pluralism, modernization, and conflict: an empirical analysis of sources of political instability in African nations. *In* Values, identities, and national integration, ed. by J. N. Paden p11-23

**Morrison, Karl Frederick**

Fragmentation and unity in "American medievalism." *In* The Past before us, ed. by M. Kammen p49-77

**Morrow, Patrick D.**

Larry McMurtry: the first phase. *In* Seasoned authors for a new season: the search for standards in popular writing, ed. by L. Filler p70-82

**Mortality**

Morowitz, H. J. Hiding in the Hammond Report. *In* Morowitz, H. J. The wine of life, and other essays on societies, energy & living things p241-45

**Morton, Adam**

Character and the emotions. *In* Explaining emotions, ed. by A. O. Rorty p153-61

**Morúa Delgado, Martin**

About

Jackson, R. L. From antislavery to anti-racism: Martin Morúa Delgado, black novelist, politician, and critic of postabolitionist Cuba. *In* Jackson, R. L. Black writers in Latin America p45-52

**Mosaic floors.** See Floors, Mosaic

**Mosaics, Byzantine**

Israel

Schapiro, M. Ancient mosaics in Israel: late antique art—pagan, Jewish, Christian. *In* Schapiro, M. Selected papers v3: Late antique, early Christian and mediaeval art p20-33

**Mosaics, Early Christian**

Israel

Schapiro, M. Ancient mosaics in Israel: late antique art—pagan, Jewish, Christian. *In* Schapiro, M. Selected papers v3: Late antique, early Christian and mediaeval art p20-33

**Moses ben Maimon**

About

Berman, L. V. The structure of the commandments of the Torah in the thought of Maimonides. *In* Studies in Jewish religious and intellectual history, ed. by S. Stein and R. Loewe p51-66

About individual works

*The guide of the perplexed*

Goshen-Gottstein, M. H. Maimonides' Guide of the perplexed: towards a critical edition. *In* Studies in Jewish religious and intellectual history, ed. by S. Stein and R. Loewe p133-42

Ethics

Fox, M. The doctrine of the mean in Aristotle and Maimonides: a comparative study. *In* Studies in Jewish religious and intellectual history, ed. by S. Stein and R. Loewe p93-120

**Moss, Howard**

About

Howard, R. Howard Moss: "Beginnings spin a web where endings spawn." *In* Howard, R. Alone with America p450-65

**Moses, Joel**

The computer in the home. *In* The Computer age: a twenty-year view, ed. by M. L. Dertouzos and J. Moses p3-20

**Mosley, Nicholas**

Human beings desire happiness. *In* Lying truths, ed. by R. Duncan and M. Weston-Smith p211-17

**Mossberg, Barbara Ann Clarke**

Reconstruction in the house of art: Emily Dickinson's "I never had a mother." *In* The Lost tradition: mothers and daughters in literature, ed. by C. N. Davidson and ,E. M. Broner p128-38

**Mother Kusters goes to heaven (Motion picture)**

Kauffmann, S. Mother Kusters goes to heaven/Jail bait. *In* Kauffmann, S. Before my eyes p218-21

**Mothers (in religion, folklore, etc.)** See Women (in religion, folklore, etc.)

**Mothers and daughters in literature**

Bannan, H. M. Spider Woman's web: mothers and daughters in Southwestern native American literature. *In* The Lost tradition: mothers and daughters in literature, ed. by C. N. Davidson and E. M. Broner p268-79

Berke, J. and Berke, L. Mothers and daughters in Wives and daughters: a study of Elizabeth Gaskell's last novel. *In* The Lost tradition: mothers and daughters in literature, ed. by C. N. Davidson and E. M. Broner p95-109

Bloom, L. Z. Heritages: dimensions of mother-daughter relationships in women's autobiographies. *In* The Lost tradition: mothers and daughters in literature, ed. by C. N. Davidson and E. M. Broner p291-303

Broe, M. L. A subtle psychic bond: the mother figure in Sylvia Plath's poetry. *In* The Lost tradition: mothers and daughters in literature, ed. by C. N. Davidson and E. M. Broner p207-16

Dash, I. G.; Kushner, D. D. and Moore, M. D. "How light a lighthouse for today's women?" *In* The Lost tradition: mothers and daughters in literature, ed. by C. N. Davidson and E. M. Broner p176-88

Davidson, C. N. Mothers and daughters in the fiction of the new Republic. *In* The Lost tradition: mothers and daughters in literature, ed. by C. N. Davidson and E. M. Broner p115-27

Demetrakopoulos, S. A. The metaphysics of matrilinearism in women's autobiography: studies of Mead's Blackberry winter, Hellman's Pentimento, Angelou's I know why the caged bird sings, and Kingston's The woman warrior. *In* Women's autobiography, ed. by E. C. Jelinek p180-205

Duncan, E. The hungry Jewish mother. *In* The Lost tradition: mothers and daughters in literature, ed. by C. N. Davidson and E. M. Broner p231-41

Elias-Button, K. The muse as Medusa. *In* The Lost tradition: mothers and daughters in literature, ed. by C. N. Davidson and E. M. Broner p193-206

Fishburn, K. The nightmare repetition: the mother-daughter conflict in Doris Lessing's Children of violence. *In* The Lost tradition: mothers and daughters in literature, ed. by C. N. Davidson and E. M. Broner p207-16

Irvine, L. A psychological journey: mothers and daughters in English-Canadian fiction. *In* The Lost tradition: mothers and daughters in literature, ed. by C. N. Davidson and E. M. Broner p242-52

Lilienfeld, J. Reentering paradise: Cather, Colette, Woolf and their mothers. *In* The Lost tradition: mothers and daughters in literature, ed. by C. N. Davidson and E. M. Broner p160-75

Macdonald, S. J. Jane Austen and the tradition of the absent mother. *In* The Lost tradition: mothers and daughters in literature, ed. by C. N. Davidson and E. M. Broner p58-69

Maglin, N. B. "Don't never forget the bridge that you crossed over on": the literature of matrilineage. *In* The Lost tradition: mothers and daughters in literature, ed. by C. N. Davidson and E. M. Broner p257-67

Mossberg, B. A. C. Reconstruction in the house of art: Emily Dickinson's "I never had a mother." *In* The Lost tradition: mothers and daughters in literature, ed. by C. N. Davidson and E. M. Broner p128-38

Ochsborn, J. Mothers and daughters in ancient Near Eastern literature. *In* The Lost tradition: mothers and daughters in literature, ed. by C. N. Davidson and E. M. Broner p5-14

Mothers and daughters in literature—*Continued*

Rosinsky, N. M. Mothers and daughters: another minority group. *In* The Lost tradition: mothers and daughters in literature, ed. by C. N. Davidson and E. M. Broner p280-90

Schotz, M. G. The great unwritten story: mothers and daughters in Shakespeare. *In* The Lost tradition: mothers and daughters in literature, ed. by C. N. Davidson and E. M. Broner p44-54

Stiller, N. Eve's orphans: mothers and daughters in medieval English literature. *In* The Lost tradition: mothers and daughters in literature, ed. by C. N. Davidson and E. M. Broner p22-32

Tintner, A. R. Mothers, daughters, and incest in the late novels of Edith Wharton. *In* The Lost tradition: mothers and daughters in literature, ed. by C. N. Davidson and E. M. Broner p147-56

Wagner, L. W. Ellen Glasgow: daughter as justified. *In* The Lost tradition: mothers and daughters in literature, ed. by C. N. Davidson and E. M. Broner p140-46

Washington, I. H. and Tobol, C. E. W. Kriemhild and Clytemnestra—sisters in crime or independent women? *In* The Lost tradition: mothers and daughters in literature, ed. by C. N. Davidson and E. M. Broner p15-21

### Bibliography

Rudenstein, G. M.; Kessler, C. F. and Moore, A. M. Mothers and daughters in literature: a preliminary bibliography. *In* The Lost tradition: mothers and daughters in literature, ed. by C. N. Davidson and E. M. Broner p309-22

Mothers in literature

Travitsky, B. S. The new mother of the English Renaissance: her writings on motherhood. *In* The Lost tradition: mothers and daughters in literature, ed. by C. N. Davidson and E. M. Broner p33-43

Motion. See Force and energy

Motion picture criticism

Kauffmann, S. Why I'm not bored. *In* Kauffmann, S. Before my eyes p432-37

Motivation (Psychology) See Expectation (Psychology)

Motten, J. P. Vander

Some problems of attribution in the canon of Sir William Killigrew's works. *In* Virginia. University. Bibliographical Society. Studies in bibliography v33 p161-68

Motto, Jerome A.

The right to suicide: a psychiatrist's view. *In* Suicide: the philosophical issues, ed. by M. P. Battin and D. J. Mayo p212-19

Moulton, Janice Marie

Sexual behavior: another position. *In* The Philosophy of sex, ed. by A. Soble p110-18

Mounin, Georges

Language, communication, chimpanzees. *In* Speaking of apes, ed. by T. A. Sebeok and J. Umiker-Sebeok p161-77

Mouzelis, Nicos

Capitalism and the development of the Greek state. *In* The State of Western Europe, ed. by R. Scase p241-73

Movie movie (Motion picture)

Kael, P. Taming the movies. *In* Kael, P. When the lights go down p501-07

Moving picture actors and actresses

### United States

Kauffmann, S. American to the world. *In* Kauffmann, S. Before my eyes p403-05

Moving-picture authorship. See Screen writers

Moving picture industry

Kauffmann, S. Money in focus. *In* Kauffmann, S. Before my eyes p425-28

Moving-picture plays

### History and criticism

Kael, P. Fear of movies. *In* Kael, P. When the lights go down p427-40

Kael, P. Where we are now. *In* Kael, P. When the lights go down p267-72

Thiher, A. Introduction. *In* Thiher, A. The cinematic muse p 1-14

Moving pictures

Kauffmann, S. Remembrance of films past. *In* Kauffmann, S. Before my eyes p425-28

*See also* Biographical films; Disasters in motion pictures; World War, 1939-1945 in motion pictures

### Aesthetics

Kauffmann, S. Why I'm not bored. *In* Kauffmann, S. Before my eyes p432-37

Thiher, A. Afterword: is film a language? *In* Thiher, A. The cinematic muse p199-206

### Dubbing

*See* Dubbing of moving-pictures

### Great Britain

Hogenkamp, B. Making films with a purpose: film-making and the working class. *In* Culture and crisis in Britain in the thirties, ed. by J. Clark and others p257-69

Moving pictures, Documentary

### Great Britain

Bond, R. Cinema in the thirties: documentary film and the labour movement. *In* Culture and crisis in Britain in the thirties, ed. by J. Clark and others p241-56

Moving-pictures, French

Thiher, A. Introduction. *In* Thiher, A. The cinematic muse p 1-14

Moving-pictures and literature. See Moving-pictures in literature

Moving-pictures in literature

Lawson, L. A. Moviegoing in The Moviegoer. *In* Walker, Percy: art and ethics, ed. by J. Tharpe p26-42

Moyles, R. G.

The text of Paradise lost: a stemma for the early editions. *In* Virginia. University. Bibliographical Society. Studies in bibliography v33 p168-82

Moynihan, Daniel Patrick

Counting our blessings

*Contents*

The advent of party in international politics

Cold dawn, high noon

Government and the ruin of private education

How much does freedom matter?

The iron law of emulation

The legacy of Woodrow Wilson

Pacem in terris

Patterns of ethnic succession

The politics of human rights

The politics of regional growth

Presenting the American case

Social science and the courts

Two tax revolts

When the Supreme Court is wrong

**Moynihan, Robert D.**
"Dwarfs of wit and learning": problems of historical time. *In* Probability, time, and space in eighteenth-century literature, ed. by P. R. Backscheider p167-85

**Mozambique**

### Politics and government

Ottaway, M. The theory and practice of Marxism-Leninism in Mozambique and Ethiopia. *In* Communism in Africa, ed. by D. E. Albright p118-44

**Mozambique Liberation Front.** See Liberation Front of Mozambique

**Mozart, Johann Chrysostom Wolfgang Amadeus**

### About

Hagstrum, J. H. Love in painting and music: an appended survey. *In* Hagstrum, J. H. Sex and sensibility p278-331

Robinson, W. P. Conceptions of Mozart in eighteenth-century periodical literature. *In* Studies in eighteenth-century culture v9 p151-65

### About individual works
*Cosi fan tutte*

Warren, R. 'Smiling at grief': some techniques of comedy in 'Twelfth night' and 'Cosi fan tutte.' *In* Shakespeare survey 32 p79-84

**Mphahlele, Ezekiel**

### About individual works
*Down Second Avenue*

Obuke, O. O. South African history, politics and literature: Mphahlele's Down Second Avenue, and Rive's Emergency. *In* African literature today no. 10: Retrospect and prospect, ed. by E. D. Jones p191-201

**Muccigrosso, Robert Henry**
Television and the urban crisis. *In* Screen and society, ed. by F J. Coppa

**Muchembled, Robert**
The witches of the Cambrésis. *In* Religion and the people, 800-1700, ed. by J. Obelkevich p221-76

**Müller, Gerhard**

### About individual works
*Sophokles. Antigone*

Knox, B. M. W. Review of Sophokles, Antigone (by Gerhard Müllar) *In* Knox, B. M. W. Word and action p165-82

**Mueller, Martin**
Children of Oedipus, and other essays in the imitation of Greek tragedy, 1550-1800

*Contents*

Athalie as displaced Oresteia and scriptural tragedy
Buchanan's Jephtha
Dido and Bérénice
Dramaturgical and thematic aspects of versions in seventeenth-century France
The fall of an ideal: Kleist's Penthesilea
The historical vision of tragedy: Garnier's Antigone
Humanist tragedy as the mediator between ancient and modern tragedy
The internalization of eighteenth-century patterns of transformation in Iphigenie auf Tauris
Moral and aesthetic tendencies in eighteenth-century adaptations of Greek tragedy
Oedipus Rex and modern analytical drama: Ibsen's Ghosts
Oedipus Rex as tragedy of fate: Corneille's Oedipe and Schiller's Die Braut von Messina
Oedipus Rex as tragedy of knowledge: Voltaire's Oedipe and Kleist's Der zerbrochene Krug
Phèdre
The scriptural tragedies of De la Taille and Garnier
The tragedy of deliverance: Samson Agonistes
The tragic epic: Paradise lost and the Iliad

**Muhammadanism.** See Islam

**Muir, Edward**

### About

Crick, J. Kafka and the Muirs. *In* The World of Franz Kafka, ed. by J. P. Stern p159-74

**Muir, Kenneth.** See Part 2 under title: Shakespeare's styles

**Muir, Willa**

### About

Crick, J. Kafka and the Muirs. *In* The World of Franz Kafka, ed. by J. P. Stern p159-74

**Mukerji, Nirmal**
The poetry of Rabindranath Tagore: the last phase. *In* Aspects of Indian writing in English, ed. by M. K. Naik p80-100

**Multilingualism**

*See also* Bilingualism

### Nigeria

Bishop, V. F. Language acquisition and value change in the Kano urban area. *In* Values, identities, and national integration, ed. by J. N. Paden

**Multinational corporations.** See International business enterprises

**Mumford, Lewis**

### About

Dow, E. "Van Wyck Brooks and Lewis Mumford: a confluence in the 'twenties." *In* Van Wyck Brooks: the critic and his critics, ed. by E. Wasserstrom p238-51

Foerster, N. "The literary prophets." *In* Van Wyck Brooks: the critic and his critics, ed. by E. Wasserstrom p56-68

**Mumming plays**
Green, A. E. Popular drama and the mummers' play. *In* Performance and politics in popular drama, ed. by D. Bradby, L. James and B. Sharratt p139-66

**Munby, Alan Noel Latimer**
The acquisition of manuscripts by institutional libraries. *In* The Bibliographical Society of America, 1904-79 p384-98

**Munch, Johan Storm**

### About

Munch, P. A. Pastor Munch of Wiota, 1827-1908. *In* Makers of an American immigrant legacy, ed. by O. S. Lovoll p62-91

**Munch, Peter A.**
Pastor Munch of Wiota, 1827-1908. *In* Makers of an American immigrant legacy, ed. by O. S. Lovoll p62-91

**Municipal finance.** See Local finance

**Munitions**
Kaldor, M. H. The significance of military technology. *In* Problems of contemporary militarism, ed. by A. Eide and M. Thee p226-29

Landgren-Bäckström, S. Arms trade and transfer of military technology to Third World countries. *In* Problems of contemporary militarism, ed. by A. Eide and M. Thee p230-47

### Underdeveloped areas

*See* Underdeveloped areas—Munitions

**Munitions trade.** See Munitions

**Munro, Ian**
George Lamming. *In* West Indian literature, ed. by B. King p126-43

**Munson, Gorham Bert**
"Van Wyck Brooks: his sphere and his encroachments." *In* Van Wyck Brooks: the critic and his critics, ed. by E. Wasserstrom p43-55

**Mural painting and decoration, Medieval**
Schapiro, M. The frescoes of Castelseprio. *In* Schapiro, M. Selected papers v3: Late antique, early Christian and mediaeval art p67-114
Schapiro, M. Notes on Castelseprio. *In* Schapiro, M. Selected papers v3: Late antique, early Christian and mediaeval art p115-42

**Murasaki, Lady.** See Murasaki Shikibu

**Murasaki Shikibu**

### About individual works

*The tale of Genji*
Pritchett, V. S. Lady Murasaki: the tale of Genji. *In* Pritchett, V. S. The tale bearers p195-205

**Murder**

### Trinidad

Naipaul, V. S. Michael X and the Black Power killings in Trinidad. *In* Naipaul, V. S. The return of Eva Perón p 1-91

**Murder on the Orient express (Motion picture)**
Kauffmann, S. A woman under the influence/Murder on the Orient express. *In* Kauffmann, S. Before my eyes p94-97

**Murphree, Wallace A.**
The necessity of humanism in the computer age. *In* Monster or messiah? Ed. by W. M. Mathews p175-84

**Murphy, Robert Francis**
Lineage and lineality in lowland South America. *In* Brazil, anthropological perspectives, ed. by M. L. Margolis and W. E. Carter p217-24

**Murphy, William M.**
Home life among the Yeatses. *In* Yeats, Sligo and Ireland, ed. by A. N. Jeffares p170-88

**Murrin, John M.**
The great inversion, or court versus country: a comparison of the revolution settlements in England (1688-1721) and America (1776-1816) *In* Three British revolutions: 1641, 1688, 1776, ed. by J. G. A. Pocock p368-453

**Murray, Lawrence Leo**
Universality and uniformity in the popular arts: the impact of television on popular culture. *In* Screen and society, ed. by F. J. Coppa p157-72

**Murrin, Michael**
The allegorical epic

*Contents*

Epilogue: The disappearance of Homer and the end of Homeric allegory: Vico and Wolf
Falerina's garden
The goddess of air
Landino's Virgil
The language of Milton's heaven
Spenser's fairyland
Tasso's enchanted wood

**Musa, Mark**
Movement and meaning in an Old Italian Poem. *In* The Interpretation of medieval lyric poetry, ed. by W. T. H. Jackson p194-204

**Museums.** See Art museums

**Music**
Botstein, L. Outside in: music on language. *In* The State of the language, ed. by L. Michaels and C. Ricks p343-61
*See also* Melody

### Historiography

*See* Musicology

### History and criticism—To 400

*See* Bible—Music

### History and criticism—20th century

Dent, E. J. Looking backward. *In* Dent, E. J. Selected essays p272-90
Dent, E. J. [The problems of modern music] *In* Dent, E. J. Selected essays p92-103
Stahl, G. Attuned to being: Heideggerian music in technological society. *In* Martin Heidegger and the question of literature, ed. by W. V. Spanos p297-324

### Philosophy and aesthetics

*See* Style, Musical

### Theory

*See* Counterpoint; Musical form

### Jews

*See* Music, Jewish

### Great Brtain

Dent, E. J. Corno di Bassetto. In Dent, E. J. Selected essays p238-49

### United States—History and criticism—17th century

Crawford, R. A. A historian's introduction to early American music. *In* American Antiquarian Society. Proceedings v89 pt2 p261-98

### United States—History and criticism—18th century

Crawford, R. A. A historian's introduction to early American music. *In* American Antiquarian Society. Proceedings v89 pt2 p261-98

**Music, Dramatic.** See Music, Incidental

**Music, English**

### History and criticism

Le Huray, P. The fair musick that all creatures made. *In* The Age of Milton, ed. by C. A. Patrides and R. B. Waddington p241-72

**Music, Incidental**
Mayer, D. The music of melodrama. *In* Performance and politics in popular drama, ed. by D. Bradby, L. James and B. Sharratt p49-63

**Music, Jewish**
Ament, S. G. Music and art of the Holocaust. *In* Encountering the Holocaust: an interdisciplinary survey, ed. by B. L. Sherwin and S. G. Ament p383-406
*See also* Bible—Music; Jews—Liturgy and ritual; Synagogue music

**Music, Religious.** See Church music

**Music, Sacred.** See Church music

**Music, Theatrical.** See Music, Incidental; Music in theaters

**Music and literature**
Fry, P. H. "Alexander's feast" and the tyranny of music. *In* Fry, P. H. The poet's calling in the English ode p49-62
Hollander, J. The sound of the music of music and sound. *In* Wallace Stevens, ed. by F. Doggett and R. Buttel p235-55
Peyre, H. Symbolism, painting, and music. *In* Peyre, H. What is symbolism? p112-27

**Music and poetry.** See Music and literature

**Music and society**

Crawford, R. A. A historian's introduction to early American music. *In* American Antiquarian Society. Proceedings v89 pt2 p261-98

**Music in theaters**

Dent, E. J. [Music for the Cambridge Greek plays] *In* Dent, E. J. Selected essays p26-36

*See also* Music, Incidental

**Musical criticism**

Carner, M. Composers as critics. *In* Carner, M. Major and minor p 1-5

**Musical form**

Dent, E. J. Binary and ternary form. *In* Dent, E. J. Selected essays p174-88

**Musical style.** See Style, Musical

**Musicology**

Dent, E. J. The historical approach to music. *In* Dent, E. J. Selected essays p189-206

**Musil, Robert**

### About

Genno, C. N. The anatomy of pre-war society in Robert Musil's Der Mann ohne Eigenschaften. *In* The First World War in German narrative prose, ed. by C. N. Genno and H. Wetzel p3-15

#### About individual works

*The man without qualities*

Genno, C. N. The anatomy of pre-war society in Robert Musil's Der Mann ohne Eigenschaften. *In* The First World War in German narrative prose, ed. by C. N. Genno

**Muslim civilization.** See Civilization, Islamic

**Muslim countries.** See Islamic countries

**Muslimism.** See Islam

**Mussulmanism.** See Islam

**Mutagen testing.** See Mutagenicity testing

**Mutagenesis.** See Mutagenicity testing

**Mutagenicity testing**

Ames, B. N. Environmental chemicals causing cancer and genetic birth defects. *In* The Condition of man, ed. by P. Hallberg p80-105

**Muth, Richard F.**

National housing policy. *In* The United States in the 1980s, ed. by P. Duignan and A. Rabushka p343-66

**Mutiso, Gideon-Cyrus Makau**

#### About individual works

*Socio-political thought in African literature*

Britwum, K. Politics and literature. *In* African literature today no. 10: Retrospect & prospect, ed, by E. D. Jones p243-47

**My love has been burning (Motion picture)**

Kauffmann, S. My love has been burning. *In* Kauffmann, S. Before my eyes p330-33

**Mycoplasmas.** See Mycoplasmatales

**Mycoplasamatales**

Morowitz, H. J. The smallest free living cell. *In* Morowitz, H. J. The wine of life, and other essays on societies, energy & living things p86-89

**Myers, Mitzi**

Harriet Martineau's autobiography: the making of a female philosopher. *In* Women's autobiography, ed. by E. C. Jelinek p53-70

Unmothered daughter and radical reformer: Harriet Martineau's career. *In* The Lost tradition: mothers and daughters in literature, ed. by C. N. Davidson and E. M. Broner p70-89

**Myers, Robert Manson** ed. The children of pride. See The children of pride

**Mylne, Vivienne**

The Bibliothèque universelle des dames. *In* Woman and society in eighteeenth-century France, ed. by E. Jacobs and others p123-38

**Mynona,** pseud. See Friedlaender, Salomo

**Mysteries and miracle-plays, English**

Robertson, D. W. The question of typology and the Wakefield Mactacio Abel. *In* Robertson, D. W. Essays in medieval culture p218-32

**Mystery stories.** See Detective and mystery stories

**Mysticism**

Daly, G. Friedrich von Hügel: experience and transcendence. *In* Daly, G. Transcendence and immanence p117-39

#### Judaism

Dan, J. The concept of knowledge in the Shi'ur qomah. *In* Studies in Jewish religious and intellectual history, ed. by S. Stein and R. Loewe p67-73

Glatzer, N. N. Was Franz Rosenzweig a mystic? *In* Studies in Jewish religious and intellectual history, ed. by S. Stein and R. Loewe p121-32

Werblowsky, R. J. Z. Jewish mysticism. *In* The Jewish world, ed. by E. Kedourie p217-23

*See also* Cabala; Golem

#### Middle Ages, 600-1500

Ozment, S. H. The spiritual traditions. *In* Ozment, S. H. The age of reform, 1250-1550 p73-134

**Myth**

Cook, A. S. Introduction. *In* Cook, A. S. Myth & language p 1-10

Cook, A. S. Language and myth. *In* Cook, A. S. Myth & language p260-83

Cook, A. S. The large phases of myth. *In* Cook, A. S. Myth & language p37-66

**Myth in literature**

Abler, L. From Angel to Orpheus: mythopoesis in the late Rilke. *In* The Binding of Proteus, ed. by M. W. McCune, T. Orbison and P. M. Withim p197-219

Aisenberg, N. Myth, fairy tale, and the crime novel. *In* Aisenberg, N. A common spring p16-67

Bateson, F. N. W. Myth—a dispensable critical term. *In* The Binding of Proteus, ed. by M. W. McCune, T. Orbison and P. M. Withim p98-109

Bernstein, G. M. The mediated vision: Eliade, Lévi-Strauss, and romantic mythopoesis. *In* The Binding of Proteus, ed. by M. W. McCune, T. Orbison and P. M. Withim p158-72

Cook, A. S. Language and myth. *In* Cook, A. S. Myth & language p260-83

Cook, A. S. The large phases of myth. *In* Cook, A. S. Myth & language p37-66

Cook, A. S. Lévi-Strauss, myth, and the Neolithic revolution. *In* Cook, A. S. Myth & language p13-36

Cook, A. S. Metaphor: literature's access to myth. *In* Cook, A. S. Myth & language p248-59

Dotterer, R. L. The fictive and the real: myth and form in the poetry of Wallace Stevens and William Carlos Williams. *In* The Binding of Proteus, ed. by M. W. McCune, T. Orbison and P. M. Withim p221-48

**Myth in literature**—*Continued*

Galand, R. Baudelaire and myth. *In* The Binding of Proteus, ed. by M. W. McCune, T. Orbison and P. M. Withim p174-95

Moorman, C. Comparative mythography: a fungo to the outfield. *In* The Binding of Proteus, ed. by M. W. McCune, T. Orbison and P. M. Withim p63-77

Nash, C. Myth and modern literature. *In* The Context of English literature, 1900-1930, ed. by M. Bell p160-85

Smith, C. F. The invention of sex in myth and literature. *In* The Binding of Proteus, ed. by M. W. McCune, T. Orbison and P. M. Withim p252-62

Uitti, K. D. The myth of poetry in twelfth- and thirteenth-century France. *In* The Binding of Proteus, ed. by M. W. McCune, T. Orbison and P. M. Withim p142-56

#### Bibliography

Nash, C. Myth and modern literature. *In* The Context of English literature, 1900-1930, ed. by M. Bell p160-85

**Mythology.** See Heroes; Symbolism

**Mythology, African**

Ray, B. The story of Kintu: myth, death, and ontology in Buganda. *In* Explorations in African systems of thought, ed. by I. C. Karp & C. S. Bird p60-79

**Mythology in literature**

Herz, J. S. The narrator as Hermes: a study of the early short fiction. *In* E. M. Forster: a human exploration, ed. by G. K. Das and J. Beer p17-27

# N

**NATO.** See North Atlantic Treaty Organization

**NDRC.** See United States. Office of Scientific Research and Development. National Defense Research Committee

**Nabokov, Vladimir Vladimirovich**

Lectures on literature

*Contents*

The art of literature and commonsense
Charles Dickens: Bleak House
Franz Kafka: "The metamorphosis"
Good readers and good writers
Gustave Flaubert: Madame Bovary
James Joyce: Ulysses
Jane Austen: Mansfield Park
Marcel Proust: The walk by Swann's place
Robert Louis Stevenson: "The strange case of Dr Jekyll and Mr Hyde"

#### About

Updike, J. Introduction. *In* Nabokov, V. V. Lectures on literature p xvii-xxvii

#### About individual works

*Lolita*

O'Connor, P. F. Lolita: a modern classic in spite of its readers. *In* Seasoned authors for a new season: the search for standards in popular writing, ed. by L. Filler p139-43

Trilling, L. The last lover. *In* Trilling, L. Speaking of literature and society p322-42

**Nagel, Thomas**

Sexual perversion. *In* The Philosophy of sex, ed. by A. Soble p76-88

**Nagler, Michael N.**

Beowulf in the context of myth. *In* Old English literature in context, ed. by J. D. Niles p143-56

**Naik, M. K.**

Idylls of the occult: the short stories of Sri Aurobindo. *In* Aspects of Indian writing in English, ed. by M. K. Naik p150-61

**Naipaul, Vidiadhar Surajprasad**

The return of Eva Perón

*Contents*

Conrad's darkness
The corpse at the iron gate
Michael X and the Black Power killings in Trinidad
A new king for the Congo: Mobutu and the nihilism of Africa

#### About

King, B. A. V. S. Naipaul. *In* West Indian literature, ed. by B. King p161-78

**Nairobi**

#### Politics and government

Ross, M. H. Political alienation, participation, and ethnicity in the Nairobi urban area. *In* Values, identities, and national integration ed. by J. N. Paden p173-81

**Naitō, Konan.** See Naitō, Torajirō

**Naitō, Torajirō**

#### About

Yue-Him Tam. An intellectual's response to Western intrusion: Naitō Konan's view of Republican China. *In* The Chinese and the Japanese, ed. by A. Iriye p161-83

**Nakamura, Takafusa**

Japan's economic thrust into North China, 1933-1938: formation of the North China Development Corporation. *In* The Chinese and the Japanese, ed. by A. Iriye p220-53

**Names.** See Names, Personal

**Names, English**

Cottle, B. Names. *In* The State of the language, ed. by L. Michaels and C. Ricks p98-107

**Names, Personal**

Kaplan, J. The naked self and other problems. *In* Telling lives, ed. by M. Pachter p36-55

**Nancy, Jean-Luc.** See Lacoue-Labarthe, P. jt. auth.

**Nandakumar, Prema**

Sri Aurobindo's 'The mother.' *In* Aspects of Indian writing in English, ed. by M. K. Naik p279-93

**Nansen, Odd**

#### About individual works

*Day after day*

Bosmajian, H. The rage for order. autobiographical accounts of the self in the nightmare of history. *In* Bosmajian, H. Metaphors of evil p27-54

**Narasimhaiah, C. D.**

R. K. Narayan's 'The guide.' *In* Aspects of Indian writing in English, ed. by M. K. Naik p172-98

**Narayan, R. K.**

English in India: the process of transmutation. *In* Aspects of Indian writing in English, ed. by M. K. Naik p19-23

#### About individual works

*The guide*

Narasimhaiah, C. D. R. K. Narayan's 'The guide'. *In* Aspects of Indian writing in English, ed. by M. K. Naik p172-98

**Narayan, Rasipuram Krishnaswamy.** See Narayan, R. K.

**Narayan, Shyamala A.**
Reality and fantasy in the novels of Sudhin N. Ghose. *In* Aspects of Indian writing in English, ed. by M. K. Naik p162-71

**Narcissism**
Collins, D. The dialectic of narcissism. *In* Collins, D. Sartre as biographer p184-94

**Naremore, James Otis**
Nature and history in The years. *In* Virginia Woolf, ed. by R. Freedman p241-62

**Narration (Rhetoric)**
De Man, P. Allegory (Julie). *In* De Man, P. Allegories of reading p188-220
De Man, P. Genesis and genealogy (Nietzsche). *In* De Man, P. Allegories of reading p79-102
Holloway, J. Conclusion: structure and the critic's art. *In* Holloway, J. Narrative and structure: exploratory essays p100-17
Holloway, J. Identity, inversion and density elements in narrative: three tales by Chekhov, James and Lawrence. *In* Holloway, J. Narrative and structure: exploratory essays p53-73
Holloway, J. Narrative process in 'Middlemarch.' *In* Holloway, J. Narrative and structure: exploratory essays p38-52
Holloway, J. Supposition and supersession: a model of analysis for narrative structure. *In* Holloway, J. Narrative and structure: exploratory essays p 1-19
Seidel, M. A. Inheritance and narrative mode. *In* Seidel, M. A. Satiric inheritance, Rabelais to Sterne p26-59

**Narrative writing.** See Narration (Rhetoric)

**Narveson, Jan**
Violence and war. *In* Matters of life and death, ed. by T. Regan p109-47

**Nash, Christopher**
Myth and modern literature. *In* The Context of English literature, 1900-1930, ed. by M. Bell p160-85

**Nash, Gerald D.**
State and local governments. *In* Encyclopedia of American economic history, ed. by G. Porter v2 p509-23

**Nash, Laura L.**
Concepts of existence: Greek origins of generational thought. *In* Generations, ed. by S. R. Graubard p 1-21

**Nashville (Motion picture)**
Kauffmann, S. Nashville. *In* Kauffmann, S. Before my eyes p35-38

**Nasty habits (Motion picture)**
Kael, P. Boss ladies. *In* Kael, P. When the lights go down p262-66

**National characteristics, American**
Inkeles, A. Continuity and change in the American national character. *In* The Third century, ed. by S. M. Lipset p389-416

**National characteristics, Brazilian**
Wagley, C. Anthropology and Brazilian national identity. *In* Brazil, anthropological perspectives, ed. by M. L. Margolis and W. E. Carter p 1-18

**National characteristics, Irish**
Plomer, W. C. F. Notes on a visit to Ireland. *In* Plomer, W. C. F. Electric delights p195-201

**National characteristics, Welsh**
Plomer, W. C. F. Kilvert's country. *In* Plomer, W. C. F. Electric delights p215-19

**National consciousness.** See Nationalism

**National Defense Research Committee.** See United States. Office of Scientific Research and Development. National Defense Research Committee

**National hysteria.** See Hysteria (Social psychology)

**National planning.** See subdivision Social policy under names of countries, e.g. Great Britain—Social policy; United States—Social policy

**National security**
Matthews, R. D. National security: propaganda or legitimate concern? *In* Problems of contemporary militarism, ed. by A. Eide and M. Thee p140-47

**National socialism**

### Germany—History

Rupp, L. J. "I don't call that Volkgemeinschaft": women, class, and war in Nazi Germany. *In* Women, war, and revolution, ed. by C. R. Berkin and C. M. Lovett p37-53

**National socialism and architecture**
Harbison, R. Tribe and race. *In* Harbison, R. Deliberate regression p180-205

**National socialism and art**
Harbison, R. Tribe and race. *In* Harbison, R. Deliberate regression p180-205

**National socialism in literature**
Bosmajian, M. Metaphors and myths of evil in history and literature: projections and reflections. *In* Bosmajian, H. Metaphors of evil p3-26

**Nationalism**
Berlin, Sir I. Nationalism: past neglect and present power. *In* Berlin, Sir I. Against the current p333-55
Isaacs, H. R. Changing arenas and identities in world affairs. *In* Propaganda and communication in world history, ed. by H. D. Lasswell, D. Lerner and H. Speier v2 p395-423
Kohn, H. Nationalism. *In* The Jew, ed. by A. A. Cohen p19-30
*See also* Nationalism and education

### Jews

Kohn, H. Nationalism. *In* The Jew, ed. by A. A. Cohen p19-30
*See also* Zionism

### Africa

Cohen, R. Epilogue: integration, ethnicity, and stratification: focus and fashion in African studies. *In* Values, identities, and national integration, ed. by J. N. Paden p361-72
Paden, J. N. Conclusion: reformation of concepts and hypotheses. *In* Values, identities, and national integration, ed. by J. N. Paden
Paden, J. N. Introduction. *In* Values, identities, and national integration, ed. by J. N. Paden p 1-7

### Cameroon

Kofele-Kale, N. The impact of environment on national political culture in Cameroon. *In* Values, identities, and national integration, ed. by J. N. Paden p151-72

### Gambia

Bayo, K. Environment and national system formation: Gambian orientations toward Senegambia. *In* Values, identities, and national integration, ed. by J. N. Paden p105-19

### Ghana

Fischer, L. F. Student orientations toward nation-building in Ghana. *In* Values, identities, and national integration, ed. by J. N. Paden p271-84

**Nationalism**—*Continued*

### Kenya

Laughlin, T. Environment, political culture, and national orientations: a comparison of settled and pastoral Masai. *In* Values, identities, and national integration, ed. by J. N. Paden p91-103

### Liberia

Sawyer, A. C. Social stratification and national orientations: students and nonstudents in Liberia. *In* Values, identities, and national integration, ed. by J. N. Paden p285-303

Sawyer, A. C. Social stratification, social change, and political socialization: students and nonstudents in Liberia. *In* Values, identities, and national integration, ed. by J. N. Paden p305-20

### Nigeria

Bishop, V. F. Language acquisition and value change in the Kano urban area. *In* Values, identities, and national integration, ed. by J. N. Paden p183-93

**Nationalism and education**

### Africa

Fischer, L. F. Mass education and national conflict in thirty African states. *In* Values, identities, and national integration, ed. by J. N. Paden p261-69

### Cameroon

Clignet, R. Teachers and national values in Cameroon: an inferential analysis from census data. *In* Values, identities, and national integration, ed. by J. N. Paden p321-36

**Nationalism and literature**

Edwards, P. Nation and empire. *In* Edwards, P. Threshold of a nation p66-109

Edwards, P. Our Irish theatre. *In* Edwards, P. Threshold of a nation p191-211

**Nations, Law of.** See International law

**Natural history**

### North America

Lutz, C. E. The American unicorn. *In* Lutz, C. E. The oldest library motto, and other library essays p115-21

**Native races.** See Ethnology

**Natural resources**

Attman, A. Man's use of nature's gifts: a historical survey. *In* The Condition of man, ed. by P. Hallberg p35-38

Kemp, G. T. H. Defense innovation and geopolitics: from the Persian Gulf to outer space. *In* National security in the 1980s: from weakness to strength, ed. by W. S. Thompson p69-87

*See also* Power resources

### Economic aspects

Davidson, P. Natural resources. *In* A Guide to post-Keynesian economics, ed. by A. S. Eichner p151-64

### United States—History

Pratt, J. A. Natural resources and energy. *In* Encyclopedia of American economic history, ed. by G. Porter v 1 p202-13

**Natural scenery.** See Landscape

**Natural selection**

Kohn, D. Theories to work by: rejected theories, reproduction, and Darwin's path to natural selection. *In* Studies in history of biology, v4. p67-170

**Natural theology.** See Philosophy of nature

**Naturalism**

Battersby, C. Hume, Newton and 'the hill called difficulty.' *In* Royal Institute of Philosophy. Philosophers of the Enlightenment p31-55

Brown, S. C. The 'principle' of natural order: or what the enlightened sceptics did not doubt. *In* Royal Institute of Philosophy. Philosophers of the Enlightment p56-76

Grimsley, R. Jean-Jacques Rousseau, philosopher of nature. *In* Royal Institute of Philosophy. Philosophers of the Enlightenment p184-98

Shea, W. M. The supernatural in the naturalists. *In* History, religion, and spiritual democracy, ed. by M. Wohlgelernter p53-75

**Naturalism in literature**

Braudy, L. B. Realists, naturalists, and novelists of manners. *In* Harvard Guide to contemporary American writing, ed. by D. Hoffman p84-152

Walker, J. A. Katai's Futon (The quilt): the birth of the I-novel. *In* Walker, J. A. The Japanese novel of the Meiji period and the ideal of individualism p93-120

*See also* Realism in literature

**Naturalists.** See Ecologists

**Nature**

### Philosophy

*See* Philosophy of nature

**Nature, Philosophy of.** See Philosophy of nature

**Nature (Aesthetics)**

Humphrey, N. K. Natural aesthetics. *In* Architecture for people, ed. by B. Mikellides p59-73

Manley, L. G. Art, nature, and convention. *In* Manley, L. G. Convention, 1500-1750 p15-25

Manley, L. G. "Conveniency to nature" and the "secrets of privitie": nature and convention in defense of poetry. *In* Manley, L. G. Convention, 1500-1750 p158-75

**Nature and nurture**

Purcell, H. D. The fallacy of environmentalism. *In* Lying truths, ed. by R. Duncan and M. Weston-Smith p85-96

**Nature in literature**

Keith, W. J. Edward Thomas. *In* Keith, W. J. The poetry of nature p141-66

Keith, W. J. Introduction. *In* Keith, W. The poetry of nature p3-10

Keith, W. J. John Clare. *In* Keith, W. J. The poetry of nature p39-66

Keith, W. J. The Georgians and after. *In* Keith, W. J. The poetry of nature p167-98

Keith, W. J. Thomas Hardy. *In* Keith, W. J. The poetry of nature p93-117

Keith, W. William Barnes. *In* Keith, W. J. The poetry of nature p67-91

Keith, W. J. William Wordsworth. *In* Keith, W. J. The poetry of nature p11-37

Rafroidi, P. Yeats, nature and the self. *In* Yeats, Sligo and Ireland, ed. by A. N. Jeffares p189-96

Sundquist, E. J. "Plowing homeward": cultivation and grafting in Thoreau and the Week. *In* Sundquist, E. J. Home as found p41-85

Uphaus, R. W. Criticism and the idea of nature. *In* Uphaus, R. W. The impossible observer p137-42

*See also* Weather in literature

**Nature in poetry.** See Nature in literature

**Nature versus nurture.** See Nature and nurture

**Nazi art.** See National socialism and art

**Nazism.** See National socialism

**Near East**

### Antiquities

Mellaart, J. Early urban communities in the Near East, c9000-3400 BC. *In* The Origins of civilization, ed. by P. S. R. Moorey p22-33

Schmandt-Besserat, D. An archaic recording system prior to writing. *In* 5000 years of popular culture, ed. by F. E. H. Schroeder p19-35

### Civilization

Hawkins, J. D. The origin and dissemination of writing in western Asia. *In* The Origins of civilization, ed. by P. S. R. Moorey p128-65

Mellaart, J. Early urban communities in the Near East, c9000-3400 BC. *In* The Origins of civilization, ed. by P. S. R. Moorey p22-33

### Historiography

Keddie, N. R. The history of the Muslim Middle East. *In* The Past before us, ed. by M. Kammen p131-56

### Literatures

*See* Near Eastern literature

### Politics and government

Duignan, P. J. and Gann, L. H. Middle East. *In* The United States in the 1980s, ed. by P. Duignan and A. Rabushka p757-96

### Study and teaching

Hourani, A. H. The present state of Islamic and Middle Eastern historiography. *In* Hourani, A. H. Europe and the Middle East p161-96

**Near Eastern literature**

Ochshorn, J. Mothers and daughters in ancient Near Eastern literature. *In* The Lost tradition: mothers and daughters in literature, ed. by C. M. Davidson and E. M. Broner p5-14

**Near Eastern studies.** See Near East

**Necessity (Philosophy)**

Sorabji, R. Causation, laws and necessity. *In* Doubt and dogmatism, ed. by M. Schofield, M. Burnyeat and J. Barnes p250-82

**Needleman, Morriss H.** See Otis, W. B. jt. auth.

**Neff, Emery Edward**

### About individual works

*Carlyle*

Trilling, L. Carlyle. *In* Trilling, L. Speaking of literature and society p77-81

**Negroes.** See Afro-Americans; Blacks

**Negroes (United States)** See Afro-Americans

**Negroponte, Nicholas**

The return of the Sunday painter. *In* The Computer age: a twenty-year view, ed. by M. L. Dertouzos and J. Moses p21-37

**Neidhart von Reuental**

### About

Hatto, A. T. Neidhart von Reuental. *In* Hatto, A. T. Essays on medieval German and other poetry p3-11

**Nelson, Clifford M. and Fryxell, Fritiof Melvin**

The ante-bellum collaboration of Meek and Hayden in stratigraphy. *In* New Hampshire Bicentennial Conference on the History of Geology, University of New Hampshire, 1976. Two hundred years of geology in America p187-200

**Nelson, Knute**

### About

Andersen, A. W. Senator Knute Nelson: Minnesota's grand old man and the Norwegian immigrant press. *In* Makers of an American immigrant legacy, ed. O. S. Lovoll p29-49

**Nelson, Marion John**

The material culture and folk arts of the Norwegians in America. *In* Perspectives on American folk art, ed. by I. M. G. Quimby and S. T. Swank p79-133

**Nemerov, Howard**

### About individual works

*Collected poems*

Vendler, H. H. Howard Nemerov. *In* Vendler, H. H. Part of nature, part of us p175-78

**Neoclassicism (Art)**

Harbison, R. The cult of death. *In* Harbison, R. Deliberate regression p25-62

**Neoclassicism (Literature)**

Manley, L. G. Real and mental theater: the complex of classicism. *In* Manley, L. G. Convention, 1500-1750 p264-90

Mueller, M. Moral and aesthetic tendencies in eighteenth-century adaptations of Greek tragedy. *In* Mueller, M. Children of Oedipus, and other essays on the imitation of Greek tragedy 1550-1800 p65-79

**Neofantastic** literature—a structuralist answer. Alazraki, J. *In* The Analysis of literary texts, ed. by R. D. Pope p286-90

**Neogrammarians**

Percival, W. K. Hermann Paul's view of the nature of language. *In* Psychology of language and thought, ed. by R. W. Rieber p187-96

**Neoplatonism**

Davidson, H. A. The principle that a finite body can contain only finite power. *In* Studies in Jewish religious and intellectual history, ed. by S. Stein and R. Loewe p75-92

*See also* Alexandrian school

**Neorealism (Literature)** See Realism in literature

**Nerval, Gérard de.** See Gérard de Nerval, Gérard Labrunie, known as

**Ness, England**

### Description

Plomer, W. C. F. A letter from the seaside. *In* Plomer, W. C. F. Electric delights p202-11

**Netherlands**

### Politics and government—1830-1898

Emmer, P. C. Anti-slavery and the Dutch: abolition without reform. *In* Anti-slavery, religion, and reform: essays in memory of Roger Anstey, ed. by C. Bolt and S. Drescher p80-98

### Politics and government—1945-

Irwin, G. A. The Netherlands. *In* Western European party systems, ed. by P. H. Merkl p161-84

**Network (Motion picture)**

Kael, P. Hot air. *In* Kael, P. When the lights go down p219-24

Kauffmann, S. Network. *In* Kauffmann, S. Before my eyes p101-04

**Neu, Jerome**

Jealous thoughts. *In* Explaining emotions, ed. by A. O. Rorty p425-63

**Neumann, Erich**
Creative man
*Contents*
C. G. Jung: 1955
Chagall and the Bible
Freud and the father image
Georg Trakl: the person and the myth
Kafka's "The trial": an interpretation through depth psychology
**Neumann, John von.** See Von Neumann, John
**Neural circuitry.** See Reflexes
**Neurophysiology.** See Reflexes
**Neuropsychology**
Changeux, J. P. Genetic determinism and epigenesis of the neuronal network: is there a biological compromise between Chomsky and Piaget. *In* Language and learning, ed. by M. Piattelli-Palmarini p185-97
**Neusner, Jacob**
Dating a Mishnah-Tractate: the case of Tamid. *In* History, religion, and spiritual democracy, ed. by M. Wohlgelernter p97-113
The Talmud. *In* The Jewish world, ed. by E. Kedourie p108-19
**New, The**
Tomlin, E. W. F. Novelty is the chief aim in art. *In* Lying truths, ed. by R. Duncan and M. Weston-Smith p231-40
**New Criticism**
Krieger, M. Theories about theories about Theory of criticism. *In* Krieger, M. Poetic presence and illusion p197-210
**The New Encyclopaedia Britannica. 15th ed.**
Morowitz, H. J. From Aalto to Zwingli. *In* Morowitz, H. J. The wine of life, and other essays on societies, energy & living things p221-24
**New England**

### History—Colonial period, ca. 1600-1775

Miller, P. The Cambridge Platform in 1648. *In* Miller, P. The responsibility of mind in a civilization of machines p45-60

### Industries—History

Soltow, J. H. Origins of small business and the relationships between large and small firms: metal fabricating and machinery making in New England, 1890-1957. *In* Small business in American life, ed. by S. W. Bruchey p192-211

### Intellectual life

Miller, P. The New England conscience. *In* Miller, P. The responsibility of mind in a civilization of machines p176-85
Miller, P. Nineteenth-century New England and its descendants. *In* Miller, P. The responsibility of mind in a civilization of machines p161-75
**New England theology**
Miller, P. Individualism and the New England tradition. *In* Miller, P. The responsibility of mind in a civilization of machines p26-44
**New York (City)**

### Industries—History

Tichenor, I. Master printer organize: the Typothetae of the City of New York, 1865-1906. *In* Small business in American life, ed. by S. W. Bruchey p169-91
**New York (City) in literature**
Festa-McCormick, D. Dos Passos's Manhattan transfer: the death of a metropolis. *In* Festa-McCormick, D. The city as catalyst p141-57

**New York (City) Public Library. Berg collection**
Gordan, J. D. A doctor's benefaction: the Berg collection at the New York Public Library. *In* The Bibliographical Society of America, 1904-79 p327-38
**New York (State)**

### Economic conditions

Moynihan, D. P. The politics of regional growth. *In* Moynihan, D. P. Counting our blessings p216-34
**New York Female Moral Reform Society.** See American Female Guardian Society and Home for the Friendless, New York
**New York, New York (Motion picture)**
Kauffmann, S. New York, New York. *In* Kauffmann, S. Before my eyes p203-05
**Newark, N.J.**

### Industries—History

Hirsch, S. E. From artisan to manufacturer: industrialization and the small producer in Newark, 1830-60. *In* Small business in American life, ed. by S. W. Bruchey p80-99
**Newcastle, Margaret (Lucas) Cavendish, Duchess of**

### About individual works

*A true relation of the birth, greeting, and life of Margaret Cavendish, Duchess of Newcastle*
Mason, M. G. The other voice: autobiographies of women writers. *In* Autobiography: essays theoretical and critical, ed. by J. Olney p207-35
**Newfoundland**

### Colonization

O'Flaherty, P. Fishers of men: three missionaries in eighteenth-century Newfoundland, 1764-98. *In* O'Flaherty, P. The rock observed p16-31

### Discovery and exploration

O'Flaherty, P. 'It passeth England': literature of discovery and early settlement, 1497-1670. *In* O'Flaherty, P. The rock observed p3-15
O'Flaherty, P. Walking new ground: books by two Newfoundland pioneers, 1770-1882. *In* O'Flaherty, P. The rock observed p32-48

### Economic conditions

O'Flaherty, P. Bridging two worlds: Margaret Duley's fiction, 1936-42. *In* O'Flaherty, P. The rock observed p127-43
O'Flaherty, P. Visions and revisions: some writers in the new Newfoundland. *In* O'Flaherty, P. The rock observed p144-83

### Historiography

O'Flaherty, P. The triumph of sentiment: History and commentary, 1793-1895. *In* O'Flaherty, P. The rock observed p49-81

### History

O'Flaherty, P. Emigrant muse: E. J. Pratt and Newfoundland, 1882-1907. *In* O'Flaherty, P. The rock observed p111-26
**Newfoundland in literature**
O'Flaherty, P. Bridging two worlds: Margaret Duley's fiction, 1936-42. *In* O'Flaherty, P. The rock observed p127-43
O'Flaherty, P. The case of George Tuff: a concluding note. *In* O'Flaherty, P. The rock observed p184-87
O'Flaherty, P. Emigrant muse: E. J. Pratt and Newfoundland, 1882-1907. *In* O'Flaherty, P. The rock observed p111-26

**Newfoundland in literature**—*Continued*

O'Flaherty. P. 'It passeth England': literature of discovery and early settlement, 1497-1670. *In* O'Flaherty, P. The rock observed p3-15

O'Flaherty, P. The lure of the north: fiction and travel literature, 1850-1905. *In* O'Flaherty, P. The rock observed p82-110

**Newman, Oscar**

Whose failure is modern architecture? *In* Architecture for people, ed. by B. Mikellides p44-58

**Newspaper publishing**

Hart, D. J. Changing relationships between publishers and journalists: an overview. *In* Newspapers and democracy, ed. by A. Smith p268-87

### Technological innovations

Smith, A. The newspaper of the late twentieth century: the U.S. model. *In* Newspapers and democracy, ed. by A. Smith p5-48

### France

Harlé, A. de. The press and the state in France. *In* Newspapers and democracy, ed. by A. Smith p127-48

### Great Britain

Curran, J.: Douglas, A. and Whannel, G. The political economy of the human-interest story. *In* Newspapers and democracy, ed. by A. Smith p288-347

### Japan

Tomita, T. The new electonic media and their place in the information market of the future. *In* Newspapers and democracy, ed. by A. Smith p49-62

### Pennsylvania—History

Adams, W. P. The colonial German-language press and the American Revolution. *In* The Press & the American Revolution, ed. by B. Bailyn and J. B. Hench p151-228

### Southern States—History

Weir, R. M. The role of the newspaper press in the Southern colonies on the eve of the Revolution. *In* The Press & the American Revolution, ed. by B. Bailyn and J. B. Hench p99-150

### Sweden

Gustafsson, K. E. The press subsidies of Sweden: a decade of experiment. *In* Newspapers and democracy, ed. by A. Smith p104-26

### United States

Bogart, L. Editorial ideals, editorial illusions. *In* Newspapers and democracy, ed. by A. Smith p247-67

Smith, A. The newspaper of the late twentieth century: the U.S. model. *In* Newspapers and democracy, ed. by A. Smith p5-48

**Newspaper reporting.** See Reporters and reporting

**Newspapers**

*See also* American newspapers; German-American newspapers; Japanese newspapers; Reporters and reporting

### United States—History

Langford, P. British correspondence in the colonial press, 1763-1775: a study in Anglo-American misunderstanding before the American Revolution. *In* The Press & the American Revolution, ed. by B. Bailyn and J. B. Hench p273-313

**Newspapers, Publishing of.** See Newspaper publishing

**Newsprint**

Wingate, P. Newsprint: from rags to riches —and back again? *In* Newspapers and democracy, ed. by A. Smith p63-89

**Newton, Sir Isaac**

### About

Battersby, C. Hume, Newton and 'the hill called difficulty.' *In* Royal Institute of Philosophy. Philosophers of the Enlightenment p31-55

Rogers G. A. J. The empiricism of Locke and Newton. *In* Royal Institute of Philosophy. Philosophers of the Enlightenment p 1-30

Schwartz, R. B. Berkeley, Newtonian space, and the question of evidence. *In* Probability, time, and space in eighteenth-century literature, ed. by P. R. Backscheider p259-73

Westfall, R. S. Isaac Newton in Cambridge: the Restoration university and scientific creativity. *In* Culture and politics from Puritanism to the Enlightenment, ed. by P. Zagorin p135-64

**Next stop, Greenwich Village (Motion picture)**

Kael, P. The artist as a young comedian. *In* Kael, P. When the lights go down p127-31

Kauffmann, S. Next stop Greenwich Village. *In* Kauffmann, S. Before my eyes p196-97

**Ngugi, James.** See Ngugi Wa Thiong'o

**Ngugi Wa Thiong'o**

### About individual works
#### A grain of wheat

Sharma, G. N. Ngugi's Christian vision: theme and pattern in A grain of wheat. *In* African literature no. 10: Retrospect & prospect, ed. by E. D. Jones p167-76

#### Petals of blood

Palmer, E. T. Ngugi's Petals of blood. *In* African literature today no. 10:Retrospect & prospect, ed. by E. D. Jones p153-66

**Nibelungenlied**

Washington, I. H. and Tobol, C. E. W. Kriemhild and Clytemnestra—sisters in crime or independent women? *In* The Lost tradition: mothers and daughters in literature, ed. by C. N. Davidson and E. M. Broner p15-21

**Nicholas of Cusa.** See Nicolaus Cusanus, Cardinal

**Nicholson, Jack**

### About individual works
#### One flew over the cuckoo's nest

Kauffmann, S. One flew over the cuckoo's nest. *In* Kauffmann, S. Before my eyes p174-77

**Nicolaus Cusanus, Cardinal**

### About individual works
#### The beryl stone

Lutz, C. E. The mystical symbol of the beryl. *In* Lutz, C. E. The oldest library motto, and other library essays p33-37

**Nicolson, Colin**

Edwardian England and the coming of the First World War. *In* The Edwardian age: conflict and stability, 1900-1914, ed. by A. O'Day p144-68

**Nielsen, Kai**

Morality and the human situation. *In* Humanist ethics, ed. by M. B. Storer p58-74

**Nietzsche, Friedrich Wilhelm**

### About

De Man, P. Rhetoric of persuasion (Nietzsche). *In* De Man, P. Allegories of reading p119-31

**Nietzsche, Friedrich W.**—About—*Continued*

De Man, P. Rhetoric of tropes (Nietzsche). *In* De Man, P. Allegories of reading p103-18

Harbison, R. Turning against history. *In* Harbison, R. Deliberate regression p147-79

Krell, D. F. Art and truth in raging discord: Heidegger and Nietzsche on the will to power. *In* Martin Heidegger and the question of literature, ed. by W. V. Spanos p39-52

### About individual works
*The birth of tragedy*

Bennett, B. Breakthrough in theory: the philosophical background of modern drama. *In* Bennett, B. Modern drama and German classicism p229-81

De Man, P. Genesis and genealogy (Nietzsche) *In* De Man, P. Allegories of reading p79-102

*Venedig*

Grundlehner, P. Friedrich Nietzsche: "Venedig." *In* Grundlehner, P. The lyrical bridge p97-107

### Influence

Wyschogrod, E. Martin Buber and the no-self perspective. *In* History, religion, and spiritual democracy, ed. by M. Wohlgelernter p130-50

### Influence—Bataille

Stoekl, A. The death of Acephale and the will to chance: Nietzsche in the text of Bataille. *In* Glyph 6 p42-67

### Relationship with women

Allen, C. G. Nietzsche's ambivalence about women. *In* The Sexism of social and political theory: women and reproduction from Plato to Nietzsche, ed. by L. M. G. Clark and L. Lange p117-33

**Nigeria**

### Ethnology

*See* Ethnology—Nigeria

**Night moves (Motion picture)**

Kauffmann, S. French connection II/Night moves. *In* Kauffmann, S. Before my eyes p131-34

**Nihilism (Philosophy)**

Ungar, P. K. I do not exist. *In* Perception and identity, ed. by G. F. Macdonald p235-51

**Niklaus, Robert**

Diderot and women. *In* Woman and society in eighteenth-century France, ed. by E. Jacobs [and others] p69-82

**Niles, John DeWitt**

The Æcerbot ritual in context. *In* Old English literature in context, ed. by J. D. Niles p44-56

**Nilo-Hamitic tribes.** See Teso tribe

**Nilson, Sten Sparre**

Mapping party competition. *In* Western European party systems, ed. by P. H. Merkl p490-508

Norway and Denmark. *In* Western European party systems, ed. by P. H. Merkl p205-34

Parties, cleavages, and the sharpness of conflict. *In* Western European party systems, ed. by P. H. Merkl p521-25

**Nimbus (Art)**

Schapiro, M. Notes on Castelseprio. *In* Schapiro, M. Selected papers v3: Late antique, early Christian and mediaeval art p115-42

**Nin, Anaïs**

### About individual works
*The diary of Anaïs Nin*

Bloom, L. Z. and Holder, O. Anaïs Nin's Diary in context. *In* Women's autobiography, ed. by E. C. Jelinek p206-20

**1900 (Motion picture)**

Kael, P. Hail, folly! *In* Kael, P. When the lights go down p323-33

Kauffmann, S. 1900. *In* Kauffmann, S. Before my eyes p298-301

**Nineteenth century.** See Civilization, Modern—19th century

**Ninon de Lenclos.** See Lenclos, Anne, called Ninon de

**Nisbet, Lee**

Kulturkampf. *In* Humanist ethics, ed. by M. B. Storer p242-52

**Nisbet, Robert Alexander**

The future of the university. *In* The Third century, ed. by S. M. Lipset p303-25

Vico and the idea of progress. *In* Conference on Vico and Contemporary Thought, New York, 1976. Vico and contemporary thought pt 1 p235-47

**Nitze, Paul Henry**

Policy and strategy from weakness. *In* National security in the 1980s: from weakness to strength, ed. by W. S. Thompson p443-56

**Nnolim, Charles E.**

Dialectic as form: pejorism in the novels of Armah. *In* African literature today no. 10: Retrospect & prospect, ed. bp E. D. Jones p207-23

**Nō plays**

### Influence

Plomer, W. C. F. The church operas. *In* Plomer, W. C. F. Electric delights p190-92

**Nodelman, Perry**

Defining children's literature. *In* Children's literature v8 p184-90

**Noll, Roger G.**

Regulation and computer services. *In* The Computer age: a twenty-year view, ed. by M. L. Dertouzos and J. Moses p254-84

**Nolte, William H.**

The literary critic. *In* On Mencken, ed. by J. Dorsey p196-205

**Nomads**

### Asia

Krader, L. The origins of the state among the nomads of Asia. *In* Soviet and Western anthropology, ed. by E. Gellner p135-47

**Nonsense-verses, American**

Ehrenpreis, I. Strange relation: Stevens' nonsense. *In* Wallace Stevens, ed. by F. Doggett and R. Buttel p219-34

**Nonverbal communication.** See Expression; Paralinguistics

**Nonverbal communication (Psychology)**

Ekman, P. Biological and cultural contributions to body and facial movement in the expression of emotions. *In* Explaining emotions, ed. by A. O. Rorty p73-101

La Barre, W. Paralinguistics, kinesics, and cultural anthropology. *In* La Barre, W. Culture in context p289-332

**Noonan, Lowell G.**

France. *In* Western European party systems, ed. by P. H. Merkl p87-121

**Nordau, Max Simon**

### About

Strauss, L. Zionism in Max Nordau. *In* The Jew, ed. by A. A. Cohen p120-26

**Norma Rae (Motion picture)**

Kauffman, S. Norma Rae. *In* Kauffmann, S. Before my eyes p245-48

**Norms, Social.** See Social norms

**Norris, David**

Imaginative response versus authority structures. A theme of the Anglo-Irish short story. *In* The Irish short story, ed. by P. Rafroidi and T. Brown p39-62

**Norris, Frank**

### About

Morace, R. A. The writer and his middle class audience: Frank Norris: a case in point. *In* Seasoned authors for a new season: the search for standards in popular writing, ed. by L. Filler p144-51

**North Atlantic Treaty Organization**

Burt, R. R. Washington and the Atlantic alliance: the hidden crisis. *In* National security in the 1980s: from weakness to strength, ed. by W. S. Thompson p109-21

West, F. J. Conventional forces beyond NATO. *In* National security in the 1980s: from weakness to strength, ed. by W. S. Thompson p319-36

**Northern Ireland**

### Population

Morowitz, H. J. Social implications of a biological principle. *In* Morowitz, H. J. The wine of life, and other essays on societies, energy & living things p159-62

**Northup, Solomon**

### About individual works

*Twelve years a slave*

Stepto, R. B. I rose and found my voice: narration, authentication, and authorial control in four slave narratives. *In* Stepto, R. B. From behind the veil p3-31

**Nortje, Arthur**

### About

Leitch, R. G. Nortje: poet at work. *In* African literature today no. 10: Retrospect & prospect, ed. by E. D. Jones p224-32

**Norton, David L.**

Equality and excellence in the democratic ideal. *In* History, religion, and spiritual democracy, ed. by M. Wohlgelernter p273-93

**Norton, Mary Beth**

Eighteenth-century American women in peace and war: the case of the Loyalists. *In* A Heritage of her own, ed. by N. F. Cott and E. H. Pleck p136-61

**Norway**

### Politics and government—1945-

Nilson, S. S. Norway and Denmark. *In* Western European party systems, ed. by P. H. Merkl p205-34

**Norwegian-American literature**

### Women authors

Christianson, J. R. Literary traditions of Norwegian-American women. *In* Makers of an American immigrant legacy, ed. by O. S. Lovoll p92-110

**Norwegian-American newspapers**

Andersen, A. W. Senator Knute Nelson: Minnesota's grand old man and the Norwegian immigrant press. *In* Makers of an American immigrant legacy, ed. by O. S. Lovoll p29-49

**Norwegian Americans**

Haugen, E. I. Norway in America: the hidden heritage. *In* Makers of an American immigrant legacy, ed. by O. S. Lovoll p15-28

### Middle West

Nelson, M. J. The material culture and folk arts of the Norwegians in America. *In* Perspectives on American folk art, ed. by I. M. G. Quimby and S. T. Swank p79-133

### Washington (State)

Arestad, S. What was Snus Hill? *In* Makers of an American immigrant legacy, ed. by O. S. Lovoll p159-72

**Norwegian language**

### Foreign elements

Haugen, E. I. Norway in America: the hidden heritage. *In* Makers of an American immigrant legacy, ed. by O. S. Lovoll p15-28

**Norwegian literature.** See Norwegian-American literature

**Norwegian newspapers.** See Norwegian-American newspapers

**Norwegians in the United States**

Haugen, E. I. Norway in America: the hidden heritage. *In* Makers of an American immigrant legacy, ed. by O. S. Lovoll p15-28

**Norwich, Lady Julian of.** See Juliana, Anchoret

**Nosworthy, James Mansfield**

The importance of being Marcade. *In* Shakespeare survey 32 p105-14

**Nothingness in literature**

Willbern, D. P. Shakespeare's nothing. *In* Representing Shakespeare, ed. by M. M. Schwartz and C. Kahn p244-63

**A nous la liberté (Motion picture)**

Thiher, A. From Entr'acte to A nous la liberté: René Clair and the order of farce. *In* Thiher, A. The cinematic muse p64-77

**Novak, Maximillian E.**

The extended moment: time, dream, history, and perspective in eighteenth-century fiction. *In* Probability, time, and space in eighteenth-century literature, ed. by P. R. Backscheider p141-66

**Novak, Michael**

On God and man. *In* Solzhenitsyn at Harvard, ed. by R. Berman p131-43

**Novalis, pseud.** See Hardenberg, Friedrich Leopold, Freiherr von

**Novelists, American**

### 20th century

Wagner, L. W. Tension and technique: the years of greatness. *In* Wagner, L. W. American modern p5-17

**Novelists, Irish**

### 19th century

Cronin, J. Introduction. *In* Cronin, J. The Anglo-Irish novel v 1 p7-18

**Noyce, Robert Norton**

Hardware prospects and limitations. *In* The Computer age: a twenty-year view, ed. by M. L. Dertouzos and J. Moses p321-37

**Nozick, Robert**

### About individual works

*Anarchy, state, utopia*

Altham, J. E. J. Reflections on the state of nature. *In* Rational action, ed. by R. Harrison p133-45

**Nuclear warfare.** See Atomic warfare

**Nuclear weapons.** See Atomic weapons

**Nugent, Jeffrey B.**
Contemporary issues in development economics. *In* Economic issues of the eighties, ed. by N. M. Kamrany and R. H. Day p262-70

**Nunn, Sam**
Defense budget and defense capabilities. *In* National security in the 1980s: from weakness to strength, ed. W. S. Thompson p375-95

**Nuns**

**France**
Léonard, J. Women, religion, and medicine. *In* Medicine and society in France, ed. by R. Forster and O. Ranum p24-47

**Nuremberg Trial of Major German War Criminals, 1945-1946**
Bassiouni, M. C. International law and the Holocaust. *In* Encountering the Holocaust: an interdisciplinary survey, ed. by B. L. Sherwin and S. G. Ament p146-88

**Nuremberg war crime trials.** See Nuremberg Trial of Major German War Criminals, 1945-1946

**Nurse midwives.** See Midwives

**Nurture and nature.** See Nature and nurture

**Nussbaum, Martha Craven**
Eleatic conventionalism and Philolaus on the conditions of thought. *In* Harvard Studies in classical philology, v83 p63-108

**Nutrition**

**Research**
Morowitz, H. J. Food for thought. *In* Morowitz, H. J. The wine of life, and other essays on societies, energy & living things p236-40

**Nwabuzor, Elonenjo Joachim O.**
Ethnic propensities for collaboration in Cameroon. *In* Values, identities, and national integration, ed. by J. N. Paden p231-58

Ethnic value distance in Cameroon. *In* Values, identities, and national integration, ed. by J. N. Paden p205-29

**Nwoga, D. I.**
Modern African poetry: the domestication of a tradition. *In* African literature today no. 10:Retrospect & prospect, ed. by E. D. Jones p32-56

**Nye, Russel B.**
Notes on photography and American culture, 1839-1890. *In* Toward a new American literary history, ed. by L. J. Budd, E. H. Cady and C. L. Anderson p244-57

# O

**ONR.** See United States. Office of Naval Research

**OPEC.** See Organization of Petroleum Exporting Countries

**OSRD.** See United States. Office of Scientific Research and Development

**Oaklander, Lester Nathan**
Sartre on sex. *In* The Philosophy of sex, ed. by A. Soble p190-206

**Oates, Joyce Carol**
The art of suicide. *In* Suicide: the philosophical issues, ed. by M. P. Battin and D. J. Mayo p161-68

**About**
Wagner, L. W. Oates: the changing shapes of her realities. *In* Wagner, L. W. American modern p67-75

**Øberg, Jan**
The new international military order: a threat to human security. *In* Problems of contemporary militarism, ed. by A. Eide and M. Thee p47-74

**Oberhelman, Steve**
Greek and Roman witches: literary conventions or agrarian fertility priestesses? *In* 5000 years of popular culture, ed. by F. E. H. Schroeder p138-53

**Oberlin College**
Madden, E. H. Asa Mahan and the Oberlin philosophy. In History, religion, and spiritual democracy, ed. by M. Wohlgelernter [and others] p155-80

**Obeso, Candelario**

**About**
Jackson, R. L. Cultural nationalism and the emergence of literary blackness in Colombia: the originality of Candelario Obeso. *In* Jackson, R. L. Black writers in Latin America p53-62

**Objectivity**
Cottrell, Sir A. Science is objective. *In* Lying truths, ed. by R. Duncan and M. Weston-Smith p159-69

**Obligation.** See Responsibility

**O'Brien, Flann,** pseud. See O'Nolan, Brian

**O'Brien, Mary**
Reproducing Marxist man. *In* The Sexism of social and political theory: women and reproduction from Plato to Nietzsche, ed. by L. M. G. Clark and L. Lange p99-116

**Obstetrics.** See Midwives

**Obuke, Okpure O.**
South African history, politics and literature: Mphahlele's Down Second Avenue, and Rive's Emergency. *In* African literature today no. 10: Retrospect & prospect, ed. by E. D. Jones p191-201

**O'Casey, Sean**

**About**
Edwards, P. Nothing is concluded. *In* Edwards, P. Threshold of a nation p229-44

**Occam, William.** See Ockham, William

**Occupational prestige**

**History**
Le Goff, J. Licit and illicit trades in the medieval West. *In* Le Goff, J. Time, work, & culture in the Middle Ages p58-70

**Occupations in literature**
Le Goff, J. Trades and professions as represented in medieval confessors' manuals. *In* Le Goff, J. Time, work, & culture in the Middle Ages p107-21

**Ocean bottom.** See Submarine geology

**Ocean currents**
Burstyn, H. L. and Schlee, S. B. The study of ocean currents in America before 1930. *In* New Hampshire Bicentennial Conference on the History of Geology, University of New Hampshire, 1976. Two hundred years of geology in America p145-55

**Ocean floor spreading.** See Sea-floor spreading

**Oceanography.** See Ocean currents; Submarine geology

**Ochshorn, Judith**
Mothers and daughters in ancient Near Eastern literature. *In* The Lost tradition: mothers and daughters in literature, ed. by C. N. Davidson and E. M. Broner p5-14

**Ockham, William**
**About**
Ozment, S. H. The scholastic traditions. *In* Ozment, S. H. The age of reform, 1250-1550 p22-72

**O'Connor, Flannery**
**About**
Kissel, S. S. Voices in the wilderness: the prophets of O'Connor, Percy, and Powers. *In* Walker Percy: art and ethics, ed. by J. Tharpe p91-98

**About individual works**
*Everything that rises must converge*
Pritchett, V. S. Flannery O'Connor: Satan comes to Georgia. *In* Pritchett, V. S. The tale bearers p164-69

**O'Connor, Frank**, pseud. See O'Donovan, Michael

**O'Connor, Philip Francis**
Lolita: a modern classic in spite of its readers. *In* Seasoned authors for a new season: the search for standards in popular writing, ed. by L. Filler p139-43

**October (Theater group)**
Bradby, D. The October group and theatre under the Front populaire. *In* Performance and politics in popular drama, ed. by D. Bradby, L. James and B. Sharratt p231-42

**O'Day, Alan**
Irish home rule and liberalism. *In* The Edwardian age: conflict and stability, 1900-1914, ed. by A. O'Day p113-32

**Odes**
**History and criticism**
Fry, P. H. Introduction: the man at the gate. *In* Fry, P. H. The poet's calling in the English ode p 1-14
Fry, P. H. Postscript: the ode after "Autumn." *In* Fry, P. H. The poet's calling in the English ode p275-78

**O'Donnell, Guillermo A.**
Tensions in the bureaucratic-authoritarian state and the question of democracy. *In* The New authoritarianism in Latin America, ed. by D. Collier p285-318

**O'Donnell, Thomas J.**
"Une exploration des déserts de ma mémoire": pastoral aspects of Lévi-Strauss's Tristes tropiques. *In* Survivals of pastoral, ed. by R. F. Hardin p87-102

**O'Donovan, John**
The first twenty years. *In* The Genius of Shaw, ed. by M. Holroyd p13-29

**O'Donovan, Michael**
**About**
Chatalic, R. Frank O'Connor and the desolation of reality. *In* The Irish short story, ed. by P. Rafroidi and T. Brown p189-204
McCrann, A. T. Frank O'Connor and the silence. *In* Irish Renaissance annual I p113-26

**About individual works**
*Guests of the nation*
Matthews, J. H. Women, war, and words: Frank O'Connor's first confessions. *In* Irish Renaissance annual I p73-112

*The saint and Mary Kate*
Matthews, J. H. Women, war, and words: Frank O'Connor's first confessions. *In* Irish Renaissance annual I p73-112

**O'Faoláin, Seán**
**About**
Le Moigne, G. Sean O'Faolain's short-stories and tales. *In* The Irish short story, ed. by P. Rafroidi and T. Brown p205-26

**Ofek, Uriel**
Tom and Laura from right to left. *In* The Arbuthnot lectures, 1970-1979 p167-85

**Office of Naval Research.** Se United States. Office of Naval Research

**Office of Scienitfc Research and Development.** See United States. Office of Scientific Research and Development

**O'Flaherty, Liam**
**About**
Kennelly, B. Liam O'Flaherty: the unchained storm. A view of his short stories. *In* The Irish short story, ed. by P. Rafroidi and T. Brown p175-87

**O'Flaherty, Patrick**
The rock observed
*Contents*
Bridging two worlds: Margaret Duley's fiction, 1936-42
The case of George Tuff: a concluding note
Emigrant muse: E. J. Pratt and Newfoundland, 1882-1907
Fishers of men: three missionaries in eighteenth-century Newfoundland, 1764-98
'It passeth England': literature of discovery and early settlement, 1497-1670
The lure of the north: fiction and travel literature, 1850-1905
The triumph of sentiment: history and commentary, 1793-1895
Visions and revisions: some writers in the new Newfoundland
Walking new ground: books by two Newfoundland pioneers, 1770-1882

**Oh, Bonnie B.**
Sino-Japanese rivalry in Korea, 1876-1885. *In* The Chinese and the Japanese, ed. by A. Iriye p37-57

**Ohaegbu, A. E.**
An approach to Ouologuem's Le devoir de violence. *In* African literature today no. 10: Retrospect & prospect, ed. by E. D. Jones p124-33

**O'Hara, Frank**
**About**
Howard, R. Frank O'Hara: "Since once we are we always will be in this life come what may." *In* Howard, R. Alone with America p466-82
Molesworth, C. "The clear architecture of the nerves": the poetry of Frank O'Hara. *In* Molesworth, C. The fierce embrace p85-97
Vendler, H. H. Frank O'Hara. *In* Vendler, H. H. Part of nature, part of us p179-94

**O'Hara, John**
**About individual works**
*Selected short stories*
Trilling, L. Social actualities. *In* Trilling, L. Speaking of literature and society p279-84

**Oil and gas law.** See Gas, Natural—Law and legislation

**Oil industry.** See Petroleum industry and trade

**Ojo-Ade, Femi**
Madness in the African novel: Awoonor's This earth, my brother. *In* African literature today no. 10: Retrospect & prospect, ed. by E. D. Jones p134-52

**Okamoto, Shumpei**

Ishibashi Tanzan and the Twenty-One Demands. *In* The Chinese and the Japanese, ed. by A. Iriye p184-98

**O'Kelly, Seumas**

### About

Clune, A. Seamus O'Kelly. *In* The Irish short story, ed. by P. Rafroidi and T. Brown p141-57

**Okonkwo, Juliet I.**

The missing link in African literature. *In* African literature today no. 10: Retrospect & prospect, ed. by E. D. Jones p86-105

**Old age, survivors and disability insurance.** See Social security

**Old English literature.** See Anglo-Saxon literature

**Old Russian literature.** See Russian literature—To 1700

**Olivella, Manuel Zapata.** See Zapata Olivella, Manuel

**Olmi, Ermanno**

### About individual works
*The tree of wooden clogs*

Kauffmann, S. The tree of wooden clogs. *In* Kauffmann, S. Before my eyes p339-41

**Olmstead, Alan L.**

The costs of economic growth. *In* Encyclopedia of American economic history, ed. by G. Porter v2 p863-81

**Olney, James Leslie**

Autobiography and the cultural moment: a thematic, historical, and bibliographical introduction. *In* Autobiography: essays theoretical and critical, ed. by J. L. Olney p3-27

Some versions of memory/some versions of bios: the ontology of autobiography. *In* Autobiography: essays theoretical and critical, ed. by J. L. Olney p236-67

**Olson, Alison Gilbert**

Parliament, Empire, and Parliamentary law, 1776. *In* Three British revolutions: 1641, 1688, 1766, ed. by J. G. A. Pocock p289-322

**Olson, Charles**

### About

Riddel, J. N. Decentering the image: the "project" of "American" poetics? *In* Textual strategies, ed. by J. V. Harari p322-58

### About individual works
*The Maximus poems*

Wagner, L. W. Call me Maximus. *In* Wagner, L. W. American modern p152-57

**Olsson, Tom**

O'Neill and the Royal Dramatic. *In* Eugene O'Neill, ed. by V. Floyd p34-60

**Olympic games**

### Records

Morowitz, H. J. De motu animalium. *In* Morowitz, H. J. The wine of life, and other essays on societies, energy & living things p24-27

**One flew over the cuckoo's nest (Motion picture)**

Kael, P. The bull goose loony. *In* Kael, P. When the lights go down p84-90

Kauffmann, S. One flew over the cuckoo's nest. *In* Kauffmann, S. Before my eyes p174-77

**One sings, the other doesn't (Motion picture)**

Kael, P. Scrambled eggs. *In* Kael, P. When the lights go down p339-42

**O'Neill, Eugene Gladstone, 1888-1953**

### About

Bergman, I. A meeting with O'Neill. *In* Eugene O'Neill, by V. Floyd p293-96

### About individual works
*Long day's journey into night*

Sewall, R. B. Long day's journey into night. *In* Sewall, R. B. The vision of tragedy p161-74

Wilson, R. N. Eugene O'Neill: the web of family. *In* Wilson, R. N. The writer as social seer p72-88

*A moon for the misbegotten*

Raleigh, J. H. The Irish atavism of A moon for the misbegotten. *In* Eugene O'Neill, ed. by V. Floyd p229-36

*Welded*

Törnqvist, E. Platonic love in O'Neill's Welded. *In* Eugene O'Neill, ed. by V. Floyd p73-83

### Characters—Mary Tyrone

Fitzgerald, G. Another neurotic Electra: a new look at Mary Tyrone. *In* Eugene O'Neill, ed. by V. Floyd p290-92

### Criticism and interpretation

Bermel, A. Poetry and mysticism in O'Neill. *In* Eugene O'Neill, ed. by V. Floyd p245-51

Egri, P. The use of the short story in O'Neill's and Chekhov's one-act plays: a Hungarian view of O'Neill. *In* Eugene O'Neill, ed. by V. Floyd p115-44

Frenz, H. Eugene O'Neill and Georg Kaiser. *In* Eugene O'Neill, ed. by V. Floyd p172-85

Jackson, E. M. O'Neill the humanist. *In* Eugene O'Neill, ed. by V. Floyd p252-56

Koreneva, M. One hundred percent American tragedy: a Soviet view. *In* Eugene O'Neill, ed. by V. Floyd p145-71

Raleigh, J. H. The last confession: O'Neill and the Catholic confessional. *In* Eugene O'Neill, ed. by V. Floyd p212-28

Rich, J. D. Exile without remedy: the late plays of Eugene O'Neill. *In* Eugene O'Neill, ed. by V. Floyd p257-76

Tiusanen, T. O'Neill's significance: a Scandinavian and European view. *In* Eugene O'Neill, ed. by V. Floyd p61-67

Wilkins, F. The pressure of Puritanism in Eugene O'Neill's New England plays. *In* Eugene O'Neill, ed. by V. Floyd p237-44

### Stage history—Czechoslovakia

Jařab, J. The lasting challenge of Eugene O'Neill: a Czechoslovak view. *In* Eugene O'Neill, ed. by V. Floyd p84-100

### Stage history—Great Britain

Leech, C. O'Neill in England—from Anna Christie to Long day's journey into night, 1923-1958. *In* Eugene O'Neill, ed. by V. Floyd p68-72

### Stage history—Hungary

Egri, P. The use of the short story in O'Neill's and Chekhov's one-act plays: a Hungarian view of O'Neill. *In* Eugene O'Neill, ed. by V. Floyd p115-44

### Stage history—Poland

Sienicka, M. O'Neill in Poland. *In* Eugene O'Neill, ed. by V. Floyd p101-14

### Stage history—Sweden

Olsson, T. O'Neill and the Royal Dramatic. *In* Eugene O'Neill, ed. by V. Floyd p34-60

**O'Neill, John**
On the history of the human senses in Vico and Marx. *In* Conference on Vico and Contemporary Thought, New York, 1976. Vico and contemporary thought pt2 p179-86

**O'Neill, Onora**
The moral perplexities of famine relief. *In* Matters of life and death, ed. by T. Regan p260-98

**Oneiromancy.** See Dreams

**Onetti, Juan Carlos**

### About individual works
*La muerte y la niña*
Terry, A. Onetti and the meaning of fiction: notes on La muerte y la niña. *In* Contemporary Latin American fiction, ed. by S. Bacarisse p54-72

**O'Nolan, Brian**

### About individual works
*A Flann O'Brien reader*
Pritchett, V. S. Flann O'Brien: Flann v. Finn. *In* Pritchett, V. S. The tale bearers p213-19

**Ontology.** See Existentialism

**Open price system.** See Competition

**Opera**
Dent, E. J. The translation of operas. *In* Dent, E. J. Selected essays p 1-25

### History and criticism
McGhee, R. D. Introduction. *In* McGhee, R. D. Marriage, duty & desire in Victorian poetry and drama p 1-28

### Great Britain
Dent, E. J. The Victorians and opera. *In* Dent, E. J. Selected essays p232-37

**Operas**
### History and criticism
*See* Opera—History and criticism

**Ophuls, Marcel**

### About individual works
*The memory of justice*
Kauffmann, S. The memory of justice. *In* Kauffmann, S. Before my eyes p248-51

**Opinion, Public.** See Public opinion

**Opland, Jeff**
From horseback to monastic cell: the impact on English literature of the introduction of writing. *In* Old English literature in context, ed. by J. D. Niles p30-43

**Oppenheim, A. Leo**
Neo-Assyrian and neo-Babylonian empires. *In* Propaganda and communication in world history, ed. by H. D. Lasswell, D. Lerner and H. Speier v 1 p111-44

**Optics, Psychological.** See Visual perception

**Oral communication.** See Conversation; Oral tradition; Speech

**Oral history**
Hareven, T. K. The search for generational memory: tribal rites in industrial society. *In* Generations, ed. by S. R. Graubard p137-49

Rosengarten, T. Stepping over cockleburs: conversations with Ned Cobb. *In* Telling lives, ed. by M. Pachter p104-31

### Historiography
Hoover, H. T. Oral history in the United States. *In* The Past before us, ed. by M. Kammen p391-407

**Oral tradition**
Coote, M. P. The singer's themes in Serbocroatian heroic song. *In* California Slavic studies v11 p201-35

Jackson, R. L. In the beginning: oral literature and the "true black experience." *In* Jackson, R. L. Black writers in Latin America p16-24

### Ireland
Kiberd, D. Story-telling: the Gaelic tradition. *In* The Irish short story, ed. by P. Rafroidi and T. Brown p13-25

### Wales
Roberts, B. F. Tales and romances. *In* A Guide to Welsh literature, ed. by A. O. H. Jarman and G. R. Hughes v 1 p203-43

**Orange, Michael**
Language and silence in A passage to India. *In* E. M. Forster: a human exploration, ed. by G. K. Das and J. Beer p142-60

**Orators**
### Greece
Dover, K. J. Classical oratory. *In* Ancient Greek literature, ed. by K. J. Dover p122-33

**Oratory**
Holloway, J. Logic, feeling and structure in nineteenth-century political oratory: a primer of analysis. *In* Holloway, J. Narrative and structure: exploratory essays p137-56

**Oratory, Ancient**
Dover, K. J. Classical oratory. *In* Ancient Greek literature, ed. by K. J. Dover p122-33

**Orbison, Theodore Tucker**
Arrabal's The solemn communion as ritual drama. *In* The Binding of Proteus, ed. by M. W. McCune, T. T. Orbison and P. M. Withim p280-96

**Orchestra rehearsal (Motion picture)**
Kauffmann, S. Orchestra rehearsal. *In* Kauffmann, S. Before my eyes p58-60

**Orders, Monastic.** See Monasticism and religious orders

**Ordinary-language philosophy**
Marin, L. On the interpretation of ordinary language: a parable of Pascal. *In* Textual strategies, ed. by J. V. Harari p239-59

**Organ, Troy Wilson**
Humanness in neo-Vedāntism. *In* Being human in a technological age, ed. by D. M. Borchert and D. Stewart p127-64

**Organization, Industrial.** See Industrial organization

**Organization, Social.** See Social structure

**Organization of Petroleum Exporting Countries**
Houthakker, H. S. World energy sources. *In* The United States in the 1980s, ed. by P. Duignan and A. Rabushka p535-58

**Organizations, Business.** See Business enterprises

**Organizations, International.** See International agencies

**Oriental literature**
### History and criticism
Hatto, A. T. Shamanism and epic poetry in northern Asia. *In* Hatto, A. T. Essays on medieval German and other poetry p117-38

**Origin of agriculture.** See Agriculture—Origin

**Origin of languages.** See Language and languages—Origin

Origin of species. See Natural selection

Originality (in literature) See Imitation (in literature)

Oromons. See Gallas

Orosius, Paulus

### About individual works
*Seven books against the pagans*

Bately, J. M. World history in the Anglo-Saxon Chronicle: its sources and its separateness from the Old English Orosius. *In* Anglo-Saxon England 8 p177-94

Orphans and orphan asylums. See Foundlings

Orr, David Gerald

Roman domestic religion: the archaeology of Roman popular art. *In* 5000 years of popular culture, ed. by F. E. H. Schroeder p156-72

Ortiz, Adalberto

### About individual works
*Juyungo*

Jackson, R. L. Adalberto Ortiz and his black Ecuadorian classic. *In* Jackson, R. L. Black writers in Latin America p122-29

Orvig, Mary

One world in children's books? *In* The Arbuthnot lectures, 1970-1979 p39-59

Orwell, George

### About

Gloversmith, F. Changing things: Orwell and Auden. *In* Class, culture and social change, ed. by F. Gloversmith p101-41

### About individual works
*1984*

Trilling, L. Orwell on the future. *In* Trilling, L. Speaking of literature and society p249-54

Osborne, Charles

The music critic. *In* The Genius of Shaw, ed. by M. Holroyd p65-76

Osek, Czechoslovakia

Wagenbach, K. Kafka's castle? *In* The World of Franz Kafka, ed. by J. P. Stern p79-86

Oser, Jacob

### About individual works
*Henry George*

Johannsen, O. B. Oser: reservations of a friendly commentator. *In* Critics of Henry George, ed. by R. V. Andelson p371-77

Osler, Margaret J.

Certainty, scepticism, and scientific optimism: the roots of eighteenth-century attitudes toward scientific knowledge. *In* Probability, time, and space in eighteenth-century literature, ed. by P. R. Backscheider p3-28

Ostriches in literature

Lutz, C. E. Some medieval impressions of the ostrich. *In* Lutz, C. E. The oldest library motto, and other library essays p101-06

Ostriker, Alicia

Body language: imagery of the body in women's poetry. *In* The State of the language, ed. by L. Michaels and C. Ricks p247-63

Ostwald, Peter F. and Rieber, Robert W.

James Rush and the theory of voice and mind. *In* Psychology of language and thought, ed. by R. W. Rieber p105-19

Otero, Lisandro

### About individual works
*La pasión de Urbino*

Lipski, J. M. Split signifiers in La pasión de Urbine. *In* The Analysis of literary texts, ed. by R. D. Pope p165-74

Otis, William Bradley, and Needleman, Morriss H.

### About individual works
*A survey-history of English literature*

Trilling, L. M., W., F. at 10. *In* Trilling, L. Speaking of literature and society p192-96

Ottaway, Marina

The theory and practice of Marxism-Leninism in Mozambique and Ethiopia. *In* Communism in Africa, ed. by D. E. Albright p118-44

Otter, Casten von. See Von Otter, Casten

Otto, Rudolf

### About individual works
*The idea of the holy*

Strauss, L. The idea of the holy (Rudolf Otto) *In* The Jew, ed. by A. A. Cohen p232-36

Ottoman Empire. See Turkey—History—Ottoman Empire, 1288-1918

Ouologuem, Yambo

### About individual works
*Bound to violence*

Ohaegbu, A. E. An approach to Ouologuem's Le devoir de violence. *In* African literature today no. 10: Retrospect & prospect, by E. D. Jones p124-33

Outdoor life. See Country life

Overland journeys to the Pacific

Faragher, J. and Stansell, C. Women and their families on the Overland trail to California and Oregon, 1842-1867. *In* A Heritage of her own, ed. by N. F. Cott and E. H. Pleck p246-67

Overtone (Linguistics) See Connotation (Linguistics)

Ovid. See Ovidius Naso, Publius

Ovidius Naso, Publius

### About

Cook, A. S. Ovid: the dialectics of recovery from atavism. *In* Cook, A. S. Myth & language p190-206

### About individual works
*Amores*

Cairns, F. Self-imitation within a generic framework: Ovid, Amores 2.9 and 3.11 and the renuntiatio amoris. *In* Creative imitation and Latin literature, ed. by D. West and T. Woodman p121-41

Gransden, K. W. Lente currite, noctis equi: Chaucer, Troilus and Criseyde 3.1422-70, Donne, The sun rising and Ovid, Amores 1.13. *In* Creative imitation and Latin literature, ed. by D. West and T. Woodman p157-71

*Metamorphoses*

Rudd, N. Pyramus and Thisbe in Shakespeare and Ovid: A midsummer night's dream and Metamorphoses 4.1-166. *In* Creative imitation and Latin literature, ed. by D. West and T. Woodman p173-93

### Influence—Chrestien de Troyes

Robertson, D. W. Chrétien's Cligés and the Ovidian spirit. *In* Robertson, D. W. Essays in medieval culture p173-82

**Owen, Gale R.**
Wynflæd's wardrobe. *In* Anglo-Saxon England 8 p195-222

**Owen, Morfydd E.**
Functional prose: religion, science, grammar, law. *In* A Guide to Welsh literature, ed. by A. O. H. Jarman and G. R. Hughes p248-76

The prose of the cywydd period. *In* A Guide to Welsh literature, ed. by A. O. H. Jarman and G. R. Hughes v2 p338-73

**Ownership.** See Property

**The Oxford Companion to film**
Kauffmann, S. The Oxford Companion to film. *In* Kauffmann, S. Before my eyes p372-76

**Ozick, Cynthia**

About

Alexander, E. The Holocaust in American Jewish fiction: a slow awakening. *In* Alexander, E. The resonance of dust p121-46

**Ozment, Steven H.**
The age of reform, 1250-1550

*Contents*

Calvin and Calvinism
Catholic reform and Counter Reformation
The ecclesiopolitical traditions
Humanism and the Reformation
The interpretation of medieval intellectual history
The legacy of the Reformation
Marriage and the ministry in the Protestant churches
The mental world of Martin Luther
Ogo-Yurugu: lord of the random, servant of wholeness
On the eve of the Reformation
Protestant resistance to tyranny: the career of John Knox
The scholastic traditions
The sectarian spectrum: radical movements within Protestantism
Society and politics in the German Reformation
The spiritual traditions
The Swiss Reformation

# P

**PMLA**
Stimpson, C. R. The power to name: some reflections on the avant-garde. *In* The Prism of sex, ed. by J. A. Sherman and E. T. Beck p55-77

**Pabisch, Peter, and Best, Alan**
The 'total novel': Heimito von Doderer and Albert Paris Gütersloh. *In* Modern Austrian writing, ed. by A. Best and H. Wolfschütz p63-78

**Pachter, Marc**
The biographer himself: an introduction. *In* Telling lives, ed. by M. Pachter p3-15

**Packard, Randall M.**
Social change and the history of misfortune among the Bashu of eastern Zaïre. *In* Explorations in African systems of thought, ed. by I. C. Karp & C. S. Bird p237-67

**Paden, John N.**
Conclusion: reformation of concepts and hypotheses. *In* Values, identities, and national integration, ed. by J. N. Paden p351-59

Introduction. *In* Values, identities, and national integration, ed. by J. N. Paden p 1-7

*See also* Hay, R. jt. auth.

**Padover, Saul Kussiel**
Karl Marx—the propagandist as prophet. *In* Propaganda and communication in world history, ed. by H. D. Lasswell, D. Lerner and H. Speier v2 p210-38

**Padre padrone (Motion picture)**
Kael, P. The sacred oak. *In* Kael, P. When the lights go down p298-304

Kauffmann, S. Padre padrone. *In* Kauffmann, S. Before my eyes p301-03

**Padua, Marsilio of.** See Marsilius of Padua

**Padua. University**

History

Le Goff, J. Academic expenses at Padua in the fifteenth century. *In* Le Goff, J. Time, work, & culture in the Middle Ages p101-06

**Paganism in literature**
Frankis, J. Paganism and pagan love in Troilus and Criseyde. *In* Essays on Troilus and Crisyde, ed. by M. Salu p57-72

**Painting**
Marin, L. Toward a theory of reading in the visual arts: Poussin's The Arcadian shepherds. *In* The Reader in the text, ed. by S. R. Suleiman and I. Crosman p293-324

Zaire—Shaba

Fabian, J. and Szombati-Fabian, I. Folk art from an anthropoligical perspective. *In* Perspectives on American folk art, ed. by I. M. G. Quimby and S. T. Swank p247-92

**Painting, Medieval**

Italy

Schapiro, M. On an Italian painting of the Flagellation of Christ in the Frick Collection. *In* Schapiro, M. Selected papers v3: Late antique, early Christian and mediaeval art p355-79

**Painting, Sienese**

History

Cole, B. The beginnings of Sienese painting. *In* Cole, B. Sienese painting p 1-23
Cole, B. Conclusion. *In* Cole, B. Sienese painting p209-14
Cole, B. Painting after mid-century. *In* Cole, B. Sienese painting p180-208

**Painting and literature.** See Art and literature

**Paintings.** See Painting

**Palacios, Arnoldo**

About

Jackson, R. L. Literary blackness in Colombia: the novels of Arnoldo Palacios. *In* Jackson, R. L. Black writers in Latin America p130-39

**Paleoanthropology.** See Man, Prehistoric

**Paleontology**

United States

Gregory, J. T. North American vertebrate paleontology, 1776-1976. *In* New Hampshire Bicentennial Conference on the History of Geology, University of New Hampshire, 1976. Two hundred years of geology in America p305-35

**Palmarini, Massimo Piattelli-.** See Piatelli-Palmarini, Massimo

**Palmer, David John**
'Twelfth night' and the myth of echo and narcissus. *In* Shakespeare survey 32 p73-78

**Palmer, Eustace Taiwo**
Ngugi's Petals of blood. *In* African literature today no. 10: Retrospect & prospect, ed. by E. D. Jones p153-66

Novels and the colonial experience. *In* African literature today no. 10: Retrospect & prospect, ed. by E. D. Jones p248-52

**Palmer, Richard E.**
The postmodernity of Heidegger. *In* Martin Heidegger and the question of literature, ed. by W. V Spanos p71-92

**Paltsits, Victor Hugo**
A plea for an anatomical method in bibliography. *In* The Bibliographical Society of America, 1904-79 p 1-2

**Pamphlets**
Adams, T. R. The British pamphlet press and the American controversy, 1764-1783. *In* American Antiquarian Society. Proceedings v89 pt 1 p33-88

**Panics.** See Depressions

**Pannuccio dal Bagno**

### About individual works

*Se quei che regna*

Musa, M. Movement and meaning in an old Italian Poem. *In* The Interpretation of medieval lyric poetry, ed. by W. T. H. Jackson p194-204

**Panuccio del Bagno.** See Pannucio dal Bagno

**Pantzer, Katharine F.**
The serpentine progress of the STC revision. *In* The Bibliographical Society of America, 1904-79 p455-69

**Papacy**

### History—To 1309

Ozment, S. H. The ecclesiopolitical traditions. *In* Ozment, S. H. The age of reform, 1250-1550 p135-81

**Papal Schism.** See Schism, The Great Western, 1378-1417

**Paper making and trade.** See Newsprint

**Paper toys**
### Collections and collecting
Coughlan, M. N. The Maxine Waldron collection of children's books and paper toys. *In* Research about nineteenth-century children and books, ed. by S. K. Richardson p61-66

**Papert, Seymour A.**
Computers and learning. *In* The Computer age: a twenty-year view, ed. by M. L. Dertouzos and J. Moses p73-86

The role of artificial intelligence in psychology. *In* Language and learning, ed. by M. Piattelli-Palmarini p90-99

**Papoušek, Hanus, and Papoušek, Mechthild**
Early ontogeny of human social interaction: its biological roots and social dimensions. *In* Human ethology, ed. by M. von Cranach [and others] p456-78

**Papoušek, Mechthild.** See Papoušek, H. jt. auth.

**Paquet, Sandra Pouchet**
The fifties. *In* West Indian literature, ed. by B. King p63-77

**Parables**
Cook, A. S. Parable. *In* Cook, A. S. Myth & language p234-47

**Parabole.** See Metaphor

**Paradox in literature**
Bullough, G. The defence of paradox. *In* Shakespeare's styles, ed. by P. Edwards, I. S. Ewbank and G. K. Hunter p163-82

**Paradise Alley (Motion picture)**
Kael, P. Rocky's knucklehead progeny. *In* Kael, P. When the lights go down p488-96

**Paradise in literature**
Schulz, M. F. Coleridge and the enchantments of earthly paradise. *In* Reading Coleridge, ed. by W. B. Crawford p116-59

**Paralinguistics**
La Barre, W. Paralinguistics, kinesics, and cultural anthropology. *In* La Barre, W. Culture in context p289-332

**Paratte, Henri-Dominique**
Patrick Boyle's tragic humanity. *In* The Irish short story, ed. by P. Rafroidi and T. Brown p275-87

**Pardo Bazán, Emilia, condesa de**

### About individual works

*Los pazos de Ulloa*

Fox-Lockert, L. Emilia Pardo Bazan. *In* Fox-Lockert, L. Women novelists in Spain and Spanish America p49-65

**Parent and child**
Papoušek, H. and Pauoussek, E. Early ontogeny of human social interaction: its biological roots and social dimensions. *In* Human ethology, ed. by M. von Cranach [and others] p456-78

Tov-Ruach, L. Jealousy, attention, and loss. *In* Explaining emotions, ed. by A. O. Rorty p465-88

*See also* Conflict of generations; Fathers

**Parent and child in literature**
Letwin, S. R. Trollope on generations without gaps. *In* Generations, ed. by S. R. Graubard p53-70

**Parent-child relations.** See Parent and child

**Paris**
### Theaters
Lawrenson, T. E. The ideal theatre in the eighteenth century: Paris and Venice. *In* Drama and mimesis, ed. by J. Redmond p51-64

**Paris in literature**
Festa-McCormick, D. Balzac's Girl with the golden eyes: Parisian masks, not faces. *In* Festa-McCormick, D. The city as catalyst p19-32

Festa-McCormick, D. Rilke's Notebooks: Paris and the phantoms of the past. *In* Festa-McCormick, D. The city as catalyst p69-88

Festa-McCormick, D. Romain's Death of a nobody: a city's collective soul. *In* Festa-McCormick, D. The city as catalyst p124-40

Festa-McCormick, D. Zola's L'assommoir: Paris's stranglehold on the lives of the poor. *In* Festa-McCormick, D. The city as catalyst p33-48

**Parker, Hershel**
Melville. *In* American literary scholarship, 1978, p43-58

**Parker, Samuel, Bp. of Oxford**
### About
Anselment, R. A. The rehearsal transpros'd. *In* Anselment, R. A. 'Betwixt jest and earnest' p94-125

**Parker, William Nelson**
Historiography of American economic history. *In* Encyclopedia of American economic history, ed. by G. Porter v 1 p3-16

**Parkinson, Richard N.**
The inheritors; or A single ticket for Howards End. *In* E. M. Forster: a human exploration, ed. by G. K. Das and J. Beer p55-68

**Parliamentary oratory.** See Political oratory

**Parmenides Eleates**

About

Nussbaum, M. C. Eleatic conventionalism and Philolaus on the conditions of thought. *In* Harvard Studies in classical philology, v83, p63-108

**Parody**
Sundquist, E. J. "At home in his words": parody and parricide in Melville's Pierre. *In* Sundquist, E. J. Home as found p143-85

**Parr, Carmen Salazar.** See Salazar Parr, Carmen

**Parra, Teresa de la**

About individual works

*Ifigenia*

Fox-Lockert, L. Teresa de la Parra (Ana Teresa Parra Sanojo). *In* Fox-Lockert, L. Women novelists in Spain and Spanish America p156-65

**Parricide in literature**
Mueller, M. Moral and aesthetic tendencies in eighteenth-century adaptations of Greek tragedy. *In* Mueller, M. Children of Oedipus, and other essays on the imitation of Greek tragedy, 1550-1800 p65-79

**Parrini, Carl P.**
Hoover and international economics. *In* Herbert Hoover, ed. by L. E. Gelfand p182-206

**Parry, Benita**
A passage to India: epitaph or manifesto? *In* E. M. Forster: a human exploration, ed. by G. K. Das and J. Beer p129-41

**Parry, Ellwood C.**
Acts of God, acts of man: geological ideas and the imaginary landscapes of Thomas Cole. *In* New Hampshire Bicentennial Conference on the History of Geology, University of New Hampshire, 1976. Two hundred years of geology in America p53-71

**Parry, Idris**
A path in autumn. *In* The World of Franz Kafka, ed. by J. P. Stern p229-37

**Parsons, Kathryn Joan Pyne**
Moral revolution. *In* The Prism of sex, ed. by J. A. Sherman and E. T. Beck p189-227

**Participation, Political.** See Political participation

**Parties, Political.** See Political parties

**Partimen.** See Jeux-partis

**Partisan Review**
Stimpson, C. R. The power to name: some reflections on the avant-garde. *In* The Prism of sex, ed. by J. A. Sherman and E. T. Beck p55-77

**Partito della democrazia cristiana**
Donolo, C. Social change and transformation of the state of Italy. *In* The State in Western Europe, ed. by R. Scase p164-96

**Pascal, Blaise**

About

Marin, L. On the interpretation of ordinary language: a parable of Pascal. *In* Textual strategies, ed. by J. V. Harari p239-59

**Pascal, Roy**
Kafka's parables. *In* The World of Franz Kafka, ed. by J. P. Stern p112-19

**Pasolini, Pier Paolo**

About individual works

*Salò*

Kauffmann, S. Salò. *In* Kauffmann, S. Before my eyes p296-98

**The passenger (Motion picture**
Kauffmann, S. The passenger/Story of a love. *In* Kauffmann, S. Before my eyes p121-26

**Passfield, Beatrice (Potter) Webb, Baroness.** See Webb, Beatrice (Potter)

**Passfield, Sidney James Webb, Baron**

About

Skidelsky, R. J. A. The Fabian ethic. *In* The Genius of Shaw, ed. by M. Holroyd p113-28

**Passions.** See Emotions

**Passmore, John Arthur**
Civil justice and its rivals. *In* Symposium on Theories of Justice in and for the Second Half of the Twentieth Century, Sydney, 1977. Justice p25-49

**Pasternak, Boris Leonidovich**

About individual works

*Doctor Zhivago*

Hosking, G. Two key works: Doctor Zhivago and One day in the life of Ivan Denisovich. *In* Hosking, G. Beyond Socialist realism p29-49

Wilson, R. N. Boris Pasternak: ideology and privacy. *In* Wilson, R. N. The writer as social seer p105-17

**Pastoral literature**

History and criticism

Gridley, R. E. Some versions of the primitive and the pastoral on the Great Plains of America. *In* Survivals of pastoral, ed. by R. F. Hardin p61-85

Hardin, R. F. The pastoral moment. *In* Survivals of pastoral, ed. by R. F. Hardin p 1-17

Ruhe, E. L. Pastoral paradigms and displacements, with some proposals. *In* Survivals of pastoral, ed. by R. F. Hardin p103-50

**Pastoral poetry, English**

History and criticism

Eversole, R. L. Collins and the end of the shepherd pastoral. *In* Survivals of pastoral, ed. by R. F. Hardin p19-32

Sutton, M. K. Truth and the pastor's vision in George Crabbe, William Barnes, and R. S. Thomas. *In* Survivals of pastoral, ed. by R. F. Hardin p33-59

**Paths of glory (Motion picture)**
Miller, G. Murder in the first degree. *In* Miller, G. Screening the novel p116-42

**Pateman, Carole**
Justifying political obligation. *In* Powers, possessions and freedom, ed. by A. Kontos p63-75

**Patient and medical personnel.** See Medical personnel and patient

**Patil, J. Birje-** See J. Birje-Patil

**Patriarchy.** See Men

**Patrides, Constantinos A.**
The experience of otherness: theology as a means of life. *In* The Age of Milton, ed. by C. A. Patrides and R. B. Waddington p170-96

Patriotism. See Nationalism

**Patron and client**

Forman, S. and Riegelhaupt, J. F. The political economy of patron-clientship: Brazil and Portugal compared. *In* Brazil, anthropological perspectives, ed. by M. L. Margolis and W. E. Carter p379-400

### Case studies

Greenfield, S. M. Patron-client exchanges in southeastern Minas Gerais. *In* Brazil, anthropological perspectives, ed. by M. L. Margolis and W. E. Carter p362-78

**Patterson, Orlando**

The black community: is there a future? *In* The Third century, ed. by S. M. Lipset p243-84

**Paul, Hermann**

#### About individual works

*Principles of the history of language*

Percival, W. K. Hermann Paul's view of the nature of language. *In* Psychology of language and thought, ed. by R. W. Rieber p187-96

**Paul, Sherman**

"The ordeal and the pilgrimage." *In* Van Wyck Brooks: the critic and his critics, ed. by W. Wasserstrom p206-10

**Paulson, Ronald**

Burke's sublime and the representation of revolution. *In* Culture and politics from Puritanism to the Enlightenment, ed. by P. Zagorin p241-69

**The pawnbroker (Motion picture)**

Miller, G. Those who walk in darkness. *In* Miller, G. Screening the novel p167-89

**Payanzo, Ntsomo**

Professional and national values among university students in Zaire. *In* Values, identities, and national integration, ed. by J. N. Paden p337-49

**Peace**

Speier, H. The chance for peace. *In* Propaganda and communication in world history, ed. by H. D. Lasswell, D. Lerner and H. Speier v2 p507-27

**Peace and women.** See Women and peace

**Peaceful coexistence.** See World politics—1945-

**Peacock, Thomas Love**

#### About

Henkle, R. B. Peacock, Thackeray, and Jerrold: the comedy of "radical" disaffection. *In* Henkle, R. B. Comedy and culture p58-110

#### About individual works

*Nightmare Abbey*

Polhemus, R. M. Peacock's Nightmare Abbey: comic communion. *In* Polhemus, R. M. Comic faith p60-87

**Peacocke, Christopher**

Holistic explanation: an outline of a theory. *In* Rational action, ed. by R. Harrison p61-74

**Pearce, Ann Philippa**

#### About

Rees, D. Achieving one's heart's desires: Philippa Pearce. *In* Rees, D. The marble in the water p36-55

**Pearce, Philippa.** See Pearce, Ann Philippa

**Pearce, Roy Harvey**

Toward decreation: Stevens and the "theory of poetry." *In* Wallace Stevens, ed. by F. Doggett and R. Buttel p286-307

**Pearl (Middle English poem)**

Robertson, D. W. The "heresy" of the Pearl. *In* Robertson, D. W. Essays in medieval culture p215-17

Robertson, D. W. The Pearl as symbol. *In* Robertson, D. W. Essays in medieval culture p209-14

**Pearlin, Leonard I.**

Life strains and psychological distress among adults. *In* Themes of work and love in adulthood, ed. by N. J. Smelser and E. H. Erikson p174-92

**Pears, David Francis**

A comparison between Ayer's views about the privileges of sense-datum statements and the views of Russell and Austin. *In* Perception and identity, ed. by G. F. Macdonald p61-83

**Pearsall, Priscilla**

Julian del Casal's portraits of women. *In* The Analysis of literary texts, ed. by R. D. Pope p78-88

**Pearson, Michael Naylor**

Art as symbolic action: Walker Percy's aesthetic. *In* Walker Percy: art and ethics, ed. by J. Tharpe, p55-64

**Peasantry**

#### Historiography

Shanin, T. The conceptual reappearance of peasantry in Anglo-Saxon social science. *In* Soviet and Western anthropology, ed. by E. Gellner p181-91

**Peasants in literature**

Hosking, G. Village prose: Vasily Belov, Valentin Rasputin. *In* Hosking, G. Beyond socialist realism p50-83

Le Goff, J. Peasants and the rural world in the literature of the early Middle Ages (fifth and sixth centuries) *In* Le Goff, J. Time, work, & culture in the Middle Ages p87-97

**Peasants' War, 1524-1525**

Ozment, S. H. Society and politics in the German Reformation. *In* Ozment, S. H. The age of reform, 1250-1550 p245-89

**Pebworth, Ted-Larry**

Cowley's Davideis and the exaltation of friendship. *In* The David myth in Western literature, ed. by R. J. Frontain and J. Wojcik p96-104

**Peckinpah, Sam**

#### About individual works

*The killer elite*

Kael, P. Notes on the nihilist poetry of Sam Peckinpah. *In* Kael, P. When the lights go down p112-19

**Pediatrics.** See Children—Care and hygiene

**Peirce, Charles Santiago Sanders**

#### About

Dusek, V. Geodesy and the earth sciences in the philosophy of C. S. Peirce. *In* New Hampshire Bicentennial Conference on the History of Geology, University of New Hampshire, 1976. Two hundred years of geology in America p265-75

Telotte, J. P. Charles Peirce and Walker Percy: from semiotic to narrative. *In* Walker Percy: art and ethics, ed. by J. Tharpe p65-79

**Pellisson-Fontanier, Paul**

#### About

Ranum, O. Pellison-Fontanier: from Protestant judge to historiographer royal. *In* Ranum, O. Artisans of glory p234-77

**Pelton, Robert D.**
The trickster in West Africa
*Contents*
Ananse: spinner of Ashanti doubleness
Interpreting the trickster
Legba: master of the Fon dialectic
Legba and Eshu: writers of destiny
Toward a theory of the trickster

**Penal law.** See Criminal law

**Penalties (Criminal law)** See Punishment

**Pencavel, John H.**
The nature of the contemporary unemployment problem. *In* The Economy in the 1980s: a program for growth and stability, ed. by M. J. Boskin p83-115

**Pendry, E. D.**
Shakespeare's life, times and stage. *In* Shakespeare survey 32 p227-37

**Pennell, Joseph Stanley**

### About individual works
*The history of Rome Hanks*
Howard, V. J. S. Pennell's The history of Rome Hanks: contributions toward perspectives. *In* Seasoned authors for a new season; the search for standards in popular writing. ed. by L. Filler p127-38

**Pennsylvania**

### History—Colonial period, 1600-1775
Adams, W. P. The colonial German-language press and the American Revolution. *In* The Press & the American Revolution, ed. by B. Bailyn and J. B. Hench p151-228

**Pennsylvania Germans**
Weiser, F. S. Baptismal certificate and gravemarker: Pennsylvania German folk art at the beginning and the end of life. *In* Perspectives on American folk art, ed. by I. M. G. Quimby and S. T. Swank p134-61

**Pensions.** See Social security

**Peoples Temple**
Reid, D. At home in the abyss: Jonestown and the language of enormity. *In* The State of the language, ed. by L. Michaels and C. Ricks p277-88

**Pepys, Samuel**

### About individual works
*The diary of Samuel Pepys*
Pritchett, V. S. Samuel Pepys: the great snail. *In* Pritchett, V. S. The tale bearers p170-76

**Perception**
Armstrong, D. M. Perception, sense data and causality. *In* Perception and identity, ed. by G. F. Macdonald p84-98
Larmore, C. Descartes' empirical epistemology. *In* Descartes, ed. by S. Gaukroger p6-22
Maull, N. L. Cartesian optics and the geometrization of nature. *In* Descartes, ed. by S. Gaukroger p23-40
Strawson, P. F. Perception and its objects. *In* Perception and identity, ed. by G. F. Macdonald p41-60
*See also* Auditory perception; Cognition

**Perception (Philosophy)**
Annas, J. Truth and knowledge. *In* Doubt and dogmatism, ed. by M. Burnyeat and J. Barnes p84-104
Rogers, G. A. J. The empiricism of Locke and Newton. *In* Royal Institute of Philosophy. Philosophers of the Enlightenment p 1-30

Taylor, C. C. W. 'All perceptions are true.' *In* Doubt and dogmatism, ed. by M. Schofield, M. Burnyeat and J. Barnes p105-24

**Perception in children.** See Space perception in children

**Perceval (Motion picture)**
Kauffmann, S. Perceval. *In* Kauffmann, S. Before my eyes p261-63

**Percival, W. Keith**
Hermann Paul's view of the nature of language. *In* Psychology of language and thought, ed. by R. W. Rieber p187-96

**Percy, Walker**

### About
Bigger, C. P. Walker Percy and the resonance of the word. *In* Walker Percy: art and ethics, ed. by J. Tharpe p43-54
Brinkmeyer, R. H. Percy's bludgeon: message and narrative strategy. *In* Walker Percy: art and ethics, ed. by J. Tharpe p80-90
Eubanks, C. L. Walker Percy: eschatology and the politics of grace. *In* Walker Percy: art and ethics, ed. by J. Tharpe p121-36
Hardy, J. E. Percy and place: some beginnings and endings. *In* Walker Percy: art and ethics, ed. by J. Tharpe p5-25
Kissel, S. S. Voices in the wilderness: the prophets of O'Connor, Percy, and Powers. *In* Walker Perry: art and ethics, ed. by J. Tharpe p55-64
Pearson, M. N. Art as a symbolic action: Walker Percy's aesthetic. *In* Walker Percy: art and ethics, ed. by J. Tharpe p55-64
Telotte, J. P. Charles Peirce and Walker Percy: from semiotic to narrative. *In* Walker Percy: art and ethics, ed. by J. Tharpe p65-79

### About individual works
*Lancelot*
Christensen, J. C. Lancelot: sign for the times. *In* Walker Percy: art and ethics, ed. by J. Tharpe p107-20
Dale, C. Lancelot and the medieval quests of Sir Lancelot and Dante. *In* Walker Percy: art and ethics, ed. by J. Tharpe p99-106

*The moviegoer*
Lawson, L. A. Moviegoing in The moviegoer. *In* Walker Percy: art and ethics, ed. by J. Tharpe p26-42

### Aesthetics
Pearson, M. N. Art as symbolic action: Walker Percy's aesthetic. *In* Walker Percy: art and ethics, ed. by J. Tharpe p55-64

### Bibliography
Weixlmann, J. and Gann, D. H. A Walker Percy bibliography. *In* Walker Percy: art and ethics, ed. by J. Tharpe p137-57

### Ethics
*See* Percy, Walker—Religion and ethics

### Knowledge—Aesthetics
*See* Percy, Walker—Aesthetics

### Knowledge—Catholic Church
*See* Percy, Walker—Religion and ethics

### Knowledge—Philosophy
*See* Percy, Walker—Philosophy

**Percy, Walker**—*Continued*

### Philosophy

Telotte, J. P. Charles Peirce and Walker Percy: from semiotic to narrative. *In* Walker Percy: art and ethics, ed. by J. Tharpe p65-79

*See also* Percy, Walker—Political and social views

### Political and social views

Eubanks, C. L. Walker Percy: eschatology and the politics of grace. *In* Walker Percy: art and ethics, ed. by J. Tharpe p121-36

### Religion and ethics

Eubanks, C. L. Walker Percy: eschatology and the politics of grace. *In* Walker Percy: art and ethics, ed. by J. Tharpe p121-36

**Percy, William Alexander**

### About

King, R. H. Repetition and despairing monumentalism: William Faulkner and Will Percy. *In* King, R. H. A Southern Renaissance p77-98

**A perfect couple (Motion picture)**

Kauffmann, S. A perfect couple. *In* Kauffmann, S. Before my eyes p48-59

**Performing arts**

### United States

Brustein, R. S. Introduction. *In* Brustein, R. S. Critical moments p xii-xx

**Periodicals, Publishing of.** See Newspaper publishing

**Periodization in history.** See History—Periodization

**Perkins, Bryce**

Education in the video age: learning via television. *In* Screen and society, ed. by F. J. Coppa p109-35

**Perkinson, Henry J.**

Vico and the methods of study of our time. *In* Conference on Vico and Contemporary Thought, New York, 1976. Vico and contemporary thought pt2 p95-109

**Perlis, Alan J.**

Current research frontiers in computer science. *In* The Computer age: a twenty-year view, ed. by M. L. Dertouzos and J. Moses p422-36

**Perón, Eva (Duarte)**

### About

Naipaul, V. S. The corpse at the iron gate. *In* Naipaul, V. S. The return of Eva Perón p95-170

**Perón, Juan Domingo, President Argentine Republic**

### About

Naipaul, V. S. The corpse at the iron gate. *In* Naipaul, V. S. The return of Eva Perón p95-170

**Perrot, Michelle**

The three ages of industrial discipline in nineteenth-century France. *In* Consciousness and class experience in nineteenth-century Europe, ed. by J. M. Merriman p149-68

**Perry, Ruth**

The veil of chastity: Mary Astell's feminism. *In* Studies in eighteenth-century culture v9 p25-43

**Perry, Theodore Anthony**

Erotic spirituality

*Contents*

Délie! an old way of dying (the meaning of Scève's title)

The Dialoghi d'amore as literature: the uses of dialogue

Erotic experiment and androgynous integration: Héroët's poetry

Ideal love and human reality: Montemayor's pastoral philosophy

John Donne's philosophy of love in "The ecstasy"

Leone Ebreo's Dialoghi d'amore: the argumen'

Pernette du Guillet's poetry of love and desire

Return and reincarnation in Scève's Délie

Withdrawal or service: the paradox of King Lear

**Pershits, A. I.**

Ethnographic reconstruction of the history of primitive society. *In* Soviet and Western anthrolopogy, ed. by E. Gellner p85-94

**Persian Gulf region**

### Foreign relations—United States

Wohlstetter, A. Half-wars and half-policies in the Persian Gulf. *In* National security in the 1980s: from weakness to strength, ed. by W. S. Thompson p123-71

### Strategic aspects

Rowen, H. S. The threatened jugular: oil supply of the West. *In* National security in the 1980s: from weakness to strength, ed. by W. S. Thompson p275-94

Wohlstetter, A. Half-wars and half-policies in the Persian Gulf. *In* National security in the 1980s: from weakness to strength, ed. by W. S. Thompson p123-71

**Personal growth.** See Self-actualization (Psychology)

**Personal liberty.** See Liberty

**Personal names.** See Names, Personal

**Personality**

Sennett, R. Destructive Gemeinschaft. *In* The Philosophy of sex, ed. by A. Soble p299-321

*See also* Character; Identity (Psychology); Individuality

**Persuasion (Psychology)** See Brain-washing; Propaganda

**Persuasion (Rhetoric)**

De Man, P. Rhetoric of persuasion (Nietzsche) *In* De Man, P. Allegories of reading p119-31

**Perversion, Sexual.** See Sexual deviation

**Pessen, Edward**

Social mobility. *In* Encyclopedia of American economic history, ed. by G. Porter v3 p1120-35

**Pessimism in literature**

Nnolim, C. E. Dialectic as form: pejorism in the novels of Armah. *In* African literature today no. 10: Retrospect & prospect, ed. by E. D. Jones p207-23

**Peters, Margot**

'As lonely as God.' *In* The Genius of Shaw, ed. by M. Holroyd p185-99

**Petersburg in literature.** See Leningrad in literature

**Petitot, Jean**

Localist hypothesis and theory of catastropres: note on the debate. *In* Language and learning, ed. by M. Piattelli-Palmarini p372-79

Petrarca, Francesco

### About individual works
*Canzoniere*

Sturm, S. Transformations of courtly love poetry: Vita nouva and Canzoniere. *In* The Expansion and transformations of courtly literature, ed. by N. B. Smith and J. T. Snow p128-40

Petroleum industry and trade

Sweeney, J. L. Energy problems and policies. *In* The Economy in the 1980s: a program for growth and stability, ed. by M. J. Boskin p353-92

### Near East

Rowen, H. S. The threatened jugular: oil supply of the West. *In* National security in the 1980s: from weakness to strength, ed. by W. S. Thompson p275-94

### Persian Gulf region

Wohlstetter, A. Half-wars and half-policies in the Persian Gulf. *In* National security in the 1980s: from weakness to strength, ed. by W. S. Thompson p123-71

Petrova-Averkieva, Yu.

Historicism in Soviet ethnographic science. *In* Soviet and Western anthropology, ed. by E. Gellner p19-27

Peyre, Henri Maurice

André Malraux and the metamorphosis of literature. *In* André Malraux, ed. by F. Dorenlot and M. Tison-Braun p27-34

Introduction. *In* Peyre, H. What is symbolism? p 1-5

On the arrogance of criticism. *In* The Analysis of literary texts, ed. by R. D. Pope p 1-8

What is symbolism?

*Contents*

Baudelaire
The heritage of symbolism in France and outside France
In search of the morbid and the strange: the decadents and Laforgue
Mallarmé
Rimbaud, or the symbolism of revolt
Symbolism, painting, and music
The symbolists
The tragic impressionism of Verlaine
The word and its antecedents

Peyton, K. M. pseud

### About

Townsend, J. R.    K. M. Peyton. *In* Townsend, J. R. A sounding of storytellers p166-78

Peyton, Kathleen Wendy. See Peyton, K. M. pseud.

Peyton, Michael. See Peyton, K. M. pseud.

Pfitzner, Hans Erich

### About

Carner, M. Pfitzner versus Berg. *In* Carner, M. Major and minor p253-57

The phantom president (Motion picture)

Kauffmann, S. The phantom president. *In* Kauffmann, S. Before my eyes p345-49

Pharisees

Buber, M. Pharisaism. *In* The Jew, ed. by A. A. Cohen p223-31

Phenomenological psychology. See Existential psychology

Phenomenology

Kurzweil, E. Paul Ricoeur: hermeneutics and structuralism. *In* Kurzweil, E. The age of structuralism p87-112

Phenomenology and literature

Lentricchia, F. Versions of phenomenology. *In* Lentricchia, F. After the New Criticism p62-100

Philanthropy. See Endowment of research

Phillips, David Graham

### About individual works
*Susan Lenox: her fall and rise*

Miller, G. The new woman gets the old treatment. *In* Miller, G. Screening the novel p19-45

Phillips curve

Scadding, J. L. Inflation: a perspective from the 1970s. *In* The Economy in the 1980s: a program for growth and stability, ed. by M. J. Boskin p53-81

Phillipson, Nicholas T.

Hume as moralist: a social historian's perspective. *In* Royal Institute of Philosophy. Philosophers of the Enlightenment p140-61

Philolaus

### About

Nussbaum, M. C. Eleatic conventionalism and Philolaus on the conditions of thought. *In* Harvard Studies in classical philology, v83 p63-108

Philosophers

Hook, S. Philosophy and public policy. *In* Hook, S. Philosophy and public policy p3-15

### Greece

Sedley, D. The protagonists. *In* Doubt and dogmatism, ed. by M. Schofield, M. Burnyeat and J. Barnes p 1-19

Philosophical anthropology. See Man—Animal nature

Philosophy

Ayer, Sir A. J. Replies. *In* Perception and identity, ed. by G. F. Macdonald p277-333

Fisch, M. H. What has Vico to say to philosophers of today? *In* Conference on Vico and Contemporary Thought, New York, 1976. Vico and contemporary thought pt 1 p9-19

Heidegger, M. The age of the world view. *In* Martin Heidegger and the question of literature, ed. by W. V. Spanos p 1-15

Hook, S. Philosophy and public policy. *In* Hook, S. Philosophy and public policy p3-15

Kristeller, P. O. Byzantine and Western Platorism in the fifteenth century. *In* Kristeller, P. O. Renaissance thought and its sources p150-63

*See also* Act (Philosophy); Agent (Philosophy); Analysis (Philosophy); Belief and doubt; Essence (Philosophy); Ethics; God; Knowledge, Theory of; Nihilism (Philosophy); Perception; Platonists; Reductionism; Self (Philosophy); Space and time; Structuralism; Truth

Philosophy, American

Madden, E. H. Asa Mahan and the Oberlin philosophy. *In* History, religion, and spiritual democracy, ed. by M. Wohlgelernter [and others] p155-80

McDermott, J. J. Spires of influence: the importance of Emerson for classical American philosophy. *In* History, religion, and spiritual democracy, ed. by M. Wohlgelernter [and others] p181-202

### 20th century

Shea, W. M. The supernatural in the naturalists. *In* History, religion, and spiritual democracy, ed. by M. Wohlgelernter [and others] p53-75

**Philosophy, Ancient**

Cook, A. S. Heraclitus and the conditions of utterance. *In* Cook, A. S. Myth & language p69-107

Dover, K. J. Classical science and philosophy. *In* Ancient Greek literature, ed. by K. J. Dover p105-21

Sedley, D. The protagonists. *In* Doubt and dogmatism, ed. by M. Schofield, M. Burnyeat and J. Barnes p 1-19

Stein, S. The concept of the "fence": observations on its origin and development. *In* Studies in Jewish religious and intellectual history, ed. by S. Stein and R. Loewe p301-29

*See also* Neoplatonism

**Philosophy, English**

**17th century**

Mintz, S. I. The motion of thought: intellectual and philosophical backgrounds. *In* The Age of Milton, ed. by C. A. Patrides and R. B. Waddington p138-69

**20th century**

Holdcroft, D. From the one to the many: philosophy, 1900-30. *In* The Context of English literature, 1900-1930, ed. by M. Bell p126-59

**Philosophy, German**

**18th century**

Berlin, Sir I. Hume and the sources of German anti-rationalism. *In* Berlin, Sir I. Against the current p162-87

**19th century**

Ashton, R. D. Coleridge and German 'aesthetics' (1802-18) *In* Ashton, R. D. The German idea p48-56

Ashton, R. P. Introduction. *In* Ashton, R. D. The German idea p 1-26

Ashton, R. D. Lewes and German philosophy. *In* Ashton, R. D. The German idea p126-31

Ashton, R. D. Lewes: one of Carlyle's 'youngmen' (1835-9) *In* Ashton, R. D. The German idea p105-11

Bennett, B. Breakthrough in theory: the philosophical background of modern drama. *In* Bennett, B. Modern drama and German classicism p229-81

**19th century—Influence**

Ashton, R. D. Carlyle and German philosophy (1824-34) *In* Ashton, R. D. The German idea p91-98

**Philosophy, Greek.** See Philosophy, Ancient

**Philosophy, Jewish**

Davidson, H. A. The principle that a finite body can contain only finite power. *In* Studies in Jewish religious and intellectual history, ed. by S. Stein and R. Loewe p75-92

Hertzberg, A. Judaism and modernity. *In* The Jewish world, ed. by E. Kedourie p301-08

Hyman, A. Jewish philosophy. *In* The Jewish world, ed. by E. Kedourie p209-16

Rabin, C. Hebrew and Arabic in medieval Jewish philosophy. *In* Studies in Jewish religious and intellectual history, ed. by S. Stein and R. Loewe p235-45

Stein, S. The concept of the "fence": observations on its origin and development. *In* Studies in Jewish religious and intellectual history, ed. by S. Stein and R. Loewe p301-29

*See also* Judaism and philosophy

**Philosophy, Medieval**

Ozment, S. H. The interpretation of medieval intellectual history. *In* Ozment, S. H. The age of reform, 1250-1550 p 1-21

Ozment, S. H. The scholastic traditions. *In* Ozment, S. H. The age of reform, 1250-1550 p22-72

*See also* Scholasticism

**Philosophy, Modern**

*See also* Phenomenology

**16th century**

*See* Philosophy, Renaissance

**18th century**

*See* Enlightenment

**20th century**

Tanner, M. The language of philosophy. *In* The State of the language, ed. by L. Michaels and C. Ricks p458-66

**Philosophy, Moral.** See Ethics

**Philosophy, Renaissance**

Kristeller, P. O. The Aristotelian tradition. *In* Kristeller, P. O. Renaissance thought and its sources p32-49

Kristeller, P. O. Renaissance philosophy and the medieval tradition. *In* Kristeller, P. O. Renaissance thought and its sources p106-33

Kristeller, P. O. Renaissance Platonism. *In* Kristeller, P. O. Renaissance thought and its sources p50-65

**Philosophy, Roman**

Stein, S. The concept of the "fence": observations on its origin and development. *In* Studies in Jewish religious and intellectual history, ed. by S. Stein and R. Loewe p301-29

**Philosophy, Scottish**

Forbes, D. Hume and the Scottish enlightenment. *In* Royal Institute of Philosophy. Philosophers of the Enlightenment p94-109

**Philosophy and Judaism.** See Judaism and philosophy

**Philosophy and religion**

Anscombe, G. E. M. What is it to believe someone? *In* Rationality and religious belief, ed. by C. F. Delaney p141-51

Gilkey, L. B. The dialectic of Christian belief: rational, incredible, credible. *In* Rationality and religious belief, ed. by C. F. Delaney p65-83

Schofield, M. Preconception, argument, and God. *In* Doubt and dogmatism, ed. by M. Schofield, M. Burnyeat and J. Barnes p283-308

Smith, J. E. Faith, belief, and the problem of rationality in religion. *In* Rationality and religious belief, ed. by C. F. Delaney p42-64

*See also* Judaism and philosophy

**Philosophy and science.** See Science—Philosophy

**Philosophy of history.** See History—Philosophy

**Philosophy of language.** See Languages—Philosophy

**Philosophy of nature**

Manley, L. G. Art, nature, and convention. *In* Manley, L. G. Convention, 1500-1750 p15-25

Manley, L. G. Neo-Stoic and Baconian nature: seventeenth century prospects. *In* Manley, L. G. Convention, 1500-1750 p133-36

Schuster, J. A. Descartes' mathesis universalis: 1619-28. *In* Descartes, ed. by S. Gaukroger p41-96

**Phoenix (Anglo-Saxon poem)**

Stanley, E. G. Two Old English poetic phrases insufficiently understood for literary criticism: þing gehegan and seonoþ gehegan. *In* Old English poetry, ed. by D. G. Calder p67-90

**Phonetic spelling**
Wollock, J. William Thornton and the practical applications of new writing systems. *In* Psychology of language and thought, ed. by R. W. Rieber p121-51

**Phonetics, Experimental**
Black, J. W. Edward Wheeler Scripture, phonetician. *In* Psychology of language and thought, ed. by R. W. Rieber p225-38

**Photography**

History—United States

Nye, R. B. Notes on photography and American culture, 1839-1890. *In* Toward a new American literary history, ed. by L. J. Budd, E. H. Cady and C. L. Anderson p244-57

**Physical anthropology.** See Human behavior

**Physical mathematics.** See Mathematical physics

**Physicians**

France

Roche, D. Talent, reason, and sacrifice: the physician during the Enlightenment. *In* Medicine and society in France, ed. by R. Forster and O. Ranum p66-88

**Physicians in literature**
Amundsen, D. W. Images of physicians in classical times. *In* 5000 years of popular culture, ed. by F. E. H. Schroeder p94-107

**Physicists**

United States

Weart, S. P. The physics business in America, 1919-1940: a statistical reconnaissance. *In* The Sciences in the American context: new perspectives, ed. by N. Reingold p295-358

**Physics**
Morowitz, H. J. Good news for humanists. *In* Morowitz, H. J. The wine of life, and other essays on societies, energy & living things p33-36

Wilson, R. R. The humanness of physics. *In* Being human in a technological age, ed. by D. M. Borchert and D. Stewart p25-35

*See also* Force and energy; Mathematical physics; Quantum theory

Philosophy

Dummett, M. A. B. Common sense and physics. *In* Perception and identity, ed. by G. F. Macdonald p 1-40

United States—History

Weart, S. P. The physics business in America, 1919-1940: a statistical reconnaissance. *In* The Sciences in the American context: new perspectives, ed. by N. Reingold p295-358

**Physiognomy.** See Facial expression

**Piaget, Jean**
Afterthoughts. *In* Language and learning. ed. by M. Piattelli-Palmarini p278-84

Introductory remarks. *In* Language and learning, ed. by M. Piattelli-Palmarini p57-61

Opening the debate: the psychogenesis of knowledge and its epistemological significance. *In* Language and learning, ed. by M. Piattelli-Palmarini p23-34

Schemes of action and language learning. *In* Language and learning, ed. by M. Piattelli-Palmarini p164-67

About

Bischof, N. Remarks on Lorenz and Piaget: how can "working hypotheses" be "necessary"? *In* Language and learning, ed. by M. Piattelli-Palmarini p233-41

Gardner, H. Foreword: Cognition comes of age. *In* Language and learning, ed. by M. Piattelli-Palmarini p xix-xxxvi

Mehler, J. Psychology and psycholinguistics: the impact of Chomsky and Piaget. *In* Language and learning, ed. by M. Piattelli-Palmarini p341-53

Mora, G. Vico and Piaget: parallels and differences. *In* Conference on Vico and Contemporary Thought, New York, 1976. Vico and contemporary thought pt2 p40-54

Piattelli-Palmarini, M. Introduction: How hard is the "hard core" of a scientific program? *In* Language and learning, ed. by M. Piattelli-Palmarini p 1-20

Putnam, H. What is innate and why: comments on the debate. *In* Language and learning, ed. by M. Piattelli-Palmarini p287-309

Thom, R. The genesis of representational space according to Piaget. *In* Language and learning, ed. by M. Piattelli-Palmarini p361-68

**Piattelli-Palmarini, Massimo**
Introduction: How hard is the "hard core" of a scientific program? *In* Language and learning, ed. by M. Piattelli-Palmarini p 1-20

**Picasso, Pablo**

About

Ashton, D. Picasso and Frenhofer. *In* Ashton, D. A fable of modern art p75-95

**Pickering, Frederick Pickering**
Essays on medieval German literature and iconography

*Contents*

Economies of history. What is fiction?
Exegesis and imagination: a contribution to the study of Rupert of Deutz
The 'fortune' of Hartmann's Erec
Goethe's 'Alexis und Dora' (1796): an interpretation
The Gothic image of Christ: the sources of medieval representations of The Crucifixion
Historical thought and moral codes in medieval epic
Justus Lipsius' De Cruce libri tres (1593) or the historian's dilemma
Notes on fate and fortune
On coming to terms with Curtius
Trinitas creator: word and image
University German and the syllabus of studies
The Western image of Byzantium in the Middle Ages

**Pickering, W. S. F.**
Theodicy and social theory: an exploration of the limits of collaboration between sociologist and theologian. *In* Sociology and theology: alliance and conflict, ed. by D. Martin, J. O. Mills [and] W. S. F. Pickering p59-79

**Pickett, Thomas E.**
James C. Booth and the first Delaware geological survey, 1837-1841. *In* New Hampshire Bicentennial Conference on the History of Geology, University of New Hampshire, 1976. Two hundred years of geology in America p167-74

**Pico della Mirandola, Giovanni**

About

Kristeller, P. O. The dignity of man. *In* Kristeller, P. O. Renaissance thought and its sources p169-81

**A piece of pleasure (Motion picture)**
Kauffmann, S. The last woman/A piece of pleasure. *In* Kauffmann, S. Before my eyes p213-16

**Pierpont Morgan Library, New York. Glazier Psalter (Ms. G. 25)**
Schapiro, M. An illuminated English psalter of the early thirteenth century. *In* Schapiro, M. Selected papers v3: Late antique, early Christian and mediaeval art p329-54

**Pierpont Morgan Library, New York, Hours of Catherine of Cleves (Ms. 945)**
Schapiro, M. A note on the Mérode altarpiece. *In* Schapiro, M. Selected papers v3: Late antique, early Christian and mediaeval art p12-19

**Piggott, Stuart**
Early towns in Europe? *In* The Origins of civilization, ed. by P. R. S. Moorey p34-53

**Pilgrims and pilgrimages.** See Christian pilgrims and pilgrimages

**Pilling, John**
Samuel Beckett: the critical heritage edited by Lawrence Graver and Raymond Federman. *In* Drama and mimesis, ed. by J. Redmond p243-47

**Pilnyak, Boris,** pseud. See Vogau, Boris Andreevich

**Pimlott, Ben.** See Seaton, J. jt. auth.

**Pincus, Jonathan J.**
Tariffs. *In* Encyclopedia of American economic history, ed. by G. Porter v 1 p439-50

**Pindar.** See Pindarus

**Pindarus**

About
Cook, A. S. Pindar: "Great deeds of prowess are always many-mythed." *In* Cook, A. S. Myth & language p108-44

About individual works
*Olympia 6*
Carne-Ross, D. S. Weaving with points of gold: Pindar's Sixth Olympian. *In* Carne-Ross, D. S. Instaurations p29-60

**Pindyck, Robert S.**
The critical issues in U.S. energy policy. *In* Economic issues of the eighties, ed. by R. M. Kamrany and R. H. Day p135-45

**Pines, Shlomo**
The Jewish religion after the destruction of Temple and state: the views of Bodin and Spinoza. *In* Studies in Jewish religious and intellectual history, ed. by S. Stein and R. Loewe p215-34

**The pink panther strikes again (Motion picture)**
Kael, P. Processing sludge. *In* Kael, P. When the lights go down p245-48

**Pinter, Harold**

About individual works
*A la recherche du temps perdu: the Proust screenplay*
Kauffmann, S. A la recherche du temps perdu: the Proust screenplay. *In* Kauffmann, S. Before my eyes p394-98

**Pioneer life.** See Frontier and pioneer life

**Pioneers.** See Frontier and pioneer life

**Piper, John**

About individual works
*Brighton aquatints*
Plomer, W. C. F. Views of Brighton. *In* Plomer, W. C. F. Electric delights p212-14

**Pipes, Richard**
In the Russian intellectual tradition. *In* Solzhenitsyn at Harvard, ed. by R. Berman p115-21

**Pipkin, James W.**
The borderers and the genesis of Wordsworth's spots of time. *In* Tennessee Studies in literature v24 p111-19

**Pirandello, Luigi**

About individual works
*Tonight we improvise*
Bassnett-McGuire, S. Art and life in Luigi Pirandello's Questa sera si recita a soggetto. *In* Drama and mimesis, ed. by J. Redmond p81-102

**Pirosmani (Motion picture)**
Kauffmann, S. The last supper/Pirosmani. *In* Kauffmann, S. Before my eyes p310-13

**Piscator, Erwin**

About individual works
*Hoppla, we're alive*
Kane, M. Erwin Piscator's 1927 production of Hoppla, we're alive. *In* Performance and politics in popular drama, ed. by D. Bradby, L. James and B. Sharratt p189-200

**Pity.** See Sympathy

**Pius X, Saint Pope**

About individual works
*Pascendi dominici gregis*
Daly, G. The integralist response (2): Pascendi and after. *In* Daly, G. Transcendence and immanence p190-217

**Pixérécourt, René Charles Guilbert de**

About
Howarth, W. D. Word and image in Pixérécourt's melodramas: the dramaturgy of the strip-cartoon. *In* Performance and politics in popular drama, ed. by R. Bradby, L. James and B. Sharratt p17-32

**Pizer, Donald**
The novels of Carl Van Vechten and the spirit of the age. *In* Toward a new American literary history, ed. by L. J. Budd, E. H. Cady and C. L. Anderson p211-29

**Plácido,** pseud. See Valdés, Gabriel de la Concepción

**Plague in literature**
West, D. A. Two plagues: Virgil, Georgics 3.478-566 and Lucretius 6.1090-1286. *In* Creative imitation and Latin literature, ed. by D. West and T. Woodman p71-88

**Plains, Great.** See Great Plains

**Planning, Economic.** See United States—Economic policy

**Planning, National.** See United States—Social policy

**Plant design.** See Factories

**Plant ecology.** See Botany—Ecology

**Plantation life**
Genovese, E. D. Life in the big house; excerpts from "Roll, Jordan, roll." *In* A Heritage of her own, ed. by N. F. Cott and E. H. Pleck p290-97

**Plantinga, Alvin**
Is belief in God rational? *In* Rationality and religious belief, ed. by C. F. Delaney p7-27

**Plants**

Ecology
*See* Botany—Ecology

**Plants in literature**
Mackenzie, E. The growth of plants: a seventeenth-century metaphor. *In* English Renaissance studies, ed. by J. Carey p194-211

**Plants in poetry.** See Plants in literature

**Plate tectonics**

Pyne, S. J. From the Grand Canyon to the Marianas Trench: the earth sciences after Darwin. *In* The Sciences in the American context: new perspectives, ed. by N. Reingold p165-92

*See also* Sea-floor spreading

**Platen, August von.** See Platen-Hallermünde, August Graf von

**Platen-Hallermünde, August Graf von**

*About individual works*

*Sonette aus Venedig (no. 36)*

Grundlehner, P. August Graf von Platen: "Ween tiefe Schwermut meine Seele wieget. . . ." *In* Grundlehner, P. The lyrical bridge p41-52

**Plath, Aurelia Schober**

*About*

Broe, M. L. A subtle psychic bond: the mother figure in Sylvia Plath's poetry. *In* The Lost tradition: mothers and daughters in literature, ed. by C. N. Davidson and E. M. Broner p207-16

**Plath, Sylvia**

*About*

Broe, M. L. A subtle psychic bond: the mother figure in Sylvia Plath's poetry. *In* The Lost tradition: mothers and daughters in literature, ed. by C. N. Davidson and E. M. Broner p207-16

Howard, R. Sylvia Plath: "And I have no face, I have wanted to efface myself. . . ." *In* Howard, R. Alone with America p483-92

*About individual works*

*Ariel [poems]*

Wagner, L. W. Plath's "Ariel": "auspicious gales." *In* Wagner, L. W. American modern p231-34

*Crossing the water*

Vendler, H. H. Sylvia Plath. *In* Vendler, H. H. Part of nature, part of us p271-76

**Plato**

*About*

Montgomery, R. L. Faculty psychology and theories of imagination: Aristotle, Plato, Augustine, and Aquinas. *In* Montgomery, R. L. The reader's eye p13-49

*About individual works*

*The Republic*

Lange, L. The function of equal education in Plato's Republic and Laws. *In* The Sexism of social and political theory: women and reproduction from Plato to Nietzsche, ed. by L. M. G. Clarke and L. Lange p3-15

*Influence*

Kristeller, P. O. Renaissance Platonism. *In* Kristeller, P. O. Renaissance thought and its sources p50-65

**Platonism.** See Platonists

**Platonists**

Kristeller, P. O. Byzantine and Western Platonism in the fifteenth century. *In* Kristeller, P. O. Renaissance thought and its sources p150-63

Kristeller, P. O. Renaissance Platonism. *In* Kristeller, P. O. Renaissance thought and its sources p50-65

*See also* Neoplatonism

**Plautus, Titus Maccius**

*About individual works*

*Bacchides*

Bain, D. Plautus uortit barbare: Plautus, Bacchides 526-61 and Menander, Dis exapaton 102-12. *In* Creative imitation and Latin literature, ed. by D. West and T. Woodman p17-34

**Plays, Bible.** See Bible plays

**Pleasure.** See Sensuality

**Pleck, Elizabeth Hafkin**

A mother's wages: income earning among married Italian and black women, 1896-1911. *In* A Heritage of her own, ed. by N. F. Cott and E. H. Pleck p367-92

**Plomer, William Charles Franklyn**

Electric delights

*Contents*

C. P. Cavafy
Charles Tennyson Turner
Christina Rossetti
The church operas
Conversation with my younger self
Edward FitzGerald
F. T. Prince
Francis Kilvert
George Gissing
Herman Melville
Ivan Bunin
John Betjeman
Kilvert's country
Lenin's favourite novel
Leonard Woolf
Let's crab an opera
A letter from the seaside
Louis Couperus
Notes on a visit to Ireland
Notes on the libretto of Gloriana
Olive Schreiner
On not answering the telephone
R. S. Thomas
Thomas Pringle
Views of Brighton
The war requiem
William Hickey
A writer's faith

*About*

Plomer, W. C. F. Conversation with my younger self. *In* Plomer, W. C. F. Electric delights p28-40

Plomer, W. C. F. A writer's faith. *In* Plomer, W. C. F. Electric delights p19-22

*About individual works*

*Gloriana* (Libretto)

Plomer, W. C. F. Notes on the libretto of Gloriana. *In* Plomer, W. C. F. Electric delights p175-79

**Plots, (Drama, novel, etc.)**

Holloway, J. Effectively complete enumeration in 'Phèdre.' *In* Holloway, J. Narrative and structure: exploratory essays p20-37

**Pluralism (Social sciences)**

Morrison, D. G. and Stevenson, H. M. Cultural pluralism, modernization, and conflict: an empirical analysis of sources of political instability in African nations. *In* Values, identities, and national integration, ed. by J. N. Paden p11-23

**Plurilingualism.** See Multilingualism

**Pocock, John Greville Agard**

Political ideas as historical events: political philosophers as historical actors. *In* Political theory and political education, ed. by M. Richter p139-58

**Pocock, John G. A.**—*Continued*

Post-Puritan England and the problem of the Enlightenment. *In* Culture and politics from Puritanism to the Enlightenment, ed. by P. Zagorin p91-111

1776: the revolution against Parliament. *In* Three British revolutions: 1641, 1688, 1776, ed. by J. G. A. Pocock p265-88

**Poe, Edgar Allan**

### About

Bickman, M. Animatopoeia: sirens of the self. *In* Bickman, M. The unsounded centre p58-79

Irwin, J. T. The hieroglyphics and the quest for origins: the myth of hieroglyphic doubling. *In* Irwin, J. T. American hieroglyphics p43-235

### About individual works

*The black cat*

Brooke-Rose, C. The readerhood of man. *In* The Reader in the text, ed. by S. R. Suleiman and I. Crosman p120-48

*Eureka*

Bickman, M. Voyages of the mind's return: three paradigmatic works. *In* Bickman, M. The unsounded centre p22-37

*The narrative of Arthur Gordon Pym of Nantucket*

Irwin   J. T. The hieroglyphics and the quest for origins: the myth of hieroglyphic doubling. *In* Irwin, J. T. American hieroglyphics p43-235

Holland, N. N. Re-covering "The purloined letter": reading as a personal transaction. *In* The Reader in the text, ed. by S. R. Suleiman and I. Crosman p350-70

*The purloined letter*

Felman, S. On reading poetry: reflections on the limits and possibilities of psychoanalytical approaches. *In* The Literary Freud: mechanisms of defense and the poetic will, ed by J. H. Smith p119-48

*The raven*

Fehrman, C. A. D. E. A. Poe and the aesthetics of work. *In* Fehrman, C. A. D. Poetic creation p73-90

### Bibliography

Stauffer, D. B. Poe. *In* American literary scholarship, 1978 p29-41

### Criticism and interpretation

Felman, S. On reading poetry: reflections on the limits and possibilities of psychoanalytical approaches. *In* The Literary Freud: mechanisms of defense and the poetic will, ed. by J. H. Smith p119-48

### Poetic works

Felman, S. On reading poetry: reflections on the limits and possibilities of psychoanalytical approaches. *In* The Literary Freud: mechanism of defense and the poetic will, ed. by J. H. Smith p119-48

**Poetics**

Holloway, J. Poetic analysis and the idea of the transformation-rule: some examples from Herbert, Wordsworth, Pope and Shakespeare. *In* Holloway, J. Narrative and structure: exploratory essays p118-36

Molesworth, C. The metaphors for the poem. *In* Molesworth, C. The fierce embrace p139-49

Sternfeld, F. W. Repetition and echo in Renaissance poetry and music. *In* English Renaissance studies, ed. by J. Carey p33-43

**Poetry**

Beaujour, M. Genus universum. *In* Glyph 7 p15-31

Bloom, H. Freud's concepts of defense and the poetic will. *In* The Literary Freud: mechanisms of defense and the poetic will, ed. by J. H. Smith p 1-28

Carne-Ross, D. S. Center of resistance. *In* Carne-Ross, D. S. Instaurations p 1-28

Donato, E. U. Divine agonies: of representation and narrative in romantic poetics. *In* Glyph 6 p90-122

Edelson, M. Two questions about psychoanalysis and poetry. *In* The Literary Freud: mechanisms of defense and the poetic will, ed. by J. H. Smith p113-18

Ferguson, M. W. Border territories of defense: Freud and defenses of poetry. *In* The Literary Freud: mechanisms of defense and the poetic will, ed. by J. H. Smith p149-80

Jayne, R. Rilke and the problem of poetic inwardness. *In* Rilke: the alchemy of alienation, ed. by F. Baron, E. S. Dick and W. R. Maurer p191-222

Miller, J. H. Theoretical and atheoretical in Stevens. *In* Wallace Stevens, ed. by F. Doggett and R. Buttel p275-85

Pearce, R. H. Toward decreation: Stevens and the "theory of poetry." *In* Wallace Stevens, ed. by F. Doggett and R. Buttel p286-307

Rosenfeld, A. H. "The being of language and the language of being": Heidegger and modern poetics. *In* Martin Heidegger and the question of literature, ed. by W. V. Spanos p195-213

*See also* Odes

### History and criticism

Bernstein, G. M. The mediated vision: Eliade, Lévi-Strauss, and romantic mythopoesis. *In* The Binding of Proteus, ed. by M. W. McCune, T. Orbison and P. M. Withim p158-72

Fehrman, C. A. D. Improvisation—rite and myth. *In* Fehrman, C. A. D. Poetic creation p35-54

Genette, G. Valéry and the poetics of language. *In* Textual strategies, ed. by J. V. Harari p359-73

Molesworth, C. Magazines and magazine verse. *In* Molesworth, C. The fierce embrace p184-95

Montgomery, R. L. Conclusion. *In* Montgomery, R. L. The reader's eye p169-85

*See also* Poetry—Themes, motives

### Philosophy

*See* Poetry

### Subjects

*See* Poetry—Themes, motives

### Technique

*See* Poetics

### Themes, motives

Keith, W. J. Introduction. *In* Keith, W. J. The poetry of nature. p3-10

**Poetry, Medieval**

Manley, L. G. The medieval redefinition. *In* Manley, L. G. Convention, 1500-1750 p54-65

### History and criticism

Hatto, A. T. The lime-tree and early German, Goliard and English lyric poetry. *In* Hatto, A. T. Essays on medieval German and other poetry p17-41

**Poetry, Medieval**—History and criticism—*Cont.*

Jackson, W. T. H. Introduction. *In* The Interpretation of medieval lyric poetry, ed. by W. T. H. Jackson p 1-21

Robertson, D. W. The doctrine of charity in medieval literary gardens: a topical approach through symbolism and allegory. *In* Robertson, D. W. Essays in medieval culture p21-50

**Poetry, Modern**

### 20th century

Molesworth, C. Reflections in place of a conclusion. *In* Molesworth, C. The fierce embrace p196-204

**Poetry and music.** See Music and literature

**Poetry and society.** See Literature and society

**Poets, American**

### 20th century

Molesworth, C. The metaphors for the poem. *In* Molesworth, C. The fierce embrace p139-49

Molesworth, C. The poet and the poet's generation. *In* Molesworth, C. The fierce embrace p77-84

Molesworth, C. "We have come this far": audience and form in contemporary poetry. *In* Molesworth, C. The fierce embrace p 1-21

**Poets, Welsh.** See Gogynfeirdd (Welsh poets)

**Poggio-Bracciolini**

### About

Marsh, D. Poggio Bracciolini and the moral debate. *In* Marsh, D. The quattrocento dialogue p38-54

**Poland**

### Intellectual life

Trilling, L. Communism and intellectual freedom. *In* Trilling, L. Speaking of literature and society p300-09

**Polanski, Roman**

### About individual works

#### Chinatown

Kauffmann, S. Chinatown. *In* Kauffmann, S. Before my eyes p16-18

**Pole, Jack Richon**

The language of American presidents. *In* The State of the language, ed. by L. Michaels and C. Ricks p421-31

Paths to the American past

*Contents*

Abraham Lincoln and the American commitment

Abraham Lincoln and the working classes of Britain

The American past: is it still usable?

Daniel J. Boorstin

The emergence of the majority principle in the American Revolution

Historians and the problem of early American democracy

The new history and the sense of social purpose in American historical writing

Of Mr. Booker T. Washington and others

Property and law in the American Republic

Representation and authority in Virginia from the Revolution to reform

Richard Hofstadter, 1916-1970

Slavery and revolution: the conscience of the rich

Slavery, race, and the debate on personality

**Polhemus, Robert M.**

Comic faith

*Contents*

Austen's Emma: the comedy of union

Carroll's Through the looking-glass: the comedy of regression

Dickens's Martin Chuzzlewit: the comedy of expression

Joyce's Finnegans wake: the comic gospel of "Shem"

Meredith's The egoist: the comedy of egoism

Peacock's Nightmare Abbey: comic communion

Thackeray's Vanity fair: the comedy of shifting perspectives

Trollope's Barchester Towers: comic reformation

**Police**

### Europe

Bayley, D. H. Police function, structure, and control in Western Europe and North America: comparative and historical studies. *In* Crime and justice v 1 p109-43

### United States

Bayley, D. H. Police function, structure, and control in Western Europe and North America: comparative and historical studies. *In* Crime and justice v 1 p109-43

Rumbaut, R. G. and Bittner, E. Changing conceptions of the police role: a sociological review. *In* Crime and justice v 1 p239-88

**Policy sciences**

Banfield, E. C. Policy science as metaphysical madness. *In* Bureaucrats, policy analysts, statesmen: who leads? Ed. by R. A. Goldwin p 1-19

Malbin, M. J. Congress, policy analysis, and natural gas deregulation: a parable about fig leaves. *In* Bureaucrats, policy anaysts, statesmen: who leads? Ed. by R. A. Goldwin p62-87

Moore, M. H. Statesmanship in a world of particular substantive choices. *In* Bureaucrats, policy analysts, statesmen: who leads? Ed. by R. A. Goldwin p20-36

Shubert, G. H. Policy analysis and public choice. *In* Bureaucrats, policy analysts, statesmen: who leads? Ed. by R. A. Goldwin p44-61

Silberman, L. H. Policy analysis: boon or curse for politicians? *In* Bureaucrats, policy analysts, statesmen: who leads? Ed by R. A. Goldwin p37-43

Storing, H. J. American statesmanship: old and new. *In* Bureaucrats, policy analysts, statesmen: who leads? Ed. by R. A. Goldwin p88-113

### Philosophy

Weale, A. Rational choice and political principles. *In* Rational action, ed. by R. Harrison p93-114

**Political behavior.** See Political psychology

**Political communication.** See Communication in politics

**Political drama.** See Political plays

**Political economy.** See Economics

**Political ethics**

Kolenda, K. Globalism vs. consensual pluralism. *In* Humanist ethics, ed. by M. B. Storer p104-21

Simpson, J. R. Toward a humanist consensus on ethics of international development. *In* Humanist ethics, ed. by M. B. Storer p122-36

**Political oratory**

### Great Britain

Robinson, I. Parliamentary expressions. *In* The State of the language, ed. by L. Michaels and C. Ricks p64-75

**Political participation**

Pateman, C. Justifying political obligation. *In* Powers, possessions and freedom, ed. by A. Kontos p63-75

### Germany, West

Hirsch, J. Developments in the political system of West Germany since 1945. *In* The State in Western Europe, ed. by R. Scase p115-41 p115-41

### Kenya—Nairobi

Ross, M. H. Political alienation, participation, and ethnicity in the Nairobi urban area. *In* Values, identities, and national integration, ed. by J. N. Paden p173-81

### United States

Barber, B. R. The undemocratic party system: citizenship in an elite/mass society. *In* Political parties in the eighties, ed. by R. A. Goldwin p34-49

**Political parties**

Fisher, S. L. The "decline of parties" thesis and the role of minor parties. *In* Western European party systems, ed. by P. H. Merkl p609-13

Mayer, L. C. A note on the aggregation of party systems. *In* Western European party systems, ed. by P. H. Merkl p515-20

Mayer, L. C. Party systems and cabinet stability. *In* Western European party systems, ed. by P. H. Merkl p335-47

Merkl, P. H. Attitudes, ideology and politics of party members. *In* Western European party systems. ed. by P. H. Markl p402-89

Nilson, S. S. Mapping party competition. *In* Western European party systems, ed. by P. H. Markl p490-508

Nilson, S. S. Parties, cleavages, and the sharpness of conflict. *In* Western European party systems, ed. by P. H. Merkl p521-25

Tate, C. N. The centrality of party in voting choice. *In* Western European party systems, ed. by P. H. Merkl p367-401

Thomas, J. C. Ideological trends in Western political parties. *In* Western European party systems, ed. by P. H. Merkl p348-66

### Austria

Mommsen-Reindl, M. Austria. *In* Western European party systems, ed. by P. H. Merkl p278-97

### Denmark

Nilson, S. S. Norway and Denmark. *In* Western European party systems, ed. by P. H. Merkl p205-34

### Europe

Merkl, P. H. Introduction: the study of party systems. *In* Western European party systems, ed. by P. H. Merkl p 1-19

Merkl, P. H. The sociology of European parties: members, voters, and social groups. *In* Western European party systems, ed. by P. H. Merkl p614-67

### Finland

Suhonen, P. Finland. *In* Western European party systems, ed. by P. H. Merkl p235-56

### France

Noonan, L. G. France. *In* Western European party systems, ed. by P. H. Merkl p87-121

### Germany, West

Kaltefleiter, W. A legitimacy crisis of the German party system? *In* Western European party systems, ed. by P. H. Merkl p597-608

Merkl, P. H. West Germany. *In* Western European party systems, ed. by P. H. Merkl p21-60

### Great Britain

Cyr, A. I. Great Britain. *In* Western European party systems, ed. by P. H. Merkl p61-86

### Ireland

Carey, M. J. Ireland. *In* Western European party systems, ed. by P. H. Merkl p257-77

### Italy

Zariski, R. Italy. *In* Western European party systems, ed. by P. H. Merkl p122-52

### Netherlands

Irwin, G. A. The Netherlands. *In* Western European party systems, ed. by P. H. Merkl p161-84

### Norway

Nilson, S. S. Norway and Denmark. *In* Western European party systems, ed. by P. H. Merkl p205-34

### Portugal

Wiarda, H. J. Spain and Portugal. *In* Western European party systems, ed. by P. H. Merkl p298-328

### Spain

Wiarda, H. J. Spain and Portugal. *In* Western European party systems, ed. by P. H. Merkl p298-328

### Sweden

Hancock, M. D. Sweden. *In* Western European party systems, ed. by P. H. Merkl p185-204

### United States

Banfield, E. C. In defense of the American party system. *In* Political parties in the eighties, ed. by R. A. Goldwin p133-49

Fraser, D. M. Democratizing the Democratic Party. *In* Political parties in the eighties, ed. by R. A. Goldwin p116-32

Ladd, E. C. The American party system today. *In* The Third century, ed. by S. M. Lipset p153-82

Licht, R. A. On the three parties in America. *In* Political parties in the eighties, ed. by R. A. Goldwin p66-96

### United States—History

Banfield, E. C. Party "reform" in retrospect. *In* Political parties in the eighties, ed. by R. A. Goldwin p20-33

Barber, B. R. The undemocratic party system: citizenship in an elite/mass society. *In* Political parties in the eighties, ed. by R. A. Goldwin p34-49

Ceaser, J. W. Political change and party reform. *In* Political parties in the eighties, ed. by R. A. Goldwin p97-115

**Political platforms.** See Political parties

**Political plays**

Sharratt, B. The politics of the popular?— From melodrama to television. *In* Performance and politics in popular drama, ed. by D. Bradby, L. James and B. Sharratt p275-95

**Political poetry, Turkish**

### History and criticism

Halman, T. S. Propaganda functions of poetry. *In* Propaganda and communication in world history, ed. by H. D. Lasswell, D. Lerner and H. Speier v 1 p493-535

**Political psychology**

Barbu, Z. The modern history of political fanaticism: a search for the roots. *In* Propaganda and communication in world history, ed. by H. D. Lasswell, D. Lerner and H. Speier v2 p112-44

*See also* Propaganda; Public opinion

**Political representation.** See Representative government and representation

**Political science**

Altham, J. E. J. Reflections on the state of nature. *In* Rational action, ed. by R. Harrison p133-45

Forbes, D. Hume and the Scottish Enlightenment. *In* Royal Institute of Philosophy. Philosophers of the Enlightenment p94-109

Hobsbawm, E. J. Pre-political movements in modern politics. *In* Powers, possessions and freedom, ed. by A. Kontos p89-106

Pocock, J. G. A. Political ideas as historical events: political philosophers as historical actors. *In* Political theory and political education, ed. by M. Richter p139-58

Sapiro, V. Women's studies and political conflict. *In* The Prism of sex, ed. by J. A. Sherman and E. T. Beck p253-65

Taylor, C. The philosophy of the social sciences. *In* Political theory and political education, ed. by M. Richter p76-93

Walzer, M. Political decision-making and political education. *In* Political theory and political education, ed. by M. Richter p159-76

Williams, B. A. O. Political philosophy and the analytical tradition. *In* Political theory and political education, ed. by M. Richter p57-75

Wolin, S. S. Political theory and political commentary. *In* Political theory and political education, ed. by M. Richter p190-203

*See also* Anarchism and anarchists; Authoritarianism; Authority; Bureaucracy; Communism; Coups d'état; Democracy; Equality; Federal government; Liberty; Nationalism; Political parties; Political psychology; Power (Social sciences); Public opinion; Representative government and representation; Revolutions; Right and left (Political science); Sovereignty; World politics

**Historiography**

Bogue, A. G. The new political history in the 1970s. *In* The Past before us, ed. by M. Kammen p231-57

**History**

Krader, L. The origins of the state among the nomads of Asia. *In* Soviet and Western anthropology, ed. by E. Gellner p135-47

**Methodology**

Elshtain, J. B. Methodological sophistication and conceptual confusion: a critique of mainstream political science. *In* The Prism of sex, ed. by J. A. Sherman and E. T. Beck p229-52

Nilson, S. S. Mapping party competition. *In* Western European party systems, ed. by P. H. Merkl p490-508

**Study and teaching**

Bloom, A. The study of texts. *In* Political theory and political education, ed. by M. Richter p113-38

**Terminology**

Pool, I. de S. The language of politics: general trends in content. *In* Propaganda and communication in world history, ed. by H. D. Lasswell, D. Lerner and H. Speier v3 p171-90

**Russia**

Lider, J. The critique of militarism in Soviet studies. *In* Problems of contemporary militarism, ed. by A. Eide and M. Thee p173-91

**Political sociology**

Pateman, C. Justifying political obligation. *In* Powers, possessions and freedom, ed. by A. Kontos p63-75

**Political violence.** See Revolutions

**Politics and culture**

Kristol, I. The adversary culture of intellectuals. *In* The Third century, ed. by L. Michaels and C. Ricks p327-43

*See also* Politics and literature

**Great Britain**

Klugmann, J. Introduction: The crises of the thirties: a view from the Left. *In* Culture and crisis in Britain in the thirties, ed. by J. Clark and others p13-36

**Politics and education**

Radest, H. B. Schooling and the search for a usable politics. *In* History, religion, and spiritual democracy, ed. by M. Wohlgelernter and others p317-40

**Politics and literature**

Cunningham, V. Neutral?: 1930s writers and taking sides. *In* Class, culture and social change, ed. by F. Gloversmith p45-69

Farrell, J. P. Revolution as tragedy; being at the center. *In* Farrell, J. Revolution as tragedy p17-68

Farrell, J. P. Tragedy and ideology. *In* Farrell, J. P. Revolution as tragedy p281-90

*See also* Politics in literature

**Great Britain**

Kettle, A. W. H. Auden: poetry and politics in the thirties. *In* Culture and crisis in Britain in the thirties, ed. by J. Clark [and others] p83-101

Margolies, D. N. Left Review and Left literature theory. *In* Culture and crisis in Britain in the thirties, ed. by J. Clark [and others] p67-82

Reid, B. The Left Book Club in the thirties. *In* Culture and crisis in Britain in the thirties, ed. by J. Clark [and others] p193-207

Wright, I. F. R. Leavis, the Scrutiny movement and the crisis. *In* Culture and crisis in Britain in the thirties, ed. by J. Clark [and others] p37-65

**Politics and religion.** See Religion and politics

**Politics and the press.** See Press and politics

**Politics in literature**

Izevbaye, D. Issues in the reassessment of the African novel. *In* African literature today no. 10: Retrospect & prospect, ed. by E. D. Jones p7-31

Last, R. Erich Fried: poetry and politics. *In* Modern Austrian writing, ed. by A. Best and H. Wolfschütz p181-96

**Pollack, Sydney**

**About individual works**

*They shoot horses, don't they?*

Miller, G. Marathon man/marathon woman. *In* Miller, G. Screening the novel p64-83

**Pollard, Alfred William**

### About individual works

*A short-title catalogue of books printed in England, Scotland, & Ireland and of English books printed abroad, 1475-1640*

Pantzer, K. F. The serpentine progress of the STC revision. *In* The Bibliographical Society of America, 1904-79 p455-69

**Polsby, Nelson W.**
The news media as an alternative to party in the Presidential selection process. *In* Political parties in the eighties, ed. by R. A. Goldwin p50-66

**Polt, John Herman Richard**
The ironic narrator in the novel: Isla. *In* Studies in eighteenth-century culture v9 p371-86

**Polyglottism.** See Multilingualism

**Pomerleau, Cynthia S.**
The emergence of women's autobiography in England. *In* Women's autobiography, ed. by E. C. Jelinek p21-38

**Pompa, Leon**
Human nature and the concept of a human science. *In* Conference on Vico and Contemporary Thought, New York, 1976. Vico and contemporary thought pt 1 p44-55

**Ponge, Francis**

### About

Strauss, W. A. Rilke and Ponge: l'objet c'est la poétique. *In* Rilke: the alchemy of alienation, ed. by F. Baron, E. S. Dick and W. R. Maurer p63-93

**Poniatowska, Elena**

### About individual works

*Hasta no verte, Jesús mío*

Fox-Lockert, L. Elena Poniatowska. *In* Fox-Lockert, L. Women novelists in Spain and Spanish America p260-77

**Pontano, Giovanni Gioviane**

### About

Marsh, D. Giovanni Pontano and the academic gathering. *In* Marsh, D. The quattrocento dialogue p100-16

**Pool, Ithiel de Sola**
The language of politics: general trends in content. *In* Propaganda and communication in world history, ed. by H. D. Lasswell, D. Lerner and H. Speier v3 p171-90

**Poor relief.** See Public welfare

**Pope, Alexander**

### About

Krieger, M. "Trying experiments upon our sensibility": the art of dogma and doubt in eighteenth-century literature. *In* Krieger, M. Poetic presence and illusion p70-91

### About individual works

*The Dunciad*

Seidel, M. A. Things unborn: Pope's The Rape of the lock and The Duncaid. *In* Seidel, M. A. Satiric inheritance, Rabelais to Sterne p226-49

*An essay on man*

Robertson, D. W. Pope and Boethius. *In* Robertson, D. W. Essays in medieval culture p332-40

*The rape of the lock*

Seidel, M. A. Things unborn: Pope's The rape of the lock and The Dunciad. *In* Seidel, M. A. Satiric inheritance, Rabelais to Sterne p226-49

*Windsor Forest*

Marshall, W. G. Pope's Windsor-Forest as providential history. *In* Tennessee Studies in literature v24 p82-93

### Characters—Eloisa

Hagstrum, J. H. Woman in love: the abandoned and passionate mistress. *In* Hagstrum, J. H. Sex and sensibility p100-32

### Characters—Women

Hagstrum, J. H. Friends and lovers: the witty and the wise. *In* Hagstrum, J. H. Sex and sensibility p133-59

**Pope, Barbara Corrado**
Revolution and retreat: upper-class French women after 1789. *In* Women, war, and revolution, ed. by C. R. Berkin and C. M. Lovett p215-36

**Popes**

### History

*See* Papacy—History

### Temporal power

Ozment, S. H. The ecclesiopolitical traditions. *In* Ozment, S. H. The age of reform, 1250-1550 p135-81

**Popkin, Richard Henry**
Jewish messianism and Christian millenarianism. *In* Culture and politics from Puritanism to the Enlightenment, ed. by P. Zagorin p67-90

**Popular arts.** See Popular culture

**Popular culture**
Lally, T. D. P. Synchronic vs diachronic popular culture studies and the Old English elegy. *In* 5000 years of popular culture, ed by F. E. H. Schroeder p203-12

Murray, L. L. Universality and uniformity in the popular arts: the impact of television on popular culture. *In* Screen and society, ed. by F. J. Coppa p157-72

Schroeder, F. E. H. Popular culture methodologies: a bibliographic afterword. *In* 5000 years of culture, ed. by F. E. H. Schroeder p319-25

### Bibliography

Schroeder, F. E. H. Popular culture methodologies: a bibliographic afterword. *In* 5000 years of culture, ed. by F. E. H. Schroeder p319-25

### History

Schroeder, F. E. H. The discovery of popular culture before printing. *In* 5000 years of popular culture, ed. by F. E. H. Schroeder p4-15

**Popular fronts**

### Great Britain

Coombes, J. British intellectuals and the Popular Front. *In* Class, culture and social change, ed. by F. Gloversmith p70-100

**Popular literature**

### Africa, East

Knight, E. Popular literature in East Africa. *In* African literature no. 10: Retrospect & prospect, ed. by E. D. Jones p177-90

**Population**
*See also* Demography

**Population**—*Continued*

### Statistics

*See* Vital statistics

**Population biology**

Morowitz, H. J. Social implications of a biological principle. *In* Morowitz, H. J. The wine of life, and other essays on societies, energy & living things p159-62

**Population geography.** See Anthropo-geography; Migration, Internal

**Pornography**

Berger, F. R. Pornography, sex and censorship. *In* The Philosophy of sex, ed. by A. Soble p322-47

**Pornography in mass media.** See Sex in mass media

**Portas, Nuno, and Gago, Serras**

Some preliminary notes on the state in contemporary Portugal. *In* The State in Western Europe, ed. by R. Scase p230-40

**Porter, Glenn**

Marketing. *In* Encyclopedia of American economic history, ed. by G. Porter v 1 p386-96

**Porter, Jack Nusan**

Social-psychological aspects of the Holocaust. *In* Encountering the Holocaust: an interdisciplinary survey, ed. by B. L. Sherwin and S. H. Ament p189-222

**Portraits.** See Self-portraits

**Portugal**

### History—Revolution, 1974

Portas, N. and Gago, S. Some preliminary notes on the state in contemporary Portugal. *In* The State in Western Europe, ed. by R. Scase p230-40

Seaton, J. and Pimlott, B. The role of the media in the Portuguese revolution. *In* Newspapers and democracy, ed. by A. Smith p174-99

### Politics and government

Forman, S. and Riegelhaupt, J. F. The political economy of patron-clientship: Brazil and Portugal compared. *In* Brazil, anthropological perspectives, ed. by M. L. Margolis and W. E. Carter p379-400

Wiarda, H. J. Spain and Portugal. *In* Western European party systems, ed. by P. H. Merkl p298-328

### Politics and government—1974

Portas, N. and Gago, S. Some preliminary notes on the state in contemporary Portugal. *In* The State in Western Europe, ed. by R. Scase p230-40

**Positivism**

Lear, J. Going native. *In* Generations, ed. by S. R. Graubard p175-88

*See also* Naturalism

**Possession, Demoniac.** See Demoniac possession

**Post, Robert C.**

Science, public policy, and popular precepts: Alexander Dallas Bache and Alfred Beach as symbolic adversaries. *In* The Sciences in the American context: new perspectives, ed. by N. Reingold p77-98

**The postman always rings twice (Motion picture)**

Miller, G. Special delivery. *In* Miller, G. Screening the novel p46-63

**Potamkin, Harry Alan**

### About individual works

*The compound cinema*

Kauffman, S. The compound cinema. *In* Kauffmann, S. Before my eyes p376-85

**Potter, Janice, and Calhoon, Robert McCluer**

The character and coherence of the loyalist press. *In* The Press & the American Revolution, ed. by B. Bailyn and J. B. Hench p229-72

**Pottle, Frederick Albert**

Printer's copy in the eighteenth century. *In* The Bibliographical Society of America, 1904-79 p108-16

**Poughkeepsie, N.Y.**

### Industries—History

Griffen, C. and Griffen, S. Small business and occupational mobility in mid-nineteenth-century Poughkeepsie. *In* Small business in American life, ed. by S. W. Bruchey p122-41

**Pouillon, Jean**

Structure and structuralism. *In* Soviet and Western anthropology, ed. by E. Gellner p275-82

**Poulet, Georges**

### About

Lentricchia, F. Versions of phenomenology. *In* Lentricchia, F. After the New Criticism p62-100

**Pound, Ezra Loomis**

### About

Duffey, B. Ezra Pound and the attainment of imagism. *In* Toward a new American literary history, ed. by L. J. Budd, E. H. Cady and C. L. Anderson p181-94

Heinzelman, K. "Getting it" in Paterson: the increment defended. *In* Heinzelman, K. The economics of the imagination p234-75

### About individual works

*The cantos*

Carne-Ross, D. S. The music of a lost dynasty: Pound in the classroom. *In* Carne-Ross, D. S. Instaurations p193-217

### Bibliography

Bornstein, G. and McDougal, S. Y. Pound and Eliot. *In* American literary scholarship, 1978 p111-25

**Poussin, Nicholas**

### About individual works

*The Arcadian shepherds*

Marin, L. Toward a theory of reading in the visual arts: Poussin's The Arcadian shepherds. *In* The Reader in the text, ed. by S. R. Suleiman and I. Crosman p293-324

**Poverty**

Smolensky, E. and Weinstein, M. M. Poverty. *In* Encyclopedia of American economic history, ed. by G. Porter v3 p1136-54

*See also* Public welfare

**Powell, John Enoch**

The language of politics. *In* The State of the language, ed. by L. Michaels and C. Ricks p432-39

**Power (Mechanics)** See Force and energy

**Power (Social sciences)**

Elshtain, J. B. Methodological sophistication and conceptual confusion: a critique of mainstream political science. *In* The Prism of sex, ed. by J. A. Sherman and E. T. Beck p229-52

**Power (Social sciences)**—*Continued*

Hook, S. The concept and realities of power. *In* Hook, S. Philosophy and public policy p38-53

Rogers, M. F. Goffman on power, hierarchy, and status. *In* The View from Goffman, ed. by J. Ditton p100-33

**Power, Executive.** See Executive power

**Power, Judicial.** See Judicial power

**Power politics.** See Balance of power

**Power resources**

Houthakker, H. S. World energy sources. *In* The United States in the 1980s, ed. by P. Duignan and A. Rabushka p535-58

*See also* Energy consumption; Energy industries

### United States

Sweeney, J. L. Energy problems and policies. *In* The Economy in the 1980s: a program for growth and stability, ed. by M. J. Boskin p353-92

**Power supply.** See Power resources

**Powers, James Farl**

### About

Kissel, S. S. Voices in the wilderness: the prophets of O'Connor, Percy, and Powers. *In* Walker Percy: art and ethics, ed. by J. Tharpe p91-98

**Powys, John Cowper**

### About

Gloversmith, F. Defining culture: J. C. Powys, Clive Bell, R. H. Tawney & T. S. Eliot. *In* Class, culture and social change, ed. by F. Gloversmith p15-44

**Prague**

### History

Carter, F. W. Kafka's Prague. *In* The World of Franz Kafka, ed. by J. P. Stern p30-43

**Prague in literature**

Stern, S. The spirit of the place. *In* The World of Franz Kafka, ed. by J. P. Stern p44-46

**Pratt, Edwin John**

### About

O'Flaherty, P. Emigrant muse: E. J. Pratt and Newfoundland, 1882-1907. *In* O'Flaherty, P. The rock observed p111-26

**Pratt, Joseph A.**

Natural resources and energy. *In* Encyclopedia of American economic history, ed. by G. Porter v 1 p202-13

**Prayer**

Matthews, G. B. Ritual and the religious feelings. *In* Explaining emotions, ed. by A. O. Rorty p339-53

**Preaching**

*See also* Communication (Theology)

### History—Middle Ages, 600-1500

Robertson, D. W. Frequency of preaching in thirteenth century England. *In* Robertson, D. W. Essays in medieval culture p114-28

**Predestination.** See Free will and determinism

**Prediction.** See Forecasting

**Prediction, Social.** See Social prediction

**Prehistoric art.** See Art, Prehistoric

**Prehistoric man.** See Man, Prehistoric

**Prehistoric religion.** See Religion, Prehistoric

**Prejudices and antipathies**

Morowitz, H. J. The roots of prejudice. *In* Morowitz, H. J. The wine of life, and other essays on societies, energy & living things p172-75

*See also* Antisemitism; Ethnocentrism

**Premack, David**

Representational capacity and accessibility of knowledge: the case of chimpanzees. *In* Language and learning, ed. by M. Piattelli-Palmarini p205-21

### About individual works

*Intelligence in ape and man*

Terrace, H. S. Is problem-solving language? *In* Speaking of apes, ed. by T. A. Sebeok and J. Umiker-Sebeok p385-405

**Preraphaelites**

Harbison, R. Turning against history. *In* Harbison, R. Deliberate regression p147-79

**Preraphaelitism.** See Preraphaelites

**Pre-Reformation.** See Reformation—Early movements

**Presidents**

### United States—Election

Ceaser, J. W. Political change and party reform. *In* Political parties in the eighties, ed. by R. A. Goldwin p97-115

### United States—Language

Pole, J. R. The language of American presidents. *In* The State of the language, ed. by L. Michaels and C. Ricks p421-31

### United States—Nomination

Bode, K. A. and Casey, C. F. Party reform: revisionism revised. *In* Political parties in the eighties, ed. by R. A. Goldwin p3-19

Polsby, N. W. The news media as an alternative to party in the Presidential selection process. *In* Political parties in the eighties, ed. by R. A. Goldwin p50-66

### United States—Powers

*See* Executive power—United States

**President's Science Advisory Committee.** See United States. President's Science Advisory Committee

**Press**

*See also* Government and the press

### Censorship

*See* Liberty of the press

### France

Tarlé, A. de. The press and the state in France. *In* Newspapers and democracy, ed. by A. Smith p127-48

### Norway

Dahl, H. The press, most national of media: a report from Norway. *In* Newspapers and democracy, ed. by A. Smith p95-103

### Scandinavia

Dahl, H. The press, most national of media: a report from Norway. *In* Newspapers and democracy, ed. by A. Smith p95-103

### Spain

Soler, J. A. M. The paradoxes of press freedom: the Spanish case. *In* Newspapers and democracy, ed. by A. Smith p153-73

### Vienna—History

Rutledge, J. S. The delayed reflex: journalism in Josephinian Vienna. *In* Studies in eighteenth-century culture v9 p79-92

**Press and government.** See Government and the press

**Press and politics**

Polsby, N. W. The news media as an alternative to party in the Presidential selection process. *In* Political parties in the eighties, ed. by R. A. Goldwin p50-66

*See also* Government and the press

### Japan

Horsley, W. The press as loyal opposition in Japan. *In* Newspapers and democracy, ed. by A. Smith p200-27

### Massachusetts—History

McCorison, M. A. Foreword. *In* The Press & the American Revolution, ed. by B. Bailyn and J. B. Hench p 1-10

### Portugal

Seaton, J. and Pimlott, B. The role of the media in the Portuguese revolution. *In* Newspapers and democracy, ed. by A. Smith p174-99

### Southern States—History

Weir, R. M. The role of the newspaper press in the Southern colonies on the eve of the Revolution. *In* The Press & the American Revolution, ed. by B. Bailyn and J. B. Hench p99-150

### Spain

Soler, J. A. M. The paradoxes of press freedom: the Spanish case. *In* Newspapers and democracy, ed. by A. Smith p153-73

### United States—History

Botein, S. Printers and the American Revolution. *In* The Press & the American Revolution, ed. by B. Bailyn and J. B. Hench p11-57

Buel, R. Freedom of the press in Revolutionary America: the evolution of libertarianism, 1760-1820. *In* The Press & the American Revolution, ed. by B. Bailyn and J. B. Hench p59-97

Plotter, J. and Calhoon, R. M. The character and coherence of the loyalist press. *In* The Press & the American Revolution, ed. by B. Bailyn and J. B. Hench p229-72

**Press censorship.** See Liberty of the press

**Pressure groups**

### Germany, West

Helm, J. A. Citizen lobbies in West Germany. *In* Western European party systems, ed. by P. H. Merkl p576-96

**Prestige.** See Social status

**Pretty baby (Motion picture)**

Kauffmann, S. Pretty baby. *In* Kauffmann, S. Before my eyes p63-66

**Prévert, Jacques, and Carné, Marcel**

#### About individual works

*Le jour se lève*

Thiher, A. Prévert and Carné's Le jour se lève: proletarian tragedy. *In* Thiher, A. The cinematic muse p113-28

**Prévost, Antoine François, called Prévost d'Exiles**

#### About individual works

*Manon Lescaut*

Miller, N. K. Love for a harlot. *In* Miller, N.K. The heroine's text. p69-82

*The life and entertaining adventures of Mr Cleveland, natural son of Oliver Cromwell, written by himself*

Stewart, P. Utopias that self-destruct. *In* Studies in eighteenth-century culture v9 p15-24

**Prévost d'Exiles.** See Prévost, Antoine Francoise, called Prévost d'Exiles

**Priamel**

Henrichs, A. Callimachus Epigram 28: a fastidious priamel. *In* Harvard Studies in classical philology, v83 p207-12

**Price theory.** See Prices

**Prices**

Kenyon, P. Pricing. *In* A Guide to post-Keynesian economics, ed. by A. S. Eichner p34-45

### United States—History

Adams, D. R. Prices and wages. *In* Encyclopedia of American economic history, ed. by G. Porter v 1 p229-46

**Prickett, Stephen**

Coleridge and the idea of the clerisy. *In* Reading Coleridge, ed. by W. B. Crawford p252-73

**Pride and vanity**

Baier, A. Master passions. *In* Explaining emotions, ed. by A. O. Rorty p403-23

Isenberg, A. Natural pride and natural shame. *In* Explaining emotions, ed. by A. O. Rorty p355-83

Taylor, G. Pride. *In* Explaining emotions, ed. by O. O. Rorty p385-402

**Primates**

#### Behavior

Kummer, H. On the value of social relationships to nonhuman primates: a heuristic scheme. *In* Human ethology, ed. by M. von Cranach [and others] p381-95

**Prince, Frank Templeton**

#### About individual works

*Soldiers bathing, and other poems*

Plomer, W. C. F.    F. T. Prince. *In* Plomer, W. C. F. Electric delights p155-57

**Prince, Gerald**

Notes on the text as reader. *In* The Reader in the text, ed. by S. R. Suleiman and I. Crosman p225-40

**Pringle, Thomas**

#### About

Plomer, W. C. F. Thomas Pringle. *In* Plomer, W. C. F. Electric delights p169-72

**Printers**

#### New York (City)—History

Tichenor, I. Master printers organize: the Typothetae of the City of New York, 1865-1906. *In* Small business in American life, ed. by S. W. Bruchey p169-91

#### United States

Botein, S. Printers and the American Revolution. *In* The Press and the American Revolution, ed. by B. Bailyn and J. B. Hench p11-57

**Printing**

#### Cancels

Wyllie, J. C. The forms of twentieth-century cancels. *In* The Bibliographical Society of America, 1904-79 p289-306

#### History—England

Jackson, W. A. Variant entry fees of the Stationers' company. *In* The Bibliographical Society of America, 1904-79 p355-62

**Propaganda, Communist**
Griffith, W. E. Communist propaganda. *In* Propoganda and communication in world history, ed. by H. D. Lasswell, D. Lerner and H. Speier v2 p239-58

**Propaganda, German**
Gombrich, Sir E. H. J. Myth and reality in German wartime broadcasts. *In* Gombrich, Sir E. H. J. Ideals and idols p93-111

**Propaganda, Greek**
Ferguson, J. Classical civilization. *In* Propaganda and communication in world history, ed. by H. D. Lasswell, D. Lerner and H. Speier v 1 p257-98

**Propaganda, Indic**
Sharma, R. S. Indian civilization. *In* Propaganda and communication in world history, ed. by H. D. Lasswell, D. Lerner and H. Speier v 1 p175-204

**Propaganda, Roman**
Ferguson, J. Classical civilization. *In* Propaganda and communication in world history, ed. by H. D. Lasswell, D. Lerner and H. Speier v 1 p257-98

**Propaganda, Turkish**
Halman, T. S. Propaganda functions of poetry. *In* Propaganda and communication in world history, ed. by H. D. Lasswell, D. Lerner and H. Speier v 1 p493-535

Godelier, M. Territory and property in primitive society. *In* Human ethology, ed. by M. von Cranach [and others] p133-55

**Propaganda in radio.** See Radio in propaganda

**Property**
Mansfield, H. C. On the political character of property in Locke. *In* Powers, possessions and freedom, ed. by A. Kontos p23-38

### Law and legisation—United States
Pole, J. R. Property and law in the American Republic. *In* Pole, J. R. Paths to the American past p75-108

### France—History
Sewell, W. H. Property, labor, and the emergence of socialism in France, 1789-1848. *In* Consciousness and class experience in nineteenth-century Europe, ed. by J. M. Merriman p45-63

**Property in literature**
Hexter, J. H. Property, monopoly, and Shakespeare's Richard II. *In* Culture and politics from Puritanism to the Enlightenment, ed. by P. Zagorin p 1-24

**Prophecy in literature**
Evans, R. W. Prophetic poetry. *In* A Guide to Welsh literature, ed. by A. O. H. Jarman and G. R. Hughes v2 p278-96

**Prophets**
Weber, M. Judaism: the psychology of the Prophets; excerpt from 'Ancient Judaism." *In* Propaganda and communication in world history, ed. by H. D. Lasswell, D. Lerner and H. Speier v 1 p299-329

**Prophethood.** See Prophets

**Proposition 13 (California property tax initiative)** See Real property tax—California

**Prostitution**
Jagger, A. M. Prostitution. *In* The Philosophy of sex, ed. by A. Soble p348-68

**Protestant dissenters.** See Dissenters, Religious

**Protestant Episcopal Church in the U.S.A.**

### About individual works
*Book of common prayer*
Doody, M. A. "How shall we sing the Lord's song upon an alien soil?": the new Episcopalian liturgy. *In* The State of the language, ed. by L. Michaels and C. Ricks p108-24

**Protestant Reformation.** See Reformation

**Protestantism**
Ozment, S. H. Humanism and the Reformation. *In* Ozment, S. H. The age of reform, 1250-1550 p290-317

Ozment, S. H. Marriage and the ministry in the Protestant churches. *In* Ozment, S. H. The age of reform, 1250-1550 p381-396
*See also* Reformation

### History
Ozment, S. H. Society and politics in the German Reformation. *In* Ozment, S. H. The age of reform, 1250-1550 p245-89

**Protestantism, Evangelical.** See Evangelicalism

**Protocols of the wise men of Zion**
Speier, H. The truth in hell: Maurice Joly on modern despotism. *In* Propaganda and communication in world history, ed. by H. D. Lasswell, D. Lerner and H. Speier v2 p301-16

**Proudfoot, Richard**
Peter Brook and Shakespeare. *In* Drama and mimesis, ed. by J. Redmond p157-89

**Proust, Marcel**

### About individual works
*Cities of the plain*
Trilling, L. Cities of the plain. *In* Trilling, L. Speaking of literature and society p10-15

*Contre Sainte-Beuve*
Trilling, L. Proust as critic and the critic as novelist. *In* Trilling, L. Speaking of literature and society p310-21

*On art and literature, 1896-1919*
Trilling, L. Proust as critic and the critic as novelist. *In* Trilling, L. Speaking of literature and society p310-21

*Remembrance of things past*
Barthes, R. Proust and names. *In* Barthes, R. New critical essays p55-68

De Man, P. Reading (Proust) *In* De Man, P. Allegories of reading p57-78

Festa-McCormick, D. Proust's Remembrance of things past: Venice and the reality within the dreams. *In* Festa-McCormick, D. The city as catalyst p89-107

Kellman, S. G. Marcel's self-begetting novel. *In* Kellman, S. G. The self-begetting novel p12-31

*Swann's way*
Nabokov, V. V. Marcel Proust: The walk by Swann's place. *In* Nabokov, V. V. Lectures on literature p207-49

**Provençal language**

### Rhyme
Ferrante, J. M. 'Ab joi mou lo vers e'l comens'. *In* The Interpretation of medieval lyric poetry p113-41

**Proverbs**
Cook, A. S. Between prose and poetry: the speech and silence of the proverb. *In* Cook, A. S. Myth and language p211-24

**Proverbs, Latin**

Lutz, C. E. A Roman proverb in sixteenth-century England. *In* Lutz, C. E. The oldest library motto, and other library essays p83-91

**Providence**

### Social conditions

Smith, J. E. Our own kind: family and community networks in Providence. *In* A Heritage of her own, ed. by N. F. Cott and E. H. Pleck p393-411

**Providence (Motion picture)**

Kael, P. Werewolf, mon amour. *In* Kael, P. When the lights go down p255-59

Kauffmann, S. Providence. *In* Kauffmann, S. Before my eyes p280-82

**Prušek, Jaroslav**

The lyrical and the epic

*Contents*

Basic problems of the history of modern Chinese literature: a review of C. T. Hsia, a history of modern Chinese fiction

The changing role of the narrator in Chinese novels at the beginning of the twentieth century

A confrontation of traditional Oriental literature with modern European literature in the context of the Chinese literary revolution

Introduction to Studies in modern Chinese literature

Lu Hsün's "Huai chiu": a precursor of modern Chinese literature

Mao Tun and Yü Ta-fu

Reality and art in Chinese literature

Subjectivism and individualism in modern Chinese literature

Yeh Shao-chün and Anton Chekhov

**Psalms**

### Music

Sarna, N. M. The psalm superscriptions and the guilds. *In* Studies in Jewish religious and intellectual history, ed. by S. Stein and R. Loewe p281-300

**Psalters**

Schapiro, M. An illuminated English psalter of the early thirteenth century. *In* Schapiro, M. Selected papers v3: Late antique, early Christian and mediaeval art p329-54

**Psathas, George**

Early Goffman and the analysis of face-to-face interaction in Strategic interaction. *In* The View from Goffman, ed. by J. Ditton p52-79

**Pseudo-romanticism.** See Romanticism

**Psychiatry**

Arieti, S. Vico and modern psychiatry. *In* Conference on Vico and Contemporary Thought, New York, 1976. Vico and contemporary thought pt2 p81-94

Morowitz, H. J. Shrinks. *In* Morowitz, H. J. The wine of life, and other essays on societies, energy & living things p149-52

Szasz, T. S. The lying truths of psychiatry. *In* Lying truths, ed. by R. Duncan and M. Weston-Smith p121-42

*See also* Existential psychology

### Philosophy

Haugsgjerd, S. Report from Norway. *In* Critical psychiatry, ed. by D. Ingleby p193-208

Ingleby, D. Understanding 'mental illness.' *In* Critical psychiatry, ed. by D. Ingleby p23-71

*See also* Antipsychiatry

**Philosophy—United States**

Kovel, J. The American mental health industry. *In* Critical psychiatry, ed. by D. Ingleby p72-101

### Great Britain—History

Treacher, A. and Baruch, G. Towards a critical history of the psychiatric profession. *In* Critical psychiatry, ed. by D. Ingleby p120-49

**Psychiatry, Social.** See Social psychiatry

**Psychoanalysis**

Kurzweil, E. Jacques Lacan: structuralist psychoanalysis. *In* Kurzweil, E. The age of structuralism p135-64

La Barre, W. Personality from a psychoanalytic viewpoint. *In* La Barre, W. Culture in context p119-40

Morris, H. The need to connect: representations of Freud's psychical apparatus. *In* The Literary Freud: mechanisms of defense and the poetic will, ed. by J. H. Smith p309-44

*See also* Child analysis; Death instinct; Dreams; Existential psychology; Psychohistory

**Psychoanalysis and literature**

Bloom, H. Freud's concepts of defense and the poetic will. *In* The Literary Freud: mechanisms of defense and the poetic will, ed. by J. H. Smith p 1-28

Dickstein, M. The price of experience: Blake's reading of Freud. *In* The Literary Freud: mechanisms of defense and the poetic will, ed. by J. H. Smith p67-111

Edelson, M. Two questions about psychoanalysis and poetry. *In* The Literary Freud: mechanisms of defense and the poetic will, ed. by J. H. Smith p113-18

Felman, S. On reading poetry: reflections on the limits and possibilities of psychoanalytical approaches. *In* The Literary Freud: mechanisms of defense and the poetic will, ed. by J. H. Smith p119-48

Gekoski, R. A. Freud and English literature, 1900-30. *In* The Context of English literature, 1900-30, ed. by M. Bell p186-217

Gohlke, M. S. "I wooed thee with my sword": Shakespeare's tragic paradigms. *In* Representing Shakespeare, ed. by M. M. Schwartz and C. Kahn p170-87

Hertz, N. H. Freud and The sandman. *In* Textual strategies, ed. by J. V. Harari p296-319

Norwood, H. N. Hermia's dream. *In* Representing Shakespeare, ed. by M. M. Schwartz and C. Kahn p 1-20

Schwartz, M. M. Shakespeare through contemporary psychoanalysis. *In* Representing Shakespeare, ed. by M. M. Schwartz and C. Kahn p21-32

Sokel, W. H. Freud and the magic of Kafka's writing. *In* The World of Franz Kafka, ed. by J. P. Stern p145-58

Sundquist, E. J. Preface. *In* Sundquist, E. J. Home as found p xi-xx

**Psychoanalysis in historiography.** See Psychohistory

**Psychoanalytic literary criticism.** See Psychoanalysis and literature

**Psychohistory**

Loewenberg, P. J. Psychohistory. *In* The Past before us, ed. by M. Kammen p408-32

Pole, J. R. Slavery, race, and the debate on personality. *In* Pole, J. R. Paths to the American past p189-219

**Psychohistory**—*Continued*

Rolle, A. F. The historic past of the unconscious. *In* Propaganda and communication in world history, ed. by H. D. Lasswell, D. Lerner and H. Speier v3 p403-60

**Psycholinguistics**

Chomsky, N. Discussion of Putnam's comments. *In* Language and learning, ed. by M. Piattelli-Palmarini p310-24

Chomsky, N. The linguistic approach. *In* Language and learning, ed. by M. Piattelli-Palmarini p109-17

Chomsky, N. Opening the debate: On cognitive structures and their development: a reply to Piaget. *In* Language and learning, ed. by M. Piattelli-Palmarini p35-54

Gardner, H. Foreword: Cognition comes of age. *In* Language and learning, ed. by M. Piattelli-Palmarini p xix-xxxvi

Inhelder, B. Language and knowledge in a constructivist framework. *In* Language and learning, ed. by M. Piattelli-Palmarini p132-37

Lenneberg, E. H. Of language knowledge, apes, and brains. *In* Speaking of apes, ed. by T. A. Sebeok and J. Umiker-Sebeok p115-40

Mehler, J. Psychology and psycholinguistics: the impact of Chomsky and Piaget. *In* Language and learning, ed. by M. Piattelli-Palmarini p341-53

Ostwald, P. F. and Rieber, R. W. James Rush and the theory of voice and mind. *In* Psychology of language and thought, ed. by R. W. Rieber p 105-19

Papert, S. The role of artificial intelligence in psychology. *In* Language and learning, ed. by M. Piattelli-Palmarini p90-99

Petitot, J. Localist hypothesis and theory of catastrophes: note on the debate. *In* Language and learning, ed. by M. Piattelli-Palmarini p372-79

Piaget, J. Afterthoughts. *In* Language and learning, ed. by M. Piattelli-Palmarini p278-84

Piaget, J. Schemes of action and language learning. *In* Language and learning, ed. by M. Piattelli-Palmarini p164-67

Premack, D. Representational capacity and accessibility of knowledge: the case of chimpanzees. *In* Language and learning, ed. by M. Piattelli-Palmarini p205-21

*See also* Language acquisition; Speech perception; Thought and thinking

### History

Rieber, T. W. and Vetter, H. J. Theoretical and historical roots of psycholinguistic research. *In* Psychology of language and thought, ed. by R. W. Rieber p3-49

Seigel, J. P. The perceptible and the imperceptible: Diderot's speculation on language in his letters on the deaf and blind. *In* Psychology of language and thought, ed. by R. W. Rieber p91-102

Stam, J. H. An historical perspective on 'linguistic relativity.' *In* Psychology of language and thought, ed. by R. W. Rieber p239-62

### Research

Reiber, T. W. and Vetter, H. J. Theoretical and historical roots of psycholinguistic research. *In* Psychology of language and thought, ed. by R. W. Rieber p3-49

**Psychological stress.** See Stress (Psychology)

**Psychology**

*See also* Aggressiveness (Psychology); Ambivalence; Cognition; Developmental psychology; Emotions; Ethnopsychology; Human behavior; Humanistic psychology; Individuality; Infant psychology; Intellect; Interpersonal relations; Personality; Psychoanalysis; Psycholinguistics; Subconsciousness; Thought and thinking

### Cross-cultural studies

*See* Ethnopsychology

### History

Sherif, C. W. Bias in psychology. *In* The Prism of sex, ed. by J. A. Sherman and E. T. Beck p93-133

**Psychology, Comparative**

Thorpe, W. H. The problem of purpose in evolution. *In* The Condition of man, ed. by P. Hallberg p128-49

*See also* Human behavior

**Psychology, Pathological.** See Mental illness; Psychiatry; Psychoanalysis

**Psychology, Physiological.** See Neuropsychology

**Psychology, Political.** See Political psychology

**Psychology, Religious**

La Barre, W. Psychoanalysis and the biology of religion. *In* La Barre, W. Culture in context p269-75

**Psychology, Sexual.** See Sex (Psychology)

**Psychology and religion.** See Psychology, Religious

**Psychology of language.** See Psycholinguistics

**Psychology of learning.** See Learning, Psychology of

**Psychopharmacology**

Conrad, P. On the medicalization of deviance and social control. *In* Critical psychiatry, ed. by D. Ingleby p102-19

**Psychotherapy**

Lakoff, R. T. When talk is not cheap: psychotherapy as conversation. *In* The State of the language, ed. by L. Michaels and C. Ricks p440-48

**Psychotropic drugs.** See Psychopharmacology

**Public administration.** See Bureaucracy; Military government

**Public assistance.** See Public welfare

**Public contracts.** See Defense contracts

**Public domain.** See Public lands

**Public finance.** See Finance, Public

**Public health**

### United States—History

Meeker, E. F. Medicine and public health. *In* Encyclopedia of American economic history, ed. by G. Porter v3 p1058-67

**Public health services.** See Public health

**Public lands**

### United States—History

Bogue, A. G. Land policies and sales. *In* Encyclopedia of American economic history ed. by G. Porter v2 p588-600

**Public opinion**

Speier, H. The rise of public opinion. *In* Propaganda and communication in world history, ed. by H. D. Lasswell, D. Lerner and H. Speier v2 p147-67

*See also* Knowledge, Sociology of; Propaganda; Public relations

Public opinion—*Continued*

### Southern States

Hero, A. O. Southern Jews and public policy. *In* Conference on Southern Jewish History, Richmond, Va. 1976. "Turn to the South" p143-50

### United States

Ladd, E. C. and Lipset, S. M. Public opinion and public policy. *In* The United States in the 1980s, ed. by P. Duignan and A. Rabushka p49-84

**Public opinions polls**

Merkl, P. H. Attitudes, ideology, and politics of party members. *In* Western European party systems, ed. by P. H. Merkl p402-89

**Public policy.** See Environmental policy; Science and state

**Public policy management.** See Policy sciences

**Public relations**

*See also* Propaganda

### United States—History

Tedlow, R. S. Advertising and public relations. *In* Encyclopedia of American economic history, ed. by G. Porter v2 p677-95

**Public speaking.** See Political oratory

**Public welfare**

### United States

Anderson, M. Welfare reform. *In* The United States in the 1980s, ed. by P Duignan and A. Rabushka p139-79

Kotlikoff, L. J. Social Security and welfare: what we have, want, and can afford. *In* The Economy in the 1980s: a program for growth and stability, ed. by M. J. Boskin p293-324

### United States—History

Trattner, W. I. Social welfare. *In* Encyclopedia of American economic history, ed. by G. Porter v3 p1155-67

**Publications of the Modern Language Association.** See PMLA

**Publicity.** See Public relations

**Publishers and authors.** See Authors and publishers

**Publishers and publishing**

*See also* Newspaper publishing

### Great Britain

Adams, T. R. The British pamphlet press and the American controversy, 1764-1783. *In* American Antiquarian Society. Proceedings v89 pt 1 p33-88

Todd, W. B. Concurrent printing: an analysis of Dodsley's Collection of poems by several hands. *In* The Bibliographical Society of America, 1904-79 p276-88

**Publishing of newspapers.** See Newspaper publishing

**Puccini, Giacomo**

### About

Carner, M. Debussy and Puccini. *In* Carner, M. Major and minor p139-47

### About individual works

*Manon Lescaut*

Carner, M. The two 'Manons.' *In* Carner, M. Major and minor p136-38

**Pugin, Augustus Welby Northmore**

### About

Harbison, R. Religion as art. *In* Harbison, R. Deliberate regression p63-93

**Punishment**

Durkheim, E. Two laws of penal evolution. *In* Durkheim, E. Emile Durkheim on institutional analysis p153-80

**Puppet plays.** See Puppets and puppet plays

**Puppets and puppet plays**

### Japan

Dunn, C.J. The Japanese puppet theatre. *In* Drama and mimesis, ed. by J. Redmond p65-80

**Purcell, Hugh Dominic**

The fallacy of environmentalism. *In* Lying truths, ed. by R. Duncan and M. Weston-Smith p85-96

**Purchasing power.** See Cost and standard of living; Income

**Puritan theology.** See Theology, Puritan

**Puritans**

Ahearn, M. L. David, the military exemplum. *In* The David myth in Western literature, ed. by D. J. Frontain and J. Wojcik p106-18

*See also* Marprelate controversy

### England

Knott, J. R. Introduction. *In* Knott, J. R. The sword of the spirit p 1-12

Knott, J. R. The Living Word. *In* Knott, J. R. The sword of the spirit p13-41

### New England

Bercovitch, S. Rhetoric and history in early New England: the Puritan errand reassessed. *In* Toward a new American literary history, ed. by L. J. Budd, E. H. Cady and C. L. Anderson p54-68

Edkins, C. Quest for community: spiritual autobiographies of eighteenth-century Quaker and Puritan women in America. *In* Women's autobiography, ed. by E. C. Jelinek p39-52

Miller, P. The Cambridge Platform in 1648. *In* Miller, P. The responsibility of mind in a civilization of machines p45-60

Miller, P. Equality in the American setting. *In* Miller, P The responsibility of mind in a civilization of machines p142-60

Miller, P. Individualism and the New England tradition. *In* Miller, P. The responsibility of mind in a civilization of machines p26-44

Miller, P. Religious background of the Bay Psalm book. *In* Miller, P. The responsibility of mind in a civilization of machines p15-25

Miller, P. The social context of the covenant. *In* Miller, P. The responsibility of mind in a civilization of machines p134-41

Ulrich, L. T. Vertuous women found: New England ministerial literature, 1668-1735. *In* A Heritage of her own, ed. by N. F. Cott and E. H. Pleck p58-80

### New England—Influence

Elliott, E. The Puritan roots of American Whig rhetoric. *In* Puritan influences in American literature, ed. by E. Elliott p107-27

**Pursell, Carroll W.**

Military-industrial complex. *In* Encyclopedia of American economic history, ed. by G. Porter v3 p926-34

Science agencies in World War II: the OSRD and its challengers. *In* The Sciences in the American context: new perspectives, ed. by N. Reingold p359-78

**Pushkin, Aleksandr Sergeevich**

### About

Katz, M. R. Dreams in Pushkin. *In* California Slavic studies v11 p71-103

**Putnam, Hilary**

Comments on Chomsky's and Fodor's replies. *In* Language and learning, ed. by M. Piattelli-Palmarini p335-40

What is innate and why: comments on the debate. *In* Language and learning, ed. by M. Piattelli-Palmerini p278-84

**Puttenham, George**

**About individual works**

*The arte of poesie*

Manley, L. G. The artlessness of art: convention in Renaissance poetics. *In* Manley, L. G. Convention, 1500-1750 p175-88

**Puzzles.** See Riddles

**Pye, Lucian W.**

Communication, development, and power. *In* Propaganda and communication in world history, ed. by H. D. Lasswell, D. Lerner and H. Speier v2 p424-45

**Pylyshyn, Zenon W.**

Complexity and the study of artificial and human intelligence. *In* Philosophical perspectives in artificial intelligence, ed. by M. Ringle p23-56

**Pynchon, Thomas**

**About individual works**

*The crying of lot 49*

Wagner, L. W. Note on Oedipa the road-runner. *In* Wagner, L. W. American modern p85-92

**Characters—Oedipa Maas**

Wagner, L. W. A note on Oedipa the road-runner. *In* Wagner, L. W. American modern p95-92

**Pyne, Stephen J.**

Certain allied problems in mechanics: Grove Karl Gilbert at the Henry Mountains. *In* New Hampshire Bicentennial Conference on the History of Geology. Two hundred years of geology in America p225-38

From the Grand Canyon to the Marianas Trench: the earth sciences after Darwin. *In* The Sciences in the American context: new perspectives, ed. by N. Reingold p165-92

**Pyne, Steve.** See Pyne, Stephen J.

**Pythagoras**

**About**

Lutz, C. E. The symbol of the Y of Pythagoras in the ninth century. *In* Lutz, C. E. The oldest library motto, and other library essays p38-46

# Q

**Quaintance, Richard E.**

Walpole's Whig interpretation of landscaping history. *In* Studies in eighteenth-century culture v9 p285-300

**Quakers.** See Friends, Society of

**Qualey, Carlton C.**

Thorstein Bunde Veblen, 1857-1929. *In* Makers of an American immigrant legacy, ed. by O. S. Llovoll p50-61

**Quantum dynamics.** See Quantum theory

**Quantum theory**

Davies, P. C. W. Reality exists outside us? *In* Lying truths, ed. by R. Duncan and M. Weston-Smith p143-58

**Quarles, Benjamin**

Black history's antebellum origins. *In* American Antiquarian Society. Proceedings v89 pt 1 p89-122

**Quesnay, Ian M. Le M. du.** See Du Quesnay, Ian M. Le M.

**Quincey, Thomas de.** See De Quincey, Thomas

**Quintet (Motion picture)**

Kael, P. The Altman bunker. *In* Kael, P. When the lights go down p548-54

Kauffmann, S. Quintet. *In* Kauffmann, S. Before my eyes p46-48

**Quirk, Randolph**

Sound barriers and Gangbangsprache. *In* The State of the language, ed. by L. Michaels and C. Ricks p3-14

**Quiroga, Elena**

**About individual works**

*Viento del norte*

Fox-Lockert, L. Elena Quiroga. *In* Fox-Lockert, L. Women novelists in Spain and Spanish America p85-93

# R

**Rabb, Theodore K.**

Population, economy and society in Milton's England. *In* The Age of Milton, ed. by C. A. Patrides and R. B. Waddington p72-101

**Rabbinical literature**

Stein, S. The concept of the "fence": observations on its origin and development. *In* Studies in Jewish religious and iltellectual history, ed. by S. Stein and R. Lowe p301-29

**Rabbis**

**Europe**

Abramsky, C. The crisis of authority within European Jewry in the eighteenth century. *In* Studies in Jewish religious and intellectual history, ed. by S. Stein and R. Loewe p13-28

**Florida—Miami**

Rosen, G. The rabbi in Miami—a case history. *In* Conference on Southern Jewish History, Richmond, Va. 1976. "Turn to the South" p33-40

**Southern States**

Spiro, J. D. Rabbi in the South: a personal view. *In* Conference on Southern Jewish History, Richmond, Va. 1976. "Turn to the South" p41-43

Stern, M. H. The role of the rabbi in the South. *In* Conference on Southern Jewish History, Richmond Va. 1976. "Turn to the South" p21-32

**Rabe, David**

**About individual works**

*In the Boom Boom Room*

Brown, J. In the Boom Boom Room. *In* Brown, J. Feminist drama p37-55

**Rabelais, François**

**About individual works**

*Gargantua and Pantagruel*

Seidel, M. A. The revisionary inheritance: Rabelais and Cervantes. *In* Seidel, M. A. Satiric inheritance, Rabelais to Sterne p60-94

**Rabin, Chaim**

Hebrew and Arabic in medieval Jewish philosophy. *In* Studies in Jewish religious and intellectual history, ed. by S. Stein and R. Loewe p235-45

**Rabinowitz, Peter J.**

"What's Hecuba to us?" The audience's experience of literary borrowing. *In* The Reader in the text, ed. by S. R. Suleiman and I. Crosman p241-63

**Rabkin, Eric S.**

### About individual works
#### The fantastic in literature

Nodelman, P. Defining children's literature. *In* Children's literature v8 p184-90

**Rabushka, Alvin**

Tax and spending limits. *In* The United States in the 1980s, ed. by P. Duignan and A. Rabushka p85-108

**Race.** See Ethnocentrism

**Race relations**

Dundes, A. The curious case of the widemouth frog. *In* Dundes, A. Interpreting folklore p62-68

*See also* Antisemitism; Pluralism (Social sciences) and subdivision Race relations under names of regions, countries, cities, e.g. Southern States—Race relations

**Race relations in literature**

Rees, D. The color of skin: Mildred Taylor. *In* Rees, D. The marble in the water p104-13

**Rachels, James**

Euthanasia. *In* Matters of life and death, ed. by T. Regan p28-66

**Racine, Jean Baptiste**

#### About

Ranum, O. Racine learns to be a historiographer. *In* Ranum, O. Artisans of glory p278-332

#### About individual works
##### Athaliah

Mueller, M. Athalie as displaced Oresteia and scriptural tragedy. *In* Mueller, M. Children of Oedipus, and other essays on the imitation of Greek tragedy, 1550-1800 p182-93

##### Bajazet

Reiss, T. J. Social truth and the will to power: Richelieu, Hobbes, Bajazet. *In* Reiss, T. J. Tragedy and truth p219-39

##### Berenice

Mueller, M. Dido and Bérénice. *In* Mueller, M. Children of Oedipus, and other essays on the imitation of Greek tragedy, 1550-1800 p230-48

##### Iphigenia

Reiss, T. J. Classicism, the individual, and economic exchange (Iphigénie). *In* Reiss, T. J. Tragedy and truth p240-58

##### Phèdre

Holloway, J. Effectively complete enumerations in 'Phèdre.' *In* Holloway, J. Narrative and structure: exploratory essays p20-37

Mueller, M. Phèdre. *In* Mueller, M. Children of Oedipus, and other essays on the imitation of Greek tragedy, 1550-1800 p46-63

Reiss, T. J. From Phèdre to history: the truths of time and the fictions of eternity. *In* Reiss, T. J. Tragedy and truth p259-81

**Racism.** See Antisemitism

**Radcliffe, Timothy**

Relativizing the relativizers: a theologian's assessment of the role of sociological explanation of religious phenomena and theology today. *In* Sciology and theology: alliance and conflict, ed. by D. Martin, J. O. Mills [and] W. S. F. Pickering p151-62

**Radest, Howard B.**

Relativism and responsibility. In Humanist ethics, ed. by M. B. Storer p228-41

Schooling and the search for a usable politics. *In* History, religion, and spiritual democracy, ed. by M. Wohlgelerntar [and others] p317-40

**Radio astronomy**

Rönnäng, B. O. Radio waves from distant galaxies, with applications to geodynamics. *In* The Condition of man, ed. by P. Hallberg p40-58

**Radio in propaganda**

Gombrich, Sir E. H. J. Myth and reality in German wartime broadcasts. *In* Gombrich, Sir E. H. J. Ideals and idols p93-111

**Radner, John B.**

The art of sympathy in eighteenth-century British moral thought. *In* Studies in eighteenth-century culture v9 p189-210

**Rae, John**

#### About individual works
##### Contemporary socialism

Fuller, A. B. Rae: a journalist out of his depth. *In* Critics of Henry George, ed. by R. V. Andelson p153-61

**Rafroidi, Patrick**

From Listowel with love: John B Keane and Bryan MacMahon. *In* The Irish short story, ed. by P. Rafroidi and T. Brown p263-73

The Irish short story in English. The birth of a new tradition. *In* The Irish short story, ed. by P. Rafroidi and T. Brown p27-38

Yeats, nature and the self. *In* Yeats, Sligo and Ireland, ed. by A. N. Jeffares p189-96

**Raghavacharyulu, D. V. K.**

The immense journey: an outline of Aswapathy's Sadhana. *In* Aspects of Indian writing in English, ed. by M. K. Naik p64-79

**Raider, Ruth**

'The flash of fervour': Daniel Deronda. *In* Reading the Victorian novel: detail into form, ed. by I. Gregory p253-73

**Railo, Eíno**

#### About individual works
##### The haunted castle

Trilling, L. A study of terror-romanticism. *In* Trilling, L. Speaking of literature and society p7-9

**Raimon de Miraval**

#### About

Cropp, G. M. The partimen between Folquet de Marseille and Tostemps. *In* The Interpretation of medieval lyric poetry, ed. by W. T. H. Jackson p91-112

**Rairndranatha Thākura.** See Tagore, Sir Rabindranath

**Raja Rao**

Books which have influenced me. *In* Aspects of Indian writing in English, ed. by M. K. Naik p45-49

#### About

Raja Rao. Books which have influenced me. *In* Aspects of Indian writing in English, ed. by M. K. Naik p45-49

**Raja Rao**—*Continued*

### About individual works

*The serpent and the rope*

Ramaswamy, S. Self and society in Raja Rao's 'The serpent and the rope'. *In* Aspects of Indian writing in English, ed. by M. K. Naik p199-208

**Raleigh, John Henry**

The Irish atavism of A moon for the misbegotten. *In* Eugene O'Neill, ed. by V. Floyd p229-36

The last confession: O'Neill and the Catholic confessional. *In* Eugene O'Neill, ed. by V. Floyd p212-28

**Ramanujan, A. K.**

### About individual works

*The striders*

Rao, K. R. Reverse romanticism: the case of A. K. Ramanujan's 'The striders'. *In* Aspects of Indian writing in English, ed. by M. K. Naik p120-25

**Ramaswamy, S.**

Self and society in Raja Rao's 'The serpent and the rope'. *In* Aspects of Indian writing in English, ed. by M. K. Naik p199-208

**Ramchand, Kenneth**

### About individual works

*An introduction to the study of West Indian literature*

Metcalf, R. West Indian literature. *In* African literature today no. 10: Retrospect & prospect, ed. by E. D. Jones p253-55

**Rameses II, King of Egypt**

Lutz, C. E. The oldest library motto. *In* Lutz, C. E. The oldest library motto, and other library essays p17-21

**Rancho deluxe (Motion picture)**

Kael, P. Poses. *In* Kael, P. When the lights go down p90-95

**Randall, John Herman, 1899-1980**

### About

Martin, J. A. The esthetic, the religious, and the natural. *In* History, religion, and spiritual democracy, ed. by M. Wohlgelernter [and others] p76-91

Shea, W. M. The supernatural in the naturalists. *In* History, religion, and spiritual democracy, ed. by M. Wohlgelernter [and others] p53-75

**Randall, Lillian M. C.**

### About individual works

*Images in the margins of Gothic manuscripts*

Schapiro, M. Marginal images and drôlerie. *In* Schapiro, M. Selected papers v3: Late antiques, early Christian and mediaeval art p197-98

**Ranum, Orest**

Artisans of glory

*Contents*

Bernard and his history

Chapelain and the royal patronage of history

Glancing backward and forward

The historiographers royal

Men of letters: sixteenth-century models of conduct

Mézerai: a libertin historiographer royal

Patronage and history from Richelieu to Colbert

Pellisson-Fontanier: from Protestant judge to historiographer royal

Racine learns to be a historiographer

Sorel: a novelist turned historiographer

**Rao, Krukundi Raghavendra**

Reverse romanticism: the case of A. K. Ramanujan's 'The striders'. *In* Aspects of Indian writing in English, ed. by M. K. Naik p120-25

**Rao, Raja.** See Raja Rao

**Rapaport, Elizabeth**

On the future of love: Rousseau, and the radical feminist. *In* The Philosophy of sex, ed. by A. Soble p369-88

**Rape**

Ketchum, S. A. The good, the bad and the perverted; sexual paradigms revisited. *In* The Philosophy of sex, ed. by A. Soble p139-57

**Raphael, David Daiches**

Adam Smith: philosophy, science, and social science. *In* Royal Institute of Philosophy. Philosophers of the Enlightenment p77-93

**Raphael, Frederic**

The language of television. *In* The State of the language, ed. by L. Michaels and C. Ricks p304-12

**Rare books.** See Bibliography—Rare books

**Rasmussen, Wayne David**

Agriculture. *In* Encyclopedia of American economic history, ed. by G. Porter v 1 p344-60

**Rasputin, Valentin Grigor'evich**

### About

Hosking, G. Village prose: Vasily Belov, Valentin Rasputin. *In* Hosking, G. Beyond Sociaist realism p50-83

Shneidman, N. N. Valentin Rasputin: village prose reconsidered. *In* Shneidman, N. N. Soviet literature in the 1970s: artistic diversity and ideological conformity p75-87

**Rationalism**

Berlin, Sir I. Hume and the sources of German anti-rationalism. *In* Berlin, Sir I. Against the current p162-87

Mavrodes, G. I. Rationality and religious belief—a perverse question. *In* Rationality and religious belief, ed. by C. F. Delaney p28-41

Plantinga, A. Is belief in God rational? *In* Rationality and religious belief, ed. by C. F. Delaney p7-27

*See also* Enlightenment; Faith and reason

**Ratner, Sidney**

Taxation. *In* Encyclopedia of American economic history, ed. by G. Porter v 1 p451-67

**Rattansi, P. M.**

The scientific background. *In* The Age of Milton, ed. by C. A. Patrides and R. B. Waddington p197-240

**Ravenna, Italy. Throne of Maximian**

Schapiro, M. The Joseph scenes on the Maximianus throne in Ravenna. *In* Schapiro, M. Selected papers v3: Late antique, early Christian and mediaeval art p35-47

**Rawicz, Piotr**

### About individual works

*Blood from the sky*

Alexander, E. The Holocaust and the God of Israel. *In* Alexander, E. The resonance of dust p195-230

**Ray, Benjamin**

The story of Kintu: myth, death, and ontology in Buganda. *In* Explorations in African systems of thought, ed. by I. C. Karp & C. S. Bird p60-79

**Ray, Gordon Norton**

The changing world of rare books. *In* The Bibliographical Society of America, 1904-79 p416-54

**Ray, Man**

### About individual works
*L'etoile de mer*

Thiher, A. The surrealist film: Man Ray and the limits of metaphor. *In* Thiher, A. The cinematic muse p38-48

**Ray, Satyajit**

### About individual works
*Distant thunder*

Kael, P. A dream of women. *In* Kael, P. When the lights go down p68-72

**Reading**

Bauschatz, C. M. Montaigne's conception of reading in the context of Renaissance poetics and modern criticism. *In* The Reader in the text, ed. by S. R. Suleiman and I. Crosman p264-91

Culler, J. Prolegomena to a theory of reading. *In* The Reader in the text, ed. by S. R. Suleiman and I. Crosman p46-66

Hartman, G. H. The work of reading. *In* Hartman, G. H. Criticism in the wilderness p161-88

Leenhardt, J. Toward a sociology of reading. *In* The Reader in the text, ed. by S. R. Suleiman and I. Crosman p205-24

Marin, L. Toward a theory of reading in the visual arts: Poussin's The Arcadian shepherds. *In* The Reader in the text, ed. by S. R. Suleiman and I. Crosman p293-324

Prince, G. Notes on the text as reader. *In* The Reader in the text, ed. by S. R. Suleiman and I. Crosman p225-40

Stierle, K. The reading of fictional texts. *In* The Reader in the text, ed. by S. R. Suleiman and I Crosman p83-105

Todorov, T. Reading as construction. *In* The Reader in the text, ed. by S. R. Suleiman and I. Crosman p67-82

**Reading, Choice of.** See Books and reading

**Reading, Psychology of**

De Man, P. Allegory (Julie). *In* De Man, P. Allegories of reading p188-220

De Man, P. Promises (Social contract). *In* De Man, P. Allegories of reading p246-77

De Man, P. Reading (Proust). *In* De Man, P. Allegories of reading p57-78

**Reading habits.** See Books and reading

**Reading research**

Leenhardt, J. Toward a sociology of reading. *In* The Reader in the text, ed. by S. R. Suleiman and I. Crosman p205-24

**Real property tax**

### California

Moynihan, D. P. Two tax revolts. *In* Moynihan, D. P. Counting our blessings p257-73

**Realism in literature**

Abramson, G. The state of Israel: Early social realism. *In* Abramson, G. Modern Hebrew drama p59-76

Braudy, L. B. Realists, naturalists, and novelists of manners. *In* Harvard Guide to contemporary American writing, ed. by D. Hoffman p84-152

Eagleton, T. Test, ideology, realism. *In* Literature and society, ed. by E. W. Said p149-73

Laing, S. Presenting 'things as they are': John Sommerfield's May Day and mass observation. *In* Class, culture and social change, ed. by F. Gloversmith p142-60

Stone, D. D. Elizabeth Gaskell, Wordsworth, and the burden of reality. *In* Stone, D. D. The romantic impulse in Victorian fiction p133-72

Trilling, L. The promise of realism. *In* Trilling, L. Speaking of literature and society p27-33

*See also* Idealism in literature

**Reality**

Annas, J. Truth and knowledge. *In* Doubt and dogmatism, ed. by M. Schofield, M. Burnyeat and J. Barnes p84-104

Davies, P. C. W. Reality exists outside us? *In* Lying truths, ed. by R. Duncan and M. Weston-Smith p143-58

*See also* Experience; Objectivity

**Reality in literature**

Prušek, J. Reality and art in Chinese literature. *In* Prušek, J. The lyrical and the epic p86-101

**Reason.** See Faith and reason

**Reason and faith.** See Faith and reason

**Reasoning**

Williams, B. A. O. Internal and external reasons. *In* Rational action, ed. by R. Harrison p17-28

*See also* Fallacies (Logic); Induction (Logic); Judgment (Logic)

**Reasoning (Psychology)**

Sousa, R. de. The rationality of emotions. *In* Explaining emotions, ed. by A. O. Rorty p127-51

*See also* Intellect

**Rebellions.** See Revolutions

**Recombinant DNA**

Morowitz, H. J. Frankenstein and recombinant DNA. *In* Morowitz, H. J. The wine of life, and other essays on societies, energy & living things p187-91

**Reconstruction (1914-1939)**

Van Meter, R. H. Herbert Hoover and the economic reconstruction of Europe, 1918-21. *In* Herbert Hoover, ed. by L. E. Gelfand p143-81

**The red desert (Motion picture)**

Arrowsmith, W. Antonioni's "Red desert": myth and fantasy. *In* The Binding of Proteus, ed. by M. W. McCune, T. Orbison and P. M. Withim p312-37

**Redding, Jay Saunders**

The Negro in American history: as scholar, as subject. *In* The Past before us, ed. by M. Kammen p292-307

**Redemption (Jewish theology)**

Thieberger, F. The Jewish conception of redemption. *In* The Jew, ed. by A. A. Cohen p149-57

**Reductionism**

Koestler, A. Nothing but . . . ? *In* Lying truths, ed. by R. Duncan and M. Weston-Smith p199-201

**Reed, John Shelton**

Ethnicity in the South: observations on the acculturation of Southern Jews. *In* Conference on Southern Jewish History, Richmond, Va. 1976. "Turn to the South" p135-42

**Rees, David**
The marble in the water
*Contents*
Achieving one's heart's desires: Philippa Pearce
The color of skin: Mildred Taylor
"The colour of saying": Paula Fox
Earthsea revisited: Ursula K. Le Guin
Hanging in their true shapes
Making the children stretch: Nina Bawden
The marble in the water: Penelope Farmer
Middle of the way: Rodie Sudbery and Beverly Cleary
Not even for a one-night stand: Judy Blume
The sadness of compromise: Robert Cormier and Jill Chaney
Time present and time past: Penelope Lively
Timor mortis conturbat me: E. B. White and Doris Buchanan Smith
Types of ambiguity: Jill Paton Walsh
Viewed from a squashed eyeball: Paul Zindel
Your arcane novelist: E. L. Konigsburg

**Reflex action.** See Reflexes

**Reflexes**
Leys, R. Background to the reflex controversy: William Alison and the doctrine of sympathy before Hall. *In* Studies in history of biology v4 p 1-66

**Reform Judaism.** See Haskalah

**Reformation**
Manley, L. G. The "duble name" of custom: the Reformation attack on convention. *In* Manley, L. G. Convention, 1500-1750 p67-90
Ozment, S. H. The legacy of the Reformation. *In* Ozment, S. H. The age of reform, 1250-1550 p434-38
Ozment, S. H. The sectarian spectrum: radical movements within Protestantism. *In* Ozment, S.H. The age of reform, 1250-1550 p340-51
Roelker, N. L. The impact of the Reformation era on communication and propaganda. *In* Propaganda and communication in world history, ed. by H. D. Lasswell, D. Lerner and H. Speier v2 p41-84

### Early movements
Ozment, S. H. On the eve of the Reformation. *In* Ozment, S. H. The age of reform, 1250-1550 p182-222

### Germany
Klassen, P. J. The role of the masses in shaping the Reformation. *In* 5000 years of popular culture, ed. by F. E. H. Schroeder p257-75
Ozment, S. H. Society and politics in the German Reformation. *In* Ozment, S. H. The age of reform, 1250-1550 p245-89
Rothkrug, L. Popular religion and holy shrines. *In* Religion and the people, 800-1700, ed. by J. Obelkevich p20-86

### History
*See* Reformation

### Scotland
Ozment, S. H. Protestant resistance to tyranny: the career of John Knox. *In* Ozment, S. H. The age of reform, 1250-1550 p419-33

### Switzerland
Ozment, S. H. The Swiss Reformation. *In* Ozment, S. H. The age of reform, 1250-1550 p318-39

### Switzerland—Geneva
Ozment, S. H. Calvin and Calvinism. *In* Ozment, S. H. The age of reform, 1250-1550 p352-80

**Reformed church.** See Calvinism

**Reformers.** See Social reformers

**Regan, Tom**
Introduction. *In* Matters of life and death, ed. by T. Regan p3-27

**Regehr, Ernie**
What is militarism? *In* Problems of contemporary militarism, ed. by A. Eide and M. Thee p127-39

**Regional economics**
Lindstrom, D. Domestic trade and regional specialization. *In* Encyclopedia of American economic history, ed. by G. Porter v 1 p264-80

**Regionalism.** See Regional economics

**Regionalism in literature**
King, R. H. Modernizers and monumentalists: social thought in the 1930s. *In* King, R. H. A Southern Renaissance p39-76

**Regulating agencies.** See Independent regulatory commissions

**Reich, Leonard S.**
Science. *In* Encyclopedia of American economic history, ed. by G. Porter v 1 p281-93

**Reid, Alec**
Test flight: Beckett's More pricks than kicks. *In* The Irish short story, ed. by P. Rafroidi and T. Brown p227-35

**Reid, Betty**
The Left Book Club in the thirties. *In* Culture and crisis in Britain in the thirties, ed. by J. Clark [and others] p193-207

**Reid, David**
At home in the abyss: Jonestown and the language of enormity. *In* The State of the language, ed. by L. Michaels and C. Ricks p277-88

**Reid, Douglas A.**
Popular theatre in Victorian Birmingham. *In* Performance and politics in popular drama, ed. by D. Bradby, L. James and B. Sharratt p65-89

**Reid, Fred**
The disintegration of Liberalism, 1895-1931. *In* The Context of English literature, 1900-1930, ed. by M. Bell p94-125

**Reilly, John M.**
Chester Himes' Harlem tough guys. *In* Seasoned authors for a new season: the search for standards in popular writing, ed. by L. Filler p58-69

**Reindl, Margareta Mommsen-** See Mommsen-Reindl, Margareta

**Reingold, Nathan**
Reflections on 200 years of science in the United States. *In* The Sciences in the American context: new perspectives, ed. by N. Reingold p9-20

**Reisler, Marsha**
Voltaire's Quaker letters as strategical truth: altering the reader's structure of perception in the service of a higher vision. *In* Studies in eighteenth-century culture v9 p429-54

**Reiss, Edmund**
Chaucer's deerne love and the medieval view of secrecy in love. *In* Chaucerian problems and perspectives, ed. by E. Vasta and Z. P. Thundy p164-79

Reiss, Timothy J.
   Tragedy and truth
      *Contents*
Buchanan, Montaigne, and the difficulty of
   speaking
Classicism, the individual, and economic ex-
   change (Iphigénie)
From Phèdre to history: the truths of time
   and the fictions of eternity
Hamlet on distraction and Fortinbras on
   knowledge
A hypothesis and its prehistory
Jodelle's Cléopâtre and the enchanted circle
Les Juifves: possession and the willful eye
The Lear of the future
A new time and the glory that was Egypt
Power and fallibility (Tamburlaine and Faus-
   tus)
Social truth and the will to power: Richelieu,
   Hobbes, Bajazet
Tragedy and truth

Reisz, Karel
   **About individual works**
      *Who'll stop the rain?*
Kauffmann, S. Who'll stop the rain? *In*
Kauffmann, S. Before my eyes p88-91

Relativism, Cultural. See Cultural relativism

Relativism, Ethical. See Ethical relativism

Relativity (Ethics) See Ethical relativism

Relativity (Linguistics) See Sapir-Whorf hypothesis

Relativity (Physics) See Quantum theory

Relics and reliquaries
   Geary, P. J. The ninth-century relic trade. *In*
Religion and the people, 800-1700, ed. by J.
Obelkevich p8-19

Relief (Aid) See Public welfare

Religion
   Bondi, Sir H. Religion is a good thing. *In*
Lying truths, ed. by R. Duncan and M. Weston-Smith p203-10
   Gilkey, L. B. The religious dilemmas of a
scientific culture: the interface of technology,
history and religion. *In* Being human in a technological age, ed. by D. M. Borchert and D.
Stewart p73-88
   *See also* Belief and doubt; Religions; Supernatural; Theology; also subdivision Religion
under names of countries, races, peoples, etc.
e.g. United States—Religion; Ashantis—Religion; and headings beginning with the word
Religious

   **Philosophy**
   Madden, E. H. Asa Mahan and the Oberlin
philosophy. *In* History, religion, and spiritual
democracy, ed. by M. Wohlgelernter [and
others] p155-80
   Rockefeller, S. C. John Dewey: the evolution of a faith. *In* History, religion, and spiritual democracy, ed. by M. Wohlgelernter [and
others] p5-34

   **Psychological aspects**
   *See* Psychology, Religious

   **Psychology**
   *See* Psychology, Religious

Religion, Prehistoric
   Sandars, N. K. The religious development
of some early societies. *In* The Origins of
civilization, ed. by P. R. S. Moorey p103-27

Religion, Primitive
   *See also* subdivision Religion under names of
ethnic groups, e.g. Ashantis—Religion

   **Africa**
   MacGaffey, W. African religions: types and
generalizations. *In* Explorations in African systems of thought, ed. by I. C. Karp & C. S.
Bird p301-28

Religion and art. See Art and religion

Religion and communism. See Communism and
   religion

Religion and culture. See Christianity and culture

Religion and humor. See Christianity and humor

Religion and law
   Manley, L. G. "Use becomes another nature": custom in sixteenth-century politics and
law. *In* Manley, L. G. Convention, 1500-1750
p90-106

Religion and literature. See Christianity and
   literature

Religion and philosophy. See Philosophy and
   religion

Religion and politics
   Berger, P. L. Religion and the American
future. *In* The Third century, ed. by S. M.
Lipset p65-77
   Hook, S. The autonomy of the democratic
faith. *In* Hook, S. Philosophy and public policy p272-78
   Lewy, G. Millenarianism as a revolutionary
force. *In* Propaganda and communication in
world history, ed. by H. D. Lasswell, D. Ler-
nr and H. Speier v2 p168-209

Religion and science
   Morowitz, H. J. Return of the six million
dollar man. *In* Morowitz, H. J. The wine of
life, and other essays on societies, energy &
living things p37-40

   **History of controversy—Great Britain**
   Turner. F. M. The Victorian conflict between science and religion: a professional dimension. *In* Consciousness and class experience
in nineteenth-century Europe, ed. by J. M.
Merriman p219-44

Religion and sociology
   Pickering, W. S. F. Theodicy and social
theory: an exploration of the limits of collaboration between sociologist and theologian. *In*
Sociology and theology: alliance and conflict,
ed. by D. Martin, J. O. Mills [and] W. S. F.
Pickering p59-79
   Radcliffe, T. Relativizing the relativizers: a
theologian's assessment of the role of sociological explanation of religious phenomena and
theology today. *In* Sociology and theology: alliance and conflict, ed. by D. Martin, J. O.
Mills [and] W. S. F. Pickering p151-62
   *See also* Sociology, Christian

Religion in literature. See Christianity in literature

Religions
   Smart, N. Religions and changing values. *In*
Value and values in evolution, ed. by E. A.
Maziarz p17-28
   *See also* Buddhism; Humanism, Religious;
Islam; Judaism; Religion; Shamanism

Religious art. See Christian art and symbolism;
   Church architecture

Religious belief. See Belief and doubt

Religious humanism. See Humanism, Religious

Religious knowledge, Theory of. See Knowledge, Theory of (Religion)

Religious life. See Monastic and religious life

**Religious literature, American**
Ulrich, L. T. Vertuous women found: New England ministerial literature, 1668-1735. *In* A Heritage of her own, ed. by N. F. Cott and E. H. Pleck p58-80

Religious music. See Church music

Religious orders. See Monasticism and religious orders

**Religious thought**

### Middle Ages, 600-1500
Le Goff, J. How did the medieval university conceive of itself? *In* Le Goff, J. Time, work, & culture in the Middle Ages p122-34
Le Goff, J. Trades and professions as represented in medieval confessors' manuals. *In* Le Goff, J. Time, work, & culture in the Middle Ages p107-21
Robertson, D. W. Historical criticism. *In* Robertson, D. W. Essays in medieval culture p3-20

### England—18th century
Pocock, J. G. A. Post-Puritan England and the problem of the Enlightenment. *In* Culture and politics from Puritanism to the Enlightenment, ed. by P. Zagorin p91-111

### Great Britain—17th century
Patrides, C. A. The experience of otherness: theology as a means of life. *In* The Age of Milton, ed. by C. A. Patrides and R. B. Waddington p170-96

**Remarque, Erich Maria**

### About
Kuxdorf, M. Mynona versus Remarque, Tucholsky, Mann, and others: not so quiet on the literary front. *In* The First World War in German narrative prose, ed. by C. N. Genno and H. Wetzel p71-92

Remodeling (Architecture) See Dwellings—Remodeling

**Renaissance**
Bouwsma, W. J. The Renaissance and the broadening of communication. *In* Propaganda and communication in world history, ed. by H. D. Lasswell, D. Lerner and H. Speier v2 p3-40
Kristeller, P. O. Paganism and Christianity. *In* Kristeller, P. O. Renaissance thought and its sources p66-81
Kristeller, P. O. The Renaissance. *In* Kristeller, P. O. Renaissance thought and its sources p242-59
Kristeller, P. O. Renaissance philosophy and the medieval tradition. *In* Kristeller, P. O. Renaissance thought and its sources p106-33
*See also* Humanism

### England
Kerrigan, W. The articulation of the ego in the English Renaissance. *In* The Literary Freud: mechanisms of defense and the poetic will, ed. by J. H. Smith p261-308

### Europe
*See* Renaissance

### Italy
Kristeller, P. O. Humanism and scholasticism in the Italian Renaissance. *In* Kristeller, P. O. Renaissance thought and its sources p85-105

### Poland
Lutz, C. E. Copernicus' stand for humanism. *In* Lutz, C. E. The oldest library motto, and other library essays p75-82

Renaissance arts. See Arts, Renaissance

Renaissance drama. See European drama—Renaissance, 1450-1600

Renaissance philosophy. See Philosophy, Renaissance

**Renaldo & Clara (Motion picture)**
Kael, P. The calvary gig. *In* Kael, P. When the lights go down p397-401

**Renner, Timothy**
Three new Homerica on papyrus. *In* Harvard Studies in classical philology v83 p311-37

**Renoir, Alain**
The inept lover and the reluctant mistress: remarks on sexual inefficiency in medieval literature. *In* Chaucerian problems and perspectives, ed. by E. Vasta and Z. P. Thundy p180-206

**Renoir, Jean**

### About
Kauffmann, S. 1894-1979. *In* Kauffmann, S. Before my eyes p401-03

### About individual works
*The grand illusion*
Thiher, A. Jean Renoir and the mimesis of history. *In* Thiher, A. The cinematic muse p92-112

*Rules of the game*
Thiher, A. Jean Renoir and the mimesis of history. *In* Thiher, A. The cinematic muse p92-112

**Renza, Louis A.**
The veto of the imagination: a theory of autobiography. *In* Autobiography: essays theoretical and critical, ed. by J. Olney p268-95

**Repentance in literature**
Huttar, C. A. Frail grass and firm tree: David as a model of repentance in the Middle Ages and early Renaissance. *In* The David myth in Western literature, ed. by R. J. Frontain and J. Wojcik p38-54

**Repetition in literature**
Sternfeld, F. W. Repetition and echo in Renaissance poetry and music. *In* English Renaissance studies, ed. by J. Carey p33-43

**Reporters and reporting**
Hart, D. J. Changing relationships between publishers and journalists: an overview. *In* Newspapers and democracy, ed. by A. Smith p268-87

**Representation (Philosophy)**
Hill, J. E. C. Covenant theology and the concept of 'a public person.' *In* Powers, possessions and freedom, ed. by A. Kontos p3-22

Representation. See Representative government and representation

**Representative government and representation**
Dannhauser, W. J. Reflections on statesmanship and bureaucracy. *In* Bureaucrats, policy analysts, statesmen: who leads? Ed. by R. A. Goldwin p114-32
Storing, H. J. American statesmanship: old and new. *In* Bureaucrats, policy analysts, statesmen: who leads? Ed. by R. A. Goldwin p88-113
*See also* Democracy

### Massachusetts—History
Pole, J. R. The emergence of the majority principle in the American Revolution. *In* Pole, J. R. Paths to the American past p41-54

**Representative government and representation**
—*Continued*

### United States

Barber, B. R. The undemocratic party system: citizenship in an elite/mass society. *In* Political parties in the eighties, ed. by R. A. Goldwin p34-49

### United States—History

Pole, J. R. The emergence of the majority principle in the American Revolution. *In* Pole, J. R. Paths to the American past p41-54

### Virginia—History

Pole, J. R. Representation and authority in Virginia from the Revolution to reform. *In* Pole, J. R. Paths to the American past p3-40

**Repression (Psychology) in literature**
Gordon, D. J. Literature and repression: the case of Shavian drama. *In* The Literary Freud: mechanisms of defense and the poetic will, ed. by J. H. Smith p181-203

**Republics.** See Federal government

**Rescher, Nicholas**
Social values and technological change. *In* Value and values in evolution, ed. by E. A. Maziarz p163-78

**Research**
Morowitz, H. J. Deep purple. *In* Morowitz, H. J. The wine of life, and other essays on societies, energy & living things p145-48

*See also* Agricultural research; Learning and scholarship

### Economic aspects

Morowitz, H. J. Grant us this day our daily bread. *In* Morowitz, H. J. The wine of life, and other essays on societies, energy & living things p133-36

### Finance

*See* Endowment of research

### United States—History

Sapolsky, H. M. Academic science and the military: the years since the Second World War. *In* The Sciences in the American context: new perspectives, ed. by N. Reingold p379-99

**Research, Endowment of.** See Endowment of research

**Research, Industrial**

### Laboratories—History

Birr, K. Industrial research laboratories. *In* The Sciences in the American context: new perspectives, ed. by N. Reingold p193-207

### United States—History

Birr, K. Industrial research laboratories. *In* The Sciences in the American context: new perspectives, ed. by N. Reingold p193-207

**Residences.** See Architecture, Domestic

**Resistance to government.** See Government, Resistance to

**Resnais, Alain**

### About individual works
*Last year at Marienbad*

Thiher, A. L'année dernière à Marienbad: the narration of narration. *In* Thiher, A. The cinematic muse p166-79

*Providence*

Kael, P. Werewolf, mon amour. *In* Kael, P. When the lights go down p255-59

**Resources, Natural.** See Natural resources

**Responsibility**
Baier, K. E. Freedom, obligation, and responsibility. *In* Humanist ethics, ed. by M. B. Storer p75-97

**Restif de La Bretonne, Nicolas Edmé**

### About

Fletcher, D. Restif de La Bretonne and woman's estate. *In* Woman and society in eighteenth-century France, ed. by E. Jacobs and others p96-109

### About individual works
*Monsieur Nicholas; or, The human heart unveiled*

Spender, S. Confessions and autobiography; excerpt from "The making of a poem." *In* Autobiography: essays theoretical and critical, ed. by J. Olney p115-22

**Retail advertising.** See Advertising

**Retail trade**

### United States—History

Hollander, S. C. The effects of industrialization of small retailing in the United States in the twentieth century. *In* Small business in American life, ed. by S. W. Bruchey p212-39

**Reuental, Neidhart von.** See Neidhart von Reuental

**Revelation**
Daly, G. George Tyrrell: revelation as experience. *In* Daly, G. Transcendence and immanence p140-64

**The Revels history of drama in English v5**
Gibbons, B. The Revels history of drama in English volume V, 1660-1750. *In* Drama and mimesis, ed. by J. Redmond p191-206

**The Revels history of drama in English v8**
Sidnell, M. J. The Revels history of drama in English volume VIII, American drama. *In* Drama and mimesis, ed. by J. Redmond p227-42

**Revenge in literature**
Veith, G. E. "Wait upon the Lord": David, Hamlet, and the problem of revenge. *In* The David myth in Western literature, ed. by R. J. Frontain and J. Wojcik p70-83

**Revenue.** See Taxation

**Reviewing (Books)** See Book reviewing

**Revival movements (Art)** See Neoclassicism (Literature)

**Revival of letters.** See Renaissance

**Revolutionary poetry**
Jackson, R. L. Folk forms and formal literature: revolution and the black poet-singer in Ecuador, Peru, and Cuba. *In* Jackson, R. L. Black writers in Latin America p160-70

**Revolutions**
Killian, L. M. The respect revolution: freedom and equality. *In* Propaganda and communication in world history, ed. by H. D. Lasswell, D. Lerner and H. Speier v3 p93-147

Lewy, G. Millenarianism as revolutionary force. *In* Propaganda and communication in world history, ed. by H. D. Lasswell, D. Lerner and H. Speier v2 p168-209

*See also* Coups d'état

**Revolutions and literature.** See Literature and revolutions

**Revolutions in literature**
Paulson, R. Burke's sublime and the representation of revolution. *In* Culture and politics from Puritanism to the Enlightenment, ed. by P. Zagorin p241-69

**Rex, Walter E.**

On the background of Rousseau's First discourse. *In* Studies in eighteenth-century culture v9 p131-50

**Rey, Georges**

Functionalism and the emotions. *In* Explaining emotions, ed. by A. O. Rorty p163-95

**Rhesus monkey**

**Psychology**

Mason, W. A. Maternal attributes and primate cognitive development. *In* Human ethology, ed. by M. von Cranach [and others] p437-55

**Rhetoric**

De Man, P. Rhetoric of tropes (Nietzsche). *In* De Man, P. Allegories of reading p103-18

De Man, P. Semiology and rhetoric. *In* De Man, P. Allegories of reading p3-19

De Man, P. Semiology and rhetoric. *In* Textual strategies, ed. by J. V. Harari p121-40

Ruegg, M. Metaphor and metonymy: the logic of structuralist rhetoric. *In* Glyph 6 p141-57

*See also* Irony; Style, Literary; subdivision Rhetoric under names of languages, e.g. English language—Rhetoric

**1500-1800**

Kristeller, P. O. The Renaissance. *In* Kristeller, P. O. Renaissance thought and its sources p242-59

Manley, L. G. The possibilities of discourse: Renaissance logic, rhetoric, and poetics. *In* Manley, L. G. Convention, 1500-1750 p137-58

**Rhetoric, Ancient**

Kristeller, P. O. Classical antiquity. *In* Kristeller, P. O. Renaissance thought and its sources p217-28

**Rhetoric, Medieval**

Kristeller, P. O. The Middle Ages. *In* Kristeller, P. O. Renaissance thought and its sources p228-42

**Rhys, Jean**

**About**

Dash, C. M. L. Jean Rhys. *In* West Indian literature, ed. by B. King p196-209

**Rice, Charles Duncan**

Literary sources and the revolution in British attitudes to slavery. *In* Anti-slavery, religion, and reform: essays in memory of Roger Anstey, ed. by C. Bolt and S. Drescher p319-34

**Rice, Lee C.**

Homosexuality and the social order. *In* The Philosophy of sex, ed. by A. Soble p256-80

**Rich, Adrienne Cecile**

**About**

Howard, R. Adrienne Rich: "What lends us anchor but the mutable?" *In* Howard, R. Alone with America p493-516

Vendler, H. H. Adrienne Rich. *In* Vendler, H. H. Part of nature, part of us p237-70

Wagner, L. W. Levertov and Rich: the later poems. *In* Wagner, L. W. American modern p221-30

**About individual works**

*Diving into the wreck*

Christ, C. P. Homesick for a woman, for ourselves: Adrienne Rich. *In* Christ, C. P. Diving deep and surfacing p 75-96

*The dream of a common language*

Christ, C. P. Homesick for a woman, for ourselves: Adrienne Rich. *In* Christ, C. P. Diving deep and surfacing p75-96

**Rich, J. Dennis**

Exile without remedy: the late plays of Eugene O'Neill. *In* Eugene O'Neill, ed. by V. Floyd p257-76

**Richard, Gaston**

**About individual works**

*Le socialisme et la science sociale*

Durkheim, E. Review of Gaston Richard, Le socialisme et la science sociale. *In* Durkheim, E. Emile Durkheim on institutional analysis p131-38

**Richards, Ivor Armstrong**

**About**

Krieger, M. The critical legacy of Matthew Arnold; or, The strange brotherhood of T. S. Eliot, I. A. Richards, and Northrop Frye. *In* Krieger, M. Poetic presence and illusion p92-107

**Richardson, Jonathan, 1665-1745**

**About**

Briggs, P. M. The Jonathan Richardsons as Milton critics. *In* Studies in eighteenth-century culture v9 p115-30

**Richardson, Jonathan, 1694-1771**

**About**

Briggs, P. M. The Jonathan Richardsons as Milton critics. *In* Studies in eighteenth-century culture v9 p115-30

**Richardson, Samuel**

**About**

Hagstrum, J. H. Richardson. *In* Hagstrum, J. H. Sex and sensibility p186-218

Wood, J. A. The chronology of the Richardson-Bradshaigh correspondence of 1751. *In* Virginia. University. Bibliographical Society. Studies in bibliography v33 p182-91

**About individual works**

*Clarissa Harlowe*

Miller, N. K. The Misfortunes of virtue: I, Clarissa. *In* Miller, N. K. The heroine's text. p83-95

Todd, J. Sentimental friendship: Samuel Richardson's Clarissa. *In* Todd, J. Women's friendship in literature p9-68

Uphaus, R. W. 'Clarissa,' 'Amelia,' and the state of probation. *In* Uphaus, R. W. The impossible observer p71-88

*Pamela*

Miller, N. K. The rewards of virtue. *In* Miller, N. K. The heroine's text p37-50

**Richelieu, Armand Jean du Plessis, Cardinal, duc de**

Ranum, O. Patronage and history from Richelieu to Colbert. *In* Ranum, O. Artisans of glory p148-68

**Richter, Harvena Conrad**

Hunting the moth: Virginia Woolf and the creative imagination. *In* Virginia Woolf, ed. by R. Freedman p13-28

**Ricks, Christopher**

Clichés. *In* The State of the language, ed. by L. Michaels and C. Ricks p54-63

**Ricoeur, Paul**

Ideology and utopia as cultural imagination. *In* Being human in a technological age, ed. by D. M. Borchert and D. Stewart p107-25

**About**

Kurzweil, E. Paul Ricoeur: hermeneutics and structuralism. *In* Kurzweil, E. The age of structuralism p87-112

**Riddel, Joseph N.**

Decentering the image: the "project" or "American" poetics? *In* Textual strategies, ed. by J. V. Harari p322-58

From Heidegger to Derrida to chance: doubling and (poetic) language. *In* Martin Heidegger and the question of literature, ed. by W. V. Spanos p231-52

Metaphoric staging: Stevens' beginning again of the "end of the book." *In* Wallace Stevens, ed. by F. Doggett and R. Buttel p308-38

**Riddles**

Cook, A. S. The self-enclosure of the riddle. *In* Cook, A. S. Myth & language p225-33

**Ridge, Martin**

Westward movement. *In* Encyclopedia of American economic history, ed. by G. Porter v2 p575-87

**Ridley, Florence H.**

Scottish transformations of courtly literature: William Dunbar and the court of James IV. *In* The Expansion and transformations of courtly literature, ed. by N. B. Smith and J. T. Snow p171-84

**Rieber, Robert W. and Vetter Harold J.**

Theoretical and historical roots of psycholinguistic research. *In* Psychology of language and thought, ed. by R. W. Rieber p3-49

**Riegelhaupt, Joyce Firstenberg.** See Forman, S. jt. auth.

**Riemenschneider, Dieter**

British characters in Indo-English fiction. *In* Aspects of Indian writing in English, ed. by M. K. Naik p137-49

**Riffaterre, Michael**

Generating Lautréamont's text. *In* Textual strategies, ed. by J. V. Harari p404-20

**Rigby, Randall L.** See Fouts, R. S. jt. auth.

**Right (Political science)** See Right and left (Political science)

**Right and left (Political science)**

Falk, R. A. Militarisation and human rights in the Third World. *In* Problems of contemporary militarism, ed. by A. Edie and M. Thee p207-25

Moynihan, D. P. Presenting the American case. *In* Moynihan, D. P. Counting our blessings p41-59

**Right to die**

Motto, J. A. The right to suicide: a psychiatrist's view. *In* Suicide: the philosophical issues, ed. by M. P. Battin and D. J. Mayo p212-19

Slater, E. Choosing the time to die. *In* Suicide: the philosophical issues, ed. by M. P. Battin and D. J. Mayo p199-204

Sullivan, A. A constitutional right to suicide. *In* Suicide: the philosophical issues, ed. by M. P. Battin and D. J. Mayo p229-53

*See also* Euthanasia; Suicide

**Right to labor**

Wilson, C. The right to work. *In* Lying truths, ed. by R. Duncan and M. Weston-Smith p8-9

**Right to work.** See Right to labor

**Rights, Civil.** See Civil rights

**Riley, Anthony W.**

The aftermath of the First World War: Christianity and revolution in Alfred Döblin's November 1918. *In* The First World War in German narrative prose, ed. by C. N. Genno and H. Wetzel p93-117

**Riley, Matilda White**

Aging, social change, and the power of ideas. *In* Generations, ed. by S. R. Graubard p39-52

**Rilke, Rainer Maria**

**About**

Ahler, L. From Angel to Orpheus: mythopoesis in the late Rilke. *In* The Binding of Proteus, ed. by M. W. McCune, T. Orbison and P. M. Withim p197-219

Ashton, D. Rilke in search of the uttermost. *In* Ashton, D. A fable of modern art p48-74

De Man, P. Tropes (Rilke). *In* De Man, P. Allegories of reading p20-56

Holthusen, H. E. The poet and the Lion of Toledo. *In* Rilke: the alchemy of alienation, ed. by F. Baron, E. S. Dick and W. R. Maurer p29-45

Jayne, R. Rilke and the problem of poetic inwardness. *In* Rilke: the alchemy of alienation, ed. by F. Baron, E. S. Dick and W. R. Maurer p191-222

Kaufmann, W. A. Rilke: Nirvana or creation. *In* Rilke: the alchemy of alienation, ed. by F. Baron, E. S. Dick and W. R. Maurer p15-28

Kopelev, L. Z. Rilke and Russia. *In* Rilke: the alchemy of alienation, ed. by F. Baron, E. S. Dick and W. R. Maurer p113-36

Sandor, A. Rilke's and Walter Benjamin's conceptions of rescue and liberation. *In* Rilke: the alchemy of alienation, ed by F. Baron, E. S. Dick and W. R. Maurer p223-42

Simenauer, E. R. M. Rilke's dreams and his conception of dreams. *In* Rilke: the alchemy of alienation, ed. by F. Baron, E. S. Dick and W. R. Maurer p243-62

Strauss, W. A. Rilke and Ponge: l'objet c'est la poétique. *In* Rilke: the alchemy of alienation, ed. by F. Baron, E. S. Dick and W. R. Maurer p63-93

Unseld, S. Rainer Maria Rilke and his publishers. *In* Unseld, S. The author and his publishers p127-89

**About individual works**

*Das Bett*

Warminski, A. Rilke's "Das Bett." *In* Rilke: the alchemy of alienation, ed. by F. Baron, E. S. Dick and W. R. Maurer p151-70

*Duino elegies*

Spender, S. Rilke and Eliot. *In* Rilke: the alchemy of alienation, ed. by F. Baron, E. S. Dick and W. R. Maurer p47-62

*Letters*

Blume, B. Rilke's Letters. *In* Rilke: the alchemy of alienation, ed. by F. Baron, E. S. Dick and W. R. Maurer p3-14

*Pont du Carrousel*

Grundlehner, P. Rainer Maria Rilke: "Pont du Carrousel." *In* Grundlehner, P. The lyrical bridge p109-18

*The notebooks of Malte Laurids Brigge*

Festa-McCormick, D. Rilke's Notebooks: Paris and the phantoms of the past. *In* Festa-McCormick, D. The city as catalyst p69-88

Sokel, W. H. The devolution of the self in The notebooks of Malte Laurids Brigge. *In* Rilke: the alchemy of alienation, ed. by F. Baron, E. S. Dick and W. R. Maurer p171-90

*Der Schwan*

Lehnert, H. Alienation and transformation: Rilke's poem "Der Schwan." *In* Rilke: the alchemy of alienation, ed. by F. Baron, E. S. Dick and W. R. Maurer p95-112

**Rilke, Rainer M.**—About individual works
—*Continued*

### Sonnets to Orpheus

Marshall, D. Reading tasting. *In* Glyph 6 p123-40

### Die Zaren

Rothe, D. Rilke's poetic cycle "Die Zaren." *In* Rilke: the alchemy of alienation, ed. by F. Baron, E. S. Dick and W. R. Maurer p137-50

**Rimbaud, Arthur.** See Rimbaud, Jean Nicolas Arthur

**Rimbaud, Jean Nicolas Arthur**

#### About

Peyre, H. Rimbaud, or the symbolism of revolt. *In* Peyre, H. What is symbolism? p33-47

**Ringel, Erwin**

Suicide prevention and the value of human life. *In* Suicide: the philosophical issues, ed. by M. P. Battin and D. J. Mayo p205-11

**Ringle, Martin**

Philosophy and artificial intelligence. *In* Philosophical perspectives in artificial intelligence, ed. by M. Ringle p 1-20

**Rites and ceremonies**

Dundes, A. Into the endzone for a touchdown: a psychoanalytic consideration of American football. *In* Dundes, A. Interpreting folklore p199-210

Niles, J. D. The Æcerbot ritual in context. *In* Old English literature in context, ed. by J. D. Niles p44-56

*See also* Initiations (in religion, folk-lore, etc.); Ritual

**Rites of passage.** See Rites and ceremonies

**Ritter, Harry**

Science and the imagination in the thought of Schiller and Marx. *In* The Quest for the new science, ed. by K. J. Fink and P. W. Marchand p28-40

**Ritual**

Eibl-Eibesfeldt, I. Ritual and ritualization from a biological perspective. *In* Human ethology, ed. by M. von Cranach [and others] p3-55

*See also* Rites and ceremonies

**Ritual in literature**

Orbison, T. T. Arrabal's The solemn communion as ritual drama. *In* The Binding of Proteus, ed. by M. W. McCune, T. T. Orbison and P. M. Withim p280-96

**Rive, Richard**

#### About individual works

##### Emergency

Obuke, O. O. South African history, politics and literature: Mphahlele's Down Second Avenue, and Rive's Emergency. *In* African literature today no. 10: Retrospect & prospect, ed. by E. D. Jones p191-201

**Rivera, Tomás**

Chicano literature: fiesta of the living. *In* The Identification and analysis of Chicano literature, ed. by F. Jiménez p19-36

**Roa Bastos, Augustus Antonio**

#### About individual works

##### Yo, el Supremo

Martin, G. Yo, el Supremo: the dictator and his script. *In* Contemporary Latin American fiction, ed. by S. Bacarisse p73-87

**Robbe-Grillet, Alain**

#### About individual works

##### Last year at Marienbad

Thiher, A. L'année dernière à Marienbad: the narration of narration. *In* Thiher, A. The cinematic muse p166-79

##### Topology of a phantom city

Mistacco, V. E. The theory and practice of reading nouveaux romans: Robbe-Grillet's Topologie d'une cité fantôme. *In* The Reader in the text, ed. by S. R. Suleiman and I. Crosman p371-400

**Robbins, John Albert**

Bibliographical addendum. *In* American literary scholarship, 1978 p489-93

**Robbins, Rossell Hope**

The Middle English court love lyric. *In* The Interpretation of medieval lyric poetry, ed. by W. T. H. Jackson p205-32

The structure of longer Middle English court poems. *In* Chaucerian problems and perspectives, ed. by E. Vasta and Z. P. Thundy p244-64

**Roberts, Brynley F.**

Historical writing. *In* A Guide to Welsh literature, ed. by A. O. H. Jarman and G. R. Hughes v 1 p244-47

Tales and romances. *In* A Guide to Welsh literature, ed. by A. O. H. Jarman and G. R. Hughes v 1 p203-43

**Roberts, Doreen**

Jane Eyre and 'the warped system of things.' *In* Reading the Victorian novel: detail into form, ed. by I. Gregor p131-49

**Robertson, Durant Waite**

Essays in medieval culture

*Contents*

The allegorist and the aesthetician

Certain theological conventions in Mannyng's treatment of the Commandments

Chaucer's franklin and his tale

Chrétien's Cligés and the Ovidian spirit

The concept of courtly love as an impediment to the understanding of medieval texts

The doctrine of charity in medieval literary gardens: a topical approach through symbolism and allegory

Five poems by Marcabru

Frequency of preaching in thirteenth century England

The "heresy" of the Pearl

Historical criticism

The historical setting of Chaucer's Book of the Duchess

The idea of fame in Chrétien's Cligés

In foraminibus petrae: a note on Leonardo's "Virgin of the rocks"

Love conventions in Marie's Equitan

A medievalist looks at Hamlet

The Partitura amorosa of Jean de Savoie

The Pearl as symbol

Pope and Boethius

The question of typology and the Wakefield Mactacio Abel

Sidney's metaphor of the ulcer

Some disputed Chaucerian terminology

Some medieval literary terminology, with special reference to Chrétien de Troyes

Some observations on method in literary studies

Two poems from the Carmina burana

**Robertson, John D.** See Kanet, R. E. jt. auth.

**Robertson, Roland**

Aspects of identity and authority in sociological theory. *In* Identity and authority, ed. by R. Robertson and B. Holzner p218-65

*See also* Holzner, B. jt. auth.

**Robespierre, Maximilien Marie Isidore de**

About

Barbu, Z. The modern history of political fanaticism: a search for the roots. *In* Propaganda and communication in world history, ed. by H. D. Lasswell, D. Lerner and H. Speier v2 p112-44

**Robin and Marian (Motion picture)**

Kael, P. Suicide is painless. *In* Kael, P. When the lights go down p157-60

**Robinson, Fred C.**

Old English literature in its most immediate context. *In* Old English literature in context, ed. by J. D. Niles p11-29

Two aspects of variation in Old English poetry. *In* Old English poetry, ed. by D. G. Calder p127-45

**Robinson, Frederick Miller**

The comedy of language

*Contents*

Afterword

The comedy of language

Faulkner: As I lay dying

Joyce: Ulysses

Samuel Beckett: Watt

Wallace Stevens: the poet as comedian

**Robinson, Ian**

Parliamentary expressions. *In* The State of the language, ed. by L. Michaels and C. Ricks p64-75

**Robinson, Roland Inwood**

The financing of small business in the United States. *In* Small business in American life, ed. by S. W. Bruchey p280-304

**Robinson, William Peter**

Conceptions of Mozart in eighteenth-century periodical literature. *In* Studies in eighteenth-century culture v9 p151-65

**Robots.** See Automation

**Roche, Daniel**

Talent, reason, and sacrifice: the physician during the Enlightenment. *In* Medicine and society in France, ed. by R. Forster and O. Ranum p66-88

**Rockefeller, Steven C.**

John Dewey: the evolution of a faith. *In* History, religion, and spiritual democracy, ed. by M. Wohlgelernter [and others] p5-34

**Rockefeller Foundation**

Kohler, R. E. Warren Weaver and the Rockefeller Foundation program in molecular biology: a case study in the management of science. *In* The Sciences in the American context: new perspectives, ed. by N. Reingold p249-93

**Rocking chairs in literature**

Aaron, M. A. Garcia Marquez' mecedor as link between passage of time and presence of mind. *In* The Analysis of literary texts, ed. by R. D. Pope p21-30

**Rockoff, Hugh**

Money supply. *In* Encyclopedia of American economic history, ed. by G. Porter v 1 p428-38

**Rocks in art**

Robertson, D. W. In foraminibus petrae: a note on Leonardo's "Virgin of the rocks." *In* Robertson, D. W. Essays in medieval culture p305-07

**Rocky (Motion picture)**

Kael, P. Stallone and Stahr. *In* Kael, P. When the lights go down p213-19

Kauffman, S. Rocky. *In* Kauffmann, S. Before my eyes p264-65

**Rocky II (Motion picture)**

Kauffmann, S. Rocky II. *In* Kauffmann, S. Before my eyes p265-66

**Rococo art.** See Art, Rococo

**Roddick, Nick**

Only the stars survive: disaster movies in the seventies. *In* Performance and politics in popular drama, ed. by D. Bradby, L. James and B. Sharratt p243-69

**Rodriguez, Richard**

An education in language. *In* The State of the language, ed. by L. Michaels and C. Ricks p129-39

**Roelker, Nancy L.**

The impact of the Reformation era on communication and propaganda. *In* Propaganda and communication in world history, ed. by H. D. Lasswell, D. Lerner and H. Speier v2 p41-84

**Roethke, Theodore**

About

Molesworth, C. "Songs of a happy man": the poetry of Theodore Roethke. *In* Molesworth, C. The fierce embrace p21-36

About individual works

*Praise to the end!*

Lewandowska, M. L. The words of their roaring: Roethke's use of the Psalms of David. *In* The David myth in Western literature, ed. by R. J. Frontain and J. Wojcik p156-67

**Rogers, G. A. J.**

The empiricism of Locke and Newton. *In* Royal Institute of Philosophy. Philosophers of the Enlightenment p 1-30

**Rogers, Henry Darwin**

About

Gerstner, P. A. Henry Darwin Rogers and William Barton Rogers on the nomenclature of the American Paleozoic rocks. *In* New Hampshire Bicentennial Conference on the History of Geology, University of New Hampshire, 1976. Two hundred years of geology in America p175-86

**Rogers, Mary Frances**

Goffman on power, hierarchy, and status. *In* The View from Goffman, ed. by J. Ditton p100-33

**Rogers, William Barton**

About

Gerstner, P. A. Henry Darwin Rogers and William Barton Rogers on the nomenclature of the American Paleozoic rocks. *In* New Hampshire Bicentennial Conference on the History of Geology, University of New Hampshire, 1976. Two hundred years of geology in America p175-86

**Rogow, Arnold A.**

Love and intimacy: mass media and phallic culture. *In* Propaganda and communication in world history, ed. by H. D. Lasswell, D. Lerner and H. Speier v3 p148-67

**Rohmer, Eric**

About individual works

*The Marquise of O . . .*

Kauffmann, S. The Marquise of O . . . . . *In* Kauffmann, S. Before my eyes p261-63

**Rohmer, Eric**—About individual works—*Cont.*

*Perceval*

Kauffmann, S. Perceval. *In* Kauffmann, S. Before my eyes p258-61

**Rolfe, Frederick William**

**About**

Pritchett, V. S. Frederick Rolfe: the crab's shell. *In* Pritchett, V. S. The tale bearers p190-94

**Rolle, Andrew F.**

The historic past of the unconscious. *In* Propaganda and communicaion in world history, ed. by H. D. Lasswell, D. Lerner and H. Speier v3 p403-60

**Rolfe, John**

**About**

Miller, P. Religious background of the Bay Psalm book. *In* Miller, P. The responsibility of mind in a civilization of machines p15-25

**Romains, Jules**

**About individual works**

*Death of a nobody*

Festa-McCormick, D. Romain's Death of a nobody: a city's collective soul. *In* Festa-McCormick, D. The city as catalyst p124-40

**Roman de la Rose**

Uitti, K. D. The myth of poetry in twelfth- and thirteenth-century France. *In* The Binding of Proteus, ed. by M. W. McCune, T. Orbison and P. M. Withim p142-56

Wimsatt, J. I. Realism in Troilus and Criseyde and the Roman de la Rose. *In* Essays on Troilus and Criseyde, ed. by M. Salu p43-56

**Roman holiday (Motion picture)**

Kauffmann, S. Roman holiday. *In* Kauffmann, S. Before my eyes p350-56

**Roman literature.** See Latin literature

**Roman philosophy.** See Philosophy, Roman

**Roman propaganda.** See Propaganda, Roman

**Romances**

Bruckner, M. T. Repetition and variation in twelfth-century French romance. *In* The Expansion and transformations of courtly literature, ed. by N. B. Smith and J. T. Snow p95-114

Uitti, K. D. The myth of poetry in twelfth- and thirteenth-century France. *In* The Binding of Proteus, ed. by M. W. McCune, T. Orbison and B. Sharratt p142-56

Vinaver, E. The questioning knight. *In* The Binding of Proteus, ed. by M. W. McCune, T. Orbison and P. M. Withim p126-40

*See also* Epic poetry

**Romances, French.** See Romances

**Romances, Welsh**

Jones, G. E. Early prose: the mabinogi. *In* A Guide to Welsh literature, ed. by A. O. H. Jarman and G. R. Hughes v 1 p189-202

Roberts, B. F. Tales and romances. *In* A Guide to Welsh literature, ed. by A. O. H. Jarman and G. R. Hughes v 1 p203-43

**The romantic Englishwoman (Motion picture)**

Kael, P. Poses. *In* Kael, P. When the lights go down p90-95

**Romanticism**

Bickman, M. One's self I sing: individuation and introjection. *In* Bickman, M. The unsounded centre p38-57

Donato, E. U. Divine agonies: of representation and narrative in romantic poetics. *In* Glyph 6 p90-122

Donoghue, D. Romantic Ireland. *In* Yeats, Sligo and Ireland, ed. by A. N. Jeffares p17-30

Fogle, R. H. Hawthorne's sketches and the English romantics. *In* Toward a new American literary history, ed. by J. L. Budd, E. H. Cady and C. L. Anderson p129-39

Lacoue-Labarthe, P. and Nancy, J. L. Genre. *In* Glyph 7 p 1-14

Mellor, A. K. A conclusion in which nothing is concluded. *In* Mellor, A. K. English romantic irony p185-89

Mellor, A. K. Fear and trembling: from Lewis Carroll to existentialism. *In* Mellor, A. K. English romantic irony p165-84

*See also* Idealism in literature

**England**

James, L. Was Jerrold's Black ey'd Susan more popular than Wordsworth's Lucy? *In* Performance and politics in popular drama, ed. by D. Bradby, L. James and B. Sharratt p3-16

Mellor, A. K. Byron: "half dust, half deity." *In* Mellor, A. K. English romantic irony p31-76

Mellor, A. K. Carlyle's Sartor resartus: a self-consuming artifact. *In* Mellor, A. K. English romantic irony p109-34

Mellor, A. K. Guilt and Samuel Taylor Coleridge. *In* Mellor, A. K. English romantic irony p137-64

Mellor, A. K. Keats and the vale of soul-making. *In* Mellor, A. K. English romantic irony p77-108

Mellor, A. K. The paradigm of romantic irony. *In* Mellor, A K. English romantic irony p3-30

Stone, D. D. Benjamin Disraeli and the romance of the will. *In* Stone, D. D. The romantic impulse in Victorian fiction p74-98

Stone, D. D. Charlotte Brontë and the perils of romance. *In* Stone, D. D. The romantic impulse in Victorian fiction p99-132

Stone, D. D. Death and circuses:: Charles Dickens and the byroads of romanticism. *In* Stone, D. D. The romantic impulse in Victorian fiction p249-83

Stone, D. D. Elizabeth Gaskell, Wordsworth, and the burden of reality. *In* Stone, D. D. The romantic impulse in Victorian fiction p133-72

Stone, D. D. George Eliot: the romantic legacy. *In* Stone, D. D. The romantic impulse in Victorian fiction p173-248

Stone, D. D. George Meredith: a romantic in spite of himself. *In* Stone, D. D. The romantic impulse in Victorian fiction p284-316

Stone, D. D. Introduction. *In* Stone, D. D. The romantic impulse in Victorian fiction p 1-45

Stone, D. D. Trollope, Byron, and the conventionalities. *In* Stone, D. D. The romantic impulse in Victorian fiction p46-73

**Germany**

Hughes, G. T. Background and backbone. *In* Hughes, G. T. Romantic German literature p 1-20

Hughes, G. T. Coda: the Swabians. *In* Hughes, G. T. Romantic German literature p127-30

Hughes, G. T. The legacy of myth: the Grimms, Brentano and Arnim. *In* Hughes, G. T. Romantic German literature p79-97

Hughes, G. T. Natural and supernatural: Eichendorff, with Görres. *In* Hughes, G. T Romantic German literature p98-111

Wohlfarth, I. The politics of prose and the art of awakening: Walter Benjamin's version of a German romantic motif. *In* Glyph 7 p13-48

**United States**

Bickman, M. Afterword. *In* Bickman, M. The unsounded centre p147-49

**Romanticism in art**
Harbison, R. Romantic localism. *In* Harbison, R. Deliberate regression p115-47

**Romanticism in literature.** See Romanticism

**Rome**

### Civilization

Brown, P. R. L. Art and society in late antiquity. *In* Age of spirituality, ed. by K. Weitzmann p17-27

Ferguson, J. Classical civilization. *In* Propaganda and communication in world history, ed. by H. D. Lasswell, D. Lerner and H. Speier v 1 p257-98

### History—Empire, 30 B.C.-476 A.D.— Historiography

Momigliano, A. After Gibbon's Decline and fall. *In* Age of spirituality, ed. by K. Weitzmann p7-16

### Religion

Orr, D. G. Roman domestic religion: the archaeology of Roman popular art. *In* 5000 years of popular culture, ed. by F. E. H. Schroeder p156-72

**Rome (City) in literature**
Festa-McCormick, D. D'Annunzio's Child of pleasure: a city's power of seduction. *In* Festa-McCormick, D. The city as catalyst p49-68

**Rome (City) Santo Stefano Rotondo**
Krautheimer, R. Success and failure in late antique church planning. *In* Age of spirituality, ed. by K. Weitzmann p121-39

**Roncaglia, Alessandro**
The Sraffian contribution. *In* A Guide to post-Keynesian economics, ed. by A. S. Eichner p87-99

**Rönnäng, Bernt O.**
Radio waves from distant galaxies, with applications to geodynamics. *In* The Condition of man, ed. by P. Hallberg p40-58

**Ronnet, Gilberte**

### About individual works

*Sophocle, poète tragique*

Knox, B. M. W. Review of Sophocle, poète tragique (by Gilberte Ronnet). *In* Knox, B. M. W. Word and action p183-93

**Rooster Cogburn (Motion picture)**
Kael, P. Horseplay. *In* Kael, P. When the lights go down p62-68

**Rorrison, Hugh**
The 'Grazer Gruppe', Peter Handke and Wolfgang Bauer. *In* Modern Austrian writing, ed. by A. Best and H. Wolfschütz p252-66

**Rorty, Amélie Oksenberg**
Agent regret. *In* Explaining emotions, ed. by A. O. Rorty p489-506

Explaining emotions. *In* Explaining emotions, ed. by A. O. Rorty p103-26

**Rosa, Enrico**

### About

Daly, G. The integralist response (1): prelude to the Roman condemnation of Modernism. *In* Daly, G. Transcendence and immanence p165-89

**Rose, Christine Brooke-** See Brooke-Rose, Christine

**Roseland (Motion picture)**
Kael, P. The unjoy of sex. *In* Kael, P. When the lights go down p354-58

**Rosen, Gladys**
The rabbi in Miami—a case history. *In* Conference on Southern Jewish History, Richmond, Va. 1976. "Turn to the South" p33-40

**Rosenbaum, Stanford Patrick**
The longest journey: E. M. Forster's refutation of idealism. *In* E. M. Forster: a human exploration, ed. by G. K. Das and J. Beer p32-54

**Rosenberg, Carroll Smith-** See Smith-Rosenberg, Carroll

**Rosenberg, Charles E.**
Rationalization and reality in shaping American agricultural research, 1875-1914. *In* The Sciences in the American context: new perspectives, ed. by N. Reingold p143-63

**Rosenberg, Nathan**
Technology. *In* Encyclopedia of American economic history, ed. by G. Porter v 1 p294-308

**Rosenblatt, Roger**
Black autobiography: life as the death weapon. *In* Autobiography: essays theoretical and critical, ed. by J. Olney p169-80

**Rosenfeld, Alvin Hirsch**
"The being of language and the language of being": Heidegger and modern poetics. *In* Martin Heidegger and the question of literature, ed. by W. V. Spanos p195-213

**Rosenfeld, Paul**
"Van Wyck Brooks": from "Port of New York." *In* Van Wyck Brooks: the critic and his critics, ed. by W. Wasserstrom p11-32

**Rosengarten, Theodore**
Stepping over cockleburs: conversations with Ned Cobb. *In* Telling lives, ed. by M. Pachter p104-31

**Rosenthal, Bernard**
Herman Melville's Wandering Jews. *In* Puritan influences in American literature, ed. by E. Elliott p167-92

**Rosenthal, Bernice Glatzer**
Eschatology and the appeal of revolution: Merezhkovsky, Bely, Blok. *In* California Slavic studies v11 p104-39

**Rosenthal, Erwin Isak Jakob**
Some observatins on Yohanan Alemanno's political ideas. *In* Studies in Jewish religious and intellectual history, ed. by S. Stein and R. Loewe p247-61

**Rosenthal, Lynne**
The development of consciousness in Lucy Boston's The children of Green Knowe. *In* Children's literature v8 p53-67

**Rosenzweig, Franz**
Apologetic thinking. *In* The Jew, ed. by A. A. Cohen p262-72

### About individual works

*The star of redemption*

Glatzer, N. N. Was Franz Rosenzweig a mystic? *In* Studies in Jewish religious and intellectual history, ed. by S. Stein and R. Loewe p121-32

Susman, M. Franz Rosenzweig's The star of redemption (a review) *In* The Jew, ed. by A. A. Cohen p273-85

### Religion

Glatzer, N. N. Was Franz Rosenzweig a mystic? *In* Studies in Jewish religious and intellectual history, ed. by S. Stein and R. Loewe p121-32

Rosinsky, Natalie M.
Mothers and daughters: another minority group. *In* The Lost tradition: mothers and daughters in literature, ed. by C. N. Davidson and E. M. Broner p280-90

Ross, D. S. Carne- See Carne-Ross, D. S.

Ross, Davis R. B. See Eichner, A. S. jt. auth.

Ross, Doran H.
Cement lions and cloth elephants: popular arts of the Fante Asafo. *In* 5000 years of popular culture, ed. by F. E. H. Schroeder p290-317

Ross, Edward Alsworth

About

Fuhrman, E. R.  Edward A. Ross. *In* Fuhrman, E. R. The sociology of knowledge in America, 1883-1915 p159-85

Ross, Marc Howard
Political alienation, participation, and ethnicity in the Nairobi urban area. *In* Values, identities, and national integration, ed. by J. N. Paden p173-81

Ross, Martin, pseud. See Martin, Violet Florence

Ross, Stephen Moodey
Faulkner's Absalom, Absalom! and the David story: a speculative contemplation. *In* The David myth in Western literature, ed. by R. J. Frontain and J. Wojcik p136-53

Ross, Thomas Edward. See Lawrence, Thomas Edward

Rossetti, Christina Georgina

About

Plomer, W. C. F.  Christina Rossetti. *In* Plomer, W. C. F. Electric delights p145-50

Rossetti, Dante Gabriel

About

McGhee, R. D. Rossetti and Meredith. *In* McGhee, R. D. Marriage, duty & desire in Victorian poetry and drama p139-76

Rossini, Gioacchino

About

Carner, M. The mass from Rossini to Dvorák. *In* Carner, M. Major and minor p122-35

Rotenstreich, Nathan
Enlightenment: between Mendelssohn and Kant. *In* Studies in Jewish religious and intellectual history, ed. by S. Stein and R. Loewe p263-79

Roth, Philip
'I always wanted you to admire my fasting', or, Looking at Kafka; excerpt from "Reading myself and others." *In* The World of Franz Kafka, ed. by J. P. Stern p202-22

About

Roth, P.  'I always wanted you to admire my fasting', or, Looking at Kafka; excerpt from "Reading myself and others." *In* The World of Franz Kafka, ed. by J. P. Stern p202-22

Rothbard, Murray Newton
Hoover's 1919 food diplomacy in retrospect. *In* Herbert Hoover, ed. by L. E. Gelfand p87-110

About

Harriss, C. L. Rothbard's anarcho-capitalist critique. *In* Critics of Henry George, ed. by R. V. Andelson p354-70

Rothe, Daria
Rilke's poetic cycle "Die Zaren." *In* Rilke: the alchemy of alienation, ed. by F. Baron, E. S. Dick and W. R. Maurer p137-50

Rothkrug, Lionel
Popular religion and holy shrines. *In* Religion and the people, 800-1700, ed. by J. Obelkevich p20-86

Rothman, Stanley
The mass media in post-industrial society. *In* The Third century, ed. by S. M. Lipset p345-88

Rothstein, Morton
Foreign trade. *In* Encyclopedia of American economic history, ed. by G. Porter v 1 p247-63

Rousseau, Jean Jacques

About

Grimsley, R. Jean-Jacques Rousseau, philosopher of nature. *In* Royal Institute of Philosophy. Philosophers of the Enlightenment p184-98

Hagstrum, J H. Rousseau. *In* Hagstrum, J. H. Sex and sensibility p219-46

Harbison, R. Nature as a child. *In* Harbison, R. Deliberate regression p3-24

Lange, L. Rousseau: women and the general will. *In* The Sexism of social and political theory: women and reproduction from Plato to Nietzsche, ed. by L. M. G. Clark and L. Lange p41-52

Rapaport, E. On the future of love: Rousseau and the radical feminists. *In* The Philosophy of sex, ed. by A. Soble p369-88

Wilson, C. Man is born free, and he is everywhere in chains. *In* Lying truths, ed. by R. Duncan and M. Weston-Smith p3-7

About individual works
*The confessions*

De Man, P. Excuses (Confessions). *In* De Man, P. Allegories of reading p278-301

Spengemann, W. C. Philosophical autobiography. *In* Spengemann, W. C. The forms of autobiography p62-109

*Discourse on the origin and the foundations of inequality among men*

De Man, P. Metaphor (Second discourse) *In* De Man, P. Allegories of reading p135-59

*Discourses on the sciences and arts*

Rex, W. E. On the background of Rousseau's First discourse. *In* Studies in eighteenth-century culture v9 p131-50

*Émile*

Jimack, P. D. The paradox of Sophie and Julie: contemporary response to Rousseau's ideal wife and ideal mother. *In* Woman and society in eighteenth-century France, ed. by E. Jacobs [and others] p152-65

*Julie; or, The new Eloise*

De Man, P. Allegory (Julie) *In* De Man, P. Allegories of reading p188-220

Miller, N. K. The misfortunes of virtue; II, La nouvelle Héloïse. *In* Miller, N. K. The heroine's text p96-115

Todd, J. Manipulative friendship: Jean-Jacques Rousseau's Julie. *In* Todd, J. Women's friendship in literature p132-67

*Narcisse*

De Man, P. Self (Pygmalion). *In* De Man, P. Allegories of reading p160-87

**Rousseau, Jean J.**—About individual works
—*Continued*

*Profession of faith of a Savoyard vicar*

De Man, P. Allegory of reading (Profession de foi). *In* De Man, P. Allegories of reading p221-45

*Pygmalion*

De Man, P. Self (Pygalion) *In* De Man, P. Allegories of reading p160-87

*The social contract*

De Man, P. Promises (Social contract). *In* De Man, P. Allegories of reading p246-77

Shklar, J. Reading The social contract. *In* Powers, possessions and freedom, ed. by A. Kontos p77-88

**Routh, Harold Victor**

### About individual works

*Towards the twentieth century*

Trilling, L. Evangelical criticism. *In* Trilling, L. Speaking of literature and society p113-15

**Rowe, Nicholas**

### Characteres—Calista

Hagstrum, J. H. Woman in love: the abandoned and passionate mistress. *In* Hagstrum, J. H. Sex and sensibility p100-32

**Rowen, Henry S.**

Defense spending and the uncertain future. *In* The Economy in the 1980s: a program for growth and stability, ed. by M. J. Boskin p325-51

The threatened jugular: oil supply of the West. *In* National security in the 1980s: from weakness to strength, ed. by W. S. Thompson p275-94

**Rowlands, Eurys I.**

The continuing tradition. *In* A Guide to Welsh literature, ed. by A. O. H. Jarman and G. R. Hughes v2 p298-320

Cynghanedd, metre, prosody. *In* A Guide to Welsh literature, ed. by A. O. H. Jarman and G. R. Hughes v2 p202-17

Tudur Aled. *In* A Guide to Welsh literature, ed. by A. O. H. Jarman and G. R. Hughes v2 p322-37

**Rowlandson, Thomas**

### About

Paulson, R. Burke's sublime and the representation of revolution. *In* Culture and politics from Puritanism to the Enlightenment, ed. by P. Zagorin p241-69

**Rowse, Alfred Leslie**

### About individual works

*Jonathan Swift*

Pritchett, V. S. Jonathan Swift: the infantilism of genius. *In* Pritchett, V. S. The tale bearers p177-83

**Roxburghe Club, London**

Granniss, R. S. What bibliography owes to private book clubs. *In* The Bibliographical Society of America, 1904-79 p51-70

**Royal Dramatic Theatre, Stockholm**

Olsson, T. O'Neill and the Royal Dramatic. *In* Eugene O'Neill, ed. by V. Floyd p34-60

**Royal flash (Motion picture)**

Kael, P. Living inside a movie. *In* Kael, P. When the lights go down p45-51

**The Royal Shakespeare Theatre Company**

Warren, R. A year of comedies: Stratford 1978. *In* Shakespeare survey 32 p201-09

**Ruach, Leila Tov-** See Tov-Ruach, Leila

**Rubinoff, Lionel**

Vico and the verification of historical interpretation. *In* Conference on Vico and Contemporary Thought, New York, 1976. Vico and contemporary thought pt 1 p94-121

**Rubinstein, Alvin Z.**

The Soviet Union and the Third World. *In* The Soviet Union since Stalin, ed. by S. F. Cohen, A. Rabinowitch, and R. Sharlet p324-31

**Rudd, Niall**

Pyramus and Thisbe in Shakespeare and Ovid: A midsummer night's dream and Metamorphoses 4.1-666. *In* Creative imitation and Latin literature, ed. by D. West and T. Woodman p173-93

**Ruddock, G. E.**

Sion Cent. *In* A Guide to Welsh literature, ed. by A. O. H. Jarman and G. R. Hughes v2 p169-87

**Rudenstein, Gail M.; Kessler, Carol Farley, and Moore, Ann M.**

Mothers and daughters in literature: a preliminary bibliography. *In* The Lost tradition: mothers and daughters in literature, ed. by C. N. Davidson and E. M. Broner p309-22

**Ruderman, Judith G.**

Tracking Lawrence's fox: an account of its composition, evolution, and publication. *In* Virginia. University. Bibliographical Society. Studies in bibliography v33 p206-21

**Ruegg, Maria**

Metaphor and metonymy: the logic of structuralist rhetoric. *In* Glyph 6 p141-57

**Ruggiers, Paul G.**

Serious Chaucer: The tale of Melibeus and The parson's tale. *In* Chaucerian problems and perspectives, ed. by E. Vasta and Z. P. Thundy p83-94

**Ruhe, Edward Lehman**

Pastoral paradigms and displacements, with some proposals. *In* Survivals of pastoral, ed. by R. F. Hardin p103-50

**Rukeyser, Muriel**

### About

Wagner, L. W. Wakoski and Rukeyser. *In* Wagner, L. W. American modern p235-37

**Rules of the game (Motion picture)**

Thiher, A. Jean Renoir and the mimesis of history. *In* Thiher, A. The cinematic muse p92-112

**Rulfo, Juan**

### About individual works

*Luvina*

Foster, D. W. Rulfo's "Luvina" and structuring figures of diction. *In* Foster, D. W. Studies in the contemporary Spanish-American short story p31-38

**Rumbat, Rubén G. and Bittner, Egon**

Changing conceptions of the police role: a sociological review. *In* Crime and justice v 1 p239-88

**Rumbaugh, Duane M.**

Language behavior of apes. *In* Speaking of apes, ed. by T. A. Sebeok and J. Umiker-Sebeok p231-59

*See also* Savage-Rumbaugh, E. S. jt. auth.

**Rumbaugh, E. Sue Savage-** See Savage-Rumbaugh, E. Sue

**Rumford, Beatrix T.**

Uncommon art of the common people: a review of trends in the collecting and exhibiting of American folk art. *In* Perspectives on American folk art, ed. by I. M. G. Quimby and S. T. Swank p13-53

**Runge, Philipp Otto**

### About

Harbison, R. The cult of death. *In* Harbison, R. Deliberate regression p25-62

**Running**

#### Physiological effect

Morowitz, H. J. Bay to Breakers. *In* Morowitz, H. J. The wine of life, and other essays on societies, energy & living things p20-23

**Ruotolo, Lucio P.**

Mrs Dalloway: the unguarded moment. *In* Virginia Woolf, ed. by R. Freedman p141-60

**Rupert of Deutz**

### About

Pickering, F P. Exegesis and imagination: a contribution to the study of Rupert of Deutz. *In* Pickering, F. P. Essays on medieval German literature and iconography p31-45

**Rupp, Leila J.**

"I don't call that Volksgemeinschaft": women, class, and war in Nazi Germany. *In* Women, war, and revolution, ed. by C. R. Berkin and C. M. Lovett p37-53

**Rural life.** See Country life

**Rural-urban migration.** See Urbanization

**Rush, James**

#### About individual works

*Brief outline of an analysis of the human intellect*

Ostwald, P. F. and Rieber, R. W. James Rush and the theory of voice and mind. *In* Psychology of language and thought, ed. by R. W. Rieber p105-19

*The philosophy of the human voice*

Ostwald, P. F. and Bieber, R. W. James Rush and the theory of voice and mind. *In* Psychology of language and thought, ed. by R. W. Rieber p105-19

**Ruskin, John**

#### About

Harbison, R. Religion as art. *In* Harbison, R. Deliberate regression p63-93

Hearn, M. P. Mr Ruskin and Miss Greenaway. *In* Children's literature v8 p22-34

Heinzelman, K. "Unreal words": language in political economy. *In* Heinzelman, K. The economics of the imagination p70-109

#### About individual works

*The king of the Golden River*

Filstrup, J. M. Thirst for enchanted views in Ruskin's The king of the Golden River. *In* Children's literature v8 p68-79

**Russell, Bertrand Russell, 3d Earl**

#### About

Holdcroft, D. From the one to the many: philosophy, 1900-30. *In* The Context of English literature, 1900-1930, ed. by M. Bell p126-59

Hook, S. Bertrand Russell and crimes against humanity. *In* Hook, S. Philosophy and public policy p207-17

**Knowledge, Theory of**

Pears, D. F. A comparison between Ayer's views about the privileges of sense-datum statements and the views of Russell and Austin. *In* Perception and identity, ed. by G. F. Macdonald p61-83

**Russell, Donald Andrew**

De imitatione. *In* Creative imitation and Latin literature, ed. by D. West and T. Woodman p 1-16

**Russia**

#### Armed forces—Appropriations and expenditures

Rowen, H. S. Defense spending and the uncertain future. *In* The Economy in the 1980s: a program for growth and stability, ed. by M. J. Boskin p325-51

#### Constitutional law

Sharlet, R. S. De-Stalinization and Soviet constitutionalism. *In* The Soviet Union since Stalin, ed. by S. F. Cohen, A. Rabinowitch, and R. Sharlet p93-110

#### Defenses

Costick, M. M. Soviet military posture and strategic trade. *In* National security in the 1980s: from weakness to strength, ed. by W. S. Thompson p189-213

Nunn, S. Defense budget and defense capabilities. *In* National security in the 1980s: from weakness to strength, ed. by W. S. Thompson p375-95

Rowen, H. S. Defense spending and the uncertain future. *In* The Economy in the 1980s: a program for growth and stability, ed. by M. J. Boskin p325-51

Zumwalt, E. R. Heritage of weakness: an assessment of the 1970s. *In* National security in the 1980s: from weakness to strength, ed. by W. S. Thompson p17-51

#### Economic conditions—1918

Taaffe, R. N. Soviet regional development. *In* The Soviet Union since Stalin, ed. by S. F. Cohen; A. Rabinowitch, and R. Sharlet p155-76

#### Economic policy—1917-

Hardt, J. P. Stages in Soviet economic development: a sixty-year record. *In* Economic issues of the eighties, ed. by N. M. Kamrany and R. H. Day p199-225

Wright, A. W. Soviet economic planning and performance. *In* The Soviet Union since Stalin, ed. by S. F. Cohen; A. Rabinowitch, and R. Sharlet p113-34

#### Foreign economic relations—United States

Costick, M. M. Soviet military posture and strategic trade. *In* National security in the 1980s: from weakness to strength, ed. by W. S. Thompson p189-213

#### Foreign relations

Gati, C. The Stalinist legacy in the Soviet foreign policy. *In* The Soviet Union since Stalin, ed. by S. F. Cohen; A. Rabinowitch, and R. Sharlet p279-301

Rubenstein, A. Z. The Soviet Union and the Third World. *In* The Soviet Union since Stalin, ed. by S. F. Cohen, A. Rabinowitch and R. Sharlet p324-31

Zimmerman, W. The Soviet Union and the West. *In* The Soviet Union since Stalin, ed. by S. F. Cohen, A Rabinowicht and R Sharlet p305-11

**Russia**—*Continued*

### Foreign relations—Africa

Albright, D. E. Moscow's African policy of the 1970s. *In* Communism in Africa, ed. by D. E. Albright p35-66

Gonzalez, E. Cuba, the Soviet Union, and Africa. *In* Communism in Africa, ed. by D. E. Albright p145-67

Legum, C. African outlooks toward the USSR. *In* Communism in Africa, ed. by D. E. Albright p7-34

Thompson, W. S. The African-American nexus in Soviet strategy. *In* Communism in Africa, ed. by D. E. Albright p189-218

Wilson, E. T. Russia's historic stake in black Africa. *In* Communism in Africa, ed. by D. E. Albright p67-92

### Foreign relations—Angola

Valenta, J. Soviet decision-making on the intervention in Angola. *In* Communism in Africa, ed. by D. E. Albright p93-117

### Foreign relations—Europe, Eastern

Kanet, R. E. and Robertson, J. D. The Soviet Union and Eastern Europe. *In* The Soviet Union since Stalin, ed by S. F. Cohen, A. Rabinowitch and R. Sharlet p312-23

### Foreign relations—United States

Burt, R. R. Washington and the Atlantic alliance: the hidden crisis. *In* National security in the 1980s: from weakness to strength, ed. by W. S. Thompson p109-21

Marshall, C. B. Strategy: the emerging dangers. *In* National security in the 1980s: from weakness to strength, ed. by W. S. Thompson p423-41

Moynihan, D. P. Pacem in terris. *In* Moynihan, D. P. Counting our blessings p60-71

Nitze, P. H. Policy and strategy from weakness. *In* National security in the 1980s: from weakness to strength, ed. by W. S. Thompson p443-56

Zumwalt, E. R. Heritage of weakness: an assessment of the 1970s. *In* National security in the 1980s: from weakness to strength, ed. by W. S. Thompson p17-51

### History—Philosophy

Gellner, E. A Russian Marxist philosophy of history. *In* Soviet and Western anthropology, ed. by E. Gellner p59-82

### History—Revolution, 1917-1921—Civilian relief

Trani, E. P. Herbert Hoover and the Russian Revolution, 1917-20. *In* Herbert Hoover, ed. by L. E. Gelfand p111-42

### History—Revolution, 1917-21—Influence

Farnsworth, B. B. Communist feminism: its synthesis and demise. *In* Women, war, and revolution, ed. by C. R. Berkin and C. M. Lovett p145-63

### Military policy

Hoeber, A. M. and Douglass, J. D. Soviet approach to global nuclear conflict. *In* The United States in the 1980s, ed. by P. Duignan and A. Rabushka p445-67

Rowen, H. S. Defense spending and the uncertain future. *In* The Economy in the 1980s: a program for growth and stability, ed. by M. J. Boskin p325-51

Welch, C. Broken eggs, but no omelete: Russia before the Revolution. *In* Lying truths, ed. by R. Duncan and M. Weston-Smith p47-60

### Politics and government—1917-

Hoffmann, E. P. Changing Soviet perspectives on leadership and administration. *In* The Soviet Union since Stalin, ed. by S. F. Cohen, A. Rabinowitch and R. Sharlet p71-92

### Politics and government—1936-1953

Medvedev, R. A. The Stalin question. *In* The Soviet Union since Stalin, ed. by S. F. Cohen, A. Rabinowitch and R. Sharlet p32-49

### Politics and government—1953-

Cohen, S. F. The friends and foes of change: reformism and conservatism in the Soviet Union. *In* The Soviet Union since Stalin, ed. by S. F. Cohen, A. Rabinowitch and R. Sharlet p11-31

### Relations (general) with Africa

Yu, G. T. Sino-Soviet rivalry in Africa. *In* Communism in Africa, ed. by D. E. Albright p168-88

### Relations (general) with the United States

Staar, R. F. Soviet Union. *In* The United States in the 1980s, ed. by P. Duignan and A. Rabushka p735-55

### Religion

Basilov, V. The study of religions in Soviet ethnography. *In* Soviet and Western anthropology, ed. by E. Gellner p231-42

### Social conditions—History

Welch, C. Broken eggs, but no omelete: Russia before the Revolution. *In* Lying truths, ed. by R. Duncan and M. Weston-Smith p47-60

### Social conditions—1945

Bushnell, J. D. The "new Soviet man" turns pessimist. *In* The Soviet Union since Stalin, ed. by S. F. Cohen, A. Rabinowitch and R. Sharlet p 179-99

**Russia in literature**

Rothe, D. Rilke's poetic cycle "Die Zaren." *In* Rilke: the alchemy of alienation, ed. by F. Baron, E. S. Dick and W. R. Maurer p137-50

**Russian fiction**

### 20th century—History and criticism

Hosking, G. The Socialist realist tradition. *In* Hosking, G. Beyond Socialist realism p1-28

Hosking, G. Village prose: Vasily Belov, Valentin Rasputin. *In* Hosking, G. Beyond Socialist realism p50-83

Shneidman, N. N. The Soviet literary scene. *In* Shneidman, N. N. Soviet literature in the 1970s: artistic diversity and ideological conformity p3-31

**Russian literature**

### To 1700—History and critcism

Grossman, J. D. Feminine images in Old Russian literature and art. *In* California Slavic studies v11 p33-70

### 20th century—History and criticism

Gibian, G. New aspects of Soviet Russsian literature. *In* The Soviet Union since Stalin, ed. by S. F. Cohen, A. Rabinowitch and R Sharlet p252-75

Slaughter, C. Literature and revolution: Trotsky. *In* Slaughter, C. Marxism, ideology & literature p86-113

**Rutherford, Reuben Clifford**

About individual works

*Henry George versus Henry George*

Collier, C. F. Rutherford: the Devil quotes scripture. *In* Critics of Henry George, ed. by R. V. Andelson p222-33

**Ruthwell Cross.** See Dumfriesshire, Scotland. Ruthwell Cross

**Rutledge, Joyce S.**

The delayed reflex: journalism in Josephinian Vienna. *In* Studies in eighteenth-century culture v9 p79-92

**Rutman, Anita H.** See Rutman, D. B. jt. auth.

**Rutman, Darrett B. and Rutman, Anita H.**

"Now-wives and sons-in-law": parental death in a seventeenth-century Virginia county. *In* The Chesapeake in the seventeenth century, ed. by T. W. Tate and D. L. Ammerman p153-82

**Ryan, John Augustine**

About individual works

*Distributive justice*

Andelson, R. V. Ryan and his domestication of natural law. *In* Critics of Henry George, ed. by R. V. Andelson p342-53

# S

**SALT.** See Strategic Arms Limitation Talks

**Sábato, Ernesto R.**

About individual works

*Abaddón, el exterminador*

Bacarisse, S. Abaddón, el exterminador: Sabato's gnostic eschatology. *In* Contemporary Latin American fiction, ed. by S. Bacarisse p88-109

**Sabin, Joseph**

About individual works

*A dictionary of books relating to America, from its discovery to the present time*

Vail, R. W. G. Sabin's Dictionary. *In* The Bibliographical Society of America, 1904-79 p117-25

**Sachs, Nelly**

About

Alexander, E. Holocaust and rebirth: Moshe Flinker, Nelly Sachs, and Abba Kovner. *In* Alexander, E. The resonance of dust p31-71

About individual works

*Landscape of screams*

Bosmajian, H. Towards the point of constriction: Nelly Sachs's "Landschaft aus Schreien" and Paul Celan's "Engführung." *In* Bosmajian, H. Metaphors of evil p183-228

**Sackville-West, Hon. Victoria Mary**

About

Love, J. O. Orlando and its genesis: venturing and experimenting in art, love, and sex. *In* Virginia Woolf, ed. by R. Freedman p188-218

**Sacred art.** See Christian art and symbolism

**Sacred music.** See Church music

**Sacrifice**

Morowitz, H. J. Sacred cows and sacrificial guinea pigs. *In* Morowitz, H. J. The wine of life, and other essays on societies, energy & living things p129-32

**Saddlemyer, Ann**

The dwarf—dramas of the early Abbey Theatre. *In* Yeats, Sligo and Ireland, ed. by A. N. Jeffares p197-215

**Sade, Donatien Alphonse François, comte, called marquis de**

About individual works

*Juliette*

Todd, J. Manipulative friendship: the Marquis de Sade's Juliette. *In* Todd, J. Women's friendship in literature p168-90

**Safety regulations.** See Industrial safety—Law and legislation

**Saggs, Henry William Frederick**

Pre-exilic Jewry. *In* The Jewish world, ed. by E. Kedourie p37-51

**Said, Edward W.**

The text, the world, the critic. *In* Textual strategies, ed. by J. V. Harari p161-88

**Saiko, George**

About

Williams, C. E. George Saiko: worlds within world. *In* Modern Austrian writing, ed. by A. Best and H. Wolfschütz p97-107

**Saine, Thomas P.**

Gotthold Ephraim Lessing's views on theological issues as reflected in his early book reviews. *In* Studies in eighteenth-century culture v9 p269-84

**St Francis, Order of.** See Franciscans

**Saint-Just, Louis Antoine Léon de**

About

Barbu, Z. The modern history of political fanaticism: a search for the roots. *In* Propaganda and communication in world history, ed. by H. D. Lasswell, D. Lerner and H. Speier v2 p112-44

**Saints**

*See also* Relics and reliquaries

Legends

Jankofsky, K. P. Entertainment, edification and popular education in the South English legendary. *In* 5000 years of popular culture, ed. by F. E. H. Schroeder p214-25

**Sakharov, Andrei Dmitrievich**

Thoughts on progress, peaceful coexistence and intellectual freedom. *In* Propaganda and communication in world history, ed by H. D. Lasswell, D. Lerner and H. Speier v2 p471-506

**Salazar Parr, Carmen**

Current trends in Chicano literary criticism. *In* The Identification and analysis of Chicano literature, ed. by F. Jiménez p134-42

**Sale, Roger H.**

Baum's magic powder of life. *In* Children's literature v8 p157-63

About individual works

*Fairy tales and after: from Snow White to E. B. White*

Nodelman, P. Defining children's literature. *In* Children's literature v8 p184-90

**Sales promotion.** See Advertising

**Salinas, Judy**
  The role of women in Chicano literature. *In* The Identification and analysis of Chicano literature, ed. by F. Jiménez p191-240

**Salinger, Jerome David**

### About individual works
#### *The catcher in the rye*
  Dessner, L. J. The Salinger story, or, Have it your way. *In* Seasoned authors for a new season: the search for standards in popular writing, ed. by L. Filler p91-97

**Salmon, Marylynn**
  "Life, liberty, and dower": the legal status of women after the American Revolution. *In* Women, war, and revolution, ed. by C. R. Berkin and C. M. Lovett p85-106

**Salò (Motion picture)**
  Kauffmann, S. Salò. *In* Kauffmann, S. Before my eyes p296-98

**Saloutos, Theodore**
  Farmers' movements. *In* Encyclopedia of American economic history, ed. by G. Porter v2 p562-74

**Salsbury, Stephen Michael**
  American business institutions before the railroad. *In* Encyclopedia of American economic history, ed. by G. Porter v2 p601-18

**Salt in animal nutrition**
  Morowitz, H. J. Lox et veritas. *In* Morowitz, H. J. The wine of life, and other essays on societies, energy & living things p256-61

**Salting of food**
  Morowitz, H. J. Lox et veritas. *In* Morowitz, H. J. The wine of life, and other essays on societies, energy & living things p256-61

**Salutations.** See Forms of address

**Salzen, Eric A.**
  Social attachment and a sense of security. *In* Human ethology, ed. by M. von Cranach [and others] p595-622

**Salzman, Jack**
  Fiction: the 1930s to the 1950s. *In* American literary scholarship, 1978 p247-82

**Samuel Beckett: the critical heritage, ed. by Lawrence Graver and Raymond Federman**
  Pilling, J. Samuel Beckett: the critical heritage, edited by Lawrence Graver and Raymond Federman. *In* Drama and mimesis, ed. by J. Redmond p243-47

**Samuel, Raphael**
  Workers' theatre, 1926-36. *In* Performance and politics in popular drama, ed. by D. Bradby, L. James and B. Sharratt p213-30

**Samuels, Marwyn S.**
  The biography of landscape: cause and culpability. *In* The Interpretation of ordinary landscapes, ed. by D. W. Meinig p51-88

**Sandars, Nancy K.**
  The religious development of some early societies. *In* The Origins of civilization, ed. by P. R. S. Moorey p103-27

**Sandburg, Carl**

### About individual works
#### *Rootabaga stories*
  Lynn, J. L. Hyacinths and biscuits in the village of liver and onions: Sandburg's Rootabaga stories. *In* Children's literature v8 p118-32

**Sander, Reinhard W.**
  The thirties and forties. *In* West Indian literature, ed. by B. King p45-62

**Sandor, Andras**
  Rilke's and Walter Benjamin's conceptions of rescue and liberation. *In* Rilke: the alchemy of alienation, ed. by F. Baron, E. S. Dick and W. R. Maurer p223-42

**Sansom, William**
  Short stories, personally speaking. *In* Royal Society of Literature of the United Kingdom, London. Essays by divers hands: innovation in contemporary literature, new ser. v40 p132-46

### About
  Sansom, W. Short stories, personally speaking. *In* Royal Society of Literature of the United Kingdom, London. Essays by divers hands: innovation in contemporary literature, new ser. v40 p132-46

**Santayana, George**

### About
  Martin, J. A. The esthetic, the religious, and the natural. *In* History, religion, and spiritual democracy, ed. by M. Wolhgelernter [and others] p76-91

### About individual works
#### *The life of reason*
  Greenlee, D. Santayana and the ideal of reason. *In* History, religion, and spiritual democracy, ed. by M. Wohlgelernter [and others] p203-30

**Santo Stefano Rotondo.** See Rome (City) Santo Stefano Rotondo

**The saphead (Motion picture)**
  Kauffmann, S. The saphead. *In* Kauffmann, S. Before my eyes p52

**Sapir-Whorf hypothesis**
  Stam, J. H. An historical perspective on 'linguistic relativity.' *In* Psychology of language and thought, ed. by R. W. Rieber p239-62

**Sapiro, Virginia**
  Women's studies and political conflict. *In* The Prism of sex, ed. by J. A. Sherman and E. T. Beck p253-65

**Sapolsky, Harvey M.**
  Academic science and the military: the years since the Second World War. *In* The Sciences in the American context: new perspectives, ed. by N. Reingold p379-99

**Sarduy, Severo**

### About individual works
#### *De donde son los cantantes*
  Ghertman, S. Language as protagonist in Sarduy's De donde son los cantantes: a linguistic approach to narrative structure. *In* The Analysis of literary texts, ed. by R. D. Pope p145-52

**Sarna, Nahum M.**
  The psalm superscriptions and the guilds. *In* Studies in Jewish religious and intellectual history, ed. by S. Stein and R. Loewe p281-300

**Sartre, Jean Paul**

### About
  Collins, D. Proteus and the rat trap. *In* Collins, D. Sartre as biographer p31-59
  Collins, D. The tribunal of crabs. *In* Collins, D. Sartre as biographer p195-201
  Collins, D. Truth and alterity. *In* Collins, D. Sartre as biographer p 1-30
  Lentricchia, F. Versions of existentialism. *In* Lentricchia, F. After the New Criticism p28-60

Sartre, Jean P.—About—*Continued*
Macdonald, I. R. Magical eclecticism: Los pasos perdidos and Jean-Paul Sartre. *In* Contemporary Latin American fiction, ed. by S. Bacarisse p 1-17

### About individual works
*Baudelaire*
Collins, D. Baudelaire and bad faith. *In* Collins, D. Sartre as biographer p60-79

*Being and nothingness*
Oaklander, L. N. Sartre on sex. *In* The Philosophy of sex, ed. by A. Soble p190-206
Taylor, R. J. Sexual experiences. *In* The Philosophy of sex, ed. by A. Soble p59-75

*L'Idiot de la famille: Gustave Flaubert de 1821-1857*
Collins, D. Flaubert and the objective neurosis. *In* Collins, D. Sartre as biographer p151-83
Collins, D. Flaubert and the subjective neurosis. *In* Collins, D. Sartre as biographer p111-50

*Nausée*
Kellman, S. G. La nausée. *In* Kellman, S. G. The self-begetting novel p32-48

*Saint Genêt, actor and martyr*
Collins, D. Genet and the just. *In* Collins, D. Sartre as biographer p80-110

*The words*
Collins, D. The dialectic of narcissism. *In* Collins, D. Sartre as biographer p184-94

Sastri, P. S.
Philosophical ideas of Swami Vivekananda. *In* Aspects of Indian writing in English, ed. by M. K. Naik p294-304

Satire
Anselment, R. A. John Milton contra Hall. *In* Anselment, R. A. 'Betwixt jest and earnest' p61-93
Anselment, R. A. The Marprelate tracts. *In* Anselment, R. A. 'Betwixt jest and earnest' p33-60
Anselment, R. A. The rehearsal transpros'd. *In* Anselment, R. A. 'Betwixt jest and earnest' p94-125
Anselment, R. A. A tale of a tub. *In* Anselment, R. A. 'Betwixt jest and earnest' p126-62
Levin, H. T. The wages of satire. *In* Literature and society, ed. by E. W. Said p 1-14
Seidel, M. A. A house divided: Marvell's last instructions and Dryden's Absalom and Achitophel. *In* Seidel, M. A. Satiric inheritance, Rabelais to Sterne p135-68
Seidel, M. A. The revisionary inheritance: Rabelais and Cervantes. *In* Seidel, M. A. Satiric inheritance, Rabelais to Sterne p60-94
Seidel, M. A. The satiric dispensation. *In* Seidel, M. A. Satiric inheritance, Rabelais to Sterne p5-25

Saturday night fever (Motion picture)
Kael, P. Nirvana. *In* Kael, P. When the lights go down p367-71
Kauffmann, S. Saturday night fever/Blue collar. *In* Kauffmann, S. Before my eyes p226-30

Saul, King of Israel
#### Poetry
Flinker, N. Saul and David in the early poetry of Yehuda Amichai. *In* The David myth in Western literature, ed. by R. J. Frontain and J. Wojcik p170-78

Saussure, Ferdinand de
#### About
Lentricchia, F. Uncovering history and the reader: structuralism. *In* Lentricchia, F. After the New Criticism p102-54

Sauvy, Alfred
#### About
Braudel, F. Demography and the scope of the human sciences. *In* Braudel, F. On history p132-61

Savage-Rumbaugh, E. Sue; Rumbaugh, Duane M. and Boysen, Sally
Linguistically mediated tool use and exchange by chimpanzees (Pan troglodytes) *In* Speaking of apes, ed. by T. A. Sebeok and J. Umiker-Sebeok p353-83

Saving and investment
#### United States—History
Davis, L. E. Savings and investment. *In* Encyclopedia of American economic history, ed. by G. Porter v 1 p183-201

Saving and thrift. See Saving and investment

Sawyer, Amos C.
Social stratification and national orientations: students and nonstudents in Liberia. *In* Values, identities, and national integration, ed. by J. N. Paden p285-303
Social stratification, social change, and political socialization: students and nonstudents in Liberia. *In* Values, identities, and national integration, ed. by J. N. Paden p305-20

Sayre, Kenneth M.
The simulation of epistemic acts. *In* Philosophical perspectives in artificial intelligence, ed. by M. Ringle p139-60

Sayre, Robert F.
Autobiography and the making of America. *In* Autobiography: essays theoretical and critical, ed. by J. Olney p146-68

Scadding, John L.
Inflation: a perspective from the 1970s. *In* The Economy in the 1980s: a program for growth and stability, ed. by M. J. Boskin p53-81

Scalapino, Robert Anthony
Asia. *In* The United States in the 1980s, ed. by P. Duignan and A. Rabushka p661-706

Scandella, Domenico
Ginzburg, C. Cheese and worms. *In* Religion and the people, 800-1700, ed. by J. Obelkevich p87-167

Scandinavian Americans. See Norwegian Americans

Scapegoat in literature
Vickery, J. B. The scapegoat in literature: some kinds and uses. *In* The Binding of Proteus, ed. by M. W. McCune, T. Orbison and P. M. Withim p264-78

Scarlatti, Alessandro
#### About
Dent, E. J. A pastoral opera by Alessandro Scarlatti. *In* Dent, E. J. Selected essays p250-60

Scase, Richard
Introduction. *In* The State in Western Europe, ed. by R. Scase p11-22

Scenery. See Landscape

Scenes from a marriage (Motion picture)
Kauffmann, S. Scenes from a marriage. *In* Kauffmann, S. Before my eyes p66-69

Scepticism. See Skepticism

Scève, Maurice

### About

Perry, T. A. Pernette du Guillet's poetry of love and desire. *In* Perry, T. A. Erotic spirituality p53-67

### About individual works
*Délie*

Perry, T. A. Délie! an old way of dying (the meaning of Scève's title) *In* Perry, T. A. Erotic spirituality p35-43

Perry, T. A. Return and reincarnation in Scève's Délie. *In* Perry, T. A. Erotic spirituality p44-52

Schachter, Oscar

Rhetoric and law in international political organs. *In* Propaganda and communication in world history, ed. by H. D. Lasswell, D. Lerner and H. Speier v2 p446-57

Schaeffle, Albert Eberhard Friedrich. See Schäffle, Albert Eberhard Friedrich

Schäffle, Albert Eberhard Friedrich

### About individual works
*Bau und Leben des sozialen Körpers*

Durkheim, E. Review of Albert Schaeffle, Bau und Leben des sozialen Körpers: erster Band. *In* Durkheim, E. Emile Durkheim on institutional analysis p93-114

Schank, Roger C.

Natural language, philosophy, and artificial intelligence. *In* Philosophical perspectives in artificial intelligence, ed. by M. Ringle p196-224

Schapiro, Meyer

Selected papers v3: Late antique, early Christian and mediaeval art

*Contents*

Ancient mosaics in Israel: late antique art—pagan, Jewish, Christian

The angel with the ram in Abraham's sacrifice: a parallel in Western and Islamic art

The Beatus Apocalypse of Gerona

The Bird's Head Haggada, an illustrated Hebrew manuscript of ca. 1300

The bowman and the bird on the Ruthwell Cross and other works: the interpretation of secular themes in early mediaeval religious art

"Cain's jawbone that did the first murder"

The Carolingian copy of the Calendar of 354

The decoration of the Leningrad manuscript of Bede

The frescoes of Castelseprio

An illuminated English psalter of the early thirteenth century

The image of the disappearing Christ

An Irish-Latin text on the angel with the ram in Abraham's sacrifice

The Joseph scenes on the Maximianus throne in Ravenna

Marginal images and drôlerie

"Muscipula diaboli," the symbolism of the Mérode altarpiece

A note on the Mérode altarpiece

A note on the wall strips of Saxon churches

Notes on Castelseprio

On an Italian painting of the Flagellation of Christ in the Frick Collection

The place of Ireland in Hiberno-Saxon art

The place of the Joshua Roll in Byzantine history

The religious meaning of the Ruthwell Cross

Schechter, Harold

The eye and the nerve: a psychological reading of James Dickey's Deliverance. *In* Seasoned authors for a new season: the search for standards in popular writing, ed. by L. Filler p4-19

Scheiber, Harry N.

Law and political institutions. *In* Encyclopedia of American economic history, ed. by G. Porter v2 p487-508

Scheick, William J.

The jawbones schema of Edward Taylor's Gods determinations. *In* Puritan influences in American literature, ed. by E. Elliott p38-54

Literature to 1800. *In* American literary scholarship, 1978 p181-97

Scheinberg, Susan

The bee maidens of the Homeric Hymn to Hermes. *In* Harvard Studies in classical philology v83 p 1-28

Schiller, Johann Christoph Friedrich von

### About

Ashton, R. D. Caryle and German philosophy (1824-34) *In* Ashton, R. D. The German idea p91-98

Bennett, B. The importance of being Egmont. *In* Bennett, B. Modern drama and German classicism p151-87

Ritter, H. Science and the imagination in the thought of Schiller and Marx. *In* The Quest for the new science, ed. by K. J. Fink and J. W. Marchand p28-40

### About individual works
*The bride of Messina*

Mueller, M. Oedipus Rex as tragedy of fate: Corneille's Oedipe and Schiller's Die Braut von Messina. *In* Mueller, M. Children of Oedipus, and other essays on the imitation of Greek tragedy 1550-1800 p129-46

*Mary Stuart*

Bennett, B. Schiller's theoretical impasse and Maria Stuart. *In* Bennett, B. Modern drama and German classicism p188-228

Schism, The Great Western, 1378-1417

Ozment, S. H. The ecclesiopolitical traditions. *In* Ozment, S. H. The age of reform, 1250-1550 p135-81

Schizophrenics

### Language

Deleuze, G. The schizophrenic and language: surface and depth in Lewis Carroll and Antonin Artaud. *In* Textual strategies, ed. by J. V. Harari p277-95

Schlee, Susan B. See Burstyn, H. L. jt. auth.

Schlegel, August Wilhelm von

### About

Hughes, G. T. Profusion and order: the brothers Schlegel. *In* Hughes, G. T. Romantic German literature p41-60

Schlegel, Friedrich von

### About

Hughes, G. T. Profusion and order: the brothers Schlegel. *In* Hughes, G. T. Romantic German literature p41-60

Mellor, A. K. The paradigm of romantic irony. *In* Mellor, A. K. English romantic irony p3-30

### About individual works
*Dialogue on poetry*

Lacoue-Labarthe, P. and Nancy, J. L. Genre. *In* Glyph 7 p 1-14

**Schmandt-Besserat, Denise**
An archaic recording system prior to writing. *In* 5000 years of popular culture, ed. by F. E. H. Schroeder p19-35

**Schmidt, Royal J.**
Hoover's reflections on the Versailles Treaty. *In* Herbert Hoover, ed. by L. E. Gelfand p61-86

**Schneider, Herbert Wallace**
Morality as an art. *In* Humanist ethics, ed. by M. B. Storer p98-103

**Schoenbaum, Samuel**
Shakespeare's Dark Lady: a question of identity. *In* Shakespeare's styles, ed. by P. Edwards, I. S. Ewbank and G. K. Hunter p221-39

**Schoenberg, Arnold.** See Schönberg, Arnold

**Schofield, Malcolm**
Preconception, argument, and God. *In* Doubt and dogmatism, ed. by M. Schofield, M. Burnyeat and J. Barnes p283-308

**Scholars.** See Women scholars

**Scholarship.** See Learning and scholarship

**Scholasticism**
Daly, G. Roman fundamental theology in the last quarter of the nineteenth century. *In* Daly, G. Transcendence and immanence p7-25

Kristeller, P. O. Humanism and scholasticism in the Italian Renaissance. *In* Kristeller, P. O. Renaissance thought and its sources p85-105

Ozment, S. H. The scholastic traditions. *In* Ozment, S. H. The age of reform, 1250-1550 p22-72

**Schönberg, Arnold**

**About**

Ashton, D. Arnold Schoenberg's ascent. *In* Ashton, D. A fable of modern art p96-120

**Schönfeld, Solomon J.**
A Hebrew source for 'The merchant of Venice.' *In* Shakespeare survey 32 p115-28

**Schor, Naomi A.**
Fiction as interpretation/interpretation as fiction. *In* The Reader in the text, ed. by S. R. Suleiman and I. Crosman p165-82

**Schorske, Carl Emil**
Generational tension and cultural change: reflections on the case of Vienna.' *In* Generations, ed. by S. R. Graubard p111-22

**Schotz, Myra Glazer**
The great unwritten story: mothers and daughters in Shakespeare. *In* The Lost tradition: mothers and daughters in literature, ed. by C. N. Davidson and E. M. Broner p44-54

**Schrade, Arlene O.**
Sex shock: the humanistic woman in the super-industrial society. *In* Monster or messiah? Ed. by W. M. Mathews p72-86

**Schramm, Wilbur Lang**
The effects of mass media in an information era. *In* Propaganda and communication in world history, ed. by H. D. Lasswell, D. Lerner and H. Speier v3 p295-345

**Schrecker, John E.**
The Reform movement of 1898 and the Meiji Restoration as ch'ing-i movements. *In* The Chinese and the Japanese, ed. by A. Iriye p96-106

**Schreiner, Olive**

**About**

Plomer, W. C. F. Olive Schreiner. *In* Plomer, W. C. F. Electric delights p113-17

**Schroeder, Fred E. H.**
The discovery of popular culture before printing. *In* 5000 years of popular culture, ed. by F. E. H. Schroeder p4-15

Popular culture methodologies: a bibliographic afterword. *In* 5000 years of culture, ed. by F. E. H. Schroeder p319-25

**Schubert, Franz Peter**

**About**

Carner, M. Schubert's orchestral music. *In* Carner, M. Major and minor p21-39

Dent, E. J. The style of Schubert. *In* Dent, E. J. Selected essays p133-41

**Schulenburg, Jane Alice Tibbetts**
Clio's European daughters: myopic modes of perception. *In* The Prism of sex, ed. by J. A. Sherman and E. T. Beck p33-53

**Schulz, Max F.**
Coleridge and the enchantments of earthly paradise. *In* Reading Coleridge, ed. by W. B. Crawford p116-59

**Schumann, Robert**

**About**

Carner, M. Mahler's re-scoring of the Schumann symphonies. *In* Carner, M. Major and minor p71-84

Carner, M. Schumann as symphonist. *In* Carner, M. Major and minor p60-70

**Schürman, Reiner**
Situating René Char: Hölderlin, Heidegger, Char and the "there is." *In* Martin Heidegger and the question of literature, ed. by W. V. Spanos p173-94

**Schuster, John A.**
Descartes' mathesis universalis: 1619-28. *In* Descartes, ed. by S. Gaukroger p41-96

**Schütze, Martin**

**About individual works**
*Academic illusions in the field of letters and the arts*
Trilling, L. The autonomy of the literary work. *In* Trilling, L. Speaking of literature and society p85-88

**Schwadron, Abraham**
The dogma of the eternal Galut: a cardinal issue in Zionist ideology. *In* The Jew, ed. by A. A. Cohen p112-19

**Schwartz, Murray M.**
Shakespeare through contemporary psychanalysis. *In* Representing Shakespeare, ed. by M. M. Schwartz and C. Kahn p21-32

**Schwartz, Richard B.**
Berkeley, Newtonian space, and the question of evidence. *In* Probability, time, and space in eighteenth-century literature, ed. by P. R. Backscheider p259-273

**Schwartz, Jack.** See Schwartzman, Jacob

**Schwartzman, Jacob**
Ingalls, Hanson, and Tucker: nineteenth-century American anarchists. *In* Critics of Henry George, ed. by R. V. Andelson p234-53

**Schwarz-Bart, André**

**About individual works**
*The last of the just*
Alexander, E. The Holocaust and the God of Israel. *In* Alexander, E. The resonance of dust p195-230

**Schwoerer, Lois G.**
The Bill of rights: epitome of the Revolution of 1688-89. *In* Three British revolutions: 1641, 1688, 1776, ed. by J. G. A. Pocock p224-43

**Schyfter, Sara E.**

Rites without passage: the adolescent world of Ana Maria Moix's Julia. *In* The Analysis of literary texts, ed. by R. D. Pope p41-50

**Science**

*See also* Chemistry

**History**

Goetzmann, W. H. Paradigm lost. *In* The Sciences in the American context: new perspectives, ed. by N. Reingold p21-34

**History—United States**

Post, R. C. Science, public policy, and popular precepts: Alexander Dallas Bache and Alfred Beach as symbolic adversaries. *In* The Sciences in the American context: new perspectives, ed. by N. Reingold p77-98

Reingold, N. Reflections on 200 years of science in the United States. *In* The Sciences in the American context: new perspectives, ed. by N. Reingold p9-20

Sinclair, B. Americans abroad: science and cultural nationalism in the early nineteenth century. *In* The Sciences in the American context: new perspectives, ed. by N. Reingold p35-53

**International cooperation**

Sinclair, B. Americans abroad: science and cultural nationalism in the early nineteenth century. *In* The Sciences in the American context: new perspectives, ed. by N. Reingold p35-53

**Methodology**

Cottrell, Sir A. Science is objective. *In* Lying truths, ed. by R. Duncan and M. Weston-Smith p159-69

Lyttleton, R. A. The Gold effect. *In* Lying truths, ed. by R. Duncan and M. Weston-Smith p181-98

Piattelli-Palmarini, M. Introduction: How hard is the "hard core" of a scientific program? *In* Language and learning, ed. by M. Piattelli-Palmarini p 1-20

**Philosophy**

Cottrell, Sir A. Science is objectives. *In* Lying truths, ed. by R. Duncan and M. Weston-Smith p159-69

Lyttleton, R. A. The Gold effect. *In* Lying truths, ed. by R. Duncan and M. Weston-Smith p181-98

Osler, M. J. Certainty, scepticism, and scientific optimism: the roots of eighteenth-century attitudes toward scientific knowledge. *In* Probability, time, and space in eighteenth-century literature, ed. by P. R. Backscheider p3-28

*See also* Naturalism

**Research**

*See* Research

**Social aspects**

Lasswell, H. D. Must science serve political power? *In* Propaganda and communication in world history, ed. by H. D. Lasswell, D. Lerner and H. Speier v3 p3-15

Malmström, B. G. Ethical implications of enzyme technology. *In* The Condition of man, ed. by P. Hallberg p162-69

**Study and teaching (Higher)—History**

Guralnick, S. M. The American scientist in higher education, 1820-1910. *In* The Sciences in the American context: new perspectives, ed. by N. Reingold p99-141

**Great Britain—History**

Rattansi, P. M. The scientific background. *In* The Age of Milton, ed. by C. A. Patrides and R B. Waddington p197-240

**Greece—History**

Dover, K.J. Classical science and philosophy. *In* Ancient Greek literature, ed. by K.J. Dover p105-21

**United States—History**

Reich, L. S. Science. *In* Encyclopedia of American economic history, ed. by G. Porter v 1 p281-93

**Science, Applied.** See Technology

**Science, Social.** See Sociology

**Science Advisory.** See United States. President's Science Advisory Committee

**Science and ethics**

Morowitz, H. J. Who are the standard bearers? *In* Morowitz, H. J. The wine of life, and other essays on societies, energy & living things p217-20

**Science and industry.** See Research, Industrial

**Science and literature.** See Literature and science

**Science and religion.** See Religion and science

**Science and society.** See Science—Social aspects

**Science and state**

Lasswell, H. D. Must science serve political power? *In* Propaganda and communication in world history, ed. by H. D. Lasswell, D. Lerner and H. Speier v3 p3-15

*See also* Technology and state

**United States**

Wiesner, J. B. The marriage of science and government. *In* Propaganda and communication in world history, ed. by H. D. Lasswell, D. Lerner, and H. Speier v3 p16-36

**Science and the humanites**

Berlin, Sir I. The divorce between the sciences and the humanities. *In* Berlin, Sir I. Against the current p80-110

**Science policy.** See Science and state

**Science research.** See Research

**Science teachers**

**United States**

Guralnick, S. M. The American scientist in higher education, 1820-1910. *In* The Sciences in the American context: new perspectives, ed. by N. Reingold p99-141

**Sciences, Social.** See Social sciences

**Scientific American**

Post, R. C. Science, public policy, and popular precepts: Alexander Dallas Bache and Alfred Beach as symbolic adversaries. *In* The Sciences in the American context: new perspectives, ed. by N. Reingold p77-98

**Scientific bureaus.** See Science and state; subdivision Scientific bureaus under names of countries, e.g. United States—Scientific bureaus

**Scientific bureaus.** See United States—Scientific bureaus

**Scientific errors.** See Errors, Scientific

**Scientific expeditions**

Goetzmann, W. H. Paradigm lost. *In* The Sciences in the American context: new perspectives, ed. by N. Reingold p21-34

**Scientific literature**

Klebs, A. C. Gleanings from incunabula of science and medicine. *In* The Bibliographical Society of America, 1904-79 p71-107

Scientific method. See Science—Methodology

Scientific research. See Research

Scientific voyages. See Scientific expeditions

Scientists
  *See also* Ecologists: Science teachers

### Great Britain
Sinclair, B. Americans abroad: science and cultural nationalism in the early nineteenth century. *In* The Sciences in the American context: new perspectives, ed. by N. Reingold p35-53

### United States
Sinclair, B. Americans abroad: science and cultural nationalism in the early nineteenth century. *In* The Sciences in the American context: new perspectives, ed. by N. Reingold p35-53

Scodel, Ruth
  ΑΔΜΗΤΟΥ ΛΟΓΟΣ and the alcestis. *In* Harvard Studies in classical philology, v83 p51-62

Scorcese, Martin

#### About individual works
*Taxi driver*
Kauffmann, S. Taxi driver. *In* Kauffmann, S. Before my eyes p200-03

Scotland

### Intellectual life
Emerson, R. L. American Indians, Frenchmen, and Scots philosophers. *In* Studies in eighteenth-century culture v9 p211-36

Scott, Franklin Daniel
  Peter Lassen: Danish pioneer of California, 1800-1859. *In* Makers of an immigrant legacy, ed. by O. S. Lovoll p186-209

Scott, Nathan A.
  Black literature. *In* Harvard Guide to contemporary American writing, ed. by D. Hoffman p287-341

Scott, Sir Walter, bart.

#### About
Stone, D. D. Introduction. *In* Stone, D. D. The romantic impulse in Victorian fiction p 1-45

#### About individual works
*The bride of Lammermoor*
Farrell, J. P. Scott: the implicit note of tragedy. *In* Farrell, J. P. Revolution as tragedy p69-129

*The heart of Midlothian*
Farrell, J. P. Scott: the implicit note of tragedy. *In* Farrell, J. P. Revolution as tragedy p69-129

*Old Mortality*
Farrell, J. P. Scott: the implicit note of tragedy. *In* Farrell, J. P. Revolution as tragedy p69-129

#### Political and social views
Farrell, J. P. Scott: the implicit note of tragedy. *In* Farrell, J. P. Revolution as tragedy p69-129

Scottish poetry

### To 1700—History and criticism
Kratzmann, G. Influences and perspectives, *In* Kratzmann, G. Anglo-Scottish literary relations, 1430-1550 p 1-32
Kratzmann, G. The two traditions. *In* Kratzmann, G. Anglo-Scottish literary relations, 1430-1550 p227-61

Scragg, Donald George
  The corpus of vernacular homilies and prose saints' lives before Ælfric. *In* Anglo-Saxon England 8 p223-77

Screen writers

### Language
Harwood, R. The language of screenwriting. *In* The State of the language, ed. by L. Michaels and C. Ricks p290-96

Scripture, Edward Wheeler

#### About individual works
*Elements of experimental phonetics*
Black, J. W. Edward Wheeler Scripture, phonetician. *In* Psychology of language and thought, ed. by R. W. Rieber p225-38

Scrutiny
  Wright, I. F. R. Leavis, the Scrutiny movement and the crisis. *In* Culture and crisis in Britain in the thirties, ed. by J. Clark [and others] p37-65

Scruton, Roger
  Emotion, practical knowledge and common culture. *In* Explaining emotions, ed. by A. O. Rorty p519-36

Scully, Terence Peter
  The sen of Chrétien de Troyes's Joie de la cort. *In* The Expansion and transformations of courtly literature, ed. by N. B. Smith and J. T. Snow p71-94

Sea-floor spreading
  Frankel, H. Why drift theory was accepted with the confirmation of Harry Hess's concept of sea-floor spreading. *In* New Hampshire Bicentennial Conference on the History of Geology, University of New Hampshire, 1976. Two hundred years of geology in America p337-53
  *See also* Plate tectonics

Sea in literature
  Caws, M. A. On one crossing-over: Valery's sea into Hart Crane's scene. *In* The Analysis of literary texts, ed. by R. D. Pope p100-06

Searle, Geoffrey Russell
  Critics of Edwardian society: the case of the Radical Right. *In* The Edwardian age: conflict and stability, 1900-1914, ed. by A. O'Day p79-96

Seaton, Jean, and Pimlott, Ben
  The role of the media in the Portuguese revolution. *In* Newspapers and democracy, ed. by A. Smith p174-99

Sebeok, Thomas Albert
  Looking in the destination for what should have been sought in the source. *In* Speaking of apes, ed. by T. A. Sebeok and J. Umiker-Sebeok p407-27
  *See also* Umiker-Sebeok, J. jt. auth.

Secret service. See Intelligence service

Secularism
  Wiener, M. Secularized religion. *In* The Jew, ed. by A. A. Cohen p215-22

Secularization (Theology). See Secularism

Securities exchange. See Stock-exchange

Security (Psychology)
  Salzen, E. A. Social attachment and a sense of security. *In* Human ethology, ed. by M. von Cranach [and others] p595-622

Security, International. See Peace

Sedition law, 1798. See Alien and Sedition laws, 1798

**Sedley, David**
The protagonists. *In* Doubt and dogmatism, ed. by M. Schofield, M. Burnyeat and J. Barnes p 1-19

**The seduction of Mimi (Motion picture)**
Kauffmann, S. The seduction of Mimi. *In* Kauffmann, S. Before my eyes p19-20

**Seelye, John**
A well-wrought Crockett: or, How the fakelorists passed through the credibility gap and discovered Kentucky. *In* Toward a new American literary history, ed. by L. J. Budd, E. H. Cady and C. L. Anderson p91-110

**Segal, Walter**
The housing crisis in Western Europe: Britain—assessment and options. *In* Architecture for people, ed. by B. Mikellides p171-75

**Segel, Elizabeth**
Domesticity and the wide, wide world. *In* Children's literature v8 p168-75

**Segerstedt, Torgny Torgnysson**
The condition of man in post-industrial society. *In* The Condition of man, ed. by P. Hallberg p152-60

**Seiber, Mátyás**

### About individual works
*Ulysses*

Carner, M. Mátyás Seiber and his Ulysses. *In* Carner, M. Major and minor p172-82

**Seibt, K. Michael**
Einfühlung, language, and Herder's philosophy of history. *In* The Quest for the new science, ed. by K. J. Fink and J. W. Marchand p17-27

**Seidel, Michael A.**
Satiric inheritance, Rabelais to Sterne
*Contents*
Fathers and sons: Swift's A tale of a tub
Gravity's inheritable line: Sterne's Tristram Shandy
A house divided: Marvell's Last instructions and Dryden's Absalom and Achitophel
Inheritance and narrative mode
The internecine romance: Butler's Hudibras
The revisionary inheritance: Rabelais and Cervantes
The satiric dispensation
Strange dispositions: Swift's Gulliver's travels
Things unborn: Pope's The rape of the lock and The Dunciad

**Seigel, Jules Paul**
The perceptible and the imperceptible: Diderot's speculation on language in his Letters on the deaf and blind. *In* Psychology of language and thought, ed. by R. W. Rieber p91-102

**Selby, Hopewell**
"Never finding full repast:" satire and self-extension in the early eighteenth century. *In* Probability, time, and space in eighteenth-century literature, ed. by P. R. Backscheider p217-47

**Selection, Natural.** See Natural selection

**Self**
Bennett, B. The assault upon the audience: types of modern drama. *In* Bennett, B. Modern drama and German classicism p282-314
Bennett, B. Egmont and the maelstrom of the self. *In* Bennett, B. Modern drama and German classicism p121-50

Kavolis, V. Logics of selfhood and modes of order: civilizational structures for individual identities. *In* Identity and authority, ed. by R. Robertson and B. Holzner p40-62
*See also* Identity (Psychology); Individuality; Will

**Self (Philosophy)**
Foster, J. In self-defence. *In* Perception and identity, ed. by G. F. Macdonald p161-85
Wollheim, R. Memory, experiential memory, and personal identity. *In* Perception and identity, ed. by G. F. Macdonald p186-234
Wyschogrod, E. Martin Buber and the no-self perspective. *In* History, religion, and spiritual democracy, ed. by M. Wohlgelernter [and others] p130-50

**Self-actualization (Psychology)**
Giele, J. Z. Adulthood as transcendence of age and sex. *In* Themes of work and love in adulthood, ed. by N. J. Smelser and E. H. Erikson p151-73
Kohn, M. L. Job complexity and adult personality. *In* Themes of work and love in adulthood, ed. by N. J. Smelser and E. H. Erikson p193-210

**Self-deception**
Sousa, E. Self-deceptive emotions. *In* Explaining emotions, ed. by A. O. Rorty p283-97

**Self-destruction.** See Suicide

**Self-determination, National.** See Sovereignty

**Self-fulfillment.** See Self-realization

**Self-government.** See Democracy; Representative government and representation

**Self in literature**
Sokel, W. H. The devolution of the self in The notebooks of Malte Laurids Brigge. *In* Rilke: the alchemy of alienation, ed. by F. Baron, E. S. Dick and W. R. Maurer p171-90

**Self-love (Psychology)** See Narcissim

**Self medication**
Morowitz, H. J. Change four sparkplugs and take two aspirin. *In* Morowitz, H. J. The wine of life, and other essays on societies, energy & living things p137-40

**Self-perception.** See Self-deception

**Self-portraits**
Howarth, W. L. Some principles of autobiography. *In* Autobiography: essays theoretical and critical, ed. by J. Olney p84-114

**Self-realization**
Marković, M. Historical praxis as the ground of morality. *In* Humanist ethics, ed. by M. B. Storer p36-57

**Self-realization (Psychology)** See Self-actualization (Psychology)

**Self-sacrifice**
Martin, R. M. Suicide and self-sacrifice. *In* Suicide: the philosophical issues, ed. by M. P. Battin and D. J. Mayo p48-68

**Self-service (Economics)**
Morowitz, H. J. Change four sparkplugs and take two aspirin. *In* Morowitz, H. J. The wine of life, and other essays on societies, energy & living things p137-40

**Seligman, Edwin Robert Anderson**

### About individual works
*Essays in taxation*

Andelson, R. V. and Gaffney, M. Seligman and his critique from social utility. *In* Critics of Henry George, ed. by R. V. Andelson p273-90

**Selling.** See Advertising; Marketing

**Selvon, Samuel**

### About

Fabre, M. H. Samuel Selvon. *In* West Indian literature, ed. by B. King p111-25

**Semantics**

Maranda, P. The dialectic of metaphor: an anthropological essay on hermeneutics. *In* The Reader in the text, ed. by S. R. Suleiman and I. Crosman p183-204

*See also* Ambiguity; Connotation (Linguistics)

**Semantics (Philosophy)**

Lear, J. Going native. *In* Generations, ed. by S. R. Graubard p175-88

*See also* Communication

**Semenov, Yu. I.**

The theory of socio-economic formations and world history. *In* Soviet and Western anthropology, ed. by E. Gellner p29-58

**Semiotics**

Holloway, J. Conclusion: structure and the critic's art. *In* Holloway, J. Narrative and structure: exploratory essays p100-17

Holloway, J. Effectively complete enumeration in 'Phèdre.' *In* Holloway, J. Narrative and structure: exploratory essays p20-37

Holloway, J. Identity, inversion and density elements in narrative: three tales by Chekhov, James and Lawrence. *In* Holloway, J. Narrative and structure: exploratory essays p53-73

Holloway, J. Logic, feeling and structure in nineteenth-century political oratory: a primer of analysis. *In* Holloway, J. Narrative and structure: exploratory essays p137-56

Holloway, J. Narrative process in 'Middlemarch.' *In* Holloway, J. Narrative and structure: exploratory essays p38-52

Holloway, J. Narrative structure and text structure: Isherwood's A meeting by the river and Muriel Spark's The prime of Miss Jean Brodie. *In* Holloway, J. Narrative and structure: exploratory essays p74-99

Holloway, J. Poetic analysis and the idea of the transformation-rule: some examples from Herbert, Wordsworth, Pope and Shakespeare. *In* Holloway, J. Narrative and structure: exploratory essays p118-36

Holloway, J. Supposition and supersession: a model of analysis for narrative structure. *In* Holloway, J. Narrative and structure: exploratory essays p 1-19

Sperber, D. Remarks on the lack of positive contributions from anthropologists to the problem of innateness. *In* Language and learning, ed. by M. Piattelli-Palmarini p245-49

*See also* Structuralism (Literary analysis)

**Semiotics and literature**

De Man, P. Semiology and rhetoric. *In* Textual strategies, ed. by J. V. Harari p121-40

*Also in* De Man, P. Allegories of reading p3-19

Frank, M. The infinite text. *In* Glyph 7 p70-101

Marshall, D. G. The ontology of the literary sign: notes toward a Heideggerian revision of semiology. *In* Martin Heidegger and the question of literature, ed. by W. V. Spanos p271-94

**Semi-tough (Motion picture)**

Kael, P. Drip-dry comedy. *In* Kael, P. When the lights go down p358-63

**Semmingsen, Ingrid**

A pioneer: Agnes Mathilde Wergeland, 1857-1914. *In* Makers of an American immigrant legacy, ed. by O. S. Lovoll p111-30

**Sen, Amartya Kumar**

Informational analysis of moral principles. *In* Rational action, ed. by R. Harrison p115-32

**Senegal**

### Foreign relations—Gambia

Bayo, K. Environment and national system formation: Gambian orientations toward Senegambia. *In* Values, identities, and national integration, ed. by J. N. Paden p105-19

**Senghaas, Dieter**

Militarism dynamics in the contemporary context of periphery capitalism. *In* Problems of contemporary militarism, ed. by A. Eide and M. Thee p195-206

**Senn, Fritz**

Bloom among the orators: the why and the wherefore and all the codology. *In* Irish Renaissance annual I p168-90

**Sennett, Richard**

Destructive Gemeinschaft. *In* The Philosophy of sex, ed. by A. Soble p299-321

**Sense data**

Armstrong, D. M. Perception, sense data and causality. *In* Perception and identity, ed. by G. F. Macdonald p84-98

Pears, D. F. A comparison between Ayer's views about the privileges of sense-datum statements and the views of Russell and Austin. *In* Perception and identity, ed. by G. F. Macdonald p61-83

Taylor, C. Sense data revisited. *In* Perception and identity, ed. by G. F. Macdonald p99-112

**Senses and sensation.** See Perception; Sense data; Sensuality; Vision

**Sensuality**

Singer, I. The sensuous and the passionate. *In* The Philosophy of sex, ed. by A. Soble p209-31

**Sentimentalism in literature**

Hagstrum, J. H. Sentimental love and marriage "esteem enliven'd by desire." *In* Hagstrum, J. H. Sex and sensibility p160-85

**Sepamla, Sydney Sipho**

### About individual works

*The Soweto I love*

February, V. Sipho Sepamla: The Soweto I love. *In* African literature today no. 10, ed.: Retrospect & prospect, by E. D. Jones p256-58

**Separation of powers**

### United States

Moynihan, D. P. The iron law of emulation. *In* Moynihan, D. P. Counting our blessings p115-37

**Sepulchral monuments**

### Pennsylvania

Weiser, F. S. Baptismal certificate and gravemarker: Pennsylvania German folk art at the beginning and the end of life. *In* Perspective on American folk art, ed. by I. M. G. Quimby and S. T. Swank p134-61

**Serban, Andrei**

### About

Knox, B. M. W. Review of Agamemnon (directed by Andrei Serban). *In* Knox, B. M. W. Word and action p70-78

**Serbocroatian poetry**

Coote, M. P. The singer's themes in Serbocroatian heroic song. *In* California Slavic studies v11 p201-35

**Serialized fiction**
### Great Britain
Andrews, M. A note on serialisation. *In* Reading the Victorian novel: detail into form, ed. by I. Gregor p243-47

**Sermons, Medieval**
Huttar, C. A. Frail grass and firm tree: David as a model of repentance in the Middle Ages and Early Renaissance. *In* The David myth in Western literature, ed. by R. J. Frontain and J. Wojcik p38-54

**Serna, Concha Espina de.** See Espina de Serna, Concha

**The serpent's egg (Motion picture)**
Kael, P. More torment, or When they broke the silence. *In* Kael, P. When the lights go down p38-92

Kauffmann, S. The serpent's egg. *In* Kauffmann, S. Before my eyes p76-79

**Serpents in literature**
Hatto, A. T. Snake-swords and boar-helms in Beowulf. *In* Hatto, A. T. Essays on medieval German and other poetry p233-54

**Serra, José Maria**
Three mistaken theses regarding the connection between industrialization and authoritarian regimes. *In* The New authoritarianism in Latin America, ed. by D. Collier p99-163

**Serres, Michel**
The algebra of literature: the wolf's game. *In* Textual strategies, ed. by J. V. Harari p260-76

**Servants, Indentured.** See Indentured servants

**Service industries**
### United States—History
Weiss, T. J. Service sector. *In* Encyclopedia of American economic history, ed. by G. Porter v 1 p413-23

**Sevčenko, Ihor**
A shadow outline of virtue: the classical heritage of Greek Christian literature (second to seventh century) *In* Age of spirituality, ed. by K. Weitzmann p53-73

**Seven beauties (Motion picture)**
Kauffmann, S. Seven beauties. *In* Kauffmann, S. Before my eyes p23-28

Kael, P. Seven fatties. *In* Kael, P. When the lights go down p135-40

**The seven-per-cent solution (Motion picture)**
Kael, P. The hundred-per-cent solution. *In* Kael, P. When the lights go down p190-95

Kauffmann, S. The seven-per-cent solution. *In* Kauffmann, S. Before my eyes p252-53

**Sevilla-Guzman, Eduardo.** See Giner, S. jt. auth.

**Seville**
### Commerce
Braudel, F. Toward a serial history: Seville and the Atlantic, 1504-1650. *In* Braudel, F. On history p91-104

**Sewall, Richard Benson**
The vision of tragedy
(See note in: List of books indexed)
*Contents*
Absalom, Absalom!
The Book of Job
The brothers Karamazov
Doctor Faustus
Dostoevski to Faulkner
King Lear
Long day's journey into night
Moby-Dick

Oedipus the King
The scarlet letter
Tragedy and Christianity
Tragedy and the modern world
The tragic form
The trial
The vision of tragedy

**Sewell, William Hamilton**
Property, labor, and the emergence of socialism in France, 1789-1848. *In* Consciousness and class experience in nineteenth-century Europe, ed. by J. M. Merriman p45-63

**Sex**
Berger, F. R. Pornography, sex and censorshop. *In* The Philosophy of sex, ed. by A. Soble p322-47

Fortunate, J. Masturbation and women's sexuality. *In* The Philosophy of sex, ed. by A. Soble p389-408

Goldman, A. H. Plain sex. *In* The Philosophy of sex, ed. by A. Soble p119-38

Gray, R. Sex and sexual perversion. *In* The Philosophy of sex, ed. by A. Soble p158-68

Ketchum, S. A. The good, the bad and the perverted: sexual paradigms revisited. *In* The Philosophy of sex, ed. by A. Soble p139-57

Moulton, J. M. Sexual behavior: another position. *In* The Philosophy of sex, ed. by A. Soble p110-18

Nagel, T. Sexual perversion. *In* The Philosophy of sex, ed. by A. Soble p76-88

Oaklander, L. N. Sartre on sex. *In* The Philosophy of sex, ed. by A. Soble p190-206

Soble, A. An introduction to the philosophy of sex. *In* The Philosophy of sex, ed. by A. Soble p 1-56

Solomon, R. C. Sexual paradigms. *In* The Philosophy of sex, ed. by A. Soble p89-98

Taylor, R. J. Sexual experiences. *In* The Philosophy of sex, ed. by A. Soble p59-75

Wilder, H. T. The language of sex and the sex of language. *In* The Philosophy of sex, ed. by A. Soble p99-109

*See also* Homosexuality; Sex customs

### Psychological aspects
*See* Sex (Psychology)

### Statistics
*See* Vital statistics

**Sex (Psychology)**
Falvey, J. Women and sexuality in the thought of La Mettrie. *In* Woman and society in eighteenth-century France, ed. by E. Jacobs and others p55-68

Gendron, B. Sexual alienation. *In* The Philosophy of sex, ed. by A. Soble p281-98

Singer, I. The sensuous and the passionate. *In* The Philosophy of sex, ed. by A. Soble p209-31

*See also* Sex difference (Psychology); Sex role

**Sex and religion**
Erickson, G. Possession, sex and hysteria; the growth of demonism in later antiquity. *In* 5000 years of popular culture, ed. by F. E. H. Schroeder p110-35

**Sex bias.** See Sexism

**Sex customs**
### United States
Rogow, A. A. Love and intimacy: mass media and phallic culture. *In* Propaganda and communication in world history, ed. by H. D. Lasswell, D. Lerner and H. Speier v3 p148-67

**Sex differences (Psychology)**

Sherif, C. W. Bias in psychology. *In* The Prism of sex, ed. by J. A. Sherman and E. T. Beck p93-133

*See also* Sex role

**Sex in literature**

Hagstrum, J. H. Richardson. *In* Hagstrum, J. H. Sex and sensibility p186-218

Hagstrum, J. H. Rousseau. *In* Hagstrum, J. H. Sex and sensibility p219-46

Rees, D. Not even for a one-night stand. *In* Rees, D. The marble in the water p173-84

Renoir, A. The inept lover and the reluctant mistress: remarks on sexual inefficiency in medieval literature. *In* Chaucerian problems and perspectives, ed. by E. Vasta and Z. P. Thundy p180-206

Wilde, A. The naturalisation of Eden. *In* E. M. Forster: a human exploration, ed. by G. K. Das and J. Beer p196-207

*See also* Incest in literature; Love in literature

**Sex in mass media**

Rogow, A. A. Love and intimacy: mass media and phallic culture. *In* Propaganda and communication in world history, ed. by H. D. Lasswell, D. Lerner and H. Speier v3 p148-67

**Sex in the arts.** See Sex in mass media

**Sex perversion.** See Sexual deviation

**Sex role**

Beidelman, T. O. Women and men in two East African societies. *In* Explorations in African systems of thought, ed. by I. C. Karp & C. S. Bird p143-64

Burns, S. A. M. The Humean female. *In* The Sexism of social and political theory: women and reproduction from Plato to Nietzsche, ed. by L. M. G. Clark and L. Lange p53-60

Clark, L. M. G. Women and Locke: who owns the apples in the Garden of Eden? *In* The Sexism and political theory: women and reproduction from Plato to Nietzsche, ed. by L. M. G. Clark and L. Lange p16-40

Cott, N. F. Passionlessness: an interpretation of Victorian sexual ideology, 1790-1850. *In* A Heritage of her own, ed. by N. F. Cott and E. H. Pleck p162-81

Ferguson, A. Androgyny as an ideal for human development. *In* The Philosophy of sex, ed. by A. Soble p232-55

La Barre, W. Anthropological perspectives on sexuality. *In* La Barre, W. Culture in context p141-62

Lange, L. The function of equal education in Plato's Republic and Laws. *In* The Sexism of social and political theory: women and reproduction from Plato to Nietzsche, ed. by L. M. G. Clark and L. Lange p3-15

Lange, L. Rousseau: women and the general will. *In* The Sexism of social and political theory: women and reproduction from Plato to Nietzsche, ed. by L. M. G. Clark and L. Lange p41-52

Marcil-Lacoste, L. Hume's method in moral reasoning. *In* The Sexism of social and political theory: women and reproduction from Plato to Nietzsche, ed. by L. M. G. Clark and L. Lange p60-73

Mills, P. J. Hegel and 'the woman question': recognition and intersubjectivity. *In* The Sexism of social and political theory: women and reproduction from Plato to Nietzsche, ed. by L. M. G. Clark and L. Lange p74-98

O'Brien, M. Reproducing Marxist man. *In* The Sexism of social and political theory: women and reproduction from Plato to Nietzsche, ed. by L. M. G. Clark and L. Lange p99-116

Schulenburg, J. A. T. Clio's European daughters: myopic modes of perception. *In* The Prism of sex, ed. by J. A. Sherman and E. T. Beck p33-53

Stimpson, C. R. Ad/d feminam: women, literature, and society. *In* Literature and society, ed. by E. W. Said p174-92

*See also* Sexism

**Sex symbolism**

Smith, C. F. The invention of sex in myth and literature. *In* The Binding of Proteus, ed. by M. W. McCune, T. Orbison and P. M. Withim p252-62

**Sexism**

Bernard, J. S. Afterword. *In* The Prism of sex, ed. by J. A. Sherman and E. T. Beck p267-75

Clark, L. M. G. Women and Locke: who owns the apples in the Garden of Eden? *In* The Sexism of social and political theory: women and reproduction from Plato to Nietzsche, ed. by L. M. G. Clark and L. Lange p16-40

Dundes, A. The crowing hen and the Easter bunny: male chauvinism in American folklore. *In* Dundes, A. Interpreting folklore p160-75

Marcil-Lacoste, L. Hume's method in moral reasoning. *In* The Sexism of social and political theory: women and reproduction from Plato to Nietzsche, ed. by L. M. G. Clark and L. Lange p60-73

Mills, P. J. Hegel and 'the woman question': recognition and intersubjectivity. *In* The Sexism of social and political theory: women and reproduction from Plato to Nietzsche, ed. by L. M. G. Clark and L. Lange p74-98

Parsons, K. J. P. Moral revolution. *In* The Prism of sex, ed. by J. A. Sherman and E. T. Beck p189-227

Sherif, C. W. Bias in psychology. *In* The Prism of sex, ed. by J. A. Sherman and E. T. Beck p93-133

*See also* Sex role

### Political aspects

Elshtain, J. B. Methodological sophistication and conceptual confusion: a critique of mainstream political science. *In* The Prism of sex, ed. by J. A. Sherman and E. T. Beck p229-52

Sapiro, V. Women's studies and political conflict. *In* The Prism of sex, ed. by J. A. Sherman and E. T. Beck p253-65.

**Sexton, Anne**

### About

Howard, R. Anne Sexton: "Some tribal female who is known but forbidden." *In* Howard, R. Alone with America p517-25

**Sextus Empiricus**

### About

Burnyeat, M. F. Can the sceptic live his scepticism? *In* Doubt and dogmatism, ed. by M. Schofield, M. Burnyeat and J. Barnes p20-53

**Sexual behavior.** See Sex; Sex customs; Sexual ethics

**Sexual behavior, Psychology of.** See Sex (Psychology)

**Sexual deviation**

Gray, R. Sex and sexual perversion. *In* The Philosophy of sex, ed. by A. Soble p 158-68

Ketchum, S. A. The good, the bad and the perverted: sexual paradigms revisited. *In* The Philosophy of sex, ed. by A. Soble p 139-57

Levy, D. Perversion and the unnatural as moral categories. *In* The Philosophy of sex, ed. by A. Soble p169-89

Nagel, T. Sexual perversion. *In* The Philosophy of sex, ed. by A. Soble p76-88

**Sexual ethics**

Goldman, A. H. Plain sex. *In* The Philosophy of sex, ed. by A. Soble p119-38

*See also* Prostitution

**Sexual perversion.** See Sexual deviation

**Sexual psychology.** See Sex (Psychology)

**Seyag (The Hebrew word)**

Stein, S. The concept of the "fence": observations on its origin and development. *In* Studies in Jewish religious and intellectual history, ed. by S. Stein and R. Loewe p301-29

**Shackleton, Robert**

Madame de Montesquieu with some considerations on Thérèse de Secondat. *In* Woman and society in eighteenth-century France, ed. by E. Jacobs and others p229-42

**Shadwell, Thomas**

#### About

Vieth, D. M. Shadwell in acrostic land: the reversible meaning of Dryden's Mac Flecknoe. *In* Studies in eighteenth-century culture v9 p503-16

**Shahane, Vasant Anant**

Jhabvala's 'Heat and dust': a cross-cultural encounter. *In* Aspects of Indian writing in English, ed. by M. K. Naik p222-31

Life's walking shadows in A passage to India. *In* E. M. Forster: a human exploration, ed. by G. K. Das and J. Beer p109-16

**Shaheen, Mohammad**

Forster's Alexandria: the transitional journey. *In* E. M. Forster: a human exploration, ed. by G. K. Das and J. Beer p79-88

**Shakespeare, William**

#### About

Bradbrook, M. C. Shakespeare's recollections of Marlowe. *In* Shakespeare's styles, ed. by P. Edwards, I. S. Ewbank and G. K. Hunter p191-204

Bullough, G. The defence of paradox. *In* Shakespeare's styles, ed. by P. Edwards, I. S. Ewbank and G. K. Hunter p163-82

Fineman, J. Fratricide and cuckoldry: Shakespeare's doubles. *In* Representing Shakespeare, ed. by M. M. Schwartz and C. Kahn p70-109

Gohlke, M. S. "I wooed thee with my sword": Shakespeare's tragic paradigms. *In* Representing Shakespeare, ed. by M. M. Schwartz and C. Kahn p170-87

Kahn C. The providential tempest and the Shakespearean family. *In* Representing Shakespeare, ed. by M. M. Schwartz, and C. Kahn p217-43

Schwartz, M. M. Shakespeare through contemporary psychoanalysis. *In* Representing Shakespeare, ed. by M. M. Schwartz and C. Kahn p21-32

Skura, M. A. Interpreting Posthumus' dream from above and below: families, psychoanalysts, and literary critics. *In* Representing Shakespeare, ed. by M. M. Schwartz and C. Kahn p203-16

Wheeler, R. P. "Since first we were dissevered": trust and autonomy in Shakespearean tragedy and romance. *In* Representing Shakespeare, ed. by M. M. Schwartz and C. Kahn p150-69

Willbern, D. P. Shakespeare's nothing. *In* Representing Shakespeare, ed. by M. M. Schwartz and C. Kahn p244-63

#### About individual works

##### All's well that ends well

Bowers, F. T. Shakespeare at work: the foul papers of All's well that ends well. *In* English Renaissance studies, ed. by J. Carey p56-73

##### Antony and Cleopatra (I,i,1-24)

Hibbard, G. R. Feliciter audax: Antony and Cleopatra, I,i,1-24. *In* Shakespeare's styles, ed. by P. Edwards, I. S. Ewbank and G. K. Hunter p95-109

Reiss, T. J. A new time and the glory that was Egypt. *In* Reiss, T. J. Tragedy and truth p204-18

##### As you like it

Hayles, N. K. Sexual disguise in 'As you like it' and 'Twelfth night.' *In* Shakespeare survey 32 p63-72

##### Coriolanus

Adelman, J. "Anger's my meat": feeding, dependency, and aggression in Coriolanus. *In* Representing Shakespeare, ed. by M. M. Schwartz and C. Kahn p129-49

##### Cymbeline

Marx, J. C. The encounter of genres: Cymbeline's structure of juxtaposition. *In* The Analysis of literary texts, ed. by R. D. Pope p138-44

Skura, M. A. Interpreting Posthumus' dream from above and below: families, psychoanalysts, and literary critics. *In* Representing Shakespeare, ed. by M. M. Schwartz and C. Kahn p203-16

Wickham, G. W. G. Riddle and emblem: a study in the dramatic structure of Cymbeline. *In* English Renaissance studies, ed. by J. Carey p94-113

##### Hamlet

Klein, J. L. 'What is't to leave betimes?' Proverbs and logic in 'Hamlet.' *In* Shakespeare survey 32 p163-76

Leverenz, D. The woman in Hamlet: an interpersonal view. *In* Representing Shakespeare, ed. by M. M. Schwartz and C. Kahn p110-28

Reiss, T. J. Hamlet on distraction and Fortinbras on knowledge. *In* Reiss, T. J. Tragedy and truth p162-82

Woodhead, M. R. Deep plots and indiscretions in 'The murder of Gonzago.' *In* Shakespeare survey 32 p151-61

##### Henry VI, Parts 1, 2 and 3

Clemen, W. H. Some aspects of style in the Henry VI plays. *In* Shakespeare's styles, ed. by P. Edwards, I. S. Ewbank and G. K. Hunter p9-24

##### King John

Champion, L. S. "Confound their skill in covetousness": the ambivalent perspective of Shakespeare's King John. *In* Tennessee Studies in literature v24 p36-55

##### King Lear

Dundes, A. "To love my father all": a psychoanalytic study of the folktale source of King Lear. *In* Dundes, A. Interpreting folklore p211-22

Shakespeare, William—*Continued*

### Bibliography

Willbern, D. P. A bibliography of psychoanalytic and psychological writings on Shakespeare: 1964-1978. *In* Representing Shakespeare, ed. by M. M. Schwartz and C. Kahn p264-86

### Biography—Bibliography

Pendry, E. D. Shakespeare's life, times and stage. *In* Shakespeare survey 32 p227-37

### Bibliography—Folios 1623

Greg, Sir W. W. The printing of Shakespeare's Troilus and Cressida in the First Folio. *In* The Bibliographical Society of America, 1904-79 p266-75

### Characters

Wheeler, R. P. "Since first we were dissevered": trust and autonomy in Shakespearean tragedy and romance. *In* Representing Shakespeare ed. by M. M. Schwartz and C. Kahn p150-69

### Characters—Caliban

Knight, G. W. Caliban as a Red Man. *In* Shakespeare's styles, ed. by P. Edwards, I. S. Ewbank and G. K. Hunter p205-20

### Characters—Coriolanus

Adelman, J. "Anger's my meat": feeding, dependency, and aggression in Coriolanus. *In* Representing Shakespeare, ed. by M. M. Schwartz and C. Kahn p129-49

### Characters—Hamlet

Leverenz, D. The woman in Hamlet: an interpersonal view. *In* Representing Shakespeare, ed. by M. M. Schwartz and C. Kahn p110-28

Robertson, D. W. A medievalist looks at Hamlet. *In* Robertson, D. W. Essays in medieval culture p312-31

Veith, G. E. "Wait upon the Lord": David, Hamlet, and the problem of revenge. *In* The David myth in Western literature, ed. by R. J. Frontain and J. Wojcik p70-83

### Characters—Hermia

Norwood, N. N. Hermia's dream. *In* Representing Shakespeare, ed. by M. M. Schwartz and C. Kahn p 1-20

### Characters—Iago

Greenblatt, S. J. Improvisation and power. *In* Literature and society, ed. by E. W. Said p57-99

### Characters—Juliet's nurse

Wells, S. W. Juliet's nurse: the uses of inconsequentiality. *In* Shakespeare's styles, ed. by P. Edwards, I. S. Ewbank and G. K. Hunter p51-66

### Characters—Kings and rulers

Edwards, P. The hidden king: Shakespeare's history plays. *In* Edwards, P. Threshold of a nation p110-30

### Characters—Leontes

Barton, A. Leontes and the spider: language and speaker in Shakespeare's last plays. *In* Shakespeare's styles, ed. by P. Edwards, I. S. Ewbank and G. K. Hunter p131-50

### Characters—Marina

Ewbank, I. S. 'My name is Marina': the language of recognition. *In* Shakespeare's styles, ed. by P. Edwards, I. S. Ewbank and G. K. Hunter p111-30

### Characters—Prospero

Sundelson, D. So rare a wonder'd father: Prospero's Tempest. *In* Representing Shakespeare, ed. by M. M. Schwartz and C. Kahn p33-53

### Characters—Shylock

Girard, R. "To entrap the wisest": a reading of The merchant of Venice. *In* Literature and society, ed. by E. W. Said p100-19

Tennenhouse, L. The counterfeit order of The merchant of Venice. *In* Representing Shakespeare, ed. by M. M. Schwartz and C. Kahn p54-69

### Characters—Women

Jackson, R. 'Perfect types of womanhood': Rosalind, Beatrice and Viola in Victorian criticism and performance. *In* Shakespeare survey 32 p15-26

Schotz, M. G. The great unwritten story: mothers and daughters in Shakespeare. *In* The Lost tradition: mothers and daughters in literature, ed. by C. N. Davidson and E. M. Broner p44-54

### Comedies

Mahood, M. M. Shakespeare's comedies: a generation of criticism. *In* Shakespeare survey 32 p 1-13

### Criticism and interpretation

Jackson, R. 'Perfect types of womanhood': Rosalind, Beatrice and Viola in Victorian criticism and performance. *In* Shakespeare survey 32 p15-26

Krieger, M. Fiction, nature, and literary kinds in Johnson's criticism of Shakespeare. *In* Krieger, M. Poetic presence and illusion p55-69

Mahood, M. M. Shakespeare's comedies: a generation of criticism. *In* Shakespeare survey 32 p 1-13

### Criticism and interpretation—Bibliography

Hill, R. F. Critical studies. *In* Shakespeare survey 32 p211-27

### Criticism, Textual

Bowers, F. T. Establishing Shakespeare's text: notes on short lines and the problem of verse division. *In* Virginia. University. Bibliographical Society. Studies in bibliography v33 p74-130

### Criticism, Textual—Bibliography

Williams, G. W. Textual studies. *In* Shakespeare survey 32 p237-47

### Histories

Edwards, P. The hidden king: Shakespeare's history plays. *In* Edwards, P. Threshold of a nation p110-30

### Influence

Krieger, M. Shakespeare and the critic's idolatry of the word. *In* Krieger, M. Poetic presence and illusion p39-54

### Language

Barton, A. Leontes and the spider: language and speaker in Shakespeare's last plays. *In* Shakespeare's styles, ed. by P. Edwards, I. S. Ewbank and G. K. Hunter p131-50

Brooke, N. Language most shows a man. . . . ? Language and speaker in Macbeth. *In* Shakespeare's styles, ed. by P. Edwards, I. S. Ewbank and G. K. Hunter p67-77

Foakes, R. A. Poetic language and dramatic significance in Shakespeare. *In* Shakespeare's styles, ed. by P. Edwards, I. S. Ewbank and G. K. Hunter p79-93

**Shakespeare, William—Language—***Continued*

Knights, L. C. Rhetoric and insincerity. *In* Shakespeare's styles, ed. by P. Edwards, I. S. Ewbank and G. K. Hunter p 1-8

Lea, K. M. Shakespeare's inner stage. *In* English Renaissance studies, ed. by J. Carey p132-40

### Manuscripts

Bowers, F. T. Shakespeare at work: the foul papers of All's well that ends well. *In* English Renaissance studies, ed. by J. Carey p56-73

### Stage history—Bibliography

Pendry, E. D. Shakespeare's life, times and stage. *In* Shakespeare survey 32 p227-37

### Stage history—Great Britain

Warren, R. A year of comedies: Stratford 1978. *In* Shakespeare survey 32 p201-09

### Stage presentation

Proudfoot, R. Peter Brook and Shakespeare. *In* Drama and mimesis, ed. by J. Redmond p157-89

### Style

Clemen, W. H. Some aspects of style in the Henry VI plays. *In* Shakespeare's styles, ed. by P. Edwards, I. S. Ewbank and G. K. Hunter p9-24

Ewbank, I. S. 'My name is Marina': the language of recognition. *In* Shakespeare's styles, ed. by P. Edwards, I. S. Ewbank and G. K. Hunter p111-30

Honigmann, E. A. J. Shakespeare's 'bombast'. *In* Shakespeare's styles, ed. by P. Edwards, I. S. Ewbank and G. K. Hunter p151-62

Wells, S. W. Juliet's nurse: the uses of inconsequentiality. *In* Shakespeare's styles, ed. by P. Edwards, I. S. Ewbank and G. K. Hunter p51-66

*See also* Shakespeare, William—Language

### Technique

Lea, K. M. Shakespeare's inner stage. *In* English Renaissance studies, ed. by J. Carey p132-40

Sprague, A. C. 'True, gallant Raleigh': some off-stage conversations in Shakespeare's plays. *In* Shakespeare's styles, ed. by P. Edwards, I. S. Ewbank and G. K. Hunter p183-90

*See also* Shakespeare, William—Style

### Tragedies

Barber, C. L. The family in Shakespeare's development: tragedy and sacredness. *In* Representing Shakespeare, ed. by M. M. Schwartz and C. Kahn p188-202

Honigmann, E. A. J. Shakespeare's 'bombast'. *In* Shakespeare's styles, ed. by P. Edwards, I. S. Ewbank and G. K. Hunter p151-62

**Shamanism**

La Barre, W. Anthropological perspectives on hallucination, hallucinogens, and the shamanic origins of religion. *In* La Barre, W. Culture in context p37-92

### Asia

Humphrey, C. Theories of North Asian shamanism. *In* Soviet and Western anthropology, ed. by E. Gellner p243-54

**Shamanism in literature**

Hatto, A. T. Shamanism and epic poetry in northern Asia. *In* Hatto, A. T. Essays on medieval German and other poetry p117-38

**Shame**

Isenberg, A. Natural pride and natural shame. *In* Explaining emotions, ed. by A. O. Rorty p355-83

**Shamir, Moshe**

### About individual works

*He walked through the fields*

Abramson, G. The state of Israel: 1948 and after. *In* Abramson, G. Modern Hebrew drama p48-58

**Shammas, Carole**

English-born and creole elites in turn-of-the-century Virginia. *In* The Chesapeake in the seventeenth century, ed. by T. W. Tate and D. L. Ammerman p274-96

**Shampoo (Motion picture)**

Kauffmann, S. Shampoo. *In* Kauffmann, S. Before my eyes p116-18

**Shange, Ntozake**

### About individual works

*For colored girls who have considered suicide, when the rainbow is enuf*

Brown, J. For colored girls who have considered suicide/when the rainbow is enuf. *In* Brown, J. Feminist drama p114-32

Christ, C. P. "i found god in myself . . . & i loved her fiercely": Ntozake Shange. *In* Christ, C. P. Diving deep and surfacing p97-117

**Shanin, Tedor**

The conceptual reappearance of peasantry in Anglo-Saxon social science. *In* Soviet and Western anthropology, ed. by E. Gellner p181-91

**Shankman, Arnold Michel**

Friend or foe? Southern blacks view the Jew, 1880-1935. *In* Conference on Southern Jewish History, Richmond, Va. 1976. "Turn to the South" p105-23

**Shao-chün Yeh.** See Yeh, Shao-chün

**Shapiro, Charles**

On our own: Trilling vs. Dreiser. *In* Seasoned authors for a new season: the search for standards in popular writing, ed. by L. Filler p152-56

**Shapiro, I. A.**

The date of a Donne elegy, and its implications. *In* English Renaissance studies, ed. by J. Carey p141-50

**Shapiro, Judith Rae**

The Tapirapé during the era of Reconstruction. *In* Brazil, anthropological perspectives, ed. by M. L. Margolis and W. E. Carter p61-85

**Shapiro, Martin M.**

Judicial activism. *In* The Third century, ed. by S. M. Lipset p109-31

**Sharlet, Robert S.**

De-Stalinization and Soviet constitutionalism. *In* The Soviet Union since Stalin, ed. by S. F. Cohen, A. Rabinowitch and R. Sharlet p93-110

**Sharma, Govind Narain**

Ngugi's Christian vision: theme and pattern in A grain of wheat. *In* African literature today no. 10: Retrospect & prospect, ed. by E. D. Jones p167-76

**Sharma, Ran S.**

Indian civilization. *In* Propaganda and communication in world history, ed. by H. D. Lasswell, D. Lerner and H. Speier v 1 p175-204

**Sharratt, Bernard**

News from nowhere: detail and desire. *In* Reading the Victorian novel: detail into form, ed. by I. Gregor p288-305

The politics of the popular?—From melodrama to television. *In* Performance and politics in popular drama, ed. by R. Bradby, L. James and B. Sharratt p275-95

**Shaw, Bernard.** See Shaw, George Bernard

**Shaw, Donald Leslie**

Narrative arrangement in La muerte de Artemio Cruz. *In* Contemporary Latin American fiction, ed. by S. Bacarisse p34-47

**Shaw, George Bernard**

### About

Brophy, B. The way of no flesh. *In* The Genius of Shaw, ed. by M. Holroyd p95-111

Gordon, D. J. Literature and repression: the case of Shavian drama. *In* The Literary Freud: mechanisms of defense and the poetic will, ed. by J. H. Smith p181-203

Green, B. A funny man. *In* The Genius of Shaw, ed. by M. Holroyd p201-11

Holroyd, M. Introduction. *In* The Genius of Shaw, ed. by M. Holroyd p9-11

O'Donovan, J. The first twenty years. *In* The Genius of Shaw, ed. by M. Holroyd p13-29

Spurling, H. The critic's critic. *In* The Genius of Shaw, ed. by M. Holroyd p129-41

Wardle, I. The plays. *In* The Genius of Shaw, ed. by M. Holroyd p143-65

White, T. de V. An Irishman abroad. *In* The Genius of Shaw, ed. by M. Holroyd p31-41

Wilson, C. A personal view. *In* The Genius of Shaw, ed. by M. Holroyd p223-[29]

### Autographs

Smoker, B. Man of letters. *In* The Genius of Shaw, ed. by M. Holroyd p213-21

### Characters—Women

Holroyd M. Women and the body politic. *In* The Genius of Shaw, ed. by M. Holroyd p167-83

### Knowledge—Art

Weintraub, S. In the picture galleries. *In* The Genius of Shaw, ed. by M. Holroyd p44-63

### Knowledge—Music

*See* Shaw, George Bernard—Music

### Music

Dent, E. J. Corno di Bassetto. *In* Dent, E. J. Selected essays p238-49

Osborne, C. The music critic. *In* The Genius of Shaw, ed. by M. Holroyd p65-76

### Political and social views

Skidelsky, R. J. A. The Fabian ethic. *In* The Genius of Shaw, ed. by M. Holroyd p113-28

### Portraits, etc.

Weintraub, S. In the picture galleries. *In* The Genius of Shaw, ed. by M. Holroyd p44-63

### Relationship with women

Holroyd, M. Women and the body politic. *In* The Genius of Shaw, ed. by M. Holroyd p167-83

Peters, M. 'As lonely as God.' *In* The Genius of Shaw, ed. by M. Holroyd p185-99

### Religion and ethics

Collis, J. S. Religion and philosophy. *In* The Genius of Shaw, ed. by M. Holroyd p79-93

### Women

*See* Shaw, George Bernard—Relationship with women

**Shaw, John Mackay**

Poetry for children of two centuries. *In* Research about nineteenth-century children and books, ed. by S. K. Richardson p133-42

**Shaw, Nate**

### About individual works

*All God's dangers; the life of Nate Shaw, [compiled by] Theodore Rosengarten*

Rosengarten, T. Stepping over cockelburs: conversations with Ned Cobb. *In* Telling lives, ed. by M. Pachter p104-31

**Shaw, Thomas Edward.** See Lawrence, Thomas Edward

**Shea, William Michael**

The supernatural in the naturalists. *In* History, religion, and spiritual democracy, ed. by M. Wohlgelernter [and others] p53-75

**Shechner, Mark Ephraim**

Jewish writers. *In* Harvard Guide to contemporary American writing, ed. by D. Hoffman p91-239

**Shelley, Mary Wollstonecraft (Godwin)**

### About individual works

*Frankenstein*

Morowitz, H. J. Frankenstein and recombinant DNA. *In* Morowitz, H. J. The wine of life, and other essays on societies, energy & living things p187-91

**Shelley, Percy Bysshe**

### About

Fry, P. H. Shelley and the celebration of power. *In* Fry, P. H. The poet's calling in the English ode p186-217

### About individual works

*The Cenci*

Twitchell, J. B. Shelley's use of vampirism in The Cenci. *In* Tennessee Studies in literature v24 p120-33

### Criticism and interpretation

Hartman, G. H. The sacred jungle 3: Frye, Burke, and some conclusions. *In* Hartman, G. H. Criticism in the wilderness p86-114

**Shen, Yen-ping**

### About

Prušek, J. Mao Tun and Yu Ta-fu. *In* Prušek, J. The lyrical and the epic p121-77

**Shen, Yien-ping.** See Shen, Yen-ping

**Shepard, Nolan E.**

Technology: messiah or monster? *In* Monster or messiah? Ed. by W. M. Mathews p145-55

**Shepherd, James F.**

Economy from the Revolution to 1815. *In* Encyclopedia of American economic history, ed. by G. Porter v 1 p51-65

**Shepherd, Massey Hamilton**

Christology: a central problem of early Christian theology and art. *In* Age of spirituality, ed. by K. Weitzmann p101-20

**Sheridan, George J.**

Household and craft in an industrializing economy: the case of the silk weavers of Lyons. *In* Consciousness and class experience in nineteenth-century Europe, ed. by J. M. Merriman p107-28

**Sheridan, Thomas, 1687-1738**

### About

Woolley, J. Thomas Sheridan and Swift. *In* Studies in eighteenth-century culture v9 p93-114

**Sherif, Carolyn Wood**
Bias in psychology. *In* The Prism of sex, ed. by J. A. Sherman and E. T. Beck p93-133

**Sherwin, Byron L.**
Ideological antecedents of the Holocaust. *In* Encountering the Holocaust: an interdisciplinary survey, ed. by B. L. Sherwin and S. G. Ament p23-51
Jewish and Christian theology encounters the Holocaust. *In* Encountering the Holocaust: an interdisciplinary survey, ed. by B. L. Sherwin and S. G. Ament p407-42
Philosophical reactions to and moral implications of the Holocaust. *In* Encountering the Holocaust: an interdisciplinary survey, ed. by B. L. Sherwin and S. G. Ament p443-72
Portrait of a romantic rebel Bernard C. Ehrenreich. *In* Conference on Southern Jewish History, Rchmond, Va. 1976. "Turn to the South" p 1-12
*See also* Weinberg, D. H. jt. auth.

**Shiloah, Amnon**
The ritual and music of the synagogue. *In* The Jewish world, ed. by E. Kedourie p120-27

**Shimazaki, Tōson**
### About
Walker, J. A. The education of a Meiji individual. *In* Walker, J. A. The Japanese novel of the Meiji period and the ideal of individualism p123-55
Walker, J. A. Shimazaki Tōson's ideal of the individual. *In* Walker, J. A. The Japanese novel of the Meiji period and the ideal of individualism p244-84
#### About individual works
*Hakai*
Walker, J. A. Hakai (Breaking the commandment): a novel of the inner life. *In* Walker, J. A. The Japanese novel of the Meiji period and the ideal of individualism p156-93
*Shinsei*
Walker, J. A. Shinsei (The new life): a novel of confession. *In* Walker, J. A. The Japanese novel of the Meiji period and the ideal of individualism p194-243

**Shiner, Roger Alfred**
Butler's theory of moral judgment. *In* Royal Institute of Philosophy. Philosophers of the Enlightenment p199-225

**Shinn, Roger Lincoln**
Toward a post-Enlightenment doctrine of human rights. *In* History, religion, and spiritual democracy, ed. by M. Wohlgelernter [and others] p294-316

**Ship-building workers**
### United States
Skold, K. B. The job he left behind: American women in the shipyards during World War II. *In* Women, war, and revolution, ed. by C. R. Berkin and C. M. Lovett p55-75

**Shipton, Clifford Kenyson**
Bibliotheca Americana. *In* The Bibliographical Society of America, 1904-79 p470-78

**Shipyard workers.** See Ship-building workers

**Shirley, Robert W.**
Law in rural Brazil. *In* Brazil, anthropological perspectives, ed. by M. L. Margolis and W. E. Carter p343-59

**Shiur komah**
Dan, J. The concept of knowledge in the Shi'ur qomah. *In* Studies in Jewish religious and intellectual history, ed. by S. Stein and R. Loewe p67-73

**Shklar, Judith**
Reading The social contract. *In* Powers, possessions and freedom, ed. by A. Kontos p77-88

**Shneidman, N. N.**
Soviet literature in the 1970s: artistic diversity and ideological conformity
*Contents*
Bondarev and Bykov: the war theme
Chingiz Aitmatov: myth and reality
Iurii Trifonov: city prose
Sergei Zalygin: innovation and variety
The Soviet literary scene
Valentin Rasputin: village prose reconsidered

**Shoot the piano player (Motion picture)**
Thiher, A. The existential play in Truffaut's early films. *In* Thiher, A. The cinematic muse p143-63

**The Shootist (Motion picture)**
Kauffmann, S. The shootist. *In* Kauffmann, S. Before my eyes. p237-40

**Short eyes (Motion picture)**
Kael, P. Contrasts. *In* Kael, P. When the lights go down p291-98

**Short stories, English**
Irish authors—History and criticism
Harmon, M. First impressions: 1968-78. *In* The Irish short story, ed. by P. Rafroidi and T. Brown p63-77
Kiberd, D. Story-telling: the Gaelic tradition. *In* The Irish short story, ed. by P. Rafroidi and T. Brown p13-25
Rafroidi, P. The Irish short story in English. The birth of a new tradition. *In* The Irish short story, ed. by P. Rafroidi and T. Brown p27-38
Irish authors—Themes, motives
Norris, D. Imaginative response versus authority structures. A theme of the Anglo-Irish short story. *In* The Irish short story, ed. by P. Rafroidi and T. Brown p39-62

**Short stories, Irish.** See Short stories, English—Irish authors

**Shoven, John B.**
Federal government taxes and tax reform. *In* The Economy in the 1980s: a program for growth and stability, ed. by M. J. Boskin p199-221

**Shrines**
Rothkrug, L. Popular religion and holy shrines. *In* Religion and the people, 800-1700, ed. by J. Obelkevich p20-86

**Shuara Indians.** See Jivaro Indians

**Shubert, Gustave H.**
Policy analysis and public choice. *In* Bureaucrats, policy analysts, statesmen: who leads? Ed. by R. A. Goldwin p44-61

**Shubik, Martin**
Computers and modeling. *In* The Computer age: a twenty-year view, ed. by M. L. Dertouzos and J. Moses p285-305

**Shuksin, Vasilii Makarovich**
### About
Hosking, G. Vasily Shukshin. *In* Hosking, G. Beyond Socialist realism p162-79

**Sibbes, Richard**
### About
Knott, J. R. Richard Sibbes and spiritual preaching. *In* Knott, J. R. The sword of the spirit p42-61

**Sicily**

### Antiquities

Momigliano, A. The rediscovery of Greek history in the eighteenth century: the case of Sicily. *In* Studies in eighteenth-century culture v9 p161-87

**Sick.** See Medical personnel and patient

**Sickness insurance.** See Insurance, Health

**Sidnell, Michael J.**
The Revels history of drama in English volume VIII, American Drama. *In* Drama and mimesis, ed. by J. Redmond p227-42

**Sidney, Sir Philip**

### About

Duncan-Jones, K. Sidney and Titian, ed. by J. Carey p 1-11

Krieger, M. Poetic presence and illusion I: Renaissance theory and the duplicity of metaphor. *In* Krieger, M. Poetic presence and illusion p3-27

### About individual works
#### An apology for poetrie

Montgomery, R. L. "The gates of popular judgments": Sidney's Apology for poetry (ca. 1581-1583). *In* Montgomery, R. L. The reader's eye p117-41

#### The defence of poesy

Manley, L. G. "Conveniency to nature" and the "secrets of privitie": nature and convention in defense of poetry. *In* Manley, L. G. Convention, 1500-1750 p158-75

Robertson, D. W. Sidney's metaphor of the ulcer. *In* Robertson, D. W. Essays in medieval culture p308-11

**Siena**

### History

Cole, B. Introduction. *In* Cole, B. Sienese painting pix-xii

**Sienese painting.** See Painting, Sienese

**Sienicka, Marta**
O'Neill in Poland. *In* Eugene O'Neill, ed. by V. Floyd p101-14

**Sight.** See Vision

**Signs and symbols.** See Symbolism

**Silberman, Laurence H.**
Policy analysis: boon or curse for politicians? *In* Bureaucrats, policy analysts, statesmen: who leads? Ed. by R. A. Goldwin p37-43

**Silent movie (Motion picture)**
Kauffmann, S. Silent movie. *In* Kauffmann, S. Before my eyes p111-13

**Silk manufacture and trade**

### France—Lyons

Sheridan, G. J. Household and craft in an industrializing economy: the case of the silk weavers of Lyons. *In* Consciousness and class experience in nineteenth-century Europe, ed. by J. M. Merriman p107-28

**Silva, Clara**

### About individual works
#### La sobreviviente

Fox-Lockert, L. Clara Silva. *In* Fox-Lockert, L. Women novelists in Spain and Spanish America p185-94

**Silver, Joan Micklin**

### About individual works
#### Hester Street

Miller, G. Jews without maners. *In* Miller, G. Screening the novel p1-18

**Silver, Nathan**
Architect talk. *In* The State of the language, ed. by L. Michaels and C. Ricks p324-30

**Silver, Rollo Gabriel**
Problems in nineteenth-century American bibliography. *In* The Bibliographical Society of America, 1904-79 p126-38

**Silverman, Jim**
A rack of journals: research in children's literature. *In* Children's literature v8 p193-204

**Simenauer, Erich**
R. M. Rilke's dreams and his conception of dream. *In* Rilke: the alchemy of alienation, ed. by F. Baron, E. S. Dick and W. R. Maurer p243-62

**Simile.** See Metaphor

**Simon, Claude**

### About individual works
#### Leçon de choses

Jiménez-Fajardo, S. A descriptive approach to Claude Simon's novel Leçon de choses. *In* The Analysis of literary texts, ed. by R. D. Pope p298-313

**Simon, Ernst**
The maturing of man and the maturing of the Jew. *In* The Jew, ed. by A. A. Cohen p127-46

**Simon, Herbert Alexander**
The consequences of computers for centralization and decentralization. *In* The Computer age: a twenty-year view, ed. by M. L. Dertouzos and J. Moses p212-28

**Simon, John Ivan**
The corruption of English. *In* The State of the language, ed. by L. Michaels and C. Ricks p35-42

### About individual works
#### Singularities

Brustein, R. S. John Simon (Uneasy stages and singularities). *In* Brustein, R. S. Critical moments p13-17

#### Uneasy stages

Brustein, R. S. John Simon (Uneasy stages and singularities). *In* Brustein, R. S. Critical moments p13-17

**Simon, Thomas William**
Philosophical objections to programs as theories. *In* Philosophical perspectives in artificial intelligence, ed. by M. Ringle p225-42

**Simone di Martino**

### About

Cole, B. Simone Martini. *In* Cole, B. Sienese painting p68-102

**Simonidēs, Kōnstantinos**

### About

Lutz, C. E. A forged manuscript in boustrophedon. *In* Lutz, C. E. The oldest library motto, and other library essays p65-72

**Simpson, James Rodney**
Toward a humanist consensus on ethics of international development. *In* Humanist ethics, ed. by M. B. Storer p122-36

**Simpson, Lewis Pearson**
Southern fiction. *In* Harvard Guide to contemporary American writing, ed. by D. Hoffman p153-90

The Southern literary vocation. *In* Toward a new American literary history, ed. by L. J. Budd, E. H. Cady and C. L. Anderson p19-35

**Simpson, Louis**

**About**

Howard, R. Louis Simpson: "The hunger in my vitals is for some credible extravaganza." *In* Howard, R. Alone with America p526-47

**Sin (Judaism)**

Werblowsky, R. J. Z. O felix culpa: a cabbalistic version. *In* Studies in Jewish religious and intellectual history, ed. by S. Stein and R. Loewe p355-62

**Sinclair, Bruce**

Americans abroad: science and cultural nationalism in the early nineteenth century. *In* The Sciences in the American context: new perspectives, ed. by N. Reingold p35-53

**Sinclair, Upton Beall**

**Characters—Lanny Budd**

Dembo, L. S. The socialist and socialite heroes of Upton Sinclair. *In* Toward a new American literary history, ed. by L. J. Budd, E. H. Cady and C. L. Anderson p164-80

**Singer, Irving**

The sensuous and the passionate. *In* The Philosophy of sex, ed. by A. Soble p209-31

**Singer, Isaac Bashevis**

**About**

Alexander, E. The destruction and resurrection of the Jews in the fiction of Isaac Bashevis Singer. *In* Alexander, E. The resonance of dust p149-69

**Singer, Jerome L.**

Vico's insight and the scientific study of the stream of consciousness. *In* Conference on Vico and Contemporary Thought, New York, 1976. Vico and contemporary thought pt2 p57-68

**Singer, Peter**

Animals and the value of life. *In* Matters of life and death, ed. by T. Regan p218-59

**Singh, Amritjit**

Contemporary Indo-English literature: an approach. *In* Aspects of Indian writing in English, ed. by M. K. Naik p 1-14

**Single tax**

Andelson, R. V. Neo-Georgism. *In* Critics of Henry George, ed. by R. V. Andelson p381-93

Wasserman, L. The essential Henry George. *In* Critics of Henry George, ed. by R. V. Andelson p29-43

**Sino-Japanese Conflict, 1937-1945**

Eastman, L. E. Facets of an ambivalent relationship: smuggling, puppets, and atrocities during the war, 1937-1945. *In* The Chinese and Japanese, ed. by A. Iriye p275-303

Marsh, S. H. Chou Fo-hai: the making of a collaborator. *In* The Chinese and the Japanese, ed. by A. Iriye p304-27

*See also* China—History—1937-1945

**Sir, Edouard Morot-** See Morot-Sir, Edouard

**Six hundred and thirteen commandments.** See Commandments, Six hundred and thirteen

**Sixteenth century.** See Reformation

**Skelton, John, 1460?-1529**

**About**

Kratzmann, G. Dunbar and Skelton. *In* Kratzmann, G. Anglo-Scottish literary relations, 1430-1550 p129-68

**About individual works**

*Magnyfycence*

Kratzmann, G. Ane satyre of the thrie estaitis and English drama. *In* Kratzmann, G. Anglo-Scottish literary relations, 1430-1550 p195-226

**Skepticism**

Battersby, C. Hume, Newton and 'the hill called difficulty.' *In* Royal Institute of Philosophy. Philosophers of the Enlightenment p31-55

Brown, S. C. The 'principle' of natural order: or what the enlightened sceptics did not doubt. *In* Royal Institute of Philosophy. Philosophers of the Enlightenment p56-76

**Skeptics (Greek philosophy)**

Barnes, J. Proof destroyed. *In* Doubt and dogmatism, ed. by M. Schofield, M. Burnyeat and J. Barnes p161-81

Burnyeat, M. F. Can the sceptic live his scepticism? *In* Doubt and dogmatism, ed. by M. Schofield, M. Burnyeat and J. Barnes p20-53

Striker, G. Sceptical strategies. *In* Doubt and dogmatism, ed. by M. Schofield, M. Burnyeat and J. Barnes p54-83

**Skidelsky, Robert Jacob Alexander**

The Fabian ethic. *In* The Genius of Shaw, ed. by M. Holroyd p113-28

Keynes and his parents. *In* Generations, ed. by S. R. Graubard p71-79

**Skinner, Burrhus Frederic**

**About**

Sutherland, N. S. The myth of mind control. *In* Lying truths, ed. by R. Duncan and M. Weston-Smith p107-20

**Skinner, Hubert C.**

Raymond Thomassy and the practical geology of Louisiana. *In* New Hampshire Bicentennial Conference on the History of Geology, University of New Hampshire, 1976. Two hundred years of geology in America p201-11

**Skinner, Quentin**

Language and social change. *In* The State of the language, ed. by L. Michaels and C. Ricks p562-78

**Skjelsbæk, Kjell**

Militarism, its dimensions and corollaries: an attempt at conceptual clarification. *In* Problems of contemporary militarism, ed. by A. Eide and M. Thee p77-105

**Skold, Karen Beck**

The job he left behind: American women in the shipyards during World War II. *In* Women, war, and revolution, ed. by C. R. Berkin and C. M. Lovett p55-75

**Skura, Meredith Anne**

Interpreting Posthumus' dream from above and below: families, psychoanalysts, and literary critics. *In* Representing Shakespeare, ed. by M. M. Schwartz and C. Kahn p203-16

Revisions and rereadings in dreams and allegories. *In* The Literary Freud: mechanisms of defense and the poetic will, ed. by J. H. Smith p345-79

**Slap shot (Motion picture)**

Kael, P. Hill's pâté. *In* Kael, P. When the lights go down p273-78

**Slater, Eliot**

Choosing the time to die. *In* Suicide: the philosophical issues, ed. by M. P. Battin and D. J. Mayo p199-204

**Slaughter, Cliff**
Marxism, ideology & literature
*Contents*
Against the stream: Walter Benjamin
Conclusions: literature and dialectical material-
ism
The hidden structure: Lucien Goldmann
The legacy of Marx
Literature and revolution: Trotsky
A man for all seasons: Georg Lukács

**Slave of love (Motion picture)**
Kauffmann, S. Slave of love. *In* Kauffmann, S. Before my eyes p317

**Slave trade**
Engerman, S. L. and Eltis, D. Economic
aspects of the abolition debate. *In* Anti-
slavery, religion, and reform: essays in memory
of Roger Anstey, ed. by C. Bolt and S.
Drescher p272-93

**Slavery**
David, D. B. Slavery and 'progress'. *In*
Anti-slavery, religion, and reform: essays in
memory of Roger Anstey, ed. by C. Bolt
and S. Drescher p351-66
Pole, J. R. Slavery and revolution: the conscience of the rich. *In* Pole, J. R. Paths to
the American past p55-74

### Economic aspects
Engerman, S. L. and Eltis, D. Economic
aspects of the abolition debate. *In* Anti-slavery,
religion, and reform: essays in memory of
Roger Anstey, ed. by C. Bolt and S. Drescher
p272-93

### History
Patterson, O. The black community: is
there a future? *In* The Third century, ed. by
S. M. Lipset p243-84

**Slavery and slaves in literature**
Jackson, R. L. Slave poetry and slave narrative: Juan Francisco Manzano and black
autobiography. *In* Jackson, R. L. Black writers in Latin America p25-35
Karcher, C. L. Lydia Maria Child and The
Juvenile Miscellany. *In* Research about nineteenth-century children and books, ed. by
S. K. Richardson p67-84
Rice, C. D. Literary sources and the revolution in British attitudes to slavery. *In* Anti-
slavery, religion, and reform: essays in
memory of Roger Anstey, ed. by C. Bolt and
S. Drescher p319-34

**Slavery and the church**
Drescher, S. Two variants of anti-slavery:
religious organization and social mobilization
in Britain and France, 1780-1870. *In* Anti-
slavery, religion, and reform: essays in
memory of Roger Anstey, ed. by C. Bolt and
S. Drescher p43-63

### Catholic Church
Daget, S. A model of the French
abolitionist movement and its variations. *In*
Anti-slavery, religion, and reform: essays in
memory of Roger Anstey, ed. by C. Bolt and
S. Drescher p64-79

### Protestant churches
Mathews, D. G. Religion and slavery—the
case of the American South. *In* Anti-slavery,
religion, and reform: essays in memory of
Roger Anstey, ed. by C. Bolt and S. Drescher
p207-32

**Slavery in Great Britain**

### Anti-slavery movements
Anstey, R. The pattern of British abolitionism in the eighteenth and nineteenth centuries.
*In* Anti-slavery, religion, and reform: essays
in memory of Roger Anstey, ed. by C. Bolt
and S. Drescher p19-42
Hollis, P. Anti-slavery and British working-
class radicalism in the years of reform. *In*
Anti-slavery, religion, and reform: essays in
memory of Roger Anstey, ed. by C. Bolt and
S. Drescher p294-315
Temperley, H. Anti-slavery as a form of
cultural imperialism. *In* Anti-slavery, religion,
and reform: essays in memory of Roger
Anstey, ed. by C. Bolt and S. Drescher p335-50
Walvin, J. The rise of British popular sentiment for abolition, 1787-1832. *In* Anti-slavery,
religion, and reform: essays in memory of
Roger Anstey, ed. by C. Bolt and S. Drescher
p149-62

**Slavery in Surinam**
Emmer, P. C. Anti-slavery and the Dutch:
abolition without reform. *In* Anti-slavery, religion, and reform: essays in memory of Roger
Anstey, ed. by C. Bolt and S. Drescher p80-98

**Slavery in the United States**

### Anti-slavery movements
Mathews, D. G. Religion and slavery—the
case of the American South. *In* Anti-slavery,
religion, and reform: essays in memory of
Roger Anstey, ed. by C. Bolt and S. Drescher
p207-32

### Fugitive slaves
Turley, D. M. 'Free air' and fugitive slaves:
British abolitionists versus government over
American fugitives, 1834-61. *In* Anti-slavery,
religion, and reform: essays in memory of
Roger Anstey, ed. by C. Bolt and S. Drescher
p163-82

### Historiography
Pole, J. R. Slavery, race, and the debate
on personality. *In* Pole, J. R. Paths to the
American past p189-219

### History
Gunderson, G. Slavery. *In* Encyclopedia of
American economic history, ed. by G. Porter
v2 p552-61

### Psychological aspects
Pole, J. R. Slavery, race, and the debate
on personality. *In* Pole, J. R. Paths to the
American past p189-219

### Southern States
Genovese, E. D. Life in the big house; excerpts from "Roll, Jordan, roll." *In* A Heritage
of her own, ed. by N. F. Cott and E. H. Pleck
p290-97
Gutman, H. G. Marital and sexual norms
among slave women. *In* A Heritage of her
own, ed. by N. F. Cott and E. H. Pleck p298-
310

**Slaves in literature.** See Slavery and slaves in
literature

**Sligo County, Ireland**
Henn, T. R. The place of shells. *In* Yeats,
Sligo and Ireland, ed. by A. N. Jeffares p73-88

**Sloane, Thomas O.**
Rhetoric, 'logic' and poetry: the formal
cause. *In* The Age of Milton, ed. by C. A.
Patrides and R. B. Waddington p307-37

**Slow dancing in the big city (Motion picture)**
Kael, P. Rocky's knucklehead progeny. *In*
Kael, P. When the lights go down p488-96

**Small, Albion Woodbury**

### About

Fuhrman, E. R. Albion W. Small. *In* Fuhrman, E. R. The sociology of knowledge in America, 1883-1915 p129-58

**Small business**

### Law and legislation—United States

Friedman, L. M. Law and small business in the United States: one hundred years of struggle and accommodation. *In* Small business in American life, ed. by S. W. Bruchey p305-18

### New England—History

Soltow, J. H. Origins of small business and the relationships between large and small firms: metal fabricating and machinery making in New England, 1890-1957. *In* Small business in American life, ed. by S. W. Bruchey p192-211

### New Jersey—Newark

Hirsch, S. E. From artisan to manufacturer: industrialization and the small producer in Newark, 1830-60. *In* Small business in American life, ed. by S. W. Bruchey p80-99

### Social aspects—New York (State)— Poughkeepsie

Griffen, C. and Griffen, S. Small business and occupational mobility in mid-nineteenth-century Poughkeepsie. *In* Small business in American life, ed. by S. W. Bruchey p122-41

### Social aspects—United States

Berthoff, R. Independence and enterprise: small business in the American dream. *In* Small business in American life, ed. by S. W. Bruchey p28-48

Ginzberg, E. The role of small business in the process of skill acquisition. *In* Small business in American life, ed. by S. W. Bruchey p366-79

### United States—Finance

Robinson, R. I. The financing of small business in the United States. *In* Small business in American life, ed. by S. W. Bruchey p280-304

### United States—History

Bensman, D. Economics and culture in the gilded age hatting industry. *In* Small business in American life, ed. by S. W. Bruchey p352-65

Brody, D. Labor and small-scale enterprise during industrialization. *In* Small business in American life, ed. by S. W. Bruchey p263-79

Bruchey, S. W. Introduction: a summary view of small business and American life. *In* Small business in American life, ed. by S. W. Bruchey p 1-27

Hammack, D. C. Small business and urban power: some notes on the history of economic policy in nineteenth-century American cities. *In* Small business in American life, ed. by S. W. Bruchey p319-37

Hollander, S. C. The effects of industrialization on small retailing in the United States in the twentieth century. *In* Small business in American life, ed. by S. W. Bruchey p212-39

Livesay, H. C. Lilliputians in Brobdingnag: small business in late-nineteenth-century America. *In* Small business in American life, ed. by S. W. Bruchey p338-51

Sylla, R. E. Small-business banking in the United States, 1780-1920. *In* Small business in American life, ed. by S. W. Bruchey p240-62

Vatter, H. G. The position of small business in the structure of American manufacturing, 1870-1970. *In* Small business in American life, ed. by S. W. Bruchey p142-68

**Small change (Motion picture)**

Kael, P. Charmed lives. *In* Kael, P. When the lights go down p167-72

Kauffmann, S. Small change. *In* Kauffmann, S. Before my eyes p187-88

**Smallpox**

### Spain—History

Dowling, J. C. Smallpox and literature in eighteenth-century Spain. *In* Studies in eighteenth-century culture v9 p59-77

**Smart, Christopher**

### About individual works

#### A song of David

Dillingham, T. F. "Blest light": Christopher Smart's myth of David. *In* The David myth in Western literature, ed. by R. J. Frontain and J. Wojcik p120-33

**Smart, Ninian**

Religions and changing values. *In* Value and values in evolution, ed. by E. A. Maziarz p17-28

**Smart, Roderic Ninian.** See Smart, Ninian

**Smelser, Neil J.**

Issues in the study of work and love in adulthood. *In* Themes of work and love in adulthood, ed. by N. J. Smelser and E. H. Erikson p 1-26

Vicissitudes of work and love in Anglo-American society. *In* Themes of work and love in adulthood, ed. by N. J. Smelser and E. H. Erikson p105-19

**Smile (Motion picture)**

Kael, P. The visceral poetry of pulp. *In* Kael, P. When the lights go down p40-45

Kauffmann, S. Smile. *In* Kauffmann, S. Before my eyes p160-63

**Smith, Adam**

### About

Raphael, D. D. Adam Smith: philosophy, science, and social science. *In* Royal Institute of Philosophy. Philosophers of the Enlightenment p77-93

**Smith, Alain**

### About

Flew, A. G. N. Intended conduct and unintended consequences. *In* Lying truths, ed. by R. Duncan and M. Weston-Smith p17-30

**Smith, Anthony**

The newspaper of the late twentieth century: the U.S. model. *In* Newspapers and democracy, ed. by A. Smith p5-48

**Smith, Bernard**

"Van Wyck Brooks"; excerpt from "After the genteel tradition." *In* Van Wyck Brooks: the critic and his critics, ed. by W. Wasserstrom p79-86

**Smith, Catherine F.**

The invention of sex in myth and literature. *In* The Binding of Proteus, ed. by M. W. McCune, T. Orbison and P. M. Within p252-62

**Smith, Dan Throop**

Issues in tax policy. *In* The United States in the 1980s, ed. by P. Duignan and A. Rabushka p109-37

**Smith, Daniel Blake**

Family. *In* Encyclopedia of American economic history, ed. by G. Porter v3 p974-87

**Smith, Daniel Scott**

Family limitation, sexual control and domestic feminism in Victorian America. *In* A Heritage of her own, ed. by N. F. Cott and E. H. Pleck p222-45

**Smith, Dave.** See Smith, David Jeddie

**Smith, David Jeddie**

**About**

Vendler, H. H. Dave Smith. *In* Vendler, H. H. Part of nature, part of us p289-302

**Smith, Doris Buchanan**

**About individual works**

*A taste of blackberries*

Rees, D. Timor mortis conturbat me: E. B. White and Doris Buchanan Smith. *In* Rees, D. The marble in the water p68-77

**Smith, Dorothy E.**

A sociology for women. *In* The Prism of sex, ed. by J. A. Sherman and E. T. Beck p135-87

**Smith, George Otis**

**About**

Manning, T. G. George Otis Smith as fourth director of the U.S. Geological Survey. *In* New Hampshire Bicentennial Conference on the History of Geology, University of New Hampshire, 1976. Two hundred years of geology in America p157-64

**Smith, John Edwin**

Faith, belief, and the problem of rationality in religion. *In* Rationality and religious belief, ed. by C. F. Delaney p42-64

**Smith, Judith E.**

Our own kind: family and community networks in Providence. *In* A Heritage of her own, ed. by N. F. Cott and E. H. Pleck p393-411

**Smith, Lillian Eugenia**

**About**

King, R. H. From therapy to morality: the example of Lillian Smith. *In* King, R. H. A Southern Renaissance p173-93

**Smith, Miranda Weston-** See Weston-Smith, Miranda

**Smith, Nathaniel B. and Snow, Joseph T.**

Courtly love and courtly literature. *In* The Expansion and transformations of courtly literature, ed. by N. B. Smith and J. T. Snow p3-14

**Smith, Peter F.**

Urban aesthetics *In* Architecture for people, ed. by B. Mikellides p74-86

**Smith, Peter M.**

Notes on the text of the fifth Homeric Hymn. *In* Harvard Studies in classical philology v83, p29-50

**Smith, Sidonie A.** See Billson, M. K. jt. auth.

**Smith-Rosenberg, Carroll**

Beauty, the beast, and the militant woman: a case study in sex roles and social stress in Jacksonian America. *In* A Heritage of her own, ed. by N. F. Cott and E. H. Pleck p197-211

The female world of love and ritual: relations between women in nineteenth-century America. *In* A Heritage of her own, ed. by N. F. Cott and E. H. Pleck p311-42

**Smitherman, Geneva**

White English in blackface, or Who do I be? *In* The State of the language, ed. by L. Michaels and C. Ricks p158-68

**Smoček, Ladislav**

**About**

Goetz-Stankiewicz, M. Ladislav Smoček. *In* Goetz-Stankiewicz, M. The silenced theatre: Czech playwrights without a stage p174-89

**Smoker, Barbara**

Man of letters. *In* The Genius of Shaw, ed. by M. Holroyd p213-21

**Smoking**

Morowitz, H. J. Fair is foul, anl foul is fair. *In* Morowitz, H. J. The wine of life, and other essays on societies, energy & living things p176-78

**Smolensky, Eugene, and Weinstein, Michael M.**

Poverty. *In* Encyclopedia of American economic history, ed. by G. Porter v3 p1136-54

**Snakes in literature.** See Serpents in literature

**Snee, Carole A.**

Working-class literature or proletarian writing? *In* Culture and crisis in Britain in the thirties, ed. by J. Clark and others p165-91

**Snodgrass, William DeWitt**

**About**

Howard, R. W. D. Snodgrass: "There's something beats the same in opposed hearts." *In* Howard, R. Alone with America p548-61

**Snow, Joseph T.** See Smith, N. B. jt. auth.

**Snyder, Gary**

**About**

Howard, R. Gary Snyder: "To hold both history and wilderness in mind." *In* Howard, R. Alone with America p562-77

**Sobel, Robert**

Exchanges. *In* Encyclopedia of American economic history, ed. by G. Porter v2 p696-706

**Soble, Alan**

An introduction to the philosophy of sex. *In* The Philosophy of sex, ed. by A. Soble p 1-56

**Social action**

Hollis, M. Rational man and social science. *In* Rational action, ed. by R. Harrison p 1-15

**Social adjustment.** See Deviant behavior

**Social alienation.** See Alienation (Social psychology)

**Social anthropology.** See Ethnology

**Social case work with children**

La Barre, M. B. "The worm in the honeysuckle": a case study of a child's hysterical blindness. *In* La Barre, W. Culture in context p233-46

**Social change**

Inkeles, A. The emerging social structure of the world. *In* Propaganda and communication in world history, ed. by H. D. Lasswell, D. Lerner and H. Speier v3 p482-515

Lerner, D. The revolutionary elites and world symbolism. *In* Propaganda and communication in world history, ed. by H. D. Lasswell, D. Lerner and H. Speier v2 p371-94

Riley, M. W. Aging, social change, and the power of ideas. *In* Generations, ed. by S. R. Graubard p39-52

*See also* Industry—Social aspects

**Social choice**

Weale, A. Rational choice and political principles. *In* Rational action, ed. by R. Harrison p93-114

**Social classes**

*See also* Middle classes

**Africa**

Cohen, R. Epilogue: integration, ethnicity, and stratification: focus and fashion in African studies. *In* Values, identities, and national integration, ed. by J. N. Paden p361-72

Social classes—*Continued*

### Brazil

Brown, D. D. Umbanda and class relations in Brazil. *In* Brazil, anthropological perspectives, ed. by M. L. Margolis and W. E. Carter p270-304

### Europe

Tilly, C. Did the cake of custom break? *In* Consciousness and class experience in nineteenth-century Europe, ed. by J. M. Merriman p17-44

### Europe—History

Le Goff, J. Licit and illicit trades in the medieval West. *In* Le Goff, J. Time, work, & culture in the Middle Ages p58-70

Le Goff, J. A note on tripartite society, monarchical ideology, and economic renewal in ninth- to twelfth-century Christendom. *In* Le Goff, J. Time, work, & culture in the Middle Ages p53-57

### Great Britain

Howkins, A. Class against class: the political culture of the Communist Party of Great Britain, 1930-35. *In* Class, culture and social change, ed. by F. Gloversmith p240-57

### Liberia

Sawyer, A. Social stratification and national orientations: students and nonstudents in Liberia. *In* Values, identities, and national integration, ed. by J. N. Paden p285-303

Sawyer, A. C. Social stratification, social change, and political socialization: students and nonstudents in Liberia. *In* Values, identities, and national integration, ed. by J. N. Paden p305-20

## Social classes in literature

Dembo, L. S. The socialist and socialite heroes of Upton Sinclair. *In* Toward a new American literary history, ed. by L. J. Budd, E. H. Cady and C. L. Anderson p164-80

## Social conflict

Isaacs, H. R. Changing arenas and identities in world affairs. *In* Propaganda and communication in world history, ed. by H. D. Lasswell, D. Lerner and H. Speier v2 p395-423

Morrison, D. G. and Stevenson, H. M. Cultural pluralism, modernization, and conflict: an empirical analysis of sources of political instability in African nations. *In* Values, identities, and national integration, ed. by J. N. Paden p11-23

Tajfel, H. Human intergroup conflict: useful and less useful forms of analysis. *In* Human ethology, ed. by M. von Cranach [and others] p396-422

*See also* Conflict of generations

## Social control

Conrad, P. On the medicalization of deviance and social control. *In* Critical psychiatry, ed. by D. Ingleby p102-19

Hepworth, M. Deviance and control in everyday life: the contribution of Erving Goffman. *In* The View from Goffman, ed. by J. Ditton p80-99

*See also* Liberty

**Social democracy.** See Socialism

**Social deviance.** See Deviant behavior

**Social equality.** See Equality

## Social ethics

Bahm, A. J. Humanist ethics as the science of oughtness. *In* Humanist ethics, ed. by M. B. Storer p210-26

Hocutt, M. Toward an ethic of mutual accommodation. *In* Humanist ethics, ed. by M. B. Storer p137-53

Kirkendall, L. A. An ethical system for now and the future. *In* Humanist ethics, ed. by M. B. Storer p193-209

Walker, P. E. Charity begins at home. *In* Lying truths, ed. by R. Duncan and M. Weston-Smith p219-29

*See also* Political ethics

**Social evolution.** See Social change

## Social groups

Tajfel, H. Human intergroup conflict: useful and less useful forms of analysis. *In* Human ethology, ed. by M. von Cranach [and others] p396-422

## Social history

Semenov, Y. I. The theory of socio-economic formations and world history. *In* Soviet and Western anthropology, ed. by E. Gellner p29-58

*See also* Social reformers

### Medieval, 500-1500

Le Goff, J. Clerical culture and folklore traditions in Merovingian civilization. *In* Le Goff, J. Time, work, & culture in the Middle Ages p153-58

Le Goff, J. Labor, techniques, and craftsmen in the value systems of the early Middle Ages (fifth to tenth centuries) *In* Le Goff, J. Time, work & culture in the Middle Ages p71-86

Le Goff, J. Licit and illicit trades in the medieval West. *In* Le Goff, J. Time, work, & culture in the Middle Ages p58-70

Le Goff, J. The medieval West and the Indian Ocean: an oneiric horizon. *In* Le Goff, J. Time, work, & culture in the Middle Ages p189-200

Le Goff, J. A note on tripartite society, monarchical ideology, and economic renewal in ninth- to twelfth-century Christendom. *In* Le Goff, J. Time, work, & culture in the Middle Ages p53-57

Le Goff, J. The symbolic ritual of vassalage. *In* Le Goff, J. Time, work, & culture in the Middle Ages p237-87

Le Goff, J. The universities and the public authorities in the Middle Ages and the Renaissance. *In* Le Goff, J. Time, work, & culture in the Middle Ages p135-49

### 16th century

Le Goff, J. The universities and the public authorities in the Middle Ages and the Renaissance. *In* Le Goff, J. Time, work, & culture in the Middle Ages p135-49

### 20th century—1945-

Marx, J. H. The ideological construction of post-modern identity models in contemporary cultural movements. *In* Identity and authority, ed. by R. Robertson and B. Holzner p145-89

### Historiography

Stearns, P. W. Toward a wider vision: trends in social history. *In* The Past before us, ed. by M. Kammen p205-30

**Social indicators.** See Social prediction

**Social institutions.** See Social structure

## Social integration

Inkeles, A. The emerging social structure of the world. *In* Propaganda and communication in world history, ed. by H. D. Lasswell, D. Lerner and H. Speier v3 p482-515

**Social interaction**
Kummer, H. On the value of social relationships to nonhuman primates: a heuristic scheme. *In* Human ethology, ed. by M. von Cranach [and others] p381-95

Psathas, G. Early Goffman and the analysis of face-to-face interaction in Strategic interaction. *In* The View from Goffman, ed. by J. Ditton p52-79

**Social justice**
Lang, W. Marxism, liberalism and justice. *In* Symposium on Theories of Justice in and for the Second Half of the Twentieth Century, Sydney, 1977. Justice p116-48

Passmore, J. A. Civil justice and its rivals. *In* Symposium on Theories of Justice in and for the Second Half of the Twentieth Century, Sydney, 1977. Justice p25-49

**Social mobility**

### United States—History
Pessen, E. Social mobility. *In* Encyclopedia of American economic history, ed. by G. Porter v3 p1120-35

**Social norms**
Hepworth, M. Deviance and control in everyday life: the contribution of Erving Goffman. *In* The View from Goffman, ed. by J. Ditton p80-99

Manley, L. G. The "duble name" of custom: the Reformation attack on convention. *In* Manley, L. G. Convention, 1500-1750 p67-90
*See also* Ethics

**Social organization.** See Social structure

**Social perception.** See Sexism

**Social policy.** See Housing policy; Medical policy; subdivision Social policy under names of countries, states, cities, etc.

**Social prediction**
Lipset, S. M. Predicting the future of post-industrial society: can we do it? *In* The Third century, ed. by S. M. Lipset p 1-35

**Social pressure.** See Propaganda

**Social problems.** See Cost and standard of living; Progress; Social ethics

**Social progress.** See Progress

**Social psychiatry**
Turkle, S. French anti-psychiatry. *In* Critical psychiatry, ed. by D. Ingleby p150-83

**Social psychology.** See Alienation (Social psychology); Exchange theory (Sociology); Hysteria (Social psychology); Interpersonal relations; Political psychology; Public opinion; Social conflict

**Social reformers**

### Great Britain
Harrison, B. A genealogy of reform in modern Britain. *In* Anti-slavery, religion, and reform: essays in memory of Roger Anstey, ed. by C. Bolt and S. Drescher p119-48

Hollis, P. Anti-slavery and British working-class radicalism in the years of reform. *In* Anti-slavery, religion, and reform: essays in memory of Roger Anstey, ed. by C. Bolt and S. Drescher p294-315

### United States
Bolt, C. The anti-slavery origins of concern for the American Indians. *In* Anti-slavery, religion, and reform: essays in memory of Roger Anstey, ed. by C. Bolt and S. Drescher p233-53

**Social role.** See Sex role

**Social science.** See Social sciences; Sociology

**Social sciences**
Barker, E. The limits of displacement: two disciplines face each other. *In* Sociology and theology: alliance and conflict, ed. by D. Martin, J. O. Mills and W. S. F. Pickering p15-23

Braudel, F. Unity and diversity in the human sciences. *In* Braudel, F. On history p55-63

Mills, J. O. Introduction: of two minds. *In* Sociology and theology: alliance and conflict, ed. by D. Martin, J. O. Mills [and] W. S. F. Pickering p 1-14
*See also* Power (Social sciences)

### Historiography
Kousser, J. M. Quantitative social-scientific history. *In* The Past before us, ed. by M. Kammen p433-56

### United States
Spengler, J. J. Social science and the collectivization of hubris. *In* Propaganda and communication in world history, ed. by H. D. Lasswell, D. Lerner and H. Speier v3 p461-81

**Social sciences and history**
Braudel, F. History and the social sciences; the longue durée. *In* Braudel, F. On history p25-54

**Social sciences and state**

### United States
Moynihan, D. P. Social science and the courts. *In* Moynihan, D. P. Counting our blessings p138-61

Spengler, J. J. Social science and the collectivization of hubris. *In* Propaganda and communication in world history, ed. by H. D. Lasswell, D. Lerner and H. Speier v3 p461-81

**Social scientists**

### United States
Spengler, J. J. Social science and the collectivization of hubris. *In* Propaganda and communication in world history, ed. by H. D. Lasswell, D. Lerner and H. Speier v3 p461-81
*See also* Women social scientists

**Social security**

### United States
Boskin, M. J. Social security and the economy. *In* The United States in the 1980s, ed. by P. Duignan and A. Rabushka p181-95

Kotlikoff, L. J. Social Security and welfare: what we have, want, and can afford. *In* The Economy in the 1980s: a program for growth and stability, ed. by M. J. Boskin p293-324

**Social service**
Mooers, G. R. Computer impact and the social welfare sector. *In* Monster or messiah? Ed. by W. M. Mathews p 113-24

Morowitz, H. J. A controlled social experiment. *In* Morowitz, H. J. The wine of life, and other essays on societies, energy & living things p163-67
*See also* Public welfare

**Social status**
La Barre, W. Social cynosure and social structure. *In* La Barre, W. Culture in context p203-14

Rogers, M. F. Goffman on power, hierarchy, and status. *In* The View from Goffman, ed. by J. Ditton p100-33
*See also* Social classes

**Social stratification.** See Social classes

**Social structure**

Inkeles, A. The emerging social structure of the world. *In* Propaganda and communication in world history, ed. by H. D. Lasswell, D. Lerner and H. Speier v3 p482-515

**Social studies.** See Social sciences

**Social welfare.** See Public welfare; Social service; related subjects referred to under these headings

**Social work.** See Social service

**Social work with children.** See Social case work with children

**Socialism**

Avineri, S. The new Jerusalem of Moses Hess. *In* Powers, possessions and freedom, ed. by A. Kontos p107-18

Flew, A. G. N. Intended conduct and unintended consequences. *In* Lying truths, ed. by R. Duncan and M. Weston-Smith p17-30

Garaudy, R. Values in a Marxist perspective. *In* Value and values in evolution, ed. by E. A. Maziarz p95-102

Hook, S. The social democratic prospect. *In* Hook, S. Philosophy and public policy p98-110

*See also* Equality; Labor and laboring classes; Women and socialism

**Socialism and art.** See Socialist realism in art

**Socialism and theater.** See Agitprop Theater

**Socialism in Great Britain**

### History

Reid, B. The Left Book Club in the thirties. *In* Culture and crisis in Britain in the thirties, ed. by J. Clark and others p193-207

**Socialism in literature**

Dembo, L. S. The socialist and socialite heroes of Upton Sinclair. *In* Toward a new American literature history, ed. by L. J. Budd, E. H. Cady and C. L. Anderson p164-80

Slaughter, C. Literature and revolution: Trotsky. *In* Slaughter, C. Marxism, ideology & literature p86-113

**Socialism in the United States**

### History

Harrington, M. Socialism. *In* Encyclopedia of American economic history, ed. by G. Porter v2 p851-62

**Socialist realism in art**

Harbison, R. Millennium. *In* Harbison, R. Deliberate regression p208-24

**Socialist realism in literature**

Hosking, G. The Socialist realist tradition. *In* Hosking, G. Beyond Socialist realism p1-28

**Socialized medicine.** See Insurance, Health

**Societies.** See Associations, institutions, etc.

**Society, Primitive**

Pershits, A. I. Ethnographic reconstruction of the history of primitive society. *In* Soviet and Western anthropology, ed. by E. Gellner p85-94

Woodburn, J. Hunters and gatherers today and reconstruction of the past. *In* Soviet and Western anthropology, ed. by E. Gellner p95-117

**Society and art.** See Art and society

**Society and education.** See Educational sociology

**Society and literature.** See Literature and society

**Society and religion.** See Religion and sociology

**Society and the arts.** See Arts and society

**Society of Jesus.** See Jesuits

**Sociolinguistics**

Goody, J. R. Thought and writing. *In* Soviet and Western anthropology, ed. by E. Gellner p119-33

Lodge, D. Where it's at: California language. *In* The State of the languge, ed. by L. Michaels and C. Ricks p503-13

Skinner, Q. Language and social change. *In* The State of the language, ed. by L. Michaels and C. Ricks p562-78

**Sociological prediction.** See Social prediction

**Sociology**

Braudel, F. History and sociology. *In* Braudel, F. On history p64-82

Coleman, J. S. Rational actors in macrosociological analysis. *In* Rational action, ed. by R. Harrison p75-91

Durkheim, E. Course in sociology: opening lecture. *In* Durkheim, E. Emile Durkheim on institutional analysis p43-70

Durkheim, E. Note on social morphology. *In* Durkheim, E. Emile Durkheim on institutional analysis p88-90

Durkheim, E. Sociology and the social sciences. *In* Durkheim, E. Emile Durkheim or institutional analysis p71-87

*See also* Communication; Crime and criminals; Exchange theory (Sociology); Family; Knowledge, Sociology of; Labor and laboring classes; Power (Social sciences); Social control; Social prediction; Social structure

### Methodology

Smith, D. E. A sociology for women. *In* The Prism of sex, ed. by J. A. Sherman and E. T. Beck p135-87

### Philosophy

Collins, R. Erving Goffman and the development of modern social theory. *In* The View from Goffman, ed. by J. Ditton p170-209

Gonos, G. The class position of Goffman's sociology: social origins of an American structuralism. *In* The View from Goffman, ed. by J. Ditton p134-69

### Russia

Drobizheva, L. Ethnic sociology of present-day life. *In* Soviet and Western anthropology, ed. by E. Gellner p171-80

### United States

Fuhrman, E. R. Social context and early American sociology: the Progressive era. *In* Fuhrman, E. R. The sociology of knowledge in America, 1883-1915 p21-43

**Sociology, Christian**

Gill, R. From sociology to theology. *In* Sociology and theology: alliance and conflict, ed. by D. Martin, J. O. Mills [and] W. S. F. Pickering p102-19

Harris, C. W. J. Displacements and reinstatements: the relations between sociology and theology considered in their changing intellectual context *In* Sociology and theology: alliance and conflict, ed. by D. Martin, J. O. Mills [and] W. S. F. Pickering p24-36

Hudson, W. D. The rational system of beliefs. *In* Sociology and theology: alliance and conflict, ed. by D. Martin, J. O. Mills [and] W. S. F. Pickering p80-101

Martin, D. A. The sociological mode and the theological vocabulary. *In* Sociology and theology: alliance and conflict, ed. by D. Martin, J. O. Mills [and] W. S. F. Pickering p46-58

Sociology, Christian—*Continued*

Mills, J. O. Introduction: of two minds. *In* Sociology and theology: alliance and conflict, ed. by D. Martin, J. O. Mills [and] W. S. F. Pickering p 1-14

Pickering, W. S. F. Theodicy and social theory: an exploration of the limits of collaboration between sociologist and theologian. *In* Sociology and theology: alliance and conflict, ed. by D. Martin, J. O. Mills [and] W. S. F. Pickering p59-79

Radcliffe, T. Relativizing the relativizers: a theologian's assessment of the role of sociological explanation of religious phenomena and theology today. *In* Sociology and theology: alliance and conflict, ed. by D. Martin, J. O. Mills [and] W. S. F. Pickering p151-62

Towler, R. Many voices. *In* Sociology and theology: alliance and conflict, ed. by D. Martin, J. O. Mills [and] W. S. F. Pickering p183-89

### Modern period, 1500-

*See* Sociology, Christian

### Sociology, Christian (Catholic)

Baum, G. The sociology of Roman Catholic theology. *In* Sociology and theology: alliance and conflict, ed. by D. Martin, J. O. Mills [and] W. S. F. Pickering p120-35

Lion, A. Theology and sociology: what point is there in keeping the distinction? *In* Sociology and theology: alliance and conflict, ed. by D. Martin, J. O. Mills [and] W. S. F. Pickering p163-82

**Sociology, Educational.** See Educational sociology

### Sociology, Military

Kučuk, E. The socio-class determinants of militarism. *In* Problems of contemporary militarism, ed. by A. Eide and M. Thee p148-72

Lumsden, M. Militarism: cultural dimensions of militarisation. *In* Problems of contemporary militarism, ed. by A. Eide and M. Thee p356-69

**Sociology, Religious.** See Religion and sociology

### Sociology, Rural

Shanin, T. The conceptual reappearance of peasantry in Anglo-Saxon social science. *In* Soviet and Western anthropology, ed. by E. Gellner p181-91

**Sociology and literature.** See Literature and society

**Sociology and religion.** See Religion and sociology

**Sociology of knowledge.** See Knowledge, Sociology

### Socrates

#### About

Frey, R. G. Did Socrates commit suicide? *In* Suicide: the philosophical issues, ed. by M. P. Battin and D. J. Mayo p35-38

**Sojo, Juan Pablo.** See Sojo R., Juan Pablo

### Sojo R., Juan Pablo

#### About individual works
##### Nochebuena negra

Jackson, R. L. Juan Pablo Sojo and the black novel in Venezuela. *In* Jackson, R. L. Black writers in Latin America p112-21

### Sokel, Walter Herbert

The devolution of the self in The notebooks of Malte Laurids Brigge. *In* Rilke: the alchemy of alienation, ed. by F. Baron, E. S. Dick and W. R. Maurer p171-90

Freud and the magic of Kafka's writing. *In* The World of Franz Kafka, ed. by J. P. Stern p145-58

### Soldiers

#### Sermons

Ahearn, M. L. David, the military exemplum. *In* The David myth in Western literature, ed. by R. J. Frontain and J. Wojcik p106-18

### Soldiers in literature

Brewer, D. S. The arming of the warrior in European literature and Chaucer. *In* Chaucerian problems and perspectives, ed. by E. Vasta and Z. P. Thundy p221-43

**The solemn** communion (criticism) Arrabal, F.

Orbison, T. T. Arrabal's The solemn communion as ritual drama. *In* The Binding of Proteus, ed. by M. W. McCune, T. T. Orbison and P. M. Withim p280-96

### Soler, José Antonio Martinez

The paradoxes of press freedom: the Spanish case. *In* Newspapers and democracy, ed. by A. Smith p153-73

### Solitude in literature

Brisman, S. H. and Brisman, L. Lies against solitude: symbolic, imaginary, and real. *In* The Literary Freud: mechanisms of defense and the poetic will, ed. by J. H. Smith p29-65

### Solmon, Lewis C. and Tierney, Michael

Education. *In* Encyclopedia of American economic history, ed. by G. Porter v3 p1012-27

### Solomon, Robert C.

Emotions and choice. *In* Explaining emotions, ed. by A. O. Rorty p251-81

Sexual paradigms. *In* The Philosophy of sex, ed. by A. Soble p89-98

### Soltow, James H.

Origins of small business and the relationships between large and small firms: metal fabricating and machinery making in New England, 1890-1957. *In* Small business in American life, ed. by S. W. Bruchey p192-211

### Soltow, Lee

Distribution of income and wealth. *In* Encyclopedia of American economic history, ed. by G. Porter v3 p1087-1119

**Solženicyn, Aleksandr.** See Solzhenifsyn, Aleksandr Isaevich

### Solzhenifsyn, Aleksandr Isaevich

A world split apart. *In* Solzhenistyn at Harvard, ed. by R. Berman p3-20

#### About individual works
##### The first circle

Hosking, G. Alexander Solzhenitsyn. *In* Hosking, G. Beyond Socialist realism p101-22

##### The Gulag Archipelago, 1918-1956

Hosking, G. Alexander Solzhenitsyn. *In* Hosking, G. Beyond Socialist realism p101-22

##### One day in the life of Ivan Denisovich

Hosking, G. Two key works: Doctor Zhivago and One day in the life of Ivan Denisovich. *In* Hosking, G. Beyond Socialist realism p29-49

#### Philosophy

Berman, H. J. The weightier matters of the law. *In* Solzhenitsyn at Harvard, ed. by R. Berman p99-113

**Solzhenifṣyn, Aleksandr I.**—Philosophy—*Cont.*

Berman, R. S. Through Western eyes. *In* Solzhenitsyn at Harvard, ed. by R. Berman p75-84

Hook, S. On Western freedom. *In* Solzhenitsyn at Harvard, ed. by R. Berman p85-97

McNeill, W. H. The decline of the West. *In* Solzhenitsyn at Harvard, ed. by R. Berman p122-30

Novak, M. On God and man. *In* Solzhenitsyn at Harvard, ed. by R. Berman p131-43

Pipes, R. In the Russian intellectual tradition. *In* Solzhenitsyn at Harvard, ed. by R. Berman p115-21

**Soma (Drug)** See Carisoprodol

**Somers, John Somers, Baron**

### About

Adams, R. M. In search of Baron Somers. *In* Culture and politics from Puritanism to the Enlightenment, ed. by P. Zagorin p165-202

**Somers, Joseph**

Critical approaches to Chicano literature. *In* The Identification and analysis of Chicano literature, ed. by F. Jiménez p143-52

**Somerville, Edith Anna Œnone, and Martin, Violet Florence**

### About individual works
#### The real Charlotte

Cronin, J. Somerville and Ross: the real Charlotte. *In* Cronin, J. The Anglo-Irish novel, v 1 p135-52

#### Some experiences of an Irish R.M.

Fehlmann, G. The composition of Somerville and Ross's Irish R.M. *In* The Irish short story, ed. by P. Rafroidi and T. Brown p103-11

**Sommerfield, John**

### About individual works
#### May Day

Laing, S. Presenting 'things as they are': John Sommerfield's May Day and mass observation. *In* Class, culture and social change, ed. by F. Gloversmith p142-60

**Song of Roland.** See Chanson de Roland

**Songs**

### History and criticism

Foley, J. M. Beowulf and traditional narrative song: the potential and limits of comparison. *In* Old English literature in context, ed. by J. D. Niles p117-36

**Songs, English**

### History and criticism

Dent, E. J. On the composition of English songs. *In* Dent, E. J. Selected essays p104-17

**Sopher, David Edward**

The landscape of home: myth, experience, social meaning. *In* The Interpretation of ordinary landscapes, ed. by D. W. Meinig p129-49

**Sophocles**

### About

Knox, B. M. W. Review of Sophocles, poète tragique (by Gilberte Ronnet). *In* Knox, B. M. W. Word and action p183-93

Knox, B. M. W. Review of Sophocles: a reading (by G. H. Gellie). *In* Knox, B. M. W. Word and action p194-97

### About individual works
#### Ajax

Knox, B. M. W. The Ajax of Sophocles. *In* Knox, B. M. W. Word and action p125-60

#### Ajax (ed. by W. B. Stanford)

Knox, B. M. W. Review of Sophocles' Ajax (ed. by W. B. Stanford). *In* Knox, B. M. W. Word and action p161-64

#### Antigone

Knox, B. M. W. Review of Sophokles, Antigone (by Gerhard Müller) *In* Knox, B. M. W. Word and action p165-82

#### Oedipus the King

Knox, B. M. W. The date of the Oedipus Tyrannus of Sophocles. *In* Knox, B. M. W. Word and action p112-24

Knox, B. M. W. Why is Oedipus called Tyrannus *In* Knox, B. M. W. Word and action p87-95

Mueller, M. Oedipus Rex as tragedy of fate: Corneille's Oedipe and Schiller's Die Braut von Messina. *In* Mueller, M. Children of Oedipus, and other essays on the imitation of Greek tragedy, 1550-1800 p129-46

Mueller, M. Oedipus Rex as tragedy of knowledge: Voltaire's Oedipe and Kleist's Der zerbrochene Krug. *In* Mueller, M. Children of Oedipus, and other essays on the imitation of Greek tragedy, 1550-1800 p109-28

#### The women of Trachis

Carne-Ross, D. S. Deianeira's dark cupboard: a question from Sophocles. *In* Carne-Ross, D. S. Instaurations p61-115

#### Characters—Oedipus

Knox, B. M. W. Sophocles' Oedipus. *In* Knox, B. M. W. Word and action p96-111

Knox, B. M. W. Why is Oedipus called Tyrannus? *In* Knox, B. M. W. Word and action p87-95

#### Influence

Mueller, M. Oedipus Rex as tragedy of fate: Corneille's Oedipe and Schiller's Die Braut von Messina. *In* Mueller, M. Children of Oedipus, and other essays on the imitation of Greek tragedy, 1550-1800 p129-46

Mueller, M. Oedipus Rex as tragedy of knowledge: Voltaire's Oedipe and Kleist's Der zerbrochene Krug. *In* Mueller, M. Children of Oedipus, and other essays on the imitation of Greek tragedy, 1550-1800 p109-28

#### Translations, English

Knox, B. M. W. Review of Sophocles, Women of Trachis (tr. by C. K. Williams and Gregory W. Dickerson) and Sophocles, Oedipus the King (tr. by Steven Berg and Diskin Clay). *In* Knox, B. M. W Word and action p198-202

**Sorabji, Richard**

Causation, laws, and necessity. *In* Doubt and dogmatism, ed. by M. Schofield, M. Burnyeat and J. Barnes p250-82

**Sorcery.** See Witchcraft

**Sorel, Charles**

### About

Ranum, O. Sorel: a novelist turned historiographer. *In* Ranum, O. Artisans of glory p129-47

**Sorel, Georges**

### About

Berlin, Sir I. Georges Sorel. *In* Berlin, Sir I. Against the current p296-332

Soriano, Elena. See Soriano Jara, Elena

Soriano Jara, Elena

### About

Fox-Lockert, L. Elena Soriano. *In* Fox-Lockert, L. Women novelists in Spain and Spanish America p94-106

Sorre, Maximilien

### About individual works

*Les fondements biologiques de la géographie humaine*

Braudel, F. Is there a geography of biological man? *In* Braudel, F. On history p105-19

Soul. See Immortality

Sound perception. See Auditory perception

Sousa, Ronald de

The rationality of emotions. *In* Explaining emotions, ed. by A. O. Rorty p127-51

Self-deceptive emotions. *In* Explaining emotions, ed. by A. O. Rorty p283-97

The South. See Southern States

South English legendary

Jankofsky, K. P. Entertainment, edification and popular education in the South English legendary. *In* 5000 years of popular culture, ed. by F. E. H. Schroeder p214-25

Southall, Ivan

Real adventure belongs to us. *In* The Arbuthnot lectures, 1970-1979 p83-101

### About

Southall, I. Real adventure belongs to us. *In* The Arbuthnot lectures, 1970-1979 p83-101

Townsend, J. R. Ivan Southall. *In* Townsend, J. R. A sounding of storytellers p179-93

Southern States

### Genealogy

Evans, E. N. Southern-Jewish history alive and unfolding. *In* Conference on Southern Jewish History, Richmond, Va. 1976. "Turn to the South" p158-67

### Historiography

Chyet, S. F. Reflections on Southern-Jewish historiography. *In* Conference on Southern Jewish History, Richmond, Va. 1976. "Turn to the South" p13-20

Evans, E. N. Southern-Jewish history alive and unfolding. *In* Conference on Southern Jewish History, Richmond, Va. 1976. "Turn to the South" p158-67

### History

King, R. H. Conclusion. *In* King, R. H. A Southern Renaissance p257-93

#### History—Colonial period, ca. 1600-1775

Weir, R. M. The role of the newspaper press in the Southern colonies on the eve of the Revolution: an interpretation. *In* The Press & the American Revolution, ed. by B. Bailyn and J. B. Hench p99-150

### Intellectual life

King, R. H. Conclusion. *In* King, R. H. A Southern Renaissance p287-93

King, R. H. Modernizers and monumentalists: social thought in the 1930s. *In* King, R. H. A Southern Renaissance p39-76

King, R. H. A Southern Renaissance. *In* King, R. H. A Southern Renaissance. p3-19

### Race relations

Hero, A. O. Southern Jews and public policy. *In* Conference on Southern Jewish History, Richmond, Va. 1976. "Turn to the South" p143-50

King, R. H. The Southern family romance and its context. *In* King, R. H. A Southern Renaissance p20-38

Shankman, A. M. Friend or foe? Southern blacks view the Jew, 1880-1935. *In* Conference on Southern Jewish History, Richmond, Va. 1976. "Turn to the South" p105-23

Spiro, J. D. Rabbi in the South: a personal view. *In* Conference on Southern Jewish History, Richmond, Va. 1976. "Turn to the South" p41-43

### Social life and customs

Bern, R. L. Utilizing the Southern-Jewish experience in literature. *In* Conference on Southern Jewish History, Richmond, Va. 1976. "Turn to the South" p151-57

Lavender, A. D. Jewish values in the Southern milieu. *In* Conference on Southern Jewish History, Richmond, Va. 1976. "Turn to the South" p124-34

Reed, J. S. Ethnicity in the South: observations on the acculturation of Southern Jews. *In* Conference on Southern Jewish History, Richmond, Va. 1976. "Turn to the South" p135-42

Whitfield, S. J. Jews and other Southerners: counterpoint and paradox. *In* Conference on Southern Jewish History, Richmond, Va. 1976. "Turn to the South" p76-104

### Social life and customs—1865-

King, R. H. The Southern family romance and its context. *In* King, R. H. A Southern Renaissance p20-38

### Social policy

King, R. H. Modernizers and monumentalists; social thought in the 1930s. *In* King, R. H. A Southern Renaissance p39-76

Southern States in literature

Simpson, L. P. Southern fiction. *In* Harvard Guide to contemporary American writing, ed. by D. Hoffman p153-90

Sovereignty

Eide, A. Militarisation with a global reach: a challenge to sovereignty, security and the international legal order. *In* Problems of contemporary militarism, ed. by A. Eide and M. Thee p299-322

Soviet literature. See Russian literature

Sower family

Adams, W. P. The colonial German-language press and the American Revolution. *In* The Press & the American Revolution, ed. by B. Bailyn and J. B. Hench p151-228

Sowerby, E. Millicent

Thomas Jefferson and his library. *In* The Bibliographical Society of America, 1904-79 p339-54

Space and time

Leclerc, I. Concepts of space. *In* Probability, time, and space in eighteenth-century literature, ed. by P. R. Backscheider p209-16

Space and time in literature

Milic, L. T. The metaphor of time as space. *In* Probability, time, and space in eighteenth-century literature, ed. by P. R. Backscheider p249-58

**Space perception in children**
Thom, R. The genesis of representational space according to Piaget. *In* Language and learning, ed. by M. Piattelli-Palmarini p361-68

**Spacks, Patricia Meyer**
Selves in hiding. *In* Women's autobiography, ed. by E. C. Jelinek p 112-32

**Spain**

History—Civil War, 1936-1939—
Campaigns and battles
Langlois, W. G. Malraux and Medellin. *In* André Malraux, ed. by F. Dorenlot and M. Tison-Braun p167-88

History—Civil War, 1936-1939—
Foreign public opinion
Cunningham, V. Neutral?: 1930s writers and taking sides. *In* Class, culture and social change, ed. by F. Gloversmith p45-69

Politics and government
Wiarda, H. J. Spain and Portugal. *In* Western European party systems, ed. by P. H. Merkl p298-328

Politics and government—20th century
Giner, S. and Sevilla-Guzman, E. From despotism to parliamentarianism: class domination and political order in the Spanish state. *In* The State in Western Europe, ed. by R. Scase p197-229

**Spanish American literature**

Black authors
Jackson, R. L. The black writer, the black press, and the black diaspora in Uruguay. *In* Jackson, R. L. Black writers in Latin America p93-111

Jackson, R. L. Conclusion: prospects for a black aesthetic in Latin America. *In* Jackson, R. L. Black writers in Latin America p191-97

Jackson, R. L. Folk forms and formal literature: revolution and the black poet-singer in Ecuador, Peru, and Cuba. *In* Jackson, R. L. Black writers in Latin America p160-70

Jackson, R. L. Introduction: the problems of literary blackness in Latin America. *In* Jackson, R. L. Black writers in Latin America p 1-14

**Spanish Americans in New York (City)**
Moynihan, D. P. Patterns of ethnic succession. *In* Moynihan, D. P. Counting our blessings p204-15

**Spanish poetry**

To 1500—History and criticism
Wardropper, B. W. Meaning in medieval Spanish folk song. *In* The Interpretation of medieval lyric poetry, ed. by W. T. H. Jackson p176-93

**Spanos, William V.**
Heidegger, Kierkegaard, and the hermeneutic circle: towards a postmodern theory of interpretation as dis-closure. *In* Martin Heidegger and the question of literature, ed. by W. V. Spanos p115-48

**Spark, Muriel**

About individual works
*The prime of Miss Jean Brodie*
Holloway, J. Narrative structure and text structure: Isherwood's A meeting by the river and Muriel Spark's The prime of Miss Jean Brodie. *In* Holloway, J. Narrative and structure: exploratory essays p74-99

**Spawn, Willman**
Notes on American bookbindings. *In* American Antiquarian Society. Proceedings v89 pt 1 p153-54

**Spears, Monroe Kirklyndorf**
Black English. *In* The State of the language, ed. by L. Michaels and C. Ricks p169-79

**A special day (Motion picture)**
Kael, P. Heart/soul. *In* Kael, P. When the lights go down p310-16

**Special section (Motion picture)**
Kael, P. Political acts. *In* Kael, P. When the lights go down p95-98

**Speculation.** See Commodity exchanges; Stock-exchange

**Speculum humanae salvationis**
Lutz, C. E. The "gentle Puritan" and the "angelic doctor." *In* Lutz, C. E. The oldest library motto, and other library essays p57-63

**Speech**
Black, J. W. Edward Wheeler Scripture, phonetician. *In* Psychology of language and thought, ed. by R. W. Rieber p225-38

Ostwald, P. F. and Rieber, R. W. James Rush and the theory of voice and mind. *In* Psychology of language and thought, ed. by R. W. Rieber p 105-19

Marler, P. Development of auditory perception in relation to vocal behavior. *In* Human ethology, ed. by M. von Cranach [and others] p663-81
*See also* Speech perception

Origin
*See* Language and languages—Origin

Psychology
*See* Psycholinguistics

**Speech, Disorders of.** See Stuttering

**Speech perception**
Liberman, A. M. An ethological approach to language through the study of speech perception. *In* Human ethology, ed. by M. von Cranach [and others] p682-704

**Speech recognition.** See Speech perception

**Speier, Hans**
The chances for peace. *In* Propaganda and communication in world history, ed. by H. D. Lasswell, D. Lerner and H. Speier v2 p507-27

The communication of hidden meaning. *In* Propaganda and communication in world history, ed. by H. D. Lasswell, D. Lerner and H. Speier v2 p261-300

The rise of public opinion. *In* Propaganda and communication in world history, ed. by H. D. Lasswell, D. Lerner and H. Speier v2 p147-67

The truth in hell: Maurice Joly on modern despotism. *In* Propaganda and communication in world history, ed. by H. D. Lasswell, D. Lerner and H. Speier v2 p301-16
*See also* Lasswell, H. D. jt. auth.

**Spender, Stephen**
Confessions and autobiography; excerpt from "The making of a poem." *In* Autobiography: essays theoretical and critical, ed. by J. Olney p115-22

Rilke and Eliot. *In* Rilke: the alchemy of alienation, ed. by F. Baron, E. S. Dick and W. R. Maurer p47-62

**Spengemann, William C.**
The forms of autobiography
*Contents*
Afterword
The formal paradigm
Historical autobiography
Philosophical autobiography
Poetic autobiography
The study of autobiography: a bibliographical essay

**Spengler, Joseph John**
Rising expectations: frustrations. *In* Propaganda and communication in world history, ed. by H. D. Lasswell, D. Lerner and H. Speier v3 p37-92

Social science and the collectivization of hubris. *In* Propaganda and communication in world history, ed. by H. D. Lasswell, D. Lerner and H. Speier v3 p461-81

**Spenser, Edmund**

About individual works
*The Faerie Queene*

Heinzelman, K. Economics in Mammon's cave. *In* Heinzelman, K. The economics of the imagination p35-69

Keaney, W. G. A courtly paradox in book IV of Spenser's Faerie Queene. *In* The Expansion and transformations of courtly literature, ed. by N. B. Smith and J. T. Snow p185-203

Murrin, M. Spenser's fairyland. *In* Murrin, M. The allegorical epic p131-52

**Sperber, Dan**
Claude Lévi-Strauss. *In* Structualism and since, ed. by J. Sturrock p19-51

Remarks on the lack of positive contributions from anthropologists to the problem of innateness. *In* Language and learning, ed. by M. Piatelli-Palmarini p245-49

**Spicehandler, Ezra**
Jewish literature: fiction. *In* The Jewish world, ed. by E. Kedourie p253-58

**Spiller, Robert E.**
The cycle and the roots: national identity in American literature. *In* Toward a new American literary history, ed. by L. J. Budd, E. H. Cady and C. L. Anderson p3-18

**Spinal cord.** See Reflexes

**Spink, John Stephenson.** See Part 2 under title: Woman and society in eighteenth-century France

**Spinoza, Benedictus de**

About individual works
*Tractatus Theologico-politicus*

Pines, S. The Jewish religion after the destruction of Temple and state: the views of Bodin and Spinoza. *In* Studies in Jewish religions and intellectual history, ed. by S. Stein and R. Loewe p215-34

Influence—Eliot, George, pseud.

Ashton, R. D. More translations: Spinoza and Feuerbach (1894-54) *In* Ashton, R. D. The German idea p155-66

**Spirits.** See Witchcraft

**Spiritual life**
Christ, C. P. Nothingness, awakening, insight, new naming. *In* Christ, C. P. Diving deep and surfacing p13-26

Christ, C. P. Toward wholeness: a vision of women's culture. *In* Christ, C. P. Diving deep and surfacing p119-31

Christ, C. P. Women's stories, women's quest. *In* Christ, C. P. Diving deep and surfacing p 1-12
*See also* Spirituality

**Spiritual-mindedness.** See Spirituality

**Spirituality**
Ghose, S. K. Sri Aurobindo and the spiritual society. *In* Aspects of Indian writing in English, ed. by M. K. Naik p268-78

**Spirituality (in religious orders, congregations, etc.)** See Monastic and religious life

**Spiro, Jack D.**
Rabbi in the South: a personal view. *In* Conference on Southern Jewish History, Richmond, Va. 1976. "Turn to the South" p41-43

**Sports**

Records
*See* Olympic games—Records

**Sprague, Arthur Colby**
'True, gallant Raleigh': some off-stage conversations in Shakespeare's plays. *In* Shakespeare's styles, ed. by P. Edwards, I. S. Ewbank and G. K. Hunter p183-90

**Springer, Arnold Reed**
Enlightened absolutism and Jewish reform: Prussia, Austria, and Russia. *In* California Slavic studies v11 p237-67

**Sprinker, John Michael**
Fictions of the self: the end of autobiography. *In* Autobiography: essays theoretical and critical, ed. by J. Olney p321-42

**Sprinker, Michael.** See Sprinker, John Michael

**Spurling, Hilary**
The critic's critic. *In* The Genius of Shaw, ed. by M. Holroyd p129-41

**Sraffia, Piero**

About
Roncaglia, A. The Sraffian contribution. *In* A Guide to post-Keynesian economics, ed. by A. S. Eichner p87-99

**Staar, Richard F.**
Soviet Union. *In* The United States in the 1980s, ed. by P. Duignan and A. Rabushka p735-55

**Stack, Carol B.**
The kindred of Viola Jackson: residence and family organization of an urban black American family. *In* A Heritage of her own, ed. by N. F. Cott and E. H. Pleck p542-54

**Stadler, Ernst Marie Richard**

About individual works
*Fahrt über die Kölner Rheinbrücke bei Nacht*

Grundlehner, P. Ernst Stadier: Fahrt über die Kölner Rheinbrücke bei Nacht." *In* Grundlehner, P. The lyrical bridge p119-29

**Staël, Madame de.** See Staël-Holstein, Anne Louise Germaine (Necker) baronne de

**Staël-Holstein, Anne Louise Germaine (Necker) baronne de**

About individual works
*Delphine*

Todd, J. Political friendship: Madame de Staël's Delphine. *In* Todd, J. Women's friendship in literature p226-45

**Stafford, William Edgar**

### About

Howard, R. William Stafford: " 'Tell us what you deserve,' the whole world said." *In* Howard, R. Alone with America p578-88

Wagner, L. W. William Stafford's plain-style. *In* Wagner, L. W. American modern p140-51

**Stagnation (Economics)** See Inflation (Finance) and unemployment

**Stahl, Gerry**

Attuned to being. Heideggerian music in technological society. *In* Martin Heidegger and the question of literature, ed. by W. V. Spanos p297-324

**Stalin, Iosif**

### About

Medvedev, R. A. The Stalin question. *In* The Soviet Union since Stalin, ed. by S. F. Cohen, A. Rabinowitch and R. Sharlet p32-49

**Stallone, Sylvester**

### About individual works
*Rocky*

Kael, P. Stallone and Stahr. *In* Kael, P. When the lights go down p213-19

**Stallybrass, Oliver**

A quorum of quotations. *In* E. M. Forster: a human exploration, ed. by G. K. Das and J. Beer p11-16

**Stam, James H.**

An historical perspective on 'linguistic relativity.' *In* Psychology of language and thought, ed. by R. W. Rieber p239-62

**Stammering.** See Stuttering

**Stamp Act, 1765**

Botein, S. Printers and the American Revolution. *In* The Press & the American Revolution, ed. by B. Bailyn and J. B. Hench p11-57

**Standard of living.** See Cost and standard of living

**Standards and standardization in education.** See Education—Standards

**Stankiewicz, Marketa Goetz-** See Goetz-Stankiewicz, Marketa

**Stanley, Eric Gerald**

Two Old English poetic phrases insufficiently understood for literary criticism: þing gehegan and seonoþ gehegan. *In* Old English poetry, ed. by D. G. Calder p67-90

**Stansell, Christine.** See Faragher, J. jt. auth.

**Stanton, Elizabeth (Cady)**

### About individual works
*Eighty years and more (1815-1897)*

Jelinek, E. C. The paradox and success of Elizabeth Cady Stanton. *In* Women's autobiography, ed. by E. C. Jelinek p71-92

**Stapleton, Darwin H.** See Lintner, S. F. jt. auth.

**A star is born (Motion picture, 1976)**

Kael, P. Contempt for the audience. *In* Kael, P. When the lights go down p240-44

**Star wars (Motion picture)**

Kael, P. Contrasts. *In* Kael, P. When the lights go down p291-98

Kauffmann, S. Star wars. *In* Kauffmann, S. Before my eyes p289-91

**Stark, Werner**

The theoretical and practical relevance of Vico's sociology for today. *In* Conference on Vico and Contemporary Thought, New York, 1976. Vico and contemporary thought pt2 p160-67

**Starobinski, Jean**

The style of autobiography. *In* Autobiography: essays theoretical and critical, ed. by J. Olney p73-83

**State, The**

Scase, R. Introduction. *In* The State in Western Europe, ed. by R. Scase p11-22

### History of theories
*See* Political science—History

**State, Welfare.** See Welfare state

**State aid to private schools**

Moynihan, D. P. When the Supreme Court is wrong. *In* Moynihan, D. P. Counting our blessings p162-90

**State and church.** See Church and state

**State and energy.** See Energy policy

**State and environment.** See Environmental policy

**State and housing.** See Housing policy

**State and industry.** See Industry and state

**State and Judaism.** See Judaism and state

**State and medicine.** See Medical policy

**State and science.** See Science and state

**State and social sciences.** See Social sciences and state

**State and technology.** See Technology and state

**State and theater.** See Theater and state

**State encouragement of science, literature, and art.** See Endowment of research

**State governments**

### United States—History

Nash, G. D. State and local governments. *In* Encyclopedia of American economic history, ed. by G. Porter v2 p509-23

**Statehood (American politics)** See State governments

**Statistics**

Frisch, O. R. You can prove anything with statistics. *In* Lying truths, ed. by R. Duncan and M. Weston- Smith p171-79

**Status, Social.** See Social status

**Stauffer, Donald B.**

Poe. *In* American literary scholarship, 1978 p29-41

**Stay hungry (Motion picture)**

Kauffmann, S. Stay hungry. *In* Kauffmann, S. Before my eyes p210-13

**Stearns, Peter N.**

Toward a wider vision: trends in social history. *In* The Past before us, ed. by M. Kammen p205-30

**Steele, Bruce**

The manuscript of D. H. Lawrence's Saga of Siegmund. *In* Virginia. University. Bibliographical Society. Studies in bibliography v33 p193-205

**Steele, Sir Richard**

### About

Hagstrum, J. H. Sentimental love and marriage "esteem enliven'd by desire." *In* Hagstrum, J. H. Sex and sensibility p160-85

**Steiger, Richard**
"Wit in a corner": hypocrisy in The country wife. *In* Tennessee Studies in literature v24 p56-70

**Steigerwalt, Albert K.**
Organized business groups. *In* Encyclopedia of American economic history, ed. by G. Porter v2 p753-71

**Stein, Gertrude**
### About
Wagner, L. W. Sherwood, Stein, the sentence, and grape sugar and oranges. *In* Wagner, L. W. American modern p31-41

### About individual works
*The autobiography of Alice B. Toklas*
Breslin, J. E. Gertrude Stein and the problems of autobiography. *In* Women's autobiography, ed. by E. C. Jelinek p149-62

### Influence—Anderson, Sherwood
Wagner, L. W. Sherwood, Stein, the sentence, and grape sugar and oranges. *In* Wagner, L. W. American modern p31-41

**Stein, Siegfried**
The concept of the "fence": observations on its origin and development. *In* Studies in Jewish religious and intellectual history, ed. by S. Stein and R. Loewe p301-29

**Steinberg, A. S.**
Dostoevski and the Jews. *In* The Jew, ed. by A. A. Cohen p158-70

**Steinson, Barbara J.**
"The mother half of humanity": American women in the peace and preparedness movements in World War I. *In* Women, war, and revolution, ed. by C. R. Berkin and C. M. Lovett p259-84

**Stepto, Robert B.**
From behind the veil
*Contents*
I rose and found my voice: narration, authentication, and authorial control in four slave narratives
Literacy and ascent: Richard Wright's Black boy
Literacy and hibernation: Ralph Ellison's Invisible man
Lost in a cause: Booker T. Washington's Up from slavery
Lost in a quest: James Weldon Johnson's The autobiography of an ex-coloured man
The quest of the weary traveler: W. E. B. Du Bois's The souls of black folk

**Stern, Malcolm H.**
The role of the rabbi in the South. *In* Conference on Southern Jewish History, Richmond, Va. 1976. "Turn to the South" p21-32

**Stern, Sheila**
The spirit of the place. *In* The World of Franz Kafka, ed. by J. P. Stern p44-46

**Sterne, Laurence**
### About
Hagstrum, J. H. The aftermath of sensibility: Sterne, Goethe, and Austen. *In* Hagstrum, J. H. Sex and sensibility p247-77

### About individual works
*Tristram Shandy*
Seidel, M. A. Gravity's inheritable line: Sterne's Tristram Shandy. *In* Seidel, M. A. Satiric inheritance, Rabelais to Sterne p250-62
Uphaus, R. W. Sterne's sixth sense. *In* Uphaus, R. W. The impossible observer p108-22

**Sternfeld, Frederick William**
Repetition and echo in Renaissance poetry and music. *In* English Renaissance studies, ed. by J. Carey p33-43

**Sternheim, Carl**
### About
Dierick, A. P. Two representative expressionist responses to the challenge of the First World War: Carl Sternheim's eigene Nuance and Leonhard Frank's utopia. *In* The First World War in German narrative prose, ed. by C. N. Genno and H. Wetzel p16-33
Robinson, F. M. Wallace Stevens: the poet as comedian. *In* Robinson, F. M. The comedy of language p89-125

**Stevens, Holly Bright**
Holidays in reality. *In* Wallace Stevens, ed. by F. Doggett and R. Buttel p105-13

### About individual works
*Souvenirs and prophecies: the young Wallace Stevens*
Miller, J. H. Theoretical and atheoretical in Stevens. *In* Wallace Stevens, ed. by F. Doggett and R. Buttel p274-85

**Stevens, Wallace**
### About
Dotterer, R. L. The fictive and the real: myth and form in the poetry of Wallace Stevens and William Carlos Williams. *In* The Binding of Proteus, ed. by M. W. McCune, T. Orbison and P. M. Withim p221-48
Ehrenpreis, I. Strange relation: Stevens' nonsense. *In* Wallace Stevens, ed. by F. Doggett and R. Buttel p219-34
Hollander, J. The sound of the music of music and sound. *In* Wallace Stevens, ed. by F. Doggett and R. Buttel p235-55
Kermode, F. Dwelling poetically in Connecticut. *In* Wallace Stevens, ed. by F. Doggett and R. Buttel p256-73
Riddel, J. N. Metaphoric staging: Stevens' beginning again of the "end of the book." *In* Wallace Stevens, ed. by F. Doggett and R. Buttel p308-38
Vendler, H. H. Stevens and Keats' "To autumn." *In* Wallace Stevens, ed. by F. Doggett and R. Buttel p171-95
Vendler, H. H. Wallace Stevens. *In* Vendler, H. H. Part of nature, part of us p 1-58

### About individual works
*Adagia*
Litz, A. W. Particles of order: the unpublished Adagia. *In* Wallace Stevens, ed. by F. Doggett and R. Buttel p57-77

*A collect of philosophy*
Brazeau, P. A. "A collect of philosophy": the difficulty of finding what would suffice. *In* Wallace Stevens, ed. by F. Doggett and R. Buttel p46-49

*The comedian as the letter C*
Martz, L. L. "From the journal of Crispin": an early version of "The comedian as the letter C." *In* Wallace Stevens, ed. by F. Doggett and R. Buttel p3-29

*Le monocle de mon oncle*
MacCaffrey, I. G. The ways of truth in "Le monocle de mon oncle." *In* Wallace Stevens, ed. by F. Doggett and R. Buttel p196-218

**Stevens, Wallace**—*Continued*

### Aesthetics

Miller, J. H. Theoretical and atheoretical in Stevens. *In* Wallace Stevens, ed. by F. Doggett and R. Buttel p274-85

Pearce, R. H. Toward decreation: Stevens and the "theory of poetry." *In* Wallace Stevens, ed. by F. Doggett and R. Buttel p286-307

### Appreciation—England

Lensing, G. S. Wallace Stevens in England. *In* Wallace Stevens, ed. by F. Doggett and R. Buttel p130-48

### Biography

Stevens, H. B. Holidays in reality. *In* Wallace Stevens, ed. by F. Doggett and R. Buttel p105-13

Taylor, W. E. Of a remembered time. *In* Wallace Stevens, ed. by F. Doggett and R. Buttel p91-104

### Biography—Character

Ellmann, R. How Wallace Stevens saw himself. *In* Wallace Stevens, ed. by F. Doggett and R. Buttel p149-70

### Books and reading

Kermode, F. Dwelling poetically in Connecticut. *In* Wallace Stevens, ed. by F. Doggett and R. Buttel p256-73

### Friends and associates

Brazeau, P. A. A trip in a balloon: a sketch of Stevens' later years in New York. *In* Wallace Stevens, ed. by F. Doggert and R. Buttel p114-29

### Psychology

*See* Stevens, Wallace—Biography—Character

**Stevenson, David R.**

Vico's Scienza nuova: an alternative to the Enlightenment mainstream. *In* The Quest for the new science, ed. by J. K. Pink and J. W. Marchand p6-16

**Stevenson, Hugh Michael.** See Morrison, D. G. jt. auth.

**Stevenson, Robert Louis**

### About individual works

*Dr Jekyll and Mr Hyde*

Nabokov, V. V. Robert Louis Stevenson: "The strange case of Dr Jekyll and Mr Hyde." *In* Nabokov, V. V. Lectures on literature p179-205

**Stewart, Philip**

Utopias that self-destruct. *In* Studies in eighteenth-century culture v9 p15-24

**Stierle, Karlheinz**

The reading of fictional texts. *In* The Reader in the text, ed. by S. R. Suleiman and I. Crosman p83-105

**Stiles, Ezra**

### About

Lutz, C. E. Abiel Holmes' life of Ezra Stiles. *In* Lutz, C. E. The oldest library motto, and other library essays p125-39

Lutz, C. E. Colonel David Humphreys and the Stiles family. *In* Lutz, C. E. The oldest library motto, and other library essays p149-55

Lutz, C. E. The "gentle Puritan" and the "angelic doctor." *In* Lutz, C. E. The oldest library motto, and other essays p57-63

**Stiles family**

Lutz, C. E. A family tablet. *In* Lutz, C. E. The oldest library motto, and other library essays p140-47

**Stiller, Nikki**

Eve's orphans: mothers and daughters in medieval English literature. *In* The Lost tradition: mothers and daughters in literature, ed. by C. N. Davidson and E. M. Broner p22-32

**Stimpson, Catharine R.**

Ad/d feminam: women, literature, and society. *In* Literature and society, ed. by E. W. Said p174-92

The power to name: some reflections on the avant-garde. *In* The Prism of sex, ed. by J. A. Sherman and E. T. Beck p55-77

**Stock-exchange**

### United States—History

Sobel, R. Exchanges. *In* Encyclopedia of American economic history, ed. by G. Porter v2 p696-706

**Stock market.** See Stock-exchange

**Stocker, Michael**

Intellectual desire, emotion, and action. *In* Explaining emotions, ed. by A. O. Rorty p323-38

**Stockholm. Dramatiska Teatern.** See Royal Dramatic Theatre, Stockholm

**Stockholm. Royal Dramatic Theatre.** See Royal Dramatic Theatre, Stockholm

**Stocks.** See Stock-exchange

**Stoekl, Allan**

The death of Acephale and the will to chance: Nietzsche in the text of Bataille. *In* Glyph 6 p42-67

**Stoics**

Annas, J. Truth and knowledge. *In* Doubt and dogmatism, ed. by M. Schofield, M. Burnyeat and J. Barnes p84-104

Barnes, J. Proof destroyed. *In* Doubt and dogmatism, ed. by M. Schofield, M. Burnyeat and J. Barnes p161-81

Brunschwig, J. Proof defined. *In* Doubt and dogmatism, ed. by M. Schofield, M. Burnyeat and J. Barnes p125-60

Frede, M. The original notion of cause. *In* Doubt and dogmatism, ed. by M. Schofield, M. Burnyeat and J. Barnes p217-49

Imbert, C. Stoic logic and Alexandrian poetics. *In* Doubt and dogmatism, ed. by M. Schofield, M. Burnyeat and J. Barnes p182-216

Schofield, M. Preconception, argument and God. *In* Doubt and dogmatism, ed. by M. Schofield, M. Burnyeat and J. Barnes p283-308

Sorabji, R. Causation, laws, and necessity. *In* Doubt and dogmatism, ed. by M. Schofield, M. Burnyeat and J. Barnes p250-82

Striker, G. Sceptical strategies. *In* Doubt and dogmatism, ed. by M. Schofield, M. Burnyeat and J. Barnes p54-83

White, N. P. The basis of Stoic ethics. *In* Harvard Studies in classical philology, v83 p143-78

**Stone, Donald David**

The romantic impulse in Victorian fiction

*Contents*

Benjamin Disraeli and the romance of the will

Charlotte Brontë and the perils of romance

Death and circuses: Charles Dickens and the byroads of romanticism

Elizabeth Gaskell, Wordsworth, and the burden of reality

George Eliot: the romantic legacy

George Meredith: a romantic in spite of himself

Trollope, Byron, and the conventionalities

**Stone, Julius**

Justice not equality. *In* Symposium on Theories of Justice in and for the Second Half of the Twentieth Century, Sydney, 1977. Justice p97-115

**Stone, Lawrence**

The results of the English revolutions of the seventeenth century. *In* Three British revolutions, 1641, 1688, 1776, ed. by J. G. A. Pocock p23-108

**Stone, Wilfred Healy**

Forster on profit and loss. *In* E. M. Forster: a human exploration, ed. by G. K. Das and J. Beer p69-78

**Stoppard, Tom**

### About individual works

*Rosencrantz and Guildenstern are dead*

Rabinowitz, P. J. "What's Hecuba to us?" The audience's experience of literary borrowing. *In* The Reader in the text, ed. by S. R. Suleiman and I. Crosman p241-63

**Storer, Morris B.**

A factual investigation of the foundations of morality. *In* Humanist ethics, ed. by M. B. Storer p281-300

**Storing, Herbert J.**

American statesmanship: old and new. *In* Bureaucrats, policy analysts, statesmen: who leads? Ed. by R. A. Goldwin p88-113

**The story of Adèle H (Motion picture)**

Kael, P. All for love. *In* Kael, P. When the lights go down p55-61

Kauffmann, S. The story of Adele H. *In* Kauffmann, S. Before my eyes p183-86

**Story-telling**

Coles, R. Children's stories: the link to a past. *In* Children's literature v8 p141-46

**Stouck, David**

Fiction: 1900 to the 1930s. *In* American literary scholarship, 1978 p229-46

**Stowe, Harriet Elizabeth (Beecher)**

### About individual works

*Uncle Tom's cabin*

Fiedler, L. A. Uncle Tom as white mother. *In* Fiedler, L. A. The inadvertent epic p29-41

Fiedler, L. A. Uncle Tom's cabin: the invisible masterpiece. *In* Fiedler, L. A. The inadvertent epic p13-27

**Strachey, John**

### About

Coombes, J. British intellectuals and the Popular Front. *In* Class, culture and social change, ed. by F. Gloversmith p70-100

**Strand, Mark**

### About

Howard, R. Mark Strand: "The mirror was nothing without you." *In* Howard, R. Alone with America p589-602

**Strand, Wilson E.**

In search of an Assyrian sense of humor. *In* 5000 years of popular culture, ed. by F. E. H. Schroeder p38-51

**Strange, Susan**

The management of surplus productive capacity. *In* Economic issues of the eighties, ed. by N. M. Kamrany and R. H. Day p226-46

**Strategic Arms Limitation Talks**

Moynihan, D. P. Cold dawn, high noon. *In* Moynihan, D. P. Counting our blessings p277-336

**Strategic forces**

### United States

Van Cleave, W. R. Quick fixes to U.S. strategic nuclear forces. *In* National security in the 1980s: from weakness to strength, ed. by W. S. Thompson p89-107

**Strategy**

Luttwak, E. N. On the meaning of strategy . . . for the United States in the 1980s. *In* National security in the 1980s: from weakness to strength, ed. by W. S. Thompson p259-73

Marshall, C. B. Strategy: the emerging dangers. *In* National security in the 1980s: from weakness to strength, ed. by W. S. Thompson p423-41

Nitze, P. H. Policy and strategy from weakness. *In* National security in the 1980s: from weakness to strength, ed. by W. S. Thompson p443-56

Thompson, W. S. Introduction. *In* National security in the 1980s: from weakness to strength, ed. by W. S. Thompson p3-16

Thompson, W. S. Toward a strategic peace. *In* National security in the 1980s: from weakness to strength, ed. by W. S. Thompson p473-88

West, F. J. Conventional forces beyond NATO. *In* National security in the 1980s: from weakness to strength, ed. by W. S. Thompson p319-36

Whaley, B. Deception—its decline and revival in international conflict. *In* Propaganda and communication in world history, ed. by H. D. Lasswell, D. Lerner and H. Speier v2 p339-67

*See also* Atomic warfare

**Stratification, Social.** See Social classes

**Strauss, Claude Lévi-** See Lévi-Strauss, Claude

**Strauss, David Friedrich**

### About individual works

*The life of Jesus critically examined*

Ashton, R. D. George Eliot, translator of Strauss (1844-6) *In* Ashton, R. D. The German idea p147-55

**Strauss, Johann**

### About

Carner, M. The secret of Johann Strauss. *In* Carner, M. Major and minor p56-59

**Strauss, Leo**

The idea of the holy (Rudolf Otto) *In* The Jew, ed. by A. A. Cohen p232-36

Zionism in Max Nordau. *In* The Jew, ed. by A. A. Cohen p120-26

**Strauss, Walter Adolf**

Rilke and Ponge: l'objet c'est la poétique. *In* Rilke: the alchemy of alienation, ed. by F. Baron, E. S. Dick and W. R. Maurer p63-93

**Strawson, Peter Frederick**

Perception and its objects. *In* Perception and identity, ed. by G. F. Macdonald p41-60

**Streeter, Thomas Winthrop**

### About

Heaney, H. J. Thomas W. Streeter, collector, 1883-1965. *In* The Bibliographical Society of America, 1904-79 p500-13

**Stress (Psychology)**

Pearlin, L. I. Life strains and psychological distress among adults. *In* Themes of work and love in adulthood, ed. by N. J. Smelser and E. H. Erikson p174-92

*See also* Anxiety

**Stricker, Frank A.**
Cookbooks and law books: the hidden history of career women in twentieth-century America. *In* A Heritage of her own, ed. by N. F. Cott and E. H. Pleck p476-98

**Striker, Gisela**
Sceptical strategies. *In* Doubt and dogmatism, ed. by M. Schofield, M. Burnyeat and J. Barnes p54-83

**Strindberg, August**

### About individual works
*Historical miniatures*
Landauer, G. Strindberg's Historical miniatures: a lecture. *In* The Jew, ed. by A. A. Cohen p171-84

**Stringer, Peter**
Models of man in Casterbridge and Milton Keynes. *In* Architecture for people, ed. by B. Mikellides p176-86

**Structural anthropology**
Maranda, P. The dialectic of metaphor: an anthropological essay on hermeneutics. *In* The Reader in the text, ed. by S. R. Suleiman and I. Crosman p183-204
Pouillon, J. Structure and structuralism. *In* Soviet and Western anthropology, ed. by E. Gellner p275-82

**Structuralism**
Kurzweil, E. Claude Lévi-Strauss: the father of structuralism. *In* Kurzweil, E. The age of structuralism p13-34
Kurzweil, E. Henri Lefebvre: a Marxist against structuralism. *In* Kurzweil, E. The age of structuralism p57-85
Kurzweil, E. Jacques Lacan: structuralist psychoanalysis. *In* Kurzweil, E. The age of structuralism p135-64
Kurzweil, E. Louis Althusser: Marxism and structuralism. *In* Kurzweil, E. The age of structuralism p35-56
Kurzweil, E. Paul Ricoeur: hermeneutics and structuralism. *In* Kurzweil, E. The age of structuralism p87-112
Pouillon, J. Structure and structuralism. *In* Soviet and Western anthropology, ed. by E. Gellner p275-82
Sturrock, J. Introduction. *In* Structuralism and since, ed. by J. Sturrock p 1-18

**Structuralism (Literary analysis)**
Banfield, A. The nature of evidence in a falsifiable literary theory. *In* The Concept of style, ed. by B. Lang p183-211
Foster, D. W. Introduction: the écriture of literary texts. *In* Foster, D. W. Studies in the contemporary Spanish-American short story p 1-12
Harari, J. V. Critical factions/critical fictions. *In* Textual strategies, ed. by J. V. Harari p17-72
Kurzweil, E. Roland Barthes: literary structuralism and erotics. *In* Kurzweil, E. The age of structuralism p165-91
Lentricchia, F. History or the abyss: post-structuralism. *In* Lentricchia, F. After the New Criticism p156-210
Lentricchia, F. Uncovering history and the reader: structuralism. *In* Lentricchia, F. After the New Criticism p 102-54
Ruegg, M. Metaphor and metonymy: the logic of structuralist rhetoric. *In* Glyph 6 p141-57
Serres, M. The algebra of literature: the wolf's game. *In* Textual strategies, ed. by J. V. Harari p260-76

Suleiman, S. R. Introduction: varieties of audience-oriented criticism. *In* The Reader in the text, ed. by S. R. Suleiman and I. Crosman p3-45
*See also* Semiotics; Semiotics and literature

### Bibliography
Crosman, I. K. Annotated bibliography of audience-oriented criticism. *In* The Reader in the text, ed. by S. R. Suleiman and I. Crosman p401-24

**Structure (Philosophy)** See Structuralism

**Struve, Gleb**
Towards a biography of Prince Peter Kozlovsky: Kozlovsky's letter to Countess Lieven. *In* California Slavic studies v11 p 1-24

### Bibliography
Hughes, R. P. comp. Gleb Struve: a bibliography. *In* California Slavic studies v11 p269-317

**Students**

### Ghana—Attitudes
Fischer, L. F. Student orientations toward nation-building in Ghana. *In* Values, identities, and national integration, ed. by J. N. Paden p271-84

### Liberia—Attitudes
Sawyer, A. C. Social stratification and national orientations: students and nonstudents in Liberia. *In* Values, identities, and national integration, ed. by J. N. Paden p285-303
Sawyer, A. C. Social stratification, social change, and political socialization: students and nonstudents in Liberia. *In* Values, identities, and national integration, ed. by J. N. Paden p305-20

**Sturm, Sara**
Transformations of courtly love poetry: Vita nuova and Canzoniere. *In* The Expansion and transformations of courtly literature, ed. by N. B. Smith and J. T. Snow p128-40

**Sturrock, John**
Introduction. *In* Structualism and since, ed. by J. Sturrock p 1-18
Roland Barthes. *In* Structualism and since, ed. by J. Sturrock p52-80

**Stuttering**
Clark, M. J. Jean Itard: a memoir on stuttering. *In* Psychology of language and thought, ed. by R. W. Rieber p153-84

**Style (The English word)**
Kubler, G. Towards a reductive theory of visual style. *In* The Concept of style, ed. by B. Lang p119-27

**Style, Literary**
Banfield, A. The nature of evidence in a falsifiable literary theory. *In* The Concept of style, ed. by B. Lang p183-211
Chatman, S. The styles of narrative codes. *In* The Concept of style, ed. by B. Lang p169-81
Hartman, G. H. Purification and danger 2: critical style. *In* Hartman, G. H. Criticism in the wilderness p133-57
Starobinski, J. The style of autobiography. *In* Autobiography: essays theoretical and critical, ed. by J. Olney p73-83
White, H. W. The problem of style in realistic representation: Marx and Flaubert. *In* The Concept of style, ed. by B. Lang p213-29
*See also* Criticism; Language and languages—Style; Letter-writing; Repetition in literature; Rhetoric

**Style, Musical**
Meyer, L. T. Toward a theory of style. *In* The Concept of style, ed. by B. Lang p3-44

**Styron, William**

### About individual works

*Lie down in darkness*

Casciato, A. D. His editor's hand: Hiram Haydn's changes in Styron's Lie down in darkness. *In* Virginia. University. Bibliographical Society. Studies in bibliography v33 p263-76

### Editors

Casciato, D. A. His editor's hand: Hiram Haydn's changes in Styron's Lie down in darkness. *In* Virginia. University. Bibliographical Society. Studies in bibliography v33 p263-76

**Subconsciousness**

Rolle, A. F. The historic past of the unconscious. *In* Propaganda and communication in world history, ed. by H. D. Lasswell, D. Lerner and H. Speier v3 p403-60

*See also* Dreams; Psychoanalysis

**Sublime, The**

Paulson, R. Burke's sublime and the representation of revolution. *In* Culture and politics from Puritanism to the Enlightenment, ed. by P. Zagorin p241-69

**Submarine geology**

Menard, H. W. Very like a spear. *In* New Hampshire Bicentennial Conference on the History of Geology, University of New Hampshire, 1976. Two hundred years of geology in America p19-30

*See also* Sea-floor spreading

**Subsidies**

### Sweden

Gustafsson, K. E. The press subsidies of Sweden: a decade of experiment. *In* Newspapers and democracy, ed. by A. Smith p104-26

**Substance (Philosophy)** See Essence (Philosophy)

**Sudbery, Rodie**

### About

Rees, D. Middle of the way: Rodie Sudbery and Beverly Cleary. *In* Rees, D. The marble in the water p90-103

**Suffering**

Kohl, M. On suffering. *In* Humanist ethics, ed. by M. B. Storer p173-78

**Suffrage**

### Virginia—History

Pole, J. R. Representation and authority in Virginia from the Revolution to reform. *In* Pole, J. R. Paths to the American past p3-40

**Suhonen, Pertti**

Finland. *In* Western European party systems, ed. by P. H. Merkl p235-56

**Suhrkamp, Peter**

### About

Unseld, S. Bertolt Brecht and his publishers. *In* Unseld, S. The author and his publisher p83-125

Unseld, S. Hermann Hesse and his publishers. *In* Unseld, S. The author and his publishers p45-81

**Suicide**

Alvarez, A. The background; excerpt from "The savage god." *In* Suicide: the philosophical issues, ed. by M. P. Battin and D. J. Mayo p7-32

Baelz, P. R. Suicide: some theological reflections. *In* Suicide: the philosophical issues, ed. by M. P. Battin and D. J. Mayo p71-83

Barrington, M. R. Apologia for suicide. *In* Suicide: the philosophical issues, ed. by M. P. Battin and D. J. Mayo p90-103

Battin, M. P. Manipulated suicide. *In* Suicide: the philosophical issues, ed. by M. P. Battin and D. J. Mayo p169-82

Battin, M. P. Suicide: a fundamental human right? *In* Suicide: the philosophical issues, ed. by M. P. Battin and D. J. Mayo p267-85

Beauchamp, T. L. Suicide. *In* Matters of life and death, ed. by T. Regan p67-108

Bogen. J. J. Suicide and virtue. *In* Suicide: the philosophical issues, ed. by M. P. Battin and D. J. Mayo p286-92

Brandt, R. B. The rationality of suicide. *In* Suicide: the philosophical issues, ed. by M. P. Battin and D. J. Mayo p117-32

Clements, C. D. The ethics of not-being: individual options for suicide. *In* Suicide: the philosophical issues, ed. by M. P. Battin and D. J. Mayo p104-14

Devine, P. E. On choosing death. *In* Suicide: the philosophical issues, ed. by M. P. Battin and D. J. Mayo p138-43

Feinberg, J. Suicide and the inalienable right to life. *In* Suicide: the philosophical issues, ed. by M. P. Battin and D. J. Mayo p223-28

Francis, L. P. Assisting suicide: a problem for the criminal law. *In* Suicide: the philosophical issues, ed. by M. P. Battin and D. J. Mayo p254-66

Frey, R. Did Socrates commit suicide? *In* Suicide: the philosophical issues, ed. by M. P. Battin and D. J. Mayo p35-38

Lebacqz, K. and Engelhardt, H. T. Suicide and covenant. *In* Suicide: the philosophical issues, ed. by M. P. Battin and D. J. Mayo p84-89

Martin, R. M. Suicide and false desires. *In* Suicide: the philosophical issues, ed. by M. P. Battin and D. J. Mayo p144-50

Martin, R. M. Suicide and self-sacrifice. *In* Suicide: the philosophical issues, ed. by M. P. Battin and D. J. Mayo p48-68

Mayo, D. J. Irrational suicide. *In* Suicide: the philosophical issues, ed. by M. P. Battin and D. J. Mayo p133-37

Oates, J. C. The art of suicide. *In* Suicide: the philosophical issues, ed. by M. P. Battin and D. J. Mayo p161-68

Szasz, T. S. The ethics of suicide. *In* Suicide: the philosophical issues, ed. by M. P. Battin and D. J. Mayo p185-98

Windt, P. Y. The concept of suicide. *In* Suicide: the philosophical issues, ed. by M. P. Battin and D. J. Mayo p39-47

Wood, D. Suicide as instrument and expression. *In* Suicide: the philosophical issues, ed. by M. P. Battin and D. J. Mayo p151-60

*See also* Right to die

### Prevention

Ringel, E. Suicide prevention and the value of human life. *In* Suicide: the philosophical issues, ed. by M. P. Battin and D. J. Mayo p205-11

**Suku (African tribe)**

### Rites and ceremonies

Kopytoff, I. Revitalization and the genesis of cults in pragmatic religion: the Kita rite of passage among the Suku. *In* Explorations in African systems of thought, ed. by I. C. Karp & C. S. Bird p183-212

**Sukuma.** See Suku (African tribe)

**Suleiman, Susan Rubin**

Introduction: varieties of audience-oriented criticism. *In* The Reader in the text, ed. by S. R. Suleiman and I. Crosman p3-45

**Sullivan, Alan**
A constitutional right to suicide. *In* Suicide: the philosophical issues, ed. by M. P. Battin and D. J. Mayo p229-53

**Sullivan, John J.**
Noam Chomsky and Cartesian linguistics. *In* Psychology of language and thought, ed. by R. W. Rieber p197-223

**Sullivan, Leonard**
Correlating national security strategy and defense investment. *In* National security in the 1980s: from weakness to strength, ed. by W. S. Thompson p337-73

**Summer in literature**
Hatto, A. T. Folk ritual and the Minnesang. *In* Hatto, A. T. Essays on medieval German and other poetry p42-63

**Summerfield, Geoffrey**
The making of The home treasury. *In* Children's literature v8 p35-52

**Summerly, Felix,** pseud. See Cole, Sir Henry

**Summers, Joseph Holmes**
'Look there, look there!' the ending of King Lear. *In* English Renaissance studies, ed. by J. Carey p74-93

**Sumner, William Graham**

About

Fuhrman, E. R. William G. Sumner. *In* Fuhrman, E. R. The sociology of knowledge in America, 1883-1915 p44-74

**Sundelson, David**
So rare a wonder'd father: Prospero's Tempest. *In* Representing Shakespeare, ed. by M. M. Schwartz and C. Kahn p33-53

**Sundquist, Eric J.**
Home as found

*Contents*

"At home in his words": parody and parricide in Melville's Pierre
"The home of my childhood": incest and imitation in Cooper's Home as found
"The home of the dead": representation and speculation in Hawthorne and The House of the Seven Gables
"Plowing homeward": cultivation and grafting in Thoreau and the Week

**The sunshine boys (Motion picture)**
Kael, P. Walking into your childhood. *In* Kael, P. When the lights go down p72-79

**Suny, Ronald Grigor**
Georgia and Soviet nationality policy. *In* The Soviet Union since Stalin, ed. by S. F. Cohen, A. Rabinowitch and R. Sharlet p200-26

**Superman (Motion picture)**
Kael, P. The package. *In* Kael, P. When the lights go down p524-28

**Supernatural**
Shea, W. M. The supernatural in the naturalists. *In* History, religion, and spiritual democracy, ed. by M. Wohlgelenter and others p53-75

**Supernatural (Theology)**
Daly, G. Lucien Laberthonnière's 'critical mysticism'. *In* Daly, G. Transcendence and immanence p91-116

**Superstition.** See Evil eye; Witchcraft

**Supply and demand.** See Demand (Economic theory)

**Supply of money.** See Money supply

**Supreme Court.** See United States. Supreme Court

**Surrey, Henry Howard, Earl of, tr.**

About individual works

*The Aeneid*

Kratzmann, G. Two Aeneid translators— Surrey's debt to Douglas: Wyatt and Henryson. *In* Kratzmann, G. Anglo-Scottish literary relations, 1430-1550 p169-94

History

Kelly, K. P. "In dispers'd country plantations": settlement patterns in sevententh-century Surry County, Virginia. *In* The Chesapeake in the seventeenth century, ed. by T. W. Tate and D. L. Ammerman p183-205

**Susan Lenox: her fall and rise (Motion picture)**
Miller, G. The new woman gets the old treatment. *In* Miller, G. Screening the novel p19-45

**Susman, Margarete**
Franz Rosenzweig's The star of redemption (a review) *In* The Jew, ed. by A. A. Cohen p273-85

**Suso, Heinrich**

About individual works

*Horologium sapientiae*

Lutz, C. E. The clock of eternal wisdom. *In* Lutz, C. E. The oldest library motto, and other library essays p25-31

**Sutherland, Norman Stuart**
The myth of mind control. *In* Lying truths, ed. by R. Duncan and M. Weston-Smith p107-20

**Sutherland, Stuart.** See Sutherland, Norman Stuart

**Sutton, Max Keith**
Truth and the pastor's vision in George Crabbe, William Barnes, and R. S. Thomas. *In* Survivals of pastoral, ed. by R. F. Hardin p33-59

**Sutton, Walter**
Apocalyptic history and the American epic: Cotton Mather and Joel Barlow. *In* Toward a new American literary history, ed. by L. J. Budd, E. H. Cady and C. L. Anderson p69-83

**Swan (in religion, folk-lore, etc.)**
Hatto, A. T. The swan maiden: a folk-tale of North Eurasian origin? *In* Hatto, A. T. Essays on medieval German and other poetry p267-97

**Swan-maidens**
Hatto, A. T. The swan maiden: a folk-tale of North Eurasian origin? *In* Hatto, A. T. Essays on medieval German and other poetry p267-97

**Swank, Scott T.**
Introduction. *In* Perspectives on American folk art, ed. by I. M. G. Quimby and S. T. Swank p 1-12

**Swanson, Guy E.**
A basis of authority and identity in post-industrial society. *In* Identity and authority, ed. by R. Robertson and B. Holzner p190-217

**Sweden**

Economic policy

Von Otter, C. Swedish welfare capitalism: the role of the state. *In* The State in Western Europe, ed. by R. Scase p142-63

**Sweden**—*Continued*

### Politics and government—1950-

Hancock, M. D. Sweden. *In* Western European party systems, ed. by P. H. Merkl p185-204

Von Otter, C. Swedish welfare capitalism: the role of the state. *In* The State in Western Europe, ed. by R. Scase p 142-63

### Social policy

Von Otter, C. Swedish welfare capitalism: the role of the state. *In* The State in Western Europe, ed. by R. Scase p142-63

**Sweeney, James Lee**

Energy problems and policies. *In* The Economy in the 1980s: a program for growth and stability, ed. by M. J. Boskin p353-92

**Swenson, May**

### About

Howard, R. May Swanson: "Turned back to the wild by love." *In* Howard, R. Alone with America p603-18

**Swept away by an unusual destiny in the blue sea of August (Motion picture)**

Kauffmann, S. Swept away. *In* Kauffmann, S. Before my eyes p20-23

**Swidler, Ann**

Love and adulthood in American culture. *In* Themes of work and love in adulthood, ed. by N. J. Smelser and E. H. Erikson p120-47

**Swift, Jonathan**

### About

Pritchett, V. S. Jonathan Swift: the infantilism of genius. *In* Pritchett, V. S. The tale bearers p177-83

Uphaus, R. W. Swift and the problematical nature of meaning. *In* Uphaus, R. W. The impossible observer p9-27

Woolley, J. Thomas Sheridan and Swift. *In* Studies in eighteenth-century culture v9 p93-114

### About individual works

*Gulliver's travels*

Seidel, M. A. Strange dispositions: Swift's Gulliver's travels. *In* Seidel, M. A. Satiric inheritance, Rabelais to Sterne p201-25

*A tale of a tub*

Anselment, R. A. A tale of a tub. *In* Anselment, R. A. 'Betwixt jest and earnest' p126-62

Seidel, M. A. Fathers and sons: Swift's A tale of a tub. *In* Seidel, M. A. Satiric inheritance, Rabelais to Sterne p169-200

### Characters—Women

Hagstrum, J. H. Friends and lovers: the witty and the wise. *In* Hagstrum, J. H. Sex and sensibility p133-59

**Swinburne, Algernon Charles**

### About

McGhee, R. D. Swinburne and Hopkins. *In* McGhee, R. D. Marriage, duty & desire in Victorian poetry and drama p177-232

**Sworakowski, Witold S.**

Herbert Hoover, launching the American Food Administration, 1917. *In* Herbert Hoover, ed. by L. E. Gelfand p40-60

**Swords in literature**

Hatto, A. T. Snake-swords and boar-helms in Beowulf. *In* Hatto, A. T. Essays on medieval German and other poetry p233-54

**Sylla, Richard Eugene**

Small-business banking in the United States, 1780-1920. *In* Small business in American life, ed. by S. W. Bruchey p240-62

**Symbol (The word)**

Peyre, H. The word and its antecedents. *In* Peyre, H. What is symbolism? p6-20

**Symbolic interaction.** See Social interaction

**Symbolism**

Bickman, M. Mythology: the symbol in Jungian thought and American romanticism. *In* Bickman, M. The unsounded centre p5-21

Campbell, J. The interpretation of symbolic forms. *In* The Binding of Proteus, ed. by M. W. McCune, T. Orbison and P. M. Withim p35-59

Eliade, M. The world, the city, and the house; excerpt from "Occultism, witchcraft, and cultural fashions." *In* Value and values in evolution, ed. by E. A. Maziarz p3-16

**Symbolism (Literary movement)**

### History and criticism

Peyre, H. Introduction. *In* Peyre, H. What is symbolism. *In* Peyre, H. What is symbolism? p 1-5

Peyre, H. Symbolism, painting, and music. *In* Peyre, H. What is symbolism? p112-27

Peyre, H. The symbolists. *In* Peyre, H. What is symbolism? p82-97

### Influence

Peyre, H. The heritage of symbolism in France and outside France. *In* Peyre, H. What is symbolism? p128-50

**Symbolism, Islamic.** See Islamic art and symbolism

**Symbolism in art.** See Christian art and symbolism; Islamic art and symbolism; Jewish art and symbolism

**Symbolism in literature**

Bickman, M. Voyage of the mind's return: three paradigmatic works. *In* Bickman, M. The unsounded centre p22-37

De Man, P. Allegory (Julie). *In* De Man, P. Allegories of reading p188-220

Peyre, H. Baudelaire. *In* Peyre, H. What is symbolism? p21-32

Peyre, H. Mallarmé. *In* Peyre, H. What is symbolism? p63-81

Peyre, H. Rimbaud, or the symbolism of revolt. *In* Peyre, H. What is symbolism? p33-47

Peyre, H. The tragic impressionism of Verlaine. *In* Peyre, H. What is symbolism? p48-62

Peyre, H. The word and its antecedents. *In* Peyre, H. What is symbolism? p6-20

*See also* Allegory

**Symbolism of numbers.** See Three (The number)

**Syme, Sir Ronald**

Ummidus Quadratus, capax imperii. *In* Harvard Studies in classical philology, v83 p287-310

**Sympathy**

Blum, L. Compassion. *In* Explaining emotions, ed. by A. O. Rorty p507-17

Radner, J. B. The art of sympathy in eighteenth-century British moral thought. *In* Studies in eighteenth-century culture v9 p189-210

**Symphony**

Carner, M. A Beethoven movement and its successors. *In* Carner, M. Major and minor p9-20

**Synagogue music**

Shiloah, A. The ritual and music of the synagogue. *In* The Jewish world, ed. by E. Kedourie p120-27

### History and criticism

*See* Bible—Music

**Synge, John Millington**

#### About

Wyatt, D. Yeats and Synge: the Cuchulain complex. *In* Wyatt, D. Prodigal sons p26-51

#### About individual works
##### The shadow of the glen

Morrissey, T. J. The Good Shepherd and the Anti-Christ in Synge's The shadow of the glen. *In* Irish Renaissance annual I p157-67

**Syrkin, Marie, and Kunzer, Ruth Goldschmidt**

Holocaust literature I: diaries and memoirs. *In* Encountering the Holocaust: an interdisciplinary survey, ed. by B. L. Sherwin and S. G. Ament p226-66

**Systems, Communication.** See Telecommunication systems

**Szasz, Thomas Stephen**

The ethics of suicide. *In* Suicide: the philosophical issues, ed. by M. P. Battin and D. J. Mayo p185-98

The lying truths of psychiatry. *In* Lying truths, ed. by R. Duncan and M. Weston-Smith p121-42

**Szombati-Fabian, Ilona.** See Fabian, J. jt. auth.

# T

**Taaffe, Robert N.**

Soviet regional development. *In* The Soviet Union since Stalin, ed. by S. F. Cohen, A. Rabinowitch and R. Sharlet p155-76

**Taboo**

La Barre, W. Obscenity: an anthropological appraisal. *In* La Barre, W. Culture in context p258-68

**Tacitus, Cornelius**

#### About individual works
##### The annals

Woodman, T. Self-imitation and the substance of history: Tacitus, Annals 1.61-5 and Histories 2.70, 5.14-15. *In* Creative imitation and Latin literature, ed. by D. West and T. Woodman p143-55

##### The histories

Woodman, T. Self-imitation and the substance of history: Tacitus, Annals 1.61-5 and Histories 2.70, 5.14-15. *In* Creative imitation and Latin literature, ed. by D. West and T. Woodman p143-55

**Tagliacozzo, Giorgio**

General education as unity of knowledge: a theory based on Vichian principles. *In* Conference on Vico and Contemporary Thought, New York, 1976. Vico and contemporary thought pt2 p110-38

**Tagore, Sir Rabindranath**

#### About

Mukerji, N. The poetry of Rabindranath Tagore: the last phase. *In* Aspects of Indian writing in English, ed. by M. K. Naik p80-100

#### About individual works
##### Red oleanders

Desai, S. K. Tagore's 'Red oleanders': a revaluation. *In* Aspects of Indian writing in English, ed. by M. K. Naik p232-47

**Taille, Jean de la.** See La Taille, Jean de

**Tailors.** See Clothing trade

**Tajfel, Henri**

Human intergroup conflict: useful and less useful forms of analysis. *In* Human ethology, ed. by M. von Cranach [and others] p396-422

**Tales, African**

Pelton, R. D. Interpreting the trickster. *In* Pelton, R. D. The trickster in West Africa p 1-24

**Tales, Welsh**

Jones, G. E. Early prose: the mabinogi. *In* A Guide to Welsh literature, ed. by A. O. H. Jarman and G. R. Hughes v 1 p189-202

Roberts, B. F. Tales and romances. *In* A Guide to Welsh literature, ed. by A. O. H. Jarman and G. R. Hughes v 1 p203-43

**Taliesin**

#### About

Jarman, A. O. H. Taliesin. *In* A Guide to Welsh literature, ed. by A. O. H. Jarman and G. R. Hughes v 1 p51-67

**Talking.** See Conversation

**Talmud**

Neusner, J. The Talmud. *In* The Jewish world, ed. by E. Kedourie p108-19

*See also* Rabbinical literature

**Tamid.** See Mishna. Tamid

**Tanner, Alain**

#### About individual works
##### The middle of the world

Kauffmann, S. The middle of the world. *In* Kauffmann, S. Before my eyes p126-28

**Tanner, Michael**

The language of philosophy. *In* The State of the language, ed. by L. Michaels and C. Ricks p458-66

**Tanselle, George Thomas**

The concept of ideal copy. *In* Virginia. University. Bibliographical Society. Studies in bibliography v33 p18-53

Some statistics on American printing, 1764-1783. *In* The Press & the American Revolution, ed. by B. Bailyn and J. B. Hench p315-63

The state of bibliography today. *In* The Bibliographical Society of America, 1904-79 p542-57

**Tanzania**

#### Ethnology

*See* Ethnology—Tanzania

**Tapirapé Indians**

Shapiro, J. R. The Tapirapé during the era of Reconstruction. *In* Brazil, anthropological perspectives, ed. by M. L. Margolis and W. E. Carter p61-85

**Taplin, Oliver Paul**

#### About individual works
##### The stagecraft of Aeschylus

Knox, B. M. W. Review of The stagecraft of Aeschylus (by Oliver Taplin). *In* Knox, B. M. W. Word and action p79-84

**Tarbet, David W.**

Reason dazzled: perspective and language in Dryden's Aureng-Zebe. *In* Probability, time, and space in eighteenth-century literature, ed. by P. R. Backscheider p187-205

**Tariff**

*Great Britain—History*

Cain, P. Political economy in Edwardian England: the tariff-reform controversy. *In* The Edwardian age: conflict and stability, 1900-1914, ed. by A. O'Day p35-59

*United States—History*

Pincus, J. J. Tariffs. *In* Encyclopedia of American economic history, ed. by G. Porter v 1 p439-50

**Tarkunde, V. M.**

Towards a fuller consensus in humanistic ethics. *In* Humanist ethics, ed. by M. B. Storer p154-72

**Tarlé, Antoine de**

The press and the state in France. *In* Newspapers and democracy, ed. by A. Smith p127-48

**Taryag mizwot.** See Commandments, Six hundred and thirteen

**Tasso, Torquato**

*About*

Montgomery, R. L. Verisimilar things: Tasso's Discourses on the heroic poem (1594). *In* Montgomery, R. L. The reader's eye p142-85

*About individual works*

*Jerusalem delivered*

Murrin, M. Tasso's enchanted wood. *In* Murrin, M. The allegorical epic p87-127

**Taste (Aesthetics)** See Aesthetics

**Tate, Allen**

*About*

King, R. H. Between repetition and recollection: Allen Tate and William Faulkner. *In* King, R. H. A Southern Renaissance p99-129

**Tate, Chester Neal**

The centrality of party in voting choice. *In* Western European party systems, ed. by P. H. Merkl p367-401

**Tate, Thadeus W.**

The seventeenth-century Chesapeake and its modern historians. *In* The Chesapeake in the seventeenth century, ed. by T. W. Tate and D. L. Ammerman p3-50

**Tatham, David**

Winslow Homer and the New England poets. *In* American Antiquarian Society. Proceedings v89 pt2 p241-60

**Tatum, Charles M.**

Contemporary Chicano prose fiction: a chronicle of misery. *In* The Identification and analysis of Chicano literature, ed. by F. Jiménez p241-53

Contemporary Chicano prose fiction: its ties to Mexican literature. *In* The Identification and analysis of Chicano literature, ed. by F. Jiménez p47-57

**Tawney, Richard Henry**

*About*

Gloversmith, F. Defining culture: J. C. Powys, Clive Bell, R. H. Tawney & T. S. Eliot. *In* Class, culture and social change, ed. by F. Gloversmith p15-44

**Tax payers' revolt.** See Taxation—Public opinion

**Taxation**

Asimakopulos, A. Tax incidence. *In* A Guide to post-Keynesian economics, ed. by A. S. Eichner p61-70

*Public opinion*

Moynihan, D. P. Two tax revolts. *In* Moynihan, D. P. Counting our blessings p257-73

*United States*

Break, G. F. State and local finance in the 1980s. *In* The Economy in the 1980s: a program for growth and stability, ed. by M. J. Boskin p233-54

Rabushka, A. Tax and spending limits. *In* The United States in the 1980s, ed. by P. Duignan and A. Rabushka p85-108

Shoven, J. B. Federal government taxes and tax reform. *In* The Economy in the 1980s: a program for growth and stability, ed. by M. J. Boskin p199-221

Smith, D. T. Issues in tax policy. *In* The United States in the 1980s, ed. by P. Duignan and A. Rabushka p109-37

*United States—History*

Ratner, S. Taxation. *In* Encyclopedia of American economic history v 1 p451-67

**Taxes.** See Taxation

**Taxi driver (Motion picture)**

Kael, P. Underground man. *In* Kael, P. When the lights go down p131-35

Kauffmann, S. Taxi driver. *In* Kauffmann, S. Before my eyes p200-03

**Tay, Alice Erh-Soon**

The sense of justice in the common law. *In* Symposium on Theories of Justice in and for the Second Half of the Twentieth Century, Sydney, 1977. Justice p79-96

**Tayama, Katai**

*About individual works*

*Futon*

Walker, J. A. Katai's Futon (The quilt): the birth of the I-novel. *In* Walker, J. A. The Japanese novel of the Meiji period and the ideal of individualism p93-120

**Taylor, Charles**

Atomism. *In* Powers, possessions and freedom, ed. by A. Kontos p39-61

The philosophy of the social science. *In* Political theory and political education, ed. by M. Richter p76-93

Sense data revisited. *In* Perception and identity, ed. by G. F. Macdonald p99-112

**Taylor, Christopher C. W.**

'All perceptions are true.' *In* Doubt and dogmatism, ed. by M. Schofield, M. Burnyeat and J. Barnes p105-24

**Taylor, Edward**

*About individual works*

*God's determinations*

Scheick, W. J. The jawbones schema of Edward Taylor's Gods determinations. *In* Puritan influences in American literature, ed. by E. Elliott p38-54

**Taylor, Gabriele**

Pride. *In* Explaining emotions, ed. by A. O. Rorty p385-402

**Taylor, Kenneth L.**

Geology in 1776: some notes on the character of an incipient science. *In* New Hampshire Bicentennial Conference on the History of Geology, University of New Hampshire, 1976. Two hundred years of geology in America p75-90

**Taylor, Laurie.** See Crook, S. jt. auth.

**Taylor, Lonn W.**
Fachwerk and Brettstuhl: the rejection of traditional folk culture. *In* Perspectives on American folk art, ed. by I. M. G. Quimby and S. T. Swank p162-76

**Taylor, Mildred D.**

### About individual works
*Roll of thunder, hear my cry*
Rees, D. The color of skin: Mildred Taylor. *In* Rees, D. The marble in the water p104-13

**Taylor, Robert H.**
Bibliothecohimatiourgomachia. *In* The Bibliographical Society of America, 1904-79 p318-26

**Taylor, Roger J.**
Sexual experiences. *In* The Philosophy of sex, ed. by A. Soble p59-75

**Taylor, Wilson E.**
Of a remembered time. *In* Wallace Stevens, ed. by F. Doggett and R. Buttel p91-104

**Tchekhoff, Anton Pavlovich.** See Chekhov, Anton Pavlovich

**Tchekhov, Anton Pavlovich.** See Chekhov, Anton Pavlovich

**Teachers**

#### Cameroon
Clignet, R. Teachers and national values in Cameroon: an inferential analysis from census data. *In* Values, identities, and national integration, ed. by J. N. Paden p321-36

**Teachers.** See Science teachers

**Teatro** Campesino, Dramatic principles of the. Jiménez, F. *In* The Identification and analysis of Chicano literature, ed. by F. Jiménez p117-32

**Technical laboratories.** See Research, Industrial—Laboratories

**Technological innovations.** See subdivision Technological innovations under subjects, e.g. Newspaper publishing—Technological innovations

**Technological transfer.** See Technology transfer

**Technology**

#### Moral and religious aspects
*See* Technology and ethics

#### Social aspects
Goldhamer, H. The social effects of communication technology. *In* Propaganda and communication in world history, ed. by H. D. Lasswell, D. Lerner and H. Speier v3 p346-400

Miller, P. The responsibility of mind in a civilization of machines. *In* Miller, P. The responsibility of mind in a civilization of machines p195-213

Rescher, N. Social values and technological change. *In* Value and values in evolution, ed. by A. A. Maziarz p163-78

Schrade, A. O. Sex-shock: the humanistic woman in the super-industrial society. *In* Monster or messiah? Ed. by W. M. Mathews p72-86

#### United States—History
Rosenberg, N. Technology. *In* Encyclopedia of American economic history, ed. by G. Porter v 1 p294-308

**Technology and civilization**
Gilkey, L. B. The religious dilemmas of a scientific culture: the interface of technology, history and religion. *In* Being human in a technological age, ed. by D. M. Borchert and D. Stewart p73-88

Murphree, W. A. The necessity of humanism in the computer age. *In* Monster or messiah? Ed. by W. M. Mathews p175-84

Williams, P. F. Reflection on computers as daughters of memory. *In* Monster or messiah? ed. by W. M. Mathews p165-74

*See also* Technology assessment

**Technology and ethics**
Bergmark, R. E. Computers and persons. *In* Monster or messiah? ed. by W. M. Mathews p47-55

Tolliver, J. E. The computer and the Protestant ethic: a conflict. *In* Monster or messiah? Ed. by W. M. Mathews p156-64

**Technology and state**

#### United States
Mansfield, E. Major issues concerning U.S. technology policy. *In* Economic issues of the eighties, ed. by N. M. Kamrany and R. H. Day p185-98

Wiesner, J. B. The marriage of science and government. *In* Propaganda and communication in world history, ed. by H. D. Lasswell, D. Lerner and H. Speier v3 p16-36

**Technology assessment**
Shepard, N. E. Technology: messiah or monster? *In* Monster or messiah? Ed. by W. M. Mathews p145-55

**Technology transfer**
Costick, M. M. Soviet military posture and strategic trade. *In* National security in the 1980s: from weakness to strength, ed. by W. S. Thompson p189-213

**Tectonics, Plate.** See Plate tectonics

**Tedlow, Richard S.**
Advertising and public relations. *In* Encyclopedia of American economic history, ed. by G. Porter v2 p677-95

Judah P. Benjamin. *In* Conference on Southern Jewish History, Richmond, Va. 1976. "Turn to the South" p44-54

**Teece, David J.**
The new social regulation: implications and alternatives. *In* The Economy in the 1980s: a program for growth and stability, ed. by M. J. Boskin p119-58

**Telecommunication**

#### International cooperation
Coppa, F. J. The global impact of television: an overview. *In* Screen and society, ed. by F. J. Coppa p 1-29

#### Social aspects
Goldhamer, H. The social effects of communication technology. *In* Propaganda and communication in world history, ed. by H. D. Lasswell, D. Lerner and H. Speier v3 p346-400

#### Japan
Tomita, T. The new electronic media and their place in the information market of the future. *In* Newspapers and democracy, ed. by A. Smith p49-62

**Telecommunication systems**
Goldhamer, H. The social effects of communication technology. *In* Propaganda and communication in world history, ed. by H. D. Lasswell, D. Lerner and H. Speier v3 p346-400

**Teleology.** See Causation

**Telephone**
Plomer, W. C. F. On not answering the telephone. *In* Plomer, W. C. F. Electric delights p23-27

**Television**

### Language

Raphael, F. The language of television. *In* The State of the language, ed. by L. Michaels and C. Ricks p304-12

### Law and legislation

Doyle, E. J. Commercial and noncommercial television in America and Europe. *In* Screen and society, ed. by F. J. Coppa p185-210

Kovaleff, T. P. Television as big business. *In* Screen and society, ed. by F. J. Coppa p173-83

**Television and sports**

Harmond, R. P. Sugar daddy or ogre? The impact of commercial television on professional sports. *In* Screen and society, ed. by F. J. Coppa p81-108

**Television audiences**

Lally, T. D. P. Synchronic vs diachronic popular culture studies and the old English elegy. *In* 5000 years of popular culture, ed. by F. E. H. Schroeder p203-12

**Television broadcasting**

*See also* Television programs

### History and criticism

*See* Television criticism

### Political aspects

*See* Television in politics

### Social aspects

Coppa, F. J. The explosion of the eye: an introduction to the promise and problems of television. *In* Screen and society, ed. by F. J. Coppa p ix-xxvii

Kirby, W. L. The influence of television on social relations: some personal reflections. *In* Screen and society, ed. by F. J. Coppa p137-56

Muccigrosso, R. H. Television and the urban crisis. *In* Screen and society, ed. by F. J. Coppa p31-57

### Europe

Doyle, E. J. Commercial and noncommercial television in America and Europe. *In* Screen and society, ed. by F. J. Coppa p185-210

### United States

Doyle, E. J. Commercial and noncommercial television in America and Europe. *In* Screen and society, ed. by F. J. Coppa p185-210

**Television broadcasting of sports.** See Television and sports

**Television criticism**

Coppa, F. J. The explosion of the eye: an introduction to the promise and problems of television. *In* Screen and society, ed. by F. J. Coppa p ix-xxvii

Coppa, F. J. The global impact of television: an overview. *In* Screen and society, ed. by F. J. Coppa p 1-29

Murray, L. L. Universality and uniformity in the popular arts: the impact of television on popular culture. *In* Screen and society, ed. by F. J. Coppa p157-72

**Television in education**

Perkins, B. Education in the video age: learning via television. *In* Screen and society, ed. by F. J. Coppa p109-35

**Television in politics**

Le Veness, F. P. The political use and abuse of television in America and abroad. *In* Screen and society, ed. by F. J. Coppa p59-80

Polsby, N. W. The news media as an alternative to party in the Presidential selection process. *In* Political parties in the eighties, ed. by R. A. Goldwin p50-66

**Television industry**

Kovaleff, T. P. Television as big business. *In* Screen and society, ed. by F. J. Coppa p173-83

### Law and legislation

*See* Television—Law and legislation

**Television programs**

Sharratt, B. The politics of the popular?— From melodrama to television. *In* Performance and politics in popular drama, ed. by D. Bradby, L. James and B. Sharratt p275-95

**Television scripts.** See Television programs

**Teller, Edward**

Technology: the imbalance of power. *In* The United States in the 1980s, ed. by P. Duignan and A. Rabushka p497-534

**Telotte, J. P.**

Charles Peirce and Walker Percy; from semiotic to narrative. *In* Walker Percy: art and ethics, ed. by J. Tharpe p65-79

**Temperament.** See Character

**Temperance.** See Alcoholism

**Temperley, Howard**

Anti-slavery as a form of cultural imperialism. *In* Anti-slavery, religion, and reform: essays in memory of Roger Anstey, ed. by C. Bolt and S. Drescher p335-50

**Ten Commandments.** See Commandments, Ten

**Tencin, Claudine Alexandrine Guérin de**

### About

Jones, S. Madame de Tencin: an eighteenth-century woman novelist. *In* Woman and society in eighteenth-century France, ed. by E. Jacobs and others p207-17

**Tendríakov, Vladimir Fedorovich**

### About

Hosking, G. Vladimir Tendryakov. *In* Hosking, G. Beyond Socialist realism p84-100

**Tendryakov, Vladimir.** See Tendríakov, Vladimir Fedorovich

**Tennenhouse, Leonard**

The counterfeit order of The merchant of Venice. *In* Representing Shakespeare, ed. by M. M. Schwartz and C. Kahn p54-69

**Tennyson, Alfred Tennyson, Baron**

### About

McGhee, R. D. Tennyson. *In* McGhee, R. D. Marriage, duty & desire in Victorian poetry and drama p29-66

**Tennyson, Charles.** See Turner, Charles Tennyson

**Tensons**

Camproux, C. On the subject of an argument between Elias and his cousin. *In* The Interpretation of medieval lyric poetry, ed. by W. T. H. Jackson p61-90

**Terrace, H. S.**

Is problem-solving language? *In* Speaking of apes, ed. by T. A. Sebeok and J. Umiker-Sebeok p385-405

**Terrace, H. S. and Bever, Thomas Gordon**

What might be learned from studying language in the chimpanzee? The importance of symbolizing oneself. *In* Speaking of apes, ed. by T. A. Sebeok and J. Umiker-Sebeok p179-89

**Terry, Arthur**

Onetti and the meaning of fiction: notes on La muerte y la niña. *In* Contemporary Latin American fiction, ed. by S. Bacarisse p54-72

**Terza, Dante Della.** See Della Terza, Dante

**Teso tribe**

**Social life and customs**

Karp, I. C. Beer drinking and social experience in an African society: an essay in formal sociology. *In* Explorations in African systems of thought, ed. by I. C. Karp & C. S. Bird p83-119

**Tetens, Johan Nicolai**

**About**

Barnouw, J. The philosophical achievement and historical significance of Johann Nicolas Tetens. *In* Studies in eighteenth-century culture v9 p301-35

**Textual criticism.** See Criticism, Textual

**Thackeray, William Makepeace**

**About**

Garrett, P. K. Thackeray: seeing double. *In* Garrett, P. K. The Victorian multiplot novel p95-134

Henkle, R. B. Peacock, Thackery, and Jerrold: the comedy of "radical" disaffection. *In* Henkle, R. B. Comedy and culture p58-110

Stone, D. D. Introduction. *In* Stone, D. D. The romantic impulse in Victorian fiction p 1-45

**About individual works**

*Vanity fair*

Kinkead-Weekes, M. The voicing of fictions. *In* Reading the Victorian novel: detail into form, ed. by I. Gregor p168-92

Polhemus, R. M. Thackeray's Vanity fair: the comedy of shifting perspectives. *In* Polhemus, R. M. Comic faith p124-65

**Thanatos.** See Death instinct

**That obscure object of desire (Motion picture)**

Kael, P. Cutting light. *In* Kael, P. When the lights go down p363-67

**Theater**

*See also* Puppets and puppet plays

**Audiences**

*See* Theater audiences

**Economic aspects**

Brustein, R. S. Art versus advocacy. *In* Brustein, R. S. Critical moments p37-43

Brustein, R. S. Can the show go on? *In* Brustein, R. S. Critical moments p44-57

Brustein, R. S. The future of the Endowments. *In* Brustein, R. S. Critical moments p58-78

**Little theater movement**

*See* Community plays, etc.

**Political aspects**

Bradby, D. The October group and theatre under the Front populaire. *In* Performance and politics in popular drama, ed. by D. Bradby, L. James and B. Sharratt p231-42

Clark, J. Agitprop and Unity Theatre: Socialist theatre in the thirties. *In* Culture and crisis in Britain in the thirties, ed. by J. Clark and others p219-39

Jiménez, F. Dramatic principles of the Teatro Campesino. *In* The Identification and analysis of Chicano literature, ed. by F. Jiménez p117-32

Samuel, R. Workers' theatre, 1926-36. *In* Performance and politics in popular drama, ed. by D. Bradby, L. James and B. Sharratt p213-30

*See also* Agitprop Theater; Political plays

**Production and direction**

*See* Theater management

**Social aspects**

Huerta, J. A. From the temple to the arena: Teatro Chicano today. *In* The Identification and analysis of Chicano literature, ed. by F. Jiménez p90-116

*See* Theater and society

**Africa**

Etherton, M. Trends in African theatre. *In* African literature today no. 10: Retrospect & prospect, ed. by E. D. Jones p57-85

**Czechoslovakia**

Goetz-Stankiewicz, M. Responses: East and West. *In* Goetz-Stankiewicz, M. The silenced theatre: Czech playwrights without a stage p14-42

**England—History**

Edwards, P. —A superfluous sort of men: the rise and fall of the professional theatre. *In* Edwards, P. Threshold of a nation p17-37

Forbes, D. Water drama. *In* Performance and politics in popular drama, ed. by D. Bradby, L. James and B. Sharratt p91-107

Mayer, D. The music of melodrama. *In* Performance and politics in popular drama, ed. by D. Bradby, L. James and B. Sharratt p49-63

Samuel, R. Workers' theatre, 1926-36. *In* Performance and politics in popular drama, ed. by D. Bradby, L. James and B. Sharratt p213-30

**England—Birmingham—History**

Reid, D. A. Popular theatre in Victorian Birmingham. *In* Performance and politics in popular drama, ed. by D. Bradby, L. James and B. Sharratt p65-89

**England—London—History**

Bratton, J. S. Theatre of war: the Crimea on the London stage, 1854-5. *In* Performance and politics in popular drama, ed. by D. Bradby, L. James and B. Sharratt p119-37

**France—History**

Bradby, D. The October group and theatre under the Front populaire. *In* Performance and politics in popular drama, ed. by D. Bradby, L. James and B. Sharratt p231-42

**Great Britain**

Anderson, M.J. Word and image: aspects of mimesis in contemporary British theatre. *In* Drama and mimesis, ed. by J. Redmond p139-53

**Great Britain—History**

Clark, J. Agitprop and Unity Theatre: Socialist theatre in the thirties. *In* Culture and crisis in Britain in the thirties, ed. by J. Clark anl others p219-39

Gyseghem, A. van. British theatre in the thirties: an autobiographical record. *In* Culture and crisis in Britain in the thirties, ed. by J. Clark and others p209-18

**Ireland—History**

Edwards, P. Our Irish theatre. *In* Edwards, P. Threshold of a nation p191-211

Edwards, P. A play-house in the waste: George Moore and the Irish theatre. *In* Edwards, P. Threshold of a nation p212-28

**Israel—History**

Abramson, G. The development of the drama: The theatres of Israel. *In* Abramson, G. Modern Hebrew drama p28-46

Theater—*Continued*

**Israel—Production and direction**

Abramson, G. The problems of the Israeli drama: The director. *In* Abramson, G. Modern Hebrew drama p197-99

**United States**

Brustein, R. S. Broadway Anglophila. *In* Brustein, R. S. Critical moments p89-94

Brustein, R. S. Theatre in the age of Einstein: the crack in the chimney. *In* Brustein, R. S. Critical moments p107-23

**Theater administration.** See Theater management

**Theater and society**

Brustein, R. S. Theatre in the age of Einstein: the crack in the chimney. *In* Brustein, R. S. Critical moments p107-23

**Theater and state**

**England—History**

Edwards, P. A superfluous sort of men: the rise and fall of the professional theatre. *In* Edwards, P. Threshold of a nation p17-37

**Theater audiences**

Bennett, B. The assault upon the audience: types of modern drama. *In* Bennett, B. Modern drama and German classicism p282-314

Brustein, R. S. The theatre audience: a house divided. *In* Brustein, R. S. Critical moments p139-47

**England**

Reid, D. A. Popular theatre in Victorian Birmingham. *In* Performance and politics in popular drama, ed. by D. Bradby, L. James and B. Sharratt p65-89

**Israel**

Abramson, G. The problems of the Israeli drama: Audiences. *In* Abramson, G. Modern Hebrew drama p200-04

**Theater critics**

Brustein, R. S. Where are the repertory critics? *In* Brustein, R. S. Critical moments p3-12

**Israel**

Abramson, G. The problems of the Israeli drama: Criticism. *In* Abramson, G. Modern Hebrew drama p190-96

**Theater management**

Brustein, R. S. Art versus advocacy. *In* Brustein, R. S. Critical moments p37-43

**Theaters**

*See also* subdivision Theaters under names of cities, e.g. Gdansk, Poland—Theaters

**Stage setting and scenery**

Forbes, D. Water drama. *In* Performance and politics in popular drama, ed. by D. Bradby, L. James and B. Sharratt p91-107

**Europe—History**

Lawrenson, T. E. The ideal theatre in the eighteenth century: Paris and Venice. *In* Drama and mimesis, ed. by J. Redmond p51-64

**Theatrical music.** See Music, Incidental; Music in theaters

**Thee, Marek**

Militarism and militarisation in contemporary international relations. *In* Problems of contemporary militarism, ed. by A. Eide and M. Thee p15-35

**Theism**

De Man, P. Allegory of reading (Profession de foi). *In* De Man, P. Allegories of reading p221-45

**Theocritus**

**About individual works**

*Idylls*

Du Quesnay, I. M. Le M. From Polyphemus to Corydon: Virgil, Eclogue 2 and the Idylls of Theocritus. *In* Creative imitation and Latin literature, ed. by D. West and T. Woodman p35-69

**Influence—Milton**

Evans, J. M. Lycidas, Daphnis, and Gallus. *In* English Renaissance studies, ed. by J. Carey p228-44

**Theodicy**

Pickering, W. S. F. Theodicy and social theory: an exploration of the limits of collaboration between sociologist and theologian. *In* Sociology and theology: alliance and conflict, ed. by D. Martin, J. O. Mills [and] W. S. F. Pickering p59-79

**Theology**

Barker, E. The limits of displacement: two disciplines face each other. *In* Sociology and theology: alliance and conflict, ed. by D. Martin, J. O. Mills [and] W. S. F. Pickering p15-23

Gill, R. From sociology to theology. *In* Sociology and theology: alliance and conflict, ed. by D. Martin, J. O. Mills [and] W. S. F. Pickering p102-19

Harris, C. W. J. Displacements and reinstatements: the relations between sociology and theology considered in their changing intellectual context. *In* Sociology and theology: alliance and conflict, ed. by D. Martin, J. O. Mills [and] W. S. F. Pickering p24-36

Hudson, W. D. The rational system of beliefs. *In* Sociology and theology: alliance and conflict, ed. by D. Martin, J. O. Mills [and] W. S. F. Pickering p80-101

Lion, A. Theology and sociology: what point is there in keeping the distinction? *In* Sociology and theology: alliance and conflict. Ed. by D. Martin, J. O. Mills [and] W. S. F. Pickering p163-82

Mills, J. O. God, man and media: on a problem arising when theologians speak of the modern world. *In* Sociology and theology: alliance and conflict, ed. by D. Martin, J. O. Mills [and] W. S. F. Pickering p136-50

Mills, J. O. Introduction: of two minds. *In* Sociology and theology: alliance and conflict, ed. by D. Martin, J. O. Mills [and] W. S. F. Pickering p 1-14

Pickering, W. S. F. Theodicy and social theory: an exploration of the limits of collaboration between sociologist and theologian. *In* Sociology and theology: alliance and conflict, ed. by D. Martin, J. O. Mills [and] W. S. F. Pickering p59-79

Radcliffe, T. Relativizing the relativizers: a theologian's assessment of the role of sociological explanation of religious phenomena and theology today. *In* Sociology and theology: alliance and conflict, ed. by D. Martin, J. O. Mills [and] W. S. F. Pickering p151-62

*See also* Religion

**Terminology**

Martin, D. A. The sociological mode and the theological vocabulary. *In* Sociology and theology: alliance and conflict, ed. by D. Martin, J. O. Mills [and] W. S. F. Pickering p46-58

**Theology, Catholic**

Baum, G. The sociology of Roman Catholic theology. *In* Sociology and theology: alliance and conflict, ed. by D. Martin, J. O. Mills [and] W. S. F. Pickering p120-35

**History**

Daly, G. The integralist response (2): Pascendi and after. *In* Daly, G. Transcendence and immanence p190-217

Daly, G. Modernism in retrospect. *In* Daly, G. Transcendence and immanence p218-31

Daly, G. Roman fundamental theology in the last quarter of the nineteenth century. *In* Daly, G. Transcendence and immanence p7-25

**Theology, Christian.** See Theology

**Theology, Doctrinal**

Daly, G. History and dogma: the debate between Alfred Loisy and Maurice Blondel. *In* Daly, G. Transcendence and immanence p69-90

Daly, G. Lucien Laberthonnière's 'critical mysticism.' *In* Daly, G. Transcendence and immanence p91-116

*See also* Fall of man; Free will and determination; God; Theodicy

**History—Middle Ages, 600-1500**

Ozment, S. H. The mental world of Martin Luther. *In* Ozment, S. H. The age of reform, 1250-1550 p223-44

Ozment, S. H. The scholastic traditions. *In* Ozment, S. H. The age of reform, 1250-1550 p22-72

Robertson, D. W. Certain theological conventions in Mannyng's treatment of the Commandments. *In* Robertson, D. W. Essays in medieval culture p105-13

**Theology, Protestant**

Briggs, E. R. Marie Huber and the campaign against eternal hell torments. *In* Woman and society in eighteenth-century France, ed. by E. Jacobs [and others] p218-28

**Theology, Puritan**

Hunsaker, O. G. Roger Williams and John Milton: the calling of the Puritan writer. *In* Puritan influences in American literature, ed. by E. Elliott p3-22

**Theology, Scholastic.** See Scholasticism

**They shoot horses, don't they? (Motion picture)**

Miller, G. Marathon man/marathon woman. *In* Miller, G. Screening the novel p64-83

**Thiébaux, Marcelle**

A mythology for women: Monique Wittig's Les guérillères. *In* The Analysis of literary texts, ed. by R. D. Pope p90-99

**Thieberger, Friedrich**

The Jewish conception of redemption. *In* The Jew, ed. by A. A. Cohen p149-57

Samson Raphael Hirsch (1808-1888) *In* The Jew, ed. by A. A. Cohen p237-50

**Thiher, Allen**

The cinematic muse

*Contents*

Afterword: is film a language?

L'année dernière à Marienbad: the narration of narration

Bresson's Un condamné à mort: the semiotics of grace

The existential play in Truffaut's early films

From Entr'acte to À nous la liberté: René Clair and the order of farce

The impressionist avant-garde

Jean Renoir and the mimesis of history

Prévert and Carné's Le jour se lève: proletarian tragedy

Postmodern dilemmas: Godard's Alphaville and Deux ou trois choses que je sais d'elle

Le sang d'un poète film as Orphism

Surrealism's enduring bite: Un chien andalou

The surrealist film: Man Ray and the limits of metaphor

Vigo's Zéro de conduite: surrealism and the myth of childhood

**Thinking.** See Thought and thinking

**Thiong'o Ngugi Wa.** See Ngugi Wa Thiong'o

**Third world.** See Underdeveloped areas

**Thom, René**

The genesis of representational space according to Piaget. *In* Language and learning, ed. by M. Piattelli-Palmarini p361-68

**Thomas Aquinas, Saint**

**About**

Montgomery, R. L. Faculty psychology and theories of imagination: Aristotle, Plato, Augustine, and Aquinas. *In* Montgomery, R. L. The reader's eye p13-49

Ozment, S. H. The scholastic traditions. *In* Ozment, S. H. The age of reform, 1250-1550 p22-72

**Thomas, Edward**

**About**

Keith, W. J. Edward Thomas. *In* Keith, W. J. The poetry of nature p141-66

**Thomas, Isaiah**

McCorison, M. A. Foreword. *In* The Press & the American Revolution, ed. by B. Bailyn and J. B. Hench p 1-10

**Thomas, John Clayton**

Ideological trends in Western political parties. *In* Western European party systems, ed. by P. H. Merkl p348-66

**Thomas, Richard F.**

New comedy, Callimachus, and Roman poetry. *In* Harvard Studies in classical philology v83 p179-206

**Thomas, Ronald Stuart**

**About**

Keith, W. J. The Georgians and after. *In* Keith, W. J. The poetry of nature p 167-98

Sutton, M. K. Truth and the pastor's vision in George Crabbe, William Barnes, and R. S. Thomas. *In* Survivals of pastoral, ed. by R. F. Hardin p33-59

**About individual works**

*Song at the year's turning*

Plomer, W. C. F. R. S. Thomas. *In* Plomer, W. C. F. Electric delights p158-61

**Thomassy, Raymond**

**About**

Skinner, H. C. Raymond Thomassy and the practical geology of Louisiana. *In* New Hampshire Bicentennial Conference on the History of Geology, University of New Hampshire, 1976. Two hundred years of geology in America p201-11

**Thompson, Brian**

Visual imagination in L'Espoir. *In* André Malraux, ed. by F. Dorenlot and M. Tison-Braun p201-08

**Thompson, Willard Scott**

The African-American nexus in Soviet strategy. *In* Communism in Africa, ed. by D. E. Albright p189-218

Introduction. *In* National security in the 1980s: from weakness to strength, ed. by W. S. Thompson p3-16

Toward a strategic peace. *In* National security in the 1980s: from weakness to strength, ed. by W. S. Thompson p473-88

**Thomson, George H.**

Where was the road from Colonus? *In* E. M. Forster: a human exploration, ed. by G. K. Das and J. Beer p28-31

**Thonga tribe**

### Rites and ceremonies

Heusch, L. de. Heat, physiology, and cosmogony: rites de passage among the Thonga. *In* Explorations in African systems of thought, ed. by I. C. Karp & C. S. Bird p27-43

**Thoreau, Henry David**

### About

Allen, G. W. How Emerson, Thoreau, and Whitman viewed the "frontier." *In* Toward a new American literary history, ed. by L. Budd, E. H. Cady and C. L. Anderson p111-28

Irwin, J. T. Thoreau: the single, basic form—patenting a leaf. *In* Irwin, J. T. American hieroglyphics p14-20

### About individual works
*Journal*

Howarth, W. L. Travelling in Concord: the world of Thoreau's Journal. *In* Puritan influences in American literature, ed. by E. Elliott p143-66

*Walden*

Heinzelman, K. "The mouth-tale of the giants": an introduction to the economics of the imagination. *In* Heinzelman, K. The economics of the imagination p3-34

*A week on the Concord and Merrimack Rivers*

Sundquist, E. J. "Plowing homeward": cultivation and grafting in Thoreau and the Week. *In* Sundquist, E. J. Home as found p41-85

### Bibliography

Glick, W. Emerson, Thoreau, and transcendentalism. *In* American literary scholarship, 1978 p3-16

**Thorlby, Anthony**

Kafka and language. *In* The World of Franz Kafka, ed. by J. P. Stern p133-44

**Thornton, William**

### About individual works
*Cadmus*

Wollock, J. William Thornton and the practical applications of new writing systems. *In* Psychology of language and thought, ed. by R. W. Rieber p121-51

**Thorpe, William Homan**

The problem of purpose in evolution. *In* The Condition of man, ed. by P. Hallberg p128-49

**Thought and thinking**

Cellérier, G. Cognitive strategies in problem solving. *In* Language and learning, ed. by M. Piattelli-Palmarini p67-72

Goody, J. R. Thought and writing. *In* Soviet and Western anthropology, ed. by E. Gellner p119-33

*See also* Cognition; Intellect; Psycholinguistics; Reasoning (Psychology)

**Three (The number)**

Dundes, A. The number three in American culture. *In* Dundes, A. Interpreting folklore p134-59

**Three days of the condor (Motion picture)**

Kael, P. The visceral poetry of pulp. *In* Kael, P. When the lights go down p40-45

**3 women (Motion picture)**

Kauffmann, S. 3 women. *In* Kauffmann, S. Before my eyes p40-43

**Throne of Maximian.** See Ravenna, Italy—Throne of Maximian

**Thucydides**

### About

Dover, K. J. The classical historians. *In* Ancient Greek literature, ed. by K. J. Dover p88-104

**Thundy, Zacharias P.**

Matheolus, Chaucer, and The wife of Bath. *In* Chaucerian problems and perspectives, ed. by E. Vasta and Z. P. Thundy p24-58

**Thurow, Lester C.**

Economic justice. *In* Economic issues of the eighties, ed. by N. M. Kamrany and R. H. Day p109-18

**Thwaites, Reuben Gold**

Bibliographical activities of historical societies of the United States. *In* The Bibliographical Society of America, 1904-79 p3-8

**Tichenor, Irene**

Master printers organize: the Typothetae of the City of New York, 1865-1906. *In* Small business in American life, ed. by S. W. Bruchey p169-91

**Tieck, Johann Ludwig**

### About

Hughes, G. T. New ways of feeling: Wackenroder, Tieck and 'the night watches.' *In* Hughes, G. T. Romantic German literature p21-40

### About individual works
*Moonlight song*

Frank, M. The infinite text. *In* Glyph 7 p70-101

**Tieck, Ludwig.** See Tieck, Johann Ludwig

**Tierney, Michael.** See Solman, L. C. jt. auth.

**Tigray (African people)** See Tigrinya (African people)

**Tigriña (African people)** See Tigrinya (African people)

**Tigrinya (African people)**

Bauer, D. F. and Hinnant, J. Normal and revolutionary divination: a Kuhnian approach to African traditional thought. *In* Explorations in African systems of thought, ed. by I. C. Karp & C. S. Bird p213-36

**Tilly, Charles**

Did the cake of custom break? *In* Consciousness and class experience in nineteenth-century Europe, ed. by J. M. Merriman p17-44

**Time**

Beck, L. W. World enough, and time. *In* Probability, time, and space in eighteenth-century literature, ed. by P. R. Backscheider p113-39

Le Goff, J. Merchant's time and church's time in the Middle Ages. p29-42

Moynihan, R. D. "Dwarfs of wit and learning": problems of historical time. *In* Probability, time, and space in eighteenth-century literature, ed. by P. R. Backscheider p167-85

### Measurement
*See* Time measurements

**Time (Theology)**
Le Goff, J. Merchant's time and church's time in the Middle Ages. *In* Le Goff, J. Time work, & culture in the Middle Ages p29-42

**Time in literature**
Aaron, M. A. Garcia Marquez' mecedor as link between passage of time and presence of mind. *In* The Analysis of literary texts, ed. by R. D. Pope p21-30

**Time measurements**
**History**
Le Goff, J. Labor time in the "crisis" of the fourteenth century: from medieval time to modern time. *In* Le Goff, J. Time, work, & culture in the Middle Ages p43-52

**Tintner, Adeline R.**
Mothers, daughters, and incest in the late novels of Edith Wharton. *In* The Lost tradition: mothers and daughters in literature, ed. by C. N. Davidson and E. M. Broner p147-56

**Tison-Braun, Micheline**
The artist as exemplar of humanity. *In* André Malraux, ed. by F. Dorenlot and D. Stewart p155-64

**Titian**
**Influence—Sidney**
Duncan-Jones, K. Sidney and Titian, ed. by J. Carey p 1-11

**Tiusanen, Timo**
O'Neill's significance: a Scandinavian and European view. *In* Eugene O'Neill, ed. by V. Floyd p61-67

**Tiziano, Vecelli.** See Titian

**Tobacco habit.** See Smoking

**Tobol, Carol E. Washington.** See Washington, I. H. jt. auth.

**Todd, Janet**
Women's friendship in literature
*Contents*
The biographical context
Erotic friendship: Denis Diderot's The nun
Erotic friendship: John Cleland's Fanny Hill
The literary context
Manipulative friendship: Jean-Jacques Rousseau's Julie
Manipulative friendship: the Marquis de Sade's Juliette
Political friendship Madam de Staël's Delphine
Political friendship: Mary Wollstonecraft's Mary, a fiction
Sentimental friendship: Samuel Richardson's Clarissa
Social friendship: Jane Austen's Emma
Social friendship: Jane Austen's Mansfield Park

**Todd, William Burton**
Concurrent printing: an analysis of Dodsley's Collection of poems by several hands. *In* The Bibliographical Society of America, 1904-79 p276-88

**Todorov, Tzvetan**
Reading as construction. *In* The Reader in the text, ed. by S. R. Suleiman and I. Crosman p67-82

**Toennies, Ferdinand.** See Tönnies, Ferdinand

**Tolkien, John Ronald Reuel**
**About individual works**
*The hobbit*
Green, W. H. The four-part structure of Bilbo's education. *In* Children's literature v8 p133-40

**Toller, Ernst**
**About individual works**
*Hoppla, we're alive*
Kane, M. Erwin Piscator's 1927 production of Hoppla, we're alive. *In* Performance and politics in popular drama, ed. by D. Bradby, L. James and B. Sharratt p189-200

**Tolliver, Johnny E.**
The computer and the Protestant ethic: a conflict. *In* Monster or messiah? Ed. by W. M. Mathews p 156-64

**Tombstones.** See Sepulchral monuments

**Tomer, Ben Zion**
**About individual works**
*The children of the shadow*
Abramson, G. Thematic development: The plays of the Holocaust. *In* Abramson, G. Modern Hebrew drama p116-40

**Tomita, Tetsuro**
The new electronic media and their place in the information market of the future. *In* Newspapers and democracy, ed. by A. Smith p49-62

**Tomlin, Eric Walter Frederick**
Novelty is the chief aim in art. *In* Lying truths, ed. by R. Duncan and M. Weston-Smith p231-40

**Tomlinson, Charles**
The poet as painter. *In* Royal Society of Literature of the United Kingdom, London. Essays by divers hands: innovation in contemporary literature, new ser. v40 p147-62

**About**
Tomlinson, C. The poet as painter. *In* Royal Society of Literature of the United Kingdom, London. Essays by divers hands: innovation in contemporary literature, new ser. v40 p147-62

**Tonga (Mozambique and South African people)** See Thonga tribe

**Tönnies, Ferdinand**
**About individual works**
*Gemeinschaft und Gesellschaft*
Durkheim, E. Review of Ferdinand Tönnies, Gemeinschaft und Gesellschaft. *In* Durkheim, E. Emile Durkheim on institutional analysis p115-22

**Topol, Josef**
**About**
Goetz-Stankiewicz, M. Josef Topol. *In* Goetz-Stankiewicz, M. The silenced theatre: Czech playwrights without a stage p146-73

**Torchiana, Donald T.**
James Joyce's method in Dubliners. *In* The Irish short story, ed. by P. Rafroidi and T. Brown p127-40

**Tories, American.** See American loyalists

**Törnqvist, Egil**
Platonic love in O'Neill's Welded. *In* Eugene O'Neill, ed. by V. Floyd p73-83

**Toulouse**
**History**
Aminzade, R. The transformation of social solidarities in nineteenth-century Toulouse. *In* Consciousness and class experience in nineteenth-century Europe, ed. by J. M. Merriman p85-105

**Touraine, Alain**

### About

Kurzweil, E. Alain Touraine: structures without structuralism. *In* Kurzweil, E. The age of structuralism p113-34

**Tourneur, Cyril**

### About individual works
*The revenger's tragedy*

Dollimore, J. Two concepts of mimesis: Renaissance literary theory and The revenger's tragedy. *In* Drama and mimesis, ed. by J. Redmond p25-50

**Tov-Ruach, Leila**
Jealousy, attention, and loss. *In* Explaining emotions, ed. by A. O. Rorty p465-88

**Towler, Robert**
Many voices. *In* Sociology and theology: alliance and conflict, ed. by D. Martin, J. O. Mills [and] W. S. F. Pickering p183-89

**Towneley plays.** See The killing of Abel

**Townsend, John Rowe**
A sounding of storytellers
*Contents*
Alan Garner
E. L. Konigsburg
Ivan Southall
Jill Paton Walsh
K. M. Peyton
Leon Garfield
Nina Bawden
Patricia Wrightson
Paula Fox
Penelope Lively
Peter Dickinson
Vera and Bill Cleaver
Virginia Hamilton
William Mayne
Standards of criticism for children's literature. *In* The Arbuthnot lectures, 1970-1979 p23-36

**Toxicity testing.** See Mutagenicity testing

**Toynbee, Arnold Joseph**

### About

Hook, S. Toynbee's City of God. *In* Hook, S. Philosophy and public policy p190-98

### About individual works
*A study of history*

Hourani, A. H. Toynbee's vision of history. *In* Hourani, A. H. Europe and the Middle East p136-60

**Toys.** See Paper toys

**Tracy, S. V.**
Athens in 100 B.C. *In* Harvard Studies in classical philology v83 p213-35

**Trade regulation.** See Antitrust law

**Trachtenberg, Alan**
Intellectual background. *In* Harvard Guide to contemporary American writing, ed. by D. Hoffman p 1-50

**Trade-unions**

### Transport workers—Ivory Coast

Lewis, B. C. Ethnicity and occupational specialization in the Ivory Coast: the Transporters' Association. *In* Values, identities, and national integration, ed. by J. N. Paden p75-87

### United States
Dunlop, J. T. The future of the American labor movement. *In* The Third century, ed. by S. M. Lipset p183-203

Kessler-Harris, A. "Where are the organized women workers?" *In* A Heritage of her own, ed. by N. F. Cott and E. H. Pleck p343-66

### United States—History
Dubofsky, M. Labor organizations. *In* Encyclopedia of American economic history, ed. by G. Porter v2 p524-51

**Tradition (Literature)** See Influence (Literary, artistic, etc.)

**Tradition, Oral.** See Oral tradition

**Tragedy**
Gelven, M. Heidegger and tragedy. *In* Martin Heidegger and the question of literature, ed. by W. V. Spanos p215-28

Robertson, D. W. Sidney's metaphor of the ulcer. *In* Robertson, D. W. Essays in medieval culture p308-11

*See also* European drama (Tragedy); Greek drama (Tragedy); and similar headings

### History and criticism
Reiss, T. J. A hypothesis and its prehistory. *In* Reiss, T. J. Tragedy and truth p 1-39

Reiss, T. J. Tragedy and truth. *In* Reiss, T. J. Tragedy and truth p282-302

**Tragic, The**
Farrell, J. Arnold: tragic vision and the third host. *In* Farrell, J. Revolution as tragedy p247-80

Farrell, J. P. Revolution as tragedy: being at the center. *In* Farrell, J. Revolution as tragedy p17-68

Farrell, J. P. Tragedy and ideology. *In* Farrell, J. P. Revolution as tragedy p281-90

Krieger, M. The tragic vision, twenty years after. *In* Krieger, M. Poetic presence and illusion p129-35

**Trakl, Georg**

### About

Harries, K. Language and silence: Heidegger's dialogue with Georg Trakl. *In* Martin Heidegger and the question of literature, ed. by W. V. Spanos p155-71

Neumann, E. Georg Trakl: the person and the myth. *In* Neumann, E. Creative man p138-231

**Trani, Eugene P.**
Herbert Hoover and the Russian Revolution, 1917-20. *In* Herbert Hoover, ed. by L. E. Gelfand p111-42

**Transcendence of God**
Daly, G. Alfred Loisy and the radicalization of the Modernist movement. *In* Daly, G. Transcendence of immanence p51-68

Daly, G. Friedrich von Hügel: experience and transcendence. *In* Daly, G. Transcendence and immanence p117-39

Daly, G. George Tyrell: revelation as experience. *In* Daly, G. Transcendence and immanence p140-64

**Transcendentalism (New England)**

### Bibliography

Glick, W. Emerson, Thoreau, and transcendentalism. *In* American literary scholarship, 1978 p3-16

**Transfer of technology.** See Technology transfer

**Transport workers.** See Trade unions—Transport workers

**Transportation**

**Ivory Coast**

Lewis, B. C. Ethnicity and occupational specialization in the Ivory Coast: the Transporters' Association. *In* Values, identities, and national integration, ed. by J. N. Paden p75-87

**United States—History**

McClelland, P. D. Transportation. *In* Encyclopedia of American economic history, ed. by G. Porter v 1 p309-34

**Transporters' Association of the Ivory Coast**

Lewis, B. C. Ethnicity and occupational specialization in the Ivory Coast: the Transporters' Association. *In* Values, identities, and national integration, ed. by J. N. Paden p75-87

**Trattner, Walter I.**

Social welfare. *In* Encyclopedia of American economic history, ed. by G. Porter v3 p1155-67

**Travel**

**Hygienic aspects**

Morowitz, H. J. High in the Andes. *In* Morowitz, H. J. The wine of life, and other essays on societies, energy & living things p251-55

**Travel hygiene.** See Travel—Hygienic aspects

**Travelers**

**Health and hygiene**

*See* Travel—Hygienic aspects

**Travels.** See Scientific expeditions

**Travitsky, Betty S.**

The new mother of the English Renaissance: her writings on motherhood. *In* The Lost tradition: mothers and daughters in literature, ed. by C. N. Davidson and E. M. Broner p33-43

**Treacher, Andrew, and Baruch, Geoff**

Towards a critical history of the psychiatric profession. *In* Critical psychiatry, ed. by D. Ingleby p120-49

**The treasure of the Sierra Madre (Motion picture)**

Miller, G. The wages of sin. *In* Miller, G. Screening the novel p84-115

**The tree of wooden clogs (Motion picture)**

Kauffmann, S. The tree of wooden clogs. *In* Kauffmann, S. Before my eyes p339-41

**Trees in poetry**

Hatto, A. T. The lime-tree and early German, Goliard and English lyric poetry. *In* Hatto, A. T. Essays on medieval German and other poetry p17-41

**Trent, Council of, 1545-1563**

Ozment, S. H. Catholic reform and Counter Reformation. *In* Ozment, S. H. The age of reform, 1250-1550 p397-418

**Trescott, Paul**

Central banking. *In* Encyclopedia of American economic history, ed. by G. Porter v2 p737-52

**Trevarthen, Colwyn**

Instincts for human understanding and for cultural cooperation: their development in infancy. *In* Human ethology, ed. by M. von Cranach [and others] p530-71

**Trials (Blasphemy)**

Ginzburg, C. Cheese and worms. *In* Religion and the people, 800-1700, ed. by J. Obelkevich p87-167

**Trials (Witchcraft)**

Midelfort, H. C. E. Witch hunting and the domino theory. *In* Religion and the people, 800-1700, ed. by J. Obelkevich p277-88

**France—Cambrésis**

Muchembled, R. The witches of the Cambrésis. *In* Religion and the people, 800-1700, ed. by J. Obelkevich p221-76

**Trickster**

Pelton, R. D. Ananse; spinner of Ashanti doubleness. *In* Pelton, R. D. The trickster in West Africa p25-70

Pelton, R. D. Interpreting the trickster. *In* Pelton, R. D. The trickster in West Africa p 1-24

Pelton, R. D. Legba and Eshu: writers of destiny. *In* Pelton, R. D. The trickster in West Africa p113-63

Pelton, R. D. Legba: master of the Fon dialetic. *In* Pelton, R. D. The trickster in West Africa p71-112

Pelton, R. D. Ogo-Yurugu: lord of the random, servant of wholeness. *In* Pelton, R. D. The trickster in West Africa p164-222

Pelton, R. D. Toward a theory of the trickster. *In* Pelton, R. D. The trickster in West Africa p223-84

**Trifonov, Iurii Valentinovich**

**About**

Hosking, G. Yury Trifonov. *In* Hosking, G. Beyond Socialist realism p180-95

Shneidman, N. N. Iurii Trifonov: city prose. *In* Shneidman, N. N. Soviet literature in the 1970s: artistic diversity and ideological conformity p88-105

**Trilling, Lionel**

Speaking of literature and society

*Contents*

The America of John Dos Passos
An American classic
An American in Spain
An American view of English literature
Another Jewish problem novel
Artists and the "societal function"
The assassination of Leon Trotsky
The autonomy of the literary work
Carlyle
The changing myth of the Jew
Cities of the plain
The Coleridge letters
A comedy of evil
Communism and intellectual freedom
D. H. Lawrence: a neglected aspect
Evangelical criticism
Family album
Fitzgerald plain
Flawed instruments
The formative years
The head and heart of Henry James
Hemingway and his critics
The last lover
Last years of a Titan
Literary pathology
Literature and power
M., W., F. at 10
Marxism in limbo
Neurosis and the health of the artist
Orwell on the future
Paradise reached for
The person of the artist
The poems of Emily Brontë
Politics and the liberal
The problem of influence
The problem of the American artist
The progressive psyche
The promise of realism
Proust as critic and the critic as novelist
Reflections on a lost cause: English literature and American education

### About
Shapiro, C. On our own: Trilling vs. Dreiser. *In* Seasoned authors for a new season: the search for standards in popular writing, ed. by L. Filler p152-56

**Tristan**
### Romances
Wiesmann-Wiedemann, F. From victim to villain: King Mark. *In* The Expansion and transformations of courtly literature, ed. by N. B. Smith and J. T. Snow p49-68

**Trivedi, H. K.**
Forster and Virginia Woolf: the critical friends. *In* E. M. Forster: a human exploration, ed. by G. K. Das and J. Beer p216-30

**Trollope, Anthony**
### About
Garrett, P. K. Trollope: eccentricities. *In* Garrett, P. K. The Victorian multiplot novel p180-220

Letwin, S. R. Trollope on generations without gaps. *In* Generation, ed. by S. R. Graubard p53-70

Stone, D. D. Trollope, Byron, and the conventionalities. *In* Stone, D. D. The romantic impulse in Victorian fiction p46-73

### About individual works
*Barchester Towers*
Polhemus, R. M. Trollope's Barchester Towers: comic reformation. *In* Polhemus, R. M. Comic faith p166-203

*Nina Balatka*
Stern, S. The spirit of the place. *In* The World of Franz Kafka, ed. by J. P. Stern p44-46

**Trotskiǐ, Lev**
### About
Hook, S. Leon Trotsky and the cunning of history. *In* Hook, S. Philosophy and public policy 181-89

Trilling, L. The assassination of Leon Trotsky. *In* Trilling, L. Speaking of literature and society p367-73

### About individual works
*Literature and revolution*
Slaughter, C. Literature and revolution; Trotsky. *In* Slaughter, C. Marxism, ideology & literature p86-113

**Trotsky, Leon.** See Trotskiǐ, Lev

**Troubadors**
Jones, L. E. Narrative transformations of twelve-century troubadour lyric. *In* The Expansion and transformations of courtly literature, ed. by N. B. Smith and J. T. Snow p118-27
*See also* Tensons

**Trowbridge, Frederick Hoyt**
White of Selborne: the ethos of probabilism. *In* Probability, time, and space in eighteenth-century literature, ed. by P. R. Backscheider p79-109

**The truck (Motion picture)**
Kael, P. Contracts. *In* Kael, P. When the lights go down p291-98

**Truehart, William B.**
Atkinson: an ill-informed assailant. *In* Critics of Henry George, ed. by R. V. Andelson p254-60

**Truffaut, François**
### About individual works
*The films in my life*
Kauffmann, S. The films in my life. *In* Kauffmann, S. Before my eyes p391-94

*The 400 blows*
Thiher, A. The existential play in Truffaut's early films. *In* Thiher, A. The cinematic muse p143-63

*Jules and Jim*
Thiher, A. The existential play in Truffaut's early films. *In* Thiher, A. The cinematic muse p143-63

*Love on the run*
Kauffmann, S. Love on the run. *In* Kauffmann, S. Before my eyes p190-93

*The man who loved women*
Kael, P. The unjoy of sex. *In* Kael, P. When the lights go down p354-58
Kauffmann, S. The man who loved women. *In* Kauffmann, S. Before my eyes p189-90

*Shoot the piano player*
Thiher, A. The existential play in Truffaut's early films. *In* Thiher, A. The cinematic muse p143-63

*Small change*
Kael, P. Charmed lives. *In* Kael, P. When the lights go down p167-22
Kauffmann, S. Small change. *In* Kauffmann, S. Before my eyes p187-88

*The story of Adèle H.*
Kauffmann, S. The story of Adèle H. *In* Kauffmann, S. Before my eyes p183-86

**Trusts, Industrial**
*See also* Consolidation and merger of corporations
### Law and legislation
*See* Antitrust law

**Truth**
Annas, J. Truth and knowledge. *In* Doubt and dogmatism, ed. by M. Schofield, M. Burnyeat and J. Barnes p84-104

Funkenstein, A. Descartes, eternal truths and the divine omnipotence. *In* Descartes, ed. by S. Gaukroger p181-95

Hacking, I. Proof and eternal truths: Descartes and Leibniz. *In* Descartes, ed. by S. Gaukroger p169-80

Kristeller, P. O. The unity of truth. *In* Kristeller, P. O. Renaissance thought and its source p196-210

Manley, L. G. "A latitude of sense": testing for truth. *In* Manley, L. G. Convention, 1500-1750 p241-64

Taylor, C. C. W. 'All perceptions are true.' *In* Doubt and dogmatism, ed. by M. Schofield, M. Burnyeat and J. Barnes p105-24
*See also* Reality

# U

Ugaki, Kazunari. See Ugaki, Kazushigi
Ugaki, Kazushigi
### About
Ikei, M. Ugaki Kazushige's view of China and his China policy, 1915-1930. *In* The Chinese and the Japanese, ed. by A. Iriye p199-219
Uitti, Karl D.
Cordemoy and 'Cartesian linguistics.' *In* Psychology of language and thought, ed. by R. W. Rieber p53-76
The myth of poetry in twelfth-and thirteenth-century France. *In* The Binding of Proteus, ed. by M. W. McCune, T. Orbison and P. M. Withim p142-56
Ulcers in literature
Robertson, D. W. Sidney's metaphor of the ulcer. *In* Robertson, D. W. Essays in medieval culture p308-11
Ulrich, Laurel Thatcher
Vertuous women found: New England ministerial literature, 1668-1735. *In* A Heritage of her own, ed. by N. F. Cott and E. H. Pleck p58-80
Umbanda (Cultus)
Brown, D. D. Umbanda and class relations in Brazil. *In* Brazil, anthropological perspectives, ed. by M. L. Margolis and W. E. Carter p270-304
Umiker-Sebeok, Jean, and Sebeok, Thomas Albert
Introduction: questioning apes. *In* Speaking of apes, ed. by T. A. Sebeok and J. Umiker-Sebeok p 1-59
Ummidii family
Syme, Sir R. Ummidius Quadratus, capax imperii. *In* Harvard Studies in classical philology, v83, p287-310
Un chien andalou (Motion picture)
Thiher, A. Surrealism's enduring bite: Un chien andalou. *In* Thiher, A. The cinematic muse p24-37
Unconsciousness. See Subconsciousness
Underdeveloped areas
Albrecht, U. Militarism and underdevelopment. *In* Problems of contemporary militarism, ed. by A. Eide and M. Thee p106-26
Kamrany, N. M. and Morgner, A. Basic needs versus developmental needs: the north-south dialogue. *In* Economic issues of the eighties, ed. by N. M. Kamrany and R. H. Day p247-61
Nugent, J. B. Contemporary issues in development economics. *In* Economic issues of the eighties, ed. by N. M. Kamrany and R. H. Day p262-70

### Armed forces—Appropriations and expenditures
Leitenberg, M. and Ball, N. The military expenditures of less developed nations as a proportion of their state budgets: a research note. *In* Problems of contemporary militarism, ed. by A. Eide and M. Thee p286-96

### Civil rights
Falk, R. A. Militarisation and human rights in the Third World. *In* Problems of contemporary militarism, ed. by A. Eide and M. Thee p207-25

### Economic assistance
*See* Economic assistance

### Economic conditions
*See* Underdeveloped areas

### Economic policy
Pye, L. W. Communication, development, and power. *In* Propaganda and communication in world history, ed. by H. D. Lasswell, D. Lerner and H. Speier v2 p424-45

### Foreign economic relations
Wolpin, M. D. Arms transfer and dependency in the Third World. *In* Problems of contemporary militarism, ed. by A. Eide and M. Thee p248-60

### Foreign relations
Rubinstein, A. Z. The Soviet Union and the Third World. *In* The Soviet Union since Stalin, ed. by S. F. Cohen; A. Rabinowitch and R. Sharlet p324-31

### Mass media
Pye, L. W. Communication, development, and power. *In* Propaganda and communication in world history, ed. by H. D. Lasswell, D. Lerner and H. Speier v2 p424-45

### Military policy
Landgren-Bäckström, S. Arms trade and transfer of military technology to Third World countries. *In* Problems of contemporary militarism, ed. by A. Eide and M. Thee p230-47

### Munitions
Kaldor, M. H. The significance of military technology. *In* Problems of contemporary militarism, ed. by A. Eide and M. Thee p226-29
Landgren-Bäckström, S. Arms trade and transfer of military technology to Third World countries. *In* Problems of contemporary militarism, ed. by A. Eide and M. Thee p230-47
Wolpin, M. D. Arms transfer and dependency in the Third World. *In* Problems of contemporary militarism, ed. by A. Eide and M. Thee p248-60

### Politics and government
Falk, R. A. Militarisation and human rights in the Third World. *In* Problems of contemporary militarism, ed. by A. Eide and M. Thee p207-25
Pye, L. W. Communication, development, and power. *In* Propaganda and communication in world history, ed. by H. D. Lasswell, D. Lerner and H. Speier v2 p424-45
Senghaas, D. Militarism dynamics in the contemporary context of periphery capitalism. *In* Problems of contemporary militarism, ed. by A. Eide and M. Thee p195-206
Underwriting. See Insurance
Unemployed
*See also* Inflation (Finance) and unemployment

### Mathematical models
*See* Phillips curve

### United States
Pencavel, J. H. The nature of the contemporary unemployment problem. *In* The Economy in the 1980s: a program for growth and stability, ed. by M. J. Boskin p83-115
Unemployment. See Labor supply; Unemployed
Ungar, Peter K.
I do not exist. *In* Perception and identity, ed. by G. F. Macdonald p235-51

**Ungerer, Gustav**
'My lady's a Catayan, we are politicians, Maluolios a Peg-a-ramsie.' *In* Shakespeare survey 32 p85-104

**Unicorns**
Lutz, C. E. The American unicorn. *In* Lutz, C. E. The oldest library motto, and other library essays p115-21

**Union, Trade.** See Trade-unions

**Unionist Party (Great Britain)** See Conservative Party (Great Britain)

**Unions, Trade.** See Trade-unions

**Unitarianism.** See Humanism, Religious

**Unitarians in the United States**
Miller, P. Individualism and the New England tradition. *In* Miller, P. The responsibility of mind in a civilization of machines p26-44

**United States**

### Appropriations and expenditures
Boskin, M. J. Federal government spending and budget policy. *In* The Economy in the 1980s: a program for growth and stability, ed. by M. J. Boskin p255-90
Rabushka, A. Tax and spending limits. *In* The United States in the 1980s, ed. by P. Duignan and A. Rabushka p85-108

### Armed forces—Appropriations and expenditures
Rowen, H. S. Defense spending and the uncertain future. *In* The Economy in the 1980s: a program for growth and stability, ed. by M. J. Boskin p325-51

### Armed Forces—Procurement
Pursell, C. W. Military-industrial complex. *In* Encyclopedia of American economic history, ed. by G. Porter v3 p926-34

### Central Intelligence Agency
Cline, R. S. The future of U.S. foreign intelligence operations. *In* The United States in the 1980s, ed. by P. Duignan and A. Rabushka p469-96

### Civilization
Dundes, A. The crowing hen and the Easter bunny: male chauvinism in American folklore. *In* Dundes, A. Interpreting folklore p160-75
Dundes, A. The number three in American culture. *In* Dundes, A. Interpreting folklore p134-59
Dundes, A. Seeing is believing. *In* Dundes, A. Interpreting folklore p86-92
Dundes, A. Thinking ahead: a folkloristic reflection of the future orientation in American worldview. *In* Dundes, A. Interpreting folklore p69-85
Miller, P. Equality in the American setting. *In* Miller, P. The responsibility of mind in a civilization of machines p142-60
Miller, P. Liberty and conformity. *In* Miller, P. The responsibility of mind in a civilization of machines p186-94
Miller, P. The responsibility of mind in a civilization of machines. *In* Miller, P. The responsibility of mind in a civilization of machines p195-213
Miller, P. The social context of the covenant. *In* Miller, P. The responsibility of mind in a civilization of machines p134-41
Sayre, R. F. Autobiography and the making of America, ed. by J. Olney p146-68
Swidler, A. Love and adulthood in American culture. *In* Themes of work and love in adulthood, ed. by N. J. Smelser and E. H. Erikson p120-47

**Civilization—1945-**
La Barre, W. Countertransference and the beatniks. *In* La Barre, W. Culture in context p276-85

### Commerce—History
Lindstrom, D. Domestic trade and regional specialization. *In* Encyclopedia of American economic history, ed. by G. Porter v 1 p264-80
Rothstein, M. Foreign trade. *In* Encyclopedia of American economic history, ed. by G. Porter v 1 p247-63

### Commercial policy
Meier, G. M. U.S. foreign economic policies. *In* The United States in the 1980s, ed. by P. Duignan and A. Rabushka p585-611
Wu, Yuan-li. U.S. foreign economic policy: politico-economic linkages. *In* United States in the 1980s, ed. by P. Duignan and A. Rabushka p613-37

### Congress
Malbin, M. J. Congress, policy analysis, and natural gas deregulation: a parable about fig leaves. *In* Bureaucrats, policy analysts, statesmen: who leads? Ed. by R. A. Goldwin p62-87

### Congress—Powers and duties
Moynihan, D. P. The iron law of emulation. *In* Moynihan, D. P. Counting our blessings p115-37

### Courts
*See* Courts—United States

### Defenses
Iklé, F. C. Arms control and national defense. *In* The United States in the 1980s, ed. by P. Duignan and A. Rabushka p419-43
Kemp, G. T. H. Defense innovation and geopolitics: from the Persian Gulf to outer space. *In* National security in the 1980s: from weakness to strength, ed. by W. S. Thompson p69-87
Moynihan, D. P. Cold dawn, high noon. *In* Moynihan, D. P. Counting our blessings p277-336
Nunn, S. Defense budget and defense capabilities. *In* National security in the 1980s: from weakness to strength, ed. by W. S. Thompson p375-95
Rowen, H. S. Defense spending and the uncertain future. *In* The Economy in the 1980s: a program for growth and stability, ed. by M. J. Boskin p325-51
Sullivan, L. Correlating national security strategy and defense investment. *In* National security in the 1980s: from weakness to strength, ed. by W. S. Thompson p337-73
Van Cleave, W. R. Quick fixes to U.S. strategic nuclear forces. *In* National security in the 1980s: from weakness to strength, ed. by W. S. Thompson p89-107
Zumwalt, E. R. Heritage of weakness: an assessment of the 1970s. *In* National security in the 1980s: from weakness to strength, ed. by W. S. Thompson p17-51

### Department of Defense—Appropriations and expenditures
Nunn, S. Defense budget and defense capabilities. *In* National security in the 1980s: from weakness to strength, ed. by W. S. Thompson p375-95
Sullivan, L. Correlating national security strategy and defense investment. *In* National security in the 1980s: from weakness to strength, ed. by W. S. Thompson p337-73

United States—*Continued*
### Emigration and immigration—History
Jones, M. A. Immigration. *In* Encyclopedia of American economic history, ed. by G. Porter v3 p1068-86

### Energy policy
*See* Energy policy—United States

### Food Administration
Sworakowski, W. S. Herbert Hoover, launching the American Food Administration, 1917. *In* Herbert Hoover, ed. by L. E. Gelfand p40-60

### Foreign economic relations
Cuddington, J. T. and McKinnon, R. I. The United States and the world economy. *In* The Economy in the 1980s: a program for growth and stability, ed. by M. J. Boskin p161-95

Meier, G. M. U.S. foreign economic policies. *In* The United States in the 1980s, ed. by P. Duignan and A. Rabushka p585-611

Wu, Yuan-li. U.S. foreign economic policy: politico-economic linkages. *In* United States in the 1980s, ed. by P. Duignan and A. Rabushka p613-37

### Foreign economic relations—Russia
Costick, M. M. Soviet military posture and strategic trade. *In* National security in the 1980s: from weakness to strength, ed. by W. S. Thompson p189-213

### Foreign relations
Hero, A. O. Southern Jews and public policy. *In* Conference on Southern Jewish history, Richmond, Va. 1976. "Turn to the South" p143-50

### Foreign relations—20th century
Moynihan, D. P. The legacy of Woodrow Wilson. *In* Moynihan, D. P. Counting our blessings p6-22

### Foreign relations—1945-
Moynihan, D. P. How much does freedom matter? *In* Moynihan, D. P. Counting our blessings p23-40

Moynihan, D. P. Pacem in terris. *In* Moynihan, D. P. Counting our blessings p60-71

Moynihan, D. P. The politics of human rights. *In* Moynihan, D. P. Counting our blessings p85-105

Moynihan, D. P. Presenting the American case. *In* Moynihan, D. P. Counting our blessings p41-59

Thompson, W. S. Introduction. *In* National security in the 1980s: from weakness to strength, ed. by W. S. Thompson p3-16

### Foreign relations—1977-
Adelman, K. L. Revitalizing alliances. *In* National security in the 1980s: from weakness to strength, ed. by W. S. Thompson p295-317

Thompson, W. S. Toward a strategic peace. *In* National security in the 1980s: from weakness to strength, ed. by W. S. Thompson p473-88

### Foreign relations—Africa
Thompson, W. S. The African-American nexus in Soviet strategy. *In* Communism in Africa, ed. by D. E. Albright p189-218

### Foreign relations—Asia
Scalapino, R. A. Asia. *In* The United States in the 1980's. ed. by P. Duignan and A. Rabushka p661-706

### Foreign relations—Europe
Grosser, A. Western Europe. *In* The United States in the 1980s, ed. by P. Duignan and A. Rabushka p707-34

### Foreign relations—Latin America
Falcoff, M. Latin America. *In* The United States in the 1980s, ed. by P. Duignan and A. Rabushka p797-826

### Foreign relations—Persian Gulf region
Wohlstetter, A. Half-wars and half-policies in the Persian Gulf. *In* National security in the 1980s: from weakness to strength, ed. by W. S. Thompson p123-71

### Foreign relations—Russia
Burt, R. R. Washington and the Atlantic alliance: the hidden crisis. *In* National security in the 1980s: from weakness to strength, ed. by W. S. Thompson p109-21

Marshall, C. B. Strategy: the emerging dangers. *In* National security in the 1980s: from weakness to strength, ed. by W. S. Thompson p423-41

Moynihan, D. P. Pacem in terris. *In* Moynihan, D. P. Counting our blessings p60-71

Nitze, P. H. Policy and strategy from weakness. *In* National security in the 1980s: from weakness to strength, ed. by W. S. Thompson p443-56

Zumwalt, E. R. Heritage of weakness: an assessment of the 1970s. *In* National security in the 1980s: from weakness to strength, ed. by W. S. Thompson p17-51

### Foreign relations—South Asia
Moynihan, D. P. How much does freedom matter? *In* Moynihan, D. P. Counting our blessings p23-40

### Genealogy
Hareven, T. K. The search for generational memory: tribal rites in industrial society. *In* Generations, ed. by S. R. Graubard p137-49

### Geological survey
Manning, T. G. George Otis as fourth director of the U.S. Geological Survey. *In* New Hampshire Bicentennial Conference on the History of Geology, University of New Hampshire, 1976. Two hundred years of geology in America p157-64

### Historiography
Dye, N. S. Clio's American daughters: male history, female reality. *In* The Prism of sex, ed. by J. A. Sherman and E. T. Beck p9-31

Pole, J. R. The American past: is it still usable? *In* Pole, J. R. Paths to the American past p250-70

Pole, J. R. Introduction. *In* Pole, J. R. Paths to the American past pxi-xxiii

### Historiography—Social aspects
Pole, J. R. The new history and the sense of social purpose in American historical writing. *In* Pole, J. R. Paths to the American past p271-98

### History—Colonial period, ca. 1600-1775
Botein, S. Printers and the American Revolution. *In* The Press & the American Revolution, ed. by B. Bailyn and J. B. Hench p11-57

Lovejoy, D. S. Two American revolutions, 1689 and 1776. *In* Three British revolutions: 1641, 1688, 1776, ed. by J. G. A. Pocock p244-62

United States—*Continued*

### History—Revolution, 1775-1783

Langford, P. British correspondence in the colonial press, 1763-1775: a study in Anglo-American misunderstanding before the American Revolution. *In* The Press & the American Revolution, ed. by B. Bailyn and J. B. Hench p273-313

Murrin, J. M. The great inversion, or court versus country: a comparison of the Revolution settlements in England (1688-1721) and America (1776-1816) *In* Three British revolutions: 1641, 1688, 1776, ed. by J. G. A. Pocock p363-453

Potter, J. and Calhoon, R. M. The character and coherence of the loyalist press. *In* The Press & the American Revolution, ed. by B. Bailyn and J. B. Hench p229-72

Tanselle, G. T. Some statistics on American printing, 1763-1783. *In* The Press & the American Revolution, ed. by B. Bailyn and J. B. Hench p315-63

### History—Revolution, 1775-1783—Causes

Olson, A. G. Parliament, Empire, and Parliamentary law, 1776. *In* Three British revolutions: 1641, 1688, 1776, ed. by J. G. A. Pocock p289-322

Pocock, J. G. A. 1776: the revolution against Parliament. *In* Three British revolutions: 1641, 1688, 1776, ed. by J. G. A. Pocock p265-88

*See also* Stamp Act, 1765

### History—Revolution, 1775-1783—Historiography

Cohen, L. H. Narrating the Revolution: ideology, language, and form. *In* Studies in eighteenth-century culture v9 p455-76

### History—Revolution, 1775-1783—Loyalists

*See* American loyalists

### History—Revolution, 1775-1783—Pamphlets

Adams, T. R. The British pamphlet press and the American controversy, 1764-1783. *In* American Antiquarian Society. Proceedings v89 pt 1 p33-88

### History—1783-1815

Murrin, J. M. The great inversion, or court versus country: a comparison of the Revolution settlements in England (1688-1721) and America (1776-1816) *In* Three British revolutions: 1641, 1688, 1776, ed. by J. G. A. Pocock p363-453

### History—Civil War, 1861-1865—Foreign public opinion, British

Pole, J. R. Abraham Lincoln and the working classes of Britain. *In* Pole, J. R. Paths to the American past p111-45

### History, Economic

*See* United States—Economic conditions

### History, Military

Goldin, C. D. War. *In* Encyclopedia of American economic history, ed. by G. Porter v3 p935-57

### Immigration

*See also* United States—Emigration and immigration

### Industries

Robinson, R. I. The financing of small business in the United States. *In* Small business in American life, ed. by S. W. Bruchey p280-304

### Industries—History

Berthoff, R. Independence and enterprise: small business in the American dream. *In* Small business in American life, ed. by S. W. Bruchey p28-48

Blumin, S. M. Black coats to white collars: economic change, nonmanual work, and the social structure of industrializing America. *In* Small business in American life, ed. by S. W. Bruchey p100-21

Brody, D. Labor and small-scale enterprise during industrialization. *In* Small business in American life, ed. by S. W. Bruchey p263-79

Bruchey, S. W. Introduction: a summary view of small business and American life. *In* Small business in American life, ed. by S. W. Bruchey p 1-27

Friedman, L. M. Law and small business in the United States: one hundred years of struggle and accommodation. *In* Small business in American life, ed. by S. W. Bruchey p305-18

Gallman, R. E. Economic growth. *In* Encyclopedia of American economic history, ed. by G. Porter v 1 p133-50

Hammack, D. C. Small business and urban power: some notes on the history of economic policy in nineteenth-century American cities. *In* Small business in American life, ed. by S. W. Bruchey p319-37

Hollander, S. C. The effects of industrialization on small retailing in the United States in the twentieth century. *In* Small business in American life, ed. by S. W. Bruchey p212-39

Livesay, H. C. Lilliputians in Brobdingnag: small business in late-nineteenth-century America. *In* Small business in American life, ed. by S. W. Bruchey p338-51

Sylla, R. E. Small-business banking in the United States, 1780-1920. *In* Small business in American life, ed. by S. W. Bruchey p240-62

Vatter, H. G. The position of small business in the structure of American manufacturing, 1870-1970. *In* Small business in American life, ed. by S. W. Bruchey p142-68

### Intellectual life

Miller, P. The responsibility of mind in a civilization of machines. *In* Miller, P. The responsibility of mind in a civilization of machines p195-213

Trachtenberg, A. Intellectual background. *In* Harvard Guide to contemporary American writing, ed. by D. Hoffman p 1-50

### Judiciary

*See* Courts—United States

### Manufactures—History

Uselding, P. J. Manufacturing. *In* Encyclopedia of American economic history, ed. by G. Porter v 1 p397-412

### Military policy

Iklé, F. C. Arms control and national defense. *In* The United States in the 1980s, ed. by P. Duignan and A. Rabushka p419-43

Luttwak, E. N. On the meaning of strategy . . . for the United States in the 1980s. *In* National security in the 1980s: from weakness to strength, ed. by W. S. Thompson p259-73

Moynihan, D. P. Cold dawn, high noon. *In* Moynihan, D. P. Counting our blessings p277-336

Regehr, E. What is militarism? *In* Problems of contemporary militarism, ed. by A. Eide and M. Thee p127-39

United States—Military policy—*Continued*

Rowen, H. S. Defense spending and the uncertain future. *In* The Economy in the 1980s: a program for growth and stability, ed. by M. J. Boskin p325-51

Thompson, W. S. Introduction. *In* National security in the 1980s: from weakness to strength, ed. by W. S. Thompson p3-16

West, F. J. Conventional forces beyond NATO. *In* National security in the 1980s: from weakness to strength, ed. by W. S. Thompson p319-36

### Moral conditions

Zimmerman, M. How "humanistic" are humanists? *In* Humanist ethics, ed. by M. B. Storer p262-71

### National security

Ellsworth, R. F. Quick fixes in intelligence. *In* National security in the 1980s: from weakness to strength, ed. by W. S. Thompson p173-87

Kemp, G. T. H. Defense innovation and geopolitics: from the Persian Gulf to outer space. *In* National security in the 1980s: from weakness to strength, ed. by W. S. Thompson p69-87

Sullivan, L. Correlating national security strategy and defense investment. *In* National security in the 1980s: from weakness to strength, ed. by W. S. Thompson p337-73

Thompson, W. S. Toward a strategic peace. *In* National security in the 1980s: from weakness to strength, ed. by W. S. Thompson p473-88

### Office of Naval Research

Sapolsky, H. M. Academic science and the military: the years since the Second World War. *In* The Sciences in the American context: new perspectives, ed. by N. Reingold p379-99

### Office of Scientific Research and Development

Pursell, C. W. Science agencies in World War II: the OSRD and its challengers. *In* The Sciences in the American context: new perspectives, ed. by N. Reingold p359-78

### Office of Scientific Research and Development. National Defense Research Committee

Pursell, C. W. Science agencies in World War II: the OSRD and its challengers. *In* The Sciences in the American context: new perspectives, ed. by N. Reinglod p359-78

### Politics and government

Banfield, E. C. In defense of the American party system. *In* Political parties in the eighties, ed. by R. A. Goldwin p133-49

Ceaser, J. W. Political change and party reform. *In* Political parties in the eighties, ed. by R. A. Goldwin p97-115

Dahl, R. A. On removing certain impediments to democracy in the United States. *In* The Moral foundations of the American Republic, ed. by R. H. Horwitz p234-56

Dannhauser, W. J. Reflections on statesmanship and bureaucracy. *In* Bureaucrats, policy analysts, statesmen: who leads? Ed. by R. A. Goldwin p114-32

Licht, R. A. On the three parties in America. *In* Political parties in the eighties, ed. by R. A. Goldwin p66-96

Moore, M. H. Statesmanship in a world of particular substantive choices. *In* Bureaucrats, policy analysts, statesmen: who leads? Ed. by R. A. Goldwin p20-36

Scheiber, H. N. Law and political institutions. *In* Encyclopedia of American economic history, ed. by G. Porter v2 p487-508

Silberman, L. H. Policy analysis: boon or curse for politicians? *In* Bureaucrats, policy analysts, statesmen: who leads? p37-43

Storing, H. J. American statesmanship: old and new. *In* Bureaucrats, policy analysts, statesmen: who leads? Ed. by R. A. Goldwin p88-113

Yeager, M. A. Bureaucracy. *In* Encyclopedia of American economic history, ed. by G. Porter v3 p894-926

### Politics and government—Colonial period, ca. 1600-1775

Elliott, E. The Puritan roots of American Whig rhetoric. *In* Puritan influences in American literature, ed. by E. Elliott p107-27

Pole, J. R. Historians and the problem of early American democracy. *In* Pole, J. R. Paths to the American past p223-49

### Politics and government—Revolution, 1775-1783

Pole, J. R. The emergence of the majority principle in the American Revolution. *In* Pole, J. R. Paths to the American past p41-54

Pole, J. R. Historians and the problem of early American democracy. *In* Pole, J. R. Paths to the American past p223-49

### Politics and government—1783-1809

Hench, J. B. ed. Letters of John Fenno and John Ward Fenno, 1779-1800—Part 1: 1779-1790. *In* American Antiquarian Society. Proceedings v89 pt2 p299-368

### Politics and government—1849-1877

Pole, J. R. Abraham Lincoln and the American commitment. *In* Pole, J. R. Paths to the American past p146-69

### Politics and government—1945-

Banfield, E. C. Party "reform" in retrospect. *In* Political parties in the eighties, ed. by R. A. Goldwin p20-33

Banfield, E. C. Policy science as metaphysical madness. *In* Bureaucrats, policy analysts, statesmen: who leads? Ed. by R. A. Goldwin p 1-19

Berger, P. Religion and the American future. *In* The Third century, ed. by S. M. Lipset p65-77

Elazar, D. J. Constitutionalism, federalism, and the post-industrial American polity. *In* The Third century, ed. by S. M. Lipset p79-107

Fraser, D. M. Democratizing the Democratic Party. *In* Political parties in the eighties, ed. by R. A. Goldwin p116-32

Ladd, E. C. The American party system today. *In* The Third century, ed. by S. M. Lipset p153-82

Shubert, G. H. Policy analysis and public choice. *In* Bureaucrats, policy analysts, statesmen: who leads? Ed. by R. A. Goldwin p44-61

### Popular culture

Brustein, R. S. Remakes: the retread culture. *In* Brustein, R. S. Critical moments p95-106

### Population—History

Easterlin, R. A. Population. *In* Encyclopedia of American economic history, ed. by G. Porter v 1 p167-82

Universities and colleges—*Continued*

### United States

Nisbet, R. A. The future of the university. *In* The Third century, ed. by S. M. Lipset p303-25

### United States—Faculty

Trilling, L. A valedictory. *In* Trilling, L. Speaking of literature and society p398-406

University students. See College students

An unmarried woman (Motion picture)

Kael, P. Empathy, and its limits. *In* Kael, P. When the lights go down p410-14

Kauffmann, S. An unmarried woman. *In* Kauffmann, S. Before my eyes p197-200

Unseld, Siegfried

The author and his publisher

*Contents*

Bertolt Brecht and his publishers
Hermann Hesse and his publishers
Rainer Maria Rilke and his publishers
The responsibilities of a literary publisher
Robert Walser and his publishers

Up in smoke (Motion picture)

Kael, P. Furry freaks. *In* Kael, P. When the lights go down p448-54

Updike, John

#### About individual works

*Rabbit redux*

Horton, A. S. Ken Kesey, John Updike and the Lone Ranger. *In* Seasoned authors for a new season: the search for standards in popular writing, ed. by L. Filler p83-90

Uphaus, Robert Walter

The impossible observer

*Contents*

'Clarissa,' 'Amelia,' and the state of probation
Criticism and the idea of nature
Defoe, deliverance, and dissimulation
The impossible observer
Johnson's equipoise and the state of man
Mandeville and the force of prejudice
Moral and tendency in 'Caleb Williams'
Sterne's sixth sense
Swift and the problematical nature of meaning

Urban economics

Hammack, D. C. Small business and urban power: some notes on the history of economic policy in nineteenth-century American cities. *In* Small business in American life, ed. by S. W. Bruchey p319-37

Urban-federal relations. See Federal-city relations

Urban policy. See Urban economics

Urban renewal

### United States

McClaughry, J. Neighborhood revitalization. *In* The United States in the 1980s, ed. by P. Duignan and A. Rabushka p367-90

Urbanization

### United States—History

Lampard, E. E. Urbanization. *In* Encyclopedia of American economic history, ed. by G. Porter v3 p1028-57

Urzidil, Johannes

Two recollections. *In* The World of Franz Kafka, ed. by J. P. Stern p56-68

Use of land. See Land use

Uselding, Paul John

Manufacturing. *In* Encyclopedia of American economic history, ed. by G. Porter v 1 p397-412

Ussel, Elias d'

#### About

Camproux, C. On the subject of an argument between Elias and his cousin. *In* The Interpretation of medieval lyric poetry, ed. by W. T. H. Jackson p61-90

Ussel, Gui d'

#### About

Camproux, C. On the subject of an argument between Elias and his cousin. *In* The Interpretation of medieval lyric poetry, ed. by W. T. H. Jackson p61-90

Utopias

Ricoeur, P. Ideology and utopia as cultural imagination. *In* Being human in a technological age, ed. by D. M. Borchert and D. Stewart p107-25

Utopias in literature

Stewart, P. Utopias that self-destruct. *In* Studies in eighteenth-century culture v9 p15-24

# V

Vail, Robert William Glenroie

Sabin's Dictionary. *In* The Bibliographical Society of America, 1904-79 p117-25

Vaizey, Lady Marina

Art language. *In* The State of the language, ed. by L. Michaels and C. Ricks p331-42

Valdes, Gabriel de la Concepcíon

#### About

Jackson, R. L. Slave societies and the free black writer: José Manuel Valdés and "Plácido." *In* Jackson, R. L. Black writers in Latin America p36-44

Valdés, José Manuel

#### About

Jackson, R. L. Slave societies and the free black writer: José Manuel Valdés and "Plácido." *In* Jackson, R. L. Black writers in Latin America p36-44

Valenta, Jiri

Soviet decision-making on the intervention in Angola. *In* Communism in Africa, ed. by D. E. Albright p93-117

Valentine, Robert Y.

Cortazar's rhetoric of reader participation. *In* The Analysis of literary texts, ed. by R. D. Pope p212-23

Valentino (Motion picture)

Kael, P. The lower trash/the higher trash. *In* Kael, P. When the lights go down p333-39

Valéry, Paul

#### About

Genette, G. Valéry and the poetics of language. *In* Textual strategies, ed. by J. V. Harari p359-73

#### About individual works

*The cemetery by the sea*

Caws, M. A. On one crossing-over: Valery's sea into Hart Crane's scene. *In* The Analysis of literary texts, ed. by R. D. Pope p100-06

Fehrman, C. A. D. Paul Valéry and Le cimetière marin. *In* Fehrman, C. A. D. Poetic creation p91-104

*The eternal virgin*

Olney, J. L. Some versions of memory/some versions of bios: the ontology of autobiography. *In* Autobiography: essays theoretical and critical, ed. by J. Olney p236-67

**Valla, Lorenzo**

About

Marsh, D. Lorenzo Valla and the rhetorical dialogue. *In* Marsh, D. The quattrocento dialogue p55-77

**Vallejo, Antonio Buero.** See Buero Vallejo, Antonio

**Values**

Boulding, K. E. Prices and values: infinite worth in a finite world. *In* Value and values in evolution, ed. by E. A. Maziarz p31-46

DeBary, W. T. Chinese values: the China problem and our problem. *In* Value and values in evolution, ed. by E. A. Maziarz p103-14

Eliade, M. The world, the city, and the house; excerpt from "Occultism, witchcraft, and cultural fashions." *In* Value and values in evolution, ed. by E. A. Maziarz p3-16

Garaudy, R. Values in a Marxist perspective. *In* Value and values in evolution, ed. by E. A. Maziarz p95-102

Levinas, E. The contemporary criticism of the idea of value and the prospects of humanism. *In* Value and values in evolution, ed. by E. A. Maziarz p179-87

Mosley, N. Human beings desire happiness. *In* Lying truths, ed. by R. Duncan and M. Weston-Smith p211-17

Rescher, N. Social values and technological change. *In* Value and values in evolution, ed. by E. A. Maziarz p163-78

Smart, N. Religions and changing values. *In* Value and values in evolution, ed. by E. A. Maziarz p17-28

*See also* Spirituality

**Vampires in literature**

Twitchell, J. B. Shelley's use of vampirism in The Cenci. *In* Tennessee Studies in literature v24 p120-33

**Van Beethoven, Ludwig.** See Beethoven, Ludwig van

**Vance, Eugene**

Roland and the poetics of memory. *In* Textual strategies, ed. by J. V. Harari p374-403

**Van Cleave, William R.**

Quick fixes to U.S. strategic nuclear forces. *In* National security in the 1980s: from weakness to strength, ed. by W. S. Thompson p89-107

**Vandeul, Marie Angélique (Diderot) de**

About

Varloot, J. Angélique Diderot and the white terror. *In* Woman and society in eighteenth-century France, ed. by E. Jacobs [and others] p243-50

**Vanek, Joann**

Time spent in housework. *In* A Heritage of her own, ed. by N. F. Cott and E. H. Pleck p499-506

**Van Gyseghem, André.** See Gyseghem, André van

**Van Hoesen, Henry Bartlett**

The Bibliographical Society of America— its leaders and activities, 1904-1939. *In* The Bibliographical Society of America, 1904-79 p139-71

**Van Meter, Robert Hardin**

Herbert Hoover and the economic reconstruction of Europe, 1918-21. *In* Herbert Hoover, ed. by L. E. Gelfand p143-81

**Van Vechten, Carl**

About

Pizer, D. The novels of Carl Van Vechten and the spirit of the age. *In* Toward a new American literary history, ed. by L. J. Budd, E. H. Cady and C. L. Anderson p211-29

**Varloot, Jean**

Angélique Diderot and the white terror. *In* Woman and society in eighteenth-century France, ed. by E. Jacobs [and others] p243-50

**Vasquez, Richard**

About individual works

*Chicano*

Grajeda, R. F. Jose Antonio Villarreal and Richard Vasquez: the novelist against himself. *In* The Identification and analysis of Chicano literature, ed. by F. Jiménez p329-57

**Vasta, Edward**

To Rosemounde: Chaucer's "gentil" dramatic monologue. *In* Chaucerian problems and perspectives, ed. by E. Vasta and Z. P. Thundy p97-113

**Vatican. Biblioteca Vaticana. Mss. (Pal. Graec. 431)**

Schapiro, M. The place of the Joshua Roll in Byzantine history. *In* Shapiro, M. Selected papers v3: Late antique, early Christian and mediaeval art p49-66

**Vatter, Harold G.**

The position of small business in the structure of American manufacturing, 1870-1970. *In* Small business in American life, ed. by S. W. Bruchey p142-68

**Vaughan, James H.**

A reconsideration of divine kingship. *In* Explorations in African systems of thought, ed. by I. C. Karp & C. S. Bird p120-42

**Veblen, Thorstein**

About

Qualey, C. C. Thorstein Bunde Veblen, 1857-1929. *In* Makers of an American immigrant legacy, ed. by O. S. Lovoll p50-61

**Vecelli, Tiziano.** See Titian

**Vedanta**

Organ, T. W. Humanness in neo-Vedāntism. *In* Being human in a technological age, ed. by D. M. Borchert and D. Stewart p127-64

**Vegio, Maffeo.** See Vegius, Mapheus

**Vegius, Mapheus**

About

Lutz, C. E. Two Renaissance dialogues in the manner of Lucian. *In* Lutz, C. E. The oldest library motto, and other library essays p92-98

**Veith, Gene Edward**

"Wait upon the Lord": David, Hamlet, and the problem of revenge. *In* The David myth in Western literature, ed. by R. J. Frontain and J. Wojcik p70-83

**Venantius Fortunatus.** See Fortunatus, Venantius Honorius Clementianus, Bp.

**Vendler, Helen Hennessy**

Four elegies. *In* Yeats, Sligo and Ireland, ed. by A. N. Jeffares p216-31

Part of nature, part of us

*Contents*

Adrienne Rich
Allen Ginsberg
Ammons, Berryman, Cummings
Broadsides
Charles Wright
Dave Smith

**Vendler, Helen H.**
Part of nature, part of us
*Contents—Continued*
Eight poets
Elizabeth Bishop
Frank O'Hara
Howard Nemerov
James Merrill
John Berryman
Louise Glück
Marianne Moore
Randall Jarrell
Robert Lowell
Robert Penn Warren
Sylvia Plath
T. S. Eliot
Ten poets
W. H. Auden
W. S. Merwin
Wallace Stevens
Stevens and Keats' "To autumn." *In* Wallace Stevens, ed. by F. Doggett and R. Buttel p171-95

**Venice**

**Theaters**
Lawrenson, T. E. The ideal theatre in the eighteenth century: Paris and Venice. *In* Drama and mimesis, ed. by J. Redmond p51-64

**Venice in literature**
Festa-McCormick, D. Proust's Remembrance of things past: Venice and the reality within the dream. *In* Festa-McCormick, D. The city as catalyst p89-107

**Venugopal, C. V.**
Asif Currimbhoy's 'The doldrummers': a glimpse into the Bombay shacks. *In* Aspects of Indian writing in English, ed. by M. K. Naik p262-67

**Verdi, Giuseppe**

**About**
Berlin, Sir I. The 'naïveté' of Verdi. *In* Berlin, Sir I. Against the current p287-95

**About**
Dent, E. J. Verdi in English. *In* Dent, E. J. Selected essays p261-71

**Vere, Aubrey Thomas de.** See De Vere, Aubrey Thomas

**Verene, Donald Phillip**
Vico's philosophy of imagination. *In* Conference on Vico and Contemporary Thought, New York, 1976. Vico and contemporary thought pt 1 p20-36

**Vergilius Maro, Publius**

**About individual works**
*The Aeneid*
Kenney, E. J. Iudicium transferendi: Virgil, Aeneid 2.469-505 and its antecedents. *In* Creative imitation and Latin literature, ed. by D. West and T. Woodman p103-20
Murrin, M. The goddess of air. *In* Murrin, M. The allegorical epic p3-25
Murrin, M. Landino's Virgil. *In* Murrin, M. The allegorical epic p27-50

*Eclogues*
Du Quesnay, I. M. Le M. From Polyphemus to Corydon: Virgil, Eclogue 2 and Idylls of Theocritus. *In* Creative imitation and Latin literature, ed. by D. West and T. Woodman p35-69

*Georgics*
West, D. A. Two plagues: Virgil, Georgics 3.478-566 and Lucretius 6.1090-1286. *In* Creative imitation and Latin literature, ed. by D. West and T. Woodman p71-88

**Influence—Milton**
Evans, J. M. Lycidas, Daphnis, and Gallus. *In* English Renaissance studies, ed. by J. Carey p228-44
Mueller, M. The tragic epic: Paradise lost and the Iliad. *In* Mueller, M. Children of Oedipus, and other essays on the imitation of Greek tragedy, 1550-1800 p213-30

**Influence—Racine**
Mueller, M. Dido and Bérénice. *In* Mueller, M. Children of Oedipus, and other essays on the imitation of Greek tragedy, 1550-1800 p230-48

**Translations, Scottish**
Kratzmann, G. Two Aeneid translators— Surrey's debt to Douglas: Wyatt and Henryson. *In* Kratzmann, G. Anglo-Scottish literary relations, 1430-1500 p104-28

**Verlaine, Paul Marie**

**About**
Peyre, H. The tragic impressionism of Verlaine. *In* Peyre, H. What is symbolism? p48-62

**Verne, Jules**

**About individual works**
*The mysterious island*
Barthes, R. Where to begin? *In* Barthes, R. New critical essays p79-89

**Vernon, Raymond, and Wortzel, Heidi**
Multinational enterprise. *In* Encyclopedia of American economic history, ed. by G. Porter v2 p652-60

**Versailles, Treaty of, June 28, 1919 (Germany)**
Schmidt, R. J. Hoover's reflections on the Versailles Treaty. *In* Herbert Hoover, ed. by L. E. Gelfand p61-86

**Vetter, Harold J.** See Rieber, T. W. jt. auth.

**Viaud, Julien**

**About individual works**
*Aziyadé*
Barthes, R. Pierre Loti: Aziyadé. *In* Barthes, R. New critical essays p105-21

**Vickery, John B.**
The scapegoat in literature: some kinds and uses. *In* The Binding of Proteus, ed. by M. W. McCune, T. Orbison and P. M. Withim p264-78

**Vico, Giambattista.** See Vico, Giovanni Battista

**Vico, Giovanni Battista**
On the heroic mind. *In* Conference on Vico and Contemporary Thought, New York, 1976. Vico and contemporary thought pt2 p228-45

**About**
Arieti, S. Vico and modern psychiatry. *In* Conference on Vico and Contemporary Thought, New York, 1976. Vico and contemporary thought pt2 p81-94
Berlin, Sir I. The divorce between the sciences and the humanities. *In* Berlin, Sir I. Against the current p80-110
Berlin, Sir I. Vico and the ideal of the Enlightenment. *In* Berlin, Sir I. Against the current p120-29

*Also in* Conference on Vico and Contemporary Thought, New York, 1976. Vico and contemporary thought pt 1 p250-63

**Vico, Giovanni B.—**About—*Continued*

Blasi, A. Vico, developmental psychology, and human nature. *In* Conference on Vico and Contemporary Thought, New York, 1976. Vico and contemporary thought pt2 p14-39

Cahnman, W. J. Vico and historical sociology. *In* Conference on Vico and Contemporary Thought, New York, 1976. Vico and contemporary thought pt2 p168-78

Fisch, M. H. What has Vico to say to philosophers of today? *In* Conference on Vico and Contemporary Thought, New York, 1976. Vico and contemporary thought pt 1 p9-19

Giorgi, A. Vico and humanistic psychology. *In* Conference on Vico and Contemporary Thought, New York, 1976. Vico and contemporary thought pt2 p69-78

Haddock, B. A. Vico and the problem of historical reconstruction. *In* Conference on Vico and Contemporary thought, New York, 1976. Vico and contemporary thought pt 1 p122-29

Haddock, B. A. Vico: the problem of interpretation. *In* Conference on Vico and Contemporary Thought, New York, 1976. Vico on contemporary thought pt 1 p145-62

Jordan, R. W. Vico and the phenomenology of the moral sphere. *In* Conference on Vico and Contemporary Thought, New York, 1976. Vico and contemporary thought pt 1 p130-41

Kelley, D. R. In Vico veritas: the true philosophy and the new science. *In* Conference on Vico and Contemporary Thought, New York, 1976. Vico and contemporary thought pt 1 p211-21

Leach, Sir E. Vico and the future of anthropology. *In* Conference on Vico and Contemporary Thought, New York, 1976. Vico and contemporary thought pt2 p149-59

Maier, J. B. Vico and critical theory. *In* Conference on Vico and Contemporary Thought, New York, 1976. Vico and contemporary thought pt2 p187-98

Mooney, M. The primacy of language in Vico. *In* Conference on Vico and Contemporary Thought, New York, 1976. Vico and contemporary thought pt 1 p191-210

Murrin, M. Epilogue: The disappearance of Homer and the end of Homeric allegory: Vico and Wolf. *In* Murrin, M. The allegorical epic p173-96

Nisbet, R. A. Vico and the idea of progress. *In* Conference on Vico and Contemporary Thought, New York, 1976. Vico and contemporary thought pt 1 p235-47

O'Neill, J. On the history of the human senses in Vico and Marx. *In* Conference on Vico and Contemporary Thought, New York, 1976. Vico and contemporary thought pt2 p179-86

Rubinoff, L. Vico and the verification of historical interpretation. *In* Conference on Vico and Contemporary Thought, New York, 1976. Vico and contemporary thought pt 1 p94-121

Singer, J. L. Vico's insight and the scientific study of the stream of consciousness. *In* Conference on Vico and Contemporary Thought, New York, 1976. Vico and contemporary thought pt2 p57-68

### About individual works
#### The new science

Dallmayr, F. R. "Natural history" and social evolution: reflections on Vico's corsi e ricorsi. *In* Conference on Vico and Contemporary Thought, New York, 1976. Vico and contemporary thought pt2 p199-215

Grassi, E. The priority of common sense and imagination: Vico's philosophical relevance today. *In* Conference on Vico and Contemporary Thought, New York, 1976. Vico and contemporary thought pt 1 p163-85

Luft, S. R. Creative activity in Vico and the secularization of providence. *In* Studies in eighteenth-century culture v9 p337-55

McMullin, E. Vico's theory of science. *In* Conference on Vico and Contemporary Thought, New York, 1976. Vico and contemporary thought pt 1 p60-90

Pompa, L. Human nature and the concept of a human science. *In* Conference on Vico and Contemporary Thought, New York, 1976. Vico and contemporary thought pt 1 p44-55

Stevenson, D. R. Vico's Scienza nuova: an alternative to the Enlightenment mainstream. *In* The Quest for the new science, ed. by K. J. Fink and J. W. Marchand p6-16

Verene, D. P. Vico's philosophy of imagination. *In* Conference on Vico and Contemporary Thought, New York, 1976. Vico and contemporary thought pt 1 p20-36

### Education

Perkinson, H. J. Vico and the methods of study of our time. *In* Conference on Vico and Contemporary Thought, New York, 1976. Vico and contemporary thought pt2 p95-109

### Knowledge, Theory of

Berlin, Sir I. Vico's concept of knowledge. *In* Berlin, Sir I. Against the current p111-19

Tagliacozzo, G. General education as unity of knowledge: a theory based on Vichian principles. *In* Conference on Vico and Contemporary Thought, New York, 1976. Vico and contemporary thought pt2 p110-38

### Political science

Costa, G. Vico's political thought in his time and ours. *In* Conference on Vico and Contemporary Thought, New York, 1976. Vico and contemporary thought pt 1 p222-34

### Psychology

Mora, G. Vico and Piaget: parallels and differences. *In* Conference on Vico and Contemporary Thought, New York, 1976. Vico and contemporary thought pt2 p40-54

### Sociology

Stark, W. The theoretical and practical relevance of Vico's sociology for today. *In* Conference on Vico and Contemporary Thought, New York, 1976. Vico and contemporary thought pt2 p160-67

**Vicq-d'Azyr, Félix**
### About

Roche, D. Talent, reason, and sacrifice: the physician during the Enlightenment. *In* Medicine and society in France, ed. by R. Forster and O. Ranum p66-88

**Vienna**
### Intellectual life

Rutledge, J. S. The delayed reflex: journalism in Josephinian Vienna. *In* Studies in eighteenth-century culture v9 p79-92

Schorske, C. E. Generational tension and cultural change: reflections on the case of Vienna. *In* Generations, ed. by S. R. Graubard p111-22

**Vieth, David M.**
Shadwell in acrostic land: the reversible meaning of Dryden's Mac Flecknoe. *In* Studies in eighteenth-century culture v9 p503-16

**Vigo, Jean**
### About individual works
*Zéro de conduite*
Thiher, A. Vigo's Zéro de conduite: surrealism and the myth of childhood. *In* Thiher, A. The cinematic muse p78-89

**Villarreal, José Antonio**
Chicano literature: art and politics from the perspective of the artist. *In* The Identification and analysis of Chicano literature, ed. by F. Jiménez p161-68

### About individual works
*Pocho*
Grajeda, R. F. Jose Antonio Villarreal and Richard Vasquez: the novelist against himself. *In* The Identification and analysis of Chicano literature, ed. by F. Jiménez p329-57

**Villarreal R., José Antonio.** See Villarreal, José Antonio

**Villon, François**
### About
Hayes, J. J. Gothic love and death: Francois Villon and the city of Paris. *In* 5000 years of popular culture, ed. by F. E. H. Schroeder p228-39

**Vinaver, Eugène**
Landmarks in Arthurian romance. *In* The Expansion and transformations of courtly literature, ed. by N. B. Smith and J. T. Snow p17-31
The questing knight. *In* The Binding of Proteus, ed. by M. W. McCune, T. Orbison and P. M. Withim p126-40

**Vincent, François, Paul, and the others (Motion picture)**
Kael, P. A piece of music. *In* Kael, P. When the lights go down p152-57

**Vinci, Leonardo.** See Leonardo da Vinci

**Violence**
### Moral and religious aspects
Narveson, J. Violence and war. *In* Matters of life and death, ed. by T. Regan p109-47

**Violence in literature**
Fineman, J. Fratricide and cuckoldry: Shakespeare's doubles. *In* Representing Shakespeare, ed. by M. M. Schwartz and C. Kahn p70-109

**Violence in moving-pictures**
Kauffmann, S. Blood on the screen. *In* Kauffmann, S. Before my eyes on p421-24

**Violent deaths.** See Murder

**Virgil.** See Vergilius Maro, Publius

**Virginia**
### Historiography
Tate, T. W. The seventeenth-century Chesapeake and its modern historians. *In* The Chesapeake in the seventeenth century, ed. by T. W. Tate and D. L. Ammerman p3-50

### History—Colonial period, ca. 1600-1775
Earle, C. V. Environment, disease, and mortality in early Virginia. *In* The Chesapeake in the seventeenth century, ed. by T. W. Tate and D. L. Ammerman p96-125
Shammas, C. English-born and creole elites in turn-of-the-century Virginia. *In* The Chesapeake in the seventeenth century, ed. by T. W. Tate and D. L. Ammerman p274-96

### Politics and government—1775-1865
Pole, J. R. Representation and authority in Virginia from the Revolution to reform. *In* Pole, J. R. Paths to the American past p3-40

**Virtue**
Grimsley, R. Jean-Jacques Rousseau, philosopher of nature. *In* Royal Institute of Philosophy. Philosophers of the Enlightenment p184-98
Shiner, R. A. Butler's theory of moral judgment. *In* Royal Institute of Philosophy. Philosophers of the Enlightenment p199-225

**Visconti, Luchino**
### About individual works
*The innocent*
Kauffmann, S. The innocent. *In* Kauffmann, S. Before my eyes p334-35

**Vision**
Dundes, A. Seeing is believing. *In* Dundes, A. Interpreting folklore p86-92
*See also* Visual perception

### Psychological aspects
*See* Visual perception

**Visser, N. W.**
The novel and the concept of social network. *In* The Analysis of literary texts, ed. by R. D. Pope p268-85

**Visual perception**
Larmore, C. Descartes' empirical epistemology. *In* Descartes, ed. by S. Gaukroger p6-22
Maull, N. L. Cartesian optics and the geometrization of nature. *In* Descartes, ed. by S. Gaukroger p23-40

**Vital, David**
Zionism and Israel. *In* The Jewish world, ed. by E. Kedourie p309-17

**Vital statistics**
Davis, K. The continuing demographic revolution in industrial societies. *In* The Third century, ed. by S. M. Lipset p37-64

**Vivas, Eliseo**
### About
Krieger, M. The theoretical contributions of Eliseo Vivas. *In* Krieger, M. Poetic presence and illusion p115-28

**Vivekânanda, Swami**
### About
Sastri, P. S. Philosophical ideas of Swami Vivekananda. *In* Aspects of Indian writing in English, ed. by M. K. Naik p294-304

**Vlach, John Michael**
Arrival and survival: the maintenance of an Afro-American tradition in folk art and craft. *In* Perspectives of American folk art, ed. by I. M. G. Quimby and S. T. Swank p177-217

**Vladimov, Georgiĭ Nikolaevich**
### About
Hosking, G. Vladimir Voinovich, Georgy Vladimov. *In* Hosking, G. Beyond Socialist realism p136-61

**Vocabulary**
Morowitz, H. J. Psychosclerosis. *In* Morowitz, H. J. The wine of life, and other essays on societies, energy & living things p225-28

**Vogau, Boris Andreevich**
### About
Chukovskiĭ, K. I. Excerpts from the diaries of Korney Chukovsky relating to Boris Pilnyak. *In* California Slavic studies v11 p187-99

**Vogelweide, Walther von der.** See Walther von der Vogelweide

**Voice.** See Speech

**Wagenbach, Klaus**

Kafka's castle? *In* The World of Franz Kafka, ed. by J. P. Stern p79-86

**Wages**

United States—History

Adams, D. R. Prices and wages. *In* Encyclopedia of American economic history, ed. by G. Porter v 1 p229-46

**Waggoner, Diana**

About individual works

*The hills of faraway: a guide to fantasy*

Nodelman, P. Defining children's literature. *In* Children's literature v8 p184-90

**Wagley, Charles**

Anthropology and Brazilian national identity. *In* Brazil, anthropological perspectives, ed. by M. L. Margolis and W. E. Carter p 1-18

**Wagner, Linda Welshimer**

American modern

Contents

Barren ground's vein of iron: Dorinda Oakley and some concepts of heroine in 1925
Berryman: from the beginning
Call me Maximus
Creeley's late poems: contexts
Damn it, Bill: they still haven't listened!
Deliverance: initiation and possibility
Faulkner and (Southern) women
Helen in Egypt: a culmination
Horace Gregory: voice in action
The latest Creeley
Levertov and Rich: the later poems
Modern American literature: the poetics of the individual voice
Nails: Gary Gildner's house of poetry
Note on Oedipa the roadrunner
Oates: the changing shapes of her realities
On David Ignatow
Personism: some notes on the she and he of it
Plath's "Ariel": "auspicious gales"
The poetry in American fiction
Sherwood, Stein, the sentence, and grape sugar and oranges
The sound of direction
"Speaking straight ahead . . ."
Spindrift: the world in a seashell
Tension and technique: the years of greatness
Wakoski and Rukeyser
William Stafford's plain-style

Ellen Glasgow: daughter as justified. *In* The Lost tradition: mothers and daughters in literature, ed. by C. N. Davidson and E. M. Broner p140-46

**Wagner, Richard**

About

Harbison, R. Turning against history. *In* Harbison, R. Deliberate regression p147-79

**Wagoner, David**

About

Howard, R. David Wagoner: "It dawns on us that we must come apart." *In* Howard, R. Alone with America p619-38

**Wake, Clive**

Poetry of the last five years. *In* African literature today no. 10: Retrospect & prospect, ed. by E. D. Jones p233-42

**Wakoski, Diane**

About

Wagner, L. W. Wakoski and Rukeyser. *In* Wagner, L. W. American modern p235-37

**Walcott, Derek**

About

Morris, M. Derek Walcott. *In* West Indian literature. ed. by B. King p144-60

**Wald, Lillian**

About

Cook, B. W. Female support networks and political activism: Lillian Wald, Crystal Eastman, Emma Goldman. *In* A Heritage of her own, ed. by N. F. Cott and E. H. Pleck p411-44

**Waldman, Milton**

About individual works

*The disinherited*

Trilling, L. Another Jewish problem novel. *In* Trilling, L. Speaking of literature and society p16-20

**Wales**

Description

Plomer, W. C. F. Kilvert's country. *In* Plomer, W. C. Electric delights p215-19

History—To 1536

Carr, A. D. The historical background, 1282-1550. *In* A Guide to Welsh literature, ed. by A. O. H. Jarman and G. R. Hughes v2 p11-33

**Walker, Francis Amasa**

About individual works

*Land and its rent*

Cord, S. B. Walker: the general leads the charge. *In* Critics of Henry George, ed. by R. V. Andelson p178-86

**Walker, Janet Anderson**

The Japanese novel of the Meiji period and the ideal of individualism

Contents

The education of a Meiji individual
Futabatei's 'Ukigumo' (The floating clouds): the first novel of the individual
Hakai (Breaking the commandment): a novel of the inner life
Katai's Futon (The quilt): the birth of the I-novel
Kitamura Tōkoku and the ideal of the inner life: the interiorization of the ideal of individualism
Shimazaki Tōson's ideal of the individual
Shinsei (The new life): a novel of confession

**Walker, Peter Edward**

Charity begins at home. *In* Lying truths, ed. by R. Duncan and M. Weston-Smith p219-29

**Wall painting.** See Mural painting and decoration, Medieval

**Wallace, John M.**

John Dryden's play and the conception of a heroic society. *In* Culture and politics from Puritanism to the Enlightenment, ed. by P. Zagorin p113-34

**Wallant, Edward Lewis**

About individual works

*The pawnbroker*

Miller, G. Those who walk in darkness. *In* Miller, G. Screening the novel p167-89

**Walpole, Horace, 4th Earl of Orford**

About

Quaintance, R. E. Walpole's Whig interpretation of landscaping history. *In* Studies in eighteenth-century culture v9 p285-300

**Walser, Martin**

On Kafka's novels. *In* The World of Franz Kafka, ed. by J. P. Stern p87-101

**Walser, Robert**

**About**

Unseld, S. Robert Walser and his publishers. *In* Unseld, S. The author and his publisher p191-273

**Walsh, Jill Paton**

**About**

Rees, D. Types of ambiguity: Jill Paton Walsh. *In* Rees, D. The marble in the water p141-54

Townsend, J. R. Jill Paton Walsh. *In* Townsend, J. R. A sounding of storytellers p153-65

**Walsh, Lorena S.**

"Till death us do part": marriage and family in seventeenth-century Maryland. *In* The Chesapeake in the seventeenth century, ed. by T. W. Tate and D. L. Ammerman p126-52

*See also* Carr, L. G. jt. auth.

**Walsh, Richard**

The revolutionary Charleston mechanic. *In* Small business in American life, ed. by S. W. Bruchey p49-79

**Walsh, William**

Small observations on a large subject. *In* Aspects of Indian writing in English, ed. by M. K. Naik p101-19

**Walther van der Vogelweide**

Hatto, A. T. Neidhart von Reuental. *In* Hatto, A. T. Essays on medieval German and other poetry p3-11

**About individual works**

*Madam, accept this garland*

Hatto, A. T. A note on Walther's song 'Madam, accept this garland' (A May dance for the court) *In* Hatto, A. T. Essays on medieval German and other poetry p12-16

**Walton, Gary M.**

The colonial economy. *In* Encyclopedia of American economic history, ed. by G. Porter v 1 p34-50

**Walton, Kendall L.**

Style and the products and processes of art. *In* The Concept of style, ed. by B. Lang p45-66

**Walvin, James**

The rise of British popular sentiment for abolition, 1787-1832. *In* Anti-slavery, religion, and reform: essays in memory of Roger Anstey, ed. by C. Bolt and S. Drescher p149-62

**Walzer, Michael**

Political decision-making and political education. *In* Political theory and political education, ed. by M. Richter p159-76

**Wandering Jew**

Rosenthal, B. Herman Melville's Wandering Jews. *In* Puritan influences in American literature, ed. by E. Elliott p167-92

**Wanyambungi (African people)** See Bashi (African people)

**Wapnewski, Peter**

Dietmar von Eist XII: 'Nu ist ez an ein Ende komen'. *In* The Interpretation of medieval lyric poetry, ed. by W. T. H. Jackson p163-75

**War**

Kende, I. Local wars 1945-76. *In* Problems of contemporary militarism, ed. by A. Eide and M. Thee p261-85

*See also* Peace; Strategy

**Moral aspects**

Narveson, J. Violence and war. *In* Matters of life and death, ed. by T. Regan p109-47

**Protection of civilians**

Bassiouni, M. C. International law and the Holocaust. *In* Encountering the Holocaust: an interdisciplinary survey, ed. by B. L. Sherwin and S. H. Ament p146-88

**War (International law)** See War—Protection of civilians

**War and literature.** See European War, 1914-1918—Literature and the war

**War and society.** See Sociology, Military

**War contracts.** See Defense contracts

**War crime trials**

**Nuremberg, 1945-1946**

*See* Nuremberg Trial of Major German War Criminals, 1945-1946

**War of 1914.** See European War, 1914-1918

**Ward, Lester Frank**

**About**

Fuhrman, E. R. Lester F. Ward. *In* Fuhrman, E. R. The sociology of knowledge in America, 1883-1913 p75-99

**Ward, Zelime Amen**

Pan-European parties: proselytes of the European Community. *In* Western European party systems, ed. by P. H. Merkl p552-75

**Wardle, Irving**

The plays. *In* The Genius of Shaw, ed. by M. Holroyd p143-65

**Wardropper, Bruce W.**

Meaning in medieval Spanish folk song. *In* The Interpretation of medieval lyric poetry, ed. by W. T. H. Jackson p176-93

**Warminski, Andrzej**

Rilke's "Das Bett." *In* Rilke: the alchemy of alienation, ed. by F. Baron, E. S. Dick and W. R. Maurer p151-70

**Warner, Deborah Jean**

Astronomy in antebellum America. *In* The Sciences in the American context: new perspectives, ed. by N. Reingold p55-75

**Warren, Robert Penn**

**About**

King, R. H. The new Southern liberalism: V. O. Key, C. Vann Woodward, Robert Penn Warren. *In* King, R. H. A Southern Renaissance p242-86

Wyatt, D. Robert Penn Warren: the critic as artist. *In* Wyatt, D. Prodigal sons p113-28

**About individual works**

*All the king's men*

King, R. H. From theme to setting: Thomas Wolfe, James Agee, Robert Penn Warren. *In* King, R. H. A Southern Renaissance p194-241

*Audubon, a vision*

Vendler, H. H. Robert Penn Warren. *In* Vendler, H. H. Part of nature, part of us p87-90

**Warren, Roger**

'Smiling at grief': some techniques of comedy in 'Twelfth night' and 'Cosi fan tutte.' *In* Shakespeare survey 32 p79-84

A year of comedies: Stratford 1978. *In* Shakespeare survey 32 p201-09

**The warriors (Motion picture)**

Kael, P. Rumbling. *In* Kael, P. When the lights go down p554-59

**Wars.** See War

Washington, Booker Taliaferro

### About individual works
*The Booker T. Washington papers*

Pole, J. R. Of Mr. Booker T. Washington and others. *In* Pole, J. R. Paths to the American past p170-88

*Up from slavery*

Stepto, R. B. Lost in a cause: Booker T. Washington's Up from slavery. *In* Stepto, R. B. From behind the veil p32-51

Wasserman, Louis

The essential Henry George. *In* Critics of Henry George, ed. by R. V. Andelson p29-43

Washington, Ida H. and Tobol, Carol E. Washington

Kriemhild and Clytemnestra—sisters in crime or independent women? *In* The Lost tradition: mothers and daughters in literature, ed. by C. N. Davidson and E. M. Broner p15-21

Wasserstrom, William

"Van Wyck Brooks." *In* Van Wyck Brooks: the critic and his critics, ed. by W. Wasserstrom p211-37

Watanabe, Shigeo

One of the dozens. *In* The Arbuthnot lectures, 1970-1979 p141-63

### About

Watanabe, S. One of the dozens. *In* The Arbuthnot lectures, 1970-1979 p141-63

Water

Morowitz, H. J. Yellow is mellow. *In* Morowitz, H. J. The wine of life, and other essays on societies, energy & living things p179-82

Water drama. Forbes, D. *In* Performance and politics in popular drama, ed. by D. Bradby, L. James and B. Sharratt p91-107

Watson, William

The city in ancient China. *In* The Origins of civilization, ed. by P. R. S. Moorey p54-77

Watteau, Antoine. See Watteau, Jean Antoine

Watteau, Jean Antoine

### About

Hagstrum, J. H. Love in painting and music: an appended survey. *In* Hagstrum, J. H. Sex and sensibility p278-331

Watts, Emily Stipes

The posy UNITY: Anne Bradstreet's search for order. *In* Puritan influences in American literature, ed. by E. Elliott p23-37

Waugh, Evelyn

### About

Pritchett, V. S. Evelyn Waugh: club and country. *In* Pritchett, V. S. The tale bearers p92-103

Wayne, John

### About

Kauffmann, S. American to the world. *In* Kauffmann, S. Before my eyes p403-05

Weale, Albert

Rational choice and political principles. *In* Rational action, ed. by R. Harrison p93-114

Weales, Gerald Clifford

Drama. *In* Harvard Guide to contemporary American writing, ed. by D. Hoffman p396-438

Wealth

Soltow, L. Distribution of income and wealth. *In* Encyclopedia of American economic history, ed. by G. Porter v3 p1087-1119

*See also* Poverty; Saving and investment

Wealth, Distribution of. See Wealth

Weapon systems. See Weapons systems

Weapons systems

Kaldor, M. H. The significance of military technology. *In* Problems of contemporary militarism, ed. by A. Eide and M. Thee p226-29

Wearmouth monastery

Meyvaert, P. Bede and the church paintings at Wearmouth—Jarrow. *In* Anglo-Saxon England 8 p63-77

Weart, Spencer P.

The physics business in America, 1919-1940: a statistical reconnaissance. *In* The Sciences in the American context: new perspectives, ed. by N. Reingold p295-358

Weather in literature

Holloway, J. How goes the weather? *In* Yeats, Sligo and Ireland, ed. by A. N. Jeffares p89-97

Weaver, Warren

### About

Kohler, R. E. Warren Weaver and the Rockefeller Foundation program in molecular biology: a case study in the management of science. *In* The Sciences in the American context: new perspectives, ed. by N. Reingold p249-93

Weavers. See Silk manufacture and trade

Webb, Beatrice (Potter)

### About

Skidelsky, R. J. A. The Fabian ethic. *In* The Genius of Shaw, ed. by M. Holroyd p113-28

Webb, Sidney. See Passfield, Sidney James Webb, Baron

Weber, Marianne (Schnitger)

### About individual works
*Ehefrau und Mutter in der Rechtsentwickelung*

Durkheim, E. Review of Marianne Weber, Ehefrau und Mutter in der Rechtsentwickelung. *In* Durkheim, E. Emile Durkheim on institutional analysis p139-44

Weber, Max

Judaism: the psychology of the Prophets; excerpt from "Ancient Judaism." *In* Propaganda and communication in world history, ed. by H. D. Lasswell, D. Lerner and H. Speier v 1 p299-329

Webster, John

### About individual works
*The Duchess of Malfi*

Whiteside, G. John Webster: a Freudian interpretation of his two great tragedies. *In* The Analysis of literary texts, ed. by R. D. Pope p201-11

*The white devil*

Whiteside, G. John Webster: a Freudian interpretation of his two great tragedies. *In* The Analysis of literary texts, ed. by R. D. Pope p201-11

A wedding (Motion picture)

Kael, P. Forty-eight characters in search of a director. *In* Kael, P. When the lights go down p440-47

Kauffmann, S. A wedding. *In* Kauffmann, S. Before my eyes p43-46

Wedding in blood (Motion picture)

Kauffmann, S. Wedding in blood. *In* Kauffmann, S. Before my eyes p8-10

Weekes, Mark Kinkead- See Kinkead-Weekes, Mark

**Weidenbaum, Murray L.**
Government power and business perform-
ance. *In* The United States in the 1980s, ed. by
P. Duignan and A. Rabushka p197-220

**Weinberg, David H.**
The Holocaust in historical perspective. *In*
Encountering the Holocaust: an interdisciplin-
ary survey, ed. by B. L. Sherwin and S. G.
Ament p52-83

**Weinberg, David H. and Sherwin, Byron L.**
The Holocaust: an historical overview. *In*
Encountering the Holocaust: an interdisciplin-
ary survey, ed. by B. L. Sherwin and S. G.
Ament p12-22

**Weiner, Sanford Louis, and Wildavsky,
Aaron B.**
The prophylactic Presidency. *In* The Third
century, ed. by S. M. Lipset p133-52

**Weinstein, Michael M.** See Smolensky, E. jt.
auth.

**Weintraub, Stanley**
In the picture galleries. *In* The Genius of
Shaw, ed. by M. Holroyd p44-63

**Weir, Robert M.**
The role of the newspaper press in the
Southern colonies on the eve of the Revolu-
tion: an interpretation. *In* The Press & the
American Revolution, ed. by B. Bailyn and
J. B. Hench p99-150

**Weiser, Frederick Sheeley**
Baptismal certificate and gravemarker:
Pennsylvania German folk art at the begin-
ning and the end of life. *In* Perspectives on
American folk art, ed. by I. M. G. Quimby
and S. T. Swank p134-61

**Weiss, Peter**

### About individual works
*The investigation*
Bosmajian, H. Rituals of judgment: Hochhuth's The Deputy and Weiss's The investigation. *In* Bosmajian, H. Metaphors of evil p147-
82

**Weiss, Theodore Russell**

### About
Howard, R. Theodore Weiss: "No shore
beyond our own." *In* Howard, R. Alone with
America p639-61

**Weiss, Thomas Joseph**
Service sector. *In* Encyclopedia of American
economic history, ed. by G. Porter v 1
p413-23

**Weitzmann, Kurt**
Introduction. *In* Age of spirituality, ed. by
K. Weitzmann p 1-5

### About individual works
*The fresco cycle of S. Maria di
Castelseprio*
Schapiro, M. The frescoes of Castelseprio.
*In* Schapiro, M. Selected papers v3: Late an-
tique, early Christian and mediaeval art p67-
114

**Weixlmann, Joe, and Gann, Daniel H.**
A Walker Percy bibliography. *In* Walker
Percy: art and ethics, ed. by J. Tharpe p137-57

**Weizenbaum, Joseph**
Once more: the computer revolution. *In* The
Computer age: a twenty-year view, ed. by
M. L. Dertouzos and J. Moses p439-58

**Welch, Colin**
Broken eggs, but no omelette: Russia be-
fore the Revolution. *In* Lying truths, ed. by
R. Duncan and M. Weston-Smith p47-60

**Welch, Robert**
Irish poetry from Moore to Yeats
*Contents*
Aubrey de Vere: an attempt at a Catholic
humanity
J. J. Callanan: a provincial romantic
James Clarence Mangan: 'apples from the
Dead sea shore'
Sir Samuel Ferguson: the two races of Ireland
Thomas Moore: an elegiac silence
William Allingham: 'the power and zest of
all appearance'
Yeats and Oisin

**Welcome to L.A. (Motion picture)**
Kael, P. Oh, anomie, I love you. *In* Kael,
P. When the lights go down p283-87
Kauffmann, S. Welcome to L.A. *In* Kauff-
mann, S. Before my eyes p286-89

**Welfare.** See Public welfare

**Welfare state**
Von Otter, C. Swedish welfare capitalism:
the role of the state. *In* The State in Western
Europe, ed. by R. Scase p142-63

**Welfare work.** See Public welfare

**Wellek, René**
"Van Wyck Brooks and a national literature." *In* Van Wyck Brooks: the critic and his
critics, ed. by H. Wasserstrom p106-15

**Welles, Orson**

### About individual works
*F is for fake*
Kauffmann, S. F is for fake. *In* Kauff-
mann, S. Before my eyes p282-84

**Wells, Herbert George**

### About
Butler, C. Mr Britling sees it through: a
view from the other side. *In* The First World
War in German narrative prose, ed. by C. N.
Genno and H. Wetzel p118-37

### About individual works
*Mr Britling sees it through*
Butler, C. Mr Britling sees it through: a
view from the other side. *In* The First World
War in German narrative prose, ed. by C. N.
Genno and H. Wetzel p118-37

**Wells, Robert V.**
Quaker marriage patterns in a colonial per-
spective. *In* A Heritage of her own, ed. by
N. F. Cott and E. H. Pleck p81-106

**Wells, Stanley W.**
Juliet's nurse: the uses of inconsequentiality.
*In* Shakespeare's styles, ed. by P. Edwards,
I. S. Ewbank and G. K. Hunter p51-66

**Welsch, Roger L.**
Beating a live horse: yet another note on
definitions and defining. *In* Perspectives of
American folk art, ed. by I. M. G. Quimby
and S. T. Swank p218-33

**Welsh language**

### Analysis and parsing
*See* Welsh language—Grammar

### Grammar
Lewis, C. W. Einion Offeiriad and the
bardic grammar. *In* A Guide to Welsh literature, ed. by A. O. H. Jarman and G. R.
Hughes v2 p58-86

### Metrics and rhytmics
*See* Welsh language—Versification

**Welsh language**—*Continued*

### Prosody

*See* Welsh language—Versification

### Versification

Lewis, C. W. Einion Offeiriad and the bardic grammar. *In* A Guide to Welsh literature, ed. by A. O. H. Jarman and G. R. Hughes v2 p58-86

Rowlands, E. I. Cynghanedd, metre, prosody. *In* A Guide to Welsh literature, ed. by A. O. H. Jarman and G. R. Hughes v2 p202-17

**Welsh national characteristics.** See National characteristics, Welsh

## Welsh poetry

### To 1550—History and criticism

Bromwich, R. The earlier cywyddwyr: poets contemporary with Dafydd ap Gwilym. *In* A Guide to Welsh literature, ed. by A. O. H. Jarman and G. R. Hughes v2 p144-67

Evans, R. W. Prophetic poetry. *In* A Guide to Welsh literature, ed. by A. O. H. Jarman and G. R. Hughes v2 p278-96

Jarman, A. O. H. The later Cynfeirdd. *In* A Guide to Welsh literature, ed. by A. O. H. Jarman and G. R. Hughes v 1 p98-122

Lewis, C. W. The content of poetry and the crisis in the bardic tradition. *In* A Guide to Welsh literature, ed. by A. O. H. Jarman and G. R. Hughes v2 p88-110

Lewis, C. W. Einion Offeiriad and the bardic grammar. *In* A Guide to Welsh literature, ed. by A. O. H. Jarman and G. R. Hughes v2 p58-86

Lewis, C. W. The historical background of early Welsh verse. *In* A Guide to Welsh literature, ed. by A. O. H. Jarman and G. R. Hughes vi p248-76

Loyd, D. M. The poets of the princes. *In* A Guide to Welsh literature, ed. by A. O. H. Jarman and G. R. Hughes v 1 p157-88

Rowlands, E. I. The continuing tradition. *In* A Guide to Welsh literature, ed. by A. O. H. Jarman and G. R. Hughes v2 p298-320

## Welsh prose literature

### History and criticism

Owen, M. E. Functional prose: religion, science, grammar, law. *In* A Guide to Welsh literature, ed. by A. O. H. Jarman and G. R. Hughes v 1 p248-76

Owen, M. E. The prose of the cywydd period. *In* A Guide to Welsh literature, ed. by A. O. H. Jarman and G. R. Hughes v2 p338-73

**Welsh romances.** See Romances, Welsh

**Welsh tales.** See Tales, Welsh

**Weltsch, Felix**

The rise and fall of the Jewish-German symbiosis: the case of Franz Kafka. *In* The World of Franz Kafka, ed. by J. P. Stern p47-55

**Wender, Wim**

### About individual works

*The goalie's anxiety at the penalty kick*

Kauffmann, S. The goalie's anxiety at the penalty kick. *In* Kauffmann, S. Before my eyes p276-79

**Wentersdorf, Karl P.**

The marriage contracts in 'Measure for measure': a reconsideration. *In* Shakespeare survey 32 p129-44

**Werblowsky, Raphael Jehudah Zwi**

Jewish mysticism. *In* The Jewish world, ed. by E. Kedourie p217-23

O felix culpa: a cabbalistic version. *In* Studies in Jewish religious and intellectual history, ed. by S. Stein and R. Loewe p355-62

**Wergeland, Agnes Mathilde**

### About

Semmingsen, I. A pioneer: Agnes Mathilde Wergeland, 1857-1914. *In* Makers of an American immigrant legacy, ed. by O. S. Lovoll p111-30

**Wertmuller, Lina**

### About individual works

*The end of the world in our usual bed in a night full of rain*

Kauffmann, S. Night full of rain. *In* Kauffmann, S. Before my eyes p29-31

*The seduction of Mimi*

Kauffmann, S. The seduction of Mimi. *In* Kauffmann, S. Before my eyes p19-20

*Seven beauties*

Kael, P. Seven fatties. *In* Kael, P. When the lights go down p135-40

Kauffmann, S. Seven beauties. *In* Kauffmann, S. Before my eyes p23-28

*Swept away by an unusual destiny in the blue sea of August*

Kauffmann, S. Swept away. *In* Kauffmann, S. Before my eyes p20-23

**Wescott, Glenway**

"Van Wyck Brooks." *In* Van Wyck Brooks: the critic and his critics, ed. by W. Wasserstrom p202-05

**West, David Alexander**

Two plagues: Virgil, Georgics 3.478-566 and Lucretius 6.1090-1286. *In* Creative imitation and Latin literature, ed. by D. West and T. Woodman p71-88

**West, Francis James**

Conventional forces beyond NATO. *In* National security in the 1980s: from weakness to strength, ed. by W. S. Thompson p319-36

**West, Martin Litchfield**

Homeric and Hesiodic poetry. *In* Ancient Greek literature, ed. by K. J. Dover p10-28

Other early poetry. *In* Ancient Greek literature, ed. by K. J. Dover p29-49

**West, Rebecca, pseud.**

### About individual works

*The meaning of treason*

Trilling, L. Treason in the modern world. *In* Trilling, L. Speaking of literature and society p230-35

**West, Victoria Mary Sackville-** See Sackville-West, Hon. Victoria Mary

## The West

### History

Ridge, M. Westward movement. *In* Encyclopedia of American economic history, ed. by G. Porter v2 p575-87

**West Germany.** See Germany, West

## The West in literature

Gridley, R. E. Some versions of the primitive and the pastoral on the Great Plains of America. *In* Survivals of pastoral, ed. by R. F. Hardin p61-85

**West Indian literature (English)**

### History and criticism

Baugh, E. Since 1960: some highlights. *In* West Indian literature, ed. by B. King p78-94

Boxill, A. The beginnings to 1929. *In* West Indian literature, ed. by B. King p30-44

Cobham, R. The background. *In* West Indian literature, ed by B. King p9-29

King, B. Introduction. *In* West Indian literature, ed. by B. King p 1-8

Metcalf, R. West Indian literature. *In* African literature today no. 10: Retrospect & prospect, ed. by E. D. Jones p253-55

Paquet, S. P. The fifties. *In* West Indian literature, ed. by B. King p63-77

Sander, R. W. The thirties and forties. *In* West Indian literature, ed. by B. King p45-62

**Western Germany.** See Germany, West

**Western Schism.** See Schism, The Great Western, 1378-1417

**Westfall, Richard S.**

Isaac Newton in Cambridge: the Restoration university and scientific creativity. *In* Culture and politics from Puritanism to the Enlightenment, ed. by P. Zagorin p135-64

**Weston-Smith, Miranda**

Mass media assist communication. *In* Lying truths, ed. by R. Duncan and M. Weston-Smith p31-33

**Wetzel, Heinz**

War and the destruction of moral principles in Arnold Zweig's Der Streit um den Sergeanten Grischa and Erziehung vor Verdun. *In* The First World War in German narrative prose, ed. by C. N. Genno and H. Wetzel p50-70

**Whalen, Richard James**

International business. *In* The United States in the 1980s, ed. by P. Duignan and A. Rabushka p639-60

**Whales**

Morowitz, H. J. Loch Ness to Lahaina. *In* Morowitz, H. J. The wine of life, and other essays on societies, energy & living things p77-80

**Whaley, Barton**

Deception—its decline and revival in international conflict. *In* Propaganda and communication in world history, ed. by H. D. Lasswell, D. Lerner and H. Speier v2 p339-67

**Whannel, Garry.** See Curran, J. jt. auth.

**Wheeler, Richard P.**

"Since first we were dissevered": trust and autonomy in Shakespearean tragedy and romance. *In* Representing, Shakespeare, ed. by M. M. Schwartz and C. Kahn p150-69

**Whitcut, Janet**

The language of address. *In* The State of the language, ed. by L. Michaels and C. Ricks p89-97

**White, Edmund**

The political vocabulary of homosexuality. *In* The State of the language, ed. by L. Michaels and C. Ricks p235-46

**White, Elwyn Brooks**

### About individual works

*Charlotte's web*

Griffith, J. Charlotte's web: a lonely fantasy of love. *In* Children's literature v8 p111-17

Rees, D. Timor mortis conturbat me: E. B. White and Doris Buchanan Smith. *In* Rees, D. The marble in the water p68-77

**White, Gilbert**

### About individual works

*The natural history of Selborne*

Trowbridge, F. H. White of Selbourne: the ethos of probabilism. *In* Probability, time, and space in eighteenth-century literature, ed. by P. R. Backscheider p79-109

**White, Hayden V.**

Michel Foucault. *In* Structuralism and since, ed. by J. Sturrock p81-115

The problem of style in realistic representation: Marx and Flaubert. *In* The Concept of style, ed. by B. Lang p213-29

**White, Ian**

Condorcet: politics and reason. *In* Royal Institute of Philosophy. Philosophers of the Enlightenment p110-39

**White, Nicholas Perry**

The basis of Stoic ethics. *In* Harvard Studies in classical philology, v83 p143-78

**White, Sheldon Harold**

Developmental psychology and Vico's concept of universal history. *In* Conference on Vico and Contemporary Thought. New York, 1976. Vico and contemporary thought pt2 p 1-13

**White, Terence de Vere**

An Irishman abroad. *In* The Genius of Shaw, ed. by M. Holroyd p31-41

**Whiteside, George**

John Webster: a Freudian interpretation of his two great tragedies. *In* The Analysis of literary texts, ed. by R. D. Pope p201-11

**Whitfield, Stephen J.**

Jews and other Southerners: counterpoint and paradox. *In* Conference on Southern Jewish History, Richmond, Va. 1976. "Turn to the South" p76-104

**Whitley, Raymond K.**

The libertine hero and heroine in the novels of John Cleland. *In* Studies in eighteenth-century culture v9 p387-404

**Whitman, Walt**

### About

Allen, G. W. How Emerson, Thoreau, and Whitman viewed the "frontier." *In* Toward a new American literary history, ed. by L. J. Budd, E. H. Cady and C. L. Anderson p111-28

Bickman, M. Words out of the sea: Walt Whitman. *In* Bickman, M. The unsounded centre p95-116

Irwin, J. T. Whitman: hieroglyphic Bibles and phallic songs. *In* Irwin, J. T. American hieroglyphics p20-40

Kaplan, J. The naked self and other problems. *In* Telling lives, ed. by M. Pachter p36-55

### About individual works

*Bivouac on a mountain side*

Withim, P. M. Mythic awareness and literary form: verbal ritual in Whitman's "Bivouac on a mountain side." *In* The Binding of Proteus, ed. by M. W. McCune, T. Orbison and P. M. Withim p111-22

*Democratic vistas*

Trilling, L. Sermon on a text from Whitman. *In* Trilling, L. Speaking of literature and society p207-16

*Passage to India*

Bickman, M. Voyages of the mind's return: three paradigmatic works. *In* Bickman, M. The unsounded centre p22-37

Whitman Walt—About individual works—*Cont.*

*Walt Whitman, poet of American democracy; selections from his poetry and prose (ed. with an introduction by Samuel Sillen)*

Trilling, L. Sermon on a text from Whitman. *In* Trilling, L. Speaking of literature and society p207-16

### Bibliography

Buckingham, W. J. Whitman and Dickinson. *In* American literary scholarship, 1978 p59-78

### Biography

Kaplan, J. The naked self and other problems. *In* Telling lives, ed. by M. Pachter p36-55

## Whitmore, William Henry

### About

Cushing, W. D. American bibliographical notes. *In* American Antiquarian Society. Proceedings v89 pt2 p371-74

## Who is killing the great chefs of Europe (Motion picture)

Kael, P. Enfant terrible. *In* Kael, P. When the lights go down p482-88

## Whole and parts (Philosophy) See Structuralism

## Who'll stop the rain (Motion picture)

Kauffmann, S. Who'll stop the rain? *In* Kauffmann, S. Before my eyes p88-91

## Whorf-Sapir thesis. See Sapir-Whorf hypothesis

## Wiarda, Howard J.

Spain and Portugal. *In* Western European party systems, ed. by P. H. Merkl p298-328

## Wickham, Glynne William Gladstone

Riddle and emblem: a study in the dramatic structure of Cymbeline. *In* English Renaissance studies, ed. by J. Carey p94-113

## Widdowson, Peter

Between the acts? English fiction in the thirties. *In* Culture and crisis in Britain in the thirties, ed. by J. Clark and others p133-64

## Wiedemann, Friederike Wiesmann- See Wiesmann-Wiedemann, Friederike

## Wiener, Max

Secularized religion. *In* The Jew, ed. by A. A. Cohen p215-22

## Wiesel, Elie

### About

Alexander, E. The incredibility of the Holocaust. *In* Alexander, E. The resonance of dust p3-28

### About individual works

*Night*

Bosmajian, H. The rage for order: autobiographical accounts of the self in the nightmare of history. *In* Bosmajian, H. Metaphors of evil p27-54

## Wiesmann-Wiedemann, Friederike

From victim to villain: King Mark. *In* The Expansion and transformations of courtly literature, ed. by N. B. Smith and J. T. Snow p49-68

## Wiesner, Jerome Bert

The marriage of science and government. *In* Propaganda and communication in world history, ed. by H. D. Lasswell, D. Lerner and H. Speier v3 p16-36

## Wiggins, David

Ayer on monism, pluralism and essence. *In* Perception and identity, ed. by G. F. Macdonald p131-60

## Wiggins, James Russell

Afterword: the legacy of the press in the American Revolution. *In* The Press & the American Revolution, ed. by B. Bailyn and J. B. Hench p365-72

## Wildavsky, Aaron B. See Weiner, S. L. jt. auth.

## Wilde, Alan

The naturalisation of Eden. *In* E. M. Forster: a human exploration, ed. by G. K. Das and J. Beer p196-207

## Wilde, Oscar

### About

Henkle, R. B. Wilde and Beerbohm: the wit of the avant-garde, the charm of failure. *In* Henkle, R. B. Comedy and culture p296-352

McGhee, R. D. Elizabeth Barrett Browning and Oscar Wilde. *In* McGhee, R. D. Marriage, duty & desire in Victorian poetry and drama p233-97

## Wilder, Hugh T.

The language of sex and the sex of language. *In* The Philosophy of sex, ed. by A. Soble p99-109

## Wilkes, Gerald Alfred

'Full of doubt I stand': the final implications of Paradise lost. *In* English Renaissance studies, ed. by J. Carey p271-78

## Wilkins, Frederick

The pressure of Puritanism in Eugene O'Neill's New England plays. *In* Eugene O'Neill, ed. by V. Floyd p237-44

## Will

Bloom, H. Freud's concepts of defense and the poetic will. *In* The Literary Freud: mechanisms of defense and the poetic will, ed. by J. H. Smith p 1-28

*See also* Free will and determinism

## Willbern, David Pierce

A bibliography of psychoanalytic and psychological writings on Shakespeare: 1964-1978. *In* Representing Shakespeare, ed. by M. M. Schwartz and C. Kahn p264-86

Shakespeare's nothing. *In* Representing Shakespeare, ed. by M. M. Schwartz and C. Kahn, p244-63

## William of Ockham. See Ockham, William

## Williams, Bernard Arthur Owen

Another time, another place, another person. *In* Perception and identity, ed. by G. F. Macdonald p252-61

Internal and external reasons. *In* Rational action, ed. by R. Harrison p17-28

Political philosophy and the analytical tradition. *In* Political theory and political education, ed. by M. Richter p57-75

### About individual works

*Problems of the self*

Harrison, R. Ethical consistency. *In* Rational action, ed. by R. Harrison p29-45

## Williams, C. E.

George Saiko: worlds within world. *In* Modern Austrian writing, ed. by A. Best and H. Wolfschütz p97-107

## Williams, George Walton

Textual studies. *In* Shakespeare survey 32 p237-47

**Williams, John Ellis Caerwyn**
Guto'r Glyn. *In* A Guide to Welsh literature, ed. by A. O. H. Jarman and G. R. Hughes v2 p218-41
Gutun Owain. *In* A Guide to Welsh literature, ed. by A. O. H. Jarman and G. R. Hughes v2 p262-77

**Williams, Polly Franklin**
Reflection on computers as daughters of memory. *In* Monster or messiah? Ed. by W. M. Mathews p 165-74

**Williams, Raymond**

**About individual works**
*Keywords: a vocabulary of culture and society*
Skinner, Q. Language and social change. *In* The State of the language, ed. by L. Michaels and C. Ricks p562-78

**Williams, Robin Murphy**
Goffman's sociology of talk. *In* The View from Goffman, ed. by J. Ditton p210-32

**Williams, Roger, 1604?-1683**

**Religion and ethics**
Hunsaker, O. G. Roger Williams and John Milton: the calling of the Puritan writer. *In* Puritan influences in American literature, ed. by E. Elliott p3-22

**Williams, Tennessee**

**About individual works**
*Letters to Donald Windham: 1940-65*
Brustein, R. S. Tennessee Williams (Letters to Donald Windham: 1940-1965) *In* Brustein, R. S. Critical moments p30-34

**Williams, William Carlos**

**About**
Dotterer, R. L. The fictive and the real: myth and form in the poetry of Wallace Stevens and William Carlos Williams. *In* The Binding of Proteus, ed. by M. W. McCune, T. Orbison and P. M. Withim p221-48
Wagner, L. W. "Speaking straight ahead . . ." *In* Wagner, L. W. American modern p115-24

**About individual works**
*Imaginations*
Wagner, L. W. Damn it, Bill: they still haven't listened! *In* Wagner, L. W. American modern p244-52

*Paterson*
Heinzelman, K. "Getting it" in Paterson: the increment defended. *In* Heinzelman, K. The economics of the imagination p234-75

**Williamson, Harold Francis**
Insurance. *In* Encyclopedia of American economic history, ed. by G. Porter v2 p727-36

**Williamson, Oliver E.**
Emergence of The visible hand: implications for industrial organization. *In* Managerial hierarchies, ed. by A. D. Chandler and H. Daems p182-202

**Wills**

**Great Britain**—History
Owen, G. R. Wynflæd's wardrobe. *In* Anglo-Saxon England 8 p195-222

**Wilmers, Mary-Kay**
The language of novel reviewing. *In* The State of the language, ed. by L. Michaels and C. Ricks p313-23

**Wilson, Angus**

**About individual works**
*Anglo-Saxon attitudes, a novel*
Pritchett, V. S. Angus Wilson: going downhill. *In* Pritchett, V. S. The tale bearers p104-14

*No laughing matter*
Pritchett, V. S. Angus Wilson: going downhill. *In* Pritchett, V. S. The tale bearers p104-14

*The strange ride of Rudyard Kipling*
Pritchett, V. S. Rudyard Kipling: a Pre-Raphaelite's son. *In* Pritchett, V. S. The tale bearers p31-42

**Wilson, Carlo Guillermo**

**About**
Jackson, R. L. Ebe yiye—"the future will be better": an update on Panama from black Cubena. *In* Jackson, R. L. Black writers in Latin America p180-90

**Wilson, Colin**
Man is born free, and he is everywhere in chains. *In* Lying truths, ed. by R. Duncan and M. Weston-Smith p3-7
A personal view. *In* The Genius of Shaw, ed. by M. Holroyd p223-[29]
The right to work. *In* Lying truths, ed. by R. Duncan and M. Weston-Smith p8-9

**Wilson, Edmund**

**About individual works**
*To the Finland station*
Pritchett, V. S. Edmund Wilson: towards revolution. *In* Pritchett, V. S. The tale bearers p138-45

**Wilson, Edward Thomas**
Russia's historic stake in black Africa. *In* Communism in Africa, ed. by D. E. Albright p67-92

**Wilson, Frank Lee**
Sources of party transformation: the case of France. *In* Western European party systems, ed. by P. H. Merkl p526-51

**Wilson, Henry**

**About**
Harbison, R. Art as religion. *In* Harbison, R. Deliberate regression p94-114

**Wilson, John Albert**
Egyptian civilization. *In* Propaganda and communication in world history, ed. by H. D. Lasswell, D. Lerner and H. Speier v 1 p145-74

**Wilson, Robert Neal**
The writer as social seer
*Contents*
Albert Camus: personality as creative struggle
Arthur Miller: the salesman and society
Boris Pasternak: ideology and privacy
Ernest Hemingway: competence and character
Eugene O'Neill: the web of family
F. Scott Fitzgerald: personality and culture
James Baldwin: relationships of love and race
Literature, society, and personality
Reflections on the sociology of literature
Samuel Beckett: the social psychology of emptiness

**Wilson, Robert Rathbun**
The humanness of physics. *In* Being Human in a technological age, ed. by D. M. Borchert and D. Stewart p25-35

**Wilson, Woodrow, President U.S.**

About

Moynihan, D. P. The legacy of Woodrow Wilson. *In* Moynihan, D. P. Counting our blessings p6-22

**Wimsatt, James I.**

Chaucer, Fortune, and Machaut's "Il m'est avis." *In* Chaucerian problems and perspectives, ed. by E. Vasta and Z. P. Thundy p119-31

Realism in Troilus and Criseyde and the Roman de la Rose. *In* Essays on Troilus and Criseyde, ed. by M. Salu p43-56

**Windeatt, Barry**

The text of the Troilus. *In* Essays on Troilus and Criseyde, ed. by M. Salu p 1-22

**Windham, Donald**

About

Brustein, R. S. Tennessee Williams (Letters to Donald Windham: 1940-1965) *In* Brustein, R. S. Critical moments p30-34

**Windt, Peter Yale**

The concept of suicide. *In* Suicide: the philosophical issues, ed. by M. P. Battin and D. J. Mayo p39-47

**Wing, Donald Goddard**

The making of the Short-title catalogue, 1641-1700. *In* The Bibliographical Society of America, 1904-79 p241-51

About individual works

*Short title catalogue of books printed in England, Scotland, Ireland, Wales and British America, and of English books printed in other countries, 1640-1700*

Wing, D. G. The making of the Short-title catalogue, 1641-1700. *In* The Bibliographical Society of America, 1904-79 p241-51

**Wingate, Pauline**

Newsprint: from rags to riches—and back again? *In* Newspapers and democracy, ed. by A. Smith p63-89

**Winograd, Terry Allen**

Toward convivial computing. *In* The Computer age: a twenty-year view, ed. by M. L. Dertouzes and J. Moses p56-72

**Winship, George Parker**

Luther S. Livingston: a biographical sketch. *In* The Bibliographical Society of America, 1904-79 p9-20

**Winstanley, Gerrard**

About

Knott, J. R. Gerrard Winstanley's Land of Righteousness. *In* Knott, J. R. The sword of the spirit p85-105

**Winston, Elizabeth**

The autobiographer and her readers: from apology to affirmation. *In* Women's autobiography, ed. by E. C. Jelinek p93-111

**Winter in literature**

Hatto, A. T. Folk ritual and the Minnesang. *In* Hatto, A. T. Essays on medieval German and other poetry p42-63

**Winterthur, Del. Henry Francis DuPont Winterthur Museum.** See Henry Francis DuPont Winterthur Museum

**Wit and humor**

Dundes, A. The curious case of the widemouth frog. *In* Dundes, A. Interpreting folklore p62-68

Jennings, P. F. Humor: the modern religion? *In* Royal Society of Literature of the United Kingdom, London. Essays by divers hands: innovation in contemporary literature, new ser. v40 p117-31

*See also* Christianity and humor; Comedy; Comic, The; Satire

**Wit and humor, Ancient**

Strand, W. E. In search of an Assyrian sense of humor. *In* 5000 years of popular culture, ed. by F. E. H. Schroeder p38-51

**Witchcraft**

*See also* Trials (Witchcraft)

Africa

MacGaffey, W. African religions: types and generalizations. *In* Explorations in African systems of thought, ed. by I. C. Karp & C. S. Bird p301-28

Tanzania

Arens, W. Taxonomy versus dynamics revisited: the interpretation of misfortune in a polyethnic community. *In* Explorations in African systems of thought, ed. by I. C. Karp & C. S. Bird p165-80

**Witchcraft in literature**

Oberhelman, S. Greek and Roman witches: literary conventions or agrarian fertility priestesses? *In* 5000 years of popular culture, ed. by F. E. H. Schroeder p138-53

**Wither, George**

About

Hill, J. E. C. George Wither and John Milton. *In* English Renaissance studies, ed. by J. Carey p212-27

**Withim, Philip M.**

Mythic awareness and literary form: verbal ritual in Whitman's "Bivouac on a mountain side." *In* The Binding of Proteus, ed. by M. W. McCune, T. Orbison and P. M. Withim p111-22

**Wittig, Monique**

About individual works

*Les guérillères*

Thiébaux, M. A mythology for women: Monique Wittig's Les guérillères. *In* The Analysis of literary texts, ed. by R. D. Pope p90-99

**The wiz (Motion picture)**

Kael, P. Saint Dorothy. *In* Kael, P. When the lights go down p469-76

**Wohlfarth, Irving**

The politics of prose and the art of awakening: Walter Benjamin's version of a German romantic motif. *In* Glyph 7 p131-48

**Wohlgelernter, Maurice**

Introduction: Joseph Leon Blau: four ways of religion and philosophy. *In* History, religion, and spiritual democracy, ed. by M. Wohlgelernter and others p xxiii-lxxiv

**Wohlstetter, Albert**

Half-wars and half-policies in the Persian Gulf. *In* National security in the 1980s: from weakness to strength, ed. by W. S. Thompson p123-71

**Wojcik, Jan**

Discrimination against David's tragedy in ancient Jewish and Christian literature. *In* The David myth in Western literature, ed. by R. J. Frontain and J. Wojcik p12-35

**Wolf, Edwin**

The reconstruction of Benjamin Franklin's library: an unorthodox jigsaw puzzle. *In* The Bibliographical Society of America, 1904-79 p399-415

**Wolf, Friedrich August**

### About

Murrin, M. Epilogue: The disappearance of Homer and the end of Homeric allegory: Vico and Wolf. *In* Murrin, M. The allegorical epic p173-96

**Wolfe, Thomas**

### About

King, R. H. From theme to setting: Thomas Wolfe, James Agee, Robert Penn Warren. *In* King, R. H. A Southern Renaissance p194-241

**Wolff, Geoffrey**

Minor lives. *In* Telling lives, ed. by M. Pachter p56-72

### About individual works
#### Black sun

Wolff, G. Minor lives. *In* Telling lives, ed. by M. Pachter p56-72

#### The Duke of deception

Wolff, G. Minor lives. *In* Telling lives, ed. by M. Pachter p56-72

**Wolfram von Eschenbach**

### About individual works
#### Parzival

Hatto, A. T. Herzeloyde's dragon-dream. *In* Hatto, A. T. Essays on medieval German and other poetry p182-99

Hatto, A. T. On Wolfram's conception of the 'Graal'. *In* Hatto, A. T. Essays on medieval German and other poetry p141-50

Hatto, A. T. Some notes on Chrétien de Troyes and Wolfram von Eschenbach. *In* Hatto, A. T. Essays on medieval German and other poetry p151-64

Hatto, A. T. Wolfram von Eschenbach and the chase. *In* Hatto, A. T. Essays on medieval German and other poetry p200-17

**Wolfschütz, Hans**

Crisis and revolt. *In* Modern Austrian writing, ed. by A. Best and H. Wolfschütz p197-213

The emergence and development of the Second Republic. *In* Modern Austrian writing, ed. by A. Best and H. Wolfschütz p 1-22

Ilse Aichinger: the sceptical narrator. *In* Modern Austrian writing, ed. by A. Best and H. Wolfschütz p156-80

Thomas Bernhard: the mask of death. *In* Modern Austrian writing, ed. by A. Best and H. Wolfschütz p214-35

**Wolin, Sheldon S.**

Political theory and political commentary. *In* Political theory and political education, ed. by M. Richter p190-203

**Wollheim, Richard**

Memory, experimental memory, and personal identity. *In* Perception and identity, ed. by G. F. Macdonald p186-234

On persons and their lives. *In* Explaining emotions, ed. by A. O. Rorty p299-321

Pictorial style: two views. *In* The Concept of style, ed. by B. Lang p129-45

Wish-fulfilment. *In* Rational action, ed. by R. Harrison p47-60

**Wollock, Jeffrey**

William Thornton and the practical applications of new writing systems. *In* Psychology of language and thought, ed. by R. W. Rieber p121-51

**Wollstonecraft, Mary.** See Godwin, Mary (Wollstonecraft)

**Wolpin, Miles D.**

Arms transfer and dependency in the Third World. *In* Problems of contemporary militarism, ed. by A. Eide and M. Thee p248-60

**A woman under the influence (Motion picture)**

Kauffmann, S. A woman under the influence/Murder on the Orient express. *In* Kauffmann, S. Before my eyes p94-97

**Women**

Allen, C. G. Nietzsche's ambivalence about women. *In* The Sexism of social and political theory: women and reproduction from Plato to Nietzsche, ed. by L. M. Clark and L. Lange p117-33

*See also* Feminism

### Education

*See* Education of women

### Employment—United States

Johnson, S. K. The future of women in America's third century. *In* The Third century, ed. by S. M. Lipset p285-301

Kessler-Harris, A. "Where are the organized women workers?" *In* A Heritage of her own, ed. by N. F. Cott and E. H. Pleck p343-66

Milkman, R. Women's work and the economic crisis: some lessons from the Great Depression. *In* A Heritage of her own, ed. by N. F. Cott and E. H. Pleck p507-41

### Employment—United States— Case studies

Pleck, E. H. A mother's wages: income earning among married Italian and black women, 1896-1911. *In* A Heritage of her own, ed. by N. F. Cott and E. H. Pleck p367-92

### Historiography

Degler, C. N. Women and the family. *In* The Past before us, ed. by M. Kammen p308-26

### Language

Carter, A. The language of sisterhood. *In* The State of the language, ed. by L. Michaels and C. Ricks p226-34

### Legal status, laws, etc.—United States

Salmon, M. "Life, liberty, and dower": the legal status of women after the American Revolution. *In* Women, war, and revolution, ed. by C. R. Berkin and C. M. Lovett p85-106

### Political activity

*See* Women in politics

### Psychology

Smith-Rosenberg, C. The female world of love and ritual: relations between women in nineteenth-century America. *In* A Heritage of her own, ed. by N. F. Cott and E. H. Pleck p311-42

### Religious life

Ulrich, L. T. Vertuous women found: New England ministerial literature, 1668-1735. *In* A Heritage of her own, ed. by N. F. Cott and E. H. Pleck p58-80

Women—*Continued*

### Sexual behavior

Cott, N. F. Passionlessness: an interpretation of Victorian sexual ideology, 1790-1850. *In* A Heritage of her own, ed. by N. F. Cott and E. H. Pleck p162-81

Fortunata, J. Masturbation and women's sexuality. *In* The Philosophy of sex, ed. by A. Soble p389-408

### Social conditions

Morowitz, H. J. Women's lib and the battle against entropy. *In* Morowitz, H. J. The wine of life, and other essays on societies, energy & living things p67-70

Schrade, A. O. Sex-shock: the humanistic woman in the super-industrial society. *In* Monster or messiah? Ed. by W. M. Mathews p72-86

Smith, D. E. A sociology for women. *In* The Prism of sex, ed. by J. A. Sherman and E. T. Beck p135-87

### Study and teaching

*See* Women's studies

### Suffrage—Great Britain—History

Holroyd, M. Women and the body politic. *In* The Genius of Shaw, ed. by M. Holroyd p167-83

### China—History

Maloney, J. M. Women in the Chinese Communist Revolution: the question of political equality. *In* Women, war, and revolution, ed. by C. R. Berkin and C. M. Lovett p165-81

### Cuba—History

Casal, L. Revolution and conciencia: women in Cuba. *In* Women, war, and revolution, ed. by C. R. Berkin and C. M. Lovett p183-206

### Europe—Historiography

Schulenburg, J. A. T. Clio's European daughters: myopic modes of perception. *In* The Prism of sex, ed. by J. A. Sherman and E. T. Beck p33-53

### France—History

Johnson, M. D. Old wine in new bottles: the institutional changes for women of the people during the French Revolution. *In* Women, war, and revolution, ed. by C. R. Berkin and C. M. Lovett p107-43

Levy, D. G. and Applewhite, H. V. B. Women of the popular classes in revolutionary Paris, 1789-1795. *In* Women, war, and revolution, ed. by C. R. Berkin and C. M. Lovett p9-35

Mylne, V. The Bibliothèque universelle des dames. *In* Woman and society in eighteenth-century France, ed. by E. Jacobs and others p123-38

Pope, B. C. Revolution and retreat: upper-class French women after 1789. *In* Women, war, and revolution, ed. by C. R. Berkin and C. M. Lovett p215-36

### France—Social conditions

Bloch, J. H. Women and the reform of the nation. *In* Woman and society in eighteenth-century France, ed. by E. Jacobs and others p3-18

Gardner, E. J. The philosophes and women: sensationalism and sentiment. *In* Woman and society in eighteenth-century France, ed. by E. Jacobs and others p19-27

Lough, J. Women in Mercier's Tableau de Paris. *In* Woman and society in eighteenth-century France, ed. by E. Jacobs and others p110-22

Mason, S. M. The riddle of Roxane. *In* Woman and society in eighteenth-century France, ed. by E. Jacobs and others p28-41

### Germany—History

Rupp, L. J. "I don't call that Volksgemeinschaft": women, class, and war in Nazi Germany. *In* Women, war, and revolution, ed. by C. R. Berkin and C. M. Lovett p37-53

### Great Britain—Employment

Lewis, J. In search of a real equality: women between the Wars. *In* Class, culture and social change, ed. by F. Gloversmith p208-39

### Great Britain—History

Buckley, S. C. The family and the role of women. *In* The Edwardian age: conflict and stability, 1900-1914, ed. by A. O'Day p133-43

### Great Britain—Social conditions

Lewis, J. In search of a real equality: women between the Wars. *In* Class, culture and social change, ed. by F. Gloversmith p208-39

Perry, R. The veil of chastity: Mary Astell's feminism. *In* Studies in eighteenth-century culture v9 p25-43

### Italy—History

Howard, J. J. Patriot mothers in the post-Risorgimento: women after the Italian revolution, ed. by C. R. Bergin and C. M. Lovett p237-58

### Maryland—History

Carr, L. G. and Walsh, L. S. The planter's wife: the experience of white women in seventeenth-century Maryland. *In* A Heritage of her own, ed. by N. F. Cott and E. H. Pleck p25-57

### New England—History

Ulrich, L. T. Vertuous women found: New England ministerial literature, 1668-1735. *In* A Heritage of her own, ed. by N. F. Cott and E. H. Pleck p58-80

### Russia—History

Farnsworth, B. B. Communist feminism: its synthesis and demise. *In* Women, war, and revolution, ed. by C. R. Berkin and C. M. Lovett p145-63

### United States—Economic conditions

Degler, C. N. Women. *In* Encyclopedia of American economic history, ed. by G. Porter v3 p988-1000

### United States—Historiography

Dye, N. S. Clio's American daughters: male history, female reality. *In* The Prism of sex, ed. by J. A. Sherman and E. T. Beck p9-31

### United States—History

Faragher, J. and Stansell, C. Women and their families on the Overland Trail to California and Oregon, 1842-1867. *In* A Heritage of her own, ed. by N. F. Cott and E. H. Pleck p246-67

Glasco, L. A. The life cycles and household structure of American ethnic groups: Irish, Germans, and native-born whites in Buffalo, New York, 1855. *In* A Heritage of her own, ed. by N. F. Cott and E. H. Pleck p268-89

**Women—United States—History—**Continued

Lerner, G. The lady and the mill girl: changes in the status of women in the age of Jackson, 1800-1840. In A Heritage of her own, ed. by N. F. Cott and E. H. Pleck p182-96

Norton, M. B. Eighteenth-century American women in peace and war: the case of the Loyalists. In A Heritage of her own, ed. by N. F. Cott and E. H. Pleck p136-61

Salmon, M. "Life, liberty, and dower": the legal status of women after the American Revolution. In Women, war, and revolution, ed. by C. R. Berkin and C. M. Lovett p85-106

Skold, K. B. The job he left behind: American women in the shipyards during World War II. In Women, war, and revolution, ed. by C. R. Berkin and C. M. Lovett p55-75

Smith, D. S. Family limitation, sexual control, and domestic feminism in Victorian America. In A Heritage of her own, ed. by N. F. Cott and E. H. Pleck p222-45

Smith-Rosenberg, C. Beauty, the beast, and the militant woman: a case study in sex roles and social stress in Jacksonian America. In A Heritage of her own, ed. by N. F. Cott and E. H. Pleck p197-221

Smith-Rosenberg, C. The female world of love and ritual: relations between women in nineteenth-century America. In A Heritage of her own, ed. by N. F. Cott and E. H. Pleck p311-42

Steinson, B. J. "The mother half of humanity": American women in the peace and preparedness movements in World War I. In Women, war, and revolution, ed. by C. R. Berkin and C. M. Lovett p259-84

Stricker, F. A. Cookbooks and law books: the hidden history of career women in twentieth-century America. In A Heritage of her own, ed. by N. F. Cott and E. H. Pleck p476-98

### United States—Sexual behavior

Johnson, S. K. The future of women in America's third century. In The Third century, ed. by S. M. Lipset p285-301

### United States—Social conditions

Johnson, S. K. The future of women in America's third century. In The Third century, ed. by S. M. Lipset p285-301

**Women (in religion, folklore, etc.)**

Bannan, H. M. Spider Woman's web: mothers and daughters in Southwestern native American literature. In The Lost tradition: mothers and daughters in literature, ed. by C. N. Davidson and E. M. Broner p268-79

Ochshorn, J. Mothers and daughters in ancient Near Eastern literature. In The Lost tradition: mothers and daughters in literature, ed. by C. N. Davidson and E. M. Broner p5-14

Washington, I. H. and Tobol, C. E. W. Kriemhild and Clytemnestra—sisters in crime or independent women? In The Lost tradition: mothers and daughters in literature, ed. by C. N. Davidson and E. M. Broner p15-21

**Women, Afro-American.** See Afro-American women

**Women, Afro-American in literature.** See Afro-American women in literature

**Women, Jewish in literature**

Duncan, E. The hungry Jewish mother. In The Lost tradition: mothers and daughters in literature, ed. by C. N. Davidson and E. M. Broner p231-41

**Women and peace**

Steinson, B. J. "The mother half of humanity": American women in the peace and preparedness movements in World War I. In Women, war, and revolution, ed. by C. R. Berkin and C. M. Lovett p259-84

**Women and religion**

Christ, C. P. Women's stories, women's quest. In Christ, C. P. Diving deep and surfacing p 1-12

See also Women—Religious life

**Women and socialism**

Casal, L. Revolution and conciencia: women in Cuba. In Women, war, and revolution, ed. by C. R. Berkin and C. M. Lovett p183-206

Farnsworth, B. B. Communist feminism: its synthesis and demise. In Women, war, and revolution, ed. by C. R. Berkin and C. M. Lovett p145-63

Maloney, J. M. Women in the Chinese Communist Revolution: the question of political equality. In Women, war, and revolution, ed. by C. R. Berkin and C. M. Lovett p165-81

**Women authors**

Lanser, S. S. and Beck, E. T. [Why] are there no great women critics? And what difference does it make? In The Prism of sex, ed. by J. A. Sherman and E. T. Beck p79-91

Mason, M. G. The other voice: autobiographies of women writers. In Autobiography: essays theoretical and critical, ed. by J. Olney p207-35

Spacks, P. M. Selves in hiding. In Women's autobiography, ed. by E. C. Jelinek p 112-32

Stimpson, C. R. Ad/d feminam: women, literature, and society. In Literature and society, ed. by E. W. Said p174-92

**Women authors, Afro-American**

Blackburn, R. In search of the black female self: African-American women's autobiographies and ethnicity. In Women's autobiography, ed. by E. C. Jelinek p 133-48

**Women authors, American**

Winston, E. The autobiographer and her readers: from apology to affirmation. In Women's autobiography, ed. by E. C. Jelinek p93-111

**Women authors, English**

Winston, E. The autobiographer and her readers: from apology to affirmation. In Women's autobiography, ed. by E. C. Jelinek p93-111

**Women authors, Norwegian-American**

Christianson, J. R. Literary traditions of Norwegian-American women. In Makers of an American immigrant legacy, ed. by O. S. Lovoll p92-110

**Women in art**

Grossman, J. D. Feminine images in Old Russian literature and art. In California Slavic studies v11 p33-70

**Women in literature**

Baruch, E. H. Women and love: some dying myths. In The Analysis of literary texts, ed. by R. D. Pope p51-65

Berke, J. and Berke, L. Mothers and daughters in Wives and daughters: a study of Elizabeth Gaskell's last novel. In The Lost tradition: mothers and daughters in literature, ed. by C. N. Davidson and E. M. Broner p95-109

Bloom, L. Z. Heritages: dimensions of mother-daughter relationships in women's autobiographies. In The Lost tradition: mothers and daughters in literature, ed. by C. N. Davidson and E. M. Broner p291-303

Women in literature—*Continued*

Christ, C. P. Toward wholeness: a vision of women's culture. *In* Christ, C. P. Diving deep and surfacing p119-31

Christ, C. P. Women's stories, women's quest. *In* Christ, C. P. Diving deep and surfacing p 1-12

Duckworth, C. D'Antraigues feminism: where fact and fantasy meet. *In* Woman and society in eighteenth-century France, ed. by E. Jacobs and others p166-82

Fineman, J. Fratricide and cuckoldry: Shakespeare's doubles. *In* Representing Shakespeare, ed. by M. M. Schwartz and C. Kahn p70-109

Fletcher, D. Resif de la Bretonne and woman's estate. *In* Woman and society in eighteenth-century France, ed. by E. Jacobs and others p96-109

Gohlke, M. S. "I wooed thee with my sword": Shakespeare's tragic paradigms. *In* Representing Shakespeare, ed. by M. M. Schwartz and C. Kahn p170-87

Grossman, J. D. Feminine images in Old Russian literature and art. *In* California Slavic studies v11 p33-70

Hagstrum, J. H. Friends and lovers: the witty and the wise. *In* Hagstrum, J. H. Sex and sensibility p133-59

Hagstrum, J. H. Woman in love: the abandoned and passionate mistress. *In* Hagstrum, J. H. Sex and sensibility p100-32

Hall, P. M. Duclos's Histoire de Madame de Luz: woman and history. *In* Woman and society in eighteenth-century France, ed. by E. Jacobs and others p139-51

Irvine, L. A psychological journey: mothers and daughters in English-Canadian fiction. *In* The Lost tradition: mothers and daughters in literature, ed. by C. N. Davidson and E. M. Broner p242-52

Jackson, R. 'Perfect types of womanhood': Rosalind, Beatrice and Viola in Victorian criticism and performance. *In* Shakespeare survey 32 p15-26

Jimack, P. D. The paradox of Sophie and Julie: contemporary response to Rousseau's ideal wife and ideal mother. *In* Woman and society in eighteenth-century France, ed. by E. Jacobs and others p152-65

Macdonald, S. P. Jane Austen and the tradition of the absent mother. *In* The Lost tradition: mothers and daughters in literature, ed. by C. N. Davidson and E. M. Broner p58-69

Mason, H. T. Women in Marivaux: journalist to dramatist. *In* Woman and society in eighteenth-century France, ed. by E. Jacobs and others p42-54

Miller, N. K. Epilogue. *In* Miller, N. K. The heroine's text p 149-58

Niklaus, R. Diderot and women. *In* Woman and society in eighteenth-century France, ed. by E. Jacobs and others p69-82

Pearsall, P. Julian del Casal's portraits of women. *In* The Analysis of literary texts, ed. by R. D. Pope p78-88

Rosinsky, N. M. Mothers and daughters: another minority group. *In* The Lost tradition: mothers and daughters in literature, ed. by C. N. Davidson and E. M. Broner p280-90

Salinas, J. The role of women in Chicano literature. *In* The Identification and analysis of Chicano literature, ed. by F. Jiménez p191-240

Schotz, M. G. The great unwritten story: mothers and daughters in Shakespeare. *In* The Lost tradition: mothers and daughters in literature, ed. by C. N. Davidson and E. M. Broner p44-54

Stiller, N. Eve's orphans: mothers and daughters in medieval English literature. *In* The Lost tradition: mothers and daughters in literature, ed. by C. N. Davidson and E. M. Broner p22-32

Stimpson, C. R. Ad/d feminam: women, literature, and society. *In* Literature and society, ed. by E. W. Said p174-92

Thiébaux, M. A mythology for women: Monique Wittig's Les guérillères. *In* The Analysis of literary texts, ed. by R. D. Pope p90-99

Todd, J. The biographical context. *In* Todd, J. Women's friendship in literature p359-402

Todd, J. Erotic friendship: Denis Diderot's The nun. *In* Todd, J. Women's friendship in literature p100-31

Todd, J. Erotic friendship: John Cleland's Fanny Hill. *In* Todd, J. Women's friendship in literature p69-100

Todd, J. The literary context. *In* Todd, J. Women's friendship in literature p305-58

Todd, J. Manipulative friendship: Jean-Jacques Rousseau's Julie. *In* Todd, J. Women's friendship in literature p132-67

Todd, J. Manipulative friendship: the Marquis de Sade's Juliette. *In* Todd, J. Women's friendship in literature p168-90

Todd, J. Political friendship. Madame de Staël's Delphine. *In* Todd, J. Women's friendship in literature p226-45

Todd, J. Political friendship: Mary Wollstonecraft's Mary, a fiction. *In* Todd, J. Women's friendship in literature p191-226

Todd, J. Sentimental friendship: Samuel Richardson's Clarissa. *In* Todd, J. Women's friendship in literature p9-68

Todd, J. Social friendship: Jane Austen's Emma. *In* Todd, J. Women's friendship in literature p274-301

Todd, J. Social friendship: Jane Austen's Mansfield Park. *In* Todd, J. Women's friendship in literature p246-74

Ulrich, L. T. Vertuous women found: New England ministerial literature. 1668-1735. *In* A Heritage of her own, ed. by N. F. Cott and E. H. Pleck p58-80

Wagner, L. W. Barren ground's vein of iron: Dorinda Oakley and some concepts of heroine in 1925. *In* Wagner, L. W. American modern p56-66

Wagner, L. W. Ellen Glasgow: daughter as justified. *In* The Lost tradition: mothers and daughters in literature, ed. by C. N. Davidson and E. M. Broner p140-46

Zimmerman, B. "The mother's history" in George Eliot's life, literature and political ideology. *In* The Lost tradition: mothers and daughters in literature, ed. by C. N. Davidson and E. M. Broner p81-94

### Bibliography

Rudenstein, G. M.; Kessler, C. F. and Moore, A. M. Mothers and daughters in literature: a preliminary bibliography. *In* The Lost tradition: mothers and daughters in literature, ed. by C. N. Davidson and E. M. Broner p302-22

**Women in politics**
Sapiro, V. Women's studies and political conflict. *In* The Prism of sex, ed. by J. A. Sherman and E. T. Beck p253-65

### China—History
Maloney, J. M. Women in the Chinese Communist Revolution: the question of political equality. *In* Women, war, and revolution, ed. by C. R. Berkin and C. M. Lovett p165-81

### Cuba—History
Casal, L. Revolution and conciencia: women in Cuba. *In* Women, war, and revolution, ed. by C. R. Berkin and C. M. Lovett p183-206

### France—History
Levy, D. G. and Applewhite, H. V. B. Women of the popular classes in revolutionary Paris, 1789-1795. *In* Women, war, and revolution, ed. by C. R. Berkin and C. M. Lovett p9-35

### Russia—History
Farnsworth, B. B. Communist feminism: its synthesis and demise. *In* Women, war, and revolution, ed. by C. R. Berkin and C. M. Lovett p145-63

**Women in the social sciences.** See Women social scientists

**Women scholars**
Bernard, J. S. Afterword. *In* The Prism of sex, ed. by J. A Sherman and E. T. Beck p267-75

Lanser, S. S. and Beck, E. T. [Why] are there no great women critics? And what difference does it make? *In* The Prism of sex, ed. by J. A. Sherman and E. T. Beck p79-91

**Women social scientists**
Smith, D. E. A sociology for women. *In* The Prism of sex, ed. by J. A. Sherman and E. T. Beck p135-87

**Women workers.** See Women—Employment

**Women's studies**
Sapiro, V. Women's studies and political conflict. *In* The Prism of sex, ed. by J. A. Sherman and E. T. Beck p253-65

**Wood, David**
Suicide as instrument and expression. *In* Suicide: the philosophical issues, ed. by M. P. Battin and D. J. Mayo p151-60

**Wood, John August**
The chronology of the Richardson-Bradshaigh correspondence of 1751. *In* Virginia. University. Bibliographical Society. Studies in bibliography v33 p182-91

**Wood-pulp.** See Newsprint

**Woodbridge, Frederick J. E.**

#### About
Shea, W. M. The supernatural in the naturalists. *In* History, religion, and spiritual democracy, ed. by M. Wohlgelernter and others p53-75

**Woodburn, James**
Hunters and gatherers today and reconstruction of the past. *In* Soviet and Western anthropology, ed. by E. Gellner p95-117

**Woodhead, M. R.**
Deep plots and indiscretions in 'The murder of Gonzago.' *In* Shakespeare survey 32 p151-61

**Woodman, Harold D.**
Economy from 1815 to 1865. *In* Encyclopedia of American economic history, ed. by G. Porter v 1 p66-90

**Woodman, Tony**
Self-imitation and the substance of history: Tacitus, Annals 1.61-5 and Histories 2.70, 5.14-15. *In* Creative imitation and Latin literature, ed. by D. West and T. Woodman p143-55

**Woodring, Carl Roy**
Sara fille: fairy child. *In* Reading Coleridge, ed. by W. B. Crawford p211-22

**Woodward, Comer Vann**

#### About
King, R. H. The new Southern liberalism: V. O. Key, Vann Woodward, Robert Penn Warren. *In* King, R. H. A Southern Renaissance p242-86

**Woodward, Ernest Llewellyn**

#### About individual works
*The age of reform, 1815-1870*
Trilling, L. The Victorians and democracy. *In* Trilling, L. Speaking of literature and society p135-40

**Wool trade and industry**

#### France—Lodève
Johnson, C. H. Patterns of proletarianization: Parisian tailors and Lodève woolens workers. *In* Consciousness and class experience in nineteenth-century Europe, ed. by J. M. Marriman p65-84

**Woolf, Leonard Sidney**

#### About individual works
*The journey, not the arrival, matters*
Plomer, W. C. F. Leonard Woolf. *In* Plomer, W. C. F. Electric delights p118-25

**Woolf, Virginia (Stephen)**

#### About
Fleishman, A. Forms of the Woolfian short story. *In* Virginia Woolf, ed. by R. Freedman p44-70

Lilienfeld, J. Reentering paradise: Cather, Colette, Woolf and their mothers. *In* The Lost tradition: mothers and daughters in literature, ed. by C. N. Davidson and E. M. Broner p160-75

Love, J. O. Orlando and its genesis: venturing and experimenting in art, love, and sex. *In* Virginia Woolf, ed. by R. Freedman p188-218

Richter, J. C. Hunting the moth: Virginia Woolf and the creative imagination. *In* Virginia Woolf, ed. by R. Freedman p13-28

#### About individual works
*Between the acts*
Fussell, B. H. Woolf's peculiar comic world: Between the acts. *In* Virginia Woolf, ed. by R. Freedman p262-83

*Jacob's room*
Freedman, R. The form of fact and fiction: Jacob's room as paradigm. *In* Virginia Woolf, ed. by R. Freedman p123-40

*Mrs Dalloway*
Ruotolo, L. P. Mrs Dalloway: the unguarded moment. *In* Virginia Woolf, ed. by R. Freedman p141-60

*Night and day*
Marcus, J. Enchanted organs, magic bells: Night and day as comic opera. *In* Virginia Woolf, ed. by R. Freedman p97-122

Woolf, Virginia S.—About individual works
—*Continued*

*Orlando*

Love, J. O. Orlando and its genesis: venturing and experimenting in art, love, and sex. *In* Virginia Woolf, ed. by R. Freedman p188-218

*To the lighthouse*

Dash, I. G.; Kushner, D. D. and Moore, D. D. "How light a lighthouse for today's women?" *In* The Lost tradition: mothers and daughters in literature, ed. by C. N. Davidson and E. M. Broner p176-88

DiBattista, M. A. To the lighthouse: Virginia Woolf's winter's tale. *In* Virginia Woolf, ed. by R. Freedman p161-88

*The voyage out*

McDowell, F. P. W. "Surely order did prevail": Virginia Woolf and The voyage out. *In* Virginia Woolf, ed. by R. Freedman p73-96

*The waves*

Moore, M. Nature and community: a study of cyclical reality in The waves. *In* Virginia Woolf, ed. by R. Freedman p219-40

*The years*

Naremore, J. O. Nature and history in The years. *In* Virginia Woolf, ed. by R. Freedman p241-62

**Characters**

Hafley, J. Virginia Woolf's narrators and the art of "life itself." *In* Virginia Woolf, ed. by R. Freedman p29-43

**Criticism and interpretation**

Freedman, R. Introduction: Virginia Woolf, the novel, and a chorus of voices. *In* Virginia Woolf, ed. by R. Freedman p3-12

Trivedi, H. K. Forster and Virginia Woolf: the critical friends. *In* E. M. Forster: a human exploration, ed. by G. K. Das and J. Beer p216-30

**Technique**

Hafley, J. Virginia Woolf's narrators and the art of "life itself." *In* Virginia Woolf, ed. by R. Freedman p29-43

**Wooley, James**

Thomas Sheridan and Swift. *In* Studies in eighteenth-century culture v9 p93-114

**Woolrych, Austin**

Political theory and political practice. *In* The Age of Milton, ed. by C. A. Patrides and R. B. Waddington p34-71

**Words, Stock of.** See Vocabulary

**Wordsworth, Dorothy**

**About individual works**

*Journals of Dorothy Wordsworth
(ed. by Ernest De Sélincourt)*

Trilling, L. The Wordsworths. *In* Trilling, L. Speaking of literature and society p177-80

**Wordsworth, William**

**About**

Beer, J. B. Coleridge and Wordsworth: the vital and the organic. *In* Reading Coleridge, ed. by W. B. Crawford p160-90

Brisman, S. H. and Brisman, L. Lies against solitude: symbolic, imaginary, and real. *In* The Literary Freud; mechanisms of defense and the poetic will, ed. by J. H. Smith p29-65

Fry, P. H. Wordsworth's severe Intimations. *In* Fry, P. H. The poet's calling in the English ode p133-61

Hartman, G. Diction and defense in Wordsworth. *In* The Literary Freud: mechanisms of defense and the poetic will, ed. by J. H. Smith p205-15

Heinzelman, K. Wordsworth's labor theory: an economics of compensation. *In* Heinzelman, K. The economics of the imagination p196-233

Keith, W. J. William Wordsworth. *In* Keith, W. J. The poetry of nature p11-37

Stone, D. D. Elizabeth Gaskell, Wordsworth, and the burden of reality. *In* Stone, D. D. The romantic impulse in Victorian fiction p133-72

**About individual works**

*The borderers*

Pipkin, J. W. The borderers and the genesis of Wordsworth's spots of time. *In* Tennessee Studies in literature v24 p111-19

*The prelude*

Spengemann, W. C. Philosophical autobiography. *In* Spengemann, W. C. The forms of autobiography p62-109

**Language**

Hartman, G. Diction and defense in Wordsworth. *In* The Literary Freud: mechanisms of defense and the poetic will, ed. by J. H. Smith p205-15

**Style**

*See* Wordsworth, William—Language

**Work**

Montgomery, D. Work. *In* Encyclopedia of American economic history, ed. by G. Porter v3 p958-73

Tolliver, J. E. The computer and the Protestant ethic: a conflict. *In* Monster or messiah? Ed. by W. M. Mathews p156-64

*See also* Labor and laboring classes

**Psychological aspects**

Kohn, M. L. Job complexity and adult personality. *In* Themes of work and love in adulthood, ed. by N. J. Smelser and E. H. Erikson p193-210

Smelser, N. J. Vicissitudes of work and love in Anglo-American society. *In* Themes of work and love in adulthood, ed. by N. J. Smelser and E. H. Erikson p105-19

**Work, Psychology of.** See Work—Psychological aspects

**Work, Right to.** See Right to labor

**Workers.** See Labor and laboring classes

**Workers' Theatre Movement (Great Britain)**

Samuel, R. Workers' theatre, 1926-36. *In* Performance and politics in popular drama, ed. by D. Bradby, L. James and B. Sharratt p213-30

**Working-classes.** See Labor and laboring classes

**Working-day.** See Hours of labor

**Working hours.** See Hours of labor

**Working men.** See Labor and laboring classes

**World history**

**Early works to 1800**

Bately, J. M. World history in the Anglo-Saxon Chronicle: its sources and its separateness from the Old English Orosius. *In* Anglo-Saxon England 8 p177-94

World politics
*See also* International relations

### 20th century
Moynihan, D. P. The advent of party in international politics. *In* Moynihan, D. P. Counting our blessings p72-84

Speier, H. The chances for peace. *In* Propaganda and communication in world history, ed. by H. D. Lasswell, D. Lerner and H. Speier v2 p507-27

### 1945-
Crozier, B. The Cold War is over. *In* Lying truths, ed. by R. Duncan and M. Weston-Smith p35-46

Isaacs, H. R. Changing arenas and identities in world affairs. *In* Propaganda and communication in world history, ed. by H. D. Lasswell, D. Lerner and H. Speier v2 p395-423

Lerner, D. The revolutionary elites and world symbolism. *In* Propaganda and communication in world history, ed. by H. D. Lasswell, D. Lerner and H. Speier v2 p371-94

Moynihan, D. P. The politics of human rights. *In* Moynihan, D. P. Counting our blessings p85-105

Moynihan, D. P. Presenting the American case. *In* Moynihan, D. P. Counting our blessings p41-59

Sakharov, A. D. Thoughts on progress, peaceful coexistence and intellectual freedom. *In* Propaganda and communication in world history, ed. by H. D. Lasswell, D. Lerner and H. Speier v2 p471-506

### 1975-1985
Adelman, K. L. Revitalizing alliances. *In* National security in the 1980s: from weakness to strength, ed. by W. S. Thompson p295-317

World War, 1914-1918. See European War, 1914-1918

World War, 1939-1945

#### Jews
*See* Holocaust, Jewish (1939-1945)

#### Personal narratives, Jewish
Syrkin, M. and Kunzer, R. G. Holocaust literature I: diaries and memoirs. *In* Encountering the Holocaust: an interdisciplinary survey, ed. by B. L. Sherwin and S. G. Ament p226-66

#### Propaganda
Gombrich, Sir E. H. J. Myth and reality in German wartime broadcasts. *In* Gombrich, Sir E. H. J. Ideals and idols p93-111

#### Women's work
Rupp, L. J. "I don't call that Volksgemeinschaft": women, class, and war in Nazi Germany. *In* Women, war and revolution, ed. by C. R. Berkin and C. M. Lovett p37-53

Skold, K. B. The job he left behind: American women in the shipyards during World War II. *In* Women, war, and revolution, ed. by C. R. Berkin and C. M. Lovett p55-75

#### United States
Skold, K. B. The job he left behind: American women in the shipyards during World War II. *In* Women, war, and revolution, ed. by C. R. Berkin and C. M. Lovett p55-75

World War, 1939-1945, in literature
Ceadel, M. Popular fiction and the next war, 1918-39. *In* Class, culture and social change, ed. by F. Gloversmith p161-84

World War, 1939-1945 in motion pictures
Lustig, A. and Lustig, J. The Holocaust and the film arts. *In* Encountering the Holocaust: an interdisciplinary survey, ed. by B. L. Sherwin and S. H. Ament p351-82

Worrall, Nick
Meyerhold and Eisenstein. *In* Performance and politics in popular drama, ed. by D. Bradley, L. James and B. Sharratt p173-87

Worry. See Anxiety

Worship. See Prayer

Worth. See Values

Wortham, Thomas
19th-century literature. *In* American literary scholarship, 1978 p199-228

Wortzel, Heidi. See Vernon, R. jt. auth.

Woyzeck (Motion picture)
Kauffmann, S. Woyzeck. *In* Kauffmann, S. Before my eyes p173-74

Wright, Arthur Frederick
Chinese civilization. *In* Propaganda and communication in world history, ed. by H. D. Lasswell, D. Lerner and H. Speier v 1 p220-56

On the spread of Buddhism to China. *In* Propaganda and communication in world history, ed. by H. D. Lasswell, D. Lerner and H. Speier v 1 p205-19

Wright, Arthur Winslow
Soviet economic planning and performance. *In* The Soviet Union since Stalin, ed. by S. F. Cohen, A. Rabinowitch and R. Sharlet p113-34

Wright, Charles, 1935-

##### About
Vendler, H. H. Charles Wright. *In* Vendler, H. H. Part of nature, part of us p277-88

Wright, Gavin
Agriculture in the South. *In* Encyclopedia of American economic history, ed. by G. Porter v 1 p371-85

Wright, Iain
F. R. Leavis, the Scrutiny movement and the crisis. *In* Culture and crisis in Britain in the thirties, ed. by J. Clark and others p37-65

Wright, James

##### About
Howard, R. James Wright: "The body wakes to burial." *In* Howard, R. Alone with America p662-78

Wright, Lulu
Antoine-Roger Bolamba. Esanzo: songs for my country. *In* African literature today no. 10: Retrospect & prospect, ed. by E. D. Jones p258-62

Wright, Richard

##### About individual works
###### Black boy
Olney, J. L. Some versions of memory/some versions of bios: the ontology of autobiography. *In* Autobiography: essays theoretical and critical, ed. by J. Olney p236-67

Stepto, R. B. Literacy and ascent: Richard Wright's Black boy. *In* Stepto, R. B. From behind the veil p128-62

## Wrightson, Francis

### About individual works

*Henry George's "Progress and poverty:"*
*the cause—the remedy*

Harrison, F. Longe and Wrightson: conservative critics of George's wage theory. *In* Critics of Henry George, ed. by R. V. Andelson p72-94

## Wrightson, Patricia

### About

Townsend, J. R. Patricia Wrightson. *In* Townsend, J. R. A sounding of storytellers p194-207

## Writing

### History

Hawkins, J. D. The origin and dissemination of writing in western Asia. *In* The Origins of civilzation, ed. by P. R. S. Moorey p128-65

Schmandt-Besserat, D. An archaic recording system prior to writing. *In* 5000 years of popular culture, ed. by F. E. H. Schroeder p19-35

### Influence

Opland, J. From horseback to monastic cell: the impact on English literature of the introduction of writing. *In* Old English literature in context, ed. by J. D. Niles p30-43

## Writing (Authorship) See Authorship

## Wroth, Lawrence Counselman

Lathrop Colgate Harper: a happy memory. *In* The Bibliographical Society of America, 1904-79 p372-83

## Wu, Yuan-li

U.S. foreign economic policy: politico-economic linkages. *In* United States in the 1980s, ed. by P. Duignan and A. Rabushka p613-37

## Wyatt, David

### Prodigal sons

*Contents*

Davies and the middle of the journey
Faulkner and the burdens of the past
Generating voice in A death in the family
Hemingway's uncanny beginnings
Modernity and paternity: James's The American
Robert Penn Warren: the critic as artist
Yeats and Synge: the Cuchulain complex

## Wyatt-Brown, Bertram

Conscience and career: young abolitionists and missionaries. *In* Anti-slavery, religion, and reform: essays in memory of Roger Anstey, ed. by C. Bolt and S. Drescher p183-203

## Wycherley, William

### About individual works

*The country wife*

Steiger, R. "Wit in a corner": hypocrisy in The country wife. *In* Tennessee Studies in literature v24 p56-70

## Wyllie, John Cook

The forms of twentieth-century cancels. *In* The Bibliographical Society of America, 1904-79 p289-306

## Wyschogrod, Edith

Martin Buber and the no-self perspective. *In* History, religion, and spiritual democracy, ed. by M. Wohlgelernter and others p130-50

# X

## Xivaro Indians. See Jivaro Indians

# Y

## Yale University

### Library

Gallup, D. C. Aldis, Foley, and the collection of American literature at Yale. *In* The Bibliographical Society of America, 1904-79 p209-28

## Yankelovich, Daniel

Two truths: the view from the social sciences. *In* Being human in a technological age, ed. by D. M. Borchert and D. Stewart p89-105

## Yanoama Indians

Harris, M. The Yanomamö and the causes of war in band and village societies. *In* Brazil, anthropological perspectives, ed. by M. L. Margolis and W. E. Carter p121-32

## Yanomamo Indians. See Yanoama Indians

## Yavetz, Zvi

The Jews and the great powers of the ancient world. *In* The Jewish world, ed. by E. Kedourie p89-107

## Yeager, Mary A.

Bureaucracy. *In* Encyclopedia of American economic history, ed. by G. Porter v3 p894-926

## Yeats, John Butler

### About

Murphy, W. M. Home life among the Yeatses. *In* Yeats, Sligo and Ireland, ed. by A. N. Jeffares p170-88

Wyatt, D. Yeats and Synge: the Cuchulain complex. *In* Wyatt, D. Prodigal sons p26-51

## Yeats, William Butler

### About

Donoghue, D. Romantic Ireland. *In* Yeats, Sligo and Ireland, ed. by A. N. Jeffares p17-30

Edwards, P. Introduction: The king's threshold. *In* Edwards, P. Threshold of a nation p 1-14

Heaney, S. Yeats as an example? *In* Yeats, Sligo and Ireland, ed. by A. N. Jeffares p56-72

Heinzelman, K. The art of labor. *In* Heinzelman, K. The economics of the imagination p137-65

Henn, T. R. The place of shells. *In* Yeats, Sligo and Ireland, ed. by A. N. Jeffares p73-88

Holloway, J. How goes the weather? *In* Yeats, Sligo and Ireland, ed. by A. N. Jeffares p89-97

Lyons, F. S. L. Yeats and Victorian Ireland. *In* Yeats, Sligo and Ireland, ed. by A. N. Jeffares p115-38

Martin, A. Hound voices were they all: an experiment in Yeats criticism. *In* Yeats, Sligo and Ireland, ed. by A. N. Jeffares p139-52

Maxwell, D. E. S. The shape-changers. *In* Yeats, Sligo and Ireland, ed. by A. N. Jeffares p153-69

Rafroidi, P. Yeats, nature and the self. *In* Yeats, Sligo and Ireland, ed. by A. N. Jeffares p189-96

Saddlemyer, A. The 'dwarf-dramas' of the early Abbey Theatre. *In* Yeats, Sligo and Ireland, ed. by A. N. Jeffares p197-215

Vendler, H. H. Four elegies. *In* Yeats, Sligo and Ireland, ed. by A. N. Jeffares p216-31

Welch, R. Yeats and Oisin. *In* Welch, R. Irish poetry from Moore to Yeats p205-27

Wyatt, D. Yeats and Synge: the Cuchulain complex. *In* Wyatt, D. Prodigal sons p26-51

**Yeats, William B.—**_Continued_
### About individual works
_Autobiographies_
Olney, J. L. Some versions of memory/some versions of bios: the ontology of autobiography. _In_ Autobiography: essays theoretical and critical, ed. by J. Olney p236-67

_Essays and introductions_
Trilling, L. Yeats as critic. _In_ Trilling, L. Speaking of literature and society p381-86

_Hound voice_
Martin, A. Hound voices were they all: an experiment in Yeats criticism. _In_ Yeats, Sligo and Ireland, ed. by A. N. Jeffares p139-52

_Leda and the swan_
Hartman, G. H. Understanding criticism. _In_ Hartman, G. H. Criticism in wilderness p19-41

_On Baile's Strand_
Wyatt, D. Yeats and Synge: the Cuchulain complex. _In_ Wyatt, D. Prodigal sons p26-51

_Per amica silentia lunae_
Hoffman, B. E. All imaginable things: Yeat's Per amica silentia lunae. _In_ Irish Renaissance annual I p56-72

### Characters—Crazy Jane
Conner, L. I. A matter of character: Red Hanrahan and Crazy Jane. _In_ Yeats, Sligo and Ireland, ed. by A. N. Jeffares p 1-16
Hardy, B. N. The wildness of Crazy Jane. _In_ Yeats, Sligo and Ireland, ed. by A. N. Jeffares p31-55

### Characters—Red Hanrahan
Conner, L. I. A matter of character: Red Hanrahan and Crazy Jane. _In_ Yeats, Sligo and Ireland, ed. by A. N. Jeffares p 1-16
**Yeats family**
Murphy, W. M. Home life among the Yeatses. _In_ Yeats, Sligo and Ireland, ed. by A. N. Jeffares p170-88
**Yeh, Shao-chün**
### About
Prušek, J. Yeh Shao-chün and Anton Chekhov. _In_ Prušek, J. The lyrical and the epic p178-94
**Yeh, Sheng-t'ao.** See Yeh, Shao-chün
**Yehoshua, Abraham B.**
### About individual works
_A night in May_
Abramson, G. Modernism: A night in May. _In_ Abramson, G. Modern Hebrew drama p181-88
**Yiddish drama**
### History and criticism
Abramson, G. The problems of the Israeli drama: Tradition. _In_ Abramson, G. Modern Hebrew drama p205-07
**Yiddish fiction**
### History and criticism
Spicehandler, E. Jewish literature: fiction. _In_ The Jewish world, ed. by E. Kedourie p253-58
**Yiddish language**
Calvary, M. Yiddish. _In_ The Jew, ed. by A. A. Cohen p31-42
Kaufmann, Y. The Hebrew language and our national future. _In_ The Jew, ed. by A. A. Cohen p97-111

**Yiddish language in the United States**
Hellerstein, K. Yiddish voices in American English. _In_ The State of the language, ed. by L. Michaels and C. Ricks p182-201
**Yiddish literature**
#### Eastern Europe—History and criticism
Alexander, E. The incredibility of the Holocaust. _In_ Alexander, E. The resonance of dust p3-28
**Yiddish poetry**
### History and criticism
Calvary, M. Yiddish. _In_ The Jew, ed. by A. A. Cohen p31-42
**Yom Kippur**
Baumgardt, D. The inner structure of the Yom Kippur liturgy. _In_ The Jew, ed. by A. A. Cohen p185-97
**Yorubas**
### Religion
Pelton, R. D. Legba and Eshu: writers of destiny. _In_ Pelton, R. D. The trickster in West Africa p113-63
**Young, Andrew, 1885-1971**
### About
Keith, W. J. The Georgians and after. _In_ Keith, W. J. The poetry of nature p167-98
**Young, Ernest P.**
Chinese leaders and Japanese aid in the early Republic. _In_ The Chinese and the Japanese, ed. by A. Iriye p124-39
**Young Frankenstein (Motion picture)**
Kauffmann, S. Young Frankenstein. _In_ Kauffmann, S. Before my eyes p110-11
**Young grammarians.** See Neogrammarians
**Youth**
### Massachusetts
Frye, J. Class, generation and social change: a case in Salem, Massachusetts, 1636-1656. _In_ 5000 years of popular culture, ed. by F. E. H. Schroeder p278-85
**Youth crime.** See Juvenile delinquency
**Youth in literature.** See Adolescence in literature; Children in literature
**Yu, George T.**
Sino-Soviet rivalry in Africa. _In_ Communism in Africa, ed. by D. E. Albright p168-88
**Yu, Ta-fu**
### About
Prušek, J. Mao Tun and Yü Ta-fu. _In_ Prušek, J. The lyrical and the epic p121-77
**Yue-Him Tam**
An intellectual's response to Western intrusion: Naito Konan's view of Republican China. _In_ The Chinese and the Japanese, ed. by A. Iriye p161-83

# Z

**Zaire**
### History—1960-
Naipaul, V. S. A new king for the Congo: Mobutu and the nihilism of Africa. _In_ Naipaul, V. S. The return of Eva Perón p173-204
### Social conditions
Naipaul, V. S. A new king for the Congo: Mobutu and the nihilism of Africa. _In_ Naipaul, V. S. The return of Eva Perón p173-204

**Zalygin, Sergei Pavlovich**

**About**

Shneidman, N. N. Sergei Zalygin: innovation and variety. *In* Shneidman, N. N. Soviet literature in the 1970s: artistic diversity and ideological conformity p61-74

**Zapata Olivella, Manuel**

**About**

Jackson, R. L. Literary blackness in Colombia: the ideological development of Manuel Zapata Olivella. *In* Jackson, R. L. Black writers in Latin America p142-52

**Zariski, Raphael**

Italy. *In* Western European party systems, ed. by P. H. Merkl p122-52

**Zayas y Sotomayor, María de**

**About**

Fox-Lockert, L. Maria de Zayas. *In* Fox-Lockert, L. Women novelists in Spain and Spanish America p25-35

**Zeitlin, Aaron**

**About**

Alexander, E. The Holocaust and the God of Israel. *In* Alexander, E. The resonance of dust p195-230

**Zejmis, Julia Brun-** See Brun-Zejmis, Julia

**Zero de conduite (Motion picture)**

Thiher, A. Vigo's Zéro de conduite: surrealism and the myth of childhood. *In* Thiher, A. The cinematic muse p78-89

**Zimmerman, Bonnie**

"The mother's history" in George Eliot's life, literature and political ideology. *In* The Lost tradition: mothers and daughters in literature, ed. by C. N. Davidson and E. M. Broner p81-94

**Zimmerman, Marvin**

How "humanistic" are humanists? *In* Humanist ethics, ed. by M. B. Storer p262-71

**Zimmerman, William**

The Soviet Union and the West. *In* The Soviet Union since Stalin, ed. by S. F. Cohen, A. Rabinowitch and R. Sharlet p305-11

**Zimring, Franklin E.**

American youth violence: issues and trends. *In* Crime and justice v 1 p67-107

**Zindel, Paul**

**About**

Rees, D. Viewed from a squashed eyeball: Paul Zindel. *In* Rees, D. The marble in the water p25-35

**Zionism**

Buber, M. Zion, the state, and humanity: remarks on Hermann Cohen's answer. *In* The Jew, ed. by A. A. Cohen p85-96

Schwadron, A. The dogma of the eternal Galut: a cardinal issue in Zionist ideology. *In* The Jew, ed. by A. A. Cohen p112-19

Strauss, L. Zionism in Max Nordau. *In* The Jew, ed. by A. A. Cohen p120-26

*See also* Nationalism—Jews

**History**

Vital, D. Zionism and Israel. *In* The Jewish world, ed. by E. Kedourie p309-17

**Zionism and Judaism**

Avineri, S. The new Jerusalem of Moses Hess. *In* Powers, possessions and freedom, ed. by A. Kontos p107-18

**Zionist movement.** See Zionism

**Zola, Émile**

**About individual works**

*L'assommoir*

Festa-McCormick, D. Zola's L'assommoir: Paris's stranglehold on the lives of the poor. *In* Festa-McCormick, D. The city as catalyst p33-48

**Zoological research**

Morowitz, H. J. Stalking the heffalump. *In* Morowitz, H. J. The wine of life, and other essays on societies, energy & living things p107-11

**Zoology**

**Research**

*See* Zoological research

**Zumthor, Paul**

A reading of a ballade by Jean Meschinot. *In* The Interpretation of medieval lyric poetry, ed. by W. T. H. Jackson p142-62

**Zumwalt, Elmo Russell**

Heritage of weakness: an assessment of the 1970s. *In* National security in the 1980s: from weakness to strength, ed. by W. S. Thompson p17-51

**Zweig, Arnold**

**About**

Wetzel, H. War and the destruction of moral principles in Arnold Zweig's Der Streit um den Sergeanten Grischa and Erziehung vor Verdun. *In* The First World War in German narrative prose, ed. by C. N. Genno and H. Wetzel p50-70

**Zwingli, Ulrich**

**About**

Ozment, S. H. The Swiss Reformation. *In* Ozment, S. H. The age of reform, 1250-1550 p318-39

**Zwingli, Huldreich.** See Zwingli, Ulrich

# List of Books Indexed

The list, arranged in one alphabet, includes both works by various authors and works by individual authors. Full information is given in the main entry for a book, with cross references from the title and the editor. For a collection of essays published in honor of a particular individual, a reference is made from the latter to the main entry. Generally, only American publishers are given. The English publisher is given when the book in question is obtainable only in an English edition.

**Abramson, Glenda.** Modern Hebrew drama. St Martins 1979 232p ISN 0-312-53988-6 LC 79-16608

**African** literature today no. 10: Retrospect & prospect. A review; ed. by Eldred Durosimi Jones. Africana Pub. Co. 1979 266p ISBN 0-8419-0397-2 LC 72-75254

**After** the New Criticism. See Lentricchia, F.

**Against** the current. See Berlin, Sir I.

The **Age** of Milton; backgrounds to seventeenth-century literature. C. A. Patrides and Raymond B. Waddington, editors. Barnes & Noble 1980 438p ISBN 0-389-20051-4

The **age** of reform, 1250-1550. See Ozment, S. H.

**Age** of spirituality; a symposium. Ed. by Kurt Weitzmann. Published in association with Princeton University Press [by] The Metropolitan Museum of Art 1980 163p ISBN 0-87099-229-5 (Metropolitan Museum of Art); ISBN 0-691-03956-9 (Princeton University Press); LC 80-11497
Papers from a symposium held in November, 1977 in conjunction with an exhibition at the Metropolitan Museum of Art entitled Age of spirituality: Late antique and early Christian art, third to seventh century

The **age** of structuralism. See Kurzweil, E.

**Aisenberg, Nadya.** A common spring; crime novel and classic. Bowling Green Univ. Pop. Press 1980 271p ISBN 0-87972-141-3 LC 79-84638

**Albright, David E.** (ed.) Communism in Africa. See Communism in Africa

**Alexander, Edward.** The resonance of dust; essays on Holocaust literature and Jewish fate. Ohio State Univ. Press 1979 256p ISBN 0-8142-0303-5 LC 79-15515

The **allegorical** epic. See Murrin, M.

**Allegories** of reading. See De Man, P.

**Alone** with America. See Howard, R.

**Altmann, Alexander.** See entry under title: Studies in Jewish religious and intellectual history

**Ament, Susan G.** (ed.) Encountering the Holocaust: an interdisciplinary survey. See Encountering the Holocaust: an interdisciplinary survey

**American Antiquarian Society, Worcester, Mass.** Proceedings of the American Antiquarian Society at the annual meeting held in Worcester, October, 17, 1979 v89 pt2. The Society 1980 394p, xxiii ISSN 0044-751X LC 5-13654

**American Antiquarian Society, Worcester, Mass.** Proceedings of the American Antiquarian Society at the semiannual meeting held in Chicago, April 18, 1979 v89 pt 1. The Society 1979 157p ISSN 0044-751X LC 5-13654

American Association for the Advancement of Science. Section on History and Philosophy of Science. The Sciences in the American context: new perspectives. *See* The Sciences in the American context: new perspectives

American hieroglyphics. See Irwin, J. T.

American Historical Association. The Past before us. *See* The Past before us

American literary scholarship, 1978; an annual. Ed. by J. Albert Robbins. Essays by Wendell Glick [and others] Duke Univ. Press 1980 528p ISBN 0-8223-0443-0 LC 65-19450

American modern. See Wagner, L. W.

Ammerman, David L. (ed.) The Chesapeake in the seventeenth century. *See* The Chesapeake in the seventeenth century

The Analysis of literary texts; current trends in methodology. Third and Fourth York College Colloquia. Ed. by Randolph D. Pope. Bilingual Press 1980 330p (Studies in literary analysis) ISBN 0-916950-14-X LC 79-54144
Partially analyzed
"Oral versions of the papers contained in this volume were presented at: Contemporary Methods of Literary Analysis: Third Colloquium on Hispanic, French and Italian Literature, held on April 29, 1977 at York College of CUNY, and Contemporary Methods of Literary Analysis: Fourth Colloquium on English, French, Italian and Spanish Literature, held on April 28, 1978 at the Graduate Center of CUNY." Verso of title page

Ancient Greek literature. K. J. Dover (editor); [contributors] E. L. Bowie, Jasper Griffin [and] M. L. West. Oxford 1980 186p ISBN 0-19-219137-3 LC 79-41627

Andelson, Robert V. (ed.) Critics of Henry George. *See* Critics of Henry George

Anderson, Carl L. (ed.) Toward a new American literary history. *See* Toward a new American literary history

André Malraux; metamorphosis and imagination. Guest editors: Françoise Dorenlot [and] Micheline Tison-Braun. N.Y. Literary Forum 1979 258p ISBN 0-931196-02-7 LC 77-18629
Partially analyzed

The Anglo-Irish novel. See Cronin, J.

Anglo-Saxon England 8; ed. by Peter Clemoes [and others]. Cambridge 1979 376p   ISBN 0-521-22788-7 LC 78-190423

Anglo-Scottish literary relations, 1430-1550. See Kratzmann, G.

Annales, économies, sociétés, civilisations. Medicine and society in France. *See* Medicine and society in France

Anselment, Raymond A. 'Betwixt jest and earnest'; Marprelate, Milton, Marvell, Swift & the decorum of religious ridicule. Univ. of Toronto Press 1979 203p ISBN 0-8020-5444-7 LC 79-12498

Anstey, Roger See entry under title: Anti-slavery, religion and reform

Anti-slavery, religion, and reform: essays in memory of Roger Anstey. Ed. by Christine Bolt [and] Seymour Drescher. Archon Bks. 1980 377p ISBN 0-208-01783-6 LC 79-41532

The Arbuthnot lectures, 1970-1979. [Sponsored by the] Association for Library Service to Children, American Library Association; with a biographical sketch of May Hill Arbuthnot by Zena Sutherland, compiler. A.L.A. 1980 203p ISBN 0-8389-3240-1 LC 79-26095

Architecture for people; explorations in a new humane environment. Ed. by Byron Mikellides. Holt 1980 192p illus ISBN 0-03-057491-9 LC 79-48067

Artisans of glory. See Ranum, O.

Ashton, Dore. A fable of modern art, with 48 illustrations. Thames & Hudson 1980 128p ISBN 0-500-23301-2 LC 79-66137

Ashton, Rosemary D. The German idea; four English writers and the reception of German thought, 1800-1860. Cambridge 1980 245p ISBN 0-521-22560-4 LC 78-75254

Aspects of Indian writing in English; essays in honour of Prof. K. R. Srinivasa Iyengar. Ed. by M. K. Naik. Humanities Press [1980 c1979] 319p

Association for Library Service to Children. The Arbuthnot lectures, 1970-1979. See The Arbuthnot lectures, 1970-1979

The author and his publisher. See Unseld, S.

Autobiography: essays theoretical and critical. Ed. by James Olney. Princeton Univ. Press 1980 360p ISBN 0-691-06412-1 LC 79-17556

Ayer, Sir Alfred Jules. See entry under title: Perception and identity

Bacarisse, Salvador (ed.) Contemporary Latin American fiction. See Contemporary Latin American fiction

Backscheider, Paula Rice (ed.) Probability, time, and space in eighteenth-century literature. See Probability, time, and space in eighteenth-century literature

Baily, Bernard (ed.) The press & the American Revolution. See The Press & the American Revolution

Barnes, Jonathan (ed.) Doubt and dogmatism. See Doubt and dogmatism

Baron, Frank (ed.) Rilke: the alchemy of alienation. See Rilke: the alchemy of alienation

Barthes, Roland. New critical essays. Trans. by Richard Howard. Hill & Wang 1980 121p ISBN 0-8090-7257-2 LC 80-12345

Battin, M. Pabst (ed.) Suicide: the philosophical issues. See Suicide: the philosophical issues

Beck, Evelyn Torton (ed.) The prisim of sex. See The Prism of sex

Beer, John B. (ed.) E. M. Forster: a human exploration. See E. M. Forster: a human exploration

Before my eyes. See Kauffmann, S.

Beichner, Paul E. See entry under title: Chaucerian problems and perspectives

Being human in a technological age; collected and ed. by Donald M. Borchert and David Stewart. Ohio Univ. Press 1979 168p ISBN 0-8214-0399-0 LC 79-4364

Bell, Michael (ed.) The context of English literature, 1900-1930. See The Context of English literature, 1900-1930

Bennett, Benjamin. Modern drama and German classicism; Renaissance from Lessing to Brecht. Cornell Univ. Press [1980 c1979] 359p ISBN 0-8014-1189-0 LC 79-14644

Berkin, Carol Ruth (ed.) Women, war, and revolution. See Women, war, and revolution

Berlin, Sir Isaiah. Against the current; essays in the history of ideas. Ed. and with a bibliography by Henry Hardy, with an introduction by Roger Hausheer. Viking 1980 liii,394p ISBN 0-670-10944-4 LC 79-22928
Companion volume to: Concepts and categories, and Russian thinkers, both analyzed in June, 1979 supplement

Berman, Ronald S. (ed.) Solzhenitsyn at Harvard. See Solzhenitsyn at Harvard

Best, Alan (ed.) Modern Austrian writing. See Modern Austrian writing

'Betwixt jest and earnest.' See Anselment, R. A.

Beyond Socialist realism. See Hosking, G.

The **Bibliographical** Society of America, 1904-79. A retrospective collection. Published for the Bibliographical Society of America by the Univ. Press of Va. 1980 557p ISBN 0-8139-0863-9 LC 80-14334

**Bicentennial Conference on the History of Geology, University of New Hampshire, 1976.** See New Hampshire Bicentennial Conference on the History of Geology, University of New Hampshire, 1976

**Bickman, Martin.** The unsounded centre; Jungian studies in American romanticism. Univ. of N.C. Press 1980 182p ISBN 0-8078-1428-8 LC 79-26042

The **Binding** of Proteus; perspectives on myth and the literary process. Ed. by Marjorie W. McCune; Tucker Orbison, and Philip M. Withim. Bucknell Univ. Press 1980 350p ISBN 0-8387-1708-X LC 76-49774
"Collected papers of the Bucknell University Program on Myth and Literature and the Bucknell-Susquehanna Colloquium on Myth in Literature held at Bucknell and Susquehanna Universities 21 and 22 March 1974"

**Bird, Charles Stephen** (ed.) Explorations in African systems of thought. *See* Explorations in African systems of thought

**Bjork, Kenneth O.** See entry under title: Makers of an American immigrant legacy

**Black** writers in Latin America. See Jackson, R. L.

**Blau, Joseph Leon.** See entry under title: History, religion, and spiritual democracy

**Bolt, Christine** (ed.) Anti-slavery, religion, and reform: essays in memory of Roger Anstey. See Anti-slavery, religion, and reform: essays in memory of Roger Anstey

**Borchert, Donald M.** (ed.) Being human in a technological age. *See* Being human in a technological age

**Boskin, Michael J.** (ed.) The economy in the 1980: a program for growth and stability. *See* The Economy in the 1980: a program for growth and stability

**Bosmajian, Hamida.** Metaphors of evil; contemporary German literature and the shadow of Nazism. Univ. of Iowa Press 1979 247p ISBN 0-87745-093-5 LC 79-22758

**Bowen, Zack** (ed.) Irish Renaissance annual I. *See* Irish Renaissance annual I

**Bowers, Fredson Thayer** (ed.) Lectures on literature. See Nabokov, V. V. Lectures on literature

**Bowers, Fredson Thayer** (ed.) Studies in bibliography v33. *See* Virginia. University. Bibliographical Society. Studies in bibliography v33

**Bradby, David** (ed.) Performance and politics in popular drama. *See* Performance and politics in popular drama

**Braudel, Fernand.** On history; tr. by Sarah Matthews. Univ. of Chicago Press 1980 226p ISBN 0-226-07150-2 LC 80-11201

**Braun, Micheline Tison-** See Tison-Braun, Micheline

**Brazil,** anthropological perspectives; essays in honor of Charles Wagley. Maxine L. Margolis and William E. Carter, editors. Columbia Univ. Press 1979 443p ISBN 0-231-04714-2 LC 79-11843

**Broner, S. M.** (ed.) The lost tradition: mothers and daughters in literature. *See* The Lost tradition: mothers and daughters in literature

**Brown, Janet.** Feminist drama; definition & critical analysis. Scarecrow Press 1979 161p ISBN 0-8108-1267-3 LC 79-22382

**Brown, Stuart C.** (ed.) Philosophers of the Enlightenment. *See* Royal Institute of Philosophy. Philosophers of the Enlightenment

**Brown, Terence** (ed.) The Irish short story. *See* The Irish short story

**Bruchey, Stuart Weems** (ed.) Small business in American life. *See* Small business in American life

**Brustein, Robert Sanford.** Critical moments; reflection on theatre & society, 1973-1979. Random House 1980 232p ISBN 0-394-51093-3 LC 79-3804
Partially analyzed

**Buber, Martin** (ed.) The Jew. *See* The Jew

**Bucknell-Susquehanna Colloquium on Myth in Literature.** The binding of Proteus. *See* The Binding of Proteus

**Budd, Louis J.** (ed.) Toward a new American literary history. *See* Toward a new American literary history

**Bureaucrats,** policy analysts, statesmen: who leads? Ed. by Robert A. Goldwin. Am. Enterprise Inst. for Public Policy Res. 1980 133p ISBN 0-8447-3383-0 LC 80-10616

**Burnyeat, Myles F.** (ed.) Doubt and dogmatism. *See* Doubt and dogmatism

**Buttel, Robert** (ed.) Wallace Stevens. *See* Wallace Stevens

**Cady, Edwin H.** (ed.) Toward a new American literary history. *See* Toward a new American literary history

**Calder, Daniel G.** (ed.) Old English poetry. *See* Old English poetry

**California** Slavic studies v11. Editors: Nicholas V. Riasanovsky, Gleb Struve [and] Thomas Eekman. Univ. of Calif. Press 1980 317p ISBN 0-520-03584-4 LC 61-1041

**Carey, John** (ed.) English Renaissance studies. *See* English Renaissance studies

**Carne-Ross, D. S.** Instaurations; essays in and out of literature: Pindar to Pound. Univ. of Calif. Press 1979 275p ISBN 0-520-03619-0 LC 77-91772

**Carner, Mosco.** Major and minor. Holmes & Meier Pub. 1980 267p ISBN 0-8419-0600-9 LC 79-27481

**Carter, William E.** (ed.) Brazil, anthropological perspectives. *See* Brazil, anthropological perspectives

**Chandler, Alfred Dupont** (ed.) Managerial hierarchies. *See* Managerial hierarchies

**Chaucerian** problems and perspectives; essays presented to Paul .E. Beichner. Ed. by Edward Vasta and Zacharias P. Thundy. Univ. of Notre Dame Press 1979 264p ISBN 0-268-00728-4 LC 78-62971

The **Chesapeake** in the seventeenth century; essays on Anglo-American society. Ed. by Thad W. Tate and David L. Ammerman. Published for the Institute of Early American History and Culture by the Univ. of N.C. Press 1979 310p ISBN 0-8078-1360-5 LC 78-31720

**Children** of Oedipus, and other essays on the imitation of Greek tragedy 1550-1800. See Mueller, M.

**Children's** literature v8; annual of The Modern Language Association Group on Children's Literature and The Children's Literature Association. Yale Univ. Press 1980 212p ISBN 0-300-02452-5 LC 79-66588

The **Children's Literature Association.** Children's literature v8. *See* Children's literature v8

The **Chinese** and the Japanese; essays in political and cultural interactions. Ed. by Akira Iriye. Contributors: Madeleine Chi [and others] Sponsored by the Joint Committee on Contemporary China of the American Council of Learned Societies and the Social Science Research Council. Princeton Univ. Press 1980 368p ISBN 0-691-03126-6 LC 80-378

**Christ, Carol P.** Diving deep and surfacing; women writers on spiritual quest. Beacon Press 1980 159p ISBN 0-8070-6362-2 LC 79-51153

The **cinematic** muse. See Thiher, A.

The **city** as catalyst. Se Festa-McCormick, D.

**Clark, Jon** (ed.) Culture and crisis in Britain in the thirties. *See* Culture and crisis in Britain in the thirties

**Clark, Lorenne M. G.** (ed.) The Sexism of social and political theory: women and reproduction from Plato to Nietzsche. *See* The Sexism of social and political theory: women and reproduction from Plato to Nietzsche

**Class,** culture and social change; a new view of the 1930s. Ed. by Frank Gloversmith; with a foreword by Asa Briggs. Humanities Press 1980 285p ISBN 0-391-01739-X

**Clemoes, Peter** (ed.) Anglo-Saxon England 8. *See* Anglo-Saxon England 8

**Cohen, Arthur Allen** (ed.) The Jew. *See* The Jew

**Cohen, Stephen Frand** (ed.) The Soviet Union since Stalin. *See* The Soviet Union since Stalin

**Cole, Bruce.** Sienese painting; from its origins to the fifteenth century. Harper 1980 243p ISBN 0-06-430901-0 LC 79-3670

**Coleman, William** (ed.) Studies in history of biology, v4. *See* Studies in history of biology, v4

**Collier, David** (ed.) The New authoritarianism in Latin America. *See* The New authoritarianism in Latin America

**Collins, Douglas.** Sartre as biographer. Harvard Univ. Press 1980 220p ISBN 0-674-78950-4 LC 79-25863

**Comedy** and culture. See Henkle, R. B.

The **comedy** of language. See Robinson, F. M.

**Comic** faith. See Polhemus, R. M.

A **common** spring. See Aisenberg, N.

**Communism** in Africa; ed. by David E. Albright. Ind. Univ. Press 1980 277p ISBN 0-253-12814-5 LC 78-13813

The **Computer** age: a twenty-year view. Ed. by Michael L. Dertouzos and Joel Moses. MIT Press 1979 491p (MIT Bicentennial studies) ISBN 0-262-04055-7 LC 79-13070

The **Concept** of style. [Contributors:] Leonard B. Meyer [and others]. Ed. by Berel Lang. Univ. of Pa. Press 1979 246p

The **Condition** of man; proceedings of an International symposium held September 8-10, 1978 in Göteborg to celebrate the 200th anniversary of The Royal Society of Arts and Sciences of Göteborg. Ed. by Paul Hallberg. Humanities Press 1980 228p ISBN 91-85252-20-4
Partially analyzed

**Conference on Southern Jewish History, Richmond, Va. 1976.** "Turn to the South"; essays on Southern Jewry. Ed. by Nathan M. Kaganoff [and] Melvin I. Urofsky. Published for the American Jewish Historical Society by the Univ. Press of Va. 1979 205p ISBN 0-8139-0742-X LC 78-9306

**Conference on the History of Geology, University of New Hampshire, 1976.** See Bicentennial Conference on the History of Geology, University of New Hampshire, 1976

**Conference** on Vico and Contemporary Thought, New York, 1976. Vico and contemporary thought. Ed. by Giorgio Tagliacozzo; Michael Mooney [and] Donald Phillip Verene and for the first time in English translation Vico's essay On the heroic mind. Humanities Press [1980 c1979] [2 pts in 1 v] ISBN 0-391-00911-7 LC 78-15669

**Consciousness** and class experience in nineteenth-century Europe. Ed. by John M. Merriman. Holmes & Meier [1980 c1979] 261p ISBN 0-8419-0444-8 LC 79-16032

**Contemporary** Latin American fiction; Carpentier, Sabato, Onetti, Roa, Donoso, Fuentes, García Márquez, seven essays. Ed. by Salvador Bacarisse. Scottish Academic Press 1980 [distributed by Columbia Univ. Press] 109p ISBN 0-7073-0255-3 "Reprinted from Forum for Modern Language Studies, Volume XV no. 2"

The **Context** of English literature, 1900-1930. Ed. by Michael Bell. Holmes & Meier Pubs. 1980 248p ISBN 0-8419-0423-5 LC 80-7792
Title on spine: 1900-1930

**Convention,** 1500-1750. See Manley, L. G.

**Cook, Albert Spaulding** Myth & language. Ind. Univ. Press 1980 332p ISBN 0-253-14027-7 LC 79-84259

**Coppa, Frank J.** (ed.) Screen and society. *See* Screen and society

**Cott, Nancy F. (ed.)** A heritage of her own. *See* A Heritage of her own

**Counting** our blessings. See Moynihan, D. P.

**Cranach, Mario von** (ed.) Human ethology. *See* Human ethology

**Crawford, Walter Byron** (ed.) Reading Coleridge. *See* Reading Coleridge

**Creative** imitation and Latin literature. Ed. by David West & Tony Woodman. Cambridge [1980 c1979] 255p ISBN 0-521-22668-6 LC 79-1181
Companion volume to the editors' Quality and pleasure in Latin poetry, analyzed in 1975-1979 cumulation

**Creative** man. See Neumann, E.

**Crime** and justice; an annual review of research v 1. Ed. by Norval Morris and Michael Tonry. Univ. of Chicago Press 1979 348p ISBN 0-226-53955-5

**Critical** moments. See Brustein, R. S.

**Critical** psychiatry; the politics of mental health. Ed. by David Ingleby. Pantheon Bks 1980 228p ISBN 0-394-42622-3 LC 79-1886

**Criticism** in the wilderness. See Hartman, G. H.

**Critics** of Henry George; a centenary appraisal of their strictures on Progress and poverty. Ed. by Robert V. Andelson. Fairleigh Dickinson Univ. Press 1979 424p ISBN 0-8386-2350-6 LC 78-066791

**Cronin, John.** The Anglo-Irish novel, v 1; the nineteenth century. Barnes & Noble 1980 157p ISBN 0-389-20014-X

**Cronin, Vincent** (ed.) Essays by divers hands: innovation in contemporary literature, new ser. v40. *See* Royal Society of Literature of the United Kingdom, London. Essays by divers hands: innovation in contemporary literature, new ser. v40

**Crosman, Inge Karalus** (ed.) The reader in the text. *See* The Reader in the text

**Culture** and crisis in Britain in the thirties; ed. by Jon Clark [and others]. Lawrence and Wishart; distributed by Humanities Press [1980 c1979] 279p ISBN 0-85315-491-0

**Dundes, Alan.** Interpreting folklore. Ind. Univ. Press 1980 304p ISBN 0-253-14307-1 LC 79-2969

**Durkheim, Emile.** Emile Durkheim on institutional analysis. Ed. tr. and with an introduction by Mark Traugott. Univ. of Chicago Press 1978 276p (The Heritage of sociology) ISBN 0-226-17330-5 LC 77-25105

**E. M. Forster:** a human exploration; centenary essays. Ed. by G. K. Das and John Beer. N.Y. Univ. Press 1979 314p ISBN 0-8147-1768-3 LC 79-84339

**Economic** issues of the eighties; ed. by Nake M. Kamrany and Richard H. Day. Johns Hopkins Univ. Press 1979 286p ISBN 0-8018-2248-3 LC 79-16772
"Based on a series of lectures presented at the University of Southern California in 1977 and 1978 as a part of the Department of Economics' colloquium 'Contemporary Economic Issues.' " Preface

The **economics** of the imagination. See Heinzelman, K.

The **Economy** in the 1980s: a program for growth and stability. Michael J. Boskin, editor. [Contributors] George F. Break [and others]. Inst. for Contemporary Studies/Transaction Bks. 1980 462p ISBN 0-87855-399-1 LC 80-80647

The **Edwardian** age: conflict and stability, 1900-1914. Ed. by Alan O'Day. Archon Bks. 1979 199p ISBN 0-208-01823-9 LC 79-11809

**Edwards, Philip** (ed.) Shakespeare's styles. See Shakespeare's styles

**Edwards, Philip.** Threshold of a nation; a study in English and Irish drama. Cambridge 1979 264p ISBN 0-521-22463-2 LC 78-72085

**Eekman, Thomas Adam** (ed.) California Slavic studies v11. See California Slavic studies v11

**Eichner, Alfred S.** (ed.) A guide to post-Keynesian economics. See A Guide to post-Keynesian economics

**Eide, Asbjørn** (ed.) Problems of contemporary militarism. See Problems of contemporary militarism

**Electric** delights. See Plomer, W. C. F.

**Elliot, Emory** (ed.) Puritan influences in American literature. See Puritan influences in American literature

**Emergence** of public opinion in the West. See Propaganda and communication in world history v2

**Encountering** the Holocaust: an interdisciplinary survey. Ed. by Byron L. Sherwin and Susan G. Ament. Impact Press 1979 [distributed by Sanhedrin Press] 502p ISBN 0-88482-936-7 LC 79-9126

**Encyclopedia** of American economic history; studies of the principal movements and ideas. 3v Ed. by Glenn Porter. Scribner 1980 ISBN set 0-684-16271-7; v 1 0-684-16510-4; v2 0-684-16511-2; v3 0-684-16512-0 LC 79-4946

**English** Renaissance studies; presented to Dame Helen Gardner in honour of her seventieth birthday [ed. by John Carey] Oxford 1980 304p ISBN 0-19-812093-1 LC 79-40839

**English** romantic irony. See Mellor, A. K.

**Ensor, Allison Rash** (ed.) Tennessee Studies in literature v24. See Tennessee Studies in literature v24

**Erikson, Erik Homburger** (ed.) Themes of work and love in adulthood. See Themes of work and love in adulthood

**Erotic** spirituality. See Perry, T. A.

The forms of autobiography. See Spengemann, W. G.

Forster, Robert (ed.) Medicine and society in France. *See* Medicine and society in France

Forum for Modern Language studies. Contemporary Latin American fiction. *See* Contemporary Latin American fiction

Foster, David William. Studies in the contemporary Spanish-American short story. Univ. of Mo. Press 1979 126p ISBN 0-8262-0279-9 LC 79-1558

Fox-Lockert, Lucía. Women novelists in Spain and Spanish America. Scarecrow 1979 347p ISBN 0-8108-1270-3 LC 79-23727

Freedman, Ralph (ed.) Virginia Woolf. *See* Virginia Woolf

From behind the veil. See Stepto, R. B.

Frontain, Raymond-Jean (ed.) The David myth in Western literature. See The David myth in Western literature

Fry, Paul H. The poet's calling in the English ode. Yale Univ. Press 1980 328p ISBN 0-300-02400-2 LC 79-20554

Fuhrman, Ellsworth R. The sociology of knowledge in America, 1883-1915. Univ. Press of Va. 1980 268p ISBN 0-8139-0785-3 LC 79-14829

Gardner, Dame Helen Louise. See entry under title: English Renaissance studies

Garrett, Peter K. The Victorian multiplot novel; studies in dialogical form. Yale Univ. Press 1980 227p ISBN 0-300-02403-7 LC 79-18658

Gasché, Rodolphe (ed.) Glyph 6. *See* Glyph 6

Gaukroger, Stephen (ed.) Descartes. *See* Descartes

Gelfand, Lawrence Emerson (ed.) Herbert Hoover. *See* Herbert Hoover

Gellner, Ernest (ed.) Soviet and Western anthropology. *See* Soviet and Western anthropology

Generations. Ed. by Stephen R. Graubard. Essays by Noel Annan [and others]. Norton [1980 c1979] 214p ISBN 0-393-01268-9 LC 79-21410

The Genius of Shaw; a symposium. Ed. by Michael Holroyd. Holt 1979 238p ISBN 0-03-043541-2 LC 78-31306

Genno, Charles N. (ed.) The First World War in German narrative prose. *See* The First World War in German narrative prose

The German idea. See Ashton, R. D.

Gloversmith, Frank (ed.) Class, culture and social change. *See* Class, culture and social change

Glyph 6; textual studies. Editors: Rodolphe Gasché, Carol Jacobs, and Henry Sussman. Johns Hopkins Univ. Press 1979 218p ISBN 0-8018-2296-3 LC 76-47370

Glyph 7; textual studies. The Strasbourg colloquium: Genre, a collection of papers. Samuel Weber, editor. Johns Hopkins Univ. Press 1980 237p ISBN 0-8018-2365-X LC 76-47370 Partially analyzed
"The papers presented in this volume are among those presented to an International Colloquium on 'Genre', held at the University of Strasbourg in July, 1979." Preface

Goetz-Stankiewicz Marketa. The silenced theatre: Czech playwrights without a stage. Univ. of Toronto Press 1979 319p ISBN 0-8020-5426-9 LC 79-13423

Goldwin, Robert Allen (ed.) Bureaucrats, policy analysts, statesmen: who leads? *See* Bureaucrats, policy analysts, statesmen: who leads?

Goldwin, Robert Allen (ed.) Political parties in the eighties. *See* Political parties in the eighties

Gombrich, Sir Ernest Hans Josef. Ideals and idols; essays on values in history and in art. Phaidon [distributed by Dutton] 1980 c1979 224p ISBN 0-7148-2009-1 LC 79-89284

Graubard, Stephen R. (ed.) Generations. *See* Generations

Gregor, Ian (ed.) Reading the Victorian novel: detail into form. *See* Reading the Victorian novel: detail into form

Griggs, Earl Leslie. See entry under title: Reading Coleridge

Grundlehner, Philip. The lyrical bridge; essays from Hölderlin to Benn. Fairleigh Dickinson Univ. Press 1979 177p ISBN 0-8386-1792-1 LC 76-46765

A Guide to post-Keynesian economics. Ed. by Alfred S. Eichner with a foreword by Joan Robinson. Sharpe [distributed by Pantheon Bks] 1979 202p ISBN 0-394-50758-4 LC 79-1971

A Guide to Welsh literature. Ed. by A. O. H. Jarman and Gwilym Rees Hughes. Davies, C. [distributed by Humanities Press] 1976-1979 2v ISBN v 1 0-7154-0124-6; v2 0-7154-0457-1

Hagstrum, Jean H. Sex and sensibility; ideal and erotic love from Milton to Mozart. Univ. of Chicago Press 1980 350p ISBN 0-226-31289-5 LC 79-20657

Hallberg, Paul (ed.) The condition of man. *See* The Condition of man

Harari, Josué V. (ed.) Textual strategies. *See* Textual strategies

Harbison, Robert. Deliberate regression. Knopf 1980 264p ISBN 0-394-50799-1 LC 79-3466

Hardin, Richard Francis (ed.) Survivals of pastoral. *See* Survivals of pastoral

Hardy, Henry (ed.) Against the current. *See* Berlin, Sir I. Against the current

Harrison, Ross (ed.) Rational action. *See* Rational action

Hartman, Geoffrey H. Criticism in the wilderness; the study of literature today. Yale Univ. Press 1980 323p ISBN 0-300-02085-6 LC 80-13491

Harvard Guide to contemporary American-writing. Daniel Hoffman, editor; with essays by Leo Braudy [and others]. The Belknap Press of Harvard Univ. Press 1979 618p ISBN 0-674-37535-1 LC 79-10930

Harvard Studies in classical philology, v83. [Ed. by Albert Henrichs] Harvard Univ. Press 1979 409p ISBN 0-674-37930-6 LC 44-32100
Partially analyzed

Hatto, Arthur Thomas Essays on medieval German and other poetry. Cambridge 1980 374p (Anglica Germanica ser 2) ISBN 0-521-22148-X LC 78-54325
Partially analyzed

Heffernan, Thomas J. A. (ed.) Tennessee Studies in literature v24. *See* Tennessee Studies in literature v24

Heinzelman, Kurt. The economics of the imagination. Univ. of Mass. Press 1979 326p ISBN 0-87023-274-6 LC 79-4019

Hench, John B. (ed.) The press & the American Revolution. *See* The Press & the American Revolution

Henkle, Roger B. Comedy and culture; England; 1820-1900. Princeton Univ. Press 1980 373p ISBN 0-691-06428-8 LC 79-3214

Henrichs, Albert (ed.) Harvard Studies in classical philology, v83. *See* Harvard Studies in classical philology, v83

Henry Francis du Pont Winterthur Museum. Perspectives on American folk art. *See* Perspectives on American folk art

Herbert Hoover; the Great War and its aftermath, 1914-23. Ed. with introduction by Lawrence E. Gelfand. Univ. of Iowa Press 1979 242p (Herbert Hoover Centennial seminars) ISBN 0-87745-095-1 LC 79-10139
"Papers presented at the Herbert Hoover Centennial Seminars"

A Heritage of her own; toward a new social history of American women. Ed. with an introduction, by Nancy F. Cott and Elizabeth H. Pleck. Simon & Schuster 1979 608p ISBN 0-671-25068-X LC 79-19565
"A Touchstone Book"

The heroine's text. See Miller, N. K.

History, religion, and spiritual democracy; essays in honor of Joseph L. Blau. Maurice Wohlgelernter, editor; James A. Martin, Jr. [and others], co-editors. Columbia Univ. Press 1980 lxxiv, 375p ISBN 0-231-04624-3 LC 79-23234

History of Science Society. The sciences in the American context: new perspectives. See The Sciences in the American context: new perspectives

Hoffman, Daniel (ed.) Harvard Guide to contemporary American writing. See Harvard Guide to contemporary American writing

Holloway, John. Narrative and structure: exploratory essays. Cambridge 1979 156p ISBN 0-521-22574-4 LC 78-20826

Holroyd, Michael (ed.) The genius of Shaw. See The Genius of Shaw

Holzner, Burkart (ed.) Identity and authority. See Identity and authority

Home as found. See Sundquist, E. J.

Hook, Sidney. Philosophy and public policy. Southern Ill. Univ. Press 1980 288p ISBN 0-8093-0937-8 LC 79-16825

Horwitz, Robert H. (ed.) The moral foundations of the American Republic. See The Moral foundations of the American Republic

Hosking, Geoffrey. Beyond Socialist realism; Soviet fiction since Ivan Denisovich. Holmes & Meier 1980 260p ISBN 0-8419-0484-7 LC 78-31891

Hourani, Albert Habib. Europe and the Middle East. Univ. of Calif. Press 1980 226p ISBN 0-520-03742-1 LC 78-059452

Howard, Richard. Alone with America; essays on the art of poetry in the United States since 1950. Enl. ed. Atheneum Pubs. 1980 687p ISBN 0-689-11000-6 LC 79-64718
1st edition analyzed in 1970-1974 cummulation

Hughes, Glyn Tegai. Romantic German literature. Holmes & Meier 1979 183p ISBN 0-8419-0521-5 LC 79-13994

Hughes, Gwilym Rees (ed.) A guide to Welsh literature. See A Guide to Welsh literature

Human ethology; claims and limits of a new discipline. Contributions to the colloquium sponsored by the Werner-Reimers-Stiftung. Ed. by M. von Cranach [and others]. Cambridge [1980 c1979] 764p ISBN 0-521-22320-2 LC 78-27330

Humanist ethics; dialogue on basics. Ed. by Morris B. Storer. Prometheus Bks. 1980 303p ISBN 0-87975-117-7 LC 80-7456

Hunter, George Kirkpatrick (ed.) Shakespeare's styles. See Shakespeares' styles

Ideals and idols. See Gombrich, Sir E. H. J.

The Identification and analysis of Chicano literature. Ed. by Francisco Jiménez. Bilingual Press 1979 411p (Studies in the language and literature of United States Hispanos) ISBN 0-916950-12-3 LC 78-67287
Partially analyzed

**Identity** and authority; explorations in the theory of society. Ed. by Roland Robertson and Burkart Holzner. St. Martins 1979 318p ISBN 0-312-40448-4 LC 79-5439
An outgrowth of the Pittsburgh Conference on Authority and Identity, 1975

**Illinois. University at Urbana-Champaign. Graduate School of Library Science.** Research about nineteenth-century children and books. *See* Research about nineteenth-century children and books

The **impossible** observer. See Uphaus, R. W.

The **inadvertent** epic. Se Fiedler, L. A.

**Ingleby, David** (ed.) Critical psychiatry. *See* Critical psychiatry

**Instaurations.** See Carne-Ross, D. S.

The **Interpretation** of medieval lyric poetry. Ed. by W. T. H. Jackson. Columbia Univ. Press 1980 239p ISBN 0-231-04490-9 LC 79-12378

The **Interpretation** of ordinary landscapes; geographical essays. D. W. Meinig, editor. [Contributors]: J. B. Jackson [and others]. Oxford 1979 255p ISBN 0-19-502536-9 LC 78-23182

**Interpreting** folklore. See Dundes, A.

**Irish** poetry from Moore to Yeats. See Welch, R.

**Irish** Renaissance annual I; ed. by Zack Bowen. Univ. of Del. Press 1980 190p ISSN 0-193-9777

The **Irish** short story; Patrick Rafroidi and Terence Brown, editors. [Contributors]: Declan Kiberd [and others]. Humanities Press 1979 308p ISBN 0-391-01703-9

**Iriye, Akira** (ed.) The Chinese and the Japanese. *See* The Chinese and the Japanese

**Irwin, John T.** American hieroglyphics; the symbol of the Egyptian hieroglyphics in the American Renaissance. Yale Univ. Press 1980 371p ISBN 0-300-02471-1 LC 80-130

**Iyengar, K. R. Srinivasa.** See entry under title: Aspects of Indian writing in English


**Jackson, Richard L.** Black writers in Latin America. Univ. of N.Mex. Press 1979 224p ISBN 0-8263-0501-6 LC 78-21431

**Jackson, W. T. H.** (ed.) The interpretation of medieval lyric poetry. *See* The Interpretation of medieval lyric poetry

**Jacobs, Carol** (ed.) Glyph 6. *See* Glyph 6

**Jacobs, Eva** (ed.) Woman and society in eighteenth-century France. *See* Woman and society in eighteenth-century France

**James, Louis** (ed.) Performance and politics in popular drama. *See* Performance and politics in popular drama

The **Japanese** novel of the Meiji period and the ideal of individualism. See Walker, J. A.

**Jarman, Alfred Owen Hughes** (ed.) A guide to Welsh literature. *See* A Guide to Welsh literature

**Jeffares, Alexander Norman** (ed.) Yeats, Sligo and Ireland. *See* Yeats, Sligo and Ireland

**Jelinek, Estelle Cohen** (ed.) Women's autobiography. *See* Women's autobiography

The **Jew;** essays from Martin Buber's journal Der Jude, 1916-1928, selected, ed. and introduced by Arthur A. Cohen. Tr. from the German by Joachim Neugroschel. Univ. of Ala. Press 1980 305p (Judaic Studies ser) ISBN 0-8173-6908-2 LC 79-10610

The **Jewish** world; history and culture of the Jewish people. Ed. by Elie Kedourie. Texts by Elie Kedourie [and others]. Abrams 1979 328p ISBN 0-8109-1154-X LC 78-31363

Jiménez, Francisco (ed.) The identification and analysis of Chicano literature. *See* The Identification and analysis of Chicano literature

Johnston, Brian. To the third empire; Ibsen's early drama. Univ. of Minn. Press 1980 328p (The Nordic ser. **v4**) ISBN 0-8166-0902-0 LC 79-28329

Jones, Eldred Durosimi (ed.) African literature today no. 10: Retrospect & prospect. See African literature today no. 10: Retrospect & prospect

Der Jude (Periodical) The Jew. *See* The Jew

Justice. See Symposium on Theories of Justice in and for the Second Half of the Twentieth Century, Sydney, 1977

Kael, Pauline. When the lights go down. Holt 1980 592p ISBN 0-03-042511-5 LC 79-19067
Partially analyzed

Kaganoff, Nathan M. (ed.) "Turn to the South." *See* Conference on Southern Jewish History, Richmond, Va. 1976. "Turn to the South"

Kahn, Coppelia (ed.) Representing Shakespeare. *See* Representing Shakespeare

Kamenka, Eugene (ed.) Justice. *See* Symposium on Theories of Justice in and for the Second Half of the Twentieth Century Sydney, 1977. Justice

Kammen, Michael G. (ed.) The past before us. *See* The Past before us

Kamrany, Nake M. (ed.) Economic issues of the eighties. *See* Economic issues of the eighties

Karp, Ivan C. (ed.) Explorations in African systems of thought. *See* Explorations in African systems of thought

Kauffmann, Stanley. Before my eyes; film criticism and comment. Harper 1980 464p ISBN 0-06-012298-6 LC 78-20171

Kedourie, Elie (ed.) The Jewish world. *See* The Jewish world

Keith, William J. The poetry of nature; rural perspectives in poetry from Wordsworth to the present. Univ. of Toronto Press 1980 219p ISBN 0-8020-5494-3 LC 79-094903-2

Kellman, Steven G. The self-begetting novel. Columbia Univ. Press 1980 161p ISBN 0-231-04782-7 LC 79-15700

King, Bruce Alvin (ed.) West Indian literature. *See* West Indian literature

King, Richard H. A Southern Renaissance; the cultural awakening of the American South, 1930-1955. Oxford 1980 350p ISBN 0-19-502664-0 LC 79-9470

Knott, John Ray. The sword of the spirit; Puritan responses to the Bible by John R. Knott, Jr. Univ. of Chicago Press 1980 194p ISBN 0-226-44848-7 LC 79-23424

Knox, Bernard MacGregor Walker. Word and action; essays on the ancient theater. Johns Hopkins Univ. Press 1979 378p ISBN 0-8018-2198-3 LC 79-11277

Kontos, Alkis (ed.) Powers, possessions and freedom. *See* Powers, possessions and freedom

Kratzmann, Gregory. Anglo-Scottish literary relations, 1430-1550. Cambridge 1980 282p ISBN 0-521-22665-1 LC 78-74537

Krieger, Murray. Poetic presence and illusion; essays in critical history and theory. Johns Hopkins Univ. Press 1979 326p ISBN 0-8018-2199-1 LC 79-14598

Kristeller, Paul Oskar. Renaissance thought and its sources. Ed. by Michael Mooney. Columbia Univ. Press 1979 347p ISBN 0-231-04512-3 LC 79-15521

Kurzweil, Edith. The age of structuralism; Lévi-Strauss to Foucault. Columbia Univ. Press 256p ISBN 0-231-04920-X LC 79-28647

McCormick, Diana Festa- See Festa-McCormick, Diana

McCune, Marjorie Wolfe (ed.) The binding of Proteus. See The Binding of Proteus

Macdonald, G. F. (ed.) Perception and identity. See Perception and identity

McGhee, Richard D. Marriage, duty & desire in Victorian poetry and drama. Regents Press of Kansas 1980 318p ISBN 0-7006-0203-8 LC 80-11962

Macpherson, Crawford Brough. See entry under title: Powers, possessions and freedom

Major and minor. See Carner, M.

Makers of an American immigrant legacy; essays in honor of Kenneth O. Bjork. Ed. by Odd S. Lovoll. Norwegian-American Historical Assoc. 1980 223p
Partially analyzed

Managerial hierarchies; comparative perspectives on the rise of modern industrial enterprise. Ed. by Alfred D. Chandler, Jr., and Herman Daems. Harvard Univ. Press 1980 237p (Harvard Studies in business history 32) ISBN 0-674-54740-3 LC 79-20396

Manley, Lawrence Gordon. Convention, 1500-1750. Harvard Univ. Press 1980 355p ISBN 0-674-17015-6 LC 79-27773

The marble in the water. See Rees, D.

Marchand, James W. (ed.) The quest for the new science. See The Quest for the new science

Margolis, Maxine L. (ed.) Brazil, anthropological perspectives. See Brazil, anthropological perspectives

Marriage, duty & desire in Victorian poetry and drama. See McGhee, R. D.

Marsh, David. The quattrocento dialogue; classical tradition and humanist innovation. Harvard Univ. Press 1980 141p (Harvard Studies in contemporary literature, 35) ISBN 0-674-74115-3 LC 79-15625

Martin, David (ed.) Sociology and theology: alliance and conflict. See Sociology and theology: alliance and conflict

Martin Heidegger and the question of literature; toward a postmodern literary hermeneutics. Ed. by William V. Spanos. Ind. Univ. Press [1980 c1979] 327p (Studies in phenomenology and existential philosophy) ISBN 0-253-17575-5 LC 79-84261
Partially analyzed

Marxism, ideology & literature. See Slaughter, C.

Mathews, Walter M. (ed.) Monster or messiah? See Monster or messiah?

Matters of life and death. [Contributors] Tom L. Beauchamp [and others]. Ed. by Tom Regan. Temple Univ. Press 1980 343p ISBN 0-87722-181-2 LC 79-3421

Maurer, Warren R. (ed.) Rilke: the alchemy of alienation. See Rilke: the alchemy of alienation

Mayo, David J. (ed.) Suicide: the philosophical issues. See Suicide: the philosophical issues

Maziarz, Edward Anthony (ed.) Value and values in evolution. See Value and values in evolution

Medicine and society in France; selections from the Annales, economies, sociétés, civilisations v6. Ed. by Robert Forster and Orest Ranum; tr. by Elborg Forster and Patricia M. Ranum. Johns Hopkins Univ. Press 1980 176p ISBN 0-8018-2305-6 LC 79-16851

Meinig, Donald William (ed.) The interpretation of ordinary landscapes. See The Interpretation of ordinary landscapes

**Mellor, Anne Kostelanetz.** English romantic irony. Harvard Univ. Press 1980 219p ISBN 0-674-25690-5 LC 80-10687

**Merkl, Peter H.** (ed.) Western European party systems. *See* Western European party systems

**Merriman, John M.** (ed.) Consciousness and class experience in nineteenth-century Europe. *See* Consciousness and class experience in nineteenth-century Europe

**Metaphors of evil.** See Bosmajian, H.

**Michaels, Leonard** (ed.) The state of the language. *See* The State of the language

**Mikellides, Byron** (ed.) Architecture for people. *See* Architecture for people

**Miller, Gabriel.** Screening the novel; rediscovered American fiction in film. With photographs. Ungar 1980 208p (Ungar Film library) ISBN 0-8044-2622-8 LC 79-48071

**Miller, Nancy K.** The heroine's text; readings in the French and English novel, 1722-1782. Columbia Univ Press 1980 185p ISBN 0-231-04910-2 LC 79-28473

**Miller, Perry.** The responsibility of mind in a civilization of machines; essays by Perry Miller. Ed. by John Crowell and Stanford J. Searl, Jr. Univ. of Mass. Press 1979 213p ISBN 0-87023-281-9 LC 79-4699

**Mills, John Orme** (ed.) Sociology and theology: alliance and conflict. See Sociology and theology: alliance and conflict

**Modern** Austrian writing; literature and society after 1945. Ed. by Alan Best and Hans Wolfschütz. Barnes & Noble 1980 307p ISBN 0-389-20038-7

**Modern** drama and German classicism. See Bennett, B.

**Modern** Hebrew drama. See Abramson, G.

**The Modern Language Association. Group on Children's Literature.** Children's literature v8. *See* Children's literature v8

**Molesworth, Charles.** The fierce embrace; a study of contemporary American poetry. Univ. of Mo. Press 1979 214p ISBN 0-8262-0278-0 LC 79-1561

**Monster** or messiah? The computer's impact on society. Editor: Walter M. Mathews. Univ. Press of Miss. 1980 222p ISBN 0-87805-108-2 LC 79-16737

**Montgomery, Robert Lawrence.** The reader's eye; studies in didactic literary theory from Dante to Tasso. Univ. of Calif. Press 1979 235p ISBN 0-520-03700-6 LC 78-57313

**Mooney, Michael** (ed.) Renaissance thought and its sources. See Kristeller, P. O. Renaissance thought and its sources

**Mooney, Michael** (ed.) Vico and contemporary thought. *See* Conference on Vico and Contemporary Thought, New York, 1976. Vico and contemporary thought

**Moorey, Peter Roger Stuart** (ed.) The origins of civilization. *See* The Origins of civilization

**The Moral** foundations of the American Republic. 2d ed. Ed. by Robert H. Horwitz. Contributors: Benjamin R. Barber [and others]. Univ. Press of Va. 1979 275p ISBN 0-8139-0853-1 LC 79-20387
First edition analyzed in 1975-1979 cummulation
This edition analyzed for new material only (one essay)

**Morowitz, Harold J.** The wine of life, and other essays on societies, energy & living things. St Martins 1979 265p ISBN 0-312-88227-0 LC 79-16404

**Morris, Norval** (ed.) Crime and justice v 1. *See* Crime and justice v 1

**Moses, Joel** (ed.) The computer age: a twenty-year view. *See* The Computer age: a twenty-year view

**Moynihan, Daniel Patrick.** Counting our blessings; reflections on the future of America. Little 1980 348p ISBN 0-316-58702-8 LC 80-13371
"An Atlantic monthly book".

**Mueller, Martin.** Children of Oedipus, and other essays on the imitation of Greek tragedy, 1550-1800. Univ. of Toronto Press 1980 282p ISBN 0-8020-5478-1 LC 79-26018

**Muir, Kenneth.** See entry under title: Shakespeare's styles

**Muir, Kenneth** (ed.) Shakespeare survey 32. *See* Shakespeare survey 32

**Murrin, Michael.** The allegorical epic; essays in its rise and decline. Univ. of Chicago Press 1980 275p ISBN 0-226-55402-3 LC 79-20832

**Myth** & language. See Cook, A. S.

**Nabokov, Vladimir Vladimirovich.** Lectures on literature. Ed by Fredson Bowers; introduction by John Updike. Harcourt 1980 xxvii, 385p ISBN 0-15-149597-1 LC 79-3690

**Naik, M. K.** (ed.) Aspects of Indian writing in English. *See* Aspects of Indian writing in English

**Naipaul, Vidiadhar Surajprasad.** The return of Eva Perón; with The killings in Trinidad. Knopf 1980 227p ISBN 0-394-50968-4 LC 79-22148

**Narrative** and structure: exploratory essays. See Holloway, J.

**National** security in the 1980s: from weakness to strength; W. Scott Thompson, editor. [Contributors] Kenneth L. Adelman [and others]. Inst. for Contemporary Studies/Transaction Bks. 1980 524p ISBN 0-87855-412-2 LC 80-80648

**Neumann, Erich.** Creative man; five essays. Tr. from the German by Eugene Rolfe. Princeton Univ. Press [1980 c1979] 264p (Bollingen ser. 61; Essays of Erich Neumann 2) ISBN 0-691-09944-8 LC 79-16711
"Published in joint sponsorship with the C. G. Jung Institute of San Francisco"
Volume 1, Art and the creative unconscious, analyzed in 1955-1959 cumulation

The **New** authoritarianism in Latin America. David Collier, editor. Contributors; Fernando Henrique Cardoso [and others]. Princeton Univ. Press [1980 c1979] 456p ISBN 0-691-07616-2 LC 79-83982
"Sponsored by the Joint Committee on Latin American studies of the Social Science Research Council and the American Council of Learned Societies"

**New** critical essays. See Barthes, R.

**New Hampshire Bicentennial Conference on the History of Geology, University of New Hampshire, 1976.** Two hundred years of geology in America; proceedings. Cecil J. Schneer, editor. Published for the University of New Hampshire by the Univ. Press of New England 1979 385p ISBN 0-87451-160-7 LC 78-63149
Partially analyzed

**New York (City) Metropolitan Museum of Art.** Age of spirituality. *See* Age of spirituality

**Newspapers** and democracy; international essays on a changing medium. Ed. by Anthony Smith. MIT Press 1980 368p ISBN 0-262-19184-9 LC 80-15665

**Niles, John DeWitt** (ed.) Old English literature in context. *See* Old English literature in context

**Obelkevich, James** (ed.) Religion and the people, 800-1700. *See* Religion and the people, 800-1700

**O'Day, Alan** (ed.) The Edwardian age: conflict and stability, 1900-1914. *See* The Edwardian age: conflict and stability, 1900-1914

**Philosophical** perspectives in artificial intelligence; ed. by Martin Ringle. Humanities Press 1979 244p ISBN 0-391-00919-2 LC 78-27899

**Philosophy** and public policy. See Hook, S.

The **Philosophy** of sex; contemporary readings. Ed. by Alan Soble. Rowman & Littlefield 1980 412p ISBN 0-8476-6292-6 LC 80-15302

**Piatelli-Palmarini, Massimo** (ed.) Language and learning. *See* Language and learning

**Pickering, Frederick Pickering.** ,Essays on medieval German literature and iconography. Cambridge 1980 228p (Anglica Germanica ser. 2) ISBN 0-521-22627-9 LC 78-73815

**Pickering, W. S. F.** (ed.) Sociology and theology: alliance and conflict. See Sociology and theology: alliance and conflict

**Pleck, Elizabeth H** .(ed.) A heritage of her own. *See* A Heritage of her own

**Plomer, William Charles Franklyn.** Electric delights; selected & introduced by Rupert Hart-Davis. Godine 1978 278p ISBN 0-87923-248-X LC 78-57682
Partially analyzed

**Pluralizing** world in formation. See Propaganda and communication in world history v3

**Pocock, James Greville Agard** (ed.) Three British revolutions: 1641, 1688, 1776. *See* Three British revolutions: 1641, 1688, 1776

**Poetic creation.** See Fehrman, C. A. D.

**Poetic** presence and illusion. See Krieger, M.

The **poetry** of nature. See Keith, W. J.

The **poet's** calling in the English ode. See Fry, P. H.

**Pole, Jack Richon.** Paths to the American past. Oxford 1979 348p ISBN 0-19-502579-2 LC 79-830

**Polhemus, Robert M.** Comic faith; the great tradition from Austen to Joyce. Univ. of Chicago Press 1980 398p ISBN 0-226-67320-0 LC 79-24856

**Political** parties in the eighties. Ed. by Robert A. Goldwin. Am. Enterprise Inst. for Public Policy Res./Kenyon College 1980 152p ISBN 0-8447-3382-2 LC 80-14977

**Political** theory and political education; ed. by Melvin Richter. Princeton Univ. Press 1980 203p ISBN 0-691-07612-X LC 79-17833

**Pope, Randolph D.** (ed.) The analysis of literary texts. *See* The Analysis of literary texts

**Porter, Glenn** (ed.) Encyclopedia of American economic history. *See* Encyclopedia of American economic history

**Powers,** possessions and freedom; essays in honour of C. B. Macpherson. Ed. by Alkis Kontos. Univ. of Toronto Press 1979 178p ISBN 0-8020-5474-9

The **Press** & the American Revolution. Ed. by Bernard Bailyn and John B. Hench. With a foreword by Marcus A. McCorison and an afterword by James Russell Wiggins. Am. Antiquarian Soc. 1980 383p ISBN 0-912296-18-6 LC 79-89434

The **Prism** of sex; essays in the sociology of knowledge. Ed. by Julia A. Sherman and Evelyn Torton Beck. Univ. of Wis. Press 1979 286p ISBN 0-299-08010-2 LC 79-3969

**Pritchett, Victor Sawdon.** The tale bearers; literary essays. Random House 1980 223p ISBN 0-394-50486-0 LC 79-5559
Companion volume to The myth makers, analyzed in 1975-1979 cumulation

The **reader's** eye. See Montgomery, R. L.

**Reading** Coleridge; approaches and applications. Ed. by Walter B. Crawford. Cornell Univ. Press 1979 288p ISBN 0-8014-1219-6 LC 79-7616
Festschrift in memory of Earl Leslie Griggs

**Reading** the Victorian novel: detail into form. Ed. by Ian Gregor. Barnes & Noble 1980 314p ISBN 0-06-492542-0

**Redmond, James** (ed.) Drama and mimesis. *See* Drama and mimesis

**Rees, David.** The marble in the water; essays on contemporary writers of fiction for children and young adults. Horn Bk. 1980 211p ISBN 0-87675-280-6 LC 80-16623

**Regan, Tom** (ed.) Matters of life and death. *See* Matters of life and death

**Reingold, Nathan** (ed.) The sciences in the American context: new perspectives. *See* The Sciences in the American context: new perspectives

**Reiss, Timothy J.** Tragedy and truth; studies in the development of a Renaissance and neoclassical discourse. Yale Univ. Press 1980 334p ISBN 0-300-02461-4 LC 80-10413

**Religion** and the people, 800-1700. Ed. by James Obelkevich. Univ. of N.C. Press 1979 336p ISBN 0-8078-1332-X LC 78-7847
"Published under the auspices of the Shelby Cullom Davis Center for Historical Studies, Princeton University"

**Renaissance** thought and its sources. See Kristeller, P. O.

**Representing** Shakespeare: new psychoanalytic essays. Ed. by Murray M. Schwartz and Coppelia Kahn. Johns Hopkins Univ. Press 1980 269p ISBN 0-8018-2302-1 LC 79-3682

**Research** about nineteenth-century children and books. Ed. by Selma K. Richardson. Univ. of Ill. at Urbana-Champaign. Graduate School of Lib. Science 1980 142p (University of Illinois. Graduate School of Library Science Monographs: no. 17) ISBN 0-87845-055-6 LC 80-19165 pa

The **resonance** of dust. See Alexander, E.

The **responsibility** of mind in a civilization of machines. See Miller, P.

The **return** of Eva Perón. See Naipaul, V. S.

**Revolution** as tragedy. See Farrell, J.

**Riasanovsky, Nicholas Valentine** (ed.) California Slavic studies v11. *See* California Slavic studies v11

**Richardson, Selma K.** (ed.) Research about nineteenth-century children and books. *See* Research about nineteenth-century children and books

**Richter, Melvin** (ed.) Political theory and political education. *See* Political theory and political education

**Ricks, Christopher** (ed.) The state of the language. *See* The State of the language

**Rieber, Robert W.** (ed.) Psychology of language and thought. *See* Psychology of language and thought

**Rilke:** the alchemy of alienation. Ed. by Frank Baron, Ernst S. Dick, and Warren R. Maurer. Regents Press of Kan. 1980 268p ISBN 0-7006-0198-8 LC 79-19759

**Ringle, Martin** (ed.) Philosophical perspectives in artificial intelligence. *See* Philosophical perspectives in artificial intelligence

**Robbins, John Albert** (ed.) American literary scholarship, 1978. *See* American literary scholarship, 1978

**Seasoned** authors for a new season: the search for standards in popular writing. [Ed. by] Louis Filler. Bowling Green Univ. Pop. Press 1980 193p  ISBN 0-87972-143-X LC 79-90128
"A question of quality #2." Volume 1 entitled: A question of quality: popularity and value in modern creative writing, analyzed in 1975-1979 cumulation under Louis Filler

**Sebeok, Jean Umiker-** See Umiker-Sebeok, Jean

**Sebeok, Thomas Albert** (ed.) Speaking of apes. *See* Speaking of apes

**Seidel, Michael A.** Satiric inheritance, Rabelais to Sterne. Princeton Univ. Press 1979 283p  ISBN 0-691-06408-3 LC 79-84016

**Selected** essays. See Dent, E. J.

**Selected** papers v3: Late antique, early Christian and mediaeval art. See Schapiro, M.

The **self**-begetting novel. See Kellman, S. G.

**Sewall, Richard Benson.** The vision of tragedy; new edition, enlarged. Yale Univ. Press 1980 209p  ISBN 0-300-02485-1 LC 79-24203
Analyzed in 1960-1964 cumulation. This edition analyzed for new material only

**Sex** and sensibility. See Hagstrum, J. H.

The **Sexism** of social and political theory: women and reproduction from Plato to Nietzsche. Ed. by Lorenne M. G. Clark and Lynda Lange. Univ. of Toronto Press 1979 141p ISBN 0-8020-5459-5 LC 79-17862

**Shakespeare** survey 32; an annual survey of Shakespearian study and production. Ed. by Kenneth Muir. Cambridge 1979 256p ISBN 0-521-22753-4 LC 49-1639

**Shakespeare's** styles; essays in honour of Kenneth Muir. Ed. by Philip Edwards; Inga-Stina Ewbank, and George Kirkpatrick Hunter. Cambridge 1980 247p ISBN 0-521-22764-X LC 79-51226

**Sharlet, Robert** (ed.) The Soviet Union since Stalin. *See* The Soviet Union since Stalin

**Sharratt, Bernard** (ed.) Performance and politics in popular drama. *See* Performance and politics in popular drama

**Sherman, Julia Ann** (ed.) The prism of sex. *See* The Prism of sex

**Sherwin, Byron L.** (ed.) Encountering the Holocaust: an interdisciplinary survey. *See* Encountering the Holocaust: an interdisciplinary survey

**Shneidman, N. N.** Soviet literature in the 1970s: artistic diversity and ideological conformity. Univ. of Toronto Press 1979 128p  ISBN 0-8020-5463-3 LC 79-14942

**Sienese** painting. See Cole, B.

The **silenced** theatre: Czech playwrights without a stage. See Goetz-Stankiewicz, M.

**Slaughter, Cliff.** Marxism, ideology & literature. Humanities Press 1980 228p (Critical social studies) ISBN 0-391-01190-1 LC 79-16392

**Small** business in American life; ed. by Stuart W. Bruchey. Columbia Univ. Press 1980 391p ISBN 0-231-04872-6 LC 80-10994

**Smelser, Neil** (ed.) Themes of work and love in adulthood. *See* Themes of work and love in adulthood

**Smith, Anthony** (ed.) Newspapers and democracy. *See* Newspapers and democracy

**Smith, Joseph H.** (ed.) The Literary Freud: mechanisms of defense and the poetic will. *See* The Literary Freud: mechanisms of defense and the poetic will

Smith, Miranda Weston- See Weston-Smith, Miranda

Smith, Nathaniel B. (ed.) The expansion and transformations of courtly literature. *See* The Expansion and transformations of courtly literature

Snow, Joseph T. (ed.) The expansion and transformations of courtly literature. *See* The Expansion and transformations of courtly literature

Soble, Alan (ed.) The philosophy of sex. *See* The Philosophy of sex

Sociology and theology: alliance and conflict. Ed. by David Martin; John Orme Mills [and] W. S. F. Pickering; with an introduction by John Orme Mills. St Martins 1980 204p ISBN 0-312-74007-7 LC 79-27012

The sociology of knowledge in America, 1883-1915. See Fuhrman, E. R.

Solzhenitsyn at Harvard; the address, twelve early response, and six later reflections. Ed. by Ronald Berman. [Contributors:] Ronald Berman [and others]. Ethics and Public Policy Center 1980 143p ISBN 0-89633-034-6 LC 79-26033 Partially analyzed

A sounding of storytellers. See Townsend, J. R.

A Southern Renaissance. See King, R. H.

Soviet and Western anthropology. Ed. by Ernest Gellner; with an introduction by Meyer Fortes. Columbia Univ. Press 1980 285p ISBN 0-231-05120-4 LC 80-11676

Soviet literature in the 1970s: artistic diversity and ideological conformity. See Shneidman, N. N.

The Soviet Union since Stalin: ed. by Stephen F. Cohen; Alexander Rabinowitch and Robert Sharlet. Ind. Univ. Press 1980 342p ISBN 0-253-32272-3 LC 79-3092

Spanos, William V. (ed.) Martin Heidegger and the question of literature. *See* Martin Heidegger and the question of literature

Speaking of apes; a critical anthology of two-way communication with man. Ed. by Thomas A. Sebeok and Jean Umiker-Sebeok. Plenum Press 1980 480p (Topics in contemporary semiotics) ISBN 0-306-40279-3 LC 79-17714

Speaking of literature and society. See Trilling, L.

Speier, Hans (ed.) Propaganda and communication in world history. *See* Propaganda and communication in world history

Spengemann, William C. The forms of autobiography; episodes in the history of a literary genre. Yale Univ. Press 1980 254p ISBN 0-300-02473-8 LC 79-22575

Spink, John Stephenson. See entry under title: Woman and society in eighteenth-century France

Stankiewicz, Marketa Goetz- See Goetz-Stankiewicz, Marketa

The State in Western Europe. ed. by Richard Scase. St. Martins 1980 282p ISBN 0-312-75610-0 LC 80-10364
Based on papers from a symposium held in Paris, Dec. 1978, under the auspices of the Franco-British programme of the Maison des sciences de l'homme and The British Social Science Research Council

The State of the language; ed. by Leonard Michaels and Christopher Ricks. Published in association with the English-Speaking Union, San Francisco Branch. Univ. of Calif. Press 1980 609p ISBN 0-520-03763-4 LC 78-62847
Partially analyzed

Stein, Siegfried (ed.) Studies in Jewish religious and intellectual history. *See* Studies in Jewish religious and intellectual history

Stepto, Robert B. From behind the veil; a study of Afro-American narrative. Univ. of Ill. Press 1979 203p ISBN 0-252-00752-2 LC 79-11283

Stern, J. P. (ed.) The world of Franz Kafka. *See* The World of Franz Kafka

Stewart, David. (ed.) Being human in a technological age. *See* Being human in a technological age

Stone, Donald David. The romantic impulse in Victorian fiction. Harvard Univ. Press 1980 396p ISBN 0-674-77932-0 LC 79-27736

Storer, Morris B. (ed.) Humanist ethics. *See* Humanist ethics

Structuralism and since; from Lévi-Strauss to Derrida. Ed. with an introduction, by John Sturrock. Oxford [1980 c1979] 190p ISBN 0-19-215839-2

Struve, Gleb (ed.) California Slavic studies v11. *See* California Slavic studies v11

Studies in eighteenth-century culture v9; ed. by Roseann Runte. Published for the American Society for Eighteenth-Century Studies by Univ. of Wis. Press 1979 550p ISBN 0-299-08020-X LC 74-25572
Partially analyzed

Studies in history of biology, v4. William Coleman and Camille Limoges, editors. Johns Hopkins Univ. Press 1980 198p ISBN 0-8018-2362-5 LC 79-47139

Studies in Jewish religious and intellectual history; presented to Alexander Altmann on the occasion of his seventieth birthday. Ed. by Siegfried Stein and Raphael Loewe. Published in association with the Institute of Jewish Studies, London by Univ. of Ala. Press 1980 [c1979] 362p ISBN 0-8173-6925-2 LC 77-7294
Partially analyzed

Studies in the contemporary Spanish-American short story. See Foster, D. W.

Sturrock, John (ed.) Structuralism and since. *See* Structuralism and since

Suicide: the philosophical issues; ed. by M. Pabst Battin and David J. Mayo. St Martins 1980 292p ISBN 0-312-77531-8 LC 79-27372

Suleiman, Susan Rubin (ed.) The reader in the text. *See* The Reader in the text

Sundquist, Eric J. Home as found; authority and genealogy in nineteenth-century American literature. Johns Hopkins Univ. Press 1979 xxi, 209p ISBN 0-8018-2241-6 LC 79-4949

Survivals of pastoral; ed. by Richard F. Hardin. Univ. of Kan. 1979 150p (University of Kansas Publications. Humanistic studies, 52)

Sussman, Henry (ed.) Glyph 6. *See* Glyph 6

Sutherland, Zena (comp.) The Arbuthnot lectures, 1970-1979. *See* The Arbuthnot lectures, 1970-1979

Swank, Scott T. (ed.) Perspectives on American folk art. *See* Perspectives on American folk art

The sword of the spirit. See Knott, J. R.

The symbolic instrument in early times. See Propaganda and communication in world history v 1

Symposium on Theories of Justice in and for the Second Half of the Twentieth Century, Sydney, 1977. Justice. Ed. by Eugene Kamenka and Alice Erh-Soon Tay. St Martins 1980 184p (Ideas and ideologies) ISBN 0-312-44945-3 LC 79-22174

Tagliacozzo, Giorgio (ed.) Vico and contemporary thought. *See* Conference on Vico and Contemporary Thought, New York, 1976. Vico and contemporary thought

The tale bearers. See Pritchett, V. S.

**Tate, Thadeus W.** (ed.) The Chesapeake in the seventeenth century. *See* The Chesapeake in the seventeenth century

**Tay, Alice Erh-Soon** (ed.) Justice. *See* Symposium on Theories of Justice in and for the Second Half of the Twentieth Century, Sydney, 1977

**Telling** lives; the biographer's art. Ed. by Marc Pachter. [Contributions] by Leon Edel [and others] New Republic Bks. 1979 151p ISBN 0-915220-54-7 LC 79-698

**Tennessee** Studies in literature v24. Editors: Allison R. Ensor [and] Thomas J. A. Heffernan. Univ. of Tenn. Press 1979 154p ISBN 0-87049-271-3 LC 58-63252
Partially analyzed

**Textual** strategies; perspectives in post-structuralist criticism. Ed. and with an introduction by Josué V. Harari. Cornell Univ. Press 1979 475p ISBN 0-8014-1218-8 LC 79-7617

**Tharpe, Jac** (ed.) Walker Percy. *See* Walker Percy

**Thee, Marek** (ed.) Problems of contemporary militarism. *See* Problems of contemporary militarism

**Themes** of work and love in adulthood. Ed. by Neil J. Smelser and Erik H. Erikson. Harvard Univ. Press 1980 297p ISBN 0-674-87750-0 LC 79-26130

**Thiher, Allen.** The cinematic muse; critical studies in the history of French cinema. Univ. of Mo. Press 1979 216p ISBN 0-8262-0277-2 LC 79-1560

The **Third** century; America as a post-industrial society. Ed. by Seymour Martin Lipset. Hoover Inst. Press 1979 471p ISBN 0-8179-7031-2 LC 78-70400

**Thompson, Willard Scott** (ed.) National security in the 1980s: from weakness to strength. *See* National security in the 1980s: from weakness to strength

**Three** British revolutions: 1641, 1688, 1776. Ed. by J. G. A. Pocock. Princeton Univ. Press 1980 468p (Folger Institute essays) ISBN 0-691-05293-X LC 79-27572

**Threshold** of a nation. See Edwards, P.

**Thundy, Zacharias P.** (ed.) Chaucerian problems and perspectives. *See* Chaucerian problems and perspectives

**Time,** work, & culture in the Middle Ages. See Le Goff, J.

**Tison-Braun, Micheline** (ed.) André Malraux. *See* André Malraux

**To** the third empire. See Johnston, B.

**Todd, Janet.** Women's friendship in literature. Columbia Univ. Press 1980 434p ISBN 0-231-04562-X LC 79-20175

**Tonry, Michael** (ed.) Crime and justice v 1. *See* Crime and justice v 1

**Toward** a new American literary history; essays in honor of Arlin Turner. Ed. by Louis J. Budd, Edwin H. Cady [and] Carl L. Anderson. Duke Univ. Press 1980 279p ISBN 0-8223-0430-9 LC 79-51499

**Townsend, John Rowe.** A sounding of storytellers; new and revised essays on contemporary writers for children. Lippincott 1979 218p ISBN 0-397-31882-0
First edition analyzed in 1970-1974 cumulation

**Tragedy** and truth. See Reiss, T. J.

**Transcendence** and immanence. See Daly, G.

**Traugott, Mark** (ed.) Emile Durkheim on institutional analysis. See Durkheim, E. Emile Durkheim on institutional analysis

The **trickster** in West Africa. See Pelton, R. D.

**Trilling, Lionel.** Speaking of literature and society. Ed. by Diana Trilling. Harcourt 1980 429p (The Works of Lionel Trilling. Uniform edition) ISBN 0-15-184710-X LC 80-7944
Partially analyzed

**"Turn** to the South." See Conference on Southern Jewish History, Richmond, Va. 1976

**Turner, Arlin.** See entry under title: Toward a new American literary history

**Two** hundred years of geology in America. See New Hampshire Bicentennial Conference on the History of Geology, University of New Hampshire, 1976

**Umiker-Sebeok, Jean** (ed.) Speaking of apes. *See* Speaking of apes

The **United** States in the 1980s. Editors: Peter Duignan [and] Alvin Rabushka; foreword: W. Glenn Campbell. Hoover Inst. Press 1980 xxxix, 868p ISBN 0-8179-7281-1 LC 79-5475

**Unseld, Siegfried.** The author and his publisher. Tr. by Hunter Hannum and Hildegarde Hannum. Univ. of Chicago Press 1980 300p ISBN 0-226-84189-8 LC 79-26021

The **unsounded** centre. See Bickman, M.

**Uphaus, Robert Walter.** The impossible observer; reason and the reader in 18th-century prose. Univ. Press of Ky. 1979 160p ISBN 0-8131-1389-X  LC 79-4014

**Urofsky, Melvin I.** (ed.) "Turn to the South." *See* Conference on Southern Jewish History, Richmond, Va. 1976. "Turn to the South"

**Value** and values in evolution; ed. by Edward A. Maziarz. Gordon & Breach 1979 196p  ISBN 0-677-15240-X LC 78-19561
"Lectures delivered at a symposium entitled 'Current evolution of man's sense of values' sponsored by Loyola University of Chicago on the occasion of its centenary celebration in 1970." Verso of title page

**Values,** identities, and national integration; empirical research in Africa. Ed. by John N. Paden. Northwestern Univ. Press 1980 397p ISBN 0-8101-0467-9 LC 77-85449

**Van Wyck Brooks:** the critic and his critics. Ed. by William Wasserstrom. Kennikat 1979 254p (National University publications. Literary criticism ser) ISBN 0-8046-9245-9 LC 79-533
Partially analyzed

**Vasta, Edward** (ed.) Chaucerian problems and perspectives. *See* Chaucerian problems and perspectives

**Vendler, Helen Hennessy.** Part of nature, part of us; modern American poets. Harvard Univ. Press 1980 376p ISBN 0-674-65475-7 LC 79-20308

**Verene, Donald Phillip** (ed.) Vico and contemporary thought. *See* Conference on Vico and Contemporary Thought, New York, 1976. Vico and contemporary thought

**Vico** and contemporary thought. See Conference on Vico and Contemporary Thought, New York, 1976

The **Victorian** multiplot novel. See Garrett, P. K.

The **View** from Goffman. Ed. by Jason Ditton. St Martins 1980 289p ISBN 0-312-84598-1 LC 79-25202

**Vinaver, Eugène.** See entry under title: The Expansions and transformations of courtly literature

**Virginia. University. Bibliographical Society.** Studies in bibliography v33; ed. by Fredson Bowers. Published for the Bibliographical Society of the University of Virginia by Univ. Press of Va. 1979 282p  LC 49-3353

Virginia Woolf; revaluation and continuity; a collection of essays. Ed. with an introduction by Ralph Freedman. Univ. of Calif. Press 1980 299p ISBN 0-520-03625-5 LC 77-91745
"This collection of essays grew out of a nucleus of papers read in 1974 at the English Institute meetings at Harvard." Preface

The vision of tragedy. See Sewall, R. B.

Von Cranach, Mario. See Cranach, Mario von

Waldington, Raymond B. (ed.) The age of Milton. *See* The Age of Milton

Wagley, Charles. See entry under title: Brazil, anthropological perspectives

Wagner, Linda Welshimer. American modern; essays in fiction and poetry. Kennikat 1980 263p (National university publications—Literary criticism ser.) ISBN 0-8046-9257-2 LC 79-18967

Walker, Janet Anderson. The Japanese novel of the Meiji period and the ideal of individualism. Princeton Univ. Press 1979 315p ISBN 0-619-06400-8 LC 79-4501

Walker Percy: art and ethics. Ed. by Jac Tharpe. Univ. Press of Miss. 1980 160p ISBN 0-87805-119-8 LC 80-12227

Wallace Stevens; a celebration. Ed. by Frank Doggett and Robert Buttel. Princeton Univ. Press 1980 361p ISBN 0-691-06414-8 LC 79-18877
Partially analyzed

Wasserstrom, William (ed.) Van Wyck Brooks: the critic and his critics. *See* Van Wyck Brooks: the critic and his critics

Weber, Samuel (ed.) Glyph 7. *See* Glyph 7

Weitzmann, Kurt (ed.) Age of spirituality. *See* Age of spirituality

Welch, Robert. Irish poetry from Moore to Yeats. Barnes & Noble 1980 248p (Irish literary studies, 5) ISBN 0-389-20000-X

West, David (ed.) Creative imitation and Latin literature. *See* Creative imitation and Latin literature

West Indian literature; ed. by Bruce King. Archon Bks. 1979 247p ISBN 0-208-01814-X LC 79-1255

Western European party systems; trends and prospects. Peter H. Merkl, editor. Free Press 1980 676p ISBN 0-02-920060-1 LC 78-22783

Weston-Smith, Miranda (comp.) Lying truths. *See* Lying truths

Wetzel, Heinz (ed.) The First World War in German narrative prose. *See* The First World War in German narrative prose

What is symbolism? See Peyre, H.

When the lights go down. See Kael, P.

Wilson, Robert Neal. The writer as social seer. Univ. of N.C. Press 1979 172p ISBN 0-8078-1363-X LC 79-455

The wine of life, and other essays on societies, energy & living things. See Morowitz, H. J.

Winterthur, Del. Henry Francis du Pont Winterthur Museum. See Henry Francis du Pont Winterthur Museum

Withim, Philip M. (ed.) The binding of Proteus. *See* The Binding of Proteus

Wohlgelernter, Maurice (ed.) History, religion, and spiritual democracy. *See* History, religion, and spiritual democracy

Wojcik, Jan (ed.) The David myth in Western literature. *See* The David myth in Western literature

**Wolfschütz, Hans** (ed.) Modern Austrian writing. *See* Modern Austrian writing

**Woman** and society in eighteenth-century France; essays in honour of John Stephenson Spink. Ed. by Eva Jacobs [and others]. Athlone Press [distributed by Humanities Press] 1979 285p ISBN 0-485-11184-5

**Women** novelists in Spain and Spanish America. See Fox-Lockert, L.

**Women,** war, and revolution. Ed. by Carol R. Berkin and Clara M. Lovett. Holmes & Meier 1980 310p ISBN 0-8419-0502-9 LC 79-26450

**Women's** autobiography; essays in criticism. Ed. with an introduction by Estelle C. Jelinek. Ind. Univ. Press 1980 274p ISBN 0-253-19193-9 LC 79-2600

**Women's** friendship in literature. See Todd, J.

**Woodman, Tony** (ed.) Creative imitation and Latin literature. *See* Creative imitation and Latin literature

**Word** and action. See Knox, B. M. W.

The **World** of Franz Kafka; ed. by J. P. Stern. Holt 1980 263p ISBN 0-03-051366-9 LC 80-23689
Partially analyzed

The **writer** as social seer. See Wilson, R. N.

**Wyatt, David.** Prodigal sons; a study in authorship and authority. Johns Hopkins Univ. Press 1980 172p ISBN 0-8018-2325-0 LC 79-22930


**Yeats,** Sligo and Ireland; essays to mark the 21st Yeats International Summer School. Ed. by A. Norman Jeffares. Barnes & Noble 1980 267p (Irish literary studies 6) ISBN 0-389-20095-6
Partially analyzed


**Zagorin, Perez** (ed.) Culture and politics from Puritanism to the Enlightenment. *See* Culture and politics from Puritanism to the Enlightenment

# Directory of Publishers and Distributors

A.L.A. American Library Association, 50 E Huron St, Chicago, Ill. 60611

AMS Press. AMS Press, 56 E 13th St, New York, N.Y. 10003

Abrams, Harry N. Abrams, Inc, 110 E 59th St, New York, N.Y. 10022

Africana Pub. Co. See Holmes & Meier Pubs.

Am. Antiquarian Soc. American Antiquarian Society, 185 Salisbury St, Worcester, Mass. 01609

American Elsevier. American Elsevier Publishers, Inc, 2 Park Av, New York, N.Y. 10016

An Enterprise Inst. for Public Policy Res. American Enterprise Institute for Public Policy Research, 1150 17th St, N.W., Washington, D. C. 20036

Archon Bks. See Shoe String

Atheneum Pubs. Atheneum Publishers, 122 E 42nd St, New York, N. Y. 10017

Barnes & Noble. See Harper

Beacon Press. Beacon Press, 25 Beacon St, Boston, Mass. 02108

Belknap Press. See Harvard Univ. Press

Bilingual Press. Bilingual Press, Department of Foreign Languages & Bilingual Studies, 106 Ford Hall, Eastern Michigan University, Ypsilanti, Mich. 48197

Bowling Green Univ. Pop. Press. Bowling Green University Popular Press, 101 University Hall, Bowling Green, Ohio 43403

Boydell Press. See Boydell & Brewer

Boydell & Brewer, Ltd, P.O. Box 9, Woodbridge, Suffolk, 1P12, 3DF, England

Braziller. George Braziller, Inc, 1 Park Av, New York, N.Y. 10016

Bucknell Univ. Press. Bucknell University Press, Lewisburg, Pa. 17837

Cambridge. Cambridge University Press, 32 E 57th St, New York, N.Y. 10022

Columbia Univ. Press, 562 W 113th St, New York, N.Y. 10025

Cornell Univ. Press, 124 Roberts Pl, Ithaca, N.Y. 14850

Duke Univ. Press. Duke University Press, Box 6697, College Station, Durham, N.C. 27708

Dutton. See American Elsevier

Ethics and Public Policy Center, 1211 Connecticut Av, N.W. Washington, D.C. 20035

Fairleigh Dickinson Univ. Press. Fairleigh Dickinson University Press, 285 Madison Av, Madison, N.J. 07940

Farrar, Straus & Giroux, Inc, 19 Union Sq. W, New York, N. Y. 10003

Free Press. The Free Press, 866 3d Av, New York, N.Y. 10022

Godine, David R. Godine Publisher Inc, 306 Dartmouth St, Boston, Mass. 02116

Gordon & Breach. Gordon & Breach, Science Publishers, Inc, 1 Park Av, New York, N.Y. 10016

Harcourt. Harcourt Brace Jovanovich, Inc, 757 3d Av, New York, N. Y. 10017

Harper. Harper & Row, Publishers, Inc, 10 E 53d St, New York, N.Y. 10022

Harvard Univ. Press. Harvard University Press, 79 Garden St, Cambridge, Mass. 02138

Hebrew Pub. Hebrew Publishing Company, 80 5th Av, New York, N.Y. 10011

Hill & Wang. See Farrar, Straus

Holmes & Meier. Holmes & Meier Publishers, Inc, 30 Irving Pl, New York, N.Y. 10003

Holt. Holt, Rinehart & Winston, 383 Madison Av, New York, N.Y. 10017

Hoover Inst. Press. Hoover Institute Press, Stanford University, Stanford, Calif. 94305

Horn Bk. The Horn Book Inc, Dept. W, Park Sq. Bldg, 31 St James Av, Boston, Mass. 02116

Humanities Press, Inc, Atlantic Highlands, N.J. 07716

Ind. Univ. Press. Indiana University Press, 10th & Morton Sts, Bloomington, Ind. 47405

Inst. for Contemporary Studies. Institute for Contemporary Studies, 260 California St, Suite 811, San Francisco, Calif. 94111

Johns Hopkins Univ. Press. Johns Hopkins University Press, Baltimore, Md. 21218

Kennikat. Kennikat Press Corporation, 90 S Bayles Av, Port Washington, N.Y. 11050

Knopf. Alfred A. Knopf, Inc, 201 E 50th St, New York, N.Y. 10022

Lippincott. J. B. Lippincott Company, E Washington Sq, Philadelphia, Pa. 19105

Little. Little, Brown & Company, 34 Beacon St, Boston, Mass. 02106

MIT Press. The MIT Press, 28 Carleton St, Cambridge, Mass. 02142

Metropolitan Museum of Art. Metropolitan Museum of Art, 5th Av & 82d St, New York, N. Y. 10028

Nelson-Hall. Nelson-Hall Publishers, 111 N Canal St, Chicago, Ill. 60606

New Republic Bks. The New Republic Books, 1220 19th St, N. W., Washington, D. C. 20036

N.Y. Literary Forum. New York Literary Forum, 21 E 79th St, New York, N.Y. 10021

N.Y. Univ. Press. New York University Press, Washington Sq, New York, N. Y. 10003

Northwestern Univ. Press. Northwestern University Press, 1735 Benson Av, Box 1093X, Evanston, Ill. 60201

Norton. W. W. Norton & Company, Inc, 500 5th Av, New York, N.Y. 10036

Ohio State Univ. Press. Ohio State University Press, Hitchcock Hall, Rm. 316, 2070 Neil Av, Columbus, Ohio 43210

Ohio Univ. Press. Ohio University Press, Scott Quadrangle, Athens, Ohio 45701

Oxford. Oxford University Press, Inc, 200 Madison Av, New York, N.Y. 10016

Pantheon Bks. Pantheon Books, Inc, 201 E 50th St, New York, N.Y. 10022

Pergamon Press. Pergamon Press, Inc, Maxwell House, Fairview Park, Elmsford, N.Y. 10523

Plenum Press. Plenum Publishing Corporation, 227 W 17th St, New York, N. Y. 10011

Princeton Univ. Press. Princeton University Press, Princeton, N.J. 08540

Prometheus Bks. Prometheus Books, 1203 Kensington Av, Buffalo, N. Y. 14215

Purdue Univ. Press. Purdue University Press, South Campus Courts-D, West Lafayette, Ind. 47907

Random House. Random House, Inc, 201 E 50th St, New York, N. Y. 10022

Regents Press of Kan. The Regents Press of Kansas, 366 Watson Library, Lawrence, Kan. 66045

Rowman & Littlefield. Rowman & Littlefield, 81 Adams Dr, Totowa, N. J. 07511

St Martin. St Martins Press, Inc, 175 5th Av, New York, N.Y. 10010

Sanhedrin Press. See Hebrew Pub.

Scarecrow Press. Scarecrow Press, Inc, 52 Liberty St, Metuchen, N.J. 08840

Scribner. Charles Scribner's Sons, 597 5th Av, New York, N. Y. 10017

Shoe String. The Shoe String Press, Inc, Box 4327, 995 Sherman Av, Hamden, Conn. 06514

Simon & Schuster. Simon & Schuster, Inc, The Simon & Schuster Bldg, 1230 Av. of the Americas, New York, N.Y. 10020

Smithsonian Inst. Press. Smithsonian Institution Press, Washington, D.C. 20560

Southern Ill. Univ. Press. Southern Illinois University Press, Box 3697, Carbondale, Ill. 62901

Temple Univ. Press. Temple University Press, Broad & Oxford Sts, Philadelphia, Pa. 19122

Thames & Hudson. Thames & Hudson, Inc, 500 5th Av, New York, N.Y. 10036

Transaction Bks. Transaction Books, Rutgers University, New Brunswick, N. J. 08903

Ungar. Frederick Ungar Publishing Company, Inc, 250 Park Av, S, New York, N.Y. 10003

Univ. of Ala. Press. University of Alabama Press, Drawer 2877, University, Ala. 35486

Univ. of Calif. Press. University of California Press, 2223 Fulton St, Berkeley, Calif. 94720

Univ. of Chicago Press. University of Chicago Press, 5801 Ellis Av, Chicago, Ill. 60637

Univ. of Del. Press. University of Delaware Press, 326 Hullihen Hall, Newark, Delaware 19711

Univ. of Ga. Press. University of Georgia Press, Athens, Ga. 30602

Univ. of Ill. Press. University of Illinois Press, 54 E Gregory Dr, Box 5081, Sta.A, Champaign, Ill. 61820

Univ. of Iowa Press. University of Iowa Press, Graphic Services Bldg, University of Iowa, Iowa City, Iowa 52242

Univ. of Kan. University of Kansas, Lawrence, Kan. 66045

Univ. of Mass. Press. University of Massachusetts Press, Box 429, Amherst, Mass. 01002

Univ. of Minn. Press. University of Minnesota Press, 2037 University Ave, S.E, Minneapolis, Minn. 55455

Univ. of Mo. Press. University of Missouri Press, 107 Swallow Hall, Columbia, Mo. 65211

Univ. of N.Mex. Press. University of New Mexico Press, Albuquerque, N.Mex. 87131

Univ. of N.C. Press. University of North Carolina, Box 2288, Chapel Hill, N.C. 27514

Univ. of Notre Dame Press. University of Notre Dame Press, Notre Dame, Ind. 46556

Univ. of Pa. Press. University of Pennsylvania Press, 3933 Walnut St, Philadelphia, Pa. 19104

Univ. of Tenn. Press. University of Tennessee Press, 293 Communications Bldg, Knoxville, Tenn. 37916

Univ. of Toronto Press. University of Toronto Press, St George Campus, Toronto, Ont. M5S 1A6, Canada

Univ. of Wis. Press. University of Wisconsin Press, 114 N Murray St, Madison, Wis. 53715

Univ. Press of Ky. University Press of Kentucky, Lexington, Ky. 40506

Univ. Press of Miss. University Press of Mississippi, 3825 Ridgewood Rd, Jackson, Miss. 39211

Univ. of New England. University Press of New England, Box 979, Hanover, N.H. 03755

Univ. Press of Va. University Press of Virginia, Box 3608, University Sta, Charlottesville, Va. 22903

Viking. The Viking Press, 625 Madison Av, New York, N.Y. 10022

Yale Univ. Press. Yale University Press, 302 Temple St, New Haven, Conn. 06511